Java Foundation Classes

Java Foundation Classes

Swing Reference

S<small>TEPHEN</small> C. D<small>RYE</small>
W<small>ILLIAM</small> C. W<small>AKE</small>

 M A N N I N G

Greenwich
(74° w. long.)

For electronic browsing and ordering of this and other Manning books,
visit http://www.manning.com. The publisher offers discounts on this book
when ordered in quantity. For more information, please contact:

Special Sales Department
Manning Publications Co.
32 Lafayette Place
Greenwich, CT 06830

Fax: (203) 661-9018
email: orders@manning.com

Library of Congress Cataloging-in-Publication Data
Drye, Stephen C., 1971
    Java foundation classes: Swing reference / Stephen C. Drye.
    William C. Wake
       p. cm.
    Includes bibliographical references and index.
    ISBN 1-884777-67-8 (alk. paper)
    1. Java (Computer program language)   2.   Java foundation classes.
 I.   Wake, William C., 1960   II. Title.
QA76.73.J38D79 1998
005.13'3--dc21   98-29935
               CIP

Manning Publications Co.   Copyeditor: Elizabeth Martin
32 Lafayette Place   Typesetter: Dottie Marsico
Greenwich, CT 06830   Cover designer: Leslie Haimes

Printed in the United States of America
1 2 3 4 5 6 7 8 9 10 – CR – 01 00 99

Dedicated to my wife Randi, the love of my life, for understanding
and being patient as this book proceeded, and for lending a hand when she could.
—Stephen Drye

Booker Tyler Wake
the most loved and respected man I know
and to
May Lyn Wake
who found out the hard way why books get dedicated to spouses.
—William Wake

contents

preface

The Java platform has been maturing rapidly. Recognizing the areas where Java needed improvement, the JavaSoft division of Sun has been quickly making changes and additions to bring Java to a level where professional applications can be developed without significant restrictions.

The improvement which will be most noticeable to end users is the Swing user interface library. A part of the Java Foundation Classes, Swing provides replacements for the AWT components. The Swing library uses the Lightweight component technology introduced by JDK 1.1 to provide components written completely in Java. Freed from the restrictions the AWT components had to deal with, Swing provides an extensive set of components that are compatible across Java virtual machines. Swing also provides the highly important *appearance* of being a professional application. Overcoming a user's initial impression is not an easy task. Swing allows a Java application to be judged on the same criteria as any other native application.

As a mature UI library, Swing can seem very complex but that is more related to its size and the sheer number of capabilities it supports. The design of Swing is quite elegant and easy to use. Even after you understand it, however, it is still hard to find the information you need to use Swing effectively without having to wade through the JavaDoc and three web sites to pull together what you need. That is where this book comes in.

Swing has come a long way from its initial public release versions. It still has room for improvement, but it is adding polish and professionalism to Java applications.

My first experience with Swing was after becoming discouraged with the available AWT controls in developing a simple office suite for a handheld device. Even with the restricted requirements of the office suite, the AWT didn't provide enough functionality. Most of the available third-party component toolkits provided some, but not all, of the components needed. Eventually, the office suite was using a collection of five different toolkits, all with their own way of doing things.

The Swing components replaced all of the other toolkits except for the spreadsheet control (which was eventually replaced with a Swing-based component). Swing also allowed the implementation of a custom user interface "look and feel," which is very significant for a consumer product.

Other developers also seem to have picked up Swing as their toolkit of choice. I have seen an increase in the number of Java applications appearing on the Internet in recent months, and most seem to be using Swing. Even older applications are beginning to be modified to use Swing. Development tools are also being updated to use Swing and a significant number of new tools are appearing that either exclusively support Swing or are even completely written using Swing.

Now that Swing has finally stabilized and integrated into the JDK, the adoption of Swing should accelerate. I hope this book will play a part in enabling developers to adopt and use Swing to its fullest.

Stephen Drye

intended audience

This book is intended for the intermediate software developer who is already familiar with Java. Knowledge of the AWT is presupposed, since most books covering Java include a significant AWT section.

This book came about as a result of trying to find a happy medium in Java books. The Java books we found in stores seemed to fall into three categories. The first category was tutorial books that we didn't need since we tended to get into new Java topics very early, long before the tutorials could be written. The second category was the minimal reference, which presents the class members without any discussion. While useful, there wasn't enough explanation there when we needed it. The third category was the huge reference, which does have more than enough information but is too large to carry around so it was never where we needed it to be.

This book is designed to strike the balance between minimal and huge reference. We believe there is enough information to settle any questions you may have quickly, but the book is still small enough to transport easily so it will be with you, whether you are at home tinkering or at the office sweating before a deadline. We believe that this book will be a handy desk-side reference.

Any Java or PersonalJava developer will benefit from learning Swing, since it has become clear that it is the future of Java. The AWT components have entered a maintenance state where they are being left in place, but not particularly improved.

Embedded Java will probably never add Swing, since it is designed for very small devices with extremely limited interfaces. PersonalJava and above will support Swing in some form or another. Enterprise Java (what is generally considered "normal" Java) already has Swing as an add-on and it has become a standard part of the language with JDK 1.2. PersonalJava does not have Swing included yet, but it is an almost foregone conclusion that it will add support for some form of Swing shortly. The reasoning behind this assumption is based on the fact that consumer devices, more than any other kind of computing device, need customized user interfaces. Swing's pluggable look and feel is the ideal solution to fulfill this need. It may be "PersonalSwing" of some sort, but PersonalJava will get Swing.

hardware and software requirements

Nothing should be too surprising in the following list of requirements for running Swing (or Java in general). If there is, then you are probably reading the wrong book.

Required Software: a JDK 1.1.2 compatible Java development environment or higher with Swing 1.0.2 or higher. If you will be implementing a look and feel you will need Swing 1.1 (or JDK 1.2) which includes the first "official" look and feel API. The Swing download package for JDK 1.1.x is available by going to http://java.sun.com and following the Java Foundation Classes link. Swing is a core part of JDK 1.2 so you do not need to separately download it if you are using that version of the JDK. Windows 95 or NT and Solaris users can also find the latest available JDK for their platforms at http://java.sun.com.

Recommended Software: Swing 1.1 or JDK 1.2. Sun's JDK 1.1.7 (or higher) on Windows 95 or NT. The recommendations for other common platforms are JDK 1.1.7 or higher on Solaris, JDK 1.1.6 or higher on Linux, JDK 1.1.6 or higher on OS/2 and JDK 1.1.5 on the Macintosh. On other platforms, check with your OS vendor to see if there is a JDK compatible with JDK 1.1.2 or higher available. JDK 1.2 is also a good choice when it is available for your platform. The recommended version of Swing is the latest version available.

Borland's JBuilder 2 was used to develop some of the examples in the book and as a testing environment on Windows. An interesting feature of JBuilder is that a significant part of its user interface was written using Swing 1.0.2. The Macintosh environment used was Metrowerks CodeWarrior.

Recommended Hardware: At least a Pentium 133MHz or equivalent with at least 32MB of memory is recommended. Using a JIT (Just-in-Time compiler) makes Java on any hardware run much faster, so try to find one that works with the JDK you are using. JDK 1.1.6 (and higher) on Windows and JDK 1.2 come with a JIT.

Recommended Browser: Your best bet for using Swing in a browser is to download the Java Plugin package from Sun. The Java Plugin is an add-in for Netscape and Internet Explorer that allows each to use the latest Sun JDK instead of the browser's built-in support. The latest versions of the Java Plugin come with Swing as part of the installation package. Swing *does* run on both Netscape 4.04 and higher with the Java 1.1 support patch and Microsoft's Internet Explorer as of version 4.01 if you wish to use the native support. A description of how to enable Swing in these browsers is available on Sun's Swing Connection web site:

`http://java.sun.com/products/jfc/swingdoc-current/index.html`.

Author Online

Purchase of *Java Foundation Classes: Swing Reference* includes free access to a private Internet forum where you can make comments about the book, ask technical questions, and receive help from the author and from other Swing users. To access the forum, point your Web browser to `http://www.manning.com/Drye`. There you will be able to subscribe to the forum. This site also provides information on how to access the forum once you are registered, what kind of help is available, and the rules of conduct on the forum.

All source code for the examples presented in *Java Foundation Classes: Swing Reference* is available to purchasers from the Manning website. The URL `http://www.manning.com/Drye` includes a link to the source code files.

how this book is organized

This book is in two parts. The first part is a brief introduction to Swing and its basic concepts. It is intended to be sufficient for an intermediate Java developer to get started with Swing. It is not intended to be an exhaustive tutorial. If you find yourself needing a more detailed tutorial, Steven Gutz has written an excellent one titled *Up to Speed With Swing: User Interfaces With Java Foundation Classes* (Manning, ISBN 1-884777-64-3). *Up to Speed With Swing* is 498 pages and includes many useful and detailed examples. It covers all of the Swing components, Swing methodology, and the details needed in developing production-quality applications or applets, such as optimization.

The second part is a detailed reference to Swing. This, the primary part of the book, includes reference information, FAQs, and examples on all of the important classes and interfaces in Swing. This part is divided into sections based on the packages in Swing. Each package forms its own section. The sections begin with a brief description of the purpose of the package, a class hierarchy diagram for the whole package, a quick summary, and FAQs about the classes in the package. The rest of the section is an alphabetical listing of all of the classes and interfaces in the package.

conventions used in this book

Various fonts are used in this book. This is what they mean:

Font	Meaning
Code	A code sample, or a reference to a Java interface, field, or method name embedded in descriptive text.
Class Member	A member of a class.
Class Member Descriptive Text	The description of the class member.

The class/interface diagrams in this book use a simple format chosen for compactness. Using UML was considered, since it is effectively "the" OO diagramming standard today, but it was rejected for two reasons. One, it doesn't handle interfaces that well (using stereotypes is the best way we have seen); and two, the available tools are very slow to work with for the number of diagrams required.

The class diagrams use the following symbols:

Purpose	Symbol
A class	Class Name
An abstract class	*AbstractClass*
An interface	InterfaceName
Extends	◄─────
Implements	◄─ ─ ─ ─

review process for this book

Manning recognizes the importance to you of accurate, relevant, and useful content in the books you buy. We, therefore, put considerable emphasis on submitting each manuscript we develop to an exhaustive technical and editorial check. This book was scrutinized in three phases: while in early manuscript form; again, after the book was mostly complete; and, finally, when a thorough tech review was conducted (just before publication).

The critique of the manuscript in its early stages led to an important realignment in the book's focus. Most initial reviewers suggested including more detail, resulting in a change in the scope of the book from a compact reference to a fully detailed and comprehensive guide to Swing. Making those changes before the manuscript had been completed saved the authors a time-consuming revision at the end.

Final manuscript reviews—in a flurry of opinion and occasional counteropinion as two beta versions of the application were released—caused us to drop from and add to the manuscript at dizzying rates that only experienced and confident Swing experts like authors Stephen Drye and William Wake could sustain. An intense review process such as this can help a draft manuscript mature quickly into a balanced, accurate, and up-to-date work ready for publication. That is obviously what happened in this case, thanks to the authors' commitment to first-rate results.

Technical comments were analyzed by Manning staff and the authors. Through multiple exchanges with the reviewers, we gained a first-hand feeling for the intense interest that Swing generates among people who know it.

While speed is critical in getting a book on a hot topic to market, consensus among the reviewers, authors, and Manning was that this book had to be right. A serious reference needs to be up-to-date as well as complete. Even the most adroit authors must have substantial experience in a technology in order to present the reader with a useful treatment, and that requires time—to which the long process of writing, reviewing, revising, and production must be sequentially added before a manuscript can become a book. In this case, the objective of producing a comprehensive and up-to-date guide at the same time that new versions of Swing were being released presented a major challenge. We believe we were up to the task.

Our manuscript review was done entirely online, saving valuable time that would otherwise have gone into transporting paper copies between us and our reviewers, especially those overseas. Online review also lets us avoid the additional delays and paperwork associated with shipping documents to overseas reviewers. This book reflects, quite literally, world-class feedback.

The following people, whose input was indispensable to the development of this book, participated in the first two rounds of reviews:

John Alegre
Eric Blood
Michael Brundage
John Clingan
Lee Crawford
Richard Crosby
Mike Hawkes
Bruce Hopkins
David Karr
Ulrich Kortenkamp
Prakash Malani
Bijal Modi
Pierre Morel
Art Muszynski
Douglas Nehring
Cameron Newham
Suresh Srinivas
Jens Steckhan
Bob Sutherland
Wong Kok Wai

In addition, Laurence Vanhelsuwe and Bob Sutherland provided the all-important last-minute checking during the technical proofing process.

about the cover illustration

"Femme de Javan" (Java Woman), the cover illustration, is from the 1805 edition of Sylvain Maréchal's four-volume collection of men's and women's regional dress customs. This book was first published in Paris in 1788, one year before the French Revolution. Its title alone required no less than 30 words:

> "Costumes Civils actuels de tous les peuples connus dessinés d'après nature gravés et coloriés, accompagnés d'une notice historique sur leurs coutumes, moeurs, religions, etc., etc., redigés par M. Sylvain Maréchal"

The four volumes include an annotation on the illustrations: "gravé à la manière noire par Mixelle d'après Desrais et colorié." Clearly, the engraver and illustrator deserved no more than mention of their last names—after all they were mere technicians. The workers who colored each illustration by hand remain nameless.

The remarkable diversity of this collection reminds us vividly of how distant and isolated the world's towns and regions were from each other just 200 years ago. Dress codes have changed everywhere and the diversity by region, so rich at the time, has practically disappeared. It is now hard to tell the inhabitant of one continent from another. Perhaps we have traded off some cultural diversity for a richer and more varied personal life—including an incredibly interesting technology environment.

Dubbed the "Java Woman Book," this is the second Manning Swing title to be illustrated with Sylvain Maréchal's people of the past. A companion volume, *Up to Speed with Swing* by Steve Gutz, known as the "Java Man Book," was released earlier in 1998. A second edition is in the works for the spring of 1999. At a time when it is hard to tell one computer book from another, Manning celebrates the inventiveness and initiative of the world of software with a new series of covers based on the rich diversity of regional life brought back to life by these pictures. Just think, Maréchal's was a world so different from ours, people would take the time to read a book title 30 words long.

special thanks

We would both like to thank the Swing team in the JavaSoft division of Sun Microsystems for providing Java applications with the fit and finish they need to go mainstream.

We would also like to thank the folks at Manning Publications for their assistance in getting this book completed and right. The Manning rogues' gallery includes: Marjan Bace, Publisher; Mary Piergies, Production Editor; Ted Kennedy, Review Editor; Dottie Marsico, typesetter; Elizabeth Martin, copyeditor; and Leslie Haimes, graphic designer.

Last, but certainly not least, we would like to thank the many reviewers of this book, listed in the section called *review process for this book*. Without them we couldn't have done this!

personal thanks

STEPHEN DRYE   I would like to thank my family for supporting me throughout the writing of this book and my coworkers in the New Concepts Group at Ericsson, for providing feedback and tons of good questions.

WILLIAM WAKE   To my family, especially my brother, Steve Wake, for his technical criticism. And to Sorin Lazareanu and Tim Spangler for our lunchtime discussions.

PART 1

An introduction to Swing

CHAPTER 1

The basics

1.1 Why Swing?

Java's AWT (Abstract Windowing Toolkit) was a remarkable feat. In response to a request from Netscape, a small group of talented programmers developed a usable user interface and graphics Application Programming Interface (API) that worked well enough across platforms to give people a taste of write once, run anywhere. A remarkable feat but, as history shows, it was just a temporary victory. It was not long after the release of Java 1.0.2 that Netscape fully understood the limitations of what it had asked Sun for and began working on its own user interface library, the Internet Foundation Classes (IFC). Not to be outdone, Microsoft developed its proprietary Application Foundation Classes (AFC) class library (replaced in early 1998 by its even more proprietary Windows Foundation Classes (WFC)).

Although it may seem so, Swing was not developed in response to either of these two user interface (UI) toolkits. In fact, the developers at Sun started down the road to Swing for the same reasons as the teams at Netscape and Microsoft. As it turned out, the fundamental requirement in AWT of supporting the controls native to the platform proved its greatest limitation. Developers quickly realized that it was impossible to write a professional application without resorting to writing their own controls because AWT supports only the controls common to all windowing toolkits. Even though the controls that were supplied existed on all platforms, the controls didn't always work the same.

Swing is being developed as part of a larger toolkit for Java, the Java Foundation Classes (JFC). The JFC is made up of several technologies: the AWT, Swing, Accessibility, and Java2D (table 1.1). These technologies are the core of Java's user interface support. Swing is the user interface component portion of the JFC. Accessibility is usually considered part of Swing because it is available as part of the Swing distribution. Accessibility is broadly described as support for assistive interface technologies such as screen magnifiers, Braille, or head-tracking devices. The AWT portion of the JFC still includes AWT components, but they have largely been replaced by Swing. Java2D is an advanced 2D drawing toolkit that extends and replaces the old 2D drawing support in AWT.

Table 1.1   The technologies included in the JFC

JFC 1.0	JFC 1.1	JFC 1.2
Java Platform 1.0 (JDK 1.0)	Java Platform 1.1 (JDK 1.1)	Java Platform 1.2 (JDK 1.2)
AWT	AWT	AWT
	Swing	Swing
	Accessibility	Accessibility
		JDK 1.2D

Swing's strength comes from four advancements over the AWT: the adoption of well-understood and highly advanced concepts from Java's predecessors in the object-oriented world; the use of the "lightweight components" concept introduced in JDK 1.1; Swing components are JavaBeans; and support for custom look and feel.

The benefits of the first advancement are immediately obvious. Many years have been spent examining how graphics and user interfaces fit into object-oriented programming models. Swing takes those ideas and builds upon them. The Swing team is made up of people from Sun, from the development team at Netscape that created the IFC, and from developers from Lighthouse Technologies, a company well known for its NeXT development work. The basic concepts of Swing will be immediately understandable to anyone who has used an object-oriented UI tool-kit, concepts such as the use of Models to separate the application's data from the data's display and using Listeners to receive messages about changes or events from other objects, or Swing's use of composition and inheritance where each is most appropriate. All of these design choices serve to provide an environment that is stable and mature, but also one that is ultimately flexible and provides a solid foundation for creativity.

The second advancement, using lightweight components, gives Swing many advantages over AWT. The most interesting advantage to most developers is compatibility. It is much, much easier to write a Java Virtual Machine (JVM) that executes the byte codes needed to render a component in Java the same way than it is to try to get platform-native components to work the same on different platforms. To understand fully how important this idea is, consider that there are operating systems (particularly in the consumer/embedded market) that do not even *have* native components. As well, many of the platform incompatibilities in Java were caused by the AWT components. Swing developers no longer worry about those problems. Lightweight components are also more flexible than their AWT brethren since they can be transparent and support pluggable hit-testing. Rounded, organic-in-appearance components are very easy to implement in Swing. As well, most Swing components do not depend on a native peer which allows them to be optimized (above and beyond the savings gained from not having to perform an OS context switch for every drawing operation, which is very expensive).

The third advancement is mostly for developers. JavaBeans are quickly making Java development much easier. In the same way that VBXs and OCXs led to the explosive growth in Visual-Basic programming, JavaBeans are causing the same growth for Java. Swing's components were designed from the beginning to be Beans, so you immediately get all of the associated benefits of Beans: for example, ease of use in the Integrated Development Environment (IDE), serialization support, and full support for the 1.1 event delegation model. As new versions of Java IDEs appear they are making use of the Bean nature of Swing to provide graphical user interface (GUI) designers that work very well. Having such designers available will help to greatly reduce the difficulty in creating professional-looking Java applications.

The benefits of the last advancement aren't at all well understood. Custom or pluggable look and feel has been tried before, most notably in Smalltalk. In that environment, it is generally considered to be of little utility. Many people have taken the Smalltalk experience with look and feel and have used it to decide that there is no benefit to them in Java, either. What is missed by that argument is that it was Smalltalk that limited the usage of custom look and feel, not the other way around. The personal computer and workstation market is of considerable size, but it still falls short of the much, much larger consumer electronics market. In consumer electronics, one of the few areas you are allowed to differentiate yourself is through your device's appearance, and a standard adage in the consumer electronics area is that you have to differentiate to sell. Java is an ideal fit for the consumer electronics market as evidenced by its quick adoption by telecommunications equipment providers and home electronics producers. In this market the concept of a pluggable look and feel makes perfect sense. The software controlling the device can remain the same while a new look and feel is used that suits the form and function of the particular device. Because Java has caught on in the consumer market, the pluggable look and feel has taken on a significant new role.

1.2   The basics

For the impatient, we now present a brief look at how to put together a simple Swing program.

```
// uncomment the following line for Swing 1.1
import java.swing.*;
// uncomment the following line for Swing 1.0.3 and before
// import com.sun.java.swing.*;
import java.awt.BorderLayout;
import java.awt.event.*;

class SwingTest
{
  public static void main(String[] args) {
    SwingTest st = new SwingTest();
  } // end main()

  public SwingTest() {
    JFrame frame = new JFrame();
    JList list = new JList();
    list.addItemListener(new ListListener());
    JTextField field = new JTextField();
    frame.getContentPane().setLayout(new BorderLayout());
    frame.getContentPane().add(list, BorderLayout.CENTER);
    frame.getContentPane().add(field, BorderLayout.NORTH);
    frame.setVisible(true);
  } // end SwingTest()

  class ListListener implements ItemListener {
    public void itemStateChanged(ItemEvent e) {
      if (e.getStateChanged() == ItemEvent.SELECTED) {
        field.setText(e.getItem().toString());
      }
    }
  } // end inner class
  } // end class
```

As you can see, a simple Swing program looks just like an AWT program that has sprouted Js. The only significant difference is in using `getContentPane().add()`, as opposed to adding just the list to the frame. It seems like such an innocent change, but not all is as it seems.

1.2.1 Where's Swing?

Notice a comment next to the import statement for the Swing package in the first example. That comment deserves some explanation, since the issue surrounding it is a source of confusion.

It is good that the Swing package has finally settled down to just one package name for both JDK 1.1 and JDK 1.2 as of Swing 1.1. It does require changing all of your application's import statements and recompiling, but Swing 1.1 is so sufficiently different from Swing 1.0 that you will probably need to recompile anyway. It's a small price to pay to get away from the turmoil the name was in for nearly all of 1998.

Table 1.2   The winding road to javax.swing

Mid 1997—Swing was only to appear in JDK 1.2 as `java.awt.swing`.

End of 1997, early 1998—Swing was going to appear in JDK 1.1 as `com.sun.java.swing` and in JDK 1.2 as `java.awt.swing`. The `com.sun.java.swing` version was also going to ship with JDK 1.2 for compatibility.

Mid 1998—Due to size, the `com.sun.java.swing` version was not going to ship with JDK 1.2.

August 1998—Swing 1.1 was going to appear in JDK 1.1 and JDK 1.2 as `com.sun.java.swing`. The `com.sun.java.swing` package name was going to become core by decree, even though it wasn't a subpackage of `java.awt`.

November 1998—Swing 1.1 ships using the `javax.swing` package for both JDK 1.1 and JDK 1.2. Packages using `javax` are defined as being allowed to be core packages in the JDK 1.2 "standard extension" specification. Swing 1.0 will remain in `com.sun.java.swing`.

If you're wondering why Sun didn't just use `javax.swing` from the beginning, it is due to the fact that the idea of standard extensions (`javax` packages) didn't exist at the time Swing was initially being developed.

Because of the double package name situation that exists as of the writing of this book, the package will simply be referred to as "swing" in the reference section (for example, `swing.plaf.basic`). Prepend "`com.sun.java.`" or "`javax.`" as appropriate for the version of Swing you are using (continuing the example, `com.sun.java.swing.plaf.basic` for Swing 1.0, or `javax.swing.plaf.basic` for Swing 1.1).

1.2.2 Porting from AWT to Swing

It is possible to write a Swing program in exactly the same way as an AWT program. Swing was designed with easy portability from AWT in mind. In fact, Swing itself was implemented using the AWT. What Swing provides is a new methodology and a new set of *components* that replaces those in the AWT. The AWT *infrastructure* is still there, and always will be. Most AWT programs can quite quickly be changed to Swing by replacing the AWT components with their Swing counterparts and then fixing any minor compilation errors that crop up. It is also possible to write a program that is made up of a combination of Swing and AWT components, but, through experience, it becomes clear that this is not recommended. While it would work, some of the program's behaviors would be, in a word, odd. The major problem in writing a combination application is that AWT components *always* draw in front of any Swing components.

This drawing problem isn't specific to Swing. It occurs whenever an AWT heavyweight component (one that uses a native peer component) is mixed with an AWT lightweight component (one that simply draws on the display area of a parent heavyweight component and therefore does not have an associated native peer). All AWT components are heavyweights and almost all Swing components are lightweight.

The following application illustrates the problem shown in figure 1.1. When you run the application, move the Swing window to the front and make it overlap the AWT `TextArea`. It is quite easy to see why this behavior is undesirable.

```
package AWTOverlap;

import java.awt.*;
//import com.sun.java.swing.*;
import javax.swing.*;

public class MainFrame extends JFrame
{
  JInternalFrame swingIF = new JInternalFrame("Swing", true, true, true,
  true);
  JInternalFrame awtIF = new JInternalFrame("AWT", true, true, true, true);
  JDesktopPane dtp = new JDesktopPane();
```

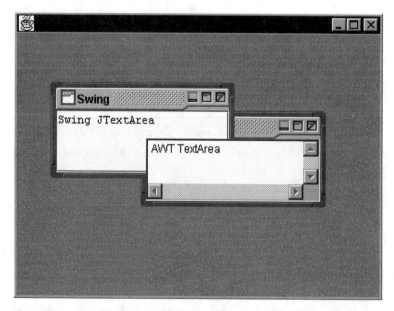

Figure 1.1   An AWT heavyweight component improperly obscuring a Swing component

```
JTextArea swingArea = new JTextArea("Swing JTextArea");
TextArea awtArea = new TextArea("AWT TextArea");

public MainFrame()
{
  setSize(new Dimension(400,300));
  getContentPane().setLayout(new BorderLayout());
  getContentPane().add(dtp, BorderLayout.CENTER);
  dtp.add(swingIF, JDesktopPane.DEFAULT_LAYER);
  swingIF.getContentPane().add(swingArea);
  swingIF.setSize(new Dimension(200,100));
  dtp.add(awtIF, JDesktopPane.DEFAULT_LAYER);
  awtIF.getContentPane().add(awtArea);
  awtIF.setSize(new Dimension(200,100));
  swingIF.toFront();
  try {
    swingIF.setSelected(true);
  }
  catch (java.beans.PropertyVetoException e) {
  }
}

public static void main(String[] args)
{
  MainFrame mainFrame1 = new MainFrame();
  mainFrame1.setVisible(true);
}
  }
```

This drawing problem has no solution, since it is a side effect of lightweights being drawn on the surface of their parent container. Since they are actually drawn *on* the container, any heavy components added to the container will always draw above the lightweights. If this weren't the case, AWT components would have to be *behind* the container holding them.

This problem makes it impossible to properly use JScrollPane to scroll AWT components, since the JViewport that it contains (which clips the components for the JScrollPane) is a lightweight component and cannot clip a heavyweight component. If you need to scroll anything containing an AWT control, even if the area contains a mix of AWT and Swing components, you need to use an AWT ScrollPane.

JInternalFrames, as shown in the example, are also unsuitable for containing AWT components.

The last place this raises issues is with pop-up components, like a JPopupMenu or the drop-down on a JComboBox. If lightweights are restricted to their parent container's drawing area, what happens when a Swing pop-up needs to draw outside the window? The answer involves using *three* different weights of components to handle the various situations. If the pop-up needs to draw outside the bounds of the parent window, it will use a JWindow (JWindow is one of the Swing components that are heavyweights). If the pop-up is completely within the window, it is drawn as a fully lightweight component and the special property lightWeightPopupEnabled is true (it is by default). This special property is used to enable the third type of pop-up, when the property is `false`, and the pop-up fits entirely within the window. This third type is used in situations where the pop-up would overlay an AWT component in the window. Since the AWT component always draws in front, the pop-up would appear to pass behind the AWT component. Setting `lightWeightPopupEnabled` to `false` forces the pop-up to use a `Panel`, which is heavyweight and will draw correctly in front of the other component.

Readers familiar with the lightweight component specification of JDK 1.1 will know that lightweight components offer some added advantages over their heavyweight brethren beyond not needing a native peer. Lightweight components can have transparent areas, which allows them to appear to be nonrectangular. Mouse events "pass through" a lightweight component to the lightweight component's parent, since lightweights are simply drawings on their parent's surface. The parent then queries all of its children to see if they contain the mouse event. This allows lightweights to implement nonrectangular hit-testing areas. Combining the transparency and flexible hit testing of lightweights allows you to create some very fancy looking components.

Because it isn't that hard to convert an AWT application completely, changing over as soon as it is feasible is recommended. Changing from Swing to AWT is not a decision you will regret. The only difficult part is custom components. If they are descended from `java.awt.Component`, then they are already lightweight components and can be used unchanged. If they are descended from `java.awt.Canvas` in the old JDK 1.02 style they will need to be rewritten.

Having said it is possible to write a Swing application in the same way that AWT applications were written, don't do it without a very strong reason. To use the older AWT style is to ignore the true power and flexibility of Swing. As you are getting used to the new style you will probably feel that it is far more complicated and question whether it is worth your while. The answer will come the first time you have to modify a Swing program you have written. Modifying a full Swing program is much easier than modifying an AWT-style program because of Swing's new style of relationship between the application's data and its display. Since modifying twenty-year-old COBOL applications has been big news in these years around the millennium, it is a safe bet that you're going to be modifying any Swing program you write at some point in its service lifetime.

1.3   *The idea behind Swing*

The standard design pattern in object-oriented user interfaces is that of the Model-View-Controller (MVC). Put simply, in this paradigm the data (the model) in the application is kept separate from the rendering of the data (the view) and the manipulation of the data (the controller) (figure 1.2).

Swing uses a common variant of MVC where the view and the controller are merged into one piece, the delegate. In practice, the view and controller are too closely related to be treated separately so merging the view and controller greatly simplifies development. This variant is also known as Document-View.

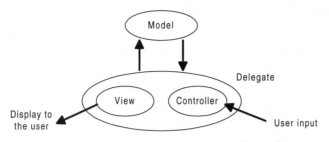

Figure 1.2 The traditional Model-Delegate model

In the Model-Delegate design, the delegate updates the model through a known interface, and the model informs the delegate when to update through an event listener. The delegate then retrieves the updated information through the same known interface. The getter/setter style of methods used with JavaBeans provides a good basis for designing the model's interface. Java's event listener system provides an ideal solution for sending the update messages.

Separating the data from the display of the data lends a great deal of flexibility to the development of a user interface. A major advantage to this model is that a single delegate class can display and update the data from several different models, with the only restriction being that the models support a common interface. This is tremendously useful because the data in an application doesn't have to be copied back and forth from the native storage to the type of storage that the user interface needs. With MVC, a developer simply implements the needed interface using the native data format of the application. This makes it much easier to maintain and update the view or views of the data correctly.

Another benefit is the reduced memory requirement due to having only one copy of the data. It may seem to be more work to implement the proper wrappers around the native application data, but after all of the code has been written to copy and update the native data from the component's default data model, the wrapper code will be much smaller and more efficient.

Also, the wrapper interfaces tend to be chosen to reflect the needs of a generic category of component (for example, a generic hierarchy for tree-style components, or a generic document for text components) so they can be used with other components of the same category with little or no modification. An example of this from Swing is `JTextField`, `JTextArea`, and `JEditor-Pane` all sharing the `Document` model.

The designers of Swing have tried to make identifying the different pieces of the MVC design easy. The models are the easiest to identify, since they all have names ending in Model, such as `ButtonModel` or `DefaultTreeModel`. To support pluggable look and feel, the view-controllers in Swing are in two parts. The items that are thought of as "the Swing components" all have names beginning with the letter J, such as `JButton`, `JTree`, and `JEditorPane`. These are the objects that actually handle the communication with the Models. Because of pluggable look and feel, these components actually delegate the view and controller responsibility to look and feel specific UI delegates. There is one delegate abstract class in the `swing.plaf` package corresponding to each type of Swing component. The concrete implementations of the delegates live in the look and feel packages, such as `swing.plaf.basic`, `swing.plaf.metal`, or any custom look and feel developed by a third party. See table 1.3.

Table 1.3   Components and their associated models

Component	Model Interfaces
JButton	ButtonModel
JToggleButton	ButtonModel
JCheckBox	ButtonModel
JRadioButton	ButtonModel
JMenu	ButtonModel
JMenuItem	ButtonModel
JCheckBoxMenuItem	ButtonModel
JRadioButtonMenuItem	ButtonModel
JComboBox	ComboBoxModel
JProgressBar	BoundedRangeModel
JScrollBar	BoundedRangeModel
JSlider	BoundedRangeModel
JTabbedPane	SingleSelectionModel
JList	ListModel, ListSelectionModel
JTable	TableModel, TableColumnModel
JTree	TreeModel, TreeSelectionModel
JEditorPane	Document
JTextPane	Document
JTextArea	Document
JTextField	Document
JPasswordField	Document

Some components use more than one model. To understand this choice, remember the rule in object-oriented programming that each object should only represent one thing. There are several models that describe selections, such as ListSelectionModel, which models the set of selected items in a list-style component. It would have been possible to have the selection managed by the component, but then code to manage a selection from a list would have been duplicated in several places. As well, the selection model represents the state of a set of *subobjects* in the component, not the state of the component itself. This subobject-object split is also seen in having the TableModel contain a set of TableColumnModels.

A more accurate diagram of how Swing implements MVC is shown in figure 1.3.

Most of the models supplied by Swing are interfaces, since they are supposed to be used to wrap existing data in an application. To lower the cost of porting to and working with Swing there are also classes provided that implement the model interface for you. Where it was possible, an abstract implementation is provided to reduce the burden of properly wrapping the data in the application. In some places default model implementations are provided but should be treated as only appropriate for prototypes. They were provided to support the AWT portability methods, and as such, they cause significant overhead through copying the data from its native application form into the form used by the default.

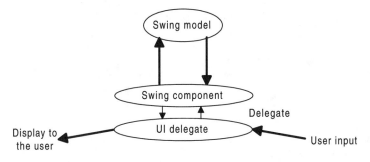

Figure 1.3   How Swing implements its version of MVC

Swing has been designed to allow the old AWT programming style, but unless you are porting an application or applet from AWT you will end up doing more work for a less efficient program. That somehow doesn't sound like a good idea. A good rule of thumb is to use the AWT compatibility methods for initially porting the application or applet from AWT and then optimize them with full Swing implementations based on profiling results. If you are starting from scratch, use Swing right from the beginning.

1.4   Swing is not AWT

Through experimenting with early, nonoptimized versions of Swing, many people have been left with the impression that Swing is slower than AWT. Swing shares one major characteristic with Java—you need to learn how to use it the way it was designed to be used. Everything in the Java world has to go through a maturation process. Java itself still has a reputation for being much slower than C++. JIT compilers keep getting better and HotSpot (if you can believe the Sun press releases) promises to allow Java to surpass C++ in terms of speed. Swing 1.0 and 1.01 were not optimized since their goal was to stabilize the APIs. Swing 1.0.2 included some optimizations and Swing 1.1 included a complete rewrite of the Swing drawing model that gave many components a considerable speed boost.

To give a concrete example of Swing being faster than AWT, consider the following example. It is a simple AWT application consisting of a `Frame` with a `List` control and a `Button` to start the test.

```
package benchmark;
import java.awt.*;
import java.awt.event.*;
//import com.sun.java.swing.*;
import javax.swing.*;

public class BenchFrame extends Frame {
  //Construct the frame
  BorderLayout borderLayout1 = new BorderLayout();
  List list1 = new List();
  Button fillButton = new Button();

  public static void main(String[] args) {
    BenchFrame bm = new BenchFrame();
  }
```

```
public BenchFrame() {
    this.setLayout(borderLayout1);
    this.setSize(new Dimension(400, 300));
    this.setTitle("AWT Benchmark");
    fillButton.addActionListener(new ActionListener() {
        public void actionPerformed(ActionEvent e) {
            fillButtonActionPerformed(e);
        }
    });
    fillButton.setLabel("Fill");
    this.add(list1, BorderLayout.CENTER);
    this.add(fillButton, BorderLayout.SOUTH);
    this.addWindowListener(new WindowAdapter() {
        public void windowClosed(WindowEvent e)
        {
            System.exit(0);
        }
    });
    setVisible(true);
}

void fillButtonActionPerformed(ActionEvent e) {
    String[] strings = new String[10000];
    for (int i = 0; i < 10000; i++) {
        strings[i] = "bob" + i;
    }
    long tmStart = System.currentTimeMillis();
    for (int j = 0; j < 10000; j++) {
        list1.add(strings[j]);
    }
    long tmEnd = System.currentTimeMillis();
    System.out.println(tmEnd - tmStart);
}
}
```

This AWT test took 40809ms (40 seconds) on a Pentium 120 with 80MB of memory. Now, convert the test to a proper Swing application.

```
package benchmark;
import java.awt.*;
import java.awt.event.*;
//import com.sun.java.swing.*;
//import com.sun.java.swing.event.ListDataListener;
import javax.swing.*;
import javax.swing.event.ListDataListener;

public class BenchFrame extends JFrame {
    //Construct the frame
    BorderLayout borderLayout1 = new BorderLayout();
    JList list1 = new JList();
    JButton fillButton = new JButton();

    public static void main(String[] args) {
```

```
      BenchFrame bm = new BenchFrame();
   }

   public BenchFrame() {
      this.getContentPane().setLayout(borderLayout1);
      this.setSize(new Dimension(400, 300));
      this.setTitle("Simple Swing Benchmark");
      fillButton.addActionListener(new ActionListener() {
         public void actionPerformed(ActionEvent e) {
            fillButtonActionPerformed(e);
         }
      });
      fillButton.setText("Fill");
      this.getContentPane().add(new JScrollPane(list1), BorderLayout.CENTER);
      this.getContentPane().add(fillButton, BorderLayout.SOUTH);
      this.setDefaultCloseOperation(JFrame.DISPOSE_ON_CLOSE);
      this.addWindowListener(new WindowAdapter() {
         public void windowClosed(WindowEvent e) {
            System.exit(0);
         }
      });
      // list1.setPrototypeCellValue("bob10000");

      setVisible(true);
   }

   void fillButtonActionPerformed(ActionEvent e) {
      ListData ld = new ListData();
      long tmStart = System.currentTimeMillis();
      list1.setModel(ld);
      list1.repaint();
      long tmEnd = System.currentTimeMillis();
      System.out.println(tmEnd - tmStart);
   }
}

class ListData extends AbstractListModel {
   String[] strings = new String[10000];
   public ListData() {
      for (int i = 0; i < 10000; i++) {
         strings[i] = "bob" + i;
      }
   }
   public int getSize() {
      return strings.length;
   }
   public Object getElementAt(int index) {
      return strings[index];
   }
}
```

This test reports taking *10 milliseconds* to run, and takes about *12 seconds* to complete displaying. Adding the call to the setPrototypeCellValue() method decreases the display time to just *1 second*. This is much better than AWT's 48 seconds, especially considering your application can go back to processing once the 10ms call to setModel() returns.

The call to setPrototypeCellValue() optimizes the display of the list by allowing Swing to precompute the sizes of the cells in the list. If this call is not made, then Swing will query every cell in the list to find out which one is the largest. The cell value passed to setPrototype-CellValue() is used to calculate the size of a single cell, which is then used as the size for all cells.

The other components in Swing also show this type of improvement when used properly. When deciding how fast or slow Swing is, remember that the methods provided for portability from AWT are there for convenience, not because they are the best way to use Swing. For example, when this test is written using this code:

```
void fillButtonActionPerformed(ActionEvent e) {
  String[] strings = new String[10000];
  for (int i = 0; i < 10000; i++)
  {
    strings[i] = "bob" + i;
  }
  long tmStart = System.currentTimeMillis();
  for (int j = 0; j < 10000; j++)
  {
    ((DefaultListModel)list1.getModel()).addElement(strings[j]);
  }
  long tmEnd = System.currentTimeMillis();
  System.out.println(tmEnd - tmStart);
}
```

it takes over *3 minutes* to run.

Explaining the extremely slow benchmark result requires understanding how the Model informs the View that it has changed. Notice that in the flawed benchmark test the Model was retrieved from the JList using getModel(). Since the Model was already attached to the list, the list had registered itself as a listener on the ListModel for ListDataEvents. So, every time a new element was added to the model using addElement(), a new ListDataEvent was sent to the list informing it that the model had changed. So that test wasn't only copying 10,000 Strings, it was also causing 10,000 event notifications to be triggered. In the correct benchmark code, no Strings were copied, and only one event message was triggered. Because of this behavior, it is always better to detach the current model from the view (by setting the model to null) before performing bulk operations on it, or create a new model instance, modify it, and then attach the new model to the view. For small or intermittent changes to a model it is safe to modify it while it is still attached to the view.

As you can clearly see, Swing is a very powerful tool where it pays to remember it is not AWT. Save the AWT methods for quick ports of existing code where you can later optimize by using Swing properly. When starting from scratch, use Swing's proper constructs and methods.

C H A P T E R   2

Into the Swing of things

The biggest limitation for Java developers in developing professional applications was its extremely restricted set of components. In implementing AWT to use the native controls of the platform, the AWT development team was forced into supplying only a very basic set. It was almost impossible to write more than a toy graphical Java application without resorting to custom controls. Swing changes Java's user interface components from toys into tools.

2.1   Swing controls similar to those in AWT

Since Swing was designed to allow for easy portability from AWT, Swing contains many components that are direct replacements for those in AWT (table 2.1).

Table 2.1   AWT components and their Swing replacements

AWT Component	Swing Component
Applet	JApplet
Button	JButton
Checkbox	JCheckBox
CheckboxGroup	ButtonGroup
Choice	JComboBox
Component	JComponent
Frame	JFrame
Label	JLabel
List	JList
Menu	JMenu
MenuItem	JMenuItem
Panel	JPanel
PopupMenu	JPopupMenu
ScrollBar	JScrollBar
ScrollPane	JScrollPane
TextArea	JTextArea
TextField	JTextField and JPasswordField

Swing makes a standard change to all controls that needs to be discussed before examining even the basic components. Components in Swing do not support scrolling directly, even if their AWT counterparts did. The way scrolling is implemented in Swing is for components to implement the Scrollable interface (p.433). This interface provides methods that a JScrollPane (p.332) will call on the component to get the information it needs to configure itself properly. This makes scrolling support in Swing standard across all components. So don't be surprised when your JList won't show a scroll bar; just put the JList into a JScrollPane and it will behave the way you expect.

2.2 Basic components in Swing

The Swing component hierarchy has many significant changes from the hierarchy in AWT. Some of these changes are simple additions of new components. Others are reorganizations that greatly improve the code sharing, functionality, and flexibility of Swing over AWT.

2.2.1 JComponent

Just as `Component` is the parent of all other components in AWT, `JComponent` (p.207) is the ancestor of all Swing components. Taking advantage of this fact, the Swing team added many new features to `JComponent`, which, in turn, apply to all of its children. `JComponent` contains the support for the pluggable look and feel, improved keyboard shortcut handling, borders, ToolTips, and the Accessibility API.

Pluggable look and feels are supported through the `JComponent` methods `getUIClassID()`, `updateUI()`, and `setUI()`. Chances are that you will never use any of these methods unless you are creating your own look and feel.

The new keyboard shortcut handling is a great improvement over what was provided in AWT. You can now assign a shortcut key to any component, and specify when the component will be able to receive the event. You can choose to have the component receive the action event when it has the focus, when a parent component has the focus, or when a parent window has the focus. You can also make a button the default button in a parent container.

Another improvement in Swing is the handling of focus switching (also known as the tab order). In the AWT the only way to control the tab order of components was the order in which they were added to the container. `JComponent`'s `setNextFocusableComponent()` method can be used to explicitly set the component to which the focus will switch next. This is very useful since the tab order can now change dynamically; for example, when components are added to or removed from an existing container.

`Borders` are powerful tools for customizing the look of your application without writing a full look and feel. Any component can have a border added to it, or have its default border changed. There are several borders available, from lines to 3D effects.

ToolTips have become a fixture in modern user interfaces. They provide a convenient way to add text to small buttons or controls without having to display the text all of the time. ToolTips were tricky to implement with AWT, so having them be standard in Swing is a boon. Any component, from buttons to elements in a `JTree`, can have a ToolTip.

`JComponents` have properties, which provide a convenient place to store instance-specific data about a component. Any `Object` can be stored into a property, and properties are set and retrieved using names as keys.

`JComponent` supplies several methods that can be used to enhance the rendering and custom development of controls. The `isOpaque()` method allows a component to declare that it fills its entire drawing area. If `isOpaque()` returns `true`, `JComponent` by default fills the background of the component with the background color. When `isOpaque()` returns `false`, the component is transparent. When a component is transparent, its background is not filled, and the components underneath the component are not clipped against the boundaries of the transparent component (allowing them to show through). `JComponent` also allows components to declare that they tile their children (any children the component has will not overlap). Tiling child components greatly improves the speed at which a component can be drawn. Lastly, `JComponent` provides support for `DebugGraphics`. The `DebugGraphics` support, when enabled, paints a component very slowly, highlighting each drawing operation in a specific color (which defaults to red). This feature allows component developers to see where drawing problems are occurring, and to also see places in the drawing process that could be optimized.

The Accessibility API is significant enough to warrant its own chapter. A significant proportion of the population has been prevented from participating in the computer revolution due to the limitations the GUI places on assistive devices like screen readers and alternate input technologies. It is a long overdue advance for making computers and electronic devices truly user friendly for all users.

2.2.2 JFrame and JDialog

`JFrame`s (p.248) are probably the first thing that trip up novice Swing programmers. To support some advanced features, the Swing team had to change how to add components to a `JFrame`. Instead of calling `add()` directly on the frame instance, developers have to call `getContentPane().add()`. The reason for this change is the `JFrame` contains a `JRootPane` (p.323) by default. A `JRootPane` is comprised of a content pane, a glass pane, and, possibly, a menu bar. The content pane is the normal place to add components and set layout managers. The purpose of the glass pane is to provide a place where components can be added that will always be on top of whatever else is in the window.

In a welcome change from AWT `Frame`s, the default layout manager for the content pane of a `JFrame` is a `BorderLayout`.

Another major change to `JFrame`s is that they now have a "default close operation." There are three constants that can be set to change this behavior. The three constants, and the behavior they cause are:

- `DO_NOTHING_ON_CLOSE`—informs the `WindowListeners` and does nothing further. The hiding and disposing of the frame must be done through the `windowClosing()` method of one of the listeners.

- `HIDE_ON_CLOSE`—informs any `WindowListeners` and then hides the frame. The frame must be disposed of by one of the listeners in its `windowClosing()` method.

- `DISPOSE_ON_CLOSE`—informs any `WindowListeners` and then automatically hides and disposes of the frame.

The default behavior is HIDE_ON_CLOSE. Usually you will want to change the default to DISPOSE_ON_CLOSE using setDefaultCloseBehavior().

JFrames are created invisible and need to have setVisible(true) called on them to make them appear.

The following code fragment illustrates the normal way a JFrame is created and configured:

```
...
ResourceBundle res = new ResourceBundle("StringResources");
JFrame mainFrame = new JFrame(res.getString("APPLICATION_TITLE"));
mainFrame.setDefaultCloseOperation(JFrame.DISPOSE_ON_CLOSE);
mainFrame.addWindowListener(new WindowAdapter() {
   public void windowClosed(WindowEvent e) {
      System.exit(0);
   }
}
mainFrame.setVisible(true);
...
```

2.2.3 JPanel

JPanel (p.305) is a lightweight container that supports double buffering. Considering how often developers had to write double-buffering code in AWT to prevent flickering, it is truly a relief to have it transparently supported. Double buffering can be enabled either as part of the constructor of JPanel or through the JComponent method setDoubleBuffered(boolean). Double buffering is enabled by default. Otherwise JPanels do not differ significantly from AWT Panels. The defaults for JPanels are a FlowLayout layout manager and they are opaque.

As of Swing 1.1, JPanels support pluggable look and feel.

2.2.4 JButton

Buttons in Swing are much improved over AWT. The button hierarchy (figure 2.1) has been changed, with several new button types being added and the functionality common to all buttons moved into an AbstractButton (p.118) superclass.

AbstractButton has several new features, most notably the ability to add an Icon (p.183) to the button. Seven different Icons can be added to a button, one each for the normal, pressed, rollover (the mouse pointer is over the button), rollover selected, selected, disabled, and disabled

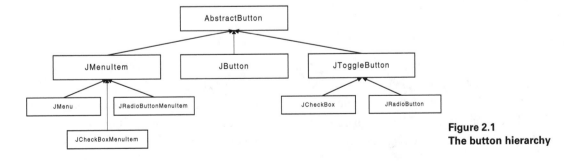

Figure 2.1
The button hierarchy

selected states. The normal state `Icon` can be set in the constructor. All of the other `Icons` must be set by calling the appropriate method inherited from `AbstractButton`. If a disabled `Icon` is not set, Swing will generate a default one by applying a graying filter to the normal state `Icon`.

The relative positions of the `Icon` and text on the button can be changed using the `horizontalAlignment`, `verticalAlignment`, `horizontalTextPosition`, and `verticalTextPosition` JavaBeans properties. The possible values for the horizontal alignment are `SwingConstants.LEFT` (left sides of the text and `Icon` are aligned), `SwingConstants.CENTER` (the default, with the center of the text and `Icon` aligned), `SwingConstants.RIGHT` (right sides of the text and `Icon` aligned), `SwingConstants.LEADING`, and `SwingConstants.TRAILING`. `LEADING` and `TRAILING` are new in Swing 1.1 and are supplied for internationalization, because languages can be read different directions. `LEADING` indicates that the beginning of the text is aligned with the `Icon` (for a left-to-right language like English, this matches `LEFT`, while for a right-to-left language this matches `RIGHT`). `TRAILING` indicates that the end of the text is aligned with the `Icon`. You should almost always use `LEADING` or `TRAILING` in preference to `LEFT` or `RIGHT`, since the alignment will work properly whether the application is internationalized or not.

For the vertical alignment, use `SwingConstants.TOP`, `SwingConstants.CENTER` (the default), and `SwingConstants.BOTTOM`. The same constants are also used for the position properties, but indicate where the text is in the button. The default value for the horizontal position is `RIGHT`.

`AbstractButton` also gives its children the ability to have a mnemonic character. This is the character that will trigger the button when it is pressed on the keyboard.

Another useful feature of `AbstractButton` is the `doClick()` method which triggers the button as if it had been pressed by the user. It is important to note that `doClick()` causes an `ActionEvent` to be sent to the listeners, while `setSelected()` does not.

```
...
ResourceBundle res = new ResourceBundle("Strings");
JButton printButton = new JButton(res.getString("PRINT"),
                new ImageIcon(getClass().getResource("images/printer.gif")));
printButton.setActionCommand("PRINT");
printButton.setMnemonic('p');
printButton.addActionListener(new ActionListener() {
   public void actionPerformed(ActionEvent e) {
     doPrint();
   }
}
...
```

Along with the normal `JButton` (p.191), Swing provides `JToggleButton` (p.385), `JRadioButton` (p.319), `JCheckBox` (p.193), and `JMenuItem` (p.291) as part of the button hierarchy.

`JToggleButton` (figure 2.2) is a new component which provides a button that is sticky. Each time the button is pressed, the button's action event is broadcast. To work with a toggle button you can either keep a `boolean` flag that you change the value of every time the `actionPerformed()`

Figure 2.2   A JToggleButton and two JButtons. The underlined characters are their mnemonics.

method is called or you can query the button's model for its state. The primary difference between a `JToggleButton` and a `JCheckBox` (or `JRadioButton`) is that a `JToggle-Button` looks like a normal `JButton` while the `JCheckBox` (or `JRadioButton`) has a distinct appearance.

A `JRadioButton` and a `JCheckBox` are quite similar in that they represent buttons which visually display one of two states. The main difference (besides the visual differences) is how they behave in a `ButtonGroup` (p.146). When added to a `ButtonGroup` with the group's `add()` method, only one `JRadioButton` in the group may be selected at a time. When one `JRadioButton` is selected, the previously selected button is deselected. Any number of `JCheckBoxes` in a `ButtonGroup` may be selected at the same time.

Figure 2.3   Three JCheckBoxes

When working with a `JCheckBox` (figure 2.3), you will want to add `ItemListeners`, not `ActionListeners`, to the `JCheckBoxes`. While an `ActionEvent` is sent every time the `JCheckBox` is clicked, what you really want to know is the selection state. An `ItemListener` is designed to give you this information. If you used an `ActionListener` you would need to check the selection state of the button every time you got an `ActionEvent`.

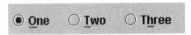

Figure 2.4   Three JRadioButtons in a ButtonGroup

A group of `JRadioButtons` only requires a single `ActionListener` instance which is added to all of the `JRadioButtons` in the same group (figure 2.4). Since only one `JRadioButton` in the group may be selected, all you need to do when you get an `ActionEvent` is ask the `ButtonGroup` (p.146) for the new selected item using the `getSelection()` method. The `getSelection()` method returns a `ButtonModel` (p.147) instance which is the model of the selected button.

2.2.5 JMenu

`JMenus` (p.281) are significantly different from `Menus` (figure 2.5) in AWT. The primary difference is that menus are now part of the `JComponent` hierarchy, unlike AWT menus which were not `Components`. In fact, menus in Swing are part of the `AbstractButton` hierarchy. Menus are generally added to a `JMenuBar` (p.288), unless they are `JPopupMenus` (p.309), in which case they can appear anywhere.

Making menus part of the `JComponent` hierarchy has some significant advantages. For one, menus can now be added to any container, not just the frame. If you have ever wanted your applets to have a menu, `JApplet` (p.186) gives you your chance. `JMenus` can also be added to `JDialogs` and `JInternalFrames`. For that matter they may be added to any class derived from `java.awt.Container` (though doing this is not really a good idea, since it is disturbing for the user. If you need a menu in a nontraditional container, use a `JPopupMenu`).

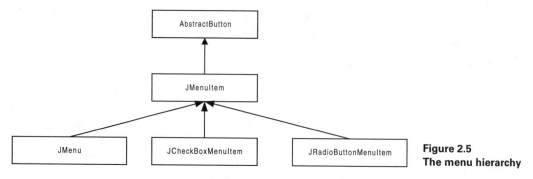

Figure 2.5
The menu hierarchy

To add a menu to a `JFrame`/`JApplet`/`JInternalFrame`/`JDialog`, use the common `set-JMenuBar()` method. This method uses the `JRootPane` contained in these classes to add the menu bar to the top of the window area.

A `JMenu` can contain five different kinds of items: `JMenuItems` (p.291), other `JMenus`, `JRadioButtonMenuItems` (p.321), `JCheckBoxMenuItems` (p.195), and arbitrary `Components`. The first four are far and away the most common, with the last being present for those rare times when the other four just won't do.

Figure 2.6   A Swing menu with JMenuItems

A `JMenuItem` (figure 2.6) is very similar to a `JButton` in functionality. Since it is also derived from `AbstractButton`, it shares many of the features provided by that class with `JButton`. The major differences in behavior are `JMenuItem` supporting the `MenuElement` interface (p.425) and `JMenuItem` supporting the concept of an accelerator key. The `MenuElement` interface provides the methods required for programmatically navigating parts of a menu in a generic way. It is used by the key- and mouse-event processing methods so that the currently selected menu can be represented as a path of `MenuElements`. An accelerator key is a `KeyStroke` (p.419) that will trigger the associated menu item even if the menu is not showing. This differs from a mnemonic (which `JMenuItem` and `JButton` both support) in that the mnemonic can only be used if the menu item is being displayed. An accelerator will usually be a combination of a character with the CTRL, SHIFT, META, or ALT keys, rather than just a single character, to prevent it from being triggered by accident.

`JRadioButtonMenuItems` are similar to `JRadioButtons` in that when more than one `JRadioButtonMenuItem` is added to a `ButtonGroup` only one can be selected at a time.

Similarly, a `JCheckBoxMenuItem` corresponds to a `JCheckBox`.

2.2.6 JList and JComboBox

After `JFrame`, `JList`, and `JComboBox` (figure 2.7) are most likely the next places where you will notice the changes Swing brings.

`JList` gets your attention by not supporting scrolling directly. Like all components in Swing, to support scrolling the `JList` must be contained in a `JScrollPane`. The pop-up for the

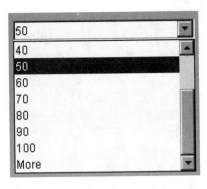

Figure 2.7   JComboBox

JComboBox *does* support scrolling by itself, thankfully (it would be very difficult to add a JScrollPane around a component created internally by the JComboBox!).

JList and JComboBox are also the first places where you will be likely to implement your own ListModel or ComboBoxModel. Instead of copying data from your application's data to the list component, it is much more efficient to write an implementor of ListModel. The ListModel wraps the way the data is stored in your application so the JList can work directly with the data. Suddenly your application is only using the memory for one set of data, not two. Another reason for implementing a ListModel is that the methods supplied by JList or JComboBox do not allow for a mutable (changeable) list of data. So, if you want to change the contents of the list you *have* to write your own model. Swing provides an AbstractListModel (p.127), a DefaultListModel (p.172), and a DefaultComboBoxModel (p.166) to make development easier.

Another new feature of Swing is the selection model. Instead of the component managing the selection directly, it delegates the responsibility to a ListSelectionModel (p.421). The selection model can be changed using the setSelectionModel() method. Generally you will not need to do this, because the setSelectionMode() (note "mode," not "model") method will do what you want. This method changes the behavior of the current selection model. The setSelectionMode() method takes one of three constants:

- ListSelectionModel.MULTIPLE_INTERVAL_SELECTION—multiple selected items are allowed and they do not need to belong to a contiguous section of the list (i.e. items 1, 4, 6, 7, and 8).

- ListSelectionModel.SINGLE_INTERVAL_SELECTION—multiple selected items are allowed but they must belong to a contiguous section of the list (i.e. items 4, 5, and 6).

- ListSelectionModel.SINGLE_SELECTION—only a single item in the list may be selected.

JComboBox is implemented using a ComboBoxModel (which extends ListModel), adding the concept of the selected item (the item that is in the text field of the JComboBox). JComboBoxes may allow for editing the entry in the text field (and also adding new items by typing them into the text field) by calling setEditable(true). A JComboBox defaults to being noneditable.

2.2.7 *JTextField and JTextArea*

JTextField (p.379) and JTextArea (p.374) are the basic text editing controls in Swing. Their underlying model is a Document (p.826), which will be explained in more detail later. For AWT compatibility they can be constructed using a String and they both have the getText(String) and setText(String) methods.

`JTextField` is a single-line text entry box. By default it only allows a single font. To control what portion of the text is visible in the field a `JTextField` uses a `BoundedRangeModel` (p.132). Horizontal alignment of the text in the field is controlled by the `setHorizontalAlignment()` and `getHorizontalAlignment()` methods.

Swing's `JTextField` does *not* support a `TextListener`, unlike the `java.awt.TextArea`. To listen for changes in the `JTextArea` you must add a `DocumentListener` (p.490) to the model returned by the `getModel()` call. A `DocumentEvent` (p.489) is sent in response to any change and contains the location and type of the change.

Customizing a `JTextField` is quite easy, but also quite different than how a `TextField` was customized. To customize a `JTextField` you change the model it is using instead of trying to intercept the keystrokes. Usually all you need to override is the `insertString()` method of the `Document` interface.

The following example illustrates how a `JTextField` which converts its contents to upper case might be implemented:

```
public class UpperField extends JTextField {

  public UpperField(int cols) {
    super(cols);
  }

  protected Document createDefaultModel() {
    return new UpperDocument();
  }

  static class UpperDocument extends PlainDocument {
    public void insertString(int offs, String str, AttributeSet a)
            throws BadLocationException
    {
      // if the String is null, there is nothing to do
      if (str == null) {
        return;
      }
      // Convert the String to upper case
      String uString = str.toUpperCase();
      // Insert the converted String into the document
      super.insertString(offs, uString, a);
    }
  }
}
```

Do not use this method to try to create a password field. Swing supplies the `JPassword-Field` (p.306) class that is designed for that purpose (it blocks copying its text to the clipboard).

`JTextArea` is a multiline edit box that supports a single font. `JTextArea` does not support scrolling directly instead, it implements the `Scrollable` interface that `JScrollPane` uses to set itself up properly.

`JTextArea` supports word wrapping that can be turned on by calling `setLineWrap(true)`. The default wrapping is probably not what you'd expect, in that it breaks the lines at the last character that will fit, instead of breaking the line at the nearest white space. To turn on breaking at white space, call `setWrapStyleWord(true)`.

```
...
JTextArea textEdit = new JTextArea();
textEdit.setLineWrap(true);
textEdit.setWrapStyleWord(true);
JScrollPane scroller = new JScrollPane(textEdit);
JPanel panel = new JPanel(scroller);
...
```

A `JTextArea` can be customized in the same way as a `JTextField`. You usually won't do that, though, since if you want a more advanced text editor you will use one of Swing's new, advanced editors (see page 46).

`JTextField` and `JTextArea` both share a new concept in Swing, the concept of using `Actions` to trigger behaviors in the component. `Actions` will be explained in more detail later.

2.2.8 JApplet

`JApplet` (p.186) exists so that applets can take advantage of the same `JRootPane` (p.323) support that `JFrames` and `JDialogs` have. The main advantage of this support is the ability to add a `JMenuBar` to the applet. There are a few other reasons related to `SecurityManager` issues as well, but don't worry about them since `JApplet` works around them. Use `JApplet` to implement applets that need to use Swing components, and everything will work as expected.

In browsers that support only JDK 1.1, use the Swing implementation for JDK 1.1. This Swing package is written to use only JDK 1.1 classes and is designed to work in both Netscape Communicator/Navigator 4 with the Java 1.1 update and Microsoft Internet Explorer 4. If you are writing for a browser that supports JDK 1.2 either natively or through Sun's new Java Plugin technology that lets the major browsers use the Sun JDK, you can use the implementation that is part of JDK 1.2. As of Swing 1.1 the class names between both implementations are the same. The JDK 1.2 implementation of Swing simply takes advantage of new features supplied by Java2D and other parts of JDK 1.2.

2.3   Going pro: advanced Swing

2.3.1 A simple application

The following simple application illustrates a number of the new features in Swing. The features will be described briefly to explain the example. The rest of this section is devoted to more detailed explanations.

```
/**********************************************
/* File: SimpleApplication\SimpleApp.java
```

```
/********************************************/
package SimpleApplication;

// Uncomment the following line for Swing 1.0.3 or before
//import com.sun.java.swing.UIManager;
// Uncomment the following line for Swing 1.1
import javax.swing.UIManager;

public class SimpleApp {
   public SimpleApp()
   {
      MainFrame frame = new MainFrame();
      frame.setVisible(true);
   }

   public static void main(String[] args)
   {
      try {
         // setLookAndFeel can throw a number of different exceptions
         // so it needs to be in a try block.
         UIManager.setLookAndFeel(UIManager.getSystemLookAndFeelClassName());
      }
      catch (Exception e)
      {
      }
      new SimpleApp();
   }
}
```

The interesting feature of this example is the use of UIManager.setLookAndFeel(), using the return value from UIManager.getSystemLookAndFeelClassName() as its parameter. All Swing applications should begin with this method call since it sets up the correct look and feel for the platform hosting the application. It is a safe call to make on all platforms, since, if it fails, the look and feel that gets set is Metal, which would have been set if the call weren't made at all. The call to getSystemLookAndFeelClassName() asks all of the look and feels that the UIManager has registered if this platform is their native platform. If the native look and feel is found, the classname of that look and feel is returned and used to set the look and feel. If none of the look and feels declare that it is the native one for this platform, this method call returns the class name of the default cross platform look and feel, the Java look and feel (also known as Metal). Using this exact method call ensures that your application looks the best that it can for the platform on which it is executing.

```
/********************************************
/* File: SimpleApplication/MainFrame.java
/********************************************/
package SimpleApplication;

import java.awt.*;
import java.awt.event.*;
import java.beans.PropertyChangeListener;
```

```
      System.exit(0);
   }
}

/*********************************************************
/* File: SimpleApplication\ExitAction.java
/*******************************************************/
package SimpleApplication;

import java.awt.event.*;
// Uncomment the following line for Swing 1.0.3 or before
//import com.sun.java.swing.*;
// Uncomment the following line for Swing 1.1
import javax.swing.*;

public class ExitAction extends AbstractAction
{
   private JFrame frame = null;

   public ExitAction() {
      putValue(Action.LONG_DESCRIPTION, "Exit the application");
      putValue(Action.NAME, "Exit");
      ImageIcon image1 = new ImageIcon(
                          getClass().getResource("blue-ball.gif"));
      putValue(Action.SMALL_ICON, image1);
   }

   public ExitAction(JFrame frame)
   {
      this();
      this.frame = frame;
   }

   public void actionPerformed(ActionEvent e)
   {
      if (frame != null) frame.dispose();
      System.exit(0);
   }
}
```

ExitAction is the Action that is added to the menu bar and toolbar in the second section of the above application. As you can see there is very little to it, since AbstractAction implements most of the required code to support the Action interface for you. The constructor of ExitAction sets up its property table with several items. The Action interface defines several constants that can be used as keys when adding items to the Action's property table. The two properties that are understood by both JMenu and JToolBar when creating a child based on an Action are Action.SMALL_ICON and Action.NAME. If you re-examine the second section of code you will notice that using the Action.LONG_DESCRIPTION property for a JToolTip on the toolbar button had to be done manually. Also notice the implementation of actionPerformed(). This method will be called when either of the menu items of the toolbar button is selected, so it is ideal for maintaining a common behavior for both.

This last section of code also introduces `ImageIcons`, which are explained in more detail below.

2.4 It don't mean a thing if it ain't got that Swing

Swing introduces several capabilities beyond just adding new controls. Since they are supported by many Swing components, they will be covered first.

2.4.1 Icons

Graphics have become very important in Swing. The Swing team recognized that imagery is very fundamental to a usable, appealing user interface, so they added support for the `Icon` interface to most components.

The `Icon` (p.183) interface contains three methods. Two are for returning the width and the height of the image. The other allows the component to ask the `Icon` to draw itself at a specific location.

Swing has one concrete implementation of the `Icon` interface—the `ImageIcon`. This class wraps the standard `java.awt.Image` class in the `Icon` interface. `ImageIcons` can be created using any of the following: a byte array, a pre-existing `Image`, a filename, or a URL. `ImageIcon` can also handle animated images.

The `Icon` interface is much more flexible than `java.awt.Image` since a class can implement the `paintIcon()` method in any way it sees fit. This means that a class could simply draw the `Icon` without needing an associated GIF or JPEG. Many of the controls supplied by the various look and feels are written this way.

2.4.2 Actions

`Action` (p.128) is a convenience interface provided to support holding the information needed for controls that trigger `ActionEvents` and also provide a common place to implement the `actionPerformed()` method for the controls. The two places Swing provides support for `Actions` are in `JMenus` and `JToolBars`. `Actions` can also be retrieved from the text components (`JTextField`, `JTextArea`, `JEditorPane`) so applications can control them programmatically. `Actions` hold arbitrary data identified by `String` keys but usually you will only use the keys that are predefined in the interface `Action`. These predefined keys allow you to store a short name, a long description (for ToolTips), and a small `Icon` (usually 16x16 pixels).

To work with `Actions`, you can either create a subclass of `AbstractAction`, or create a class that implements `Action` directly. `AbstractAction` provides convenience methods to set the default fields and support `PropertyChangeListeners`, so all that remains to be added is an implementation of the `actionPerformed()` method (since `Action` implements `ActionListener`).

There is no way to directly create a `JToolBar` (p.388) button or a `JMenuItem` (p.291) using an `Action`. To create one of these components using an `Action` you add the `Action` to the parent `JMenu` or `JToolBar`. The parent will then create the appropriate control using the information from the `Action`. The control will also add itself to the `Action` as a `PropertyChangeListener` so the control can be enabled or disabled based on the enabled/disabled state of the `Action`. In return, the `Action` is registered as an `ActionListener` on the control so its `actionPerformed()` method gets called when the control is selected. If you want to further modify the properties of the created `JMenuItem` or `JButton`, you need to keep the reference returned by the call to `JMenu.add(Action)` or `JToolBar.add(Action)`.

The same `Action` can be used to create both a toolbar button and a menu item. This is very helpful, since then the menu item and toolbar button can be enabled or disabled at the same time by changing the state of the `Action`. The `Action` also provides a common place to handle the `ActionEvents` from both controls, so the controls behave exactly the same.

2.4.3 Borders

All components in Swing support `Borders` (p.465). `JComponent` supplies two methods, `getBorder()` and `setBorder(Border)`, to change the border on a component.

The `Border` interface and several implementations are in the `swing.border` package. `Borders` have a useful characteristic in that they can be shared among components. Most of the methods in `Border` take a `JComponent`, which allows them to discover the information they need to render themselves when they need it.

Swing provides several `Border` implementations, all defined in the `swing.border` package. The borders it supplies are the common ones used in standard user interfaces, such as single-pixel width lines, 3D lines, etched lines, and titled borders. It also supplies a `CompoundBorder` (p.466) which can be used to combine borders to form a more complex border.

There is a class in the Swing package called `BorderFactory` (p.129) that should be used where possible to get instances of the different `Borders`. As a factory class it creates shared instances of the different borders.

In a significant change from AWT components, Swing components actually define their insets in terms of their border. You shouldn't call `setInsets()` on a Swing component. Create an `EmptyBorder` instead, and make it the border of the component. To support this change, the `getInsets()` method is overridden by `JComponent` to call its border's `getBorderInsets()` method. This change was required due to the border of a component occupying space that previously would have been reserved by the insets.

`AbstractBorder` is supplied to simplify creating your own borders. Subclassing from this class means that you only have to implement three methods. The `paintBorder()` method is the primary method, since it is responsible for drawing the border. The other two are `getBorderInsets()` and `isBorderOpaque()`.

You do need to be careful when using borders, since some components (such as buttons) have borders that implement look and feel-specific behaviors. It is safe to arbitrarily change the border of a JPanel or derivative. See the "Other Keys" table in Appendix B (p.1017) to find these look and feel-specific borders.

```
// Uncomment the following line for Swing 1.0.3 or before
//import com.sun.java.swing.border.*;
// Uncomment the following line for Swing 1.1
import javax.swing.border.*;
import java.awt.*;

public class RedLineBorder extends AbstractBorder
{
   public RedLineBorder() {
   }

   public void paintBorder(Component c, Graphics g, int x, int y, int width,
     int height)
   {
     g.setColor(Color.red);
     g.drawRect(x, y, width-1, height-1);
   }

   public Insets getBorderInsets(Component c) {
     return new Insets(1,1,1,1);
   }

   public boolean isBorderOpaque() {
     return false;
   }
}
```

2.4.4 Scrollable

As you will quickly notice, Swing components do not natively support scrolling. In a remarkable example of the efficiency that can be gained through using good object-oriented design, all components in Swing use the JScrollPane (p.332) component to enable scrolling.

To support scrolling, all a component has to do is implement the Scrollable (p.433) interface. This interface supplies several methods to set up the JScrollPane properly.

There are four important methods in Scrollable; the fifth is irrelevant depending on the parent container's layout manager. The four methods are:

- int getScrollableBlockIncrement(java.awt.Rectangle visibleSize, int orientation, int direction)

  This method allows components that display logical rows or columns (a table or a text editor, for example) to scroll by a page. A reasonable value to return from this method for vertical scrolling is (visibleSize.height / rowHeight) * rowHeight, which scrolls a distance equal to the height of all of the full rows in the viewport. If the component doesn't display logical rows or columns, have this method return a value that is approximately three-fourths of the visibleSize. That way there still is a piece of the previous view visible afterwards, so the user doesn't lose his or her bearings on where they are in the component.

- `boolean getScrollableTracksViewportHeight()`,
  `boolean getScrollableTracksViewportWidth()`

  These methods let the `JScrollPane`'s `JViewport` know in which direction it needs to scroll. If you return `true` from one or both of these methods the component in the viewport will squash or stretch to match the height or width of the visible area of the `JScrollPane`, instead of allowing scrolling. A `JComboBox`'s drop-down would be an example of a component that would return `true` from `getScrollableTracksViewportWidth()` and `false` from `getScrollableTracksViewportHeight()`, since it should only be able to scroll vertically.

- `int getScrollableUnitIncrement(Rectangle visibleSize,`
  `int orientation, int direction)`

  This method returns the distance (in pixels) used for scrolling one line. Try to not return 1 from this method, since most users find one pixel scrolling far too slow. Use a reasonable value like one-fourth of the `visibleSize`, or one-twentieth of the total size of what you are scrolling. Users generally don't want to click several hundred times, or hold the mouse button down for an interminable length of time trying to get from one end of the data to the other.

2.5   The new containers

2.5.1 JLayeredPane

This component is much more useful than it would initially appear. To understand how important it is requires remembering that there isn't any easy way to control the Z-order (stacking) of components in Java after the components have been added. That is the void that `JLayeredPane` (p.268) fills.

   `JLayeredPane` allows components to be added to specific layers, indicated by `Integers`. When this pane is painted, it forces the layers to be drawn from bottom to top, or vice versa. Components can be moved from layer to layer by calling the `setLayer(Component, Integer)` method on the `JLayeredPane`. `JLayeredPane` also allows for having components that float on top of all of the other components in an application, by adding the component to a high-numbered pane.

   There are several constants defined in `JLayeredPane` to indicate commonly used layers. The constants define the following layers (from back to front):

- `FRAME_CONTENT_LAYER`—always the furthest back pane, with an `Integer` value of `-30000`. This layer is used by `JRootPane` for the components you would normally consider to be part of the window, such as the `JMenuBar`. You should probably never use this layer.

- `DEFAULT_LAYER`—the standard layer. Most components should go here.

- `PALETTE_LAYER`—the layer for floating toolbars and palettes.

- MODAL_LAYER—the layer for modal dialogs. Using this layer ensures the dialog is not obscured by another component.

- POPUP_LAYER—the pop-up layer is used by components such as JComboBox's pop-up list. This layer's level is such that the pop-up will appear in front if the JComboBox is in a modal dialog.

- DRAG_LAYER—the highest layer of all. Components in this layer appear in front of all other components that are not in the DRAG_LAYER. It is called the DRAG_LAYER since this behavior is what is needed during drag-and-drop operations.

Components can be added to a specific layer by passing the layer Integer as the constraint to the JLayeredPane.add() call. After they have been added they can be moved between layers using the setLayer() method.

Within a single layer, components can be stacked relative to each other using the moveTo-Front(), moveToBack(), and setPosition() methods. The setPosition() method takes an int ranging from –1 to one less than the number of components in the same layer. –1 specifies the bottom (back) position and 0 is always the top (front). For the other allowed values, the higher-numbered components appear *behind* the lower-numbered components.

It is important to remember that the components in the JLayeredPane are still all in the same container, so if a layout manager is set on the JLayeredPane all components will be arranged by it irregardless of their layers.

2.5.2 JDesktopPane

JDesktopPane (p.224) is a welcome addition to Java's containers. A desktop pane, in general terms, is a JLayeredPane (p.268) that supports windows inside itself and provides a manager class to handle JInternalFrames (p.254). For those familiar with Microsoft Windows, this allows a developer to implement the Multiple Document Interface (MDI) style of application where the main frame contains secondary frames inside itself.

When a JInternalFrame is placed inside a JDesktopPane, the frame is supposed to delegate all window activities to the DesktopManager (p.180) of the JDesktopPane. A window activity is minimization, maximization, closing, and so forth. This allows the JDesktopPane to manage tasks like showing the JInternalFrame's JDesktopIcon when the frame is minimized and removing the frame from the JDesktopPane when it is closed.

JInternalFrames provide several helper methods for use in JDesktopPanes (actually, the methods will work in all JLayeredPanes, but they are intended for JDesktopPanes). The more useful of these methods are toFront() and toBack(), which move the JInternalFrame to the front or the back of the Z-order. Note that this reordering is only relative to the other components in the same layer so floating toolbars in the PALETTE_LAYER would be unaffected by a change in the DEFAULT_LAYER.

Another useful method in `JInternalFrame` is `getDesktopPane()`, which searches the `JInternalFrame`'s parents for the nearest `JDesktopPane`.

When a `JInternalFrame` is minimized, the `JDesktopPane` gets the appropriate `JDesktopIcon` using the `getDesktopIcon()` method of `JInternalFrame`.

2.5.3 JSplitPane

Most recent UIs involve split panes. A split pane provides a split bar (also known as a divider) between components; this divider can be moved to change the relative sizes of the components. Swing supports both horizontal (the components to the right and left) and vertical splitting (the components one on top of the other).

`JSplitPane` (p.346) interacts with the `maximumSize`, `minimumSize`, and `preferredSize` component properties. The `maximumSize` and `minimumSize` act as bounds on how far the divider can be moved. When the user moves the divider to a point that one of the components reaches its minimum or maximum size, the divider will not move further. The `JSplitPane` also provides a way to reset the components to their preferred sizes.

Moving the divider will usually be left up to the user, but the divider can also be moved programmatically using the `setDividerLocation()` method. The `setDividerLocation()` method comes in two forms, one which takes a pixel location and one that takes a float value that represents the percentage of the `JSplitPane` allocated to the left or top component.

2.5.4 JTabbedPane

`JTabbedPane` (p.351) is a major improvement over using a `CardLayout`. `JTabbedPane` provides the logic and the means to switch between its child panes, which had to be coded by hand with the `CardLayout`.

New panes or pages are added to the `JTabbedPane` using the `addTab()` or `insertTab()` methods. Each page is indicated by a tab which can contain a `String`, an `Icon`, or both. `JTabbedPane` supports drawing the tabs on any of its four sides.

An application can listen for when tabs are chosen by adding itself as a `ChangeListener` (p.488) on the `JTabbedPane` or on its model. This is useful because the components on pages which have not been shown yet are not yet realized. By listening to the tab `ChangeEvents`, an application can create the pages when they are first shown. If the pages are never shown, the application does not have to incur the overhead of creating them.

Pages in a `JTabbedPane` can be added and removed dynamically using the `addTab()`, `insertTab()`, and `removeTabAt()` methods. Tabs may also be enabled and disabled using the `setEnabledAt()` method.

Tabs also may be colored independently.

2.6   The new components

2.6.1 JTree

JTree (p.393) fills a significant void in the controls supplied by Java. Almost all modern UIs have a need for a tree-type component since displaying hierarchical data is so common.

The two main ways to work with JTree (figure 2.8) are implementing your own Tree-Model (p.987) using the native data formats in your application, or using the DefaultTree-Model (p.975) and implementing the TreeNode (p.988) interface using the data in your application.

TreeModel is a simple interface, with only eight methods to implement. If your data is in the form of a hierarchy, including the ability to manage the interrelationships between the items, implement TreeModel in a wrapper class for your data.

Swing provides two classes that implement TreeNode. DefaultTreeNode implements a tree node that cannot be modified. DefaultMutableTreeNode implements a node that can be modified. Both classes have a data member that holds an Object. To store your data in the tree, you simply put a reference to your data into this data member. When JTree displays the node, TreeNode calls toString() on the data you added to it, so you have to make sure your class' toString() returns a String appropriate for a user to see. This behavior can be overridden using a custom TreeCellRenderer (p.985).

JTree supports TreeCellRenderers (p.985) and TreeCellEditors (p.985), which allow you to change how each node in the tree is drawn and allow you to edit the data in the model for the respective cell.

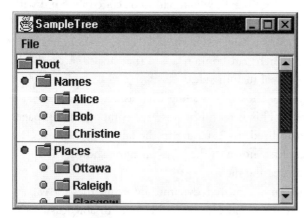

Figure 2.8   A JTree in the metal look and feel

One thing to be careful of with JTree is related to updating the model. To have the JTree reflect the updates made to the model, you must update the tree through the model. For example, if you have used DefaultMutableTree-Nodes to build the model, you have two choices. The first is to use the Default-TreeModel's insert() and remove() methods, not the DefaultMutable-TreeNodes'. The second choice is to update the TreeNodes, create the appropriate update events and then call the fireXXXEvent() methods in the TreeModel. You can call the DefaultTreeModel's reload(TreeNode) method if you are using the DefaultTreeModel, but as its name implies, that method causes the entire tree below the given node to be rebuilt and reset to nonexpanded. After calling reload(), the tree's nodes need to be reset to their previous expansion state. The overhead from calling `reload()` greatly outweighs the simplicity of the reload call, so try using the appropriate events.

The following example shows how to use a `JTree` to browse a `UIDefaults` (p.452) table. The tree uses a custom `TreeModel` to set itself up to display the different categories of UIResources in the `UIDefaults` table as different nodes in the tree.

```java
// File: TreeExample\TreeFrame.java
package TreeExample;

import com.sun.java.swing.*;
import java.awt.*;
import java.awt.event.*;

public class TreeFrame extends JFrame {
  JScrollPane jScrollPane1 = new JScrollPane();
  JTree jTree1 = new JTree(new UIDefaultsTreeModel());
  public TreeFrame() {
    try {
      initUI();
    }
    catch (Exception e)
    {
      e.printStackTrace();
    }
  }

  public static void main(String[] args) {
    TreeFrame treeFrame1 = new TreeFrame();
    treeFrame1.setVisible(true);
  }

  private void initUI() throws Exception {
    this.setSize(new Dimension(400,300));
    this.addWindowListener(new WindowAdapter() {
      public void windowClosed(WindowEvent e) {
        System.exit(0);
      }
    });
    this.setDefaultCloseOperation(WindowConstants.DISPOSE_ON_CLOSE);
    this.getContentPane().add(jScrollPane1, BorderLayout.CENTER);
    jScrollPane1.getViewport().add(jTree1, null);
  }
}

// File: TreeExample\UIDefaultsTreeModel.java
package TreeExample;

import java.util.*;
import com.sun.java.swing.*;
import com.sun.java.swing.tree.*;
import com.sun.java.swing.event.TreeModelListener;

public class UIDefaultsTreeModel implements TreeModel {
```

```
DefaultTreeModel innerModel;
DefaultMutableTreeNode rootNode = new DefaultMutableTreeNode("UIDefaults");
DefaultMutableTreeNode colorNode =
        new DefaultMutableTreeNode("Color Resources");
DefaultMutableTreeNode borderNode =
        new DefaultMutableTreeNode("Border Resources");
DefaultMutableTreeNode fontNode =
        new DefaultMutableTreeNode("Font Resources");
DefaultMutableTreeNode iconNode =
        new DefaultMutableTreeNode("Icon Resources");
DefaultMutableTreeNode otherNode =
        new DefaultMutableTreeNode("Other Resources");

public UIDefaultsTreeModel() {
  innerModel = new DefaultTreeModel(rootNode);
  innerModel.insertNodeInto(colorNode, rootNode, 0);
  innerModel.insertNodeInto(borderNode, rootNode, 1);
  innerModel.insertNodeInto(fontNode, rootNode, 2);
  innerModel.insertNodeInto(iconNode, rootNode, 3);
  innerModel.insertNodeInto(otherNode, rootNode, 4);
  UIDefaults defaults = UIManager.getDefaults();
  Enumeration elems = defaults.keys();
  String keyName;
  Object valueForKey;
  while (elems.hasMoreElements()) {
    DefaultMutableTreeNode newKeyNode;
    DefaultMutableTreeNode newValueNode;
    try {
      keyName = (String)elems.nextElement();
      valueForKey = defaults.get(keyName);

      newKeyNode = new DefaultMutableTreeNode(keyName);
      newValueNode = new DefaultMutableTreeNode(valueForKey);

      if (valueForKey instanceof java.awt.Color)
      {
        innerModel.insertNodeInto(newKeyNode, colorNode, 0);
      }
      else if (valueForKey instanceof com.sun.java.swing.border.Border)
      {
        innerModel.insertNodeInto(newKeyNode, borderNode, 0);
      }
      else if (valueForKey instanceof java.awt.Font)
      {
        innerModel.insertNodeInto(newKeyNode, fontNode, 0);
      }
      else if (valueForKey instanceof javax.swing.Icon)
      {
        innerModel.insertNodeInto(newKeyNode, iconNode, 0);
      }
      else
      {
        innerModel.insertNodeInto(newKeyNode, otherNode, 0);
      }
```

```
        innerModel.insertNodeInto(newValueNode, newKeyNode, 0);
    }
    catch (NullPointerException e)
    {
    }
  }
}

// all of these methods delegate to the contained DefaultTreeModel
public Object getRoot() {
  return innerModel.getRoot();
}

public Object getChild(Object parm1, int parm2) {
  return innerModel.getChild(parm1, parm2);
}

public int getChildCount(Object parm1) {
  return innerModel.getChildCount(parm1);
}

public boolean isLeaf(Object parm1) {
  return innerModel.isLeaf(parm1);
}

public void valueForPathChanged(TreePath parm1, Object parm2) {
  innerModel.valueForPathChanged(parm1, parm2);
}

public int getIndexOfChild(Object parm1, Object parm2) {
  return innerModel.getIndexOfChild(parm1, parm2);
}

public void addTreeModelListener(TreeModelListener parm1) {
  innerModel.addTreeModelListener(parm1);
}

public void removeTreeModelListener(TreeModelListener parm1) {
  innerModel.removeTreeModelListener(parm1);
}
}
```

2.6.2 JTable

JTable (p.357) is a very useful component. To understand how to use JTable, it helps to first understand that it is not a spreadsheet. JTable's role is to simply present tabular data.

The columns of a JTable must present data all of one type (or at least data sharing a common base class. By default the common base class is Object).

Selection in a JTable is based on selecting a complete row or column. JTable does support selecting a single cell, but it is defined as being equivalent to simultaneously selecting a row and a column. When just row or column selection is allowed JTable allows for either single or multiple selection, based on the ListSelectionModel (p.421) supplied.

Cells in a JTable are addressed using row and column indexes. An important detail to remember is that because JTable supports reordering the columns in the view (by dragging the column headers) the indexes for the JTable methods may be different than the ones for the model methods. The methods in the model tend to be the least confusing to use since the columns never change their order. Column one in the model is always column one, and column four is always column four. If you find the need to get the column index in the JTable view that corresponds to a given column index in the model, JTable supplies the convertColumnIndexToView() and convertColumnIndexToModel() methods.

To simplify creating data models, Swing provides AbstractTableModel (p.735), which makes it very easy to create a wrapper model class appropriate for your data. In about the same amount of code that is required to copy the data back and forth from a DefaultTableModel (using twice the memory in the process), a wrapper class for the existing data structure used in your application can be created.

The other piece to the JTable puzzle is the TableColumnModel (p.764). Since all columns in a JTable contain the same data type, the behavior of a column can be encapsulated in a single helper class. The TableColumnModel is the model that contains the TableColumns (p.761) for the view. A TableColumn encapsulates all of the attributes of a column in a JTable, from the mapping to a column in the model to the column width, editor, and renderer. When columns are moved around in a JTable, it is actually the TableColumn that gets moved. Since the mapping to the column in the model stored in the TableColumn doesn't change, the moved column still renders the same column. The renderer and editor entries in a TableColumn may be null, in which case the default renderer or editor set in the JTable for the class of data stored in the column will be used. The default editor and renderer is set on a per-class basis for the JTable using the setDefaultRenderer(Class, TableCellRenderer) and setDefaultEditor(Class, TableCellEditor) methods.

TableCellRenderers (p.760) are very useful in improving the professionalism of your application. If you have data that represents a yes or no, true or false concept, then you could choose to use a JCheckBox to represent that item. Or you could use a JLabel subclass to draw an Icon in the column representing the severity of a problem, thereby allowing the user to scan quickly for the fatal problems. A TableCellRenderer is simply any component that gets used to display the contents of a cell. The simplest starting point for implementing a custom TableCellRenderer is the DefaultTableCellRenderer (p.742) class. This class extends JLabel, and supports all of the capabilities of that class.

The real power of JTable appears when you start to use TableCellEditors (p.758). Editors allow the user to change the data in place. If the field were represented by a JCheckBox, the user could click on the cell and have the change in state reflected in the model automatically. In a similar fashion to cell renderers, Swing provides a DefaultCellEditor (p.164) class. This class can act as a wrapper for a JCheckBox, JComboBox, or JTextField editor.

Other ways the drawing of a JTable can be modified are by turning off the grid lines and changing the way the columns automatically resize.

The display of the grid lines can be changed using the setShowGrid(), setShowHorizontalLines(), and setShowVerticalLines() methods. The color of all of the grid lines can be changed using the setGridColor() method.

Column sizing is set either through the constructor or the setAutoResizeMode() method. The parameters this method can take are the following:

- AUTO_RESIZE_ALL_COLUMNS—Resizes all columns equally to fill the space available. If this mode is set the JTable will not scroll horizontally.

- AUTO_RESIZE_LAST_COLUMN—Resizes the last column to fill the space left after all other columns have been created. If this mode is set the JTable will not scroll horizontally.

- AUTO_RESIZE_NEXT_COLUMN—Resizes the column immediately following the column being adjusted. If this mode is set the JTable will not scroll horizontally.

- AUTO_RESIZE_SUBSEQUENT_COLUMNS—Resizes the columns following the column being adjusted. If this mode is set the JTable will not scroll horizontally.

- AUTO_RESIZE_OFF—All columns use their default sizes, or the widths set using their associated TableColumns. If this mode is set the JTable will scroll horizontally as needed.

In any of these modes you can set the width of an individual column by calling

```
TableColumn tc = getColumn(getColumnName(indexOfColumn));
tc.setWidth(desiredWidthInPixels);
```

The demos supplied with Swing provide an excellent view of the capabilities of a JTable. If you have not examined them before, you should take the time to, since that research will save you a great deal of time during your own development.

2.6.3 JToolBar

Figure 2.9   A Swing toolbar

JToolBar (p.388) is a toolbar (figure 2.9) component. It contains a set of JButtons or components added by passing Actions or Components to JToolBar's add() method. When one of the buttons is pressed, the action-Performed() method of the Action is called. For Components which have been added, the buttons behave as if they had simply been added to a container with a BoxLayout.

JToolBar provides a method call, addSeparator(), that adds a gap between controls on the toolbar. The width of the gap can be controlled using the addSeparator(int) method, but you will generally not want to do that so your user interface stays consistent with the look and feel.

A JToolBar can be dragged away from the edge of a window to become a floating window inside the parent container. This floating behavior can be ended by dragging the JToolBar close to one of the edges of the parent container, which causes the toolbar to "dock." The docking code has been written so that the toolbar can be docked to any side of a panel, not just the top. The ability to dock can also be disabled programmatically. When the toolbar is near a place where it can dock, the border changes so that the user has a visual cue. To aid in the dragging of the toolbar, only use JToolBar in containers that use BorderLayout and do not fill any of the other cardinal directions of the layout with components. Add components only to the CENTER. This allows the JToolBar to add() itself to the NORTH, SOUTH, EAST, or WEST as needed.

A JMenu can have the same Action instances added to it as were added to the JToolBar. This lets you add the same Action to both the menu of your application and a toolbar. By doing this, you can have the listener code and enabling/disabling code for both be the exact same code. By using an Action, both the button and the menu stay in perfect sync.

You cannot share a Component on a JToolBar with another container due to the restriction in AWT of not being able to add() a Component to two different containers.

2.6.4 JOptionPane

This new component adds the concept of system message boxes to Java. Using JOptionPane (p.294) allows your application to share the same look and feel for its message boxes.

JOptionPane supplies four different standard message boxes which are created using one of four static methods:

- showConfirmDialog()
- showInputDialog()
- showMessageDialog()
- showOptionDialog()

There are also versions of these functions that create the dialogs inside an internal frame (see JInternalFrame on p.254).

2.6.5 JSlider

Figure 2.10   A JSlider with text and snap-to ticks

JSlider (p.341) (figure 2.10) is the ideal component for allowing users to choose from a range of numeric values. Considering that the only way in AWT to implement this control was to use a Scrollbar, JSlider is an extremely useful component.

The appearance and behavior of a JSlider can be changed to suit how it is being used. For a range of discrete values, the slider knob can be made to snap to the displayed ticks using the setSnapToTicks() method. By default, the JSlider assumes that its maximum value is to the right (or top, depending on the slider's orientation). This default can be changed using the set-Inverted() method.

The values displayed on the ticks are set using the `setLabelTable()` method. This method takes a dictionary (usually a hash table) containing (key, value) pairs where the key is the `Integer` value, and the value is a `Component` used for the label. A `JSlider` may have major and minor tick labels, and may be set so it doesn't show any labels at all using the `setPaintLabels()` method. Similarly, the `JSlider` can be set so it does not paint any ticks using the `setPaintTicks()` method.

`JSlider` provides the utility methods `createStandardLabels(int increment)` and `createStandardLabels(int increment, int startValue)` to help create a hash table which can be used in the `setLabelTable()` method.

2.6.6 JProgressBar

`JProgressBar` (figure 2.11) can be considered a sibling of `JSlider`, since they both represent a value from a range of values. The main difference is that progress bars are read-only. `JProgressBar` exists so that the user interface of the two components can be different.

Since the long operation that the progress bar is representing will usually be running in another thread, it is important to remember the nonthread-safe nature of Swing (see Multithreading and Swing on page 53). To update the state of the progress bar from the other thread, use the `SwingUtilities.invokeLater(Runnable)` method.

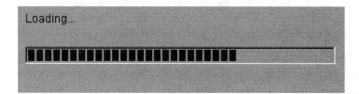

Figure 2.11
A JProgressBar

Swing also provides the `ProgressMonitor` (p.429) and `ProgressMonitorInputStream` (p.430) utility classes which use the `JProgressBar` class. A `ProgressMonitor` is a standard `JDialog` that contains a message, a `JProgressBar`, and a Cancel button. The `ProgressMonitor` can be informed of how far along the process it is associated with is by using the `setProgress()` method. An application using this class must check the `isCanceled()` method as often as it can to make sure the user has not canceled the activity. If the Cancel button has been pressed, the `isCanceled()` method will return `true`, and the application should stop the associated activity and clean up.

A `ProgressMonitorInputStream` is a `FilterInputStream` that displays a `ProgressMonitor`. This class manages the display and update of the `ProgressMonitor` by itself, and throws an `InterruptedIOException` if the Cancel button is pressed.

```
InputStream in = new BufferedInputStream(
        new ProgressMonitorInputStream(
                parentComponent,
```

```
"Loading " + fileName,
    new FileInputStream(fileName)));
```

2.7   The Swing text components

JTextField (p.379) and JTextArea (p.374) were covered previously as components similar to those in AWT. As it turns out, that isn't completely true. As Swing text components, they are far more powerful and flexible than their AWT counterparts. It is a testament to the design of Swing that the complexity stays hidden until it is needed.

The text components in Swing are made up of several pieces. The components themselves are JTextField, JPasswordField (p.306), JTextArea, JEditorPane (p.232), and JTextPane (p.383). All Swing components inherit from JTextComponent (p.838). The other pieces are a Document (p.826), which defines the model for the text; a View (p.893) (or set of Views) to display the Document; an EditorKit (p.829), which is used to process the text; Action implementors to handle text commands; and a Keymap (p.846), which is used to supply keystroke handling.

A Document represents a sequence of characters. The coordinate system used by a Document is a zero-based offset into the sequence. When the Document changes it issues a DocumentEvent (p.489) that carries information about the change. The Document may also send an Undoable-EditEvent (p.515), if it supports undo. The section of the Document that changed is represented by an offset and a length, which together represent a range. A Position (p.860) is a special offset into the sequence that tracks any changes to the Document so it maintains its relative position in the sequence of characters. Obviously, if a Position is in a range that is removed, it cannot continue to represent that relative position. In that case the Position is moved to represent the character immediately after the range that was moved. Swing provides an AbstractDocument (p.778) class to implement most of the common functionality needed by Documents. The content storage and management is configuarable and is usually created as a subclass of AbstractDocument.Content (p.788). Swing 1.0.x supplied a StringContent (p.877) class that used a character array to store the Document content. Swing 1.1 uses a GapContent (p.833) class which is a more efficient storage implementation, especially when changes are being made to the Document.

Documents use Elements (p.830) to support marking up the text. The marking up of the text is kept separate from the storage so that a more efficient storage mechanism can be used if needed without disturbing the markup classes. An Element represents a range in the Document, with an AttributeSet (p.794) for the markup. Elements form a hierarchy. For example, in the DefaultStyledDocument (p.820) the Elements form a hierachy made of character Elements, paragraph Elements, and section Elements. Predefined values for attributes are defined in the StyleConstants class (p.865).

The View abstract class is extended by classes that display Elements in a Document. Swing provides a hierarchy of views consisting of BoxView (p.797), ParagraphView (p.853), Label-View (p.847), ComponentView (p.802), and IconView (p.837). BoxView represents the entire document and contains subviews, arranged vertically. Usually those subviews are Paragraph-Views, which also contain subviews. LabelViews, ComponentViews, and IconViews are views which display text, arbitrary components, or Icons. To create a view which knows how to represent a custom attribute, first create the custom attribute in the same manner as the predefined attributes in StyleConstants. Next, create a subclass of a View, usually a LabelView subclass that understands the new attribute. A View is responsible for assisting in layout, rendering an Element or Elements in the Document, translating between model and view coordinates, and listening for changes in the model.

An EditorKit is responsible for creating a Document appropriate for the type of text content it handles. It also provides a factory for creating appropriate Views, appropriate command processing, and the ability to read and write an IOStream or Reader/Writer.

The commands (used to control the JEditorPane) supplied by an EditorKit are implementors of the Action interface. All of the text commands supplied with Swing are subclasses of the TextAction (p.891) class. Usually the actions are triggered through a Keymap, but they can also be attached to menus or toolbars.

A Keymap maps between KeyStrokes and Actions. The following lines of code bind the Windows and Macintosh standard CTRL-X, CTRL-C, and CTRL-V (COMMAND-X, COMMAND-C, COMMAND-V on the Mac) keystrokes to the default Swing cut, copy, and paste actions.

```
...
   // Set up a table of KeyBindings between the KeyStrokes and the Actions
   static JTextComponent.KeyBinding[] editBindings = {
      new JTextComponent.KeyBinding(KeyStroke.getKeyStroke(KeyEvent.VK_C,
Event.CTRL_MASK), DefaultEditorKit.copyAction),
      new JTextComponent.KeyBinding(KeyStroke.getKeyStroke(KeyEvent.VK_V,
Event.CTRL_MASK), DefaultEditorKit.pasteAction),
      new JTextComponent.KeyBinding(KeyStroke.getKeyStroke(KeyEvent.VK_X,
Event.CTRL_MASK), DefaultEditorKit.cutAction),
   };
   JTextPane tp = new JTextPane();
   Keymap km = tp.getKeymap();
   JTextComponent.loadKeymap(km, defaultBindings, tp.getActions());
...
```

The important idea to remember after reading about all of these capabilities in the Swing text API is that you will almost never directly use them. The text components in Swing expose this functionality in a much simpler form. You generally will only need to delve this deep to customize the functionality of the text components; for example, to create an EditorKit that does color syntax highlighting, or a Document that does on-the-fly spellchecking.

JEditorPane best exhibits these new capabilities in Swing, so it will be described more fully.

2.7.1 JEditorPane

JEditorPane (p.232) is a component that provides almost the full capabilities of a word processor. In the 1.1 implementation of Swing, it provides the capability to edit plain text, HTML, and

RTF. It supports different kinds of documents through the use of EditorKits. Except for writing your own, you generally will never use an EditorKit directly since most of the functionality is accessible through the JEditorPane. To change the type of document you are editing, call setContentType(String mimeType) on the JEditorPane. This call uses the MIME type to look up the appropriate EditorKit and install it. The default MIME types are "text/plain", "text/html", and "text/rtf". The HTML support supports most of HTML 3.2, including forms. If you want to edit an existing document, set the content type of the editor pane and then call read() to read the document. Saving is done through the write() method. Swing 1.1 also includes the setPage(String url) and setPage(java.net.URL url) methods. These methods handle setting the content type based on the stream being read, along with actually reading the content.

JEditorPane, along with JTextField, JTextPane, and JTextArea, uses Actions to implement its behaviors. Using Actions makes it very easy to create a JToolBar (or JMenu) that supports all of the available functionality of the editor and also lets the EditorKits add new Actions to the list dynamically and have them immediately available (see table 2.2).

Table 2.2   The Actions for JEditorPane using the default EditorKit (which is DefaultEditorKit)

Action Name	Purpose
"caret-backward"	Moves the caret logically backward one position.
"beep"	Causes the system to emit a beep.
"caret-begin"	Moves the caret to the beginning of the document.
"caret-begin-line"	Moves the caret to the beginning of the current line.
"caret-begin-paragraph"	Moves the caret to the beginning of the current paragraph.
"caret-begin-word"	Moves the caret to the beginning of the current word (the position after the first white space to be found before the current caret position).
"copy-to-clipboard"	Places a copy of the selected text into the system clipboard.
"cut-to-clipboard"	Removes the selected text from the document and places it in the system clipboard.
"default-typed"	The action to perform when a key is typed and there isn't a Keymap entry for it.
"delete-next"	Deletes the character that is immediately after the current caret position.
"delete-previous"	Deletes the character that is immediately before the current caret position.
"caret-down"	Moves the caret logically downward one position (usually forward a line's worth of content).
"caret-end"	Moves the caret to the end of the document.
"caret-end-line"	Moves the caret to the end of the current line.
"caret-end-paragraph"	Moves the caret to the end of the current paragraph.
"caret-end-word"	Moves the caret to the end of the current word (the position before the first white space to be found after the current caret position).
"caret-forward"	Moves the caret logically forward one position.
"insert-break"	Inserts a line or paragraph break into the document, replacing the selected text if there is any.

Action Name	Purpose
"insert-content"	Inserts text into the document, replacing the selected text if, there is any.
"insert-tab"	Inserts a tab character into the document, replacing the selected text, if there is any.
"caret-next-word"	Moves the caret to the beginning of the next word.
"page-down"	Scrolls the View down a page.
"page-up"	Scrolls the View up a page.
"paste-from-clipboard"	Inserts the contents of the system clipboard into the document, replacing the selected text, if there is any.
"caret-previous-word"	Moves the caret to the beginning of the previous word.
"set-read-only"	Makes the editor read-only.
"select-all"	Selects the entire document.
"selection-backward"	Changes the selection by moving the caret logically backward one position.
"selection-begin"	Changes the selection by moving the caret to the beginning of the document.
"selection-begin-line"	Changes the selection by moving the caret to the beginning of the current line.
"selection-begin-paragraph"	Changes the selection by moving the caret to the beginning of the current paragraph.
"selection-begin-word"	Changes the selection by moving the caret to the beginning of the current word.
"selection-down"	Changes the selection by moving the caret logically downward one position (usually forward a line's worth of content).
"selection-end"	Changes the selection by moving the caret to the end of the document.
"selection-end-line"	Changes the selection by moving the caret to the end of the current line.
"selection-end-paragraph"	Changes the selection by moving the caret to the end of the current paragraph.
"selection-end-word"	Changes the selection by moving the caret to the end of the current word.
"selection-forward"	Changes the selection by moving the caret logically forward one position.
"selection-next-word"	Changes the selection by moving the caret to the beginning of the next word.
"selection-previous-word"	Changes the selection by moving the caret to the beginning of the previous word.
"selection-up"	Changes the selection by moving the caret logically upward one position (usually backward a line's worth of content).
"select-line"	Selects the line the caret is on.
"select-paragraph"	Selects the paragraph the caret is in.
"select-word"	Selects the word the caret is in.
"caret-up"	Moves the caret logically upward one position (usually backwards a line's worth of content).
"set-writable"	Makes the editor editable.

2.8 *The new layout managers*

The new components in Swing are not the only new features. Swing also comes with some new layout managers.

The only layout manager in Swing directly usable by developers is the BoxLayout (p.144). The other layouts are used to support various components in Swing.

`BoxLayout` forces a panel to lay itself out either horizontally or vertically. The orientation of the layout is set using a parameter to the constructor, either `BoxLayout.X_AXIS`, or `BoxLayout.Y_AXIS`. There is a helper class in Swing, the `Box` (p.134) class, which implements a panel that uses `BoxLayout` by default and also provides several useful `static` methods. The `static` methods in `Box` give the developer the ability to create space-filling components that can be used to adjust the location of components in the panel. The first space filler is known as "glue." It is truly a space filler, in that it will expand or contract to fill the leftover space in the panel. The other space filler is a "strut," which provides a fixed-size component and is usually used to create aesthetic gaps between components.

Be careful with the constructor to `BoxLayout`. The component parameter it takes is the panel it will be laying out. So, for example,

```
public class TestBox extends JPanel {
  public TestBox() {
    super();
    this.setLayout(new BoxLayout(this, BoxLayout.X_AXIS));
  }
}
...
```

will correctly lay out an instance of `TestBox`, while

```
public class BadTestBox extends JPanel {
  public BadTestBox() {
    JPanel innerBoxPanel = new JPanel();
    innerBoxPanel.setLayout(new BoxLayout(this, BoxLayout.X_AXIS));
    add(innerBoxPanel);
  }
}
```

will not correctly lay out `innerBoxPanel` (in fact, it will fail at run time). The reason the second example fails is that the first parameter passed to the `BoxLayout` constructor should have been `innerBoxPanel`, not `this`, which is an instance of `BadTestBox`. The way to remember this is the first parameter of the `BoxLayout` constructor should always match the component which is having `setLayout()` called. Note that this means that instances of `BoxLayout` cannot be shared among components.

2.9   The undo package

Swing provides a set of classes and interfaces which support a generalized undo/redo mechanism. In Swing it is used only by the text classes, but it was implemented in such a way as to be extensible for any use.

To use the undo support with the text classes, remember that `Documents` trigger `Undoable-EditEvents` when they are modified. To support undo in your application, create an instance of `UndoManager` (p.1008) and add it as an `UndoableEditListener` (p.516) to the `Documents` you wish to be able to undo. That way whenever the Document changes the UndoManager will be notified and keep track of the changes.

UndoManager provides methods to get information about the UndoableEditEvents that it is storing. It also provides methods to undo or redo a change in its list. The UndoManager retains all events in its list until they are explicitly retired using the trimEdits(), trimEditsFor-Limit(), or discardAllEdits() methods. This allows the UndoManager to redo() events which have previously been undone.

To support undo/redo in your own models, have them contain an instance of a subclass of UndoableEditSupport. This class is specially designed to handle managing and notifying lists of UndoableEditListeners. Your model should delegate calls to add/removeUndoable-EditListeners() to the UndoableEditSupport subclass instance. The postEdit() method of UndoableEditSupport notifies listeners about a single update. The beginUpdate() and endUpdate() methods are used to form a compound edit. When endUpdate() is called, it automatically calls postEdit() to notify the listeners about the compound update.

To create your custom UndoableEdit, you have two possible approaches. The first is to use StateEdit, which uses hash tables to store the information needed to distinguish the before and after edit states of the model. To work with StateEdit, your model must support the State-Editable interface. The second method is to create a subclass of AbstractUndoableEdit and have your model handle creating a new instance of the subclass whenever the model changes.

Once you complete those steps, your model will have undo, the all-time favorite feature of users.

2.10 Swing, color, and the UIDefaults table

In another change from the AWT, Swing uses its own method for discovering user interface colors. This change was made for two reasons. The first is that SystemColors in AWT are unreliable in JDK 1.1 due to some difficulties querying the platform for them. The second and more useful reason is this new method for specifying colors allowed for user interface Themes of different colors and other UI resources.

Swing uses a lookup table for all of its graphical resources. Colors in Swing are identified by Strings, which are used as the lookup keys in the resource table. When looking up a color, Swing looks in three different tables: one for user defaults, one for look and feel defaults, and one for system defaults.

The user table contains colors set by the user or by an application using UIManager.set-Color(). The look and feel table contains colors defined for the current look and feel. Switching the look and feel only affects the look and feel table, so colors that applications or users have set remain constant. The system table contains defaults for the JVM and appears to be mostly used to hold the Swing equivalent of SystemColors. The default keys in this table are the names of the SystemColor member variables.

A standard set of color key names is available in all current look and feels. The System-Color names are still available from the system table, but these new key names are much more descriptive. Each general component type (i.e., Desktop, Button, Tree) has its own set of keys of the form ComponentName.part. So the background of a JMenuItem is defined by the key "MenuItem.background".

The table in appendix B (p.1013) presents a list of all of the color keys defined in Basic-LookAndFeel. This set is complete in all other look and feels, with minor exceptions in the form of new keys for UI elements that don't exist in Basic. If you look at the table carefully you will see that there are colors used which are not SystemColors, so using these keys is the best way to match your own custom renderers to the standard UI colors.

As an example of how to use these keys, examine the following method from a subclass of DefaultTableCellRenderer:

```
public Component getTableCellRendererComponent(JTable table, Object value,
   boolean isSelected, boolean isFocussed, int row, int column)
{
   if (hasFocus)
     setBorder(setBorder(UIManager.getBorder(
                        "Table.focusCellHighlightBorder")));
   else
     setBorder(null);

   try {
     if (isSelected) {
       setBackground(UIManager.getColor("Table.selectionBackground"));
       setForeground(UIManager.getColor("Table.selectionForeground"));
       setOpaque(true);
       setText(value.toString() + " I'm selected");
     } else {
       setBackground(UIManager.getColor("Table.background"));
       setForeground(UIManager.getColor("Table.foreground"));
       setOpaque(false);
       setText(value.toString());
     }
   }
   catch (NullPointerException e)
   {
   }
   return this;
}
```

As seen in the preceding example, when the border is changed, the resource table does indeed hold other kinds of UIResources than just Colors. The actual name of the table is the UIDefaults table. UIManager provides methods to look up Borders (getBorder()), Colors (getColor()), Dimensions (getDimension()), Fonts (getFont()), Icons (getIcon()), Insets (getInsets()), ints (getInt()), and Strings (getString()). A generic get() method is provided to retrieve any other kind of object you wish to store in the table. Adding entries to the table is done using the `put(Object key, Object value)` method, so anything descended from `Object` can be added to the table. Appendix B (p.1017) also contains a table listing the other interesting keys defined by the Basic look and feel.

`Themes` are a way for a Swing application to provide a number of pleasant (or at least appropriate to the platform) palettes of colors which can be dynamically changed. Currently only the Java look and feel (also known as Metal) and the no-longer-supported Organic look and feel support `Themes`. One would expect `Themes` to become standard in all look and feels that don't have to match the native platform's look and feel. If you go to such great lengths to match an existing OS's look, it is understandable why you might not want users to be able to make your application look different using `Themes`, so leaving `Theme` support out is reasonable.

When implementing a look and feel, you use this new method of defining resources by filling the defaults table with the `Colors` and other resources you want. You do not have to use a unique `Color` for each key name, as long as each key name has a `Color` assigned to it. Other resources besides `Colors` should be unique unless they can be safely shared (like `Borders`).

The cleanest way to work with `Themes` is to create a `Theme` object that defines "getter" methods for all of the resource keys it contains. Then when the `Theme` object changes, the appropriate method in the `Theme` can be called to retrieve the resource or color. You can then have a number of these `Theme` objects with different color and resource schemes and the same code can be used to fill the defaults table using the current `Theme`. One `Theme` will have to be made the default theme, either in code or by reading a properties file, so the default colors and resources can be assigned the first time the look and feel is being configured.

2.11 Multithreading and Swing

The use of multiple threads in any application above the level of a toy is almost a given in the Java community. Developers wanting to use Swing need to be aware of the issues surrounding the use of multiple threads and Swing components.

Swing components are *not* thread safe. This is a common choice made by user interface APIs, including Windows95 (Windows NT's APIs are thread safe), X11, and the Mac. There are several reasons for this, the first and foremost being that making a user interface component thread safe usually makes it dramatically slower. As a secondary issue, requiring thread safety makes it much more difficult to develop custom components due to the added complexity.

Since Swing is not thread safe, almost all Swing calls must be made from the event dispatching thread. The only methods which can safely be called from another thread are the `repaint()`, `revalidate()`, and `invalidate()` methods of `JComponent`. All of these methods indicate a state change to the event-dispatching thread. The actual work of updating the display to reflect the state change is handled by the event-dispatching thread.

It is also safe to make Swing method calls before the components are realized. Realization occurs when the components are actually created for display on the screen, usually in response to show() or pack() (pack() needs the components realized so it can get their actual sizes). It is this fact which makes it safe to set up components and containers from the main thread of the application, before calling show() or pack().

This limitation is not as severe as it seems. After components are set up and shown, almost all interaction with the components occurs in event listeners. Event listeners, conveniently enough, are executed in the event-dispatching thread. So generally this limitation only has to be dealt with when writing code that explicitly is run in a separate thread.

Swing provides a mechanism to allow other threads to call code that needs to be executed in the event-dispatching thread. Careful examination of the SwingSet sample source code reveals the common use of a method in the SwingUtilities class, invokeLater(). This is the method used to perform this magic.

To use invokeLater(), place the code needing to execute in the event-dispatching thread in the run() method of a class that implements the Runnable interface. Then pass the Runnable as the parameter to invokeLater(). For example:

```
JButton stopButton = new JButton(); // button created in main thread

// this code is from a thread doing a long operation that
// can be stopped by a button click.  When the thread ends,
// the button to stop the thread must be disabled
...
Runnable disableStopButton = new Runnable() {
    public void run() {
        stopButton.setEnabled(false);
    }
}

if (threadIsDone) {
    SwingUtilities.invokeLater(disableStopButton);
}
...
```

2.12   About Swing bugs

Writing about bugs in Swing is a tricky issue. For one, the bugs in Swing change from release to release. Another issue is that a Swing bug may actually be a bug in the underlying JDK. An example of this second issue is the inability to set the icon for a JFrame that was found in Swing 1.0.1. As it turned out, that bug was actually a problem with JDK 1.1.5 that was fixed in JDK 1.1.6. Another example is the focus difficulties in Swing, which are actually problems in JDK 1.1.6, which are fixed in JDK 1.1.7.

The best way to approach bugs in Swing is to make use of the fact that the Swing distribution provides source code. It is extremely helpful to rebuild a version of Swing yourself that includes debugging information. Using the special debug version you can trace into the Swing code from your code to better understand the behavior of Swing. Since Swing is complex, it may turn out to be the case that the intent of the Swing code is different than what you thought it was, thereby explaining the unexpected results.

The other advantage of having a debug version is in discovering why the Swing code isn't working correctly. It is much easier to get Sun to fix a bug when you can point its developers to the exact offending portion of code with a description of why the code is incorrect and how it should work. You can also usually use the information gained from this exercise to find a temporary workaround.

The next step after finding and confirming a Swing bug is to check the Java Developer's Connection Bug Parade page (`http://developer.javasoft.com/developer/bugParade/index.html`) to see if someone else has already reported it. The Bug Parade page provides a limited search engine that works reasonably well. The most reliable way of confirming the existence of a bug report related to your problem is to use the name of the faulty component as the search criteria. This method returns a lot of bug reports that you have to examine, but it guarantees that you will find the report if it exists. You can also be certain you are reporting something new if you can't find a match. If you're lucky, you may find it has already been marked as fixed.

If you find a match you can use the Bug Parade's voting mechanism to increase the chances of the bug being fixed promptly. Each registered user of the Developer's Connection has three votes which can be applied to any bug in the bug database. The three votes can be applied to the same or different bugs and can be changed at any time. The Swing team is using the vote totals from this mechanism to help prioritize when they fix the reported bugs.

C H A P T E R   3

Pluggable look and feel

3.1 Using predefined pluggable look and feels

Using look and feels in Swing is quite simple, but can become tricky unless care is taken.

When a Swing application or applet starts, it uses the Java (Metal) look and feel by default. You would expect it to try to use the native look and feel, but it doesn't. The reasoning behind this decision is that the default look and feel Swing sets on startup should be a look and feel that is guaranteed to be available. The Java look and feel is the only one supplied in `swing.jar`, so it necessarily had to be the one chosen.

Sometimes you may have a specialized need that cannot bear the overhead of installing and then immediately garbage collecting the default look and feel (for example, a consumer device where the look and feel is custom and fixed). The default look and feel can be overridden by setting values in the `$JAVA_HOME/lib/swing.properties` file. `$JAVA_HOME` is defined as being the location where the JDK (or JRE) is installed. The `swing.properties` file (figure 3.1) is not automatically created by the Swing installation; it must be created by the end user or a specialized installation program. To override the default look and feel you need to set the `swing.defaultlaf` key. The look and feel name given on that line must be one of the names set for the `swing.installedlafs` key.

```
swing.installedlafs=Metal,MyCustomLAF
swing.installedlaf.Metal.name=Metal
swing.installedlaf.Metal.class=
   com.sun.java.swing.plaf.metal.MetalLookAndFeel
swing.installedlaf.MyCustomLAF.name=Consumo
swing.installedlaf.MyCustomLAF.class=
   com.mycompany.plaf.consumo.ConsumoLookAndFeel
swing.defaultlaf=com.mycompany.plaf.consumo.ConsumoLookAndFeel
```

Figure 3.1 A sample swing.properties file

Setting a default look and feel in this way is a safe operation, since Swing will always revert to Metal if it cannot load the look and feel specified in the file.

Two methods are supplied in `UIManager` to get the native, or the default, cross-platform. Those two methods are `getSystemLookAndFeelClassName()` and `getCrossPlatformLook-AndFeelClassName()`. The `Strings` returned from these methods can be passed to the `UIManager`'s `setLookAndFeel()` method to change the current look and feel.

`UIManager` also supplies a method, `getInstalledLookAndFeels()`, to return an array of `UIManager.LookAndFeelInfo` (p.457) instances describing all of the look and feels installed with the JDK. Using the information returned from this call you can set a look and feel as follows:

```
UIManager.LookAndFeelInfo[] info = UIManager.getInstalledLookAndFeels();
UIManager.setLookAndFeel(info[0].getClassName());
```

Use the `LookAndFeelInfo.getName()` method to get the names of the returned look and feels to display to the user.

To use a look and feel other than the ones that can be returned by those methods, pass the full class name of the class that extends `LookAndFeel` in the other look and feel. By convention this class is always named using the form `XLookAndFeel`, where `X` is the look and feel name. For example, the class name to pass to set the Motif look and feel on a non-Motif platform is `com.sun.java.swing.plaf.motif.MotifLookAndFeel`.

When changing the look and feel, all instantiated components need to be informed of the change. If you are intending to just use one look and feel for the life of the application or applet, it is best to set the look and feel before you start creating components. Then when the components are created they will use the correct look and feel.

If the look and feel is changed after components are created, you must notify all components of the change using their `updateUI()` method. The `SwingUtilities` class provides a method, `updateComponentTreeUI(root)`, which calls `updateUI()` on any components in the component tree rooted at `root`.

Individual components interact with the look and feel through a UI delegate. The standard UI delegates Swing supplies are shared among all instances of the same type of component. So, for example, there is only one `ButtonUI` UI delegate for all `JButtons`. It is actually the UI delegate that is responsible for handling painting the component and receiving input for the component.

The `JComponent` class defines several methods to support the UI delegate concept. The methods are `getUIClassID()`, which returns the `String` used to look up the correct UI delegate in the `UIDefaults` table; `setUI()`, which sets a new UI delegate for the component; and `updateUI()`, which is called to inform the component that its default UI delegate may have changed in the `UIDefaults` table. When `updateUI()` is called, the component will call `setUI()` with the return value from `UIManager.getUI(this)`.

Custom cell renderers and editors require special attention because of pluggable look and feel. See the section "Swing, color, and the `UIDefaults` table" (p.452) for more information on how to write a renderer or editor to take into account the current look and feel.

3.1.1 Custom painting components

If you need to change the look of a component in your application you do not need to go to all of the effort of creating a new look and feel for it.

`JComponent` is responsible for asking the UI delegate to paint the component, so you can take over the painting by creating a subclass of `JComponent` (or one of the other Swing components, of course). In Swing you can override the `paint()` method if you want to do all of the work yourself.

`JComponent`'s `paint()` method calls three separate methods to do the actual work of painting the whole component: `paintComponent()`, `paintBorder()`, and `paintChildren()`.

The `paintComponent()` method is responsible for painting the nonborder area of the component. This is most likely the only one of the three methods you will override. The default behavior of this method is to delegate its painting to the UI delegate, if it is non-`null`.

It is quite important in overriding `paintComponent()` that you do not use the `Graphics` object which is passed in directly. The reasoning behind this is that all Swing components render into the same `Graphics` object, so you do not want to make irrevocable changes (such as `translate()`) on the `Graphics` object. To get a `Graphics` object which you can use, call the `SwingGraphics.createSwingGraphics(g.create())` method. Using `createSwingGraphics()` is a bit safer than simply calling `g.create()`, since `createSwingGraphics()` will handle situations where `g` is a normal AWT `Graphics` instance. Remember to `dispose()` of the returned `Graphics` object when you are done with it! The easiest way to ensure that the object is disposed of at the end of painting is to wrap the painting into a try/finally statement. That way, even if an exception is thrown while painting, the `finally` clause will get called and dispose of the `Graphics` object.

The second method, `paintBorder()`, is responsible for painting the border of the component. There is no need to override this method, since you can change the way the border is painted by changing the border itself using the `setBorder()` method.

The third method, `paintChildren()`, should probably never be overridden. Chances are very, very good that you don't want to change the way the child components of this component are drawn. If you did, you would override the `paintComponent()` method of the child.

3.2   Pluggable Picasso: writing a custom look and feel

Custom look and feel implementation is relatively easy, due to the significant support provided by Swing. At its most elementary, you simply subclass `BasicLookAndFeel` and any other classes in the Basic look and feel package that you want to implement new looks and/or feels for. When you have chosen the set of classes you want to override, update `YourLookAndFeel`'s `getDefaults()` method to fill the lookup table used to choose the classes to render the components.

To illustrate, examine the following limited look and feel, Very Light Interface Widgets (VLIW). The requirements for this look and feel are minimal drawing operations, only black and white are to be used, no support for `Icons`, and no floating point math.

Only a sampling of all possible controls will be illustrated here. The sample controls are a button and a progress bar.

The `VLIWLookAndFeel` class holds the methods used to describe, install, uninstall, and configure the look and feel. This `LookAndFeel` class represents the smallest worthwhile implementation, including the four mandatory methods (the first four) and the `initClassDefaults()` method (which has to be overridden if you want your look and feel to be different). You do not have to extend `BasicLookAndFeel`, but if you want your look and feel to be transparently usable

by third parties, you should, since it sets up a number of default resources and entries in the
UIDefaults table that Swing application writers will expect to be present.

```
// File: lookandfeel\VLIW\VLIWLookAndFeel.java
package lookandfeel.VLIW;
import javax.swing.plaf.basic.*;
import javax.swing.plaf.*;
import javax.swing.*;
import javax.swing.border.*;

import java.awt.*;

public class VLIWLookAndFeel extends BasicLookAndFeel
{
    public String getName() {
      return "VLIW"; // this should be localized, if necessary
    }
    public String getID() {
      return "VLIW";
    }
    public String getDescription() {
      return "VLIW, the Very Light Interface Widgets";
    }
```

The name, ID, and description properties are used to distinguish this look and feel from others. The getName() method should return a short name, such as Windows, Motif/CDE, or VLIW, that is appropriate for presenting to a user. The getID() method is used as the fixed, unique, identifying name of the look and feel. The getDescription() method allows you to more fully describe the look and feel. You should expect the name and the description to be used to describe your look and feel to a user, so you will probably want to localize at least the description.

```
    public boolean isNativeLookAndFeel() {
      // this isn't the native look and feel for any platform
      return false;
    }
    public boolean isSupportedLookAndFeel() {
      // it is supported on all platforms
      return true;
    }
```

The two isXLookAndFeel() methods allow the look and feel to indicate whether it is the preferred look and feel for the current platform and whether it is even supported on the platform. The isNativeLookAndFeel() method should return true if this look and feel is the default for the platform, as the Windows look and feel is for Windows95 and WindowsNT. The second method, isSupportedLookAndFeel(), was added as a direct result of Sun not wanting to be sued by Microsoft over using the Windows look. The Windows and Macintosh look and feels both return false on anything other than their native platform. If you don't want your look and feel supported on a particular platform, or on a platform other than its native one, return `false` from this method. Usually, you will return `true` unless your look and feel uses native code.

```
protected void initClassDefaults(UIDefaults table) {
    String vliwPackageName = "lookandfeel.VLIW.";

    // Fill the table with the default Basic L&F
    // controls.  We'll override the ones we implement
    // later
    super.initClassDefaults(table);

    Object[] uiDefaults = {
        "ButtonUI", vliwPackageName + "VLIWButtonUI",
        "ProgressBarUI",
        "javax.swing.plaf.basic.BasicProgressBarUI",
    };
    table.putDefaults(uiDefaults);
}

protected void initComponentDefaults(UIDefaults table) {
    super.initComponentDefaults(table);
    ColorUIResource black = new ColorUIResource(Color.black);
    ColorUIResource white = new ColorUIResource(Color.white);
    Object buttonBorder = new UIDefaults.LazyValue() {
        public Object createValue(UIDefaults table) {
            return new BorderUIResource(new CompoundBorder(
                            BorderFactory.createEmptyBorder(3,3,3,3),
                            BorderFactory.createLineBorder(Color.black)));
        }
    };

    Object progressBarBorder = new
                    BorderUIResource.LineBorderUIResource(Color.white, 2);

    Object[] defaults = {
        "Button.border", buttonBorder,
        "Button.background", black,
        "Button.foreground", wnite,
        "Button.focus", white,
        "Button.pressed", white,
        "ProgressBar.foreground", white,
        "ProgressBar.background", black,
        "ProgressBar.border", progressBarBorder,
        "ProgressBar.cellLength", new Integer(4),
        "ProgressBar.cellSpacing", new Integer(1)
    };
    table.putDefaults(defaults);
}
```

Supporting `initClassDefaults()` is a requirement if you want to do anything with your look and feel other than just rename someone else's. This method gets called by Swing when the look and feel is installed and it is where you add your own `ComponentUI` subclasses to the UIDefaults table. The standard implementation of this method calls `super.initClassDefaults()`, creates an array of UI key names and the `ComponentUIs` this look and feel wants to use, and then puts this information into the table. For the `VLIWLookAndFeel` you may have noticed that this method adds its own button implementation, but uses the Basic look and feel `BasicProgressBarUI`. `BasicProgressBarUI` is implemented so that it can support almost all types of linear progress bars. To change how the progress bar draws, simply set values into the `UIDefaults` table in `initComponentDefaults()` and the `BasicProgressBarUI` will use them.

```java
// File: com\manning\swing\plaf\vliw\VLIWButtonUI.java
package com.manning.swing.plaf.vliw;
import java.awt.*;
import javax.swing.*;

public class VLIWButtonUI extends BasicButtonUI implements Serializable {
    // Colors
    protected Color getSelectColor() {
        return UIManager.getColor("Button.pressed");
    }
    protected Color getDisabledColor() {
        return UIManager.getColor("Button.disabled");
    }
    protected Color getDisabledTextColor()
    {
        return UIManager.getColor("Button.disabledText");
    }
    protected Color getFocusColor() {
        return UIManager.getColor("Button.focus");
    }

    // Borders
    private final static Insets defaultMargin = new Insets(2,14,2,14);

    // protected static ButtonUI buttonUI; // inherited from BasicButtonUI

    public static ComponentUI createUI(JComponent c) {
        if(buttonUI == null) {
            buttonUI = new VLIWButtonUI();
        }
        return buttonUI;
    }

    public void paint(Graphics gr, JComponent comp) {
        Color foreground = UIManager.getColor("Button.foreground");
        Color background = UIManager.getColor("Button.background");
        AbstractButton button = (AbstractButton)comp;
        ButtonModel model = button.getModel();
        Dimension size = button.getSize();
        FontMetrics fm = gr.getFontMetrics();
        Insets insets = comp.getInsets();
        Rectangle viewRect = new Rectangle(size);
        viewRect.x += insets.left;
        viewRect.y += insets.top;
```

```
viewRect.width -= (insets.right + viewRect.x);
viewRect.height -= (insets.bottom + viewRect.y);
Rectangle textRect = new Rectangle();
// not used, but needed by layoutCompoundLabel
Rectangle iconRect = new Rectangle();
Font f = comp.getFont();
gr.setFont(f);
// layout the text on the button
String text = SwingUtilities.layoutCompoundLabel(
   fm, button.getText(), null,
   button.getVerticalAlignment(),
   button.getHorizontalAlignment(),
   button.getVerticalTextPosition(),
   button.getHorizontalTextPosition(),
   viewRect, iconRect, textRect,
   button.getText() == null ? 0 : defaultTextIconGap
);

// When the button is pressed, the colors invert
if (model.isArmed() && model.isPressed()) {
   foreground = UIManager.getColor("Button.background");
   background = UIManager.getColor("Button.foreground");
}
// Paint background
gr.setColor(background);
gr.fillRect(0,0, size.width, size.height);
// Paint the border
gr.setColor(foreground);
gr.drawRect(0, 0, size.width, size.height);

// Draw the Text
if(text != null && !text.equals("")) {
   if(model.isEnabled()) {
      // *** paint the text normally
      gr.setColor(foreground);
      BasicGraphicsUtils.drawString(gr,text,
          model.getMnemonic(),
          textRect.x + getTextShiftOffset(),
          textRect.y + fm.getAscent() +
          getTextShiftOffset());
   } else {
      // *** paint the text disabled
      gr.setColor(foreground);
      BasicGraphicsUtils.drawString(gr,
         text,model.getMnemonic(),
         textRect.x, textRect.y + fm.getAscent());
         gr.setColor(background);
      BasicGraphicsUtils.drawString(gr,
         text,model.getKeyAccelerator(),
         textRect.x - 1,
         textRect.y + fm.getAscent() - 1);
   }
}
if (button.isFocusPainted() && button.hasFocus()) {
```

```
         // paint the focus, which is just a rectangle
         // inset three pixels from the border
         g.setColor(foreground);
         g.drawRect(8, 8, size.width - 16, size.height - 16);
      }
   }
}
```

You may have noticed that the only two methods overridden from `BasicButtonUI` were `createUI()` and `paint()`. This is generally the case, since `BasicLookAndFeel` implements sensible behaviors for most platforms. The `createUI()` method needs to be overridden for all component subclasses, since it is the factory method that returns an instance of the correct subclass. If it weren't overridden, the `BasicButtonUI.createUI()` method would be called and the button would have been from the Basic look and feel.

Most of the information needed to paint is retrieved from the `ButtonModel`, which holds the state information about the button. This feature is what makes it simple to replace a look and feel, since the look and feel does not know anything about the button beyond what it retrieves (or sets: remember that the `ComponentUI` delegates are both the View and Controller) from the `ButtonModel`. To be a correct look and feel implementation, the paint code should get its colors from the `UIDefaults` table using the "Button.pressed," "Button.disabled," "Button.disabled-Text," and "Button.focus" keys. These keys would have been set to the correct colors for this look and feel by overriding the `initComponentDefaults()` method in the `LookAndFeel` subclass.

Creating similar components for the rest of the look and feel follows the same pattern. First, check to see if the Basic look and feel can be reconfigured through the `UIDefaults` table to do what you want. The Metal look and feel only subclasses a subset of the Basic look and feel components because of this. If the Basic look and feel component can't do what you need, then create a subclass of the Basic component to implement the behavior you want.

When your look and feel is complete, it can be used in exactly the same way as any other Swing look and feel.

```java
// File lookandfeel\TestFrame.java
package lookandfeel;

import java.awt.*;
import java.awt.event.*;
import javax.swing.*;

public class TestFrame extends JFrame {

   public TestFrame() {
      this.setDefaultCloseOperation(DISPOSE_ON_CLOSE);
      this.addWindowListener(new WindowAdapter()
      {
         public void windowClosed(WindowEvent e)
         {
            System.exit(0);
```

```
        }
    });
    JPanel fringe = new JPanel(new BorderLayout());
    fringe.setBorder(BorderFactory.createEmptyBorder(10,10,10,10));
    this.getContentPane().add(fringe);
    fringe.add(new JButton("Hi, I'm a different looking button"),
            BorderLayout.CENTER);
    JProgressBar prog = new JProgressBar();
    prog.setValue(75);
    this.getContentPane().add(prog , BorderLayout.SOUTH);
}

public static void main(String[] args) {
    try {
        UIManager.setLookAndFeel("lookandfeel.VLIW.VLIWLookAndFeel");
    }
    catch (Exception e)
    {}
    TestFrame testFrame1 = new TestFrame();
    testFrame1.setSize(640,480);
    testFrame1.setVisible(true);
}
}
```

3.3 Themes

The Java (Metal) look and feel introduces a useful new concept to look and feels, the *Theme*. The simplest description of a Theme is that it is a named collection of Fonts and Colors which can be changed as a group.

From a technical perspective, a Theme is implemented by defining an abstract superclass for Themes in this look and feel. This superclass defines the interface and supplies default values for each UIResource. There doesn't have to be an exact one-to-one correspondence between methods in this Theme and keys in the UIDefaults table since many components share common characteristics (e.g., controls usually have the same background color). Each of the methods in the Theme class returns a UIResource (usually a Font or a Color). Then, to create other Themes you can either create subclasses of the superclass Theme to return different UIResources, or you can provide setter methods for the properties in the Theme and use multiple instances of the Theme object.

As an example, this is the base class used for Themes in the Metal look and feel:

```
public abstract class MetalTheme extends java.lang.Object
{
  // Constructors
  public MetalTheme();

  // Methods
  public void addCustomEntriesToTable(UIDefaults);
  public ColorUIResource getAcceleratorForeground();
  public ColorUIResource getAcceleratorSelectedForeground();
```

```
   protected ColorUIResource getBlack();
   public ColorUIResource getControl();
   public ColorUIResource getControlDarkShadow();
   public ColorUIResource getControlDisabled();
   public ColorUIResource getControlHighlight();
   public ColorUIResource getControlInfo();
   public ColorUIResource getControlShadow();
   public ColorUIResource getControlTextColor();
   public abstract FontUIResource getControlTextFont();
   public ColorUIResource getDesktopColor();
   public ColorUIResource getFocusColor();
   public ColorUIResource getHighlightedTextColor();
   public ColorUIResource getInactiveControlTextColor();
   public ColorUIResource getInactiveSystemTextColor();
   public ColorUIResource getMenuBackground();
   public ColorUIResource getMenuDisabledForeground();
   public ColorUIResource getMenuForeground();
   public ColorUIResource getMenuSelectedBackground();
   public ColorUIResource getMenuSelectedForeground();
   public abstract FontUIResource getMenuTextFont();
   public abstract String getName();
   protected abstract ColorUIResource getPrimary1();
   protected abstract ColorUIResource getPrimary2();
   protected abstract ColorUIResource getPrimary3();
   public ColorUIResource getPrimaryControl();
   public ColorUIResource getPrimaryControlDarkShadow();
   public ColorUIResource getPrimaryControlHighlight();
   public ColorUIResource getPrimaryControlInfo();
   public ColorUIResource getPrimaryControlShadow();
   protected abstract ColorUIResource getSecondary1();
   protected abstract ColorUIResource getSecondary2();
   protected abstract ColorUIResource getSecondary3();
   public ColorUIResource getSeparatorBackground();
   public ColorUIResource getSeparatorForeground();
   public abstract FontUIResource getSubTextFont();
   public ColorUIResource getSystemTextColor();
   public abstract FontUIResource getSystemTextFont();
   public ColorUIResource getTextHighlightColor();
   public ColorUIResource getUserTextColor();
   public abstract FontUIResource getUserTextFont();
   protected ColorUIResource getWhite();
   public ColorUIResource getWindowBackground();
   public ColorUIResource getWindowTitleBackground();
   public abstract FontUIResource getWindowTitleFont();
   public ColorUIResource getWindowTitleForeground();
   public ColorUIResource getWindowTitleInactiveBackground();
   public ColorUIResource getWindowTitleInactiveForeground();
}
```

A Theme is used to fill in the values for the UIDefaults table. Instead of adding an explicit UIResource to the table, you instead call the appropriate method in the Theme and store the UIResource it returns. This way, another Theme can be used by the look and feel simply by passing it to the method that fills the table instead of the default theme.

The standard way this is done is for the `LookAndFeel` class of the Theme-supporting look and feel to implement a method to set the current look and feel. It also provides static methods to return the correct color using the current look and feel. These static methods are what are called in the `initX` methods in the `LookAndFeel` class to retrieve the correct `UIResource`.

In the `initComponentDefaults()` method of the `MetalLookAndFeel` class, the following line is used in the definition of the defaults table to initialize the background color of the `ButtonUI` delegate:

```
"Button.background", getControl()
```

The `getControl()` method is defined by `MetalLookAndFeel` as

```
public static ColorUIResource getControl() {
    return currentTheme.getControl();
}
```

`MetalLookAndFeel` also supplies a method to create the default Theme. This is required since a Theme needs to be supplied when the look and feel is installed for the first time. Which Theme is the default is a purely arbitrary choice.

Themes should supply a descriptive (or at least unique among Themes in this look and feel) name which can be presented to the user. This allows the user to change the Theme of the look and feel dynamically at run time. When changing the theme, set the current Theme before updating the UI, as follows:

```
MyLookAndFeel.setCurrentTheme(selectedTheme);
try {
    UIManager.setLookAndFeel("com.manning.MyLookAndFeel");
} catch (Exception ex) {
    System.out.println(ex);
}
```

Changing the current Theme needs to be done first so that the `UIDefaults` table is filled correctly when the look and feel is being used to fill it. Calling `UIManager.setLookAndFeel()` will *always* reinitialize the look and feel, even if the look and feel being set is the same as the current one.

3.4   About the Multi look and feel

If you have been working with look and feels, you have probably examined the Multi look and feel. You also probably have no idea what it is for since it isn't exactly obvious (or documented).

The Multi look and feel isn't a look and feel per-se; it is actually a mechanism for supporting more than one simultaneous look and feel. This is used for Accessibility technologies. The second (or *auxiliary* look and feel) will generally not be a full look and feel; it also really shouldn't be a second *visual* look and feel.

The auxiliary look and feel would, as an example, be one which supported Braille or audible feedback. As an example of how the auxiliary look and feel could be used, imagine a normal application using the Metal look and feel being put onto a device which used a touch screen instead of a mouse. Touch screen devices can use audible feedback to let users know they have used a component successfully (making a click noise when a button is pressed, for example). You wouldn't want this audible feedback on a device with a mouse, since it would be out of place, and you also wouldn't want to create a full subclass of Metal to just add the sound. You would have to completely reimplement the sound-enabled subclass if you later changed from the Metal look and feel.

The way an auxiliary look and feel would be used in this case would be to create an auxiliary look and feel which provided just the sound. Continuing the example, the auxiliary look and feel would have a JButton UI delegate that made a click noise when pressed. The auxiliary JButton would not paint itself, leaving the visuals to the primary look and feel. By implementing the auxiliary look and feel this way, you could reuse it with any other primary look and feel you wanted, without changing it at all.

To install the auxiliary look and feel you need to use the swing.properties file (figure 3.2). In the properties file you would define the swing.auxiliarylaf key and set its value to be a comma-separated list of look and feel class names.

```
swing.auxiliarylaf=com.mycompany.plaf.AudioFeedbackLookAndFeel,
    com.mycompany.plaf.BrailleLookAndFeel
```

Figure 3.2 Setting auxiliary look and feels in the swing.properties file

When Swing initializes itself it looks for this key. If it finds it, it automatically sets the Multi look and feel and informs the Multi look and feel about the default primary look and feel and all auxiliary ones. The Multi look and feel keeps a list of the primary and auxiliary look and feels and when one of its component UI delegate methods gets called it calls the same method in each of the look and feels it knows about. Of course, all of this will work only if the Multi look and feel can be found on the class path. To ensure that it is, you can either use swingall.jar or swing.jar and multi.jar.

The way the default Multi look and feel works is quite straightforward. When initializing, the default look and feel is the first one created. The default look and feel is always the one returned from UIManager.getLookAndFeel() even if the Multi look and feel is installed. After initializing the default look and feel, the auxiliary look and feels are initialized in the order they are found on the swing.auxiliarylaf line. The auxiliary look and feels are returned by the UIManager.getAuxiliaryLookAndFeels() method. The elements in the LookAndFeel array returned by this method are in the same order as they were initialized. When information is requested from a JComponent (for example, through the getInsets() method) the Multi look and feel calls the appropriate method on the default look and feel's matching UI delegate. The auxiliary look and feel's UI delegates are *not* queried. When a method which does not return information is called on a JComponent (such as installUI()), the Multi look and feel calls that method on the default look and feel and on all auxiliary look and feels.

Developing an auxiliary look and feel is no more difficult (and in some cases it is easier) than developing a primary look and feel. The first simplifying factor for auxiliary look and feels is they do not need to be complete. The Multi look and feel is designed to expect this and quietly handle it. The main problem is the UIDefaults class which writes a message to System.err and throws an Error if it can't find a UI delegate for a given component. The way around this is to create a UIDefaults subclass and return it from the auxiliary look and feel's getDefaults() method.

```
public class AuxiliaryLookAndFeel extends LookAndFeel {
...
  public UIDefaults getDefaults() {
    UIDefaults table = new AuxiliaryUIDefaults();
    Object[] uiDefaults = {
      "ButtonUI", "ClickingButtonUI",
    }
    table.putDefaults(uiDefaults);
    return table;
  }
}

class AuxiliaryUIDefaults extends UIDefaults {
  protected void getUIError(String msg) {
    // leave empty to eliminate message
  }
}
```

With an auxiliary look and feel the main methods are installUI() and uninstallUI(). These methods are where the look and feel can add or remove its listeners from the component and the component's data model.

Auxiliary look and feels should directly subclass the classes in the swing.plaf package instead of extending Basic or one of the other visual look and feels. If you inherit from one of the visual look and feels you may accidentally create a situation where the auxiliary look and feel is disturbing the default look and feel by painting or changing input. The auxiliary look and feel UI delegate should also override *all* methods in its superclass. The reason for this suggestion is to eliminate the chance of missing a situation like that of ComponentUI's update() method. ComponentUI's update() fills the background of any opaque component as its default behavior. If you didn't override this method, all opaque components in the default look and feel would be overpainted with a blank rectangle by the auxiliary look and feel. Unless you are implementing a "scratch off square to win a prize" look and feel, this isn't what you want to have happen.

CHAPTER 4

The Accessibility API

Accessibility is all about understanding your customer and meeting their needs. All user interface design is geared towards making an application easy to use. Accessibility takes that ease-of-use idea up the next logical step in making interfaces usable by all people, regardless of any disability which prevents them from using a standard, traditional means of interaction.

Accessibility is a tremendously important issue, but also one almost universally overlooked by applications developers. The presence of a standardized accessibility API will be a tremendous asset in getting Java adopted by industries such as banking, telecommunications, and consumer electronics. These industries in particular have requirements for accessibility that have been created by laws or an awareness of the substantial size of the potential market for accessible applications.

Accessibility opens a whole new market to a product. It is estimated that the market for accessible products is approximately 40 million people in the United States alone. Considering that the population of Canada is (as of 1998) just over 30 million people, a market of 40 million people is a very healthy one to target.

Beyond the market size issues, it is interesting that programs that are accessible also tend to be easier for fully able users to use. Working with accessibility requires thinking about ideas such as keyboard access and reducing the number of steps to perform an action. Both of these make your application easier for everyone.

The term "accessibility technology" covers a very wide range of devices. The best way to characterize them is by describing the issues they are designed to deal with. There are three broad categories of disability:

- *Vision* Users with sight limitations need support in several areas. Both low- and no-sight users need keyboard means of performing any operation that would normally be done with a mouse. The reason for this isn't that a keyboard is easier for the user, it is that keyboard-style input is easier for a speech-style input system to use. This area is the easiest to test for, since you need only to unplug your mouse and try to use the application. Similarly, blind or low-vision users also need to know where the focus is and when it changes, as well as what the default action is and how to trigger it. These users also need text descriptions for both graphics and video. For videos it is important if an action is being shown to also describe it. Online documentation is also advantageous to both of these types of users, since it is much more convenient using text-to-speech than having to have Braille or large-print versions of paper documentation (for both the developer and the user).

  Low-vision users can also benefit from screen magnifiers and high-contrast color Themes.

- *Hearing* Restricted-hearing users' needs can be summarized in a simple concept: don't use only sound to indicate something important. Don't just have a ringing noise for an incoming call; have a visual cue as well, such as flashing the "answer" icon. Text descriptions of any audio are also useful. Video should provide the information needed by a closed-captioning style service.

- *Mobility*   Mobility-impaired users have needs that are less in the area of the application developer and more in the area of the assistive-technology vendor. The primary responsibility of an applications vendor is to provide a simple, rational system for choosing actions. Actions should not be buried so deeply it takes a concerted effort for a user to get to them. The last sentence should have caught your attention, since it is good user interface design applicable to *all* users. Online documentation is also beneficial to this category of user.

Supporting all of these variations may seem like a daunting task, so you'll probably be happy to find out it isn't completely your responsibility to implement all of it. Because Swing components support the Accessibility API, you are responsible only for providing the *information* needed by these technologies. Implementing the actual technologies is the responsibility of accessibility technology companies. You still have some details to think about, but consider it as simply paying more attention to the usability of your application.

Java is a significant improvement over most previous technologies in that its accessibility requirements are being considered very early in its life. Legacy operating systems generally added accessibility support much later in their life cycles (with the exception of the Macintosh, which did address many of these issues early on). Java also benefits from a full object-oriented structure, in which components are already subdivided into easily understandable parts. Java does not have to support applications written in procedural languages, unlike the existing operating system APIs. Swing is also a significant improvement for Java, since it mostly eliminates the native peers of the AWT. The transition from JVM to native component meant that accessibility technologies previously lost access to a significant amount of information.

Java isn't perfect in this area, and it is still evolving, but the cost to a developer of supporting accessibility is much lower than ever.

4.1   Using the Accessibility API

Making a Swing application accessible requires about the same degree of effort as internationalization. The application developer is responsible for providing the information that will be presented to the user by appropriate accessibility technologies.

Since `JComponent` implements `Accessible` (p.85), all Swing components are at least partially accessible. At its simplest, all that needs to be done to support accessibility with a Swing component is to set the `accessibleName` or `accessibleDescription` properties, or both.

For components that display text titles such as a `JLabel` or the tabs in a `JTabbedPane`, the `accessibleName` property will be set by default to the component's text. Situations where just an `Icon` is displayed (for example a `JButton` with just its `Icon` set) will require explicitly setting the `accessibleName`. If you ever wondered what the second parameter in the constructor for `ImageIcon` (p.184) was, your answer is that it is the information provided to the accessibility engine to describe the `Icon` (see figure 4.1).

```
printButton = new JButton(iconOfAPrinter);
printButton.setToolTipText("Print the current document");
printButton.getAccessibleContext().setAccessibleName("Print");
printButton.setMnemonic('p');
```

Figure 4.1   Setting the basic Accessibility information for an Icon-only JButton

Conveniently, the developers of Swing chose to make the ToolTip text of a control (if any) the default `accessibleDescription`. So, if you are already supplying ToolTips for your controls, you are pretty much finished setting the description. If a ToolTip is not supplied, the `accessibleDescription` needs to be explicitly set using `AccessibleContext`'s (p.90) `setAccessibleDescription()` method. `JLabels` (p.264) are a special case in that they have a `setLabelFor()` method that tells the accessibility engine what component this `JLabel` is describing. The `setLabelFor()` method information is also used by accessibility focus management so it can put the focus in the correct component (since the `JLabel` may be above or to the side of its associated component).

Naming `JPanels` is actually quite helpful. You, as the applications developer, are using the `JPanel` to group together related controls. Naming the panel and giving it a description (based on why you are grouping the controls it contains) provides an excellent way to give a disabled user more information about the purpose of the components it contains. Containers with a `TitledBorder` will use the text from the title as their name.

Swing 1.1 supplies keyboard support for most controls. The keys bound to the different actions are implemented by the installed look and feel. This leaves adding accelerator keys and mnemonics to the developer. As a rule, *all* menu items should have a way to select them using the keyboard. This support does not need to be a full accelerator keystroke, but should, at the very least, be a series of menu items with mnemonic characters leading to the desired menu item. Also, toolbar or floating palette buttons should have menu items that correspond to them and which also pass the keyboard access test.

Focus management needs to be implemented as well. The rule of thumb in this case is to have the focus on the component with which the user first needs to interact. If the activity in a panel is entering a name, have the focus placed in the text area for the first part of the name when the panel appears. A blind user can't use the mouse to click in a text area to establish focus. The default means Swing has of identifying the next component after the current one is the order in which components were added to the container. So, make sure that the order in which `add()` is called is consistent with the order that the focus should traverse the components. If you want to explicitly override the default component the focus will change to, `JComponent` supplies the `setNextFocusableComponent()` method. `JComponent` also supplies the `isFocusTraversable()` method, which can disable the ability of a component to get the focus if it returns `false`. You should not override this to return `false` in a subclass unless the component does not have an associated action or you have explicitly supplied a keyboard means of triggering the action. Otherwise a user without a mouse would not be able to use the component.

Notifying the user about status or errors (through a JDialog or some form of status bar) should be implemented using Swing components so that the accessibility engine can notice these events and report them to the user.

4.2   Understanding the Accessibility API

The Accessibility API provides several classes and interfaces for use by traditional applications. The main interface is the Accessible interface (p.85).

The Accessible interface is very simple, containing the getAccessibleContext() method. The AccessibleContext (p.90) is the core of the Accessibility API, providing methods (table 4.1) to get all of the other information required. As such, it contains a large number of methods. Don't let that overwhelm you, since most of the methods are implemented to simply return null, indicating that the component does not support that kind of accessibility information. For example, a JScrollBar's associated AccessibleContext will return an Accessible-Value (p.104) object from its getAccessibleValue() method, but it will return null from its getAccessibleText() method. JLabel is just the opposite, in that it returns an Accessible-Text (p.103) object from its getAccessibleText() method and null from its getAccessibleValue() method. Most components in Swing implement their AccessibleContext using an inner class.

Table 4.1   Methods in AccessibleContext supporting accessibility features

Method	Description
getAccessibleAction()	Returns the AccessibleAction (p.86) associated with this component.
getAccessibleChild(int index)	Returns the Accessible child at *index* in the component.
getAccessibleChildrenCount()	Returns the number of Accessible children in the component.
getAccessibleComponent()	Returns the AccessibleComponent (p.87) associated with this AccessibleContext.
getAccessibleDescription()	Returns the accessibleDescription property of this object.
getAccessibleIndexInParent()	Returns the 0-based index of this component in its Accessible parent.
getAccessibleName()	Returns the accessibleName property of this component.
getAccessibleParent()	Returns the Accessible parent of this component.
getAccessibleRole()	Returns the role of this component.
getAccessibleSelection()	Returns the AccessibleSelection (p.98) associated with this component.
getAccessibleStateSet()	Returns the AccessibleStateSet (p.101) of this component.
getAccessibleText()	Returns the AccessibleText (p.103) associated with this component.

Table 4.1   Methods in AccessibleContext supporting accessibility features (continued)

Method	Description
`getAccessibleValue()`	Returns the `AccessibleValue` (p.104) associated with this component.
`setAccessibleDescription(String description)`	Sets the localized `accessibleDescription` of this component.
`setAccessibleName(String name)`	Sets the localized `accessibleName` of this component.
`setAccessibleParent(Accessible parent)`	Sets the `Accessible` parent of this component.

`AccessibleContext` supports `PropertyChangeListeners` as well. It has a number of property events (table 4.2) that it can generate so that accessibility technologies can be informed when the component changes; conversely, the component can be updated when the accessibility technology causes a change.

Table 4.2   Property names defined by AccessibleContext

Property	Description
`ACCESSIBLE_ACTIVE_DESCENDANT_PROPERTY`	Property name used when the focused child in a `JTable`, `JList`, or `JTree` changes.
`ACCESSIBLE_CARET_PROPERTY`	Property name used when the `accessibleText` caret has changed.
`ACCESSIBLE_CHILD_PROPERTY`	Property name used when accessible children are added to or removed from the object.
`ACCESSIBLE_DESCRIPTION_PROPERTY`	Property name used when the `accessibleDescription` property has changed.
`ACCESSIBLE_NAME_PROPERTY`	Property name used when the `accessibleName` property has changed.
`ACCESSIBLE_SELECTION_PROPERTY`	Property name used when the `accessibleSelection` has changed.
`ACCESSIBLE_STATE_PROPERTY`	Property name used when the `accessibleStateSet` property has changed.
`ACCESSIBLE_TEXT_PROPERTY`	Property name used when the `accessibleText` has changed.
`ACCESSIBLE_VALUE_PROPERTY`	Property name used when the `accessibleValue` property has changed.
`ACCESSIBLE_VISIBLE_DATA_PROPERTY`	Property name used when the visual appearance of the object has changed.

The `accessibleName` property is the name of the object. It is usually implemented to return the text contained in the control, if it has any. Since the contained text is displayed, it should be localized. For example, a "yes" button would have "Yes" as its `accessibleName` in the en_US (English-US) locale and "Oui" in the fr_FR (French-France) locale.

For complex controls that contain a number of items, such as a `JTable` or `JList`, the `accessibleName` needs to be explicitly set using the `setAccessibleName()` method. A `JTable` displaying the contents of a company's orders database could have a localized `accessibleName` such as "Orders" in the en_US locale.

When the `accessibleName` property changes, an `ACCESSIBLE_NAME_PROPERTY` PropertyChangeEvent is fired.

The second important property is `accessibleDescription`. This property is a localized description of an object's purpose. The `JTable` from the `accessibleName` example could have an `accessibleDescription` such as "The Wallace Company's Grommet Order Database." By default, Swing components will use their ToolTip text (if they have any) as their `accessibleDescription`.

Changing the `accessibleDescription` property causes an `ACCESSIBLE_DESCRIPTION_PROPERTY` `PropertyChangeEvent` to be fired.

An `AccessibleValue` (p.104) tends to be used for classes that represent a range of values, such as a `JScrollBar` or `JSlider`. There are a few exceptions to this rule, which can be understood once you see what the value is representing. An `AbstractButton` (p.118) subclass uses its `accessibleValue` property to represent its pressed state. A `JSplitPane` (p.346) uses it to represent the location of the divider. Other components that use the associated `AccessibleValue` (p.104) interface are `JInternalFrame` (p.254), `JInternalFrame.JDesktopIcon` (p.263), and `JProgressBar` (p.315). The associated `PropertyChangeEvent` to this property is `ACCESSIBLE_VALUE_CHANGE`.

`AccessibleSelection` (p.98) is a collection of the selected `Accessible` children in the component. `AccessibleSelection` maintains an internal vector of selected items. The last item in this vector (at index n-1, since the vector is 0 based) is the last selected item. `AccessibleSelection` is extremely important to the user. It tells the user what is currently selected and it is supported by any component that allows its children to be selected, such as `JLists`, `JMenus`, or `JTrees`. A `JDesktopPane` should be subclassed to implement this interface when it is managing several child windows (it does not support this interface by default). `AccessibleSelection` does not handle text selections. Use the `AccessibleText` interface for that kind of selection.

`AccessibleComponent` (p.87) is the `Accessible` component associated with this `AccessibleContext`. `AccessibleComponent` defines a standard interface for the accessibility engine to directly interact with the component. The methods it implements mirror those found in `JComponent`.

`AccessibleText` (p.103) provides support for complex text manipulation. This interface also provides methods for controlling the text `Caret` when the text is editable. This interface is not for use by simple, noneditable components that contain text. For example, `JTextField`'s `AccessibleContext` returns an instance of an object supporting this interface, but `JButton` and `JLabel`'s `AccessibleContexts` return `null` from `getAccessibleText()`. The components that can be manipulated using this interface are the components that have a `Document` as their model. As long as any `Document` you create uses the `StyleConstants` (p.865) attributes, the component using the `Document` will be able to be manipulated through this interface. Note that text selections are manipulated though this interface, not the `AccessibleSelection` interface. The property changes fired by changes made using this interface are the `ACCESSIBLE_TEXT_PROPERTY` (content changes), `ACCESSIBLE_SELECTION_PROPERTY` (selection changes), and ACCESSIBLE_CARET_PROPERTY (the Caret moved). Even though it is a change in the appearance of the component, changing the text contents of a Document does not fire the ACCESSIBLE_VISIBLE_DATA_PROPERTY event.

Since hypertext has become so common, a subinterface of AccessibleText is supplied by the Accessibility API. The AccessibleHypertext (p.94) interface has methods to simplify working with hypertext documents. Objects implementing this interface are still retrieved using the getAccessibleText() method. You can test the returned object using instanceof to see if it supports AccessibleHypertext once you have a reference to it.

The accessibleParent and accessibleChildren properties are handled transparently for you by Swing. As Swing components are added to and removed from each other, the appropriate accessibleParent/accessibleChild relationships are maintained.

The accessibleRole property of an object is a generic way of expressing what an accessible object is. The constants for the different roles are all defined in the AccessibleRole (p.95) class. Note that a single object can only have one role. A JComboBox has a role of Accessible-Role.COMBO_BOX, not AccessibleRole.TEXT and AccessibleRole.LIST. If you are subclassing a component for a more specific purpose, do not define your own AccessibleRole. Use the accessibleDescription to distinguish the new component from its parent class instead. The reason for this is that the accessibility technology doesn't care that the purpose of the component is different as long as it still behaves in roughly the same way.

The accessibleState property of an object expresses its current state. For example, a JCheckBox can be checked or not checked. A single object may have many AccessibleStates (p.99) and they are all combined into an instance of the AccessibleStateSet (p.101) class. The previously mentioned JCheckBox may also have the AccessibleState.ENABLED and AccessibleState.FOCUSED states in its AccessibleStateSet along with the Accessi-bleState.CHECKED state.

Components that trigger an Action will have an AccessibleContext that returns an AccessibleAction (p.86) object. An AccessibleAction contains a list mapping between actions and their descriptions. The list will be presented to the user, and the user can then choose to trigger one of the actions by its index. This makes it possible to use JToolBar and JMenu without a mouse. Web pages can present their image maps in the form of an AccessibleAction as well, where each image map hotspot is represented as an entry in the list. The description would indicate where the hotspot would take the user and the associated action would be triggering the hyperlink. In fact this is a common-enough usage of AccessibleAction that there is a subinterface of AccessibleAction named AccessibleHyperlink (p.93). The getAccessibleAction() interface is used to retrieve objects that implement AccessibleHyperlink. Once you have a reference to an object returned by getAccessibleAction() you can test it (using instanceof) to see if it implements the extended AccessibleHyperlink interface.

4.3 Accessibility through pluggable look and feel

A second way accessibility can be implemented is through writing a custom look and feel. This method is appropriate for situations where the user interface needs radical changes to support the accessibility technology, such as a pure speech interface, or a puffer/headtracker interface.

A full, new look and feel could be written to support a new technology, but a much better solution has been provided. As discussed in the chapter on look and feel, the Multi look and feel is designed primarily to support accessibility technologies. If you are trying to provide a new input mechanism for the user, all you need to implement using the Multi look and feel is the input part of the look and feel. You can use an existing look and feel (such as Metal) for the visual output. A look and feel designed for the Multi look and feel is known as an auxiliary look and feel. Auxiliary look and feels can also be transparently combined, so an input look and feel can be combined with an output look and feel (such as a screen reader).

For more information about how the Multi look and feel works, see chapter 3.

4.4 The end result

Accessibility, like internationalization, may seem at times to be more trouble than it is worth. With accessibility, you are enabling people to use your product who may not have *any* other choices. That's worth a lot.

Beyond the warm fuzzy reasons, there are also sound business reasons. There are very large lobby groups committed to accessibility, and very large industries that have already seen the positive business aspects to supporting these technologies. That is even beyond having a market which wants applications and until now hasn't had many choices.

Swing makes it relatively easy to support accessibility in your applications. Since you are already doing most of the work of supporting accessibility through adding text and ToolTips to your application (without even knowing it), doing the rest of the work is well worth it.

PART 2

Swing Reference

Package accessibility

Accessibility is best described as the support for assistive technologies such as screen readers, magnifiers, Braille displays, and alternative input methods. Speech input is not covered in this category, since it has its own API, JavaSpeech.

The accessibility package is technically not part of the Swing section of the Java Foundation Classes (JFC). It *is* distributed as part of the Swing distribution and all Swing components support it, so it is covered in this reference.

The designers of the Accessibility API have tried to make it as general—and as simple—as possible, to enable accessibility in your applications. Enabling accessibility in a Swing application generally involves making one or possibly two method calls on each component. The two calls set the name and the description of the component.

Making your own custom components accessible is also very easy, since the basic interface, `Accessible`, only involves one method call. The method call in `Accessible` returns an instance of `AccessibleContext` which describes the component. The abstract `Accessible-Context` class only requires implementing six simple methods in a subclass.

Accessibility extends/implements hierarchy

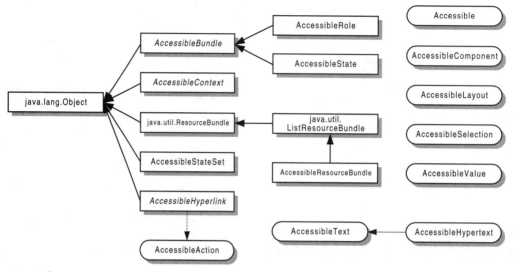

Quick summary

The Main Interface	`Accessible` (p.85).

The Main Class	`AccessibleContext` (p.90). The sole method in `Accessible` returns an instance of this class. Through the methods of this class you can find out all of the other available pieces of information.
How to Use	If you are implementing a class not descended from `JComponent`, make the class implement `Accessible`. If you are using an accessible class, at a minimum make sure you set the `accessibleName` and `accessibleDescription` properties.
Other Classes	• `AccessibleRole` (p.95) describes the role (purpose) of this object in a general way. • `AccessibleState` (p.99) describes the state of the object.
Other Interfaces	• `AccessibleAction` (p.86) describes and/or manipulates an `Action`. • `AccessibleComponent` (p.87) describes a component. • `AccessibleSelection` (p.98) describes and allows the modification of a (nontext) selection. • `AccessibleText` (p.103) describes text and allows the manipulation of any selection in it. • `AccessibleValue` (p.104) describes a value. Instances of classes implementing these interfaces are retrieved through the corresponding methods in `AccessibleContext`.

FAQs

How do I make my component accessible?

Conveniently, the Swing components are all accessible since `JComponent` provides default accessibility support. To make a Swing component fully accessible, all you need do is set the `accessibleName` or `accessibleDescription`. By default the `accessibleName` is set to the text on the component, for components that have simple text labels like JButtons or JMenuItems (if the text is set; if the component is only displaying an Icon, you will have to set the name). Components such as JMenuBar and JTextArea that don't have simple text labels need to have the accessibleName explicitly set. To set the accessibleName or accessibleDescription, get the AccessibleContext for the object and use the methods it provides, as follows:

```
JTextArea noteArea = new JTextArea();
noteArea.getAccessibleContext().setAccessibleName("Notes");
noteArea.getAccessibleContext().setAccessibleDescription("The notes you
    want to take");
```

I don't have a Swing component. How do I make the component accessible then?

Make your component implement the interface Accessible which has one method, getAccessibleContext(), that returns an instance of AccessibleContext. AccessibleContext is an abstract class that has six methods you will need to implement, at a minimum. Override the other methods in AccessibleContext as needed. For example, if your class was a form of a text area, perhaps a custom scrolling marquee, you would override the getAccessibleText() method to return an instance of AccessibleText. AccessibleText provides methods so that assistive technologies can retrieve more detailed information about the text; for example, finding individual words in the text.

accessibility.Accessible

INTERFACE   (Accessible)

This is the main interface for the JFC's accessibility support. All components that support accessibility must implement this interface.

public interface Accessible

Methods
public abstract AccessibleContext getAccessibleContext()
> Returns the AccessibleContext associated with this object. The only time this method may return null is if it is in a non-Accessible subclass of a class which is Accessible. In that case this method can be overridden to return null.

Implemented by   Box (p.134), CellRendererPane (p.151), JApplet (p.186), JButton (p.191), JCheckBox (p.193), JCheckBoxMenuItem (p.195), JComboBox (p.200), JComboBox.AccessibleJComboBox. (p.206), JDesktopPane (p.224), JDialog (p.226), JFrame (p.248), JInternalFrame (p.254), JInternalFrame.JDesktopIcon (p.263), JLabel (p.264), JLayeredPane (p.268), JList (p.271), JList.AccessibleJList.AccessibleJListChild (p.279), JMenu (p.281), JMenuBar (p.288), JMenuItem (p.291), JPanel (p.305), JPopupMenu (p.309), JProgressBar (p.315), JRadioButton (p.319), JRadioButtonMenuItem (p.321), JRootPane (p.323), JScrollBar (p.328), JScrollPane (p.332), JSeparator (p.338), JSlider (p.341), JSplitPane (p.346), JTabbedPane (p.351), JTable (p.357), JTable.AccessibleJTable.AccessibleJTableCell (p.372),

JTableHeader (p.752), JTableHeader.AccessibleJTableHeader.AccessibleJTableHeaderEntry (p.755), JTextComponent (p.838), JToggleButton (p.385), JToolBar (p.388), JToolTip (p.391), JTree (p.393), JTree.AccessibleJTree.AccessibleJTreeNode (p.404), JViewport (p.410), JWindow (p.414).

See also   AccessibleContext (p.90).

accessibility.AccessibleAction

INTERFACE   AccessibleAction

This interface is to be implemented by any object that can perform `Actions`. After discovering the number of `Actions` available, the assistive technology (for example, a screen reader) can present the descriptions of the `Actions` to the user. Once the user chooses an `Action` to perform, `doAccessibleAction()` can be called to perform the `Action`.

`public interface AccessibleAction`

Methods

`public abstract boolean doAccessibleAction(int index)`

Performs the action represented by the given *index*. If the action was performed successfully this method should return `true`. If the action fails, or the *index* is not valid for this object, this method should return `false`.

`public abstract int getAccessibleActionCount()`

Returns the number of accessible actions available in this object. If there is more than one, the first one is the default action. Note that the actions are numbered from zero, not one.

`public abstract String getAccessibleActionDescription(`
`int index)`

Returns a localized description of the specified action which can be presented to the user.

Implemented by   AbstractButton.AccessibleAbstractButton (p.125), AccessibleHyperlink (p.93), JComboBox.AccessibleJComboBox (p.206), JTree.AccessibleJTree.AccessibleJTreeNode (p.404).

Returned by   AbstractButton.AccessibleAbstractButton.getAccessibleAction() (p.125), AccessibleContext.getAccessibleAction() (p.90), JComboBox.AccessibleJComboBox.getAccessibleAction() (p.206), JList.AccessibleJList.AccessibleJListChild.getAccessibleAction() (p.279), JTable.AccessibleJTable.AccessibleJTableCell.getAccessibleAction() (p.372), JTableHeader.AccessibleJTableHeader.AccessibleJTableHeaderEntry.getAccessibleAction() (p.755), JTree.AccessibleJTree.AccessibleJTreeNode.getAccessibleAction() (p.402).

accessibility.AccessibleBundle

CLASS   java.lang.Object ◄─── AccessibleBundle

A base class provided to support a strongly typed enumeration.

`public abstract class AccessibleBundle`

Constructors
`public AccessibleBundle()`
> Default constructor.

Methods
`public String toDisplayString()`
> Returns a localized string describing the key for the user, using the default `Locale`.

`public String toDisplayString(java.util.Locale locale)`
> Returns a description of the key as a `String` appropriate to the given `locale`. If there isn't a localized description available, the contents of the key field will be returned.

`public String toString()`
> See `toDisplayString()`.

Protected Fields
`protected String key`
> The `String` used internally as the key. This string may be returned by `toDisplayString()` if a localized value is not supplied.

Protected Methods
`protected String toDisplayString(String resourceBundleName,`
`    java.util.Locale locale)`
> Obtains the key as a localized string from the `ResourceBundle resourceBundleName`. If a localized string cannot be found for this object's key, the contents of the key field will be returned. This method is provided so subclasses can provide `ResourceBundle`s for their own keys.

Extended by   AccessibleRole (p.95), AccessibleState (p.99).

accessibility.AccessibleComponent

INTERFACE   (AccessibleComponent)

This interface should be supported by any component that wishes to be `Accessible`. `JComponent` does not implement this interface, but all Swing components (including `Box`) implement it to provide accessibility.

`public interface AccessibleComponent`

Methods
`public abstract void addFocusListener(`
`    java.awt.event.FocusListener listener)`
> Adds a focus listener to be notified about `FocusEvents` by this component.

`public abstract boolean contains(java.awt.Point point)`
> Returns `true` if the `point` is inside this component. The coordinates of `point` must be relative to the origin of this component.

public abstract Accessible getAccessibleAt(java.awt.Point point)
Returns the `Accessible` child at the given `point`. If there isn't an `Accessible` child at `point`, returns `null`. The coordinate system used for `point` must be relative to the origin of this component.

public abstract java.awt.Color getBackground()
Gets the background `Color` of this object. This method can return `null` if this component does not support a background `Color`.

public abstract java.awt.Rectangle getBounds()
Returns the width, height, and location of this component relative to its parent. This method may return `null` if the component is not on screen.

public abstract java.awt.Cursor getCursor()
Returns the `Cursor` used for this component. If the component does not support a non-default `Cursor`, this method should return `null`.

public abstract java.awt.Font getFont()
Returns the `Font` used for this component. If the component does not support a non-default `Font`, this method should return `null`.

public abstract java.awt.FontMetrics getFontMetrics(java.awt.Font font)
Returns the `FontMetrics` for the given `Font` when used by this component. If the component does not support `Fonts`, this method should return `null`.

public abstract java.awt.Color getForeground()
Returns the foreground `Color` of this component. If a foreground `Color` is not supported by the component, this method should return `null`.

public abstract java.awt.Point getLocation()
Returns the location of this component relative to its parent's origin. If the component or its parent are not on screen, this method may return `null`.

public abstract java.awt.Point getLocationOnScreen()
Returns the location of the component relative to the screen. If the component is not on screen, this method may return `null`.

public abstract java.awt.Dimension getSize()
Returns the component's width and height. If the component is not on screen, this method may return `null`.

public abstract boolean isEnabled()
Returns `true` if the component is enabled, `false` otherwise. Objects which are enabled also have `AccessibleState.ENABLED` added to their `AccessibleStateSet`.

public abstract boolean isFocusTraversable()
Returns `true` if this component can accept the focus. An example of a component that cannot accept the focus would be a `JLabel`. Objects which are focus traversable also have `AccessibleState.FOCUSABLE` added to their `AccessibleStateSet`.

public abstract boolean isShowing()
Returns `true` if the component is `showing`. The `showing` property is determined by checking the visibility of the object and ancestors of the component. This method will return `true` even if the component is partially or fully covered by another. Objects which are showing also have `AccessibleState.SHOWING` added to their `AccessibleStateSet`.

public abstract boolean isVisible()
Returns `true` if the component is visible. Note that this method can return `true` even if the component cannot be seen on screen as a result of one of its ancestors being hidden. Objects which are visible also have `AccessibleState.VISIBLE` added to their `AccessibleStateSet`.

`public abstract void removeFocusListener(java.awt.event.FocusListener listener)`

Removes the `listener` from the list of objects to notify about this component's `FocusEvents`.

`public abstract void requestFocus()`

Requests the `focus` for this component. The `FocusManager` may reject this request by simply ignoring it.

`public abstract void setBackground(java.awt.Color color)`

Sets the background `Color` of this component, if a background `Color` is supported.

`public abstract void setBounds(java.awt.Rectangle rect)`

Sets the `bounds` of this component. The bounds specify this object's width, height, and location relative to its parent.

`public abstract void setCursor(java.awt.Cursor cursor)`

Sets the `Cursor` of this component.

`public abstract void setEnabled(boolean b)`

Sets the `enabled` state of this component.

`public abstract void setFont(java.awt.Font font)`

Sets the `Font` of this component, if it supports `Fonts`.

`public abstract void setForeground(java.awt.Color color)`

Sets the `foreground` color of this component, if it supports a foregound color.

`public abstract void setLocation(java.awt.Point p)`

Sets the `location` of the component relative to the parent.

`public abstract void setSize(java.awt.Dimension d)`

Resizes this component.

`public abstract void setVisible(boolean show)`

Shows or hides the component depending on the value of `show`.

Implemented by   Box.AccessibleBox (p.137), Box.Filler.AccessibleBoxFiller (p.141), CellRendererPane.AccessibleCellRendererPane (p.152), JApplet.AccessibleJApplet (p.189), JComponent.AccessibleJComponent (p.221), JDialog.AccessibleJDialog (p.230), JFrame.AccessibleJFrame (p.252), JList.AccessibleJList.AccessibleJListChild (p.230), JTable.AccessibleJTable.AccessibleJTableCell (p.372), JTableHeader.AccessibleJTableHeader.AccessibleJTableHeaderEntry (p.755), JTree.AccessibleJTree.AccessibleJTreeNode (p.404), JWindow.AccessibleJWindow (p.417).

Returned by   AccessibleContext.getAccessibleComponent() (p.90), Box.AccessibleBox.getAccessibleComponent() (p.137), Box.Filler.AccessibleBoxFiller.getAccessibleComponent() (p.141), CellRendererPane.AccessibleCellRendererPane.getAccessibleComponent() (p.152), JApplet.AccessibleJApplet.getAccessibleComponent() (p.189), JComponent.AccessibleJComponent.getAccessibleComponent() (p.221), JDialog.AccessibleJDialog.getAccessibleComponent() (p.230), JFrame.AccessibleJFrame.getAccessibleComponent() (p.252), JList.AccessibleJList.AccessibleJListChild.getAccessibleComponent() (p.279), JTable.AccessibleJTable.AccessibleJTableCell.getAccessibleComponent() (p.372), JTableHeader.AccessibleJTableHeader.AccessibleJTableHeaderEntry.getAccessibleComponent() (p.755), JTree.AccessibleJTree.AccessibleJTreeNode.getAccessibleComponent() (p.404), JWindow.AccessibleJWindow.getAccessibleComponent() (p.417).

See also   Accessible (p.85), AccessibleContext (p.90).

accessibility.AccessibleContext

CLASS

```
java.lang.Object  ◄─── AccessibleContext
```

An `AccessibleContext` holds the information that all accessible classes need to supply. All accessible classes need to supply—at a minimum—an accessible name, a description of the object for the user, a role (a general indicator of the purpose of the object), the state of the object, and information about the parent and child accessible objects of the object.

This class also contains methods for retrieving more specific information about the object using `getAccessibleAction()`, `getAccessibleComponent()`, `getAccessibleSelection()`, `getAccessibleStateSet()`, `getAccessibleText()`, and `getAccessibleValue()`.

```
public abstract class AccessibleContext
```

Fields

```
public static final String ACCESSIBLE_ACTIVE_DESCENDANT_PROPERTY =
    "AccessibleActiveDescendant"
```
Property name used when the "active descendant" has changed. This property is used by components which have transient children, such as a `JTable` or `JTree`. The old value will be the `Accessible` which was previously active, and the new value will be the `Accessible` which is currently active.

```
public static final String ACCESSIBLE_CARET_PROPERTY =
    "AccessibleCaret"
```
Property name used when the `accessibleText Caret` is changed. The old value is an `Integer` representing the previous `Caret` position, and the new value is an `Integer` representing the current position of the `Caret`.

```
public static final String ACCESSIBLE_CHILD_PROPERTY =
    "AccessibleChild"
```
Property name used when the `accessibleChildren` of an object have been changed. When a new child is added, the old value is `null` and the new value holds the added child. When a child is removed, the old value will be the removed child and the new value will be `null`.

```
public static final String ACCESSIBLE_DESCRIPTION_PROPERTY =
    "AccessibleDescription"
```
Property name used when the `accessibleDescription` changes. The old and new values are the old and new `accessibleDescriptions`, respectively.

```
public static final String ACCESSIBLE_NAME_PROPERTY = "AccessibleName"
```
Property name used when the `accessibleName` changes. The old and new values are the old and new `accessibleNames`, respectively.

```
public static final String ACCESSIBLE_SELECTION_PROPERTY =
    "AccessibleSelection"
```
Property name used when the `accessibleSelection` changes. The old and new values are currently unused.

`public static final String ACCESSIBLE_STATE_PROPERTY = "AccessibleState"`

Property name used when the `accessibleStateSet` property changes. One event is sent for each change to the set. The old value will be the value in the set before the change, and the new value will be the value in the set after the change. Either value may be `null`, indicating an `AccessibleState` being added or removed, rather than changed.

`public static final String ACCESSIBLE_TEXT_PROPERTY = "AccessibleText"`

Property name used when the `accessibleText` changes. The old and new values are currently unused.

`public static final String ACCESSIBLE_VALUE_PROPERTY = "AccessibleValue"`

Property name used when the `accessibleValue` changes. The old value will be a `Number` representing the previous value and the new value will be a `Number` representing the new value.

`public static final String ACCESSIBLE_VISIBLE_DATA_PROPERTY = "AccessibleVisibleData"`

Property name used when the visible state of the object changes, in particular when the `Caret` moves. The old value is an `Integer` representing the old `Caret` position and the new value is an `Integer` representing the new `Caret` position.

Constructors

`public AccessibleContext()`

Default constructor.

Methods

`public void addPropertyChangeListener(`
`    java.beans.PropertyChangeListener listener)`

Adds a `PropertyChangeListener` to the listener list and registers it against all properties.

`public void firePropertyChange(String propertyName, Object oldValue,`
`    Object newValue)`

Fires a new `PropertyChangeEvent` on behalf of an accessible object. This method only fires the event if the old and new values are actually different and there is at least one listener registered.

`public AccessibleAction getAccessibleAction()`

Gets the `AccessibleAction` associated with this object. If the object does not support an `AccessibleAction` this method returns `null`.

`public abstract Accessible getAccessibleChild(int i)`

Returns the specified `Accessible` child of the object.

`public abstract int getAccessibleChildrenCount()`

Returns the number of accessible children in the object.

`public AccessibleComponent getAccessibleComponent()`

Gets the `AccessibleComponent` information associated with this object. If the object does not support `AccessibleComponent` this method returns `null`.

`public String getAccessibleDescription()`

Gets the `accessibleDescription` of this object. If the object does not have a description, this method returns `null`. This `String` is intended for the user, so it should be localized.

`public abstract int getAccessibleIndexInParent()`

Returns the index of this object in its accessible parent. This method returns `-1` if this object does not have an accessible parent.

`public String getAccessibleName()`

Gets the `accessibleName` of this object. An object is allowed to have a `null String` for its name. This `String` is intended for the user, so it should be localized.

`public Accessible getAccessibleParent()`

Gets the `accessibleParent` of this object. This method returns `null` if this object does not have an accessible parent.

`public abstract AccessibleRole getAccessibleRole()`

Gets the role of this object.

`public AccessibleSelection getAccessibleSelection()`

Gets the `accessibleSelection` associated with this object if one exists. If this object does not support an `AccessibleSelection`, this method should return `null`.

`public abstract AccessibleStateSet getAccessibleStateSet()`

Gets the state set of this object.

`public AccessibleText getAccessibleText()`

Gets the `accessibleText` associated with this object if one exists. If this object does not support an `AccessibleText` object, this method should return `null`.

`public AccessibleValue getAccessibleValue()`

Gets the `accessibleValue` associated with this object if one exists. If this object does not support an `AccessibleValue`, this method should return `null`.

`public abstract java.util.Locale getLocale()`

    `throws java.awt.IllegalComponentStateException`

Gets the locale of the component. By default, `Accessible` children inherit the locale of their `Accessible` parent, if they have a parent.

Throws: `IllegalComponentStateException` if the `Component` does not have its own locale and has not yet been added to an `Accessible` parent that does have a locale set.

`public void removePropertyChangeListener(`

    `java.beans.PropertyChangeListener listener)`

Removes a `PropertyChangeListener` from the listener list.

`public void setAccessibleDescription(String s)`

Sets the `accessibleDescription` of this object.

`public void setAccessibleName(String s)`

Sets the `accessibleName` of this object. This `String` should be localized since it is intended for the user.

`public void setAccessibleParent(Accessible a)`

Sets the `accessibleParent` of this object. By default the accessible parent is the `Component` that this object was added to. This method should only be called by the parent `Component`, and only in situations where it has another object it is using to handle accessibility issues.

Protected Fields

`protected String accessibleDescription`

A localized `String` containing the description of the object.

`protected String accessibleName`

A localized `String` containing the name of the object.

`protected Accessible accessibleParent`

The accessible parent of this object.

Extended by   Box.AccessibleBox (p.137), Box.Filler.AccessibleBoxFiller (p.141), CellRendererPane.AccessibleCellRendererPane (p.152), JApplet.AccessibleJApplet (p.189), JComponent.AccessibleJComponent (p.221), JDialog.AccessibleJDialog (p.230), JFrame.AccessibleJFrame (p.252), JList.AccessibleJList.AccessibleJListChild (p.279), JTable.AccessibleJTable.AccessibleJTableCell (p.372), JTableHeader.AccessibleJTableHeader.AccessibleJTableHeaderEntry (p.755), JTree.AccessibleJTree.AccessibleJTreeNode (p.404), JWindow.AccessibleJWindow (p.417).

Returned by   Many.

See also   Accessible (p.85), AccessibleAction (p.86), AccessibleComponent (p.87), AccessibleRole (p.95), AccessibleSelection (p.98), AccessibleState (p.99), AccessibleStateSet (p.101), AccessibleText (p.103), AccessibleValue (p.104).

accessibility.AccessibleHyperlink

ABSTRACT
CLASS

The `AccessibleHyperlink` interface is used to allow assistive technologies to navigate and identify hyperlinks, for example in an HTML document.

```
public abstract class AccessibleHyperlink extends java.lang.Object
    implements AccessibleAction
```

Constructors
`public AccessibleHyperlink()`

Default constructor.

Methods
`public abstract boolean doAccessibleAction(int i)`

Performs the specified `Action` on the object. If the `Action` is performed, returns `true`.

Implements: doAccessibleAction in interface `AccessibleAction`.

`public abstract Object getAccessibleActionAnchor(int i)`

Returns an `Object` which is the link anchor. For links which have text as their anchor, this method will return a `String`. Links which use an image will have the image returned as an `ImageIcon`. The `getAccessibleActionDescription()` method can be used to get the descriptive text (the `alt=` parameter in the tag) for the image.

`public abstract int getAccessibleActionCount()`

Returns the number of `Actions` associated with this link. In situations where there is more than one `Action` associated with a link (such as in an image map), the `Actions` for the link are not in a priority order, which implies link 0 is *not* the "default" link.

Implements: getAccessibleActionCount in interface `AccessibleAction`.

`public abstract String getAccessibleActionDescription(int i)`

Returns the text associated with an anchor. For text links, this is the same as the value returned from `getAccessibleActionAnchor()`. For image anchors, the text returned is the `alt=` text.

Implements: getAccessibleActionDescription in interface `AccessibleAction`.

public abstract Object getAccessibleActionObject(int i)
Returns the hyperlink itself. It should usually return a `java.net.URL`.

public abstract int getEndIndex()
Returns the offset in the document where the text for this link ends.

public abstract int getStartIndex()
Returns the offset in the document where the text for this link begins.

public abstract boolean isValid()
When the `Document` changes, any links in it become invalid. This method returns `true` if this `AccessibleHyperlink` is still valid.

Extended by   JEditorPane.JEditorPaneAccessibleHypertextSupport.HTMLLink (p.238).
Returned by   AccessibleHypertext.getLink() (p.94),
JEditorPane.JEditorPaneAccessibleHypertextSupport.getLink() (p.237).

accessibility.AccessibleHypertext

INTERFACE

This interface provides the support needed to handle hypertext. It extends the `AccessibleText` interface by providing a means to enumerate and retrieve the links contained within the document.

To discover if an object supports `AccessibleHypertext`, get the object's `AccessibleContext` and call its `getAccessibleText()` method. If the value returned is non-null and it is an instance of `AccessibleHypertext`, it supports this interface.

public interface AccessibleHypertext extends AccessibleText

Methods
public abstract AccessibleHyperlink getLink(int n)
Returns the link at index *n* (zero based) in the object.

public abstract int getLinkCount()
Returns the number of links within this object.

public abstract int getLinkIndex(int charIndex)
Returns the index of the link which appears at the given *charIndex* in the text. If the index given is not inside text that defines a link, this method should return `null`.

Implemented by   JEditorPane.JEditorPaneAccessibleHypertextSupport (p.237).

accessibility.AccessibleResourceBundle

CLASS

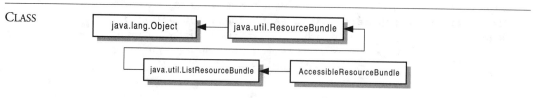

A resource bundle containing the localized strings in the accessibility package. This class is not intended for use by developers. It is purely for use by the other classes in the accessibility package.

```
public class AccessibleResourceBundle
    extends java.util.ListResourceBundle
```

Constructors
public AccessibleResourceBundle()
Default constructor.

Methods
public Object[][] getContents()
Overrides: getContents in class ListResourceBundle.

accessibility.AccessibleRole

CLASS

This class provides a way to generically describe the purpose of an object.

The way to use this class is to use one of the predefined constants, or a variable referencing one of them. To get a localized String describing the role to the user, call toDisplayString() on the role constant. For example,

```
String stringToShowUser = AccessibleRole.DIALOG.toDisplayString();
```

This information will generally be used by the assistive technology. From an application developer's standpoint setting up the instance of AccessibleContext returned from the object with the correct role is the only real use for this class.

If the roles provided do not match the role of a component (most likely for a custom component), then create a subclass of this class and provide a set of constants to describe the component's role. The constructor of this class is declared protected to allow for this type of extension. As an example, to provide a role for a component which only displays images, define a class:

```
public class ImageAccessibleRole extends AccessibleRole {
    public static final AccessibleRole IMAGE = new AccessibleRole("Image");
    protected ImageAccessibleRole() { }
}
```

public class AccessibleRole extends AccessibleBundle

Constants
public static final AccessibleRole ALERT
This object is used to alert the user.
public static final AccessibleRole AWT_COMPONENT
This object is an AWT component that has no accessible information.
public static final AccessibleRole CHECK_BOX
This object can have one of two states and presents a separate indicator revealing the current state.

public static final AccessibleRole COLOR_CHOOSER
This object allows a user to choose a color.

public static final AccessibleRole COLUMN_HEADER
This object is the header for a column of information.

public static final AccessibleRole COMBO_BOX
This object is a list of items users can select from, or optionally enter their own item.

public static final AccessibleRole DESKTOP_ICON
This object is an iconized INTERNAL_FRAME in a DESKTOP_PANE.

public static final AccessibleRole DESKTOP_PANE
This object is a PANEL that can support INTERNAL_FRAMEs.

public static final AccessibleRole DIALOG
This object is a top-level window with a title and a border. It is similar to, but less flexible than, a FRAME.

public static final AccessibleRole DIRECTORY_PANE
This object is a PANEL that can be used to navigate a file system.

public static final AccessibleRole FILE_CHOOSER
This object allows the user to select a file.

public static final AccessibleRole FILLER
This object simply fills up space to fine-tune a layout. It has no interactive use.

public static final AccessibleRole FRAME
This object is a top-level window with a title bar, a content area, and, potentially, a menu bar. It predominantly is used as the main window for an application.

public static final AccessibleRole GLASS_PANE
This object is a PANEL which is guaranteed to be displayed on top of all other PANELs.

public static final AccessibleRole INTERNAL_FRAME
This object is a frame-like panel which is managed and constrained by a DESKTOP_PANE.

public static final AccessibleRole LABEL
This object is a read-only area used to optionally display a String and an Icon.

public static final AccessibleRole LAYERED_PANE
This object is a PANEL which renders its children in a configurable stacking order (Z-order).

public static final AccessibleRole LIST
This object is a list of items the user can choose from. It is usually held in a SCROLL_PANE.

public static final AccessibleRole MENU
This object contains a set of MENU_ITEMs.

public static final AccessibleRole MENU_BAR
This object contains a set of MENUs, and is usually attached to a FRAME or INTERNAL_FRAME.

public static final AccessibleRole MENU_ITEM
This object is usually contained in a MENU or POPUP_MENU and triggers an action when selected.

public static final AccessibleRole OPTION_PANE
This object is a specialized form of a DIALOG.

public static final AccessibleRole PAGE_TAB
This object is contained in a PAGE_TAB_LIST and presents a PANEL to the user when selected.

public static final AccessibleRole PAGE_TAB_LIST
This object contains a list of PAGE_TABs.

public static final AccessibleRole PANEL
This object is a container used to hold other components.

public static final AccessibleRole PASSWORD_TEXT

This object is used for password fields where the text is not displayed to the user.

public static final AccessibleRole POPUP_MENU

This object is a transient window that presents a set of MENUs and MENU_ITEMs to the user and disappears when a MENU_ITEM is selected.

public static final AccessibleRole PROGRESS_BAR

This object displays in some manner how much of a task has been completed.

public static final AccessibleRole PUSH_BUTTON

This object triggers an action when selected.

public static final AccessibleRole RADIO_BUTTON

This object is a special CHECK_BOX that will deselect all other RADIO_BUTTONs in its group when selected.

public static final AccessibleRole ROOT_PANE

This object is a PANEL that has a LAYERED_PANE and a GLASS_PANE as its children.

public static final AccessibleRole ROW_HEADER

This object is the header for a row of data.

public static final AccessibleRole SCROLL_BAR

This object allows the user to choose a portion of data to display. It is usually contained in a SCROLL_PANE.

public static final AccessibleRole SCROLL_PANE

This object contains SCROLL_BARs and a VIEWPORT to allow a user to select a portion of data to display.

public static final AccessibleRole SEPARATOR

This object is a nonselectable member of a MENU which provides a logical separation between MENU_ITEMs or sub-MENUs.

public static final AccessibleRole SLIDER

This object allows the selection of a value from a range of values.

public static final AccessibleRole SPLIT_PANE

This object is a PANEL that contains two sub-PANELs that can be resized relative to each other using a provided "divider" component.

public static final AccessibleRole SWING_COMPONENT

This object is a Swing/JFC component that does not supply any accessibility information.

public static final AccessibleRole TABLE

This object presents data in rows and columns.

public static final AccessibleRole TEXT

This object presents text to the user, and is usually editable. Generally it provides more text than a LABEL.

public static final AccessibleRole TOGGLE_BUTTON

This object can take on one of two states, and indicates the selected state by modifying how it displays itself.

public static final AccessibleRole TOOL_BAR

This object displays a set of components representing the most commonly used features of an application. The components displayed are usually PUSH_BUTTONs or TOGGLE_BUTTONs.

public static final AccessibleRole TOOL_TIP

This object displays information about another object, usually in a "floating" panel in the vicinity of the other object.

public static final AccessibleRole TREE

This object displays data that takes the form of a hierarchy.

public static final AccessibleRole UNKNOWN

This object represents a screen element that no information is available about.

public static final AccessibleRole VIEWPORT

This object is almost universally used in a SCROLL_PANE, and displays the region of the data that the user has chosen to display.

public static final AccessibleRole WINDOW

This object is a top-level window without any decorations.

Protected Constructors

protected AccessibleRole(String key)

Creates a new AccessibleRole using the given locale independent key. This method is protected so it can only be used to create the constants in this class, which makes the class a strongly typed enumeration. Subclasses may use this method to extend the list of values.

See also   AccessibleBundle (p.86).

accessibility.AccessibleSelection

INTERFACE   AccessibleSelection

This interface is used by objects that support the concept of selected items. It can be used both to retrieve information about and modify a selection. Note that AccessibleText (p.103) handles the concept of selected text.

public interface AccessibleSelection

Methods

public abstract void addAccessibleSelection(int index)

Adds the accessible child at *index* to the set of selected items.

public abstract void clearAccessibleSelection()

Clears the list of selected items in the object.

public abstract Accessible getAccessibleSelection(int index)

Returns an Accessible representing the item at *index* in the list of selected items. If the index is out of range, this method should return null instead of throwing an exception.

public abstract int getAccessibleSelectionCount()

Returns the number of items in this object which are selected.

public abstract boolean isAccessibleChildSelected(int index)

Returns true if the accessible child at *index* is selected and false if it is not. If *index* is out of range, this method should simply return false.

public abstract void removeAccessibleSelection(int index)

Removes the item at *index* from the selected list, if it is selected. If the item is not selected, this method should simply return. If the index is out of range, this method should simply return instead of throwing an exception.

`public abstract void selectAllAccessibleSelection()`

Selects all of the object's children, if the object supports multiple selected items. If it does not support multiple selection, this method should simply return.

Returned by   AccessibleContext.getAccessibleSelection() (p.90),
JList.AccessibleJList.AccessibleJListChild.getAccessibleSelection() (p.279),
JList.AccessibleJList.getAccessibleSelection() (p.277),
JMenu.AccessibleJMenu.getAccessibleSelection() (p.286),
JMenuBar.AccessibleJMenuBar.getAccessibleSelection() (p.290),
JTabbedPane.AccessibleJTabbedPane.getAccessibleSelection() (p.356),
JTable.AccessibleJTable.AccessibleJTableCell.getAccessibleSelection() (p.372),
JTable.AccessibleJTable.getAccessibleSelection() (p.369),
JTableHeader.AccessibleJTableHeader.AccessibleJTableHeaderEntry.getAccessibleSelection() (p.755),
JTree.AccessibleJTree.AccessibleJTreeNode.getAccessibleSelection() (p.404),
JTree.AccessibleJTree.getAccessibleSelection() (p.402).

Implemented by   JList.AccessibleJList (p.277), JMenu.AccessibleJMenu (p.286),
JMenuBar.AccessibleJMenuBar (p.290), JTabbedPane.AccessibleJTabbedPane (p.356),
JTable.AccessibleJTable (p.369), JTree.AccessibleJTree (p.402),
JTree.AccessibleJTree.AccessibleJTreeNode (p.404).

See also   Accessible (p.85), AccessibleContext (p.90), AccessibleText (p.103).

accessibility.AccessibleState

CLASS

This class provides a set of constants used to describe the state of an object. The `AccessibleContext` method `getAccessibleStateSet()` returns a set of these states to fully define the current state of an object.

The correct way to use this class is to interact with the predefined constants, or a variable referencing one of the constants. Use the `toDisplayString()` method to return a `String` describing the state to the user, as follows:

```
String stringToShow = AccessibleState.BUSY.toDisplayString();
```

If this set of states is insufficient to describe the state of a component (usually because the component is a custom component), create a subclass of this class and create a set of constants sufficient to describe the extra state information. For example,

```
public class VeryBadComponentState extends AccessibleState {
   public static final AccessibleState FUBAR =
                     new AccessibleState("You don't want to know");
   protected VeryBadComponent() {}
}
```

`public class AccessibleState extends AccessibleBundle`

Fields

public static final AccessibleState ACTIVE

This state indicates that a window is currently active. This state is also applied to the "active descendant" in components which have one, such as `JTable` or `JTree`. The "active descendant" is the subcomponent which has the focus in the component.

public static final AccessibleState ARMED

This state indicates that an object is armed. It is contained in the state set of buttons when they are pressed and the mouse pointer is still within their bounds. Note that this does not apply to a toggle button's `SELECTED` state.

public static final AccessibleState BUSY

This state indicates the object is active. Used by `JProgressBars`, `JSliders`, and `JScrollBars`.

public static final AccessibleState CHECKED

This state indicates that the object is checked. It is usually set on `JToggleButton` and its descendants.

public static final AccessibleState COLLAPSED

This state indicates that the object is collapsed. It is usually used with tree nodes ot other collapsable hierarchies.

public static final AccessibleState EDITABLE

This state indicates the object is editable. It is not used on objects which are always editable when enabled. It is usually used on text components.

public static final AccessibleState ENABLED

This state indicates the object is enabled and can be manipulated by the user.

public static final AccessibleState EXPANDABLE

This state indicates the object can be "expanded" to show more information or "collapsed" to reduce the amount of information it is displaying.

public static final AccessibleState EXPANDED

This state indicates the object is expanded. It is usually used with tree nodes or other expandable hierarchies.

public static final AccessibleState FOCUSABLE

This state indicates the object can accept the focus.

public static final AccessibleState FOCUSED

This state indicates the object currently has the focus.

public static final AccessibleState HORIZONTAL

This state indicates that the object is oriented horizontally.

public static final AccessibleState ICONIFIED

This state indicates that the object is in an iconic state. It is usually used with `JFrames` and `JInternalFrames`.

public static final AccessibleState MODAL

This state indicates that this object is the only object which can be interacted with. It also implies that there is a way to complete the task associated with this object.

public static final AccessibleState MULTISELECTABLE

This state indicates that the object can have more than one selected child.

public static final AccessibleState MULTI_LINE

This state indicates that the object can hold multiple lines of text.

public static final AccessibleState OPAQUE

This state indicates that the object completely fills its alotted area.

public static final AccessibleState PRESSED

This state indicates the object is pressed. This usually indicates the user has pressed a controller button while the controller cursor was over this object and the user has not released the button.

public static final AccessibleState RESIZABLE

This state indicates that the size and shape of the object may be modified by the user.

public static final AccessibleState SELECTABLE

This state indicates that this object is selectable.

public static final AccessibleState SELECTED

This state indicates that this object is selected.

public static final AccessibleState SHOWING

This state indicates that the object intends to be visible on the display and all of its parent components are also SHOWING, It may be obscured by another object.

public static final AccessibleState SINGLE_LINE

This state indicates the object can hold a single line of text.

public static final AccessibleState TRANSIENT

This state indicates that an accessibility technology should not keep a reference to this object either directly or through a listener. This state is used for objects that are generated dynamically to support Accessibility, such as a cell renderer in a JTable where one component supports an entire column of cells.

public static final AccessibleState VERTICAL

This state indicates the object is oriented vertically.

public static final AccessibleState VISIBLE

This state indicates the object intends to be visible on the display, but one of its parents is not SHOWING.

Protected Constructors

protected AccessibleState(String key)

Creates an `AccessibleState` using the given locale independent key. This method is protected to allow this class to behave as if it were a strongly typed enumeration. Subclasses can use this method to extend the set of values in the enumeration.

Returned by   AccessibleStateSet.toArray() (p.101).
See also   AccessibleBundle (p.86).

accessibility.AccessibleStateSet

CLASS

An `AccessibleStateSet` is exactly what one would imagine, a set of `AccessibleStates`. Use this class to maintain and provide access to all of the `AccessibleStates` that define the overall state of an object.

public class AccessibleStateSet

Constructors

public AccessibleStateSet()

    Creates an empty state set.

public AccessibleStateSet(AccessibleState[] states)

    Creates a state set containing the given set of AccessibleStates.

Methods

public boolean add(AccessibleState state)

    Adds a new AccessibleState to the current set if it is not already present. If the state is already in the set, the new state is not added and this method returns false.

public void addAll(AccessibleState[] states)

    Adds all of the *states* to the set. Any AccessibleStates which are already in the set are ignored.

public void clear()

    Empties the set of all states.

public boolean contains(AccessibleState state)

    Returns true if *state* is already in the set, false if it is not.

public boolean remove(AccessibleState state)

    Removes *state* from the set. If *state* is not in the set, nothing is done and this method returns false.

public AccessibleState[] toArray()

    Returns the set as an array of AccessibleStates.

public String toString()

    Returns a comma-separated list of localized strings representing the AccessibleStates in the set. *Overrides:* toString in class Object.

Protected Fields

protected java.util.Vector states

    Contains the AccessibleState instances defining the overall state of the object.

    Returned by   AbstractButton.AccessibleAbstractButton.getAccessibleStateSet() (p.125), AccessibleContext.getAccessibleStateSet() (p.90), Box.AccessibleBox.getAccessibleStateSet() (p.137), Box.Filler.AccessibleBoxFiller.getAccessibleStateSet() (p.141), CellRendererPane.AccessibleCellRendererPane.getAccessibleStateSet() (p.152), JApplet.AccessibleJApplet.getAccessibleStateSet() (p.189), JComponent.AccessibleJComponent.getAccessibleStateSet() (p.221), JDialog.AccessibleJDialog.getAccessibleStateSet() (p.230), JEditorPane.AccessibleJEditorPane.getAccessibleStateSet() (p.236), JFrame.AccessibleJFrame.getAccessibleStateSet() (p.252), JList.AccessibleJList.AccessibleJListChild.getAccessibleStateSet() (p.279), JList.AccessibleJList.getAccessibleStateSet() (p.277), JMenuBar.AccessibleJMenuBar.getAccessibleStateSet() (p.290), JProgressBar.AccessibleJProgressBar.getAccessibleStateSet() (p.319), JScrollBar.AccessibleJScrollBar.getAccessibleStateSet() (p.332), JSlider.AccessibleJSlider.getAccessibleStateSet() (p.345), JSplitPane.AccessibleJSplitPane.getAccessibleStateSet() (p.350), JTable.AccessibleJTable.AccessibleJTableCell.getAccessibleStateSet() (p.372),

JTableHeader.AccessibleJTableHeader.AccessibleJTableHeaderEntry.getAccessibleStateSet() (p.755),
JTextArea.AccessibleJTextArea.getAccessibleStateSet() (p.379),
JTextComponent.AccessibleJTextComponent.getAccessibleStateSet() (p.844),
JTextField.AccessibleJTextField.getAccessibleStateSet() (p.383),
JToolBar.AccessibleJToolBar.getAccessibleStateSet() (p.390),
JTree.AccessibleJTree.AccessibleJTreeNode.getAccessibleStateSet() (p.404),
JWindow.AccessibleJWindow.getAccessibleStateSet() (p.417),
SwingUtilities.getAccessibleStateSet() (p.443).
See also AccessibleState (p.99).

accessibility.AccessibleText

INTERFACE AccessibleText

Implementing `AccessibleText` allows components that display text to be manipulated by an accessibility technology.

public interface AccessibleText

Fields
public static final int CHARACTER = 1
public static final int SENTENCE = 3
public static final int WORD = 2
   Constants to use for the *what* parameter in the methods of this interface.

Methods
public abstract String getAfterIndex(int what, int index)
   Returns a `String` representing the first full character, word, or sentence immediately after *index*. The static final members of this interface define the acceptable values for *what*.
public abstract String getAtIndex(int what, int index)
   Returns a `String` representing the character, word, or sentence at *index*. The static final members of this interface define the acceptable values for *what*.
public abstract String getBeforeIndex(int what, int index)
   Returns a `String` representing the first full character, word, or sentence immediately before *index*. The static final members of this interface define the acceptable values for *what*.
public abstract int getCaretPosition()
   Returns the index in the text that represents the caret location. In the view representation of the text, the character will be immediately before the character at *index* in the text. Note that the caret may be to the left or to the right of the character, depending on the direction of text in the current locale.
public abstract int getCharCount()
   Returns the number of characters in the text. Gives an upper bound on valid indices for the text.
public abstract AttributeSet getCharacterAttribute(int index)
   Returns the `AttributeSet` of the character at *index* in the text.

`public abstract java.awt.Rectangle getCharacterBounds(int index)`

Returns the bounding box occupied by the character at *index* in the text. The coordinates returned are relative to the origin of the component displaying the text. Returns `null` from this method if the given index is invalid (greater than the return value of `getCharCount() - 1`).

`public abstract int getIndexAtPoint(java.awt.Point point)`

Returns the index of the character under `point`. Returns `-1` if there isn't any text at *point*.

`public abstract String getSelectedText()`

Returns any selected text.

`public abstract int getSelectionEnd()`

Returns the index of the end of the selected text. Note that if there isn't any text selected, this method should be implemented to return the location of the caret.

`public abstract int getSelectionStart()`

Returns the index of the start of the selected text. Note that if there isn't any text selected, this method should be implemented to return the location of the caret.

Returned by AccessibleContext.getAccessibleText() (p.90),
JComboBox.AccessibleJComboBox.AccessibleJComboBoxList.getAccessibleText() (p.207),
JList.AccessibleJList.AccessibleJListChild.getAccessibleText() (p.279),
JTable.AccessibleJTable.AccessibleJTableCell.getAccessibleText() (p.372),
JTableHeader.AccessibleJTableHeader.AccessibleJTableHeaderEntry.getAccessibleText() (p.755),
JTextComponent.AccessibleJTextComponent.getAccessibleText() (p.844),
JTree.AccessibleJTree.AccessibleJTreeNode.getAccessibleText() (p.404).

Implemented by JTextComponent.AccessibleJTextComponent (p.844).

See also Accessible (p.85), AccessibleContext (p.90), AttributeSet (p.794).

accessibility.AccessibleValue

INTERFACE (AccessibleValue)

An `AccessibleValue` is an accessible representation of a numeric value. The value can be of any of the subclasses of `java.lang.Number`, such as `Integer` or `Float`.

`public interface AccessibleValue`

Methods

`public abstract java.lang.Number getCurrentAccessibleValue()`

Returns the value of this object as a `Number`.

`public abstract java.lang.Number getMaximumAccessibleValue()`

Gets the maximum value of this object as a `Number`, or returns `null` if this object does not have an upper bound.

`public abstract java.lang.Number getMinimumAccessibleValue()`

Gets the minimum value of this object as a `Number`, or returns `null` if this object does not have a lower bound.

```
public abstract boolean setCurrentAccessibleValue(
    java.lang.Number newNumber)
```
Sets the value of this object to newNumber. To have a read-only AccessibleValue this method may return false and ignore this request.

Returned by   AbstractButton.AccessibleAbstractButton.getAccessibleValue() (p.125), AccessibleContext.getAccessibleValue() (p.90), JComboBox.AccessibleJComboBox.AccessibleJComboBoxList.getAccessibleValue() (p.206), JInternalFrame.AccessibleJInternalFrame.getAccessibleValue() (p.262), JInternalFrame.JDesktopIcon.AccessibleJDesktopIcon.getAccessibleValue() (p.264), JList.AccessibleJList.AccessibleJListChild.getAccessibleValue() (p.279), JProgressBar.AccessibleJProgressBar.getAccessibleValue() (p.319), JScrollBar.AccessibleJScrollBar.getAccessibleValue() (p.332), JSlider.AccessibleJSlider.getAccessibleValue() (p.345), JSplitPane.AccessibleJSplitPane.getAccessibleValue() (p.350), JTable.AccessibleJTable.AccessibleJTableCell.getAccessibleValue() (p.372), JTableHeader.AccessibleJTableHeader.AccessibleJTableHeaderEntry.getAccessibleValue() (p.755), JTree.AccessibleJTree.AccessibleJTreeNode.getAccessibleValue() (p.404).

Implemented by   AbstractButton.AccessibleAbstractButton (p.125), JInternalFrame.AccessibleJInternalFrame (p.262), JInternalFrame.JDesktopIcon.AccessibleJDesktopIcon (p.264), JProgressBar.AccessibleJProgressBar (p.319), JScrollBar.AccessibleJScrollBar (p.332), JSlider.AccessibleJSlider (p.345), JSplitPane.AccessibleJSplitPane (p.350).

See also   Accessible (p.85), AccessibleContext (p.90).

Package swing

Swing extends/implements hierarchy

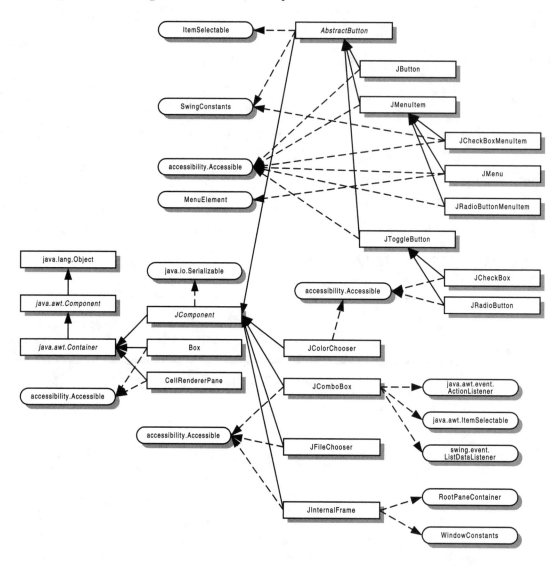

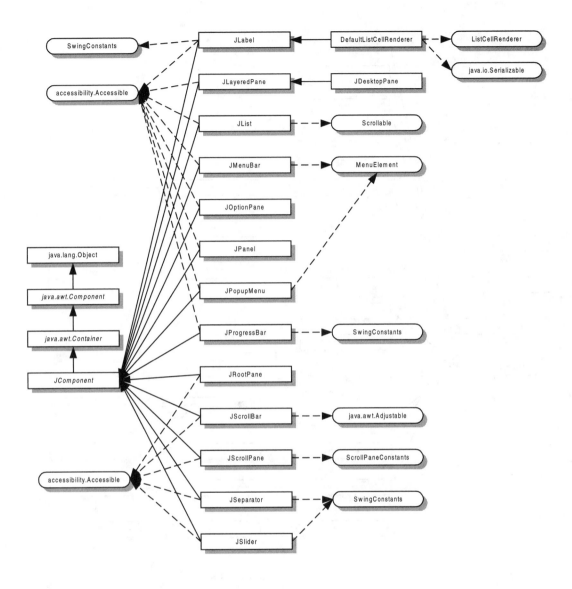

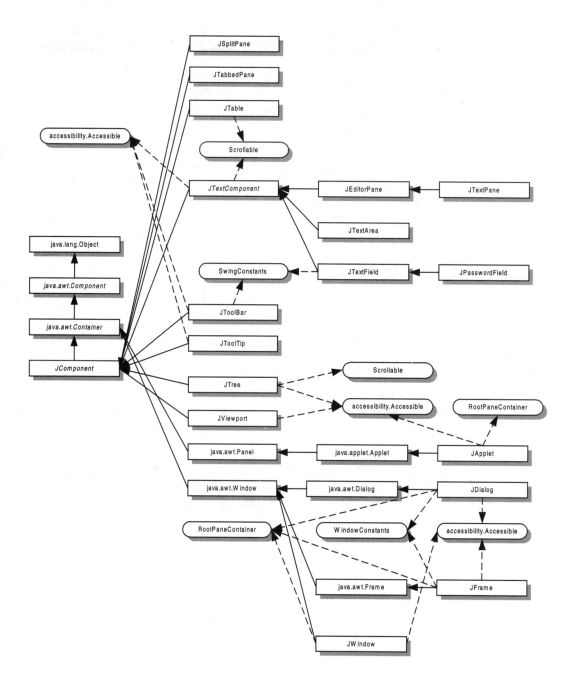

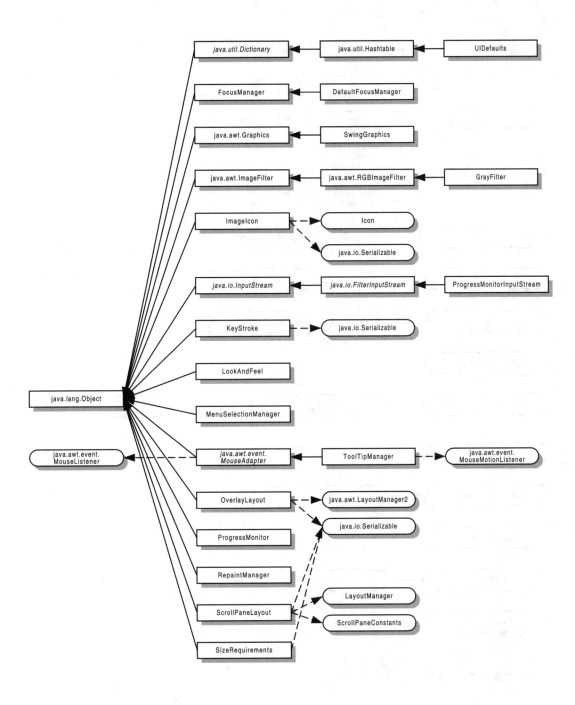

Swing extends/implements hierarchy 111

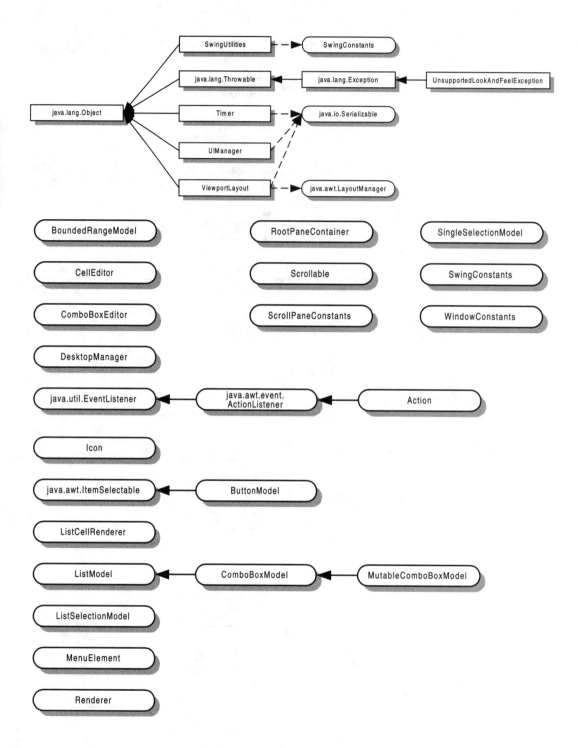

Swing extends/implements hierarchy

Quick summary

The main part of this chapter is devoted to an alphabetical, class-by-class description. It is also helpful to consider clusters of classes. The following tables will orient you in using classes together.

Action summary

Interface	`Action` (p.128) defines functionality that can be controlled in a one place. (If you disable the action, it is disabled in any menus or toolbars in which it appears.)
Abstract class	`AbstractAction` (p.115) provides a default implementation.
Used by	`JMenu` (p.281) can put an `Action` on the menu; `JToolBar` (p.388) can display it in a toolbar.
How to use	Create your action: subclass `AbstractAction`, override `actionPerformed()` (and others as needed), and register it with menus and/or toolbars. Keep track of your action so you can enable and disable it as needed.

Button summary

Model	`ButtonModel` (p.147) tracks the state of buttons. `DefaultButtonModel` (p.161) provides an implementation of the model.
Abstract view	`AbstractButton` (p.118) provides a default view/controller implementation that handles basic state and notification.
Concrete views	`JButton` (p.191) is a simple pushbutton. `JToggleButton` (p.385) represents boolean values; it has subclasses `JCheckBox` (p.193) and `JRadioButton` (p.319). `JCheckBox` is for a single boolean value. `JRadioButton`, in conjunction with a `ButtonGroup` (p.146), provides 1-of-n selection.
Menus	Menus are also part of the button hierarchy. See the Menu summary.

Layout summary

Box	`BoxLayout` (p.144) stacks objects vertically or horizontally. A `Box` (p.134) provides a panel with a built-in `BoxLayout`.
Overlay	`OverlayLayout` (p.428) lays objects over the top of each other (like stacked overhead projector sheets).
Specialty layouts	(These layouts are special purpose, not likely to be used by a typical application program.) `ScrollPaneLayout` (p.437) knows how to arrange the various components associated with a `JScrollPane` (p.332). `ViewportLayout` (p.458) lays objects within a viewport, depending on the relative size of the viewport and the objects.

List summary

Model	`ListModel` (p.421) defines what it means to be a list. `AbstractListModel` (p.127) provides a minimal implementation, and `DefaultListModel` (p.172) provides the default implementation. `ComboBoxModel` (p.156) extends `ListModel` for combo boxes.
Concrete views	`JList` (p.271) is a basic list. `JComboBox` (p.200) is a cross between a pop-up list and a textfield, that allows both selection and editing. (Used read-only, it implements a drop-down list.)

Selection   ListSelectionModel (p.421) defines selection in a list (single element, range, or arbitrary). DefaultListSelectionModel (p.175) provides an implementation.

Display   ListCellRenderer (p.420) displays each row in a list. ComboBoxEditor (p.155) edits the selected item in a combo box.

Menu summary

Interface   MenuElement (p.425) provides the basic interface for menu-like objects.

Implementation   A JMenuBar (p.288) is the top-level container for menus; it usually appears at the top of the frame or the screen. JPopupMenu (p.309) provides a pop-up menu. The top-level entries in these are each a JMenu (p.281). They, in turn, contain objects of the JMenuItem (p.291), JCheckBoxMenuItem (p.195), JRadioButtonMenuItem (p.321) (used with a ButtonGroup (p.146)), or JSeparator (p.338) classes.

Related classes   A JToolBar (p.388) acts like a menu too. An Action (p.128) can be used wth a menu item. (See the Action summary.) Drop-down menus can be implemented via a read-only JComboBox (p.200). (See the List summary.)

Selection   A MenuSelectionManager (p.426) tracks menu selection.

Panel summary

Splitter   JSplitPane (p.346) allows you to put a moveable divider between two panels.

Tabs   JTabbedPane (p.351) provides "notebook tab" panels. It essentially replaces java.awt.CardLayout, since it provides the UI elements necessary to make a stack-style layout useful.

Layers   JRootPane (p.323) and JLayeredPane (p.268) allow for panes appearing in layers. (For example, this is used by pop-up menus to allow the pop-up to appear above its frame.)

Scrolling   JScrollPane (p.332) allows you to easily set up scrolling for a component. (see the Scrolling summary.)

Bounded Range summary

Model   BoundedRangeModel (p.132) describes a range between two endpoints. DefaultBoundedRangeModel (p.159) provides an implementation.

Views   JSlider (p.341) provides a view of a point in a range. JProgressBar (p.315) (possibly in conjunction with ProgressMonitor (p.429) or ProgressMonitorInputStream (p.430)) shows a proportion of progress. JScrollBar (p.328) shows a scrolling position (see the Scrolling summary).

Scrolling summary

Basics   Scrollable (p.433) defines the interface which objects that want to be scrolled must support. JScrollPane (p.332) provides a widget that will scroll its contents.

Parts   JScrollBar (p.328) defines the scroll bar itself. ScrollPaneLayout (p.437) defines how a scroll pane is composed. ViewportLayout (p.458) and JViewport (p.410) define the main viewing area.

Other   ScrollPaneConstants (p.436) defines constants used by scrolling-related objects.

Text summary

Model   `Document` (p.826). See the `swing.text` package.

Views   `JTextComponent` (p.838) is the superclass of the text editing views. `JTextField` (p.379) provides a one-line text entry box; `JPasswordField` (p.306) does the same but hides the input characters. `JTextArea` (p.374) provides a multiline area for text with only one style; `JTextPane` (p.383) provides the same for multiple styles. `JEditorPane` (p.232) provides a multiline, multistyle editor that supports various file types.

Container summary

Concrete classes   `JApplet` (p.186), `JFrame` (p.248), `JInternalFrame` (p.254), and `JWindow` (p.414) provide basic windows. `JDialog` (p.226) and `JOptionPane` (p.294) provide dialogs and message boxes, respectively.

Panes   `JLayeredPane` (p.268) and `JRootPane` (p.323) handle the 2½D layering of panes.

Internal frames `JInternalFrame` (p.254) and its inner class `JDesktopIcon` (p.263) can be contained in a `JDesktopPane` (p.224) to support a multiple document style interface. `DefaultDesktopManager` (p.168) (an implementation of `DesktopManager` (p.180)) handles window operations for internal frames.

Models, implementations, and views

Model	Implementation	Views
`BoundedRangeModel` (p.132)	`DefaultBoundedRangeModel` (p.159)	`JProgressBar` (p.315), `JScrollBar` (p.328), `JSlider` (p.341)
`ButtonModel` (p.147)	`DefaultButtonModel` (p.161)	`AbstractButton` (p.118), `JButton` (p.191), `JCheckBox` (p.193), `JRadioButton` (p.319), `JToggleButton` (p.385)
`ListModel` (p.421)	`AbstractListModel` (p.127) `DefaultListModel` (p.172)	`JComboBox` (p.200), `JList` (p.271)
`ListSelectionModel` (p.421)	`DefaultListSelectionModel` (p.175)	`JComboBox` (p.200), `JList` (p.271)
`SingleSelectionModel` (p.440)	`DefaultSingleSelectionModel` (p.179)	`JPopupMenu` (p.309)

swing.AbstractAction

ABSTRACT
CLASS

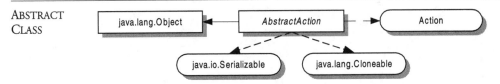

This class provides a default implementation of the `Action` interface.

Example

```
// File action\ActionTest.java
package action;

import java.awt.*;
import java.awt.event.*;
// Uncomment the following line for Swing 1.0.3 and before
//import com.sun.java.swing.*;
// Uncomment the following line for Swing 1.1 and JDK 1.2
import javax.swing.*;

public class ActionTest extends JFrame {
  JToolBar toolBar = new JToolBar();
  JMenuBar menuBar = new JMenuBar();
  JMenu testMenu = new JMenu("Test");
  MyAction theAction = new MyAction(this);

  public ActionTest() {
    this.setJMenuBar(menuBar);
    menuBar.add(testMenu);

    // create a JMenuItem and JToolbar button using the Action
    testMenu.add(theAction);
    toolBar.add(theAction);

    // add a menu item which disables the Action, which
    // disables the JMenuItem and JToolbar button created with it.
    JMenuItem disableActionItem = new JMenuItem("Disable the Action");
    testMenu.addSeparator();
    testMenu.add(disableActionItem);
    disableActionItem.addActionListener(new ActionListener() {
      public void actionPerformed(ActionEvent e) {
        theAction.setEnabled(false);
      }
    });
    this.getContentPane().add(toolBar, BorderLayout.NORTH);
    this.setDefaultCloseOperation(JFrame.DISPOSE_ON_CLOSE);
    this.addWindowListener(new WindowAdapter() {
      public void windowClosed(WindowEvent e) {
        System.exit(0);
      }
    });
    this.getContentPane().setBackground(Color.red);
    this.setSize(320, 200);
    this.setVisible(true);
  }
  public static void main(String[] args) {
    ActionTest t = new ActionTest();
  }
} // end ActionTest

class MyAction extends AbstractAction {
  JFrame f;
  boolean toggle = true;

  public MyAction(JFrame f) {
    super("Change Color");
```

```
        this.f = f;
    }
    public void actionPerformed (ActionEvent e) {
      if (toggle) {
        f.getContentPane().setBackground(Color.blue);
        toggle = false;
      } else {
        f.getContentPane().setBackground(Color.red);
        toggle = true;
      }
      f.repaint();
    }
} // end MyAction
```

public abstract class AbstractAction extends java.lang.Object
implements Action, java.lang.Cloneable, java.io.Serializable

Constructors

public AbstractAction()
public AbstractAction(String name)
public AbstractAction(String name, Icon icon)

Creates an abstract action with the specified name and icon. If no name is specified, an empty string is used. If no icon is provided, a default icon is created.

Methods

public synchronized void addPropertyChangeListener(
java.beans.PropertyChangeListener listener)

Adds listener for any changes in the properties of this action.

Implements: addPropertyChangeListener in interface Action.

public Object getValue(String key)

Returns the Object associated with key in this Action's dictionary, if a corresponding Object exists.

Implements: getValue in interface Action.

public boolean isEnabled()

Returns true if this action is enabled.

Implements: isEnabled in interface Action.

public synchronized void putValue(String key, Object newValue)

Adds a new (key, newValue) pair to the value Dictionary of this Action.

Implements: putValue in interface Action.

public synchronized void removePropertyChangeListener(
java.beans.PropertyChangeListener listener)

Removes listener from the list of listeners.

Implements: removePropertyChangeListener in interface Action.

public synchronized void setEnabled(boolean shouldEnable)

Sets whether the action is enabled. If the enabled state changes, notifies the listeners.

Implements: setEnabled in interface Action.

Protected Fields

protected SwingPropertyChangeSupport changeSupport

The list of listeners to be notified of a property change.

protected boolean enabled

The enabled property for this `AbstractAction`.

Protected Methods

protected Object clone()

throws java.lang.CloneNotSupportedException

Overrides `clone()` so that the clone gets its own copy of the dictionary. The default `clone()` operation performs a bitwise copy, so the clone would have shared the same table.

Overrides: clone in class `Object`.

protected void firePropertyChange(String property, Object oldValue, Object newValue)

Handles notification of property changes.

Extended by   BasicFileChooserUI.ApproveSelectionAction (p.591), BasicFileChooserUI.CancelSelectionAction (p.592), BasicFileChooserUI.ChangeToParentDirectoryAction (p.593), BasicFileChooserUI.GoHomeAction (p.593), BasicFileChooserUI.NewFolderAction (p.594), BasicFileChooserUI.UpdateAction (p.595), BasicInternalFrameTitlePane.CloseAction (p.600), BasicInternalFrameTitlePane.IconifyAction (p.600), BasicInternalFrameTitlePane.MaximizeAction (p.601), BasicInternalFrameTitlePane.MoveAction (p.601), BasicInternalFrameTitlePane.RestoreAction (p.602), BasicInternalFrameTitlePane.SizeAction (p.603), BasicSliderUI.ActionScroller (p.660), BasicTreeUI.TreeCancelEditingAction (p.725), BasicTreeUI.TreeIncrementAction (p.727), BasicTreeUI.TreeHomeAction (p.726), BasicTreeUI.TreePageAction (p.728), BasicTreeUI.TreeToggleAction (p.729), BasicTreeUI.TreeTraverseAction (p.729), TextAction (p.891).

See also   Action (p.128), Icon (p.183), SwingPropertyChangeSupport (p.506).

swing.AbstractButton

CLASS

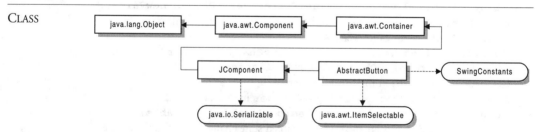

This is the generic Swing class for buttons. The buttons such as `JButton` or `JRadioButton` inherit from it. In a change from AWT, Swing `JMenus` and `JMenuItems` also inherit from this class. Many of these methods delegate to the `ButtonModel`.

An abstract button allows for both text and an icon. For text, use:

`getText()` and `setText()`.

For icons, there are many methods to handle the various states:

```
getDisabledIcon(), setDisabledIcon()
getDisabledSelectedIcon(), setDisabledSelectedIcon()
getIcon(), setIcon()
getRolloverIcon(), setRolloverIcon()
getRolloverSelectedIcon(), setRolloverSelectedIcon()
getSelectedIcon(), setSelectedIcon().
```

Example

```
// Put the text to the left of the icon; set up a rollover
// image and a mnemonic.
AbstractButton b = new JButton("Test");
b.setHorizontalTextPosition(SwingConstants.LEFT);
b.setIcon (new ImageIcon(getClass().getResource("red-ball.gif")));
b.setRolloverIcon(
   new ImageIcon(getClass().getResource("blue-ball.gif")));
b.setRolloverEnabled(true);
b.setMnemonic('t');          // Click on Alt-t
getContentPane().add(b);
```

public abstract class AbstractButton extends JComponent
    implements java.awt.ItemSelectable, SwingConstants

Fields

public static final String BORDER_PAINTED_CHANGED_PROPERTY
    Property name for the borderPainted property.
public static final String CONTENT_AREA_FILLED_CHANGED_PROPERTY
    Property name for the contentAreaFilled property.
public static final String DISABLED_ICON_CHANGED_PROPERTY
    Property name for the disabledIcon property.
public static final String DISABLED_SELECTED_ICON_CHANGED_PROPERTY
    Property name for the disabledSelectedIcon property.
public static final String FOCUS_PAINTED_CHANGED_PROPERTY
    Property name for the focusPainted property.
public static final String HORIZONTAL_ALIGNMENT_CHANGED_PROPERTY
    Property name for the horizontalAlignment property.
public static final String HORIZONTAL_TEXT_POSITION_CHANGED_PROPERTY
    Property name for the horizontalTextPosition property.
public static final String ICON_CHANGED_PROPERTY
    Property name for the icon property.
public static final String MARGIN_CHANGED_PROPERTY
    Property name for the margin property.
public static final String MNEMONIC_CHANGED_PROPERTY
    Property name for the mnemonic property.
public static final String MODEL_CHANGED_PROPERTY
    Property name for the model property.

public static final String PRESSED_ICON_CHANGED_PROPERTY
Property name for the `pressedIcon` property.
public static final String ROLLOVER_ENABLED_CHANGED_PROPERTY
Property name for the `rolloverEnabled` property.
public static final String ROLLOVER_ICON_CHANGED_PROPERTY
Property name for the `rolloverIcon` property.
public static final String ROLLOVER_SELECTED_ICON_CHANGED_PROPERTY
Property name for the `rolloverSelectedIcon` property.
public static final String SELECTED_ICON_CHANGED_PROPERTY
Property name for the `selectedIcon` property.
public static final String TEXT_CHANGED_PROPERTY
Property name for the `text` property.
public static final String VERTICAL_ALIGNMENT_CHANGED_PROPERTY
Property name for the `verticalAlignment` property.
public static final String VERTICAL_TEXT_POSITION_CHANGED_PROPERTY
Property name for the `verticalTextPosition` property.

Constructors
public AbstractButton()
Default constructor.

Methods
public void addActionListener(java.awt.event.ActionListener listener)
Adds `listener` to the list of objects to be notified when an action event occurs.
public void addChangeListener(ChangeListener listener)
Adds `listener` to the list of objects to be notified about changes in the state of the button.
public void addItemListener(java.awt.event.ItemListener listener)
Adds `listener` to the list of objects to be notified about changes in the item list (for radio buttons and check boxes).
Implements: `addItemListener` in interface `ItemSelectable`.
public void doClick()
Programmatically clicks on the button. This method causes an `ActionEvent` to be sent to all registered `ActionListeners`. If you need to set the selected state of the button without causing an `ActionEvent`, see the `setSelected()` method.
public void doClick(int milliseconds)
Programmatically clicks on the button; shows it pressed for `milliseconds`. This method causes an `ActionEvent` to be sent to all registered `ActionListeners`. If you need to set the selected state of the button without causing an `ActionEvent`, see the `setSelected()` method.
public String getActionCommand()
Gets the action command string associated with this button. See `setActionCommand()`.
public Icon getDisabledIcon()
Returns the icon shown when this button is disabled. See the icon methods mentioned in the class description above.
public Icon getDisabledSelectedIcon()
Returns the icon shown when this button is both disabled and selected. See the icon methods mentioned in the class description above.

public int getHorizontalAlignment()

Returns the alignment of the icon and text of the button, relative to the button as a whole. The return value will be SwingConstants.LEFT, SwingConstants.CENTER, or SwingConstants.RIGHT. Default: CENTER.

public int getHorizontalTextPosition()

Returns the position of the text relative to the icon. The result will be SwingConstants.LEFT, SwingConstants.CENTER, or SwingConstants.RIGHT. Default: RIGHT.

public Icon getIcon()

Returns the icon associated with this button. See the icon methods mentioned in the class description above.

public String getLabel()

Deprecated, use getText().

public java.awt.Insets getMargin()

Returns the margin between the border and the button itself.

public int getMnemonic()

Returns the mnemonic key associated with the button.

public ButtonModel getModel()

Returns the model associated with this button.

public Icon getPressedIcon()

Returns the icon shown when the button is pressed.

public Icon getRolloverIcon()

Returns the rollover icon shown when the mouse is over the button. See the icon methods mentioned in the class description above.

public Icon getRolloverSelectedIcon()

Returns the rollover icon shown when the mouse is over the button and the button is selected. See the icon methods mentioned in the class description above.

public Icon getSelectedIcon()

Returns the icon shown when the button is selected. See the icon methods mentioned in the class description above.

public synchronized Object[] getSelectedObjects()

Gets an array of the selected items (for radio buttons and check boxes).

Implements: getSelectedObjects in interface ItemSelectable.

public String getText()

Returns the text for this button.

public ButtonUI getUI()

Gets the UI (look and feel) of this button. See the chapter on look and feel for more information.

public int getVerticalAlignment()

Returns the vertical alignment of the icon and text relative to the button as a whole. Return value will be SwingConstants.TOP, SwingConstants.CENTER, or SwingConstants.BOTTOM. *Default:* CENTER.

public int getVerticalTextPosition()

Returns the position of the text relative to the icon. Return value will be SwingConstants.TOP, SwingConstants.CENTER, or SwingConstants.BOTTOM. *Default:* CENTER.

public boolean isBorderPainted()

Returns true if the border should be painted.

public boolean isContentAreaFilled()

Returns `true` if the content area (the button face) area should be filled. For buttons, the `content-AreaFilled` property should be used in preference to the `opaque` property.

public boolean isFocusPainted()

Returns `true` if the focus should be painted.

public boolean isRolloverEnabled()

Returns `true` if the button changes when the mouse is over it.

public boolean isSelected()

Returns `true` if the button is selected (applies only to `JToggleButton` and its subclasses).

public void removeActionListener(java.awt.event.ActionListener listener)

Removes `listener` from the list of listeners for actions.

public void removeChangeListener(ChangeListener listener)

Removes `listener` from the list of listeners for changes.

public void removeItemListener(java.awt.event.ItemListener listener)

Removes `listener` from the list of item listeners.

Implements: `removeItemListener` in interface `ItemSelectable`.

public void setActionCommand(String command)

Sets the action command. This is a locale-independent string that can be associated with the button. By making your code depend on the action command rather than the button's title, you won't need to change your code for localization.

public void setBorderPainted(boolean shouldPaint)

Sets whether the border should be painted. See `paintBorder()`.

public void setContentAreaFilled(boolean b)

Sets whether the button's face is filled. This property is subtly different than the `opaque` property, and should be used in preference to `setOpaque()`. Look and feels use this property to control whether they paint rollover and pressed effects which fill the background. For example, Basic uses this property to set the `opaque` property, while Metal uses it to decide whether to paint the background "flash" effect when a button is pressed.

public void setDisabledIcon(Icon icon)

Sets the icon to be used when the button is disabled. See the icon methods mentioned in the class description above.

public void setDisabledSelectedIcon(Icon icon)

Sets the icon to be used when the button is disabled and selected. See the icon methods mentioned in the class description above.

public void setEnabled(boolean shouldEnable)

Sets whether the button is enabled (active).

Overrides: `setEnabled` in class Component.

public void setFocusPainted(boolean shouldPaint)

Sets whether the focus should be painted.

public void setHorizontalAlignment(int alignment)

Sets the alignment of the text and icon relative to the button as a whole. The alignment must be `SwingConstants.LEFT`, `SwingConstants.CENTER`, `SwingConstants.RIGHT`, `SwingConstants.LEADING`, or `SwingConstants.TRAILING`. LEADING, CENTER, or TRAILING are preferred in Swing 1.1 or later, since they support internationalization.

public void setHorizontalTextPosition(int position)

Sets the position of the text relative to the icon. The alignment must be SwingConstants.LEFT, SwingConstants.CENTER, SwingConstants.RIGHT, SwingConstants.LEADING, or SwingConstants.TRAILING. LEADING, CENTER, or TRAILING are preferred in Swing 1.1 or later, since they support internationalization.

public void setIcon(Icon icon)

Sets the default icon for the button. See the icon methods mentioned in the class description above.

public void setLabel(String text)

Deprecated. See SetText for more information.

public void setMargin(java.awt.Insets margin)

Sets the margin between the border and the button interior.

public void setMnemonic(int key)

public void setMnemonic(char key)

Sets the mnemonic key for the button.

public void setModel(ButtonModel model)

Sets the model for the button. (Note that most of the AbstractButton methods are delegated to the model.)

public void setPressedIcon(Icon icon)

Sets the icon used when the button is pressed. See the icon methods mentioned in the class description above.

public void setRolloverEnabled(boolean isEnabled)

Sets whether rollover is enabled. (Rollover is the state when the mouse is moved over the button, before it is clicked.)

public void setRolloverIcon(Icon icon)

Sets the icon used when the mouse is over the button (if rollover is enabled). See the icon methods mentioned in the class description above.

public void setRolloverSelectedIcon(Icon icon)

Sets the icon used when the mouse is over a selected button (if rollover is enabled). See the icon methods mentioned in the class description above.

public void setSelected(boolean isSelected)

Sets whether the button is selected (for radio buttons and check boxes). Note that calling this method *does not* cause an ActionEvent to be sent to listeners. If you need an ActionEvent to be sent, see the doClick() method.

public void setSelectedIcon(Icon icon)

Sets the icon used when the button is selected. See the icon methods mentioned in the class description above.

public void setText(String text)

Sets the text for the button.

public void setUI(ButtonUI ui)

Sets the UI to ui. Usually called by updateUI().

public void setVerticalAlignment(int alignment)

Sets the vertical alignment of the text and icon relative to the button as a whole. The alignment parameter must be SwingConstants.TOP, SwingConstants.CENTER, or SwingConstants.BOTTOM. *Default:* CENTER.

public void setVerticalTextPosition(int position)

Sets the vertical position of the text relative to the icon. The position must be `SwingCon-stants.TOP`, `SwingConstants.CENTER`, or `SwingConstants.BOTTOM`. *Default:* CENTER.

public void updateUI()

Tells the button to update its appearance with the new look and feel. Subclasses should override this to retrieve the UI appropriate for themselves.
Overrides: `updateUI` in class `JComponent`.

Protected Fields

protected java.awt.event.ActionListener actionListener

The list of listeners for actions.

protected transient ChangeEvent changeEvent

The event used to notify listeners about changes in the state of the button.

protected ChangeListener changeListener

The list of listeners for changes in the state of the button.

protected java.awt.event.ItemListener itemListener

The listener for changes in the items associated with a button—for radio buttons and check boxes only.

protected ButtonModel model

The model associated with this button.

Protected Methods

protected int checkHorizontalKey(int key, String message)

Verifies that `key` is `SwingConstants.LEFT`, `SwingConstants.CENTER`, `SwingCon-stants.RIGHT`, `SwingConstants.LEADING`, or `SwingConstants.TRAILING`. Throw an exception using `message` if it is not.

protected int checkVerticalKey(int key, String message)

Verifies that `key` is `SwingConstants.TOP`, `SwingConstants.CENTER`, or `SwingCon-stants.BOTTOM`. Throw an exception using `message` if it is not.

protected java.awt.event.ActionListener createActionListener()

Creates the action listener attached to the model.

protected ChangeListener createChangeListener()

Creates the change listener attached to the model.

protected java.awt.event.ItemListener createItemListener()

Creates the item listener attached to the model.

protected void fireActionPerformed(java.awt.event.ActionEvent event)

Notifies action listeners of event.

protected void fireItemStateChanged(java.awt.event.ItemEvent ie)

Notifies item listeners of event.

protected void fireStateChanged()

Notifies change listeners that the state has changed.

protected void init(String text, Icon icon)

Sets the text and icon for the button.

protected void paintBorder(java.awt.Graphics g)

Paints the border onto `g` (this happens only if `isBorderPainted()` is true).
Overrides: `paintBorder` in class `JComponent`.

protected String paramString()

Returns a string representation of an AbstractButton for use in debugging. It includes information from JComponent.paramString() as well as information specific to this class and its descendants.

Overrides: paramString in class JComponent.

Inner Classes

protected class AbstractButton.ButtonChangeListener
protected abstract class AbstractButton.AccessibleAbstractButton

> *Extended by* JButton (p.191), JMenuItem (p.291), JToggleButton (p.385).
> *See also* ButtonModel (p.147), ButtonUI (p.528), ChangeEvent (p.487),
> ChangeListener (p.488), Icon (p.183), JComponent (p.207), SwingConstants (p.442).

swing.AbstractButton.AccessibleAbstractButton

INNER CLASS

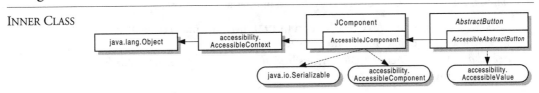

General accessibility support for all types of buttons.

protected abstract class AbstractButton.AccessibleAbstractButton
    extends JComponent.AccessibleJComponent
    implements AccessibleValue

Methods

public boolean doAccessibleAction(int actionIndex)

Performs the specified Action on the object.

Implements: doAccessibleAction in interface AccessibleAction.

public AccessibleAction getAccessibleAction()

Returns the default AccessibleAction associated with this object if one exists. Otherwise return null.

public int getAccessibleActionCount()

Returns the number of Actions supported by this button. If there is more than one Action, the first one is the default action.

Implements: getAccessibleActionCount in interface AccessibleAction.

public String getAccessibleActionDescription(int i)

Returns a description of the specified action of the object.

Implements: getAccessibleActionDescription in interface AccessibleAction.

public String getAccessibleName()

Returns the accessibleName of this button, if it has one. If it does not have an accessibleName, this method returns null.

Overrides: getAccessibleName in JComponent.AccessibleJComponent.

public AccessibleStateSet getAccessibleStateSet()

Returns a set of AccessibleStates that describe the current state of the object.

public AccessibleValue getAccessibleValue()

Gets the `AccessibleValue` associated with this object if one exists. Otherwise returns `null`.

public java.lang.Number getCurrentAccessibleValue()

Returns `Integer(0)` if this button isn't selected or `Integer(1)` if it is selected.

Implements: `getCurrentAccessibleValue` in interface `AccessibleValue`.

See also: isSelected.

public java.lang.Number getMaximumAccessibleValue()

Gets the maximum value of this object as a `Number`. Returns `Integer(1)`.

Implements: `getMaximumAccessibleValue` in interface `AccessibleValue`.

public java.lang.Number getMinimumAccessibleValue()

Gets the minimum value of this object as a `Number`. Returns `Integer(0)`.

Implements: `getMinimumAccessibleValue` in interface `AccessibleValue`.

public boolean setCurrentAccessibleValue(java.lang.Number n)

Sets the value of this object as a `Number`. Returns `true` if the value was set.

Implements: `setCurrentAccessibleValue` in interface `AccessibleValue`.

Extended by   JButton.AccessibleJButton (p.192), JMenuItem.AccessibleJMenuItem (p.294), JToggleButton.AccessibleJToggleButton (p.387).

See also   AccessibleAction (p.86), AccessibleStateSet (p.101), AccessibleValue (p.104), JComponent.AccessibleJComponent (p.221).

swing.AbstractButton.ButtonChangeListener

INNER CLASS

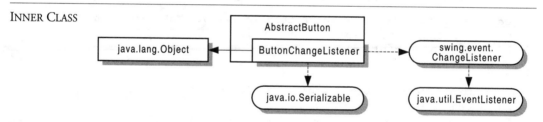

Extends `ChangeListener` to be serializable. This is required so that `AbstractButton` can be properly serialized.

```
protected class AbstractButton.ButtonChangeListener
    extends java.lang.Object
    implements ChangeListener, java.io.Serializable
```

Methods

public void stateChanged(ChangeEvent e)

Implements: `stateChanged` in interface `ChangeListener`.

See also   ChangeEvent (p.487), ChangeListener (p.488).

swing.AbstractListModel

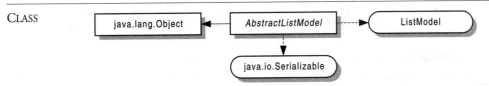

This class provides a default implementation of the ListModel interface for use with classes such as JList.

```
public class AbstractListModel implements ListModel,
    java.io.Serializable
```

Constructors
public AbstractListModel()
Creates a new abstract list model.

Methods
public void addListDataListener(ListDataListener listener)
Adds listener as a listener for changes in the list.

public void removeListDataListener(ListDataListener listener)
Removes listener as a listener for changes in the list.

Protected Fields
protected EventListenerList listenerList
The list of listeners.

Protected Methods
protected void fireContentsChanged(Object source, int index1, int index2)
Subclasses of AbstractListModel must call this method after they change the contents of the list. The source is the model that has changed (and is usually this). The range is from min(index1, index2) to max(index1, index2), inclusive on both ends.

protected void fireIntervalAdded(Object source, int index1, int index2)
Subclasses of AbstractListModel must call this method after they add new items to the list. The source is the model that has changed (and is usually this). The range is from min(index1, index2) to max(index1, index2), inclusive on both ends.

protected void fireIntervalRemoved(Object source, int index1, int index2)
Subclasses of AbstractListModel must call this method after they remove part of the list. The source is the model that has changed (and is usually this). The range is from min(index1, index2) to max(index1, index2), inclusive on both ends.

Extended by   BasicDirectoryModel (p.585), DefaultComboBoxModel (p.166), DefaultListModel (p.172).

See also   EventListenerList (p.491), JList (p.271), ListDataListener (p.499), ListModel (p.421).

swing.Action

An `Action` encapsulates a program function so it can be controlled in one place, even though it might be used in several places. For instance, an `Action` might be both on a menu and on a toolbar. By having a single object, both places can be enabled or disabled at once. Also, all associated components can call the `Action`'s `actionPerformed()` method to trigger a common behavior.

`Action` maintains a list of property values, and notifies listeners when these change. You can use the constants as standard keys, or define your own.

When a container that knows about `Action`s (such as `JToolBar` (p.388) or `JMenu` (p.281)) has an `Action` added, it uses the property information to configure itself. For example, the toolbar might display the icon and use the short description in a `JToolTip` (p.391), while the menu might use the icon and/or the name. Both would monitor the `Action` for its enabled status, and adjust their presentation if it changes.

Example: See `AbstractAction` (p.115).

```
public interface Action
    implements java.awt.event.ActionListener
```

Fields

```
public static final String DEFAULT = "Default"
```
A predefined property key representing the default information for this action.
```
public static final String LONG_DESCRIPTION = "LongDescription"
```
The property name for a full description of this action. Usually used for context-sensitive help pop-ups.
```
public static final String NAME = "Name"
```
The property name for the name of this action. Usually used for a menu item or button text.
```
public static final String SHORT_DESCRIPTION = "ShortDescription"
```
The property name for a short description of this action. Usually used for ToolTip text.
```
public static final String SMALL_ICON = "SmallIcon"
```
The property name for the `Icon` to use for this action. `JMenuItem` and `JToolBar` use this icon.

Methods

```
public abstract void addPropertyChangeListener(
    java.beans.PropertyChangeListener listener)
```
Adds `listener` for any changes in the properties of this action.
```
public abstract Object getValue(String key)
```
Gets the `Object` stored in this `Action` using `key`.
```
public abstract boolean isEnabled()
```
Returns `true` if this action is enabled.
```
public abstract void putValue(String key, Object value)
```
Stores the `value` in the `Action`'s table using `key`.

public abstract void removePropertyChangeListener(
  java.beans.PropertyChangeListener listener)
  Removes `listener` from the list of listeners.
public abstract void setEnabled(boolean shouldEnable)
  Sets whether the action is enabled. If the enabled state changes, this method notifies the listeners. Components created using the `Action` are expected to enable or disable themselves in response to the notification.

  Implemented by   AbstractAction (p.115).
  Returned by   BasicFileChooserUI.getApproveSelectionAction() (p.591),
  BasicFileChooserUI.getCancelSelectionAction() (p.592),
  BasicFileChooserUI.getChangeToParentDirectoryAction() (p.593),
  BasicFileChooserUI.getGoHomeAction() (p.593),
  BasicFileChooserUI.getNewFolderAction() (p.594),
  BasicFileChooserUI.getUpdateAction() (p.595), DefaultEditorKit.getActions() (p.810),
  EditorKit.getActions() (p.829), HTMLEditorKit.getActions() (p.922),
  JTextComponent.getActions() (p.838), JTextField.getActions() (p.379),
  Keymap.getAction() (p.846), Keymap.getBoundActions() (p.846),
  Keymap.getDefaultAction() (p.846), StyledEditorKit.getActions() (p.878),
  TextAction.augmentList() (p.891).
  See also   Icon (p.183).

swing.BorderFactory

CLASS

The `BorderFactory` provides factory methods for creating borders (see package `swing.border` on page 461). Most borders are immutable—once created they cannot be changed. The `BorderFactory` will reuse borders where it can, thereby minimizing the number of borders that are created.

Example

```
package BorderFactorySample;

import com.sun.java.swing.*;
import com.sun.java.swing.border.*;
import java.awt.event.*;
import java.awt.*;

public class Sample extends JFrame {
  public Sample() {
    this.addWindowListener(new WindowAdapter() {
      public void windowClosing(WindowEvent e) {
      Sample.this.dispose();
      System.exit(0);
    }
    });
```

```
   JPanel panel = new JPanel();
   JLabel label;

   label = new JLabel ("Beveled (like a button)");
   label.setBorder(BorderFactory.createBevelBorder(BevelBorder.RAISED));
   panel.add(label);

   label = new JLabel ("Compound - red inside green lines");
   label.setBorder (BorderFactory.createCompoundBorder (
      new LineBorder(Color.green), new LineBorder(Color.red)));
   panel.add(label);

   label = new JLabel ("Empty");
   label.setBorder(BorderFactory.createEmptyBorder(10,20,10,20));
   panel.add(label);

   label = new JLabel ("Etched");
   label.setBorder(BorderFactory.createEtchedBorder());
   panel.add(label);

   label = new JLabel ("Titled border");
   label.setBorder(BorderFactory.createTitledBorder("Titled"));
   panel.add(label);

   getContentPane().add(panel);
   pack();
   }
   public static void main(String[] args) {
      Sample s = new Sample();
      s.setVisible(true);
   }
}
```

public class BorderFactory

Methods

public static Border createBevelBorder(int bevelType)

Creates a BevelBorder which will use brighter and darker variants of the component's own colors to draw the bevel effect. The bevelType may either be BevelBorder.LOWERED or BevelBorder.RAISED.

public static Border createBevelBorder(int bevelType,
java.awt.Color highlight, java.awt.Color shadow)

Creates a BevelBorder. The bevelType may either be BevelBorder.LOWERED or BevelBorder.RAISED. The highlight color is used for one side, the shadow for the other (depending on whether it is lowered or raised).

public static Border createBevelBorder(int bevelType,
java.awt.Color outerHighlight, java.awt.Color innerHighlight,
java.awt.Color outerShadow, java.awt.Color innershadow)

Creates a BevelBorder. The bevelType may either be BevelBorder.LOWERED or BevelBorder.RAISED. The bevel is built from two lines: outerHighlight and innerHighlight on one side, outerShadow and innerShadow on the other.

public static CompoundBorder createCompoundBorder()

Creates a new compound border from two null Borders.

```
public static CompoundBorder createCompoundBorder(
    Border outerBorder, Border innerBorder)
```
Creates a new compound border built from `outerBorder` and `innerBorder`.

```
public static Border createEmptyBorder()
```
Creates an empty border with 0 for all insets.

```
public static Border createEmptyBorder(int top, int left,
    int bottom, int right)
```
Creates an empty border with the specified inset on each side.

```
public static Border createEtchedBorder()
```
Creates an etched border using lighter and darker variations of the component's background color.

```
public static Border createEtchedBorder(java.awt.Color highlight,
    java.awt.Color shadow)
```
Creates an etched border with the specified highlight and shadow colors.

```
public static Border createLineBorder(java.awt.Color lineColor)
```
Creates a one-pixel-thick line border with the specified color.

```
public static Border createLineBorder(java.awt.Color lineColor,
    int thickness)
```
Creates a `LineBorder` with the specified color and thickness.

```
public static Border createLoweredBevelBorder()
```
Creates a `BevelBorder` of type `BevelBorder.LOWERED`.

```
public static MatteBorder createMatteBorder(int top, int left,
    int bottom, int right, Icon icon)
```
Creates a `MatteBorder` with the thickness specified for `top`, `left`, `bottom`, and `right`. It is produced from repeating `icon`.

```
public static MatteBorder createMatteBorder(int top, int left,
    int bottom, int right, java.awt.Color color)
```
Creates a `MatteBorder` with the thickness specified for `top`, `left`, `bottom`, and `right`. It is produced from solid color specified by `color`.

```
public static Border createRaisedBevelBorder()
```
Creates a `BevelBorder` of type `BevelBorder.RAISED`, using lighter and darker variants of the component's background color to create the bevel effect.

```
public static TitledBorder createTitledBorder(String title)
```
Creates a `TitledBorder` with the title `title`. The border and font used by a `TitledBorder` is defined by the look and feel.

```
public static TitledBorder createTitledBorder(Border border)
```
Creates a `TitledBorder` based on `border`.

```
public static TitledBorder createTitledBorder(Border border, String title)
```
Creates a `TitledBorder` based on `border` with the chosen `title`.

```
public static TitledBorder createTitledBorder(Border border,
    String title, int titleJustification, int titlePosition)
```
Creates a `TitledBorder` with the specified `border` and `title`. See `TitledBorder` for the values for `titleJustification` and `titlePosition`.

```
public static TitledBorder createTitledBorder(Border border, String title,
    int titleJustification, int titlePosition, java.awt.Font font)
```
Creates a `TitledBorder` with the specified `border`, `title`, and `font`. See `TitledBorder` for the values for `titleJustification` and `titlePosition`.

```
public static TitledBorder createTitledBorder(Border border, String title,
    int titleJustification, int titlePosition, java.awt.Font font,
    java.awt.Color color)
```
Creates a `TitledBorder` with the specified `border` and `title`, with the title in the specified `font` and `color`. See `TitledBorder` for the values for `titleJustification` and `titlePosition`.

See also   BevelBorder (p.463), Border (p.465), CompoundBorder (p.466), EmptyBorder (p.467), EtchedBorder (p.468), LineBorder (p.470), MatteBorder (p.471), TitledBorder (p.473).

swing.BoundedRangeModel

INTERFACE   BoundedRangeModel

A `BoundedRangeModel` is the data model used by components such as sliders and scroll bars. It represents a value between a minimum and a maximum. It also has an extent associated with it, which is the "width" of the value. For example, in a scroll bar, the value will be the position of the top of the scroll bar, and the extent is the height of its thumb (in look and feels that have a proportionally sized thumb).

The values in the model meet these constraints:

```
minimum <= value <= (value + extent) <= maximum
```

To enforce these constraints, a `BoundedRangeModel` may change the other three properties when one is changed. The maximum property will try to change the minimum, value, and extent properties (in that order) to maintain the constraints. Similarly, the minimum property will do the same with the maximum, value, and extent properties. The maximum and minimum values are "hard" limits, so changes to the value and extent will only modify the value or extent to fit.

Example

```
package BoundedRangeModelEx;

import java.awt.*;
import java.awt.event.*;
import com.sun.java.swing.*;
import com.sun.java.swing.event.*;

public class Main extends JFrame {
  JSlider slider = new JSlider();
  BoundedRangeModel model = slider.getModel();

  public Main () {
    this.addWindowListener(new WindowAdapter() {
      public void windowClosing(WindowEvent e) {
        Main.this.dispose();
        System.exit(0);
      }
    });
    getContentPane().add(slider, BorderLayout.CENTER);

    model.addChangeListener (new ChangeListener() {
```

132   swing.BoundedRangeModel

```
      public void stateChanged (ChangeEvent e) {
        System.out.println ("Value: " + model.getValue());
      }
    });
    pack();
    setVisible(true);
  }
  public static void main (String arg[]) {
    new Main();
  }
}
```

public interface BoundedRangeModel

Methods

public abstract void addChangeListener(ChangeListener listener)

Adds `listener` as a listener to the list of those to be notified when any values change.

public abstract int getExtent()

Returns the extent.

public abstract int getMaximum()

Returns the maximum value allowed in the model. The actual maximum is defined by maximum–extent.

public abstract int getMinimum()

Returns the minimum value allowed in the model.

public abstract int getValue()

Returns the current value.

public abstract boolean getValueIsAdjusting()

Returns `true` when the value is in the middle of a series of changes (knowing this may let you avoid unnecessary updates).

public abstract void removeChangeListener(ChangeListener listener)

Removes `listener` from the list of listeners to be notified of changes in the model.

public abstract void setExtent(int extent)

Sets the extent value. If `extent` is negative, or `value + extent > maximum`, this method should change the values to fit. Listeners are notified of any change in values.

public abstract void setMaximum(int newValue)

Sets the new maximum value. If the minimum or current values are greater than `newValue`, they are silently set to `newValue`. Listeners are notified of any change in values.

public abstract void setMinimum(int newValue)

Sets the new minimum value. If the current value or maximum are less than `newValue`, they are silently set to `newValue`. Listeners are notified of any change in values.

public abstract void setRangeProperties(int newValue,
int newExtent, int newMin, int newMax, boolean isAdjusting)

Sets all values. All constraints are enforced. If any properties are changed, listeners are notified.

public abstract void setValue(int newValue)

Sets the current value. If `newValue < minimum` or `newValue > maximum`, an `Illegal-ArgumentException` is thrown. If necessary, the extent is adjusted so `newValue + extent <= maximum`. Listeners are notified of any change in values.

public abstract void setValueIsAdjusting(boolean isAdjusting)

Sets whether the value is in the midst of a series of changes.

swing.Box

CLASS

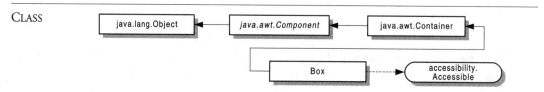

A Box is a container with a predefined layout BoxLayout. It can be oriented horizontally or vertically. The Box class can also provide invisible glue and strut components, that can be used to modify the arrangement of objects in Box or other containers.

Glue is a stretchy, invisible component. If you add it to a container, it has no effect when space is tight. When there is extra space, space is distributed to the glue just as it is to any other component that can stretch. In this way, you can place objects that will spread apart naturally as space becomes plentiful.

Struts are also invisible, but they are of a fixed size. They can be used to keep components a fixed distance from each other, without worrying about borders or insets.

Example 1

```
package BoxExample;

import com.sun.java.swing.*;
import java.awt.event.*;
import java.awt.*;

public class Ex1 extends JFrame {
   public Ex1() {
      JPanel p = new JPanel(new GridLayout(3, 1));

      JPanel p1 = new JPanel();
      Box box1 = new Box(BoxLayout.X_AXIS);
      box1.add(Box.createHorizontalGlue());
      box1.add(new JButton("glue-strut"));
      box1.add(Box.createHorizontalStrut(15));
      box1.add(new JButton("strut-glue"));
      box1.add(Box.createHorizontalGlue());
      p1.add(box1);
      p1.setBorder(BorderFactory.createRaisedBevelBorder());

      JPanel p2 = new JPanel();
      Box box2 = new Box(BoxLayout.X_AXIS);
      box2.add(Box.createHorizontalStrut(25));
      box2.add(new JButton("strut-glue"));
      box2.add(Box.createHorizontalGlue());
      box2.add(new JButton("glue-strut"));
```

```
      box2.add(Box.createHorizontalStrut(25));
      p2.add(box2);
      p2.setBorder(BorderFactory.createRaisedBevelBorder());

      JPanel p3 = new JPanel();
      Box box3 = new Box(BoxLayout.X_AXIS);
      box3.add(Box.createHorizontalStrut(25));
      box3.add(new JButton("strut-glue"));
      box3.add(Box.createHorizontalGlue());
      box3.add(new JButton("glue-glue"));
      box3.add(Box.createHorizontalGlue());
      p3.add(box3);
      p3.setBorder(BorderFactory.createRaisedBevelBorder());

      p.add(p1);
      p.add(p2);
      p.add(p3);
      getContentPane().add(p);
      addWindowListener(new WindowAdapter() {
         public void windowClosing(WindowEvent e) {
            Ex1.this.dispose();
            System.exit(0);
         }
      });
      pack();
   }

   public static void main(String[] args) {
      Ex1 ex1 = new Ex1();
      ex1.setVisible(true);
   }
}
```

Example 2

```
package BoxExample;

import com.sun.java.swing.*;
import java.awt.event.*;
import java.awt.*;

public class Ex2 extends JFrame {
   public Ex2() {
      // Shows a box with vertical components
      Box box = new Box(BoxLayout.Y_AXIS);
      box.add (new JButton("Test button"));
      box.add (new JSlider());
      box.add (new JTextField("Text field with some text", 20));
      box.add (new JButton("Another, bigger button"));

      getContentPane().add(box);
      addWindowListener(new WindowAdapter() {
         public void windowClosing(WindowEvent e) {
            Ex2.this.dispose();
            System.exit(0);
         }
      });
      pack();
```

```
      }
   public static void main(String[] args) {
      Ex2 ex2 = new Ex2();
      ex2.setVisible(true);
   }
}
```

public class Box extends java.awt.Container
    implements Accessible

Constructor

public Box(int axis)

Creates a box, with orientation specified by axis (either `BoxLayout.X_AXIS` or `BoxLayout.Y_AXIS`). A Box always uses a BoxLayout.

Methods

public static java.awt.Component createGlue()

Creates glue that is willing to stretch both horizontally and vertically. See the discussion on glue above, and `createHorizontalGlue()` and `createVerticalGlue()`.

public static Box createHorizontalBox()

Creates and returns a Box oriented horizontally.

public static java.awt.Component createHorizontalGlue()

Creates glue that is willing to stretch horizontally only. See the discussion on glue above, and `createGlue()` and `createVerticalGlue()`.

public static java.awt.Component createHorizontalStrut(int width)

Creates a horizontal strut of width `width` and height 0. This strut could be used in a horizontal box to maintain a fixed distance between components, or in a vertical box to ensure that the box maintains a minimum width. See the discussion on struts above, and `createRigidArea()` and `createVerticalStrut()`.

public static java.awt.Component createRigidArea(
    java.awt.Dimension d)

Creates a two-dimensional strut of height and width specified by d. See the discussion on struts above, and `createHorizontalStrut()` and `createVerticalStrut()`.

public static Box createVerticalBox()

Creates and returns a Box oriented vertically.

public static java.awt.Component createVerticalGlue()

Creates glue that is willing to stretch vertically only. See the discussion on glue above, and `createGlue()` and `createHorizontalGlue()`.

public static java.awt.Component createVerticalStrut(int height)

Creates a horizontal strut of width 0 and height `height`. This strut could be used in a horizontal box to ensure that the box maintains a minimum height, or in a vertical box to maintain a fixed vertical distance between components. See the discussion on struts above, and `createRigidArea()` and `createVerticalStrut()`.

public AccessibleContext getAccessibleContext()

Returns the accessible context for this box. See the chapter on accessibility.
Implements: getAccessibleContext in interface `Accessible`.

public void setLayout(java.awt.LayoutManager notAllowed)

> Do not call this method. It is part of the `Container` interface, but a `Box` is not allowed to change its layout manager. This method will throw an AWTError if called.

Protected Fields

protected AccessibleContext accessibleContext

> See the chapter on accessibility.

> *Returned by* Box.createHorizontalBox() (p.134), Box.createVerticalBox() (p.134).
> *See also* Accessible (p.85), AccessibleContext (p.90), BoxLayout (p.144).

swing.Box.AccessibleBox

INNER CLASS

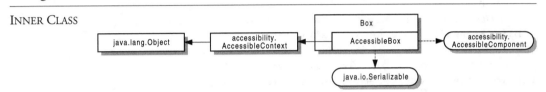

This class supports accessibility for a `Box`. It is what gets returned from `Box.getAccessible Context()`.

**protected class Box.AccessibleBox extends AccessibleContext
    implements java.io.Serializable, AccessibleComponent**

Constructors

public AccessibleBox()

> Default constructor.

Methods

public void addFocusListener(java.awt.event.FocusListener l)

> Adds a `FocusListener` to this component.
> *Implements:* addFocusListener in interface `AccessibleComponent`.

public boolean contains(java.awt.Point p)

> Returns `true` if p is within this component's bounds. The coordinates of p are assumed to be relative to this component.
> *Implements:* contains in interface `AccessibleComponent`.

public Accessible getAccessibleAt(java.awt.Point p)

> If there is an accessible child component at the given point p in this component, it is returned. If there isn't a child there, `null` is returned. The coordinates of point p are assumed to be relative to this component.
> *Implements:* getAccessibleAt in interface `AccessibleComponent`.

public Accessible getAccessibleChild(int i)

> Returns the ith Accessible child of the object.
> *Overrides:* getAccessibleChild in class `AccessibleContext`.

public int getAccessibleChildrenCount()

> Returns the number of accessible children in the object.
> *Overrides:* getAccessibleChildrenCount in class `AccessibleContext`.

public AccessibleComponent getAccessibleComponent()

Returns the `AccessibleComponent` associated with this object. If there isn't one this method returns `null`.

Overrides: getAccessibleComponent in class `AccessibleContext`.

public int getAccessibleIndexInParent()

Returns the index of this object in its `Accessible` parent. If this object does not have an `Accessible` parent, this method returns −1.

Overrides: getAccessibleIndexInParent in class `AccessibleContext`.

See also: getAccessibleParent.

public Accessible getAccessibleParent()

Returns `getParent()` if its parent is `Accessible`. If its parent is not `Accessible`, this method returns `null`.

Overrides: getAccessibleParent in class `AccessibleContext`.

public AccessibleRole getAccessibleRole()

Returns the `AccessibleRole` of this object.

Overrides: getAccessibleRole in class `AccessibleContext`.

public AccessibleStateSet getAccessibleStateSet()

Returns the `AccessibleStateSet` of this object.

Overrides: getAccessibleStateSet in class `AccessibleContext`.

public java.awt.Color getBackground()

Returns the background color of the object, if it supports one.

Implements: getBackground in interface `AccessibleComponent`.

public java.awt.Rectangle getBounds()

Returns the bounds of this object. The coordinates in the returned `Rectangle` are relative to this object's parent. If the object is not on screen, this method returns `null`.

Implements: getBounds in interface `AccessibleComponent`.

public java.awt.Cursor getCursor()

Returns the `Cursor` to use for this object, if one is supported. If a `Cursor` is not supported, this method returns `null`.

Implements: getCursor in interface `AccessibleComponent`.

public java.awt.Font getFont()

Returns the `Font` to use for this object. The returned value may be `null` if the object does not support `Font`s.

Implements: getFont in interface `AccessibleComponent`.

public java.awt.FontMetrics getFontMetrics(java.awt.Font f)

Returns the `FontMetrics` for the given font, if this object supports `Font`s.

Implements: getFontMetrics in interface `AccessibleComponent`.

See also: getFont.

public java.awt.Color getForeground()

Returns the foreground `Color` of this object if it supports one.

Implements: getForeground in interface `AccessibleComponent`.

public java.util.Locale getLocale()

Returns the `Locale` of this object.

Overrides: getLocale in class `AccessibleContext`.

public java.awt.Point getLocation()

Returns the location of this object's origin in its parent, in coordinates relative to its parent.

Implements: getLocation in interface AccessibleComponent.

public java.awt.Point getLocationOnScreen()

Returns the location of this object on screen, or null if the object is not on the screen.

Implements: getLocationOnScreen in interface AccessibleComponent.

public java.awt.Dimension getSize()

Returns the size of the object.

Implements: getSize in interface AccessibleComponent.

public boolean isEnabled()

Returns true if the object is enabled.

Implements: isEnabled in interface AccessibleComponent.

public boolean isFocusTraversable()

Returns true if the object can accept the focus.

Implements: isFocusTraversable in interface AccessibleComponent.

public boolean isShowing()

Returns true if the object is showing. Note that this method can return true even if the object is covered by another.

Implements: isShowing in interface AccessibleComponent.

public boolean isVisible()

Returns true if the object intends to be visible. This method may return true even if the object is hidden as a result of its parent being hidden.

Implements: isVisible in interface AccessibleComponent.

public void removeFocusListener(java.awt.event.FocusListener l)

Removes the given FocusListener.

Implements: removeFocusListener in interface AccessibleComponent.

public void requestFocus()

Gets the focus for this object.

Implements: requestFocus in interface AccessibleComponent.

public void setBackground(java.awt.Color c)

Sets the background color.

Implements: setBackground in interface AccessibleComponent.

public void setBounds(java.awt.Rectangle r)

Sets the bounds of this object. Note that the coordinates used in r are relative to the object's parent.

Implements: setBounds in interface AccessibleComponent.

public void setCursor(java.awt.Cursor cursor)

Sets the Cursor of this object.

Implements: setCursor in interface AccessibleComponent.

public void setEnabled(boolean b)

Sets the enabled state of the object.

Implements: setEnabled in interface AccessibleComponent.

public void setFont(java.awt.Font f)

Sets the Font of this object.

Implements: setFont in interface AccessibleComponent.

public void setForeground(java.awt.Color c)

Sets the foreground color of this object.

Implements: setForeground in interface AccessibleComponent.

```
public void setLocation(java.awt.Point p)
```
Sets the location of the object relative to the parent.
Implements: setLocation in interface AccessibleComponent.

```
public void setSize(java.awt.Dimension d)
```
Resizes the object.
Implements: setSize in interface AccessibleComponent.

```
public void setVisible(boolean b)
```
Sets the visible state of the object.
Implements: setVisible in interface AccessibleComponent.

See also   Accessible (p.85), AccessibleComponent (p.87), AccessibleContext (p.90), AccessibleRole (p.95), AccessibleStateSet (p.101).

swing.Box.Filler

INNER CLASS

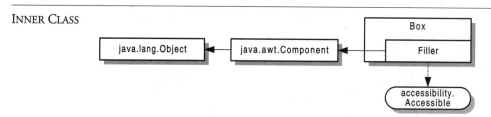

An implementation of a lightweight component that participates in layout but has no view.

```
public static class Box.Filler extends java.awt.Component
    implements Accessible
```

Constructors
```
public Filler(java.awt.Dimension min, java.awt.Dimension pref,
    java.awt.Dimension max)
```
Constructor to create shape with the given size ranges.

Methods
```
public void changeShape(java.awt.Dimension min,
    java.awt.Dimension pref, java.awt.Dimension max)
```
Changes the size requests for this shape. An invalidate() is propagated upward as a result so that layout will eventually happen with using the new sizes.

```
public AccessibleContext getAccessibleContext()
```
Gets the AccessibleContext associated with this Component.

```
public java.awt.Dimension getMaximumSize()
```
Overrides: getMaximumSize in class Component.

```
public java.awt.Dimension getMinimumSize()
```
Overrides: getMinimumSize in class Component.

```
public java.awt.Dimension getPreferredSize()
```
Overrides: getPreferredSize in class Component.

Protected Fields
```
protected AccessibleContext accessibleContext
```

Inner Classes
protected class Box.Filler.AccessibleBoxFiller

See also   Accessible (p.85), AccessibleContext (p.90).

swing.Box.Filler.AccessibleBoxFiller

Inner Class

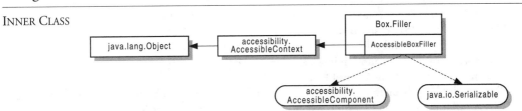

```
protected class Box.Filler.AccessibleBoxFiller
    extends AccessibleContext implements java.io.Serializable,
    AccessibleComponent
```

Methods
public void addFocusListener(java.awt.event.FocusListener l)

Adds the specified focus listener to receive focus events from this Component.

Implements: addFocusListener in interface AccessibleComponent.

public boolean contains(java.awt.Point p)

Checks whether the specified point is within this object's bounds, where the point's *x* and *y* coordinates are defined to be relative to the coordinate system of the object.

Implements: contains in interface AccessibleComponent.

public Accessible getAccessibleAt(java.awt.Point p)

Returns the Accessible child, if one exists, contained at the local coordinate p.

Implements: getAccessibleAt in interface AccessibleComponent.

public Accessible getAccessibleChild(int n)

Returns the nth Accessible child of the object.

Overrides: getAccessibleChild in class AccessibleContext.

public int getAccessibleChildrenCount()

Returns the number of Accessible children in the object. If all of the children of this object implement Accessible, then this method returns the number of children of this object.

Overrides: getAccessibleChildrenCount in class AccessibleContext.

public AccessibleComponent getAccessibleComponent()

Returns the AccessibleComponent associated with this object if one exists. Otherwise, it returns null.

Overrides: getAccessibleComponent in class AccessibleContext.

public int getAccessibleIndexInParent()

Returns the index of this object in its accessible parent. This method returns −1 if this object does not have an accessible parent.

Overrides: getAccessibleIndexInParent in class AccessibleContext.

public Accessible getAccessibleParent()

Returns the Accessible parent of this object. If the parent of this object implements Accessible, this method should simply return getParent().

Overrides: getAccessibleParent in class AccessibleContext.

public AccessibleRole getAccessibleRole()

Returns AccessibleRole.FILLER.

Overrides: getAccessibleRole in class AccessibleContext.

public AccessibleStateSet getAccessibleStateSet()

Returns the state of this object.

Overrides: getAccessibleStateSet in class AccessibleContext.

public java.awt.Color getBackground()

Returns the background color of this object or null if it does not support one.

Implements: getBackground in interface AccessibleComponent.

public java.awt.Rectangle getBounds()

Returns the bounds of this object in the form of a Rectangle object. The bounds specify this object's width, height, and location relative to its parent. If the object is not on screen this method can return null.

Implements: getBounds in interface AccessibleComponent.

public java.awt.Cursor getCursor()

Returns the Cursor of this object, if it supports one.

Implements: getCursor in interface AccessibleComponent.

public java.awt.Font getFont()

Returns the Font of this object, or null if it does not support one.

Implements: getFont in interface AccessibleComponent.

public java.awt.FontMetrics getFontMetrics(java.awt.Font f)

Returns the FontMetrics of this object.

Implements: getFontMetrics in interface AccessibleComponent.

public java.awt.Color getForeground()

Returns the foreground color of this object or null if the component does not support a foreground color.

Implements: getForeground in interface AccessibleComponent.

public java.util.Locale getLocale()

Returns the locale of this object.

Overrides: getLocale in class AccessibleContext.

public java.awt.Point getLocation()

Returns the location of the object relative to the parent in the form of a point specifying the object's top-left corner in the screen's coordinate space.

Implements: getLocation in interface AccessibleComponent.

public java.awt.Point getLocationOnScreen()

Returns the location of the object on the screen. Returns null if the object is not on screen.

Implements: getLocationOnScreen in interface AccessibleComponent.

public java.awt.Dimension getSize()

Returns the size of this object in the form of a Dimension object. The height field of the Dimension object contains this object's height, and the width field of the Dimension object contains this object's width.

Implements: getSize in interface AccessibleComponent.

public boolean isEnabled()

Returns true if the object is enabled.

Implements: isEnabled in interface AccessibleComponent.

public boolean isFocusTraversable()

Returns whether this object can accept focus or not.

Implements: isFocusTraversable in interface AccessibleComponent.

public boolean isShowing()

Returns true if the object is showing. This is determined by checking the visibility of the object and ancestors of the object. Note that this method will return true even if the object is obscured by another (for example, it happens to be underneath a menu that was pulled down).

Implements: isShowing in interface AccessibleComponent.

public boolean isVisible()

Returns true if the object is visible. Note that this means that the object *intends* to be visible. It may not in fact be showing on the screen because one of the objects that this object is contained by is not visible. To determine if an object is showing on the screen, use isShowing().

Implements: isVisible in interface AccessibleComponent.

public void removeFocusListener(java.awt.event.FocusListener l)

Removes the specified focus listener so it no longer receives focus events from this component.

Implements: removeFocusListener in interface AccessibleComponent.

public void requestFocus()

Requests focus for this object.

Implements: requestFocus in interface AccessibleComponent.

public void setBackground(java.awt.Color c)

Sets the background color of this object.

Implements: setBackground in interface AccessibleComponent.

public void setBounds(java.awt.Rectangle r)

Sets the bounds of this object in the form of a Rectangle object. The bounds specify this object's width, height, and location relative to its parent.

Implements: setBounds in interface AccessibleComponent.

public void setCursor(java.awt.Cursor cursor)

Sets the Cursor of this object.

Implements: setCursor in interface AccessibleComponent.

public void setEnabled(boolean b)

Sets the enabled state of the object.

Implements: setEnabled in interface AccessibleComponent.

public void setFont(java.awt.Font f)

Sets the Font of this object.

Implements: setFont in interface AccessibleComponent.

public void setForeground(java.awt.Color c)

Sets the foreground color of this object.

Implements: setForeground in interface AccessibleComponent.

public void setLocation(java.awt.Point p)

Sets the location of the object relative to the parent.

Implements: setLocation in interface AccessibleComponent.

public void setSize(java.awt.Dimension d)

Resizes this object so that it has width and height.

Implements: setSize in interface AccessibleComponent.

public void setVisible(boolean b)

Sets the visible state of the object.

Implements: setVisible in interface AccessibleComponent.

Protected Constructors

protected AccessibleBoxFiller()
Default constructor.

See also   Accessible (p.85), AccessibleComponent (p.87), AccessibleContext (p.90), AccessibleRole (p.95), AccessibleStateSet (p.101).

swing.BoxLayout

CLASS

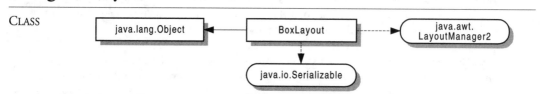

A BoxLayout arranges components horizontally or vertically. In a horizontal layout, it puts them left-to-right, using their preferred widths, but with the height determined by the tallest component. If a component can't be stretched vertically, it is centered vertically according to layoutAlignmentY.

In a vertical box, preferred heights are honored, but widths are stretched horizontally if possible, or centered according to layoutAlignmentX.

See the Box (p.134) class for a container with a built-in BoxLayout.

**public class BoxLayout extends java.lang.Object
    implements java.awt.LayoutManager2, java.io.Serializable**

Fields

public static final int X_AXIS = 0
public static final int Y_AXIS = 1
These constants are for use in the constructor, and tell whether the layout should be oriented horizontally left-to-right (X_AXIS) or vertically top-to-bottom (Y_AXIS).

Constructors

public BoxLayout(java.awt.Container c, int axis)
Creates a box layout for container c oriented according to axis. See Box (p.134) for a container with a built-in BoxLayout.
Throws: AWTError if axis is not a valid constant.

Methods

**public void addLayoutComponent(java.awt.Component component,
    Object constraints)**
An empty method.
Implements: addLayoutComponent in interface LayoutManager2.
public void addLayoutComponent(String name, java.awt.Component component)
An empty method.

Implements: addLayoutComponent in interface LayoutManager.

public float getLayoutAlignmentX(java.awt.Container c)

Returns the alignment along the *x* axis for the container. If the box is horizontal, the default alignment will be returned. Otherwise, the alignment needed to place the children along the *x* axis will be returned.

Throws: AWTError if the target isn't the container specified to the BoxLayout constructor.

Implements: getLayoutAlignmentX in interface LayoutManager2.

public float getLayoutAlignmentY(java.awt.Container c)

Returns the alignment along the *y* axis for the container. If the box is vertical, the default alignment will be returned. Otherwise, the alignment needed to place the children along the *y* axis will be returned.

Throws: AWTError if the target isn't the container specified to the BoxLayout constructor.

Implements: getLayoutAlignmentY in interface LayoutManager2.

public void invalidateLayout(java.awt.Container c)

Indicates that a child has changed its layout-related information, and thus any cached calculations should be flushed.

Throws: AWTError if the target isn't the container specified to the BoxLayout constructor.

Implements: invalidateLayout in interface LayoutManager2.

public void layoutContainer(java.awt.Container c)

Called by AWT when the specified container needs to be laid out.

Throws: AWTError if the target isn't the container specified to the BoxLayout constructor.

public java.awt.Dimension maximumLayoutSize(java.awt.Container c)

Returns the minimum dimensions needed to lay out the components contained in the specified target container.

Throws: AWTError if the target isn't the container specified to the BoxLayout constructor.

Implements: maximumLayoutSize in interface LayoutManager2.

public java.awt.Dimension minimumLayoutSize(java.awt.Container c)

Returns the minimum dimensions needed to lay out the components contained in the specified target container.

Throws: AWTError if the target isn't the container specified to the BoxLayout constructor.

public java.awt.Dimension preferredLayoutSize(java.awt.Container c)

Returns the preferred dimensions for this layout, given the components in the specified target container.

Throws: AWTError if the target isn't the container specified to the BoxLayout constructor.

public void removeLayoutComponent(java.awt.Component component)

An empty method.

Implements: removeLayoutComponent in interface LayoutManager.

Extended by DefaultMenuLayout (p.731).

See also Box (p.134).

swing.ButtonGroup

CLASS

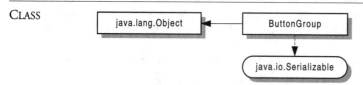

A button group manages a set of buttons to make sure that only one of them is selected at a time. Most commonly, you would use it with JRadioButton (p.319) to get full radio button behavior.

To start, all buttons are unselected. When a button is selected, all other buttons in the group become unselected. After the first time a button in the group is selected (either by the user or through setSelected()) there will always be one button selected. Beyond destroying and recreating the group there is no way to return to the initial "all unselected" state of the group.

Example: (see JRadioButton (p.319) and JRadioButtonMenuItem (p.321) for other examples).

```
package ButtonGroupExample;
import com.sun.java.swing.*;
import java.awt.event.*;

public class Example extends JFrame {
   public Example() {
      this.addWindowListener(new WindowAdapter() {
         public void windowClosing(WindowEvent e) {
            Example.this.dispose();
            System.exit(0);
         }
      });
      Box p = new Box(BoxLayout.Y_AXIS);

      ButtonGroup group = new ButtonGroup();
      // "group.getSelection()" will have selected ButtonModel

      JRadioButton b = new JRadioButton("Blues");
      group.add(b);    // Add to group
      p.add(b);          // and then to the container

      b = new JRadioButton("Country");
      group.add(b);
      p.add(b);

      b = new JRadioButton("Jazz");
      group.add(b);
      p.add(b);

      b = new JRadioButton("Rock");
      group.add(b);
      p.add(b);

      b = new JRadioButton("Not in ButtonGroup - try it");
      p.add(b);

      getContentPane().add(p);
      pack();
   }
```

```
  public static void main(String[] args) {
    Example ex = new Example();
    ex.setVisible(true);
  }
}
```

public class ButtonGroup extends java.lang.Object
    implements java.io.Serializable

Constructors
public ButtonGroup()
    Creates a new button group.

Methods
public void add(AbstractButton button)
    Adds a button to the set of buttons managed by the button group.
public java.util.Enumeration getElements()
    Gets an enumeration of all buttons in the button group. Each element in the group will be an AbstractButton.
public ButtonModel getSelection()
    Gets the model of the currently selected button.
public boolean isSelected(ButtonModel model)
    Tells whether model is selected.
public void remove(AbstractButton button)
    Removes button from the list of buttons managed by this button group.
public void setSelected(ButtonModel model, boolean shouldSelect)
    Sets model to be selected or not, as indicated by shouldSelect.

Protected Fields
protected java.util.Vector buttons
    The set of buttons for this group.

    See also   AbstractButton (p.118), ButtonModel (p.147).

swing.ButtonModel

INTERFACE

This is the model for all buttons, including radio buttons and check boxes.
    Buttons have several associated states:

- armed—the mouse has clicked but not yet released, and the mouse is currently over the button. If the mouse is released over the button, the button is pressed or selected. If the mouse moves off of the button before it is released, most look and feels disarm the button without pressing or selecting it.
- enabled—the user is allowed to manipulate the button.

- pressed—the mouse has been released over a `JButton`. For example, a button may activate only if the click and release are in the button. While the *mouse* button is pressed over the Swing button it is "armed." If the mouse button is then released over the `JButton`, the `JButton` will have `setPressed(true)` called.
- rollover—the mouse is over the button (but hasn't clicked).
- selected—the button is selected (only for check box and radio buttons).

Example

```
package buttonmodel;

import java.awt.*;
import java.awt.event.*;
import com.sun.java.swing.*;
import com.sun.java.swing.event.*;
public class Main extends JFrame {
    JButton b = new JButton("Test");
    ButtonModel model = b.getModel();
    public Main () {
        this.addWindowListener(new WindowAdapter() {
            public void windowClosing(WindowEvent e) {
                Main.this.dispose();
                System.exit(0);
            }
        });
        model.addChangeListener (new ChangeListener() {
            public void stateChanged (ChangeEvent e) {
                System.out.println("Armed: " + model.isArmed()
                + " Enabled: " + model.isEnabled()
                + " Pressed: " + model.isPressed());
            }
        });
        getContentPane().add(b, BorderLayout.CENTER);
        pack();
        setVisible(true);
    }
    public static void main (String arg[]) {
        new Main();
    }
}
```

`public interface ButtonModel extends java.awt.ItemSelectable`

Methods

`public abstract void addActionListener(`
`java.awt.event.ActionListener listener)`
    Adds `listener` to the list of listeners for actions.

`public abstract void addChangeListener(ChangeListener listener)`
    Adds `listener` to the list of listeners for changes in the button status.

`public abstract void addItemListener(java.awt.event.ItemListener listener)`

> Adds `listener` to the list of listeners for changes in the items (for radio buttons and check boxes).
> *Inherited from:* interface `ItemSelectable`.

`public abstract String getActionCommand()`

> Gets the action command associated with this button.

`public abstract int getMnemonic()`

> Gets the character used as the accelerator key for this button.

`public abstract boolean isArmed()`

> Returns `true` if the button is armed, which indicates it is "pressed" but the mouse button is still being held down.

`public abstract boolean isEnabled()`

> Returns `true` if the button is enabled, which indicates that it can be selected or pressed by the user.

`public abstract boolean isPressed()`

> Returns `true` if the button is pressed.

`public abstract boolean isRollover()`

> Returns `true` if the mouse is over the button (but hasn't yet clicked).

`public abstract boolean isSelected()`

> Returns `true` if the button is selected (radio buttons and check boxes only).

`public abstract void removeActionListener(`
`    java.awt.event.ActionListener listener)`

> Removes `listener` from the list of listeners for action events.

`public abstract void removeChangeListener(ChangeListener listener)`

> Removes `listener` from the list of listeners for changes in the button state.

`public abstract void removeItemListener(`
`    java.awt.event.ItemListener listener)`

> Removes `listener` from the list of listeners for changes in selection status (radio buttons and check boxes only).
> *Inherited from:* interface `java.awt.ItemSelectable`.

`public abstract void setActionCommand(String command)`

> Sets the action command string.

`public abstract void setArmed(boolean newValue)`

> Sets the armed state as indicated by `newValue`. Notifies any change listeners if the state changes.

`public abstract void setEnabled(boolean newValue)`

> Sets the enabled state as indicated by `newValue`. Notifies any change listeners if the state changes.

`public abstract void setGroup(ButtonGroup group)`

> Makes this button part of `group`. Only one button in a group can be active at any time. See `ButtonGroup` for more information.

`public abstract void setMnemonic(int key)`

> Sets the new key accelerator for this button.

`public abstract void setPressed(boolean newValue)`

> Sets the pressed state as indicated by `newValue`. Notifies any change listeners if the state changes.

`public abstract void setRollover(boolean newValue)`

> Sets the rollover state as indicated by `newValue`. Notifies any change listeners if the state changes.

`public abstract void setSelected(boolean newValue)`

> Sets the selected state as indicated by `newValue`. Notifies any change listeners or item listeners if the state changes.

Implemented by   DefaultButtonModel (p.161).
Returned by   AbstractButton.getModel() (p.118), ButtonGroup.getSelection() (p.146).
See also   ButtonGroup (p.146), ChangeListener (p.488).

swing.CellEditor

INTERFACE   CellEditor

This interface is supported by editors for the cells in tables and trees (and other such components introduced in the future). It notifies listeners of type `CellEditorListener` (p.486) of any changes it makes.

This interface is used to insulate the component using the editor from the actual editor implementation. This allows editors to be as simple or as complex as the developer wants, as long as they support this interface. See `DefaultCellEditor` (p.164) for a sample class implementing this interface. Note that `DefaultCellEditor` actually encapsulates *three* different editors in one class but it can be used transparently by a component which uses `CellEditors`.

For the viewing (as opposed to editing) of a table cell, see `TableCellRenderer` (p.760). For the viewing of a tree cell, see `TreeCellRenderer` (p.985).

```
public interface CellEditor
```

Methods
`public abstract void addCellEditorListener(CellEditorListener listener)`
Adds `listener` to the list of listeners to be notified of changes in the cell editor.
`public abstract void cancelCellEditing()`
Tells the editor to cancel editing and restore the cell value to what it was before editing. Notifies any listeners.
`public abstract Object getCellEditorValue()`
Gets the value that the editor has produced (for example, a `String`).
`public abstract boolean isCellEditable(java.util.EventObject event)`
Returns `true` if the cell allows editing. The `event` is in the coordinate system of the component that called this method. The editor may not, however, assume that the cell has been installed in the component hierarchy. This lets cells avoid being instantiated until they are absolutely needed. See `shouldSelectCell()`.
`public abstract void removeCellEditorListener(CellEditorListener listener)`
Stops `listener` from receiving any more notifications of cell editor activity.
`public abstract boolean shouldSelectCell(java.util.EventObject event)`
Tells the editor to select the cell for editing. The `event` is in the coordinate system of the component that called this method, and identifies the cell to be edited. This method returns `true` if the cell should be selected. (You may sometimes might want to just edit a cell without selecting it.)
`public abstract boolean stopCellEditing()`
Stops editing. Notifies any listeners that editing has stopped.

Extended by   TableCellEditor (p.758), TreeCellEditor (p.985).
See also   CellEditorListener (p.486).

swing.CellRendererPane

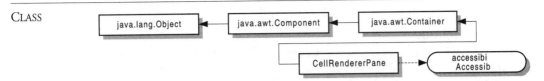

`CellRendererPane` is a support class used for cell rendering by `JList`, `JTable`, and `JTree`. It exists to control the propagation of `repaint` and `invalidate` calls, ensuring that it retains control of the repaint rather than letting its parent take ownership.

```
public class CellRendererPane extends java.awt.Container
    implements Accessible
```

Constructors

public CellRendererPane()

Creates a cell renderer pane.

Methods

public AccessibleContext getAccessibleContext()

Returns the accessible context for this pane. See the chapter on `accessibility`.

Implements: `getAccessibleContext` in interface `Accessible`.

public void invalidate()

Does nothing (this prevents invalidate from being propagated up the tree).

Overrides: `invalidate` in class `Container`.

public void paint(java.awt.Graphics g)

Not used. Do not call.

Overrides: `paint` in class `Container`.

public void paintComponent(java.awt.Graphics g, java.awt.Component c,
java.awt.Container parent, java.awt.Rectangle rect)

Equivalent to `paintComponent(g, renderer, parent, rectangle.x, rectangle.y, rectangle.width, rectangle.height, false)`.

public void paintComponent(java.awt.Graphics gr,
java.awt.Component renderer, java.awt.Container parent, int x,
int y, int width, int height)

Equivalent to `paintComponent(g, renderer, parent, x, y, width, height, false)`.

public void paintComponent(java.awt.Graphics gr,
java.awt.Component renderer, java.awt.Container parent, int x,
int y, int width, int height, boolean shouldValidate)

Paints the `renderer` onto `gr` at (x,y) with `width` and `height`. The `parent` is the component on which the cell is being drawn. First, if `shouldValidate` is `true`, validates `renderer`. Then it makes `this` be the parent of `renderer`, and relocates `renderer` to the proper position. Finally, it paints `renderer`.

public void update(java.awt.Graphics g)

Not used. Do not call.

Overrides: `update` in `Container`.

Protected Fields

`protected AccessibleContext accessibleContext`
    The accessible context.

Protected Methods

`protected void addImpl(java.awt.Component c, Object constraints, int index)`
    Adds `component` at `index`, according to `constraint`. This enforces the content pane constraint.
    Overrides: `addImpl` in `Container`.

    Returned by   BasicTreeUI.createCellRendererPane() (p.710).
    See also   Accessible (p.85), AccessibleContext (p.90).

swing.CellRendererPane.AccessibleCellRendererPane

Inner Class

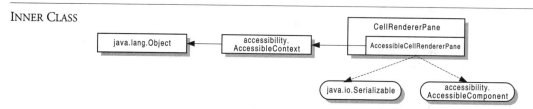

`protected class CellRendererPane.AccessibleCellRendererPane`
    `extends AccessibleContext`
    `implements AccessibleComponent, java.io.Serializable`

Methods

`public void addFocusListener(java.awt.event.FocusListener l)`
    Adds the specified focus listener to receive focus events from this component.
    Implements: `addFocusListener` in interface `AccessibleComponent`.

`public boolean contains(java.awt.Point p)`
    Checks whether the specified point is within this object's bounds, where the point's x and y coordinates are defined to be relative to the coordinate system of the object.
    Implements: `contains` in interface `AccessibleComponent`.

`public Accessible getAccessibleAt(java.awt.Point p)`
    Returns the `Accessible` child, if one exists, contained at the local coordinate `Point`.
    Implements: `getAccessibleAt` in interface `AccessibleComponent`.

`public Accessible getAccessibleChild(int i)`
    Returns the ith `Accessible` child of the object.
    Overrides: `getAccessibleChild` in class `AccessibleContext`.

`public int getAccessibleChildrenCount()`
    Returns the number of accessible children in the object. If all of the children of this object implement `Accessible`, then this method should return the number of children of this object.
    Overrides: `getAccessibleChildrenCount` in class `AccessibleContext`.

`public AccessibleComponent getAccessibleComponent()`
    Gets the `AccessibleComponent` associated with this object if one exists. Otherwise returns `null`.
    Overrides: `getAccessibleComponent` in class `AccessibleContext`.

public int getAccessibleIndexInParent()

Returns the index of this object in its accessible parent. This method returns −1 if this object does not have an accessible parent.

Overrides: getAccessibleIndexInParent in class AccessibleContext.

See also: getAccessibleParent.

public Accessible getAccessibleParent()

Gets the Accessible parent of this object. If the parent of this object implements Accessible, this method should simply return getParent().

Overrides: getAccessibleParent in class AccessibleContext.

public AccessibleRole getAccessibleRole()

Returns the role of this object.

Overrides: getAccessibleRole in class AccessibleContext.

public AccessibleStateSet getAccessibleStateSet()

Returns the state of this object.

Overrides: getAccessibleStateSet in class AccessibleContext.

public java.awt.Color getBackground()

Returns the background color of this object.

Implements: getBackground in interface AccessibleComponent.

public java.awt.Rectangle getBounds()

Returns the bounds of this object in the form of a Rectangle object. The bounds specify this object's width, height, and location relative to its parent.

Implements: getBounds in interface AccessibleComponent.

public java.awt.Cursor getCursor()

Returns the Cursor of this object.

Implements: getCursor in interface AccessibleComponent.

public java.awt.Font getFont()

Returns the Font of this object.

Implements: getFont in interface AccessibleComponent.

public java.awt.FontMetrics getFontMetrics(java.awt.Font f)

Returns the FontMetrics of this object.

Implements: getFontMetrics in interface AccessibleComponent.

See also: getFont.

public java.awt.Color getForeground()

Gets the foreground color of this object.

Implements: getForeground in interface AccessibleComponent.

public java.util.Locale getLocale()

Returns the locale of this object.

Overrides: getLocale in class AccessibleContext.

public java.awt.Point getLocation()

Returns the location of the object relative to the parent in the form of a point specifying the object's top-left corner in the screen's coordinate space.

Implements: getLocation in interface AccessibleComponent.

public java.awt.Point getLocationOnScreen()

Returns the location of the object on the screen.

Implements: getLocationOnScreen in interface AccessibleComponent.

public java.awt.Dimension getSize()

Returns the size of this object in the form of a `Dimension` object. The height field of the `Dimension` object contains this object's height, and the width field of the `Dimension` object contains this object's width.

Implements: `getSize` in interface `AccessibleComponent`.

public boolean isEnabled()

Returns `true` if the object is enabled.

Implements: `isEnabled` in interface `AccessibleComponent`.

public boolean isFocusTraversable()

Returns whether this object can accept focus or not.

Implements: `isFocusTraversable` in interface `AccessibleComponent`.

public boolean isShowing()

Returns `true` if the object is showing. This is determined by checking the visibility of the object and ancestors of the object. Note: this will return `true` even if the object is obscured by another (for example, it happens to be underneath a menu that was pulled down).

Implements: `isShowing` in interface `AccessibleComponent`.

public boolean isVisible()

Returns `true` if the object is visible. Note: this means that the object intends to be visible; however, it may not, in fact, be showing on the screen because one of the objects that this object is contained by is not visible. To determine if an object is showing on the screen, use `isShowing()`.

Implements: `isVisible` in interface `AccessibleComponent`.

public void removeFocusListener(java.awt.event.FocusListener 1)

Removes the specified focus listener so it no longer receives focus events from this component.

Implements: `removeFocusListener` in interface `AccessibleComponent`.

public void requestFocus()

Requests focus for this object.

Implements: `requestFocus` in interface `AccessibleComponent`.

public void setBackground(java.awt.Color c)

Sets the background color of this object.

Implements: `setBackground` in interface `AccessibleComponent`.

public void setBounds(java.awt.Rectangle r)

Sets the bounds of this object in the form of a `Rectangle` object. The bounds specify this object's width, height, and location relative to its parent.

Implements: `setBounds` in interface `AccessibleComponent`.

public void setCursor(java.awt.Cursor cursor)

Sets the cursor of this object.

Implements: `setCursor` in interface `AccessibleComponent`.

public void setEnabled(boolean b)

Sets the enabled state of the object.

Implements: `setEnabled` in interface `AccessibleComponent`.

public void setFont(java.awt.Font f)

Sets the font of this object.

Implements: `setFont` in interface `AccessibleComponent`.

public void setForeground(java.awt.Color c)

Sets the foreground color of this object.

Implements: `setForeground` in interface `AccessibleComponent`.

```
public void setLocation(java.awt.Point p)
```
Sets the location of the object relative to the parent.
Implements: setLocation in interface AccessibleComponent.
```
public void setSize(java.awt.Dimension d)
```
Resizes this object so that it has width and height.
Implements: setSize in interface AccessibleComponent.
```
public void setVisible(boolean b)
```
Sets the visible state of the object.
Implements: setVisible in interface AccessibleComponent.

Protected Constructors
```
protected AccessibleCellRendererPane()
```
Default constructor.

See also   Accessible (p.85), AccessibleComponent (p.87), AccessibleContext (p.90).

swing.ComboBoxEditor

INTERFACE   (ComboBoxEditor)

The ComboBoxEditor controls the editing of a combo box item (a combo box acts as a drop-down box whose chosen value can be edited).

```
public interface ComboBoxEditor
```

Methods
```
public void addActionListener(java.awt.event.ActionListener listener)
```
Adds listener to the list of objects notified when the edited item changes.
```
public java.awt.Component getEditorComponent()
```
Returns the component that actually does the editing.
```
public Object getItem()
```
Gets the item as edited.
```
public void removeActionListener(java.awt.event.ActionListener listener)
```
Removes listener from the list of objects notified when the edited item changes.
```
public void selectAll()
```
Selects all characters of the item, and begins editing.
```
public void setItem(Object newItem)
```
Sets the item to be edited. If something is already being edited, cancels its editing and begins editing newItem instead.

Implemented by   BasicComboBoxEditor (p.563).
Returned by   JComboBox.getEditor() (p.200).
See also   JComboBox (p.200).

swing.ComboBoxModel

INTERFACE

The model for a combo box is like a `ListModel`, but it adds the notion of a currently selected item.

```
public interface ComboBoxModel extends ListModel
```

Methods
public Object getSelectedItem()
Gets the currently selected item.
public void setSelectedItem(Object anItem)
Sets the currently selected item to `item`.

Extended by   MutableComboBoxModel (p.427).
Returned by   JComboBox.getModel() (p.200).
See also   ListModel (p.421).

swing.DebugGraphics

CLASS

`DebugGraphics` provides an alternative graphics context that a `JComponent` can install to help you see what's going on in your drawing code. `JComponent` provides a method to properly configure and start using an instance of `DebugGraphics` (`setDebugGraphicsOptions()`), so you will rarely directly create an instance of this class.

For `DebugGraphics` to work properly, double buffering must be turned off completely, not just for the component you are interested in. To completely disable double buffering, add the following lines to your code:

```
RepaintManager rpm = RepaintManager.currentManager(theComponent);
rpm.setDoubleBufferingEnabled(false);
```

The reason for this is that a parent component that is using double buffering will prevent the intermediate `DebugGraphics` updates from showing.

```
public class DebugGraphics extends java.awt.Graphics
```

Fields
```
public static final int BUFFERED_OPTION = 4
public static final int FLASH_OPTION = 2
public static final int LOG_OPTION = 1
public static final int NONE_OPTION = -1
```
These constants are used by `getDebugOptions()` and `setDebugOptions()`. For BUFFERED_OPTION, graphics operations (even offscreen ones) are shown in a separate frame. For FLASH_OPTION, each operation will be done several times in alternate colors, to make it obvious what is

changing. For LOG_OPTION, graphic operations will be logged to a PrintStream. For NONE_OPTION, all options will be turned off. When passing these constants to `getDebugOptions()`, they are OR'd together with any constants in use, except that if NONE_OPTION is used all options are turned off.

Constructors

`public DebugGraphics()`

Creates an instance of the `DebugGraphics` class.

`public DebugGraphics(java.awt.Graphics g)`

Creates an instance of `DebugGraphics` that actually draws on g.

`public DebugGraphics(java.awt.Graphics g, JComponent component)`

Creates an instance of `DebugGraphics` that draws on g, and uses the options set for `component`.

Methods Unique to DebugGraphics

`public static java.awt.Color flashColor()`

Tells the color that will be used for the flashed drawing when FLASH_OPTION is set.

`public static int flashCount()`

Tells how many times the drawing will be flashed when FLASH_OPTION is set.

`public static int flashTime()`

Tells how many milliseconds will be between flashes when FLASH_OPTION is set.

`public int getDebugOptions()`

Returns the set of current options (OR'd together). They are from the constants above. The value is 0 if no options are in effect.

`public boolean isDrawingBuffer()`

Returns `true` if this object is drawing from a buffer.

`public static java.io.PrintStream logStream()`

Tells where the log output will be sent when LOG_OPTION is set.

`public void setDebugOptions(int options)`

Sets the debugging options. The `options` are OR'd together with the current options. (However, if the option is NONE_OPTION, then all options are cleared.)

`public static void setFlashColor(java.awt.Color c)`

Sets the color that will be used for the flashed drawing when FLASH_OPTION is set.

`public static void setFlashCount(int count)`

Sets the number of times the drawing will be flashed when FLASH_OPTION is set.

`public static void setFlashTime(int msec)`

Sets the number of milliseconds between flashes when FLASH_OPTION is set.

`public static void setLogStream(PrintStream p)`

Sets where the log output will be sent when LOG_OPTION is set.

Methods

`public void clearRect(int x, int y, int width, int height)`
`public void clipRect(int x, int y, int width, int height)`
`public void copyArea(int x, int y, int width, int height, int newX,`
`    int newY)`
`public java.awt.Graphics create()`
`public java.awt.Graphics create(int x, int y, int width, int height)`
`public void dispose()`
`public void draw3DRect(int x, int y, int width, int height,`
`    boolean isRaised)`

```
public void drawArc(int x, int y, int width, int height,
    int startAngle, int arcAngle)
public void drawBytes(byte[] data, int dataStart, int dataLength,
    int x, int y)
public void drawChars(char[] data, int dataStart, int dataLength,
    int x, int y)
public boolean drawImage(java.awt.Image image, int x1Dest, int y1Dest,
    int x2Dest, int y2Dest, int x1Source, int y1Source, int x2Source,
    int y2Source, java.awt.Color color, java.awt.ImageObserver obs)
public boolean drawImage(java.awt.Image image, int x1Dest, int y1Dest,
    int x2Dest, int y2Dest, int x1Source, int y1Source, int x2Source,
    int y2Source, java.awt.ImageObserver obs)
public boolean drawImage(java.awt.Image image, int x, int y, int width,
    int height, java.awt.Color color, java.awt.ImageObserver obs)
public boolean drawImage(java.awt.Image image, int x, int y,
    int width, int height, java.awt.ImageObserver obs)
public boolean drawImage(java.awt.Image image, int x, int y,
    java.awt.Color color, java.awt.ImageObserver obs)
public boolean drawImage(java.awt.Image image, int x, int y,
    java.awt.ImageObserver obs)
public void drawLine(int x1, int y1, int x2, int y2)
public void drawOval(int x, int y, int width, int height)
public void drawPolygon(int[] xPoints, int[] yPoints, int numberOfPoints)
public void drawPolyline(int[] xPoints, int[] yPoints, int numberOfPoints)
public void drawRect(int x, int y, int width, int height)
public void drawRoundRect(int x, int y, int width, int height, int arcWidth,
    int arcHeight)
public void drawString(String string, int x, int y)
public void fill3DRect(int x, int y, int width, int height,
    boolean isRaised)
public void fillArc(int x, int y, int width, int height,
    int startAngle, int Angle)
public void fillOval(int x, int y, int width, int height)
public void fillPolygon(int[] xPoints, int[] yPoints, int numberOfPoints)
public void fillRect(int x, int y, int width, int height)
public void fillRoundRect(int x, int y, int width, int height,
    int arcWidth, int arcHeight)
public java.awt.Shape getClip()
public Rectangle getClipBounds()
public java.awt.Color getColor()
public java.awt.Font getFont()
public java.awt.FontMetrics getFontMetrics()
public java.awt.FontMetrics getFontMetrics(java.awt.Font)
public void setClip(int x, int y, int width, int height)
public void setClip(java.awt.Shape shape)
public void setColor(java.awt.Color color)
public void setFont(java.awt.Font font)
public void setPaintMode()
public void setXORMode(java.awt.Color color)
```

```
public void translate(int x, int y)
```
These methods are all overridden from `java.awt.Graphics`. Recall that (0,0) is the upper left corner.

See also JComponent (p.207).

swing.DefaultBoundedRangeModel

CLASS

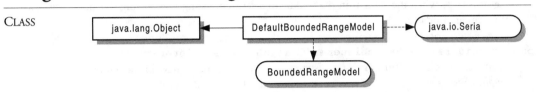

This is an implementation of the `BoundedRangeModel`, which is used by classes such as `JSlider` and `JScrollBar`.

A bounded range is a value between a minimum and a maximum. It also has an extent associated with it, which is the "width" of the value. For example, in a vertical scroll bar, the value might be the position of the top of the scroll bar, and the extent its height of its thumb/slider.

The values meet these constraints:

```
minimum <= value <= maximum
0 <= extent <= (maximum - value)
```
(Note that the value plus the extent cannot exceed the maximum.)

```
public class DefaultBoundedRangeModel extends java.lang.Object
    implements BoundedRangeModel, java.io.Serializable
```

Constructors
```
public DefaultBoundedRangeModel()
```
Creates a `DefaultBoundedRangeModel` using the following default values: max=100, min=0, value=0, extent=0.
```
public DefaultBoundedRangeModel(int value, int extent, int min, int max)
```
Initializes `value`, `extent`, `minimum`, and `maximum` to the given values.
Throws: `IllegalArgumentException` if the constraints aren't satisfied.

Methods
```
public void addChangeListener(ChangeListener listener)
```
Adds `listener` as a listener to the list of those to be notified when any values change.
Implements: `addChangeListener` in interface `BoundedRangeModel`.
```
public int getExtent()
```
Returns the extent (the "width").
Implements: `getExtent` in interface `BoundedRangeModel`.
```
public int getMaximum()
```
Returns the maximum value.
Implements: `getMaximum` in interface `BoundedRangeModel`.

public int getMinimum()

Returns the minimum value.

Implements: getMinimum in interface BoundedRangeModel.

public int getValue()

Returns the current value.

Implements: getValue in interface BoundedRangeModel.

public boolean getValueIsAdjusting()

Returns true when the value is in the middle of a series of changes. Knowing this may let you avoid unnecessary updates.

Implements: getValueIsAdjusting in interface BoundedRangeModel.

public void removeChangeListener(ChangeListener listener)

Removes listener from the list of listeners to be notified of changes in the model.

Implements: removeChangeListener in interface BoundedRangeModel.

public void setExtent(int newValue)

Sets the extent value. If newValue is negative, it will be set to 0. If value + newValue > maximum, it sets extent to maximum - value. Listeners are notified of any change in values.

Implements: setExtent in interface BoundedRangeModel.

public void setMaximum(int newValue)

Sets the new maximum value. If the minimum or current values are greater than newValue, they are silently set to newValue. Listeners are notified of any change in values.

Implements: setMaximum in interface BoundedRangeModel.

public void setMinimum(int newValue)

Sets the new minimum value. If the current value or maximum is less than newValue, they are silently set to newValue. Listeners are notified of any change in values.

Implements: setMinimum in interface BoundedRangeModel.

public void setRangeProperties(int newValue, int newExtent, int newMin, int newMax, boolean isAdjusting)

Sets all values. All constraints are enforced. If this changes any of the properties, listeners are notified using a single ChangeEvent.

Implements: setRangeProperties in interface BoundedRangeModel.

public void setValue(int newValue)

Sets the current value. If newValue < minimum then value will be set to minimum. If newValue > maximum, value will be set to maximum. If necessary, the extent is adjusted so newValue + extent <= maximum. Listeners are notified of any change in values.

Implements: setValue in interface BoundedRangeModel.

public void setValueIsAdjusting(boolean isAdjusting)

Sets whether the value is in the midst of a series of changes. This is usually set to true for situations where the component representing the range is being dragged, and it is set back to false when the dragging completes.

Implements: setValueIsAdjusting in interface BoundedRangeModel.

public String toString()

Returns a string that represents all of the BoundedRangeModel properties.

Overrides: toString in class Object.

Protected Fields

protected transient ChangeEvent changeEvent

    This event is used to notify listeners about changes in the model.

protected EventListenerList listenerList

    The list of listeners.

    See also   BoundedRangeModel (p.132), ChangeEvent (p.487), ChangeListener (p.488), EventListenerList (p.491), JScrollBar (p.328), JSlider (p.341).

swing.DefaultButtonModel

CLASS

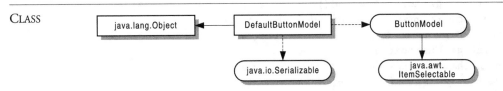

This is a default implementation of ButtonModel. It is used by the button components when they have not had a specialized ButtonModel set as their model.

    Buttons have several associated states:

- armed—the mouse has been clicked on the button but not released, and the mouse is currently over the button.
- enabled—the button is currently active.
- pressed—the button is in the midst of being used. (For example, a button may activate only if tease are in the button. During the time between click and release, it will be in the pressed state.)
- rollover—the mouse is over the button but it hasn't clicked.
- selected—the button is selected. (Only used for check box and radio buttons.)

```
public class DefaultButtonModel extends java.lang.Object
    implements ButtonModel, java.io.Serializable
```

Fields

```
public static final int ARMED = 1
public static final int ENABLED = 8
public static final int PRESSED = 4
public static final int ROLLOVER = 16
public static final int SELECTED = 2
```

    These constants are used to track the states of the button (as described above). Their values are set in stateMask, which is accessible to subclasses.

Constructors

public DefaultButtonModel()

    Creates a button model.

Methods

public void addActionListener(java.awt.event.ActionListener listener)

Adds `listener` to the list of listeners for actions.

Implements: addActionListener in interface ButtonModel.

public void addChangeListener(ChangeListener listener)

Adds `listener` to the list of listeners for changes in the button status.

Implements: addChangeListener in interface ButtonModel.

public void addItemListener(java.awt.event.ItemListener listener)

Adds `listener` to the list of listeners for changes in the items.

Implements: addItemListener in interface ButtonModel.

public String getActionCommand()

Gets the action command associated with this button.

Implements: getActionCommand in interface ButtonModel.

public int getMnemonic()

Gets the character used as the accelerator key for this button.

Implements: getMnemonic in interface ButtonModel.

public Object[] getSelectedObjects()

Returns `null`.

public boolean isArmed()

Returns `true` if the button is armed (the button will be selected or pressed if the mouse button is released while the mouse cursor is still over the button).

Implements: isArmed in interface ButtonModel.

public boolean isEnabled()

Returns `true` if the button is enabled.

Implements: isEnabled in interface ButtonModel.

public boolean isPressed()

Returns `true` if the button is pressed.

Implements: isPressed in interface ButtonModel.

public boolean isRollover()

Returns `true` if the mouse is over the button but the mouse button is not pressed.

Implements: isRollover in interface ButtonModel.

public boolean isSelected()

Returns `true` if the button is selected (radio buttons and check boxes only).

Implements: isSelected in interface ButtonModel.

**public void removeActionListener(
java.awt.event.ActionListener listener)**

Removes `listener` from the list of listeners for action events.

Implements: removeActionListener in interface ButtonModel.

public void removeChangeListener(ChangeListener listener)

Removes `listener` from the list of listeners for changes in the button state.

Implements: removeChangeListener in interface ButtonModel.

public void removeItemListener(java.awt.event.ItemListener listener)

Removes `listener` from the list of listeners for changes in selection status.

Implements: removeItemListener in interface ButtonModel.

public void setActionCommand(String command)

Sets the action command string.

Implements: `setActionCommand` in interface `ButtonModel`.

`public void setArmed(boolean newValue)`

Sets the armed state as indicated by `newValue`. Notifies any change listeners if the state changes.

Implements: `setArmed` in interface `ButtonModel`.

`public void setEnabled(boolean newValue)`

Sets the enabled state as indicated by `newValue`. Notifies any change listeners if the state changes.

Implements: `setEnabled` in interface `ButtonModel`.

`public void setGroup(ButtonGroup group)`

Makes this button part of a group. Only one button in a group can be active at any time. See `ButtonGroup` for more information.

Implements: `setGroup` in interface `ButtonModel`.

`public void setMnemonic(int key)`

Sets the new key accelerator for this button.

Implements: `setMnemonic` in interface `ButtonModel`.

`public void setPressed(boolean newValue)`

Sets the pressed state as indicated by `newValue`. Notifies any change listeners if the state changes.

Implements: `setPressed` in interface `ButtonModel`.

`public void setRollover(boolean newValue)`

Sets the rollover state as indicated by `newValue`. Notifies any change listeners if the state changes.

Implements: `setRollover` in interface `ButtonModel`.

`public void setSelected(boolean newValue)`

Sets the selected state as indicated by `newValue`. Notifies any change listeners or item listeners if the state changes.

Implements: `setSelected` in interface `ButtonModel`.

Protected Fields

`protected String actionCommand`

The action command string. See `getActionCommand()` and `setActionCommand()`.

`protected transient ChangeEvent changeEvent`

The change event used to notify change listeners (changes always refer to the same model, so the event can be reused).

`protected ButtonGroup group`

The group set by `setButtonGroup()` (or `null`).

`protected EventListenerList listenerList`

The list of all listeners.

`protected int mnemonic`

The accelerator key for this button. See `getMnemonic()` and `setMnemonic()`.

`protected int stateMask`

The state of the model, built by OR-ing together the above public constants.

Protected Methods

`protected void fireActionPerformed(`
`    java.awt.event.ActionEvent event)`

Notifies action listeners that `event` has occurred.

`protected void fireItemStateChanged(java.awt.event.ItemEvent event)`

Notifies item listeners that `event` has occurred.

```
protected void fireStateChanged()
```
Notifies change listeners that a change event has occurred.

Extended by JToggleButton.ToggleButtonModel (p.387).
See also ButtonGroup (p.146), ButtonModel (p.147), ChangeEvent (p.487), ChangeListener (p.488), EventListenerList (p.491).

swing.DefaultCellEditor

CLASS

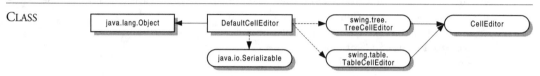

The `DefaultCellEditor` is an implementation of `CellEditor` capable of editing table or tree cells.

If your editor depends on the position of the cell in the table or tree, you can override `get-TableCellEditorComponent()` or `getTreeCellEditorComponent()` to set the editor's characteristics based on the position.

```
public class DefaultCellEditor extends java.lang.Object
    implements TableCellEditor, TreeCellEditor,
    java.io.Serializable
```

Constructors
```
public DefaultCellEditor(JCheckBox check)
public DefaultCellEditor(JComboBox combo)
public DefaultCellEditor(JTextField text)
```
Creates a cell editor that will use the specified component for editing.

Methods
```
public void addCellEditorListener(CellEditorListener listener)
```
Adds `listener` to be notified of cell editing events.
```
public void cancelCellEditing()
```
Cancels the edit in progress (without saving any changes). Calls `fireEditingCanceled()` to notify any listeners.
```
public Object getCellEditorValue()
```
Gets the result of the edit (for example, a `String` or `Boolean`).
```
public int getClickCountToStart()
```
Gets the number of clicks required to initiate editing in this cell. See `clickCountToStart` and `setClickCountToStart()`.
```
public java.awt.Component getComponent()
```
Gets the editing component established in the constructor.
```
public java.awt.Component getTableCellEditorComponent(JTable table,
    Object cellValue, boolean isSelected, int row, int column)
```
Gets the component to be used to edit the `cellValue` in `table`. The selection status and position are available to the editor.

public java.awt.Component getTreeCellEditorComponent(JTree tree,
    Object cellValue, boolean isSelected,
    boolean isExpanded, boolean isLeaf, int rowNumber)

Gets the component to be used to edit the cellValue in tree. The selection, expansion, and leaf status are available, as is rowNumber.

public boolean isCellEditable(java.awt.event.EventObject event)

Returns true if the cell allows editing. The event is in the coordinate system of the component that called this method. The editor may not, however, assume that the cell has been installed in the component hierarchy (this lets cells avoid being instantiated until they are absolutely needed).

public void removeCellEditorListener(CellEditorListener listener)

Makes listener no longer receive notification of cell editing.

public void setClickCountToStart(int clicks)

Sets the number of clicks required to initiate editing. See clickCountToStart and getClickCountToStart().

public boolean shouldSelectCell(java.awt.event.EventObject event)

Tells the editor to select the cell for editing. The event is in the coordinate system of the component that called this method, and identifies the cell to be edited. This method returns true if the cell should be selected. (You may sometimes might want to just edit a cell without selecting it.)

public boolean stopCellEditing()

Tells the editor to complete editing the cell (and use the result). Calls fireEditingStopped() to notify listeners of the completed edit.

Protected Fields

protected transient ChangeEvent changeEvent

The event used to notify CellEditorListener objects of changes.

protected int clickCountToStart

The number of clicks required to activate the editor. For example, if a JTextField is in a JTable, the first click selects the item, but the second click starts the editor. In that case, clickCountToStart would be set to 2.

protected DefaultCellEditor.EditorDelegate delegate

A "hidden" implementation used to support the particular editor type.

protected JComponent editorComponent

The editing component passed in to the constructor.

protected EventListenerList listenerList

The list of listeners to be notified of cell editing events.

Protected Methods

protected void fireEditingCanceled()

Notifies any listeners that the edit was canceled. Usually called by cancelCellEditing().

protected void fireEditingStopped()

Notifies any listeners that editing is complete. Usually called by stopCellEditing().

See also CellEditorListener (p.486), ChangeEvent (p.487), ChangeListener (p.488), DefaultCellEditor.EditorDelegate (p.164), EventListenerList (p.491), JCheckBox (p.193), JComboBox (p.200), JComponent (p.207), JTable (p.357), JTextField (p.379), JTree (p.393), TableCellEditor (p.758), TreeCellEditor (p.985).

INNER CLASS

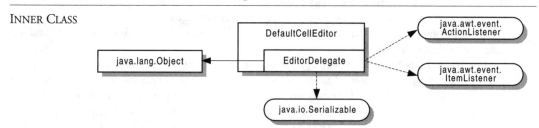

```
protected class DefaultCellEditor.EditorDelegate
    extends java.lang.Object
    implements java.awt.event.ActionListener,
    java.awt.event.ItemListener, java.io.Serializable
```

Methods

public void actionPerformed(java.awt.event.ActionEvent e)
Implements: actionPerformed in interface java.awt.event.ActionListener.

public void cancelCellEditing()
Cancels editing. This causes the editor to revert the edited value back to its original value.

public java.lang.Object getCellEditorValue()
Retrieves the value from the editor.

public boolean isCellEditable(java.util.EventObject anEvent)
Returns true if the editor can start editing in response to the given event.

public void itemStateChanged(java.awt.event.ItemEvent e)
Implements: itemStateChanged in interface java.awt.event.ItemListener.

public void setValue(java.lang.Object x)
Sets the value the editor is editing.

public boolean startCellEditing(java.util.EventObject anEvent)
Starts editing.

public boolean stopCellEditing()
Stops editing. The editor retains the changed value.

Protected Fields

protected java.lang.Object value
The value being edited.

swing.DefaultComboBoxModel

CLASS

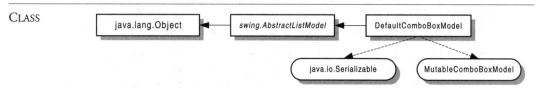

This model is the default model for JComboBoxes. It is important to note that it is a mutable model, meaning that it can have elements added or removed.

```
public class DefaultComboBoxModel extends AbstractListModel
    implements MutableComboBoxModel, java.io.Serializable
```

Constructors

public DefaultComboBoxModel()

> Constructs an empty DefaultComboBoxModel.

public DefaultComboBoxModel(Object[] items)

> Constructs a model containing the items in the given array.

public DefaultComboBoxModel(java.util.Vector v)

> Constructs a model containing the items in the given Vector.

Methods

public void addElement(Object anObject)

> Adds a new element to the end of the model.
>
> *Implements:* addElement in interface MutableComboBoxModel.

public Object getElementAt(int index)

> Returns the object at the given index in the model.
>
> *Implements:* getElementAt in interface ListModel.

public int getIndexOf(Object anObject)

> Returns the position of the given object in the model. This method returns −1 if the object is not found.

public Object getSelectedItem()

> Returns the selected item from the model.

public int getSize()

> Returns the number of elements in the model.
>
> *Implements:* getSize in interface ListModel.

public void insertElementAt(Object anObject, int index)

> Inserts the given element into the model at the given index. The element which used to be at the index is pushed back to index + 1.
>
> *Implements:* insertElementAt in interface MutableComboBoxModel.

public void removeAllElements()

> Empties the model of all elements.

public void removeElement(Object anObject)

> Removes the given element from the model.
>
> *Implements:* removeElement in interface MutableComboBoxModel.

public void removeElementAt(int index)

> Removes the element at the given index from the model.
>
> *Implements:* removeElementAt in interface MutableComboBoxModel.

public void setSelectedItem(Object anObject)

> Sets the element in the model that is the "selected" item; that is, the item displayed in the text field of the combo box.
>
> *See also*   AbstractListModel (p.127), MutableComboBoxModel (p.427).

swing.DefaultDesktopManager

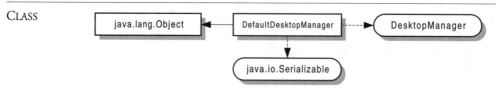

A `DesktopManager` provides support for window operations on internal frames. `DefaultDesktopManager` provides a basic implementation of `DesktopManager`. The `DesktopManager` used by a `JInternalFrame` will usually be the one which is supplied by a parent `JDesktopPane`. In situations where a `JInternalFrame` is not contained in a `JDesktopPane` you can create an instance of this class and use it to control the behaviors of the `JInternalFrame`.

```
public class DefaultDesktopManager extends java.lang.Object
    implements DesktopManager, java.io.Serializable
```

Constructors
public DefaultDesktopManager()

Creates a desktop manager.

Public Methods
public void activateFrame(JInternalFrame frame)

Shows that `frame` has been selected and has the focus. This method is called after the internal frame has been selected (and has verifed that nothing has vetoed the change).

Implements: `activateFrame` in interface `DesktopManager`.

public void beginDraggingFrame(JComponent internalFrame)

Notifies the desktop manager that `internalFrame` is about to be dragged. The manager can do any necessary setup. (It will be followed by calls to `dragFrame()` and `endDraggingFrame()`.)

Implements: `beginDraggingFrame` in interface `DesktopManager`.

public void beginResizingFrame(JComponent internalFrame, int direction)

Notifies the desktop manager that `internalFrame` is about to be resized in `direction`. (This call will be followed by calls to `resizeFrame()` and `endResizingFrame()`.) The direction will be one of the values in `SwingConstants` (such as `SwingConstants.NORTH`.)

Implements: `beginResizingFrame` in interface `DesktopManager`.

public void closeFrame(JInternalFrame frame)

Closes the frame and removes it from its desktop pane.

Implements: `closeFrame` in interface `DesktopManager`.

public void deactivateFrame(JInternalFrame frame)

Notifies the desktop manager that `frame` has lost the focus. This method is called after the internal frame has been deselected (and has verifed that nothing has vetoed the change).

Implements: `deactivateFrame` in interface `DesktopManager`.

public void deiconifyFrame(JInternalFrame frame)

Makes `frame` no longer iconified. Returns it to the position and size it had before it was iconified.

Implements: `deiconifyFrame` in interface `DesktopManager`.

public void dragFrame(JComponent internalFrame, int newX, int newY)

Drags `internalFrame` to newX, newY using `setBoundsForFrame()`. This is called after `beginDraggingFrame()` and before `endDraggingFrame()`.

Implements: `dragFrame` in interface `DesktopManager`.

public void endDraggingFrame(JComponent internalFrame)

Completes the dragging of `internalFrame`. This is called so you can finalize anything needed after a repositioning. (See `beginDraggingFrame()` and `dragFrame()`.)

Implements: `endDraggingFrame` in interface `DesktopManager`.

public void endResizingFrame(JComponent internalFrame)

Completes the resizing of `internalFrame`. This is called after `beginResizingFrame()` and `resizeFrame()`.

Implements: `endResizingFrame` in interface `DesktopManager`.

public void iconifyFrame(JInternalFrame frame)

Iconifies this frame: removes it from its parent and replaces it with the frame in icon form.

Implements: `iconifyFrame` in interface `DesktopManager`.

public void maximizeFrame(JInternalFrame frame)

Makes `frame` as large as possible (up to the size of its parent's bounds).

Implements: `maximizeFrame` in interface `DesktopManager`.

public void minimizeFrame(JInternalFrame frame)

Returns `frame` to the size it had before it was maximized.

Implements: `minimizeFrame` in interface `DesktopManager`.

public void openFrame(JInternalFrame frame)

Displays `frame`. This method is not usually used. Instead, the creator of a `JInternalFrame` will add *frame* to the appropriate parent.

Implements: `openFrame` in interface `DesktopManager`.

public void resizeFrame(JComponent internalFrame, int x, int y, int width, int height)

Resizes `internalFrame` to the indicated position and `size`. This call is preceded by `beginResizeFrame()` and eventually followed by `endResizeFrame()`.

Implements: `resizeFrame` in interface `DesktopManager`.

public void setBoundsForFrame(JComponent internalFrame, int x, int y, int width, int height)

Sets `internalFrame` to the indicated position and size.

Implements: `setBoundsForFrame` in interface `DesktopManager`.

Protected Methods

protected java.awt.Rectangle getBoundsForIconOf(JInternalFrame frame)

This method is called by `iconifyFrame()` to determine the bounds of the `JDesktopIcon` that will replace `frame`.

protected java.awt.Rectangle getPreviousBounds(JInternalFrame frame)

Gets the bounds `frame` had before it was maximized.

protected void removeIconFor(JInternalFrame frame)

Removes the desktop icon for the given internal frame.

protected void setPreviousBounds(JInternalFrame frame, Rectangle rect)

Stores the bounds of `frame` (taken from `rect`) before it is maximized. This is a bound property.

protected void setWasIcon(JInternalFrame frame, Boolean wasIcon)
   Tracks whether `frame` was an icon. This is a bound property.

protected boolean wasIcon(JInternalFrame frame)
   Tells whether `frame` was ever iconified.

   See also   DesktopManager (p.180), JComponent (p.207), JDesktopPane (p.224), JInternalFrame (p.254), SwingConstants (p.442).

swing.DefaultFocusManager

CLASS

The `DefaultFocusManager` provides a concrete implementation of the `FocusManager` (p.181) class.

public class DefaultFocusManager extends FocusManager

Constructors
public DefaultFocusManager()
   Creates an instance of the default focus manager.

Methods
public boolean compareTabOrder(java.awt.Component c1, java.awt.Component c2)
   Returns `true` if `c1` precedes `c2` in the tab order. The default tab order is left-to-right and top-to-bottom. To change the order, override this method.

public void focusNextComponent(java.awt.Component component)
   Moves focus to the next component (just after `component`).
   Overrides: `focusNextComponent` in class `FocusManager`.

public void focusPreviousComponent(java.awt.Component component)
   Moves focus to the previous component (just before `component`).

public java.awt.Component getComponentAfter(
   java.awt.Container container, java.awt.Component component)
   Gets the component after `component` that should receive the focus (in `container`).

public java.awt.Component getComponentBefore(
   java.awt.Container container, java.awt.Component component)
   Gets the component that should receive focus before `component` (in `container`).

public java.awt.Component getFirstComponent(java.awt.Container container)
   Gets the first component in `container` that can receive focus.

public java.awt.Component getLastComponent(java.awt.Container container)
   Gets the last component in `container` that can receive focus.

public void processKeyEvent(java.awt.Component component,
   java.awt.event.KeyEvent event)
   Handles `event` on `component`. This method is called by `JComponent` so that the focus manager has the first chance to intercept keys that change the focus (usually `Tab` and `Shift-Tab`). If the focus manager wants to intercept the key, it calls `event.consume()` so that the event is not propagated further. This method is called for both `KeyEvent.KEY_PRESSED`, `KeyEvent.KEY_TYPED`, and

`KeyEvent.KEY_RELEASED`; it should take care to consume or ignore all events for a particular keystroke.

Overrides: `processKeyEvent` in class `FocusManager`.

See also   FocusManager (p.181), JComponent (p.207).

swing.DefaultListCellRenderer

CLASS

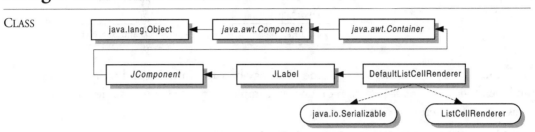

This class is the default implementation of `ListCellRenderer`. Since it extends `JLabel` it can display an `Icon` and text. It differs from `JLabel` by being opaque and having a border.

```
public class DefaultListCellRenderer extends JLabel
    implements ListCellRenderer, java.io.Serializable
```

Constructors
```
public DefaultListCellRenderer()
```
Instantiates `noFocusBorder`, makes it the border of this component, and then sets this component to be opaque.

Methods
```
public java.awt.Component getListCellRendererComponent(JList list,
    Object value, int index, boolean isSelected, boolean cellHasFocus)
```
Implements: `getListCellRendererComponent` in interface `ListCellRenderer`.

Protected Fields
```
protected static Border noFocusBorder
```
This border is an `EmptyBorder` with all insets 1 pixel.

Inner Classes
```
public static class DefaultListCellRenderer.UIResource
```

Extended by   DefaultListCellRenderer.UIResource (p.172).

swing.DefaultListCellRenderer.UIResource

INNER CLASS

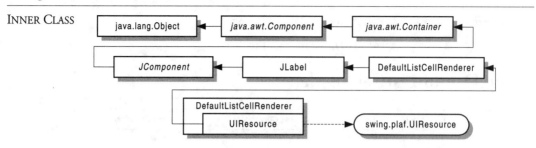

This inner class implements UIResource so it may be safely installed and uninstalled by a look and feel. DefaultListCellRenderer does not implement UIResource so developers may use it as a basis for their own custom renderers.

```
public static class DefaultListCellRenderer.UIResource
    extends DefaultListCellRenderer
    implements UIResource
```

Constructors
```
public UIResource()
```
    Default constructor.

    See also   UIResource (p.544).

swing.DefaultListModel

CLASS

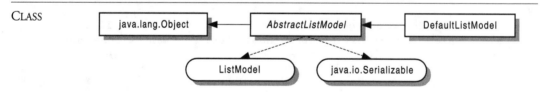

This provides an implementation of ListModel. This class uses a java.util.Vector internally for storage. Listeners are notified of any changes to the list.

Example

```
package defaultlistmodel;

import java.awt.*;
import java.awt.event.*;
import com.sun.java.swing.*;
import com.sun.java.swing.event.*;

public class Main extends JFrame {
    private class MyListModel extends DefaultListModel {
        protected int[] count = new int[100];

        public Object getElementAt(int index) {
```

```
      if (index < 100) {
         count[index]++;
      }
      return super.elementAt(index);
   }

   public void dump() {
      System.out.println("Frequency of use:\ni\tcount[i]\telement[i]");
      for (int i = 0; i < 100; i++) {
         if (count[i] != 0) {
           System.out.println(i + "\t" + count[i] + "\t\t" + elementAt(i));
         }
      }
      System.out.println();
   }
}

MyListModel model = new MyListModel();

public Main () {
   for (int i = 0; i < 25; i++) {
      model.addElement("A" + i);
   }
   JList list = new JList(model);
   getContentPane().add(new JScrollPane(list), BorderLayout.CENTER);

   addWindowListener (new WindowAdapter() {
      public void windowClosing(WindowEvent e) {
         model.dump();
         e.getWindow().dispose();
         System.exit(0);
      }
   });

   pack();
   setVisible(true);
}

public static void main (String arg[]) {
   new Main();
}
}
```

public class DefaultListModel extends AbstractListModel

Constructors
public DefaultListModel()
Creates a new default list model.

Methods
public void add(int index, Object element)
Adds element to the list at index.
Throws: ArrayIndexOutOfBoundsException if the index is outside of the range 0 <= index
<= getSize().
public void addElement(Object element)
Adds element to the end of the list.

public int capacity()

Returns the number of elements that can be added without resizing the list.

public void clear()

Removes all elements from the list.

public boolean contains(Object object)

Returns `true` if the list contains `object`.

public void copyInto(Object[] array)

Copies all elements of `array` into the list.

Throws: `ArrayIndexOutOfBoundsException` if the array is too small to contain this list's elements.

public Object elementAt(int index)

Returns the element at `index`. Eventually this method will be deprecated in favor of `get()`, which is the standard method used by the Java Collections API.

public java.util.Enumeration elements()

Returns an enumeration of the elements in the list.

public void ensureCapacity(int newCapacity)

Tells the list to ensure there is space for `newCapacity` items. If necessary this method will increase the size of the list but this method will not shrink the list if `newCapacity` is smaller than `size()`.

public Object firstElement()

Returns the first element of the list.

public Object get(int index)

Returns the `Object` at index.

Throws: `ArrayIndexOutOfBoundsException` if index is outside the range 0 <= index <= get-Size().

public Object getElementAt(int index)

Returns the element at `index`. The `get()` method should be used in preference to this one, since `get()` is the standard method name used by the Java Collections API.

Throws: `ArrayIndexOutOfBoundsException` if index is outside the range 0 <= index <= get-Size().

public int getSize()

Returns the number of elements in the list.

public int indexOf(Object object)

Returns the position of `object` in the list, or –1 if it is not present.

public int indexOf(Object object, int nth)

Returns the nth occurrence of `object` in the list, or –1 if it is not present.

public void insertElementAt(Object element, int index)

Inserts `element` at index. Other elements are moved, if necessary, to make room. The `add()` method should be used in preference to this method to ensure future compatibility with the Java Collections API.

public boolean isEmpty()

Returns `true` if the list has no elements.

public Object lastElement()

Returns the last element in the list.

public int lastIndexOf(Object object)

Returns the position of the last occurrence of `object`, or –1 if it is not present.

public int lastIndexOf(Object object, int nth)

Returns the position of the nth-to-last occurrence of `object`, or –1 if it is not present.

public Object remove(int index)

Removes and returns the object at index.

public void removeAllElements()

Removes all elements from the list. The `clear()` method should be used in preference to this method to ensure future compatibility with the Java Collections API.

public boolean removeElement(Object object)

Removes `object` from the list; returns `true` if it was present.

public void removeElementAt(int index)

Removes the element at index from the list. The `remove()` method should be used in preference to this method to ensure future compatibility with the Java Collections API.

Throws: `ArrayIndexOutOfBoundsException` if index is outside the range 0 <= index <= getSize()

public void removeRange(int index1, int index2)

Removes all elements from index1 to index2 (inclusive).

Throws: `ArrayIndexOutOfBoundsException` if either index is invalid, `IllegalArgumentException` if index1 > index2.

public Object set(int index, Object element)

Replaces the object at index with element.

Throws: `ArrayIndexOutOfBoundsException` if index is outside the range 0 <= index <= getSize().

public void setElementAt(Object element, int index)

Sets the element at index to element (replacing whatever is there). The `set()` method should be used in preference to this method.

Throws: `ArrayIndexOutOfBoundsException` if index is outside the range 0 <= index <= getSize().

public void setSize(int newSize)

Sets the size of the list to newSize. If necessary, elements are removed or null elements are added.

public int size()

Returns the size of the list.

public Object[] toArray()

Creates and returns a list of all elements in the list.

public String toString()

Returns a string that displays the properties of this object.

Overrides: `toString` in class `Object`.

public void trimToSize()

Tells the list that its capacity can be reduced to the current size of the list.

See also   AbstractListModel (p.127), ListModel (p.421).

swing.DefaultListSelectionModel

CLASS

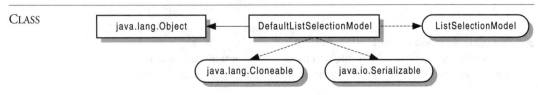

A list selection consists of a set of indexes that represents the items selected. In general, this is a set of intervals. For example, in a list with 7 items, {[0,2], [6,6]} would indicate that elements 0, 1, 2, and 6 are selected.

Many of the methods refer to `index1` and `index2`. The value for `index1` need not be less than the value for `index2`—the selection may go from "high" to "low."

Some look and feels have the notion of an anchor and a lead index. These are based on the most recently added selection interval. The anchor is the item which was selected first in the interval; the lead is the item selected last.

See `ListSelectionModel` (p.421) for the selection mode constants.

```
public class DefaultListSelectionModel extends java.lang.Object
    implements ListSelectionModel, java.lang.Cloneable,
    java.io.Serializable
```

Constructors
public DefaultListSelectionModel()
Creates a default list selection model.

Methods
public void addListSelectionListener(ListSelectionListener listener)
Adds `listener` as a listener for changes in the list selection.
Implements: addListSelectionListener in interface `ListSelectionModel`.

public void addSelectionInterval(int index1, int index2)
Causes the range from `index1` to `index2` to be added to the selection. Listeners are notified if this changes the selection.
Implements: addSelectionInterval in interface `ListSelectionModel`.

public void clearSelection()
Causes the selection to become empty. Listeners are notified if this changes the selection.
Implements: clearSelection in interface `ListSelectionModel`.

public Object clone() throws CloneNotSupportedException
Clones this model.
Throws: CloneNotSupportedException if the object does not implement the `Cloneable` interface and also does not have a `clone()` method.
Overrides: clone in class `Object`.

public int getAnchorSelectionIndex()
Gets the `index1` value from the most recently added selection interval. See `addSelectionInterval()`.
Implements: getAnchorSelectionIndex in interface `ListSelectionModel`.

public int getLeadSelectionIndex()
Gets the `index2` value from the most recently added selection interval. See `addSelectionInterval()`.
Implements: getLeadSelectionIndex in interface `ListSelectionModel`.

public int getMaxSelectionIndex()
Returns the maximum index in the selection, or –1 if nothing is selected.
Implements: getMaxSelectionIndex in interface `ListSelectionModel`.

public int getMinSelectionIndex()

Returns the minimum index in the selection, or –1 if nothing is selected.

Implements: getMinSelectionIndex in interface ListSelectionModel.

public int getSelectionMode()

Returns one of the following selection mode constants: ListSelectionModel.SINGLE_SELEC-TION, ListSelectionModel.SINGLE_INTERVAL_SELECTION, or ListSelectionModel.MULTIPLE_INTERVAL_SELECTION.

Implements: getSelectionMode in interface ListSelectionModel.

public boolean getValueIsAdjusting()

Returns true if further changes are expected in the selection (for example, while the selection is in the middle of an update).

Implements: getValueIsAdjusting in interface ListSelectionModel.

public void insertIndexInterval(int index, int length, boolean before)

Inserts length values into the selection, starting at index. The values are from index-length+1 to index if before is true, and from index to index+length-1 if before is false. This method can be used to make the selection correspond to changes in the underlying model. Listeners are notified if this changes the selection.

Implements: insertIndexInterval in interface ListSelectionModel.

public boolean isLeadAnchorNotificationEnabled()

Returns true if changes in the lead and anchor should be sent to listeners (as well as changes in the selection, which are always sent on). The model always tracks the lead and anchor internally even if this value is false.

public boolean isSelectedIndex(int index)

Returns true if index is in the set of selected index values.

Implements: isSelectedIndex in interface ListSelectionModel.

public boolean isSelectionEmpty()

Returns true if the selection is empty.

Implements: isSelectionEmpty in interface ListSelectionModel.

public void removeIndexInterval(int index1, int index2)

Removes indexes from index1 to index2 inclusive from the selection. This method can be used to make the selection correspond to changes in the underlying model. Listeners are notified if this changes the selection.

Implements: removeIndexInterval in interface ListSelectionModel.

public void removeListSelectionListener(ListSelectionListener listener)

Removes listener from the list of listeners to be notified of selection changes.

Implements: removeListSelectionListener in interface ListSelectionModel.

public void removeSelectionInterval(int index1, int index2)

Causes the range from index1 to index2 to be removed from the selection interval. Listeners are notified if this changes the selection.

Implements: removeSelectionInterval in interface ListSelectionModel.

public void setAnchorSelectionIndex(int anchorIndex)

Sets the anchor selection index, leaving all selection values unchanged. If leadAnchorNotificationEnabled is true, it sends a notification covering the old and new anchor cells.

Implements: setAnchorSelectionIndex in interface ListSelectionModel.

public void setLeadAnchorNotificationEnabled(boolean flag)

Sets the value of the leadAnchorNotificationEnabled property.

public void setLeadSelectionIndex(int leadIndex)

Sets the lead selection index and changes the elements between the lead index and the anchor to all selected or all deselected.

There are two different cases handled by this method. The first is when the anchor is selected. In this case, this method deselects any elements between the anchor and the old lead. It then selects all elements between the anchor and the new lead. The second case is when the anchor is not selected. In the unselected case, this method will select any items between the anchor and the old lead and deselect any items between the anchor and the new lead.

A single event is generated as a result of the changes made by this method. The indices in the event are the end elements of the range of elements involved in the changes.

Implements: setLeadSelectionIndex in interface ListSelectionModel.

public void setSelectionInterval(int index1, int index2)

Causes the selection to consist only of elements from index1 to index2 inclusive. Listeners are notified if this changes the selection.

Implements: setSelectionInterval in interface ListSelectionModel.

public void setSelectionMode(int mode)

Sets the mode; mode must be SINGLE_SELECTION, SINGLE_INTERVAL_SELECTION, or MULTIPLE_INTERVAL_SELECTION. Those modes are defined in ListSelectionModel.

Implements: setSelectionMode in interface ListSelectionModel.

public void setValueIsAdjusting(boolean valueIsAdjusting)

Sets whether the selection is in the middle of an adjustment. This way, listeners don't need to make intermediate adjustments, but can wait for the final selection.

Implements: setValueIsAdjusting in interface ListSelectionModel.

public String toString()

Returns a string that represents this object's properties.

Overrides: toString in class Object.

Protected Fields

protected boolean leadAnchorNotificationEnabled

Returns true if listeners should be notified about changes in the lead and anchor (as well as changes in the selection).

protected EventListenerList listenerList

The list of listeners.

Protected Methods

protected void fireValueChanged(boolean isAdjusting)

Notifies listeners that the model is about to change (or has just finished changing).

protected void fireValueChanged(int index1, int index2)

Notifies listeners that the selection from index1 to index2 (inclusive) has changed.

protected void fireValueChanged(int index1, int index2,
boolean doneAdjusting)

Notifies listeners that the selection from index1 to index2 (inclusive) has changed. If doneAdjusting is true, this is the last in a series of changes.

See also   EventListenerList (p.491), ListSelectionListener (p.500), ListSelectionModel (p.421).

swing.DefaultSingleSelectionModel

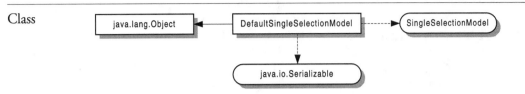

This class provides a simple implementation of SingleSelectionModel (p.440), which allows, at most, one selected item.

```
public class DefaultSingleSelectionModel extends java.lang.Object
    implements SingleSelectionModel, java.io.Serializable
```

Constructors
public DefaultSingleSelectionModel()
    Creates a single selection model.

Methods
public void addChangeListener(ChangeListener listener)
    Adds listener to the list of listeners notified when the model changes.
    Implements: addChangeListener in interface SingleSelectionModel.

public void clearSelection()
    Deselects any selected item and informs listeners that the selection is now empty.
    Implements: clearSelection in interface SingleSelectionModel.

public int getSelectedIndex()
    Gets the index of the currently selected item, or –1 if no item is selected.
    Implements: getSelectedIndex in interface SingleSelectionModel.

public boolean isSelected()
    Returns true if any item is selected.
    Implements: isSelected in interface SingleSelectionModel.

public void removeChangeListener(ChangeListener listener)
    Removes listener from the list of items notified when the model changes.
    Implements: removeChangeListener in interface SingleSelectionModel.

public void setSelectedIndex(int index)
    Makes the item at index be the currently selected item; notifies listeners if this is a change.
    Implements: setSelectedIndex in interface SingleSelectionModel.

Protected Fields
protected transient ChangeEvent changeEvent
    The event used to notify listeners of changes.

protected EventListenerList listenerList
    The list of listeners.

Protected Methods
protected void fireStateChanged()
    Notifies listeners of a change in state.

See also   ChangeEvent (p.487), ChangeListener (p.488), EventListenerList (p.491), SingleSelectionModel (p.440).

swing.DesktopManager

INTERFACE   DesktopManager

A `DesktopManager` provides support for window operations on internal frames. A `JDesktopPane` owns the desktop manager. A `JInternalFrame` should delegate its window operations like this:

```
myFrame.getDesktopPane().getDesktopManager().closeFrame(myFrame);
```

```
public interface DesktopManager
```

Methods

`public void activateFrame(JInternalFrame frame)`
Shows that `frame` has been selected and has the focus. This method is called after the internal frame has been selected (and has verifed that nothing has vetoed the change).

`public void beginDraggingFrame(JComponent internalFrame)`
Notifies the desktop manager that `internalFrame` is about to be dragged. The manager can do any necessary setup. (It will be followed by calls to `dragFrame()` and `endDraggingFrame()`.)

`public void beginResizingFrame(JComponent internalFrame, int direction)`
Notifies the desktop manager that `internalFrame` is about to be resized in `direction`. (This method will be followed by calls to `resizeFrame()` and `endResizingFrame()`.) The direction will be one of the values in `SwingConstants` (such as `SwingConstants.NORTH`).

`public void closeFrame(JInternalFrame frame)`
Closes `frame` and removes it from its desktop pane.

`public void deactivateFrame(JInternalFrame frame)`
Notifies the desktop manager that `frame` has lost the focus. This method is called after the internal frame has been deselected (and has verifed that nothing has vetoed the change).

`public void deiconifyFrame(JInternalFrame frame)`
Makes `frame` no longer iconified. Returns it to the position and size it had before it was iconified.

`public void dragFrame(JComponent internalFrame, int newX, int newY)`
Drags `internalFrame` to `newX`, `newY`. This is called after `beginDraggingFrame()` and before `endDraggingFrame()`.

`public void endDraggingFrame(JComponent internalFrame)`
Completes the dragging of `internalFrame`. This is called so you can finalize anything needed after a repositioning. (See `beginDraggingFrame()` and `dragFrame()`.)

`public void endResizingFrame(JComponent internalFrame)`
Completes the resizing of `internalFrame`. This is called after `begingResizingFrame()` and `resizeFrame()`.

`public void iconifyFrame(JInternalFrame frame)`
Iconifies `frame`: removes it from its parent and replaces it with the frame in icon form.

`public void maximizeFrame(JInternalFrame frame)`
Makes `frame` as large as possible (up to the size of its parent's bounds).

`public void minimizeFrame(JInternalFrame frame)`
Returns `frame` to the size it had before it was maximized.

```
public void openFrame(JInternalFrame frame)
```
Displays `frame`. This method is not usually used. Instead, the creator of a `JInternalFrame` will add `frame` to the appropriate parent.
```
public void resizeFrame(JComponent frame, int x, int y, int width,
    int height)
```
Resizes `frame` to the indicated position and size. This call is preceded by `beginResizeFrame()` and eventually followed by `endResizeFrame()`.
```
public void setBoundsForFrame(JComponent frame, int x, int y,
    int width, int height)
```
Sets `frame` to the indicated position and size.

Implemented by   DefaultDesktopManager (p.168).
Returned by   BasicInternalFrameUI.createDesktopManager() (p.605),
BasicInternalFrameUI.getDesktopManager() (p.605), JDesktopPane.getDesktopManager() (p.180).
See also   JComponent (p.207), JDesktopPane (p.224), JInternalFrame (p.254),
SwingConstants (p.442).

swing.FocusManager

ABSTRACT
CLASS

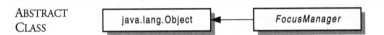

The `FocusManager` class handles the way focus moves from component to component. (Focus is the idea of a default component. For example, a button with focus might be activated if the RETURN key is pressed.) Usually, the TAB key moves forward from component to component, and SHIFT+TAB moves backwards. See `JComponent` for information about focus and components, and `DefaultFocusManager` for an implementation.

Focus is handled according to thread groups. All threads in a group share a single focus manager.

```
public abstract class FocusManager extends java.lang.Object
```

Fields
```
public static String FOCUS_MANAGER_CLASS_PROPERTY = "FocusManagerClassName"
```
Provides the name of the class that is the focus manager for the current look and feel.

Constructors
```
public FocusManager()
```
Creates a new focus manager.

Methods
```
public static void disableSwingFocusManager()
```
Tells the system to disable the use of the Swing focus manager. You would do this if you use regular AWT components, which have their own focus manager.

public abstract void focusNextComponent(java.awt.Component component)
Moves focus to the next component (just after component).

public abstract void focusPreviousComponent(java.awt.Component component)
Moves focus to the previous component (just before component).

public static FocusManager getCurrentManager()
Gets the focus manager in effect for the thread group of the caller. (Each thread group has its own focus manager.)

public static boolean isFocusManagerEnabled()
Returns true if the focus manager is in effect. See disableSwingFocusManager().

public abstract void processKeyEvent(java.awt.Component focusedComponent, java.awt.event.KeyEvent anEvent)
Allows a FocusManager to implement keyboard-based focus switching. This method is called by JComponent when it receives a KeyEvent. If the KeyEvent is used for switching focus, anEvent should be consumed. This method receives KEY_PRESSED, KEY_RELEASED, and KEY_TYPED events. If one of them is used for focus switching, the other two events corresponding to the same keystroke should be consumed as well.

public static void setCurrentManager(FocusManager manager)
Sets the focus manager for threads in the thread group of the caller.

Extended by   DefaultFocusManager (p.170).
Returned by   FocusManager.getCurrentManager() (p.181).

swing.GrayFilter

CLASS

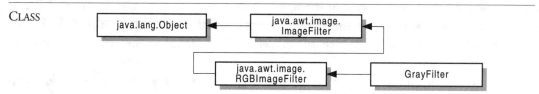

A gray filter is an image filter that makes an icon look disabled by turning it into a grayscale image and brightening or dimming its pixels.

Example

```
package grayfilter;
import java.awt.*;
import java.awt.event.*;
import com.sun.java.swing.*;
public class Main extends JFrame {
   public Main () {
      addWindowListener(new WindowAdapter() {
         public void windowClosing(WindowEvent e) {
            Main.this.dispose();
            System.exit(0);
         }
      });

      JPanel p = new JPanel();
```

```
    ImageIcon icon = new ImageIcon(getClass().getResource(
      "red-ball.gif"));

    JButton b1 = new JButton("Regular", icon);
    p.add(b1);

    Image image = GrayFilter.createDisabledImage(icon.getImage());
    JButton b2 = new JButton("GrayFilter", new ImageIcon(image));
    p.add(b2);

    getContentPane().add(p);

    pack();
    setVisible(true);
  }
  public static void main (String arg[]) {
    new Main();
  }
}
```

public class GrayFilter extends java.awt.image.RGBImageFilter

Constructors
public GrayFilter(boolean shouldBrighten, int percent)
Creates a filter that will brighten or dim pixels by `percent` (depending on whether should-Brighten is `true`).

Methods
public static java.awt.Image createDisabledImage(java.awt.Image image)
Creates a filtered image from `image`, with grayscale pixels 50 percent brighter.
public int filterRGB(int x, int y, int rgb)
Converts color `rgb` (at `(x,y)`) to its corresponding output color.
Overrides: `filterRGB` in class `RGBImageFilter`.

swing.Icon

INTERFACE

An `Icon` is a picture that has a fixed width and height. It has the ability to paint itself.

public interface Icon

Methods
public abstract int getIconHeight()
Returns the `height` of the icon.
public abstract int getIconWidth()
Returns the `width` of the icon.
public abstract void paintIcon(java.awt.Component component, java.awt.Graphics g, int x, int y)
Draws the icon onto graphics context `g` at `(x,y)`. The `component` may be used for information about the context, such as background color.

Implemented by   IconUIResource (p.534), ImageIcon (p.184).
Returned by   Many.

swing.ImageIcon

CLASS

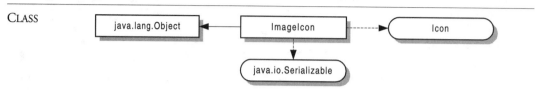

An image icon is an image encapsulated in an `Icon`. The image can be loaded from a `java.awt.Image`, from a byte array, or from a URL. A MediaTracker is used to monitor the image loading process.

Example

```
package imageicon;

// See also the GrayFilter example
import java.awt.*;
import java.awt.event.*;
import com.sun.java.swing.*;

public class Main extends JFrame {
   public Main () {
      addWindowListener(new WindowAdapter() {
         public void windowClosing(WindowEvent e) {
            Main.this.dispose();
            System.exit(0);
         }
      });
      ImageIcon icon = new ImageIcon(getClass().getResource(
         "blue-ball.gif"));
      JButton button = new JButton("ImageIcon", icon);
      getContentPane().add(button);

      pack();
      setVisible(true);
   }
   public static void main (String arg[]) {
      new Main();
   }
}
```

```
public class ImageIcon extends java.lang.Object
   implements Icon, java.io.Serializable
```

Constructors
```
public ImageIcon()
```
   Creates a new image icon, with no image specified.
```
public ImageIcon(byte[] imageData)
```

```
public ImageIcon(byte[] imageData, String description)
```
Creates a new image icon, with data provided from `imageData`. This data must be in a supported format (for example, GIF or JPEG). The `description` (defaulting to an empty string) may also be provided. The `description` is used by accessibility, so it should be provided.
```
public ImageIcon(java.awt.Image image)
public ImageIcon(java.awt.Image image, String description)
```
Creates a new image icon, based on `image`. The `description` (defaulting to an empty string) may also be provided. The `description` is used by accessibility, so it should be provided.
```
public ImageIcon(String filename)
public ImageIcon(String filename, String description)
```
Creates a new image icon, loaded from file `filename`. The filename will be converted to a URL, so it is safe to use "/" in place of `File.separator`. The `description` (defaulting to an empty string) may also be provided. The `description` is used by accessibility, so it should be provided.
```
public ImageIcon(java.net.URL url)
public ImageIcon(java.net.URL url, String description)
```
Creates a new image icon, loaded from `url`. The `description` (defaulting to an empty string) may also be provided. The `description` is used by accessibility, so it should be provided.

Methods
```
public String getDescription()
```
Gets the description string for the image.
```
public int getIconHeight()
```
Gets the height of the icon.

Implements: `getIconHeight` in interface `Icon`.
```
public int getIconWidth()
```
Gets the width of the icon.

Implements: `getIconWidth` in interface `Icon`.
```
public java.awt.Image getImage()
```
Gets the image associated with the icon.
```
public int getImageLoadStatus()
```
Returns the status of the image loading operation, which will be one of the following: `MediaTracker.ABORTED`, `MediaTracker.ERRORED`, or `MediaTracker.COMPLETE`.
```
public java.awt.image.ImageObserver getImageObserver()
```
Provides an image observer for the image.
```
public synchronized void paintIcon(java.awt.Component component,
    java.awt.Graphics gr, int x, int y)
```
Paints `component` onto context `gr`, at `(x,y)`. `(0,0)` is the upper left-hand corner.

Implements: `paintIcon` in interface `Icon`.
```
public void setDescription(String description)
```
Sets the textual description for the image. This provides a nonvisual way to describe or index the content.
```
public void setImage(java.awt.Image image)
```
Sets (and loads) the image for the icon.
```
public void setImageObserver(java.awt.image.ImageObserver observer)
```
Sets the image observer for the image. The observer is notified about properties as they become available, rather than requiring the image to be fully loaded. If the image is animated, an image observer should be added.

Protected Fields

protected static final java.awt.Component component
Used in creating the image.

protected static final java.awt.MediaTracker tracker
The tracker used to monitor the image loading.

Protected Methods

protected void loadImage(java.awt.Image image)
Loads the image into the icon (waits for the image to load completely).

See also   Icon (p.183).

swing.JApplet

CLASS

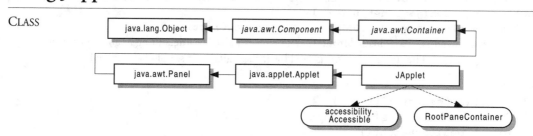

`JApplet` is the Swing version of `Applet`. It provides a root pane so components can be layered and a `JMenu` can be added. See `JRootPane` and `JLayeredPane` for more information.

A consequence of the use of a root pane is a change in the way objects are added to the applet. Instead of adding them directly to the applet, add them to the content pane like this:

```
myApplet.getContentPane().add(object, constraints);
```

The content pane is always present; it may be replaced but never deleted. The default content pane uses a `BorderLayout`.

`JApplet` prints a harmless but distracting message to the console window when it starts up. The reason it does this is a Swing applet checks the system event queue to see if it is allowed to access it. Netscape and Internet Explorer both deny `JApplet`s access to the system event queue, which is why the message is printed. To prevent this message from appearing, you can explicitly tell the applet to not perform this check. To do this, add the following lines of code to your `JApplet`'s `init()` method:

```
JRootPane rp = myJApplet.getRootPane();
rp.putClientProperty("defeatSystemEventQueueCheck", Boolean.TRUE);
```

Example: Place the following text in TestApplet.html:

```
<html><head><title>Test applet</title></head>
<body>
    <applet code="japplet.TestApplet.class" height="100" width="300">
        <param NAME="param" VALUE="test parameter">
        Sorry, can't run test
```

```
    </applet>
</body>
</html>
```

The following code is the code for the applet itself.

```
package japplet;

import java.awt.event.*;
import com.sun.java.swing.*;

public class TestApplet extends JApplet {
  JButton button = new JButton("A very minimal applet");

  public void init() {
    System.out.println("parameter="+getParameter("param"));

    button.addActionListener(new ActionListener() {
      public void actionPerformed(ActionEvent e) {
        System.out.println("Button was clicked");
      }
    });

    getContentPane().add(button);
  }
}
```

**public class JApplet extends java.applet.Applet
    implements Accessible, RootPaneContainer**

Constructors
public JApplet()
> Creates a new applet.

Methods
public AccessibleContext getAccessibleContext()
> Gets the accessible context.
> *Implements:* getAccessibleContext in interface Accessible.

public java.awt.Container getContentPane()
> Gets the content pane. This is the pane to which contained objects should be added.
> *Implements:* getContentPane in interface RootPaneContainer.

public java.awt.Component getGlassPane()
> Gets the glass pane associated with this applet.
> *Implements:* getGlassPane in interface RootPaneContainer.

public JMenuBar getJMenuBar()
> Gets the menu bar associated with this applet (or null if not present).

public JLayeredPane getLayeredPane()
> Gets the layered pane for this applet. This will contain the content pane and optionally the menu bar.
> *Throws:* IllegalComponentStateException if the layered pane parameter is null.
> *Implements:* getLayeredPane in interface RootPaneContainer.

public JRootPane getRootPane()
> Gets the root pane for this applet. It contains all panes.
> *Implements:* getRootPane in interface RootPaneContainer.

public void setContentPane(java.awt.Container container)

Sets the content pane for this applet. An applet always has a content pane; attempting to set it to null will cause an error.

Throws: IllegalComponentStateException if the content pane parameter is null.

Implements: setContentPane in interface RootPaneContainer.

public void setGlassPane(java.awt.Component component)

Sets the glass pane for the applet. This is an upper pane where pop-up menus and other floating content can be displayed.

Implements: setGlassPane in interface RootPaneContainer.

public void setJMenuBar(JMenuBar menubar)

Sets the menu bar for this applet. If present, the menu bar is managed by the content pane. See JRootPane (p.323).

public void setLayeredPane(JLayeredPane layeredPane)

Sets the layered pane. This pane contains the content pane and the optional menu bar.

Implements: setLayeredPane in interface RootPaneContainer.

public void setLayout(java.awt.LayoutManager manager)

The layout of a JApplet may not be changed. The actual place the layout needs to be changed is in the contentPane.

Throws: Error if called with rootPaneChecking true.

Overrides: setLayout in class Container.

public void update(java.awt.Graphics gr)

Calls paint() without filling the background.

Overrides: update in class Container.

Protected Fields

protected AccessibleContext accessibleContext

The accessible context. See the chapter on accessibility.

protected JRootPane rootPane

A cached reference to the root pane since it is frequently used.

protected boolean rootPaneCheckingEnabled

If true, checks are made to prevent components from being added directly to the JApplet instead of to the contentPane. The setLayout() method also performs a check when this is true.

Protected Methods

protected void addImpl(java.awt.Component component,
**   Object constraint, int index)**

Adds component at index, according to constraint. This enforces the content pane constraint.

protected JRootPane createRootPane()

Creates the root pane for this applet.

protected boolean isRootPaneCheckingEnabled()

Returns true if add() and setLayout() will throw an exception.

protected void setRootPaneCheckingEnabled(boolean enabled)

If enabled is true, then calls to add() and setLayout() will throw an exception.

protected void processKeyEvent(java.awt.event.KeyEvent event)

Handles keystrokes for this applet.

Overrides: processKeyEvent in class Component.

```
protected void setRootPane(JRootPane rootPane)
```
Sets the root pane. This contains all the other panes of the applet.

See also   Accessible (p.85), AccessibleContext (p.90), JLayeredPane (p.268), JMenuBar (p.288), JRootPane (p.323), RootPaneContainer (p.433).

swing.JApplet.AccessibleJApplet

INNER CLASS

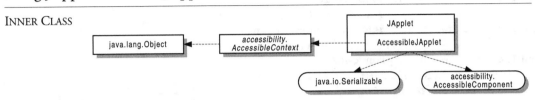

Provides the accessibility support for JApplet.

```
protected class JApplet.AccessibleJApplet
    extends AccessibleContext
    implements java.io.Serializable, AccessibleComponent
```

Methods
```
public void addFocusListener(java.awt.event.FocusListener l)
```
    Implements: addFocusListener in interface AccessibleComponent.
```
public boolean contains(java.awt.Point p)
```
    Implements: contains in interface AccessibleComponent.
```
public Accessible getAccessibleAt(java.awt.Point p)
```
    Implements: getAccessibleAt in interface AccessibleComponent.
```
public Accessible getAccessibleChild(int i)
```
    Overrides: getAccessibleChild in class AccessibleContext.
```
public int getAccessibleChildrenCount()
```
    Overrides: getAccessibleChildrenCount in class AccessibleContext.
```
public AccessibleComponent getAccessibleComponent()
```
    Overrides: getAccessibleComponent in class AccessibleContext.
```
public int getAccessibleIndexInParent()
```
    Overrides: getAccessibleIndexInParent in class AccessibleContext.
```
public Accessible getAccessibleParent()
```
    Overrides: getAccessibleParent in class AccessibleContext.
```
public AccessibleRole getAccessibleRole()
```
    Overrides: getAccessibleRole in class AccessibleContext.
```
public AccessibleStateSet getAccessibleStateSet()
```
    Overrides: getAccessibleStateSet in class AccessibleContext.
```
public java.awt.Color getBackground()
```
    Implements: getBackground in interface AccessibleComponent.
```
public java.awt.Rectangle getBounds()
```
    Implements: getBounds in interface AccessibleComponent.
```
public java.awt.Cursor getCursor()
```
    Implements: getCursor in interface AccessibleComponent.
```
public java.awt.Font getFont()
```
    Implements: getFont in interface AccessibleComponent.

```
public java.awt.FontMetrics getFontMetrics(java.awt.Font f)
```
Implements: getFontMetrics in interface AccessibleComponent.
```
public java.awt.Color getForeground()
```
Implements: getForeground in interface AccessibleComponent.
```
public java.util.Locale getLocale()
```
Overrides: getLocale in class AccessibleContext.
```
public java.awt.Point getLocation()
```
Implements: getLocation in interface AccessibleComponent.
```
public java.awt.Point getLocationOnScreen()
```
Implements: getLocationOnScreen in interface AccessibleComponent.
```
public java.awt.Dimension getSize()
```
Implements: getSize in interface AccessibleComponent.
```
public boolean isEnabled()
```
Implements: isEnabled in interface AccessibleComponent.
```
public boolean isFocusTraversable()
```
Implements: isFocusTraversable in interface AccessibleComponent.
```
public boolean isShowing()
```
Implements: isShowing in interface AccessibleComponent.
```
public boolean isVisible()
```
Implements: isVisible in interface AccessibleComponent.
```
public void setBackground(java.awt.Color c)
```
Implements: setBackground in interface AccessibleComponent.
```
public void setBounds(java.awt.Rectangle r)
```
Implements: setBounds in interface AccessibleComponent.
```
public void setCursor(java.awt.Cursor cursor)
```
Implements: setCursor in interface AccessibleComponent.
```
public void setEnabled(boolean b)
```
Implements: setEnabled in interface AccessibleComponent.
```
public void setFont(java.awt.Font f)
```
Implements: setFont in interface AccessibleComponent.
```
public void setForeground(java.awt.Color c)
```
Implements: setForeground in interface AccessibleComponent.
```
public void setLocation(java.awt.Point p)
```
Implements: setLocation in interface AccessibleComponent.
```
public void setSize(java.awt.Dimension d)
```
Implements: setSize in interface AccessibleComponent.
```
public void setVisible(boolean b)
```
Implements: setVisible in interface AccessibleComponent.
```
public void removeFocusListener(java.awt.event.FocusListener l)
```
Implements: removeFocusListener in interface AccessibleComponent.
```
public void requestFocus()
```
Implements: requestFocus in interface AccessibleComponent.

See also Accessible (p.85), AccessibleComponent (p.87), AccessibleContext (p.90), AccessibleRole (p.95), AccessibleStateSet (p.101), JApplet (p.186).

swing.JButton

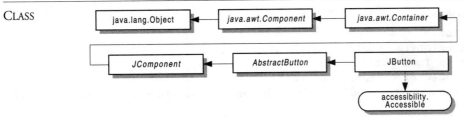

JButton implements a simple pushbutton.

JButton is one of the few components where you generally won't use the model; the component methods are sufficient. The reason for this is that a JButton doesn't keep any significant *application* state. The state it maintains is related to its own state; all an application cares about is the ActionEvents it generates. Even JCheckBox, which is only slightly more complex, can have its model represent a boolean in an application.

Example

```
package jbutton;
import java.awt.*;
import java.awt.event.*;
import com.sun.java.swing.*;
public class Main extends JFrame {
  public Main () {
    addWindowListener(new WindowAdapter() {
      public void windowClosing(WindowEvent e) {
        Main.this.dispose();
        System.exit(0);
      }
    });

    JButton button = new JButton("Button");

    // Can be used like a JDK 1.1 Button
    button.addActionListener (new ActionListener() {
      public void actionPerformed (ActionEvent e) {
        System.out.println("Button clicked");
      }
    });
    // It's also a JComponent (and an AbstractButton)
    button.setToolTipText("Click the button");

    getContentPane().add(button);

    pack();
    setVisible(true);
  }
  public static void main (String arg[]) {
    new Main();
  }
}
```

```
public class JButton extends AbstractButton
    implements Accessible
```

Constructors

```
public JButton()
public JButton(String text)
public JButton(Icon icon)
public JButton(String text, Icon icon)
```
    Creates a button with `text` and `icon`. If either is omitted, it will default to `null` and not be shown.

Methods

public AccessibleContext getAccessibleContext()
    Gets the accessible context.
    Overrides: `getAccessibleContext` in class `JComponent`.
    Implements: `getAccessibleContext` in interface `Accessible`.

public String getUIClassID()
    Returns "ButtonUI".
    Overrides: `getUIClassID` in class `JComponent`.

public boolean isDefaultButton()
    Returns `true` if this button is the default button for its parent RootPane.

public boolean isDefaultCapable()
    Returns `true` if this button is capable of being the default button for its parent RootPane.

protected String paramString()
    Returns a string representation of this `JButton`.
    Overrides: `paramString` in class `AbstractButton`.

public void setDefaultCapable(boolean defaultCapable)
    Sets whether this button is capable of being the default button for its parent RootPane.

public void updateUI()
    Updates the button to reflect the current look and feel.

    Extended by   BasicArrowButton (p.550).
    Returned by   BasicComboBoxUI.createArrowButton() (p.565),
BasicFileChooserUI.getApproveButton() (p.587), BasicScrollBarUI.createDecreaseButton() (p.642),
BasicScrollBarUI.createIncreaseButton() (p.642),
BasicSplitPaneDivider.createLeftOneTouchButton() (p.664),
BasicSplitPaneDivider.createRightOneTouchButton() (p.664),
JRootPane.getDefaultButton() (p.323), JToolBar.add() (p.388).
    See also   Accessible (p.85), AccessibleContext (p.90), ButtonGroup (p.146), Icon (p.183).

swing.JButton.AccessibleJButton

INNER CLASS

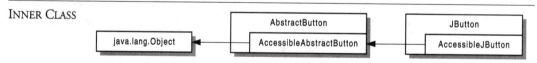

This class provides a correct `AccessibleRole` for a `JButton`.

```
protected class JButton.AccessibleJButton
    extends AbstractButton.AccessibleAbstractButton
```

Methods

`public AccessibleRole getAccessibleRole()`

Returns `AccessibleRole.PUSH_BUTTON`.

Overrides: `getAccessibleRole` in class `JComponent.AccessibleJComponent`.

See also   AbstractButton.AccessibleAbstractButton (p.125), AccessibleRole (p.95).

swing.JCheckBox

CLASS

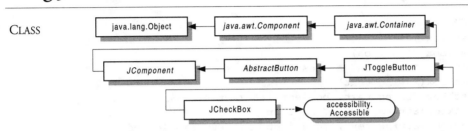

A `JCheckBox` is a button that can either be selected or not (usually it is displayed with an X or checkmark to indicate it is selected).

The main use of a `JCheckBox`'s model (a `ButtonModel`) is to represent a two-state (on/off, true/false) value in an application. A very common use of this is as a cell renderer and/or cell editor for a `boolean` value in a `JTable`. Using the `ButtonModel` allows the changes to the button's state to be updated automatically, instead of the application using an `ActionListener` and calling the set methods of `JCheckBox`. Using the `boolean` as the model prevents keeping two parallel variables representing the same value.

Example

```
package jcheckbox;
import java.awt.*;
import java.awt.event.*;
import com.sun.java.swing.*;
public class Main extends JFrame {
  JCheckBox check = new JCheckBox ("Checkbox", false);

  public Main () {
    addWindowListener(new WindowAdapter() {
      public void windowClosing(WindowEvent e) {
        Main.this.dispose();
        System.exit(0);
      }
    });
    check.addItemListener (new ItemListener() {
      public void itemStateChanged (ItemEvent e) {
        System.out.println("Checked? "+check.isSelected());
      }
    });
    getContentPane().add(check);
```

```
      pack();
      setVisible(true);
   }
   public static void main (String arg[]) {
      new Main();
   }
}
```

public class JCheckBox extends JToggleButton
    implements Accessible

Constructors
public JCheckBox()
public JCheckBox(Icon icon)
public JCheckBox(Icon icon, boolean isSelected)
public JCheckBox(String text)
public JCheckBox(String text, boolean isSelected)
public JCheckBox(String text, Icon icon)
public JCheckBox(String text, Icon icon, boolean isSelected)
> Creates a check box, with specified `text`, `icon`, and initial selection status. *Default:* no text, no icon, and not selected.

Methods
public AccessibleContext getAccessibleContext()
> Returns the accessible context. See the chapter on accessibility.

public String getUIClassID()
> Returns "CheckBoxUI". See the chapter on look and feel.

public void updateUI()
> Updates the button according to the current look and feel.

Protected Methods
protected String paramString()
> Returns a string representation of this properties of this `JCheckBox`. The string may be empty but will not be `null`.
> *Overrides:* `paramString` in class `JToggleButton`.

Inner Classes
protected class JCheckBox.AccessibleJCheckBox

> *See also*   Accessible (p.85), AccessibleContext (p.90), Icon (p.183), JRadioButton (p.319).

swing.JCheckBox.AccessibleJCheckBox

INNER CLASS

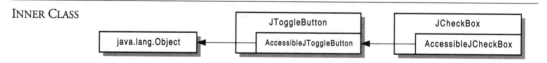

Returns the correct `AccessibleRole` for a `JCheckBox`.

protected class JCheckBox.AccessibleJCheckBox
    extends JToggleButton.AccessibleJToggleButton

Methods
`public AccessibleRole getAccessibleRole()`

Returns `AccessibleRole.CHECK_BOX`.

Overrides: `getAccessibleRole` in class `JToggleButton.AccessibleJToggleButton`.

See also AccessibleRole (p.95), JToggleButton.AccessibleJToggleButton (p.387).

swing.JCheckBoxMenuItem

CLASS

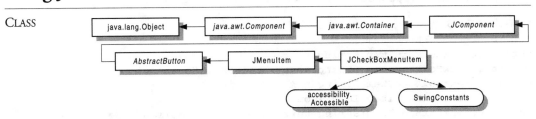

A `JCheckBoxMenuItem` is a menu item that can take one of two states: `checked` or `unchecked`. It is similar to a `JRadioButtonMenuItem`, but differs in that it is intended to be used by itself, while a `JRadioButtonMenuItem` is used as part of a `ButtonGroup` in the menu.

Example

```
package jcbmenu;

import java.awt.*;
import java.awt.event.*;
import com.sun.java.swing.*;
public class Main extends JFrame {
  JCheckBoxMenuItem check = new JCheckBoxMenuItem ("Check");

  public Main () {
    addWindowListener(new WindowAdapter() {
      public void windowClosing(WindowEvent e) {
        Main.this.dispose();
        System.exit(0);
      }
    });

    JMenuBar bar = new JMenuBar();
    JMenu menu = new JMenu("Checkable");
    bar.add (menu);
    menu.add(check);

    check.addItemListener (new ItemListener() {
      public void itemStateChanged (ItemEvent e) {
        System.out.println("Checked? "+check.isSelected());
      }
    });

    setJMenuBar(bar);
    getContentPane().add(new JLabel("A placeholder"));

    pack();
```

```
      setSize (300, 300);
      setVisible(true);
   }
   public static void main (String arg[]) {
      new Main();
   }
}
```

public class JCheckBoxMenuItem extends JMenuItem
implements SwingConstants, Accessible

Constructors

public JCheckBoxMenuItem()
public JCheckBoxMenuItem(String text)
public JCheckBoxMenuItem(String text, boolean isSelected)
public JCheckBoxMenuItem(String text, Icon icon)
public JCheckBoxMenuItem(Icon icon)
public JCheckBoxMenuItem(String text, Icon icon, boolean isSelected)

Creates a check box usable as a MenuItem. You can specify the text, icon, and whether it is initially selected. *Default:* empty text, no icon, not selected.

Methods

public AccessibleContext getAccessibleContext()

Returns the accessible context. See the chapter on accessibility.

Overrides: getAccessibleContext in class JMenuItem.

Implements: getAccessibleContext in interface Accessible.

public synchronized Object[] getSelectedObjects()

If this check box is selected, returns an array with one item: the text of this check box. If not selected, returns null.

Overrides: getSelectedObjects in class AbstractButton.

Implements: getSelectedObjects in interface ItemSelectable.

public boolean getState()

Returns the selection state of this check box. In Swing, the preferred method would be getSelected().

public String getUIClassID()

Returns "CheckBoxMenuItemUI".

Overrides: getUIClassID in class JMenuItem.

public void requestFocus()

Requests that the focus manager set the focus to this component.

Overrides: requestFocus in class JComponent.

public synchronized void setState(boolean isSelected)

Sets the state of the check box. In Swing, it is preferable to use the setSelected() method for this function.

public void updateUI()

Tells the check box to update itself with the current look and feel.

Overrides: updateUI in class JMenuItem.

Protected Methods

protected void init(String text, Icon icon)

Sets the text and icon for this check box.

Overrides: init in class JMenuItem.

protected String paramString()

Returns a string representing the properties of this JCheckBoxMenuItem. The returned string may be empty but will not be null.

Overrides: paramString in class JMenuItem.

Inner Classes

protected class JCheckBoxMenuItem.AccessibleJCheckBoxMenuItem

See also   Accessible (p.85), AccessibleContext (p.90), Action (p.128), CheckBoxMenuItemUI (p.529), Icon (p.183), JMenuItem (p.291), SwingConstants (p.442).

swing.JCheckBoxMenuItem.AccessibleJCheckBoxMenuItem

INNER CLASS

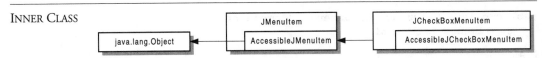

Returns the correct AccessibleRole for a JCheckBoxMenuItem.

protected class JCheckBoxMenuItem.AccessibleJCheckBoxMenuItem
  extends JMenuItem.AccessibleJMenuItem

Methods

public AccessibleRole getAccessibleRole()

Returns AccessibleRole.CHECK_BOX.

Overrides: getAccessibleRole in class JMenuItem.AccessibleJMenuItem.

See also   AccessibleRole (p.95), JMenuItem.AccessibleJMenuItem (p.294).

swing.JColorChooser

CLASS

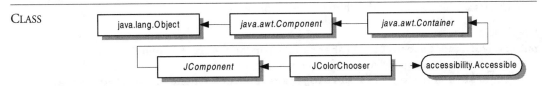

JColorChooser allows a user to choose a Color. It is a component similar to JOptionPane and JFileChooser in providing a preconfigured complex component.

It is important to note that a JColorChooser component does not have a container by default. Static methods are provided to wrap the JColorChooser in a JDialog, but the chooser can appear elsewhere (as the drop down of a JComboBox, for example). Because of this, a JColorChooser does *not* have predefined OK or Cancel buttons. This component is strictly the color choosing portion.

This class provides two static utility methods to create a `JDialog` wrapped around a `JColorChooser`. The first method, `showDialog()`, does everything itself, and simply returns the chosen `Color` when the dialog is dismissed. It adds OK, Cancel, and Reset (resets the selected `Color` to the specified initial `Color`) buttons to the `JDialog` but does not allow the application to interact with them.

The second utility method wraps an application-created `JColorChooser` in a `JDialog` with OK, Cancel, and Reset buttons. This allows the application to preconfigure the `JColorChooser` the way it wants (for example, adding a custom chooser for a different color space model, such as CMYK). This method also allows the application to provide listeners for the OK and Cancel buttons. When either of those buttons is pressed, the dialog is hidden, but not disposed of.

The other way to use this class is to create a new instance and add it to the container of your choice. This allows for more advanced functions, like an "apply" button, or having the chooser update itself in response to an "eye-dropper" style control.

```
public class JColorChooser extends JComponent
    implements Accessible
```

Fields

```
public static final String CHOOSER_PANELS_PROPERTY = "chooserPanels"
```
The `chooserPanel` array property name.
```
public static final String PREVIEW_PANEL_PROPERTY = "previewPanel"
```
The `previewPanel` property name.
```
public static final String SELECTION_MODEL_PROPERTY = "selectionModel"
```
The `selectionModel` property name.

Constructors

```
public JColorChooser()
```
Creates a color chooser panel with an initial color of `Color.white`.
```
public JColorChooser(ColorSelectionModel model)
```
Creates a color chooser panel with the specified `ColorSelectionModel`.
```
public JColorChooser(java.awt.Color initialColor)
```
Creates a color chooser panel with the specified initial color.

Methods

```
public void addChooserPanel(AbstractColorChooserPanel panel)
```
Adds a color chooser panel to the color chooser.
```
public static JDialog createDialog(java.awt.Component c, String title,
    boolean modal, JColorChooser chooserPane,
    java.awt.event.ActionListener okListener,
    java.awt.event.ActionListener cancelListener)
```
Creates and returns a new dialog containing the specified ColorChooser pane along with OK, Cancel, and Reset buttons. If the OK or Cancel buttons are pressed, the dialog is automatically hidden (but not disposed of). If the Reset button is pressed, the ColorChooser's color will be reset to the color which was set the last time `show()` was invoked on the dialog and the dialog will remain showing.

public AccessibleContext getAccessibleContext()

Gets the AccessibleContext associated with this JColorChooser.

Overrides: getAccessibleContext in class JComponent.

Implements: getAccessibleContext in interface Accessible.

public AbstractColorChooserPanel[] getChooserPanels()

public java.awt.Color getColor()

Gets the current color value from the color chooser. By default, this delegates to the model.

public JComponent getPreviewPanel()

public ColorSelectionModel getSelectionModel()

public ColorChooserUI getUI()

Returns the look and feel object that renders this component.

public String getUIClassID()

Returns "ColorChooserUI".

Overrides: getUIClassID in class JComponent.

**public AbstractColorChooserPanel removeChooserPanel(
    AbstractColorChooserPanel panel)**

Removes the specified color panel.

public void setChooserPanels(AbstractColorChooserPanel[] panels)

public void setColor(int c)

Sets the current color of the color chooser to the specified color.

public void setColor(int r, int g, int b)

Sets the current color of the color chooser to the specified RGB color.

public void setColor(java.awt.Color color)

Sets the current color of the color chooser to the specified color. This will fire a PropertyChangeEvent for the property named color.

public void setPreviewPanel(JComponent preview)

Sets the current preview panel. This will fire a PropertyChangeEvent for the property preview-Panel.

public void setSelectionModel(ColorSelectionModel newModel)

Sets the model containing the selected color.

public void setUI(ColorChooserUI ui)

**public static java.awt.Color showDialog(java.awt.Component component,
    String title, java.awt.Color initialColor)**

Shows a modal color-chooser dialog and blocks until the dialog is hidden. If the user presses the OK button, then this method hides/disposes of the dialog and returns the selected color. If the user presses the Cancel button or closes the dialog without pressing OK, then this method hides/disposes of the dialog and returns null.

public void updateUI()

Notification from the UIManager that the look and feel has changed. Replaces the current UI object with the latest version from the UIManager.

Overrides: updateUI in class JComponent.

Protected Fields

protected AccessibleContext accessibleContext

Protected Methods

protected String paramString()

Returns a `String` representation of the properties of this `JColorChooser`. The returned string may be empty but will not be `null`.

Overrides: `paramString` in class `JComponent`.

Inner Classes

protected class JColorChooser.AccessibleJColorChooser

See also   AbstractColorChooserPanel (p.478), AccessibleContext (p.90), ColorSelectionModel (p.479), JComponent (p.207), JDialog (p.226).

swing.JColorChooser.AccessibleJColorChooser

INNER CLASS

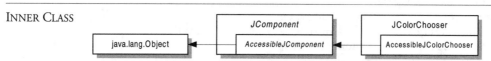

This inner class provides the `AccessibleContext` for a `JColorChooser`.

protected class JColorChooser.AccessibleJColorChooser
    extends AccessibleJComponent

Constructors

public AccessibleJColorChooser()

Default constructor.

Methods

public AccessibleRole getAccessibleRole()

Returns the correct `AccessibleRole` for a `JColorChooser`, which is `Accessible-Role.COLOR_CHOOSER`.

See also   AccessibleRole (p.95), JComponent.AccessibleJComponent (p.221).

swing.JComboBox

CLASS

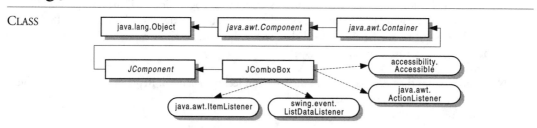

A combo box is a component that lets you select a value from a drop-down list or enter a text value directly. The editing feature can be turned off so that it acts as a pure drop-down list.

The combo box has two kinds of listeners: `ActionListener` for changes in the selection and `ItemListener` for changes in the list contents.

Swing 1.1 finally supplies a usable model for a JComboBox, the MutableComboBoxModel. Previously there was only a ComboBoxModel, which didn't provide methods for changing the contents of the model. To use a mutable model before Swing 1.1, you were stuck with using DefaultComboBoxModel.

Using a MutableComboBoxModel is very useful, especially when the number of items in the combo box is large. Imagine having a list of large cities, for example, to use in choosing a timezone by finding the nearest city. If the list is world-wide, you really don't want to have to have the main copy of the list (which may be a Red-Black tree so the list is sorted) and also the copy used by the DefaultComboBoxModel. Now you can give the user the ability to add new cities by typing them into the edit field, which would require a sorted insertion in both the tree and the DefaultComboBoxModel. Wrapping the tree with the MutableComboBoxModel interface allows the tree to be used directly by the JComboBox.

Example

```
package combobox;

import java.awt.*;
import java.awt.event.*;
import com.sun.java.swing.*;

public class Main extends JFrame {
  JComboBox combo = new JComboBox();

  public Main () {
    addWindowListener(new WindowAdapter() {
      public void windowClosing(WindowEvent e) {
        Main.this.dispose();
        System.exit(0);
      }
    });

    combo.addItem("Art");
    combo.addItem("History");
    combo.addItem("Philosophy");
    combo.setEditable(true);
    System.out.println("#items="+combo.getItemCount());

    combo.addActionListener(new ActionListener() {
      public void actionPerformed(ActionEvent e) {
        System.out.println(
          "Selected index="+combo.getSelectedIndex()
          + " Selected item="+combo.getSelectedItem());
      }
    });

    getContentPane().add(combo);
    pack();
    setVisible(true);
  }

  public static void main (String arg[]) {
    new Main();
  }
}
```

```
public class JComboBox extends JComponent
    implements Accessible, java.awt.event.ActionListener,
    java.awt.ItemSelectable, ListDataListener
```

Constructors

public JComboBox()

Creates an empty JComboBox, using a DefaultComboBoxModel.

public JComboBox(ComboBoxModel model)

Creates a JComboBox which will use the given ComboBoxModel.

public JComboBox(Object[] items)

Creates a JComboBox using a DefaultComboBoxModel that contains the elements in the given array.

public JComboBox(java.util.Vector items)

Creates a JComboBox using a DefaultComboBoxModel that contains the elements in the given Vector.

Methods

public void actionPerformed(java.awt.event.ActionEvent event)

Not for public use—do not call or override.

Implements: actionPerformed in interface ActionListener.

public void addActionListener(java.awt.event.ActionListener listener)

Adds listener to the list of objects to be notified when a selection is made.

public void addItem(Object item)

Adds item to the list of items in the combo box. This method requires the model be an instance of MutableComboBoxModel.

Throws: java.lang.Error if the model is not an instance of MutableComboBoxModel.

public void addItemListener(java.awt.event.ItemListener listener)

Adds listener to the list of objects to be notified when the list of items changes.

Implements: addItemListener in interface ItemSelectable.

public void configureEditor(ComboBoxEditor editor, Object value)

Begins editing value using editor.

public void contentsChanged(swing.event.ListDataEvent event)

Not for public use—do not call or override.

Implements: contentsChanged in interface ListDataListener.

public AccessibleContext getAccessibleContext()

Gets the accessible context. See the chapter on accessibility.

Overrides: getAccessibleContext in class JComponent.

Implements: getAccessibleContext in interface Accessible.

public String getActionCommand()

Gets the string that is the command sent to listeners when the action is performed.

public ComboBoxEditor getEditor()

Gets the editor used to edit the combo box.

public Object getItemAt(int index)

Gets the item at index.

public int getItemCount()

Returns the number of items in the combo box list.

public JComboBox.KeySelectionManager getKeySelectionManager()

Gets the current key manager. See createKeySelectionManager().

public int getMaximumRowCount()

Returns the number of items the combo box can display without requiring a scroll bar. (The scroll bar will be added automatically.)

public ComboBoxModel getModel()

Gets the model for the combo box.

public ListCellRenderer getRenderer()

Gets the component responsible for displaying the combo box list of items.

public int getSelectedIndex()

Returns the position of the currently selected object, or –1 if there is no current selection or it is not in the list.

public Object getSelectedItem()

Gets the currently selected item.

public Object[] getSelectedObjects()

If there is a selected object, returns a one-element array containing that object. If no object is selected, returns an empty array.

Implements: getSelectedObjects in interface ItemSelectable.

public ComboBoxUI getUI()

Gets the look and feel for this component. See the chapter on look and feel.

public String getUIClassID()

Returns "ComboBoxUI".

Overrides: getUIClassID in class JComponent.

public void hidePopup()

Closes the pop-up window of the drop-down list.

public void insertItemAt(Object item, int index)

Adds item at index. Notifies any ItemListeners of the change. Requires the model be an instance of MutableComboBoxModel.

Throws: java.lang.Error if the model is not an instance of MutableComboBoxModel.

public void intervalAdded(ListDataEvent event)

Invoked (by the model) when items have been added to the combo box model.

Implements: intervalAdded in interface ListDataListener.

public void intervalRemoved(ListDataEvent event)

Invoked (by the model) when items have been removed from the combo box model.

Implements: intervalRemoved in interface ListDataListener.

public boolean isEditable()

Returns true if the combo box permits the item in the text field portion to be edited. If false, it acts like a drop-down list, where the item can only be changed by selecting a new choice from the list.

public boolean isFocusTraversable()

Returns false if the combo box is editable, so the editor will receive focus instead of the whole JComboBox. Returns true if the combo box is not editable.

Overrides: isFocusTraversable in class JComponent.

public boolean isLightWeightPopupEnabled()

Returns true if lightweight pop-ups are in use, or false if heavyweight (AWT) pop-ups are being used. This method has been used since Swing 1.0.2.

public boolean isPopupVisible()

Returns true if the pop-up is showing.

public void processKeyEvent(java.awt.event.KeyEvent event)

Processes the event through the key map of the combo box's text field.

Overrides: processKeyEvent in class JComponent.

public void removeActionListener(java.awt.event.ActionListener listener)

Removes listener from the list of objects notified when an item is selected.

public void removeAllItems()

Removes all items from the list of items. Notifies any ItemListeners of the change. Requires the model be an instance of MutableComboBoxModel.

Throws: java.lang.Error if the model is not an instance of MutableComboBoxModel.

public void removeItem(Object item)

Removes item from the list of items. Notifies any ItemListeners of the change.

Throws: java.lang.Error if the model is not an instance of MutableComboBoxModel.

public void removeItemAt(int index)

Removes the item at index from the list of items. Notifies any ItemListeners of the change.

Throws: java.lang.Error if the model is not an instance of MutableComboBoxModel.

public void removeItemListener(java.awt.event.ItemListener listener)

Removes listener from the list of objects notified when the list of items changes.

Implements: removeItemListener in interface ItemSelectable.

public boolean selectWithKeyChar(char ch)

Selects the first item in the list beginning with ch. See createKeySelectionManager().

public void setActionCommand(String action)

Sets the string to be sent to any ActionListener when the selection changes.

public void setEditable(boolean mayEdit)

Sets whether editing of the text field portion is allowed. If editing is not allowed, the combo box acts like a drop-down list.

public void setEditor(ComboBoxEditor editor)

Sets the editor used to display the item in the field. If the JComboBox is editable, this component both renders and edits the field area. If the JComboBox is not editable, the ListCellRenderer is used to render the field area.

public void setEnabled(boolean isEnabled)

Sets whether the combo box is enabled (allowed to change or edit its selection).

Overrides: setEnabled in class JComponent.

public void setKeySelectionManager(JComboBox.KeySelectionManager manager)

Sets the manager that handles typing of a key which makes the selection move to the item starting with that letter.

public void setLightWeightPopupEnabled(boolean aFlag)

When displaying the pop-up list, JComboBox can use a lightweight pop-up if it will fit inside the parent window. You would call this method with false to disable the use of lightweight pop-ups if you need to mix lightweight and heavyweight components in a window. If you don't turn off the lightweight pop-up, it will draw *behind* any heavyweight components it intersects with. This method has been used since Swing 1.0.2.

public void setMaximumRowCount(int count)

Sets the number of rows allowed before the combo box introduces scroll bars.

public void setModel(ComboBoxModel model)

Sets the model for the combo box. (The model tracks the list and the current selection.)

public void setPopupVisible(boolean v)

Shows or hides the pop-up.

public void setRenderer(ListCellRenderer renderer)

Sets the component responsible for displaying the item's combo box. The ListCellRenderer added should be able to handle a cell index of −1, which should cause it to return the renderer for the field. The renderer is only used for the field when the JComboBox is not editable. If it is editable, the ComboBoxEditor is used for editing and rendering the field.

public void setSelectedIndex(int index)

Sets the current selection to the item at index.

public void setSelectedItem(Object item)

Sets the current selection to be item.

public void setUI(ComboBoxUI ui)

Sets the UI (look and feel) for the combo box. See the chapter on look and feel.

public void showPopup()

Shows the pop-up menu for the combo box list. See hidePopup().

public void updateUI()

Tells the combo box to update itself according to the current look and feel. See the chapter on look and feel.

Overrides: updateUI in class JComponent.

Protected Fields

protected String actionCommand

The command string sent to listeners when the action is performed.

protected ComboBoxModel dataModel

The model for the combo box. (Keeps track of the current item.)

protected ComboBoxEditor editor

The editor for the combo box.

protected boolean isEditable

Returns true if editing is permitted. If false, this acts like a pure drop-down list.

protected JComboBox.KeySelectionManager keySelectionManager

The component that matches items to keys. See createKeySelectionManager().

protected boolean lightWeightPopupEnabled

Returns true if the JComboBox is allowed to use a lightweight component for its pop-up.

protected int maximumRowCount

The number of items that can be displayed without requiring a scroll bar.

protected ListCellRenderer renderer

The object that draws the combo box.

protected Object selectedItemReminder

The previously selected item.

Protected Methods

protected JComboBox.KeySelectionManager createDefaultKeySelectionManager()

Creates a manager that matches up items to keys. This way, when you type a character, the combo box may be able to select a value that starts with that letter.

protected void fireActionEvent()

Notifies any registered ActionListener that the selected item has changed.

protected void fireItemStateChanged(java.awt.event.ItemEvent)

Notifies any registered `ItemListener` that the list of items has changed.

protected void installAncestorListener()

Installs the listener for changes in the `JComboBox`'s parent. This listener is used to hide the popup when the state of the parent changes.

protected String paramString()

Returns a string representation of the properties of this `JComboBox`. The returned string may be empty but will not be `null`.

Overrides: paramString in class JComponent.

protected void selectedItemChanged()

Called when the selected item has changed. Notifies any `ItemListeners` of the change.

See also   Accessible (p.85), AccessibleContext (p.90), ComboBoxEditor (p.155), ComboBoxModel (p.156), ComboBoxUI (p.530), ListCellRenderer (p.420), ListDataEvent (p.498), ListDataListener (p.499), MutableComboBoxModel (p.427).

swing.JComboBox.AccessibleJComboBox

INNER CLASS

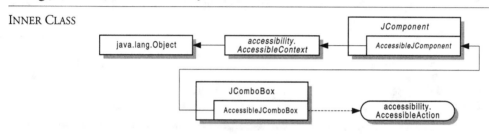

```
protected class JComboBox.AccessibleJComboBox
    extends JComponent.AccessibleJComponent
    implements AccessibleAction
```

Methods

public boolean doAccessibleAction(int i)

Performs the specified `Action` on the object.

Implements: doAccessibleAction in interface AccessibleAction.

public AccessibleAction getAccessibleAction()

Gets the `AccessibleAction` associated with this object if one exists. Otherwise returns `null`.

public int getAccessibleActionCount()

Returns the number of `Actions` available in this object. If there is more than one, the first one is the "default" action.

Implements: getAccessibleActionCount in interface AccessibleAction.

public String getAccessibleActionDescription(int i)

Returns a description of the specified action of the object.

Implements: getAccessibleActionDescription in interface AccessibleAction.

public AccessibleRole getAccessibleRole()

Returns `AccessibleRole.COMBO_BOX`.

See also   Accessible (p.85), AccessibleAction (p.86), AccessibleStateSet (p.101), JComponent.AccessibleJComponent (p.221).

INNER
INTERFACE

JComboBox

KeySelectionManager

```
public static interface JComboBox.KeySelectionManager
```

Methods

```
public abstract int selectionForKey(char aKey,
    ComboBoxModel aModel)
```

For a given character, returns the row index which should be selected. This method should return −1 if a row is not selected. Having this functionality presented through an interface allows the behavior to be pluggable. Some examples of common behaviors are having the selection iterate through all list rows that begin with the character, or making a more accurate selection as more characters of a word are typed.

Returned by   JComboBox.createDefaultKeySelectionManager() (p.200), JComboBox.getKeySelectionManager() (p.200).

swing.JComponent

CLASS

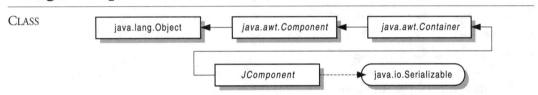

java.lang.Object ← java.awt.Component ← java.awt.Container

JComponent ----→ java.io.Serializable

JComponent is the root class of much of the Swing library—most of Swing's visual components are subclasses of JComponent. It is an extremely complex class; it supports many behaviors. It is also an abstract class—you cannot create instances directly; you must use (or create) a subclass.

DebugGraphics

You can use setDebugGraphicsOptions() to set debugging behavior. (Also see class Debug-Graphics for more information.) DebugGraphics.LOG_OPTION causes a text message to be written to System.out before each significant graphics activity. DebugGraphics.FLASH_OPTION causes the drawing to flash while drawing (so you can see components as they are painted). DebugGraphics.BUFFERED_OPTION causes a window to appear that shows drawing operations as they are performed on the offscreen buffer.

Focus

The *focus* is how Swing manages the notion of a default component. For example, a button with focus would be specially highlighted, and could be activated with the RETURN key rather than requiring a mouse click. JComponents can assist in managing focus.

If a component wants to manage focus, it can override `isManagingFocus()` to return true. It might indicate that it manages its own cycle of focus by returning `true` for `isFocusCycleRoot()`.

You can manage whether or not a component can receive the focus when it requests it (which it does via `requestFocus`). If `isRequestFocusEnabled()` is true, focus may be requested. You can change this with `setRequestFocusEnabled()`. While a component has focus, `hasFocus()` is true. There is also a `grabFocus()` method for use by focus managers.

The focus manager can use `isFocusTraversable` to determine whether a component should receive the focus, and `requestDefaultFocus()` to request that a component be given the focus. Method `getNextFocusableComponent()` will tell which component will next have the focus; `setNextFocusableComponent()` sets that value.

See the `FocusManager` abstract class for more information.

Keystrokes

Keystrokes are managed by these methods: `getActionForKeystroke()`, `getConditionForKeystroke()`, `getRegisteredKeyStrokes()`, `registerKeyboardAction()`, `resetKeyboardAction()`, and `unregisterKeyboardAction()`. For each possible keystroke, there may be an `ActionListener` to be notified when the keystroke happens according to a condition. The condition can be UNDEFINED_CONDITION, WHEN_FOCUSED, WHEN_ANCESTOR_OF_FOCUSED_COMPONENT, or WHEN_IN_FOCUSED_WINDOW.

The conditions determine the scope of the keystroke. For WHEN_FOCUSED, the keystroke applies when this component has the focus. For WHEN_ANCESTOR_OF_FOCUSED_COMPONENT, the keystroke applies when this component or any of its children has the focus. For WHEN_IN_FOCUSED_WINDOW, the keystroke applies when any component in the window has focus (for the window in which this component is located).

Painting

Painting in `JComponent` is a little more complicated than in AWT. The `JComponent paint()` routine first calls `paintComponent()`, then `paintBorder()`, then `paintChildren()`, to ensure that the parts of this component are painted properly. A subclass would typically override only `paintComponent()`. The default behavior of these methods is to call the associated method in the component's UI delegate in the installed look and feel.

Sizes

A component has three sizes associated with it: minimum, preferred, and maximum. In AWT, component sizes are determined by the layout manager. In Swing, the process is more complex.

In Swing, when a `JComponent`'s size is requested, it tries several methods. If a size has been explicitly set, that size is returned. If no size was set, the UI (look and feel) is asked for the size. If it returns a size, that size is used. If not (if it returns `null`), the layout manager determines the size.

The important methods are `getMinimumSize()`, `setMinimumSize()`, `getPreferred-Size()`, `setPreferredSize()`, `getMaximumSize()`, and `setMaximumSize()`. (See the `swing.plaf` chapter for more information on look and feel, and methods `updateUI()`, `setUI()`, and `getUIClassID()` in `JComponent`.)

There are many methods which get information about various aspects of the size and location:

- Both position and size—`getBounds()`/`setBounds()`.
- Position only—`getLocation()`/`setLocation()`, `getX()`/`setX()`, `getY()`/`setY()`.
- Size only—`getSize()`/`setSize()`, `getHeight()`/`setHeight()`, `getWidth()`/`set-Width()`.

ToolTips

Each `JComponent` may have a ToolTip associated with it. This is a small pop-up text window that appears when the mouse pauses over the component. The simplest way to use a ToolTip is to use `setToolTipText()` to establish the text and `getToolTipText()` to retrieve it.

A more sophisticated component can make the ToolTip depend on the mouse location. A subclass can override `getToolTipLocation()` to determine exactly where the ToolTip should be put. A subclass can override `getToolTipText(MouseEvent)` to set the text according to the mouse location. Finally, `createToolTip()` can be overriden to make a subclass of ToolTip become the ToolTip for that component.

JComponent Beans properties

Property	Type
accessibleContext	AccessibleContext
alignmentX	float
alignmentY	float
autoscrolls	boolean
background	java.awt.Color
border	Border
component	indexed
componentCount	int
debugGraphicsOptions	int
doubleBuffered	boolean
enabled	boolean
focusCycleRoot	boolean
focusTraversable	boolean
font	java.awt.Font

JComponent Beans properties (continued)

Property	Type
foreground	java.awt.Color
graphics	java.awt.Graphics
height	int
insets	java.awt.Insets
layout	java.awt.LayoutManager
managingFocus	boolean
maximumSize	java.awt.Dimension
minimumSize	java.awt.Dimension
name	String
nextFocusableComponent	java.awt.Component
opaque	boolean
optimizedDrawingEnabled	boolean
paintingTile	boolean
preferredSize	java.awt.Dimension
registeredKeyStrokes	Keystroke[]
requestFocusEnabled	boolean
rootPane	JRootPane
toolTipText	String
topLevelAncestor	java.awt.Container
ui	ComponentUI
uiClassID/UIClassID	String
validateRoot	boolean
visible	boolean
visibleRect	java.awt.Rectangle
width	int
x	int
y	int

Events generated by JComponent

Events generated

AncestorEvent
ComponentEvent (from Component)
ContainerEvent (from Container)
FocusListener (from Component)
KeyListener (from Component)
MouseListener (from Component)
MouseMotionListener (from Component)
PropertyChangeEvent
VetoableChangeEvent

Example

```
package jcomponent;

import java.awt.*;
import java.awt.event.*;
import com.sun.java.swing.*;
import com.sun.java.swing.border.*;
public class Main extends JFrame {
  JComponent comp = new JLabel ("Test label");

  public Main () {
    addWindowListener(new WindowAdapter() {
      public void windowClosing(WindowEvent e) {
        Main.this.dispose();
        System.exit(0);
      }
    });

    comp.setToolTipText("Some tooltip text for component");
    comp.setBorder (new TitledBorder("Button"));

    System.out.println("X:"+comp.getX() + " Y:"+comp.getY()
        + " width:" + comp.getWidth() + " height:" + comp.getHeight());

    getContentPane().add(comp);
    pack();
    System.out.println("X:"+comp.getX() + " Y:"+comp.getY()
        + " width:" + comp.getWidth() + " height:" + comp.getHeight());

    setVisible(true);
  }
  public static void main (String arg[]) {
    new Main();
  }
}
```

FAQs

How do I do animation in Swing?

Simple animation is quite easy in Swing, since double-buffering is already implemented. The key is to override paintComponent(), not paint()/update(). The two ways to implement this feature are to subclass JPanel or JComponent.

The two ways to do simple animation are subtly different. Subclassing JPanel simply requires overriding paintComponent(), since double-buffering is turned on by default. The catch is that in paintComponent(), super.paintComponent() must be called first. Subclassing JComponent requires having the constructor call setDoubleBuffered(true), but does not require calling super.paintComponent() from paintComponent(). So, either choice involves about the same amount of work.

Threaded animation is a bit harder, since you can't get at the double-buffer created by Swing. You need to create your own offscreen buffer in the same way as it was done with an AWT `Canvas` (by calling `Component.getGraphics()` after the `Component` has been realized through calling `show()` or `pack()` on it), and then you draw to the off-screen buffer from the thread. Once the thread is done painting the buffer it can call `repaint()` (which is safe to call from a background thread). `paintComponent()` can then just blit the off-screen buffer into the main buffer. Since you are supplying your own buffer, you can turn Swing's own double-buffering support off.

```
public abstract class JComponent extends java.awt.Container
    implements java.io.Serializable
```

Fields

`public static final String TOOL_TIP_TEXT_KEY = "ToolTipText"`

A ToolTip is a small text description that appears over a component when the mouse stops moving over it. This string is used as a property key to get the ToolTip text for the component. See `getClientProperties()`, `getClientProperty()`, and `setClientProperty()` for information on properties. See `createToolTip()`, `getToolTipLocation()`, `getToolTipText()`, and `setToolTipText()` for information on ToolTips.

`public static final int UNDEFINED_CONDITION = -1`
`public static final int WHEN_ANCESTOR_OF_FOCUSED_COMPONENT = 1`
`public static final int WHEN_FOCUSED = 0`
`public static final int WHEN_IN_FOCUSED_WINDOW = 2`

See `getConditionForKeyStroke()` and `registerKeyboardAction()`, and the discussion on keystrokes above.

Constructors

`public JComponent()`

Creates a `JComponent` with a `null` layout manager.

Methods

`public void addAncestorListener(AncestorListener listener)`

Registers `listener` to receive an `AncestorEvent` when this component or one of its ancestors either moves or changes visibility.

`public void addNotify()`

Notifies this component that it now has a parent, and establishes the chain of `KeyboardAction` listeners.

Overrides: `addNotify` in class `Container`.

`public synchronized void addPropertyChangeListener(`
`java.beans.PropertyChangeListener listener)`

Registers `listener` to receive a `PropertyChangeEvent` when this component changes a bound property.

`public synchronized void addVetoableChangeListener(`
`java.beans.VetoableChangeListener listener)`

Registers `listener` to receive a `VetoableChangeEvent` when this component wants to change a vetoable bound property.

`public void computeVisibleRect(java.awt.Rectangle result)`

Intersects this component's visible rectangle with that of all its ancestors, and returns the value in `result`.

`public boolean contains(int x, int y)`

Calls the `contains()` method in the associated UI delegate to allow for nonrectangular shapes.

Overrides: contains in class `Component`.

`public JToolTip createToolTip()`

Creates the ToolTip for this component. You could override this method to return a particular subclass of `JToolTip`. See the discussion on ToolTips.

`public void firePropertyChange(String property, boolean oldValue,`
`    boolean newValue)`

`public void firePropertyChange(String property, byte oldValue,`
`    byte newValue)`

`public void firePropertyChange(String property, char oldValue,`
`    char newValue)`

`public void firePropertyChange(String property, double oldValue,`
`    double newValue)`

`public void firePropertyChange(String property, float oldValue,`
`    float newValue)`

`public void firePropertyChange(String property, int oldValue,`
`    int newValue)`

`public void firePropertyChange(String property, long oldValue,`
`    long newValue)`

`public void firePropertyChange(String property, short oldValue,`
`    short newValue)`

These methods differ only in the type of `oldValue` and `newValue`. Each method compares old-Value to newValue. If they differ, then the `PropertyChangeListeners` in `listenerList` are sent a `PropertyChangeEvent` for *property* (the name of a bound property), with `oldValue` and `newValue` included. A subclass of `JComponent` should use one of these methods to notify listeners of changes in bound properties.

`public AccessibleContext getAccessibleContext()`

Returns the context for this component.

`public java.awt.event.ActionListener getActionForKeyStroke(`
`    KeyStroke keystroke)`

Gets the `ActionListener` currently associated with `keystroke`. See the discussion on keystrokes above.

`public float getAlignmentX()`

Returns the horizontal alignment for this component, ranging from 0.0 (all the way left) to 1.0 (all the way right). This tells where the component should be positioned if there is leftover space.

Overrides: getAlignmentX in class `Container`.

`public float getAlignmentY()`

Returns the vertical alignment for this component, ranging from 0.0 (all the way up) to 1.0 (all the way down). This tells where the component should be positioned if there is leftover space.

Overrides: getAlignmentY in class `Container`.

`public boolean getAutoscrolls()`

Returns `true` if this component supports automatic scrolling. For example, you would like a text editor to autoscroll to a new position if you're selecting text that extends past the current window.

public Border getBorder()

Gets the border for this component. See the chapter on `swing.border`. Returns `null` if no border has been set.

public java.awt.Rectangle getBounds(Rectangle result)

Gets the bounds (position and size) for this component, sets these values in `result`, and then returns `result`.

public final Object getClientProperty(Object key)

Gets the value of the property for `key`, or `null` if none has been set.

public int getConditionForKeyStroke(KeyStroke keystroke)

Returns the constant established as the condition for `keystroke`: it will be `UNDEFINED_CONDITION`, `WHEN_ANCESTOR_OF_FOCUSED_COMPONENT`, `WHEN_FOCUSED`, or `WHEN_IN_FOCUSED_WINDOW`. See the discussion on keystrokes above.

public int getDebugGraphicsOptions()

Gets the debugging graphics options currently set. See `setDebugGraphicsOptions()` and class `DebugGraphics` (p.156) for more information.

public java.awt.Graphics getGraphics()

Gets a `Graphics` context object, so you can draw on this component.

public int getHeight()

Returns the current height in pixels of the component. This method is equivalent to (but more efficient than) `getSize ().height`.

public java.awt.Insets getInsets()

Returns the insets. If there is a border, asks the border for the insets. If not, returns the insets computed by `Container.getInsets()`.

Overrides: `getInsets` in class `Container`.

public java.awt.Insets getInsets(java.awt.Insets insets)

Attempts to reuse the passed-in `insets` object to return the insets values. Note that the returned `Insets` instance is *not* guaranteed to be the same as the one passed in so an application must still use the reference returned by this method.

public java.awt.Point getLocation(java.awt.Point result)

Gets the location (x and y) of this component, sets them in `result`, and returns `result`. If `result` is `null`, a new `Point` instance will be allocated and used.

public java.awt.Dimension getMaximumSize()

Returns the maximum size for the component. See the discussion on sizes above. If a size has been set using `setMaximumSize()`, it will be used. If the UI provides a (non-`null`) size, that will be used. Otherwise, the layout manager determines the size.

Overrides: `getMaximumSize` in class `Container`.

public java.awt.Dimension getMinimumSize()

Returns the minimum size for the component. See the discussion on sizes above. If a size has been set using `setMinimumSize()`, it will be used. If the UI provides a (non-`null`) size, that will be used. Otherwise, the layout manager determines the size.

Overrides: `getMinimumSize` in class `Container`.

public java.awt.Component getNextFocusableComponent()

Tells which component will get focus after this one (for example, if the TAB key is pressed). See `setNextFocusableComponent()` and the discussion on focus above.

public java.awt.Dimension getPreferredSize()

Returns the preferred size for the component. See the discussion on sizes above. If a size has been set using setPreferredSize(), it will be used. If the UI provides a (non-null) size, that will be used. Otherwise, the layout manager determines the size.

Overrides: getPreferredSize in class Container.

public KeyStroke[] getRegisteredKeyStrokes()

Returns an array of all keystrokes registered with this component. See the discussion on keystrokes above.

public JRootPane getRootPane()

Returns the root pane for this component. See JRootPane (p.323).

public java.awt.Dimension getSize(java.awt.Dimension result)

Gets the size (width and height) of this component, sets them in result, and returns result. If result is null, this method will allocate a new Dimension instance and return it.

public java.awt.Point getToolTipLocation(
java.awt.event.MouseEvent e)

Returns the origin for the ToolTip associated with the location of the event e. See the discussion on ToolTips above.

public String getToolTipText()

Returns the current ToolTip text for this component. See the discussion on ToolTips above.

public String getToolTipText(java.awt.event.MouseEvent e)

Returns the ToolTip text associated with event e. This allows the ToolTip to depend on the mouse location. See the discussion on ToolTips above.

public java.awt.Container getTopLevelAncestor()

Returns the top-level window or applet containing this component, or null if none does.

public String getUIClassID()

Returns "ComponentUI". This method must be overridden by any subclass that supports pluggable look and feel. Subclasses should return the string that represents the name of the ComponentUI subclass that provides the look and feel for the component. See the chapter on look and feel for more information.

public java.awt.Rectangle getVisibleRect()

Returns the visible rectangle for this component: the intersection of its bounds with those of all its ancestors. See also computeVisibleRect().

public int getWidth()

Returns the current width in pixels of the component. This method is equivalent to (but more efficient than) getSize().width.

public int getX()

Returns the *x* coordinate of the component. (0,0) is at the top left. This method is equivalent to (but more efficient than) getLocation().x.

public int getY()

Returns the *y* coordinate of the component. (0,0) is at the top left. This method is equivalent to (but more efficient than) getLocation().y.

public void grabFocus()

Used by focus managers to force this component to have the focus. (A component would usually use requestFocus to request the focus.) See the discussion on focus above.

public boolean hasFocus()

Returns true if the component currently has the focus. See the discussion on focus above.

swing

public boolean isDoubleBuffered()

Returns `true` if the component should use double buffering for its painting. (Double buffering paints first to an offscreen buffer, and then paints the offscreen buffer to the screen, to minimize flickering.) See `setDoubleBuffered()`.

public boolean isFocusCycleRoot()

Returns `true` if this component manages a focus cycle. (For example, a form might arrange for tab to move from the last subcomponent to the first one.) This returns `false` for JComponent, but a subclass might override it.

public boolean isFocusTraversable()

Returns `true` if the component is able to accept the focus. (A disabled component would return `false`.) See the discussion on focus above.

public static boolean isLightweightComponent(Component c)

Returns `true` if c is lightweight (has no peer).

public boolean isManagingFocus()

Overrides this method to `true` if your component manages its own focus. When set, the component will receive TAB key events. JComponent returns `false` by default. See the description on focus above.

public boolean isOpaque()

Returns `true` if the component is opaque (covers every pixel of its region). JComponent always returns `false`, but a subclass that promises to paint its whole area can return `true`.

public boolean isOptimizedDrawingEnabled()

Returns `true` if this component paints its components without overlap (tiles them). JComponent returns `true`, but a subclass that allows overlapping components would return `false`. Drawing is much faster if overlapping is not a possibility.

public boolean isPaintingTile()

Returns `true` during painting, if the current painting rectangle is only a tile of the whole component. On the last tile (or if tiling is not used), this method returns `false`.

public boolean isRequestFocusEnabled()

Returns `true` if a component is allowed to request the focus using `requestFocus`. You can change this value using `setRequestFocusEnabled()`. See also the discussion on focus above.

public boolean isValidateRoot()

A subclass of JComponent should return `true`, if whenever a descendant calls `revalidate()`, everything from this component down should be validated. JComponent (and most subclasses) return `false`, but JScrollPane returns `true` to support scrolling behavior. See `validate()`.

public void paint(java.awt.Graphics g)

As in AWT, `paint()` handles the display of the component. The JComponent `paint()` works a little differently. It first calls `paintComponent()`, then `paintBorder()`, then `paintChildren()`. (They are called in this order to ensure that children components appear on top.) To change the appearance of the component, override `paintComponent()`.

Overrides: paint in class Container.

public void paintImmediately(int x, int y, int width, int height)
public void paintImmediately(java.awt.Rectangle r)

Paints the component and all its descendants right away. It's usually more efficient to call `repaint()`, which will schedule a `paint()` in the future, and may be able to consolidate painting to make things even faster.

public final void putClientProperty(Object key, Object value)

Adds `value` for property `key`. Each JComponent maintains a small dictionary of property values, that other objects can use to hold information about this object. See `getClientProperty()`, `getClientProperties()`, and `setClientProperties()`.

public void registerKeyboardAction(ActionListener listener, KeyStroke keystroke, int condition)

public void registerKeyboardAction(ActionListener anAction, String aCommand, KeyStroke aKeyStroke, int aCondition)

Establishes `listener` to receive an `ActionEvent` when `keystroke` is typed, according to condition. The value for `condition` may be one of the following: `WHEN_FOCUSED`, to apply only if `keystroke` is typed while this component has focus; `WHEN_IN_FOCUSED_WINDOW`, to apply if `keystroke` is typed anywhere in the window currently having focus (regardless of the containment hierarchy); or `WHEN_ANCESTOR_OF_FOCUSED_COMPONENT`, to apply if this component or one of its contained components has the focus when `keystroke` is typed. If this exact `keystroke` already has a listener, that listener will be replaced by `listener`. See `resetKeyboardAction()`, `unregisterKeyboardAction()`, and the discussion above.

public void removeAncestorListener(AncestorListener listener)

Removes `listener` from the list of listeners for `AncestorEvents`. See `addAncestorListener()`.

public void removeNotify()

Notifies this component that it no longer has a parent. Any `KeyboardAction` set for this component will be removed from the parent.

Overrides: removeNotify in class `Container`.

public synchronized void removePropertyChangeListener(java.beans.PropertyChangeListener listener)

Removes `listener` from the list of listeners.

public synchronized void removeVetoableChangeListener(java.beans.VetoableChangeListener listener)

Removes `listener` from the list of listeners.

public void repaint(java.awt.Rectangle r)

public void repaint(long time, int x, int y, int width, int height)

Adds the rectangle (specified either way) to the list of dirty regions, and requests that a repaint be scheduled within `time` milliseconds (default 0).

public boolean requestDefaultFocus()

Attempts to set the default focus to this component, and returns `true` if it was able to accept it. A component will try to pass the focus recursively to the (first) lowest level component that will accept it. See the discussion on focus above.

public void requestFocus()

Requests the focus for this component. See the discussion on focus above.

public void resetKeyboardActions()

Removes all keystroke bindings associated with this component. See the discussion on keystrokes above.

public void reshape(int x, int y, int w, int h)

Moves and resizes this component.

Overrides: reshape in class `Component`.

public void revalidate()

First calls `invalidate()`. If the component returns `true` for `isValidateRoot()`, then the root (a `JScrollPane`-like object) will be added to a list of components to be validated (when there is a little free time in event handling). See `isValidateRoot()`.

public void scrollRectToVisible(Rectangle)

By default, `scrollRectToVisible()` is deferred to the component's parent. Components such as `JViewPort` that do scroll will override this method and perform the scrolling themselves.

public void setAlignmentX(float newAlignment)

Sets the desired horizontal alignment for this component. Argument `newalignment` may range from `0.0` (all the way left) to `1.0` (all the way right).

public void setAlignmentY(float)

Sets the desired vertical alignment for this component. Argument `newalignment` may range from `0.0` (all the way up) to `1.0` (all the way down).

public void setAutoscrolls(boolean shouldAutoscroll)

Sets whether this component should autoscroll. See `getAutoscrolls()`.

public void setBackground(java.awt.Color bg)

Sets the background color of this component.

Overrides: `setBackground` in class `Component`.

public void setBorder(Border newBorder)

Sets the border for this component. (Use `null` to indicate no border should be used.) See `getBorder()`, and the chapter on `swing.border`.

public void setDebugGraphicsOptions(int newOptions)

Sets the options for debugging of graphics. (See class `DebugGraphics` (p.156) for more information.) If `newOptions` is `DebugGraphics.NONE_OPTION`, debugging is turned off. Otherwise, the specified option is added to the current set. `DebugGraphics.LOG_OPTION` causes a text message to be written to System.out before each significant graphics activity. `DebugGraphics.FLASH_OPTION` causes the drawing to flash while drawing (so you can see components as they are painted). `DebugGraphics.BUFFERED_OPTION` causes a window to appear that shows drawing operations as they are performed on the offscreen buffer.

public void setDoubleBuffered(boolean shouldBuffer)

If set, the component should use double buffering for its painting. (Double buffering paints first to an offscreen buffer, and then paints the offscreen buffer to the screen, to minimize flickering.) If an ancestor component has a buffer available, that buffer will be used rather than a new one allocated. See `isDoubleBuffered()`.

public void setEnabled(boolean enabled)

Sets whether or not this component is enabled.

Overrides: `setEnabled` in class `Component`.

public void setFont(java.awt.Font font)

Sets the font for this component.

Overrides: `setFont` in class `Component`.

public void setForeground(java.awt.Color fg)

Sets the foreground color of this component.

Overrides: `setForeground` in class `Component`.

public void setMaximumSize(java.awt.Dimension newSize)

Sets the maximum size for this component. See the discussion on sizes above.

public void setMinimumSize(java.awt.Dimension newSize)

Sets the minimum size for this component. See the discussion on sizes above.

public void setNextFocusableComponent(java.awt.Component nextFocusedComponent)

Sets which component should get the focus after this one (for example, when the TAB key is pressed). See `getNextFocusableComponent()`, and the discussion above.

public void setOpaque(boolean isOpaque)

Returns `true` if the component's background will be filled with the background color during `update()`. The default value of this property is `false`.

public void setPreferredSize(java.awt.Dimension newSize)

Sets the preferred size for this component. See the discussion on sizes above.

public void setRequestFocusEnabled(boolean shouldAllowFocus)

Sets whether the component may use `requestFocus` to obtain focus. See also `isRequestFocusEnabled()`, and the discussion on focus above.

public void setToolTipText(String text)

Sets the ToolTip text for this component. See the discussion on ToolTips above.

public void setVisible(boolean aFlag)

Shows or hides the component.

Overrides: `setVisible` in class `Component`.

public void unregisterKeyboardAction(KeyStroke keystroke)

If there is an `ActionListener` in place for `keystroke`, removes it (effectively deactivating the keystroke for this component).

public void update(java.awt.Graphics g)

Calls `paint()` to draw the component. Unlike the AWT version, `update()` does not clear the background first—it defers this to `paintComponent()`.

Overrides: `update` in class `Container`.

public void updateUI()

Called by the `UIFactory` to notify the component that the look and feel has changed. The component needs to call `UIManager.getUI()` to determine the new UI, and `setUI()` to set it for this component.

Protected Fields

protected AccessibleContext accessibleContext

Subclasses of `JComponent` should provide the support for accessibility.

protected EventListenerList listenerList

The list of `EventListeners` for this component (to support `AncestorListener`, `PropertyChangeListener`, and `VetoableChangeListener`).

protected transient ComponentUI ui

The UI delegate for this component.

Protected Methods

protected void firePropertyChange(String property, Object oldValue, Object newValue)

This method is like the preceding `firePropertyChange` methods, except it operates on `Object` values.

protected void fireVetoableChange(String property,
    Object oldValue, Object newValue) throws PropertyVetoException

If `oldValue` and `newValue` differ, notify any `VetoableChangeListener` of a `Property-ChangeEvent`. The exception is thrown if one of the listeners vetos the change. (This is for support of Java beans' constrained properties: the property change occurs only if no listener vetos the change.)

protected java.awt.Graphics getComponentGraphics(java.awt.Graphics g)

If `debugGraphicsOptions` indicates that debugging is desired, a new `DebugGraphics` (p.156) is returned. Otherwise, g is returned.

protected void paintBorder(java.awt.Graphics g)

Called by `paint()` to paint the border for this component.

protected void paintChildren(java.awt.Graphics g)

Called by `paint()` to paint the children of this component.

protected void paintComponent(java.awt.Graphics g)

Called by `paint()` to paint the component itself. (The painting is handled by the UI if one is there is one.) Override this method to change the component's appearance.

protected String paramString()

Returns a string representation of the properties of this `JComponent`.

Overrides: `paramString` in class `Container`.

protected void processComponentKeyEvent(java.awt.event.KeyEvent e)

Processes any key events that the component itself recognizes. This will be called after the focus manager and any interested `KeyListeners` and before the look and feel keyboard support. The implementation of this method in this class does nothing. If a subclass overrides this method to process an event, it should `consume()` the event.

protected void processFocusEvent(java.awt.event.FocusEvent e)

Notifies any registered `FocusListener` about event e. Overridden to remove the overhead of thread-safety, which is unsupported in Swing.

Overrides: `processFocusEvent` in class `Component`.

protected void processKeyEvent(java.awt.event.KeyEvent e)

Notifies any registered `KeyListener` about event e. Overridden to remove the overhead of thread safety, which is unsupported in Swing.

Overrides: `processKeyEvent` in class `Component`.

protected void processMouseMotionEvent(java.awt.event.MouseEvent e)

Notifies any `MouseListeners` about event e. Overridden to remove the overhead of thread safety, which is unsupported in Swing.

Overrides: `processMouseMotionEvent` in class `Component`.

protected void setUI(ComponentUI newUI)

Sets the UI for this component. See the chapter on look and feel for more information.

Extended by AbstractButton (p.118), BasicInternalFrameTitlePane (p.597), JColorChooser (p.197), JComboBox (p.200), JFileChooser (p.239), JInternalFrame (p.254), JInternalFrame.JDesktopIcon (p.263), JLabel (p.264), JLayeredPane (p.268), JList (p.271), JMenuBar (p.288), JOptionPane (p.294), JPanel (p.305), JPopupMenu (p.309), JProgressBar (p.315), JRootPane (p.323), JScrollBar (p.328), JScrollPane (p.332), JSeparator (p.338), JSlider (p.341), JSplitPane (p.346), JTabbedPane (p.351), JTable (p.357), JTableHeader (p.752), JTextComponent (p.838), JToolBar (p.388), JToolTip (p.391), JTree (p.393), JViewport (p.410).

Returned by AncestorEvent.getComponent() (p.484),
BasicInternalFrameUI.createEastPane() (p.605), BasicInternalFrameUI.createNorthPane() (p.605),
BasicInternalFrameUI.createSouthPane() (p.605), BasicInternalFrameUI.createWestPane() (p.605),
BasicInternalFrameUI.getEastPane() (p.605), BasicInternalFrameUI.getNorthPane() (p.605),
BasicInternalFrameUI.getSouthPane() (p.605), BasicInternalFrameUI.getWestPane() (p.605),
ColorChooserComponentFactory.getPreviewPanel (p.479),
JColorChooser.getPreviewPanel() (p.197), JFileChooser.getAccessory() (p.239),
JToolTip.getComponent() (p.391).
See also AccessibleContext (p.90), AncestorEvent (p.484), AncestorListener (p.485),
Border (p.465), ComponentUI (p.530), JRootPane (p.323), KeyStroke (p.419).

swing.JComponent.AccessibleJComponent

INNER CLASS

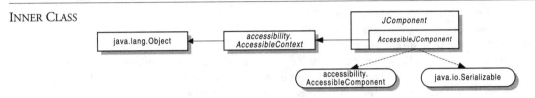

This class provides default accessibility support for Swing components.

```
public abstract class JComponent.AccessibleJComponent
    extends AccessibleContext
    implements java.io.Serializable, AccessibleComponent
```

Methods

public void addFocusListener(java.awt.event.FocusListener l)
Adds the specified focus listener to receive focus events from this component.
Implements: addFocusListener in interface AccessibleComponent.

public void addPropertyChangeListener(
java.beans.PropertyChangeListener listener)
Adds a PropertyChangeListener to the listener list.
Overrides: addPropertyChangeListener in class AccessibleContext.

public boolean contains(java.awt.Point p)
Checks whether the specified point is within this object's bounds, where p's *x* and *y* coordinates are
relative to the origin of this object.
Implements: contains in interface AccessibleComponent.

public Accessible getAccessibleAt(java.awt.Point p)
Returns the Accessible child below the given point if one exists.
Implements: getAccessibleAt in interface AccessibleComponent.

public Accessible getAccessibleChild(int i)
Returns the ith Accessible child of this object.
Overrides: getAccessibleChild in class AccessibleContext.

public int getAccessibleChildrenCount()
Returns the number of accessible children in the object.
Overrides: getAccessibleChildrenCount in class AccessibleContext.

public AccessibleComponent getAccessibleComponent()

Returns this object, since it implements AccessibleComponent.

Overrides: getAccessibleComponent in class AccessibleContext.

public java.lang.String getAccessibleDescription()

Returns a localized String describing the object from a user's perspective. This method defaults to returning accessibleDescription if it is set. Failing that, this method will return the object's ToolTip text, which may not always be appropriate.

Overrides: getAccessibleDescription in class AccessibleContext.

public int getAccessibleIndexInParent()

Gets the index of this object in its accessible parent.

Overrides: getAccessibleIndexInParent in class AccessibleContext.

public java.lang.String getAccessibleName()

Returns the accessibleName. If that is null, tries to find a TitledBorder and returns its text. If it can't find either, this method returns null.

Overrides: getAccessibleName in class AccessibleContext.

public Accessible getAccessibleParent()

Returns the accessibleParent. If that is null, and the component returned by getParent() is Accessible, this method returns the parent component. As a last resort this method returns null.

Overrides: getAccessibleParent in class AccessibleContext.

public AccessibleRole getAccessibleRole()

Returns AccessibleRole.SWING_COMPONENT.

Overrides: getAccessibleRole in class AccessibleContext.

public AccessibleStateSet getAccessibleStateSet()

Overrides: getAccessibleStateSet in class AccessibleContext.

public java.awt.Color getBackground()

Implements: getBackground in interface AccessibleComponent.

public java.awt.Rectangle getBounds()

Gets the bounds of this object in the form of a Rectangle object.

Implements: getBounds in interface AccessibleComponent.

public java.awt.Cursor getCursor()

Implements: getCursor in interface AccessibleComponent.

public java.awt.Font getFont()

Implements: getFont in interface AccessibleComponent.

public java.awt.FontMetrics getFontMetrics(java.awt.Font f)

Implements: getFontMetrics in interface AccessibleComponent.

public java.awt.Color getForeground()

Implements: getForeground in interface AccessibleComponent.

public java.util.Locale getLocale()

Overrides: getLocale in class AccessibleContext.

public java.awt.Point getLocation()

Implements: getLocation in interface AccessibleComponent.

public java.awt.Point getLocationOnScreen()

Implements: getLocationOnScreen in interface AccessibleComponent.

public java.awt.Dimension getSize()

Implements: getSize in interface AccessibleComponent.

public boolean isEnabled()

Implements: isEnabled in interface AccessibleComponent.

public boolean isFocusTraversable()

Implements: isFocusTraversable in interface AccessibleComponent.

public boolean isShowing()

Implements: isShowing in interface AccessibleComponent.

public boolean isVisible()

Implements: isVisible in interface AccessibleComponent.

public void removeFocusListener(java.awt.event.FocusListener l)

Implements: removeFocusListener in interface AccessibleComponent.

public void removePropertyChangeListener(
java.beans.PropertyChangeListener listener)

Removes a PropertyChangeListener from the listener list.

Overrides: removePropertyChangeListener in class AccessibleContext.

public void requestFocus()

Implements: requestFocus in interface AccessibleComponent.

public void setBackground(java.awt.Color c)

Implements: setBackground in interface AccessibleComponent.

public void setBounds(java.awt.Rectangle r)

Implements: setBounds in interface AccessibleComponent.

public void setCursor(java.awt.Cursor cursor)

Implements: setCursor in interface AccessibleComponent.

public void setEnabled(boolean b)

Implements: setEnabled in interface AccessibleComponent.

public void setFont(java.awt.Font f)

Implements: setFont in interface AccessibleComponent.

public void setForeground(java.awt.Color c)

Implements: setForeground in interface AccessibleComponent.

public void setLocation(java.awt.Point p)

Implements: setLocation in interface AccessibleComponent.

public void setSize(java.awt.Dimension d)

Implements: setSize in interface AccessibleComponent.

public void setVisible(boolean b)

Implements: setVisible in interface AccessibleComponent.

Protected Constructors

protected AccessibleJComponent()

Default constructor.

Protected Methods

protected String getBorderTitle(Border b)

Recursively searches through the border hierarchy (if it exists) for a TitledBorder with a non-null title. This is used in finding the accessibleName.

Extended by AbstractButton.AccessibleAbstractButton (p.125),
JComboBox.AccessibleJComboBox (p.206), JDesktopPane.AccessibleJDesktopPane (p.226),
JInternalFrame.AccessibleJInternalFrame (p.262),
JInternalFrame.JDesktopIcon.AccessibleJDesktopIcon (p.264),
JLabel.AccessibleJLabel (p.268), JLayeredPane.AccessibleJLayeredPane (p.271),
JList.AccessibleJList (p.277), JMenuBar.AccessibleJMenuBar (p.290),

JPanel.AccessibleJPanel (p.306), JPopupMenu.AccessibleJPopupMenu (p.314),
JProgressBar.AccessibleJProgressBar (p.319), JRootPane.AccessibleJRootPane (p.327),
JScrollBar.AccessibleJScrollBar (p.332), JScrollPane.AccessibleJScrollPane (p.337),
JSeparator.AccessibleJSeparator (p.340), JSlider.AccessibleJSlider (p.345),
JSplitPane.AccessibleJSplitPane (p.350), JTabbedPane.AccessibleJTabbedPane (p.356),
JTable.AccessibleJTable (p.369), JTableHeader.AccessibleJTableHeader (p.755),
JTextComponent.AccessibleJTextComponent (p.844),
JToolBar.AccessibleJToolBar (p.390), JToolTip.AccessibleJToolTip (p.393),
JTree.AccessibleJTree (p.402), JViewport.AccessibleJViewport (p.413).

swing.JComponent.AccessibleJComponent.AccessibleContainerHandler

INNER CLASS

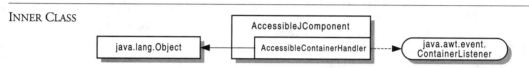

This inner class listens for `ContainerEvents` and fires `PropertyChangeEvents` when children
are added or removed.

```
protected class AccessibleContainerHandler
    extends java.lang.Object implements ContainerListener
```

Methods
`public void componentAdded(java.awt.event.ContainerEvent e)`
   Implements: componentAdded in interface ContainerListener.
`public void componentRemoved(java.awt.event.ContainerEvent e)`
   Implements: componentRemoved in interface ContainerListener.

swing.JDesktopPane

CLASS

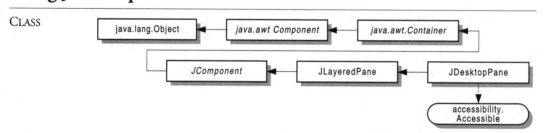

A `JDesktopPane` provides a single point of containment for a set of `JInternalFrames`. This
allows them to be related to a `DesktopManager` object. The `JInternalFrame` and `JInternal-`
`Frame.JDesktopIcon` objects should delegate their window-manipulation methods (such as
close or resize) to the `DesktopManager`.

Example: See `JInternalFrame` and `Scrollable`.

```
public class JDesktopPane extends JLayeredPane
    implements Accessible
```

Constructors
`public JDesktopPane()`

Creates desktop pane.

Methods
`public AccessibleContext getAccessibleContext()`

Gets the accessible context for this pane. See the chapter on accessibility.

`public JInternalFrame[] getAllFrames()`

Gets an array of all the internal frames associated with this desktop pane (including any minimized frames).

`public JInternalFrame[] getAllFramesInLayer(int layer)`

Gets an array of all frames at a particular layer of the desktop pane (including any minimized frames). See `JLayeredPane` for a discussion of layers.

`public DesktopManager getDesktopManager()`

Gets the desktop manager for this pane. The look and feel of a `JInternalFrame` or `JDesktopIcon` contained in the desktop manager should delegate window-handling events to the desktop manager.

`public DesktopPaneUI getUI()`

Returns the look and feel for the desktop manager.

`public String getUIClassID()`

Returns "DesktopPaneUI".

Overrides: `getUIClassID` in class `JLayeredPane`.

`public boolean isOpaque()`

Returns `true` if the the desktop pane is opaque (paints its background).

`public void setDesktopManager(DesktopManager manager)`

Sets the desktop manager for the desktop pane.

`public void setUI(DesktopPaneUI ui)`

Sets the UI (look and feel) to `ui`. See the chapter on look and feel.

`public void updateUI()`

Updates the desktop pane to the current look and feel.

Protected Methods
`protected String paramString()`

Returns a string representation of the properties of this `JDesktopPane`. The returned string may be empty but will not be `null`.

Overrides: `paramString` in class `JLayeredPane`.

Inner Classes
`protected class JDesktopPane.AccessibleJDesktopPane`

Returned by   JInternalFrame.getDesktopPane() (p.254),
JInternalFrame.JDesktopIcon.getDesktopPane() (p.263),
JOptionPane.getDesktopPaneForComponent() (p.294).

See also   Accessible (p.85), AccessibleContext (p.90), DesktopManager (p.180),
DesktopPaneUI (p.532), JInternalFrame (p.254).

swing.JDesktopPane.AccessibleJDesktopPane

INNER CLASS

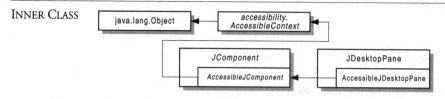

Returns a correct `AccessibleRole` for a `JDesktopPane`.

```
protected class JDesktopPane.AccessibleJDesktopPane extends
    JComponent.AccessibleJComponent
```

Methods

`public AccessibleRole getAccessibleRole()`

Returns `AccessibleRole.DESKTOP_PANE`.

Overrides: `getAccessibleRole` in class `JComponent.AccessibleJComponent`.

swing.JDialog

CLASS

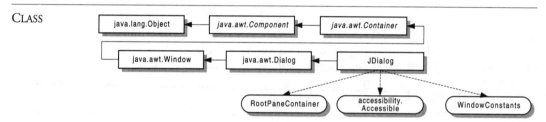

The `JDialog` is one of the basic window classes in Swing, corresponding to `Dialog` in AWT. `JDialogs` may be *modal*, in which case they block input to anything other than the dialog until the dialog is dismissed. It is important to note that if a `JDialog` is to be modal it should not contain any heavyweight components. This requirement is needed to work around a limitation in the AWT. This restriction means that `JComboBoxes`, `JPopupMenus`, and `JMenuBars` will all be forced to use lightweight components for their pop-ups. Because all pop-ups will be lightweight, a heavyweight component in the `JDialog` would overlap the pop-up when it was shown.

`JDialogs` contain a single child, a `JRootPane`. Because of this they behave slightly differently than `Dialogs`. In fact, they behave exactly the same as all other components that contain `JRootPanes`, such as `JWindow` and `JFrame`/`JInternalFrame`.

Components are not added directly to the dialog; instead, they are added to the content pane: `myDialog.getContentPane().add(component, constraints);`. The dialog will warn you at run time if you try to add directly to it. See `JRootPane` for more information on the way panes are arranged in dialogs.

A `JDialog` can control its behavior when the close box is clicked. See `getDefaultClose-Operation()` and `setDefaultCloseOperation()`.

For other types of windows, see JFrame (p.248), JInternalFrame (p.254), JOptionPane (p.294), and JWindow (p.414).

Example

```
package jdialog;

import java.awt.*;
import java.awt.event.*;
import com.sun.java.swing.*;
public class Test extends JFrame {
   JDialog d = new JDialog(this, "Dialog title", true);

   public Test() {
      addWindowListener(new WindowAdapter() {
         public void windowClosing(WindowEvent e) {
            Test.this.dispose();
            System.exit(0);
         }
      });
      d.getContentPane().add(new JLabel("Click the OK button"),
                           BorderLayout.CENTER);
      JButton closeIt = new JButton("OK");
      closeIt.addActionListener(new ActionListener() {
         public void actionPerformed(ActionEvent e) {
            System.out.println("Closing dialog");
            d.dispose();
         }
      });
      d.getContentPane().add(closeIt, BorderLayout.SOUTH);
      d.setDefaultCloseOperation(WindowConstants.DISPOSE_ON_CLOSE);
      d.pack();

      getContentPane().add(new JLabel("Placeholder label"));
      pack();
      setSize(200,200);
      setVisible(true);
      d.setVisible(true);      // Show dialog
   }
   public static void main (String[] args) {
      new Test();
   }
}
```

FAQs

What's the easiest way to create a dialog?

Use a JOptionPane.

```
public class JDialog extends java.awt.Dialog
    implements WindowConstants, Accessible, RootPaneContainer
```

Constructors

public JDialog()

Creates a default nonmodal dialog with an invisible Frame as its parent.

public JDialog(java.awt.Frame parent)

Constructs a JDialog with the given Frame as its parent. The JDialog will be created without a title and will be modeless.

public JDialog(java.awt.Frame parent, String title)

Constructs a JDialog with the given Frame as its parent and with the given title. The JDialog will be modeless.

public JDialog(java.awt.Frame parent, boolean isModal)

Constructs a JDialog with the given Frame as its parent and without a title. If isModal is true, the JDialog will be modal. Keep in mind that a modal JDialog may not contain heavyweight components.

public JDialog(java.awt.Frame parent, String title, boolean isModal)

Creates a JDialog with parent frame parent, and the given title title. If isModal is true, the JDialog will be modal. Keep in mind that a modal JDialog may not contain heavyweight components.

Methods

public AccessibleContext getAccessibleContext()

Gets the accessible context for this dialog. See the chapter on accessibility.

Implements: getAccessibleContext in interface Accessible.

public java.awt.Container getContentPane()

Gets the content pane. This is the pane to which contained objects should be added.

Implements: getContentPane in interface RootPaneContainer.

public int getDefaultCloseOperation()

Returns DISPOSE_ON_CLOSE, DO_NOTHING_ON_CLOSE, or HIDE_ON_CLOSE.

public java.awt.Component getGlassPane()

Gets the glass pane associated with this dialog.

Implements: getGlassPane in interface RootPaneContainer.

public JMenuBar getJMenuBar()

Returns the menu bar set on this dialog.

public JLayeredPane getLayeredPane()

Gets the layered pane for this dialog. This will contain the content pane.

Implements: getLayeredPane in interface RootPaneContainer.

public JRootPane getRootPane()

Gets the root pane for this dialog (the root pane contains all other panes).

Implements: getRootPane in interface RootPaneContainer.

public void setContentPane(java.awt.Container container)

Sets the content pane for this dialog. A dialog always has a content pane; attempting to set it to null will cause an error.

Implements: setContentPane in interface RootPaneContainer.

Throws: java.awt.IllegalComponentStateException if the content pane parameter is null.

public void setDefaultCloseOperation(int closeOption)

Sets the default behavior when the close box is clicked. The closeOption must be DISPOSE_ON_ CLOSE, DO_NOTHING_ON_CLOSE, or HIDE_ON_CLOSE. *Default:* HIDE_ON_CLOSE. See Window-Constants.

public void setGlassPane(java.awt.Component component)

Sets the glass pane for the dialog. This is an upper pane where pop-up menus and other floating content can be displayed.

Implements: setGlassPane in interface RootPaneContainer.

public void setJMenuBar(JMenuBar menu)

Sets the menubar for the dialog.

public void setLayeredPane(JLayeredPane layeredPane)

Sets the layered pane. This pane contains the content pane and the optional menu bar.

Implements: setLayeredPane in interface RootPaneContainer.

Throws: java.awt.IllegalComponentStateException—(a run time exception) if the layered pane parameter is null.

public void setLayout(java.awt.LayoutManager manager)

By default the layout of this component may not be set. The layout of its contentPane should be set instead. For example:

```
thisComponent.getContentPane().setLayout(new BorderLayout());
```

An attempt to set the layout of this component will cause a run-time exception to be thrown. Subclasses can disable this behavior.

Throws: java.lang.Error if called with rootPaneChecking true.

Overrides: setLayout in class java.awt.Container.

public void setLocationRelativeTo(Component component)

Sets the dialog's location to be relative to component. If component is not visible, center the dialog on the screen.

public void update(java.awt.Graphics g)

This method was overridden to prevent an unneccessary call to clear the background.

Overrides: update in class java.awt.Container.

Protected Fields

protected AccessibleContext accessibleContext

The accessible context. See the chapter on accessibility.

protected JRootPane rootPane

The root pane for the dialog. See JRootPane.

protected boolean rootPaneCheckingEnabled

If true, add() and setLayout() will throw an exception.

Protected Methods

protected void addImpl(java.awt.Component comp,
java.lang.Object constraints, int index)

By default, children may not be added directly to this component; they must be added to its contentPane instead.

Throws: java.lang.Error if called with rootPaneChecking set to true.

Overrides: addImpl in class java.awt.Container.

protected JRootPane createRootPane()

Creates the root pane for this dialog. The root pane holds the glass pane and the content pane. See JRootPane.

protected void dialogInit()

Called by the constructor to finish initializing the dialog.

protected boolean isRootPaneCheckingEnabled()

Returns true if add() and setLayout() throw exceptions when called.

protected String paramString()

Returns a string representation of the properties of this JDialog. The returned string may be empty but will not be null.

Overrides: paramString in class Dialog.

protected void processWindowEvent(WindowEvent event)

Handles window events. If the event is a window closing, it handles it according to defaultClose-Operation.

Overrides: processWindowEvent in class java.awt.Window.

protected void setRootPane(JRootPane rootPane)

Sets the root pane. This contains all the other panes of the frame.

protected void setRootPaneCheckingEnabled(boolean enable)

If enable is true, add() and setLayout() will throw exceptions when called.

Returned by JOptionPane.createDialog() (p.294).

See also Accessible (p.85), AccessibleContext (p.90), JLayeredPane (p.268), JMenuBar (p.288), JOptionPane (p.294), JRootPane (p.323), RootPaneContainer (p.433), WindowConstants (p.459).

swing.JDialog.AccessibleJDialog

INNER CLASS

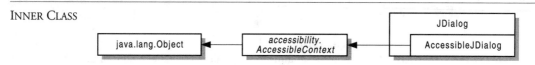

Returns a correct AccessibleRole for a JDialog. See AccessibleComponent (p.87) and AccessibleContext (p.90) for a description of the other methods.

```
protected class JDialog.AccessibleJDialog
    extends AccessibleContext
    implements java.io.Serializable, AccessibleComponent
```

Methods

public void addFocusListener(java.awt.event.FocusListener l)

Implements: addFocusListener in interface AccessibleComponent.

public boolean contains(java.awt.Point p)

Implements: contains in interface AccessibleComponent.

public Accessible getAccessibleAt(java.awt.Point p)

Implements: getAccessibleAt in interface AccessibleComponent.

public Accessible getAccessibleChild(int i)

Overrides: getAccessibleChild in class AccessibleContext.

public int getAccessibleChildrenCount()

Overrides: getAccessibleChildrenCount in class AccessibleContext.

public AccessibleComponent getAccessibleComponent()
Overrides: getAccessibleComponent in class AccessibleContext.
public int getAccessibleIndexInParent()
Overrides: getAccessibleIndexInParent in class AccessibleContext.
public java.lang.String getAccessibleName()
Overrides: getAccessibleName in class AccessibleContext.
public AccessibleRole getAccessibleRole()
Returns AccessibleRole.DIALOG.
Overrides: getAccessibleRole in class AccessibleContext.
public Accessible getAccessibleParent()
Overrides: getAccessibleParent in class AccessibleContext.
public AccessibleStateSet getAccessibleStateSet()
Overrides: getAccessibleStateSet in class AccessibleContext.
public java.awt.Color getBackground()
Implements: getBackground in interface AccessibleComponent.
public java.awt.Rectangle getBounds()
Implements: getBounds in interface AccessibleComponent.
public java.awt.Cursor getCursor()
Implements: getCursor in interface AccessibleComponent.
public java.awt.Font getFont()
Implements: getFont in interface AccessibleComponent.
public java.awt.FontMetrics getFontMetrics(java.awt.Font f)
Implements: getFontMetrics in interface AccessibleComponent.
public java.awt.Color getForeground()
Implements: getForeground in interface AccessibleComponent.
public java.util.Locale getLocale()
Overrides: getLocale in class AccessibleContext.
public java.awt.Point getLocation()
Implements: getLocation in interface AccessibleComponent.
public java.awt.Point getLocationOnScreen()
Implements: getLocationOnScreen in interface AccessibleComponent.
public java.awt.Dimension getSize()
Implements: getSize in interface AccessibleComponent.
public boolean isEnabled()
Implements: isEnabled in interface AccessibleComponent.
public boolean isFocusTraversable()
Implements: isFocusTraversable in interface AccessibleComponent.
public boolean isShowing()
Implements: isShowing in interface AccessibleComponent.
public boolean isVisible()
Implements: isVisible in interface AccessibleComponent.
public void removeFocusListener(java.awt.event.FocusListener l)
Implements: removeFocusListener in interface AccessibleComponent.
public void requestFocus()
Implements: requestFocus in interface AccessibleComponent.
public void setBackground(java.awt.Color c)
Implements: setBackground in interface AccessibleComponent.

```
public void setBounds(java.awt.Rectangle r)
```
Implements: setBounds in interface AccessibleComponent.
```
public void setCursor(java.awt.Cursor cursor)
```
Implements: setCursor in interface AccessibleComponent.
```
public void setEnabled(boolean b)
```
Implements: setEnabled in interface AccessibleComponent.
```
public void setFont(java.awt.Font f)
```
Implements: setFont in interface AccessibleComponent.
```
public void setForeground(java.awt.Color c)
```
Implements: setForeground in interface AccessibleComponent.
```
public void setLocation(java.awt.Point p)
```
Implements: setLocation in interface AccessibleComponent.
```
public void setSize(java.awt.Dimension d)
```
Implements: setSize in interface AccessibleComponent.
```
public void setVisible(boolean b)
```
Implements: setVisible in interface AccessibleComponent.

See also Accessible (p.85), AccessibleComponent (p.87), AccessibleContext (p.90), AccessibleRole (p.95), AccessibleStateSet (p.101).

swing.JEditorPane

CLASS

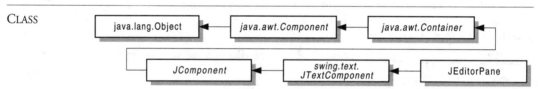

A JEditorPane is a type of text editing pane that works with various types of content. It uses an EditorKit to provide editor parts.

The model for a JEditorPane is a Document. This component (and the other text components) are different from the rest of Swing in that the model is created through an EditorKit, not directly by an application. The reason behind this is that a Document is tied very closely to the means provided to edit and display it. Since the EditorKits are what know how to modify and display a Document, they are responsible for returning an instance of the Document type they understand.

The exception to the "EditorKits create the Document" rule is when you want to create a filtered (i.e., numbers-only) Document. Since doing that requires using a Document subclass, you have to instantiate it and set it into the JEditorPane. Doing this also requires that the installed EditorKit understands the type of the installed document, so match the superclass you derived the custom Document from to its corresponding EditorKit. Generally, filtered Documents are extended from PlainDocument or DefaultStyledDocument, which correspond to Default-EditorKit and StyledEditorKit.

Using a `JEditorPane` as a web browser requires you to call `setEditable(false)` on the `JEditorPane` before loading the HTML content with `read()` or `setPage()`. If you don't call `setEditable(false)`, you will get an HTML editor which doesn't allow the user to click on links to follow them. When the `JEditorPane` is non-editable, it sends `HyperlinkEvents` to any registered `HyperlinkListeners`. If the `HyperlinkEvent` is of type `HyperlinkEvent.Event-Type.ACTIVATED`, call `setPage()` on the `JEditorPane` with the URL returned from `Hyper-linkEvent.getURL()`.

Example: See the `swing.text` package (p.769).

```
public class JEditorPane extends JTextComponent
```

Constructors
```
public JEditorPane()
public JEditorPane(String url) throws IOException
public JEditorPane(java.net.URL url) throws IOException
```
Creates an editor pane. The `url` is used to look up the initial contents of the editor; an `IOException` is thrown if the URL cannot be accessed. The type of the file named by the URL is used to configure the `EditorKit`.

```
public JEditorPane(String MIMEtype, String text)
```
A convenience constructor that calls the `setContentType()` and `setText()` methods with the provided information.

Methods
```
public synchronized void addHyperlinkListener(HyperlinkListener listener)
```
Adds `listener` to the list of objects to be notified of any hyperlink transitions.

```
public static EditorKit createEditorKitForContentType(String mimeType)
```
Returns the `EditorKit` that will be used for a particular MIME type (for example, `"text/rtf"` or `"text/html"`).

```
public static EditorKit createEditorKitForContentType(String type)
```
Returns an `EditorKit` instance appropriate for the given MIME type. `EditorKit` keeps a static registry of `EditorKit` types so that they can be cloned instead of being instantiated. If the primordial instance of a particular type of `EditorKit` has not already been loaded it will be loaded, stored in the registry, and then cloned.

```
public void fireHyperlinkUpdate(HyperlinkEvent event)
```
Notifies all hyperlink listeners that `event` has occurred. (This method is usually called by the `EditorKit`.)

```
public AccessibleContext getAccessibleContext()
```
Gets the `AccessibleContext` associated with this `JEditorPane`. A new context is created if necessary.
Overrides: `getAccessibleContext` in class `JTextComponent`.
Implements: `getAccessibleContext` in interface `Accessible`.

```
public final String getContentType()
```
Gets the MIME content type that the current editor handles (for example, `"text/rtf"`).

```
public final EditorKit getEditorKit()
```
Gets the `EditorKit` in use for the current document.

public EditorKit getEditorKitForContentType(String mimeType)

Gets the EditorKit that would be used for mimeType. First tries to locate an EditorKit set for that type previously set via setEditorKitForContent(). If there is none registered for the JEditorPane instance, it tries the class method createEditorKitForContent(). If that fails, it uses a DefaultEditorKit.

public java.net.URL getPage()

Gets the URL of the current document (or null if the document was not created using a URL and has had none assigned using setPage()).

public java.awt.Dimension getPreferredSize()

Adjusts the preferredSize to match the minimumSize when the containing JScrollPane becomes small. This is done to allow items in the Document that have a fixed minimum size to not be made smaller than that size.

Overrides: getPreferredSize in class JComponent.

public boolean getScrollableTracksViewportHeight()

If the height of the containing viewport is between the minimum and maximum heights for this component, returns true to enable scrolling.

Overrides: getScrollableTracksViewportHeight in class JTextComponent.

Implements: getScrollableTracksViewportHeight in interface Scrollable.

public boolean getScrollableTracksViewportWidth()

If the width of the containing viewport is between the minimum and maximum widths for this component, returns true to enable scrolling.

Overrides: getScrollableTracksViewportWidth in class JTextComponent.

Implements: getScrollableTracksViewportWidth in interface Scrollable.

public String getText()

Returns the text in terms of the content type of this editor. If an exception is thrown while attempting to retrieve the text, null will be returned. This method calls JTextComponent.write() with a StringWriter.

Overrides: getText in class JTextComponent.

public String getUIClassID()

Returns "EditorPaneUI".

Overrides: getUIClassID in class JComponent.

public boolean isManagingFocus()

Returns true, which turns off tab traversal once focus is gained to allow the TAB key to be used in the document.

Overrides: isManagingFocus in class JComponent.

public void read(java.io.InputStream in, Object desc) throws IOException

Initializes the JEditorPane from a stream. This method allows you to pass in an HTMLDocument for the desc parameter and if the current EditorKit is an HTMLEditorKit it will use the editor kit to read the contents into the HTMLDocument. Otherwise this method simply defers to the superclass read(Reader, Object) method.

Throws: IOException if it is thrown by the stream.

public static void registerEditorKitForContentType(String mimeType, String className)

Sets the EditorKit to be used for mimeType to be className. The class will be dynamically loaded when the first document of that type is created, and then cloned to create further instances.

public static void registerEditorKitForContentType(String type,
    String classname, java.lang.ClassLoader loader)
Sets the `EditorKit` to be used for `mimeType` to be `className`. The class will be dynamically loaded using the given `ClassLoader` when the first document of that type is created, and then cloned to create further instances.

public synchronized void removeHyperlinkListener(HyperlinkListener listener)
Removes `listener` from the list of listeners notified of hyperlink activity.

public void replaceSelection(String content)
Replaces the current selection in the document with the given `String`. When there isn't a current selection, this method inserts the text at the caret location. If `content` is empty (but *not* `null`) and there is a selection, this method effectively removes the selected text from the document. The inserted text will assume the attributes of the text at the point where it is inserted. If the document is not editable, this method beeps and does nothing further. If the document or *content* is `null`, this method does nothing. This method is thread safe.
Overrides: `replaceSelection` in class `JTextComponent`.

public final void setContentType(String mimeType)
Sets the MIME type for this document. See `getContentType()`.

public void setEditorKit(EditorKit kit)
Sets the `EditorKit` for this document.

public void setEditorKitForContentType(String mimeType, EditorKit kit)
Sets the `EditorKit` for `mimeType` to be `kit`. See `getEditorKitForContentType()`.

public void setPage(String url) throws IOException
public void setPage(URL url) throws IOException
Sets the document to edit the page identified by `url`. Depending on the document being used by the `EditorKit` this method may load the content of the URL in a background thread. If a background thread is used, this method will not throw an exception even if the loading fails.
Throws: `IOException` if the URL can't be used to read the page and the page is being loaded synchronously.

public void setText(String content)
Sets the text of this editor to the specified `content`, which should be in the format understood by the current `EditorKit`. This method is thread safe.
Overrides: `setText` in class `JTextComponent`.

Protected Methods

protected EditorKit createDefaultEditorKit()
Returns the `EditorKit` to use when one is not set either directly, or by specifying a content type.

protected java.io.InputStream getStream(java.net.URL page)
    throws IOException
Returns the stream to be used by the `setPage()` method. If this method is overridden to add additional functionality (such as adding a `ProgressMonitorInputStream`) it is also expected to set the content type and `EditorKit` correctly. The simplest way to assure this is to call `super.getStream()` and then add the additional behaviors using the returned stream where needed.

protected String paramString()
Returns a string representation of the properties of this `JEditorPane`. The returned string may be empty but it will not be `null`.
Overrides: `paramString` in class `JTextComponent`.

protected void processComponentKeyEvent(java.awt.event.KeyEvent e)

Consumes the TAB and SHIFT-TAB key events to prevent the AWT from responding to them and changing the focus when it shouldn't.

Overrides: processComponentKeyEvent in class JTextComponent.

protected void scrollToReference(String reference)

Scrolls the document so the given reference point is visible. This method only understands HTML style references (i.e., the 1984 in http://doublespeak.com/quack.html#1984). Subclasses can override this method to support other reference types.

Inner Classes

protected class JEditorPane.AccessibleJEditorPane
protected class JEditorPane.AccessibleJEditorPaneHTML
protected class JEditorPane.JEditorPaneAccessibleHypertextSupport

Extended by JTextPane (p.383).

See also Accessible (p.85), EditorKit (p.829), HyperlinkEvent (p.494), HyperlinkListener (p.495), JTextComponent (p.838), Scrollable (p.433).

swing.JEditorPane.AccessibleJEditorPane

INNER CLASS

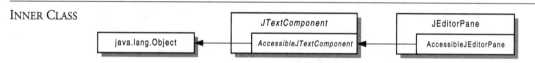

Overrides methods to behave appropriately for a JEditorPane.

protected class JEditorPane.AccessibleJEditorPane
extends AccessibleJTextComponent

Methods

public java.lang.String getAccessibleDescription()

Returns the accessibleDescription of this editor. If the accessibleDescription is null this method will return the content type of the JEditorPane.

Overrides: getAccessibleDescription in class AccessibleJComponent.

public AccessibleStateSet getAccessibleStateSet()

Adds the AccessibleState.MULTI_LINE state to the default state set.

Overrides: getAccessibleStateSet in class AccessibleJTextComponent.

Extended by JEditorPane.AccessibleJEditorPaneHTML (p.237), JEditorPane.JEditorPaneAccessibleHypertextSupport (p.237).

See also JComponent.AccessibleJComponent (p.221), JTextComponent.AccessibleJTextComponent (p.844).

swing.JEditorPane.AccessibleJEditorPaneHTML

INNER CLASS

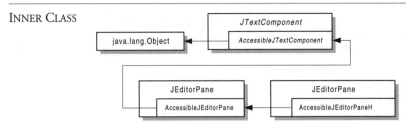

This inner class supports the `AccessibleHypertext` interface for a `JEditorPane` that is using an `HTMLEditorKit`.

```
protected class AccessibleJEditorPaneHTML
    extends JEditorPane.AccessibleJEditorPane
```

Methods

```
public AccessibleText getAccessibleText()
```
Returns the `AccessibleText` instance representing the text in the `Document`.

See also   AccessibleHypertext (p.94), AccessibleText (p.103), HTMLEditorKit (p.922).

swing.JEditorPane.JEditorPaneAccessibleHypertextSupport

INNER CLASS

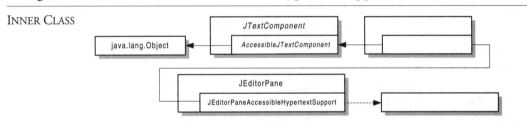

This inner class is returned by the `getAccessibleText()` method of `AccessibleJEditor-PaneHTML`.

```
protected class JEditorPaneAccessibleHypertextSupport
    extends JEditorPane.AccessibleJEditorPane
    implements AccessibleHypertext
```

Constructors

```
public JEditorPaneAccessibleHypertextSupport()
```
Default constructor.

Methods

```
public AccessibleHyperlink getLink(int linkIndex)
```
Returns the hyperlink at `linkIndex`, if it exists. Returns `null` if it does not exist.
Implements: `getLink` in interface `AccessibleHypertext`.

public int getLinkCount()
> Returns the number of hyperlinks within this document.
> *Implements:* getLinkCount in interface `AccessibleHypertext`.

public int getLinkIndex(int charIndex)
> Returns the index of the hyperlink at `charIndex`, or `-1` if there isn't a hyperlink at that offset into the document.
> *Implements:* getLinkIndex in interface `AccessibleHypertext`.

public String getLinkText(int linkIndex)
> Returns the text which is used to display the hyperlink at the given index.

Inner Classes

public class JEditorPane.JEditorPaneAccessibleHypertextSupport.HTMLLink

> *See also* AccessibleHyperlink (p.93), AccessibleHypertext (p.94).

swing.JEditorPane.JEditorPaneAccessibleHypertextSupport.HTMLLink

Inner Class

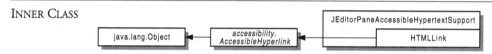

public class HTMLLink extends AccessibleHyperlink

Constructors

public HTMLLink(Element e)
> Constructs an `HTMLLink` from the text in the given `Element`.

Methods

public boolean doAccessibleAction(int i)
> Performs the specified `Action` on this object. This usually involves following the link.
> *Overrides:* doAccessibleAction in class `AccessibleHyperlink`.
> *Implements:* doAccessibleAction in interface `AccessibleAction`.

public Object getAccessibleActionAnchor(int i)
> Returns an object that visually represents the link anchor to the user. Generally this is either text or an image.
> *Overrides:* getAccessibleActionAnchor in class `AccessibleHyperlink`.

public int getAccessibleActionCount()
> Returns the number of `Action`s that can be performed on this link. For a normal link anchor there will be only one `Action`; an image map may have more than one.
> *Overrides:* getAccessibleActionCount in class `AccessibleHyperlink`.
> *Implements:* getAccessibleActionCount in interface `AccessibleAction`.

public String getAccessibleActionDescription(int i)
> Returns a `String` description of this particular link action. This is similar to getAccessible-ActionAnchor(), but for images it returns their associated text instead.
> *Overrides:* getAccessibleActionDescription in class `AccessibleHyperlink`.
> *Implements:* getAccessibleActionDescription in interface `AccessibleAction`.

public Object getAccessibleActionObject(int i)
> Returns a `java.net.URL` object that represents the link.

Overrides: getAccessibleActionObject in class AccessibleHyperlink.

public int getEndIndex()

Returns the offset into the Document where the text forming this link ends.

Overrides: getEndIndex in class AccessibleHyperlink.

public int getStartIndex()

Returns the offset into the Document where the text forming this link ends.

Overrides: getStartIndex in class AccessibleHyperlink.

public boolean isValid()

Returns true if the Document associated with this link has not changed since the reference to the link was retrieved.

Overrides: isValid in class AccessibleHyperlink.

See also   AccessibleHyperlink (p.93), Element (p.830).

swing.JFileChooser

CLASS

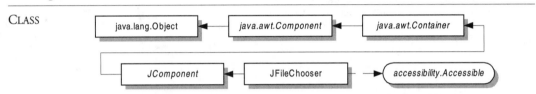

JFileChooser provides the concept of a file dialog to Swing. A JFileChooser uses three classes to provide a view of the underlying platform's filesystem. The main class of the three is a File-SystemView which understands the platform specifics of the filesystem (such as drive letters under Windows versus a single unified file system under UNIX). The other two classes are FileFilter and FileView. FileFilter can be used to restrict the types of files which will be displayed in the JFileChooser. FileView is used to handle the platform specifics of files, in particular how they should be displayed, and what information is supplied by the underlying filesystem.

It is important to note that the default classes installed as the FileSystemView and File-View are supplied by the installed look and feel.

Example

```
package jfilechooser;

import java.awt.*;
import java.io.*;
import java.awt.event.*;
import com.sun.java.swing.*;
import com.sun.java.swing.filechooser.*;

public class Frame1 extends JFrame {
    JScrollPane scroller = new JScrollPane();
    JEditorPane editor = new JEditorPane();
    JMenuBar menuBar = new JMenuBar();
    JMenu fileMenu = new JMenu();
    JMenuItem openItem = new JMenuItem();
    JMenuItem exitItem = new JMenuItem();
```

```
public Frame1() {
  this.setDefaultCloseOperation(WindowConstants.DISPOSE_ON_CLOSE);
  this.addWindowListener(new WindowAdapter() {
    public void windowClosed(WindowEvent e) {
      System.exit(0);
    }
  });
  this.setTitle("JFileChooser Example");
  fileMenu.setText("File");
  fileMenu.setMnemonic('m');
  fileMenu.setActionCommand("FILE");
  openItem.setText("Open");
  openItem.setMnemonic('o');
  openItem.setActionCommand("OPEN");
  openItem.addActionListener(new OpenHandler());

  exitItem.setText("Exit");
  exitItem.setMnemonic('x');
  exitItem.addActionListener(new ActionListener() {
    public void actionPerformed(ActionEvent e) {
      Frame1.setVisible(false);
      Frame1.dispose();
      System.exit(0);
    }
  });

  menuBar.add(fileMenu);
  fileMenu.add(openItem);
  fileMenu.addSeparator();
  fileMenu.add(exitItem);
  this.setJMenuBar(menuBar);

  this.getContentPane().add(scroller, BorderLayout.CENTER);
  scroller.getViewport().add(editor, null);

  this.setSize(new Dimension(400,300));
  this.setVisible(true);
}
public static void main(String[] args) {
  Frame1 frame11 = new Frame1();
}
/** This is the section that uses the JFileChooser.
 * It constructs a JFileChooser and then overrides the default FileFilter
 * and FileView.
 * Note that on Windows this example will cause a "please close the drive
 * door" pop-up to occur if you have a removable drive (such as a Zip
 * drive).
 * This is due to Java not having proper support for enumerating drives,
 * so the default FileSystemView on Windows makes a reasonable attempt
 * to find the drives by trying the letters C through Z.  It just
 * assumes drive A: exists.  A custom FileSystemView which uses native
 * methods to identify the drives is the only way around this in the
 */ current versions of Java.
protected class OpenHandler implements ActionListener {
  public void actionPerformed(ActionEvent e) {
    JFileChooser chooser = new JFileChooser();
```

```
         FileFilter filter = new DotFileFilter();
         chooser.setFileFilter(filter);
         FileView fileView = new LowerCaseFileView();
         chooser.setFileView(fileView);
         int returnVal = chooser.showOpenDialog(Frame1.this);

         // If the button chosen to dismiss the dialog is the "approve"
         //  button, load the file as plain text into the editor.
         if(returnVal == JFileChooser.APPROVE_OPTION) {
            try {
               editor.read(
                  new FileInputStream(chooser.getSelectedFile()), null);
            }
            catch (IOException ioe) {
            }
         }
      }
   }

// This file filter accepts directories and all files that
// do not begin with a '.', similar to how UNIX hides files
// that begin with a '.'.
protected class DotFileFilter extends FileFilter {
   public DotFileFilter() {
   }

   public boolean accept(File f) {
      if(f != null) {
         if(f.isDirectory()) {
            return true;
         }
         if(!(f.getName().startsWith("."))) {
            return true;
         }
      }
      return false;
   }

   public String getDescription() {
      return "Hides files that begin with a dot";
   }
} // end DotFileFilter
/**
 * This FileView displays all filenames as lowercase.
 */
protected class LowerCaseFileView extends FileView {
   public String getName(File f) {
      return f.getName().toLowerCase();
   }

   public String getDescription(File f) {
      return null;
   }

   public String getTypeDescription(File f) {
      return null;
```

```
        }
      public Icon getIcon(File f) {
         return null;
      }

      public Boolean isHidden(File f) {
         return Boolean.FALSE;
      }

      public Boolean isTraversable(File f) {
         if(f.isDirectory()) {
            return Boolean.TRUE;
         } else {
            return Boolean.FALSE;
         }
      }
   } // end LowerCaseFileView
} // end Frame1
```

```
public class JFileChooser extends JComponent
   implements Accessible
```

Chooser Type Fields

`public static final int OPEN_DIALOG = 0`
   Used to create an Open dialog.
`public static final int SAVE_DIALOG = 1`
   Used to create a Save dialog.
`public static final int CUSTOM_DIALOG = 2`
   Used to create a dialog that supports a custom operation, such as "Run."

Return Value Fields

`public static final int APPROVE_OPTION = 0`
   Return value if the approve (OK) button is chosen.
`public static final int CANCEL_OPTION = 1`
   Return value if the cancel button is chosen or the dialog is dismissed.
`public static final int ERROR_OPTION = -1`
   Return value if an error occured.

Chooser Display Options Fields

`public static final int DIRECTORIES_ONLY = 1`
   Used to cause the file chooser to only display directories.
`public static final int FILES_AND_DIRECTORIES = 2`
   Used to cause the file chooser to display both files and directories.
`public static final int FILES_ONLY = 0`
   Used to cause the file chooser to display only files.

Chooser Action Names Fields

`public static final String APPROVE_SELECTION = "ApproveSelection"`
   The action name used when the approve (OK) button is selected.
`public static final String CANCEL_SELECTION = "CancelSelection"`
   The action name used when the cancel button is selected.

Property Name Fields

`public static final String ACCESSORY_CHANGED_PROPERTY =`
    `"AccessoryChangedProperty"`

The property name used when the `accessoryPanel` is changed.

`public static final String APPROVE_BUTTON_MNEMONIC_CHANGED_PROPERTY =`
    `"ApproveButtonMnemonicChangedProperty"`

The property name used when the approve button's mnemonic character is changed.

`public static final String APPROVE_BUTTON_TEXT_CHANGED_PROPERTY =`
    `"ApproveButtonTextChangedProperty"`

The property name used when the approve button's text is changed.

`public static final`
    `String APPROVE_BUTTON_TOOL_TIP_TEXT_CHANGED_PROPERTY =`
    `"ApproveButtonToolTipTextChangedProperty"`

The property name used when the approve button's ToolTip text is changed.

`public static final`
    `String CHOOSABLE_FILE_FILTER_CHANGED_PROPERTY =`
    `"ChoosableFileFilterChangedProperty"`

The property name used when the list of file filters that the user can choose from is changed.

`public static final String DIALOG_TITLE_CHANGED_PROPERTY =`
    `"DialogTitleChangedProperty"`

The property name used when the chooser's title changes.

`public static final String DIALOG_TYPE_CHANGED_PROPERTY =`
    `"DialogTypeChangedProperty"`

The property name used when the type of file chooser is changed.

`public static final String DIRECTORY_CHANGED_PROPERTY = "directoryChanged"`

The property name used when the current directory is changed.

`public static final String FILE_FILTER_CHANGED_PROPERTY =`
    `"fileFilterChanged"`

The property name used when the currently selected file filter is changed.

`public static final String FILE_HIDING_CHANGED_PROPERTY =`
    `"FileHidingChanged"`

The property name used when the display of hidden files property is changed.

`public static final String FILE_SELECTION_MODE_CHANGED_PROPERTY =`
    `"fileSelectionChanged"`

The property name used when the file selection mode is changed.

`public static final String FILE_SYSTEM_VIEW_CHANGED_PROPERTY =`
    `"FileSystemViewChanged"`

The property name used when the selected file system is changed.

`public static final String FILE_VIEW_CHANGED_PROPERTY = "fileViewChanged"`

The property name used when the object used to retrieve file information is changed.

`public static final String`
    `MULTI_SELECTION_ENABLED_CHANGED_PROPERTY "fileFilterChanged"`

The property name used when multiple selection is turned on or off.

`public static final String SELECTED_FILE_CHANGED_PROPERTY =`
    `"SelectedFileChangedProperty"`

The property name used when the single selection file selection changes.

```
public static final String SELECTED_FILES_CHANGED_PROPERTY =
    "SelectedFilesChangedProperty"
```
The property name used when a change occurs in the set of multiply selected files.

Constructors

public JFileChooser()

Creates a `JFileChooser` pointing to the user's home directory.

public JFileChooser(FileSystemView fileSystemView)

Creates a `JFileChooser` using the given `FileSystemView`.

public JFileChooser(java.io.File currentDirectory)

Creates a `JFileChooser` using the given `File` as the path. Passing in a `null` file causes the file chooser to point to the user's home directory.

public JFileChooser(java.io.File currentDirectory,
FileSystemView fileSystemView)

Creates a `JFileChooser` using the given current directory and `FileSystemView`.

public JFileChooser(String currentDirectoryPath)

Creates a `JFileChooser` using the given path. Passing in a `null` string causes the file chooser to point to the user's home directory.

public JFileChooser(String currentDirectoryPath,
FileSystemView fileSystemView)

Creates a `JFileChooser` using the given current directory path and `FileSystemView`.

Methods

public boolean accept(java.io.File f)

Returns `true` if the given file will be shown, based on the current file filter.

public void addActionListener(java.awt.event.ActionListener l)

Adds an `ActionListener` to the approve and cancel buttons. The source of the event can be discovered from the `actionCommand` in the event.

public void addChoosableFileFilter(FileFilter filter)

Adds a filter to the list of user-choosable file filters.

public void approveSelection()

Causes the `JFileChooser` to act as if the approve (Open or Save) button had been pressed. This method is called by the associated `FileChooserUI` when the user presses the approve button.

public void cancelSelection()

Causes the `JFileChooser` to act as if the cancel button had been pressed.

public void changeToParentDirectory()

Changes the current directory to point to one level higher in the directory hierarchy.

public void ensureFileIsVisible(java.io.File f)

Changes the display in the `JFileChooser` (by scrolling, expanding tree nodes, etc.) to make sure that the given file is visible to the user.

public FileFilter getAcceptAllFileFilter()

Returns the `FileFilter`, which does not filter out any files.

public AccessibleContext getAccessibleContext()

Gets the `AccessibleContext` associated with this `JFileChooser`.

Overrides: `getAccessibleContext` in class `JComponent`.

Implements: `getAccessibleContext` in interface `Accessible`.

public JComponent getAccessory()

Returns the accessory component, which can be used to add extra controls (such as a preview panel) to the file chooser.

public int getApproveButtonMnemonic()

Returns the approve button's mnemonic.

public String getApproveButtonText()

Returns the text used in the approveButton (the Open or Save button) in the FileChooserUI. If null, the UI delegate will return the default String used by the look and feel.

public String getApproveButtonToolTipText()

Returns the ToolTip text used in the approveButton.

public FileFilter[] getChoosableFileFilters()

Returns an array containing the file filters the user can choose from.

public java.io.File getCurrentDirectory()

Returns the current directory.

public String getDescription(java.io.File f)

Returns the description of the given file. The return value may be null.

public String getDialogTitle()

Returns the string that is displayed in the JFileChooser's titlebar.

public int getDialogType()

Returns the type of this dialog, which will be one of the following: OPEN_DIALOG, SAVE_DIALOG, or CUSTOM_DIALOG.

public FileFilter getFileFilter()

Returns the currently selected file filter.

public int getFileSelectionMode()

Returns which kinds of Files may be selected in the chooser, which will be one of the following: FILES_ONLY, DIRECTORIES_ONLY, or FILES_AND_DIRECTORIES.

public FileSystemView getFileSystemView()

Returns the current FileSystemView being used.

public FileView getFileView()

Returns the current FileView.

public Icon getIcon(java.io.File f)

Returns the Icon to use for this file. The return value may be null.

public String getName(java.io.File f)

Returns the name of the given file.

public java.io.File getSelectedFile()

Returns the selected file.

public java.io.File[] getSelectedFiles()

Returns the list of selected files if the file chooser allows multiple selection.

public String getTypeDescription(java.io.File f)

Returns a text description of the type of the given file. The return value may be null.

public FileChooserUI getUI()

Returns the current UI delegate used for JFileChoosers.

public String getUIClassID()

Returns "FileChooserUI".

Overrides: getUIClassID in class JComponent.

public boolean isDirectorySelectionEnabled()

Returns true if directories are allowed to be selected based on the current file selection mode.

```
public boolean isFileHidingEnabled()
```
Returns `true` if hidden files are not shown in the file chooser. What defines a hidden file is controlled by the `FileView`.
```
public boolean isFileSelectionEnabled()
```
Returns `true` if files are allowed to be selected based on the current file selection mode.
```
public boolean isMultiSelectionEnabled()
```
Returns `true` if multiple selection is allowed.
```
public boolean isTraversable(java.io.File f)
```
Returns `true` if the given directory is accessible to the user.
```
public void removeActionListener(java.awt.event.ActionListener l)
```
Removes an `ActionListener` from the approve and cancel buttons.
```
public boolean removeChoosableFileFilter(FileFilter f)
```
Removes a filter from the list of user-choosable file filters.
```
public void rescanCurrentDirectory()
```
Refreshes the viewer based on the contents of the current directory.
```
public void resetChoosableFileFilters()
```
Resets the file filters list to just contain the "accept all" filter.
```
public void setAccessory(JComponent newAccessory)
```
Sets the accessory component. This component can be used to support any additional functionality you desire, such as a preview panel.
```
public void setApproveButtonMnemonic(char mnemonic)
public void setApproveButtonMnemonic(int mnemonic)
```
Sets the approve button's mnemonic.
```
public void setApproveButtonText(String approveButtonText)
```
Sets the text used in the `approveButton` in the `FileChooserUI`. If this value is set to `null`, the UI delegate will use the default text for the look and feel.
```
public void setApproveButtonToolTipText(String toolTipText)
```
Sets the ToolTip text used in the `approveButton`. If this value is set to `null`, the UI delegate will use the default text for the look and feel.
```
public void setCurrentDirectory(java.io.File dir)
```
Changes the current directory displayed to `dir`, or the parent of `dir` if `dir` is actually a file. If `dir` is inaccessible to the user (due to insufficient permissions), the current directory will be set to the nearest parent directory the user is allowed to see.
```
public void setDialogTitle(String dialogTitle)
```
Sets the string that goes in the `JFileChooser` window's title bar.
```
public void setDialogType(int dialogType)
```
Sets the type of this dialog. This parameter will usually be set through the constructor. The allowed values for dialogType are `OPEN_DIALOG`, `SAVE_DIALOG`, or `CUSTOM_DIALOG`.
```
public void setFileFilter(FileFilter filter)
```
Sets the `FileFilter`, which is used to control which files the user sees.
```
public void setFileHidingEnabled(boolean b)
```
Enables or disables the hiding of files in the `JFileChooser`. Choosing which files are to be hidden is the responsibility of the `FileView`.
```
public void setFileSelectionMode(int mode)
```
Sets the `JFileChooser` to allow the user to just select files (`FILES_ONLY`), just select directories (`DIRECTORIES_ONLY`), or select both files and directories (`FILES_AND_DIRECTORIES`).

public void setFileSystemView(FileSystemView fileSystemView)

Sets the file system view which the JFileChooser uses to access and create file system resouces, such as finding the floppy drive and getting a list of root drives.

public void setFileView(FileView fileView)

Sets the FileView, which is used to control the information displayed about a file (such as its name, description, and Icon). The FileView also controls which files are hidden if file hiding is enabled.

public void setMultiSelectionEnabled(boolean b)

Sets the JFileChooser to allow multiple selections.

public void setSelectedFile(java.io.File selectedFile)

Sets the selected file. This method calls ensureFileIsVisible() to make the selected file visible to the user.

public void setSelectedFiles(java.io.File[] selectedFiles)

Sets the list of selected files if the file chooser is set to allow multiselection.

public int showDialog(java.awt.Component parent,
String approveButtonText)

Shows a JFileChooser dialog using the given approve button text.

public int showOpenDialog(java.awt.Component parent)

Shows a JFileChooser dialog using the default "open" text (as defined by the look and feel) for the approve button.

public int showSaveDialog(java.awt.Component parent)

Shows a JFileChooser dialog using the default "save" text (as defined by the look and feel) for the approve button.

public void updateUI()

Updates the look and feel from the UIDefaults table to match the currently installed look and feel. *Overrides:* updateUI in class JComponent.

Protected Fields

protected AccessibleContext accessibleContext

The accessibleContext for the JFileChooser.

Protected Methods

protected void fireActionPerformed(String command)

Notifies all ActionListeners when a button is pressed. The command string is required because the approve and cancel buttons share this method.

protected void setup(FileSystemView view)

Performs common constructor initialization and setup.

Inner Classes

protected class JFileChooser.AccessibleJFileChooser

Returned by   BasicFileChooserUI.getFileChooser() (p.587).
See also   Accessible (p.85), AccessibleContext (p.90), FileChooserUI (p.533), FileFilter (p.518), FileSystemView (p.518), FileView (p.520), Icon (p.183), JComponent (p.207).

swing.JFileChooser.AccessibleJFileChooser

INNER CLASS

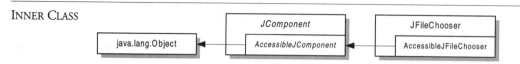

This inner class subclasses `AccessibleJComponent` to return the correct `accessibleRole` for a `JFileChooser`.

protected class JFileChooser.AccessibleJFileChooser
    extends AccessibleJComponent

Methods
public AccessibleRole getAccessibleRole()
    Returns `AccessibleRole.FILE_CHOOSER`.

See also   AccessibleRole (p.95), JComponent.AccessibleJComponent (p.221).

swing.JFrame

CLASS

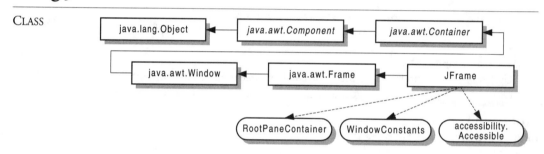

The JFrame is one of the basic window classes in Swing, corresponding to `Frame` in the AWT. Swing frames are `RootPaneContainers` like `JDialog` and `JWindow`: their child window is a `JRootPane` which consists of a content pane and the menu bar (if present), and a glass pane overlaying the whole frame. The glass pane is used for things such as pop-up menus that appear to float over the surface of the frame.

Components are not added directly to the frame; instead they are added to the content pane:

```
myFrame.getContentPane().add(component, constraints);
```

The JFrame will warn you at run time if you try to add directly to the frame (if `isRoot-PaneCheckingEnabled()`, which it is by default). See `JRootPane` for more information on the way panes are arranged in frames.

A JFrame can control its behavior when the close box is clicked. See `getDefaultCloseOperation()` and `setDefaultCloseOperation()`.

For other types of windows, see JDialog (p.226), JInternalFrame (p.254), JOptionPane (p.294), and JWindow (p.414).

Example: See almost any component example. For example, see `JMenuBar` (p.288) or `JComponent` (p.207).

FAQs

Why do I get complaints when I add components to a frame?

To support some of the new, advanced features of Swing top-level windows, you don't add directly to the window. Instead, you need to add to the `JFrame`'s `contentPane` like this:

`myWindow.getContentPane.add(component)`

See `JRootPane` (p.323) for further explanation. `JInternalFrame`, `JWindow`, and `JDialog` also behave in this way.

How do I add a menu to a JFrame?

Use `setJMenuBar(JMenu)`.

My JFrame closes when I click on the exit button, but my application doesn't exit. Why?

In Swing, the default behavior of a `JFrame` is to `HIDE_ON_CLOSE`. This means that the `JFrame` will disappear, but it never finishes closing. You have two options to fix this. You can leave things the way they are and override `WindowListener.windowClosing()` to call `dispose()` on the `JFrame` and then exit the application. Your other choice is to change the behavior by calling `setDefaultCloseOperation(JFrame.DISPOSE_ON_CLOSE)` and then overriding `Window-Listener.windowClosed()` to exit the application.

How to I get a JFrame to respect the current look and feel?

You don't, since a `JFrame` is a native window, not a lightweight Swing component. The closest you can come is to use a `JWindow` to hold a `JInternalFrame` of the same size as the `JWindow`. This is tricky to do, since you need to update the `JWindow` when the `JInternalFrame` is resized or dragged. Handling the minimization of the `JInternalFrame` is even more problematic, since you can't (yet) minimize native windows from Java.

```
public class JFrame extends java.awt.Frame
    implements WindowConstants, Accessible, RootPaneContainer
```

Fields (from WindowConstants)

```
public static final int DISPOSE_ON_CLOSE = 2
public static final int DO_NOTHING_ON_CLOSE = 0
public static final int HIDE_ON_CLOSE = 1
```

These fields describe how the window is to be handled when closed using the close box. See `WindowConstants` (p.459) for more information.

Constructors

```
public JFrame()
```

public JFrame(String title)

Builds a frame (with optional title). The frame is not visible until you call `setVisible(true)`.

Methods

public AccessibleContext getAccessibleContext()

Gets the accessible context.

Implements: `getAccessibleContext` in interface `Accessible`.

public java.awt.Container getContentPane()

Returns the content pane. This is the pane to which contained objects should be added.

Implements: `getContentPane` in interface `RootPaneContainer`.

public int getDefaultCloseOperation()

Returns `DISPOSE_ON_CLOSE`, `DO_NOTHING_ON_CLOSE`, or `HIDE_ON_CLOSE`.

public java.awt.Component getGlassPane()

Returns the glass pane associated with this frame.

Implements: `getGlassPane` in interface `RootPaneContainer`.

public JMenuBar getJMenuBar()

Returns the menu bar associated with this frame (or `null` if not present).

public JLayeredPane getLayeredPane()

Returns the layered pane for this frame. This will contain the content pane and, optionally, the menu bar.

Implements: `getLayeredPane` in interface `RootPaneContainer`.

public JRootPane getRootPane()

Returns the root pane for this frame. It contains all panes. See `JRootPane`.

public void setContentPane(java.awt.Container container)

Sets the content pane for this frame. A frame always has a content pane; attempting to set it to `null` will cause an error.

Throws: `java.awt.IllegalComponentStateException` if the content pane parameter is `null`.

Implements: `setContentPane` in interface `RootPaneContainer`.

public void setDefaultCloseOperation(int closeOption)

Sets the default behavior when the close box is clicked. The `closeOption` must be `DISPOSE_ON_CLOSE`, `DO_NOTHING_ON_CLOSE`, or `HIDE_ON_CLOSE`. Default: `HIDE_ON_CLOSE`. See `Window-Constants`.

public void setGlassPane(java.awt.Component component)

Sets the glass pane for the frame. This is an upper pane where pop-up menus and other floating content can be displayed.

Implements: `setGlassPane` in interface `RootPaneContainer`.

public void setJMenuBar(JMenuBar menubar)

Sets the menu bar for this frame. If present, the menu bar is managed by the content pane. See `JRootPane`.

public void setLayeredPane(JLayeredPane layeredPane)

Sets the layered pane. This pane contains the content pane and the optional menu bar.

Throws: `java.awt.IllegalComponentStateException` if the layered pane parameter is `null`.

Implements: `setLayeredPane` in interface `RootPaneContainer`.

public void setLayout(java.awt.LayoutManager manager)

By default the layout of this component may not be set; the layout of its contentPane should be set instead. For example:

```
thisComponent.getContentPane().setLayout(new BorderLayout())
```

An attempt to set the layout of this component will cause a run-time exception to be thrown. Subclasses can disable this behavior.

Throws: java.lang.Error if called with rootPaneChecking true.

Overrides: setLayout in class Container.

public void update(java.awt.Graphics gr)

Overridden to simply call paint(), since drawing the background is handled as part of the normal painting process.

Overrides: update in class Container.

Protected Fields

protected AccessibleContext accessibleContext

The accessible context. See the chapter on accessibility.

protected JRootPane rootPane

The root pane for this frame.

protected boolean rootPaneCheckingEnabled

Set to true if the frame can have children added. This is used to enforce the constraint that components be added to the content pane only.

Protected Methods

protected void addImpl(java.awt.Component component,
   Object constraint, int index)

Adds component at index, according to constraint. This enforces the content pane constraint.

Throws: java.lang.Error if called with rootPaneChecking true.

Overrides: addImpl in class Container.

protected JRootPane createRootPane()

Creates the root pane for this frame. See JRootPane.

protected void frameInit()

Called by the constructors to complete initialization of the frame.

protected boolean isRootPaneCheckingEnabled()

Returns whether calls to add and setLayout cause an exception to be thrown.

protected String paramString()

Returns a string representation of the properties of this JFrame. The returned string may be empty but will not be null.

Overrides: paramString in class Frame.

protected void processKeyEvent(java.awt.event.KeyEvent event)

Handles keystrokes for this frame.

Overrides: processKeyEvent in class Component.

protected void processWindowEvent(
   java.awt.event.WindowEvent event)

Handles window events. If the event is a window closing, handles it according to defaultClose-Operation.

Overrides: processWindowEvent in class Window.

protected void setRootPane(JRootPane rootPane)
> Sets the root pane. This contains all the other panes of the frame.

protected void setRootPaneCheckingEnabled(boolean enabled)
> Determines whether calls to add and setLayout cause an exception to be thrown.

Returned by   BasicToolBarUI.createFloatingFrame() (p.702).

See also   Accessible (p.85), JLayeredPane (p.268), JMenuBar (p.288), JRootPane (p.323), RootPaneContainer (p.433).

swing.JFrame.AccessibleJFrame

INNER CLASS

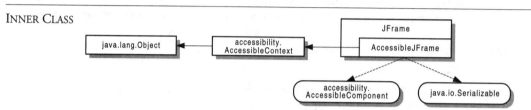

Returns a correct AccessibleRole for this component

protected class JFrame.AccessibleJFrame extends AccessibleContext
  implements java.io.Serializable, AccessibleComponent

Methods
public void addFocusListener(java.awt.event.FocusListener l)
> *Implements:* addFocusListener in interface AccessibleComponent.

public boolean contains(java.awt.Point p)
> *Implements:* contains in interface AccessibleComponent.

public Accessible getAccessibleAt(java.awt.Point p)
> *Implements:* getAccessibleAt in interface AccessibleComponent.

public Accessible getAccessibleChild(int i)
> *Overrides:* getAccessibleChild in class AccessibleContext.

public int getAccessibleChildrenCount()
> *Overrides:* getAccessibleChildrenCount in class AccessibleContext.

public AccessibleComponent getAccessibleComponent()
> *Overrides:* getAccessibleComponent in class AccessibleContext.

public int getAccessibleIndexInParent()
> *Overrides:* getAccessibleIndexInParent in class AccessibleContext.

public java.lang.String getAccessibleName()
> *Overrides:* getAccessibleName in class AccessibleContext.

public AccessibleRole getAccessibleRole()
> Returns AccessibleRole.FRAME.
> *Overrides:* getAccessibleRole in class AccessibleContext.

public Accessible getAccessibleParent()
> *Overrides:* getAccessibleParent in class AccessibleContext.

public AccessibleStateSet getAccessibleStateSet()
> *Overrides:* getAccessibleStateSet in class AccessibleContext.

public java.awt.Color getBackground()
> *Implements:* getBackground in interface AccessibleComponent.

```
public java.awt.Rectangle getBounds()
```
Implements: getBounds in interface AccessibleComponent.
```
public java.awt.Cursor getCursor()
```
Implements: getCursor in interface AccessibleComponent.
```
public java.awt.Font getFont()
```
Implements: getFont in interface AccessibleComponent.
```
public java.awt.FontMetrics getFontMetrics(java.awt.Font f)
```
Implements: getFontMetrics in interface AccessibleComponent.
```
public java.awt.Color getForeground()
```
Implements: getForeground in interface AccessibleComponent.
```
public java.util.Locale getLocale()
```
Overrides: getLocale in class AccessibleContext.
```
public java.awt.Point getLocation()
```
Implements: getLocation in interface AccessibleComponent.
```
public java.awt.Point getLocationOnScreen()
```
Implements: getLocationOnScreen in interface AccessibleComponent.
```
public java.awt.Dimension getSize()
```
Implements: getSize in interface AccessibleComponent.
```
public boolean isEnabled()
```
Implements: isEnabled in interface AccessibleComponent.
```
public boolean isFocusTraversable()
```
Implements: isFocusTraversable in interface AccessibleComponent.
```
public boolean isShowing()
```
Implements: isShowing in interface AccessibleComponent.
```
public boolean isVisible()
```
Implements: isVisible in interface AccessibleComponent.
```
public void removeFocusListener(java.awt.event.FocusListener l)
```
Implements: removeFocusListener in interface AccessibleComponent.
```
public void requestFocus()
```
Implements: requestFocus in interface AccessibleComponent.
```
public void setBackground(java.awt.Color c)
```
Implements: setBackground in interface AccessibleComponent.
```
public void setBounds(java.awt.Rectangle r)
```
Implements: setBounds in interface AccessibleComponent.
```
public void setCursor(java.awt.Cursor cursor)
```
Implements: setCursor in interface AccessibleComponent.
```
public void setEnabled(boolean b)
```
Implements: setEnabled in interface AccessibleComponent.
```
public void setFont(java.awt.Font f)
```
Implements: setFont in interface AccessibleComponent.
```
public void setForeground(java.awt.Color c)
```
Implements: setForeground in interface AccessibleComponent.
```
public void setLocation(java.awt.Point p)
```
Implements: setLocation in interface AccessibleComponent.
```
public void setSize(java.awt.Dimension d)
```
Implements: setSize in interface AccessibleComponent.

```
public void setVisible(boolean b)
```
Implements: setVisible in interface AccessibleComponent.

See also   Accessible (p.85), AccessibleComponent (p.87), AccessibleContext (p.90), AccessibleRole (p.95), AccessibleStateSet (p.101).

swing.JInternalFrame

CLASS

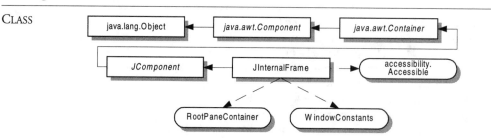

An internal frame is a type of window that can be contained within a desktop area. This is sometimes called an MDI (Multiple Document Interface) style user interface. A text editor might use this approach: a large window (a JFrame, for example) contains the JMenuBar and a JDesktopPane, and each document being edited is given a JInternalFrame within the JDesktopPane.

An internal frame can behave much like a normal JFrame: it may be closed, resized, minimized (iconified), or maximized. Each internal frame may be at a particular layer in the JDesktopPane. A JInternalFrame uses root panes and content panes like other Swing "top level" windows.

The major difference between a JInternalFrame and a JFrame is that an internal frame is a lightweight object while a JFrame is heavyweight. This allows the internal frame to have a UI delegate and to be properly contained in a Swing container like a JDesktopPane or a JScrollPane.

JInternalFrames will usually be contained in a JDesktopPane.

JInternalFrame Beans properties

Property	Type	Property Type
contentPane	java.awt.Container	Bound
glassPane	java.awt.Component	Bound
isClosed	boolean	Constrained
isIcon	boolean	Constrained
isMaximum	boolean	Constrained
isSelected	boolean	Constrained
layeredPane	JLayeredPane	Bound
menuBar	JMenuBar	Bound
rootPane	JRootPane	Bound
title	String	Bound

Example

```java
// File jinternalfrm/Main.java
package jinternalfrm;

import java.awt.*;
import java.awt.event.*;
import com.sun.java.swing.*;

public class Main extends JFrame {
  public Main() {
    addWindowListener(new WindowAdapter() {
      public void windowClosing(WindowEvent e) {
        Main.this.dispose();
        System.exit(0);
      }
    });

    JDesktopPane desk = new JDesktopPane();
    desk.setPreferredSize (new Dimension(1000, 1000));
    getContentPane().add (new JScrollPane(desk), BorderLayout.CENTER);

    JInternalFrame f1 = new JInternalFrame ("Frame 1");
    f1.getContentPane().add(new JLabel("This is frame f1"));
    f1.setResizable(true);
    f1.pack();
    f1.setVisible(true);
    desk.add(f1, new Integer(10)); // Layer 10

    JInternalFrame f2 = new JInternalFrame("Frame 2");
    f2.getContentPane().add (new JLabel("Content for f2"));
    f2.setResizable(true);
    f2.pack();
    f2.setVisible(true);
    desk.add(f2, new Integer(20)); // Layer 20 (above 10)

    JInternalFrame f3 = new JInternalFrame("Frame 3");
    f3.getContentPane().add (new JLabel("Content for f3"));
    f3.setResizable(true);
    f3.pack();
    f3.setVisible(true);
    desk.add(f3, new Integer(20));
    f3.toFront();
    try {
      f3.setSelected(true);
    }
    catch (java.beans.PropertyVetoException ignored) {
    }
    pack();
    setSize(300, 300);
    setVisible(true);
  }
  public static void main (String arg[]) {
    new Main();
  }
}
```

```
public class JInternalFrame extends JComponent
    implements Accessible, WindowConstants, RootPaneContainer
```

Fields

```
public static final String CONTENT_PANE_PROPERTY = "contentPane"
public static final String FRAME_ICON_PROPERTY = "frameIcon"
public static final String GLASS_PANE_PROPERTY = "glassPane"
public static final String LAYERED_PANE_PROPERTY "layeredPane"
public static final String MENU_BAR_PROPERTY = "menuBar"
public static final String ROOT_PANE_PROPERTY = "rootPane"
public static final String TITLE_PROPERTY = "title"
```
Property names for the bound properties.
```
public static final String IS_CLOSED_PROPERTY = "isClosed"
public static final String IS_ICON_PROPERTY = "isIcon"
public static final String IS_MAXIMUM_PROPERTY = "isMaximum"
public static final String IS_SELECTED_PROPERTY = "isSelected"
```
Property names for the constrained (vetoable) properties.

Constructors

```
public JInternalFrame()
public JInternalFrame(String title)
public JInternalFrame(String title, boolean mayResize)
public JInternalFrame(String title, boolean mayResize, boolean mayClose)
public JInternalFrame(String title, boolean mayResize,
    boolean mayClose, boolean mayMaximize)
public JInternalFrame(String title, boolean mayResize,
    boolean mayClose, boolean mayMaximize, boolean mayIconify)
```
Creates an internal frame. The title defaults to an empty string; the boolean values default to `false`.

Methods

```
public synchronized void addInternalFrameListener(InternalFrameListener l)
```
Adds the specified internal frame listener to receive internal frame events from this internal frame.
```
public void dispose()
```
Disposes of this internal frame. If the frame is not already closed, a `windowClosing` event is posted.
```
public AccessibleContext getAccessibleContext()
```
Returns the accessible context for the internal frame.

Overrides: `getAccessibleContext` in class `JComponent`.

Implements: `getAccessibleContext` in interface `Accessible`.
```
public java.awt.Color getBackground()
```
Gets the background color of the internal frame.

Overrides: `getBackground` in class `Component`.
```
public java.awt.Container getContentPane()
```
Creates the content pane associated with the internal frame. See `JRootPane` for a discussion of how panes work with windowlike objects. The content pane is the one to which components should usually be added.

Implements: `getContentPane` in interface `RootPaneContainer`.
```
public int getDefaultCloseOperation()
```
Returns the default operation which occurs when the user initiates a `close` on this window.

public JInternalFrame.JDesktopIcon getDesktopIcon()

Gets the icon used when the frame is minimized. (See `getFrameIcon()` for the icon in the upper left-hand corner of the frame's window.)

public JDesktopPane getDesktopPane()

Gets the `JDesktopPane` associated with the internal frame.

public java.awt.Color getForeground()

Gets the foreground color associated with this frame.

Overrides: `getForeground` in class `Component`.

public Icon getFrameIcon()

Gets the icon used in the upper left-hand corner of the window for the internal frame. (See `get-DesktopIcon()` for the icon used when the frame is minimized.)

public java.awt.Component getGlassPane()

Gets the glass pane associated with this internal frame. See `JRootPane` for more information.

Implements: `getGlassPane` in interface `RootPaneContainer`.

public JMenuBar getJMenuBar()

Gets the menu bar associated with the internal frame.

public int getLayer()

Gets the layer of this frame. See `JLayeredPane`.

public JLayeredPane getLayeredPane()

Gets the layered pane associated with the internal frame. See `JLayeredPane` and `JRootPane` for more information.

Implements: `getLayeredPane` in interface `RootPaneContainer`.

public JMenuBar getMenuBar()

Deprecated. Use `getJMenuBar()`.

public JRootPane getRootPane()

Gets the root pane for the internal frame. See `JRootPane` for more information.

Overrides: `getRootPane` in class `JComponent`.

Implements: `getRootPane` in interface `RootPaneContainer`.

public String getTitle()

Gets the title of the internal frame.

public InternalFrameUI getUI()

Gets the the UI (look and feel) associated with this internal frame.

public String getUIClassID()

Returns "InternalFrameUI".

Overrides: `getUIClassID` in class `JComponent`.

public final String getWarningString()

Gets the warning string that is displayed with this window when it is shown in a browser. Since an internal frame is always fully contained within a window which might need a warning string, this method always returns `null`.

public boolean isClosable()

Returns `true` if the internal frame may be closed.

public boolean isClosed()

Returns `true` if the internal frame is currently closed.

public boolean isIcon()

Returns `true` if the internal frame is minimized.

public boolean isIconifiable()

Returns `true` if the internal frame can be minimized.

public boolean isMaximizable()

Returns `true` if the internal frame can be maximized.

public boolean isMaximum()

Returns `true` if the internal frame is currently maximized.

public boolean isResizable()

Returns `true` if the internal frame may be resized.

public boolean isSelected()

Returns `true` if the internal frame is currently selected.

public void moveToBack()

Moves the internal frame to the back of all the internal frames contained in its parent `JLayered-Pane` (if that's what its parent is).

public void moveToFront()

Moves the internal frame to the front of all the internal frames contained in its parent `JLayered-Pane` (if that's what its parent is).

public void pack()

Lays out the components in the internal frame.

**public synchronized void removeInternalFrameListener(
InternalFrameListener l)**

Removes the specified internal frame listener so that it no longer receives internal frame events from this internal frame.

public void reshape(int x, int y, int width, int height)

Resizes the internal frame to the indicated position and size. This method also causes a relayout to update the title and menu bars.

Overrides: `reshape` in class `JComponent`.

public void setBackground(java.awt.Color color)

Sets the background color for this internal frame.

Overrides: `setBackground` in class `JComponent`.

public void setClosable(boolean mayClose)

Sets whether the internal frame may be closed.

public void setClosed(boolean doClose) throws PropertyVetoException

Attempts to close the internal frame, subject to veto.

Throws: `PropertyVetoException` when the attempt to set the property is vetoed by one of the listeners.

public void setContentPane(Container container)

Sets the content pane for the internal frame. It may not be set to `null`. Components for display should be added to the content pane, not directly to the internal frame. See `JRootPane`.

Throws: `IllegalComponentStateException` if the content pane parameter is `null`.

Implements: `setContentPane` in interface `RootPaneContainer`.

public void setDefaultCloseOperation(int operation)

Sets the operation which will happen by default when the user initiates a close on this window. The possible choices are `DO_NOTHING_ON_CLOSE`, `HIDE_ON_CLOSE`, or `DISPOSE_ON_CLOSE`. The default value is `HIDE_ON_CLOSE`.

public void setDesktopIcon(JInternalFrame.JDesktopIcon icon)

Sets the icon used when the frame is minimized (see setFrameIcon() for the icon used in the upper left-hand corner of the internal frame's window).

public void setForeground(java.awt.Color color)

Sets the foreground color for the internal frame.

Overrides: setForeground in class JComponent.

public void setFrameIcon(Icon icon)

Sets the icon in the upper left-hand corner of the internal frame's window. (See setDesktop-Icon() for the icon used when the frame is minimized.)

public void setGlassPane(Component component)

Sets the glass pane used by the internal frame. See JRootPane.

Implements: setGlassPane in interface RootPaneContainer.

public void setIcon(boolean doIconify)
throws PropertyVetoException

Attempts to minimize the internal frame, subject to veto.

Throws: PropertyVetoException when the attempt to set the property is vetoed by one of the listeners.

public void setIconifiable(boolean mayIconify)

Sets whether the internal frame may be minimized.

public void setJMenuBar(JMenuBar b)

Sets the menu for this JInternalFrame.

public void setLayer(Integer layer)

Sets the layer number for this frame. (See JLayeredPane for typical values for layer.)

public void setLayeredPane(JLayeredPane layeredPane)

Sets the JLayeredPane that will be used by the internal frame. (See JRootPane for a discussion of how the panes are arranged.)

Throws: IllegalComponentStateException if the layered pane parameter is null.

Implements: setLayeredPane in interface RootPaneContainer.

public void setLayout(java.awt.LayoutManager manager)

By default the layout of this component may not be set; the layout of its contentPane should be set instead. For example:

```
thisComponent.getContentPane().setLayout(new BorderLayout());
```

An attempt to set the layout of this component will cause a run-time exception to be thrown. Subclasses can disable this behavior.

Throws: Error if called with rootPaneChecking true.

Overrides: setLayout in class Container.

public void setMaximizable(boolean mayMaximize)

Sets whether the internal frame may be maximized.

public void setMaximum(boolean doMaximize) throws PropertyVetoException

Attempts to maximize the internal frame, subject to veto.

Throws: PropertyVetoException when the attempt to set the property is vetoed by one of the listeners.

public void setMenuBar(JMenuBar menubar)

Deprecated. Use setJMenuBar().

public void setResizable(boolean mayResize)

Sets whether the internal frame may be resized.

public void setSelected(boolean doSelect) throws PropertyVetoException

Attempts to select the internal frame, subject to veto.

Throws: PropertyVetoException when the attempt to set the property is vetoed by one of the listeners.

public void setTitle(String title)

Sets the title for this internal frame.

public void setUI(InternalFrameUI ui)

Sets the UI (look and feel) for this internal frame to ui.

public void setVisible(boolean b)

Sets the visible state of the object.

Overrides: setVisible in class JComponent.

public void show()

Shows this internal frame, and brings it to the front. If this window is not yet visible, show makes it visible. If this window is already visible, then this method brings it to the front.

Overrides: show in class Component.

public void toBack()

Sends this internal frame to the back. Places this internal frame at the bottom of the stacking order and makes the corresponding adjustment to other visible windows.

public void toFront()

Brings this internal frame to the front. Places this internal frame at the top of the stacking order and makes the corresponding adjustment to other visible windows.

public void updateUI()

Tells the internal frame to update itself to use the current look and feel.

Overrides: updateUI in class JComponent.

Protected Fields

protected boolean closable

Set to true if the internal frame may be closed.

protected JInternalFrame.JDesktopIcon desktopIcon

The desktop icon associated with this internal frame. (This is the icon shown when the frame is minimized.)

protected Icon frameIcon

The icon to use while the frame is not minimized. Where this icon appears depends on the look and feel. For example, in Metal/Java and Windows, the icon is in the top left-hand corner.

protected boolean iconable

Returns true if the internal frame may be minimized (iconified).

protected boolean isClosed

Returns true if the internal frame is currently closed.

protected boolean isIcon

Returns true if the internal frame is iconified.

protected boolean isMaximum

Returns true if the internal frame is currently maximized.

protected boolean isSelected

Returns true if the internal frame is currently selected.

protected boolean maximizable

Returns true if the internal frame is permitted to be maximized (and has a maximization box).

protected boolean resizable

Returns `true` if the frame is permitted to be resized.

protected JRootPane rootPane

The root pane of the internal frame. (See `JRootPane`.)

protected boolean rootPaneCheckingEnabled

If `true`, then calls to `add` and `setLayout` cause an exception to be thrown.

protected String title

The title of the internal frame.

Protected Methods

protected void addImpl(java.awt.Component comp, Object constraints, int index)

By default, children may not be added directly to this component; they must be added to its `contentPane` instead. For example:

```
thisComponent.getContentPane().add(child)
```

An attempt to add directly to this component will cause a run-time exception to be thrown. Subclasses can disable this behavior.

Throws: `Error` if called with `rootPaneChecking` true.

Overrides: `addImpl` in class `Container`.

protected JRootPane createRootPane()

Creates the root pane associated with the internal frame. See `JRootPane` for a discussion of how panes work with windowlike objects.

protected void fireInternalFrameEvent(int id)

Fires an event when the state of this internal frame changes.

protected boolean isRootPaneCheckingEnabled()

Returns whether calls to `add` and `setLayout` cause an exception to be thrown.

protected String paramString()

Returns a string representation of the properties of this `JInternalFrame`. The returned string may be empty but will not be `null`.

Overrides: `paramString` in class `JComponent`.

protected void setRootPane(JRootPane root)

Sets the `rootPane` property. This method is called by the constructor.

protected void setRootPaneCheckingEnabled(boolean enabled)

Determines whether calls to `add` and `setLayout` cause an exception to be thrown.

Returned by   JDesktopPane.getAllFrames() (p.224),
JDesktopPane.getAllFramesInLayer() (p.224),
JInternalFrame.JDesktopIcon.getInternalFrame() (p.263),
JOptionPane.createInternalFrame() (p.294).

See also   DesktopManager (p.180), Icon (p.183), InternalFrameUI (p.535),
JComponent (p.207), JDesktopPane (p.224), JInternalFrame.JDesktopIcon (p.263),
JLayeredPane (p.268), JMenuBar (p.288), JRootPane (p.323), RootPaneContainer (p.433),
WindowConstants (p.459).

swing.JInternalFrame.AccessibleJInternalFrame

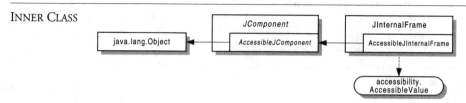

Returns a correct `AccessibleRole` for a `JInternalFrame`, and provides accessibility support for inspecting and modifying the `JInternalFrame`'s layer property.

```
protected class JInternalFrame.AccessibleJInternalFrame
    extends JComponent.AccessibleJComponent
    implements AccessibleValue
```

Methods

public java.lang.String getAccessibleName()
> Tries to return the `accessibleName`. If that is `null`, tries to return the window's `title`.
> *Overrides:* `getAccessibleName` in class `JComponent.AccessibleJComponent`.

public AccessibleRole getAccessibleRole()
> Returns `AccessibleRole.INTERNAL_FRAME`.
> *Overrides:* `getAccessibleRole` in class `JComponent.AccessibleJComponent`.

public AccessibleValue getAccessibleValue()
> Returns `this`.
> *Overrides:* `getAccessibleValue` in class `AccessibleContext`.

public java.lang.Number getCurrentAccessibleValue()
> Returns the layer the `JInternalFrame` is in.
> *Implements:* `getCurrentAccessibleValue` in interface `AccessibleValue`.

public boolean setCurrentAccessibleValue(java.lang.Number n)
> If `n` is an Integer, sets the layer property of the `JInternalFrame`.
> *Implements:* `setCurrentAccessibleValue` in interface `AccessibleValue`.

public java.lang.Number getMaximumAccessibleValue()
> Returns `Integer.MAX_VALUE`.
> *Implements:* `getMaximumAccessibleValue` in interface `AccessibleValue`.

public java.lang.Number getMinimumAccessibleValue()
> Returns `Integer.MIN_VALUE`.
> *Implements:* `getMinimumAccessibleValue` in interface `AccessibleValue`.

See also   AccessibleContext (p.90), AccessibleRole (p.95), AccessibleValue (p.104), JComponent.AccessibleJComponent (p.221).

swing.JInternalFrame.JDesktopIcon

INNER CLASS

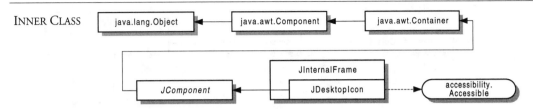

This class represents the minimized form of a `JInternalFrame`. This class is used by the look and feel classes. There is no reason to use it directly, since the only configurable item, the icon, can be set through the `setDesktopIcon()` method in `JInternalFrame`.

```
public static class JInternalFrame.JDesktopIcon extends JComponent
    implements Accessible
```

Constructor

`public JDesktopIcon(JInternalFrame f)`

Creates a desktop icon for an internal frame.

Methods

`public AccessibleContext getAccessibleContext()`

Implements: getAccessibleContext in interface `Accessible`.

Overrides: getAccessibleContext in class `JComponent`.

`public JDesktopPane getDesktopPane()`

Returns the utility method for finding the desktop which contains the desktop icon.

`public JInternalFrame getInternalFrame()`

Returns the `JInternalFrame` associated with this desktop icon.

`public DesktopIconUI getUI()`

Returns the UI delegate for this class.

`public java.lang.String getUIClassID()`

Returns "DesktopIconUI".

Overrides: getUIClassID in class `JComponent`.

`public void setInternalFrame(JInternalFrame f)`

Changes the `JInternalFrame` this desktop icon is associated with.

`public void setUI(DesktopIconUI ui)`

Sets the UI delegate for this class.

`public void updateUI()`

Overrides: updateUI in class `JComponent`.

See also   DesktopIconUI (p.531), JComponent (p.207), JDesktopPane (p.224),
JInternalFrame (p.254).

swing.JInternalFrame.JDesktopIcon.AccessibleJDesktopIcon

INNER CLASS

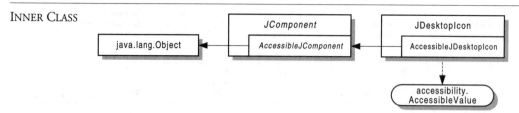

```
protected class JInternalFrame.JDesktopIcon.AccessibleJDesktopIcon
    extends JComponent.AccessibleJComponent
    implements AccessibleValue
```

Methods

`public AccessibleRole getAccessibleRole()`
Returns `AccessibleRole.DESKTOP_ICON`.
Overrides: `getAccessibleRole` in class `AccessibleJComponent`.

`public AccessibleValue getAccessibleValue()`
Overrides: `getAccessibleValue` in class `AccessibleContext`.

`public java.lang.Number getCurrentAccessibleValue()`
Returns the layer of the desktop that contains the `JDesktopIcon`.
Implements: `getCurrentAccessibleValue` in interface `AccessibleValue`.

`public boolean setCurrentAccessibleValue(java.lang.Number n)`
Implements: `setCurrentAccessibleValue` in interface `AccessibleValue`.

`public java.lang.Number getMaximumAccessibleValue()`
Implements: `getMaximumAccessibleValue` in interface `AccessibleValue`.

`public java.lang.Number getMinimumAccessibleValue()`
Implements: `getMinimumAccessibleValue` in interface `AccessibleValue`.

See also AccessibleContext (p.90), AccessibleRole (p.95), AccessibleValue (p.104), JComponent.AccessibleJComponent (p.221).

swing.JLabel

CLASS

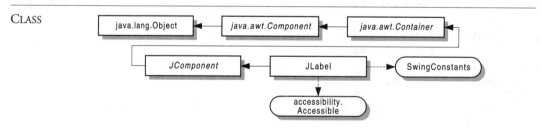

A label is an icon, text, or both. It is not active—it does not receive events. It may have a mnemonic character, in which case the component defined using the `setLabelFor()` method will get the focus.

The position of the icon and/or text relative to the label as a whole and to each other can be controlled.

It is useful to note that a JLabel is non-opaque by default, so calling setBackground() doesn't appear to do anything. To show the changed background color you need to call setOpaque(true) on the JLabel.

Example

```
package jlabel;

import java.awt.*;
import java.awt.event.*;
// Uncomment the following line for Swing 1.0.3 and before
//import com.sun.java.swing.*;
// Uncomment the following line for Swing 1.1 and JDK 1.2
import javax.swing.*;

public class Main extends JFrame {

   public Main () {
      addWindowListener(new WindowAdapter() {
        public void windowClosing(WindowEvent e) {
          Main.this.dispose();
          System.exit(0);
        }
      });
      JLabel label = new JLabel("Some label text");
      label.setBorder(BorderFactory.createLineBorder(Color.green));
      label.setFont(new Font("Serif", Font.ITALIC, 16));

      getContentPane().add(label);
      pack();
      setVisible(true);
   }
   public static void main (String arg[]) {
      new Main();
   }
}
```

public class JLabel extends JComponent
**   implements SwingConstants, Accessible**

Constructors
public JLabel()
   Creates a label with no text or icon. By default it is left-aligned and vertically centered.
public JLabel(Icon icon)
   Creates a label with icon. The icon is centered horizontally and vertically.
public JLabel(Icon icon, int alignment)
   Creates a label with icon. The label is centered vertically. Horizontal position is determined by alignment, JLabel.LEFT, JLabel.CENTER, or JLabel.RIGHT.
public JLabel(String text)
   Creates a label with text. The label is left-aligned and vertically centered.

public JLabel(String text, int alignment)

Creates a label with `text`. The label is centered vertically. Horizontal position is determined by `alignment`, `JLabel.LEFT`, `JLabel.CENTER`, or `JLabel.RIGHT`.

public JLabel(String text, Icon icon, int alignment)

Creates a label with `icon` to the left of `text`. The label is centered vertically. Horizontal position is determined by `alignment`, `JLabel.LEFT`, `JLabel.CENTER`, or `JLabel.RIGHT`.

Methods

public AccessibleContext getAccessibleContext()

Returns the `AccessibleContext` for the label.

public Icon getDisabledIcon()

Returns the icon used when the label is disabled. If none has been set via `setDisabledIcon()`, a grayed out version of the icon is created (see `GrayFilter`) and returned.

public int getDisplayedMnemonic()

Gets the character for the shortcut key for this label. When this key is pressed the focus will be requested by the component set using `setLabelFor()`.

public int getHorizontalAlignment()

Returns the horizontal alignment, which is one of the following: `JLabel.LEFT`, `JLabel.CENTER`, or `JLabel.RIGHT`.

public int getHorizontalTextPosition()

Returns the position of the text relative to the icon, which is one of the following: `JLabel.LEFT`, `JLabel.CENTER`, or `JLabel.RIGHT`.

public Icon getIcon()

Gets the icon associated with this label.

public int getIconTextGap()

Gets the gap (in pixels) between the icon and the text. *Default:* 4 pixels.

public java.awt.Component getLabelFor()

Returns the component for which this is the label. This is the component which will get the focus if the `JLabel`'s mnemonic character is pressed.

public String getText()

The text associated with this label.

public LabelUI getUI()

The UI (look and feel) for this label.

public String getUIClassID()

The UI string—always "LabelUI".

public int getVerticalAlignment()

Gets the vertical alignment. Returns `JLabel.TOP`, `JLabel.CENTER`, or `JLabel.BOTTOM`.

public int getVerticalTextPosition()

Gets the position of the text relative to the icon. Returns `JLabel.TOP`, `JLabel.CENTER`, or `JLabel.BOTTOM`.

public void setDisabledIcon(Icon icon)

Sets the icon to use when the label is disabled. See `getDisabledIcon()` and `setEnabled()` (in `JComponent`). This is a bound property.

public void setDisplayedMnemonic(char c)
public void setDisplayedMnemonic(int c)

Sets the character to be displayed as the accelerator key for this label.

public void setHorizontalAlignment(int alignment)

Sets the horizontal alignment. The `alignment` must be `JLabel.LEFT`, `JLabel.CENTER`, or `JLabel.RIGHT`. This is a bound property.

public void setHorizontalTextPosition(int alignment)

Sets the position of the text relative to the icon. The `alignment` must be `JLabel.LEFT`, `JLabel.CENTER`, or `JLabel.RIGHT`.

public void setIcon(Icon icon)

Sets the icon for the label. This is a bound property.

public void setIconTextGap(int gap)

Sets the gap (in pixels) between the icon and the text. This is a bound property.

public void setLabelFor(java.awt.Component component)

Associates the label with `component`. When the mnemonic character of the `JLabel` is pressed, the focus will be requested by `component`.

public void setText(String text)

Sets the text for the label. This is a bound property.

public void setUI(LabelUI ui)

Sets the UI object for the label. See the chapter on look and feel.

public void setVerticalAlignment(int alignment)

Sets the vertical alignment. The `alignment` must be `JLabel.TOP`, `JLabel.CENTER`, or `JLabel.BOTTOM`. This is a bound property.

public void setVerticalTextPosition(int)

Sets the position of the text relative to the icon. The `alignment` must be `JLabel.TOP`, `JLabel.CENTER`, or `JLabel.BOTTOM`. This is a bound property.

public void updateUI()

Tells the label to update itself with the current UI.

Overrides: `updateUI` in class `JComponent`.

Protected Fields

protected java.awt.Component labelFor

Tracks the component for which this is the label. See `getLabelFor()` and `setLabelFor()`.

Protected Methods

protected int checkHorizontalKey(int alignment, String messageString)

Verifies that `alignment` is `JLabel.LEFT`, `JLabel.CENTER`, or `JLabel.RIGHT`. If not, it throws an exception with `messageString`.

protected int checkVerticalKey(int alignment, String messageString)

Verifies that `alignment` is `JLabel.TOP`, `JLabel.CENTER`, or `JLabel.BOTTOM`. If not, it throws an exception with `messageString`.

protected String paramString()

Returns a string representation of the properties of this `JLabel`. The returned string may be empty but will not be `null`.

Overrides: `paramString` in class `JComponent`.

Extended by BasicComboBoxRenderer (p.564), DefaultListCellRenderer (p.171), DefaultTableCellRenderer (p.742), DefaultTreeCellRenderer (p.972).

See also Accessible (p.85), AccessibleContext (p.90), Icon (p.183), JComponent (p.207), LabelUI (p.535).

swing.JLabel.AccessibleJLabel

INNER CLASS

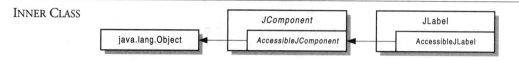

```
protected class JLabel.AccessibleJLabel
    extends JComponent.AccessibleJComponent
```

Methods
public java.lang.String getAccessibleName()
  Overrides: getAccessibleName in class JComponent.AccessibleJComponent.
public AccessibleRole getAccessibleRole()
  Returns AccessibleRole.LABEL.
  Overrides: getAccessibleRole in class JComponent.AccessibleJComponent.

  See also   AccessibleRole (p.95), JComponent.AccessibleJComponent (p.221).

swing.JLayeredPane

CLASS

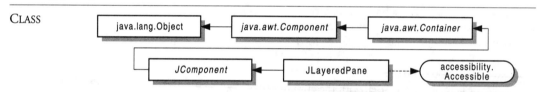

A JLayeredPane is a stack of see-through panes. Each pane may contain components. The panes are similar to the cells used in 2½D animation: the content on each pane acts independently, but they are viewed as if "stacked" so the transparent portion of higher panes lets lower panes show through. Panes are used for components that typically float above other ones, such as dialog boxes and pop-up menus.

There are three integers associated with components in a pane: the layer, the overall position, and the position within the layer. (Be careful to keep these in mind with the methods below.) The layer may be any integer, but there are predefined constants for typical cases. The panes are stacked from lowest layer number to highest.

Layout managers use the overall position (without any awareness of the layers).

A component's layer can be set in one of two ways. One way is to use an Integer constraint when you add it to the layered pane:

```
myPane.add(component, new Integer(50));
```

(The constants in this class define Integer values that are useful for this style.)

The second way is to set the layer before adding it to the pane:

```
myPane.setLayer(component, 50);
myPane.add(component);
```

```
public class JLayeredPane extends JComponent
    implements Accessible
```

Fields
```
public static final String LAYER_PROPERTY = "layeredContainerLayer"
```
The property name for an object's layer.
```
public static final Integer DEFAULT_LAYER = Integer(0)
public static final Integer DRAG_LAYER = Integer(400)
public static final Integer FRAME_CONTENT_LAYER = Integer(-30000)
public static final Integer MODAL_LAYER = Integer(200)
public static final Integer PALETTE_LAYER = Integer(100)
public static final Integer POPUP_LAYER = Integer(300)
```
These constants define `Integer` values that can be used as constraints when adding a component to the layered pane. Layers with a high value display above layers with a lower value. Notice the low value on `FRAME_CONTENT_LAYER`: that is the layer used for the content pane and the menu bar (see `JRootPane`).

Constructors
```
public JLayeredPane()
```
Builds a layered pane.

Methods
```
public AccessibleContext getAccessibleContext()
```
Gets the accessible context for this object.

Overrides: getAccessibleContext in class JComponent.

Implements: getAccessibleContext in interface Accessible.
```
public int getComponentCountInLayer(int layer)
```
Returns the number of components in `layer`.
```
public java.awt.Component[] getComponentsInLayer(int layer)
```
Gets an array of all components in `layer`.
```
public int getIndexOf(java.awt.Component component)
```
Gets the `index` of `component` in the layered pane. (This is the index in the whole pane, not restricted to its own layer.)
```
public static int getLayer(JComponent component)
```
Gets the layer value for `component`. A component that doesn't explicitly have a value is assumed to be in `DEFAULT_LAYER`. You would usually call the instance method `getLayer()` instead of this class method.
```
public int getLayer(java.awt.Component component)
```
Gets the layer `component` is in.
```
public static JLayeredPane getLayeredPaneAbove(java.awt.Component c)
```
Convenience method that returns the first `JLayeredPane` which contains the specified component. Note that all `JFrames` have a `JLayeredPane` at their root, so any component in a `JFrame` will have a `JLayeredPane` parent.
```
public int getPosition(java.awt.Component component)
```
Returns the position of `component` within its layer.
```
public int highestLayer()
```
Returns the highest layer number of the contained components, or 0 if there are none.

public boolean isOptimizedDrawingEnabled()

Returns `true` if there is no layering (and painting can be tiled).

Overrides: `isOptimizedDrawingEnabled` in class `JComponent`.

public int lowestLayer()

Returns the lowest layer number of the contained components, or 0 if there are none.

public void moveToBack(java.awt.Component component)

Moves `component` to the back of its current layer.

public void moveToFront(java.awt.Component component)

Moves `component` to the front of its current layer.

public void paint(java.awt.Graphics gr)

Paints the pane onto the graphics context `gr`, taking into account all layering.

Overrides: `paint` in class `JComponent`.

public static void putLayer(JComponent component, int layerNumber)

Sets the layer property for this component. You would usually call the instance method `putLayer()`. Unlike the instance method, this method does not add or remove the component, or force a repaint.

public void remove(int overallIndex)

Removes the `component` at `overallIndex`.

Overrides: `remove` in class `Container`.

public void setLayer(java.awt.Component component, int layer)

Sets the layer for `component`. This should be called before the component is added to the layered pane.

public void setLayer(java.awt.Component component,
int layerNumber, int index)

Sets the layer for `component` to `layerNumber`, with the component at `index`.

public void setPosition(java.awt.Component component, int position)

Sets the `component` to be at `position` within the current layer. Position –1 puts the component at the back of its layer.

Protected Methods

protected void addImpl(java.awt.Component component,
Object constraint, int layerIndex)

Adds the `component` with `constraint` at `layerIndex`.

Overrides: `addImpl` in class `Container`.

protected java.util.Hashtable getComponentToLayer()

The hash table mapping non-Swing components to their layers. The key is `LAYER_PROPERTY`.

protected Integer getObjectForLayer(int layerNumber)

Returns the `Integer` corresponding to `layerNumber`. Note that `layerNumber` is not restricted to the constant values above—you may use other layer numbers if you like.

protected int insertIndexForLayer(int layer, int positionWithinLayer)

Determines the overall index for a component, based on the desired `layer` and `positionWithinLayer`.

protected String paramString()

Returns a string representation of the properties of this `JLayeredPane`. The returned string may be empty but will not be `null`.

Overrides: `paramString` in class `JComponent`.

Inner Classes
protected class JLayeredPane.AccessibleJLayeredPane

> *Extended by*   JDesktopPane (p.224).
> *Returned by*   JApplet.getLayeredPane() (p.186), JDialog.getLayeredPane() (p.226),
> JFrame.getLayeredPane() (p.248), JInternalFrame.getLayeredPane() (p.254),
> JLayeredPane.getLayeredPaneAbove() (p.268), JRootPane.createLayeredPane() (p.323),
> JRootPane.getLayeredPane() (p.323), JWindow.getLayeredPane() (p.414),
> RootPaneContainer.getLayeredPane() (p.433).
> *See also*   Accessible (p.85), AccessibleContext (p.90).

swing.JLayeredPane.AccessibleJLayeredPane

INNER CLASS

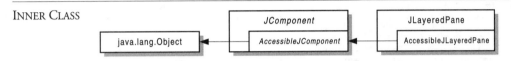

Returns the correct AccessibleRole for a JLayeredPane.

protected class JLayeredPane.AccessibleJLayeredPane
   extends JComponent.AccessibleJComponent

Methods
public AccessibleRole getAccessibleRole()

> Returns AccessibleRole.LAYERED_PANE.
> *Overrides:* getAccessibleRole in class JComponent.AccessibleJComponent.
>
> *See also*   AccessibleRole (p.95), JComponent.AccessibleJComponent (p.221).

swing.JList

CLASS

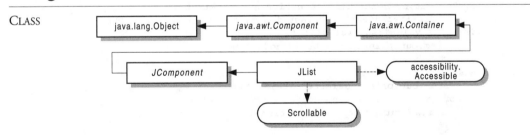

JList is a component that can show and select from a list of items. See ListSelectionModel for more information on selection. See ListCellRenderer for information on how the items are displayed.

The easiest way to work with a JList's model is to create an "adapter" class for your data by subclassing AbstractListModel. AbstractListModel provides implementations of some helper methods you can use to send the correct events when you update the list data, and it also provides methods to maintain the listener list. The adapter class should take a reference to the list's data structure in its constructor and then implement the `getElementAt()` and `getSize()` methods to call the appropriate methods in the data structure.

Example

```
package jlist;

import java.awt.*;
import java.awt.event.*;
// Uncomment the following two lines for Swing 1.0.3 and before
//import com.sun.java.swing.*;
//import com.sun.java.swing.event.*;
// Uncomment the following two lines for Swing 1.1 and JDK 1.2
import javax.swing.*;
import javax.swing.event.*;
public class Main extends JFrame {
    JList list = new JList(new Object[] {
        "This", "Is", "A", "Test", "Of", "JList"
        }
    );

    public Main () {
        addWindowListener(new WindowAdapter() {
            public void windowClosing(WindowEvent e) {
                Main.this.dispose();
                System.exit(0);
            }
        });
        list.setSelectionMode(ListSelectionModel.SINGLE_INTERVAL_SELECTION);
        list.addListSelectionListener(new ListSelectionListener() {
            public void valueChanged(ListSelectionEvent e) {
                JList sourceList = (JList)e.getSource();
                Object[] selection = sourceList.getSelectedValues();
                System.out.println("List selection event: First index: "
                    + e.getFirstIndex() + " Last index: " + e.getLastIndex());
                if (e.getValueIsAdjusting()) {
                    System.out.println("value is adjusting.");
                }
                else {
                    System.out.print("Selected items: ");
                    for (int i = 0; i < selection.length; i++) {
                        System.out.print(" "+selection[i]);
                    }
                    System.out.println();
                }
            }
        });

        getContentPane().add(new JScrollPane(list));
        pack();
        setVisible(true);
    }
    public static void main(String arg[]) {
```

```
        new Main();
    }
}
```

FAQs

Where are the scroll bars on my JList?

Swing components don't implement scrolling behavior directly. All scrolling has been encapsulated in the `JScrollPane` class. To get scroll bars on the `JList` (or any Swing component where it is logical for it to support scrolling), wrap it in a `JScrollPane`.

For example, to add a `JList` to the content area of a `JFrame` and have it support scrolling, do the following:

```
theFrame.getContentPane().add(new JScrollPane(theJList));
```

Components that don't implement `Scrollable` will get the default behavior supplied by `JScrollPane`.

```
public class JList extends JComponent
    implements Scrollable, Accessible
```

Constructors

public JList()

Creates a list component. An empty `AbstractListModel` anonymous inner class is used for the model.

public JList(ListModel model)

Creates a list component with `model` as its model.

public JList(final Object[] array)

Creates a list component with an `AbstractListModel` anonymous inner class initialized with `array`.

public JList(final java.util.Vector vector)

Creates a list component with an `AbstractListModel` anonymous inner class initialized with `vector`.

Methods

public void addListSelectionListener(ListSelectionListener listener)

Adds `listener` as a listener for changes in the list selection.

public void addSelectionInterval(int index1, int index2)

Causes the range from `index1` to `index2` to be added to the selection. Listeners are notified if this changes the selection.

public void clearSelection()

Makes the list selection empty.

public void ensureIndexIsVisible(int index)

If the list is in a `JViewPort`, scrolls it so the item at `index` is visible.

public AccessibleContext getAccessibleContext()

Gets the accessible context.

Overrides: `getAccessibleContext` in class `JComponent`.

Implements: `getAccessibleContext` in interface `Accessible`.

public int getAnchorSelectionIndex()

Gets the index1 value from the most recently added selection interval. See addSelectionInterval() and ListSelectionModel.

public java.awt.Rectangle getCellBounds(int index1, int index2)

Returns the bounds of the list from index1 to index2, or null if the range is invalid.

public ListCellRenderer getCellRenderer()

Returns the renderer responsible for drawing list items. See ListCellRenderer for more information.

public int getFirstVisibleIndex()

Returns the index of the first (at least partially) visible cell in the list. Returns -1 if there is no such cell.

public int getFixedCellHeight()

Returns the height of each cell in the list. If this value is 0, each cell's height is computed on its own. If the value is greater than 0, it specifies the same height to be used for each cell. This is a bound property.

public int getFixedCellWidth()

Returns the width of each cell in the list. If this value is 0, each cell's width is computed on its own. If the value is greater than 0, it specifies the same width to be used for each cell. This is a bound property.

public int getLastVisibleIndex()

Returns the index of the last (at least partially) visible cell in the list. Returns -1 if there is no such cell.

public int getLeadSelectionIndex()

Returns the index of the lead selection. See ListSelectionModel for more information.

public int getMaxSelectionIndex()

Gets the highest index in the selection, or -1 if there is no selection.

public int getMinSelectionIndex()

Gets the lowest index in the selection, or -1 if there is no selection.

public ListModel getModel()

Gets the model associated with this component.

public java.awt.Dimension getPreferredScrollableViewportSize()

Gets the size of the viewport that would be needed to display getVisibleRowCount() rows. This is part of the Scrollable interface.

To determine the size: If the fixedCellHeight and fixedCellWidth properties are set (either directly, or implicitly by a prototypeCellValue), they are used to calculate the height and width. Otherwise, if the model list is not empty, the height is computed from the height of the first row times the number of visible rows, and the width is the width of the widest list element. Otherwise, there is nothing in the model, so it defaults to 16 pixels high (times the number of visible rows), and 100 pixels wide.

Implements: getPreferredScrollableViewportSize in interface Scrollable.

public Object getPrototypeCellValue()

Gets the prototype cell value, used to provide fixed width and height boundaries for the entire list. Setting a prototypeCellValue is a useful optimization for large lists. The prototype value should have a width and height that are the maximum that will be found in the list.

public int getScrollableBlockIncrement(java.awt.Rectangle r, int orientation, int direction)

Returns the number of pixels to use for scrolling, either r.width or r.height. The orientation must be SwingConstants.HORIZONTAL or SwingConstants.VERTICAL. This is part of the Scrollable interface. The direction is positive to scroll right or down, or negative for left or up.

Implements: getScrollableBlockIncrement in interface Scrollable.

public boolean getScrollableTracksViewportHeight()

Returns `false`, which enables vertical scrolling.

Implements: `getScrollableTracksViewportHeight` in interface `Scrollable`.

public boolean getScrollableTracksViewportWidth()

Returns `false`, which enables horizontal scrolling.

Implements: `getScrollableTracksViewportWidth` in interface `Scrollable`.

public int getScrollableUnitIncrement(java.awt.Rectangle r, int orientation, int direction)

Returns the number of pixels required to show the next or previous row. (Which one is determined by `direction`: `direction>0` asks for the distance to the next row.) If the first row is only partially visible, the distance is only enough to show or hide the first row; if the first row is fully visible, it returns the distance to the next or previous row.

Implements: `getScrollableUnitIncrement` in interface `Scrollable`.

public int getSelectedIndex()

Returns the first index in the selection, or –1 if there is none.

public int[] getSelectedIndices()

Returns an array of all selected indexes, in increasing order.

public Object getSelectedValue()

Returns the first selected value, or `null` if there is none.

public Object[] getSelectedValues()

Returns an array of all selected values, ordered by increasing index.

public java.awt.Color getSelectionBackground()

Returns the background color used for selected cells.

public java.awt.Color getSelectionForeground()

Returns the foreground color used for selected cells.

public int getSelectionMode()

Returns the selection mode which is one of the following: `ListSelectionModel.SINGLE_SELECTION`, `ListSelectionModel.SINGLE_INTERVAL_SELECTION`, or `ListSelectionModel.MULTIPLE_INTERVAL_SELECTION`.

public ListSelectionModel getSelectionModel()

Returns the current selection model. This is a bound property.

public ListUI getUI()

Returns the UI object responsible for the look and feel of this component.

public String getUIClassID()

Returns "ListUI".

Overrides: `getUIClassID` in class `JComponent`.

public boolean getValueIsAdjusting(boolean isAdjusting)

Returns `true` if the list is in the middle of a series of changes.

public int getVisibleRowCount()

Gets the preferred number of visible rows.

public java.awt.Point indexToLocation(int index)

Returns the location of the item at `index` in `JList` coordinates.

public boolean isSelectedIndex(int index)

Returns `true` if the item at `index` is currently selected.

public boolean isSelectionEmpty()

Returns `true` if nothing is currently selected.

```
public int locationToIndex(java.awt.Point p)
```
Converts point p (in JList coordinates) to the index of that item, or −1 if there's no such item.

```
public void removeListSelectionListener(ListSelectionListener listener)
```
Removes listener from the list of selection listeners.

```
public void removeSelectionInterval(int index1, int index2)
```
Removes items from index1 to index2 from the selection list (index1 need not be less than index2).

```
public void setCellRenderer(ListCellRenderer renderer)
```
Sets the renderer used to display all cells. This is a bound property.

```
public void setFixedCellHeight(int newValue)
```
Sets the default height for all cells. (If newValue is 0 or less, the height will be computed rather than fixed.) This is a bound property.

```
public void setFixedCellWidth(int newValue)
```
Sets the default width for all cells. (If newValue is 0 or less, the width will be computed rather than fixed.) This is a bound property.

```
public void setListData(Object[] array)
```
Builds a DefaultListModel from the elements in array, and calls setModel() on it.

```
public void setListData(java.util.Vector vector)
```
Builds a DefaultListModel from the elements in vector, and calls setModel() on it.

```
public void setModel(ListModel model)
```
Sets the model. This is a bound property.

```
public void setPrototypeCellValue(Object proto)
```
Sets the prototype cell value. When a prototype value is available, it is used to compute cell sizes. Setting a prototypeCellValue is a useful optimization for large lists. The prototype value should have a width and height that are the maximum that will be found in the list. When the prototype cell is set, the fixedCellHeight and fixedCellWidth properties are affected, but no property change event is triggered for them. This is a bound property.

```
public void setSelectedIndex(int selectedIndex)
```
Sets which (single) item should be selected.

```
public void setSelectedIndices(int[] selectedIndices)
```
Sets which items should be selected.

```
public void setSelectedValue(Object value, boolean scrollToVisible)
```
Selects value. If scrollToVisible is true, it makes the newly selected item visible.

```
public void setSelectionBackground(java.awt.Color color)
```
Sets the background color of the selection. This is a bound property.

```
public void setSelectionForeground(java.awt.Color)
```
Sets the foreground color of the selection. This is a bound property.

```
public void setSelectionInterval(int index1, int index2)
```
Sets the selection interval to be from index1 to index2 inclusive (index1 may be larger than index2).

```
public void setSelectionMode(int mode)
```
Sets the selection mode to one of the following: ListSelectionModel.SINGLE_SELECTION, ListSelectionModel.SINGLE_INTERVAL_SELECTION, or ListSelectionModel.MULTIPLE_INTERVAL_SELECTION.

```
public void setSelectionModel(ListSelectionModel selectionModel)
```
Sets the selection model. This is a bound property.

`public void setUI(ListUI ui)`

Sets the look and feel for this component.

`public void setValueIsAdjusting(boolean stillAdjusting)`

Sets whether the selection is in the middle of an update.

`public void setVisibleRowCount(int numRows)`

Sets the number of rows that are desired to be visible. Default: 8 rows. This is a bound property.

`public void updateUI()`

Tells the list to update its look and feel.

Overrides: `updateUI` in class `JComponent`.

Protected Methods

`protected ListSelectionModel createSelectionModel()`

Creates a selection model for this list. The default selection model created is a `DefaultListSelectionModel`, but subclasses could use a different one.

`protected void fireSelectionValueChanged(int index1, int index2,`
`boolean valueIsAdjusting)`

Notifies listeners that the selection has changed in the interval from `index1` to `index2`. If `valueIsAdjusting` is `true`, the listener should expect more changes.

`protected String paramString()`

Returns a string representation of the properties of this `JList`. The returned string may be empty but will not be `null`.

Overrides: `paramString` in class `JComponent`.

Inner Classes

`protected class JList.AccessibleJList`

Returned by BasicComboBoxUI.createListBox() (p.565), BasicComboBoxUI.getList() (p.565), BasicComboPopup.createList() (p.572), ComboBoxUI.getList() (p.530).

See also AbstractListModel (p.127), Accessible (p.85), AccessibleContext (p.90), DefaultListModel (p.172), DefaultListSelectionModel (p.175), JComponent (p.207), ListCellRenderer (p.420), ListModel (p.421), ListSelectionListener (p.500), ListSelectionModel (p.421), ListUI (p.535), Scrollable (p.433).

swing.JList.AccessibleJList

INNER CLASS

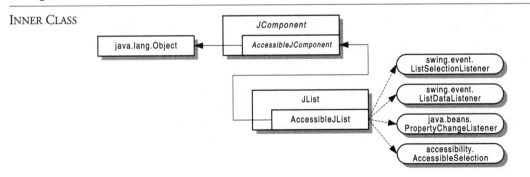

Implements the accessibility behavior for a `JList`.

```
protected class JList.AccessibleJList
    extends JComponent.AccessibleJComponent
    implements AccessibleSelection, ListSelectionListener, ListDataListener
```

Constructor

`public AccessibleJList()`

Creates a new instance of this class and adds it as a listener to the associated `JList`.

Methods

`public void addAccessibleSelection(int i)`

Implements: addAccessibleSelection in interface AccessibleSelection.

`public void clearAccessibleSelection()`

Implements: clearAccessibleSelection in interface AccessibleSelection.

`public void contentsChanged(ListDataEvent e)`

Called when the contents of the list change.

Implements: contentsChanged in interface ListDataListener.

`public Accessible getAccessibleAt(java.awt.Point p)`

Overrides: getAccessibleAt in class AccessibleJComponent.

`public Accessible getAccessibleChild(int i)`

Overrides: getAccessibleChild in class AccessibleJComponent.

`public int getAccessibleChildrenCount()`

Overrides: getAccessibleChildrenCount in class AccessibleJComponent.

`public AccessibleRole getAccessibleRole()`

Returns AccessibleRole.LIST.

Overrides: getAccessibleRole in class AccessibleJComponent.

`public AccessibleSelection getAccessibleSelection()`

Overrides: getAccessibleSelection in class AccessibleContext.

`public Accessible getAccessibleSelection(int i)`

Implements: getAccessibleSelection in interface AccessibleSelection.

`public int getAccessibleSelectionCount()`

Implements: getAccessibleSelectionCount in interface AccessibleSelection.

`public AccessibleStateSet getAccessibleStateSet()`

Overrides: getAccessibleStateSet in class AccessibleJComponent.

`public void intervalAdded(ListDataEvent e)`

Called when an interval is added to the list.

Implements: intervalAdded in interface ListDataListener.

`public void intervalRemoved(ListDataEvent e)`

Called when an interval is removed from the list.

Implements: intervalRemoved in interface ListDataListener.

`public boolean isAccessibleChildSelected(int i)`

Implements: isAccessibleChildSelected in interface AccessibleSelection.

`public void propertyChange(PropertyChangeEvent e)`

Implements: propertyChange in interface PropertyChangeListener.

`public void removeAccessibleSelection(int i)`

Implements: removeAccessibleSelection in interface AccessibleSelection.

public void selectAllAccessibleSelection()

    Implements: selectAllAccessibleSelection in interface AccessibleSelection.

public void valueChanged(ListSelectionEvent e)

    Called when the list selection changes.

    Implements: valueChanged in interface ListSelectionListener.

Inner Classes

protected class JList.AccessibleJList.AccessibleJListChild

    See also   Accessible (p.85), AccessibleRole (p.95), AccessibleSelection (p.98), AccessibleStateSet (p.101), JComponent.AccessibleJComponent (p.221), ListDataListener (p.499), ListSelectionListener (p.500).

swing.JList.AccessibleJList.AccessibleJListChild

INNER CLASS

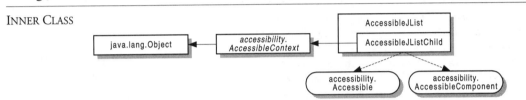

Provides accessibility support for items in a JList.

```
protected class JList.AccessibleJList.AccessibleJListChild
    extends AccessibleContext
    implements Accessible, AccessibleComponent
```

Constructor

public AccessibleJListChild(JList parent, int indexInParent)

    Constructs an Accessible representing an item in a JList.

Methods

public void addFocusListener(java.awt.event.FocusListener l)

    Implements: addFocusListener in interface AccessibleComponent.

public void addPropertyChangeListener(java.beans.PropertyChangeListener l)

    Overrides: addPropertyChangeListener in class AccessibleContext.

public boolean contains(java.awt.Point p)

    Implements: contains in interface AccessibleComponent.

public AccessibleAction getAccessibleAction()

    Overrides: getAccessibleAction in class AccessibleContext.

public Accessible getAccessibleAt(java.awt.Point p)

    Implements: getAccessibleAt in interface AccessibleComponent.

public Accessible getAccessibleChild(int i)

    Overrides: getAccessibleChild in class AccessibleContext.

public int getAccessibleChildrenCount()

    Overrides: getAccessibleChildrenCount in class AccessibleContext.

public AccessibleComponent getAccessibleComponent()

    Overrides: getAccessibleComponent in class AccessibleContext.

public AccessibleContext getAccessibleContext()
    Implements: getAccessibleContext in interface Accessible.
public java.lang.String getAccessibleDescription()
    Overrides: getAccessibleDescription in class AccessibleContext.
public int getAccessibleIndexInParent()
    Overrides: getAccessibleIndexInParent in class AccessibleContext.
public java.lang.String getAccessibleName()
    Overrides: getAccessibleName in class AccessibleContext.
public AccessibleRole getAccessibleRole()
    Returns the role of the JList child this instance represents.
    Overrides: getAccessibleRole in class AccessibleContext.
public AccessibleSelection getAccessibleSelection()
    Overrides: getAccessibleSelection in class AccessibleContext.
public AccessibleStateSet getAccessibleStateSet()
    Overrides: getAccessibleStateSet in class AccessibleContext.
public AccessibleText getAccessibleText()
    Overrides: getAccessibleText in class AccessibleContext.
public AccessibleValue getAccessibleValue()
    Overrides: getAccessibleValue in class AccessibleContext.
public java.awt.Color getBackground()
    Implements: getBackground in interface AccessibleComponent.
public java.awt.Rectangle getBounds()
    Implements: getBounds in interface AccessibleComponent.
public java.awt.Cursor getCursor()
    Implements: getCursor in interface AccessibleComponent.
public java.awt.Font getFont()
    Implements: getFont in interface AccessibleComponent.
public java.awt.FontMetrics getFontMetrics(java.awt.Font f)
    Implements: getFontMetrics in interface AccessibleComponent.
public java.awt.Color getForeground()
    Implements: getForeground in interface AccessibleComponent.
public java.util.Locale getLocale()
    Overrides: getLocale in class AccessibleContext.
public java.awt.Point getLocation()
    Implements: getLocation in interface AccessibleComponent.
public java.awt.Point getLocationOnScreen()
    Implements: getLocationOnScreen in interface AccessibleComponent.
public java.awt.Dimension getSize()
    Implements: getSize in interface AccessibleComponent.
public boolean isEnabled()
    Implements: isEnabled in interface AccessibleComponent.
public boolean isFocusTraversable()
    Implements: isFocusTraversable in interface AccessibleComponent.
public boolean isShowing()
    Implements: isShowing in interface AccessibleComponent.
public boolean isVisible()
    Implements: isVisible in interface AccessibleComponent.

```
public void removeFocusListener(java.awt.event.FocusListener l)
```
Implements: removeFocusListener in interface AccessibleComponent.
```
public void removePropertyChangeListener(
    java.beans.PropertyChangeListener l)
```
Overrides: removePropertyChangeListener in class AccessibleContext.
```
public void requestFocus()
```
Implements: requestFocus in interface AccessibleComponent.
```
public void setAccessibleDescription(java.lang.String s)
```
Overrides: setAccessibleDescription in class AccessibleContext.
```
public void setAccessibleName(java.lang.String s)
```
Overrides: setAccessibleName in class AccessibleContext.
```
public void setBackground(java.awt.Color c)
```
Implements: setBackground in interface AccessibleComponent.
```
public void setBounds(java.awt.Rectangle r)
```
Implements: setBounds in interface AccessibleComponent.
```
public void setCursor(java.awt.Cursor c)
```
Implements: setCursor in interface AccessibleComponent.
```
public void setEnabled(boolean b)
```
Implements: setEnabled in interface AccessibleComponent.
```
public void setFont(java.awt.Font f)
```
Implements: setFont in interface AccessibleComponent.
```
public void setForeground(java.awt.Color c)
```
Implements: setForeground in interface AccessibleComponent.
```
public void setLocation(java.awt.Point p)
```
Implements: setLocation in interface AccessibleComponent.
```
public void setSize(java.awt.Dimension d)
```
Implements: setSize in interface AccessibleComponent.
```
public void setVisible(boolean b)
```
Implements: setVisible in interface AccessibleComponent.

See also   Accessible (p.85), AccessibleComponent (p.87), AccessibleContext (p.90), AccessibleRole (p.95), AccessibleStateSet (p.101), AccessibleText (p.103).

swing.JMenu

CLASS

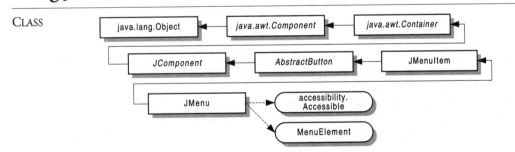

A JMenu is a container for JMenuItems. In a menu bar, a JMenu corresponds to the top-level menus—for example, the File, Edit, or Help menus on most platforms. The most helpful way to think of a menu in Swing is as a button which brings up a JPopupMenu which contains the JMenu's child JMenuItems and JMenus.

Note that the layout manager of a JMenu (and JPopupMenu) can be changed to allow for custom menus such as multicolumn menus. Due to the nature of Swing JMenus you need to change the layout on the component returned from getPopupMenu() to actually "change the layout of the menu."

Example

```
package jmenu;

import java.awt.*;
import java.awt.event.*;
// Uncomment the following line for Swing 1.0.3 and before
//import com.sun.java.swing.*;
// Uncomment the following line for Swing 1.1 and JDK 1.2
import javax.swing.*;

public class Main extends JFrame {
    public Main () {
        addWindowListener(new WindowAdapter() {
            public void windowClosing(WindowEvent e) {
                Main.this.dispose();
                System.exit(0);
            }
        });
        JMenuBar bar = new JMenuBar();
        JMenu menu = new JMenu("File");
        menu.setMnemonic('f');
        bar.add (menu);

        JMenuItem exit = new JMenuItem("Exit");
        exit.setMnemonic('x');
        exit.addActionListener(new ActionListener() {
            public void actionPerformed (ActionEvent e) {
                System.out.println ("Exit performed");
                Main.this.dispose();
                System.exit(0);
            }
        });
        menu.add(exit);

        menu = new JMenu("Edit");
        menu.setMnemonic('e');
        bar.add(menu);

        EditListener l = new EditListener();
        JMenuItem mi;
        mi = menu.add(new JMenuItem("Cut", 't'));
        mi.setAccelerator(KeyStroke.getKeyStroke(KeyEvent.VK_X,
                        Event.CTRL_MASK));
        mi.addActionListener(l);
        mi = menu.add(new JMenuItem("Copy", 'c'));
        mi.setAccelerator(KeyStroke.getKeyStroke(KeyEvent.VK_C,
                        Event.CRTL_MASK));
```

```
         mi.addActionListener(l);
         mi = menu.add(new JMenuItem("Paste", 'p'));
         mi.setAccelerator(KeyStroke.getKeyStroke(KeyEvent.VK_V,
                        Event.CTRL_MASK));
         mi.addActionListener(l);

         setJMenuBar(bar);
         getContentPane().add(new JLabel("A placeholder"));

         pack();
         setSize (300, 300);
         setVisible(true);
      }
      private class EditListener implements ActionListener {
         public void actionPerformed(ActionEvent e) {
            System.out.println(e.getActionCommand());
         }
      }
      public static void main (String arg[]) {
         new Main();
      }
   }
```

public class JMenu extends JMenuItem
implements Accessible, MenuElement

Constructors

public JMenu()

Creates a menu with an empty name.

public JMenu(String name)

Creates a menu with name.

public JMenu(String name, boolean canTear)

Creates a menu with name, that can be torn off if canTear is true. Not implemented as of Swing 1.1.

Methods

public JMenuItem add(Action action)

Creates a new menu item for action, and adds it to the menu.

public JMenuItem add(JMenuItem menuItem)

Adds menuItem to the menu.

public java.awt.Component add(java.awt.Component component)

Adds component to the menu.

Overrides: add in class Container.

public void add(String name)

Creates a new menu item with name, and adds it to the menu.

public void addMenuListener(MenuListener listener)

Adds listener to the list of listeners to be notified when the menu changes.

public void addSeparator()

Adds a separator to the menu (usually shown as a line or blank area).

public void doClick(int pressTime)

Programatically "clicks" the menu. This method extends the superclass doClick() to pop up the menu.

Overrides: doClick in class AbstractButton.

public AccessibleContext getAccessibleContext()

Gets the accessible context for this menu.

Overrides: getAccessibleContext in class JMenuItem.

Implements: getAccessibleContext in interface Accessible.

public java.awt.Component getComponent()

Gets the component with which this menu is associated.

Overrides: getComponent in class JMenuItem.

Implements: getComponent in interface MenuElement.

public int getDelay()

Gets the delay (in milliseconds) between when a menu is selected and when it pops up the JPopup-
Menu.

public JMenuItem getItem(int index)

Gets the submenu at index.

Throws: IllegalArgumentException if the value of index is less than 0.

public int getItemCount()

Tells how many items are on this menu, including separators. Included for AWT compatibility; use
getMenuComponentCount() instead.

public java.awt.Component getMenuComponent(int index)

Gets the component at index.

public int getMenuComponentCount()

Tells how many items are on this menu.

public java.awt.Component[] getMenuComponents()

Gets a list of all items in the menu.

public JPopupMenu getPopupMenu()

Returns the pop-up menu associated with this menu.

public MenuElement[] getSubElements()

Returns an array consisting of the submenus contained in this menu.

Overrides: getSubElements in class JMenuItem.

Implements: getSubElements in interface MenuElement.

public String getUIClassID()

Returns "MenuUI".

Overrides: getUIClassID in class JMenuItem.

public JMenuItem insert(Action action, int index)

Creates a new JMenuItem from action, and inserts it at index.

public JMenuItem insert(JMenuItem menuItem, int index)

Inserts menuItem at index.

public void insert(String name, int index)

Creates a new JMenuItem with name, and inserts it at index.

public void insertSeparator(int index)

Inserts a separator at index.

Throws: IllegalArgumentException if the value of index is less than 0.

public boolean isMenuComponent(java.awt.Component component)

Returns true if component is part of this menu's child hierarchy.

public boolean isPopupMenuVisible()

Returns true if the pop-up for this menu is visible.

public boolean isSelected()

Returns true if this menu is selected.

Overrides: `isSelected` in class `AbstractButton`.

`public boolean isTearOff()`

Returns `true` if this is a tear-off menu. Not yet implemented as of Swing 1.1.

`public boolean isTopLevelMenu()`

Returns `true` if this is a top-level menu.

`public void menuSelectionChanged(boolean selected)`

Sets the menu selection state to `selected`.

Overrides: `menuSelectionChanged` in class `JMenuItem`.

Implements: `menuSelectionChanged` in interface `MenuElement`.

`public void remove(java.awt.Component menuItem)`

Removes `menuItem` from the menu.

Overrides: `remove` in class `Container`.

`public void remove(int index)`

Removes the item at `index` from the menu.

Throws: `IllegalArgumentException` if the value of index is less than 0.

Overrides: `remove` in class `Container`.

`public void removeAll()`

Removes all items from the menu.

Overrides: `removeAll` in class `Container`.

`public void removeMenuListener(MenuListener listener)`

Removes `listener` from the list of objects notified about menu events.

`public void setAccelerator(KeyStroke keyStroke)`

This method does not do anything for a `JMenu`. Use `setMnemonic()` instead.

Overrides: `setAccelerator` in class `JMenuItem`.

`public void setDelay(int delayMilliseconds)`

Sets the delay for how long it takes a pop-up to appear.

Throws: `IllegalArgumentException` if the value of d is less than 0.

`public void setMenuLocation(int x, int y)`

Sets the location for this menu (relative to the component in which it is contained).

`public void setModel(ButtonModel model)`

Sets the model for this menu.

Overrides: `setModel` in class `AbstractButton`.

`public void setPopupMenuVisible(boolean isVisible)`

Sets whether or not the pop-up is visible.

`public void setSelected(boolean isSelected)`

Sets whether or not the menu is selected.

Overrides: `setSelected` in class `AbstractButton`.

`public void updateUI()`

Notifies this object to update its look and feel. This class actually has two parts to its UI. It uses a `MenuItemUI` to act as the `JMenu` itself, and it uses a `PopupMenuUI` to act as the pop-up portion of the menu.

Overrides: `updateUI` in class `JMenuItem`.

Protected Fields

`protected JMenu.WinListener popupListener`

A listener for window events affecting pop-ups.

Protected Methods

protected java.beans.PropertyChangeListener createActionChangeListener(JMenuItem b)

Creates the listener used to keep the JMenuItems created using an Action (b) in synch with the changes to the Action.

protected JMenu.WinListener createWinListener(JPopupMenu popup)

Creates a window listener for popup.

protected void fireMenuCanceled()

Notifies all listeners that the menu has been canceled without a selection.

protected void fireMenuDeselected()

Notifies listeners that the menu is no longer selected.

protected void fireMenuSelected()

Notifies listeners that the menu is now selected.

protected String paramString()

Returns a string that tells the state of the menu. The string returned may be empty, but will not be null.
Overrides: paramString in class JMenuItem.

protected void processKeyEvent(java.awt.event.KeyEvent event)

Handles a key event by passing it to the default MenuSelectionManager.
Overrides: processKeyEvent in class JComponent.

Returned by BasicInternalFrameTitlePane.createSystemMenu() (p.597), JMenuBar.add() (p.288), JMenuBar.getHelpMenu() (p.288), JMenuBar.getMenu() (p.288).
See also Accessible (p.85), JMenuBar (p.288), JMenuItem (p.291), JMenu.WinListener (p.287), JPopupMenu (p.309), JSeparator (p.338), MenuElement (p.425), MenuItemUI (p.536), MenuListener (p.504), MenuSelectionManager (p.426), PopupMenuUI (p.538).

swing.JMenu.AccessibleJMenu

INNER CLASS

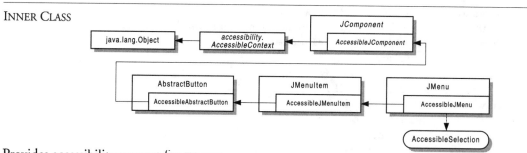

Provides accessibility support for JMenus.

```
protected class JMenu.AccessibleJMenu
    extends JMenuItem.AccessibleJMenuItem
    implements AccessibleSelection
```

Methods

public void addAccessibleSelection(int i)

Selects the ith item in the menu. If the item is a submenu, this will cause it to open.
Implements: addAccessibleSelection in interface AccessibleSelection.

public void clearAccessibleSelection()

Clears the menu selection.

Implements: clearAccessibleSelection in interface AccessibleSelection.

public int getAccessibleChildrenCount()

Overrides: getAccessibleChildrenCount in class JComponent.AccessibleJComponent.

public Accessible getAccessibleChild(int i)

Overrides: getAccessibleChild in class JComponent.AccessibleJComponent.

public AccessibleRole getAccessibleRole()

Overrides: getAccessibleRole in class JMenuItem.AccessibleJMenuItem.

public AccessibleSelection getAccessibleSelection()

Overrides: getAccessibleSelection in class AccessibleContext.

public Accessible getAccessibleSelection(int i)

Implements: getAccessibleSelection in interface AccessibleSelection.

public int getAccessibleSelectionCount()

Implements: getAccessibleSelectionCount in interface AccessibleSelection.

public boolean isAccessibleChildSelected(int i)

Implements: isAccessibleChildSelected in interface AccessibleSelection.

public void removeAccessibleSelection(int i)

Unselects the ith menu item, if it is selected. If the item is a submenu, this will cause it to close.

Implements: removeAccessibleSelection in interface AccessibleSelection.

public void selectAllAccessibleSelection()

This method does nothing, since it makes no sense in a menu.

Implements: selectAllAccessibleSelection in interface AccessibleSelection.

swing.JMenu.WinListener

INNER CLASS

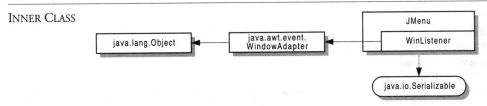

Listens for the pop-up representing a menu closing. When the menu closes, this class deselects the associated menu item.

```
protected class JMenu.WinListener
    extends java.awt.event.WindowAdapter
    implements java.io.Serializable
```

Constructor

public JMenu.WinListener(JPopupMenu p)

Constructs a window listener for the specified JPopupMenu.

Methods

public void windowClosing(java.awt.event.WindowEvent e)

Deselects the menu when the pop-up is closed.

Overrides: windowClosing in class WindowAdapter.

swing.JMenuBar

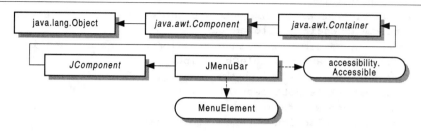

JMenuBar provides menu bars. These are horizontal lists of menus, usually at the top of a screen or window.

Example: See JMenu.

FAQs

How do I add a menu to a JFrame?

Use setJMenuBar(JMenu).

```
public class JMenuBar extends JComponent
    implements Accessible, MenuElement
```

Constructors

public JMenuBar()
    Creates a menu bar.

Methods

public JMenu add(JMenu menu)
    Adds menu to the menu bar.

public void addNotify()
    Overrides JComponent.addNotify() to register this menu bar with the current KeyboardManager.
    Overrides: addNotify in class JComponent.

public AccessibleContext getAccessibleContext()
    Gets the accessible context for this menu.
    Overrides: getAccessibleContext in class JComponent.
    Implements: getAccessibleContext in interface Accessible.

public java.awt.Component getComponent()
    Returns this, since a JMenuBar is a top-level menu item.
    Implements: getComponent in interface MenuElement.

public java.awt.Component getComponentAtIndex(int index)
    Gets the menu element at index.

public int getComponentIndex(java.awt.Component component)
    Finds the index for component.

public JMenu getHelpMenu()

Gets the help menu if available. Not implemented as of Swing 1.1.

public java.awt.Insets getMargin()

Returns the margin between the pop-up menu and its menu elements.

public JMenu getMenu(int index)

Returns the top-level menu at position index.

public int getMenuCount()

Returns the number of top-level menus on the menu bar.

public SingleSelectionModel getSelectionModel()

Gets the selection model for this pop-up.

public MenuElement[] getSubElements()

Returns all of the JMenus contained in this JMenuBar.

Implements: getSubElements in interface MenuElement.

public MenuBarUI getUI()

Gets the UI (look and feel) for this menu bar.

public String getUIClassID()

Returns "MenuBarUI".

Overrides: getUIClassID in class JComponent.

public boolean isBorderPainted()

Returns true if the border should be painted.

public boolean isManagingFocus()

Returns true if the menu bar manages its own focus cycle, which it does.

Overrides: isManagingFocus in class JComponent.

public boolean isSelected()

Returns true if a component in the menu bar is currently selected.

public void menuSelectionChanged(boolean wasAdded)

This method is not used by JMenuBar; it is provided only because it is required by interface MenuElement.

Implements: menuSelectionChanged in interface MenuElement.

public void processKeyEvent(java.awt.event.KeyEvent event, MenuElement[] path, MenuSelectionManager manager)

This method has no effect; it is provided only because it is required by interface MenuElement.

Implements: processKeyEvent in interface MenuElement.

public void processMouseEvent(java.awt.event.MouseEvent event, MenuElement[] path, MenuSelectionManager manager)

This method has no effect; it is provided only because it is required by interface MenuElement.

Implements: processMouseEvent in interface MenuElement.

public void removeNotify()

Overrides JComponent.removeNotify() to unregister this menu bar with the current KeyboardManager.

Overrides: removeNotify in class JComponent.

public void setBorderPainted(boolean shouldPaint)

Sets whether the border should be painted.

public void setHelpMenu(JMenu helpMenu)

Makes helpMenu be the help menu for this menu bar. Not implemented as of Swing 1.1.

public void setMargin(java.awt.Insets margin)

Sets the margin between the menu bar's border and its contained menus.

public void setSelected(Component selection)

Makes `selection` be the new current selection. Propagates this to the selection model.

public void setSelectionModel(SingleSelectionModel model)

Sets the selection model for this `JMenuBar`.

public void setUI(MenuBarUI ui)

Sets the UI (look and feel) for this menu bar. See the chapter on look and feel.

public void updateUI()

Notification that the menu should update itself to the current look and feel.

Overrides: `updateUI` in class `JComponent`.

Protected Methods

protected void paintBorder(java.awt.Graphics g)

Paints the menu bar's border if the `borderPainted` property is `true`.

Overrides: `paintBorder` in class `JComponent`.

protected String paramString()

Returns a string representation of the properties of this `JMenuBar`. The returned string may be empty but will not be null.

Overrides: `paramString` in class `JComponent`.

Extended by   BasicInternalFrameTitlePane.SystemMenuBar (p.603).

Returned by   BasicInternalFrameTitlePane.createSystemMenuBar() (p.597),
JApplet.getJMenuBar() (p.186), JDialog.getJMenuBar() (p.226),
JFrame.getJMenuBar() (p.248), JInternalFrame.getJMenuBar() (p.254),
JRootPane.getJMenuBar() (p.323).

See also   Accessible (p.85), AccessibleContext (p.90), JMenu (p.281),
JMenuItem (p.291), JPopupMenu (p.309), MenuBarUI (p.536), MenuElement (p.425),
MenuSelectionManager (p.426), SingleSelectionModel (p.440).

swing.JMenuBar.AccessibleJMenuBar

INNER CLASS

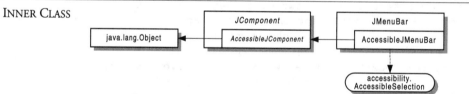

protected class JMenuBar.AccessibleJMenuBar
    extends JComponent.AccessibleJComponent
    implements AccessibleSelection

Methods

public void addAccessibleSelection(int i)

Selects the ith menu in the menu bar, forcing it to show.

Implements: `addAccessibleSelection` in interface `AccessibleSelection`.

public void clearAccessibleSelection()

Closes any open menu on this `JMenuBar`.

Implements: `clearAccessibleSelection` in interface `AccessibleSelection`.

public AccessibleRole getAccessibleRole()

Returns `AccessibleRole.MENU_BAR`.

Overrides: `getAccessibleRole` in class `AccessibleJComponent`.

public AccessibleSelection getAccessibleSelection()

Returns `this`, since this class implements `AccessibleSelection`.

Overrides: `getAccessibleSelection` in class `AccessibleContext`.

public Accessible getAccessibleSelection(int i)

Returns the currently selected menu, or returns `null` if there isn't a selection.

Implements: `getAccessibleSelection` in interface `AccessibleSelection`.

public int getAccessibleSelectionCount()

Returns 1 if a menu item in this menu bar is selected, 0 otherwise.

Implements: `getAccessibleSelectionCount` in interface `AccessibleSelection`.

public AccessibleStateSet getAccessibleStateSet()

Calls the superclass method and returns the result.

Overrides: `getAccessibleStateSet` in class `AccessibleJComponent`.

public boolean isAccessibleChildSelected(int i)

Returns `true` if the accessible child at the given index `i` is the current selection.

Implements: `isAccessibleChildSelected` in interface `AccessibleSelection`.

public void removeAccessibleSelection(int i)

Deselects the ith menu if it is selected. Deselecting a menu will force it to close.

Implements: `removeAccessibleSelection` in interface `AccessibleSelection`.

public void selectAllAccessibleSelection()

This method does nothing, since select all is meaningless for menus.

Implements: `selectAllAccessibleSelection` in interface `AccessibleSelection`.

See also Accessible (p.85), AccessibleRole (p.95), AccessibleSelection (p.98), AccessibleStateSet (p.101).

swing.JMenuItem

CLASS

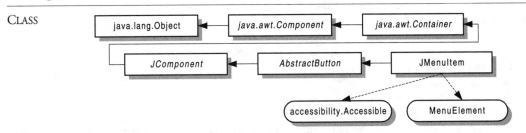

A `JMenuItem` is a single entry on a menu. It is usually contained in a `JMenu` or a `JPopupMenu`. In a menu on the menu bar such as Edit, the menu items might be Cut and Copy.

A mnemonic is a character in the menu item name which, when pressed while the menu is open triggers the corresponding menu item's action. An accelerator is a `KeyStroke` (usually some combination of the CONTROL, ALT, or META keys with another key) which will trigger the menu item regardless of whether the menu is showing, as long as it is part of the current menu hierarchy for the window. For example, the mnemonic for the Cut menu item is usually 't', while the accelerator is CTRL-X (COMMAND-X on the Mac).

Example: See JMenu.

```
public class JMenuItem extends AbstractButton
    implements Accessible, MenuElement
```

Constructors
```
public JMenuItem()
public JMenuItem(String text)
public JMenuItem(Icon icon)
public JMenuItem(String text, Icon icon)
```
Builds a menu item with the indicated text and icon. The default values are no text and no icon.
```
public JMenuItem(String text, int mnemonic)
```
Builds a menu item with the given text and the specified mnemonic key.

Methods
```
public void addMenuDragMouseListener(MenuDragMouseListener l)
```
Adds a MenuDragMouseListener to the menu item.
```
public void addMenuKeyListener(MenuKeyListener l)
```
Adds a MenuKeyListener to the menu item.
```
public KeyStroke getAccelerator()
```
Returns the KeyStroke for the accelerator.
```
public AccessibleContext getAccessibleContext()
```
Gets the accessible context.
Overrides: getAccessibleContext in class JComponent.
Implements: getAccessibleContext in interface Accessible.
```
public java.awt.Component getComponent()
```
Returns the component used to render this menu item. This component is also used for hit-testing mouse events.
Implements: getComponent in interface MenuElement.
```
public MenuElement[] getSubElements()
```
For hierarchical menus, returns an array of the menu's submenus.
Implements: getSubElements in interface MenuElement.
```
public String getUIClassID()
```
Returns "MenuItemUI".
Overrides: getUIClassID in class JComponent.
```
public boolean isArmed()
```
Returns true if this menu item is armed (the mouse has clicked over the item but not released, and the mouse is over the item).
```
public void menuSelectionChanged(boolean wasAdded)
```
Returns notification that the menu selection has changed. Parameter wasAdded is true if the menu element has been added, or false if it has been removed.
Implements: menuSelectionChanged in interface MenuElement.
```
public void processKeyEvent(java.awt.event.KeyEvent event,
    MenuElement[] path, MenuSelectionManager manager)
```
Handles a key event directed at this menu element. Delegated to the UI.

Implements: processKeyEvent in interface MenuElement.

public void processMenuDragMouseEvent(MenuDragMouseEvent e)

Handles mouse drag in a menu.

public void processMenuKeyEvent(MenuKeyEvent e)

Handles a keystroke in a menu.

public void processMouseEvent(java.awt.event.MouseEvent event,
MenuElement[] path, MenuSelectionManager manager)

Handles a mouse event. The event's source is the component associated with this menu element. The path is the path through a hierarchical menu, ending at this menu element. Use manager to change the menu selection. The manager will continue forwarding this event to submenus if necessary.

Implements: processMouseEvent in interface MenuElement.

public void removeMenuDragMouseListener(MenuDragMouseListener l)

Removes a MenuDragMouseListener from the menu item.

public void removeMenuKeyListener(MenuKeyListener l)

Removes a MenuKeyListener from the menu item.

public void setAccelerator(KeyStroke keyStroke)

Sets the KeyStroke which will trigger this menu item's action.

public void setArmed(boolean newState)

Sets the armed state of this menu item.

public void setEnabled(boolean newState)

Sets the enabled state of this menu item.

Overrides: setEnabled in class AbstractButton.

public void setUI(MenuItemUI ui)

Sets the look and feel to ui.

public void updateUI()

Updates this component with the current UI (look and feel).

Overrides: updateUI in class AbstractButton.

Protected Methods

protected void fireMenuDragMouseDragged(MenuDragMouseEvent event)

Called from processMenuDragMouseEvent().

protected void fireMenuDragMouseEntered(MenuDragMouseEvent event)

Called from processMenuDragMouseEvent().

protected void fireMenuDragMouseExited(MenuDragMouseEvent event)

Called from processMenuDragMouseEvent().

protected void fireMenuDragMouseReleased(MenuDragMouseEvent event)

Called from processMenuDragMouseEvent().

protected void fireMenuKeyPressed(MenuKeyEvent event)

Called from processMenuKeyEvent().

protected void fireMenuKeyReleased(MenuKeyEvent event)

Called from processMenuKeyEvent().

protected void fireMenuKeyTyped(MenuKeyEvent event)

Called from processMenuKeyEvent().

protected void init(String text, Icon icon)

Sets the menu element to use the specified text and icon.

Overrides: init in class AbstractButton.

```
protected String paramString()
```
Returns a string representation of the properties of this `JMenuItem`. The returned string may be empty, but it will not be `null`.

Overrides: `paramString` in class `AbstractButton`.

Extended by   JCheckBoxMenuItem (p.195), JMenu (p.281), JRadioButtonMenuItem (p.321).
Returned by   JMenu.add() (p.281), JMenu.getItem() (p.281), JMenu.insert() (p.281), JPopupMenu.add() (p.309).
See also   AbstractButton (p.118), Accessible (p.85), AccessibleContext (p.90), JCheckBoxMenuItem (p.195), JMenu (p.281), JPopupMenu (p.309), JRadioButtonMenuItem (p.321), KeyStroke (p.419), MenuDragMouseEvent (p.501), MenuElement (p.425), MenuKeyEvent (p.503), MenuSelectionManager (p.426).

swing.JMenuItem.AccessibleJMenuItem

INNER CLASS

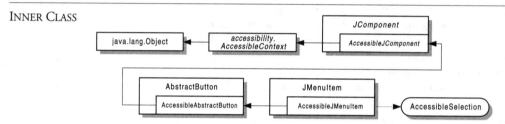

Provides appropriate implementations for `AccessibleSelection` and `getAccessibleRole()`.

```
protected class AccessibleJMenuItem
    extends AbstractButton.AccessibleAbstractButton
    implements ChangeListener
```

Methods

```
public AccessibleRole getAccessibleRole()
```
Returns `AccessibleRole.MENU_ITEM`.
Overrides: `getAccessibleRole` in class `JComponent.AccessibleJComponent`.

```
public void stateChanged(ChangeEvent e)
```
Implements: `stateChanged` in interface `ChangeListener`.

Extended by   JCheckBoxMenuItem.AccessibleJCheckBoxMenuItem (p.197), JMenu.AccessibleJMenu (p.286), JRadioButtonMenuItem.AccessibleJRadioButtonMenuItem (p.323).

swing.JOptionPane

CLASS

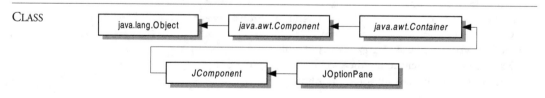

`JOptionPane` allows you to create simple to moderately complex dialogs.

The easiest way to use this class is to use the static methods. There are predefined methods for eight dialog types which are defined by the possible combinations of Confirm, Input, Message, and Option dialogs with two different kinds of frames, both heavyweight and lightweight.

The four basic kinds of dialogs are defined as follows:

- Confirm—allows the user to accept or reject a request (for example, "Save file?").

- Input—accepts input from the user.

- Message—displays a message for the user to acknowledge.

- Option—combines the Confirm, Input, and Message forms.

`JOptionPane` also gives you the ability to create custom dialogs by instantiating a `JOption-Pane` directly and then creating a container for it using the `createDialog()` or `createInternalFrame()` methods.

Example 1—Confirmation Dialog

```
package joptionpane;
import java.awt.event.*;
// Uncomment the following line for Swing 1.0.3 and before
//import com.sun.java.swing.*;
// Uncomment the following line for Swing 1.1 and JDK 1.2
import javax.swing.*;

public class Test extends JFrame {
   public Test() {
      addWindowListener(new WindowAdapter() {
         public void windowClosing(WindowEvent e) {
            Test.this.dispose();
            System.exit(0);
         }
      });
      getContentPane().add(new JLabel("Placeholder label"));
      pack();
      setSize(200,200);
      setVisible(true);

      int replaced = JOptionPane.showConfirmDialog(this,
                           "Replace existing selection?");

      String result = "?";
      switch(replaced) {
         case JOptionPane.CANCEL_OPTION: result = "Canceled"; break;
         case JOptionPane.CLOSED_OPTION: result = "Closed"; break;
         case JOptionPane.NO_OPTION: result = "No"; break;
         case JOptionPane.YES_OPTION: result = "Yes"; break;
         default: ;
      }
      System.out.println ("Replace? " + result);
   }
   public static void main (String[] args) {
```

```
      new Test();
    }
}
```

Example 2—Option Dialog

```
package joptionpane;

import java.awt.event.*;
// Uncomment the following line for Swing 1.0.3 and before
//import com.sun.java.swing.*;
// Uncomment the following line for Swing 1.1 and JDK 1.2
import javax.swing.*;

public class Test2 extends JFrame {
    public Test2() {
        addWindowListener(new WindowAdapter() {
            public void windowClosing(WindowEvent e) {
                Test2.this.dispose();
                System.exit(0);
            }
        });

        getContentPane().add(new JLabel("Placeholder label"));
        pack();
        setSize(200,200);
        setVisible(true);

        Object msg[] = {"Complex Message",
                        new JButton("A component"),
                        new Object[] {"  Nested", "  Array"},
                        "for JOptionPane"};
        Object type[] = {"Animal", "Vegetable", "Mineral"};
        int result = JOptionPane.showOptionDialog(
                        this, msg, "Choose", JOptionPane.YES_NO_OPTION,
                        JOptionPane.QUESTION_MESSAGE, null, type, null);

        System.out.println ("Result (index)= " + result + " ("
                            + type[result] + ")");
    }

    public static void main (String[] args) {
        new Test2();
    }
}
```

public class JOptionPane extends JComponent

Fields

public static final int ERROR_MESSAGE = 0
public static final int INFORMATION_MESSAGE = 1
public static final int PLAIN_MESSAGE = -1
public static final int QUESTION_MESSAGE = 3
public static final int WARNING_MESSAGE = 2

The type of the message. The UI will usually provide a different icon (and possibly a different layout style) for each message type.

public static final int DEFAULT_OPTION = -1

```
public static final int OK_CANCEL_OPTION = 2
public static final int YES_NO_CANCEL_OPTION = 1
public static final int YES_NO_OPTION = 0
```

The type of option buttons made available in a confirmation or option dialog. (There are also forms of the constructors and class methods that let you provide your own set of options.)

```
public static final int CANCEL_OPTION = 2
public static final int CLOSED_OPTION = -1
public static final int NO_OPTION = 1
public static final int OK_OPTION = 0
public static final int YES_OPTION = 0
```

These values are returned by the class methods that return integer values corresponding to a selected option. CLOSED_OPTION indicates that the dialog was closed without selecting an option; this should usually be interpreted as CANCEL_OPTION or NO_OPTION.

```
public static final String ICON_PROPERTY = "icon"
public static final String INITIAL_SELECTION_VALUE_PROPERTY =
    "initialSelectionValue"
public static final String INITIAL_VALUE_PROPERTY = "initialValue"
public static final String INPUT_VALUE_PROPERTY = "inputValue"
public static final String MESSAGE_PROPERTY = "message"
public static final String MESSAGE_TYPE_PROPERTY = "messageType"
public static final String OPTIONS_PROPERTY = "options"
public static final String OPTION_TYPE_PROPERTY = "optionType"
public static final String SELECTION_VALUES_PROPERTY = "selectionValues"
public static final String VALUE_PROPERTY = "value"
public static final String WANTS_INPUT_PROPERTY = "wantsInput"
```

These correspond to the various properties of an option pane.

```
public static final Object UNINITIALIZED_VALUE
```

This is the value returned when no selection is made.

Constructors

```
public JOptionPane()
public JOptionPane(Object message)
public JOptionPane(Object message, int messageType)
public JOptionPane(Object message, int messageType, int optionType)
public JOptionPane(Object message, int messageType,
    int optionType, Icon icon)
public JOptionPane(Object message, int messageType,
    int optionType, Icon icon, Object[] options)
public JOptionPane(Object message, int messageType, int optionType,
    Icon icon, Object[] options, Object initialValue)
```

Creates an instance of an option pane. (Usually, you can use the class methods to create one for you.)

- message—message to display. If message is an array, each value in the array will be converted (recursively) and the results stacked vertically; if message is a Component, it will be used as is; if message is an Icon, it will be displayed in a JLabel; anything else will be converted to a String, and the string will be used as the title of a JLabel. (In its simplest form, message is just a String.)

- messageType—one of the following: ERROR_MESSAGE, INFORMATION_MESSAGE, WARNING_MESSAGE, QUESTION_MESSAGE, or PLAIN_MESSAGE.
- optionType—one of the following: DEFAULT_OPTION, YES_NO_OPTION, YES_NO_CANCEL_OPTION, or OK_CANCEL_OPTION.
- icon—the icon to draw. (Each message type has a default icon.)
- options—an array of values to be used for the buttons. A value of type Component is used as is; an Icon will be displayed in a JButton; anything else will be converted to a String, and the string will be used as the label of a JButton. (Usually, each value is just a String.)
- initialValue—the default selection.

Methods

public JDialog createDialog(java.awt.Component component, String title)

Creates a modal dialog with title, with its parent the frame corresponding to component. The contents of the dialog will be the option pane that creates it. The dialog will be disposed of when it is closed.

public JInternalFrame createInternalFrame(
java.awt.Component component, String title)

Creates an internal frame as a modal dialog, with title, whose parent corresponds to component. The contents of the dialog will be the option pane that creates it. The internal frame will be owned by the same JDesktopPane that owns the internal frame containing component.

public AccessibleContext getAccessibleContext()

Gets the AccessibleContext associated with this JComponent.

Overrides: getAccessibleContext in class JComponent.

Implements: getAccessibleContext in interface Accessible.

public static JDesktopPane getDesktopPaneForComponent(
java.awt.Component component)

Returns the JDesktopPane that contains component, or returns null if it is not part of a JInternalFrame.

public static java.awt.Frame getFrameForComponent(
java.awt.Component component)

Gets the frame containing component. If none is available, uses the one provided by getRootFrame().

public Icon getIcon()

Returns the icon of the option pane.

public Object getInitialSelectionValue()

Returns the value that will initially be selected.

public Object getInitialValue()

Returns the value initially set for this dialog.

public Object getInputValue()

Returns the input value obtained from the user (only if getWantsInput() is true).

public int getMaxCharactersPerLineCount()

Returns the number of characters to use per line for the message. Default: Integer.MAX_VALUE.

public Object getMessage()

Returns the message for this option pane.

public int getMessageType()

Returns the message type: ERROR_MESSAGE, INFORMATION_MESSAGE, WARNING_MESSAGE, QUESTION_MESSAGE, or PLAIN_MESSAGE.

public int getOptionType()

Returns the type of options used in this dialog: DEFAULT_OPTION, YES_NO_OPTION, YES_NO_CANCEL_OPTION, or OK_CANCEL_OPTION. .

public Object[] getOptions()

Gets the list of all options (for example, buttons) the user can select.

public static java.awt.Frame getRootFrame()

Gets a frame to be used as the parent of a dialog, in the case where none has been provided.

public Object[] getSelectionValues()

Gets the list of all selection values available as input.

public OptionPaneUI getUI()

Returns the UI (look and feel) for this option pane.

public String getUIClassID()

Returns "OptionPaneUI".

public Object getValue()

Returns the value selected by the user. If the user hasn't yet selected anything, returns UNINITIALIZED_VALUE. If the user closed the dialog without selecting anything, returns null.

public boolean getWantsInput()

Returns true if the dialog expects input from the user.

public void selectInitialValue()

Requests that the initial value be selected. This should be done after the option pane has been created and given a parent, but before it is displayed.

public void setIcon(Icon icon)

Sets the icon for the option pane.

public void setInitialSelectionValue(Object selectionValue)

Sets the value to be initially selected.

public void setInitialValue(Object value)

Sets the initial value for the user's input.

public void setInputValue(Object value)

Sets the value corresponding to the user's input.

public void setMessage(Object message)

Sets the message for the dialog. (See the discussion on the constructors and class methods.)

public void setMessageType(int messageType)

Sets the message type: ERROR_MESSAGE, INFORMATION_MESSAGE, WARNING_MESSAGE, QUESTION_MESSAGE, or PLAIN_MESSAGE.

public void setOptionType(int optionType)

Sets the type of options used in this dialog: DEFAULT_OPTION, YES_NO_OPTION, YES_NO_CANCEL_OPTION, or OK_CANCEL_OPTION.

public void setOptions(Object[] options)

Sets the list of options the user can click (for example, the buttons).

public static void setRootFrame(java.awt.Frame frame)

Sets the frame to be used as the default parent of a dialog, used when none has been provided.

public void setSelectionValues(Object[] selectionValues)

Sets the list of selection values the user has available for input.

public void setUI(OptionPaneUI ui)

Sets the UI (look and feel) to ui. See the chapter on look and feel.

public void setValue(Object selectedValue)

Sets the value selected by the user.

```
public void setWantsInput(boolean wantsInput)
```
Sets whether the dialog expects input.
```
public static int showConfirmDialog(java.awt.Component parent,
    Object message)
public static int showConfirmDialog(java.awt.Component parent,
    Object message, String title, int optionType)
public static int showConfirmDialog(java.awt.Component parent,
    Object message, String title, int optionType, int messageType)
public static int showConfirmDialog(java.awt.Component parent,
    Object message, String title, int optionType, int messageType,
    Icon icon)
```
Produces a confirmation modal dialog. The return value is CANCEL_OPTION, CLOSE_OPTION, NO_OPTION, OK_OPTION, or YES_OPTION.

- parent—the component whose frame is the parent of the dialog.
- message—the message to display. If message is an array, each value in the array will be converted (recursively) and the results stacked vertically; if message is a Component, it will be used as is; if message is an Icon, it will be displayed in a JLabel; anything else will be converted to a String, and the string will be used as the title of a JLabel (Usually, message is just a String).
- title—the title of the dialog. The default title is Select an Option.
- optionType—one of the following: DEFAULT_OPTION, YES_NO_OPTION, YES_NO_CANCEL_OPTION, or OK_CANCEL_OPTION. The default value for optionType is YES_NO_CANCEL_OPTION.
- messageType—one of the following: ERROR_MESSAGE, INFORMATION_MESSAGE, WARNING_MESSAGE, QUESTION_MESSAGE, or PLAIN_MESSAGE. *Default:* QUESTION_MESSAGE.
- icon— the icon to draw (each message type has a default icon).

```
public static String showInputDialog(Object message)
public static String showInputDialog(java.awt.Component parent,
    Object message)
public static String showInputDialog(java.awt.Component parent,
    Object message, String title, int messageType)
public static Object showInputDialog(java.awt.Component parent,
    Object message, String title, int messageType, Icon icon,
    Object[] selectionValues, Object initiallySelectedValue)
```
Produces a modal dialog requesting input.

- parent—the component whose frame is the parent of the dialog.
- message—the message to display. If message is an array, each value in the array will be converted (recursively) and the results will be stacked vertically; if message is a Component, it will be used as is; if message is an Icon, it will be displayed in a JLabel; anything else will be converted to a String, and the string will be used as the title of a JLabel (usually, message is just a String).
- title—the title of the dialog. The default title of an input dialog is Input.
- messageType—one of the following: ERROR_MESSAGE, INFORMATION_MESSAGE, WARNING_MESSAGE, QUESTION_MESSAGE, or PLAIN_MESSAGE. *Default:* QUESTION_MESSAGE.
- icon—the icon to draw (each message type has a default icon).

- selectionValues—an array of values to be used for input. The UI decides how to display the selectionValues; usually it will use a JComboxBox, a JList, or a JTextField. The default is null, meaning that any value can be input, usually in a JTextField.
- selectedValue—the default selection (see selectionValues[]).

```
public static int showInternalConfirmDialog(
    java.awt.Component parent, Object message)
public static int showInternalConfirmDialog(
    java.awt.Component parent, Object message, String title, int optionType)
public static int showInternalConfirmDialog(
    java.awt.Component parent, Object message, String title,
    int optionType, int messageType)
public static int showInternalConfirmDialog(
    java.awt.Component parent, Object message, String title,
    int optionType, int messageType, Icon icon)
```
Produces a confirmation modal dialog for an internal frame. The return value is one of CANCEL_OPTION, CLOSE_OPTION, NO_OPTION, OK_OPTION, or YES_OPTION.

- parent—the component whose frame is the parent of the dialog.
- message—the message to display. If message is an array, each value in the array will be converted (recursively) and the results will be stacked vertically; if message is a Component, it will be used as is; if message is an Icon, it will be displayed in a JLabel; anything else will be converted to a String, and the string will be used as the title of a JLabel. (Usually, message is just a String.)
- title—the title of the dialog. *Default:* Select an Option.
- optionType—one of the following: DEFAULT_OPTION, YES_NO_OPTION, YES_NO_CANCEL_OPTION, or OK_CANCEL_OPTION. *Default:* YES_NO_CANCEL_OPTION.
- messageType—one of the following: ERROR_MESSAGE, INFORMATION_MESSAGE, WARNING_MESSAGE, QUESTION_MESSAGE, or PLAIN_MESSAGE. *Default:* QUESTION_MESSAGE.
- icon—the icon to draw. (Each message type has a default icon.)

```
public static String showInternalInputDialog(
    java.awt.Component parent, Object message)
public static String showInternalInputDialog(java.awt.Component parent,
    Object message, String title, int messageType)
public static Object showInternalInputDialog(java.awt.Component parent,
    Object message, String title, int messageType, Icon icon,
    Object[] selectionValues, Object selectedValue)
```
Produces a modal dialog requesting input for an internal frame.

- parent—the component whose frame is the parent of the dialog.
- message—the message to display. If message is an array, each value in the array will be converted (recursively) and the results will be stacked vertically; if message is a Component, it will be used as is; if message is an Icon, it will be displayed in a JLabel; anything else will be converted to a String, and the string will be used as the title of a JLabel. (Usually, message is just a String.)
- title—the title of the dialog. *Default:* Input.
- messageType—one of the following: ERROR_MESSAGE, INFORMATION_MESSAGE, WARNING_MESSAGE, QUESTION_MESSAGE, or PLAIN_MESSAGE. *Default:* QUESTION_MESSAGE.

- icon—the icon to draw. (Each message type has a default icon.)
- selectionValues—an array of values to be used for input. The UI decides how to display the selectionValues; usually it will use a JComboxBox, a JList, or a JTextField. *Default:* null, meaning that any value can be input (usually in a JTextField).
- selectedValue—the default selection (selectionValues[]).

```
public static void showInternalMessageDialog(
    java.awt.Component parent, Object message)
public static void showInternalMessageDialog(java.awt.Component parent,
    Object message, String title, int messageType)
public static void showInternalMessageDialog(
    java.awt.Component parent, Object message, String title,
    int messageType, Icon icon)
```
Produces a modal dialog for an internal frame, with a message for the user to acknowledge.

- parent—the component whose frame is the parent of the dialog.
- message—the message to display. If message is an array, each value in the array will be converted (recursively) and the results will be stacked vertically; if message is a Component, it will be used as is; if message is an Icon, it will be displayed in a JLabel; anything else will be converted to a String, and the string will be used as the title of a JLabel. (Usually, message is just a String.)
- title—the title of the dialog. *Default:* Confirm.
- messageType—one of the following: ERROR_MESSAGE, INFORMATION_MESSAGE, WARNING_MESSAGE, QUESTION_MESSAGE, or PLAIN_MESSAGE. *Default:* QUESTION_MESSAGE.
- icon—the icon to draw. (Each message type has a default icon.)

```
public static int showInternalOptionDialog(ava.awt.Component parent,
    Object message, String title, int optionType, int messageType,
    Icon icon,Object[] selectionValues, Object selectedValue)
```
Produces a modal dialog for an internal frame. It allows input values and has buttons for the user to choose.

- parent—the component whose frame is the parent of the dialog.
- message—the message to display. If message is an array, each value in the array will be converted (recursively) and the results will be stacked vertically; if message is a Component, it will be used as is; if message is an Icon, it will be displayed in a JLabel; anything else will be converted to a String, and the string will be used as the title of a JLabel. (Usually, message is just a String.)
- title—the title of the dialog.
- optionType—one of the following: DEFAULT_OPTION, YES_NO_OPTION, YES_NO_CANCEL_OPTION, or OK_CANCEL_OPTION. *Default:* YES_NO_CANCEL_OPTION.
- messageType—one of the following: ERROR_MESSAGE, INFORMATION_MESSAGE, WARNING_MESSAGE, QUESTION_MESSAGE, or PLAIN_MESSAGE.
- icon—the icon to draw. (Each message type has a default icon.)
- selectionValues—an array of values to be used for input. The UI decides how to display the selectionValues. Usually it will use a JComboxBox, a JList, or a JTextField. *Default:* null, meaning that any value can be input (usually in a JTextField).
- selectedValue—the default selection (one of the selectionValues[]).

```
public static void showMessageDialog(java.awt.Component parent,
    Object message)
public static void showMessageDialog(java.awt.Component parent,
    Object message, String title, int messageType)
public static void showMessageDialog(java.awt.Component parent,
    Object message, String title, int messageType, Icon icon)
```
Produces a modal dialog with a message for the user to acknowledge.

- `parent`—the component whose frame is the parent of the dialog.
- `message`—the message to display. If `message` is an array, each value in the array will be converted (recursively) and the results will be stacked vertically; if `message` is a Component, it will be used as is; if `message` is an Icon, it will be displayed in a `JLabel`; anything else will be converted to a `String`, and the string will be used as the title of a `JLabel`. (Usually, `message` is just a `String`.)
- `title`—the title of the dialog. *Default:* Confirm.
- `messageType`—one of the following: ERROR_MESSAGE, INFORMATION_MESSAGE, WARNING_MESSAGE, QUESTION_MESSAGE, or PLAIN_MESSAGE. *Default:* QUESTION_MESSAGE.
- `icon`—the icon to draw. (Each message type has a default icon.)

```
public static int showOptionDialog(java.awt.Component parent,
    Object message, String title, int optionType, int messageType,
    Icon icon, Object[] selectionValues, Object selectedValue)
```
Produces a modal dialog that allows input values, and buttons the user may choose.

- `parent`—the component whose frame is the parent of the dialog.
- `message`—the message to display. If `message` is an array, each value in the array will be converted (recursively) and the results will be stacked vertically; if `message` is a Component, it will be used as is; if `message` is an Icon, it will be displayed in a `JLabel`; anything else will be converted to a `String`, and the string will be used as the title of a `JLabel`. (Usually, `message` is just a `String`.)
- `title`—the title of the dialog.
-
- —one of the following: DEFAULT_OPTION, YES_NO_OPTION, YES_NO_CANCEL_OPTION, or OK_CANCEL_OPTION. *Default:* YES_NO_CANCEL_OPTION.
- `messageType`—one of the following: ERROR_MESSAGE, INFORMATION_MESSAGE, WARNING_MESSAGE, QUESTION_MESSAGE, or PLAIN_MESSAGE.
- `icon`—the icon to draw. (Each message type has a default icon.)
- `selectionValues`—an array of values to be used for input. The UI decides how to display the `selectionValues`. Usually it will use a `JComboxBox`, a `JList`, or a `JTextField`. *Default:* null, meaning that any value can be input (usually in a `JTextField`).
- `selectedValue`—the default selection (one of the `selectionValues[]`).

```
public void updateUI()
```
Updates the appearance according to the current look and feel.
Overrides: updateUI in class `JComponent`.

Protected Fields
```
protected transient Icon icon
```
The icon for this option pane.

protected transient Object initialSelectionValue
> The value that will initially be selected among the options.

protected transient Object initialValue
> The initial value for the user's input.

protected transient Object inputValue
> The value input by the user.

protected transient Object message
> The message for this option pane.

protected int messageType
> The message type: ERROR_MESSAGE, INFORMATION_MESSAGE, WARNING_MESSAGE, QUESTION_MESSAGE, or PLAIN_MESSAGE.

protected int optionType
> The option type: DEFAULT_OPTION, YES_NO_OPTION, YES_NO_CANCEL_OPTION, or OK_CANCEL_OPTION.

protected transient Object[] options
> The options (for example, buttons) to display to the user.

protected transient Object[] selectionValues
> The values available for selection.

protected transient Object value
> The currently selected value: one of the selection values, or UNINITIALIZED_VALUE, or null.

protected boolean wantsInput
> Set to true if a widget needs to be provided for user input.

Inner Classes
protected class JOptionPane.AccessibleJOptionPane

> *See also*   JComponent (p.207), JDesktopPane (p.224), Icon (p.183), OptionPaneUI (p.537).

swing.JOptionPane.AccessibleJOptionPane

INNER CLASS

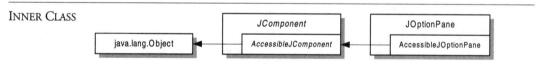

protected class JOptionPane.AccessibleJOptionPane
    extends AccessibleJComponent

Methods
public AccessibleRole getAccessibleRole()
> Returns AccessibleRole.OPTION_PANE.

> *See also*   AccessibleRole (p.95).

swing.JPanel

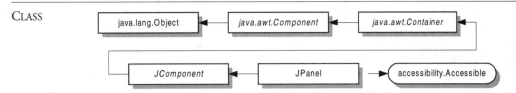

A `JPanel` is the Swing analog to `Panel`. The key addition is the ability to double buffer drawing done in the panel. Double buffering is turned on using the constructor.

In Swing 1.1, `JPanel` also supports a UI delegate.

FAQs

How do I do animation in Swing?

Simple animation is quite easy in Swing, since double-buffering is already implemented. The key is to override `paintComponent()`, not `paint()`/`update()`. The two ways to implement this feature are to subclass `JPanel` or `JComponent`.

The two ways to do simple animation are subtly different. Subclassing `JPanel` simply requires overriding `paintComponent()`, since double-buffering is turned on by default. The catch is that in `paintComponent()`, `super.paintComponent()` must be called first. Subclassing `JComponent` requires having the constructor call `setDoubleBuffered(true)`, but does not require calling `super.paintComponent()` from `paintComponent()`. So, either choice involves about the same amount of work.

Threaded animation is a bit harder, since you can't get at the double-buffer created by Swing. You need to create your own offscreen buffer in the same way as it was done with an AWT `Canvas` (by calling `Component.getGraphics()` after the `Component` has been realized through calling `show()` or `pack()` on it), and then you draw to the off-screen buffer from the thread. Once the thread is done painting the buffer it can call `repaint()` (which is safe to call from a background thread). `paintComponent()` can then just blit the off-screen buffer into the main buffer. Since you are supplying your own buffer, you can turn Swing's own double-buffering support off.

```
public class JPanel extends JComponent
    implements Accessible
```

Constructors
```
public JPanel()
public JPanel(java.awt.LayoutManager layout)
public JPanel(boolean doubleBuffered)
public JPanel(java.awt.LayoutManager layout, boolean doubleBuffered)
```
Creates a new panel with layout manager `layout`, double buffered if `doubleBuffered` is true. *Default:* `FlowLayout`, double buffered.

Methods

`public AccessibleContext getAccessibleContext()`
>   Gets the accessible context.
>   *Overrides:* `getAccessibleContext` in class `JComponent`.
>   *Implements:* `getAccessibleContext` in interface `Accessible`.

`public String getUIClassID()`
>   Returns "PanelUI".
>   *Overrides:* `getUIClassID` in class `JComponent`.

`public void updateUI()`
>   Notifies the panel to update itself according to the current UI (look and feel).
>   *Overrides:* `updateUI` in class `JComponent`.

Protected Methods

`protected String paramString()`
>   Returns a string representation of the properties of this `JPanel`. The returned string may be empty but it will not be `null`.
>   *Overrides:* `paramString` in class `JComponent`.

Inner Classes

`protected class JPanel.AccessibleJPanel`

>   *Extended by*   AbstractColorChooserPanel (p.478).
>   *See also*   Accessible (p.85), AccessibleContext (p.90), JComponent (p.207).

swing.JPanel.AccessibleJPanel

INNER CLASS

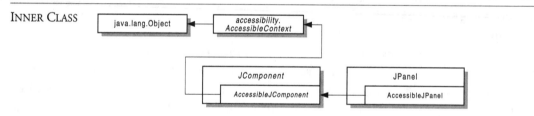

`protected class JPanel.AccessibleJPanel`
`   extends JComponent.AccessibleJComponent`

Methods

`public AccessibleRole getAccessibleRole()`
>   Returns `AccessibleRole.PANEL`.
>   *Overrides:* `getAccessibleRole` in class `AccessibleJComponent`.

swing.JPasswordField

CLASS

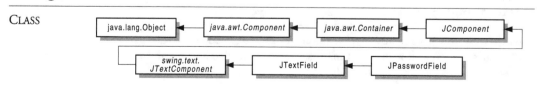

JPasswordField is a JTextField customized to handle text strings that should not be displayed to the user (for example, passwords). Note that this class is implemented so that the password text cannot be cut or copied to the clipboard, but a password can be pasted into the field.

Unlike the JDK 1.1 AWT, this functionality is separate from JTextField. This makes it easier for a look and feel to avoid the mistake of assuming all textfield characters should always be displayed.

Example

```
package jpasswordfield;

import java.awt.*;
import java.awt.event.*;
// Uncomment the following line for Swing 1.0.3 and before
//import com.sun.java.swing.*;
// Uncomment the following line for Swing 1.1 and JDK 1.2
import javax.swing.*;

public class Main extends JFrame {
   JPasswordField field = new JPasswordField("*", 10);

   public Main () {
     addWindowListener(new WindowAdapter() {
       public void windowClosing(WindowEvent e) {
         Main.this.dispose();
         System.exit(0);
       }
     });

     field.addActionListener(new ActionListener() {
       public void actionPerformed(ActionEvent e) {
         System.out.println("Field="+field.getText());
       }
     });

     getContentPane().add(field);
     pack();
     setVisible(true);
   }
   public static void main (String arg[]) {
     new Main();
   }
}
```

public class JPasswordField extends JTextField

Constructors
public JPasswordField()
public JPasswordField(String initialText)
public JPasswordField(int numColumns)
public JPasswordField(String initialText, int numColumns)
public JPasswordField(Document document, String initialText, int numColumns)
   Creates a new password field.
   Defaults: document: a newly created PlainDocument; initialText: empty; numColumns: 0.

Methods

public void copy()

Overrides so that the password text cannot be copied to the clipboard.

Overrides: copy in class JTextComponent.

public void cut()

Overrides so that the password text cannot be cut to the clipboard.

Overrides: cut in class JTextComponent.

public boolean echoCharIsSet()

Returns true if this text field has an echo character set; for example, setEchoChar() was previously called.

public AccessibleContext getAccessibleContext()

Returns the AccessibleContext associated with this JPasswordField. A new context is created as necessary.

Overrides: getAccessibleContext in class JTextField.

Implements: getAccessibleContext in interface Accessible.

public char getEchoChar()

Returns the echo character that was set.

public char[] getPassword()

Returns the text contained in the field. To prevent having the password remain in memory for a potentially long period of time before being garbage collected, you should overwrite the characters in the password array after you have used the password.

public String getText()

Deprecated. Use getPassword().

Overrides: getText in class JTextComponent.

public String getText(int offs, int len) throws BadLocationException

Deprecated. Use getPassword().

Throws: BadLocationException if the offset or length are invalid.

Overrides: getText in class JTextComponent.

public String getUIClassID()

Returns "PasswordFieldUI".

public void setEchoChar(char echo)

Sets the echo character for the password. (A UI is not required to follow this choice; for example, it might use small squares rather than the chosen character.)

Protected Methods

protected String paramString()

Returns a string representation of the properties of this JPasswordField. The returned string may be empty but it will not be null.

Overrides: paramString in class JTextField.

See also   Document (p.826), JTextComponent (p.838), JTextField (p.379), PlainDocument (p.857).

swing.JPasswordField.AccessibleJPasswordField

INNER CLASS

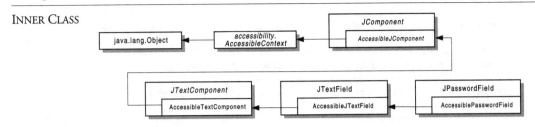

```
public class AccessibleJPasswordField
    extends JTextField.AccessibleJPasswordField
```

Method
```
public AccessibleRole getAccessibleRole()
```
Returns `AccessibleRole.PASSWORD_TEXT`.

Overrides: `getAccessibleRole` in class `AccessibleJTextComponent`.

See also   AccessibleRole (p.95), JTextField.AccessibleJTextField (p.383).

swing.JPopupMenu

CLASS

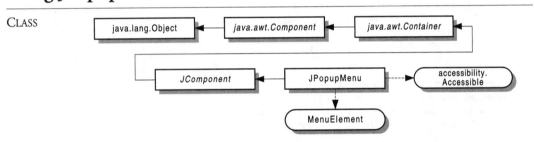

`JPopupMenu` provides pop-up menus. When used directly, these are typically in-place menus, triggered by a right-click on an item. `JPopupMenu` is also transparently used by `JMenu` to provide the piece that pops up when you press the `JMenu`'s label component.

Note that the layout manager of a `JPopupMenu` can be changed to create custom menus, such as multicolumn menus.

Example

```
package jpopupmenu;
import java.awt.*;
import java.awt.event.*;
// Uncomment the following line for Swing 1.0.3 and before
//import com.sun.java.swing.*;
// Uncomment the following line for Swing 1.1 and JDK 1.2
import javax.swing.*;

public class Test extends JFrame {
    JPopupMenu menu = new JPopupMenu("Popup");
```

```
class MyLabel extends JLabel {
  public MyLabel(String text) {
    super(text);
    addMouseListener(new PopupTriggerListener());
  }
  // NOTE: to use isPopupTrigger(), you _must_ check it
  // on both mousePressed and mouseReleased!  Which one
  // is the popupTrigger depends on the underlying OS.
  protected class PopupTriggerListener extends MouseAdapter {
    public void mousePressed(MouseEvent ev) {
      if (ev.isPopupTrigger()) {
        menu.show(ev.getComponent(), ev.getX(), ev.getY());
      }
    }
    public void mouseReleased(MouseEvent ev) {
      if (ev.isPopupTrigger()) {
        menu.show (ev.getComponent(), ev.getX(), ev.getY());
      }
    }
  }
}

JLabel label = new MyLabel("Popup shows when this label is right-clicked");
public Test() {
  addWindowListener(new WindowAdapter() {
    public void windowClosing(WindowEvent e) {
      Test.this.dispose();
      System.exit(0);
    }
  });
  JMenuItem item = new JMenuItem("Test1");
  item.addActionListener(new ActionListener() {
    public void actionPerformed(ActionEvent e) {
      System.out.println("Menu item Test1");
    }
  });
  menu.add(item);

  item = new JMenuItem("Test2");
  item.addActionListener(new ActionListener() {
    public void actionPerformed(ActionEvent e) {
      System.out.println("Menu item Test2");
    }
  });
  menu.add(item);

  getContentPane().add(label);
  pack();
   setSize(300,100);
}
public static void main (String[] args) {
  new Test().setVisible(true);
}
}
```

```
public class JPopupMenu extends JComponent
    implements Accessible, MenuElement
```

Constructors

public JPopupMenu()

Creates a pop-up menu.

public JPopupMenu(String label)

Creates a pop-up menu with label as a title.

Methods

public JMenuItem add(Action action)

Creates a JMenuItem corresponding to action, and adds it to the pop-up menu.

public JMenuItem add(JMenuItem menuItem)

Adds menuItem to the end of the pop-up menu.

public JMenuItem add(String itemLabel)

Adds component to the end of this menu.

public void addPopupMenuListener(PopupMenuListener listener)

Adds listener to the list of listeners to be notified of significant events for this menu.

public void addSeparator()

Adds a separator to the menu, usually shown as a line or blank area. See JSeparator.

public AccessibleContext getAccessibleContext()

Returns the accessible context for this menu.

Overrides: getAccessibleContext in class JComponent.

Implements: getAccessibleContext in interface Accessible.

public java.awt.Component getComponent()

Returns the component with which this menu is associated.

Implements: getComponent in interface MenuElement.

public java.awt.Component getComponentAtIndex(int index)

Returns the menu element at index.

public int getComponentIndex(java.awt.Component component)

Finds the index for component.

public static boolean getDefaultLightWeightPopupEnabled()

Returns the default value for the lightWeightPopupEnabled property.

public java.awt.Component getInvoker()

Returns the component which owns this pop-up menu and is currently invoking it.

public String getLabel()

Returns the pop-up menu's label.

public java.awt.Insets getMargin()

Returns the margin between the pop-up menu and its menu elements.

public SingleSelectionModel getSelectionModel()

Gets the selection model for this pop-up.

public MenuElement[] getSubElements()

For hierarchical pop-ups, gets a list of all children menu elements.

Implements: getSubElements in interface MenuElement.

public PopupMenuUI getUI()

Returns the UI (look and feel) for this menu.

public String getUIClassID()

    Returns "PopupMenuUI".

    Overrides: getUIClassID in class JComponent.

public void insert(Action action, int index)

    Adds action to the pop-up menu at index.

public void insert(java.awt.Component component, int index)

    Adds component to the pop-up menu at index.

public boolean isBorderPainted()

    Returns true if the border should be painted.

public boolean isLightWeightPopupEnabled()

    Returns true if Swing is allowed to use lightweight pop-ups. See setLightWeightPopupEnabled().

public boolean isVisible()

    Returns true if the pop-up is visible.

    Overrides: isVisible in class Component.

public void menuSelectionChanged(boolean wasAdded)

    Returns a notification that the menu selection has changed. Parameter wasAdded is true if the menu element has been added, or false if it has been removed.

    Implements: menuSelectionChanged in interface MenuElement.

public void pack()

    Lays out the pop-up.

public void processKeyEvent(java.awt.event.KeyEvent event, MenuElement[] path, MenuSelectionManager manager)

    Handles a key event directed at this menu element.

    Implements: processKeyEvent in interface MenuElement.

public void processMouseEvent(java.awt.event.MouseEvent event, MenuElement[] path, MenuSelectionManager manager)

    Handles a mouse event. The event's source is the component associated with this menu element. The path is the path through a hierarchical menu, ending at this menu element. Uses manager to change the menu selection. The manager will continue forwarding this event to submenus if necessary.

    Implements: processMouseEvent in interface MenuElement.

public void remove(java.awt.Component comp)

    Removes the given component from this pop-up menu.

    Overrides: remove in class Container.

public void removePopupMenuListener(PopupMenuListener listener)

    Removes listener from the list so it is no longer notified of changes in this menu.

public void setBorderPainted(boolean shouldPaint)

    Sets whether the border should be painted.

public void setDefaultLightWeightPopupEnabled(boolean beLightweight)

    Usually, you will leave this true, indicating that you want to use the more efficient lightweight menus when you can. If you are mixing lightweight and heavyweight components, you must set this false to ensure that pop-ups are visible above the heavyweight components.

public void setInvoker(java.awt.Component component)

    Sets the component that should be regarded as the invoker of the menu.

public void setLabel(String label)

    Sets the pop-up menu's label. Different look and feels may choose to display or not to display this.

```
public void setLightWeightPopupEnabled(boolean aFlag)
```
When displaying the pop-up, JPopupMenu chooses to use a lightweight pop-up if it fits. This method allows you to disable this feature when you are mixing light- and heavyweight components.
```
public void setLocation(int x, int y)
```
Sets the desired location for this menu. (0,0) is the upper left-hand corner.

Overrides: setLocation in class Component.
```
public void setPopupSize(int width, int height)
public void setPopupSize(java.awt.Dimension dim)
```
Sets the size of this pop-up menu.
```
public void setSelected(java.awt.Component selection)
```
Makes selection be the new current selection. Propagates this to the selection model.
```
public void setSelectionModel(SingleSelectionModel model)
```
Sets the selection model for this pop-up.
```
public void setUI(PopupMenuUI ui)
```
Sets the UI (look and feel) for this menu. See the chapter on look and feel.
```
public void setVisible(boolean isVisible)
```
Sets whether this pop-up should be visible.

Overrides: setVisible in class JComponent.
```
public void show(java.awt.Component component, int x, int y)
```
Shows this menu attached to component at (x,y). (Coordinates are relative to the component.)
```
public void updateUI()
```
Returns notification that the menu should update itself to the current look and feel.

Overrides: updateUI in class JComponent.

Protected Methods
```
protected java.beans.PropertyChangeListener
    createActionChangeListener(JMenuItem b)
```
Creates the PropertyChangeListener needed when a JMenuItem is added using an Action.
```
protected void firePopupMenuCanceled()
```
Notifies listeners that the pop-up menu was canceled.
```
protected void firePopupMenuWillBecomeInvisible()
```
Notifies listeners that this pop-up menu will become invisible.
```
protected void firePopupMenuWillBecomeVisible()
```
Notifies listeners that this pop-up menu will become visible.
```
protected void paintBorder(java.awt.Graphics g)
```
Paints the border onto graphics context g.
```
protected String paramString()
```
Returns a string representation of the properties of this JPopupMenu. The returned string may be empty, but it will not be null.

Overrides: paramString in class JComponent.

Inner Classes
```
protected class JPopupMenu.AccessibleJPopupMenu
public static class JPopupMenu.Separator
```

Extended by   BasicComboPopup (p.572).
Returned by   JMenu.getPopupMenu() (p.281).

See also   Accessible (p.85), AccessibleContext (p.90), Action (p.128), JMenuItem (p.291), MenuElement (p.425), MenuSelectionManager (p.426), PopupMenuListener (p.506), PopupMenuUI (p.538), SingleSelectionModel (p.440).

swing.JPopupMenu.AccessibleJPopupMenu

INNER CLASS

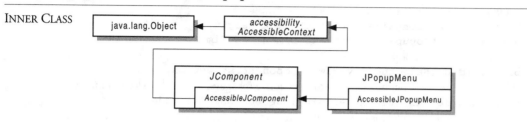

```
protected class JPopupMenu.AccessibleJPopupMenu
    extends JComponent.AccessibleJComponent
```

Methods
```
public AccessibleRole getAccessibleRole()
```
   Returns `AccessibleRole.POPUP_MENU`.
   Overrides: getAccessibleRole in class `AccessibleJComponent`.

See also   AccessibleRole (p.95), JComponent.AccessibleJComponent (p.221).

swing.JPopupMenu.Separator

INNER CLASS

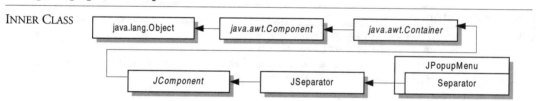

A separator component for `JPopupMenus`.

```
public static class JPopupMenu.Separator extends JSeparator
```

Constructors
```
public Separator()
```
   Constructs a horizontal separator.

Methods
```
public String getUIClassID()
```
   Returns "PopupMenuSeparatorUI".
   Overrides: getUIClassID in class `JSeparator`.

See also   JSeparator (p.338).

swing.JProgressBar

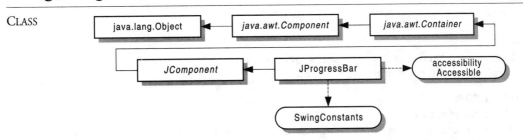

A `JProgressBar` is a component that is suitable for things such as showing the percentage done. It monitors a `BoundedRangeModel`, and updates itself whenever the model significantly changes. It maintains minimum, current, and maximum values such that

minimum <= current <= maximum

at all times.

Example

```
package jprogressbar;

import java.awt.*;
import java.awt.event.*;
// Uncomment the following line for Swing 1.0.3 and before
//import com.sun.java.swing.*;
// Uncomment the following line for Swing 1.1 and JDK 1.2
import javax.swing.*;

public class Main extends JFrame {
  JProgressBar bar = new JProgressBar();
  JButton step = new JButton("Step");

  public Main () {
    addWindowListener(new WindowAdapter() {
      public void windowClosing(WindowEvent e) {
        Main.this.dispose();
        System.exit(0);
      }
    });
    step.addActionListener(new ActionListener() {
      public void actionPerformed(ActionEvent e) {
        int value = bar.getValue() + 7;
        if (value > bar.getMaximum()) {
          value = bar.getMaximum();
        }
        bar.setValue(value);
      }
    });

    getContentPane().add(bar, BorderLayout.NORTH);
    getContentPane().add(step, BorderLayout.EAST);
    pack();
    setVisible(true);
```

```
    }
    public static void main (String arg[]) {
       new Main();
    }
}
```

public class JProgressBar extends JComponent
    implements SwingConstants, Accessible

Constructors

public JProgressBar()

Creates a horizontal progress bar using a default `BoundedRangeModel` ranging from 0 to 100. No string is displayed and the border is painted.

public JProgressBar(BoundedRangeModel newModel)

Creates a horizontal progress bar using the given `BoundedRangeModel`. No string is displayed and the border is painted.

public JProgressBar(int orient)

Creates a progress bar with the specified orientation, which can be either `VERTICAL` or `HORIZON-TAL`. A default `BoundedRangeModel` ranging from 0 to 100 is used. No string is displayed and the border is painted.

public JProgressBar(int min, int max)

Creates a horizontal progress bar using a `BoundedRangeModel` initialized to the given `min` and `max`. No string is displayed and the border is painted.

public JProgressBar(int orientation, int min, int max)

Creates a progress bar using the specified `orientation`, `min`, and `max`. No string is displayed and the border is painted.

Methods

public void addChangeListener(ChangeListener newListener)

Adds a new change listener.

public AccessibleContext getAccessibleContext()

Returns the accessible context. See the chapter on accessibility for more information.

Overrides: `getAccessibleContext` in class `JComponent`.

Implements: `getAccessibleContext` in interface `Accessible`.

public int getMaximum()

Returns the maximum value for the progress bar. See `setMaximum()`, `getMinimum()`, `setMinimum()`, `getValue()`, and `setValue()`.

public int getMinimum()

Returns the minimum value for the progress bar. See `getMaximum()`, `setMaximum()`, `setMinimum()`, `getValue()`, and `setValue()`.

public BoundedRangeModel getModel()

Gets the model for this progress bar. See the `BoundedRangeModel` class for more information.

public int getOrientation()

Returns either `JProgressBar.HORIZONTAL` or `JProgressBar.VERTICAL`.

public double getPercentComplete()

Returns the percent complete for the progress bar as a floating point value ranging from 0.0 to 1.0.

public String getString()

Returns the current value of the string which is displayed in the progress bar if isStringPainted is true. The default value is the percent complete as a String.

public ProgressBarUI getUI()

Returns the UI (look and feel) object responsible for this object. See the chapter on look and feel for more information.

public String getUIClassID()

Always returns "ProgressBarUI".

Overrides: getUIClassID in class JComponent.

public int getValue()

Returns the current value of the progress bar (minimum <= current <= maximum). See getMaximum(), setMaximum(), getMinimum(), setMinimum(), and setValue().

public boolean isBorderPainted()

Returns true if the progress bar should have a border.

public boolean isStringPainted()

Returns true if the progress bar will render a string onto the representation of the progress bar. The default value is false. The default string used is the percent complete as a string.

public void removeChangeListener(ChangeListener listener)

Removes listener from the list of listeners listening for changes in the progress bar.

public void setBorderPainted(boolean shouldPaintBorder)

Sets whether the border should be painted.

public void setMaximum(int newMax)

Sets the maximum value for the progress bar. If the minimum or the current value is greater than newMax, it will be set to newMax. See getMaximum(), getMinimum(), setMinimum(), getValue(), and setValue().

public void setMinimum(int newMin)

Sets the minimum value for the progress bar. If the current value or the maximum is less than newMin, it will be set to newMin. See getMaximum(), setMaximum(), getMinimum(), getMinimum(), getValue(), and setValue().

public void setModel(BoundedRangeModel newModel)

Sets the model for the progress bar.

public void setOrientation(int axis)

Sets the orientation to either JProgressBar.HORIZONTAL or JProgressBar.VERTICAL.

Throws: IllegalArgumentException if axis is an illegal value.

public void setString(String s)

Allows you to set a custom string to display inside the progress bar. If you specify a string through this method it will remain fixed until you change it. The default string is null, which causes the JProgressBar to use the percent complete as a String as the displayed string.

public void setStringPainted(boolean b)

If set to true, the progress bar will paint the string set through setString() (or the default string) inside the progress bar. This property defaults to false.

public void setUI(ProgressBarUI newUI)

Sets the UI object that is responsible for the look and feel of the progress bar. See the chapter on look and feel for more information.

public void setValue(int newValue)

Sets the current value of the progress bar. You must have minimum <= newValue <= maximum or an exception will be thrown. See getMaximum(), setMaximum(), getMinimum(), setMinimum(), and getValue().

public void updateUI()

Tells the progress bar to replace its look and feel. See the chapter on look and feel for more information.

Overrides: updateUI in class JComponent.

Protected Fields

protected transient ChangeEvent changeEvent

The ChangeEvent for this progress bar. (A single event can be used for all notifications for a particular progress bar, rather than constructing one each time.)

protected ChangeListener changeListener

The listener that is notified of changes in the model so the progress bar can be updated.

protected BoundedRangeModel model

The model for this progress bar.

protected int orientation

The orientation of the progress bar, either JProgressBar.HORIZONTAL or JProgress-Bar.VERTICAL.

protected boolean paintBorder

Set to true if the border should be painted.

protected boolean paintString

Set to true if the progress bar should paint the progressString inside the progress bar.

protected String progressString

The string to paint inside the progress bar. Defaults to null, which causes the JProgressBar to use the String value of the percent complete as the progressString.

Protected Methods

protected ChangeListener createChangeListener()

Creates a change listener for this progress bar (provided so subclasses can use a different listener if they want).

protected void fireStateChanged()

Notifies all listeners about the new state.

protected void paintBorder(java.awt.Graphics g)

Paints the border for the progress bar.

Overrides: paintBorder in class JComponent.

protected String paramString()

Returns a string representation of the properties of this JProgressBar. The returned string may be empty but it will not be null.

Overrides: paramString in class JComponent.

See also   Accessible (p.85), AccessibleContext (p.90), BoundedRangeModel (p.132), ChangeEvent (p.487), ChangeListener (p.488), ProgressBarUI (p.538).

INNER CLASS

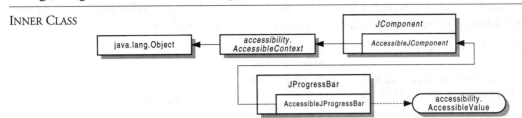

```
protected class JProgressBar.AccessibleJProgressBar
    extends JComponent.AccessibleJComponent
    implements AccessibleValue
```

Methods

public AccessibleRole getAccessibleRole()

Returns `AccessibleRole.PROGRESS_BAR`.

Overrides: getAccessibleRole in class JComponent.AccessibleJComponent.

public AccessibleStateSet getAccessibleStateSet()

Overrides: getAccessibleStateSet in class JComponent.AccessibleJComponent.

public AccessibleValue getAccessibleValue()

Overrides: getAccessibleValue in class AccessibleContext.

public java.lang.Number getCurrentAccessibleValue()

Implements: getCurrentAccessibleValue in interface AccessibleValue.

public java.lang.Number getMaximumAccessibleValue()

Implements: getMaximumAccessibleValue in interface AccessibleValue.

public java.lang.Number getMinimumAccessibleValue()

Implements: getMinimumAccessibleValue in interface AccessibleValue.

public boolean setCurrentAccessibleValue(java.lang.Number n)

Implements: setCurrentAccessibleValue in interface AccessibleValue.

See also   AccessibleRole (p.95), AccessibleStateSet (p.101), AccessibleValue (p.104), JComponent.AccessibleJComponent (p.207).

swing.JRadioButton

CLASS

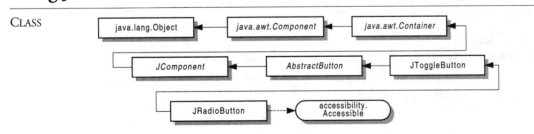

A JRadioButton is a button that can either be selected or unselected. It differs primarily from a JToggleButton in the way that it is rendered. A JRadioButton is usually part of a ButtonGroup, which ensures that only one button in the group is selected at a time.

Example: See ButtonGroup.

```
public class JRadioButton extends JToggleButton
    implements Accessible
```

Constructors

```
public JRadioButton()
public JRadioButton(Icon icon)
public JRadioButton(Icon icon, boolean isSelected)
public JRadioButton(String text)
public JRadioButton(String text, boolean isSelected)
public JRadioButton(String text, Icon icon)
public JRadioButton(String text, Icon icon, boolean isSelected)
```
Creates a radio button with the specified text, icon, and initial selection status. Default values: no text, no icon, and/or not selected.

Methods

```
public AccessibleContext getAccessibleContext()
```
Gets the accessible context.
Overrides: getAccessibleContext in class JToggleButton.
Implements: getAccessibleContext in interface Accessible.

```
public String getUIClassID()
```
Returns "RadioButtonUI".
Overrides: getUIClassID in class JToggleButton.

```
public void updateUI()
```
Updates the button according to the current look and feel.
Overrides: updateUI in class JToggleButton.

Protected Methods

```
protected String paramString()
```
Returns a string representation of the properties of this JRadioButton. The returned string may be empty but it may not be null.
Overrides: paramString in class JToggleButton.

Inner Classes

```
protected class JRadioButton.AccessibleJRadioButton
```

See also   Accessible (p.85), AccessibleContext (p.90), ButtonGroup (p.146), Icon (p.183), JCheckBox (p.193), JToggleButton (p.385).

swing.JRadioButton.AccessibleJRadioButton

INNER CLASS

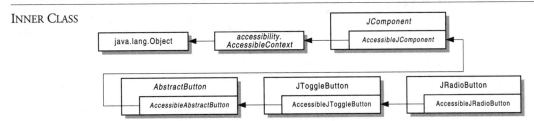

Returns a correct `AccessibleRole` for a `JRadioButton`.

```
protected class JRadioButton.AccessibleJRadioButton
    extends JToggleButton.AccessibleJToggleButton
```

Method

```
public AccessibleRole getAccessibleRole()
```
Returns `AccessibleRole.RADIO_BUTTON`.
Overrides: `getAccessibleRole` in class `AccessibleJToggleButton`.

swing.JRadioButtonMenuItem

CLASS

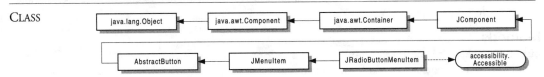

Creates a radio button suitable for use as a menu item. (It must still be grouped using `Button-Group` to acquire radio button behavior.)

Example

```
import java.awt.*;
import java.awt.event.*;
// Uncomment the following line for Swing 1.0.3 and before
//import com.sun.java.swing.*;
// Uncomment the following line for Swing 1.1 and JDK 1.2
import javax.swing.*;

public class Main extends JFrame {
    public Main () {
        JMenuBar bar = new JMenuBar();
        JMenu menu = new JMenu("File");
        bar.add (menu);

        ButtonGroup group = new ButtonGroup();
        JRadioButtonMenuItem item = new JRadioButtonMenuItem("Cat");
        group.add(item);
        menu.add(item);

        item = new JRadioButtonMenuItem("Dog");
        group.add(item);
```

```
        menu.add(item);
        group.setSelected(item.getModel(), true);

        setJMenuBar(bar);
        getContentPane().add(new JLabel("A placeholder"));
    pack();
    setSize (300, 300);
      setVisible(true);
    }
    public static void main (String arg[]) {new Main();}
}
```

public class JRadioButtonMenuItem extends JMenuItem
    implements com.sun.java.accessibility.Accessible

Constructors

public JRadioButtonMenuItem()
public JRadioButtonMenuItem(String text)
public JRadioButtonMenuItem(String text, boolean selected)
public JRadioButtonMenuItem(Icon icon)
public JRadioButtonMenuItem(Icon icon, boolean selected)
public JRadioButtonMenuItem(String text, Icon icon)
public JRadioButtonMenuItem(String text, Icon icon, boolean selected)

Creates a radio button menu item, with text and/or icon. Default values: empty text, no icon, and not selected.

Methods

public AccessibleContext getAccessibleContext()

Returns the accessible context for this menu item.

Overrides: getAccessibleContext in class JMenuItem.

Implements: getAccessibleContext in interface Accessible.

public String getUIClassID()

Returns "RadioButtonMenuItemUI".

Overrides: getUIClassID in class JMenuItem.

public void requestFocus()

Requests focus for this component.

Overrides: requestFocus in class JComponent.

public void updateUI()

Updates the component with the current look and feel. See the chapter on look and feel.

Overrides: updateUI in class JMenuItem.

Protected Methods

protected void init(String text, Icon icon)

Initializes the text and icon for this menu item.

Overrides: init in class JMenuItem.

protected String paramString()

Returns a string representation of the properties of this JRadioButtonMenuItem. The returned string may be empty but it will not be null.

Overrides: paramString in class JMenuItem.

See also Accessible (p.85), AccessibleContext (p.90), ButtonGroup (p.146), Icon (p.183), MenuItemUI (p.536).

swing.JRadioButtonMenuItem.AccessibleJRadioButtonMenuItem

INNER CLASS

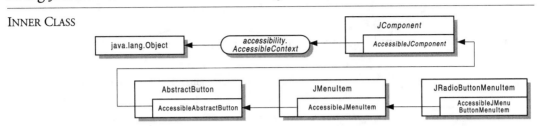

```
protected class
    JRadioButtonMenuItem.AccessibleJRadioButtonMenuItem
    extends JMenuItem.AccessibleJMenuItem
```

Methods

```
public AccessibleRole getAccessibleRole()
```
Returns `AccessibleRole.RADIO_BUTTON`.
Overrides: `getAccessibleRole` in class `JMenuItem.AccessibleJMenuItem`.

See also AccessibleRole (p.95), JMenuItem.AccessibleJMenuItem (p.294).

swing.JRootPane

CLASS

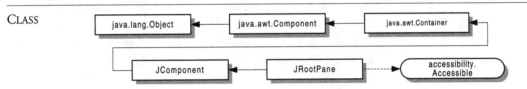

`JRootPane` manages a set of panes (usually for a Swing window of some sort). As the name implies, panes are see-through objects that can be stacked. They are similar to the cells used in 2½D animation: the content on each pane acts independently, but they are viewed as if stacked so the transparent portion of higher panes lets lower panes show through. The layers of a pane are used for components that typically float above other ones, such as dialog boxes and pop-up menus.

Several components in Swing contain `JRootPane`s. The components are the ones which are usually thought of as top-level windows. They are `JWindow`, `JDialog`, `JInternalFrame`, `JFrame`, and `JApplet`. All of these components implement the `RootPaneContainer` interface so that visual design tools can recognize that they should not use the `add()` method. When implementing your own components that contain a `JRootPane`, it is advisable to implement the `RootPaneContainer` interface for the same reason.

A `JRootPane` manages several other panes: it contains a glass pane (a lightweight, transparent, transparent component) and a layered pane (see `JLayeredPane`). The layered pane contains a content pane with an optional menu bar above it.

This is the containment hierarchy:

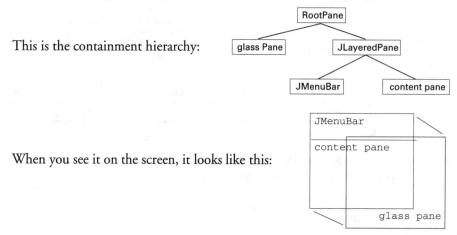

When you see it on the screen, it looks like this:

(The glass pane is in front, and the layered pane containing the menu bar and content pane is present but invisible.)

`JRootPane` is strict about what is beneath it. The glass pane, the layered pane, and the content pane are always present. The menu bar is optional. The glass pane is always the first child of the `JRootPane`, the layered pane is always the second child, and there are never other direct children. You may replace these panes but you may not set them to `null`.

The glass pane is the first child of the `JRootPane`, so it gets the first chance at all events. The glass pane is usually not visible. You can use `myRootPane.getGlassPane().setVisible(true)` when you want it to be visible.

The layered pane contains the content pane and the menu bar, at the layer indicated by `JLayeredPane.FRAME_CONTENT_LAYER`. See `JLayeredPane` for more information.

When you want to add components, you must add them to the content pane, like this:
`myRootPane.getContentPane().add(object, constraints);`

The content pane has a `java.awt.BorderLayout` by default.

The `JRootPane` itself has a custom layout manager, a `RootLayout`. It makes sure the glass pane and the layered pane cover the whole area not occupied by the menu bar, and that the menu bar (if present) is above the content pane.

Example: See `JInternalFrame` (p.254).

```
public class JRootPane extends JComponent
    implements Accessible
```

Constructors

public JRootPane()

Constructs a JRootPane, setting up its various pieces.

Public Methods

public void addNotify()

Overrides: addNotify in class JComponent.

public AccessibleContext getAccessibleContext()

Gets the accessible context for this JRootPane. See the chapter on accessibility.

Overrides: getAccessibleContext in class JComponent.

Implements: getAccessibleContext in interface Accessible.

public java.awt.Container getContentPane()

Gets the content pane. This is the pane to which contained objects should be added.

public JButton getDefaultButton()

Returns the current default button for this JRootPane.

public java.awt.Component getGlassPane()

Gets the glass pane associated with this window. This method really should not return Component, since Component's add method accepts only a PopupMenu. To use the result of this method, downcast it to a Container first.

public JLayeredPane getLayeredPane()

Gets the layered pane for this window. This will contain the content pane.

public JMenuBar getJMenuBar()

Returns the menu bar for the JRootPane.

public JMenuBar getMenuBar()

Deprecated. Use getJMenuBar().

public boolean isFocusCycleRoot()

Returns true, causing tabbing to only move between components in the JRootPane when the focus is set on the root pane.

Overrides: isFocusCycleRoot in class JComponent.

public boolean isValidateRoot()

If a child of this JRootPane calls revalidate() (which propagates up the parent chain of the component), stops propagating the call and validates from here down.

Overrides: isValidateRoot in class JComponent.

public void removeNotify()

Overrides: removeNotify in class JComponent.

public void setContentPane(java.awt.Container container)

Sets the content pane for this window. A JRootPane always has a content pane; attempting to set it to null will cause an error.

Throws: IllegalComponentStateException if the content pane parameter is null.

public void setDefaultButton(JButton defaultButton)

Sets the default button for this JRootPane. A default button is the button which will be triggered by a look and feel defined event (usually the ENTER/RETURN key being pressed) regardless of whether the button has the focus. To understand what this is doing, think about the default button in a dialog box. If the focus is on a component which consumes the event, such as a JTextArea, the button will not be triggered. To disable the default button feature, call this method with null.

```
public void setGlassPane(java.awt.Component component)
```
Sets the glass pane for the window. This is an upper pane where pop-up menus and other floating content can be displayed. It should be a lightweight component since it should be transparent.

```
public void setLayeredPane(JLayeredPane layeredPane)
```
Sets the layered pane. This pane contains the content pane.

```
public void setJMenuBar()
```
Sets the menu bar for the `JRootPane`.

```
public void setMenuBar(JMenuBar menu)
```
Deprecated. Use `setJMenuBar()`.

Protected Fields

```
protected java.awt.Container contentPane
```
The content pane.

```
protected JButton defaultButton
```
The default button to trigger when a look and feel defined event occurs.

```
protected JRootPane.DefaultAction defaultPressAction
```
The action to take when the defaultButton is pressed.

```
protected JRootPane.DefaultAction defaultReleaseAction
```
The action to take when the defaultButton is released.

```
protected java.awt.Component glassPane
```
The glass pane.

```
protected JLayeredPane layeredPane
```
The layered pane.

```
protected JMenuBar menuBar
```
The menu bar.

Protected Methods

```
protected void addImpl(java.awt.Component component,
    Object constraints, int index)
```
Adds `component` to the pane. It ensures that the glass pane is the first child.
Overrides: `addImpl` in class `Container`.

```
protected java.awt.Container createContentPane()
```
Creates the content pane: a `JComponent` with a `BorderLayout` layout manager.

```
protected java.awt.Component createGlassPane()
```
Creates the glass pane: a `JComponent` with `setVisible(false)`.

```
protected JLayeredPane createLayeredPane()
```
Creates the layered pane: a `JLayeredPane`.

```
protected java.awt.LayoutManager createRootLayout()
```
Creates the custom layout manager.

Returned by JApplet.createRootPane() (p.186), JApplet.getRootPane() (p.186), JComponent.getRootPane() (p.207), JDialog.createRootPane() (p.226), JDialog.getRootPane() (p.226), JFrame.createRootPane() (p.248), JFrame.getRootPane() (p.248), JInternalFrame.createRootPane() (p.254), JInternalFrame.getRootPane() (p.254), JWindow.createRootPane() (p.414), JWindow.getRootPane() (p.414), RootPaneContainer.getRootPane() (p.433), SwingUtilities.getRootPane() (p.443).

See also   Accessible (p.85), AccessibleContext (p.90), BoxLayout (p.144), JApplet (p.186), JButton (p.191), JComponent (p.207), JDialog (p.226), JFrame (p.248), JInternalFrame (p.254), JLayeredPane (p.268), JMenuBar (p.288), JWindow (p.414), RootPaneContainer (p.433).

swing.JRootPane.AccessibleJRootPane

INNER CLASS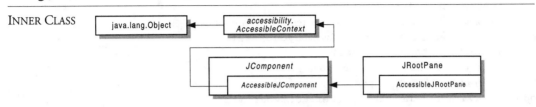

```
protected class JRootPane.AccessibleJRootPane
    extends JComponent.AccessibleJComponent
public AccessibleRole getAccessibleRole()
```
Returns `AccessibleRole.ROOT_PANE`.
Overrides: `getAccessibleRole` in class `JComponent.AccessibleJComponent`.

See also   AccessibleRole (p.95), JComponent.AccessibleJComponent (p.221).

swing.JRootPane.RootLayout

INNER CLASS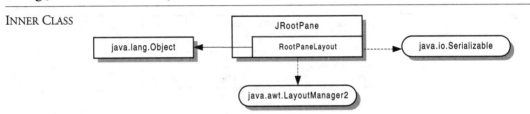

A layout manager for laying out the `contentPane`, `glassPane`, and menu bar.

```
protected class JRootPane.RootLayout
    implements java.awt.LayoutManager2, java.io.Serializable
```

Methods
```
public void addLayoutComponent(java.awt.Component comp,
    java.lang.Object constraints)
```
Implements: `addLayoutComponent` in interface `LayoutManager2`.
```
public void addLayoutComponent(java.lang.String name,
    java.awt.Component comp)
```
Adds a component to the layout.
Implements: `addLayoutComponent` in interface `LayoutManager`.
```
public float getLayoutAlignmentX(java.awt.Container target)
```
Implements: `getLayoutAlignmentX` in interface `LayoutManager2`.
```
public float getLayoutAlignmentY(java.awt.Container target)
```
Implements: `getLayoutAlignmentY` in interface `LayoutManager2`.

public void invalidateLayout(java.awt.Container target)
> *Implements:* invalidateLayout in interface LayoutManager2.

public void layoutContainer(java.awt.Container parent)
> Performs the layout.
> *Implements:* layoutContainer in interface LayoutManager.

public java.awt.Dimension maximumLayoutSize(
java.awt.Container target)
> *Implements:* maximumLayoutSize in interface LayoutManager2.

public java.awt.Dimension minimumLayoutSize(
java.awt.Container parent)
> Returns the minimum size for the layout.
> *Implements:* minimumLayoutSize in interface LayoutManager.

public java.awt.Dimension preferredLayoutSize(
java.awt.Container parent)
> Returns the preferred size the layout wants in the given container.
> *Implements:* preferredLayoutSize in interface LayoutManager.

public void removeLayoutComponent(java.awt.Component comp)
> Removes a component from the layout.
> *Implements:* removeLayoutComponent in interface LayoutManager.

swing.JScrollBar

CLASS

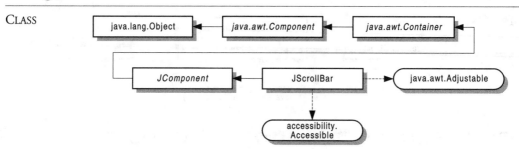

A scroll bar provides a visual representation of a position and extent. See BoundedRangeModel—in many ways it is like that model.

A JScrollBar's constraints are a little stricter than a regular BoundedRangeModel:

> minimum <= value < maximum

> 1 <= extent <= (maximum - value)

A scroll bar maintains two increment values: a unit increment (for by-line scrolling) and a block increment (for by-page scrolling).

public class JScrollBar extends JComponent
implements java.awt.Adjustable, Accessible

Fields
public static final int HORIZONTAL

```
public static final int VERTICAL
```
These two values are inherited from `Adjustable`. They refer to the orientation of the scroll bar.

Constructors

```
public JScrollBar()
```
Creates a (`VERTICAL`) scroll bar. The default values for the other scroll bar attributes are minimum 0, maximum 100, value 0, and extent 10.

```
public JScrollBar(int orientation)
```
Creates a scroll bar with the specified orientation (`HORIZONTAL` or `VERTICAL`) and minimum 0, maximum 100, value 0, and extent 10.

```
public JScrollBar(int orientation, int value, int extent,
    int minimum, int maximum)
```
Creates a scroll bar with the specified orientation (`HORIZONTAL` or `VERTICAL`) and values.

Methods

```
public void addAdjustmentListener(
    java.awt.event.AdjustmentListener listener)
```
Adds `listener` as a listener looking for `AdjustmentEvents`.
Implements: addAdjustmentListener in interface `Adjustable`.

```
public AccessibleContext getAccessibleContext()
```
Returns the accessibility context for the scroll bar.
Overrides: getAccessibleContext in class `JComponent`.
Implements: getAccessibleContext in interface `Accessible`.

```
public int getBlockIncrement()
```
Implements: getBlockIncrement in interface `Adjustable`.

```
public int getBlockIncrement(int orientation)
```
Returns the block increment for this scroll bar.

```
public int getMaximum()
```
Returns the maximum value for the scroll bar.
Implements: getMaximum in interface `Adjustable`.

```
public java.awt.Dimension getMaximumSize()
```
Gets the maximum size for this scroll bar. Horizontal scroll bars have a fixed height but try to be as wide as possible; vertical scroll bars have a fixed width but are as tall as possible.
Overrides: getMaximumSize in class `JComponent`.

```
public int getMinimum()
```
Returns the minimum value for this scroll bar.
Implements: getMinimum in interface `Adjustable`.

```
public java.awt.Dimension getMinimumSize()
```
Returns the minimum size for this scroll bar.
Overrides: getMinimumSize in class `JComponent`.

```
public BoundedRangeModel getModel()
```
Returns the model for this scroll bar.

```
public int getOrientation()
```
Returns the orientation (`HORIZONTAL` or `VERTICAL`) of this scroll bar.
Implements: getOrientation in interface `Adjustable`.

```
public ScrollBarUI getUI()
```
Returns the UI (look and feel) for the scroll bar.

public String getUIClassID()

Always returns "ScrollBarUI".

Overrides: getUIClassID in class JComponent.

public int getUnitIncrement()

Implements: getUnitIncrement in interface Adjustable.

public int getUnitIncrement(int orientation)

Returns the unit increment (by line) for this scroll bar.

public int getValue()

Returns the current value of the scroll bar.

Implements: getValue in interface Adjustable.

public boolean getValueIsAdjusting()

Returns true if the scroll bar is in the middle of adjusting its value.

public int getVisibleAmount()

Gets the extent of this scroll bar.

Implements: getVisibleAmount in interface Adjustable.

**public void removeAdjustmentListener(
java.awt.event.AdjustmentListener listener)**

Removes the adjustment listener listener from the list of listeners.

Implements: removeAdjustmentListener in interface Adjustable.

public void setBlockIncrement(int newValue)

Sets the size of the block increment.

Implements: setBlockIncrement in interface Adjustable.

public void setEnabled(boolean shouldEnable)

Enables or disables the scroll bar.

Overrides: setEnabled in class JComponent.

public void setMaximum(int newValue)

Sets the maximum value (in the model). Notifies listeners of any changes.

Implements: setMaximum in interface Adjustable.

public void setMinimum(int newValue)

Sets the minimum value (in the model). Notifies listeners of any changes.

Implements: setMinimum in interface Adjustable.

public void setModel(BoundedRangeModel model)

Sets the model for this scroll bar.

public void setOrientation(int axis)

Sets the orientation to either HORIZONTAL or VERTICAL.

Throws: IllegalArgumentException if the orientation is not VERTICAL or HORIZONTAL.

public void setUnitIncrement(int newValue)

Sets the unit increment to newValue.

Implements: setUnitIncrement in interface Adjustable.

public void setValue(int newValue)

Sets the current value to newValue. Notifies listeners of any changes.

Implements: setValue in interface Adjustable.

public void setValueIsAdjusting(boolean isAdjusting)

Sets whether the value is adjusting (in the model).

```
public void setValues(int newValue, int newExtent, int newMinimum,
    int newMaximum)
```
Sets the values in the model (taking into account the constraints above). Notifies listeners of any changes.

```
public void setVisibleAmount(int newValue)
```
Sets the extent.

Implements: setVisibleAmount in interface Adjustable.

```
public void updateUI()
```
Tells the scroll bar to update itself according to its (new) UI. See the chapter on look and feel.

Overrides: updateUI in class JComponent.

Protected Fields

```
protected int blockIncrement
```
The by-page increment.

```
protected BoundedRangeModel model
```
The model for this scroll bar.

```
protected int orientation
```
Either HORIZONTAL or VERTICAL.

```
protected int unitIncrement
```
The by-line increment.

Protected Methods

```
protected void fireAdjustmentValueChanged(
    java.awt.event.AdjustmentEvent e)
```
Sends an AdjustmentEvent to all listeners.

```
protected String paramString()
```
Returns a string representation of the properties of this JScrollBar. The returned string may be empty but it will not be null.

Overrides: paramString in class JComponent.

Inner Classes

```
protected class JScrollBar.AccessibleJScrollBar
```

Extended by   JScrollPane.ScrollBar (p.337).

Returned by   JScrollPane.createHorizontalScrollBar() (p.332),
JScrollPane.createVerticalScrollBar() (p.332), JScrollPane.getHorizontalScrollBar() (p.332),
JScrollPane.getVerticalScrollBar() (p.332), ScrollPaneLayout.getHorizontalScrollBar() (p.437),
ScrollPaneLayout.getVerticalScrollBar() (p.437).

See also   Accessible (p.85), AccessibleContext (p.90), BoundedRangeModel (p.132),
JComponent (p.207), ScrollBarUI (p.538).

swing.JScrollBar.AccessibleJScrollBar

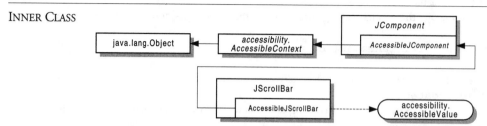

```
protected class JScrollBar.AccessibleJScrollBar
    extends JComponent.AccessibleJComponent
    implements AccessibleValue
```

Methods

public AccessibleRole getAccessibleRole()
  Overrides: getAccessibleRole in class JComponent.AccessibleJComponent.
public AccessibleStateSet getAccessibleStateSet()
  Overrides: getAccessibleStateSet in class JComponent.AccessibleJComponent.
public AccessibleValue getAccessibleValue()
  Overrides: getAccessibleValue in class AccessibleContext.
public java.lang.Number getCurrentAccessibleValue()
  Implements: getCurrentAccessibleValue in interface AccessibleValue.
public java.lang.Number getMaximumAccessibleValue()
  Implements: getMaximumAccessibleValue in interface AccessibleValue.
public java.lang.Number getMinimumAccessibleValue()
  Implements: getMinimumAccessibleValue in interface AccessibleValue.
public boolean setCurrentAccessibleValue(java.lang.Number n)
  Implements: setCurrentAccessibleValue in interface AccessibleValue.

  See also   AccessibleRole (p.95), AccessibleStateSet (p.101), AccessibleValue (p.104), JComponent.AccessibleJComponent (p.221).

swing.JScrollPane

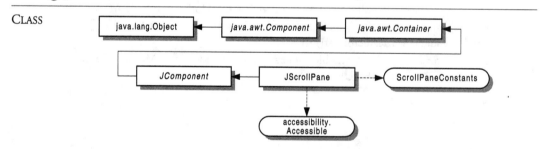

JScrollPane provides a container that supports scrolling. It has a main scrolling area, containing the component to be scrolled, but it also provides for the scroll bars, column and row headers, and corners.

Example

```
package jscrollpane;

import java.awt.*;
import java.awt.event.*;
// Uncomment the following line for Swing 1.0.3 and before
// import com.sun.java.swing.*;
// Uncomment the following line for Swing 1.1 and JDK 1.2
import javax.swing.*;

public class Test extends JFrame {
  public Test() {
    addWindowListener(new WindowAdapter() {
      public void windowClosing(WindowEvent e) {
        Test.this.dispose();
        System.exit(0);
      }
    });
    JPanel panel = new JPanel(new GridLayout(5, 10));
    for (int i = 0; i < 50; i++) {
      panel.add (new JLabel(" Label " + i));
    }

    JScrollPane scrolled = new JScrollPane(panel);
    scrolled.setRowHeaderView(new JLabel("Labels: "));

    getContentPane().add (scrolled, BorderLayout.CENTER);

    pack();
    setSize(300, 100);
    setVisible(true);
  }
  public static void main (String[] args) {
    new Test();
  }
```

```
public class JScrollPane extends JComponent
    implements Accessible, ScrollPaneConstants
```

Constructors

```
public JScrollPane()
public JScrollPane(java.awt.Component component)
public JScrollPane(int verticalPolicy, int horizontalPolicy)
public JScrollPane(java.awt.Component component,
    int verticalPolicy, int horizontalPolicy)
```
Creates a new scroll pane for component (default null). The verticalPolicy must be VERTICAL_SCROLLBAR_ALWAYS, VERTICAL_SCROLLBAR_AS_NEEDED, or VERTICAL_SCROLLBAR_NEVER (defaulting to VERTICAL_SCROLLBAR_AS_NEEDED). The horizontalPolicy must be HORIZONTAL_SCROLLBAR_ALWAYS, HORIZONTAL_SCROLLBAR_AS_NEEDED, or HORIZONTAL_SCROLLBAR_NEVER (defaulting to HORIZONTAL_SCROLLBAR_AS_NEEDED).

Methods

public JScrollBar createHorizontalScrollBar()

Used by the UI (look and feel) to produce the horizontal scroll bar.

public JScrollBar createVerticalScrollBar()

Used by the UI (look and feel) to produce the vertical scroll bar.

public AccessibleContext getAccessibleContext()

Gets the accessible context.

Overrides: getAccessibleContext in class JComponent.

Implements: getAccessibleContext in interface Accessible.

public JViewport getColumnHeader()

Gets the column header (the nonscrolling area at the top of the scroll pane).

public java.awt.Component getCorner(String cornerName)

Gets the specified corner. The cornerName must be LOWER_LEFT_CORNER, LOWER_RIGHT_CORNER, UPPER_LEFT_CORNER, or UPPER_RIGHT_CORNER.

public JScrollBar getHorizontalScrollBar()

Gets the horizontal scroll bar.

public int getHorizontalScrollBarPolicy()

Returns HORIZONTAL_SCROLLBAR_ALWAYS, HORIZONTAL_SCROLLBAR_AS_NEEDED, or HORIZONTAL_SCROLLBAR_NEVER.

public JViewport getRowHeader()

Gets the row header (the label area at the top of the scroll pane).

public ScrollPaneUI getUI()

Gets the UI (look and feel) for the scroll pane. See the chapter on look and feel.

public String getUIClassID()

Returns "ScrollPaneUI".

public JScrollBar getVerticalScrollBar()

Gets the vertical scroll bar.

public int getVerticalScrollBarPolicy()

Returns VERTICAL_SCROLLBAR_ALWAYS, VERTICAL_SCROLLBAR_AS_NEEDED, or VERTICAL_SCROLLBAR_NEVER.

public JViewport getViewport()

Gets the viewport (main scrolling area).

public Border getViewportBorder()

Gets the border for the viewport. Borders for this component are nonstandard, as they are not attached directly to the viewport. This is a bound property.

public java.awt.Rectangle getViewportBorderBounds()

Returns the bounding rectangle of the viewport border.

public boolean isOpaque()

Returns true if the viewport contains a component that is opaque and which fills the entire viewport area. Otherwise returns false.

Overrides: isOpaque in class JComponent.

public boolean isValidateRoot()

Returns true. This ensures that a revalidate() of any descendant of the scroll pane will cause the whole scroll pane and all its descendants to be validated.

Overrides: isValidateRoot in class JComponent.

public void setColumnHeader(JViewport header)

   Sets the column header (the nonscrolling label at the top of the scroll pane).

public void setColumnHeaderView(java.awt.Component component)

   Wraps component in a JViewport and makes it the column header. See setColumnHeader().

public void setCorner(String cornerName, java.awt.Component component)

   Makes component be the corner corresponding to cornerName. The cornerName must be LOWER_LEFT_CORNER, LOWER_RIGHT_CORNER, UPPER_LEFT_CORNER, or UPPER_RIGHT_ CORNER.

public void setHorizontalScrollBar(JScrollBar horizontalScrollBar)

   Sets the horizontal scroll bar to horizontalScrollBar. You would only ever use this if you wanted to install a custom JScrollBar, usually a JScrollBar subclass.

public void setHorizontalScrollBarPolicy(int policy)

   The policy must be HORIZONTAL_SCROLLBAR_ALWAYS, HORIZONTAL_SCROLLBAR_AS_ NEEDED, or HORIZONTAL_SCROLLBAR_NEVER.

public void setLayout(java.awt.LayoutManager layout)

   Overridden to ensure that only subclasses of ScrollPaneLayout can be installed.

   Throws: ClassCastException if layout is not a ScrollPaneLayout.

   Overrides: setLayout in class Container.

public void setRowHeader(JViewport header)

   Sets the row header (the nonscrolling label at the left of the scroll pane).

public void setRowHeaderView(java.awt.Component component)

   Wraps component in a JViewport and makes it the row header. See setRowHeader().

public void setUI(ScrollPaneUI)

   Sets the UI (look and feel) for this component. See the chapter on look and feel.

public void setVerticalScrollBar(JScrollBar verticalScrollBar)

   Sets the vertical scroll bar to verticalScrollBar. You would only ever use this if you wanted to install a custom JScrollBar, usually a JScrollBar subclass.

public void setVerticalScrollBarPolicy(int policy)

   The policy must be VERTICAL_SCROLLBAR_ALWAYS, VERTICAL_SCROLLBAR_AS_NEEDED, or VERTICAL_SCROLLBAR_NEVER.

public void setViewport(JViewport viewport)

   Sets the viewport to be used for the main scrolling area.

public void setViewportBorder(Border border)

   Fakes a border around the viewport. (JViewport doesn't support borders because they complicate scrolling.) This is a bound property.

public void setViewportView(java.awt.Component component)

   Creates the viewport (if none has been created yet), and puts component inside it in the main scrolling area.

public void updateUI()

   Tells the scroll pane to update itself according to the current look and feel. See the chapter on look and feel.

   Overrides: updateUI in class JComponent.

Protected Fields

protected JViewport columnHeader

   The column header viewport. Defaults to null.

protected JScrollBar horizontalScrollBar

The scroll pane's horizontal scrollbar. Defaults to a JScrollBar.

protected int horizontalScrollBarPolicy

The display policy for the horizontal scroll bar. Defaults to HORIZONTAL_SCROLLBAR_AS_ NEEDED.

protected java.awt.Component lowerLeft

The component to display in the lower left corner. Defaults to null.

protected java.awt.Component lowerRight

The component to display in the lower right corner. Defaults to null.

protected JViewport rowHeader

The row header. Defaults to null.

protected java.awt.Component upperLeft

The component to display in the upper left corner. Defaults to null.

protected java.awt.Component upperRight

The component to display in the upper right corner. Defaults to null.

protected JScrollBar verticalScrollBar

The scroll pane's vertical scroll bar. Defaults to a JScrollBar.

protected int verticalScrollBarPolicy

The display policy for the vertical scroll bar. Defaults to VERTICAL_SCROLLBAR_AS_NEEDED.

protected JViewport viewport

The scroll pane's main viewport. Defaults to an empty JViewport.

Protected Methods

protected JViewport createViewport()

Creates the viewport (the main scrolling area).

protected String paramString()

Returns a string representation of the properties of this JScrollPane. The returned string may be empty but it will not be null.

Overrides: paramString in class JComponent.

Inner Classes

protected class JScrollPane.ScrollBar

protected class JScrollPane.AccessibleJScrollPane

Returned by   BasicComboPopup.createScroller() (p.572), BasicTreeUI.ComponentHandler.getScrollPane() (p.720), JTable.createScrollPaneForTable() (p.357).

See also   Accessible (p.85), AccessibleContext (p.90), JComponent (p.207), JScrollBar (p.328), JViewport (p.410), ScrollPaneConstants (p.436), ScrollPaneUI (p.539).

swing.JScrollPane.AccessibleJScrollPane

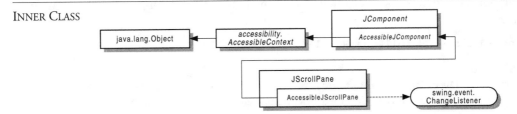

```
protected class JScrollPane.AccessibleJScrollPane
    extends JComponent.AccessibleJComponent
    implements ChangeListener
```

Constructors
public AccessibleJScrollPane()
Default constructor.

Methods
public AccessibleRole getAccessibleRole()
Returns `AccessibleRole.SCROLL_PANE`.
Overrides: `getAccessibleRole` in class `JComponent.AccessibleJComponent`.

public void resetViewPort()
Resets the viewport to its original state.

public void stateChanged(ChangeEvent e)
Fires a property change when the viewport state changes.
Implements: `stateChanged` in interface `ChangeListener`.

Protected Fields
protected JViewport viewPort
The viewport contained in the associated `JScrollPane`.

See also ChangeEvent (p.487), ChangeListener (p.488).

swing.JScrollPane.ScrollBar

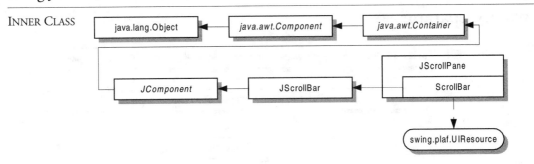

This class overrides the `getUnitIncrement()` and `getBlockIncrement()` methods to query the component in the viewport for the information. This is done to support `Scrollable` items in the viewport.

```
protected class JScrollPane.ScrollBar extends JScrollBar
```

Constructor

`public ScrollBar(int orientation)`

Creates a scroll bar with the specified orientation, either `ScrollPaneConstants.VERTICAL_SCROLLBAR` or `ScrollPaneConstants.HORIZONTAL_SCROLLBAR`.

Methods

`public int getBlockIncrement(int direction)`

If the viewport contains a `Scrollable`, asks it for the appropriate value. If the viewport's content is not `Scrollable`, the `blockIncrement` equals the viewport's width or height. If a viewport has not been created, returns `super.getBlockIncrement()`.

Overrides: `getBlockIncrement` in class `JScrollBar`.

`public int getUnitIncrement(int direction)`

If the viewport contains a `Scrollable`, asks it for the appropriate value. Otherwise returns `super.getUnitIncrement()`.

Overrides: `getUnitIncrement` in class `JScrollBar`.

`public void setBlockIncrement(int blockIncrement)`

Calls `JScrollBar.setBlockIncrement()` to set the value and then sets a flag so that future calls to `getBlockIncrement()` won't query the viewport.

Overrides: `setBlockIncrement` in class `JScrollBar`.

Implements: `setBlockIncrement` in interface `Adjustable`.

`public void setUnitIncrement(int unitIncrement)`

Calls `JScrollBar.setUnitIncrement()` to set the value and then sets a flag so that future calls to `getUnitIncrement()` won't query the viewport.

Overrides: `setUnitIncrement` in class `JScrollBar`.

Implements: `setUnitIncrement` in interface `Adjustable`.

See also   JScrollBar (p.328), ScrollPaneConstants (p.436), UIResource (p.544).

swing.JSeparator

CLASS

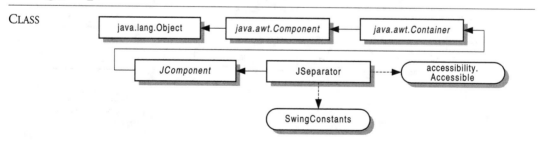

A separator is used between menu items, to provide a visual grouping of related items. It is usually shown as a line or blank area between two items.

Example

```
package jseparator;

import java.awt.*;
import java.awt.event.*;
// Uncomment the following line for Swing 1.0.3 or earlier
//import com.sun.java.swing.*;
// Uncomment the following line for Swing 1.1 and JDK 1.2
import javax.swing.*;

public class Main extends JFrame {
   public Main () {
      addWindowListener(new WindowAdapter() {
         public void windowClosing(WindowEvent e) {
            Main.this.dispose();
            System.exit(0);
         }
      });
      JMenuBar bar = new JMenuBar();
      JMenu menu = new JMenu("File");
      bar.add (menu);

      menu.add(new JMenuItem("Close"));
      menu.add(new JSeparator());            // SEPARATOR
      menu.add(new JMenuItem("Exit"));

      setJMenuBar(bar);
      getContentPane().add(new JLabel("A placeholder"));

      pack();
      setSize(300, 300);
      setVisible(true);
   }
   public static void main (String arg[]) {
      new Main();
   }
}
```

public class JSeparator extends JComponent
implements Accessible, SwingConstants

Constructors
public JSeparator()
> Creates a horizontal separator.

public JSeparator(int orientation)
> Creates a new separator with either HORIZONTAL or VERTICAL orientation. A vertical separator could be used in a multicolumn menu (the layout of a JPopupMenu can be changed!).

Methods
public AccessibleContext getAccessibleContext()
> Returns the accessible context.
> *Overrides:* getAccessibleContext in class JComponent.
> *Implements:* getAccessibleContext in interface Accessible.

public int getOrientation()
>   Returns the orientation.

public SeparatorUI getUI()
>   Returns the look and feel for the separator.

public String getUIClassID()
>   Returns "SeparatorUI".
>   *Overrides:* getUIClassID in class JComponent.

public boolean isFocusTraversable()
>   Always returns false.
>   *Overrides:* isFocusTraversable in class JComponent.

public void setOrientation(int orientation)
>   Sets the orientation of the separator.

public void setUI(SeparatorUI ui)
>   Set the UI (look and feel) to a new value. (Usually called by updateUI().)

public void updateUI()
>   Notifies the separator to update itself to the current look and feel.
>   *Overrides:* updateUI in class JComponent.

Protected Methods

protected String paramString()
>   Returns a string representation of the properties of this JSeparator. The returned string may be empty but it will not be null.
>   *Overrides:* paramString in class JComponent.

Inner Classes

protected class JSeparator.AccessibleJSeparator

>   *See also*   Accessible (p.85), AccessibleContext (p.90), JComponent (p.207), SeparatorUI (p.539).

swing.JSeparator.AccessibleJSeparator

INNER CLASS

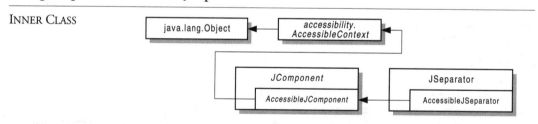

protected class JSeparator.AccessibleJSeparator
       extends JComponent.AccessibleJComponent

Method

public AccessibleRole getAccessibleRole()
>   Returns AccessibleRole.SEPARATOR.
>   *Overrides:* getAccessibleRole in class JComponent.AccessibleJComponent.

>   *See also*   AccessibleRole (p.95), JComponent.AccessibleJComponent (p.221).

swing.JSlider

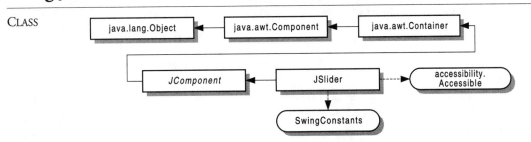

A slider selects a value from a bounded range of options. The model for a slider is the Bounded-RangeModel. A JSlider can include major and minor tick marks and numeric labels.

Example

```
package jslider;

import java.awt.*;
import java.awt.event.*;
import java.util.*;
// Uncomment the following two lines for Swing 1.0.3 and before
//import com.sun.java.swing.*;
//import com.sun.java.swing.event.*;
// Uncomment the following two lines for Swing 1.1 and JDK 1.2
import javax.swing.*;
import javax.swing.event.*;
public class Test extends JFrame {
   JSlider slider1 = new JSlider();
   JSlider slider2 = new JSlider(JSlider.HORIZONTAL, -100, 100, 0);

   public Test() {
      addWindowListener(new WindowAdapter() {
         public void windowClosing(WindowEvent e) {
            Test.this.dispose();
            System.exit(0);
         }
      });
      getContentPane().setLayout(new GridLayout(2,1));

      slider1.addChangeListener(new ChangeListener() {
         public void stateChanged(ChangeEvent e) {
            System.out.println("Slider1: " + slider1.getValue());
         }
      });
      getContentPane().add (slider1);

      slider2.setPaintTicks(true);
      slider2.setMajorTickSpacing(50);
      slider2.setMinorTickSpacing(10);
      slider2.setPaintLabels(true);
      Hashtable ht = slider2.createStandardLabels(50);
      slider2.setLabelTable(ht);
```

```
      slider2.addChangeListener (new ChangeListener() {
        public void stateChanged (ChangeEvent e) {
          System.out.println("Slider2: " + slider2.getValue());
        }
      });
      getContentPane().add(slider2);
      pack();
    }
    public static void main (String[] args) {
      new Test().setVisible(true);
    }
}
```

public class JSlider extends JComponent
   implements SwingConstants, Accessible

Fields
public static final int HORIZONTAL
public static final int VERTICAL
   Values for orientation.

Constructors
public JSlider()
   Creates a HORIZONTAL slider with range 0 to 100, initial value 50.
public JSlider(BoundedRangeModel brm)
   Creates a horizontal slider using the given BoundedRangeModel.
public JSlider(int orientation)
   Creates a slider using the given orientation with the range 0 to 100 and a value of 50.
public JSlider(int min, int max)
   Creates a horizontal slider using the given min and max with a value of 50.
public JSlider(int min, int max, int value)
   Creates a horizontal slider using the given min, max, and value.
public JSlider(int orientation, int minimum, int maximum, int initialValue)
   Creates a slider with corresponding minimum, maximum, and initialValue. The orientation must either be HORIZONTAL or VERTICAL.
   Throws: IllegalArgumentException if orientation is not VERTICAL or HORIZONTAL.

Methods
public void addChangeListener(ChangeListener listener)
   Adds listener as a listener for changes in range or current value.
public java.util.Hashtable createStandardLabels(int increment)
   Returns the same value as createStandardLabels(increment, getMinimum()).
public java.util.Hashtable createStandardLabels(int increment, int start)
   Builds a table of labels. The key values are for start, start+increment, start+2*increment, and so forth. The values are converted to type Integer and used as keys in the table. The values stored with them are labels (of type JLabel), the string values of those keys. Once you have a label table, use setLabelTable() to put it in force.

public AccessibleContext getAccessibleContext()

Gets the accessible context.

Overrides: getAccessibleContext in class JComponent.

Implements: getAccessibleContext in interface Accessible.

public int getExtent()

Returns the extent (see BoundedRangeModel).

public boolean getInverted()

Returns true if the slider is oriented so that the range is from maximum to minimum instead of the normal minimum to maximum.

public java.util.Dictionary getLabelTable()

Gets the label table. See setLabelTable() and createStandardLabels() for more information.

public int getMajorTickSpacing()

Returns the spacing in pixels between major tick marks.

public int getMaximum()

Returns the maximum value.

public int getMinimum()

Returns the minimum value.

public int getMinorTickSpacing()

Returns the spacing in pixels between minor tick marks.

public BoundedRangeModel getModel()

Returns the model for this slider.

public int getOrientation()

Returns HORIZONTAL or VERTICAL depending on the orientation.

public boolean getPaintLabels()

Returns true if labels should be painted.

public boolean getPaintTicks()

Returns true if ticks should be painted.

public boolean getPaintTrack()

Returns true if the track area should be painted.

public boolean getSnapToTicks()

Returns true if the slider value should be snapped to the tick marks.

public SliderUI getUI()

Gets the current UI (look and feel). See the chapter on look and feel.

public String getUIClassID()

Returns "SliderUI".

Overrides: getUIClassID in class JComponent.

public int getValue()

Gets the current value of the slider.

public boolean getValueIsAdjusting()

Returns true if the value is in the midst of an adjustment. (This can let listeners avoid intermediate updates.)

public void removeChangeListener(swing.event.ChangeListener listener)

Removes listener as a listener.

public void setExtent(int)

Sets the extent (see BoundedRangeModel). Notifies listeners of the change.

```
public void setInverted(boolean shouldInvert)
```
Sets whether the slider should be inverted. This orients the slider so the user sees it as ranging from maximum to minimum, not the usual minimum to maximum.

```
public void setLabelTable(java.util.Dictionary dictionary)
```
Establishes `dictionary` as the set of label values. The format of entries is (`Integer` key, `Component` labelValue).

```
public void setMajorTickSpacing(int newSpacing)
```
Sets the major tick spacing (in pixels).

```
public void setMaximum(int newValue)
```
Sets the maximum value for the slider. Notifies listeners of the change.

```
public void setMinimum(int newValue)
```
Sets the minimum value for the slider. Notifies listeners of the change.

```
public void setMinorTickSpacing(int newSpacing)
```
Sets the minor tick spacing (in pixels).

```
public void setModel(BoundedRangeModel model)
```
Sets `model` as the new model.

```
public void setOrientation(int orientation)
```
Sets whether the slider is `HORIZONTAL` or `VERTICAL`.

Throws: `IllegalArgumentException` if orientation is not `VERTICAL` or `HORIZONTAL`.

```
public void setPaintLabels(boolean shouldPaint)
```
Tells whether labels should be shown.

```
public void setPaintTicks(boolean shouldPaint)
```
Tells whether tick marks should be shown.

```
public void setPaintTrack(boolean b)
```
Tells whether the track should be painted.

```
public void setSnapToTicks(boolean shouldSnap)
```
Tells whether the slider value should snap to the values corresponding to the tick marks.

```
public void setUI(SliderUI ui)
```
Sets the UI (look and feel) for this slider. See the chapter on look and feel.

```
public void setValue(int newValue)
```
Sets the value for the slider. Notifies any listeners of the change.

```
public void setValueIsAdjusting(boolean isAdjusting)
```
Sets whether the value is in the midst of a series of updates. (Listeners might use this to avoid painting intermediate versions.)

```
public void updateUI()
```
Sets the UI to the current look and feel. See the chapter on look and feel for more information.

Overrides: `updateUI` in class `JComponent`.

Protected Fields

```
protected transient ChangeEvent changeEvent
```
The event used to notify listeners of changes.

```
protected ChangeListener changeListener
```
Tracks listeners for changes in the value.

```
protected int majorTickSpacing
```
The spacing in pixels between major tick marks.

```
protected int minorTickSpacing
```
The spacing in pixels between minor tick marks.

protected int orientation

Either HORIZONTAL or VERTICAL.

protected BoundedRangeModel sliderModel

The model for the slider.

protected boolean snapToTicks

Returns true if the values should be restricted to matching the values at the tick marks.

Protected Methods

protected ChangeListener createChangeListener()

Creates the listener that will be attached to the model.

protected void fireStateChanged()

Notifies listeners that the state has changed.

protected String paramString()

Returns a string representation of the properties of this JSlider. The returned string may be empty but it will not be null.

Overrides: paramString in class JComponent.

protected void updateLabelUIs()

Updates the UI (look and feel) of any labels (see createStandardLabels() and setLabelTable()).

Inner Classes

protected class JSlider.AccessibleJSlider

See also   Accessible (p.85), AccessibleContext (p.90), BoundedRangeModel (p.132), ChangeEvent (p.487), ChangeListener (p.488), JComponent (p.207), SliderUI (p.539), SwingConstants (p.442).

swing.JSlider.AccessibleJSlider

INNER CLASS

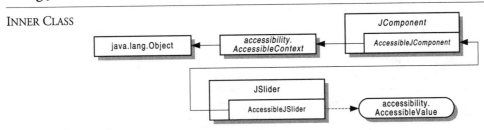

protected class JSlider.AccessibleJSlider
    extends JComponent.AccessibleJComponent
    implements AccessibleValue

Methods

public AccessibleRole getAccessibleRole()

Overrides: getAccessibleRole in class JComponent.AccessibleJComponent.

public AccessibleStateSet getAccessibleStateSet()

Overrides: getAccessibleStateSet in class JComponent.AccessibleJComponent.

public AccessibleValue getAccessibleValue()

Overrides: getAccessibleValue in class AccessibleContext.

```
public java.lang.Number getCurrentAccessibleValue()
```
Implements: getCurrentAccessibleValue in interface AccessibleValue.
```
public java.lang.Number getMaximumAccessibleValue()
```
Implements: getMaximumAccessibleValue in interface AccessibleValue.
```
public java.lang.Number getMinimumAccessibleValue()
```
Implements: getMinimumAccessibleValue in interface AccessibleValue.
```
public boolean setCurrentAccessibleValue(java.lang.Number n)
```
Implements: setCurrentAccessibleValue in interface AccessibleValue.

See also   AccessibleRole (p.95), AccessibleStateSet (p.101), AccessibleValue (p.104), JComponent.AccessibleJComponent (p.221).

swing.JSplitPane

CLASS

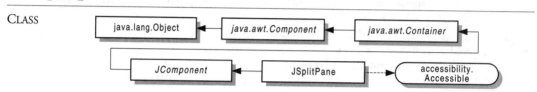

A split pane provides a panel which holds two components and a divider bar that controls their relative sizes. The split may either be horizontal or vertical.

The divider is not permitted to violate the component's minimum or maximum size constraints. Its initial position is based on the component's preferred size. See JComponent for information on changing these values. (If you don't set the minimum and/or preferred sizes, the split pane will probably not work the way you expect.)

Example

```
package jsplitpane;

import java.awt.*;
import java.awt.event.*;
// Uncomment the following line for Swing 1.0.3 and before
//import com.sun.java.swing.*;
// Uncomment the following line for Swing 1.1 and JDK 1.2
import javax.swing.*;

public class Test extends JFrame {
   public Test() {
      addWindowListener(new WindowAdapter() {
        public void windowClosing(WindowEvent e) {
           Test.this.dispose();
           System.exit(0);
        }
      });
      JPanel panel1 = new JPanel(new GridLayout(1,5));
      for (int i = 0; i < 5; i++) {
        panel1.add (new JLabel("Left " + i));
      }
```

```
        panel1.setPreferredSize(new Dimension(250,50));

        JPanel panel2 = new JPanel(new GridLayout(1,5));
        for (int i = 0; i < 5; i++) {
           panel2.add (new JLabel("Right " + i));
        }
        panel2.setPreferredSize(new Dimension(250,50));

        JSplitPane split = new JSplitPane(
                            JSplitPane.HORIZONTAL_SPLIT, panel1, panel2);
        split.setContinuousLayout(true);
        getContentPane().add(split, BorderLayout.CENTER);
        pack();
        setSize(500,100);
    }
    public static void main (String[] args) {
        new Test().setVisible(true);
    }
}
```

public class JSplitPane extends JComponent
   implements Accessible

Fields

public static final String CONTINUOUS_LAYOUT_PROPERTY
public static final String DIVIDER_SIZE_PROPERTY
public static final String LAST_DIVIDER_LOCATION_PROPERTY
public static final String ONE_TOUCH_EXPANDABLE_PROPERTY
public static final String ORIENTATION_PROPERTY

The names of the bound properties of the JSplitPane.

public static String BOTTOM
public static String LEFT
public static String RIGHT
public static String TOP
public static String DIVIDER

The valid constraint values for addImpl().

public static int HORIZONTAL_SPLIT
public static int VERTICAL_SPLIT

These constants define whether the pane is split horizontally or vertically. See orientation, getOrientation(), and setOrientation().

Constructors

public JSplitPane()
public JSplitPane(int orientation)
public JSplitPane(int orientation, boolean continuousLayout)
public JSplitPane(int orientation, java.awt.Component leftOrTop,
   java.awt.Component rightOrBottom)
public JSplitPane(int orientation, boolean continuousLayout,
   java.awt.Component leftOrTop, java.awt.Component rightOrBottom)

Creates a new split pane. The orientation must be either HORIZONTAL_SPLIT or VERTICAL_SPLIT (the default is VERTICAL_SPLIT). The continuousLayout defaults to false. The components default to null.

Methods

public AccessibleContext getAccessibleContext()

Gets the accessible context for this pane.

Overrides: getAccessibleContext in class JComponent.

Implements: getAccessibleContext in interface Accessible.

public java.awt.Component getBottomComponent()

Gets the component on the bottom (or the right).

public int getDividerLocation()

Gets the current location of the divider.

public int getDividerSize()

Returns the size of the divider in pixels.

public int getLastDividerLocation()

Returns the last location of the divider before its current position.

public java.awt.Component getLeftComponent()

Returns the left (or upper) component.

public int getMaximumDividerLocation()

Gets the maximum divider location allowed. This is determined by the minimum and maximum sizes of the components involved. (The divider will not be allowed to violate a component's minimum or maximum size.)

public int getMinimumDividerLocation()

Gets the minimum divider location allowed. This is determined by the minimum and maximum sizes of the components involved. (The divider will not be allowed to violate a component's minimum or maximum size.)

public int getOrientation()

Returns either HORIZONTAL_SPLIT or VERTICAL_SPLIT.

public java.awt.Component getRightComponent()

Returns the right (or bottom) component.

public java.awt.Component getTopComponent()

Returns the top (or left) component.

public SplitPaneUI getUI()

Gets the UI (look and feel) for this pane. See the chapter on look and feel.

public String getUIClassID()

Returns "SplitPaneUI".

Overrides: getUIClassID in class JComponent.

public boolean isContinuousLayout()

Returns true if the components will be continuously redrawn; returns false if redrawing will wait until the divider is done moving.

public boolean isOneTouchExpandable()

Returns true if the divider has a widget to directly collapse and restore the divider.

public void remove(int index)

Removes the component at index, where 1 represents the left/top component and 2 represents the right/bottom component.

Overrides: remove in class Container.

public void remove(java.awt.Component component)

Removes component.

Overrides: remove in class Container.

public void removeAll()
    Removes both components.
    Overrides: removeAll in class Container.
public void resetToPreferredSizes()
    Returns the divider to the original location (based on the preferred sizes of its two components).
public void setBottomComponent(java.awt.Component component)
    Sets the bottom (or right) component.
public void setContinuousLayout(boolean shouldLayoutContinuously)
    Sets whether the display should update while the divider is moving, or waits until it is done.
public void setDividerLocation(double proportion)
    Sets the divider's location. The proportion must be between 0.0 and 1.0 inclusive. It tells what proportion of the divider will be used for the top (or left) component.
    Throws: IllegalArgumentException if the specified location is < 0 or > 1.0.
public void setDividerLocation(int location)
    Sets the divider's location.
public void setDividerSize(int size)
    Sets the size of the divider in pixels.
public void setLastDividerLocation(int oldLocation)
    Records the previous divider location as oldLocation.
public void setLeftComponent(java.awt.Component component)
    Sets the left (or top) component.
public void setOneTouchExpandable(boolean shouldBeExpandable)
    Sets whether the divider has a widget to collapse and expand the partitions.
public void setOrientation(int orientation)
    Sets the orientation to either HORIZONTAL_SPLIT or VERTICAL_SPLIT.
public void setRightComponent(java.awt.Component component)
    Sets the right (or bottom) component.
public void setTopComponent(java.awt.Component component)
    Sets the top (or left) component.
public void setUI(SplitPaneUI ui)
    Sets the UI (look and feel) to ui. See the chapter on look and feel.
public void updateUI()
    Notifies the pane to update itself to the current look and feel.
    Overrides: updateUI in class JComponent.

Protected Fields
protected boolean continuousLayout
    Tells whether the layout will be updated as the divider bar is moved, or not until it is in its new place.
protected int dividerSize
    The width of the divider in pixels.
protected int lastDividerLocation
    The previous location of the divider.
protected java.awt.Component leftComponent
    The left-hand (or upper) component.
protected boolean oneTouchExpandable
    Returns true if the divider provides a widget to collapse the pane.

protected int orientation
> Tells whether the pane is split horizontally or vertically; has one of the values `HORIZONTAL_SPLIT` or `VERTICAL_SPLIT`.

protected java.awt.Component rightComponent
> The right-hand (or lower) component.

Protected Methods

protected void addImpl(java.awt.Component component,
    Object constraint, int index)
> Adds `component` at `index` according to `constraint`. The `constraint` must be `TOP`, `LEFT`, `BOTTOM`, `RIGHT`, or `DIVIDER`. The `index` is 1 for left/top, 2 for right/bottom.
>
> *Throws:* `IllegalArgumentException` is thrown if the constraints object does not match an existing component.
>
> *Overrides:* `addImpl` in class `Container`.

protected void paintChildren(java.awt.Graphics gr)
> Paints the border, the components, and the divider.
>
> *Overrides:* `paintChildren` in class `JComponent`.

protected String paramString()
> Returns a string representation of the properties of this `JSplitPane`. The returned string may be empty but it will not be `null`.
>
> *Overrides:* `paramString` in class `JComponent`.

Inner Classes

protected class JSplitPane.AccessibleJSplitPane

> *Returned by*   BasicSplitPaneUI.getSplitPane() (p.668).
>
> *See also*   Accessible (p.85), AccessibleContext (p.90), JComponent (p.207), SplitPaneUI (p.540).

swing.JSplitPane.AccessibleJSplitPane

INNER CLASS

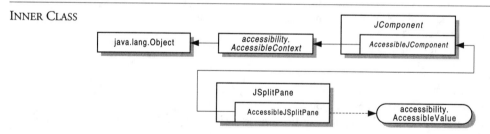

protected class JSplitPane.AccessibleJSplitPane
    extends JComponent.AccessibleJComponent
    implements AccessibleValue

Methods

public AccessibleRole getAccessibleRole()
> Returns `AccessibleRole.SPLIT_PANE`.
>
> *Overrides:* `getAccessibleRole` in class `JComponent.AccessibleJComponent`.

```
public AccessibleStateSet getAccessibleStateSet()
```
   Overrides: getAccessibleStateSet in class JComponent.AccessibleJComponent.
```
public AccessibleValue getAccessibleValue()
```
   Overrides: getAccessibleValue in class AccessibleContext.
```
public java.lang.Number getCurrentAccessibleValue()
```
   Returns the divider location.
   Implements: getCurrentAccessibleValue in interface AccessibleValue.
```
public java.lang.Number getMaximumAccessibleValue()
```
   Implements: getMaximumAccessibleValue in interface AccessibleValue.
```
public java.lang.Number getMinimumAccessibleValue()
```
   Implements: getMinimumAccessibleValue in interface AccessibleValue.
```
public boolean setCurrentAccessibleValue(java.lang.Number n)
```
   Sets the divider location.
   Implements: setCurrentAccessibleValue in interface AccessibleValue.

See also   AccessibleRole (p.95), AccessibleStateSet (p.101), AccessibleValue (p.104), JComponent.AccessibleJComponent (p.221).

swing.JTabbedPane

CLASS

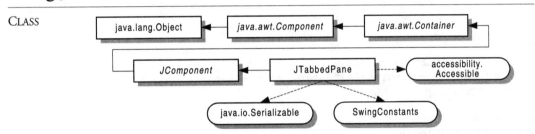

A tabbed pane is a component that provides a set of tabs, each having its own associated panel. Only one tab's associated panel is visible at a time. The tabs are labeled (with both text and Icons) and you can change tabs by clicking on a label. This layout is effectively a java.awt.CardLayout which includes all of the support you had to write yourself previously.

   The model for a tabbed pane is a SingleSelectionModel (p.440).

Example

```
package jtabbedpane;
import java.awt.*;
import java.awt.event.*;
// Uncomment the follwing two lines for Swing 1.0.3 and before
//import com.sun.java.swing.*;
//import com.sun.java.swing.event.*;
// Uncomment the following two lines for Swing 1.1 and JDK 1.2
import javax.swing.*;
import javax.swing.event.*;
public class Test extends JFrame {
   JTabbedPane tabs = new JTabbedPane();
```

```
  public Test() {
    addWindowListener(new WindowAdapter() {
      public void windowClosing(WindowEvent e) {
        Test.this.dispose();
        System.exit(0);
      }
    });
    JPanel p = new JPanel();
    p.add (new JButton("Button on Tab 0"));
    tabs.addTab("Tab 0", p);

    p = new JPanel();
    p.add(new JTextField("Text on Tab 1"));
    tabs.addTab("Tab 1", p);

    tabs.addChangeListener(new ChangeListener() {
      public void stateChanged(ChangeEvent e) {
        System.out.println("Tab="+tabs.getSelectedIndex());
      }
    });
    getContentPane().add (tabs, "Center");
    pack();
  }
  public static void main (String[] args) {
    new Test().setVisible(true);
  }
}
```

public class JTabbedPane extends JComponent
    implements java.io.Serializable, Accessible,
    SwingConstants

Constructors

public JTabbedPane()

    Creates a tabbed pane with no tabs.

public JTabbedPane(int tabPlacement)

    Creates an empty tabbed pane with the tabs on the tabPlacement side. The tabPlacement parameter is TOP, BOTTOM, LEFT, or RIGHT.

Methods

public java.awt.Component add(java.awt.Component component)

    Adds a new page containing component with a tab title defaulting to the name of the component. This method simply calls insertTab(). This method was added to help graphical UI design tools. Developers should try to use addTab() for clarity.

    Overrides: add in class Container.

public java.awt.Component add(java.awt.Component component, int index)

    Adds a new page containing component at the given tab index with a tab title defaulting to the name of the component. This method simply calls insertTab(). This method was added to help graphical UI design tools. Developers should try to use addTab() for clarity.

    Overrides: add in class Container.

public void add(java.awt.Component component, Object constraints)

Adds a new page containing component to the tabbed pane. If constraints is a String or an Icon, it will be used for the tab title; otherwise, the component's name will be used as the tab title. This method simply calls insertTab(). This method was added to help graphical UI design tools. Developers should try to use addTab() for clarity.

Overrides: add in class Container.

public void add(java.awt.Component component, Object constraints, int index)

Adds a new page containing component at the specified tab index. If constraints is a String or an Icon, it will be used for the tab title; otherwise, the component's name will be used as the tab title. This method simply calls insertTab(). This method was added to help graphical UI design tools. Developers should try to use addTab() for clarity.

Overrides: add in class Container.

public java.awt.Component add(String title, java.awt.Component component)

Adds a new page containing component with the specified tab title title. This method simply calls insertTab(). This method was added to help graphical UI design tools. Developers should try to use addTab() for clarity.

Overrides: add in class Container.

public void addChangeListener(ChangeListener listener)

Adds listener to the list of objects to be notified of a change in properties of the tabbed pane.

public void addTab(String title, Icon icon, java.awt.Component body)

public void addTab(String title, Icon icon, java.awt.Component body, String tooltip)

public void addTab(String title, java.awt.Component body)

Creates a new tab from body. It is labeled with title and icon (icon defaults to null). It may have a ToolTip string, tooltip, for the tab (default none).

public AccessibleContext getAccessibleContext()

Returns the accessible context for this component. See the chapter on accessibility.

Overrides: getAccessibleContext in class JComponent.

Implements: getAccessibleContext in interface Accessible.

public java.awt.Color getBackgroundAt(int index)

Returns the background color of the tab at index.

public java.awt.Rectangle getBoundsAt(int index)

Returns the bounds of the tab at index. If there is no UI set on this tabbed pane, then it returns null.

public java.awt.Component getComponentAt(int index)

Returns the component corresponding to the index tab.

public Icon getDisabledIconAt(int index)

Returns the disabled icon for the tab at index.

public java.awt.Color getForegroundAt(int index)

Returns the foreground color of the tab at index.

public Icon getIconAt(int index)

Returns the icon corresponding to the index tab.

public SingleSelectionModel getModel()

Gets the model for the tabbed pane.

public java.awt.Component getSelectedComponent()

Returns the component for the currently selected pane.

public int getSelectedIndex()

Returns the index of the currently selected pane.

public int getTabCount()

Returns the number of tabs.

public int getTabPlacement()

Returns the placement of the tabs for this JTabbedPane.

public int getTabRunCount()

Returns the number of tab runs currently used to display the tabs. A tab run is a row for TOP and BOTTOM tabs, and a column for LEFT or RIGHT tabs.

public String getTitleAt(int index)

Gets the title corresponding to the index tab.

public String getToolTipText(java.awt.event.MouseEvent event)

Gets the ToolTip text associated with event (in the currently selected pane).

public TabbedPaneUI getUI()

Gets the look and feel used for this component. See the chapter on look and feel.

public String getUIClassID()

Returns "TabbedPaneUI".

Overrides: getUIClassID in class JComponent.

public int indexOfComponent(java.awt.Component component)

Finds component in the set of tabs, and returns its index, or –1 if not found.

public int indexOfTab(Icon icon)

Finds the index of the first tab showing icon. Returns –1 if not found.

public int indexOfTab(String title)

Finds the index of the first tab labeled title. Titles are compared using String.equals(). Returns –1 if not found.

public void insertTab(String title, Icon icon, java.awt.Component body, String tooltip, int index)

Inserts a tab at index, built from body, labeled with title and icon, and with tooltip.

public boolean isEnabledAt(int index)

Returns whether or not the tab at index is currently enabled.

public void remove(java.awt.Component component)

Removes the tab which corresponds to the specified component.

Overrides: remove in class Container.

public void removeAll()

Removes all tabs.

Overrides: removeAll in class Container.

public void removeChangeListener(ChangeListener listener)

Removes listener from the list of objects to be notified of changes in the model.

public void removeTabAt(int index)

Deletes the tab at index, moving other tabs to fill in the space.

public void setBackgroundAt(int index, java.awt.Color background)

Sets the background color at index to background which can be null, in which case the tab's background color will default to the background color of the tabbed pane.

public void setComponentAt(int index, java.awt.Component body)

Sets the component at index to be body.

public void setDisabledIconAt(int index, Icon disabledIcon)
  Sets the disabled icon on the tab at at index to disabledIcon, which can be null.
public void setEnabledAt(int index, boolean enabled)
  Sets whether or not the tab at index is enabled.
public void setForegroundAt(int index, java.awt.Color foreground)
  Sets the foreground color for the tab at index to foreground, which can be null. If foreground is null, the color defaults to the foreground color of the JTabbedPane.
public void setIconAt(int index, Icon icon)
  Sets the Icon on the tab at index to be icon.
public void setModel(SingleSelectionModel model)
  Sets the model for the tabbed pane.
public void setSelectedComponent(java.awt.Component body)
  Selects the tab whose component is body.
public void setSelectedIndex(int index)
  Selects the tab at index.
public void setTabPlacement(int tabPlacement)
  Sets where the tabs are drawn for this JTabbedPane. The tabPlacement must be one of the following: SwingConstants.TOP (the default), SwingConstants.BOTTOM, SwingConstants.LEFT, or SwingConstants.RIGHT.
public void setTitleAt(int index, String title)
  Sets the title for the tab at index to be title.
public void setUI(TabbedPaneUI ui)
  Sets the look and feel for this tabbed pane. See the chapter on look and feel.
public void updateUI()
  Updates the tabbed pane to reflect the current UI (look and feel). See the chapter on look and feel.

Protected Fields
protected transient ChangeEvent changeEvent
  The event used to notify listeners of changes in properties of the tabbed pane.
protected ChangeListener changeListener
  The listener added to the model.
protected SingleSelectionModel model
  The model.
protected int tabPlacement
  The location where the tabs are drawn. See setTabPlacement().

Protected Methods
protected ChangeListener createChangeListener()
  Creates the changeListener field. (A subclass may want to do this differently.)
protected void fireStateChanged()
  Notifies listeners that the model has changed.
protected String paramString()
  Returns a string representation of the properties of this JTabbedPane. The returned string may be empty but it will not be null.
  Overrides: paramString in class JComponent.

See also   Accessible (p.85), AccessibleContext (p.90), ChangeListener (p.488), Icon (p.183), SingleSelectionModel (p.440), SwingConstants (p.442), TabbedPaneUI (p.540).

swing.JTabbedPane.AccessibleJTabbedPane

INNER CLASS

This class implements accessibility features for JTabbedPane.

```
protected class JTabbedPane.AccessibleJTabbedPane
    extends JComponent.AccessibleJComponent
    implements AccessibleSelection, ChangeListener
```

Methods

public void addAccessibleSelection(int i)
  Implements: addAccessibleSelection in interface AccessibleSelection.
public void clearAccessibleSelection()
  Implements: clearAccessibleSelection in interface AccessibleSelection.
public Accessible getAccessibleAt(java.awt.Point p)
  Implements: getAccessibleAt in interface AccessibleComponent.
public Accessible getAccessibleChild(int i)
  Overrides: getAccessibleChild in class AccessibleContext.
public int getAccessibleChildrenCount()
  Overrides: getAccessibleChildrenCount in class JComponent.AccessibleJComponent.
public AccessibleRole getAccessibleRole()
  Returns AccessibleRole.TABBED_PANE.
  Overrides: getAccessibleChildrenCount in class JComponent.AccessibleJComponent.
public AccessibleSelection getAccessibleSelection()
  Overrides: getAccessibleSelection in class AccessibleContext.
public Accessible getAccessibleSelection(int i)
  Returns the index of the currently selected tab.
  Implements: getAccessibleSelection in interface AccessibleSelection.
public int getAccessibleSelectionCount()
  Returns 1 because a tab is always selected in a JTabbedPane.
  Implements: getAccessibleSelectionCount in interface AccessibleSelection.
public boolean isAccessibleChildSelected(int i)
  Implements: isAccessibleChildSelected in interface AccessibleSelection.
public void removeAccessibleSelection(int i)
  Implements: removeAccessibleSelection in interface AccessibleSelection.

public void selectAllAccessibleSelection()

An empty method, since this does not make sense in a JTabbedPane.

Implements: selectAllAccessibleSelection in interface AccessibleSelection.

public void stateChanged(ChangeEvent e)

Listens for the selected tab changing in the associated JTabbedPane.

Implements: stateChanged in interface ChangeListener.

See also   Accessible (p.85), AccessibleRole (p.95), AccessibleSelection (p.98), ChangeEvent (p.487), ChangeListener (p.488), JComponent.AccessibleJComponent (p.221).

swing.JTabbedPane.ModelListener

INNER CLASS

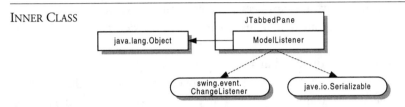

This class takes ChangeEvents from the JTabbedPane and forwards them along as ChangeEvents which have the JTabbedPane as the source, not the model.

**protected class JTabbedPane.ModelListener extends java.lang.Object
    implements ChangeListener, java.io.Serializable**

Methods
public void stateChanged(ChangeEvent e)

Implements: stateChanged in interface ChangeListener.

See also   ChangeEvent (p.487), ChangeListener (p.488).

swing.JTable

CLASS

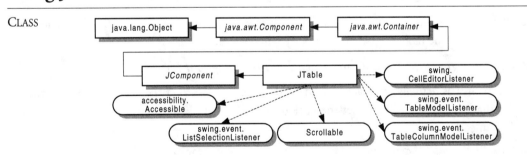

A table represents a 2-dimensional grid. The Swing JTable does not try to cover every use of a table (such as spreadsheets), but it is a workaday implementation that supports access to large data sets, so it can be used for things like displaying part of a database. See the swing.table package for more information on tables.

The models—There are several models used by `JTable`. The data model is a `TableModel`, and it contains the contents of the cells. The column model is a `TableColumnModel`, and it tracks information about the columns (including column selection). The row selection information is tracked by a `ListSelectionModel`.

Selection—Tables may be allowed to select columns, rows, or both. They may be defined to allow single selection, selection of contiguous items, or arbitrary multiple selection.

Coordinates—There are two coordinate systems in use: the model's and the view's. Most methods of `JTable` use the view's coordinate system. (The methods of `TableModel` use the model's coordinate system.) Events of type `TableModelEvent` come from the model, so they use the model's coordinate system. There are two systems because of column reordering. Reordering is a feature of the view, and the model is unaware of it. Thus "column 1" in the view may correspond to "column 3" in the model.

Header—Header information is maintained in a `JTableHeader`.

Rendering and editing—The `TableColumnModel` may provide the renderer (that draws a cell) or the editor (that changes a cell). If not, the `JTable` may define these based on the class of the cell. To change the background color of specific cells only, you need to provide a customized renderer. (Renderers have access to the cell contents, row, and value, and can use this information to decide how to draw the cell.)

As of Swing 1.0.2, `JTables` no longer need to use the static `createScrollPaneForTable()` method to properly add themselves to a `JScrollPane`. Just add the `JTable` to the `JScrollPane` in the same way as any other component and the `JTable` will recognize this and properly configure itself.

Example: See the `swing.table` package.

FAQs

I put my table in a JScrollPane; why don't I have any column headers?

Use `JTable.createScrollPaneForTable()`; it sets up the headers. Swing 1.0.2 deprecates this method and has the table set itself up properly when it is added to a `JScrollPane`.

Where is that gray area coming from when I put my table in a JScrollPane?

That gray area is actually the background of the `JScrollPane`'s `JViewport` since the table is smaller than the `JViewport`. To set the background of the `JViewport` to the correct color, add this line of code:

```
theScrollPane.getViewport().setBackground(theTable.getBackground());
```

How do I change the color of a cell (or row, or column) in a JTable?

Provide a renderer that changes the background color of the renderer component based on the row and/or column index. The trick is to make sure that the component is opaque, so that the background is painted.

```
public class JTable extends JComponent
    implements Accessible, CellEditorListener,
    ListSelectionListener, Scrollable, TableColumnModelListener,
    TableModelListener
```

Fields

public static final int AUTO_RESIZE_ALL_COLUMNS = 4

When a column is grown or shrunk, this gets the space needed by performing the opposite operation on all of the other columns in the table.

public static final int AUTO_RESIZE_LAST_COLUMN = 3

When a column is grown or shrunk, this gets the space needed by performing the opposite operation on the last column.

public static final int AUTO_RESIZE_NEXT_COLUMN = 1

When a column is grown or shrunk, this gets the space needed by performing the opposite operation on the single column immediately after it.

public static final int AUTO_RESIZE_OFF = 0

Does not automatically change the size of any columns in the table. Leaves them at their defaults or the size set by the user, and supplies a scroll bar as necessary.

public static final int AUTO_RESIZE_SUBSEQUENT_COLUMNS = 2

When a column is grown or shrunk, this gets the space needed by performing the opposite operation on the columns after it in the table.

Constructors

public JTable()
public JTable(TableModel dataModel)
public JTable(TableModel dataModel, TableColumnModel columnModel)
public JTable(TableModel dataModel, TableColumnModel columnModel,
    ListSelectionModel selectionModel)

Creates a table object, using the specified models.

Defaults: dataModel created by createDefaultDataModel() (by default a DefaultTableModel), columnModel created by createDefaultColumnModel() (by default a DefaultTableColumnModel), and selectionModel created by createDefaultSelectionModel() (by default a DefaultListSelectionModel).

public JTable(int numColumns, int numRows)

Creates a table with its model a DefaultTableModel. The model has the specified number of columns and rows. The columns are labeled "A," "B," "C," ..., "AA," "AB," and so forth.

public JTable(Object[][] array, Object[] columnNames)

Creates a table with its model a DefaultTableModel. The model is initialized with the data in array, and given the specified columnNames. Note that array[r][c] specifies the data at a particular row and column.

Throws: IllegalArgumentException is thrown if array is null, or if the number of columns in array doesn't equal the number of columns in columnNames.

public JTable(java.util.Vector data, java.util.Vector columnNames)

Creates a table with a DefaultTableModel. The data is a Vector of Vectors which contain the data objects. Note that ((Vector)data.elementAt(r)).elementAt(c) specifies the data at a particular row and column.

Throws: IllegalArgumentException is thrown if array is null, or if the number of columns in array doesn't equal the number of columns in columnNames.

Methods

`public void addColumn(TableColumn column)`

Adds a new column to the table (the model and the view).

`public void addColumnSelectionInterval(int start, int finish)`

Adds the columns from `start` to `finish` (inclusive) to the set of selected columns.

`public void addNotify()`

Calls `configureEnclosingScrollPane()` when the `JTable` detects it has been added to a `JScrollPane`.

Overrides: `addNotify` in class `JComponent`.

`public void addRowSelectionInterval(int start, int finish)`

Adds the rows from `start` to `finish` (inclusive) to the set of selected rows.

`public void clearSelection()`

Removes all rows (or columns) from the selection. (If a selection is required, selects the first row.)

`public void columnAdded(TableColumnModelEvent event)`

Allows the table to receive events when a column is added to the table.

Implements: `columnAdded` in interface `TableColumnModelListener`.

`public int columnAtPoint(java.awt.Point p)`

Locates the index of the column containing p, or −1 if there is no such point in the table's area.

`public void columnMarginChanged(ChangeEvent event)`

Allows the table to receive events when the width of a column is changed.

Implements: `columnMarginChanged` in interface `TableColumnModelListener`.

`public void columnMoved(TableColumnModelEvent event)`

Allows the table to receive events when a column in the table is moved.

Implements: `columnMoved` in interface `TableColumnModelListener`.

`public void columnRemoved(TableColumnModelEvent event)`

Allows the table to receive events when a column is removed from the table.

Implements: `columnRemoved` in interface `TableColumnModelListener`.

`public void columnSelectionChanged(ListSelectionEvent event)`

Allows the table to receive events when the selection changes.

Implements: `columnSelectionChanged` in interface `TableColumnModelListener`.

`public int convertColumnIndexToModel(int viewColumn)`

Converts the column number in view coordinates to the column number in model coordinates. (The model is unaware of column reordering in the view.) If `viewColumn` < 0, it is returned as is. See also `convertColumnIndexToView()`.

`public int convertColumnIndexToView(int modelColumn)`

Converts the column number in model coordinates to the column number in view coordinates, or −1 if the model column is not displayed. If `modelColumn` < 0, it is returned as is. (The model is unaware of column reordering in the view.) See also `convertColumnIndexToModel()`.

`public void createDefaultColumnsFromModel()`

Tells the table to first discard any column information it has, and then refresh it by going to the model, using `getColumnCount()` and `getColumnType()`. This happens only if `autoCreateColumnsFromModel` is `true`.

`public static JScrollPane createScrollPaneForTable(JTable table)`

Deprecated as of Swing 1.0.2. A `JTable` now configures itself correctly when it is added to a `JScrollPane`.

public boolean editCellAt(int row, int column)

Starts a cell editor to edit the specified cell. Returns `true` if the cell can be edited.

Throws: `IllegalArgumentException` if `row` or `column` are not in the valid range.

public boolean editCellAt(int row, int column,
java.awt.event.EventObject event)

Starts a cell editor to edit the specified cell. The `event` is passed to `shouldSelectCell()` and `isCellEditable()` of `TableCellEditor`. Returns `true` if the cell can be edited.

Throws: `IllegalArgumentException` if `row` or `column` are not in the valid range.

public void editingCanceled(ChangeEvent event)

Notifies the table that the editing of the cell was canceled, without making a change to the cell.

Implements: `editingCanceled` in interface `CellEditorListener`.

public void editingStopped(ChangeEvent event)

Notifies the table that the editing of the cell has stopped, and a change was made. Supports the `CellEditorListener` interface.

Implements: `editingStopped` in interface `CellEditorListener`.

public AccessibleContext getAccessibleContext()

Gets the accessible context for the component.

Overrides: `getAccessibleContext` in class `JComponent`.

Implements: `getAccessibleContext` in interface `Accessible`.

public boolean getAutoCreateColumnsFromModel()

Tells whether columns will be determined from the model. If so, when a new model is provided via `setModel()`, or if the whole table is marked as changed in the `tableChanged()` notification, the model will be queried for columns. Otherwise, the existing columns will be used. See also `create-DefaultColumnsFromModel()` and `setAutoCreateColumnsFromModel()`. *Default:* true.

public int getAutoResizeMode()

Gets the resize policy for cells when the table size is adjusted. Returns one of the `AUTO_RESIZE_X` constants defined in this class. *Default:* `AUTO_RESIZE_ALL_COLUMNS`. See also `setAutoResize-Mode()`.

public TableCellEditor getCellEditor()

Gets the default editor used to edit cells.

public TableCellEditor getCellEditor(int row, int column)

Returns the editor to use for editing the cell at (`row`, `column`). This method doesn't work quite as you would expect, since it needs to be compatible with Swing 1.0.3 and before. For compatibility, the `TableColumn` is checked first for a non-null editor. If one is found, it is returned. Only if the `TableColumn`'s editor is null is the type of data in the column checked (using `getColumn-Class()`) and used to find a default editor that matches.

public java.awt.Rectangle getCellRect(int row, int column,
boolean includeSpacing)

Returns the bounding rectangle (in screen coordinates) for the specified cell. If `includeSpacing` is true, the rectangle includes the `intercellSpacing` surrounding the cell. If `false`, it includes only half the intercell spacing (and neighboring cells would include the other half). See also `getInter-cellSpacing()`. (Uses `JTable` view coordinates.)

Throws: `IllegalArgumentException` if `row` or `column` are not in the valid range.

public boolean getCellSelectionEnabled()

Returns `true` if a cell may be selected (and not whole columns or rows only).

public TableColumn getColumn(Object object)

Gets the first column c, for which `getColumnName(c).equals(object)`.

Throws: `IllegalArgumentException` if object is `null`, or if no column has a matching identifier.

public Class getColumnClass(int column)

Gets the class associated with `column`. See `TableModel`.

public int getColumnCount()

Gets the number of columns.

public TableColumnModel getColumnModel()

Gets the model containing all column information.

public String getColumnName(int column)

Gets the name associated with `column`. (Uses `JTable` view column indices.)

public boolean getColumnSelectionAllowed()

Returns `true` if columns may be selected. See `setColumnSelectionAllowed()`, `getCellSelectionEnabled()`, `setCellSelectionEnabled()`, `getRowSelectionAllowed()`, and `setRowSelectionAllowed()`.

public TableCellEditor getDefaultEditor(Class class)

Gets the editor used by default for items of type `class`. By default, `JTable` provides editors for `Boolean`, `Number`, and `Object`. If no editor is found for `class`, its superclasses are tested until an editor is found for one of them. If you want a specific editor for a column, use the `TableColumn` to install it. See `getColumnClass()`, `setDefaultEditor()`, and `TableColumn`.

public TableCellRenderer getDefaultRenderer(Class class)

Gets the renderer (display object) used by default for items of type `class`. By default, `JTable` provides renderers for `Boolean`, `Number`, and `Object`. If no renderer is found for `class`, its superclasses are tested until an editor is found for one of them. If you want a specific renderer for a column, use the `TableColumn` to install it. See `getColumnClass()`, `setDefaultRenderer()`, and `TableColumn`.

public int getEditingColumn()

Returns the index of the column being edited, using the view column index.

public int getEditingRow()

Returns the index of the row being edited.

public java.awt.Component getEditorComponent()

If `isEditing()` is `true`, returns the component acting as the editor.

public java.awt.Color getGridColor()

Gets the color used for grid lines (drawn to separate cells). *Default:* `gray`.

public java.awt.Dimension getIntercellSpacing()

Returns the spacing used between cells. *Default:* 3 pixels horizontally, 2 pixels vertically.

public TableModel getModel()

Returns the model representing the table's data.

public java.awt.Dimension getPreferredScrollableViewportSize()

Gets the ideal size for the viewport. This is, by default, a fairly large value, but it can be adjusted by `setPreferredScrollableViewPortSize()`.

Implements: `getPreferredScrollableViewportSize` in interface `Scrollable`.

public int getRowCount()

Returns the number of rows.

```
public int getRowHeight()
```
Gets the height of the rows. If 0, each row's height is calculated independently (otherwise they are all assumed to be identical). *Default:* 16 pixels. See `setRowHeight()`.

```
public int getRowMargin()
```
Returns the gap, in pixels, between rows. This returns the same value as `getIntercellSpacing().height`.

```
public boolean getRowSelectionAllowed()
```
Returns `true` if whole rows may be selected.

```
public int getScrollableBlockIncrement(java.awt.Rectangle visible,
    int orientation, int direction)
```
Calculates how far to scroll for one block, typically to move by one screenful of text. The `visible` rectangle is the section of the object visible in the viewport. The `orientation` is either `SwingConstants.HORIZONTAL` or `SwingConstants.VERTICAL`. The direction is negative to scroll left (or up), or positive to scroll right (or down). The result is the number of pixels to scroll in the specified direction.

Implements: `getScrollableBlockIncrement` in interface `Scrollable`.

```
public boolean getScrollableTracksViewportHeight()
```
Always returns `false`.

Implements: `getScrollableTracksViewportHeight` in interface `Scrollable`.

```
public boolean getScrollableTracksViewportWidth()
```
Returns `false` if the resize mode is `AUTO_RESIZE_OFF`, returns `true` otherwise.

Implements: `getScrollableTracksViewportWidth` in interface `Scrollable`.

```
public int getScrollableUnitIncrement(java.awt.Rectangle visible,
    int orientation, int direction)
```
Calculates how far to scroll one unit. For example, a unit scroll would typically scroll by one row of the table. The `visible` rectangle is the section of the object visible in the viewport. The `orientation` is either `SwingConstants.HORIZONTAL` or `SwingConstants.VERTICAL`. The direction is negative to scroll left (or up), or positive to scroll right (or down). The result is the number of pixels to scroll in the specified direction.

Implements: `getScrollableUnitIncrement` in interface `Scrollable`.

```
public int getSelectedColumn()
```
Returns the index of the last column added to the selection, or –1 if no columns are selected.

```
public int getSelectedColumnCount()
```
Returns the number of selected columns.

```
public int[] getSelectedColumns()
```
Returns an array containing the column indexes of all the selected columns. The array will have no elements if there are no selected columns.

```
public int getSelectedRow()
```
Returns the index of the last row added to the selection, or –1 if no rows are selected.

```
public int getSelectedRowCount()
```
Returns the number of selected rows.

```
public int[] getSelectedRows()
```
Returns an array containing the row indexes of all the selected rows. The array will have no elements if there are no selected rows.

```
public java.awt.Color getSelectionBackground()
```
Returns the background color for selected cells.

public java.awt.Color getSelectionForeground()

Returns the foreground color for selected cells.

public ListSelectionModel getSelectionModel()

Returns the selection model for rows. (The column selection model is maintained in the column model; see `getColumnModel()`.) If row selection is not allowed, this returns `null`.

public boolean getShowHorizontalLines()

Returns `true` if the horizontal lines between cells are drawn. *Default:* `true`.

public boolean getShowVerticalLines()

Returns `true` if the vertical lines between cells are drawn. *Default:* `true`.

public JTableHeader getTableHeader()

Returns the table header (which maintains the column labels). See `swing.table.JTableHeader`.

public String getToolTipText(java.awt.event.MouseEvent event)

Gets the text for the ToolTip when the mouse is at `event`. See also `setToolTipText()` in `JComponent`. The `initializeLocalVars()` method registers the table with `ToolTipManager`; if `setToolTipText(null)` is called, the table will be deregistered and ToolTips will no longer work.
Overrides: `getToolTipText` in class `JComponent`.

public TableUI getUI()

Gets the UI (look and feel) for the table. See the chapter on look and feel.

public String getUIClassID()

Returns "TableUI".
Overrides: `getUIClassID` in class `JComponent`.

public Object getValueAt(int row, int column)

Returns the value at the specified `row` and `column`. (These are in the coordinates of the view.)

public boolean isCellEditable(int row, int column)

Returns `true` if the specified cell may be edited. (If `false`, you can't click on the cell to edit it, and `setValueAt()` will have no effect.)

public boolean isCellSelected(int row, int column)

Returns `true` if the specified cell is selected.
Throws: `IllegalArgumentException` if `row` or `column` are not in the valid range.

public boolean isColumnSelected(int column)

Returns `true` if the specified column is selected.
Throws: `IllegalArgumentException` if `column` is not in the valid range.

public boolean isEditing()

Returns `true` while an editor is active in the table.

public boolean isManagingFocus()

Returns `true`, so the table can use `TAB` and `SHIFT-TAB` to move the focus inside the table.
Overrides: `isManagingFocus` in class `JComponent`.

public boolean isRowSelected(int row)

Returns `true` if the specified row is selected. While `true`, `editingColumn()` and `editingRow()` are defined.
Throws: `IllegalArgumentException` if row is not in the valid range.

public void moveColumn(int column, int newColumn)

Moves `column` to become `newColumn`. The column formerly at `newColumn` is moved left if `column < newColumn`, or right if `column > newColumn`. Note that this only affects the view—tables are not rearranged in the model.

```
public java.awt.Component prepareEditor(TableCellEditor editor,
    int row, int column)
```
Sets up the cell editor so that it is ready to edit the specified cell.

```
public java.awt.Component prepareRenderer(
    TableCellRenderer renderer, int row, int column)
```
Sets up the renderer to paint the given row and column, based on the data and selection models.

```
public void removeColumn(TableColumn column)
```
Removes the specified column from the view. (It is still present in the model, and can be added back to the JTable view via addColumn().)

```
public void removeColumnSelectionInterval(int column1, int column2)
```
Removes column1 to column2 (inclusive) from the selection. If empty column selections are not allowed, one of the columns will remain selected. (The column1 is permitted to be larger than column2.)

```
public void removeEditor()
```
Makes the editor no longer used by the table. (See getCellEditor().)

```
public void removeRowSelectionInterval(int row1, int row2)
```
Removes row1 to row2 (inclusive) from the row selection. If the row selection is not allowed to be empty, one of the rows will remain selected. (The row1 is permitted to be larger than row2.)

```
public void reshape(int x, int y, int width, int height)
```
Uses sizeColumnsToFit() to relayout the table after it has been resized.

Overrides: reshape in class JComponent.

```
public int rowAtPoint(java.awt.Point point)
```
Gets the index of the row that contains point, or –1 if none does.

```
public void selectAll()
```
Stops any editing and then selects all rows and columns in the table.

```
public void setAutoCreateColumnsFromModel(boolean doAutoCreate)
```
Returns true if the columns will be determined from the model (following setModel(), or a full table structure change).

```
public void setAutoResizeMode(int mode)
```
Sets how table resizing works. The mode is one of the values AUTO_RESIZE_ALL_COLUMNS, AUTO_RESIZE_NEXT_COLUMN, AUTO_RESIZE_SUBSEQUENT_COLUMNS, AUTO_RESIZE_LAST_COLUMN, or AUTO_RESIZE_OFF.

```
public void setCellEditor(TableCellEditor editor)
```
Sets the default cell editor.

```
public void setCellSelectionEnabled(boolean maySelectBoth)
```
Sets whether a cell can be selected (for example, both a row and a column at the same time.)

```
public void setColumnModel(TableColumnModel model)
```
Sets the table column model for the JTable itself and the JTableHeader. The table will listen to the model for column information.

Throws: IllegalArgumentException if newModel is null.

```
public void setColumnSelectionAllowed(boolean maySelectColumn)
```
Sets whether columns may be selected.

```
public void setColumnSelectionInterval(int column1, int column2)
```
If column selection is allowed, selects from column1 to column2 (inclusive).

public void setDefaultEditor(Class class, TableCellEditor editor)

Sets the `editor` to be used by cells of `class` (unless one is provided by the `TableColumn`). To remove the default editor for a class, call it with that class and `null` for the `editor`.

public void setDefaultRenderer(Class class, TableCellRenderer renderer)

Sets the `renderer` to be used to display cells of type `class` (unless one is provided by the `Table-Column`). To remove the default renderer for a class, call this method with that class and `null` for the `renderer`.

public void setEditingColumn(int column)

Sets the editing column (in effect while the `isEditing()` is true). See `editingColumn()`.

public void setEditingRow(int row)

Sets the editing row (in effect while `isEditing()` is true). See `editingRow()`.

public void setGridColor(java.awt.Color color)

Sets the color for the grid lines drawn between cells.

Throws: `IllegalArgumentException` if `color` is `null`.

public void setIntercellSpacing(java.awt.Dimension dim)

Sets the spacing between cells (horizontal and vertical). *Default:* 3 pixels horizontally, 2 pixels vertically.

public void setModel(TableModel model)

Sets the data model for the table.

Throws: `IllegalArgumentException` if `newModel` is `null`.

public void setPreferredScrollableViewportSize(
java.awt.Dimension dimension)

Sets the ideal size for the viewport. This is, by default, a fairly large value. See also `getPreferred-ScrollableViewPortSize()`. This supports the `Scrollable` interface.

public void setRowHeight(int height)

Sets the height to be used for all rows (must be at least 1 pixel).

Throws: `IllegalArgumentException` if `height` is less than 1.

public void setRowMargin(int rowMargin)

Sets the gap, in pixels, between rows.

public void setRowSelectionAllowed(boolean maySelect)

If `maySelect` is `true`, rows may be selected.

public void setRowSelectionInterval(int row1, int row2)

If rows may be selected, selects from `row1` to `row2` (inclusive).

public void setSelectionBackground(java.awt.Color selectionBackground)

Sets the background color for selected cells.

public void setSelectionForeground(java.awt.Color selectionForeground)

Sets the foreground color for selected cells.

public void setSelectionMode(int mode)

Sets how selections may be made. The mode is one of the following: `ListSelection-Model.SINGLE_SELECTION`, `ListSelectionModel.SINGLE_INTERVAL_SELECTION`, or `ListSelectionModel.MULTIPLE_INTERVAL_SELECTION`.

public void setSelectionModel(ListSelectionModel model)

Sets the model used to track row selections.

Throws: `IllegalArgumentException` if `newModel` is `null`.

public void setShowGrid(boolean shouldShow)

If `shouldShow` is `true`, a grid is drawn between cells.

public void setShowHorizontalLines(boolean b)

If b is true, lines between the rows in the table should be drawn.

public void setShowVerticalLines(boolean b)

If b is true, lines between the columns in the table should be drawn.

public void setTableHeader(JTableHeader header)

Sets the header for the table, which may be null. See JTableHeader.

public void setUI(TableUI ui)

Sets a new UI (look and feel) for the table.

public void setValueAt(Object value, int row, int column)

Sets the value of the specified cell.

public void sizeColumnsToFit(boolean fitFromLastColumn)

Deprecated as of Swing 1.0.3. Use sizeColumnsToFit(int).

public void sizeColumnsToFit(int resizingColumn)

Resizes none, some, or all of the columns in the table so that the total width of the columns is the same as the width of the table. When the table is resized, resizingColumn will be –1. In this case all columns get an even proportion of the change in size, whether it is an increase or decrease.

If one of the columns in the table is resized, resizingColumn will be the view index of the column which is changing. The autoResizeMode is used to decide how to alter the other columns to adjust for the change. With AUTO_RESIZE_OFF, all columns keep their same size. If the table is in a JScrollPane, a scroll bar will be created as needed. When the mode is AUTO_RESIZE_NEXT_COLUMN the column immediately after the one being resized will grow or shrink to absorb the change. All other columns will stay the same size. AUTO_RESIZE_SUBSEQUENT_COLUMNS mode distributes the change among all columns after the resizing one in the table. AUTO_RESIZE_LAST_COLUMN adjusts the last column in the table. The AUTO_RESIZE_ALL_COLUMNS mode distributes the change among all columns, *including* the one being resized.

When resizing, a column will never shrink or grow past its maximum or minimum width. This may cause either an empty area to the right of the table to be shown, or the last column(s) may be clipped by the parent container. You should almost always place a JTable inside a JScrollPane for this reason.

public void tableChanged(TableModelEvent event)

Notifies the JTable that the model has changed. The event is in model coordinates; the coordinates are converted to view coordinates by this routine.

Implements: tableChanged in interface TableModelListener.

public void updateUI()

Updates the table to reflect the current UI (look and feel). See the chapter on look and feel.

Overrides: updateUI in class JComponent.

public void valueChanged(ListSelectionEvent event)

Repaints the rows as necessary because of row selections.

Implements: valueChanged in interface ListSelectionListener.

Protected Fields

protected boolean autoCreateColumnsFromModel

If true, query the model for the columns.

protected int autoResizeMode

Controls how extra space is allocated to the table when it is resized. See the constants above.

`protected transient TableCellEditor cellEditor`

Returns the editor for the cell currently being edited.

`protected boolean cellSelectionEnabled`

Returns `true` if both a row and column may be selected to select a single cell.

`protected TableColumnModel columnModel`

Returns the model for the columns of the table.

`protected TableModel dataModel`

Returns the model for the data in the table.

`protected transient java.util.Hashtable defaultEditorsByColumnClass`

Maps from a `Class` object to the editor for that class.

`protected transient java.util.HashtabledefaultRenderersByColumnClass`

Maps from a `Class` object to a renderer for that class.

`protected transient int editingColumn`

Returns the column currently being edited.

`protected transient int editingRow`

Returns the row currently being edited.

`protected transient java.awt.Component editorComp`

If currently editing, this is the editor.

`protected java.awt.Color gridColor`

Returns the color of the grid.

`protected java.awt.Dimension preferredViewportSize`

Tells the `Scrollable` interface the preferred size of the viewport.

`protected int rowHeight`

Returns the height of all rows in the table (in pixels).

`protected int rowMargin`

Returns the distance between rows (in pixels).

`protected boolean rowSelectionAllowed`

Returns `true` if rows may be selected.

`protected java.awt.Color selectionBackground`

Returns the background color of selected cells.

`protected java.awt.Color selectionForeground`

Returns the foreground color of selected cells.

`protected ListSelectionModel selectionModel`

Returns the model for the currently selected rows.

`protected boolean showHorizontalLines`

Returns `true` if lines between rows will be painted.

`protected boolean showVerticalLines`

Returns `true` if lines between columns will be painted.

`protected JTableHeader tableHeader`

Returns the table header for the table.

Protected Methods

`protected void configureEnclosingScrollPane()`

Called by `addNotify()` to properly set up the table when it is added to a `JScrollPane`.

`protected TableColumnModel createDefaultColumnModel()`

Causes the table to create a default column model. Creates a `DefaultColumnModel` by default. (See the constructors.)

protected TableModel createDefaultDataModel()

Causes the table to create a default data model. Creates a `DefaultTableModel` by default. (See the constructors.)

protected void createDefaultEditors()

Tells the table to create default editors for all columns. Consults the type of the column to determine which editor to use.

protected void createDefaultRenders()

Tells the table to create default renderers for all columns. Consults the type of the column to determine which renderer to use.

protected ListSelectionModel createDefaultSelectionModel()

Creates a default selection model. Creates a `DefaultListSelectionModel` by default. (See the constructors.)

protected JTableHeader createDefaultTableHeader()

Tells the table to create its default table headers (a `JTableHeader`).

protected void initializeLocalVars()

Common routine called by the constructors to set up the table.

protected String paramString()

Returns a string representation of the properties of this `JTable`. The returned string may be empty but it will not be `null`.

Overrides: paramString in class JComponent.

protected void resizeAndRepaint()

Helper method that simply calls `revalidate()` and `repaint()`.

Inner Classes

protected class JTable.AccessibleJTable

See also Accessible (p.85), AccessibleContext (p.90), CellEditorListener (p.486), JTableHeader (p.752), ListSelectionEvent (p.499), ListSelectionListener (p.500), ListSelectionModel (p.421), Scrollable (p.433), TableCellEditor (p.758), TableColumnModel (p.764), TableColumnModelListener (p.508), TableModel (p.766), TableModelListener (p.513), TableUI (p.541).

swing.JTable.AccessibleJTable

INNER CLASS

The class used to obtain the accessible role for this object. It also handles updating the `Accessi-bleSelection` as the table changes and updating the table as the `AccessibleSelection` changes.

```
protected class AccessibleJTable
    extends JComponent.AccessibleJComponent
    implements AccessibleSelection, ListSelectionListener,
    TableModelListener, TableColumnModelListener,
    CellEditorListener, PropertyChangeListener
```

Constructors

`public AccessibleJTable()`

Default constructor.

Methods

`public void addAccessibleSelection(int i)`

Adds the given accessible child to the selection (or makes it the selection). Cell selection must be enabled in the table for this to work, since the accessible children of a `JTable` are its cells.

Implements: addAccessibleSelection in interface AccessibleSelection.

`public void clearAccessibleSelection()`

Clears the selection.

Implements: clearAccessibleSelection in interface AccessibleSelection.

`public void columnAdded(TableColumnModelEvent e)`

Fires an ACCESSIBLE_VISIBLE_DATA_PROPERTY property change event.

Implements: columnAdded in interface TableColumnModelListener.

`public void columnMarginChanged(ChangeEvent e)`

Fires an ACCESSIBLE_VISIBLE_DATA_PROPERTY property change event.

Implements: columnMarginChanged in interface TableColumnModelListener.

`public void columnMoved(TableColumnModelEvent e)`

Fires an ACCESSIBLE_VISIBLE_DATA_PROPERTY property change event.

Implements: columnMoved in interface TableColumnModelListener.

`public void columnRemoved(TableColumnModelEvent e)`

Fires an ACCESSIBLE_VISIBLE_DATA_PROPERTY property change event.

Implements: columnRemoved in interface TableColumnModelListener.

`public void columnSelectionChanged(ListSelectionEvent e)`

Does nothing as of Swing 1.1. It is supposed to switch the `TableColumnModel` listener over to the new column.

Implements: columnSelectionChanged in interface TableColumnModelListener.

`public void editingCanceled(ChangeEvent e)`

Does nothing.

Implements: editingCanceled in interface CellEditorListener.

`public void editingStopped(ChangeEvent e)`

Fires an ACCESSIBLE_VISIBLE_DATA_PROPERTY property change event.

Implements: editingStopped in interface CellEditorListener.

`public Accessible getAccessibleAt(java.awt.Point p)`

Returns the `Accessible` child, if one exists, contained at the local coordinate p.

Overrides: getAccessibleAt in class JComponent.AccessibleJComponent.

public Accessible getAccessibleChild(int i)

Returns the ith Accessible child of the object.

Overrides: getAccessibleChild in class JComponent.AccessibleJComponent.

public int getAccessibleChildrenCount()

Returns the number of accessible children in the object. If all of the children of this object implement Accessible, then this method should return the number of children of this object.

Overrides: getAccessibleChildrenCount in class JComponent.AccessibleJComponent.

public AccessibleRole getAccessibleRole()

Returns AccessibleRole.TABLE.

Overrides: getAccessibleRole in class JComponent.AccessibleJComponent.

public AccessibleSelection getAccessibleSelection()

Returns the current AccessibleSelection, which is this.

Overrides: getAccessibleSelection in class AccessibleContext.

public Accessible getAccessibleSelection(int i)

Returns the ith selected cell.

Implements: getAccessibleSelection in interface AccessibleSelection.

public int getAccessibleSelectionCount()

Returns the number of cells selected in the table.

Implements: getAccessibleSelectionCount in interface AccessibleSelection.

public boolean isAccessibleChildSelected(int i)

Returns true if the cell at i is selected. Cell indices are calculated by row * numColumns + column index.

Implements: isAccessibleChildSelected in interface AccessibleSelection.

public void propertyChange(java.beans.PropertyChangeEvent e)

When a property in the JTable is changed (such as the model), this method updates the listeners to get events from the new object.

Implements: propertyChange in interface PropertyChangeListener.

public void removeAccessibleSelection(int i)

Deselects the cell at the given index, i. Cell indices are calculated by row * numColumns + col. Cell selection must be enabled in the table for this to work.

Implements: removeAccessibleSelection in interface AccessibleSelection.

public void selectAllAccessibleSelection()

If the table has cell selection enabled, and allows multiple selections, this method selects the entire table.

Implements: selectAllAccessibleSelection in interface AccessibleSelection.

public void tableChanged(TableModelEvent e)

Fires an ACCESSIBLE_VISIBLE_DATA_PROPERTY property change event.

Implements: tableChanged in interface TableModelListener.

public void tableRowsDeleted(TableModelEvent e)

Fires an ACCESSIBLE_VISIBLE_DATA_PROPERTY property change event.

public void tableRowsInserted(TableModelEvent e)

Fires an ACCESSIBLE_VISIBLE_DATA_PROPERTY property change event.

public void valueChanged(ListSelectionEvent e)

Fires an ACCESSIBLE_SELECTION_PROPERTY property change event to inform listeners of the change in selection and an ACCESSIBLE_ACTIVE_DESCENDANT_PROPERTY to inform listeners about the cell that now has the focus.

Implements: valueChanged in interface ListSelectionListener.

Inner Classes
protected class JTable.AccessibleJTable.AccessibleJTableCell

> *See also*   Accessible (p.85), AccessibleRole (p.95), AccessibleSelection (p.98),
> CellEditorListener (p.486), ListSelectionEvent (p.499), ListSelectionListener (p.500),
> JComponent.AccessibleJComponent (p.221), TableColumnModelEvent (p.507),
> TableColumnModelListener (p.508), TableModelEvent (p.508),
> TableModelListener (p.510).

swing.JTable.AccessibleJTable.AccessibleJTableCell

INNER CLASS

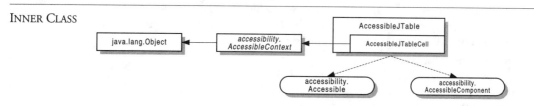

Provides Accessiblity support for a table cell. See Accessible (p.85), AccessibleComponent
(p.87), and AccessibleContext (p.90) for descriptions of the methods.

```
protected class JTable.AccessibleJTable.AccessibleJTableCell
    extends AccessibleContext
    implements Accessible, AccessibleComponent
```

Constructor
public AccessibleJTableCell(JTable t, int row, int column, int i)
> Constructs an AccessibleJTableCell for the given row and column, and makes it child index
> i in the AccessibleJTable.

Methods
public void addFocusListener(java.awt.event.FocusListener l)
> *Implements:* addFocusListener in interface AccessibleComponent.

public void addPropertyChangeListener(java.beans.PropertyChangeListener l)
> *Overrides:* addPropertyChangeListener in class AccessibleContext.

public boolean contains(java.awt.Point p)
> *Implements:* contains in interface AccessibleComponent.

public AccessibleAction getAccessibleAction()
> *Overrides:* getAccessibleAction in class AccessibleContext.

public Accessible getAccessibleAt(java.awt.Point p)
> *Implements:* getAccessibleAt in interface AccessibleComponent.

public Accessible getAccessibleChild(int i)
> *Overrides:* getAccessibleChild in class AccessibleContext.

public int getAccessibleChildrenCount()
> *Overrides:* getAccessibleChildrenCount in class AccessibleContext.

public AccessibleComponent getAccessibleComponent()
> *Overrides:* getAccessibleComponent in class AccessibleContext.

public AccessibleContext getAccessibleContext()
    Implements: getAccessibleContext in interface Accessible.
public java.lang.String getAccessibleDescription()
    Overrides: getAccessibleDescription in class AccessibleContext.
public int getAccessibleIndexInParent()
    Overrides: getAccessibleIndexInParent in class AccessibleContext.
public java.lang.String getAccessibleName()
    Overrides: getAccessibleName in class AccessibleContext.
public Accessible getAccessibleParent()
    Overrides: getAccessibleParent in class AccessibleContext.
public AccessibleRole getAccessibleRole()
    Overrides: getAccessibleRole in class AccessibleContext.
public AccessibleSelection getAccessibleSelection()
    Overrides: getAccessibleSelection in class AccessibleContext.
public AccessibleStateSet getAccessibleStateSet()
    Overrides: getAccessibleStateSet in class AccessibleContext.
public AccessibleText getAccessibleText()
    Overrides: getAccessibleText in class AccessibleContext.
public AccessibleValue getAccessibleValue()
    Overrides: getAccessibleValue in class AccessibleContext.
public java.awt.Color getBackground()
    Implements: getBackground in interface AccessibleComponent.
public java.awt.Rectangle getBounds()
    Implements: getBounds in interface AccessibleComponent.
public java.awt.Cursor getCursor()
    Implements: getCursor in interface AccessibleComponent.
public java.awt.Font getFont()
    Implements: getFont in interface AccessibleComponent.
public java.awt.FontMetrics getFontMetrics(java.awt.Font f)
    Implements: getFontMetrics in interface AccessibleComponent.
public java.awt.Color getForeground()
    Implements: getForeground in interface AccessibleComponent.
public java.util.Locale getLocale()
    Overrides: getLocale in class AccessibleContext.
    Throws: java.awt.IllegalComponentStateException if the component has not had its Locale set and it does not have an ancestor with a Locale.
public java.awt.Point getLocation()
    Implements: getLocation in interface AccessibleComponent.
public java.awt.Point getLocationOnScreen()
    Implements: getLocationOnScreen in interface AccessibleComponent.
public java.awt.Dimension getSize()
    Implements: getSize in interface AccessibleComponent.
public boolean isEnabled()
    Implements: isEnabled in interface AccessibleComponent.
public boolean isFocusTraversable()
    Implements: isFocusTraversable in interface AccessibleComponent.

public boolean isShowing()
> *Implements:* isShowing in interface AccessibleComponent.

public boolean isVisible()
> *Implements:* isVisible in interface AccessibleComponent.

public void removeFocusListener(java.awt.event.FocusListener l)
> *Implements:* removeFocusListener in interface AccessibleComponent.

public void removePropertyChangeListener(
java.beans.PropertyChangeListener l)
> *Overrides:* removePropertyChangeListener in class AccessibleContext.

public void requestFocus()
> *Implements:* requestFocus in interface AccessibleComponent.

public void setAccessibleDescription(java.lang.String s)
> *Overrides:* setAccessibleDescription in class AccessibleContext.

public void setAccessibleName(java.lang.String s)
> *Overrides:* setAccessibleName in class AccessibleContext.

public void setBackground(java.awt.Color c)
> *Implements:* setBackground in interface AccessibleComponent.

public void setBounds(java.awt.Rectangle r)
> *Implements:* setBounds in interface AccessibleComponent.

public void setCursor(java.awt.Cursor c)
> *Implements:* setCursor in interface AccessibleComponent.

public void setEnabled(boolean b)
> *Implements:* setEnabled in interface AccessibleComponent.

public void setFont(java.awt.Font f)
> *Implements:* setFont in interface AccessibleComponent.

public void setForeground(java.awt.Color c)
> *Implements:* setForeground in interface AccessibleComponent.

public void setLocation(java.awt.Point p)
> *Implements:* setLocation in interface AccessibleComponent.

public void setSize(java.awt.Dimension d)
> *Implements:* setSize in interface AccessibleComponent.

public void setVisible(boolean b)
> *Implements:* setVisible in interface AccessibleComponent.

See also Accessible (p.85), AccessibleComponent (p.87), AccessibleContext (p.90), AccessibleRole (p.95), AccessibleSelection (p.98), AccessibleStateSet (p.101), AccessibleText (p.103), AccessibleValue (p.104).

swing.JTextArea

CLASS

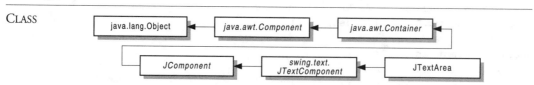

A `JTextArea` displays plain text in one or more lines. It implements the `Scrollable` interface, so it can be placed in a `JScrollPane` if scrolling is desired. `JTextArea` is a lightweight component, but it is almost source-compatible with `java.awt.TextArea`.

A `JTextArea` displays all characters in a single font. For styled editing, see `JEditorPane`. For a single line of text, use a `JTextField`.

Example

```
package jtextarea;

import java.awt.*;
import java.awt.event.*;
// Uncomment the following two lines for Swing 1.0.3 and before
//import com.sun.java.swing.*;
//import com.sun.java.swing.event.*;
// Uncomment the following two lines for Swing 1.1 and JDK 1.2
import javax.swing.*;
import javax.swing.event.*;

public class Test extends JFrame {
    JTextArea text = new JTextArea(10,40);

    public Test() {
        addWindowListener(new WindowAdapter() {
            public void windowClosing(WindowEvent e) {
                Test.this.dispose();
                System.exit(0);
            }
        });
        // A JTextArea defaults to no word wrap, so turn it on.
        text.setLineWrap(true);
        // It also defaults to wrapping in the middle of words, so tell it to
        // wrap at whitespace.
        text.setWrapStyleWord(true);

        text.getDocument().addDocumentListener(new DocumentListener() {
            public void showSize(DocumentEvent e) {
                System.out.println("Doc size: " + e.getDocument().getLength());
            }
            public void insertUpdate(DocumentEvent e) {showSize(e);}
            public void removeUpdate(DocumentEvent e) {showSize(e);}
            public void changedUpdate(DocumentEvent e){showSize(e);}
        });
// Place the text area in a scrollpane.
// Note the use of HORIZONTAL_SCROLLBAR_NEVER, to allow word-wrap to work.
        getContentPane().add(
        new JScrollPane(text, JScrollPane.VERTICAL_SCROLLBAR_AS_NEEDED,
                        JScrollPane.HORIZONTAL_SCROLLBAR_NEVER),
                        BorderLayout.CENTER);
        pack();
        setSize(200, 200);
    }

    public static void main (String[] args) {
```

```
        new Test().setVisible(true);
    }
}
```

FAQs

Where are the scroll bars on my JTextArea?

Swing components don't implement scrolling behavior directly. All scrolling has been encapsulated in the `JScrollPane` class. To get scroll bars on the `JTextArea` (or any Swing component where it is logical for it to support scrolling), wrap it in a `JScrollPane`.

For example, to add a `JTextArea` to the content area of a `JFrame` and have it support scrolling, do the following:

```
theFrame.getContentPane().add(new JScrollPane(theJTextArea));
```

Components that don't implement `Scrollable` will get the default behavior supplied by `JScrollPane`.

public class JTextArea extends JTextComponent

Constructors

public JTextArea()
Creates a new text area using an empty `PlainDocument` and no preferred size.

public JTextArea(Document document)
Creates a new text area using the given `Document`, which must be a `PlainDocument` or derivative.

public JTextArea(String initialText)
Creates a new text area using a new `PlainDocument`, which is filled with the given text.

public JTextArea(int rows, int columns)
Creates a new text area using an empty `PlainDocument`, and assigns it the given preferred size.

public JTextArea(String initialText, int rows, int columns)
Creates a new text area using a new `PlainDocument`, which is filled with the given text. The text area has a preferred size based on the given number of `rows` and `columns`.

public JTextArea(Document document, String initialText, int rows, int columns)
Creates a new text area using the given `Document` (which must be a `PlainDocument` or derivative). The `Document` contains the given text and the text area has a preferred size based on the given number of `rows` and `columns`.

Public Methods

public void append(String text)
Appends `text` to the end of the document.

public AccessibleContext getAccessibleContext()
Gets the `AccessibleContext` associated with this `JTextArea`. Creates a new context if necessary.
Overrides: getAccessibleContext in class `JTextComponent`.
Implements: getAccessibleContext in interface `Accessible`.

public int getColumns()
Gets the number of columns.

public int getLineCount()

Determines the number of lines contained in the area.

public int getLineEndOffset(int line) throws BadLocationException

Determines the offset of the end of the given line.

Throws: BadLocationException is thrown if the line is less than zero or greater than or equal to the number of lines contained in the document (as reported by getLineCount).

public int getLineOfOffset(int offset) throws BadLocationException

Translates an offset into the component's text to a line number.

Throws: BadLocationException is thrown if the offset is less than zero or greater than the document length.

public int getLineStartOffset(int line) throws BadLocationException

Determines the offset of the start of the given line.

Throws: BadLocationException is thrown if the line is less than zero or greater than or equal to the number of lines contained in the document (as reported by getLineCount).

public boolean getLineWrap()

Gets the line-wrapping policy of the text area.

public java.awt.Dimension getPreferredScrollableViewportSize()

Returns the preferred size (in pixels) when this text area is included in a viewport. If they have been set, uses the row and columns and their sizes.

Overrides: getPreferredScrollableViewportSize in class JTextComponent.

Implements: getPreferredScrollableViewportSize in interface Scrollable.

public java.awt.Dimension getPreferredSize()

Returns the preferred size of the text area. This is the maximum size needed to display the text and the size requested for the viewport.

Overrides: getPreferredSize in class JComponent.

public int getRows()

Returns the number of rows in the JTextArea.

public boolean getScrollableTracksViewportWidth()

Returns true if a viewport should always force the width of this Scrollable to match the width of the viewport. This is implemented to return true if the line wrapping policy is true, and false if lines are not being wrapped.

Overrides: getScrollableTracksViewportWidth in class JTextComponent.

Implements: getScrollableTracksViewportWidth in interface Scrollable.

public int getScrollableUnitIncrement(
java.awt.Rectangle rectangle, int orientation, int direction)

Returns the number of pixels to be scrolled in the given direction (so one "line" will be scrolled at a time). The rectangle is the visible area in the scrolling viewport. The orientation must be either SwingConstants.VERTICAL or SwingConstants.HORIZONTAL. The direction will be negative for scrolling left or up, positive for scrolling right or down. Uses getRowHeight() and getColumnWidth() to determine the scrolling distance.

Throws: IllegalArgumentException for an invalid orientation.

Overrides: getScrollableUnitIncrement in class JTextComponent.

Implements: getScrollableUnitIncrement in interface Scrollable.

public int getTabSize()

Returns the number of characters corresponding to a tab. Defaults to 8.

public String getUIClassID()

Returns "TextAreaUI".

Overrides: getUIClassID in class JComponent.

public boolean getWrapStyleWord()

Gets the style of wrapping used if the text area is wrapping lines. If set to true the lines will be wrapped at word boundaries (such as white space) if they are too long to fit within the allocated width. If set to false, the lines will be wrapped at character boundaries.

public void insert(String text, int position)

Inserts text into the document after position characters. This method is thread safe.

Throws: IllegalArgumentException if position is an invalid position in the model.

public boolean isManagingFocus()

Returns true, as it captures tab keystrokes once it has the focus.

Overrides: isManagingFocus in class JComponent.

public void replaceRange(String text, int start, int end)

Replaces the characters from start to end with text. This method is thread safe.

Throws: IllegalArgumentException if part of the range is an invalid position in the model.

public void setColumns(int numColumns)

Sets the number of columns.

Throws: IllegalArgumentException if numColumns is less than 0.

public void setFont(java.awt.Font font)

Sets the font for the text area. (This component uses a single font for its whole contents.)

Overrides: setFont in class Component.

public void setLineWrap(boolean wrap)

Sets the line-wrapping policy of the text area. If set to true the lines will be wrapped if they are too long to fit within the allocated width. If set to false, the lines will always be unwrapped. A PropertyChangeEvent is fired when this property is changed. By default, the wrapping will occur at the character nearest the end of the line. To break at white space, see setWrapStyleWord().

public void setRows(int numRows)

Sets the number of rows.

Throws: IllegalArgumentException if numRows is less than 0.

public void setTabSize(int numCharacters)

Sets the number of characters each tab character expands to. (In a variable width font, it will use the width of the widest character.)

public void setWrapStyleWord(boolean word)

Sets the style of wrapping used if the text area is wrapping lines. If set to true the lines will be wrapped at word boundaries (such as white space) if they are too long to fit within the allocated width. If set to false, the lines will be wrapped at character boundaries.

Protected Methods

protected Document createDefaultModel()

Creates a new document, with a default type of PlainDocument.

protected int getColumnWidth()

Gets the width of a column (in pixels). This is typically the width of the "m" character.

protected int getRowHeight()

Returns the height of the row. *Default:* height of the font.

protected String paramString()

Returns a String containing the properties of this JTextArea. The returned String may be empty, but it will not be null.

Overrides: paramString in class Container.

protected void processComponentKeyEvent(java.awt.event.KeyEvent e)

Consumes TAB and SHIFT-TAB characters so they can be used for editing, not focus traversal.

Overrides: processComponentKeyEvent in class JTextComponent.

See also AccessibleContext (p.90), Document (p.826), JTextComponent (p.838), PlainDocument (p.857).

swing.JTextArea.AccessibleJTextArea

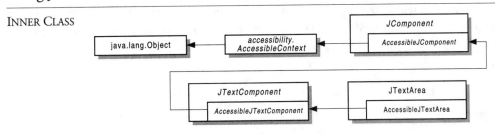

**protected class JTextArea.AccessibleJTextArea
    extends JTextComponent.AccessibleJTextComponent**

Method

public AccessibleStateSet getAccessibleStateSet()

Adds AccessibleState.MULTI_LINE to the AccessibleJTextComponent AccessibleStateSet.

Overrides: getAccessibleStateSet in class JTextComponent.AccessibleJTextComponent.

See also AccessibleStateSet (p.101), JTextComponent.AccessibleJTextComponent (p.844).

swing.JTextField

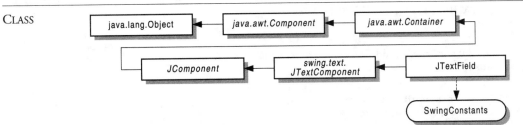

A JTextField is a lightweight component that allows the user to view and edit a single line of text. JTextField is almost source-compatible with java.awt.TextArea. For password fields, use JPasswordField (p.306).

For compatibility with `TextArea`, this component does not work the way a normal Swing component works with respect to default buttons. Usually in Swing, when the RETURN/ENTER key is pressed, the default button for the enclosing `JRootPane` is triggered. If a `JTextField` has the focus when the RETURN/ENTER key is pressed it will send an `ActionEvent` to its listeners instead. To have it behave as a normal Swing component, remove the VK_ENTER key binding as follows:

```
KeyStroke enter = KeyStroke.getKeyStroke(KeyEvent.VK_ENTER, 0);
JTextField field = new JTextField();
Keymap keyMap = field.getKeymap();
keyMap.removeKeyStrokeBinding(enter);
```

To filter the content allowed by the field (for example, for a numeric entry field), create a subclass of `PlainDocument` and override the `insertString()` method. See the FAQ for the text package (p.777) for more information.

Example

```
package jtextfield;

import java.awt.*;
import java.awt.event.*;
// Uncomment the following line for Swing 1.0.3 and before
//import com.sun.java.swing.*;
// Uncomment the following line for Swing 1.1
import javax.swing.*;

public class Test extends JFrame {
    JTextField text = new JTextField("Press Return", 40);

    public Test() {
        addWindowListener(new WindowAdapter() {
            public void windowClosing(WindowEvent e) {
                Test.this.dispose();
                System.exit(0);
            }
        });
        text.addActionListener (new ActionListener() {
            public void actionPerformed (ActionEvent e) {
                System.out.println("Text="+text.getText());
            }
        });
        getContentPane().add (text, BorderLayout.CENTER);
        pack();
    }

    public static void main (String[] args) {
        new Test().setVisible(true);
    }
}

public class JTextField extends JTextComponent
    implements SwingConstants
```

Constants

public static final String notifyAction

The name of the action sent when the RETURN key is pressed in the field.

Constructors

public JTextField()
public JTextField(String initialText)
public JTextField(int numColumns)
public JTextField(String initialText, int numColumns)
public JTextField(Document document, String initialText, int numColumns)

Creates a text field.

Default values: document: a new PlainDocument; initialText: empty; numColumns: 0. If numColumns is 0, the text field will accept whatever width it is given.

Public Methods

public synchronized void addActionListener(
java.awt.event.ActionListener listener)

Adds listener to the list of listeners to be notified when the RETURN/ENTER key is pressed.

public AccessibleContext getAccessibleContext()

Gets the AccessibleContext associated with this JTextField. Creates a new context if necessary.

Overrides: getAccessibleContext in class JTextComponent.

Implements: getAccessibleContext in interface Accessible.

public Action[] getActions()

Returns the list of all actions supported by this component. Includes those of the UI as well as those of the text field itself.

Overrides: getActions in class JTextComponent.

public int getColumns()

Gets the number of columns.

public int getHorizontalAlignment()

Returns the alignment of the text field. SwingConstants.LEFT, SwingConstants.CENTER, or SwingConstants.RIGHT. *Default:* LEFT.

public BoundedRangeModel getHorizontalVisibility()

Gets a range model corresponding to the view of the text field. This represents the visible portion, as the text field scrolls horizontally during typing.

public java.awt.Dimension getPreferredSize()

Returns the preferred size of the text field. If getColumns()!=0, this is getColumns()*getColumnWidth(). Otherwise, there is no preferred size.

Overrides: getPreferredSize in class JComponent.

public int getScrollOffset()

The starting position of the visible part of the text. (See getHorizontalVisibility().)

public String getUIClassID()

Returns "TextFieldUI".

Overrides: getUIClassID in class JComponent.

public boolean isValidateRoot()

Calls to revalidate that come from within the textfield itself will be handled by validating the textfield.

Overrides: isValidateRoot in class JComponent.

public void postActionEvent()

Sends any action events to registered action listeners.

public synchronized void removeActionListener(
java.awt.event.ActionListener listener)

Removes listener from the list of listeners.

public void scrollRectToVisible(Rectangle rectangle)

Scrolls the text field (horizontally) until rectangle is visible.

Overrides: scrollRectToVisible in class JComponent.

public void setActionCommand(String action)

Sets the action command string (sent when the RETURN key is pressed).

public void setColumns(int numColumns)

Sets the number of columns.

Throws: IllegalArgumentException if numColumns is less than 0.

public void setFont(java.awt.Font font)

Sets the font for the text area. (This component uses a single font for its whole contents.)

Overrides: setFont in class Component.

public void setHorizontalAlignment(int alignment)

Sets the alignment of the text field. It will be SwingConstants.LEFT, SwingConstants.CEN-TER, or SwingConstants.RIGHT. *Default:* LEFT.

Throws: IllegalArgumentException if the alignment specified is not a valid key.

public void setScrollOffset(int offset)

Sets the position of the scrolling. See also getScrollOffset() and getHorizontalVisibility().

Protected Methods

protected Document createDefaultModel()

Creates a new document, with a default PlainDocument.

protected void fireActionPerformed()

Notifies listeners that the RETURN key has been pressed.

protected int getColumnWidth()

Returns the width of a column (in pixels). This is typically the width of the "m" character.

protected String paramString()

Returns the parameter string for the text area, which is the number of columns and the command string.

Overrides: paramString in class Container.

Inner Classes

protected class JTextField.AccessibleJTextField

See also Action (p.128), BoundedRangeModel (p.132), Document (p.826), PlainDocument (p.857).

swing.JTextField.AccessibleJTextField

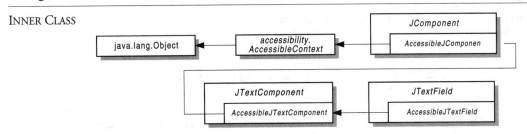

```
protected class AccessibleJTextField
    extends JTextComponent.AccessibleJTextComponent
```

Methods

`public AccessibleStateSet getAccessibleStateSet()`

    Adds `AccessibleState.SINGLE_LINE` to the `AccessibleJTextComponent` Accessible-
StateSet.

    Overrides: `getAccessibleStateSet` in class `JTextComponent.AccessibleJTextCompo-
nent`.

    Extended by   JPasswordField.AccessibleJPasswordField (p.309).

    See also   AccessibleStateSet (p.101), JTextComponent.AccessibleJTextComponent (p.844).

swing.JTextPane

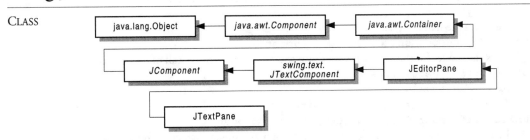

`JTextPane` provides a component that can edit styled text. See the `swing.text` package
(p.769).

    The `Document` type for this editor is `StyledDocument` (p.877), which supports three kinds
of formatting: character-level, paragraph-level, and logical. Logical styles needn't be tied to the
paragraph/character hierarchy.

    To edit text with a single style, use a `JTextArea`. To edit specific file types (for example,
HTML or RTF), use a `JEditorPane`. The major difference between this class and `JEditorPane`
is the addition of helper methods to work with styles and the use of a `StyledDocument`.

```
public class JTextPane extends JEditorPane
```

Constructors

public JTextPane()

public JTextPane(StyledDocument document)

Builds a new text pane, with a new StyledDocument or with the specified document.

Methods

public Style addStyle(String styleName, Style parentStyle)

Creates a new named style, styleName. (If styleName is null, the style cannot be manipulated by name). The new style has a parentStyle, used to resolve attributes that aren't specifically mentioned by the new style. (If parentStyle is null, the style stands alone.) For example, if a new style specifies italic, and doesn't override the font, while the parent style specifies 10-point font, the result when this style is applied will be a 10-point italic font. See getStyle() and removeStyle().

public AttributeSet getCharacterAttributes()

Gets the character-level attributes at the current position in the document.

public MutableAttributeSet getInputAttributes()

Returns the attributes to use for inserted text. Note that as the Caret moves the set can change, so you need to keep calling this method.

public Style getLogicalStyle()

Gets the logical style associated with the current paragraph.

public AttributeSet getParagraphAttributes()

Gets the paragraph-level attributes of the current paragraph.

public boolean getScrollableTracksViewportWidth()

Always returns true, indicating that the text pane should be as wide as possible in its containing view.
Overrides: getScrollableTracksViewportWidth in class JEditorPane.
Implements: getScrollableTracksViewportWidth in interface Scrollable.

public Style getStyle(String)

Retrieves the named style. See addStyle().

public StyledDocument getStyledDocument()

Gets the model for this text pane. (See also the getDocument() call of JTextComponent.)

public String getUIClassID()

Returns "TextPaneUI".
Overrides: getUIClassID in class JEditorPane.

public void insertComponent(Component component)

Inserts component into the document, treating it as a single character. To insert text, use replaceSelection(). This method is thread safe.

public void insertIcon(Icon icon)

Inserts icon into the document, treating it as a single character. To insert text, use replaceSelection(). This method is thread safe.

public void removeStyle(String styleName)

Deletes the named style. See addStyle().

public void replaceSelection(String replacement)

Replaces the current selection. This is the mechanism used to insert and delete text. (If the current selection is empty, text is merely inserted; if the replacement is empty, the selection is deleted.) Also see getInputAttributes(). This method is thread safe.
Overrides: replaceSelection in class JEditorPane.

public void setCharacterAttributes(AttributeSet attributes, boolean replace)

Sets the character attributes for the current selection (or the next input). If `replace` is `true`, replaces the current attributes with the new ones; otherwise, it adds the new ones to the existing ones. This method is thread safe.

public void setDocument(Document d)

Sets the model for this text pane. The document must be an instance of class `StyledDocument`.

Throws: `IllegalArgumentException` if d isn't a `StyledDocument` or a subclass.

Overrides: `setDocument` in class `JTextComponent`.

public final void setEditorKit(EditorKit kit)

Sets the editor kit. The kit must be a `StyledEditorKit` or a subclass.

Throws: `IllegalArgumentException` if kit is not a `StyledEditorKit`.

Overrides: `setEditorKit` in class `JEditorPane`.

public void setLogicalStyle(Style style)

Sets the logical style for the current paragraph. A logical style is in effect if there are no character or paragraph styles. See `getLogicalStyle()` and `Style`. This method is thread safe.

public void setParagraphAttributes(AttributeSet attrs, boolean replace)

Sets the paragraph attributes for the current selection (or the next input). If `replace` is `true`, replaces the current attributes with the new ones; otherwise, it adds the new ones to the existing ones. This method is thread safe.

public void setStyledDocument(StyledDocument document)

Sets the model for this text pane (similar to `setDocument()`, except with the argument type customized).

Protected Methods

protected EditorKit createDefaultEditorKit()

Creates and returns a `StyledEditorKit`.

Overrides: `createDefaultEditorKit` in class `JEditorPane`.

protected final StyledEditorKit getStyledEditorKit()

Returns the editor kit.

protected String paramString()

Returns a string representation of the properties of this `JTextPane`. The returned string may be empty but it will not be `null`.

Overrides: `paramString` in class `JEditorPane`.

See also   AttributeSet (p.794), Document (p.826), Style (p.865), StyledEditorKit (p.878), StyledDocument (p.877), TextUI (p.542).

swing.JToggleButton

CLASS

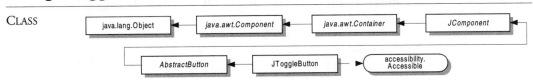

`JToggleButton` has functionality common to check boxes and radio buttons—the ability to hold two states (selected or not).

Example: See `JCheckBox` and `JRadioButton`.

```
public class JToggleButton extends AbstractButton
    implements Accessible
```

Constructors

```
public JToggleButton()
public JToggleButton(Icon icon)
public JToggleButton(Icon icon, boolean isSelected)
public JToggleButton(String text)
public JToggleButton(String text, boolean isSelected)
public JToggleButton(String text, Icon icon)
public JToggleButton(String text, Icon icon, boolean isSelected)
```
Creates a toggle button, with specified text, icon, and initial selection status. *Default:* no text, no icon, and/or not selected. You would usually use one of `JToggleButton`'s subclasses: `JCheckBox` or `JRadioButton`.

Public Methods

```
public AccessibleContext getAccessibleContext()
```
The accessible context.
Overrides: `getAccessibleContext` in class `JComponent`.
Implements: `getAccessibleContext` in interface `Accessible`.
```
public String getUIClassID()
```
Returns "ToggleButtonUI".
Overrides: `getUIClassID` in class `JComponent`.
```
public void updateUI()
```
Updates the button according to the current look and feel.
Overrides: `updateUI` in class `AbstractButton`.

Protected Methods

```
protected String paramString()
```
Returns a string representation of the properties of this `JToggleButton`. The returned string may be empty but it will not be `null`.
Overrides: `paramString` in class `AbstractButton`.

Inner Classes

```
protected class JToggleButton.AccessibleJToggleButton
public static class JToggleButton.ToggleButtonModel
```

Extended by   JCheckBox (p.193), JRadioButton (p.319).
See also   AbstractButton (p.118), AccessibleContext (p.90), Icon (p.183).

swing.JToggleButton.AccessibleJToggleButton

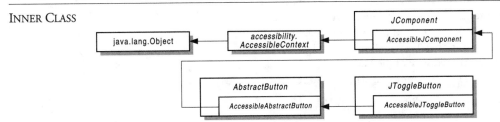

```
protected class AccessibleJToggleButton
    extends AbstractButton.AccessibleAbstractButton
```

Constructor
public AccessibleJToggleButton()
 Default constructor.

Methods
public AccessibleRole getAccessibleRole()
 Returns AccessibleRole.TOGGLE_BUTTON.
 Overrides: getAccessibleRole in class JComponent.AccessibleJComponent.

public void itemStateChanged(java.awt.event.ItemEvent e)
 Fires AccessibleContext.ACCESSIBLE_STATE_PROPERTY property events indicating that the property is now AccessibleState.SELECTED (when the button is selected) or null when the button is deselected.

 Extended by JCheckBox.AccessibleJCheckBox (p.194), JRadioButton.AccessibleJRadioButton (p.321).
 See also AbstractButton.AccessibleAbstractButton (p.125), AccessibleRole (p.95).

swing.JToggleButton.ToggleButtonModel

The button model for a toggle button. These methods need to be overridden because JToggle-Buttons can be in ButtonGroups.

```
public static class ToggleButtonModel extends DefaultButtonModel
```

Constructor
public ToggleButtonModel()
 Constructs a new ToggleButtonModel.

Methods
public boolean isSelected()
 Checks if the button is selected.

Overrides: `isSelected` in class `DefaultButtonModel`.

`public void setPressed(boolean isPressed)`
Sets the pressed state of the toggle button.
Overrides: `setPressed` in class `DefaultButtonModel`.

`public void setSelected(boolean isSelected)`
Sets the selected state of the button.
Overrides: `setSelected` in class `DefaultButtonModel`.

See also   DefaultButtonModel (p.161).

swing.JToolBar

CLASS

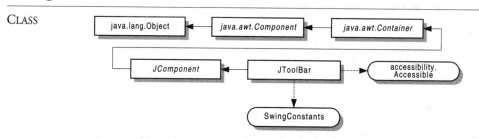

A toolbar is a palette of buttons, each corresponding to an action. Depending on the look and feel, a toolbar may be movable and resizable as a floating palette, or it may be forced to remain on the edge of a window.

A `JToolBar` can contain any component, not just `Actions`. It inherits the `add(Component)` method from `JComponent`, and supplies its own version to add `Actions`.

By default a `JToolBar` uses a `BoxLayout`. The `LayoutManager` can be changed using `setLayout()`, but any future call to `setOrientation()` will reset the layout to `BoxLayout`.

Example: See `AbstractAction`.

```
public class JToolBar extends JComponent
    implements Accessible
```

Constructors
`public JToolBar()`
Creates a toolbar.
`public JToolBar(int orientation)`
Creates a toolbar in the given orientation (which is either `HORIZONTAL` or `VERTICAL`).

Public Methods
`public JButton add(Action action)`
Adds `action` to the toolbar, and returns the corresponding button object.
`public void addSeparator()`
Adds a separator (space with no action attached) to the end of the toolbar.
`public void addSeparator(ava.awt.Dimension size)`
Adds a separator of the given size to the end of the toolbar.

public AccessibleContext getAccessibleContext()

Gets the accessible context for the toolbar.

Overrides: getAccessibleContext in class JComponent.

Implements: getAccessibleContext in interface Accessible.

public java.awt.Component getComponentAtIndex(int index)

Returns the component at index.

public int getComponentIndex(java.awt.Component component)

Locates the index of component, or –1 if component is not found.

public java.awt.Insets getMargin()

Returns the margin between the toolbar and its buttons. See setMargin().

public int getOrientation()

Returns the orientation of the toolbar, which is either HORIZONTAL or VERTICAL.

public ToolBarUI getUI()

Gets the look and feel associated with this component.

public String getUIClassID()

Returns "ToolBarUI".

Overrides: getUIClassID in class JComponent.

public boolean isBorderPainted()

Returns true if the border should be painted.

public boolean isFloatable()

Returns true if the toolbar can be dragged out by the user.

public void remove(java.awt.Component comp)

Removes comp from the toolbar.

Overrides: remove in class Container.

public void setBorderPainted(boolean shouldPaint)

Sets whether the border should be painted.

public void setFloatable(boolean b)

Sets whether the toolbar can be dragged by the user.

public void setMargin(java.awt.Insets newMargin)

Sets the margin between the toolbar and its buttons. Note: if a border has been explicitly set on this toolbar, that border is also responsible for the margins. In that case, setMargin() will have no effect.

public void setOrientation(int o)

Sets the orientation of the toolbar to either HORIZONTAL or VERTICAL.

public void setUI(ToolBarUI ui)

Sets the look and feel to a new value (usually called by updateUI()).

public void updateUI()

Tells the toolbar to update itself according to the current look and feel.

Overrides: updateUI in class JComponent.

Protected Methods

protected void addImpl(java.awt.Component comp,
Object constraints, int index)

Overrides this method so that buttons in the toolbar cannot be the default buttons.

Overrides: addImpl in class Container.

protected PropertyChangeListener createActionChangeListener(JButton b)
Creates the listener that listens for changes in the button and the associated action and updates the other when one changes.

protected void paintBorder(java.awt.Graphics graphicsContext)
Paints the border onto `graphicsContext`.

protected String paramString()
Returns a string representation of the properties of this `JToolBar`. The returned string may be empty but it will not be `null`.
Overrides: `paramString` in class `JComponent`.

Inner Classes

protected class JToolBar.AccessibleJToolBar
public static class JToolBar.Separator

See also   Accessible (p.85), AccessibleContext (p.90), Action (p.128), JButton (p.191), JComponent (p.207), ToolBarUI (p.543).

swing.JToolBar.AccessibleJToolBar

INNER CLASS

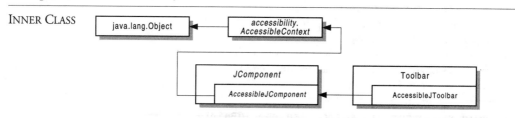

protected class JToolBar.AccessibleJToolBar extends JComponent.AccessibleJComponent

Methods

public AccessibleRole getAccessibleRole()
Returns `AccessibleRole.TOOL_BAR`.
Overrides: `getAccessibleRole` in class `JComponent.AccessibleJComponent`.

public AccessibleStateSet getAccessibleStateSet()
Uses `SwingUtilities.getAccessibleStateSet()` to build the state set.
Overrides: `getAccessibleStateSet` in class `JComponent.AccessibleJComponent`.

See also   AccessibleRole (p.95), AccessibleStateSet (p.101), JComponent.AccessibleJComponent (p.221), SwingUtilities (p.443).

swing.JToolBar.Separator

INNER CLASS

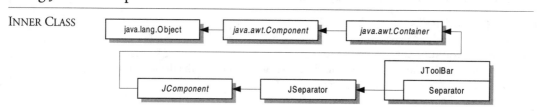

This class represents the space-filling separator that can be added to `JToolBar`s.

`public class JToolBar.Separator extends JSeparator`

Constructor
`public Separator()`
> Constructs the separator.

`public Separator(java.awt.Dimension size)`
> Constructs a separator of the given size.

Methods
`public java.awt.Dimension getMaximumSize()`
> Returns the maximum size for the separator.
> *Overrides:* `getMaximumSize` in class `Component`.

`public java.awt.Dimension getMinimumSize()`
> Returns the minimum size for the separator.
> *Overrides:* `getMinimumSize` in class `Component`.

`public java.awt.Dimension getPreferredSize()`
> Returns the preferred size for the separator.
> *Overrides:* `getPreferredSize` in class `Component`.

`public java.awt.Dimension getSeparatorSize()`
> Returns the size of the separator. Does not modify the returned value, as it is the actual internal variable holding the size. Uses `setSeparatorSize()` to change the size.

`public String getUIClassID()`
> Returns "ToolBarSeparatorUI".
> *Overrides:* `getUIClassID` in class `JSeparator`.

`public void setSeparatorSize(java.awt.Dimension size)`
> Sets the size of the separator.

> *See also* JSeparator (p.338), JToolBar (p.388).

swing.JToolTip

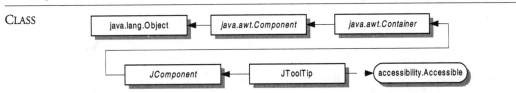

A `JToolTip` is a small window of help text associated with a component. It appears when the mouse pauses over the component to which it is attached. A component gets a ToolTip by using the `createToolTip()` method of `JComponent`. See class `ToolTipManager` for information on controlling the delay times associated with ToolTips.

Example

```
package jtooltip;
import java.awt.event.*;
```

```
// Uncomment the following line for Swing 1.0.3 or before
//import com.sun.java.swing.*;
// Uncomment the following line for Swing 1.1
import javax.swing.*;

public class Test extends JFrame {
   public Test() {
      addWindowListener(new WindowAdapter() {
         public void windowClosing(WindowEvent e) {
            Test.this.dispose();
            System.exit(0);
         }
      });
      JButton b = new JButton("Test");
      b.setToolTipText("Help text for the button");    // VERY EASY!
      getContentPane().add (b, BorderLayout.CENTER);
      pack();
   }
   public static void main (String[] args) {
      new Test().setVisible(true);
   }
}
```

public class JToolTip extends JComponent
   implements Accessible

Constructors
public JToolTip()
   Creates a ToolTip with empty text.

Public Methods
public AccessibleContext getAccessibleContext()
   Returns the AccessibleContext for this component.
   Overrides: getAccessibleContext in class JComponent.
   Implements: getAccessibleContext in interface Accessible.
public JComponent getComponent()
   Returns the component with which this ToolTip is associated.
public String getTipText()
   Returns the text for this ToolTip.
public ToolTipUI getUI()
   Returns the UI (look and feel) for this ToolTip.
public String getUIClassID()
   Returns the string "ToolTipUI". See the chapter on look and feel.
   Overrides: getUIClassID in class JComponent.
public void setComponent(JComponent c)
   Sets the component with which this ToolTip should be associated.
public void setTipText(String tipText)
   Sets the message for this ToolTip.
public void updateUI()
   Tells the ToolTip to update its UI (look and feel). See the chapter on look and feel.

Overrides: updateUI in class JComponent.

Protected Methods

protected String paramString()

Returns a string representation of the properties of this JToolTip. The returned string may be empty but it will not be null.

Overrides: paramString in class JComponent.

See also   Accessible (p.85), AccessibleContext (p.90), JComponent (p.207), ToolTipUI (p.543).

swing.JToolTip.AccessibleJToolTip

INNER CLASS

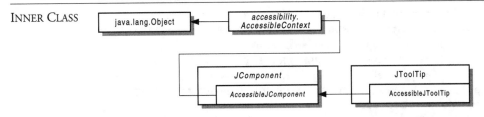

protected class AccessibleJToolTip
    extends JComponent.AccessibleJComponent

Methods

public java.lang.String getAccessibleDescription()

Returns the ToolTip text if the accessibleDescription is null.

Overrides: getAccessibleDescription in class JComponent.AccessibleJComponent.

public AccessibleRole getAccessibleRole()

Returns AccessibleRole.TOOL_TIP.

Overrides: getAccessibleRole in class JComponent.AccessibleJComponent.

See also   AccessibleRole (p.95), JComponent.AccessibleJComponent (p.221).

swing.JTree

CLASS

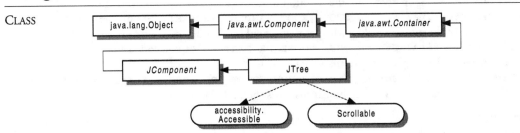

JTree supports a hierarchical or outline view of the tree it contains. See the swing.tree package (p.107).

FAQs

How do I prevent the expansion (or collapsing) of a node?

Add a `TreeWillExpandListener`, which is new in Swing 1.1. This type of listener is notified before the change occurs, and it can throw a `javax.swing.tree.ExpandVetoException` to prevent the change.

```
public class JTree extends JComponent
    implements Accessible, Scrollable
```

Fields

`public static final String CELL_EDITOR_PROPERTY = "cellEditor"`
   The name of the property for the cell editor. See `getCellEditor()`.

`public static final String CELL_RENDERER_PROPERTY = "cellRenderer"`
   The name of the property for the cell renderer. See `getCellRenderer()`.

`public static final String EDITABLE_PROPERTY = "editable"`
   The name of the property telling whether the tree may be edited. See `isEditable()`.

`public static final String INVOKES_STOP_CELL_EDITING_PROPERTY =`
   `"messagesStopCellEditing"`
   The name of the property telling whether to stop editing (and accept changes) or cancel editing (and reject them) when the selection changes without confirming the change first. See `getInvokes-StopCellEditing()`.

`public static final String LARGE_MODEL_PROPERTY = "largeModel"`
   The name of the property telling whether the tree is expected to be large (and perhaps generate its cells on the fly). See `isLargeModel()`.

`public static final String ROOT_VISIBLE_PROPERTY = "rootVisible"`
   The name of the property telling whether the top-level node is visible. See `isRootVisible()`.

`public static final String ROW_HEIGHT_PROPERTY = "rowHeight"`
   The name of the property telling the height of the rows. See `getRowHeight()`.

`public static final String SCROLLS_ON_EXPAND_PROPERTY = "scrollsOnExpand"`
   The name of the property indicating whether the tree should scroll to ensure all newly expanded nodes are visible. See `getScrollsOnExpand()`.

`public static final String SELECTION_MODEL_PROPERTY = "selectionModel"`
   The name of the property telling the selection model. See `getSelectionModel()`.

`public static final String SHOWS_ROOT_HANDLES_PROPERTY = "showsRootHandles"`
   The name of the property telling whether there should be handles displayed on top-level nodes.

`public static final String TREE_MODEL_PROPERTY = "treeModel"`
   The name of the property for the tree's data model.

`public static final String VISIBLE_ROW_COUNT_PROPERTY = "visibleRowCount"`
   The name of the property telling how many rows should be displayed.

Constructors

`public JTree()`
`public JTree(TreeModel model)`
   Creates a tree using `model` (or a `DefaultTreeModel`).
`public JTree(TreeNode node)`

public JTree(TreeNode node, boolean askAllowsChildren)

Creates a tree based on `node`, which decides if it should ask for leaves using lack of children (`askAllowsChildren false`), or by asking the node directly (`askAllowsChildren true`).

public JTree(Object[] list)
public JTree(java.util.Hashtable list)
public JTree(java.util.Vector list)

These constructors create a new tree. The model is a new `DefaultTreeModel`—it has a dummy root node, and its top-level children are taken from the list. The `rootVisible` property is `false`, and `showsRootHandles` is `true`.

Methods

public void addSelectionInterval(int row1, int row2)

Adds to the selection the paths contained in the rows from `row1` to `row2` inclusive.

public void addSelectionPath(TreePath path)

Adds `path` to the selection. All nodes in the path are made visible.

public void addSelectionPaths(TreePath[] paths)

Adds all paths in the array to the selection. All nodes in all paths are made visible.

public void addSelectionRow(int row)

Adds the path containing `row` to the selection.

public void addSelectionRows(int[] rows)

Adds to the selection the paths corresponding to the items in `rows`.

public void addTreeExpansionListener(TreeExpansionListener listener)

Adds `listener` to the list of objects to be notified when the tree opens or closes a node.

public void addTreeSelectionListener(TreeSelectionListener listener)

Adds `listener` to the list of objects to be notified when the selection changes.

public void addTreeWillExpandListener(TreeWillExpandListener tel)

Adds a listener that gets `TreeExpansionEvents` before the node actually expands so the expansion can be vetoed.

public void cancelEditing()

If the tree is being edited, cancels the editing session.

public void clearSelection()

Deselects all rows (and notifies any selection listeners).

public void collapsePath(TreePath path)

Causes all nodes in the path, except for the last, to be visible and expanded, with the last node in the path collapsed (does not show its children).

public void collapseRow(int row)

Causes the node at `row` to be collapsed (i.e., not show its children).

public String convertValueToText(Object value, boolean isSelected, boolean isExpanded, boolean isLeaf, int row, boolean hasFocus)

Converts a node to its text. This method is called by the renderer; the default implementation returns `value.toString()`.

public void expandPath(TreePath path)

Causes all nodes in the path to be visible and expanded, and makes sure the last node in the path is expanded (shows its children).

public void expandRow(int row)

Causes the node at `row` to be expanded (show its children).

public void fireTreeCollapsed(TreePath path)

Notifies tree listeners that the node at `path` has collapsed.

public void fireTreeExpanded(TreePath path)

Notifies tree listeners that the node at `path` has expanded.

public void fireTreeWillCollapse(TreePath path) throws ExpandVetoException

Notifies tree expansion listeners that the node at the end of the path is about to collapse.

public void fireTreeWillExpand(TreePath path) throws ExpandVetoException

Notifies tree expansion listeners that the node at the end of the path is about to expand.

public AccessibleContext getAccessibleContext()

Gets the accessible context.

Overrides: `getAccessibleContext` in class `JComponent`.

Implements: `getAccessibleContext` in interface `Accessible`.

public TreeCellEditor getCellEditor()

Gets the editor used to edit rows of the tree. See also `cellEditor` and `setCellEditor()`.

public TreeCellRenderer getCellRenderer()

Gets the renderer used to display rows of the tree. See also `cellRenderer` and `setCellRenderer()`.

public TreePath getClosestPathForLocation(int x, int y)

Locates the node closest to (`x,y`), and returns its path. If there is no tree model, or if no nodes are visible, returns `null`. Note that the node need not contain the specified point. See also `getPathForLocation()`.

public int getClosestRowForLocation(int x, int y)

Locates the node closest to (`x,y`), and returns its row index. If there is no tree model, or if no nodes are visible, returns −1. Note that the node need not contain the specified point. See also `getRowForLocation()`.

public TreePath getEditingPath()

If `isEditing()` is `true`, returns the path of the node currently being edited.

public java.util.Enumeration getExpandedDescendants(TreePath parent)

Returns an `Enumeration` of the descendants (as `TreePaths`) of `parent` that are expanded. If `parent` is not expanded, this method returns `null`.

public boolean getInvokesStopCellEditing()

If `true`, when the user selects a different row, editing changes on the current row are accepted (by calling `stopCellEditing()`). If `false`, when the user selects a different row, editing changes on the current row are ignored (by calling `cancelCellEditing()`). *Default:* `false` (that is, changing rows without pressing RETURN to accept the value causes the partial change to be ignored).

public Object getLastSelectedPathComponent()

Returns the deepest component in the selected path.

public TreePath getLeadSelectionPath()

Gets the lead selection path: the last one added to the selection.

public int getLeadSelectionRow()

Gets the lead selection row: the last one added to the selection.

public int getMaxSelectionRow()

Gets the maximum row in the selection, or −1 if no rows are selected.

public int getMinSelectionRow()

Gets the minimum row in the selection, or −1 if no rows are selected.

public TreeModel getModel()

Gets the tree data model.

public java.awt.Rectangle getPathBounds(TreePath path)

Returns the bounding box for the last element in path.

public TreePath getPathForLocation(int x, int y)

Gets the path containing (x,y), or null if none does.

public TreePath getPathForRow(int row)

Gets the path corresponding to row. Returns null if row is not visible.

public java.awt.Dimension getPreferredScrollableViewportSize()

Returns the size the JTree would prefer to be when contained in a scroll pane. This is based on the preferred width, getRowHeight(), and getVisibleRowCount().

Implements: getPreferredScrollableViewportSize in interface Scrollable.

public java.awt.Rectangle getRowBounds(int row)

Returns the bounds rectangle for row.

public int getRowCount()

Gets the number of rows in the tree.

public int getRowForLocation(int x, int y)

Gets the row containing the specified point. Returns –1 if no row contains (x,y). See also get-ClosestRowForLocation().

public int getRowForPath(TreePath path)

Gets the row containing path. Returns –1 if there is no such row visible.

public int getRowHeight()

Gets the standard (fixed) height for each row. If it is 0, the height is not fixed, and it must be computed by the renderer on a row-by-row basis.

public int getScrollableBlockIncrement(java.awt.Rectangle visible, int orientation, int direction)

Computes the distance to scroll by one block (page). The visible rectangle tells what portion of the tree is currently visible. The orientation is either SwingConstants.HORIZONTAL or SwingConstants.VERTICAL. The direction is positive to scroll right (or down), and negative to scroll left (or up).

Implements: getScrollableBlockIncrement in interface Scrollable.

public boolean getScrollableTracksViewportHeight()

Returns false (the tree's height is independent of the scroll pane).

Implements: getScrollableTracksViewportHeight in interface Scrollable.

public boolean getScrollableTracksViewportWidth()

Returns false (the tree's width is independent of the scroll pane).

Implements: getScrollableTracksViewportWidth in interface Scrollable.

public int getScrollableUnitIncrement(java.awt.Rectangle visible, int orientation, int direction)

Computes the distance to scroll by one row. (If the first or last row is not completely visible, it will show the rest of it; otherwise, it will go to the next row.) The visible rectangle tells what portion of the tree is currently visible. The orientation is either SwingConstants.HORIZONTAL or SwingConstants.VERTICAL. The direction is positive to scroll right (or down), and negative to scroll left (or up).

Implements: getScrollableUnitIncrement in interface Scrollable.

public boolean getScrollsOnExpand()

Returns `true` if the tree scrolls to ensure newly expanded child nodes are visible.

public int getSelectionCount()

Returns the number of currently selected nodes.

public TreeSelectionModel getSelectionModel()

Returns the model for selection. See also `setSelectionModel()`.

public TreePath getSelectionPath()

Returns the path to the first selected node, or `null` if no path is selected.

public TreePath[] getSelectionPaths()

Gets the paths of all selected rows, or returns `null` if no paths are selected.

public int[] getSelectionRows()

Gets the row numbers of all selected items.

public boolean getShowsRootHandles()

Returns `true` if root handles should be shown. (These indicate that the top-level items have children.)

public String getToolTipText(java.awt.event.MouseEvent event)

Gets the ToolTip text for `event`. ToolTips for nodes are not active unless the JTree itself has been explicitly registered with the ToolTipManager. To do this, simply call `ToolTipManager.shared-Instance().registerComponent(tree)`.

Overrides: `getToolTipText` in class `JComponent`.

public TreeUI getUI()

Gets the UI (look and feel) for this component. See the chapter on look and feel.

public String getUIClassID()

Returns "TreeUI".

Overrides: `getUIClassID` in class `JComponent`.

public int getVisibleRowCount()

Gets the number of rows that should be visible. Helps support the `Scrollable` interface.

public boolean hasBeenExpanded(TreePath path)

Returns `true` if the node identified by the `path` has *ever* been expanded.

public boolean isCollapsed(TreePath path)

Returns `true` if the node at the end of `path` is collapsed (if it is visible and its children are not displayed).

public boolean isCollapsed(int row)

Returns `true` if the node at `row` is collapsed (doesn't display its children).

public boolean isEditable()

Returns `true` if editing is permitted on the tree.

public boolean isEditing()

Returns `true` if currently editing a node.

public boolean isExpanded(TreePath path)

Returns `true` if the nodes along `path` are visible, and the last node has its children visible (if any).

public boolean isExpanded(int row)

Returns `true` if the node at `row` has its children visible (if any).

public boolean isFixedRowHeight()

Returns `true` if each row is the same size. (Allows more efficient computation of position.)

public boolean isLargeModel()

If `true`, the model is "large," and parts of it may be created on the fly. (A look and feel might be able to take this characteristic into account.)

`public boolean isPathEditable(TreePath path)`

Returns true if path may be edited. The default implementation just returns isEditable(), but a subclass could override this to control editing on a node-by-node basis.

`public boolean isPathSelected(TreePath path)`

Returns true if all nodes on path are currently selected.

`public boolean isRootVisible()`

Returns true if the root of the tree should be displayed. See setRootVisible().

`public boolean isRowSelected(int row)`

Returns true if row is currently selected.

`public boolean isSelectionEmpty()`

Returns true if no rows are selected.

`public boolean isVisible(TreePath path)`

Returns true if all nodes on path are visible.

`public void makeVisible(TreePath path)`

Tells the tree to make each node in path visible.

`public void removeSelectionInterval(int row1, int row2)`

Removes from the selection list each path from row1 to row2.

`public void removeSelectionPath(TreePath path)`

Removes the named path from the selection.

`public void removeSelectionPaths(TreePath[] paths)`

Removes all paths in paths from the selection.

`public void removeSelectionRow(int row)`

Removes the path corresponding to row from the selection.

`public void removeSelectionRows(int[] rows)`

Removes each of the paths corresponding to the rows from the selection.

`public void removeTreeExpansionListener(TreeExpansionListener listener)`

Removes listener from the list of nodes to be notified when nodes are collapsed or expanded.

`public void removeTreeSelectionListener(TreeSelectionListener listener)`

Removes listener from the list of nodes to be notified when nodes are selected or deselected.

`public void removeTreeWillExpandListener(TreeWillExpandListener tel)`

Removes a listener from the list which receives TreeExpansionEvent events before the node is expanded.

`public void scrollPathToVisible(TreePath path)`

Makes sure each node in the path (up to but not including the last) is expanded and visible.

`public void scrollRowToVisible(int row)`

Scrolls the tree until row is visible. (This only applies when the tree is in a scroll pane.)

`public void setCellEditor(TreeCellEditor editor)`

Sets the editor for the tree.

`public void setCellRenderer(TreeCellRenderer renderer)`

Sets the renderer, which actually draws each row. To change the appearance of the row (perhaps to change the icon or provide a unique background color), you should create a custom renderer.

`public void setEditable(boolean mayEdit)`

Returns true if the tree rows may be edited.

```
public void setInvokesStopCellEditing(
    boolean shouldAutomaticallyAcceptEdits)
```
If set `true`, when the selected node changes, pending edits will be accepted (by calling `editing-Stopped()` on `CellEditorListener`). If `false`, partial edits will be canceled (by a call to `editingCanceled()` on `CellEditorListener`).

```
public void setLargeModel(boolean isLarge)
```
Sets whether the model should be listed as "large." See `isLargeModel()`. This is a bound property.

```
public void setModel(TreeModel model)
```
Set the data model for the tree.

```
public void setRootVisible(boolean makeRootVisible)
```
Sets whether the top root node will be visible. This is a bound property.

```
public void setRowHeight(int height)
```
Sets the height for each row. If the height is 0, each row's height must be computed separately.

```
public void setScrollsOnExpand(boolean newValue)
```
Sets whether newly expanded child nodes will be scrolled to make them visible. Defaults to `true`.

```
public void setSelectionInterval(int row1, int row2)
```
Makes the selection consist of the paths corresponding to `row1` to `row2` (inclusive) to the selection.

```
public void setSelectionModel(TreeSelectionModel selectionModel)
```
Sets the selection model for the tree. If `selectionModel` is `null`, the tree creates a selection model that always reports itself as empty.

```
public void setSelectionPath(TreePath path)
```
Makes the selection consist of only `path`. The path is made visible if necessary.

```
public void setSelectionPaths(TreePath[] paths)
```
Makes the selection consist of all paths in `paths`. Makes each node of each path visible.

```
public void setSelectionRow(int row)
```
Makes the selection be the path corresponding to `row`.

```
public void setSelectionRows(int[] rows)
```
Makes the selection be the paths corresponding to each row in `rows`.

```
public void setShowsRootHandles(boolean shouldShowHandles)
```
Sets whether root handles should be shown for top-level nodes. (This should usually be set `true` when `isRootVisible()` is `false`, so that it is obvious that those nodes have children.) This is a bound property.

```
public void setUI(TreeUI ui)
```
Sets the UI (look and feel) for the tree. See the chapter on look and feel.

```
public void setVisibleRowCount(int rows)
```
Sets the number of rows to be visible when the tree is contained in a scroll pane.

```
public void startEditingAtPath(TreePath path)
```
Attempts to start the `CellEditor` editing the last node in the path.

```
public boolean stopEditing()
```
Tells the tree to stop editing the currently edited node. (This method is ignored if no node is being edited.) Accepts any changes to the node. (See also `setInvokesStopCellEditing()` and the `CellEditorListener` class.)

```
public void treeDidChange()
```
Notifies the tree that its bounds changed, and that it should be resized and repainted.

```
public void updateUI()
```
Tells the tree to update itself according to the current UI (look and feel).

Overrides: `updateUI` in class `JComponent`.

Protected Fields
protected transient TreeCellEditor cellEditor
> The editor used to edit each cell.

protected transient TreeCellRenderer cellRenderer
> The renderer used to display each cell.

protected boolean editable
> Returns `true` if the tree may be edited.

protected boolean invokesStopCellEditing
> If `true`, when the user selects a different row, editing changes on the current row are accepted (by calling `stopCellEditing()`). If `false`, when the user selects a different row, editing changes on the current row are ignored (by calling `cancelCellEditing()`).

protected boolean largeModel
> Returns `true` if the model should be regarded as a large model (so big it doesn't load the whole tree at once). This is for the benefit of the look and feel (but it is not required to do anything special because of this property).

protected boolean rootVisible
> Set to `true` if the single root of the tree is displayed, `false` if the root's children are the top-level view.

protected int rowHeight
> The height of each row. If `rowHeight <= 0`, the height will be determined on a row-by-row basis. (A fixed height is more efficient to work with, however.)

protected boolean scrollsOnExpand
> If `true`, the tree will scroll to make all newly expanded nodes visible.

protected transient TreeSelectionModel selectionModel
> The model for the selected nodes of the tree.

protected transient JTree.TreeSelectionRedirector selectionRedirector
> An auxiliary variable, used to distribute selection events properly.

protected boolean showsRootHandles
> If `true`, the expansion icons are shown for the top-level items displayed. (If `rootVisible` is `false`, this should usually be `true`.)

protected int toggleClickCount
> The number of mouse clicks on a node before it is expanded.

protected transient TreeModel treeModel
> The model for the tree's data.

protected transient TreeModelListener treeModelListener
> Updates `expandedState`.

protected int visibleRowCount
> The number of rows that should be simultaneously visible. (Used by the `Scrollable` interface.)

Protected Methods
protected void clearToggledPaths()
> Empties the cache holding previously expanded nodes.

protected static TreeModel createTreeModel(Object object)
> Creates a `DefaultTreeModel` from `object`. If `object` is of type `Object[]`, `Hashtable`, or `Vector`, it creates a dummy root and members of the list as its children. Used by the constructors when no `TreeModel` is provided.

protected TreeModelListener createTreeModelListener()
> Creates and returns an instance of the inner class `TreeModelHandler`.

protected void fireValueChanged(TreeSelectionEvent event)
Notifies tree listeners that the node has changed.

protected static TreeModel getDefaultTreeModel()
Creates a tree with dummy data in a `TreeModel`. Used by the `JTree()` no-arguments constructor.

protected java.util.Enumeration getDescendantToggledPaths(TreePath parent)
Returns an `Enumeration` of all children of `parent` that have previously been expanded at least once.

protected TreePath[] getPathBetweenRows(int row1, int row2)
Gets the path of all nodes between `row1` and `row2`.

protected String paramString()
Returns a string representation of the properties of this `JTree`. The returned string may be empty but it will not be `null`.
Overrides: `paramString` in class `JComponent`.

protected void removeDescendantToggledPaths(java.util.Enumeration toRemove)
Removes any descendants of the `TreePaths` in `toRemove` that have ever been expanded from the cache of expanded nodes.

protected void setExpandedState(TreePath path, boolean state)
Sets the expansion state of the node at the end of `path`. If `state` is true, all nodes in `path` are marked as expanded. If `state` is `false`, all nodes in `path` are expanded, except for the last node, which is collapsed.

Inner Classes

```
protected class JTree.AccessibleJTree
public static class JTree.DynamicUtilTreeNode
protected static class JTree.EmptySelectionModel
protected class JTree.TreeModelHandler
protected class JTree.TreeSelectionRedirector
```

See also   Accessible (p.85), AccessibleContext (p.90), JTree.TreeSelectionRedirector (p.410), TreeCellEditor (p.985), TreeCellRenderer (p.985), TreeExpansionListener (p.511), TreeModel (p.987), TreePath (p.989), TreeSelectionEvent (p.513), TreeSelectionListener (p.514), TreeSelectionModel (p.990), TreeUI (p.543).

swing.JTree.AccessibleJTree

INNER CLASS

```
protected class AccessibleJTree
    extends JComponent.AccessibleJComponent
```

```
implements AccessibleSelection, TreeModelListener,
TreeSelectionListener, TreeExpansionListener
```

Constructor
public AccessibleJTree()
> Default constructor.

Methods
public void addAccessibleSelection(int i)
> *Implements:* addAccessibleSelection in interface AccessibleSelection.

public void clearAccessibleSelection()
> *Implements:* clearAccessibleSelection in interface AccessibleSelection.

public void fireVisibleDataPropertyChange()
> Fires a visible data property change notification.

public Accessible getAccessibleAt(java.awt.Point p)
> *Overrides:* getAccessibleAt in class JComponent.AccessibleJComponent.

public Accessible getAccessibleChild(int i)
> *Overrides:* getAccessibleChild in class JComponent.AccessibleJComponent.

public int getAccessibleChildrenCount()
> Returns the number of top-level children nodes of this JTree.
> *Overrides:* getAccessibleChildrenCount in class JComponent.AccessibleJComponent.

public int getAccessibleIndexInParent()
> Gets the index of this object in its parent.

public AccessibleRole getAccessibleRole()
> Returns AccessibleRole.TREE.
> *Overrides:* getAccessibleRole in class JComponent.AccessibleJComponent.

public AccessibleSelection getAccessibleSelection()
> *Overrides:* getAccessibleSelection in class AccessibleContext.

public Accessible getAccessibleSelection(int i)
> *Implements:* getAccessibleSelection in interface AccessibleSelection.

public int getAccessibleSelectionCount()
> *Implements:* getAccessibleSelectionCount in interface AccessibleSelection.

public boolean isAccessibleChildSelected(int i)
> *Implements:* isAccessibleChildSelected in interface AccessibleSelection.

public void removeAccessibleSelection(int i)
> *Implements:* removeAccessibleSelection in interface AccessibleSelection.

public void selectAllAccessibleSelection()
> *Implements:* selectAllAccessibleSelection in interface AccessibleSelection.

public void treeCollapsed(TreeExpansionEvent e)
> Notification from the model that a tree node was collapsed.
> *Implements:* treeCollapsed in interface TreeExpansionListener.

public void treeExpanded(TreeExpansionEvent e)
> Notification from the model that a tree node was expanded.
> *Implements:* treeExpanded in interface TreeExpansionListener.

public void treeNodesChanged(TreeModelEvent e)
> Notification from the model that tree nodes changed.
> *Implements:* treeNodesChanged in interface TreeModelListener.

public void treeNodesInserted(TreeModelEvent e)
    Notification from the model that tree nodes were inserted.
    Implements: treeNodesInserted in interface TreeModelListener.
public void treeNodesRemoved(TreeModelEvent e)
    Notification from the model that tree nodes were removed.
    Implements: treeNodesRemoved in interface TreeModelListener.
public void treeStructureChanged(TreeModelEvent e)
    Notification from the model that the tree structure changed.
    Implements: treeStructureChanged in interface TreeModelListener.
public void valueChanged(TreeSelectionEvent e)
    Implements: valueChanged in interface TreeSelectionListener.

Inner Classes
protected class JTree.AccessibleJTree.AccessibleJTreeNode

    See also   Accessible (p.85), AccessibleRole (p.95), AccessibleSelection (p.98), JComponent.AccessibleJComponent (p.221), TreeModelEvent (p.511), TreeSelectionEvent (p.513).

swing.JTree.AccessibleJTree.AccessibleJTreeNode

INNER CLASS

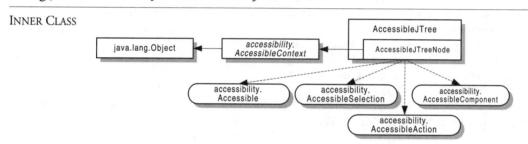

protected class AccessibleJTreeNode extends AccessibleContext
    implements Accessible, AccessibleComponent,
    AccessibleSelection, AccessibleAction

Constructor
public AccessibleJTreeNode(JTree tree, TreePath path, Accessible parent)
    Constructs an AccessibleJTreeNode representing the end node in path, with the accessibleParent *parent*.

Methods
public void addAccessibleSelection(int i)
    Implements: addAccessibleSelection in interface AccessibleSelection.
public void addFocusListener(java.awt.event.FocusListener l)
    Implements: addFocusListener in interface AccessibleComponent.
public void addPropertyChangeListener(java.beans.PropertyChangeListener l)
    Overrides: addPropertyChangeListener in class AccessibleContext.
public void clearAccessibleSelection()
    Implements: clearAccessibleSelection in interface AccessibleSelection.

public boolean contains(java.awt.Point p)

Implements: contains in interface AccessibleComponent.

public boolean doAccessibleAction(int i)

Implements: doAccessibleAction in interface AccessibleAction.

public AccessibleAction getAccessibleAction()

Overrides: getAccessibleAction in class AccessibleContext.

public int getAccessibleActionCount()

Returns the number of AccessibleActions supported by this tree node. This list includes those defined by the TreeCellRenderer and adds one more for toggling the node's expanded state if the node is not a leaf.

Implements: getAccessibleActionCount in interface AccessibleAction.

public java.lang.String getAccessibleActionDescription(int i)

Implements: getAccessibleActionDescription in interface AccessibleAction.

public Accessible getAccessibleAt(java.awt.Point p)

Implements: getAccessibleAt in interface AccessibleComponent.

public Accessible getAccessibleChild(int i)

Overrides: getAccessibleChild in class AccessibleContext.

public int getAccessibleChildrenCount()

Overrides: getAccessibleChildrenCount in class AccessibleContext.

public AccessibleComponent getAccessibleComponent()

If the associated node is not on screen, or its parent isn't expanded, this method returns null.

Overrides: getAccessibleComponent in class AccessibleContext.

public AccessibleContext getAccessibleContext()

Returns the accessibleContext for this TreeNode.

Implements: getAccessibleContext in interface Accessible.

public java.lang.String getAccessibleDescription()

Overrides: getAccessibleDescription in class AccessibleContext.

public int getAccessibleIndexInParent()

Overrides: getAccessibleIndexInParent in class AccessibleContext.

public java.lang.String getAccessibleName()

Overrides: getAccessibleName in class AccessibleContext.

public Accessible getAccessibleParent()

Overrides: getAccessibleParent in class AccessibleContext.

public AccessibleRole getAccessibleRole()

Overrides: getAccessibleRole in class AccessibleContext.

public AccessibleSelection getAccessibleSelection()

Overrides: getAccessibleSelection in class AccessibleContext.

public Accessible getAccessibleSelection(int i)

Implements: getAccessibleSelection in interface AccessibleSelection.

public int getAccessibleSelectionCount()

Implements: getAccessibleSelectionCount in interface AccessibleSelection.

public AccessibleStateSet getAccessibleStateSet()

Overrides: getAccessibleStateSet in class AccessibleContext.

public AccessibleText getAccessibleText()

Overrides: getAccessibleText in class AccessibleContext.

public AccessibleValue getAccessibleValue()
> *Overrides:* getAccessibleValue in class AccessibleContext.

public java.awt.Color getBackground()
> *Implements:* getBackground in interface AccessibleComponent.

public java.awt.Rectangle getBounds()
> *Implements:* getBounds in interface AccessibleComponent.

public java.awt.Cursor getCursor()
> *Implements:* getCursor in interface AccessibleComponent.

public java.awt.Font getFont()
> *Implements:* getFont in interface AccessibleComponent.

public java.awt.FontMetrics getFontMetrics(java.awt.Font f)
> *Implements:* getFontMetrics in interface AccessibleComponent.

public java.awt.Color getForeground()
> *Implements:* getForeground in interface AccessibleComponent.

public java.util.Locale getLocale()
> *Throws:* IllegalComponentStateException if the Component does not have its own locale and also does not have an ancestor with a defined locale.
> *Overrides:* getLocale in class AccessibleContext.

public java.awt.Point getLocation()
> *Implements:* getLocation in interface AccessibleComponent.

public java.awt.Point getLocationOnScreen()
> *Implements:* getLocationOnScreen in interface AccessibleComponent.

public java.awt.Dimension getSize()
> *Implements:* getSize in interface AccessibleComponent.

public boolean isAccessibleChildSelected(int i)
> *Implements:* isAccessibleChildSelected in interface AccessibleSelection.

public boolean isEnabled()
> *Implements:* isEnabled in interface AccessibleComponent.

public boolean isFocusTraversable()
> *Implements:* isFocusTraversable in interface AccessibleComponent.

public boolean isShowing()
> *Implements:* isShowing in interface AccessibleComponent.

public boolean isVisible()
> *Implements:* isVisible in interface AccessibleComponent.

public void removeAccessibleSelection(int i)
> *Implements:* removeAccessibleSelection in interface AccessibleSelection.

public void removeFocusListener(java.awt.event.FocusListener l)
> *Implements:* removeFocusListener in interface AccessibleComponent.

public void removePropertyChangeListener(
java.beans.PropertyChangeListener l)
> *Overrides:* removePropertyChangeListener in class AccessibleContext.

public void requestFocus()
> *Implements:* requestFocus in interface AccessibleComponent.

public void selectAllAccessibleSelection()
> *Implements:* selectAllAccessibleSelection in interface AccessibleSelection.

public void setAccessibleDescription(java.lang.String s)
> *Overrides:* setAccessibleDescription in class AccessibleContext.

```
public void setAccessibleName(java.lang.String s)
```
   Overrides: setAccessibleName in class AccessibleContext.
```
public void setBackground(java.awt.Color c)
```
   Implements: setBackground in interface AccessibleComponent.
```
public void setBounds(java.awt.Rectangle r)
```
   Implements: setBounds in interface AccessibleComponent.
```
public void setCursor(java.awt.Cursor c)
```
   Implements: setCursor in interface AccessibleComponent.
```
public void setEnabled(boolean b)
```
   Implements: setEnabled in interface AccessibleComponent.
```
public void setFont(java.awt.Font f)
```
   Implements: setFont in interface AccessibleComponent.
```
public void setForeground(java.awt.Color c)
```
   Implements: setForeground in interface AccessibleComponent.
```
public void setLocation(java.awt.Point p)
```
   Implements: setLocation in interface AccessibleComponent.
```
public void setSize(java.awt.Dimension d)
```
   Implements: setSize in interface AccessibleComponent.
```
public void setVisible(boolean b)
```
   Implements: setVisible in interface AccessibleComponent.

Protected Methods
```
protected java.awt.Point getLocationInJTree()
```
   Used by getBounds() to identify the location of the node's parent.

   See also   Accessible (p.85), AccessibleAction (p.86), AccessibleComponent (p.87),
   AccessibleContext (p.90), AccessibleSelection (p.98), AccessibleStateSet (p.101),
   AccessibleText (p.103), AccessibleValue (p.104).

swing.JTree.DynamicUtilTreeNode

INNER CLASS

A TreeNode that creates its children as necessary from an array, a vector, or a hash table.

```
public static class DynamicUtilTreeNode
    extends DefaultMutableTreeNode
```

Constructors
```
public DynamicUtilTreeNode(Object value, Object children)
```
   Creates a new TreeNode with the given user object and set of children. The children parameter
   cannot be null if the node is *ever* to have children. It must be one of the allowed data structures,
   even if it is empty.

Methods

public java.util.Enumeration children()
> Subclassed to load the children as needed.
> *Overrides:* children in class DefaultMutableTreeNode.

public static void createChildren(DefaultMutableTreeNode parent,
Object children)
> Adds all of the children to the node.

public TreeNode getChildAt(int index)
> Subclassed to load the children as needed.
> *Overrides:* getChildAt in class DefaultMutableTreeNode.

public int getChildCount()
> Returns the number of children.
> *Overrides:* getChildCount in class DefaultMutableTreeNode.

public boolean isLeaf()
> Returns false (the node is not a leaf) if the node was created with a valid children object, even if it is empty.
> *Overrides:* isLeaf in class DefaultMutableTreeNode.

Protected Fields

protected Object childValue
> The array, vector, or hash table to create the children from when the node is expanded.

protected boolean hasChildren
> Returns true if this node has children.

protected boolean loadedChildren
> Returns true if the children of the node have been created.

Protected Methods

protected void loadChildren()
> Loads the children based on childValue. If childValue is a vector or array, each element is added as a child; if childValue is a hash table, each key/value pair is added in the order that Enumeration returns the keys.

> *See also*   DefaultMutableTreeNode (p.961).

swing.JTree.EmptySelectionModel

INNER CLASS

A TreeSelectionModel that does not allow a selection.

protected static class EmptySelectionModel
extends DefaultTreeSelectionModel

Methods

public void addSelectionPaths(TreePath[] paths)
> Ignores all calls.

Overrides: addSelectionPaths in class DefaultTreeSelectionModel.

Implements: addSelectionPaths in interface TreeSelectionModel.

public void removeSelectionPaths(TreePath[] paths)

Ignores all calls.

Overrides: removeSelectionPaths in class DefaultTreeSelectionModel.

Implements: removeSelectionPaths in interface TreeSelectionModel.

public void setSelectionPaths(TreePath[] pPaths)

Ignores all calls.

Overrides: setSelectionPaths in class DefaultTreeSelectionModel.

Implements: setSelectionPaths in interface TreeSelectionModel.

public static JTree.EmptySelectionModel sharedInstance()

Returns a reference to a shared instance of EmptySelectionModel. Use this method in preference to the constructor, since all instances of this model are exactly the same.

Protected Fields

protected static final JTree.EmptySelectionModel sharedInstance

The shared instance of this TreeSelectionModel.

Returned by JTree.EmptySelectionModel.sharedInstance() (p.408).

See also DefaultTreeSelectionModel (p.978), TreePath (p.989).

swing.JTree.TreeModelHandler

INNER CLASS

Updates the expandedState of the JTree as nodes change in the tree model.

```
protected class JTree.TreeModelHandler extends java.lang.Object
    implements TreeModelListener
```

Constructors

public TreeModelHandler()

Default constructor.

Methods

public void treeNodesChanged(TreeModelEvent e)

Implements: treeNodesChanged in interface TreeModelListener.

public void treeNodesInserted(TreeModelEvent e)

Implements: treeNodesInserted in interface TreeModelListener.

public void treeNodesRemoved(TreeModelEvent e)

Implements: treeNodesRemoved in interface TreeModelListener.

public void treeStructureChanged(TreeModelEvent e)

Implements: treeStructureChanged in interface TreeModelListener.

See also TreeModelEvent (p.511), TreeModelListener (p.513).

swing.JTree.TreeSelectionRedirector

INNER CLASS

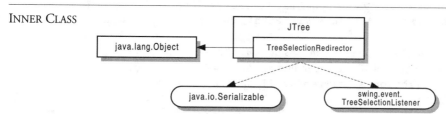

Listens for TreeSelectionEvents from the model and forwards them along with the JTree set as the source.

```
protected class JTree.TreeSelectionRedirector
    extends java.lang.Object
    implements java.io.Serializable, TreeSelectionListener
```

Method
```
public void valueChanged(TreeSelectionEvent e)
```
Called by the TreeSelectionModel when the selection changes.
Implements: valueChanged in interface TreeSelectionListener.

See also   TreeSelectionEvent (p.513), TreeSelectionListener (p.514).

swing.JViewport

CLASS

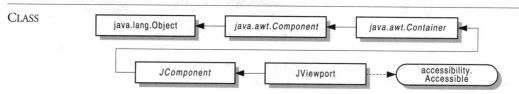

JViewport manages the actual scrolling of a component in a JScrollPane (or any custom component that knows how to manipulate a JViewport). See also JScrollPane, ScrollPaneLayout, and ViewportLayout.

```
public class JViewport extends JComponent
    implements Accessible
```

Constructors
```
public JViewport()
```
Creates a viewport.

Methods
```
public void addChangeListener(ChangeListener listener)
```
Adds listener to the list of objects to be notified when the size or position of the view or the viewport has changed.

public AccessibleContext getAccessibleContext()

Returns the accessible context for the component. See the chapter on accessibility.

Overrides: getAccessibleContext in class JComponent.

Implements: getAccessibleContext in interface Accessible.

public java.awt.Dimension getExtentSize()

Returns the size of the visible portion of the viewport.

public final java.awt.Insets getInsets()

Always returns a zero inset. This simplifies size calculations, but means that a viewport may need to be wrapped in a separate panel with a border when borders or insets are needed.

Overrides: getInsets in class JComponent.

public final java.awt.Insets getInsets(java.awt.Insets insets)

Returns the insets of the viewport using the passed-in insets. The insets object will be filled with zeroes for all sides.

Overrides: getInsets in class JComponent.

public java.awt.Component getView()

Returns the main scrolling view object.

public java.awt.Point getViewPosition()

Returns the position of the top-left corner of the viewport, in view coordinates.

public java.awt.Rectangle getViewRect()

Returns the visible part of the view, in view coordinates.

public java.awt.Dimension getViewSize()

Returns the size of the view. If there is no view, returns (0,0). If there is a view, and its size has been explicitly set, returns that size; otherwise, returns the view's preferred size.

public boolean isBackingStoreEnabled()

Returns true if the viewport is using a backing store (offscreen buffer).

public boolean isOptimizedDrawingEnabled()

Returns false, to ensure that the viewport's paint() method will be explicitly called.

Overrides: isOptimizedDrawingEnabled in class JComponent.

public void paint(java.awt.Graphics gr)

Paints the visible part of the view. Uses the backing store if possible.

Overrides: paint in class JComponent.

public void remove(java.awt.Component component)

Makes component no longer be the view object.

Overrides: remove in class Container.

public void removeChangeListener(ChangeListener listener)

Makes listener no longer receive notifications of changes in the view or viewport.

public void repaint(long time, int x, int y, int width, int height)

Schedules a repaint. Specifies the area to be repainted in the parent view's coordinates (if there is a parent view). This may let the RepaintManager consolidate some changes.

Overrides: repaint in class JComponent.

public void reshape(int x, int y, int w, int h)

Sets the bounds of the viewport, informing any listeners if the width or height changes.

Overrides: reshape in class JComponent.

public void scrollRectToVisible(java.awt.Rectangle rectangle)

Scrolls the specified rectangle (of the view) to be visible (in the viewport).

Overrides: scrollRectToVisible in class JComponent.

`public void setBackingStoreEnabled(boolean shouldEnable)`

Sets whether the viewport should maintain a backing store (offscreen image). If most scrolling is of a short distance in the x or y direction (and not diagonal), this will improve drawing speeds.

`public final void setBorder(Border border)`

Blocks a border from being set. (See `getInsets()`.) To put a border around a scroll pane, put the scroll pane in a panel, and put a border around the panel.

`public void setExtentSize(java.awt.Dimension dimension)`

Sets the size of the visible part of the viewport (in view coordinates). Notifies any change listeners.

`public void setView(java.awt.Component component)`

Sets the main scrolling view.

`public void setViewPosition(java.awt.Point point)`

Sets the position of the upper left-hand corner of the viewport, relative to the view, in view coordinates. Notifies any change listeners.

`public void setViewSize(java.awt.Dimension newSize)`

Sets the size of the view. Notifies any change listeners.

`public java.awt.Dimension toViewCoordinates(java.awt.Dimension dimension)`

Converts `dimension` in viewport coordinates to view coordinates. A subclass could override this to introduce its own coordinate system.

`public java.awt.Point toViewCoordinates(java.awt.Point point)`

Converts `point` in viewport coordinates to view coordinates. A subclass could override this to introduce its own coordinate system.

Protected Fields

`protected boolean backingStore`

Returns `true` if the backing store is in use.

`protected java.awt.Image backingStoreImage`

The backing store.

`protected boolean isViewSizeSet`

Returns `true` if an explicit size has been set for the view.

`protected java.awt.Point lastPaintPosition`

Tells how much of the backing store is in use.

`protected boolean scrollUnderway`

Returns `true` if in the middle of autoscrolling.

Protected Methods

`protected void addImpl(java.awt.Component component, Object constraints, int index)`

Sets the viewport's view to be `component`.

`protected boolean computeBlit(int dx, int dy, java.awt.Point resultFrom, java.awt.Point resultTo, java.awt.Dimension resultSize, java.awt.Rectangle resultPainted)`

Computes the blit for a scroll by `dx` and `dy`. The `resultFrom` and `resultTo` tell the points where to start and end; `resultSize` tells the size of the resulting rectangle; `resultPainted` tells the rectangle to paint. The return value of this routine is `true` if a fast copy can be made according to the `resultXxx` parameters.

`protected java.awt.LayoutManager createLayoutManager()`

Creates the layout manager for the viewport.

protected JViewport.ViewListener createViewListener()

    Creates a view listener, which detects when the component has changed size, and then fires a state change notification.

protected void fireStateChanged()

    Notifies all listeners that the size or position of the view or viewport has changed.

protected String paramString()

    Returns a string representation of this JViewport. The returned string may be empty but it will not be null.

    Overrides: paramString in class JComponent.

Inner Classes

protected class JViewport.AccessibleJViewport
protected class JViewport.ViewListener

    Returned by   JScrollPane.createViewport() (p.332), JScrollPane.getColumnHeader() (p.332), JScrollPane.getRowHeader() (p.332), JScrollPane.getViewport() (p.332), ScrollPaneLayout.getColumnHeader() (p.437), ScrollPaneLayout.getRowHeader() (p.437), ScrollPaneLayout.getViewport() (p.437).

    See also   Accessible (p.85), AccessibleContext (p.90), Border (p.465), ChangeListener (p.488), JComponent (p.207), JScrollPane (p.332), ScrollPaneLayout (p.437), ViewportLayout (p.458).

swing.JViewport.AccessibleJViewport

INNER CLASS

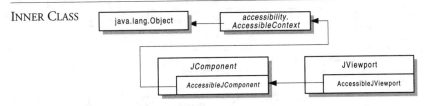

protected class AccessibleJViewport
    extends JComponent.AccessibleJComponent

Methods

public AccessibleRole getAccessibleRole()

    Returns AccessibleRole.VIEWPORT.

    Overrides: getAccessibleRole in JComponent.AccessibleJComponent.

    See also   AccessibleRole (p.95), JComponent.AccessibleJComponent (p.221).

swing.JViewport.ViewListener

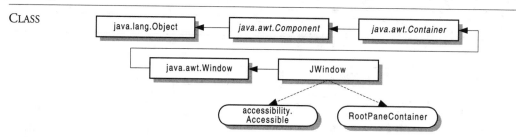

Listens to changes in the viewport.

```
protected class ViewListener
    extends java.awt.event.ComponentAdapter
    implements java.io.Serializable
```

Methods

```
public void componentResized(java.awt.ComponentEvent e)
```
Overrides: componentResized in class ComponentAdapter.
Implements: componentResized in interface ComponentListener.

Returned by JViewport.createViewListener() (p.410).

swing.JWindow

CLASS

JWindow is one of the basic window classes in Swing, corresponding to Window in the AWT. Swing windows are layered: there is a layered pane consisting of the content pane and the menu bar (if present), and there is a glass pane overlaying the whole window. (The glass pane is used for things such as pop-up menus that appear to float over the surface of the window.)

Components are not added directly to the window; instead, they are added to the content pane:

```
myWindow.getContentPane().add (component, constraints);
```

The JWindow will warn you at run time if you try to add directly to the window. See JRoot-Pane for more information on the way panes are arranged in windows.

For other types of windows, see JDialog, JFrame, JInternalPane, and JOptionPane.

Example

```
package jwindow;
```

```
import java.awt.*;
import java.awt.event.*;
// Uncomment the following line for Swing 1.0.3 and before
//import com.sun.java.swing.*;
// Uncomment the following line for Swing 1.1
import javax.swing.*;
public class Test extends JFrame {
   JWindow window = new JWindow(this);

   public Test() {
      addWindowListener(new WindowAdapter() {
         public void windowClosing(WindowEvent e) {
            Test.this.dispose();
            System.exit(0);
         }
      });
      window.getContentPane().add(new JLabel("About this app"),
                         BorderLayout.NORTH);
      window.getContentPane().add(new JLabel("Not much to tell",
                         SwingConstants.CENTER), BorderLayout.CENTER);
      JButton b = new JButton("Close");
      window.getContentPane().add(b, BorderLayout.SOUTH);
      b.addActionListener(new ActionListener () {
         public void actionPerformed (ActionEvent e) {
            window.setVisible(false);
         }
      });
      window.pack();
      window.setBounds(50,50,200,200);

      b = new JButton("About...");
      b.addActionListener(new ActionListener() {
         public void actionPerformed (ActionEvent e) {
            window.setVisible(true);
         }
      });
      getContentPane().add(b);
      pack();
   }
   public static void main (String[] args) {
      new Test().setVisible(true);
   }
}
```

public class JWindow extends java.awt.Window
   implements Accessible, RootPaneContainer

Constructors
public JWindow()
   Constructs a JWindow using a hidden JFrame as its parent.
public JWindow(JFrame frame)
   Builds a window owned by frame. The window is not visible until you call setVisible(true).

Methods

public AccessibleContext getAccessibleContext()

Returns the accessible context.

Implements: getAccessibleContext in interface Accessible.

public java.awt.Container getContentPane()

Returns the content pane. This is the pane to which contained objects should be added.

Implements: getContentPane in interface RootPaneContainer.

public java.awt.Component getGlassPane()

Returns the glass pane associated with this window.

Implements: getGlassPane in interface RootPaneContainer.

public JLayeredPane getLayeredPane()

Returns the layered pane for this window. This will contain the content pane and the menu bar.

Implements: getLayeredPane in interface RootPaneContainer.

public JRootPane getRootPane()

Returns the root pane for this frame. It contains all panes.

Implements: getRootPane in interface RootPaneContainer.

public void setContentPane(java.awt.Container container)

Sets the content pane for this window. A JWindow always has a content pane; attempting to set it to null will cause an error.

Throws: IllegalComponentStateException if the content pane parameter is null.

Implements: setContentPane in interface RootPaneContainer.

public void setGlassPane(java.awt.Component component)

Sets the glass pane for the window. This is an upper pane where pop-up menus and other floating content can be displayed.

Implements: setGlassPane in interface RootPaneContainer.

public void setLayeredPane(JLayeredPane layeredPane)

Sets the layered pane. This pane contains the content pane.

Throws: IllegalComponentStateException if the content pane parameter is null.

Implements: setLayeredPane in interface RootPaneContainer.

public void setLayout(java.awt.LayoutManager manager)

By default the layout of this component may not be set. The layout of its contentPane should be set instead. For example:

```
thisComponent.getContentPane().setLayout(new BorderLayout());
```

An attempt to set the layout of this component will cause a run-time exception to be thrown. Subclasses can disable this behavior.

Throws: Error if called with rootPaneChecking true.

Overrides: setLayout in class Container.

Protected Fields

protected AccessibleContext accessibleContext

The accessible context.

protected JRootPane rootPane

The root pane for this window.

protected boolean rootPaneCheckingEnabled

If true, then calls to add and setLayout cause an exception to be thrown.

Protected Methods

protected void addImpl(java.awt.Component comp,
 Object constraints, int index)

By default, children may not be added directly to this component; they must be added to its `contentPane` instead. For example:

```
thisComponent.getContentPane().add(child)
```

An attempt to add to directly to this component will cause a run-time exception to be thrown. Subclasses can disable this behavior.

Throws: `Error` if called with `rootPaneChecking` true.

Overrides: `addImpl` in class `Container`.

protected JRootPane createRootPane()

Creates the root pane for this window. See `JRootPane`.

protected boolean isRootPaneCheckingEnabled()

Returns whether calls to `add` and `setLayout` cause an exception to be thrown.

protected String paramString()

Returns a string representation of the properties of this `JWindow`. The returned string may be empty but it will not be `null`.

Overrides: `paramString` in class `Container`.

protected void setRootPane(JRootPane rootPane)

Sets the root pane. This contains all the other panes of the window.

protected void setRootPaneCheckingEnabled(boolean enabled)

Determines whether calls to `add` and `setLayout` cause an exception to be thrown.

protected void windowInit()

Uses the return value from `createRootPane()` to set the default root pane, and it also calls `setRootPaneCheckingEnabled(true)`.

Inner Classes

protected class JWindow.AccessibleJWindow

See also Accessible (p.85), AccessibleContext (p.90), JLayeredPane (p.268), JRootPane (p.323), RootPaneContainer (p.433).

swing.JWindow.AccessibleJWindow

INNER CLASS

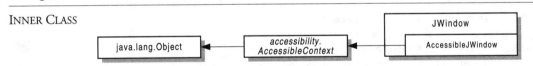

protected class AccessibleJWindow extends AccessibleContext
 implements java.io.Serializable, AccessibleComponent

Methods

public void addFocusListener(java.awt.event.FocusListener l)

Adds `l` to receive focus events from this component.

Implements: `addFocusListener` in interface `AccessibleComponent`.

public boolean contains(java.awt.Point p)

Implements: `contains` in interface `AccessibleComponent`.

```
public Accessible getAccessibleAt(java.awt.Point p)
```
Implements: getAccessibleAt in interface AccessibleComponent.
```
public Accessible getAccessibleChild(int i)
```
Overrides: getAccessibleChild in class AccessibleContext.
```
public int getAccessibleChildrenCount()
```
Overrides: getAccessibleChildrenCount in class AccessibleContext.
```
public AccessibleComponent getAccessibleComponent()
```
Overrides: getAccessibleComponent in class AccessibleContext.
```
public int getAccessibleIndexInParent()
```
Overrides: getAccessibleIndexInParent in class AccessibleContext.
```
public Accessible getAccessibleParent()
```
Overrides: getAccessibleParent in class AccessibleContext.
```
public AccessibleRole getAccessibleRole()
```
Overrides: getAccessibleRole in class AccessibleContext.
```
public AccessibleStateSet getAccessibleStateSet()
```
Overrides: getAccessibleStateSet in class AccessibleContext.
```
public java.awt.Color getBackground()
```
Implements: getBackground in interface AccessibleComponent.
```
public java.awt.Rectangle getBounds()
```
Implements: getBounds in interface AccessibleComponent.
```
public java.awt.Cursor getCursor()
```
Implements: getCursor in interface AccessibleComponent.
```
public java.awt.Font getFont()
```
Implements: getFont in interface AccessibleComponent.
```
public java.awt.FontMetrics getFontMetrics(java.awt.Font f)
```
Implements: getFontMetrics in interface AccessibleComponent.
```
public java.awt.Color getForeground()
```
Implements: getForeground in interface AccessibleComponent.
```
public java.util.Locale getLocale()
```
Overrides: getLocale in class AccessibleContext.
```
public java.awt.Point getLocation()
```
Implements: getLocation in interface AccessibleComponent.
```
public java.awt.Point getLocationOnScreen()
```
Implements: getLocationOnScreen in interface AccessibleComponent.
```
public java.awt.Dimension getSize()
```
Implements: getSize in interface AccessibleComponent.
```
public boolean isEnabled()
```
Implements: isEnabled in interface AccessibleComponent.
```
public boolean isFocusTraversable()
```
Implements: isFocusTraversable in interface AccessibleComponent.
```
public boolean isShowing()
```
Implements: isShowing in interface AccessibleComponent.
```
public boolean isVisible()
```
Implements: isVisible in interface AccessibleComponent.
```
public void removeFocusListener(java.awt.FocusListener l)
```
Implements: removeFocusListener in interface AccessibleComponent.

public void requestFocus()
> *Implements:* requestFocus in interface AccessibleComponent.

public void setBackground(java.awt.Color c)
> *Implements:* setBackground in interface AccessibleComponent.

public void setBounds(java.awt.Rectangle r)
> *Implements:* setBounds in interface AccessibleComponent.

public void setCursor(java.awt.Cursor cursor)
> *Implements:* setCursor in interface AccessibleComponent.

public void setEnabled(boolean b)
> *Implements:* setEnabled in interface AccessibleComponent.

public void setFont(java.awt.Font f)
> *Implements:* setFont in interface AccessibleComponent.

public void setForeground(java.awt.Color c)
> *Implements:* setForeground in interface AccessibleComponent.

public void setLocation(java.awt.Point p)
> *Implements:* setLocation in interface AccessibleComponent.

public void setSize(java.awt.Dimension d)
> *Implements:* setSize in interface AccessibleComponent.

public void setVisible(boolean b)
> *Implements:* setVisible in interface AccessibleComponent.

See also Accessible (p.85), AccessibleComponent (p.87), AccessibleContext (p.90), AccessibleRole (p.95), AccessibleStateSet (p.101), AccessibleValue (p.104).

swing.KeyStroke

CLASS

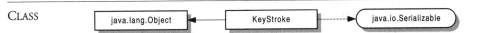

A keystroke encapsulates a combination of a key and its modifiers, as typed. You can register keystrokes with a JComponent or on JMenuItems using the setAccelerator() method.

You don't build a keystroke directly—its constructor is private. Instead, use one of the class methods to create one for you. These methods guarantee that a particular keystroke is created only once.

```
public class KeyStroke extends java.lang.Object
    implements java.io.Serializable
```

Methods
public boolean equals(Object keystroke)
> Returns true if two keystrokes are the same.
> *Overrides:* equals in class Object.

public char getKeyChar()
> Returns the character for this keystroke.

public int getKeyCode()
> Returns the key code associated with this keystroke.

```
public static KeyStroke getKeyStroke(char key)
```
Factory method to produce a unique KeyStroke for character key.
```
public static KeyStroke getKeyStroke(char keyChar, boolean onKeyRelease)
```
Deprecated. Use getKeyStroke(char).
```
public static KeyStroke getKeyStroke(int key, int modifiers)
```
Factory method to produce a unique KeyStroke for character key with modifiers. (Modifiers are things like CTRL_MASK or ALT_MASK.) The modifiers are defined in java.awt.event.InputEvent.
```
public static KeyStroke getKeyStroke(int key, int modifiers,
    boolean onRelease)
```
Factory method to produce a unique KeyStroke for character key with modifiers. (Modifiers are things like CTRL_MASK or ALT_MASK.) The modifiers are defined in java.awt.event.InputEvent. If onRelease is true, the KeyStroke takes effect when the key is released rather than when it is pressed. *Default:* false.
```
public static KeyStroke getKeyStroke(String stringRepresentation)
```
Factory method to produce a unique KeyStroke for the keystroke represented by stringRepresentation. Not implemented as of Swing 1.1, so it returns null.
```
public static KeyStroke getKeyStrokeForEvent(java.awt.event.KeyEvent event)
```
Factory method to produce a unique KeyStroke based on the event.
```
public int getModifiers()
```
Returns the modifiers associated with this keystroke. See java.awt.event.InputEvent for their values (which are OR'd together).
```
public int hashCode()
```
Returns a hashcode for this keystroke.
Overrides: hashCode in class Object.
```
public boolean isOnKeyRelease()
```
Returns true if the keystroke applies when the key is released (rather than when it is pressed).
```
public String toString()
```
Returns a string that displays this object's properties.
Overrides: toString in class Object.

See also   JComponent (p.207), JMenuItem (p.291).

swing.ListCellRenderer

INTERFACE   (ListCellRenderer)

The renderer is responsible for displaying an item of the list. This design allows a single drawing component to be shared by all items in the list.

```
public interface ListCellRenderer
```

Method
```
public abstract
```

```
java.awt.Component getListCellRendererComponent(JList list,
Object value, int index, boolean isSelected, boolean cellHasFocus)
```
Returns a component that can be used to display a list entry. (See JList.) The value is the object to be displayed; it is from `list.getModel().getElementAt(index)`. The isSelected and hasFocus flags let the renderer know whether it must do anything special to indicate that an item is selected and/or has the current focus. The returned component's paint() method will be called to do the actual display.

Implemented by BasicComboBoxRenderer (p.564), DefaultListCellRenderer (p.171).
Returned by BasicComboBoxUI.createRenderer() (p.565), JComboBox.getRenderer() (p.200), JList.getCellRenderer() (p.271).
See also JList (p.271).

swing.ListModel

INTERFACE   (ListModel)

This interface is the model interface used by JLists.

```
public interface ListModel
```

Methods
```
public abstract void addListDataListener(ListDataListener listener)
```
Adds listener as a listener for changes in the list.
```
public abstract Object getElementAt(int index)
```
Returns the element at index.
```
public abstract int getSize()
```
Returns the number of elements in the list.
```
public abstract void removeListDataListener(ListDataListener listener)
```
Removes listener as a listener for changes in the list.

Extended by ComboBoxModel (p.156).
Returned by JList.getModel() (p.271).
Implemented by AbstractListModel (p.127).
See also ListDataListener (p.499).

swing.ListSelectionModel

INTERFACE   (ListSelectionModel)

A list selection consists of a set of indexes that represent the items selected. In general, this is a set of intervals. For example, in a list with 7 items, the set { [0,2], [6,6]} would indicate that elements 0, 1, 2, and 6 are selected.

Many of the methods refer to index1 and index2. The value for index1 need not be less than the value for index2—the selection may go from high to low.

Some look and feels have the notion of an anchor and a lead index. These are based on the most recently added selection interval. The anchor is the first index in that interval; the lead is the second.

```
public interface ListSelectionModel
```

Fields

```
public static final int SINGLE_SELECTION = 0
public static final int SINGLE_INTERVAL_SELECTION = 1
public static final int MULTIPLE_INTERVAL_SELECTION = 2
```

These constants describe the type of selection allowed. A SINGLE_SELECTION allows only one element to be selected. A SINGLE_INTERVAL_SELECTION allows only a contiguous range of items to be selected. A MULTIPLE_INTERVAL_SELECTION allows arbitrary selections (as a set of selected ranges).

Methods

```
public abstract void addListSelectionListener(
    ListSelectionListener listener)
```

Adds listener as a listener for changes in the list selection.

```
public abstract void addSelectionInterval(int index1, int index2)
```

Causes the range from index1 to index2 to be added to the selection. Listeners are notified if this changes the selection.

```
public abstract void clearSelection()
```

Causes the selection to become empty. Listeners are notified if this changes the selection.

```
public abstract int getAnchorSelectionIndex()
```

Gets the anchor: the index1 value from the most recently added selection interval. See addSelectionInterval().

```
public abstract int getLeadSelectionIndex()
```

Gets the lead: the index2 value from the most recently added selection interval. See addSelectionInterval().

```
public abstract int getMaxSelectionIndex()
```

Returns the maximum index in the selection, or -1 if nothing is selected.

```
public abstract int getMinSelectionIndex()
```

Returns the minimum index in the selection, or -1 if nothing is selected.

```
public abstract int getSelectionMode()
```

Returns SINGLE_SELECTION, SINGLE_INTERVAL_SELECTION, or MULTIPLE_INTERVAL_SELECTION.

```
public abstract boolean getValueIsAdjusting()
```

Returns true if further changes are expected in the selection (for example, while the selection is in the middle of an update).

```
public abstract void insertIndexInterval(int index, int length,
    boolean before)
```

Inserts length values into the selection, starting at index. The values are from index-length+1 to index if before is true, and from index to index+length-1 if before is false. This method can be used to make the selection correspond to changes in the underlying model. Listeners are notified if this changes the selection.

public abstract boolean isSelectedIndex(int index)

Returns true if index is in the set of selected index values.

public abstract boolean isSelectionEmpty()

Returns true if the selection is empty.

public abstract void removeIndexInterval(int index1, int index2)

Removes indexes from index1 to index2 (inclusive) from the selection. This method can be used to make the selection correspond to changes in the underlying model. Listeners are notified if this changes the selection.

public abstract void removeListSelectionListener(
ListSelectionListener listener)

Removes listener from the list of listeners to be notified of selection changes.

public abstract void removeSelectionInterval(int index1, int index2)

Causes the range from index1 to index2 to be removed from the selection interval. Listeners are notified if this changes the selection.

public abstract void setAnchorSelectionIndex(int index)

Sets the index that will be the "beginning" of the selected range. Calling this method should be equivalent to calling addSelectionInterval() with a new index1 and the most recently used index2.

public abstract void setLeadSelectionIndex(int index)

Sets the index that will be the "end" of the selected range. Calling this method should be equivalent to calling addSelectionInterval() with the old index1 and a new index2.

public abstract void setSelectionInterval(int index1, int index2)

Causes the selection to consist only of elements from index1 to index2 inclusive. Listeners are notified if this changes the selection.

public abstract void setSelectionMode(int mode)

Sets the mode; mode must be SINGLE_SELECTION, SINGLE_INTERVAL_SELECTION, or MULTIPLE_INTERVAL_SELECTION.

public abstract void setValueIsAdjusting(boolean valueIsAdjusting)

Sets whether the selection is in the middle of an adjustment. (This way, listeners don't need to make intermediate adjustments, but they can wait for the final selection.)

See also   ListSelectionListener (p.500).

swing.LookAndFeel

ABSTRACT
CLASS

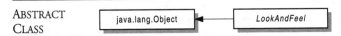

LookAndFeel provides the information needed to describe a look and feel. See UIDefaults and UIManager, and the chapter on look and feel.

It is helpful to understand the typical sequence of calls to this class:

1 new LookAndFeel()

2 getName(), getDescription(), isSupportedLookAndFeel(), isNativeLookAndFeel() (any order)

```
3 initialize()
4 getDefaults()
5 uninitialize()
```

Notice that a look and feel may be created, and then never used. (Perhaps it is not supported on the platform.) To minimize resources used, do as little as possible in the constructor (and in static initializers). Instead, do that work in the `initialize()` method, which is called after it has been determined that this look and feel will be used. Similarly, resources may be freed in `uninitialize()`, which is called when it is determined that this look and feel will be retired (for now, anyway).

public abstract class LookAndFeel extends java.lang.Object

Constructors
public LookAndFeel()
Creates a look and feel.

Methods
public UIDefaults getDefaults()
Called once (by a UIManager) to get the default mapping information for the look and feel. (The `initialize()` method is called prior to this method being called.) See above.

public abstract String getDescription()
A one-line description of the look and feel to be presented to the user (for example, in a tool tip). This string should be localized. See also `getName()`.

public abstract string getID()
Returns a String that can be used by applications to identify statndard look and feels. A look and feel that extends another without significantly changing any behavior or appearance should not override this method.

public abstract String getName()
Returns a short name for the look and feel to be presented to the user (for example, in a menu). This string should be localized. See also `getDescription()`.

public void initialize()
Called once (by a UIManager) to initialize the look and feel. See above.

public static void installBorder(JComponent component,
String borderPropertyName)
If `component` has no border, or its border is a `UIResource` (a tagging interface indicating it was installed by a look and feel), use `UIManager` to look up the border corresponding to `borderPropertyName`, and set the border to that value.

public static void installColors(JComponent component,
String foregroundColorPropertyName, String backgroundColorPropertyName)
For both foreground and background colors, if `component` has no color assigned, or its color is a `UIResource` (a tagging interface indicating it was installed by a look and feel), use `UIManager` to look up the color corresponding to `foregroundColorPropertyName` (or `backgroundColorPropertyName`) and set the color to that value.

```
public static void installColorsAndFont(JComponent component,
    String foregroundColorPropertyName,
    String backgroundColorPropertyName, String fontPropertyName)
```
For both foreground and background colors, if `component` has no color assigned, or its color is a `UIResource` (a tagging interface indicating it was installed by a look and feel), use `UIManager` to look up the color corresponding to `foregroundColorPropertyName` (or `backgroundColorPropertyName`) and set the color to that value. Similarly, if `component` has no font assigned or its font is a `UIResource`, look up `fontPropertyName` and set the font of the component to that value.

```
public abstract boolean isNativeLookAndFeel()
```
Returns `true` if this is the look and feel for the current platform.

```
public abstract boolean isSupportedLookAndFeel()
```
Returns `true` if the look and feel is supported on the current platform. For example, the Macintosh look and feel may not be supported on a Windows system.

```
public static Object makeIcon(Class, String gifFilename)
```
Builds a `UIDefaults.LazyValue` that will create an `ImageIcon` (tagged as a `UIResource`) corresponding to the specified GIF or JPEG file.

```
public static JTextComponent.KeyBinding[]
    makeKeyBindings(Object[] keyBindingList)
```
Utility method for building sets of `KeyBindings`. Returns an array of `KeyBindings`, one for each (`KeyStroke`, `Action`) pair in `keyBindingList`.

```
public String toString()
```
Returns a string that displays this object's properties.
Overrides: `toString` in class `Object`.

```
public void uninitialize()
```
Called when a look and feel is about to be "retired." This call gives the look and feel an opportunity to free resources it no longer needs.

```
public static void uninstallBorder(JComponent component)
```
If the border on `component` is a `UIResource` (indicating it was installed by a look and feel), remove the border (for example, set it to `null`).

Extended by   BasicLookAndFeel (p.621).
Returned by   UIManager.getAuxiliaryLookAndFeels() (p.455),
UIManager.getLookAndFeel() (p.455).
See also   JComponent (p.207), UIDefaults (p.452), UIManager (p.455).

swing.MenuElement

INTERFACE   MenuElement

This is the parent interface for many menu-type objects.

```
public interface MenuElement
```

Methods

public abstract java.awt.Component getComponent()
> Returns the component with which this menu element is associated.

public abstract MenuElement[] getSubElements()
> For hierarchical menus, returns an array of the menu's submenus.

public abstract void menuSelectionChanged(boolean wasAdded)
> Returns a notification that the menu selection has changed. Parameter wasAdded is true if the menu element has been added, or false if it has been removed.

public abstract void processKeyEvent(java.awt.event.KeyEvent event, MenuElement[] path, MenuSelectionManager manager)
> Handles a key event directed at this menu element.

public abstract void processMouseEvent(java.awt.event.MouseEvent event, MenuElement[] path, MenuSelectionManager manager)
> Handles a mouse event. The event's source is the component associated with this menu element. The path is the path through a hierarchical menu, ending at this menu element. Use manager to change the menu selection. The manager will continue forwarding this event to submenus if necessary.

Returned by BasicMenuItemUI.getPath() (p.624), JMenuBar.getSubElements() (p.288), JMenu.getSubElements() (p.281), JMenuItem.getSubElements() (p.291), JPopupMenu.getSubElements() (p.309), MenuDragMouseEvent.getPath() (p.501), MenuElement.getSubElements() (p.425), MenuKeyEvent.getPath() (p.503), MenuSelectionManager.getSelectedPath() (p.426).

Implemented by JMenu (p.281), JMenuBar (p.288), JMenuItem (p.291), JPopupMenu (p.309).

See also MenuSelectionManager (p.426).

swing.MenuSelectionManager

CLASS

```
java.lang.Object  ◄──  MenuSelectionManager
```

This class tracks the currently selected menu item.

public class MenuSelectionManager extends java.lang.Object

Constructors

public MenuSelectionManager()
> Creates a menu selection manager. (Usually you would use the one from defaultManager() rather than creating a new one.)

Methods

public void addChangeListener(ChangeListener l)
> Adds a ChangeListener to be informed when the selection changes.

public void clearSelectedPath()
> Makes there be no selected path.

```
public java.awt.Component componentForPoint(
    java.awt.Component source, java.awt.Point sourcePoint)
```
Returns the component in the currently selected path which contains sourcePoint. The coordinates are specified relative to the origin of source.

```
public static synchronized MenuSelectionManager defaultManager()
```
This factory method provides an instance of the default menu selection manager.

```
public MenuElement[] getSelectedPath()
```
Gets an array of menu elements, comprising the path to the currently selected menu element.

```
public boolean isComponentPartOfCurrentMenu(java.awt.Component component)
```
Returns true if component is part of the menu currently in use.

```
public void processKeyEvent(java.awt.event.KeyEvent event)
```
Handles a key event that a menu element might receive. (May select the appropriate menu element.)

```
public void processMouseEvent(java.awt.event.MouseEvent event)
```
Handles a mouse event that a menu element might receive. (May select the appropriate menu element.)

```
public void removeChangeListener(ChangeListener l)
```
Removes a ChangeListener from the manager.

```
public void setSelectedPath(MenuElement[] path)
```
Makes path be the currently selected path.

Protected Methods
```
protected void fireStateChanged()
```
Informs listeners when the selection changes.

Returned by   MenuDragMouseEvent.getMenuSelectionManager() (p.501),
MenuKeyEvent.getMenuSelectionManager() (p.503), MenuSelectionManager.defaultManager().
See also   MenuElement (p.425).

swing.MutableComboBoxModel

 INTERFACE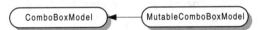

A ComboBoxModel that can be altered after it has been created.

```
public interface MutableComboBoxModel extends ComboBoxModel
```

Methods
```
public abstract void addElement(Object obj)
```
Adds an item to the end of the model.

```
public abstract void insertElementAt(Object obj, int index)
```
Adds an item at a specific index

```
public abstract void removeElement(Object obj)
```
Adds an item to the end of the model.

```
public abstract void removeElementAt(int index)
```
Removes an item at a specific index.

Implemented by   DefaultComboBoxModel (p.166).

swing.OverlayLayout

CLASS

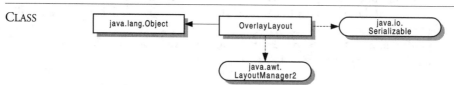

An overlay layout arranges a set of components overlapping on top of each other. (Imagine the layers of a 2½D cartoon, where the characters can be moved independently of the background.) The total size is as large as the largest item in the container.

```
public class OverlayLayout extends java.lang.Object
    implements java.awt.LayoutManager2, java.io.Serializable
```

Constructors

public OverlayLayout(java.awt.Container c)
Creates an overlay layout for container c.

Methods

public void addLayoutComponent(java.awt.Component component,
    Object constraints)
Adds the given component using the constraints.
Implements: addLayoutComponent in interface LayoutManager2.

public void addLayoutComponent(String name, java.awt.Component component)
Not used.
Implements: addLayoutComponent in interface LayoutManager.

public float getLayoutAlignmentX(java.awt.Container c)
Implements: getLayoutAlignmentX in interface LayoutManager2.

public float getLayoutAlignmentY(java.awt.Container c)
Implements: getLayoutAlignmentY in interface LayoutManager2.

public void invalidateLayout(java.awt.Container c)
Implements: invalidateLayout in interface LayoutManager2.

public void layoutContainer(java.awt.Container c)
Called by the AWT.
Implements: layoutContainer in interface LayoutManager.

public java.awt.Dimension maximumLayoutSize(java.awt.Container c)
Implements: maximumLayoutSize in interface LayoutManager2.

public java.awt.Dimension minimumLayoutSize(java.awt.Container c)
Implements: minimumLayoutSize in interface LayoutManager.

public java.awt.Dimension preferredLayoutSize(java.awt.Container c)
Implements: preferredLayoutSize in interface LayoutManager.

public void removeLayoutComponent(java.awt.Component component)
Not used.
Implements: removeLayoutComponent in interface LayoutManager.

swing.ProgressMonitor

CLASS

java.lang.Object ◄── ProgressMonitor

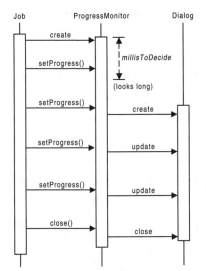

A progress monitor exists to inform a user of a potentially lengthy operation. If the operation is short, there is no notification; if it takes long, a dialog box is popped up. The dialog box consists of a message, a (potentially changing) note, and a progress bar.

The monitor tracks a value relative to a minimum and maximum. The job to be monitored must update the note and the value regularly.

There are two time values: `millisToDecideToPopup` and `millisToPopup`. After `millisToDecideToPopup` has passed, the `setProgress()` calls will cause the monitor to make an estimate of the time for the whole operation. If it looks like it will take more than `millisToPopup`, or if `millisToPopup` has already passed, the dialog is displayed.

```
public class ProgressMonitor extends java.lang.Object
```

Constructors
```
public ProgressMonitor(java.awt.Component parent, Object message,
    String note, int min, int max)
```
Creates a new progress monitor, with `parent` as the root of any dialog presented. The `message` is interpreted as in `JOptionPane` (see that class for more information); in its simplest form it can be a `String`. The `message` is constant once the dialog is presented. The `note`, however, can vary (see `setNote()`). If `note` is `null` in the constructor, no note will be present on the dialog and `setNote()` will have no effect. The `min` and `max` values represent the endpoints used to measure progress.

See `JProgressBar` for information on how progress is shown. See `ProgressMonitorInputStream` for an input stream that behaves much like this class.

Methods
```
public void close()
```
Indicates that the action is finished and the monitor may be closed. This will also be called when the current value is >= the maximum.
```
public int getMaximum()
```
Returns the maximum value.
```
public int getMillisToDecideToPopup()
```
Returns how long to wait before evaluating whether a dialog box will be needed.
```
public int getMillisToPopup()
```
Returns how long to wait before popping up the dialog box.

```
public int getMinimum()
```
Returns the minimum value.
```
public String getNote()
```
Gets the current note.
```
public boolean isCanceled()
```
Returns `true` if the operation is canceled (for example, by the Cancel button on the dialog).
```
public void setMaximum(int newValue)
```
Sets a new maximum value.
```
public void setMillisToDecideToPopup(int delay)
```
Sets how long to wait before deciding whether a dialog box will be needed. *Default:* 500 milliseconds.
```
public void setMillisToPopup(int delay)
```
Sets how long to wait before popping up a dialog box (once it is decided one is needed). *Default:* 2,000 milliseconds.
```
public void setMinimum(int newValue)
```
Sets the minimum value.
```
public void setNote(String note)
```
Sets the new note value (and updates it on the dialog box). This only works if a non-`null` note were used in the constructor.
```
public void setProgress(int newValue)
```
Sets the current progress value. If it is >= the maximum, the action is complete and the monitor will be closed.

Returned by   ProgressMonitorInputStream.getProgressMonitor() (p.430).
See also   JProgressBar (p.315).

swing.ProgressMonitorInputStream

CLASS

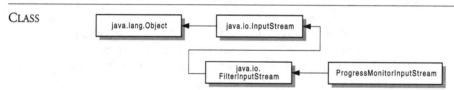

This creates a stream that combines an `InputStream` with a `ProgressMonitor`. If the read takes a while, the progress monitor will pop up a dialog box. If the CANCEL button is pressed, future reads will return an I/O exception. See `ProgressMonitor` for more information.

Example
```
InputStream fileStream = new FileInputStream (filename);
InputStream stream = new ProgressMonitorInputStream (
                    parent, "Reading " + filename, fileStream);
```

```
public class ProgressMonitorInputStream
    extends java.io.FilterInputStream
```

Constructors

`public ProgressMonitorInputStream(java.awt.Component parent,`
`    Object message, java.io.InputStream stream)`

Creates an input stream with an associated progress monitor. The `parent` is the owner of the dialog box. The `message` is used as described in `ProgressMonitor` or `JOptionPane`. The `stream` is the stream that the monitoring stream should wrap around.

Methods

`public void close() throws IOException`

Closes the I/O stream.

`public ProgressMonitor getProgressMonitor()`

Gets the progress monitor associated with this stream. See class `ProgressMonitor`.

`public int read() throws IOException`

Reads a single byte. (Returns −1 if at end-of-file.) The exception may be thrown for the usual I/O reasons, or because the CANCEL button has been pressed.

`public int read(byte[] buffer) throws IOException`

Reads an array of bytes. Returns the number of bytes read, or −1 if at end-of-file. The exception may be thrown for the usual I/O reasons, or because the CANCEL button has been pressed.

`public int read(byte[] buffer, int offset, int length) throws IOException`

Reads a partial array of bytes, from `buffer[offset]` to at most `buffer[offset+length-1]`. Returns the number of bytes read, or −1 if at end-of-file. The exception may be thrown for the usual I/O reasons, or because the CANCEL button has been pressed.

`public synchronized void reset() throws IOException`

Returns the stream to a marked point. (See `java.io.InputStream`.)

`public long skip(long bytesToSkip) throws IOException`

Skips the specified number of bytes.

See also   JOptionPane (p.294), ProgressMonitor (p.429).

swing.Renderer

INTERFACE   (Renderer)

The interface for a generic `Renderer`.

`public interface Renderer`

Methods

`public abstract java.awt.Component getComponent()`

Gets the renderer component.

`public abstract void setValue(Object value, boolean isSelected)`

Sets the value the renderer is to display.

swing.RepaintManager

CLASS   java.lang.Object ◄── RepaintManager

The `RepaintManager` tries to optimize the painting that is done to update `components`' appearance. To do this, it maintains a list of components that are invalid (need to be laid out again) and those that are dirty (need to be repainted). When a new repaint request is added to the list, it is examined to see if it can be merged with another request.

```
public class RepaintManager extends java.lang.Object
```

Constructors
```
public RepaintManager()
```
Creates a `RepaintManager`. This is not usually called by user code; use `currentManager()` instead.

Methods
```
public synchronized void addDirtyRegion(JComponent component,
    int x, int y, int width, int height)
```
Adds the specified rectangle of `component` to the dirty components list (to be repainted). If `component` is already on the list, the rectangle may be merged into the existing entry.
```
public synchronized void addInvalidComponent(JComponent component)
```
Marks `component` as dirty, and adds it to the list for validation (relay out).
```
public static RepaintManager currentManager(JComponent component)
```
Returns the repaint manager for `component` in the current thread.
```
public static RepaintManager currentManager(Component c)
```
Returns the repaint manager for `component` in the current thread.
```
public java.awt.Rectangle getDirtyRegion(JComponent component)
```
Finds the dirty rectangle of `component`, or an empty rectangle if `component` is not on the list of dirty components.
```
public java.awt.Dimension getDoubleBufferMaximumSize()
```
Gets the size of the image allocated as a double buffer.
```
public java.awt.Image getOffscreenBuffer(
    java.awt.Component component, int width, int height)
```
Gets an image for use as an offscreen buffer in painting `component`. The `width` and `height` are the proposed size of the buffer, but the manager may return a smaller buffer.
```
public boolean isCompletelyDirty(JComponent component)
```
Returns `true` if `component` must be fully repainted. (Some components must work hard to calculate dirty areas; this lets them avoid that step, if possible.)
```
public boolean isDoubleBufferingEnabled()
```
Returns `true` if double buffering is enabled.
```
public void markCompletelyClean(JComponent component)
```
Removes `component` from the list of dirty components.
```
public void markCompletelyDirty(JComponent component)
```
Adds `component` to the list of dirty components, with its whole area marked dirty.
```
public void paintDirtyRegions()
```
Paints all `components` on the dirty components list.
```
public synchronized void removeInvalidComponent(JComponent component)
```
Removes `components` from the list of invalid components.
```
public static void setCurrentManager(RepaintManager manager)
```
Makes `manager` be the repaint manager for the threads in the thread group of the calling thread.

```
public void setDoubleBufferMaximumSize(java.awt.Dimension limits)
```
Sets the maximum size for the offscreen buffer.
```
public void setDoubleBufferingEnabled(boolean isEnabled)
```
Sets whether double buffering is enabled.
```
public synchronized String toString()
```
Returns a string that displays this object's properties.
Overrides: toString in class Object.
```
public void validateInvalidComponents()
```
Validates all components that need to be validated.

See also JComponent (p.207).

swing.RootPaneContainer

This interface serves as a tag interface so automated graphical UI designers can identify where they need to use getContentPane().add() instead of just add(). See JRootPane (p.323) for more information.

```
public interface RootPaneContainer
```

Methods
```
public abstract java.awt.Container getContentPane()
```
Gets the content pane of the RootPaneContainer.
```
public abstract java.awt.Component getGlassPane()
```
Gets the glass pane of the RootPaneContainer.
```
public abstract JLayeredPane getLayeredPane()
```
Gets the layered pane of the RootPaneContainer.
```
public abstract JRootPane getRootPane()
```
Gets the JRootPane of the container.
```
public abstract void setContentPane(java.awt.Container cp)
```
Sets the content pane of the RootPaneContainer.
```
public abstract void setGlassPane(java.awt.Component gp)
```
Sets the glass pane of the RootPaneContainer.
```
public abstract void setLayeredPane(JLayeredPane lp)
```
Sets the layered pane of the RootPaneContainer.

Implemented by   JApplet (p.186), JDialog (p.226), JFrame (p.248), JInternalFrame (p.254), JWindow (p.414).
See also   JRootPane (p.323).

swing.Scrollable

The Scrollable interface is implemented by components that tend to be included in a
JScrollPane so they can be scrolled properly. For example, JTree supports this interface
because trees almost always require the ability to scroll.

Example

```
package scrollable;

import java.awt.*;
import java.awt.event.*;
// Uncomment the following line for Swing 1.0.3 and before
//import com.sun.java.swing.*;
// Uncomment the following line for Swing 1.1
import javax.swing.*;

public class Main extends JFrame {
    // Compare this to the JInternalFrame example.
    private class ScrollDesktop extends JDesktopPane implements Scrollable {
        public Dimension getPreferredScrollableViewportSize() {
            return getPreferredSize();
        }
        // Make the arrows move the picture faster
        public int getScrollableUnitIncrement(Rectangle r, int axis, int dir) {
            return 50;
        }
        public int getScrollableBlockIncrement (Rectangle r, int axis,
            int dir) {
            return 200;
        }
        public boolean getScrollableTracksViewportWidth() {
            return false;
        }
        public boolean getScrollableTracksViewportHeight() {
            return false;
        }
    }

    public Main () {
        addWindowListener(new WindowAdapter() {
            public void windowClosing(WindowEvent e) {
                Main.this.dispose();
                System.exit(0);
            }
        });
        JDesktopPane desk = new ScrollDesktop();
        desk.setPreferredSize (new Dimension(1000, 1000));
        getContentPane().add (new JScrollPane(desk), "Center");
        JInternalFrame f1 = new JInternalFrame ("Frame 1");
        f1.getContentPane().add (new JLabel("This is frame f1"));
        f1.setResizable(true);
        f1.pack();
        f1.setVisible(true);
        desk.add (f1, new Integer(10)); // Layer 10

        JInternalFrame f2 = new JInternalFrame("Frame 2");
        f2.getContentPane().add (new JLabel("Content for f2"));
```

```
      f2.setResizable(true);
      f2.pack();
      f2.setVisible(true);
      desk.add (f2, new Integer(20)); // Layer 20 (above 10)

      JInternalFrame f3 = new JInternalFrame("Frame 3");
      f3.getContentPane().add (new JLabel("Content for f3"));
      f3.setResizable(true);
      f3.pack();
      f3.setVisible(true);
      desk.add (f3, new Integer(20));

      f3.toFront();
      try {
         f3.setSelected(true);
      } catch (java.beans.PropertyVetoException ignored) {
      }

      pack();
      setSize(300, 300);
      setVisible(true);
   }
   public static void main (String arg[]) {
      new Main();
   }
}
```

public interface Scrollable

Methods

public java.awt.Dimension getPreferredScrollableViewportSize()

Gets the ideal size for the viewport, based on the scrollable object. For many objects, this will be their preferred size, but this needn't be true. For example, the preferred size of a JList is based on its total number of rows, but its preferred viewport size is based on the number of rows it prefers to show.

public int getScrollableBlockIncrement(java.awt.Rectangle visible, int orientation, int direction)

Calculates how far to scroll for one block. For example, a block scroll in a text document might move to the next screenful of text. The visible rectangle is the section of the object visible in the viewport. The orientation is either SwingConstants.HORIZONTAL or SwingConstants.VERTICAL. The direction is negative to scroll left (or up), or positive to scroll right (or down). The result is the number of pixels to scroll in the specified direction. See also setBlockIncrement() of JScrollBar.

public boolean getScrollableTracksViewportHeight()

Returns true if the height of this object should match the height of the viewport that contains it. (If true, there will be no need for vertical scroll bars.) For example, we might be displaying a set of bar graphs with a common baseline; we wouldn't want to split them across lines because that would make it more difficult to compare graphs.

public boolean getScrollableTracksViewportWidth()

Returns true if the width of this object should match the width of the viewport that contains it. (If true, there will be no need for horizontal scroll bars.) For example, an editor with word wrapping would return true, so that word wrapping would be based on the viewport's size rather than the object's natural size.

```
public int getScrollableUnitIncrement(java.awt.Rectangle visible,
    int orientation, int direction)
```
Calculates how far to scroll one unit. For example, a unit scroll in a text document might move to the next line of text. This routine should attempt to fully show the current unit before scrolling to the next one. For example, if the last line of text is a partial line, it would be better to first scroll up to show the whole line before scrolling to the next line.

The `visible` rectangle is the section of the object visible in the viewport. The `orientation` is either `SwingConstants.HORIZONTAL` or `SwingConstants.VERTICAL`. The direction is negative to scroll left (or up), or positive to scroll right (or down). The result is the number of pixels to scroll in the specified direction. See also `setUnitIncrement()` of `JScrollBar`.

Implemented by JList (p.271), JTable (p.357), JTextComponent (p.838), JTree (p.393).
See also JScrollPane (p.332), JViewport (p.410).

swing.ScrollPaneConstants

INTERFACE   (ScrollPaneConstants)

This interface consists entirely of constants. It is implemented by classes that want to use these constants to describe scroll bars.

```
public interface ScrollPaneConstants
```

Fields
```
public static final String HORIZONTAL_SCROLLBAR = "HORIZONTAL_SCROLLBAR"
public static final String VERTICAL_SCROLLBAR = "VERTICAL_SCROLLBAR"
```
These constants identify a scroll bar as horizontal or vertical. They are used as constraints on `addLayoutComponent()` of `ScrollPaneLayout`.
```
public static final String LOWER_LEFT_CORNER = "LOWER_LEFT_CORNER"
public static final String LOWER_RIGHT_CORNER = "LOWER_RIGHT_CORNER"
public static final String UPPER_LEFT_CORNER = "UPPER_LEFT_CORNER"
public static final String UPPER_RIGHT_CORNER = "UPPER_RIGHT_CORNER"
```
These constants identify a corner. They are used as constraints on `addLayoutComponent()` of `ScrollPaneLayout`.
```
public static final String VERTICAL_SCROLLBAR_POLICY =
    "VERTICAL_SCROLLBAR_POLICY"
public static final String HORIZONTAL_SCROLLBAR_POLICY =
    "HORIZONTAL_SCROLLBAR_POLICY"
public static final int HORIZONTAL_SCROLLBAR_ALWAYS =
    "HORIZONTAL_SCROLLBAR_ALWAYS"
public static final int HORIZONTAL_SCROLLBAR_AS_NEEDED =
    "HORIZONTAL_SCROLLBAR_AS_NEEDED"
public static final int HORIZONTAL_SCROLLBAR_NEVER =
    "HORIZONTAL_SCROLLBAR_NEVER"
public static final int VERTICAL_SCROLLBAR_ALWAYS =
    "VERTICAL_SCROLLBAR_ALWAYS"
```

```
public static final int VERTICAL_SCROLLBAR_AS_NEEDED =
    "VERTICAL_SCROLLBAR_AS_NEEDED"
public static final int VERTICAL_SCROLLBAR_NEVER =
    "VERTICAL_SCROLLBAR_NEVER"
```
These constants define when a scroll bar should be provided.
```
public static final String COLUMN_HEADER = "COLUMN_HEADER"
public static final String ROW_HEADER = "ROW_HEADER"
public static final String VIEWPORT = "VIEWPORT"
```
These constants define parts of components related to scroll bars. They are used as constraints on `addLayoutComponent()` of `ScrollPaneLayout`.

Implemented by   BasicScrollPaneUI (p.650), JScrollPane (p.332), ScrollPaneLayout (p.437).

swing.ScrollPaneLayout

CLASS

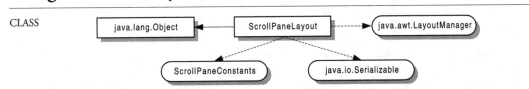

The `ScrollPaneLayout` manages the components that make up a `JScrollPane`: the viewport, the scroll bars, row and column headers, and optional corners. Usually you would use the `JScrollPane` methods directly.

The row and column headers are not scrolled—they stay in place while the viewport is scrolled. For example, a `JTable` uses column headers for the column labels.

```
public class ScrollPaneLayout extends java.lang.Object
    implements java.awt.LayoutManager, ScrollPaneConstants,
    java.io.Serializable
```

Constructors
```
public ScrollPaneLayout()
```
Creates a scroll pane layout.

Methods
```
public void addLayoutComponent(String constraint,
    java.awt.Component component)
```
Adds the component to the layout. The `constraint` must be COLUMN_HEADER, HORIZONTAL_ SCROLLBAR, LOWER_LEFT_CORNER, LOWER_RIGHT_CORNER, ROW_HEADER, UPPER_LEFT_ CORNER, UPPER_RIGHT_CORNER, VERTICAL_SCROLLBAR, or VIEWPORT. (These constants are defined in `ScrollPaneConstants`.)
Implements: addLayoutComponent in interface LayoutManager.
```
public JViewport getColumnHeader()
```
Gets the column header. (See colHead.)

public java.awt.Component getCorner(String cornerName)
Gets the specified component. The cornerName must be LOWER_LEFT_CORNER, LOWER_RIGHT_CORNER, UPPER_LEFT_CORNER, or UPPER_RIGHT_CORNER.

public JScrollBar getHorizontalScrollBar()
Gets the horizontal scroll bar. (See hsb.)

public int getHorizontalScrollBarPolicy()
Returns HORIZONTAL_SCROLLBAR_ALWAYS, HORIZONTAL_SCROLLBAR_AS_NEEDED, or HORIZONTAL_SCROLLBAR_NEVER. (See hsbPolicy.)

public JViewport getRowHeader()
Gets the row header. (See rowHead.)

public JScrollBar getVerticalScrollBar()
Gets the vertical scroll bar. (See vsb.)

public int getVerticalScrollBarPolicy()
Returns VERTICAL_SCROLLBAR_ALWAYS, VERTICAL_SCROLLBAR_AS_NEEDED, or VERTICAL_SCROLLBAR_NEVER. (See vsbPolicy.)

public JViewport getViewport()
Gets the viewport (the main scrolling view).

**public java.awt.Rectangle getViewportBorderBounds(
JScrollPane scrollpane)**
Deprecated as of Swing 1.1. Use JScrollPane.getViewportBorderBounds().

public void layoutContainer(java.awt.Container container)
Lays out the components of the scroll pane in container. The space is arranged like this:

- If the row header is not null, and is visible, it is given its preferred height and made as wide as the viewport.
- If the column header is not null, and is visible, it is given its preferred width and made as tall as the viewport.
- If a vertical scroll bar is needed (either because the viewport is shorter than the view, or the vertical scroll bar policy is VERTICAL_SCROLLBAR_ALWAYS), it is given its preferred width and made as tall as the viewport.
- If a horizontal scroll bar is needed (either because the viewport is less wide than the view, or the horizontal scroll bar policy is HORIZONTAL_SCROLLBAR_ALWAYS), it is given its preferred height and made as wide as the viewport.
- If there is a scroll pane border, space is given to it.
- Any leftover space is available for the main scrolling viewport.
- If they exist and are needed, the corners are placed on the headers and/or the scroll bars.

Implements: layoutContainer in interface LayoutManager.

public java.awt.Dimension minimumLayoutSize(java.awt.Container container)
Calculates the minimum acceptable size for the scroll pane.
Implements: minimumLayoutSize in interface LayoutManager.

**public java.awt.Dimension preferredLayoutSize(
java.awt.Container container)**
Calculates the preferred size for the scroll pane.
Implements: preferredLayoutSize in interface LayoutManager.

public void removeLayoutComponent(java.awt.Component component)
Removes component from the layout.

Implements: removeLayoutComponent in interface LayoutManager.

public void setHorizontalScrollBarPolicy(int policy)

The policy must be HORIZONTAL_SCROLLBAR_ALWAYS, HORIZONTAL_SCROLLBAR_AS_ NEEDED, or HORIZONTAL_SCROLLBAR_NEVER. (See hsbPolicy.)

public void setVerticalScrollBarPolicy(int policy)

The policy must be VERTICAL_SCROLLBAR_ALWAYS, VERTICAL_SCROLLBAR_AS_NEEDED, or VERTICAL_SCROLLBAR_NEVER. (See vsbPolicy.)

public void syncWithScrollPane(JScrollPane sp)

This method must be called on any layout used for a JScrollPane immediately after it has been added. It makes sure the layout matches what is defined in the JScrollPane.

Protected Fields

protected JViewport colHead

The column header (in place at the top of the scrolling area, but not itself scrolled).

protected JScrollBar hsb

The horizontal scroll bar.

protected int hsbPolicy

The policy of the horizontal scroll bar: HORIZONTAL_SCROLLBAR_ALWAYS, HORIZONTAL_ SCROLLBAR_AS_NEEDED, or HORIZONTAL_SCROLLBAR_NEVER.

protected java.awt.Component lowerLeft

The lower-left corner.

protected java.awt.Component lowerRight

The lower-right corner.

protected JViewport rowHead

The row header (in place at the left of the scrolling area, but not itself scrolled).

protected java.awt.Component upperLeft

The upper-left corner.

protected java.awt.Component upperRight

The upper-right corner.

protected JViewport viewport

The main scrolling area.

protected JScrollBar vsb

The vertical scroll bar.

protected int vsbPolicy

The scrolling policy for the vertical scroll bar: VERTICAL_SCROLLBAR_ALWAYS, VERTICAL_ SCROLLBAR_AS_NEEDED, or VERTICAL_SCROLLBAR_NEVER.

Protected Methods

protected java.awt.Component addSingletonComponent(
java.awt.Component oldComponent, java.awt.Component newComponent)

Replaces oldComponent with newComponent. This is used instead of individual setXxx() methods for the various components.

Inner Classes

public static class ScrollPaneLayout.UIResource

See also   JScrollBar (p.328), JScrollPane (p.332), JViewport (p.410), ScrollPaneConstants (p.436).

swing.ScrollPaneLayout.UIResource

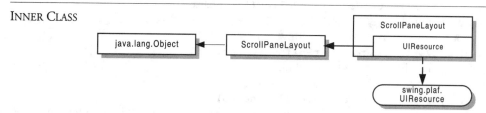

A `UIResource` wrapped inner class that can be used safely by a look and feel.

```
public static class ScrollPaneLayout.UIResource
    extends ScrollPaneLayout
    implements UIResource
```

Constructors
```
public UIResource()
```
   Default constructor.

swing.SingleSelectionModel

SingleSelectionModel

This model allows, at most, one selected item. (In this way, it is similar to the `ButtonGroup` which forces radio button behavior.) This model is used by `JPopupMenu` to ensure that a single item is selected.

```
public interface SingleSelectionModel
```

Methods
```
public void addChangeListener(ChangeListener listener)
```
   Adds `listener` to the list of listeners notified when the model changes.
```
public void clearSelection()
```
   Makes sure there is no selected item; notifies listeners if this is a change.
```
public int getSelectedIndex()
```
   Gets the index of the currently selected item, or −1 if no item is selected.
```
public boolean isSelected()
```
   Returns `true` if any item is selected.
```
public void removeChangeListener(ChangeListener listener)
```
   Removes `listener` from the list of items notified when the model changes.
```
public void setSelectedIndex(int index)
```
   Makes the item at `index` be the currently selected item; notifies listeners if this is a change.

   Implemented by   DefaultSingleSelectionModel (p.179).
   See also   ChangeListener (p.488), JPopupMenu (p.309).

swing.SizeRequirements

This class is used by layout managers. Its values represent the width or height of a component, and there are utility methods that calculate positions based on its values.

There are two layout approaches supported by the class methods: aligned and tiled. The aligned layouts are based on the preferred alignment of components. The tiled layouts put the components one after the other, so that they fill the allotted space.

```
public class SizeRequirements extends java.lang.Object
    implements java.io.Serializable
```

Fields
public float alignment
The alignment ranges from `0.0` (top or left) to `1.0` (bottom or right), inclusive.

public int maximum
The maximum width or height this component would like. Should be equal to `getMaximumSize().width` or `getMaximumSize().height`. (See `JComponent`.)

public int minimum
The minimum width or height this component should have. Should be equal to `getMinimumSize().width` or `getMinimumSize().height`. (See `JComponent`.)

public int preferred
The width or height that is natural or best for this component. Should be equal to `getPreferredSize().width` or `getPreferredSize().height`. (See `JComponent`.)

Constructors
public SizeRequirements()
public SizeRequirements(int minimum, int preferred, int maximum, float alignment)
Creates a `SizeRequirements` object. If the values aren't specified, they default to 0 for `minimum`, `preferred`, and `maximum`, and `0.5` (centered) for `alignment`.

Methods
public static int[] adjustSizes(int delta, SizeRequirements[] children)
Adjusts a specified array of sizes by a given `delta`.

public static void calculateAlignedPositions(int toBeAllocated, SizeRequirements total, SizeRequirements[] components, int[] offsets, int[] spans)
Given the total space `toBeAllocated`, and the required space for all components `total`, and the requirements for each of the `components`, computes `offsets` and `spans`. The components are laid out according to their preferred alignment. The components may overlap.

```
public static void calculateTiledPositions(int toBeAllocated,
    SizeRequirements total, SizeRequirements[] components,
    int[] offsets, int[] spans)
```
Given the total space `toBeAllocated`, and the required space for all components `total`, and the requirements for each of the `components`, computes `offsets` and `spans`. The components are laid out in a tiled manner, one after the other, with the first offset starting at 0.

```
public static SizeRequirements getAlignedSizeRequirements (
    SizeRequirements[] components)
```
Computes the size required to place the `components` according to their alignment. (They may overlap, but each will have its alignment honored.)

```
public static SizeRequirements getTiledSizeRequirements(
    SizeRequirements[] components)
```
Computes the size required to place the `components` one after the other with no space between. (Think of a `java.awt.FlowLayout`.) Computes all three values in parallel: minimum, preferred, and maximum. The alignment is ignored on input, and set to 0.5 (centered) in the result.

```
public String toString()
```
Returns a string containing the minimum, preferred, and maximum size requirements, along with the alignment.

Overrides: `toString` in class `Object`.

swing.SwingConstants

INTERFACE   SwingConstants

This interface defines constants for the compass point directions, for positions, and for orientation.

```
public interface SwingConstants
```

Fields

```
public static final int CENTER = 0
public static final int EAST = 3
public static final int NORTH = 1
public static final int NORTH_EAST = 2
public static final int NORTH_WEST = 8
public static final int SOUTH = 5
public static final int SOUTH_EAST = 4
public static final int SOUTH_WEST = 6
public static final int WEST = 7
```
These constants define compass points. (Note that `CENTER` is used as both a compass point value and as a relative position value. It is only defined once in this interface, but it is shown here and below for clarity.)

```
public static final int TOP = 1
public static final int BOTTOM = 3
public static final int LEFT = 2
public static final int RIGHT= 4
```

```
public static final int CENTER = 0
```
These values define positions. (Note that CENTER is used as both a relative position value and as a compass point value. It is only defined once in this interface, but it is shown here and above for clarity.)

```
public static final int HORIZONTAL = 0
public static final int VERTICAL = 1
```
These values define orientations (for sliders, etc.).

```
public static final int LEADING = 10
public static final int TRAILING = 11
```
These values are used by buttons and labels to compensate for the reading direction of languages. If LEADING is used, the text will be placed logically "before" the Icon, and if TRAILING is used, the text will be placed logically "after."

Implemented by   AbstractButton (p.118), BasicArrowButton (p.550), BasicInternalFrameUI.BorderListener (p.609), BasicScrollBarUI (p.642), BasicTabbedPaneUI (p.679), BasicToolbarUI (p.702), JCheckBoxMenuItem (p.195), JLabel (p.264), JProgressBar (p.315), JSeparator (p.338), JSlider (p.341), JTabbedPane (p.351), JTextField (p.379), JToolBar (p.388), SwingUtilities (p.443).

swing.SwingUtilities

CLASS

A variety of utility methods: rectangle arithmetic, coordinate conversion, accessibility, deferred operations, and others.

- Rectangle arithmetic—computeDifference(), computeIntersection(), compute-Union(), isRectangleContainingRectangle().

- Coordinate conversion—convertMouseEvent(), convertPoint(), convertPointFrom-Screen(), convertPointToScreen(), convertRectangle(), getLocalBounds().

- Accessibility—getAccessibleAt(), getAccessibleChild(), getAccessibleChil-drenCount(), getAccessibleIndexInParent(), getAccessibleStateSet().

- Deferred operations—invokeAndWait(), invokeLater().

- Other—computeStringWidth(), findFocusOwner(), getAncestorNamed(), get-AncestorOfClass(), getDeepestComponentAt(), getRootPane(), isDescending-From(), isLeftMouseButton(), isMiddleMouseButton(), isRightMouseButton(), layoutCompoundLabel(), layoutMenuItem(), paintComponent(), updateComponent-TreeUI(), windowForComponent().

```
public class SwingUtilities extends java.lang.Object
    implements SwingConstants
```

Methods

`public static java.awt.Rectangle[] computeDifference(`
    `java.awt.Rectangle r1, java.awt.Rectangle r2)`
Computes the difference of `r1 - r2`.

`public static java.awt.Rectangle computeIntersection(int x, int y,`
    `int width, int height, java.awt.Rectangle r)`
Computes the intersection of the rectangle `(x,y,width,height)` and `r`.

`public static int computeStringWidth(java.awt.FontMetrics`
    `fontInfo, String s)`
Computes the (display) width of `s` using `fontInfo`.

`public static java.awt.Rectangle computeUnion(int x, int y,`
    `int width, int height, java.awt.Rectangle r)`
Computes the union of the rectangles `(x,y,width,height)` and `r`.

`public static java.awt.event.MouseEvent convertMouseEvent(`
    `java.awt.Component source, java.awt.event.MouseEvent event,`
    `java.awt.Component destination)`
Returns a new `MouseEvent`, based on `event`, but with the coordinates translated. The coordinates are assumed to be in the coordinate system of `source`, and they are converted to the coordinate system of `destination`. The source for the new event is set to `destination`, unless it is `null`, in which case it remains `source`.

`public static java.awt.Point convertPoint(`
    `java.awt.Component source, int x, int y, java.awt.Component destination)`
Translates `(x,y)` (in the coordinate system of `source`) to the coordinate system of `destination`. If `destination` is `null`, translates the point to the coordinate system of the root component of `source`. If both `source` and `destination` are `null`, returns the point corresponding to `(x,y)`.

`public static java.awt.Point convertPoint(java.awt.Component source,`
    `java.awt.Point point, java.awt.Component destination)`
Translates `point` (in the coordinate system of `source`) to the coordinate system of `destination`. If `destination` is `null`, translates the point to the coordinate system of the root component of `source`. If both `source` and `destination` are `null`, returns `point`.

`public static void convertPointFromScreen(java.awt.Point point,`
    `java.awt.Component component)`
Converts `point` from the screen coordinate system to the coordinate system of `component`. (The point value is modified.)

`public static void convertPointToScreen(java.awt.Point point,`
    `java.awt.Component component)`
Converts `point` from the coordinate system of `component` to the screen coordinate system. (The point value is modified.)

`public static java.awt.Rectangle convertRectangle(java.awt.Component source,`
    `java.awt.Rectangle rectangle, java.awt.Component destination)`
Translates `rectangle` (in the coordinate system of `source`) to the coordinate system of `destination`. If `destination` is `null`, translates `rectangle` to the coordinate system of the root component of `source`. If both `source` and `destination` are `null`, returns `rectangle`.

`public static java.awt.Component findFocusOwner(`
    `java.awt.Component component)`
Finds the `component` that has the focus, either in `component` or below. Returns `null` if it fails to find such a component. (Note that this call may fail in applets because of security restrictions.)

```
public static Accessible getAccessibleAt(
    java.awt.Component component, java.awt.Point point)
```
Given `point` in the coordinate system of `component`, finds the corresponding `Accessible` object. See the chapter on accessibility.

```
public static Accessible getAccessibleChild(
    java.awt.Component component, int nth)
```
Of the children of component, returns the nth accessible. See the chapter on accessibility.

```
public static int getAccessibleChildrenCount(java.awt.Component component)
```
Gets the number of accessible children of `component`. See the chapter on accessibility.

```
public static int getAccessibleIndexInParent(java.awt.Component component)
```
For component, returns the position of it in its parent (counting `Accessible` components only). See the chapter on accessibility.

```
public static AccessibleStateSet
    getAccessibleStateSet(java.awt.Component component)
```
Gets the `AccessibleStateSet` corresponding to `component`. See `java.accessibility.AccessibleStateSet` and the chapter on accessibility.

```
public static java.awt.Container getAncestorNamed(String name,
    java.awt.Component component)
```
Searches above `component` for the first ancestor named `name`.

```
public static java.awt.Container getAncestorOfClass(Class class,
    java.awt.Component component)
```
Searches above `component` for the first ancestor of class `class`.

```
public static java.awt.Component
    getDeepestComponentAt(java.awt.Component component, int x, int y)
```
Returns the deepest descendant of `component` which is at `(x,y)`. (Note that if `component` is not a `Container`, it is already the deepest component, and is returned directly.)

```
public static java.awt.Rectangle getLocalBounds(
    java.awt.Component component)
```
Returns the rectangle `(0,0, component.getBounds().width, component.get-Bounds().height)` for `component`. (This is the bounds rectangle in the coordinate system of `component`.)

```
public static java.awt.Component getRoot(java.awt.Component c)
```
Returns the `applet` or other top-level component that is an ancestor of the given `component`.

```
public static JRootPane getRootPane(java.awt.Component component)
```
Gets the root pane that contains `component`. See `JRootPane`.

```
public static void invokeAndWait(Runnable runnable)
    throws InterruptedException, InvocationTargetException
```
This method is only used by threads other than the main event thread. The `runnable` is scheduled to run in the main event thread (after other pending events have been handled). The calling thread is blocked until the `run()` is completed. If another thread interrupts the calling thread, an `InterruptedException` is thrown. If any errors are thrown in the `run()` method, `InvocationTargetException` is thrown in the calling thread.

This method is used because of a Swing policy that only the main event thread is permitted to modify Swing components during execution. This method lets another thread schedule such a modification in the Swing event thread. See also `invokeLater()`.

```
public static void invokeLater(Runnable runnable)
```
The `runnable` is scheduled to run in the main event thread after pending events have been handled. The calling thread is not blocked. (The calling thread may be any thread, including the main event thread.) This method may be used to meet the constraint that only methods in the main event thread may modify Swing components. See also `invokeAndWait()`.

```
public static boolean isDescendingFrom(java.awt.Component c1,
    java.awt.Component c2)
```
Returns `true` if `c1` is a descendant of (contained in) `c2`.

```
public static boolean isEventDispatchThread()
```
Returns `true` if the current thread is the event dispatch thread (the main event thread).

```
public static boolean isLeftMouseButton(java.awt.event.MouseEvent event)
```
Returns `true` if `event` involves the left mouse button.

```
public static boolean isMiddleMouseButton(java.awt.event.MouseEvent event)
```
Returns `true` if `event` involves the middle mouse button.

```
public static final boolean isRectangleContainingRectangle(
    java.awt.Rectangle r1, java.awt.Rectangle r2)
```
Returns `true` if `r1` contains `r2`.

```
public static boolean isRightMouseButton(java.awt.event.MouseEvent event)
```
Returns `true` if `event` involves the right mouse button.

```
public static String layoutCompoundLabel(JComponent c, java.awt.FontMetrics
    fm, String text, Icon icon, int verticalAlignment,
    int horizontalAlignment, int verticalTextPosition,
    int horizontalTextPosition, java.awt.Rectangle coordinates,
    java.awt.Rectangle returnedIconR, java.awt.Rectangle returnedTextRect,
    int textIconGap)
```
Computes the positions for the icon and text of a label. This method stores the resulting values in the two "returned" parameters. The returned values are relative to `coordinates`. This method understands the LEADING and TRAILING relative position indicators so it should be used in preference to the other version of this method. See `JLabel` (p.264) for a description of the alignment and position constants.

```
public static String layoutCompoundLabel(java.awt.FontMetrics metrics,
    String string, Icon icon, int verticalAlignment,
    int horizontalAlignment, int verticalTextPosition,
    int horizontalTextPosition, java.awt.Rectangle coordinates,
    java.awt.Rectangle iconResult, java.awt.Rectangle textResult,
    int textIconGap)
```
This version of this method does not understand the LEADING and TRAILING position constants. The other version of this method should be used instead.

```
public static void paintComponent(java.awt.Graphics gr,
    java.awt.Component component, java.awt.Container parent, int x,
    int y, int width, int height)
```
Paints `component` on `gr`, limited to painting within the rectangle (`x,y,width,height`). During painting, `component` is wrapped within a special component whose parent is `parent`, that prevents `repaint()` and `validate()` calls from propagating up the container tree.

```
public static void paintComponent(java.awt.Graphics gr,
    java.awt.Component component, java.awt.Container parent,
    java.awt.Rectangle rectangle)
```
Paints component on gr, limited to painting within rectangle. During painting, component is wrapped within a special component whose parent is parent, that prevents repaint() and validate() calls from propagating up the container tree.

```
public static void updateComponentTreeUI(java.awt.Component component)
```
Tells component and its descendants to update themselves to the current look and feel, by calling their updateUI() methods.

```
public static java.awt.Window windowForComponent(
    java.awt.Component component)
```
Tells which window contains component.

swing.Timer

CLASS

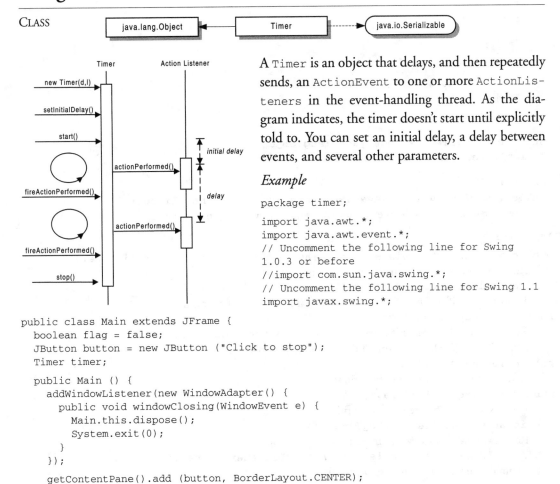

A Timer is an object that delays, and then repeatedly sends, an ActionEvent to one or more ActionListeners in the event-handling thread. As the diagram indicates, the timer doesn't start until explicitly told to. You can set an initial delay, a delay between events, and several other parameters.

Example

```
package timer;

import java.awt.*;
import java.awt.event.*;
// Uncomment the following line for Swing
1.0.3 or before
//import com.sun.java.swing.*;
// Uncomment the following line for Swing 1.1
import javax.swing.*;

public class Main extends JFrame {
  boolean flag = false;
  JButton button = new JButton ("Click to stop");
  Timer timer;

  public Main () {
    addWindowListener(new WindowAdapter() {
      public void windowClosing(WindowEvent e) {
        Main.this.dispose();
        System.exit(0);
      }
    });

    getContentPane().add (button, BorderLayout.CENTER);
```

```
    // Stop timer when button clicked
    button.addActionListener (new ActionListener() {
      public void actionPerformed (ActionEvent e) {
        timer.stop();
        button.setBackground (Color.red);
      }
    });

    // Blink button once per second.
    // Timer fires in event-handling
    // thread, so it's ok to modify components.
    timer = new Timer (1000, new ActionListener() {
      public void actionPerformed (ActionEvent e) {
        button.setBackground (flag ? Color.green : Color.yellow);
        flag = !flag;
        repaint();
      }
    });

    timer.start();

    pack();
    setVisible(true);
  }
  public static void main (String arg[]) {
    new Main();
  }
}
```

public class Timer extends java.lang.Object
    implements java.io.Serializable

Constructors

public Timer(int delay, java.awt.event.ActionListener listener)
    Creates a timer that sends an event to `listener` every `delay` milliseconds.

Methods

public void addActionListener(java.awt.event.ActionListener listener)
    Adds a listener to be informed when the timer expires.

public boolean isCoalesce()
    Returns `true` if the timer coalesces events that don't get sent promptly.

public boolean isRunning()
    Returns `true` if the timer is currently running. It is running when it has been started and has not had stop called and/or has not expired if it is a nonrepeating timer.

public int getDelay()
    Returns the delay between notifications.

public int getInitialDelay()
    Returns the delay before the first notification.

public static boolean getLogTimers()
    Returns `true` if timer events are sent to `System.out`.

public void removeActionListener(ActionListener listener)
    Maintains the list of listeners to be notified.

public boolean repeats()

Returns `true` if the timer repeats.

public void restart()

After setting the parameters, use `start()` to start the timer running. At this point, `isRunning()` will return `true`. The timer will wait for the initial delay, and then notify listeners using `fireActionPerformed()`. If repeating is on, the timer will repeatedly wait for the delay interval and `fireActionPerformed()` until `stop()` is called. If `restart()` is called, the timer will clear any pending events, wait the initial delay, and begin again.

public void setCoalesce(boolean shouldCoalesce)

Sets whether pending notifications will be merged. When coalescing, "extra" notifications will be dropped. (Coalescing could occur if the timer interval is so small or the system is so busy that there is not a chance to complete all notifications before the next event.) (*Default:* `true`.)

Multimedia applications such as animation or video often find coalescing events to be the best way to degrade quality when the CPU is overloaded. For example, delayed frames of a video can be dropped, rather than engaging in a futile effort to display the intervening frames. (The video would be jerky either way; dropping the frames lets the system move on.)

public void setDelay(int delay)

Sets the delay (in milliseconds) between notifications. (*Default:* set in `constructor`.)

public void setInitialDelay(int initialDelay)

Sets the delay (in milliseconds) until the first notification. (*Default:* uses `delay` from `constructor`.)

public static void setLogTimers(boolean shouldLogEvents)

Sets whether timer activity should be logged to `System.out`.

public void setRepeats(boolean shouldRepeat)

If `true`, the timer repeats. If `false`, the timer is one-shot. (*Default:* `true.`)

public void start()

Starts the timer.

public void stop()

Stops the timer. Does not notify any listeners.

Protected Fields

protected EventListenerList listenerList

The list of listeners for this timer.

Protected Methods

protected void fireActionPerformed(
java.awt.event.ActionEvent event)

Routine to walk the list of listeners and send `event` to each one.

swing.ToolTipManager

CLASS

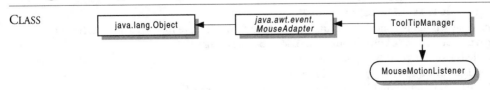

The `ToolTipManager` manages all ToolTips (see class `JToolTip`). It has no publicly available constructor—the Swing package takes care of creating it.

When you move the mouse over a component for which ToolTips are active, there is an initial delay before any ToolTip is shown, and it is shown for the time indicated by the dismiss delay. If the mouse stays there, the ToolTip is shown again after the reshow delay, and the process repeats.

```
public class ToolTipManager extends java.awt.event.MouseAdapter
    implements java.awt.event.MouseMotionListener
```

Methods

public int getDismissDelay()
Returns the delay (in milliseconds) the ToolTip remains shown.

public int getInitialDelay()
Returns the delay (in milliseconds) the mouse must sit in a ToolTip-enabled region before the Tool-Tip is shown.

public int getReshowDelay()
Gets the delay (in milliseconds) before reshowing the ToolTip.

public boolean isEnabled()
Returns `true` if ToolTips are enabled.

public boolean isLightWeightPopupEnabled()
Returns `true` if lightweight ToolTips are in use or `false` if heavyweight ToolTips are being used.

public void mouseDragged(java.awt.event.MouseEvent e)
Implements: mouseDragged in interface `java.awt.event.MouseMotionListener`.

public void mouseEntered(MouseEvent event)
Overrides: mouseEntered in class `MouseAdapter`.
Implements: mouseEntered in interface `MouseListener`.

public void mouseExited(MouseEvent event)
Overrides: mouseExited in class `MouseAdapter`.
Implements: mouseExited in interface `MouseListener`.

public void mouseMoved(java.awt.event.MouseEvent e)
Implements: mouseMoved in interface `java.awt.event.MouseMotionListener`.

public void mousePressed(java.awt.event.MouseEvent e)
Overrides: mousePressed in class `java.awt.event.MouseAdapter`.

public void registerComponent(JComponent component)
Registers component with the ToolTipManager (enabling any ToolTip it might have).

public void setDismissDelay(int dismissDelay)
Sets the delay (in milliseconds) telling how long to show the ToolTip.

public void setEnabled(boolean shouldEnable)
Sets whether or not ToolTips are enabled.

public void setInitialDelay(int delay)
Sets the delay (in milliseconds) determining how long to wait before first showing the ToolTip.

public void setLightWeightPopupEnabled(boolean aFlag)
Deprecated. Use `setToolTipWindowUsePolicy(int)`.

public void setReshowDelay(int delay)
Sets the delay (in milliseconds) between repeated showings of the ToolTip.

```
public static ToolTipManager sharedInstance()
```
    Returns the (single) ToolTipManager object.
```
public void unregisterComponent(JComponent component)
```
    Unregisters component from the ToolTip manager (thus disabling any ToolTips for it).

Protected Fields
```
protected boolean heavyWeightPopupEnabled
protected boolean lightWeightPopupEnabled
```
    If either field is true, allows the ToolTip window algorithm to use that kind of window.

Inner Classes
```
protected class ToolTipManager.insideTimerAction
protected class ToolTipManager.outsideTimerAction
protected class ToolTipManager.stillInsideTimerAction
```

    See also   JToolTip (p.391).

swing.ToolTipManager.insideTimerAction

INNER CLASS

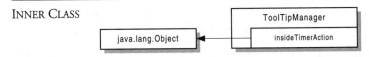

The timer event sent when the timer expires, letting the ToolTip know it has been inside the component for long enough to show.
```
protected class insideTimerAction extends java.lang.Object
    implements java.awt.event.ActionListener
```

Methods
```
public void actionPerformed(java.awt.event.ActionEvent e)
```
    Implements: actionPerformed in interface ActionListener.

swing.ToolTipManager.outsideTimerAction

INNER CLASS

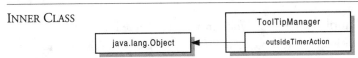

The timer event sent when the timer expires, letting the ToolTip know it has been outside the component for long enough to disappear.
```
protected class outsideTimerAction extends java.lang.Object
    implements java.awt.event.ActionListener
```

Methods
```
public void actionPerformed(java.awt.event.ActionEvent e)
```
    Implements: actionPerformed in interface ActionListener.

swing.ToolTipManager.stillInsideTimerAction

INNER CLASS

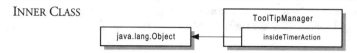

The timer event sent when the timer expires, letting the ToolTip know it has been inside the component and showing for long enough to disappear.

```
protected class stillInsideTimerAction extends java.lang.Object
    implements java.awt.event.ActionListener
```

Methods
```
public void actionPerformed(java.awt.event.ActionEvent e)
```
Implements: `actionPerformed` in interface `ActionListener`.

swing.UIDefaults

CLASS

These provide a mapping of default values for look and feel. Use `UIManager` to change these values.

The `getUI()` method is the heart of the look and feel approach: for a given component, it locates the look and feel class that will do the work of displaying that component.

See the chapter on look and feel for more information.

To keep from having to build copies of every object that could potentially be used by a look and feel, this class defines two public interfaces:

```
public interface UIDefaults.LazyValue {
   Object createValue(UIDefaults table); }
public interface UIDefaults.ActiveValue {
   Object createValue(UIDefaults table); }
```

A `LazyValue` is not created until it is needed. Once created, the value is stored for the next time. An `ActiveValue` is created each time it is requested. (See `get()` below.) To use these, you might use an anonymous inner class like this:

```
Object myObject = new LazyValue {
   Object createValue(UIDefaults table) { return new JButton("test");}
} ;
myDefaults.put("button", myObject);
```

When `get()` is called, it will call the `createValue()` routine, and get the new button.

```
public class UIDefaults extends java.util.Hashtable
```

Constructors
```
public UIDefaults()
```
Creates a `UIDefaults` which defines no mapping.

```
public UIDefaults(Object[] mapPairs)
```
Creates a `UIDefaults` with an initial mapping. The `mapPairs` should be a sequence of values—a `String` which is the key, followed by an object which is the value. (You may use any number of keys and values.)

Methods

```
public synchronized void addPropertyChangeListener(
    java.beans.PropertyChangeListener listener)
```
Adds `listener` to be notified when any property changes.

```
public synchronized Object get(Object key)
```
Gets the value for `key`. If the value is a `LazyValue`, instantiates it and replaces the table value by the instantiated value (and returns the instantiated value). If the value is an `ActiveValue`, instantiates it and returns the instantiated value (but leaves the `ActiveValue` in the table).

```
public Border getBorder(Object borderKey)
```
If the value associated with `borderKey` is a `swing.border.Border` object, returns it; otherwise, returns `null`.

```
public java.awt.Color getColor(Object colorKey)
```
If the value associated with `colorKey` is a `java.awt.Color` object, returns it; otherwise, returns `null`.

```
public java.awt.Dimension getDimension(Object key)
```
If the value associated with `key` is a `Dimension`, returns it; otherwise, returns `null`.

```
public java.awt.Font getFont(Object fontKey)
```
If the value associated with `fontKey` is a `java.awt.Font` object, returns it; otherwise, returns `null`.

```
public Icon getIcon(Object iconKey)
```
If the value associated with `iconKey` is an `Icon` object, returns it; otherwise, returns `null`.

```
public java.awt.Insets getInsets(Object key)
```
If the value associated with `key` is an `Insets`, returns it; otherwise, returns `null`.

```
public int getInt(Object key)
```
If the value associated with `key` is an `Integer`, returns its integer value; otherwise, returns `0`.

```
public String getString(Object stringKey)
```
If the value associated with `stringKey` is a `java.lang.String` object, returns it; otherwise, returns `null`.

```
public ComponentUI getUI(JComponent component)
```
Locates the look and feel delegate object associated with `component`. To do this, first use the `getUIClassID()` method of `JComponent`. (For example, `someButton.getUIClassID()` returns `ButtonUI`.) The look and feel will provide a mapping from that string to the name of the corresponding `ComponentUI` class. This method will use the class method `createUI()` to construct the actual `ComponentUI` instance that is returned. (See `getUIClass()`, `getUIError()`, and the chapter on look and feel.)

```
public Class getUIClass(String classKey)
```
Locates the class corresponding to `(String) classKey`. Returns `Class.forName(get(classKey))`. If there is no class corresponding to `classKey`, returns `null`.

```
public Class getUIClass(String uiClassID, ClassLoader uiClassLoader)
```
Locates the class corresponding to `(String) uiClassID`. Returns `Class.forName(get(uiClassID))`. If there is no class corresponding to `uiClassID`, returns `null`.

public synchronized Object put(Object key, Object value)

Associates `value` with `key`. Notifies any listeners if the value is new (or changed).

public synchronized void putDefaults(Object[] mapPairs)

As in the constructor, `mapPairs` is a list of keys and values. Rather than notifying for each property individually, this method sends one change notice with `UIDefaults` as the value of the property.

public synchronized void removePropertyChangeListener (
java.beans.PropertyChangeListener listener)

Removes `listener` from the set of objects notified of property value changes.

Protected Methods

protected void firePropertyChange(String property,
Object oldValue, Object newValue)

Notifies any listeners that `property` has changed from `oldValue` to `newValue`.

protected void getUIError(String errorMessage)

Called by `getUI()` if it is unable to find a suitable `ComponentUI`. Prints the `errorMessage`.

Inner Classes

public static interface UIDefaults.ActiveValue
public static interface UIDefaults.LazyValue

Returned by   BasicLookAndFeel.getDefaults() (p.621), LookAndFeel.getDefaults() (p.423), UIManager.getDefaults() (p.455), UIManager.getLookAndFeelDefaults() (p.455).

See also   Border (p.465), ComponentUI (p.530), Icon (p.183).

swing.UIDefaults.ActiveValue

INNER
INTERFACE

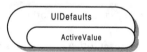

This interface allows creating objects for the `UIDefaults` table that will return a new instance every time they are retrieved from the table. The best way to use this interface is to use it in the creation of an anonymous inner class as shown in the example.

Example: This segment of code shows how to create an `ActiveValue` that returns new instances of `BasicComboBoxEditor` every time it is looked up in the `UIDefaults` table.

```
Object comboBoxEditorActiveValue = new UIDefaults.ActiveValue() {
  public Object createValue(UIDefaults table) {
    return new BasicComboBoxEditor.UIResource();
  }
};
uiDefaultsTable.put("MultiInstanceComboBoxEditor",
  comboBoxEditorActiveValue);
```

public static interface UIDefaults.ActiveValue

Methods

public abstract Object createValue(UIDefaults table)

Override this method to create and return a new instance of the value.

swing.UIDefaults.LazyValue

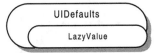

This interface allows creating objects for the `UIDefaults` table that will only be created when needed, and will only be created once per entry in the table. The best way to use this interface is to use it in the creation of an anonymous inner class as shown in the example.

Example: Here's an example of a `LazyValue` that constructs a shared `MatteBorder`:

```
Object matteBorderLazyValue = new UIDefaults.LazyValue() {
  public Object createValue(UIDefaults table) {
    return new BorderFactory.createMatteBorder(5,5,5,5,java.awt.Color.red);
  }
};
uiDefaultsTable.put("RedBorder", matteBorderLazyValue);
```

public static interface UIDefaults.LazyValue

Methods

public abstract Object createValue(UIDefaults table)

Creates and returns an instance of the implementing class. This method will only be called once per table entry, since its return value will actually replace the object in the table. The object returned should not implement this interface. If you want a new instance of the object to be returned every time the key is looked up, use the `UIDefaults.ActiveValue` interface.

swing.UIManager

CLASS

This class manages the current look and feel and the three `UIDefaults` tables. The three `UIDefaults` tables are for defaults set by the user, set by the look and feel, and those set by the system. When looking for a given key, the tables are searched in that order. It is important to note that changing the look and feel only changes the middle (look and feel) table. This means that any custom values that may have been set by an application are preserved when the look and feel changes.

public class UIManager extends java.lang.Object
    implements java.io.Serializable

Constructors

public UIManager()

Creates a `UIManager`. Only one is needed; most of the interesting methods are static.

Methods

public static void addAuxiliaryLookAndFeel(LookAndFeel laf)

Adds a `LookAndFeel` to the list of auxiliary look and feels.

public static synchronized void addPropertyChangeListener(
java.beans.PropertyChangeListener listener)

Adds `listener` to the list of objects to be notified when any property changes its value.

public static Object get(Object key)

Gets the value associated with `key`.

public static LookAndFeel[] getAuxiliaryLookAndFeels()

For the Multi look and feel, returns a list of the other look and feels beside the default one to be used in creating the multiplexed look and feel.

public static Border getBorder(Object borderKey)

If the value associated with `borderKey` is a `swing.border.Border` object, returns it; otherwise, returns `null`.

public static java.awt.Color getColor(Object colorKey)

If the value associated with `colorKey` is a `java.awt.Color` object, returns it; otherwise, returns `null`.

public static String getCrossPlatformLookAndFeelClassName()

Returns the name of the cross platform look and feel.

public static UIDefaults getDefaults()

Gets the object that manages the default look and feel, used if none other is provided.

public static java.awt.Dimension getDimension(Object key)

Returns a `Dimension` from the defaults table.

public static java.awt.Font getFont(Object fontKey)

If the value associated with `fontKey` is a `java.awt.Font` object, returns it; otherwise, returns `null`.

public static Icon getIcon(Object iconKey)

If the value associated with `iconKey` is an `Icon` object, returns it; otherwise, returns `null`.

public static Insets getInsets(Object key)

Returns an `Insets` object from the defaults table.

public static UIManager.LookAndFeelInfo[] getInstalledLookAndFeels()

Returns an array of information about the look and feels known to Swing.

public static int getInt(Object key)

Returns an `int` from the defaults table.

public static LookAndFeel getLookAndFeel()

Gets the current look and feel.

public static UIDefaults getLookAndFeelDefaults()

Returns the current `UIDefaults` table.

public static String getString(Object stringKey)

If the value associated with `stringKey` is a `java.lang.String` object, returns it; otherwise, returns `null`.

public static String getSystemLookAndFeelClassName()

Returns the name of the look and feel native to the underlying platform. If none is found, the cross platform look and feel's name is returned.

public static ComponentUI getUI(JComponent component)

Locates the look and feel delegate object associated with `component`. To do this, first uses the `getUIClassID()` method of `JComponent`. (For example, `someButton.getUIClassID()`

returns `ButtonUI`.) The look and feel will provide a mapping from that string to the name of the corresponding `ComponentUI` class. This method uses the class method `createUI()` to construct the actual `ComponentUI` instance that is returned. (See `UIDefaults`, and the chapter on look and feel.)

public static void installLookAndFeel(UIManager.LookAndFeelInfo info)
Installs the look and feel defined by `info`.

public static void installLookAndFeel(String name,
String className)
Installs the look and feel defined by `name` and `className`.

public static Object put(Object key, Object value)
Associates `value` with `key`. Notifies any listeners if the value is new (or changed).

public static boolean removeAuxiliaryLookAndFeel(LookAndFeel laf)
Removes `laf` from the list of installed auxiliary look and feels.

public static synchronized void removePropertyChangeListener(
java.beans.PropertyChangeListener listener)
Removes `listener` from the list of objects to be notified when a property changes.

public static void setInstalledLookAndFeels(
UIManager.LookAndFeelInfo[] infos) throws java.lang.SecurityException
Replaces the current list of installed look and feels.

public static void setLookAndFeel(LookAndFeel laf)
throws UnsupportedLookAndFeelException
Makes `laf` be the new look and feel. Notifies any listeners if this is a change. If the look and feel is not supported on this platform, throws the exception.

public static void setLookAndFeel(String lafName)
throws ClassNotFoundException, InstantiationException,
IllegalAccessException, UnsupportedLookAndFeelException
Looks up `lafName` to locate the corresponding look and feel, and makes that be the new look and feel. Notifies any listeners if this is a change. Several things could go wrong:

- If the named class cannot be found, throws `java.lang.ClassNotFoundException`.
- If the named class cannot be instantiated, throws `java.lang.InstantiationException` or `java.lang.IllegalAccessException` as appropriate.

Throws: `UnsupportedLookAndFeelException` if the look and feel is not supported on this platform.

Inner Classes
public static class UIManager.LookAndFeelInfo

See also Border (p.465), ComponentUI (p.530), Icon (p.183), LookAndFeel (p.423), UIDefaults (p.452).

swing.UIManager.LookAndFeelInfo

INNER CLASS

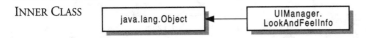

public static class UIManager.LookAndFeelInfo
extends java.lang.Object

Constructors
public LookAndFeelInfo(String name, String className)
> Constructs a new LookAndFeelInfo instance with the given name and class name.

Methods
public String getClassName()
> Returns the fully qualified class name of the associated look and feel.

public String getName()
> Returns the name of the look and feel.

public String toString()
> *Overrides:* toString in class Object.

> *Returned by* UIManager.getInstalledLookAndFeels() (p.455).
> *See also* LookAndFeel (p.423).

swing.UnsupportedLookAndFeelException

CLASS

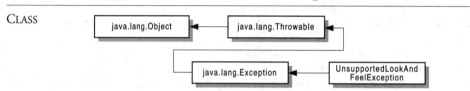

This exception is thrown when you try to set a look and feel on a platform it doesn't support. For example, the Windows and Macintosh look and feels cause this exception to be thrown on any platform other than their native one.

```
public class UnsupportedLookAndFeelException
    extends java.lang.Exception
```

Method
public UnsupportedLookAndFeelException(String s)
> This exception is thrown should you attempt to use a look and feel that isn't supported on your platform. (For example, the Windows look and feel might not be permitted under UNIX.)

> *Thrown by* UIManager.setLookAndFeel() (p.455).

swing.ViewportLayout

CLASS

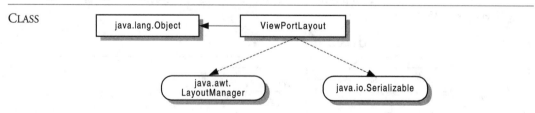

ViewportLayout is the default layout manager for JViewport. When the viewport is smaller than the contents, the contents are kept flush with the bottom of the viewport. When the viewport is larger than the contents, the contents are kept flush with the top of the viewport.

```
public class ViewportLayout extends java.lang.Object
    implements java.awt.LayoutManager, java.io.Serializable
```

Constructors
```
public ViewportLayout()
```
Creates a ViewportLayout, the default for a JViewPort.

Methods
```
public void addLayoutComponent(String name, java.awt.Component component)
```
Implements: addLayoutComponent in interface LayoutManager.
```
public void layoutContainer(java.awt.Container parent)
```
Implements: layoutContainer in interface LayoutManager.
```
public java.awt.Dimension minimumLayoutSize(java.awt.Container parent)
```
Implements: minimumLayoutSize in interface LayoutManager.
```
public java.awt.Dimension preferredLayoutSize(java.awt.Container parent)
```
Implements: preferredLayoutSize in interface LayoutManager.
```
public void removeLayoutComponent(java.awt.Component component)
```
Implements: removeLayoutComponent in interface LayoutManager.

swing.WindowConstants

INTERFACE   WindowConstants

```
public interface WindowConstants
```

Fields
```
public static final int DISPOSE_ON_CLOSE = 2
public static final int DO_NOTHING_ON_CLOSE = 0
public static final int HIDE_ON_CLOSE = 1
```
These constants are values for the setDefaultCloseOperation() in the implementing classes. They describe how the window should react to its close box being clicked. For DISPOSE_ON_CLOSE, any WindowListeners are notified, and the window is automatically hidden and closed. For DO_NOTHING_ON_CLOSE, WindowListeners are notified but there is no other action. For HIDE_ON_CLOSE, WindowListeners are notified and the window is merely hidden. *Default:* HIDE_ON_CLOSE.

Implemented by   JDialog (p.226), JInternalFrame (p.254), JFrame (p.248).

Package swing.border

All components in Swing can have borders attached. This offers the developer a high degree of design flexibility in changing the application's appearance even without resorting to a custom look and feel. Swing gives a developer the ability to have buttons with rounded corners, sunken or raised panels, or whatever combination of effects the developer wants.

Border extends/implements hierarchy

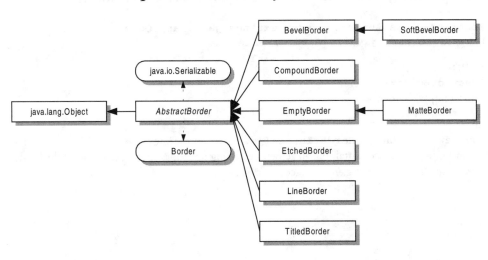

461

Quick summary

Key interface	`Border` (p.465) draws a border around a component. Use the `setBorder()` method in `JComponent` (p.207) to install a border.
How to use	If possible, use `BorderFactory` (p.129) to create an instance of `Border` since it will reuse border instances when it is able to do so.
Implementation	`AbstractBorder` (p.462) provides a basic border implementation as a basis for custom borders.
Concrete classes	`BevelBorder` (p.463), `CompoundBorder` (p.466), `EmptyBorder` (p.467), `EtchedBorder` (p.468), `LineBorder` (p.470), `MatteBorder` (p.471), `SoftBevelBorder` (p.472), `TitledBorder` (p.473).
Notes	Swing uses `EmptyBorder`s instead of `java.awt.Insets` to reserve space around components.

FAQs

My JButton stops working properly when I put a different Border on it. Why?

Some components have specialized `Border`s supplied by the look and feel which really shouldn't be replaced. `JButton` is one of them. See the Other keys table in *appendix B: UIDefaults Table Standard Keys* on page 1017 for a list of the components which have a default look and feel border.

swing.border.AbstractBorder

ABSTRACT
CLASS

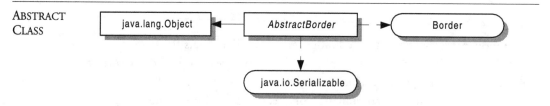

This class fully implements the `Border` interface, so it is a convenient basis for new borders you might create. It provides an empty border; its subclasses provide an actual border.

```
public abstract class AbstractBorder extends java.lang.Object
    implements Border, java.io.Serializable
```

Constructors
```
public AbstractBorder()
```
Creates an (empty) border.

Methods
```
public java.awt.Insets getBorderInsets(java.awt.Component c)
```
Returns an `Insets` instance containing all zeroes, indicating no empty space is left around the border. *Implements:* `getBorderInsets` in interface `Border`.

```
public java.awt.Insets getBorderInsets(java.awt.Component component,
    java.awt.Insets insets)
```
Sets the values in the insets parameter to this Border's current Insets. The component is the component associated with this Border. It is required because a single Border can be shared among many components.

```
public java.awt.Rectangle getInteriorRectangle(java.awt.Component c,
    int x, int y, int width, int height)
```
An auxiliary method that subtracts the insets from the rectangle, so a component can be told what space is safe to draw in.

```
public static java.awt.Rectangle getInteriorRectangle(
    java.awt.Component c, Border b, int x, int y, int width, int height)
```
An auxiliary method that subtracts the insets from the rectangle, so a component can be told what space is safe to draw in.

```
public boolean isBorderOpaque()
```
Always returns false (subclasses may change this).
Implements: isBorderOpaque in interface Border.

```
public void paintBorder(java.awt.java.awt.Component c,
    java.awt.Graphics g, int x, int y, int width, int height)
```
Called by the associated component to paint the border when required.
Implements: paintBorder in interface Border.

Extended by   BasicBorders.ButtonBorder (p.551), BasicBorders.FieldBorder (p.552), BasicBorders.MarginBorder (p.553), BasicBorders.MenuBarBorder (p.553), BevelBorder (p.463), CompoundBorder (p.466), EmptyBorder (p.467), EtchedBorder (p.468), LineBorder (p.470), MatteBorder (p.471), SoftBevelBorder (p.472), TitledBorder (p.473).
See also   Border (p.465).

swing.border.BevelBorder

CLASS

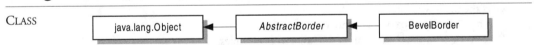

A beveled border resembles a picture frame. In a RAISED bevel, the top and left are light colors (highlight), and the bottom and right are dark (shadow). In a LOWERED bevel, the opposite is true. The bevel is built from two lines (inner and outer). If you don't specify a color, the color is based on the background of the component being painted.

```
public class BevelBorder extends AbstractBorder
```

Constants
```
public static final int LOWERED = 1
public static final int RAISED = 0
```
These values are passed to the constructor as the bevelType.

Constructors

`public BevelBorder(int bevelType)`

Constructs a BevelBorder of the given type that will create the highlight and shadow colors from the component's background color.

`public BevelBorder(int bevelType, java.awt.Color highlight,`
`java.awt.Color shadow)`

`public BevelBorder(int bevelType, java.awt.Color outerHighlight,`
`java.awt.Color innerHighlight, java.awt.Color outerShadow,`
`java.awt.Color innerShadow)`

Creates a beveled border with type specified by `bevelType`, and with the chosen highlight and shadow colors.

Methods

`public int getBevelType()`

Returns `BevelBorder.LOWERED` or `BevelBorder.RAISED`.

`public java.awt.Insets getBorderInsets(java.awt.Component c)`

Overrides: `getBorderInsets` in class `AbstractBorder`.

Implements: `getBorderInsets` in interface `Border`.

`public java.awt.Insets getBorderInsets(java.awt.Component component,`
`java.awt.Insets insets)`

Sets the values in the `insets` parameter to this `Border`'s current `Insets`. The `component` is the component associated with the `Border`. It is required because a single `Border` can be shared among many components.

Overrides: `getBorderInsets` in class `AbstractBorder`.

`public java.awt.Color getHighlightInnerColor(java.awt.Component c)`

`public java.awt.Color getHighlightOuterColor(java.awt.Component c)`

Gets the highlight colors.

`public java.awt.Color getShadowInnerColor(java.awt.Component c)`

`public java.awt.Color getShadowOuterColor(java.awt.Component c)`

Gets the shadow colors.

`public boolean isBorderOpaque()`

Returns `true` if the border paints the full area it occupies.

Overrides: `isBorderOpaque` in class `AbstractBorder`.

Implements: `isBorderOpaque` in interface `Border`.

`public void paintBorder(java.awt.java.awt.Component c,`
`java.awt.Graphics g, int x, int y, int width, int height)`

Overrides: `paintBorder` in class `AbstractBorder`.

Implements: `paintBorder` in interface `Border`.

Protected Fields

`protected int bevelType`

`LOWERED` or `RAISED`.

`protected java.awt.Color highlightInner`
`protected java.awt.Color highlightOuter`
`protected java.awt.Color shadowInner`
`protected java.awt.Color shadowOuter`

The colors used by the border.

Protected Methods

protected void paintLoweredBevel(java.awt.Component component,
    java.awt.Graphics g, int x, int y, int width, int height)
    Paints a lowered bevel onto g for component, of the specified size.

protected void paintRaisedBevel(java.awt.Component component,
    java.awt.Graphics g, int x, int y, int width, int height)
    Paints a raised bevel border onto g for component, of the specified size.

Extended by   BorderUIResource.BevelBorderUIResource (p.525), SoftBevelBorder (p.472).
See also   AbstractBorder (p.462), Border (p.465).

swing.border.Border

INTERFACE   (Border)

This is the main interface all Border objects must implement.

Example

```
Border border = BorderFactory.createTitledBorder("Title");
JLabel label = new JLabel("Test label");
label.setBorder(border);
```

public interface Border
public abstract java.awt.Insets getBorderInsets(java.awt.Component c)
    Computes how much space the border requires.
public abstract boolean isBorderOpaque()
    Returns true if the border promises to paint its own background.
public abstract void paintBorder(java.awt.Component component,
    java.awt.Graphics g, int x, int y, int width, int height)
    Paints the border of component onto g, at the specified position and size.

Implemented by   AbstractBorder (p.462), BasicBorders.SplitPaneBorder (p.554)
BorderUIResource (p.524).
Returned by   BorderFactory.createBevelBorder() (p.129),
BorderFactory.createEmptyBorder() (p.129), BorderFactory.createEtchedBorder() (p.129),
BorderFactory.createLineBorder() (p.129), BorderFactory.createLoweredBevelBorder() (p.129),
BorderFactory.createRaisedBevelBorder() (p.129),
BorderUIResource.getBlackLineBorderUIResource() (p.524),
BorderUIResource.getEtchedBorderUIResource() (p.524),
BorderUIResource.getLoweredBevelBorderUIResource() (p.524),
BorderUIResource.getRaisedBevelBorderUIResource() (p.524),
CompoundBorder.getInsideBorder() (p.466), CompoundBorder.getOutsideBorder() (p.466),
DefaultTreeCellEditor.DefaultTextField.getBorder() (p.968), JComponent.getBorder() (p.207),
JScrollPane.getViewportBorder() (p.332), LineBorder.createBlackLineBorder() (p.470),
LineBorder.createGrayLineBorder() (p.470), TitledBorder.getBorder() (p.473),
UIDefaults.getBorder() (p.452), UIManager.getBorder() (p.455).

border

swing.border.CompoundBorder

A compound border creates a `Border` from two other `Borders` for more advanced effects.

Example

```
package compborder;

import java.awt.*;
import java.awt.event.*;
import com.sun.java.swing.*;
import com.sun.java.swing.border.*;

public class Main extends JFrame {
  JLabel label = new JLabel("A label with some borders");

  public Main () {
    addWindowListener(new WindowAdapter() {
      public void windowClosing(WindowEvent e) {
        Main.this.dispose();
        System.exit(0);
      }
    });
    // Stack up a few borders via CompoundBorder
    Border border1 = new CompoundBorder (
                LineBorder.createBlackLineBorder(),
                BorderFactory.createLineBorder(Color.red, 20));
    Border border2 = new CompoundBorder (
                border1, BorderFactory.createLoweredBevelBorder());

    label.setBorder (border2);
    getContentPane().add(label, BorderLayout.CENTER);
    pack();
  }
  public static void main (String arg[]) {
    Main m = new Main();
    m.setVisible(true);
  }
}
```

public class CompoundBorder extends AbstractBorder

Constructors
public CompoundBorder()
   Creates a compound border, with both inside and outside borders `null`.
public CompoundBorder(Border outsideBorder, Border insideBorder)
   Constructs a compound border using the two given borders. One or both of the borders may already be a CompoundBorder to create complex border effects.

Methods

public java.awt.Insets getBorderInsets(java.awt.Component c)

Returns the sum of the `Insets` for both `Borders`.

Overrides: `getBorderInsets` in class `AbstractBorder`.

Implements: `getBorderInsets` in interface `Border`.

public java.awt.Insets getBorderInsets(java.awt.Component component, java.awt.Insets insets)

Sets the values in the `insets` parameter with the sum of the insets of both `Borders`. The `component` parameter is required because a single `Border` may be shared among many components.

Overrides: `getBorderInsets` in class `AbstractBorder`.

public Border getInsideBorder()

Returns the `Border` being used as the inner border.

public Border getOutsideBorder()

Returns the `Border` being used as the outer border.

public boolean isBorderOpaque()

Only returns `true` if both `Borders` are opaque.

Overrides: `isBorderOpaque` in class `AbstractBorder`.

Implements: `isBorderOpaque` in interface `Border`.

public void paintBorder(java.awt.Component c, java.awt.Graphics g, int x, int y, int width, int height)

Implements: `paintBorder` in interface `Border`.

Protected Fields

protected Border insideBorder
protected Border outsideBorder

The two borders.

Extended by   BorderUIResource.CompoundBorderUIResource (p.525).

Returned by   BorderFactory.createCompoundBorder() (p.129).

See also   AbstractBorder (p.462), Border (p.465).

swing.border.EmptyBorder

CLASS

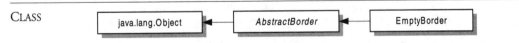

An empty border takes the space indicated in its constructor, but is transparent. If you need a border that occupies space, but is filled, use a `MatteBorder` (p.471).

This class is the preferred way in Swing to give a component an empty margin. Instead of setting the `Insets` on a component, give it an `EmptyBorder`, or a `CompoundBorder` with an `EmptyBorder` as one of its parts.

```
public class EmptyBorder extends AbstractBorder
```

Constructors

public EmptyBorder(int top, int left, int bottom, int right)

```
public EmptyBorder(java.awt.Insets insets)
```
Creates an empty border, with sides of the indicated sizes.

Methods
```
public java.awt.Insets getBorderInsets(java.awt.Component c)
```
Returns an `Insets` object containing the sizes specified in the constructor.
Overrides: `getBorderInsets` in class `AbstractBorder`.
Implements: `getBorderInsets` in interface `Border`.
```
public java.awt.Insets getBorderInsets(java.awt.Component c,
    java.awt.Insets insets)
```
Sets the values in the given insets object to the sizes specified in the constructor.
Overrides: `getBorderInsets` in class `AbstractBorder`.
```
public boolean isBorderOpaque()
```
Returns `false`.
Overrides: `isBorderOpaque` in class `AbstractBorder`.
Implements: `isBorderOpaque` in interface `Border`.
```
public void paintBorder(java.awt.Component c, java.awt.Graphics g,
    int x, int y, int width, int height)
```
Overrides: `paintBorder` in class `AbstractBorder`.
Implements: `paintBorder` in interface `Border`.

Protected Fields
```
protected bottom
protected left
protected top
protected right
```
The sizes of the border margins.

Extended by   BorderUIResource.EmptyBorderUIResource (p.526), MatteBorder (p.471).
See also   AbstractBorder (p.462), Border (p.465), CompoundBorder (p.466).

swing.border.EtchedBorder

CLASS

An etched border looks like a groove. It uses a highlight and shadow color, derived from the component if none is specified.

```
public class EtchedBorder extends AbstractBorder
```

Fields
```
public static final int LOWERED = 1
public static final int RAISED = 0
```
Constants for specifying whether the etching appears raised or lowered.

Constructors

`public EtchedBorder()`

    Creates a lowered etched border which will derive its colors from the background of the component.

`public EtchedBorder(java.awt.Color highlight, java.awt.Color shadow)`

    Creates a lowered etched border that will use the given colors.

`public EtchedBorder(int etchType)`

    Creates an etched border of the given type (either `RAISED` or `LOWERED`) which will derive its colors from the component's background.

`public EtchedBorder(int etchType, java.awt.Color highlight,`
`java.awt.Color shadow)`

    Creates an etched border of the given type (either `RAISED` or `LOWERED`) which will use the given colors.

Methods

`public java.awt.Insets getBorderInsets(java.awt.Component c)`

    Overrides: `getBorderInsets` in class `AbstractBorder`.

    Implements: `getBorderInsets` in interface `Border`.

`public java.awt.Insets getBorderInsets(java.awt.Component c,`
`java.awt.Insets insets)`

    Fills the `insets` parameter with this `Border`'s `Insets`.

    Overrides: `getBorderInsets` in class `AbstractBorder`.

`public int getEtchType()`

    Returns either `EtchedBorder.RAISED` or `EtchedBorder.LOWERED`.

`public java.awt.Color getHighlightColor(java.awt.Component c)`

    Returns the current highlight color.

`public java.awt.Color getShadowColor()`

    Returns the current shadow color.

`public boolean isBorderOpaque()`

    Overrides: `isBorderOpaque` in class `AbstractBorder`.

    Implements: `isBorderOpaque` in interface `Border`.

`public void paintBorder(java.awt.Component c, java.awt.Graphics g,`
`int x, int y, int width, int height)`

    Overrides: `paintBorder` in class `AbstractBorder`.

    Implements: `paintBorder` in interface `Border`.

Protected Fields

`protected int etchType`

    Either `RAISED` or `LOWERED`. Defaults to `LOWERED`.

`protected java.awt.Color highlight`
`protected java.awt.Color shadow`

    The highlight and shadow colors.

    Extended by   BorderUIResource.EtchedBorderUIResource (p.526).

    See also   AbstractBorder (p.462), Border (p.465).

swing.border.LineBorder

CLASS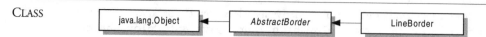

A line border has a specified color and thickness, which is the same on all four sides. The static methods provide a one-pixel-thick black or gray border. If you want the edges to have different thicknesses, use a `MatteBorder` (p.471).

```
public class LineBorder extends AbstractBorder
```

Constructors
public LineBorder(java.awt.Color lineColor)
    Creates a one-pixel-wide `LineBorder` using the given color.
public LineBorder(java.awt.Color lineColor, int thickness)
    Creates a `LineBorder` of the given color and line width.

Methods
public static Border createBlackLineBorder()
    Returns a one-pixel-thick `Color.black` border.
public static Border createGrayLineBorder()
    Returns a one-pixel-thick `Color.gray` border.
public java.awt.Insets getBorderInsets(java.awt.Component c)
    Overrides: `getBorderInsets` in class `AbstractBorder`.
    Implements: `getBorderInsets` in interface `Border`.
public java.awt.Insets getBorderInsets(java.awt.Component c, java.awt.Insets insets)
    Sets the values of the given `insets` parameter to the current `Border` insets.
    Overrides: `getBorderInsets` in class `AbstractBorder`.
public java.awt.Color getLineColor()
    Returns the line color of this border.
public int getThickness()
    Returns the thickness, in pixels, of this border.
public boolean isBorderOpaque()
    Returns `true`.
    Overrides: `isBorderOpaque` in class `AbstractBorder`.
    Implements: `isBorderOpaque` in interface `Border`.
public void paintBorder(java.awt.Component c, java.awt.Graphics g, int x, int y, int width, int height)
    Overrides: `paintBorder` in class `AbstractBorder`.
    Implements: `paintBorder` in interface `Border`.

Protected Fields
protected java.awt.Color lineColor
    The color of the line.
protected boolean roundedCorners
    Default: `false`. This value is currently unused.

```
protected int thickness
```
The thickness of the line (in pixels).

Extended by   BorderUIResource.LineBorderUIResource (p.527).
See also   AbstractBorder (p.462), Border (p.465).

swing.border.MatteBorder

CLASS

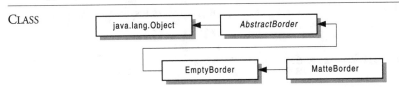

A matte border is a border of either solid color or a repeated `Icon`. When using a solid color, it is similar to a line border but each edge's thickness may be specified independently. (In a LineBorder (p.470), each edge has the same thickness.)

```
public class MatteBorder extends EmptyBorder
```

Constructors
```
public MatteBorder(int top, int left, int bottom, int right,
    java.awt.Color color)
public MatteBorder(int top, int left, int bottom, int right, Icon icon)
```
Creates a border of the specified thickness and fills it with the given `Color` or `Icon`.

Methods
```
public java.awt.Insets getBorderInsets(java.awt.Component c)
```
Overrides: `getBorderInsets` in class `EmptyBorder`.
Implements: `getBorderInsets` in interface `Border`.
```
public boolean isBorderOpaque()
```
Returns `true` when using a `Color`, returns `false` if one of the `Colors` is `null`.
Overrides: `isBorderOpaque` in class `EmptyBorder`.
Implements: `isBorderOpaque` in interface `Border`.
```
public void paintBorder(java.awt.Component c, java.awt.Graphics g,
    int x, int y, int width, int height)
```
Overrides: `paintBorder` in class `EmptyBorder`.
Implements: `paintBorder` in interface `Border`.

Protected Fields
```
protected java.awt.Color color
```
The color of the border.
```
protected Icon tileIcon
```
The `Icon` used to tile the border area.

Extended by   BorderUIResource.MatteBorderUIResource (p.527).
Returned by   BorderFactory.createMatteBorder() (p.129).
See also   AbstractBorder (p.462), Border (p.465), EmptyBorder (p.467), Icon (p.183).

swing.border.SoftBevelBorder

CLASS

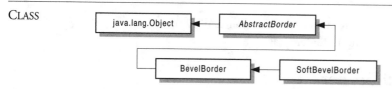

A soft bevel border is similar to a `BevelBorder` (p.463), but it appears less indented or extruded by using thinner lines.

```
public class SoftBevelBorder extends BevelBorder
```

Constructors
```
public SoftBevelBorder(int bevelType)
public SoftBevelBorder(int bevelType, java.awt.Color highlight,
    java.awt.Color shadow)
public SoftBevelBorder(int bevelType, java.awt.Color highlightOuter,
    java.awt.Color highlightInner, java.awt.Color shadowOuter,
    java.awt.Color shadowInner)
```
Creates a bevel border with softer corners. The `bevelType` must be `BevelBorder.LOWERED` or `BevelBorder.RAISED`. By default, the colors are derived from the background color of the component for which this is a border if they are not specified.

Methods
```
public java.awt.Insets getBorderInsets(java.awt.Component c)
```
Overrides: `getBorderInsets` in class `BevelBorder`.
```
public boolean isBorderOpaque()
```
Overrides: `isBorderOpaque` in class `BevelBorder`.
```
public void paintBorder(java.awt.java.awt.Component c,
    java.awt.Graphics g, int x, int y, int width, int height)
```
Overrides: `paintBorder` in class `BevelBorder`.

Protected Fields
```
protected int bevelType
```
`LOWERED` or `RAISED`.
```
protected java.awt.Color highlightInner
protected java.awt.Color highlightOuter
protected java.awt.Color shadowInner
protected java.awt.Color shadowOuter
```
The border colors.

Protected Methods
```
protected void paintLoweredBevel(java.awt.Component c,
    java.awt.Graphics g, int x, int y, int width, int height)
```
Overrides: `paintLoweredBevel` in class `BevelBorder`.

```
protected void paintRaisedBevel(java.awt.Component c,
    java.awt.Graphics g, int x, int y, int width, int height)
```
Overrides: paintRaisedBevel in class BevelBorder.

See also AbstractBorder (p.462), BevelBorder (p.463), Border (p.465).

swing.border.TitledBorder

CLASS

A titled border places a title string on some other border. By default, a title is placed over an etched border, but you can use any border you choose (even another TitledBorder). The title can be placed in one of several vertical positions, and can be placed at left, center, or right.

Subclasses of TitledBorder have access to EDGE_SPACING, TEXT_INSET_H, and TEXT_SPACING so they can use the default spacings and just change how the border is painted.

TitledBorder is unusual. It is the only border that can be changed after it is created.

```
public class TitledBorder extends AbstractBorder
```

Fields
```
public static final int ABOVE_BOTTOM = 4
public static final int ABOVE_TOP = 1
public static final int BELOW_BOTTOM = 6
public static final int BELOW_TOP = 3
public static final int BOTTOM = 5
public static final int CENTER = 2
public static final int DEFAULT_JUSTIFICATION = 0
public static final int DEFAULT_POSITION = 0
public static final int LEFT = 1
public static final int RIGHT = 3
public static final int TOP = 2
```
Constants for representing justification (CENTER, LEFT, or RIGHT) and alignment (ABOVE_TOP, TOP, BELOW_TOP, ABOVE_BOTTOM, BOTTOM, or BELOW_BOTTOM).

Constructors
```
public TitledBorder(String title)
public TitledBorder(Border border)
public TitledBorder(Border border, String title)
public TitledBorder(Border border, String title,
    int titleJustification, int titlePosition)
public TitledBorder(Border border, String title,
    int titleJustification, int titlePosition, java.awt.Font titleFont)
public TitledBorder(Border border, String title, int titleJustification,
    int titlePosition, java.awt.Font titleFont, java.awt.Color titleColor)
```
Creates a titled border.

Defaults: border—etched border, title—empty, titleJustification—LEFT, titlePo-sition—TOP, titleFont—determined by UI, titleColor—determined by UI.

Methods

`public Border getBorder()`
Returns the border part of the compound TitleBorder.

`public java.awt.Insets getBorderInsets(java.awt.Component c)`
Implements: getBorderInsets in interface Border.

`public java.awt.Insets getBorderInsets(java.awt.Component c,`
`    java.awt.Insets insets)`
Fills the values in the insets parameter with the current Border insets.
Overrides: getBorderInsets in class AbstractBorder.

`public java.awt.Dimension getMinimumSize(java.awt.Component c)`
Returns the minimum space needed by the border and the title.

`public String getTitle()`
Returns the title string.

`public java.awt.Color getTitleColor()`
Returns the color of the title string.

`public java.awt.Font getTitleFont()`
Returns the font being used for the title string.

`public int getTitleJustification()`
Returns the horizontal justification of the title: CENTER, LEFT, or RIGHT.

`public int getTitlePosition()`
Returns the vertical position of the title: ABOVE_TOP, TOP, BELOW_TOP, ABOVE_BOTTOM, BOTTOM, or BELOW_BOTTOM.

`public boolean isBorderOpaque()`
Overrides: isBorderOpaque in class AbstractBorder.
Implements: isBorderOpaque in interface Border.

`public void paintBorder(java.awt.Component c, java.awt.Graphics g,`
`    int x, int y, int width, int height)`
Overrides: paintBorder in class AbstractBorder.
Implements: paintBorder in interface Border.

`public void setBorder(Border border)`
Sets the border to use with the string.

`public void setTitle(String title)`
Sets the title string.

`public void setTitleColor(java.awt.Color titleColor)`
Sets the color used to display the title string.

`public void setTitleFont(java.awt.Font titleFont)`
Sets the font used to display the title string.

`public void setTitleJustification(int titleJustification)`
Sets the justification of the title string: CENTER, LEFT, or RIGHT.

`public void setTitlePosition(int titlePosition)`
Sets the position of the title string: ABOVE_TOP, TOP, BELOW_TOP, ABOVE_BOTTOM, BOTTOM, or BELOW_BOTTOM.

Protected Fields

```
protected static final int EDGE_SPACING
protected static final int TEXT_INSET_H
protected static final int TEXT_SPACING
```

Constants defining the size in pixels of various dimensions of the border.

```
protected Border border
protected String title
protected java.awt.Color titleColor
protected java.awt.Font titleFont
protected int titleJustification
protected int titlePosition
```

Values set in the constructor.

Protected Methods

```
protected java.awt.Font getFont(java.awt.Component component)
```

The title font for the border on component.

Extended by   BorderUIResource.TitledBorderUIResource (p.528).
Returned by   BorderFactory.createTitledBorder() (p.129).
See also   AbstractBorder (p.462), Border (p.465).

Package swing.colorchooser

The classes and interfaces in this package support the JColorChooser component.

Colorchooser extends/implements hierarchy

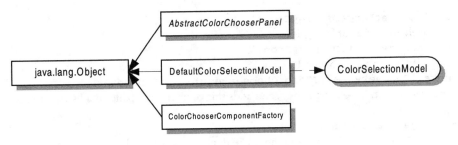

Quick summary

Key interface	ColorSelectionModel (p.479) is the data model interface for the JColorChooser (p.197).
Useful classes	ColorChooserComponentFactory (p.479) constructs and returns an array of standard Color chooser panels.

FAQs

How do I use these classes?

Use a JColorChooser.

swing.colorchooser.AbstractColorChooserPanel

ABSTRACT
CLASS

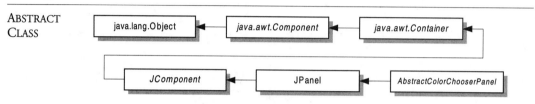

This class is the superclass for all panels which can be used in a JColorChooser.

```
public abstract class AbstractColorChooserPanel extends JPanel
```

Constructors
```
public AbstractColorChooserPanel()
```
Default constructor.

Methods
```
public ColorSelectionModel getColorSelectionModel()
```
Returns the model of the associated JColorChooser, which is the model that will be modified by this color chooser panel.

```
public abstract String getDisplayName()
```
Returns the localized String name to be put on the tab of the tab page which holds this panel in the JColorChooser.

```
public abstract Icon getLargeDisplayIcon()
```
Apparently completely unused as of Swing 1.1.

```
public abstract Icon getSmallDisplayIcon()
```
Apparently completely unused as of Swing 1.1.

```
public void installChooserPanel(JColorChooser enclosingChooser)
```
Calls buildChooser(), updateChooser(), and adds this color chooser panel as a listener to the model of the given JColorChooser.

```
public void paint(java.awt.Graphics g)
```
Simply calls updateChooser(). All painting should be done in that method.
Overrides: paint in class JComponent.

```
public void uninstallChooserPanel(JColorChooser enclosingChooser)
```
Removes this color chooser as a listener list of the JColorChooser.

```
public abstract void updateChooser()
```
This method is where any painting or updating of the panel should occur. To perform the initial update this method is called from installChooserPanel(). It is also called whenever the model of the associated JColorChooser changes and when the paint() method is called.

Protected Methods
protected abstract void buildChooser()
> Use to construct the chooser panel initially.

protected java.awt.Color getColorFromModel()
> Returns the selected `Color` from the associated `JColorChooser`.

> *Returned by* BasicColorChooserUI.createDefaultChoosers() (p.561),
> ColorChooserComponentFactory.getDefaultChooserPanels() (p.479),
> JColorChooser.getChooserPanels() (p.197),
> JColorChooser.removeChooserPanel() (p.197).

> *See also* ColorSelectionModel (p.479), Icon (p.183), JColorChooser (p.197), JPanel (p.305).

swing.colorchooser.ColorChooserComponentFactory

CLASS

This factory class creates a set of `AbstractColorChooserPanel`s that support the standard color models in Java (currently only RGB and HSB, but it is reasonable to expect that the class supplied with JDK 1.2 will support the new models it supplies).

public class ColorChooserComponentFactory extends java.lang.Object

Methods
public static AbstractColorChooserPanel[] getDefaultChooserPanels()
> Returns an array of color chooser panels which support the standard Java color models.

public static JComponent getPreviewPanel()
> Returns an instance of the package class `DefaultPreviewPanel`, which provides a rectangular area that has its background filled in with the selected color, and some sample text for contrast.

> *See also* AbstractColorChooserPanel (p.478), JComponent (p.207).

swing.colorchooser.ColorSelectionModel

INTERFACE ColorSelectionModel

A model that supports selecting a `Color`.

public interface ColorSelectionModel

Methods
public abstract void addChangeListener(ChangeListener listener)
> Adds a listener that gets notified when the model changes.

public abstract java.awt.Color getSelectedColor()
> Returns the selected `Color` from the model.

public abstract void removeChangeListener(ChangeListener listener)
> Removes the given listener from the model.

```
public abstract void setSelectedColor(java.awt.Color color)
```
Sets the model's selected color to `color`. Notifies any listeners if the new color is different than the old color.

Returned by   AbstractColorChooserPanel.getColorSelectionModel() (p.478),
JColorChooser.getSelectionModel() (p.197).
Implemented by   DefaultColorSelectionModel (p.480).

swing.colorchooser.DefaultColorSelectionModel

CLASS

A generic implementation of `ColorSelectionModel`.

```
public class DefaultColorSelectionModel extends java.lang.Object
    implements ColorSelectionModel, java.io.Serializable
```

Constructors
```
public DefaultColorSelectionModel()
```
Default constructor. Initializes `selectedColor` to `Color.white`.
```
public DefaultColorSelectionModel(java.awt.Color color)
```
Initializes `selectedColor` to `color`.

Methods
```
public void addChangeListener(ChangeListener 1)
```
Adds a `ChangeListener` to the model.
Implements: `addChangeListener` in interface `ColorSelectionModel`.
```
public java.awt.Color getSelectedColor()
```
Implements: `getSelectedColor` in interface `ColorSelectionModel`.
```
public void removeChangeListener(ChangeListener 1)
```
Removes a `ChangeListener` from the model.
Implements: `removeChangeListener` in interface `ColorSelectionModel`.
```
public void setSelectedColor(java.awt.Color color)
```
Implements: `setSelectedColor` in interface `ColorSelectionModel`.

Protected Fields
```
protected transient ChangeEvent changeEvent
```
Caches the single instance of `ChangeEvent` that is needed because the source never changes.
```
protected EventListenerList listenerList
```
The list of current listeners.

Protected Methods
```
protected void fireStateChanged()
```
Calls each listener's `stateChanged()` method.

Package swing.event

Events are the tie between models and views.

In the MVC design, views register with models for notification when the model changes. In Swing, the view will usually be a listener of some sort (for example, a JComboBox is an Action-Listener). When a model changes, it creates an event describing the change, and sends the event to each registered listener.

In most cases listeners can add themselves to either the component or the model. Adding a listener to a component is more familiar to AWT programmers, but adding to the model is more flexible. Remember that the same model can represent a category of components, so, if you ever needed to, you could change the component without disturbing the listener code.

The events generally try to describe the change in enough detail that the view can update itself efficiently. For example, TableModelEvent can represent changes ranging in complexity from a change in a single cell to a revision of the whole table structure. In this way, the view needn't examine the whole model for simple changes, but can do so when it is necessary.

ChangeEvent is the exception to this sufficient detail rule. It is intended for components or models which can change value rapidly, such as a JScrollBar, JSlider, or their model BoundedRangeModel. In a ChangeEvent, the only value that ever changes is the source, and it will stay constant for each instance of ChangeEvent. Since it never changes, the same ChangeEvent instance can be reused and the overhead of object creation is removed. This greatly improves the performance of notifying listeners of a change. The caveat of this is that the listeners then have to actively get the new value from the source component or model.

Event extends/inherits hierarchy

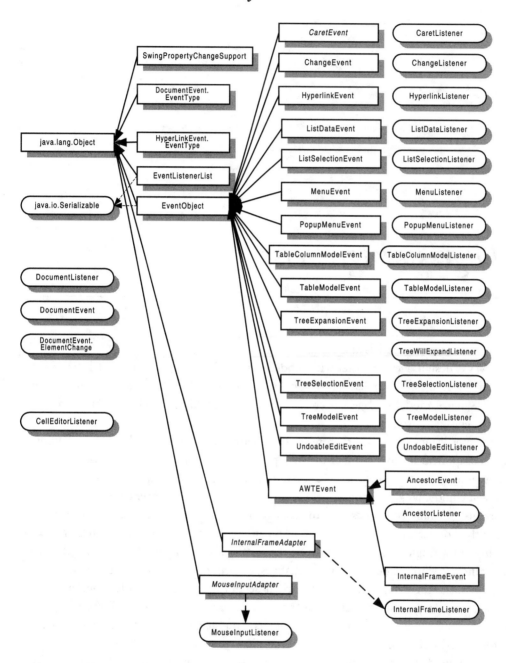

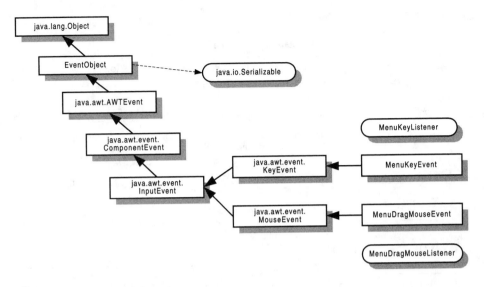

Summary

Event sources and their listeners:

Event sources

Event source	Event/listener interface
JComponent (p.207)	AncestorEvent (p.484)/AncestorListener (p.485)
JTextComponent (p.838)	CaretEvent (p.485)/CaretListener (p.486)
DefaultCellEditor (p.164)	ChangeEvent (p.487)/CellEditorListener (p.486)
AbstractButton (p.118) DefaultBoundedRangeModel (p.159) DefaultButtonModel (p.161) DefaultCaret (p.806) DefaultSingleSelectionModel (p.179) JProgressBar (p.315) JSlider (p.341) JTabbedPane (p.351) JViewport (p.410) StyleContext (p.872)	ChangeEvent (p.487)/ChangeListener (p.488)
AbstractDocument (p.778)	DocumentEvent (p.489)/DocumentListener (p.490)
JEditorPane (p.232)	HyperlinkEvent (p.494)/HyperlinkListener (p.495)
JInternalFrame (p.254)	InternalFrameEvent (p.497)/InternalFrameListener (p.498)
AbstractListModel (p.127)	ListDataEvent (p.498)/ListDataListener (p.499)
DefaultListSelectionModel (p.175) JList (p.271)	ListSelectionEvent (p.499)/ListSelectionListener (p.500)
JMenuItem (p.291)	MenuDragMouseEvent (p.501)/MenuDragMouseListener (p.502)
JMenu (p.281)	MenuEvent (p.502)/MenuListener (p.504)
JMenuItem (p.291)	MenuKeyEvent (p.503)/MenuKeyListener (p.503)

event

Event sources (continued)

Event source	Event/listener interface
JPopupMenu (p.309)	PopupMenuEvent (p.505)/PopupMenuListener (p.506)
DefaultTableColumnModel (p.744)	TableColumnModelEvent (p.507)/TableColumnModelListener (p.508)
AbstractTableModel (p.735)	TableModelEvent (p.508)/TableModelListener (p.510)
JTree (p.357)	TreeExpansionEvent (p.511)/TreeExpansionListener (p.511)/TreeWillExpandListener (p.515)
DefaultTreeModel (p.975)	TreeModelEvent (p.511)/TreeModelListener (p.513)
DefaultTreeSelectionModel (p.978) JTree (p.393)	TreeSelectionEvent (p.513)/TreeSelectionListener (p.514)
UndoableEditSupport (p.1006)	UndoableEditEvent (p.515)/UndoableEditListener (p.516)

swing.event.AncestorEvent

CLASS

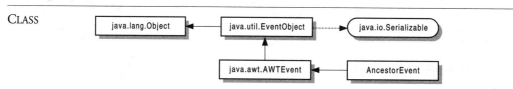

A JComponent (p.207) uses an AncestorEvent to notify listeners when components are added, moved, removed, or made visible or invisible. AncestorListener (p.485) is the interface corresponding to this event.

```
public class AncestorEvent extends java.awt.AWTEvent
```

Constants

```
public static final int ANCESTOR_ADDED = 1
public static final int ANCESTOR_MOVED = 3
public static final int ANCESTOR_REMOVED = 2
```

These are the values for the event ID. See the getID() method of java.awt.AWTEvent.

Constructors

```
public AncestorEvent(JComponent source, int id, java.awt.Container
    ancestor, java.awt.Container parent)
```

Creates an event, indicating that ancestor (an ancestor of source) is participating in an event of type id. The ancestor's parent is also made available.

Methods

```
public java.awt.Container getAncestor()
```

Gets the changing ancestor of the notifying component.

```
public java.awt.Container getAncestorParent()
```

Gets the parent of the ancestor that has changed. You can't just ask the ancestor for this value because if the ancestor were removed it wouldn't know its former parent.

```
public JComponent getComponent()
```
Gets the component that caused the notification. (Use addAncestorListener() on JCompo-nent to request these notifications.)

See also   AncestorListener (p.485), JComponent (p.207).

swing.event.AncestorListener

INTERFACE

An AncestorListener can register interest in what happens to the containment (parent) hierar-chy of a JComponent. See JComponent (p.207) for methods to register an AncestorListener for notifications, and AncestorEvent (p.484) for information about the event.

```
public interface AncestorListener extends java.util.EventListener
```

Methods
```
public abstract void ancestorAdded(AncestorEvent event)
```
Called when an ancestor is made visible by having setVisible(true) called or by being added to a visible containment hierarchy.
```
public abstract void ancestorMoved(AncestorEvent event)
```
Called when an ancestor is moved.
```
public abstract void ancestorRemoved(AncestorEvent event)
```
Called when an ancestor becomes invisible by having setVisible(false) called or by being removed from a visible hierarchy. You will probably want to use AncestorEvent.getAncestor-Parent() to find out about the ancestor's former parent.

See also   AncestorEvent (p.484), JComponent (p.207).

swing.event.CaretEvent

ABSTRACT
CLASS

The caret tracks the text cursor.

The dot is the point where text will next be inserted. The mark is the anchor point of a selection (it may precede or follow the dot). When there is no selection, the dot and the mark are at the same point. When there is a selection, it is the text from the mark to the dot that is selected, and the next typing will replace that selection.

The Craft of Text Editing by Craig Finseth (Springer-Verlag, 1991) describes this approach in detail.

```
public abstract class CaretEvent extends java.util.EventObject
```

Constructors
```
public CaretEvent(Object source)
```
The source is the object reporting the event.

Methods

`public abstract int getDot()`

Returns the point where text will be inserted (after the specified character position).

`public abstract int getMark()`

Returns the start of the current selection; same as the dot when there is no selection.

swing.event.CaretListener

INTERFACE

A `CaretListener` can be attached to a `Document`. It is notified whenever the state of the `Document`'s caret changes.

`public interface CaretListener extends java.util.EventListener`

Methods

`public abstract void caretUpdate(CaretEvent event)`

Receives notifications of a change in the caret (dot and/or mark).

Implemented by   JTextComponent.AccessibleJTextComponent (p.844).
See also   CaretEvent (p.485), Document (p.826).

swing.event.CellEditorListener

INTERFACE

This listener is used by trees and tables for their cells. It detects when editing is canceled (for example, by clicking on a different row) or stopped (with the changes accepted, for example, by pressing RETURN).

`public interface CellEditorListener extends java.util.EventListener`

Methods

`public void editingCanceled(ChangeEvent event)`

Editing has been canceled; the original cell contents should be restored. The `event` describes the object that was being edited.

`public void editingStopped(ChangeEvent event)`

Editing has been stopped, and the changed contents are accepted. The `event` describes the object that was being edited.

Implemented by   BasicTreeUI.CellEditorHandler (p.719), JTable (p.357), JTable.AccessibleJTable (p.369).
Returned by   BasicTreeUI.createCellEditorListener() (p.710).
See also   ChangeEvent (p.487), JTable (p.357), JTree (p.393).

swing.event.ChangeEvent

CLASS

This event describes changes in objects. It is often used to let a view monitor a model object for simple changes. (Many Swing objects generate this event when their important properties change.) It is used as a lightweight notification, since the same event instance can be used for all changes. Do not confuse this event with the `java.beans.PropertyChangeEvent` used by Java-Beans.

Example: Listening to a `JSlider` as it is dragged.

```
package changeevt;

import java.awt.event.*;
// Uncomment the following two lines for Swing 1.0.3 and before
//import com.sun.java.swing.*;
//import com.sun.java.swing.event.*;
// Uncomment the following two lines for Swing 1.1 and JDK 1.2
import javax.swing.*;
import javax.swing.event.*;
public class Main extends JFrame {
   public Main() {
      addWindowListener(new WindowAdapter() {
         public void windowClosing(WindowEvent e) {
            Main.this.dispose();
            System.exit(0);
         }
      });
      JSlider slider = new JSlider();
      BoundedRangeModel model = slider.getModel();
      model.addChangeListener(new ChangeListener() {
         public void stateChanged(ChangeEvent e) {
            // The source of the change is the model.  If we had attached
            // ourselves to the component, the component would
            // be the source instead.
            BoundedRangeModel m = (BoundedRangeModel)e.getSource();
            System.out.println("Slider position changed to " + m.getValue());
         }
      });
      getContentPane().add(slider);
      pack();
   }
   public static void main(String[] args) {
      Main m = new Main();
      m.setVisible(true);
   }
}
```

public class ChangeEvent extends java.util.EventObject

Constructors

public ChangeEvent(Object source)

Creates an event that says a property of source has changed.

See also   ChangeListener (p.488).

swing.event.ChangeListener

This interface allows an object to listen for changes in values of another object. (Many Swing objects generate change events.)

Note that a ChangeListener is not the same as a PropertyChangeListener used by Java-Beans. The PropertyChangeListener listens for changes on a bound property; the Change-Listener listens for state changes on the model object. A ChangeListener is often used by Swing to build the notification mechanism between model and view: the view registers as a ChangeListener on the model, so it receives notifications when the model changes. The view may have listeners as well; the view may propagate the changes to its listeners, perhaps even to a JavaBeans PropertyChangeListener (see JButton (p.191), ButtonModel (p.147), and DefaultButtonModel (p.161) for an example of this listener).

public interface ChangeListener extends java.util.EventListener

Methods

public abstract void stateChanged(ChangeEvent event)

The source object (contained in event) has changed.

Implemented by   AbstractButton.ButtonChangeListener (p.118), BasicButtonListener (p.556), BasicMenuUI.ChangeHandler (p.627), BasicProgressBarUI.ChangeHandler (p.638), BasicScrollBarUI.ModelListener (p.642), BasicScrollPaneUI.HSBChangeListener (p.652), BasicScrollPaneUI.ViewportChangeHandler (p.653), BasicScrollPaneUI.VSBChangeListener (p.653), BasicSliderUI.ChangeHandler (p.661), BasicTabbedPaneUI.TabSelectionHandler (p.687), JMenuItem.AccessibleJMenuItem (p.291), JScrollPane.AccessibleJScrollPane (p.337), JTabbedPane.AccessibleJTabbedPane (p.356), JTabbedPane.ModelListener (p.357).

Returned by   AbstractButton.createChangeListener() (p.118), BasicMenuBarUI.createChangeListener() (p.622), BasicMenuUI.createChangeListener() (p.627), BasicScrollPaneUI.createHSBChangeListener() (p.650), BasicScrollPaneUI.createViewportChangeListener() (p.650), BasicScrollPaneUI.createVSBChangeListener() (p.650), BasicSliderUI.createChangeListener() (p.655), BasicTabbedPaneUI.createChangeListener() (p.679), JProgressBar.createChangeListener() (p.315), JSlider.createChangeListener() (p.341), JTabbedPane.createChangeListener() (p.351).

See also   ChangeEvent (p.487).

swing.event.DocumentEvent

INTERFACE 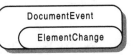 DocumentEvent

This event details the changes made to an element of a document. See the chapter on the swing.text package (p.769), as well as DocumentEvent.ElementChange (p.489), and DocumentEvent.EventType (p.490).

```
public interface DocumentEvent
```

Methods
public DocumentEvent.ElementChange getChange(Element element)
>   Gets the details of changes made to element. (If no changes were made, the result is null.)

public abstract Document getDocument()
>   Returns the document that changed.

public abstract UndoableEdit getEdit()
>   Fetches the undo/redo record associated with this edit.

public abstract int getLength()
>   Returns the length of the change.

public abstract int getOffset()
>   Returns the starting point of the change, relative to the start of the document.

public DocumentEvent.EventType getType()
>   Returns the type of the change. The return value will be DocumentEvent.EventType.CHANGE, DocumentEvent.EventType.INSERT, or DocumentEvent.EventType.REMOVE.

Inner Classes
```
public static interface DocumentEvent.ElementChange
public static class DocumentEvent.ElementType
```

>   *Implemented by*   AbstractDocument.DefaultDocumentEvent (p.789).
>   *See also*   DocumentListener (p.488), Element (p.830).

swing.event.DocumentEvent.ElementChange

INNER
INTERFAC   DocumentEvent
ElementChange

Describes changes made to an element.

```
public static interface DocumentEvent.ElementChange
```

Methods
public abstract Element[] getChildrenAdded()
>   Returns the children that were added to the base element. The elements in the list are sorted according to increasing offset of their start position.

```
public abstract Element[] getChildrenRemoved()
```
Returns the children that were removed from the base element. The elements in the list are sorted according to increasing offset of their start position.
```
public abstract Element getElement()
```
Returns the base element for which the change is being described.
```
public abstract int getIndex()
```
Returns the starting point of the change, relative to the start of the base element.

Implemented by AbstractDocument.ElementEdit (p.790).
Returned by AbstractDocument.DefaultDocumentEvent.getChange() (p.789), DocumentEvent.getChange() (p.489).
See also Element (p.830).

swing.event.DocumentEvent.EventType

INNER CLASS

This type is used by `DocumentEvent` to describe the type of an edit.

```
public static final class DocumentEvent.EventType
```

Constants
```
public static final DocumentEvent.EventType CHANGE
public static final DocumentEvent.EventType INSERT
public static final DocumentEvent.EventType REMOVE
```
These constants define the type of an editing event.

See also DocumentEvent (p.489).

swing.event.DocumentListener

INTERFACE

Receives notification of changes in a document. See `DocumentEvent` (p.489), and the `swing.text` package (p.769).

```
public interface DocumentListener extends java.util.EventListener
```

Methods
```
public abstract void changedUpdate(DocumentEvent event)
```
Returns elements were changed in the document (described by `event`).
```
public abstract void insertUpdate(DocumentEvent event)
```
Returns elements were inserted into the document (described by `event`).
```
public abstract void removeUpdate(DocumentEvent event)
```
Returns elements were deleted from the document (described by `event`).

See also DocumentEvent (p.489).

swing.event.EventListenerList

EventListenerList is a utility class to track listeners. It can accommodate several types of listeners in a single list; when you notify listeners you must take care to notify listeners of the appropriate type.

Why not just keep a list of listeners, without tracking their listener class? Because an object may implement several interfaces; we only want to notify objects that registered in their role as a listener for a particular listener type.

Example

```
package listenerlist;

// Main.java
import java.awt.*;
import java.awt.event.*;
// Uncomment the following two lines for Swing 1.0.3 and before
//import com.sun.java.swing.*;
//import com.sun.java.swing.event.*;
// Uncomment the following two lines for Swing 1.1 and JDK 1.2
import javax.swing.*;
import javax.swing.event.*;

public class Main {
   private class DualListener implements ActionListener, ChangeListener {
      public void actionPerformed(ActionEvent e) {
         System.out.println("dual: Action " + e);
      }

      public void stateChanged(ChangeEvent e) {
         System.out.println("dual: Change " + e);
      }
   }

   public Main() {
      MyPair pair = new MyPair("This is 'a'", "This is 'b'");

      ActionListener al = new ActionListener() {
         public void actionPerformed(ActionEvent e) {
            System.out.println("al: Action " + e);
         }
      };

      DualListener dual = new DualListener();
      pair.addActionListener(al);
      pair.addChangeListener(dual);
      System.out.println("Change a: should see 'al'");
      pair.setA("new A");
      System.out.println("Change b: should see 'dual'");
      pair.setB("new B");
      System.out.println("Add dual as an ActionListener too");
      pair.addActionListener(dual);
      System.out.println("Should see 'al' and 'dual' on 'a'");
```

```java
      pair.setA("another A");
      System.out.println("Remove dual as an ActionListener");
      pair.removeActionListener(dual);
      System.out.println("Dual should still fire for 'b'");
      pair.setB("another B");
      System.out.println("Only al should fire for 'a'");
      pair.setA("final A");
   }

   public static void main (String arg[]) {
      new Main();
   }
}

/////////////////////////////////////////////////////////////////
// MyPair.java
package listenerlist;
import java.awt.*;
import java.awt.event.*;
// Uncomment the following two lines for Swing 1.0.3 and before
//import com.sun.java.swing.*;
//import com.sun.java.swing.event.*;
// Uncomment the following two lines for Swing 1.1 and JDK 1.2
import javax.swing.*;
import javax.swing.event.*;

public class MyPair {
   // Represent an ordered pair
   Object a=null, b=null;
   // Notify ActionListeners when 'a' changes,
   // ChangeListeners when 'b' changes.
   // Notice that both ActionListeners and ChangeListeners
   // are put on the same EventListenerList.
   EventListenerList events = new EventListenerList();
   // ActionListeners: delegate to EventListenerList
   public void addActionListener(ActionListener listener) {
      events.add(ActionListener.class, listener);
   }
   public void removeActionListener(ActionListener listener) {
      events.remove(ActionListener.class, listener);
   }
   // ChangeListeners: delegate to EventListenerList
   public void addChangeListener(ChangeListener listener) {
      events.add(ChangeListener.class, listener);
   }
   public void removeChangeListener(ChangeListener listener) {
      events.remove(ChangeListener.class, listener);
   }
   // Access to 'a' and 'b'
   public Object getA() {return a;}
   public void setA(Object newA) {a = newA; fireAChanged();}

   public Object getB() {return b;}
   public void setB(Object newB) {b = newB; fireBChanged();}

   // Notification for 'a'
   ActionEvent actionEvent;     // start null, create as needed
```

```
      // Notify ActionListeners. Notice that we walk the list
      // in reverse order, that events[i] has the class and
      // events[i+1] the listener, and we create the event only if
      // needed.
      protected void fireAChanged() {
        Object[] listeners = events.getListenerList();
        for (int i = listeners.length-2; i>=0; i-=2) {
          if (listeners[i]==ActionListener.class) {
            if (actionEvent == null) {
              actionEvent = new ActionEvent(
                this,ActionEvent.ACTION_PERFORMED, "a");
            }
            ((ActionListener)listeners[i+1]).actionPerformed(actionEvent);
          }
        }
      }

      // Notification for 'b'
      ChangeEvent changeEvent;    // start null, create as needed

      protected void fireBChanged() {
        Object[] listeners = events.getListenerList();
        for (int i = listeners.length-2; i>=0; i-=2) {
          if (listeners[i]==ChangeListener.class) {
            if (changeEvent == null) {
              changeEvent = new ChangeEvent(this);
            }
            ((ChangeListener)listeners[i+1]).stateChanged(changeEvent);
          }
        }
      }
      public MyPair(Object a1, Object b1) {
        a = a1; b = b1;
      }
    }
```

**public class EventListenerList extends java.lang.Object
    implements java.io.Serializable**

Constructors
public EventListenerList()
    Creates a listener list.

Methods
**public synchronized void add(java.lang.Class class,
    java.util.EventListener listener)**
    Adds listener of type class to the list.
public int getListenerCount()
    Gets the number of listeners.
public int getListenerCount(java.lang.Class class)
    Gets the number of listeners of type class.

public Object[] getListenerList()

Gets the `listenerList` array. This array is always non-`null`, but it may have 0 elements. You should not modify the elements of the returned array, since it is a reference to the actual list. If you really need to modify the elements in the array, use a copy of the array instead.

public synchronized void remove(java.lang.Class class,
java.util.EventListener listener)

Removes the `listener` for `class` from the list. (The `listenerList` may be empty but it will not become `null`.)

public String toString()

Returns a string representation of the `EventListenerList`.

Overrides: `toString` in class `Object`.

Protected Fields

protected transient Object[] listenerList

The list of listeners. The class is stored in `listenerList[2*i]`; its corresponding listener is stored in `listenerList[2*i+1]`. This array is never `null` (though it may have 0 elements).

swing.event.HyperlinkEvent

CLASS

This event describes things that may happen to a hyperlink.

public class HyperlinkEvent extends java.util.EventObject

Constructors

public HyperlinkEvent(Object source, HyperlinkEvent.EventType type,
java.net.URL url)

Creates a hyperlink event for `source`, of `type`, and related to `url`.

Methods

public HyperlinkEvent.EventType getEventType()

Returns the type of link activity: `HyperlinkEvent.EventType.ACTIVATED`, `ENTERED`, or `EXITED`.

public java.net.URL getURL()

Returns the URL for the event.

Inner Classes

public static final class HyperlinkEvent.EventType

See also   HyperlinkEvent.EventType (p.495), HyperlinkListener (p.495).

swing.event.HyperlinkEvent.EventType

INNER CLASS

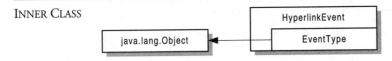

These constants describe things that happen to hyperlinks.

```
public static final class HyperlinkEvent.EventType
    extends java.lang.Object
```

Constants

```
public static final HyperlinkEvent.EventType ACTIVATED
```
Indicates that the link has been activated (e.g., by a mouse click).

```
public static final HyperlinkEvent.EventType ENTERED
```
Indicates that the link has been entered (as when the mouse moves over the link, without clicking). (This would allow you to add rollover effects.)

```
public static final HyperlinkEvent.EventType EXITED
```
Indicates that the link has been left (as when the mouse moves off the link, without clicking). (This would allow you to add rollover effects.)

Methods

```
public String toString()
```
Overrides: toString in class Object.

Returned by   HyperlinkEvent.getEventType() (p.494).
See also   HyperlinkEvent (p.494), HyperlinkListener (p.495).

swing.event.HyperlinkListener

INTERFACE

A notification of hyperlink activity.

```
public interface HyperlinkListener extends java.util.EventListener
```

Methods

```
public abstract void hyperlinkUpdate(HyperlinkEvent e)
```
Returns notification that something has happened to a hyperlink.

See also   HyperlinkEvent (p.494), HyperlinkEvent.EventType (p.495).

swing.event.InternalFrameAdapter

CLASS

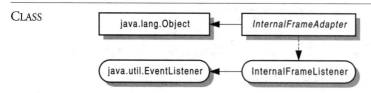

This is a fully implemented abstract class (all its methods are fully implemented; you just need to declare a subclass). By subclassing it, you can define handlers for the particular internal frame event(s) you want to handle, rather than being required to handle them all.

```
public abstract class InternalFrameAdapter
    implements InternalFrameListener
```

Constructors

```
public InternalFrameAdapter()
```
Creates the adapter.

Methods

```
public void internalFrameActivated(InternalFrameEvent event)
```
The frame is now the active (focused) window.

Implements: internalFrameActivated in interface InternalFrameListener.

```
public void internalFrameClosed(InternalFrameEvent event)
```
The frame has closed.

Implements: internalFrameClosed in interface InternalFrameListener.

```
public void internalFrameClosing(InternalFrameEvent event)
```
The frame is about to close. (It will only actually close if hide() or dispose() is called on the frame. This allows for things like a frame that can only close if the user has saved changes.)

Implements: internalFrameClosing in interface InternalFrameListener.

```
public void internalFrameDeactivated(InternalFrameEvent event)
```
The frame is no longer the active window.

Implements: internalFrameDeactivated in interface InternalFrameListener.

```
public void internalFrameDeiconified(InternalFrameEvent event)
```
The frame has deiconified, meaning it has been returned to full size after it was an icon.

Implements: internalFrameDeiconified in interface InternalFrameListener.

```
public void internalFrameIconified(InternalFrameEvent event)
```
The frame has been iconified.

Implements: internalFrameIconified in interface InternalFrameListener.

```
public void internalFrameOpened(InternalFrameEvent event)
```
The frame has been opened, created, and made visible. (This event happens only once in the lifetime of a frame.)

Implements: internalFrameOpened in interface InternalFrameListener.

See also   InternalFrameEvent (p.497), InternalFrameListener (p.498).

swing.event.InternalFrameEvent

CLASS

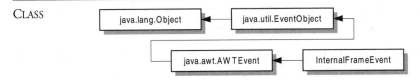

This event type describes things that happen to an internal frame. See `InternalFrameAdapter` and `InternalFrameListener`, and also `java.awt.event.WindowEvent` (as this event is a close relative of that one).

`public class InternalFrameEvent extends java.awt.AWTEvent`

Constants

`public static final int INTERNAL_FRAME_ACTIVATED = 25554`
  The frame is now the active window (it receives keystrokes and actions).

`public static final int INTERNAL_FRAME_CLOSED = 25551`
  The frame has closed.

`public static final int INTERNAL_FRAME_CLOSING = 25550`
  The frame is closing. Sent before the frame is actually closed; the listener must call `dispose()` or `hide()` to actually close the frame.

`public static final int INTERNAL_FRAME_DEACTIVATED = 25555`
  The frame is no longer the active window.

`public static final int INTERNAL_FRAME_DEICONIFIED = 25553`
  The frame is no longer iconified.

`public static final int INTERNAL_FRAME_FIRST = 25549`
  This constant corresponds to the least `INTERNAL_FRAME_xxx` constant.

`public static final int INTERNAL_FRAME_ICONIFIED = 25552`
  The frame has been iconified.

`public static final int INTERNAL_FRAME_LAST = 25555`
  This constant corresponds to the greatest `INTERNAL_FRAME_xxx` constant.

`public static final int INTERNAL_FRAME_OPENED = 25549`
  The frame has been opened. (This occurs only once in the frame's lifetime.)

Constructors

`public InternalFrameEvent(JInternalFrame source, int id)`
  Creates an internal frame event, of type `id`, that applies to the frame `source`. You can obtain the `source` from the event by the `getSource()` method of `java.util.EventObject`, and the `id` by the `getID()` method of java.awt.AWTEvent.

Methods

`public String paramString()`
  Returns a `String` containing the properties of this event. The returned `String` may be empty but it will not be `null`.
  Overrides: `paramString` in class `AWTEvent`.

  See also   InternalFrameAdapter (p.496), InternalFrameListener (p.498).

event

swing.event.InternalFrameListener

INTERFACE

java.util.EventListener ◄— InternalFrameListener

This listener receives notification of events on internal frames. See `InternalFrameAdapter`, which implements an abstract class for this listener type, and `InternalFrameEvent`.

```
interface InternalFrameListener extends java.util.EventListener
```

Methods

public void internalFrameActivated(InternalFrameEvent event)
> The frame is now the active (focused) window.

public void internalFrameClosed(InternalFrameEvent event)
> The frame has closed.

public void internalFrameClosing(InternalFrameEvent event)
> The frame is about to close. (It will only actually close if `hide()` or `dispose()` is called on the frame. This allows you to program a frame that can only close if the user has saved changes.)

public void internalFrameDeactivated(InternalFrameEvent event)
> The frame is no longer the active window.

public void internalFrameDeiconified(InternalFrameEvent event)
> The frame has deiconified, meaning it has been returned to full size after it was an icon.

public void internalFrameIconified(InternalFrameEvent event)
> The frame has been iconfied.

public void internalFrameOpened(InternalFrameEvent event)
> The frame has been opened, created, and made visible. (This event only happens once in the lifetime of a frame.)

> *Implemented by*   InternalFrameAdapter (p.496),
> BasicInternalFrameUI.BasicInternalFrameListener (p.609).
> *See also*   InternalFrameAdapter (p.496), InternalFrameEvent (p.497).

swing.event.ListDataEvent

CLASS

java.lang.Object ◄— java.util.EventObject ◄— ListDataEvent

This event describes changes in a list.

```
public class ListDataEvent extends java.util.EventObject
```

Fields

```
public static final int CONTENTS_CHANGED = 0
public static final int INTERVAL_ADDED = 1
public static final int INTERVAL_REMOVED = 2
```
> These constants correspond to the type of the event.

Constructors

`public ListDataEvent(Object source, int type, int index0, int index1)`

Creates an event indicating that the `source` list has changed from `index0` to `index1` (inclusive). The change `type` is `CONTENTS_CHANGED`, `INTERVAL_ADDED`, or `INTERVAL_REMOVED`.

Methods

`public int getIndex0()`

Returns the starting row for changes.

`public int getIndex1()`

Returns the ending row for changes. (The range is from `index0` to `index1`, inclusive.)

`public int getType()`

Returns the type of the change; it will be `CONTENTS_CHANGED`, `INTERVAL_ADDED`, or `INTERVAL_REMOVED`.

See also   ListDataListener (p.499).

swing.event.ListDataListener

INTERFACE

`public interface ListDataListener extends java.util.EventListener`

Methods

`public void contentsChanged(ListDataEvent event)`

The list has changed: rows `event.getIndex0()` to `event.getIndex1()` have changed their contents. The change may merely be changes in the values of list items, or it may include rows being added or deleted.

`public void intervalAdded(ListDataEvent event)`

The list has changed: rows `event.getIndex0()` to `event.getIndex1()` are new.

`public void intervalRemoved(ListDataEvent event)`

The list has changed: rows `event.getIndex0()` to `event.getIndex1()` have been deleted.

Returned by   BasicComboBoxUI.createListDataListener() (p.565), BasicComboPopup.createListDataListener() (p.572), BasicListUI.createListDataListener() (p.614). *Implemented by*   BasicComboBoxUI.ListDataHandler (p.571), BasicComboPopup.ListDataHandler (p.577), BasicListUI.ListDataHandler (p.614), JComboBox (p.200), JList.AccessibleJList (p.277).

swing.event.ListSelectionEvent

CLASS

This event describes changes in a list selection.

`public class ListSelectionEvent extends java.util.EventObject`

Constructors
public ListSelectionEvent(java.lang.Object source, int firstIndex,
    int lastIndex, boolean isAdjusting)

In the list `source`, the selection from `firstIndex` to `lastIndex` (inclusive, `firstIndex <= lastIndex`) may have changed. The *source* must be consulted to find the exact status of each of these items. If `isAdjusting` is `true`, more changes are expected (as when a mouse drag is selecting a number of items).

Methods
public int getFirstIndex()

Gets the position of the first entry that has changed its selection status.

public int getLastIndex()

Gets the position of the last entry that has changed its selection status.

public boolean getValueIsAdjusting()

Returns `True` if more changes are likely.

public String toString()

Overrides: `toString` in class `EventObject`.

See also   ListSelectionListener (p.500).

swing.event.ListSelectionListener

INTERFACE

This listener is notified that the associated list's selection has changed.

Example: listening for changes of selection in a `JList`.

```
package sellistener;
import java.awt.*;
import java.awt.event.*;
// Uncomment the following two lines for Swing 1.0.3 and before
//import com.sun.java.swing.*;
//import com.sun.java.swing.event.*;
// Uncomment the following two lines for Swing 1.1 and JDK 1.2
import javax.swing.*;
import javax.swing.event.*;

public class Main extends JFrame {
    public Main() {
        addWindowListener(new WindowAdapter() {
            public void windowClosing(WindowEvent e) {
                Main.this.dispose();
                System.exit(0);
            }
        });

        String items[] = {"Alice", "Bob", "Charles", "Donna" };
        JList list = new JList(items);
        ListSelectionModel selModel = list.getSelectionModel();

        selModel.addListSelectionListener(new ListSelectionListener() {
```

```
    public void valueChanged(ListSelectionEvent e) {
      // The getValueIsAdjusting check is used to prevent this
      // listener from recognizing selection changes that are part of
      //a larger change
      if (!e.getValueIsAdjusting()) {
        System.out.println("selection changed: " + e.getFirstIndex());
      }
    }
  });
  getContentPane().add(list);
  pack();
  setVisible(true);
  }
  public static void main(String[] args) {
    Main m = new Main();
  }
}
public interface ListSelectionListener
    extends java.util.EventListener
```

Methods

public abstract void valueChanged(ListSelectionEvent event)

The selection has changed. See event for information about the change.

Returned by   BasicComboPopup.createListSelectionListener() (p.572),
BasicFileChooserUI.createListSelectionListener() (p.587),
BasicListUI.createListSelectionListener() (p.614).

Implemented by   BasicComboPopup.ListSelectionHandler (p.579),
BasicFileChooserUI.SelectionListener (p.594), BasicListUI.ListSelectionHandler (p.614),
DefaultTableColumnModel (p.744), JList.AccessibleJList (p.277), JTable (p.357),
JTable.AccessibleJTable (p.369).

See also   ListSelectionEvent (p.499), ListSelectionModel (p.421).

swing.event.MenuDragMouseEvent

CLASS

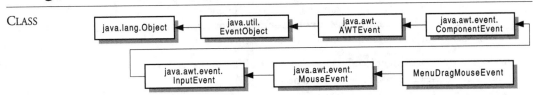

A MenuDragMouseEvent is used to notify listeners that a given menu item has received a mouse
event while the mouse is being dragged. An example of the need for this event is in the Basic look
and feel, where the mouse changes the selection as it is being dragged.

public class MenuDragMouseEvent extends java.awt.event.MouseEvent

Constructors

```
public MenuDragMouseEvent(java.awt.Component source, int type,
    long timeOccurred, int modifiers, int xPos, int yPos,
    int clickCount, boolean isPopupTrigger,
    MenuElement[] pathToMenuItem, MenuSelectionManager m)
```
Constructs a `MenuDragMouseEvent` object. The `type` parameter is one of the following: `MOUSE_CLICKED`, `MOUSE_DRAGGED`, `MOUSE_ENTERED`, `MOUSE_EXITED`, `MOUSE_MOVED`, `MOUSE_PRESSED`, or `MOUSE_RELEASED`. The `modifiers` parameter is one of the following: `ALT_MASK`, `CTRL_MASK`, `META_MASK`, or `SHIFT_MASK`.

Methods

```
public MenuSelectionManager getMenuSelectionManager()
```
Returns the menu selection manager for this event.
```
public MenuElement[] getPath()
```
Returns the path to the menu item.

See also   MenuElement (p.425), MenuSelectionManager (p.426).

swing.event.MenuDragMouseListener

INTERFACE

This listener is notified when the mouse is dragged through a menu.

```
public interface MenuDragMouseListener
    extends java.util.EventListener
```

Methods

```
public abstract void menuDragMouseDragged(MenuDragMouseEvent e)
```
Called when the mouse is dragged inside a menu component.
```
public abstract void menuDragMouseEntered(MenuDragMouseEvent e)
```
Called when the mouse is dragged into a menu component.
```
public abstract void menuDragMouseExited(MenuDragMouseEvent e)
```
Called when the mouse is dragged out of a menu component.
```
public abstract void menuDragMouseReleased(MenuDragMouseEvent e)
```
Called when the mouse is released while it is inside a menu component.

Returned by   BasicMenuItemUI.createMenuDragMouseListener() (p.624),
BasicMenuUI.createMenuDragMouseListener() (p.627).

swing.event.MenuEvent

CLASS

This event is used to inform listeners that a menu has changed its state.

```
public class MenuEvent extends java.util.EventObject
```

Constructors

public MenuEvent(Object source)

Creates an event for menu `source`.

See also MenuListener (p.504).

swing.event.MenuKeyEvent

CLASS

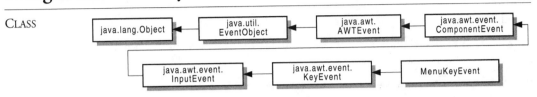

`MenuKeyEvent` is used to notify interested parties that the menu element has received a `KeyEvent` forwarded to it in a menu tree.

public class MenuKeyEvent extends java.awt.event.KeyEvent

Constructors

public MenuKeyEvent(java.awt.event.Component source, int type, long when, int modifiers, int keyCode, char keyChar, MenuElement[] pathToAffectedMenuItem, MenuSelectionManager m)

Constructs a `MenuKeyEvent` object. The `type` parameter is one of `KEY_PRESSED`, `KEY_RELEASED`, or `KEY_TYPED`.

Methods

public MenuSelectionManager getMenuSelectionManager()

Returns the menu selection manager for this event.

public MenuElement[] getPath()

Returns the path to the menu item affected by this event.

See also MenuElement (p.425), MenuKeyListener (p.503), MenuSelectionManager (p.426).

swing.event.MenuKeyListener

INTERFACE

public interface MenuKeyListener extends java.util.EventListener

Methods

public abstract void menuKeyPressed(MenuKeyEvent e)

Called when a key has been pressed in the menu.

public abstract void menuKeyReleased(MenuKeyEvent e)

Called when a key has been released in the menu.

public abstract void menuKeyTyped(MenuKeyEvent e)

Called when a key has been typed (pressed and released) in the menu.

Returned by   BasicMenuItemUI.createMenuKeyListener() (p.624),
BasicMenuUI.createMenuKeyListener() (p.627).

swing.event.MenuListener

INTERFACE

Notification of events that happen to menus.

```
public interface MenuListener extends java.util.EventListener
```

Methods
```
public abstract void menuCanceled(MenuEvent event)
```
The menu was canceled.
```
public abstract void menuDeselected(MenuEvent event)
```
The menu that had been selected is no longer selected.
```
public abstract void menuSelected(MenuEvent event)
```
The menu was selected.

See also   MenuEvent (p.502).

swing.event.MouseInputAdapter

CLASS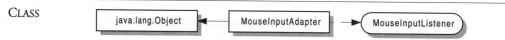

This is the standard adapter class for the `MouseInputListener` interface. It supplies empty implementations of all methods in the interface so that classes extending from this one only need to override the methods they are interesed in.

```
public abstract class MouseInputAdapter extends java.lang.Object
    implements MouseInputListener
```

Constructors
```
public MouseInputAdapter()
```
Default constructor.

Methods
```
public void mouseClicked(java.awt.event.MouseEvent e)
```
Implements: mouseClicked in interface MouseInputListener.
```
public void mouseDragged(java.awt.event.MouseEvent e)
```
Implements: mouseDragged in interface MouseInputListener.
```
public void mouseEntered(java.awt.event.MouseEvent e)
```
Implements: mouseEntered in interface MouseInputListener.
```
public void mouseExited(java.awt.event.MouseEvent e)
```
Implements: mouseExited in interface MouseInputListener.

```
public void mouseMoved(java.awt.event.MouseEvent e)
```
Implements: mouseMoved in interface MouseInputListener.
```
public void mousePressed(java.awt.event.MouseEvent e)
```
Implements: mousePressed in interface MouseInputListener.
```
public void mouseReleased(java.awt.event.MouseEvent e)
```
Implements: mouseReleased in interface MouseInputListener.

Extended by BasicDesktopIconUI.MouseInputHandler (p.581),
BasicInternalFrameUI.BorderListener (p.609), BasicSliderUI.TrackListener (p.663).
Returned by BasicInternalFrameUI.createBorderListener() (p.605).

swing.event.MouseInputListener

INTERFACE

This interface is a utility interface. It extends the MouseListener and MouseMotionListener interfaces to provide one interface that handles all mouse events.

```
public interface MouseInputListener
    extends java.awt.event.MouseListener,
    java.awt.event.MouseMotionListener
```

Implemented by BasicInternalFrameUI.GlassPaneDispatcher (p.611),
BasicListUI.MouseInputHandler (p.619), BasicMenuItemUI.MouseInputHandler (p.627),
BasicTableHeaderUI.MouseInputHandler (p.689), BasicTableUI.MouseInputHandler (p.693),
BasicToolBarUI.DockingListener (p.706), BasicTreeUI.MouseInputHandler (p.722),
MouseInputAdapter (p.504).
Returned by BasicDesktopIconUI.createMouseInputListener() (p.580),
BasicInternalFrameUI.createGlassPaneDispatcher() (p.605),
BasicListUI.createMouseInputListener() (p.614),
BasicMenuItemUI.createMouseInputListener() (p.624),
BasicMenuUI.createMouseInputListener() (p.627),
BasicTableHeaderUI.createMouseInputListener() (p.688),
BasicTableUI.createMouseInputListener() (p.690), BasicToolBarUI.createDockingListener() (p.702).

swing.event.PopupMenuEvent

CLASS

This event is used to inform listeners that a pop-up menu has changed its state.

```
public class PopupMenuEvent extends java.util.EventObject
```

Constructors

public PopupMenuEvent(Object source)

    Creates an event for the pop-up menu source.

See also   PopupMenuListener (p.505).

swing.event.PopupMenuListener

INTERFACE

Notification of events that happen to pop-up menus.

public interface PopupMenuListener extends java.util.EventListener

Methods

public abstract void popupMenuCanceled(PopupMenuEvent event)

    The pop-up menu was canceled.

**public abstract void popupMenuWillBecomeInvisible(
PopupMenuEvent event)**

    The pop-up menu is about to become invisible.

public abstract void popupMenuWillBecomeVisible(PopupMenuEvent event)

    The pop-up menu is about to become visible.

See also   PopupMenuEvent (p.505).

swing.event.SwingPropertyChangeSupport

CLASS

This class is a reimplementation of the PropertyChangeSupport class to remove thread-safety and list copying from the methods which fire the events to listeners. Since Swing is not thread-safe, the overhead of locking those methods is unnecessary.

**public final class SwingPropertyChangeSupport
    extends java.beans.PropertyChangeSupport**

Constructors

public SwingPropertyChangeSupport(Object sourceBean)

    Constructs a SwingPropertyChangeSupport instance which will use sourceBean as its source.

Methods

**public synchronized void addPropertyChangeListener(
PropertyChangeListener listener)**

    Adds a PropertyChangeListener to the listener list. The listener will be notified when any property in the source object changes.

    Overrides: addPropertyChangeListener in class PropertyChangeSupport.

```
public synchronized void addPropertyChangeListener(String
    propertyName, PropertyChangeListener listener)
```
Adds a PropertyChangeListener to the listener list. The listener will be notified only when the
property named propertyName changes.
```
public void firePropertyChange(PropertyChangeEvent evt)
```
Sends the given PropertyChangeEvent to all registered listeners. If the events old and new values
are the same and not null, the event will *not* be sent.
```
public void firePropertyChange(String propertyName, Object oldValue,
    Object newValue)
```
Sends a PropertyChangeEvent to all listeners registered for the given property. If oldValue and
newValue are equal and not null the event will *not* be sent.

Overrides: firePropertyChange in class PropertyChangeSupport.
```
public synchronized boolean hasListeners(String propertyName)
```
Returns true if there are any listeners registered for the given property.
```
public synchronized void removePropertyChangeListener(
    java.beans.PropertyChangeListener listener)
```
Removes the given PropertyChangeListener from the listener list.

Overrides: removePropertyChangeListener in class PropertyChangeSupport.
```
public synchronized void removePropertyChangeListener(String
    propertyName, java.beans.PropertyChangeListener listener)
```
Removes a PropertyChangeListener for a specific property from the listener list.

swing.event.TableColumnModelEvent

event

CLASS

This event describes what happens when a column is added, deleted, or moved.

```
public class TableColumnModelEvent extends java.util.EventObject
```

Constructors
```
public TableColumnModelEvent(TableColumnModel source, int fromIndex,
    int toIndex)
```
Creates an event for source. (See the field descriptions above for fromIndex and toIndex.)

Methods
```
public int getFromIndex()
public int getToIndex()
```
Returns the indices of the affected columns. (See their field descriptions above.)

Protected Fields
```
protected int fromIndex
```
For an added column, this field is unused. For a deleted column, this is the column number of the
deleted column. For a moved column, this is the former index of the moved column.

```
protected int toIndex
```
For an added column, this is the index of the new column. For a deleted column, this field is unused. For a moved column, this is the new index of the moved column.

See also   JTable (p.357), TableColumn (p.761), TableColumnModelListener (p.508).

swing.event.TableColumnModelListener

INTERFACE

Notification of events that happen to a table's column model.

```
public interface TableColumnModelListener
    extends java.util.EventListener
```

Methods

```
public abstract void columnAdded(TableColumnModelEvent event)
```
A column has been added to the table. The event tells which column model was affected, and the index of the new column.

```
public abstract void columnMarginChanged(ChangeEvent event)
```
A change in the size of the margin. The event tells which column model has changed.

```
public abstract void columnMoved(TableColumnModelEvent event)
```
A column has moved in the table. The event tells which column model was affected, and the old and new indices of that column.

```
public abstract void columnRemoved(TableColumnModelEvent event)
```
A column has been removed from the table. The event tells which column model was affected, and the index of the removed column.

```
public abstract void columnSelectionChanged(ListSelectionEvent event)
```
The column selection has changed. The event tells which column model was affected, and the range of indices that could be affected.

Implemented by   JTable (p.357), JTable.AccessibleJTable (p.369), JTableHeader (p.752).
See also   ChangeEvent (p.487), ListSelectionEvent (p.499), TableColumnModelEvent (p.507).

swing.event.TableModelEvent

CLASS

This event describes changes in the data or structure of a table. In order to allow the view to efficiently update itself, the event allows for fine-grained description of changes.

Type of change	Sample event
One cell	`TableModelEvent(source, row, row, column)`
One row	`TableModelEvent(source, row)`

Type of change	Sample event
One column	`TableModelEvent(source, 0, last, column)`
Partial column	`TableModelEvent(source, first, last, column)`
Range of rows	`TableModelEvent(source, first, last)`
All data changed	`TableModelEvent(source)`
Table structure	`TableModelEvent(source, HEADER_ROW)`

(These examples covered the UPDATE type; you can also specify that DELETE or INSERT occurred.)

```
public class TableModelEvent extends java.util.EventObject
```

Fields

```
public static final int ALL_COLUMNS = -1
```
When used as the value for the column, implies all columns have changed.

```
public static final int HEADER_ROW = -1
```
When used as the value for the row, implies that the column structure has changed.

```
public static final int DELETE = -1
public static final int INSERT = 1
public static final int UPDATE = 0
```
These values describe the type of a change.

Constructors

```
public TableModelEvent(TableModel source, int firstRow, int lastRow,
    int column, int type)
```
Says that the source has changed, from firstRow to lastRow (inclusive) in the named column. If firstRow is HEADER_ROW, this implies that the whole table has changed, including the column structure (so the table must be completely refreshed). The column may be ALL_COLUMNS to indicate that all columns have changed. The type of change is one of DELETE, INSERT, or UPDATE. (For DELETE, the range of rows is the deleted rows; for INSERT, it is the newly inserted rows; for UPDATE, it is the changed rows.)

```
public TableModelEvent(TableModel source)
```
Says the contents of the whole table have changed (but not its structure). Equivalent to: `TableModelEvent(source, 0, source.getRowCount()-1, ALL_COLUMNS, UPDATE)`.

```
public TableModelEvent(TableModel source, int firstRow)
```
Says that the contents of a particular row have changed. If that row is HEADER_ROW, it implies that the whole structure of the table has changed. Equivalent to:
`TableModelEvent(source, firstRow, firstRow, ALL_COLUMNS, UPDATE)`.

```
public TableModelEvent(TableModel source, int firstRow, int lastRow)
```
Says that the contents of a range of rows have changed. If firstRow is HEADER_ROW, the whole table structure has changed. Equivalent to:
`TableModelEvent(source, firstRow, lastRow, ALL_COLUMNS, UPDATE)`.

```
public TableModelEvent(TableModel source, int firstRow, int lastRow,
    int column)
```
Says that the contents of a range of rows have changed, but only in a particular column. If firstRow is HEADER_ROW, the whole table structure has changed. If column is ALL_COLUMNS, it indicates

that all columns in the affected rows have changed. Equivalent to:

```
TableModelEvent(source, firstRow, lastRow, column, UPDATE).
```

Methods

public int getColumn()

Gets the affected column. If this value is ALL_COLUMNS, all columns are affected.

public int getFirstRow()

Gets the start of the range of affected rows. If this value is HEADER_ROW, the whole table structure has changed; there may be a completely new set of columns (HEADER_ROW would not be used if only the table's data has changed).

public int getLastRow()

Gets the end of the range of affected rows.

public int getType()

Gets the type of the change; this value will be one of DELETE, INSERT, or UPDATE.

Protected Fields

protected int column

The affected column. May have the value ALL_COLUMNS, implying all columns have changed.

protected int firstRow

The first affected row. May have the value HEADER_ROW, implying that the table structure has changed.

protected int lastRow

The last affected row.

protected int type

The type of change; one of DELETE, INSERT, or UPDATE.

See also   JTable (p.357), TableModel (p.766), TableModelListener (p.510).

swing.event.TableModelListener

INTERFACE

This listener is notified when a table's data have changed.

public interface TableModelListener extends java.util.EventListener

Methods

public abstract void tableChanged(TableModelEvent event)

The table has changed its data. The event tells which table was affected, and the rows and/or columns that changed.

Implemented by   JTable (p.357), JTable.AccessibleJTable (p.369).
See also   TableModel (p.766), TableModelEvent (p.508).

swing.event. TreeExpansionEvent

CLASS

This event describes a tree node expanding or collapsing.

```
public class TreeExpansionEvent extends java.util.EventObject
```

Constructors
```
public TreeExpansionEvent(Object source, TreePath path)
```
Creates an expansion event. The same event covers both expanding and collapsing; see `TreeExpan-sionListener`. The `source` is a `JTree`; the `path` is the path to the node that has changed.

Methods
```
public TreePath getPath()
```
Returns the `path` that has been expanded or collapsed.

Protected Fields
```
protected TreePath path
```
Returns the `path` that has been expanded or collapsed.

See also JTree (p.393), TreeExpansionListener (p.511), TreePath (p.989).

swing.event. TreeExpansionListener

INTERFACE

Notification that a tree node has collapsed or expanded. Listeners of this type are notified after the change has occurred. `TreeWillExpandListener` listeners are informed before the change occurs.

```
public interface TreeExpansionListener
    extends java.util.EventListener
```

Methods
```
public abstract void treeCollapsed(TreeExpansionEvent event)
```
The tree described in `event` has collapsed (its subtree is now hidden).
```
public abstract void treeExpanded(TreeExpansionEvent event)
```
The tree described in `event` has expanded (its subtree is now exposed).

See also TreeExpansionEvent (p.511).

swing.event. TreeModelEvent

CLASS

Describes a change in the model of a tree. The event describes the parent of the nodes that have changed.

```
public class TreeModelEvent extends java.util.EventObject
```

Constructors

```
public TreeModelEvent(Object source, TreePath path)
```
The tree source has changed. The path is the path to the parent of the affected nodes.

```
public TreeModelEvent(Object source, TreePath path,
    int[] childIndices, Object[] children)
```
The tree source has changed. The path is to the parent of the affected nodes. The nodes are at childIndices under the parent, and their actual values are children.

```
public TreeModelEvent(Object source, Object[] path)
```
The tree source has changed. The path is the path of nodes to the parent of the affected nodes.

```
public TreeModelEvent(Object source, Object[] path,
    int[] childIndices, Object[] children)
```
The tree source has changed. The path is the path of nodes to the parent of the affected nodes. The nodes are at childIndices under the parent, and their actual values are children.

Methods

```
public int[] getChildIndices()
```
Gets the indices of the affected nodes (under the parent identified by the path). The indices are in ascending order.

```
public Object[] getChildren()
```
Returns the affected children nodes, corresponding to the childIndices. (However, in a deletion, the children will no longer be present, and childIndices will indicate their former position.)

```
public Object[] getPath()
```
Returns the path to the parent of the affected nodes (found by looking up each node in the tree path).

```
public TreePath getTreePath()
```
Returns the path to the parent of the affected nodes.

```
public String toString()
```
Returns a string that displays this object's properties.
Overrides: toString in class EventObject.

Protected Fields

```
protected int[] childIndices
```
The positions of the nodes that have changed (beneath the parent). The indices are in increasing order.

```
protected Object[] children
```
The children of the affected node. (Looked up via the childIndices.)

```
protected TreePath path
```
The path to the affected node.

See also JTree (p.393), TreeModelListener (p.513), TreePath (p.989).

swing.event.TreeModelListener

INTERFACE

Notification of changes in a tree's data model.

```
public interface TreeModelListener extends java.util.EventListener
```

Methods
public abstract void treeNodesChanged(TreeModelEvent event)
   Returns nodes in the tree that have changed their value, but not their position or their children. The child indices in the event indicate the positions of the changed nodes.

public abstract void treeNodesInserted(TreeModelEvent event)
   Returns nodes that have been inserted into the tree. The child indices indicate the positions of the new nodes.

public abstract void treeNodesRemoved(TreeModelEvent event)
   Returns nodes that have been removed from the tree. The child indices indicate the former positions of the deleted nodes. This notification need only occur once, describing the topmost node of a deleted subtree (and need not occur for each subtree of the deleted node).

public abstract void treeStructureChanged(TreeModelEvent event)
   The tree's structure has changed too much to be described by the other methods. All nodes beneath the path may have changed; if the path has only one node, that is now the root of the tree.

   Implemented by BasicTreeUI.TreeModelHandler (p.727), JTree.AccessibleJTree (p.402), JTree.TreeModelHandler (p.409).
   Returned by BasicTreeUI.createTreeModelListener() (p.710), JTree.createTreeModelListener() (p.393).
   See also DefaultTreeModel (p.975), JTree (p.393), TreeModel (p.987).

swing.event.TreeSelectionEvent

CLASS

Describes a change in the selected nodes of a tree. The selection is described as a set of paths.

```
public class TreeSelectionEvent extends java.util.EventObject
```

Constructors
public TreeSelectionEvent(Object source, TreePath path,
   boolean isNew, TreePath oldLeadSelectionPath,
   TreePath newLeadSelectionPath)
   Creates an event describing a change in the selection for the tree `source`. The `path` is to be added to the selection if `isNew` is `true`, or deleted if `false`. Tells the `path` to use as the lead selection before and after the `path` is added.

```
public TreeSelectionEvent(Object source, TreePath[] paths,
    boolean[] areNew, TreePath oldLeadSelectionPath,
    TreePath newLeadSelectionPath)
```
Creates an event describing a change in the selection for the tree source. The paths are to be added to the selection if areNew is true (for the corresponding position), or deleted if false. Tells the path to use as the lead selection before and after the path is added.

Methods

```
public Object cloneWithSource(Object newSource)
```
Clones the event, but replaces the source with newSource.

```
public TreePath getNewLeadSelectionPath()
```
Gets the current lead selection path.

```
public TreePath getOldLeadSelectionPath()
```
Gets the previous lead selection path.

```
public TreePath getPath()
```
Returns the first path (in paths[]).

```
public TreePath[] getPaths()
```
Returns the list of all paths that are to change their selection status.

```
public boolean isAddedPath()
```
Returns true if the first path is to be added to the selection; returns false if it is to be deleted from the selection.

```
public boolean isAddedPath(TreePath path)
```
Returns true if path is to be added to the selection; returns false if it is to be deleted from the selection.

Protected Fields

```
protected boolean[] areNew
```
For each path in paths[], tell if it is to be added (if true) or deleted.

```
protected TreePath newLeadSelectionPath
```
Tells the path to be the lead selection path after the event takes place. May be null.

```
protected TreePath oldLeadSelectionPath
```
Tells the path to be the lead selection path before the event takes place. May be null.

```
protected TreePath[] paths
```
The set of paths to change their selection status. See areNew().

See also   TreeModelListener (p.513), TreePath (p.989), TreeSelectionModel (p.990).

swing.event.TreeSelectionListener

INTERFACE

Notification that the tree's selection has changed.

```
public interface TreeSelectionListener
    extends java.util.EventListener
```

Methods

`public abstract void valueChanged(TreeSelectionEvent event)`

Notification that the tree's selection has changed, as described by event.

Implemented by BasicTreeUI.TreeSelectionHandler (p.728), DefaultTreeCellEditor (p.968), JTree.AccessibleJTree (p.402), JTree.TreeSelectionRedirector (p.410).
Returned by BasicTreeUI.createTreeSelectionListener() (p.710).
See also JTree (p.393), TreeSelectionEvent (p.513), TreeSelectionModel (p.990).

swing.event.TreeWillExpandListener

INTERFACE

This listener is notified just *before* a tree expands or collapses a node. `TreeExpansionListener` listeners are notified of the change after it occurs. The major difference is that listeners of this type are allowed to veto the change.

```
public interface TreeWillExpandListener
    extends java.util.EventListener
```

Methods

`public abstract void treeWillCollapse(TreeExpansionEvent event)`
`   throws ExpandVetoException`
Invoked whenever a node in the tree is about to be collapsed.
`public abstract void treeWillExpand(TreeExpansionEvent event)`
`   throws ExpandVetoException`
Invoked whenever a node in the tree is about to be expanded.

See also ExpandVetoException (p.982), TreeExpansionEvent (p.511), TreeExpansionListener (p.511).

swing.event.UndoableEditEvent

CLASS

Describes an undoable edit.

`public class UndoableEditEvent extends java.util.EventObject`

Constructors

`public UndoableEditEvent(java.lang.Object source, UndoableEdit edit)`
Creates an event, indicating that edit took place on source.

Methods

`public UndoableEdit getEdit()`
Gets the edit that occurred.

See also UndoableEdit (p.1005), UndoableEditListener (p.516).

swing.event.UndoableEditListener

INTERFACE

Notification of an undoable edit.

```
public interface UndoableEditListener extends java.util.EventListener
```

Methods
```
public abstract void undoableEditHappened(UndoableEditEvent event)
```
Indicates that an undoable edit happened, as described by event.

Implemented by   UndoManager (p.1008).
See also   UndoableEditEvent (p.515).

Package swing.filechooser

The classes in this package exist to support the `JFileChooser` component.

Filechooser extends/implements hierarchy

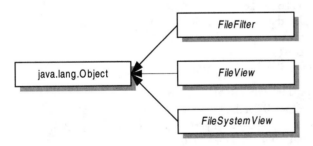

Quick summary

Key classes	This package defines only three classes. Of the three, you will generally mostly use `FileFilter` (p.518) which changes which files are shown in the `JFileChooser` (p.239).

FAQs

How do I use these classes?

See the example given with the `JFileChooser` class (p.239).

swing.filechooser.FileFilter

ABSTRACT
CLASS

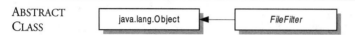

The `FileFilter` class is used by a `JFileChooser` to control what the user sees in the chooser. The main part of `FileFilter` is its `accept()` method. A file or directory will only be shown in the chooser if this method returns `true`. The `getDescription()` method is used to get the `String` to display in the file chooser's list of available filters.

Note that a default implementation of this class is not supplied. `JFileChooser` does supply a `getAcceptAllFileFilter()` method to return a subclass of this class that does not reject any files or directories.

Example: See `JFileChooser` (p.239).

```
public abstract class FileFilter extends java.lang.Object
```

Constructors
```
public FileFilter()
```
Default constructor.

Methods
```
public abstract boolean accept(java.io.File f)
```
Returns `true` if the file chooser is to display the given file. Note that the `FileSystemView` class can still make the file hidden.
```
public abstract String getDescription()
```
Returns a localized `String` describing which files this filter accepts.

Extended by : BasicFileChooserUI.AcceptAllFileFilter (p.587).
Returned by BasicFileChooserUI.getAcceptAllFileFilter() (p.587),
FileChooserUI.getAcceptAllFileFilter() (p.533), JFileChooser.getAcceptAllFileFilter() (p.239),
JFileChooser.getChoosableFileFilters() (p.239), JFileChooser.getFileFilter() (p.239).

swing.filechooser.FileSystemView

ABSTRACT
CLASS

`FileSystemView` provides a way for `JFileChooser` to find out about the filesystem of the current underlying platform.

It supports a few generic concepts, such as a "home" directory and finding the root (or roots) of the filesystem.

The current implementation of this class makes a reasonable effort to discover and support the features of Windows, UNIX, and the Macintosh. The term "reasonable" is used because the current set of `io` classes in Java provide very little information about the filesystem. In particular, the `io` classes provide no support for platform-specific ideas such as "drive letters" under Windows.

A reasonable idea until Java provides greater support for identifying and using platform-specific filesystem features would be to create a subclass of this class which uses native methods. You could reasonably create one subclass for each major platform and/or the platforms you know you are going to run on. In situations where the platform cannot be identified you could then fall back to the support provided in this class.

```
public abstract class FileSystemView extends java.lang.Object
```

Constructors
```
public FileSystemView()
```
Default constructor.

Methods
```
public java.io.File createFileObject(java.io.File dir, String filename)
```
Creates a `File` of the given name in the given directory.
```
public java.io.File createFileObject(String path)
```
Creates a `File` of the given name in the current directory.
```
public abstract java.io.File createNewFolder(
    java.io.File containingDir) throws IOException
```
Creates a `File` representing a directory using a standard name (in this class, "New Folder" is used).
```
public static FileSystemView getFileSystemView()
```
Returns a `FileSystemView` representing the underlying filesystem. Currently this factory method will return a Windows, UNIX, Macintosh, or generic `FileSystemView`, depending on what it can discover.
```
public java.io.File[] getFiles(java.io.File dir, boolean useFileHiding)
```
Returns an array of the `Files` in the given directory. If *useFileHiding* is true, the `isHidden-File()` method will be called and any `Files` that have `false` returned will not be included in the array.
```
public java.io.File getHomeDirectory()
```
Returns the user's home directory, or the directory the `JFileChooser` will default to when opened.
```
public java.io.File getParentDirectory(java.io.File dir)
```
Returns the parent directory of the given `File`, or `null` if *dir* represents the root directory.
```
public abstract java.io.File[] getRoots()
```
Returns any filesystem root directories. Under UNIX this method returns a single `File` for '/', while Windows and the Macintosh return an entry for each of their drives.
```
public abstract boolean isHiddenFile(java.io.File f)
```
Returns `true` if *f* should not be shown.
```
public abstract boolean isRoot(java.io.File f)
```
Returns `true` if *f* is the root directory of a drive.

Returned by　JFileChooser.getFileSystemView() (p.239),
FileSystemView.getFileSystemView() (p.518).

swing.filechooser.FileView

CLASS

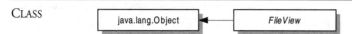

The `FileView` class controls how a `File` is displayed in the `JFileChooser`. This class controls which `Icon` gets displayed, the displayed name of the file, a description of the file and its type, and whether the `File` is traversable.

```
public abstract class FileView extends java.lang.Object
```

Constructors
```
public FileView()
```
Default constructor.

Methods
```
public abstract String getDescription(java.io.File f)
```
Returns a localized description of the *contents* of the file, if one is available. If a description is not available, this method returns `null`.

```
public abstract Icon getIcon(java.io.File f)
```
Returns the `Icon` to be displayed next to the file's name in the `JFile-Chooser`.

```
public abstract String getName(java.io.File f)
```
Returns the name of the file. Normally the `String` returned would be the returned `String` from `f.getName()` but if you wanted to lowercase the name, for example, you would do it here.

```
public abstract String getTypeDescription(java.io.File f)
```
Returns a localized `String` describing the `type` of the file.

```
public abstract Boolean isTraversable(java.io.File f)
```
Returns `true` if the directory is traversable (the user is allowed to see its contents). An example of a directory that would return `false` is one which the user does not have privileges on under UNIX or Windows NT.

Extended by　BasicFileChooserUI.BasicFileView (p.592).
Returned by　BasicFileChooserUI.getFileView() (p.587), FileChooserUI.getFileView() (p.533), JFileChooser.getFileView() (p.239).
See also　Icon (p.183).

Package swing.plaf

This package defines the standard interfaces for Swing's pluggable look and feel support.

Each type of component has its own associated UI delegate which is defined by a class in this package. Almost all classes in this package are abstract, since they exist to define a contract with the components. Concrete implementations of these classes are defined by a look and feel. The few concrete classes in this package are `UIResource` classes which are used by the UI delegates to safely set and unset appearance properties in the components (such as fonts and background colors).

The class which is associated with a component is discovered by calling the `getUIClassID()` method in the component. The return value from this method is a `String` that matches the unqualified class name in this package.

plaf

Plaf extends/implements hierarchy

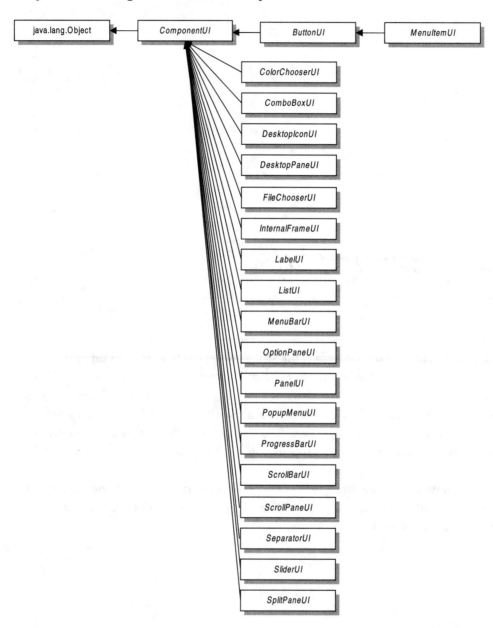

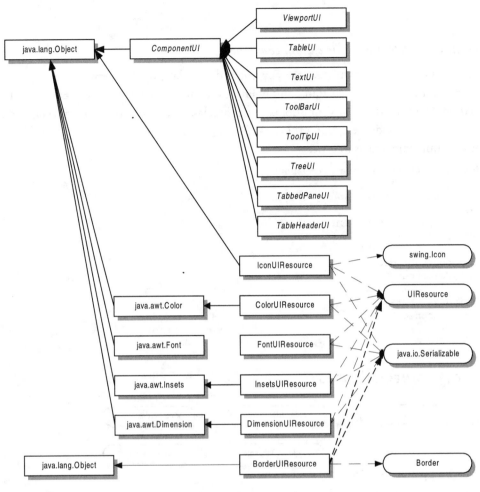

Quick summary

The main class	ComponentUI (p.530) is the abstract base class for most of the classes in this package. It defines the minimal requirements for all Swing UI delegates.
The main interface	The main interface in this package is the UIResource (p.544) interface. It is a "tag" interface designed to allow UI delegates to safely change properties in components.
How to use	Unless you are creating a very unusual look and feel you will usually subclass the classes in the Basic look and feel (p.547). Most of the behavior of the delegates in that package can be used as-is, leaving just the painting of the components to be overridden. The classes in this package do not, for the most part, implement any behaviors at all.

FAQs

How do I create a UI delegate for my custom component?

Have your component extend from JComponent (or a descendant of JComponent). Create a subclass of ComponentUI for your custom component, overriding at least the createUI() and paint() methods. Four methods of your JComponent subclass need to be overridden to enable the new UI. The four methods are updateUI(), setUI(), getUI(), and getUIClassID(). The four methods get implemented as follows:

```
public class MyComponent extends JComponent {
  public void updateUI() {
    setUI((MyComponentUI)UIManager.getUI(this));
  }
  public void setUI(MyComponentUI newUI) {
    super.setUI(newUI);
  }
  public MyComponentUI getUI() {
    return (MyComponentUI)ui;
  }
  public String getUIClassID() {
    return "MyComponentUI";
  }
}
```

swing.plaf.BorderUIResource

CLASS

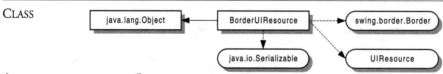

A UIResource wrapper for Border.

**public class BorderUIResource extends java.lang.Object
    implements Border, UIResource**

Constructors
public BorderUIResource(Border delegate)
Creates a BorderUIResource object which wraps a Border instance.

Methods
public static BorderUIResource getBlackLineBorderUIResource()
Returns a BorderUIResource which wraps a black LineBorder.
public java.awt.Insets getBorderInsets(java.awt.Component c)
Implements: getBorderInsets in interface Border.
public static BorderUIResource getEtchedBorderUIResource()
Returns a BorderUIResource which wraps an EtchedBorder.
public static BorderUIResource getLoweredBevelBorderUIResource()
Returns a BorderUIResource which wraps a lowered BevelBorder.

public static BorderUIResource getRaisedBevelBorderUIResource()

Returns a BorderUIResource which wraps a raised BevelBorder.

public boolean isBorderOpaque()

Implements: isBorderOpaque in interface Border.

public void paintBorder(java.awt.Component c, java.awt.Graphics g,
int x, int y, int width, int height)

Implements: paintBorder in interface Border.

See also   BevelBorder (p.463), Border (p.465), EtchedBorder (p.468), LineBorder (p.470),
UIResource (p.544).

swing.plaf.BorderUIResource.BevelBorderUIResource

INNER CLASS

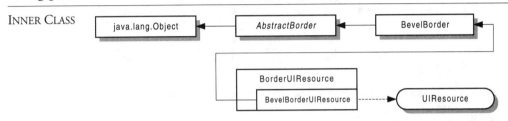

public static class BorderUIResource.BevelBorderUIResource
extends BevelBorder
implements UIResource

Constructors

public BevelBorderUIResource(int bevelType)

Calls super(bevelType).

public BevelBorderUIResource(int bevelType, java.awt.Color highlight,
java.awt.Color shadow)

Calls super(bevelType, highlight, shadow).

public BevelBorderUIResource(int bevelType, java.awt.Color highlightOuter,
java.awt.Color highlightInner, java.awt.Color shadowOuter,
java.awt.Color shadowInner)

Calls super(bevelType, highlightOuter, highlightInner, shadowOuter, shadow-
Inner).

See also   BevelBorder (p.463), UIResource (p.544).

swing.plaf.BorderUIResource.CompoundBorderUIResource

INNER CLASS

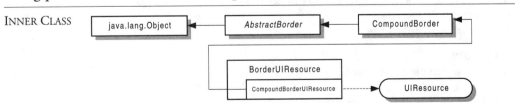

```
public static class BorderUIResource.CompoundBorderUIResource
    extends CompoundBorder
    implements UIResource
```

Constructors

```
public CompoundBorderUIResource(Border outsideBorder, Border insideBorder)
```
Calls super(outsideBorder, insideBorder).

See also   Border (p.465), CompoundBorder (p.466), UIResource (p.544).

swing.plaf.BorderUIResource.EmptyBorderUIResource

INNER CLASS

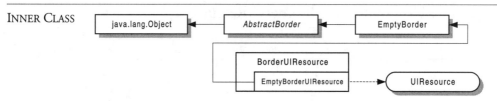

```
public static class BorderUIResource.EmptyBorderUIResource
    extends EmptyBorder
    implements UIResource
```

Constructors

```
public EmptyBorderUIResource(int top, int left, int bottom, int right)
```
Calls super(top, left, bottom, right).
```
public EmptyBorderUIResource(java.awt.Insets insets)
```
Calls super(insets).

See also   EmptyBorder (p.467), UIResource (p.544).

swing.plaf.BorderUIResource.EtchedBorderUIResource

INNER CLASS

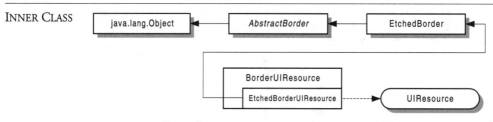

```
public static class BorderUIResource.EtchedBorderUIResource
    extends EtchedBorder
    implements UIResource
```

Constructors

```
public EtchedBorderUIResource()
```
Calls super().
```
public EtchedBorderUIResource(int etchType)
```
Calls super(etchType).

```
public EtchedBorderUIResource(int etchType, java.awt.Color highlight,
    java.awt.Color shadow)
```
Calls super(etchType, highlight, shadow).
```
public EtchedBorderUIResource(java.awt.Color highlight,
    java.awt.Color shadow)
```
Calls super(highlight, shadow).

See also   EtchedBorder (p.468), UIResource (p.544).

swing.plaf.BorderUIResource.LineBorderUIResource

INNER CLASS

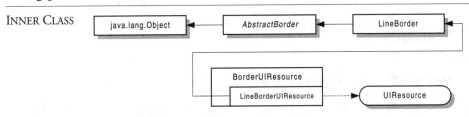

```
public static class LineBorderUIResource extends LineBorder
    implements UIResource
```

Constructors
```
public LineBorderUIResource(java.awt.Color color)
```
Calls super(color).
```
public LineBorderUIResource(java.awt.Color color, int thickness)
```
Calls super(color, thickness).

See also   LineBorder (p.470), UIResource (p.544).

swing.plaf.BorderUIResource.MatteBorderUIResource

INNER CLASS

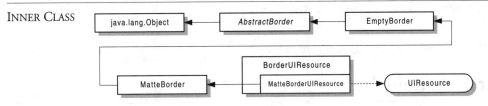

```
public static class MatteBorderUIResource extends MatteBorder
    implements UIResource
```

Constructors
```
public MatteBorderUIResource(Icon tileIcon)
```
Calls super(tileIcon).
```
public MatteBorderUIResource(int top, int left, int bottom,
    int right, Icon tileIcon)
```
Calls super(top, left, bottom, right, tileIcon).
```
public MatteBorderUIResource(int top, int left, int bottom,
    int right, java.awt.Color color)
```
Calls super(top, left, bottom, right, color).

See also MatteBorder (p.471), UIResource (p.544).

swing.plaf.BorderUIResource.TitledBorderUIResource

INNER CLASS

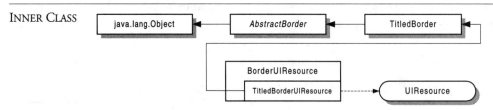

```
public static class TitledBorderUIResource extends TitledBorder
    implements UIResource
```

Constructors

```
public TitledBorderUIResource(Border border)
```
Calls super(border).

```
public TitledBorderUIResource(Border border, String title)
```
Calls super(border, title).

```
public TitledBorderUIResource(Border border, String title,
    int titleJustification, int titlePosition)
```
Calls super(border, title, titleJustification, titlePosition).

```
public TitledBorderUIResource(Border border, String title,
    int titleJustification, int titlePosition, java.awt.Font titleFont)
```
Calls super(border, title, titleJustification, titlePosition, titleFont).

```
public TitledBorderUIResource(Border border, String title,
    int titleJustification, int titlePosition,
    java.awt.Font titleFont, java.awt.Color titleColor)
```
Calls super(border, title, titleJustification, titlePosition, titleFont, titleColor).

```
public TitledBorderUIResource(String title)
```
Calls super(title).

See also TitledBorder (p.473), UIResource (p.544).

swing.plaf.ButtonUI

ABSTRACT
CLASS

The UI delegate interface for the AbstractButton class. This UI delegate is used by all of AbstractButton's subclasses except for JMenuItem and its subclasses, which use MenuItemUI.

```
public abstract class ButtonUI extends ComponentUI
```

Constructors

```
public ButtonUI()
```
Default constructor.

Extended by   BasicButtonUI (p.557), MenuItemUI (p.536).
Returned by   AbstractButton.getUI() (p.118).
See also   AbstractButton (p.118), ComponentUI (p.530), JComponent (p.207).

swing.plaf.ColorChooserUI

ABSTRACT
CLASS

The UI delegate interface for the `JColorChooser` component.

```
public abstract class ColorChooserUI extends swing.plaf.ComponentUI
```

Constructors
```
public ColorChooserUI()
```
Default constructor.

> *Extended by*   BasicColorChooserUI (p.561).
> *Returned by*   JColorChooser.getUI() (p.197).
> *See also*   ComponentUI (p.530), JComponent (p.207).

swing.plaf.ColorUIResource

CLASS
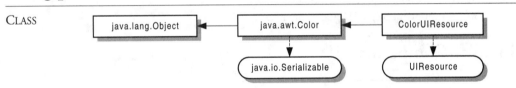

A `UIResource` wrapper for a `java.awt.Color`.

```
public class ColorUIResource extends java.awt.Color
    implements swing.plaf.UIResource
```

Constructors
```
public ColorUIResource(java.awt.Color c)
```
Constructs a `ColorUIResource` wrapping the given `Color`.
```
public ColorUIResource(int rgb)
public ColorUIResource(int r, int g, int b)
public ColorUIResource(float r, float g, float b)
```
Constructs a `Color` using the given information and then calls the first constructor, which wraps a `Color`.

> *See also*   UIResource (p.544).

plaf

swing.plaf.ComboBoxUI

The UI delegate interface for the `JComboBox` component.

```
public abstract class ComboBoxUI extends ComponentUI
```

Constructors
`public ComboBoxUI()`
> Default constructor.

Methods
`public abstract boolean isFocusTraversable()`
> Returns whether the whole combo box can be traversed by the focus, not whether the individual parts of the combo box can.

`public abstract boolean isPopupVisible()`
> Returns `true` if the `ComboPopup` is visible.

`public abstract void setPopupVisible()`
> Called to cause the UI to show the `ComboPopup`.

> *Extended by* BasicComboBoxUI (p.565).
> *Returned by* JComboBox.getUI() (p.200).
> *See also*   ComboPopup (p.731), ComponentUI (p.530).

swing.plaf.ComponentUI

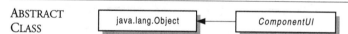

The abstract base class for all other component UI delegates.

```
public abstract class ComponentUI extends java.lang.Object
```

Constructors
`public ComponentUI()`
> Default constructor.

Methods
`public boolean contains(JComponent c, int x, int y)`
> Returns `true` if the `point (x, y)` is inside the bounds of the given component. Equivalent to `contains(Point p)` in `java.awt.Component`.

`public static ComponentUI createUI(JComponent c)`
> Returns the factory method which must be overridden by subclasses to return the correct UI delegate. `ComponentUI`'s implementation of this method throws an `Error` indicating that this method has not been implemented.

plaf

public Accessible getAccessibleChild(JComponent c, int i)

Returns the ith `Accessible` child of the object. This method is provided to allow user interfaces to provide components that act as if they were composed of multiple components, even though they are actually a single component.

public int getAccessibleChildrenCount(JComponent c)

Returns the number of "components" which make up this component. See `getAccessible-Child()`.

public java.awt.Dimension getMaximumSize(JComponent c)

This method can be overridden by subclasses to return a maximum size. `ComponentUI`'s implementation of this method returns `getPreferredSize()`.

public java.awt.Dimension getMinimumSize(JComponent c)

This method can be overridden by subclasses to return a minimum size. `ComponentUI`'s implementation of this method returns `getPreferredSize()`.

public java.awt.Dimension getPreferredSize(JComponent c)

This method can be overridden by subclasses to return a preferred size. `ComponentUI`'s implementation of this method returns `null`.

public void installUI(JComponent c)

This method should be overridden by subclasses to install their UI into the given `JComponent`. `ComponentUI`'s implementation of this method does nothing.

public void paint(java.awt.Graphics g, JComponent c)

This method should be overridden by subclasses to paint their UI. `ComponentUI`'s implementation of this method does nothing.

public void uninstallUI(JComponent c)

This method should be overridden by subclasses to uninstall their UI from the given `JComponent`. `ComponentUI`'s implementation of this method does nothing.

public void update(java.awt.Graphics g, JComponent c)

This method will usually not be overridden by subclasses, since `ComponentUI` implements a reasonable behavior. If the given `JComponent`'s `isOpaque()` method returns `true`, the background is filled with the `c.getBackground()` color. This method then calls `paint(g, c)`.

Extended by   ButtonUI (p.528), ColorChooserUI (p.529), ComboBoxUI (p.530), DesktopIconUI (p.531), DesktopPaneUI (p.532), FileChooserUI (p.533), InternalFrameUI (p.535), LabelUI (p.535), ListUI (p.535), MenuBarUI (p.536), OptionPaneUI (p.537), PanelUI (p.537), PopupMenuUI (p.538), ProgressBarUI (p.538), ScrollBarUI (p.538), ScrollPaneUI (p.539), SeparatorUI (p.539), SliderUI (p.539), SpinnerUI (p.539), SplitPaneUI (p.540), TabbedPaneUI (p.540), TableHeaderUI (p.541), TableUI (p.541), TextUI (p.542), ToolBarUI (p.543), ToolTipUI (p.543), TreeUI (p.543).
Returned by   Many.
See also   JComponent (p.207).

swing.plaf.DesktopIconUI

ABSTRACT
CLASS

The UI delegate interface for the `JInternalFrame.JDesktopIcon` component.

`public abstract class DesktopIconUI extends ComponentUI`

Constructors
`public DesktopIconUI()`
> Default constructor.

> *Extended by*   BasicDesktopIconUI (p.580).
> *Returned by*   JInternalFrame.JDesktopIcon.getUI() (p.263).
> *See also*   ComponentUI (p.530), JInternalFrame.JDesktopIcon (p.263).

swing.plaf.DesktopPaneUI

ABSTRACT
CLASS

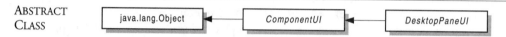

The UI delegate interface for the `JDesktopPane` component.

`public abstract class DesktopPaneUI extends ComponentUI`

Constructors
`public DesktopPaneUI()`
> Default constructor.

> *Extended by*   BasicDesktopPaneUI (p.582).
> *Returned by*   JDesktopPane.getUI() (p.224).
> *See also*   ComponentUI (p.530), JDesktopPane (p.224).

swing.plaf.DimensionUIResource

CLASS

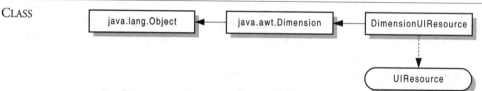

`UIResource` wrapper for a `java.awt.Dimension`.

`public class DimensionUIResource extends java.awt.Dimension`
`    implements UIResource`

Constructors
`public DimensionUIResource(int width, int height)`
> Default constructor.

> *See also*   UIResource (p.544).

swing.plaf.FileChooserUI

ABSTRACT
CLASS

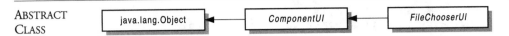

The UI delegate interface for the `JFileChooser` component.

```
public abstract class FileChooserUI extends ComponentUI
```

Constructors
`public FileChooserUI()`
  Default constructor.

Methods
`public abstract void ensureFileIsVisible(JFileChooser fc, java.io.File f)`
  When this method is called the UI will ensure (by scrolling, expanding nodes in a tree, etc.) that the given file is visible to the user in the given file chooser.
`public abstract FileFilter getAcceptAllFileFilter(JFileChooser fc)`
  Returns a `FileFilter` appropriate to the current look and feel that allows all files to be shown.
`public abstract String getApproveButtonText(JFileChooser fc)`
  Returns the default text to use for the approve button, based on the type and mode of the JFileChooser.
`public abstract String getDialogTitle(JFileChooser fc)`
  Returns the default dialog title for the current look and feel based on the type and mode of the JFileChooser.
`public abstract FileView getFileView(JFileChooser fc)`
  Returns the default `FileView` for the look and feel.
`public abstract void rescanCurrentDirectory(JFileChooser fc)`
  Updates the UI to reflect the current contents of the current directory.

Extended by   BasicFileChooserUI (p.587).
Returned by   JFileChooser.getUI() (p.239).
See also   ComponentUI (p.530).

swing.plaf.FontUIResource

CLASS

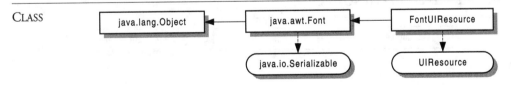

A UIResource wrapper for a `java.awt.Font`.

```
public class FontUIResource extends java.awt.Font
    implements swing.plaf.UIResource
```

Constructors

public FontUIResource(java.awt.Font font)

Constructs a FontUIResource wrapping the given font.

public FontUIResource(String name, int style, int size)

Using the supplied information this constructor creates a Font and then calls the first constructor.

See also   UIResource (p.544).

swing.plaf.IconUIResource

CLASS

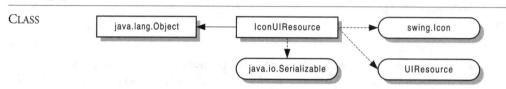

A UIResource wrapper for implementors of the Icon interface.

```
public class IconUIResource extends java.lang.Object
    implements Icon, UIResource, java.io.Serializable
```

Constructors

public IconUIResource(Icon delegate)

Creates a UIResource icon object which wraps an existing Icon instance.

Methods

public int getIconHeight()

Implements: getIconHeight in interface Icon.

public int getIconWidth()

Implements: getIconWidth in interface Icon.

public void paintIcon(java.awt.Component c, java.awt.Graphics g, int x, int y)

Implements: paintIcon in interface Icon.

See also   Icon (p.183), UIResource (p.544).

swing.plaf.InsetsUIResource

CLASS

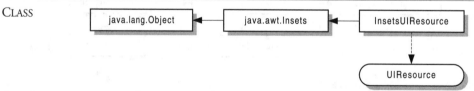

A UIResource wrapper for a java.awt.Insets.

```
public class InsetsUIResource extends java.awt.Insets
    implements UIResource
```

Constructors

public InsetsUIResource(int top, int left, int bottom, int right)
    Default constructor.

    See also   UIResource (p.544).

swing.plaf.InternalFrameUI

ABSTRACT
CLASS

The UI delegate interface for the `JInternalFrame` component.

public abstract class InternalFrameUI extends ComponentUI

Constructors

public InternalFrameUI()
    Default constructor.

    Extended by   BasicInternalFrameUI (p.605).
    Returned by   JInternalFrame.getUI() (p.254).
    See also   ComponentUI (p.530), JInternalFrame (p.254).

swing.plaf.LabelUI

ABSTRACT
CLASS

The UI delegate interface for the `JLabel` component.

public abstract class LabelUI extends ComponentUI

Constructors

public LabelUI()
    Default constructor.

    Extended by   BasicLabelUI (p.613).
    Returned by   JLabel.getUI() (p.264).
    See also   ComponentUI (p.530), JLabel (p.264).

swing.plaf.ListUI

ABSTRACT
CLASS

The UI delegate for the `JList` component. The `ListUI` interface adds new methods related to mapping from mouse coordinates to cells in the `JList`.

public abstract class ListUI extends ComponentUI

Constructors
public ListUI()
>Default constructor.

Methods
public abstract Rectangle getCellBounds(JList list, int index1, int index2)
>Returns the coordinates of the rectangle containing the range of cells between index1 and index2. The coordinates returned are relative to the JList. If either index is invalid, this method returns null. The implementation of this method also accepts index1 and index2 in any order (lowest to highest or highest to lowest).

public abstract java.awt.Point indexToLocation(JList list, int index)
>Returns the origin of the cell at index in coordinates relative to the JList. If *index* is out of range, this method returns null.

public abstract int locationToIndex(JList list, java.awt.Point location)
>Given a point in coordinates relative to the JList, this method returns the index of the cell which contains the point. If location references an empty section of the JList, this method returns –1.

>*Extended by*   BasicListUI (p.614).
>*Returned by*   JList.getUI() (p.271).
>*See also*   ComponentUI (p.530), JList (p.271).

swing.plaf.MenuBarUI

ABSTRACT
CLASS

The UI delegate for the JMenuBar component.

```
public abstract class MenuBarUI extends swing.plaf.ComponentUI
```

Constructors
public MenuBarUI()
>Default constructor.

>*Extended by*   BasicMenuBarUI (p.622).
>*Returned by*   JMenuBar.getUI() (p.288).
>*See also*   ComponentUI (p.530), JMenuBar (p.288).

swing.plaf.MenuItemUI

ABSTRACT
CLASS

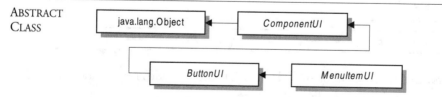

The UI delegate interface for the JMenuItem component.

plaf

```
public abstract class MenuItemUI extends ButtonUI
```

Constructors
```
public MenuItemUI()
```
   Default constructor.

   Extended by   BasicMenuItemUI (p.624).
   See also   ButtonUI (p.528), JMenuItem (p.291).

swing.plaf.OptionPaneUI

ABSTRACT
CLASS

The UI delegate for the JOptionPane component.

```
public abstract class OptionPaneUI extends swing.plaf.ComponentUI
```

Constructors
```
public OptionPaneUI()
```
   Default constructor.

Methods
```
public abstract boolean containsCustomComponents()
```
   Returns true if the JOptionPane is using user-supplied Components for either the options or the message.
```
public abstract void selectInitialValue(JOptionPane op)
```
   Requests the focus for the default component in the option pane.

   Extended by   BasicOptionPaneUI (p.630).
   Returned by   JOptionPane.getUI() (p.294).
   See also   ComponentUI (p.530), JOptionPane (p.294).

swing.plaf.PanelUI

ABSTRACT
CLASS

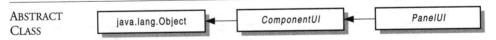

The UI delegate for a JPanel.

```
public abstract class PanelUI extends ComponentUI
```

Constructors
```
public PanelUI()
```
   Default constructor.

   Extended by   BasicPanelUI (p.634).
   See also   ComponentUI (p.530).

plaf

swing.plaf.PopupMenuUI

ABSTRACT
CLASS

The UI delegate interface for the `JPopupMenu` component.

```
public abstract class PopupMenuUI extends swing.plaf.ComponentUI
```

Constructors
`public PopupMenuUI()`
> Default constructor.

> *Extended by*   BasicPopupMenuUI (p.636).
> *Returned by*   JPopupMenu.getUI() (p.309).
> *See also*   ComponentUI (p.530), JPopupMenu (p.309).

swing.plaf.ProgressBarUI

ABSTRACT
CLASS

The UI delegate interface for the `JProgressBar` component.

```
public abstract class ProgressBarUI extends swing.plaf.ComponentUI
```

Constructors
`public ProgressBarUI()`
> Default constructor.

> *Extended by*   BasicProgressBarUI (p.638).
> *Returned by*   JProgressBar.getUI() (p.315).
> *See also*   ComponentUI (p.530), JProgressBar (p.315).

swing.plaf.ScrollBarUI

ABSTRACT
CLASS

The UI delegate interface for the `JScrollBar` component.

```
public abstract class ScrollBarUI extends swing.plaf.ComponentUI
```

Constructors
`public ScrollBarUI()`
> Default constructor.

> *Extended by*   BasicScrollBarUI (p.642).
> *Returned by*   JScrollBar.getUI() (p.328).

See also   ComponentUI (p.530), JScrollBar (p.328).

swing.plaf.ScrollPaneUI

ABSTRACT
CLASS

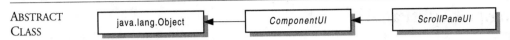

The UI delegate interface for the `JScrollPane` component.

`public abstract class ScrollPaneUI extends swing.plaf.ComponentUI`

Constructors
`public ScrollPaneUI()`
Default constructor.

Extended by   BasicScrollPaneUI (p.650).
Returned by   JScrollPane.getUI() (p.332).
See also   ComponentUI (p.530), JScrollPane (p.332).

swing.plaf.SeparatorUI

ABSTRACT
CLASS

The UI delegate for the `JSeparator` component.

`public abstract class SeparatorUI extends swing.plaf.ComponentUI`

Constructors
`public SeparatorUI()`
Default constructor.

Extended by   BasicSeparatorUI (p.654).
Returned by   JSeparator.getUI() (p.338).
See also   ComponentUI (p.530), JSeparator (p.338).

swing.plaf.SliderUI

ABSTRACT
CLASS

The UI delegate interface for the `JSlider` component.

`public abstract class SliderUI extends swing.plaf.ComponentUI`

Constructors
`public SliderUI()`
Default constructor.

plaf

Extended by　BasicSliderUI (p.655).
Returned by　JSlider.getUI() (p.341).
See also　ComponentUI (p.530), JSlider (p.341).

swing.plaf.SplitPaneUI

ABSTRACT
CLASS

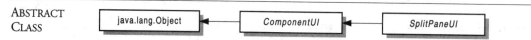

The UI delegate interface for the `JSplitPane` component.

```
public abstract class SplitPaneUI extends swing.plaf.ComponentUI
```

Constructors
```
public SplitPaneUI()
```
　　Default constructor.

Methods
```
public abstract void finishedPaintingChildren(JSplitPane jc,
    java.awt.Graphics g)
```
　　Called by `JSplitPane` after it has finished painting its children.
```
public abstract int getDividerLocation()
```
　　Returns the location of the divider. The int returned is either the x or y coordinate of the divider, relative to the `JSplitPane`. Whether the x or y is returned is dependent upon whether the `JSplitPane` is a horizontal or a vertical splitter.
```
public abstract int getMaximumDividerLocation()
```
　　Returns the maximum possible location for the divider, based on the maximum and minimum preferred sizes of the `JSplitPane`'s child components and the various insets and widths of the components forming the `JSplitPane`.
```
public abstract int getMinimumDividerLocation()
```
　　Returns the minimum possible location for the divider.
```
public abstract void resetToPreferredSizes()
```
　　Called to have the UI reset the `JSplitPane`'s children to their preferred sizes.
```
public abstract void setDividerLocation(int location)
```
　　Moves the divider to a specific location, if allowed by the maximum or minimum divider location.

Extended by　BasicSplitPaneUI (p.668).
Returned by　JSplitPane.getUI() (p.346).
See also　ComponentUI (p.530), JSplitPane (p.346).

swing.plaf.TabbedPaneUI

ABSTRACT
CLASS

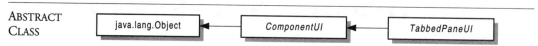

The UI delegate interface for the `JTabbedPane` component.

plaf

```
public abstract class TabbedPaneUI extends ComponentUI
```

Constructors
```
public TabbedPaneUI()
```
> Default constructor.

Methods
```
public abstract java.awt.Rectangle getTabBounds(JTabbedPane pane, int index)
```
> Returns the bounding rectangle for the tab at *index*.
```
public abstract int getTabRunCount(JTabbedPane pane)
```
> Returns the number of "runs" (rows) of tabs.
```
public abstract int tabForCoordinate(JTabbedPane pane, int x, int y)
```
> Returns the index of the tab at (x, y).

> *Extended by*   BasicTabbedPaneUI (p.679).
> *Returned by*   JTabbedPane.getUI() (p.351).
> *See also*   ComponentUI (p.530), JTabbedPane (p.351).

swing.plaf.TableHeaderUI

ABSTRACT
CLASS

The UI delegate for the JTableHeader component.

```
public abstract class TableHeaderUI extends swing.plaf.ComponentUI
```

Constructors
```
public TableHeaderUI()
```
> Default constructor.

> *Extended by*   BasicTableHeaderUI (p.688).
> *Returned by*   JTableHeader.getUI() (p.752).
> *See also*   ComponentUI (p.530), JTableHeader (p.752).

swing.plaf.TableUI

ABSTRACT
CLASS

The UI delegate for the JTable component.

```
public abstract class TableUI extends swing.plaf.ComponentUI
```

Constructors
```
public TableUI()
```
> Default constructor.

> *Extended by*   BasicTableUI (p.690).

plaf

Returned by   JTable.getUI() (p.357).

See also   ComponentUI (p.530), JTable (p.357).

swing.plaf.TextUI

ABSTRACT
CLASS

The UI delegate for the text components.

```
public abstract class TextUI extends swing.plaf.ComponentUI
```

Constructors

```
public TextUI()
```
Default constructor.

Methods

```
public abstract void damageRange(JTextComponent c, int p0, int p1)
```
Causes the view area representing the given range in the model to repaint.

```
public abstract void damageRange(JTextComponent t, int p0, int p1,
    Position.Bias firstBias, Position.Bias secondBias)
```
Causes the view area representing the given range in the model to repaint.

```
public abstract EditorKit getEditorKit()
```
Returns the current EditorKit. Note that there should be a default EditorKit for each type of text component.

```
public abstract int getNextVisualPositionFrom(JTextComponent t, int pos,
    Position.Bias b, int direction, Position.Bias[] biasRet)
    throws BadLocationException
```
Returns the next offset into the Document that can be represented visually and allows the cursor into its region. The direction parameter is relative to the current location of the Caret in the display. The direction parameter is one of SwingConstants.NORTH, SwingConstants.SOUTH, SwingConstants.EAST, or SwingConstants.WEST.

Throws: IllegalArgumentException for an invalid direction.

```
public abstract View getRootView(JTextComponent c)
```
Returns a View from which all parts of the Document model can be reached.

```
public abstract java.awt.Rectangle modelToView(JTextComponent c,
    int pos) throws BadLocationException
```
Returns the Rectangle bounding the element at pos in the model.

Throws: BadLocationException if the pos does not represent a valid location in the model.

```
public abstract int viewToModel(JTextComponent c, java.awt.Point pt)
```
Returns the position in the model which is the closest match to the point pt.

```
public abstract int viewToModel(JTextComponent t, java.awt.Point pt,
    Position.Bias[] biasReturn)
```
Returns the position in the model which is the closest match to the point pt. The biasReturn parameter is an *output* parameter which indicates whether the offset refers to the character before or after the offset (for bidirectional text).

Extended by   BasicTextUI (p.696).

Returned by JTextComponent.getUI() (p.838).
See also BadLocationException (p.796), ComponentUI (p.530), EditorKit (p.829), JTextComponent (p.838), Position.Bias (p.860).

swing.plaf. ToolBarUI

ABSTRACT
CLASS

The UI delegate interface for the `JToolBar` component.

`public abstract class ToolBarUI extends swing.plaf.ComponentUI`

Constructors
`public ToolBarUI()`
    Default constructor.

Extended by BasicToolBarUI (p.702).
Returned by JToolBar.getUI() (p.388).
See also ComponentUI (p.530), JToolBar (p.388).

swing.plaf. ToolTipUI

ABSTRACT
CLASS

The UI delegate interface for the `JToolTip` component.

`public abstract class ToolTipUI extends swing.plaf.ComponentUI`

Constructors
`public ToolTipUI()`
    Default constructor.

Extended by BasicToolTipUI (p.709).
Returned by JToolTip.getUI() (p.391).
See also ComponentUI (p.530), JToolTip (p.391).

swing.plaf. TreeUI

ABSTRACT
CLASS

The UI delegate interface for the `JTree` component.

`public abstract class TreeUI extends ComponentUI`

plaf

Constructors

`public TreeUI()`

Default constructor.

Methods

`public abstract void cancelEditing(JTree tree)`

Cancels any editing that is happening in the tree. This method returns `true` if the editor allows the editing to stop.

`public abstract TreePath getClosestPathForLocation(JTree t, int x, int y)`

Returns the path to the node closest to `(x, y)`, where `(x, y)` is relative to the `JTree`. This method always returns a valid path as long as any node is visible. If no nodes are visible, then this method returns null. To test if the returned tree node contains `(x, y)`, you must get the bounds for that tree node and compare them to `(x, y)`.

`public abstract TreePath getEditingPath(JTree t)`

Returns the `path` to the node being edited.

`public abstract java.awt.Rectangle getPathBounds(JTree t, TreePath path)`

Returns the `Rectangle` bounding the label of the last node in the path. This method returns `null` if any node in the `path` is not visible.

`public abstract TreePath getPathForRow(JTree t, int row)`

Returns the `path` whose last element is in `row`. If `row` is not visible, this method returns `null`.

`public abstract java.awt.Rectangle getRowBounds(int row)`

Returns the `Rectangle` bounding the label of the tree node at `row`.

`public abstract int getRowCount(JTree t)`

Returns the number of displayed rows.

`public abstract int getRowForPath(JTree t, TreePath path)`

Returns the `row` occupied by the last item in `path`. This method returns -1 if any node in `path` is not visible.

`public abstract boolean isEditing(JTree t)`

Returns `true` if a node in the tree is being edited. Use `getEditingPath()` to return the node being edited.

`public abstract void startEditingAtPath(JTree t, TreePath path)`

Selects the node at the end of `path` and tries to start editing it. This method fails if the `CellEditor` for the tree does not allow editing of the node.

`public abstract boolean stopEditing(JTree t)`

Stops any editing in the tree. This method returns `true` if the `CellEditor` allows editing to stop. Stopping editing differs from canceling editing in that the results are preserved, rather than discarded.

Extended by   BasicTreeUI (p.710).
Returned by   JTree.getUI() (p.393).
See also   ComponentUI (p.530), JTree (p.393), TreePath (p.989).

swing.plaf.UIResource

INTERFACE   ⬭ UIResource ⬭

The `UIResource` interface is a tag interface used to mark objects as being created by a UI delegate. This interface is needed so that the UI delegates do not overwrite properties set into components by the user.

This tag can be used in the `ComponentUI` methods `installUI()` and `uninstallUI()`. In `installUI()`, if the property is `null` the property can be set using an instance of an appropriate `UIResource` implementor. Then, in `uninstallUI()`, the property can be checked to see if it is an `instanceof UIResource`. If it is, then the property can be reset to `null`. If it is not, then the property has been set by the user and should not be changed.

This methodology works for all properties except the `font`, `foregroundColor`, and `backgroundColor` properties of `java.awt.Component`. For those properties, if they are `null`, the component inherits them from its container. For those properties, simply check them to see if they are instances of `UIResource` in `installUI()`. If they are, then do not change the property. Remember that (`null instanceof AnyClass`) is always `true`.

As an example of this, the `installUI()` method for JButton would use the following check:

```
Color bg = button.getBackgroundColor();
if (bg == null || bg instanceof UIResource) {
    button.setBackground(UIManager.getColor("Button.background"));
}
```

The `LookAndFeel` (p.423) class provides helper methods which perform this check before setting these properties.

public interface UIResource

Implemented by   BasicBorders.ButtonBorder (p.551), BasicBorders.FieldBorder (p.552), BasicBorders.MarginBorder (p.553), BasicBorders.MenuBarBorder (p.553), BasicBorders.SplitPaneBorder (p.554), BasicComboBoxEditor.UIResource (p.564), BasicComboBoxRenderer.UIResource (p.565), BasicTextUI.BasicCaret (p.700), BasicTextUI.BasicHighlighter (p.700), BorderUIResource (p.524), BorderUIResource.BevelBorderUIResource (p.525), BorderUIResource.CompoundBorderUIResource (p.525), BorderUIResource.EmptyBorderUIResource (p.526), BorderUIResource.EtchedBorderUIResource (p.526), BorderUIResource.LineBorderUIResource (p.527), BorderUIResource.MatteBorderUIResource (p.527), BorderUIResource.TitledBorderUIResource (p.528), ColorUIResource (p.529), DefaultListCellRenderer.UIResource (p.172), DefaultMenuLayout (p.731), DefaultTableCellRenderer.UIResource (p.744), DimensionUIResource (p.532), FontUIResource (p.533), IconUIResource (p.534), InsetsUIResource (p.534), JScrollPane.ScrollBar (p.337), ScrollPaneLayout.UIResource (p.440).

plaf

swing.plaf.ViewportUI

ABSTRACT
CLASS

The UI delegate for a `JViewport`.

```
public abstract class ViewportUI extends ComponentUI
```

Constructors
`public ViewportUI()`
> Default constructor.

> *Extended by*   BasicViewportUI (p.730).
> *See also*   ComponentUI (p.530), JViewport (p.410).

plaf

Package *swing.plaf.basic*

The Basic look and feel is intended as the common ancestor of all visual primary look and feels. It defines behaviors that match those that have become de-facto standards for most common mouse-based user interfaces. Because the class `BasicLookAndFeel` is abstract, this look and feel cannot be used directly. The UI delegates, on the other hand, are designed to be used directly in a look and feel subclassed from `BasicLookAndFeel`.

There are two different ways the UI delegates defined in this package can be used. The first way is to use them directly, and change the resources they retrieve from the `UIDefaults` table to customize them to your needs. The second way is to create a subclass and override what you need. The designers of the classes in this look and feel have helpfully implemented most behaviors using inner classes returned by `createX()` methods. The "look" for a UI delegate is implemented using `paintX()` methods. So, when creating a subclass, it is usually just those particular methods that need to be overridden.

The information in this section covers only the APIs defined starting in Swing 1.1 (JDK 1.2). Swing 1.1 was the first release with an "official" API, which was significantly different from the previous versions.

For more information on implementing a look and feel, whether a visual one extended from Basic or an auxiliary look and feel to be used by the Multi look and feel, see chapter 3 (p.57).

Basic extends/implements hierarchy

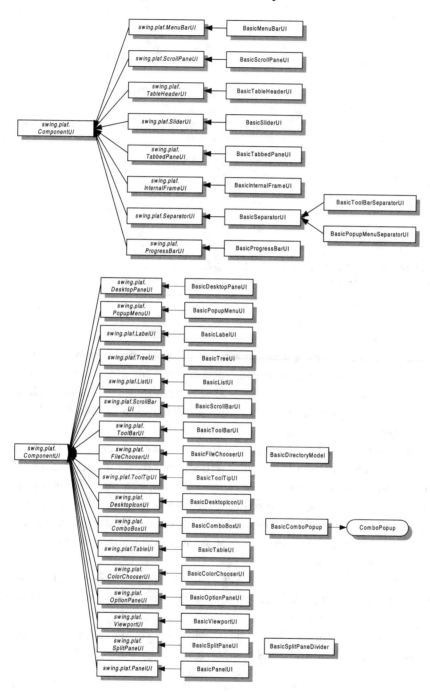

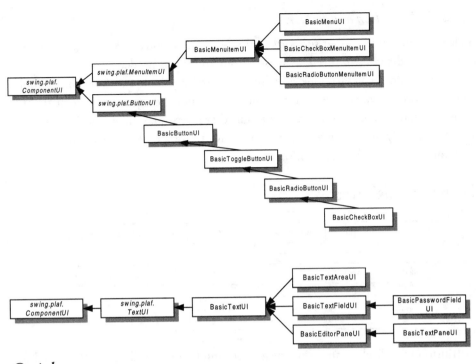

Quick summary

Main class	BasicLookAndFeel (p.621). Subclasses of this class form the basis for a new look and feel. This class provides implementations of the methods defined in LookAndFeel (p.423) which can be overridden or used to install the classes and resources for your own look and feel.
Classes to subclass in creating a new look and feel	Any class that ends with "UI" is a UI delegate and can be subclassed. All of the other classes are support classes, which may be subclassed as needed.

FAQs

How do I customize the behavior of a UI delegate for my look and feel?

The obvious answer to this question is to create a subclass and override the methods you need to. This solution will work in all cases, but the designers of Swing have helpfully made it easier than that in many cases. Most of the UI delegates in this package take an appreciable part of their appearance from resources defined in the UIDefaults table. This is why the Metal look and feel defines so many fewer classes than the Basic look and feel. Metal uses some of the classes from Basic and simply changes their resources.

More information on this topic is available in chapter 3 (p.57).

What resources are defined in the UIDefaults table?

See appendix B: UIDefaults table standard keys (p.1013) for a list of the keys defined by the Basic look and feel.

What on earth is the Multi look and feel for?

Multi is a specialized look and feel that supports multiple, simultaneous look and feels. You will never try to set Multi as the look and feel; Swing sets it for you if it is needed.

Multi is a way to add secondary look and feels to a primary look and feel. For example, Multi allows you to write a look and feel that only produces sounds for specific events (e.g., button clicks). Then the sound look and feel can be installed as a secondary look and feel to whatever primary look and feel you want, whether it is Metal, Motif, or a custom look and feel.

For more information, see chapter 3 (p.57).

swing.plaf.basic.BasicArrowButton

CLASS

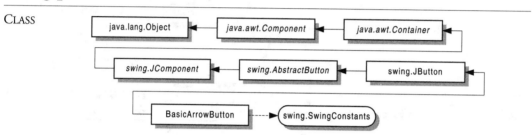

This class is a JButton that displays an arrow image pointing in a given direction. It is used for scroll bar arrows or combo box drop-down arrows, for example.

```
public class BasicArrowButton extends JButton
    implements SwingConstants
```

Constructors

```
public BasicArrowButton(int direction)
```
Constructs a `BasicArrowButton` with the arrow pointing in the given direction.

Methods

```
public int getDirection()
```
Returns the direction the arrow is pointing.
```
public java.awt.Dimension getMaximumSize()
```
Overrides: getMaximumSize in class JComponent.
```
public java.awt.Dimension getMinimumSize()
```
Overrides: getMinimumSize in class JComponent.
```
public java.awt.Dimension getPreferredSize()
```
Overrides: getPreferredSize in class JComponent.
```
public boolean isFocusTraversable()
```
Overrides: isFocusTraversable in class JComponent.
```
public void paint(java.awt.Graphics g)
```
Overrides: paint in class JComponent.
```
public void paintTriangle(java.awt.Graphics g, int x, int y,
    int size, int direction, boolean isEnabled)
```
Paints the arrow image onto the button.

plaf.basic

public void requestFocus()
> *Overrides:* requestFocus in class JComponent.

public void setDirection(int dir)
> Changes the direction the arrow points, and repaints the button.

public void updateUI()
> Overrides this method to ignore changes in the look and feel.
> *Overrides:* updateUI in class JButton.

Protected Fields
protected int direction
> Stores the direction the arrow is pointing.

swing.plaf.basic.BasicBorders

CLASS

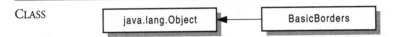

A Border factory that creates the standard borders used by the Basic look and feel components.

public class BasicBorderFactory extends java.lang.Object

Constructors
public BasicBorders()
> Default constructor.

Inner Classes
public static class BasicBorders.ButtonBorder
public static class BasicBorders.FieldBorder
public static class BasicBorders.MarginBorder
public static class BasicBorders.MenuBarBorder
public static class BasicBorders.RadioButtonBorder
public static class BasicBorders.SplitPaneBorder
public static class BasicBorders.ToggleButtonBorder

swing.plaf.basic.BasicBorders.ButtonBorder

INNER CLASS

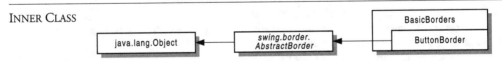

public static class BasicBorders.ButtonBorder extends AbstractBorder
   implements UIResource

Constructors
public ButtonBorder(java.awt.Color shadow, java.awt.Color darkShadow,
   java.awt.Color highlight, java.awt.Color lightHighlight)

Methods
public java.awt.Insets getBorderInsets(java.awt.Component c)
> *Overrides:* getBorderInsets in class AbstractBorder.
> *Implements:* getBorderInsets in interface Border.

public void paintBorder(java.awt.Component c, java.awt.Graphics g, int x, int y, int width, int height)
> *Overrides:* paintBorder in class AbstractBorder.
> *Implements:* paintBorder in interface Border.

Protected Fields
protected java.awt.Color darkShadow
protected java.awt.Color highlight
protected java.awt.Color lightHighlight
protected java.awt.Color shadow

> *Extended by* BasicBorders.RadioButtonBorder (p.554), BasicBorders.ToggleButtonBorder (p.555).
>
> *See also* AbstractBorder (p.462), Border (p.465), UIResource (p.544).

swing.plaf.basic.BasicBorders.FieldBorder

INNER CLASS

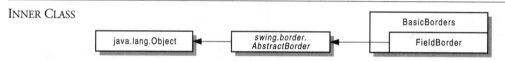

public static class BasicBorders.FieldBorder extends AbstractBorder implements UIResource

Constructors
public FieldBorder(java.awt.Color shadow, java.awt.Color darkShadow, java.awt.Color highlight, java.awt.Color lightHighlight)

Methods
public java.awt.Insets getBorderInsets(java.awt.Component c)
> *Overrides:* getBorderInsets in class AbstractBorder.
> *Implements:* getBorderInsets in interface Border.

public void paintBorder(java.awt.Component c, java.awt.Graphics g, int x, int y, int width, int height)
> *Overrides:* paintBorder in class AbstractBorder.
> *Implements:* paintBorder in interface Border.

Protected Fields
protected java.awt.Color darkShadow
protected java.awt.Color highlight
protected java.awt.Color lightHighlight
protected java.awt.Color shadow

> *See also* AbstractBorder (p.462), Border (p.465), UIResource (p.544).

swing.plaf.basic.BasicBorders.MarginBorder

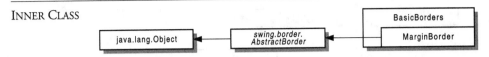

```
public static class BasicBorders.MarginBorder extends AbstractBorder
    implements UIResource
```

Constructors
```
public MarginBorder()
```
Default constructor.

Methods
```
public java.awt.Insets getBorderInsets(java.awt.Component c)
```
Overrides: getBorderInsets in class AbstractBorder.
Implements: getBorderInsets in interface Border.

See also   AbstractBorder (p.462), Border (p.465), UIResource (p.544).

swing.plaf.basic.BasicBorders.MenuBarBorder

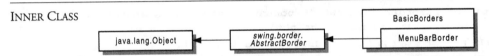

```
public static class BasicBorders.MenuBarBorder extends AbstractBorder
    implements UIResource
```

Constructors
```
public MenuBarBorder(java.awt.Color shadow, java.awt.Color highlight)
```
Constructs the standard border used for menus.

Methods
```
public java.awt.Insets getBorderInsets(java.awt.Component c)
```
Overrides: getBorderInsets in class AbstractBorder.
Implements: getBorderInsets in interface Border.
```
public void paintBorder(java.awt.Component c, java.awt.Graphics g,
    int x, int y, int width, int height)
```
Overrides: paintBorder in class AbstractBorder.
Implements: paintBorder in interface Border.

See also   AbstractBorder (p.462), Border (p.465), UIResource (p.544).

plaf.basic

swing.plaf.basic.BasicBorders.RadioButtonBorder

 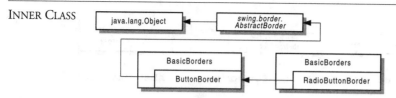

```
public static class BasicBorders.RadioButtonBorder
    extends BasicBorders.ButtonBorder
```

Constructors

```
public RadioButtonBorder(java.awt.Color shadow,
    java.awt.Color darkShadow, java.awt.Color highlight,
    java.awt.Color lightHighlight)
```
Constructs the border used for JRadioButtons.

Methods

```
public java.awt.Insets getBorderInsets(java.awt.Component c)
```
Overrides: getBorderInsets in class BasicBorders.ButtonBorder.
Implements: getBorderInsets in interface Border.

```
public void paintBorder(java.awt.Component c, java.awt.Graphics g,
    int x, int y, int width, int height)
```
Overrides: paintBorder in class BasicBorders.ButtonBorder.
Implements: paintBorder in interface Border.

See also AbstractBorder (p.462), BasicBorders.ButtonBorder (p.551), Border (p.465).

swing.plaf.basic.BasicBorders.SplitPaneBorder

 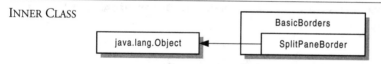

This Border is used around the components in a JSplitPane. This class does not inherit from AbstractBorder due to it having to draw around the whole JSplitPane area and then around the two child components.

```
public static class BasicBorders.SplitPaneBorder
    extends java.lang.Object
    implements Border, UIResource
```

Constructors

```
public SplitPaneBorder(java.awt.Color highlight, java.awt.Color shadow)
```
Constructs a SplitPaneBorder using the given Colors to create a 3D effect.

Methods

public java.awt.Insets getBorderInsets(java.awt.Component c)

Returns new Insets(1,1,1,1).

Implements: getBorderInsets in interface Border.

public boolean isBorderOpaque()

Returns true.

Implements: isBorderOpaque in interface Border.

public void paintBorder(java.awt.Component c, java.awt.Graphics g,
int x, int y, int width, int height)

Paints a border around the whole JSplitPane (passed in as *c*), then around each of the child components if they exist.

Implements: paintBorder in interface Border.

Protected Fields

protected java.awt.Color highlight
protected java.awt.Color shadow

> *See also* Border (p.465), UIResource (p.544).

swing.plaf.basic.BasicBorders.ToggleButtonBorder

INNER CLASS

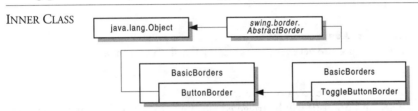

public static class BasicBorders.ToggleButtonBorder
extends BasicBorders.ButtonBorder

Constructors

public ToggleButtonBorder(java.awt.Color shadow, java.awt.Color darkShadow,
java.awt.Color highlight, java.awt.Color lightHighlight)

Constructs the standard border used for JToggleButtons.

Methods

public java.awt.Insets getBorderInsets(java.awt.Component c)

Overrides: getBorderInsets in class BasicBorders.ButtonBorder.

Implements: getBorderInsets in interface Border.

public void paintBorder(java.awt.Component c, java.awt.Graphics g,
int x, int y, int width, int height)

Overrides: paintBorder in class BasicBorders.ButtonBorder.

Implements: paintBorder in interface Border.

> *See also* AbstractBorder (p.462), BasicBorders.ButtonBorder (p.551), Border (p.465).

swing.plaf.basic.BasicButtonListener

CLASS

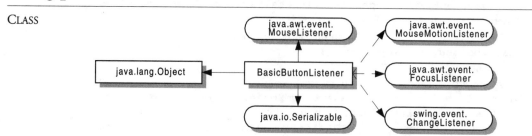

The `Listener` class creates the behavior of buttons in the Basic look and feel. It also provides some shared functionality among all buttons (for example, handling of the Spacebar being pressed and released).

```
public class BasicButtonListener extends java.lang.Object
    implements java.awt.event.MouseListener,
    java.awt.event.MouseMotionListener,
    java.awt.event.FocusListener, ChangeListener,
    java.beans.PropertyChangeListener
```

Constructors

public BasicButtonListener(AbstractButton b)

Creates a `BasicButtonListener` to get events triggered by the given button *b*.

Methods

public void focusGained(java.awt.event.FocusEvent e)

Makes this button the default button (it will be triggered when enter is pressed) if the button is an child of a `JRootPane`.

Implements: focusGained in interface `FocusListener`.

public void focusLost(java.awt.event.FocusEvent e)

Repaints the button.

Implements: focusLost in interface `FocusListener`.

public void installKeyboardActions(JComponent c)

Installs the default key actions. In the Basic look and feel, there are two: programmatically clicking the button when the Spacebar is pressed and the action for the same mnemonic key.

public void mouseClicked(java.awt.event.MouseEvent e)

Empty.

Implements: mouseClicked in interface `MouseListener`.

public void mouseDragged(java.awt.event.MouseEvent e)

Checks for the mouse entering or exiting the button while a mouse button is depressed. Uses this check to set the armed property.

Implements: mouseDragged in interface `MouseMotionListener`.

public void mouseEntered(java.awt.event.MouseEvent e)

If rollover is enabled, sets the rollover property to `true`.

Implements: mouseEntered in interface `MouseListener`.

public void mouseExited(java.awt.event.MouseEvent e)

If rollover is enabled, sets the rollover property to `false`.

plaf.basic

Implements: mouseExited in interface MouseListener.

public void mouseMoved(java.awt.event.MouseEvent e)

Empty.

Implements: mouseMoved in interface MouseMotionListener.

public void mousePressed(java.awt.event.MouseEvent e)

Sets the armed and pressed button properties to true, and tries to get the focus.

Implements: mousePressed in interface MouseListener.

public void mouseReleased(java.awt.event.MouseEvent e)

Sets the pressed button property to false.

Implements: mouseReleased in interface MouseListener.

public void propertyChange(java.beans.PropertyChangeEvent e)

Implements: propertyChange in interface PropertyChangeListener.

public void stateChanged(ChangeEvent e)

Implements: stateChanged in interface ChangeListener.

public void uninstallKeyboardActions(JComponent c)

Uninstalls the keyboard actions installed in installKeyboardActions.

Protected Methods

protected void checkOpacity(AbstractButton b)

Sets the opaque property based on the value of b.isContentAreaFilled().

Returned by   BasicButtonUI.createButtonListener() (p.557).

See also   AbstractButton (p.118), ChangeEvent (p.487), ChangeListener (p.488), JComponent (p.207).

swing.plaf.basic.BasicButtonUI

CLASS

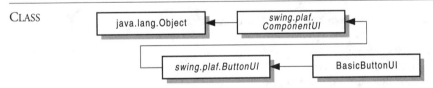

Basic look and feel Button implementation. This class keeps a static reference to a shared BasicButtonUI instance that is used by all buttons in the user interface.

This class provides a considerable amount of support for its subclasses. Because of this it provides a method, getPropertyPrefix(), which is used by this class and subclasses to retrieve resources from the UIDefaults table. The property prefix String is prepended to the common key names so each class can have its own resources. The property prefix String should end with a '.' character.

UIDefaults table key	Description
getPropertyPrefix() + "background"	The Color used for the button background.
getPropertyPrefix() + "border"	The Border used around the button.
getPropertyPrefix() + "font"	The Font used for the button text.

UIDefaults table key	Description
getPropertyPrefix() + "foreground"	The Color used for the button text.
getPropertyPrefix() + "margin"	The Insets around the button.
getPropertyPrefix() + "textIconGap"	The gap, in pixels, between the button's text and Icon.
getPropertyPrefix() + "textShiftOffset"	The number of pixels to shift the text when the button is pressed.

`public class BasicButtonUI extends ButtonUI`

Constructors

`public BasicButtonUI()`

Default constructor.

Methods

`public static ComponentUI createUI(JComponent c)`

Returns a BasicButtonUI instance.

Overrides: createUI in class ComponentUI.

`public int getDefaultTextIconGap(AbstractButton b)`

Returns the default gap between the text and the icon on the button face.

`public java.awt.Dimension getMaximumSize(JComponent c)`

Overrides: getMaximumSize in class ComponentUI.

`public java.awt.Dimension getMinimumSize(JComponent c)`

Overrides: getMinimumSize in class ComponentUI.

`public java.awt.Dimension getPreferredSize(JComponent c)`

Overrides: getPreferredSize in class ComponentUI.

`public void installUI(JComponent c)`

Installs the font and color into the JComponent.

Overrides: installUI in class ComponentUI.

`public void paint(java.awt.Graphics g, JComponent c)`

Paints the BasicButtonUI.

Overrides: paint in class ComponentUI.

`public void uninstallUI(JComponent c)`

Uninstalls the font and colors from the JComponent.

Overrides: uninstallUI in class ComponentUI.

Protected Fields

`protected int defaultTextIconGap`

The gap between the text and the icon on the button.

`protected int defaultTextShiftOffset`

The number of pixels to offset the button's contents to get a "pressed" effect.

Protected Methods

`protected void clearTextShiftOffset()`

Resets the textShiftOffset to its default zero pixels.

`protected BasicButtonListener createButtonListener(JComponent c)`

Creates and sets up the BasicButtonListener instance associated with this ButtonUI instance.

`protected String getPropertyPrefix()`

Returns "Button." (note the period character at the end).

protected int getTextShiftOffset()
Returns the value in pixels to shift the text. The value is controlled by the `clearTextShiftOff-set()` and `setTextShiftOffset()` methods.

protected void installDefaults(AbstractButton c)
Installs the font and colors into the `JComponent`.

protected void installKeyboardActions(AbstractButton c)
Sets up the keyboard actions for this button.

protected void installListeners(AbstractButton c)
Makes the listener listen to the appropriate events from the `JComponent`.

protected void paintButtonPressed(java.awt.Graphics g, AbstractButton b)
Paints the button in its pressed state.

protected void paintFocus(java.awt.Graphics g, AbstractButton b, java.awt.Rectangle viewRect, java.awt.Rectangle textRect, java.awt.Rectangle iconRect)
Paints the focus indicator (an inset rectangle drawn with a dotted line) when the button has the focus.

protected void paintIcon(java.awt.Graphics g, JComponent c, java.awt.Rectangle rect)
Paints the button's icon.

protected void paintText(java.awt.Graphics g, JComponent c, java.awt.Rectangle textRect, String text)
Paints the button's text.

protected void setTextShiftOffset(int i)
Returns the distance to shift the text when the button is pressed.

protected void uninstallDefaults(AbstractButton b)
Uninstalls the font and colors from the `JComponent`.

protected void uninstallKeyboardActions(AbstractButton b)
Uninstalls the keyboard actions for this button from the `JComponent`.

protected void uninstallListeners(AbstractButton b)
Removes this UI delegate from the listener lists installed on the given `AbstractButton` in `installListeners()`.

Extended by   BasicToggleButtonUI (p.701).
See also   AbstractButton (p.118), ButtonUI (p.528), ComponentUI (p.530), JComponent (p.207).

swing.plaf.basic.BasicCheckBoxMenuItemUI

CLASS

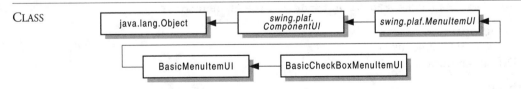

The Basic look and feel UI delegate for `JCheckBoxMenuItems`.

UIDefaults table key	Description
CheckBoxMenuItem.checkIcon	The Icon used to display the check.

`public class BasicCheckBoxMenuItemUI extends BasicMenuItemUI`

Constructors

`public BasicCheckBoxMenuItemUI()`
Default constructor.

Methods

`public static ComponentUI createUI(JComponent c)`
Returns an instance of BasicCheckBoxMenuItemUI.
Overrides: createUI in class BasicMenuItemUI.

`public void processMouseEvent(JMenuItem item, java.awt.event.MouseEvent e, MenuElement[] path, MenuSelectionManager manager)`
Updates the menu selection based on the mouse event.

Protected Methods

`protected String getPropertyPrefix()`
Returns "CheckBoxMenuItem.".
Overrides: getPropertyPrefix in class BasicMenuItemUI.

`protected void installDefaults()`
Overrides: installDefaults in class BasicMenuItemUI.

See also BasicMenuItemUI (p.624), MenuElement (p.425), MenuSelectionManager (p.426).

swing.plaf.basic.BasicCheckBoxUI

CLASS

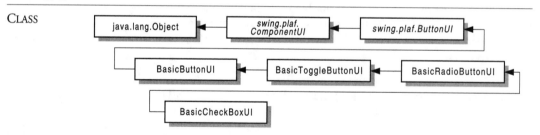

Basic look and feel implementation of CheckBoxUI for JCheckBoxes.

`public class BasicCheckBoxUI extends BasicRadioButtonUI`

Constructors

`public BasicCheckBoxUI()`
Default constructor.

Methods

`public static ComponentUI createUI(JComponent b)`
Returns an instance of BasicCheckBoxUI.

Overrides: createUI in class BasicRadioButtonUI.

public String getPropertyPrefix()

    Returns "CheckBox.".

    See also   BasicRadioButtonUI (p.641), JCheckBox (p.193), JComponent (p.207).

swing.plaf.basic.BasicColorChooserUI

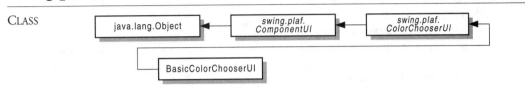

The Basic look and feel for a JColorChooser. This provides a container that can hold either a single ColorChooserPanel or a set of ColorChooserPanels in a tabbed pane.

UIDefaults table key	Description
ColorChooser.background	The background Color for the color chooser.
ColorChooser.font	The Font for the color chooser.
ColorChooser.foreground	The foreground Color for the color chooser.
ColorChooser.previewText	The text used for the TitledBorder around the preview panel.

public class BasicColorChooserUI extends ColorChooserUI

Constructors
public BasicColorChooserUI()

    Default constructor.

Methods
public static ComponentUI createUI(JComponent c)

    Creates a new BasicColorChooserUI instance.

    Overrides: createUI in class ComponentUI.

public void installUI(JComponent c)

    Overrides: installUI in class ComponentUI.

public void uninstallUI(JComponent c)

    Overrides: uninstallUI in class ComponentUI.

Protected Fields
protected AbstractColorChooserPanel[] defaultChoosers

    Holds a list of the default ColorChooserPanels returned from ColorChooserComponent-Factory.

protected ChangeListener previewListener

    Listens to the ColorSelectionModel of the component in the preview panel.

protected PropertyChangeListener propertyChangeListener

    Listens for changes in the associated JColorChooser.

Protected Methods

protected AbstractColorChooserPanel[] createDefaultChoosers()
Retrieves the default ColorChooserPanels from ColorChooserComponentFactory.

protected java.beans.PropertyChangeListener createPropertyChangeListener()
Creates the listener for changes in the associated JColorChooser's chooserPanels property.

protected void installDefaults()
Installs this UI's defaults into the JComponent.

protected void installListeners()
Adds the listeners to the JComponent.

protected void installPreviewPanel()
Installs the component to use as the preview panel into the associated JColorChooser. Retrieves this panel from the ColorChooserComponentFactory.

protected void uninstallDefaultChoosers()
Removes the default ColorChooserPanels from the associated JColorChooser.

protected void uninstallDefaults()
Uninstalls this UI's defaults from the JComponent.

protected void uninstallListeners()
Removes the listeners from the JComponent.

Inner Classes

public class BasicColorChooserUI.PropertyHandler

See also AbstractColorChooserPanel (p.478), ChangeListener (p.488), ColorChooserComponentFactory (p.479), ColorChooserUI (p.529), JColorChooser (p.197), JComponent (p.207).

swing.plaf.basic.BasicColorChooserUI.PropertyHandler

INNER CLASS

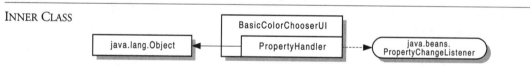

This inner class listens for PropertyChangeEvents in the associated JColorChooser on behalf of the BasicColorChooserUI.

This inner class should be treated as a protected inner class, since it will be changed to protected after a compiler bug is resolved.

```
public class BasicColorChooserUI.PropertyHandler
    extends java.lang.Object
    implements java.beans.PropertyChangeListener
```

Constructors

public PropertyHandler()
Default constructor.

Methods

public void propertyChange(java.beans.PropertyChangeEvent pce)
Implements: propertyChange in interface PropertyChangeListener.

swing.plaf.basic.BasicComboBoxEditor

CLASS

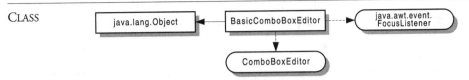

The Basic look and feel `ComboBoxEditor` implementation. It is used as the default editor in editable `JComboBox`es.

```
public class BasicComboBoxEditor extends java.lang.Object
    implements ComboBoxEditor, java.awt.event.FocusListener
```

Constructors
public BasicComboBoxEditor()

Constructs and configures a new `BasicComboBoxEditor`.

Methods
public void addActionListener(java.awt.event.ActionListener l)

Implements: addActionListener in interface ComboBoxEditor.

public void focusGained(java.awt.event.FocusEvent e)

This is an empty method.

Implements: focusGained in interface FocusListener.

public void focusLost(java.awt.event.FocusEvent e)

Triggers an `ActionEvent`.

Implements: focusLost in interface FocusListener.

public java.awt.Component getEditorComponent()

Returns `editor`.

Implements: getEditorComponent in interface ComboBoxEditor.

public Object getItem()

Returns the text in the editor.

Implements: getItem in interface ComboBoxEditor.

public void removeActionListener(java.awt.event.ActionListener l)

Implements: removeActionListener in interface ComboBoxEditor.

public void selectAll()

Selects all of the text in the `editor` and requests the focus.

Implements: selectAll in interface ComboBoxEditor.

public void setItem(Object anObject)

Sets the text in the `editor` to `anObject.toString()`.

Implements: setItem in interface ComboBoxEditor.

Protected Fields
protected JTextField editor

The editor.

Inner Classes
public static class BasicComboBoxEditor.UIResource

Extended by   BasicComboBoxEditor.UIResource (p.564).
See also   ComboBoxEditor (p.155).

swing.plaf.basic.BasicComboBoxEditor.UIResource

INNER CLASS

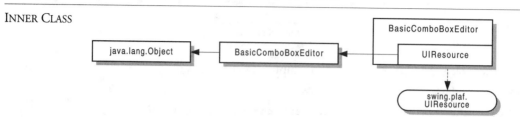

A subclass of `BasicComboBoxEditor` that implements `UIResource`.

```
public static class BasicComboBoxEditor.UIResource
    extends BasicComboBoxEditor
    implements UIResource
```

Constructors
```
public UIResource()
```
Default constructor.

> *See also*   BasicComboBoxEditor (p.563), UIResource (p.544).

swing.plaf.basic.BasicComboBoxRenderer

CLASS

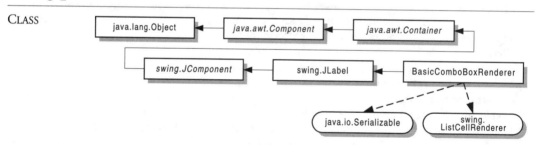

Basic look and feel's default combo box renderer implementation. It is an opaque `JLabel` that uses a single pixel `EmptyBorder`.

```
public class BasicComboBoxRenderer extends JLabel
    implements ListCellRenderer, java.io.Serializable
```

Constructors
```
public BasicComboBoxRenderer()
```

Methods
```
public java.awt.Component getListCellRendererComponent(JList list,
    Object value, int index, boolean isSelected, boolean cellHasFocus)
```
Implements: getListCellRendererComponent in interface `ListCellRenderer`.

plaf.basic

Protected Fields
protected static Border noFocusBorder
 The border to use when the renderer doesn't have the focus.

Inner Classes
public static class BasicComboBoxRenderer.UIResource

Extended by   BasicComboBoxRenderer.UIResource (p.565).

See also   Border (p.465), EmptyBorder (p.467), JLabel (p.264), ListCellRenderer (p.420).

swing.plaf.basic.BasicComboBoxRenderer.UIResource

INNER CLASS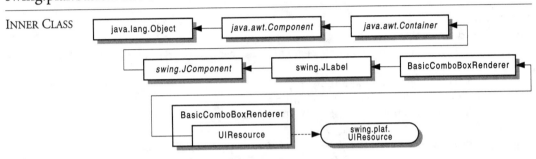

A subclass of BasicComboBoxRenderer that implements UIResource.

```
public static class BasicComboBoxRenderer.UIResource
    extends BasicComboBoxRenderer
    implements UIResource
```

Constructors
public UIResource()
 Default constructor.

See also   BasicComboBoxRenderer (p.564), UIResource (p.544).

swing.plaf.basic.BasicComboBoxUI

CLASS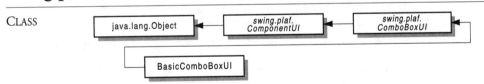

Basic look and feel's implementation of a UI for JComboBox. This class manages the editor and the arrow button (the button that shows or hides the pop-up). See the inner classes' documentation for the handlers for other aspects of the ComboBoxUI.

UIDefaults table key	Description
ComboBox.background	The background Color for the combo box.

plaf.basic

UIDefaults table key	Description
ComboBox.border	The Border for the combo box.
ComboBox.font	The Font for the combo box.
ComboBox.foreground	The foreground Color for the combo box.

`public class BasicComboBoxUI extends ComboBoxUI`

Constructors

`public BasicComboBoxUI()`

Default constructor.

Methods

`public void addEditor()`

Installs the editor at construction time or after the user has changed the editor. This method also calls configureEditor().

`public void configureArrowButton()`

Adds the listeners to the pop-up's arrow button.

`public static ComponentUI createUI(JComponent c)`

Overrides: createUI in class ComponentUI.

`public Accessible getAccessibleChild(JComponent c, int i)`

Overrides: getAccessibleChild in class ComponentUI.

`public int getAccessibleChildrenCount(JComponent c)`

Overrides: getAccessibleChildrenCount in class ComponentUI.

`public java.awt.Dimension getMaximumSize(JComponent c)`

Overrides: getMaximumSize in class ComponentUI.

`public java.awt.Dimension getMinimumSize(JComponent c)`

Overrides: getMinimumSize in class ComponentUI.

`public java.awt.Dimension getPreferredSize(JComponent c)`

Overrides: getPreferredSize in class ComponentUI.

`public void installUI(JComponent c)`

Overrides: installUI in class ComponentUI.

`public boolean isFocusTraversable()`

Returns true if the combo box is editable, false if it is not.

Overrides: isFocusTraversable in class ComboBoxUI.

`public boolean isPopupVisible(JComboBox c)`

Returns true if the pop-up is currently visible (even if it showing, but obscured by another component).

Overrides: isPopupVisible in class ComboBoxUI.

`public void paint(java.awt.Graphics g, JComponent c)`

Overrides: paint in class ComponentUI.

`public void paintCurrentValue(java.awt.Graphics g,`
`    java.awt.Rectangle bounds, boolean hasFocus)`

Paints the currently selected item.

`public void paintCurrentValueBackground(java.awt.Graphics g,`
`    java.awt.Rectangle bounds, boolean hasFocus)`

Paints the background of the currently selected item.

public void removeEditor()

Removes the editor from the JComboBox in preparation for adding a new one (usually a custom editor). This method calls unconfigureEditor() as part of its processing.

public void setPopupVisible(JComboBox c, boolean v)

Shows or hides the pop-up depending on the value of *v*.

Overrides: setPopupVisible in class ComboBoxUI.

public void unconfigureArrowButton()

Removes the listeners that were added to the pop-up's arrow button.

public void uninstallUI(JComponent c)

Overrides: uninstallUI in class ComponentUI.

Protected Fields

```
protected JButton arrowButton
protected java.awt.Dimension cachedMinimumSize
protected JComboBox comboBox
protected CellRendererPane currentValuePane
protected java.awt.Component editor
protected java.awt.event.FocusListener focusListener
protected boolean hasFocus
protected boolean isMinimumSizeDirty
protected java.awt.event.ItemListener itemListener
protected java.awt.event.KeyListener keyListener
protected JList listBox
protected ListDataListener listDataListener
protected ComboPopup popup
protected java.awt.event.KeyListener popupKeyListener
protected java.awt.event.MouseListener popupMouseListener
protected java.awt.event.MouseMotionListener popupMouseMotionListener
protected java.beans.PropertyChangeListener propertyChangeListener
```

Protected Methods

protected void configureEditor()

Sets the editor's font and adds listeners.

protected JButton createArrowButton()

Returns an instance of BasicArrowButton, which can be overridden by subclasses.

protected ComboBoxEditor createEditor()

Creates the ComboBoxEditor that is to be used in editable combo boxes. This method gets called only if a custom editor has not already been installed in the JComboBox.

protected java.awt.event.FocusListener createFocusListener()

Creates the FocusListener. The default FocusListener returned is an instance of BasicComboBoxUI.FocusHandler which hides the pop-up when the focus is lost.

protected java.awt.event.ItemListener createItemListener()

Creates the ItemListener. The default ItemListener returned is an instance of BasicComboBoxUI.ItemHandler which updates the editor when the selection changes.

protected java.awt.event.KeyListener createKeyListener()

Creates the KeyListener. The default KeyListener returned is an instance of BasicComboBoxUI.KeyHandler which handles type-ahead.

protected java.awt.LayoutManager createLayoutManager()

Creates the LayoutManager. The default LayoutManager returned is an instance of BasicComboBoxUI.ComboBoxLayoutManager which lays out the arrow button at the right end of the editor.

protected ListDataListener createListDataListener()

Creates the ListDataListener that is used for caching the preferred sizes. The default ListDataListener returned is an instance of BasicComboBoxUI.ListDataHandler.

protected ComboPopup createPopup()

Creates an instance of a class that implements the ComboPopup interface. The default ComboPopup implementor returned is BasicComboPopup.

protected java.beans.PropertyChangeListener createPropertyChangeListener()

Creates the listener for property changes in the combo box. The important properties to listen for are the model and the editor. Other properties to listen for are the editable, enabled, and maxiumumRowCount properties. The default property change listener returned is BasicComboBoxUI.PropertyChangeHandler.

protected ListCellRenderer createRenderer()

Creates and installs the default renderer (if a custom renderer has not been installed).

protected java.awt.Dimension getDefaultSize()

Returns the default size to use when the combo box editor and list are empty of all data.

protected java.awt.Dimension getDisplaySize()

Returns the size of the largest element in the combo box if there are any elements. Otherwise, it returns getDefaultSize().

protected java.awt.Insets getInsets()

Returns the insets of the associated JComboBox.

protected void installComponents()

Installs the editor and arrow button into the JComboBox.

protected void installDefaults()

Installs the default colors, font, renderer, and editor into the JComboBox.

protected void installKeyboardActions()

Adds the keyboard actions to the JComboBox. This class supplies actions for ENTER and ESCAPE. Subclasses can add more actions as they see fit.

protected void installListeners()

Attaches listeners to the JComboBox and ComboBoxModel.

protected boolean isNavigationKey(int keyCode)

Returns true if the given key is one used for navigation. This method is used for optimization, since keys it returns true for are not passed to the type-ahead KeyListener. Subclasses need to override this if they change which keys are used for navigation. This default implementation only returns true for VK_UP and VK_DOWN.

protected java.awt.Rectangle rectangleForCurrentValue()

Returns the bounding box for the currently selected item.

protected void selectNextPossibleValue()

Selects the next item in the list, if there is one.

protected void selectPreviousPossibleValue()

Selects the previous item in the list, if there is one.

protected void toggleOpenClose()

Toggles the hiding/showing state of the pop-up.

protected void unconfigureEditor()
    Removes the listeners from the editor.
protected void uninstallComponents()
    Calls removeAll() on the JComboBox.
protected void uninstallDefaults()
    Uninstalls the default colors, default font, and default renderer from the JComboBox.
protected void uninstallKeyboardActions()
    Removes the keyboard actions added by installKeyboardActions().
protected void uninstallListeners()
    Removes the listeners from the JComboBox and ComboBoxModel.

Inner Classes
```
public class BasicComboBoxUI.ComboBoxLayoutManager
public class BasicComboBoxUI.FocusHandler
public class BasicComboBoxUI.ItemHandler
public class BasicComboBoxUI.KeyHandler
public class BasicComboBoxUI.ListDataHandler
public class BasicComboBoxUI.PropertyChangeHandler
```

See also   Accessible (p.85), ComboPopup (p.731), ComponentUI (p.530), JButton (p.191), JComboBox (p.200), JComponent (p.207), JList (p.271), ListCellRenderer (p.420), ListDataListener (p.499).

swing.plaf.basic.BasicComboBoxUI.ComboBoxLayoutManager

INNER CLASS

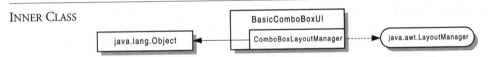

This layout manager handles laying out the combo box in the "standard" way, with the arrow button to the right of the editor.

```
public class BasicComboBoxUI.ComboBoxLayoutManager
    extends java.lang.Object implements java.awt.LayoutManager
```

Constructors
public ComboBoxLayoutManager()
    Default constructor.

Methods
public void addLayoutComponent(String name, java.awt.Component comp)
    Empty method.
    Implements: addLayoutComponent in interface LayoutManager.
public void layoutContainer(java.awt.Container parent)
    Lays out the arrow button and the editor.
    Implements: layoutContainer in interface LayoutManager.
public java.awt.Dimension minimumLayoutSize(java.awt.Container parent)
    Returns the minimum size of the JComboBox.
    Implements: minimumLayoutSize in interface LayoutManager.

plaf.basic

`public java.awt.Dimension preferredLayoutSize(java.awt.Container parent)`
> Returns the preferred size of the `JComboBox`.
>
> *Implements:* `preferredLayoutSize` in interface `LayoutManager`.

`public void removeLayoutComponent(java.awt.Component comp)`
> Empty method.
>
> *Implements:* `removeLayoutComponent` in interface `LayoutManager`.

swing.plaf.basic.BasicComboBoxUI.FocusHandler

INNER CLASS

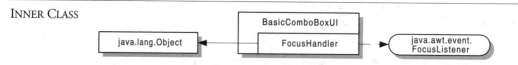

This class listens for focus changes related to a `BasicComboBoxUI`.

```
protected class BasicComboBoxUI.ComboBoxFocusListener
    extends java.lang.Object
    implements java.awt.event.FocusListener
```

Constructors
`public FocusHandler()`
> Default constructor.

Methods
`public void focusGained(java.awt.event.FocusEvent fe)`
> Repaints the combo box.
>
> *Implements:* `focusGained` in interface `FocusListener`.

`public void focusLost(java.awt.event.FocusEvent fe)`
> Hides the pop-up if it is showing and repaints the combo box.
>
> *Implements:* `focusLost` in interface `FocusListener`.

swing.plaf.basic.BasicComboBoxUI.ItemHandler

INNER CLASS

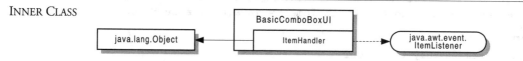

This class listens for selection changes in a `JComboBox`.

```
protected class BasicComboBoxUI.ComboBoxItemListener
    extends java.lang.Object
    implements java.awt.event.ItemListener
```

Constructors
`public ItemHandler()`
> Default constructor.

Methods
`public void itemStateChanged(java.awt.event.ItemEvent e)`
> Updates the editor if there is one, and repaints the combo box.
> *Implements:* `itemStateChanged` in interface `ItemListener`.

swing.plaf.basic.BasicComboBoxUI.KeyHandler

INNER CLASS

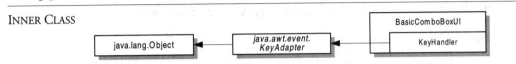

This class filters out navigation keys before forwarding the key along to the `JComboBox`'s `selectWithKeyChar` method.

`protected class BasicComboBoxUI.KeyHandler`
`    extends java.awt.event.KeyAdapter`

Constructors
`public KeyHandler()`
> Default constructor.

Methods
`public void keyPressed(java.awt.event.KeyEvent e)`
> *Overrides:* `keyPressed` in class `KeyAdapter`.
> *Implements:* `keyPressed` in interface `KeyListener`.

swing.plaf.basic.BasicComboBoxUI.ListDataHandler

INNER CLASS

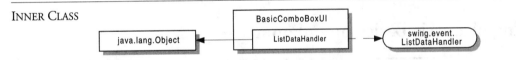

This class invalidates any cached size information in the `BasicComboBoxUI` when the data in the combo box changes.

`protected class BasicComboBoxUI.ComboBoxListDataListener`
`    extends java.lang.Object`
`    implements ListDataListener`

Constructors
`public ListDataHandler()`
> Default constructor.

Methods
`public void contentsChanged(ListDataEvent e)`
> Sets the `isMinimumSizeDirty` flag in `BasicComboBoxUI`.
> *Implements:* `contentsChanged` in interface `ListDataListener`.

`public void intervalAdded(ListDataEvent e)`
> Calls `contentsChanged`.

Implements: intervalAdded in interface ListDataListener.

public void intervalRemoved(ListDataEvent e)

Calls contentsChanged.

Implements: intervalRemoved in interface ListDataListener.

See also   ListDataEvent (p.498), ListDataListener (p.499).

swing.plaf.basic.BasicComboBoxUI.PropertyChangeHandler

INNER CLASS

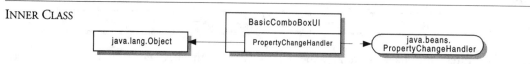

This class listens for bound properties changing in the JComboBox. It looks for the model or editor being changed and updates the BasicComboBoxUI. It also looks for changes in the editable, enabled, and maximumRowCount properties.

```
public class BasicComboBoxUI.PropertyChangeHandler
    extends java.lang.Object
    implements java.beans.PropertyChangeListener
```

Constructors

public PropertyChangeHandler()

Default constructor.

Methods

public void propertyChange(java.beans.PropertyChangeEvent e)

Implements: propertyChange in interface PropertyChangeListener.

swing.plaf.basic.BasicComboPopup

CLASS

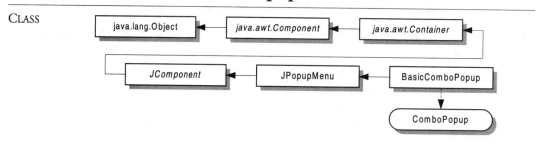

This class provides an implementation of the ComboPopup interface for the Basic look and feel. It extends JPopupMenu since most common UIs use something similar in appearance and behavior to a pop-up menu for their combo box pop-ups.

Most common UIs will only have to override the createX methods in this class to adapt it to their needs.

```
public class BasicComboPopup extends JPopupMenu
    implements ComboPopup
```

Constructors

public BasicComboPopup(JComboBox combo)

Constructs the pop-up for the given combo box.

Methods

public java.awt.event.KeyListener getKeyListener()

Implements: getKeyListener in interface ComboPopup.

public JList getList()

Implements: getList in interface ComboPopup.

public java.awt.event.MouseListener getMouseListener()

Implements: getMouseListener in interface ComboPopup.

public java.awt.event.MouseMotionListener getMouseMotionListener()

Implements: getMouseMotionListener in interface ComboPopup.

public void hide()

Overrides: hide in class Component.

Implements: hide in interface ComboPopup.

public boolean isFocusTraversable()

Returns false.

Overrides: isFocusTraversable in class JComponent.

public void show()

Overrides: show in class Component.

Implements: show in interface ComboPopup.

public void uninstallingUI()

Since this pop-up isn't in the component tree, it won't yet have uninstallUI() called on it, so this method is provided to fill that role. It removes the listeners that were added in addComboBoxListeners.

Implements: uninstallingUI in interface ComboPopup.

Protected Fields

protected static final int SCROLL_DOWN

protected static final int SCROLL_UP

Constants used in the scrollDirection field.

protected Timer autoscrollTimer

protected JComboBox comboBox

protected boolean hasEntered

protected boolean isAutoScrolling

protected java.awt.event.ItemListener itemListener

protected java.awt.event.KeyListener keyListener

protected JList list

protected ListDataListener listDataListener

protected java.awt.event.MouseListener listMouseListener

protected java.awt.event.MouseMotionListener listMouseMotionListener

protected ListSelectionListener listSelectionListener

protected java.awt.event.MouseListener mouseListener

protected java.awt.event.MouseMotionListener mouseMotionListener

protected java.beans.PropertyChangeListener propertyChangeListener

protected int scrollDirection

protected JScrollPane scroller

protected boolean valueIsAdjusting

Protected Methods

protected void autoScrollDown()

Continues autoscrolling downwards in the list.

protected void autoScrollUp()

Continues autoscrolling upwards in the list.

protected java.awt.Rectangle computePopupBounds(int px, int py, int pw, int ph)

Returns the bounding rectangle for the pop-up.

protected void configureList()

Configures the list created by `createList()`.

protected void configurePopup()

Configures this object.

protected void configureScroller()

Configures the `JScrollPane` created by `createScroller()`.

protected java.awt.event.MouseEvent convertMouseEvent(java.awt.event.MouseEvent e)

Converts the location of the given mouse event from the source container's coordinate system to the pop-up's.

protected java.awt.event.ItemListener createItemListener()

Creates an item listener that watches for selection changes in the `JComboBox`. Returns an instance of `BasicComboPopup.ItemHandler`.

protected java.awt.event.KeyListener createKeyListener()

Creates the key listener that is returned by `getKeyListener()`. This class returns an instance of `BasicComboPopup.InvocationKeyHandler`.

protected JList createList()

Creates the `JList` that is used to display the items in the model.

protected java.awt.event.MouseListener createListMouseListener()

Creates a mouse listener that watches for mouse events in the pop-up's list. Returns an instance of `BasicComboPopup.ListMouseHandler`.

protected java.awt.event.MouseMotionListener createListMouseMotionListener()

Creates a mouse motion listener that watches for mouse motion events in the pop-up's list. Returns an instance of `BasicComboPopup.ListMouseMotionHandler`.

protected ListSelectionListener createListSelectionListener()

Creates a list selection listener that watches for selection changes in the pop-up's list. Returns an instance of `BasicComboPopup.ListSelectionHandler`.

protected java.awt.event.MouseListener createMouseListener()

Creates the mouse listener that is returned by `getMouseListener()`. Returns an instance of `Basic-ComboPopup.InvocationMouseHandler`.

protected java.awt.event.MouseMotionListener createMouseMotionListener()

Creates the mouse motion listener that is returned by `getMouseMotionListener()`. Returns an instance of `BasicComboPopup.InvocationMouseMotionHandler`.

protected java.beans.PropertyChangeListener createPropertyChangeListener()

Creates a property change listener that watches for changes in the bound properties in the `JComboBox`. Returns an instance of `BasicComboPopup.PropertyChangeHandler`.

protected JScrollPane createScroller()

Creates the `JScrollPane` that is used in the pop-up to hold the list.

protected void delegateFocus(java.awt.event.MouseEvent e)

This is a utility method that helps event handlers figure out where to send the focus when the pop-up is brought up. This implementation delegates the focus to the editor if the combo box is editable or to the JComboBox if the editor is not editable.

protected int getPopupHeightForRowCount(int maxRowCount)

Returns the height that the pop-up needs for the given number of rows.

protected void installComboBoxListeners()

Adds a PropertyChangeListener and ItemListener to the associated JComboBox. This method also calls installComboBoxModelListeners().

protected void installComboBoxModelListeners(ComboBoxModel model)

Adds a ListDataListener to the model of the associated JComboBox.

protected void installListListeners()

Called by configureList() to add the necessary listeners to the list.

protected void startAutoScrolling(int direction)

Called by BasicComboPopup.InvocationMouseMotionListener to start autoscrolling the list in the given direction.

protected void stopAutoScrolling()

Called by BasicComboPopup.InvocationMouseMotionListener to stop autoscrolling the list.

protected void togglePopup()

Toggles the hidden/showing state of the pop-up.

protected void uninstallComboBoxModelListeners(ComboBoxModel model)

Removes the listeners added in installComboBoxListeners().

protected void updateListBoxSelectionForEvent(
java.awt.event.MouseEvent anEvent, boolean shouldScroll)

Called by the event listeners to change the list selection to the item underneath the given mouse event coordinates.

Inner Classes

public class BasicComboPopup.InvocationKeyListener
protected class BasicComboPopup.InvocationMouseListener
protected class BasicComboPopup.InvocationMouseMotionListener
protected class BasicComboPopup.ListSelListener
protected class BasicComboPopup.ListMouseListener
protected class BasicComboPopup.ListMouseMotionListener
protected class BasicComboPopup.ComboItemListener
protected class BasicComboPopup.ComboPropertyChangeListener

See also   ComboBoxModel (p.156), ComboPopup (p.731), JComboBox (p.200), JList (p.271), JScrollPane (p.332), ListSelectionListener (p.500).

swing.plaf.basic.BasicComboPopup.InvocationKeyHandler

INNER CLASS

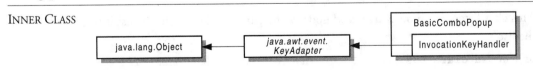

plaf.basic

This class listens for the Spacebar being pressed and shows/hides the pop-up accordingly.

```
public class BasicComboPopup.InvocationKeyHandler
    extends java.awt.event.KeyAdapter
```

Constructors
```
public InvocationKeyHandler()
```
Default constructor.

Methods
```
public void keyReleased(java.awt.event.KeyEvent e)
```
Overrides: keyReleased in class KeyAdapter.
Implements: keyReleased in interface KeyListener.

swing.plaf.basic.BasicComboPopup.InvocationMouseHandler

INNER CLASS

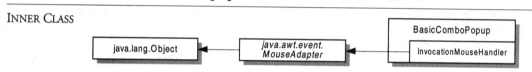

This class listens for mouse events and handles showing or hiding the list and drag selections in the list.

```
protected class BasicComboPopup.InvocationMouseHandler
    extends java.awt.event.MouseAdapter
```

Constructors
```
public InvocationMouseHandler()
```
Default constructor.

Methods
```
public void mousePressed(java.awt.event.MouseEvent e)
```
Overrides: mousePressed in class MouseAdapter.
Implements: mousePressed in interface MouseListener.
```
public void mouseReleased(java.awt.event.MouseEvent e)
```
Overrides: mouseReleased in class MouseAdapter.
Implements: mouseReleased in interface MouseListener.

swing.plaf.basic.BasicComboPopup.InvocationMouseMotionHandler

INNER CLASS

This class listens for mouse drags and updates the current selection in the list if the drag is inside the list.

```
protected class BasicComboPopup.InvocationMouseMotionHandler
    extends java.awt.event.MouseMotionAdapter
```

plaf.basic

Constructors
public InvocationMouseMotionHandler()
> Default constructor.

Methods
public void mouseDragged(java.awt.event.MouseEvent e)
> *Overrides:* mouseDragged in class MouseMotionAdapter.
> *Implements:* mouseDragged in interface MouseMotionListener.

swing.plaf.basic.BasicComboPopup.ItemHandler

INNER CLASS

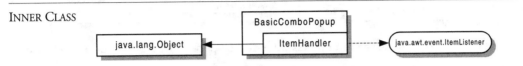

This class listens for changes in the JComboBox's selection. It updates the list accordingly when it is notified.

```
protected class BasicComboPopup.ItemHandler extends java.lang.Object
    implements java.awt.event.ItemListener
```

Constructors
public ItemHandler()
> Default constructor.

Methods
public void itemStateChanged(java.awt.event.ItemEvent e)
> Selects the new selected item, and makes sure it is visible.
> *Implements:* itemStateChanged in interface ItemListener.

swing.plaf.basic.BasicComboPopup.ListDataHandler

INNER CLASS

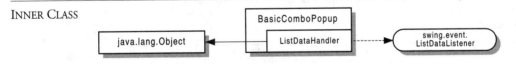

Updates the JComboBox's selection to match the selection in the pop-up.

```
public class BasicComboPopup.ListDataHandler extends java.lang.Object
    implements ListDataListener
```

Constructors
public ListDataHandler()
> Default constructor.

Methods
public void contentsChanged(ListDataEvent e)
> *Implements:* contentsChanged in interface ListDataListener.

plaf.basic

```
public void intervalAdded(ListDataEvent e)
```
Implements: intervalAdded in interface ListDataListener.
```
public void intervalRemoved(ListDataEvent e)
```
Implements: intervalRemoved in interface ListDataListener.

See also   ListDataEvent (p.498), ListDataListener (p.499).

swing.plaf.basic.BasicComboPopup.ListMouseHandler

INNER CLASS

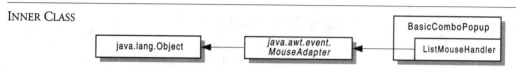

This class listens for mouseReleased events and hides the pop-up when the mouse is released in the list.

```
protected class BasicComboPopup.ListMouseHandler
    extends java.awt.event.MouseAdapter
```

Constructors
```
public ListMouseHandler()
```
Default constructor.

Methods
```
public void mousePressed(java.awt.event.MouseEvent e)
```
Overrides: mousePressed in class MouseAdapter.
Implements: mousePressed in interface MouseListener.
```
public void mouseReleased(java.awt.event.MouseEvent anEvent)
```
Overrides: mouseReleased in class MouseAdapter.
Implements: mouseReleased in interface MouseListener.

swing.plaf.basic.BasicComboPopup.ListMouseMotionHandler

INNER CLASS

This listener changes the selected item as you move the mouse over the list. The selection change is not committed to the model—this simply provides visual feedback. The selection is committed to the model when the mouse is released.

```
protected class BasicComboPopup.ListMouseMotionHandler
    extends java.awt.event.MouseMotionAdapter
```

Constructors
```
public ListMouseMotionHandler()
```
Default constructor.

Methods
public void mouseMoved(java.awt.event.MouseEvent anEvent)

Overrides: mouseMoved in class MouseMotionAdapter.

Implements: mouseMoved in interface MouseMotionListener.

swing.plaf.basic.BasicComboPopup.ListSelectionHandler

INNER CLASS

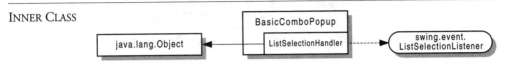

This class listens for changes in the list's selection and forwards them to the combo box.

protected class BasicComboPopup.ListSelListener
   extends java.lang.Object implements ListSelectionListener

Constructors
public ListSelectionHandler()

Default constructor.

Methods
public void valueChanged(ListSelectionEvent e)

Implements: valueChanged in interface ListSelectionListener.

See also   ListSelectionEvent (p.499), ListSelectionListener (p.500).

swing.plaf.basic.BasicComboPopup.PropertyChangeHandler

INNER CLASS

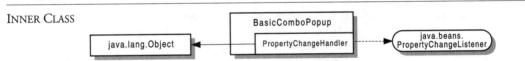

This class listens for bound property changes in the associated JComboBox. If the model or the renderer changes, the pop-up hides itself.

protected class BasicComboPopup.PropertyChangeHandler
   extends java.lang.Object
   implements java.beans.PropertyChangeListener

Constructors
public PropertyChangeHandler()

Default constructor.

Methods
public void propertyChange(java.beans.PropertyChangeEvent e)

Implements: propertyChange in interface PropertyChangeListener.

plaf.basic

swing.plaf.basic.BasicDesktopIconUI

CLASS

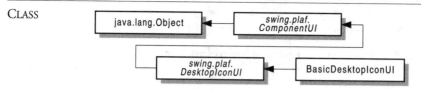

The Basic look and feel implementation of a `JInternalFrame` which is minimized.

UIDefaults table key	Description
DesktopIcon.border	The Border used by the desktop icon.

```
public class BasicDesktopIconUI extends DesktopIconUI
```

Constructors
public BasicDesktopIconUI()
> Constructs a new BasicDesktopIconUI.

Methods
public static ComponentUI createUI(JComponent c)
> *Overrides:* createUI in class ComponentUI.

public void deiconize()
> Restores the JInternalFrame from the desktop icon.

public java.awt.Insets getInsets(JComponent c)
> Returns the insets the desktop icon should use.

public java.awt.Dimension getMaximumSize(JComponent c)
> *Overrides:* getMaximumSize in class ComponentUI.

public java.awt.Dimension getMinimumSize(JComponent c)
> *Overrides:* getMinimumSize in class ComponentUI.

public java.awt.Dimension getPreferredSize(JComponent c)
> *Overrides:* getPreferredSize in class ComponentUI.

public void installUI(JComponent c)
> *Overrides:* installUI in class ComponentUI.

public void uninstallUI(JComponent c)
> *Overrides:* uninstallUI in class ComponentUI.

Protected Fields
protected JInternalFrame.JDesktopIcon desktopIcon
> The JDesktopIcon from the associated JInternalFrame.

protected JInternalFrame frame
> The associated JInternalFrame.

Protected Methods
protected MouseInputListener createMouseInputListener()
> Returns the MouseInputListener for this desktop icon.

protected void installComponents()
> Installs the layout manager and the components that make up the desktop icon.

protected void installDefaults()
Installs the border onto the desktop icon.
protected void installListeners()
Adds a MouseInputListener to the desktop icon.
protected void uninstallComponents()
Uninstalls the components and layout manager for the desktop icon.
protected void uninstallDefaults()
Uninstalls the border from the desktop icon.
protected void uninstallListeners()
Removes the MouseInputListener.

See also   ComponentUI (p.530), JComponent (p.207), JInternalFrame (p.254),
JInternalFrame.JDesktopIcon (p.263), MouseInputListener (p.505).

swing.plaf.basic.BasicDesktopIconUI.MouseInputHandler

INNER CLASS

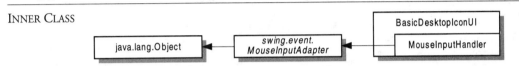

This class listens for mouse movements and acts on them.

```
public class BasicDesktopIconUI.MouseInputHandler
    extends MouseInputAdapter
```

Constructors
public MouseInputHandler()
Default constructor.

Methods
public void mouseDragged(java.awt.event.MouseEvent)
Moves and repaints the desktop icon as it is dragged.
Implements: mouseDragged in interface MouseMotionListener.
public void mouseMoved(java.awt.event.MouseEvent)
Empty method.
Implements: mouseDragged in interface MouseMotionListener.
public void mousePressed(java.awt.event.MouseEvent)
Selects the desktop icon and moves it to the front. If the click count is more than a single click, this
method will deiconize() the desktop icon.
Overrides: mousePressed in class MouseAdapter.
public void mouseReleased(java.awt.event.MouseEvent)
Resets the starting coordinates used for drags.
Overrides: mousePressed in class MouseAdapter.
**public void moveAndRepaint(JComponent f, int newX, int newY,
    int newWidth, int newHeight)**
Moves the desktop icon to a new location and repaints the display as necessary.

See also   JComponent (p.207), MouseInputAdapter (p.504).

plaf.basic

swing.plaf.basic.BasicDesktopPaneUI

CLASS

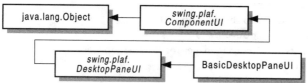

The Basic look and feel JDesktopPane UI delegate.

UIDefaults table key	Description
Desktop.background	The background Color for the desktop pane.

```
public class BasicDesktopPaneUI extends DesktopPaneUI
```

Constructors
```
public BasicDesktopPaneUI()
```
Constructs a new BasicDesktopPaneUI.

Methods
```
public static ComponentUI createUI(JComponent c)
```
Overrides: createUI in class ComponentUI.
```
public java.awt.Dimension getMaximumSize(JComponent c)
```
Overrides: getMaximumSize in class ComponentUI.
```
public java.awt.Dimension getMinimumSize(JComponent c)
```
Overrides: getMinimumSize in class ComponentUI.
```
public java.awt.Dimension getPreferredSize(JComponent c)
```
Overrides: getPreferredSize in class ComponentUI.
```
public void installUI(JComponent c)
```
Overrides: installUI in class ComponentUI.
```
public void paint(java.awt.Graphics g, JComponent c)
```
Overrides: paint in class ComponentUI.
```
public void uninstallUI(JComponent c)
```
Overrides: uninstallUI in class ComponentUI.

Protected Fields
```
protected KeyStroke closeKey
```
The KeyStroke which closes a JInternalFrame.
```
protected JDesktopPane desktop
```
The associated JDesktopPane.
```
protected DesktopManager desktopManager
```
The associated DesktopManager.
```
protected KeyStroke maximizeKey
```
The KeyStroke which will maximize a JInternalFrame.
```
protected KeyStroke minimizeKey
```
The KeyStroke which will minimize a JInternalFrame.

protected KeyStroke navigateKey

The KeyStroke which moves forwards through the set of JInternalFrames.

protected KeyStroke navigateKey2

The KeyStroke which moves backwards through the set of JInternalFrames.

Protected Methods

protected void installDefaults(JComponent c)

Installs the default colors and border into the JDesktopPane.

protected void installDesktopManager()

Installs the default look and feel desktop manager into the desktop pane if a custom desktop manager has not been set.

protected void installKeyboardActions()

Installs the KeyStrokes used to control the JInternalFrames held by this component.

protected void registerKeyboardActions()

Registers the KeyStrokes with the JDesktopPane.

protected void uninstallDefaults()

Removes the colors and border installed in installDefaults.

protected void uninstallDesktopManager()

Uninstalls the desktop manager if one was installed in installDesktopManager.

protected void uninstallKeyboardActions()

Uninstalls the KeyStrokes.

protected void unregisterKeyboardActions()

Unregisters the KeyStrokes from the JDesktopPane.

Inner Classes

protected class BasicDesktopPaneUI.MinimizeAction
protected class BasicDesktopPaneUI.MaximizeAction
protected class BasicDesktopPaneUI.CloseAction
protected class BasicDesktopPaneUI.NavigateAction

See also   ComponentUI (p.530), DesktopManager (p.180), DesktopPaneUI (p.532), JComponent (p.207), JDesktopPane (p.224).

swing.plaf.basic.BasicDesktopPaneUI.CloseAction

INNER CLASS

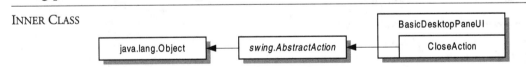

protected class BasicDesktopPaneUI.CloseAction extends AbstractAction

Constructors

public CloseAction()

Default constructor.

Methods

public void actionPerformed(java.awt.event.ActionEvent e)

```
public boolean isEnabled()
```
Overrides: isEnabled in class AbstractAction.
Implements: isEnabled in interface Action.

See also   AbstractAction (p.115).

swing.plaf.basic.BasicDesktopPaneUI.MaximizeAction

INNER CLASS

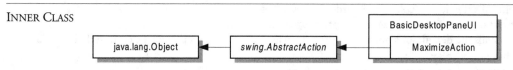

```
protected class BasicDesktopPaneUI.MaximizeAction
    extends AbstractAction
```

Constructors
```
public MaximizeAction()
```
Default constructor.

Methods
```
public void actionPerformed(java.awt.event.ActionEvent e)
public boolean isEnabled()
```
Overrides: isEnabled in class AbstractAction.
Implements: isEnabled in interface Action.

See also   AbstractAction (p.115).

swing.plaf.basic.BasicDesktopPaneUI.MinimizeAction

INNER CLASS

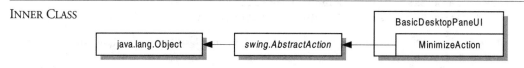

```
protected class BasicDesktopPaneUI.MaximizeAction
    extends AbstractAction
```

Constructors
```
public MaximizeAction()
```
Default constructor.

Methods
```
public void actionPerformed(java.awt.event.ActionEvent e)
public boolean isEnabled()
```
Overrides: isEnabled in class AbstractAction.
Implements: isEnabled in interface Action.

See also   AbstractAction (p.115).

swing.plaf.basic.BasicDesktopPaneUI.NavigateAction

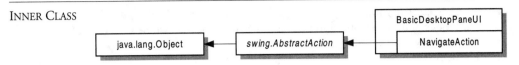

```
protected class BasicDesktopPaneUI.NavigateAction
    extends AbstractAction
```

Constructors
```
public NavigateAction()
```
Default constructor.

Methods
```
public void actionPerformed(java.awt.event.ActionEvent e)
public boolean isEnabled()
```
Overrides: isEnabled in class AbstractAction.
Implements: isEnabled in interface Action.

See also AbstractAction (p.115).

swing.plaf.basic.BasicDirectoryModel

CLASS

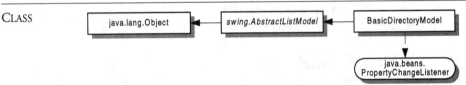

This class is the model used by the BasicFileChooserUI.

```
public class BasicDirectoryModel extends AbstractListModel
    implements java.beans.PropertyChangeListener
```

Constructors
```
public BasicDirectoryModel(JFileChooser filechooser)
```
Constructs a model of the directory structure based on the information in the given JFileChooser.

Methods
```
public boolean contains(Object o)
```
Returns true if the current directory contains the given object (which should be a File).
```
public void fireContentsChanged()
```
Informs listeners that the list of Files has changed.
```
public java.util.Vector getDirectories()
```
Returns a Vector of the directories in the current directory.
```
public Object getElementAt(int index)
```
Implements: getElementAt in interface ListModel.
```
public java.util.Vector getFiles()
```
Returns a Vector of the files in the current directory.

plaf.basic

public int getSize()

Implements: getSize in interface ListModel.

public int indexOf(Object o)

Returns the index of the given object in the file cache. The object is assumed to be a File.

public void intervalAdded(ListDataEvent e)

Not implemented yet.

public void intervalRemoved(ListDataEvent e)

Not implemented yet.

public void invalidateFileCache()

Empties the file cache.

public void propertyChange(java.beans.PropertyChangeEvent e)

Reloads the file cache, if necessary, due to a change in the associated JFileChooser.

Implements: propertyChange in interface PropertyChangeListener.

public void validateFileCache()

Reloads the file cache with the current directory's information.

Protected Methods

protected boolean lt(java.io.File a, java.io.File b)

Returns true if file a is "before" file b in the filesystem. The decision is based on comparing the file names of the two files.

protected void sort(java.util.Vector v)

Uses Quicksort to sort the given Vector. This method assumes the Vector contains Files.

Returned by   BasicFileChooserUI.getModel() (p.587).
See also   JFileChooser (p.239), ListDataEvent (p.498).

swing.plaf.basic.BasicEditorPaneUI

CLASS

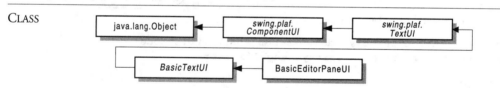

The Basic look and feel UI delegate for JEditorPane.

public class BasicEditorPaneUI extends BasicTextUI

Constructors

public BasicEditorPaneUI()

Constructs a new BasicEditorPaneUI.

Methods

public static ComponentUI createUI(JComponent c)

Creates and returns a UI for the JEditorPane.

Overrides: createUI in class BasicTextUI.

public EditorKit getEditorKit()

Retrieves the EditorKit to be used by the UI delegate from the JEditorPane.

Overrides: `getEditorKit` in class `BasicTextUI`.

Protected Methods

protected String getPropertyPrefix()

Returns "EditorPane. ". The `propertyPrefix` is prepended to all keys used to retrieve values from the `UIDefaults` table.

Overrides: `getPropertyPrefix` in class `BasicTextUI`.

See also   BasicTextUI (p.696), ComponentUI (p.530), EditorKit (p.829), JComponent (p.207), JEditorPane (p.232).

swing.plaf.basic.BasicFileChooserUI

CLASS

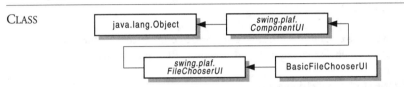

The Basic look and feel UI delegate for the `JFileChooser` component.

This class uses the following set of keys in the `UIDefaults` table. Subclassed look and feels can use these values to change the appearance of the `JFileChooser` with minimal effort.

Key name	Description
FileChooser.cancelButtonText	The text to use on a Cancel button.
FileChooser.cancelButtonToolTipText	The ToolTip text for a Cancel button.
FileChooser.detailsViewIcon	The icon for the button which switches the JFileChooser into details view.
FileChooser.helpButtonText	The text for a Help button.
FileChooser.helpButtonToolTipText	The ToolTip text for a Help button.
FileChooser.homeFolderIcon	The icon for the button that triggers the GoHome action.
FileChooser.listViewIcon	The icon for the button which switches the JFileChooser into list view.
FileChooser.newFolderIcon	The icon for the button which triggers the NewFolder action.
FileChooser.openButtonText	The text to use on an Open button.
FileChooser.openButtonToolTipText	The ToolTip text for an Open button.
FileChooser.saveButtonText	The text to use on a Save button.
FileChooser.saveButtonToolTipText	The ToolTip text for a Save button.
FileChooser.updateButtonText	The text for an Update (Refresh) button.
FileChooser.updateButtonToolTipText	The ToolTip text for an Update button.
FileChooser.upFolderIcon	The icon for the button which triggers the ChangeToParentDirectory action.
FileView.computerIcon	The icon used for the root of all filesystems.
FileView.directoryIcon	The icon used to represent a directory.

Key name	Description
FileView.fileIcon	The icon used to represent a file.
FileView.floppyDriveIcon	The icon used to represent a floppy disk drive.
FileView.hardDriveIcon	The icon used to represent a hard disk drive.

public class BasicFileChooserUI extends FileChooserUI

Constructors

public BasicFileChooserUI(JFileChooser b)

Constructs a BasicFileChooserUI.

Methods

public void clearIconCache()

Unloads all of the Icons currently being used in the JFileChooser.

public ListSelectionListener createListSelectionListener(JFileChooser fc)

Creates the listener used to listen for changes in the selection. Returns a BasicFileChooser-UI.SelectionListener.

public java.beans.PropertyChangeListener createPropertyChangeListener(JFileChooser fc)

Creates the listener used to listen for changes in the JFileChooser's properties. Returns null.

public void ensureFileIsVisible(JFileChooser fc, java.io.File f)

Scrolls the file list of the JFileChooser so that the given file is visible.

Overrides: ensureFileIsVisible in class FileChooserUI.

public FileFilter getAcceptAllFileFilter(JFileChooser fc)

Returns the default FileFilter, which does not filter any files.

Overrides: getAcceptAllFileFilter in class FileChooserUI.

public JPanel getAccessoryPanel()

Returns the accessoryPanel, a panel which can be used to hold components to extend the behavior of the JFileChooser.

public int getApproveButtonMnemonic(JFileChooser fc)

Returns the character (as an integer value) used as the mnemonic character on the Approve button.

public String getApproveButtonText(JFileChooser fc)

Returns the text which is used for the Approve button. This text changes based on what kind of JFileChooser is being used.

Overrides: getApproveButtonText in class FileChooserUI.

public String getApproveButtonToolTipText(JFileChooser fc)

Returns the text for the Approve button.

public Action getApproveSelectionAction()

Returns the Action triggered by the Approve button.

public Action getCancelSelectionAction()

Returns the Action triggered by the Cancel button.

public Action getChangeToParentDirectoryAction()

Returns the Action triggered by the Up Folder button.

public String getDialogTitle(JFileChooser fc)

Returns the title of the JFileChooser.

Overrides: getDialogTitle in class FileChooserUI.

plaf.basic

```
public String getDirectoryName()
```
Returns the name of the current directory.
```
public JFileChooser getFileChooser()
```
Returns the associated JFileChooser.
```
public String getFileName()
```
Returns the name of the currently selected file.
```
public FileView getFileView(JFileChooser fc)
```
Returns the view to be used in displaying the filesystem hierarchy.

Overrides: getFileView in class FileChooserUI.
```
public Action getGoHomeAction()
```
Returns the Action triggered by the Go Home button.
```
public BasicDirectoryModel getModel()
```
Returns the model to use to store the filesystem information.
```
public Action getNewFolderAction()
```
Returns the Action triggered by the New Folder button.
```
public Action getUpdateAction()
```
Returns the Action triggered by the Update button.
```
public void installComponents(JFileChooser fc)
```
An empty method.
```
public void installUI(JComponent c)
```
Overrides: installUI in class ComponentUI.
```
public void rescanCurrentDirectory(JFileChooser fc)
```
Overrides: rescanCurrentDirectory in class FileChooserUI.
```
public void setDirectoryName(String dirname)
```
An empty method.
```
public void setFileName(String filename)
```
An empty method.
```
public void uninstallComponents(JFileChooser fc)
```
An empty method.
```
public void uninstallUI(JComponent c)
```
Overrides: uninstallUI in class ComponentUI.

Protected Fields

```
protected String cancelButtonText
protected String cancelButtonToolTipText
protected Icon computerIcon
protected Icon detailsViewIcon
protected Icon directoryIcon
protected Icon fileIcon
protected Icon floppyDriveIcon
protected Icon hardDriveIcon
protected int helpButtonMnemonic
protected String helpButtonText
protected String helpButtonToolTipText
protected Icon homeFolderIcon
protected Icon listViewIcon
protected Icon newFolderIcon
protected int openButtonMnemonic
```

```
protected String openButtonText
protected String openButtonToolTipText
protected int saveButtonMnemonic
protected String saveButtonText
protected String saveButtonToolTipText
protected Icon upFolderIcon
protected int updateButtonMnemonic
protected String updateButtonText
protected String updateButtonToolTipText
```

Protected Methods

protected java.awt.event.MouseListener createDoubleClickListener(
    JFileChooser fc, JList list)
Returns the listener used to respond to double clicks in the FileView.

protected void createModel()
Creates the model used to store the filesystem information for the JFileChooser.

protected JButton getApproveButton(JFileChooser fc)
Returns the Approve button.

protected void installDefaults(JFileChooser fc)
Installs the Icons and the Strings into the JFileChooser.

protected void installIcons(JFileChooser fc)
Installs the Icons into the JFileChooser. Called by installDefaults().

protected void installListeners(JFileChooser fc)
Adds the PropertyChangeListener to the JFileChooser.

protected void installStrings(JFileChooser fc)
Installs the Strings into the JFileChooser. Called by installDefaults().

protected void uninstallDefaults(JFileChooser fc)
Uninstalls the Icons and the Strings.

protected void uninstallIcons(JFileChooser fc)
Uninstalls the Icons. Called from uninstallDefaults.

protected void uninstallListeners(JFileChooser fc)
Uninstalls the PropertyChangeListener.

protected void uninstallStrings(JFileChooser fc)
Uninstalls the Strings. Called from uninstallDefaults().

Inner Classes

```
protected class BasicFileChooserUI.AcceptAllFileFilter
protected class BasicFileChooserUI.ApproveSelectionAction
protected class BasicFileChooserUI.BasicFileView
protected class BasicFileChooserUI.CancelSelectionAction
protected class BasicFileChooserUI.ChangeToParentDirectoryAction
protected class BasicFileChooserUI.DoubleClickListener
protected class BasicFileChooserUI.GoHomeAction
protected class BasicFileChooserUI.NewFolderAction
protected class BasicFileChooserUI.SelectionListener
protected class BasicFileChooserUI.UpdateAction
```

plaf.basic

See also Action (p.128), BasicDirectoryModel (p.585), FileView (p.520), Icon (p.183), JComponent (p.207), JFileChooser (p.239), JList (p.271), JPanel (p.305), ListSelectionListener (p.500).

swing.plaf.basic.BasicFileChooserUI.AcceptAllFileFilter

INNER CLASS

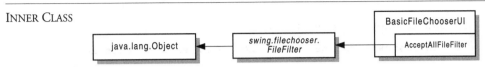

A file filter that doesn't filter any files.

```
protected class BasicFileChooserUI.AcceptAllFileFilter
    extends FileFilter
```

Constructors
```
public AcceptAllFileFilter()
```

Methods
```
public boolean accept(java.io.File f)
```
Overrides: accept in class FileFilter.
```
public String getDescription()
```
Overrides: getDescription in class FileFilter.

See also FileFilter (p.518).

swing.plaf.basic.BasicFileChooserUI.ApproveSelectionAction

INNER CLASS

Responds to an Open or Save request.

```
protected class BasicFileChooserUI.ApproveSelectionAction
    extends AbstractAction
```

Constructors
```
public ApproveSelectionAction()
```
Default constructor.

Methods
```
public void actionPerformed(java.awt.event.ActionEvent e)
```

See also AbstractAction (p.115).

plaf.basic

INNER CLASS

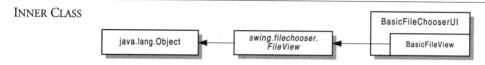

The Basic look and feel implementation of `FileView`.

```
protected class BasicFileChooserUI.BasicFileView extends FileView
```

Constructors
```
public BasicFileView()
```

Methods
```
public void cacheIcon(java.io.File f, Icon i)
```
    Caches an association between the given file and the `Icon`.
```
public void clearIconCache()
```
    Empties the `Icon` cache.
```
public Icon getCachedIcon(java.io.File f)
```
    Returns the `Icon` previously associated with the given file.
```
public String getDescription(java.io.File f)
```
    Overrides: `getDescription` in class `FileView`.
```
public Icon getIcon(java.io.File f)
```
    Overrides: `getIcon` in class `FileView`.
```
public String getName(java.io.File f)
```
    Overrides: `getName` in class `FileView`.
```
public String getTypeDescription(java.io.File f)
```
    Overrides: `getTypeDescription` in class `FileView`.
```
public Boolean isHidden(java.io.File f)
```
    Returns `true` if the given file is hidden.
```
public Boolean isTraversable(java.io.File f)
```
    Overrides: `isTraversable` in class `FileView`.

Protected Fields
```
protected java.util.Hashtable iconCache
```

    See also   Icon (p.183).

swing.plaf.basic.BasicFileChooserUI.CancelSelectionAction

INNER CLASS

```
protected class BasicFileChooserUI.CancelSelectionAction
    extends AbstractAction
```

Constructors
```
public CancelSelectionAction()
```

Methods

`public void actionPerformed(java.awt.event.ActionEvent e)`

> *Overrides:* actionPerformed in class AbstractAction.

> *See also* AbstractAction (p.115).

swing.plaf.basic.BasicFileChooserUI.ChangeToParentDirectoryAction

INNER CLASS

`protected class BasicFileChooserUI.ChangeToParentDirectoryAction`
   `extends AbstractAction`

Constructors

`public ChangeToParentDirectoryAction()`

Methods

`public void actionPerformed(java.awt.event.ActionEvent e)`

> *Overrides:* actionPerformed in class AbstractAction.

> *See also* AbstractAction (p.115).

swing.plaf.basic.BasicFileChooserUI.DoubleClickListener

INNER CLASS

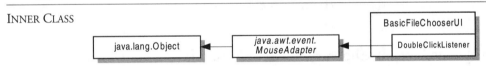

`protected class BasicFileChooserUI.DoubleClickListener`
   `extends java.awt.event.MouseAdapter`

Constructors

`public DoubleClickListener(JList list)`

Methods

`public void mouseClicked(MouseEvent e)`

> *Overrides:* mouseClicked in class MouseAdapter.
> *Implements:* mouseClicked in interface MouseListener.

swing.plaf.basic.BasicFileChooserUI.GoHomeAction

INNER CLASS

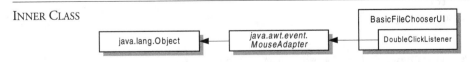

`protected class BasicFileChooserUI.GoHomeAction`
   `extends AbstractAction`

Constructors
`protected GoHomeAction()`

Methods
`public void actionPerformed(java.awt.event.ActionEvent e)`
    Overrides: actionPerformed in class AbstractAction.

    See also   AbstractAction (p.115).

swing.plaf.basic.BasicFileChooserUI.NewFolderAction

INNER CLASS

This `Action` creates a new subfolder inside the current folder.

`protected class BasicFileChooserUI.NewFolderAction`
    `extends AbstractAction`

Constructors
`protected NewFolderAction()`

Methods
`public void actionPerformed(java.awt.event.ActionEvent e)`
    Overrides: actionPerformed in class AbstractAction.

    See also   AbstractAction (p.115).

swing.plaf.basic.BasicFileChooserUI.SelectionListener

INNER CLASS

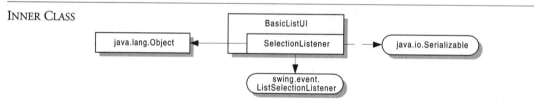

`protected class BasicFileChooserUI.SelectionListener`
    `extends java.lang.Object`
    `implements ListSelectionListener`

Constructors
`public SelectionListener()`
    Default constructor.

Methods
`public void valueChanged(ListSelectionEvent e)`
    Implements: valueChanged in interface ListSelectionListener.

    See also   ListSelectionEvent (p.499), ListSelectionListener (p.500).

swing.plaf.basic.BasicFileChooserUI.UpdateAction

INNER CLASS

This `Action` updates the `FileChooserUI` with the up-to-date contents of the current folder.

```
protected class BasicFileChooserUI.UpdateAction
    extends AbstractAction
```

Constructors
```
protected UpdateAction()
```

Methods
```
public void actionPerformed(java.awt.event.ActionEvent e)
```
Overrides: `actionPerformed` in class `AbstractAction`.

See also   AbstractAction (p.115).

swing.plaf.basic.BasicGraphicsUtils

CLASS

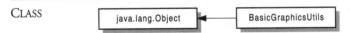

Utility methods that are shared among the various classes in this package.

```
public class BasicGraphicsUtils extends java.lang.Object
```

Constructors
```
public BasicGraphicsUtils()
```
This should not be called. Use the static methods.

Methods
```
public static void drawBezel(java.awt.Graphics g, int x, int y,
    int w, int h, boolean isPressed, boolean hasFocus)
```
Draws the standard 3D border.
```
public static void drawDashedRect(java.awt.Graphics g, int x, int y,
    int width, int height)
```
Draws the dashed rectangle used to indicate focus.
```
public static void drawEtchedRect(java.awt.Graphics g, int x, int y,
    int w, int h)
```
Draws an etched rectangle.
```
public static void drawGroove(java.awt.Graphics g, int x, int y,
    int w, int h)
```
Draws a groove.
```
public static void drawLoweredBezel(java.awt.Graphics g, int x,
    int y, int w, int h)
```
Draws a 3D recessed border.

```
public static void drawString(java.awt.Graphics g, String text,
    int underlinedChar, int x, int y)
```
Draws a String starting at (*x*, *y*). Underlines the first occurrence of underlinedChar in the String (for JMenuItem mnemonics).

```
public static java.awt.Insets getEtchedInsets()
```
Returns the amount of space taken up by a border drawn by drawEtchedRect().

```
public static java.awt.Insets getGrooveInsets()
```
Returns the amount of space taken up by a border drawn by drawGroove().

```
public static java.awt.Dimension getPreferredButtonSize(
    AbstractButton b, int textIconGap)
```
Returns the preferred size for the given button using the given gap between the icon and the text.

swing.plaf.basic.BasicIconFactory

CLASS

This class generates icons which are appropriate to the Basic look and feel.

```
public class BasicIconFactory extends java.lang.Object
    implements java.io.Serializable
```

Constructors
```
public BasicIconFactory()
```
Never call this. Use the static methods.

Methods
```
public static Icon createEmptyFrameIcon()
```
Returns an Icon which is an empty area.

```
public static Icon getCheckBoxIcon()
```
Returns the Icon used for a JCheckBox.

```
public static Icon getCheckBoxMenuItemIcon()
```
Returns the Icon used for a JCheckBoxMenuItem.

```
public static Icon getMenuArrowIcon()
```
Returns the Icon used for the arrows on a JMenu.

```
public static Icon getMenuItemArrowIcon()
```
Returns the Icon used for the arrows on a JMenuItem.

```
public static Icon getMenuItemCheckIcon()
```
Returns the Icon used for placing a check mark on a JMenuItem.

```
public static Icon getRadioButtonIcon()
```
Returns the Icon used for a JRadioButton.

```
public static Icon getRadioButtonMenuItemIcon()
```
Returns the Icon used for a JRadioButtonMenuItem.

See also   Icon (p.183).

swing.plaf.basic.BasicInternalFrameTitlePane

CLASS

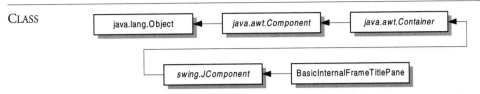

This class manages and renders the title area on a `JInternalFrame` for the Basic look and feel.

UIDefaults key name	Description
`InternalFrame.activeTitleBackground`	The `Color` for the title area background when the window is selected.
`InternalFrame.activeTitleForeground`	The `Color` for the title area foreground when the window is selected.
`InternalFrame.closeIcon`	The `Icon` used by the Close button.
`InternalFrame.icon`	The `Icon` used for the System menu.
`InternalFrame.iconifyIcon`	The `Icon` used by the Minimize button.
`InternalFrame.inactiveTitleBackground`	The `Color` for the title area background when the window is not selected.
`InternalFrame.inactiveTitleForeground`	The `Color` for the title area foreground when the window is not selected.
`InternalFrame.maximizeIcon`	The `Icon` used by the Maximize button.
`InternalFrame.minimizeIcon`	The `Icon` used for the "restore from maximized state" control.
`InternalFrame.titleFont`	The `Font` used for the title text.

```
public class BasicInternalFrameTitlePane extends JComponent
```

Constructors
```
public BasicInternalFrameTitlePane(JInternalFrame f)
```
Constructs a `BasicInternalFrameTitlePane` for the given `JInternalFrame`.

Methods
```
public void paintComponent(java.awt.Graphics g)
```
Overrides: `paintComponent` in class `JComponent`.

Protected Fields
```
protected static final String CLOSE_CMD = "Close"
protected static final String ICONIFY_CMD = "Minimize"
protected static final String MAXIMIZE_CMD = "Maximize"
protected static final String MOVE_CMD = "Move"
protected static final String RESTORE_CMD = "Restore"
protected static final String SIZE_CMD = "Size"
```
These constants are used as the values for the `Action.NAME` property in the associated `Action`. Note that these `Strings` are not internationalized in Swing 1.0.x. The `Actions` which use these `Strings` are all created in `createActions()`, so they may be safely modified in an overridden version of that method after calling `super.createActions()`.

protected Action closeAction

The Action used to close the JInternalFrame. Used by the closeButton and the System menu.

protected JButton closeButton

The button on the title bar which triggers the closeAction.

protected Icon closeIcon

The Icon used on the closeButton.

protected JInternalFrame frame

The associated JInternalFrame.

protected JButton iconButton

The Minimize button.

protected Icon iconIcon

The Icon used on the iconButton.

protected Action iconifyAction

The Action which will iconify the window to its JDesktopIcon form. Used by the iconButton and the System menu.

protected JButton maxButton

The Maximize button.

protected Icon maxIcon

The Icon used on the maxButton.

protected Action maximizeAction

The Action which will maximize the window. Used by the maxButton and the System menu.

protected JMenuBar menuBar

The System menu bar, which contains only the windowMenu.

protected Icon minIcon

The Icon used by the restore-from-maximized button.

protected Action moveAction

The Action which initiates moving the window using the keyboard. Used by the System menu.

protected java.awt.Color notSelectedTextColor

The text color when the JInternalFrame is not selected.

protected java.awt.Color notSelectedTitleColor

The background color when the JInternalFrame is not selected.

protected java.beans.PropertyChangeListener propertyChangeListener

The listener for property changes in the associated JInternalFrame.

protected Action restoreAction

The Action which restores the window from a minimized state. Used by the System menu.

protected java.awt.Color selectedTextColor

The text color when the JInternalFrame is selected.

protected java.awt.Color selectedTitleColor

The background color when the JInternalFrame is selected.

protected Action sizeAction

The Action used to initiate window resizing using the keyboard. Used by the System menu.

protected JMenu windowMenu

The System menu.

Protected Methods

protected void addSubComponents()

As of Swing 1.1 this method doesn't do anything (although it looks like it does). The layout manager of this UI delegate is an inner class and directly manipulates the components contained in this class, so the add() method is ignored.

protected void addSystemMenuItems(JMenu systemMenu)

Adds the Actions to the System menu.

protected void assembleSystemMenu()

Adds the System menu to its menu bar.

protected void createActions()

Creates the Actions used by this class.

protected void createButtons()

Creates the buttons for the title area.

protected java.awt.LayoutManager createLayout()

Creates the layout manager, which is an instance of BasicInternalFrame-TitlePane.TitlePaneLayout.

protected java.beans.PropertyChangeListener createPropertyChangeListener()

Creates the property change listener used by this class.

protected JMenu createSystemMenu()

Constructs the System JMenu.

protected JMenuBar createSystemMenuBar()

Constructs the JMenuBar used to hold the System menu.

protected void enableActions()

Sets the appropriate enabled/disabled state on all Actions based on the current state of the JInternalFrame.

protected void installDefaults()

Installs the Icons and Colors into the JInternalFrame.

protected void installListeners()

Adds the property change listener to the JInternalFrame.

protected void installTitlePane()

Installs the title pane (this) into the JInternalFrame.

protected void postClosingEvent(JInternalFrame frame)

Posts a fake WINDOW_CLOSING event to the JInternalFrame. This allows the JInternalFrame to behave like a JFrame.

protected void setButtonIcons()

Sets the correct Icons on their associated buttons.

protected void uninstallDefaults()

Uninstalls the Icons and Colors installed in installDefaults().

Inner Classes

```
public class BasicInternalFrameTitlePane.CloseAction
public class BasicInternalFrameTitlePane.IconifyAction
public class BasicInternalFrameTitlePane.MaximizeAction
public class BasicInternalFrameTitlePane.MoveAction
public class BasicInternalFrameTitlePane.PropertyChangeHandler
public class BasicInternalFrameTitlePane.RestoreAction
```

```
public class BasicInternalFrameTitlePane.SizeAction
public class BasicInternalFrameTitlePane.SystemMenuBar
public class BasicInternalFrameTitlePane.TitlePaneLayout
```

See also   Action (p.128), Icon (p.183), JButton (p.191), JInternalFrame (p.254), JMenu (p.281), JMenuBar (p.288).

swing.plaf.basic.BasicInternalFrameTitlePane.CloseAction

INNER CLASS

This `Action` is triggered by the `JInternalFrame`'s Close button and System menu Close item.

As of Swing 1.1 this class was `public` due to a compiler bug in JDK 1.1.6. It should be treated as `protected`.

```
public class BasicInternalFrameTitlePane.CloseAction
    extends AbstractAction
```

Constructors
```
public CloseAction()
```
   Constructs a `CloseAction`, setting its NAME to `BasicInternalFrameTitlePane.CLOSE_CMD`.

Methods
```
public void actionPerformed(java.awt.event.ActionEvent e)
```
   If the `JInternalFrame` `isCloseable()`, this calls its `setClosed()` method.

   See also   AbstractAction (p.115).

swing.plaf.basic.BasicInternalFrameTitlePane.IconifyAction

INNER CLASS

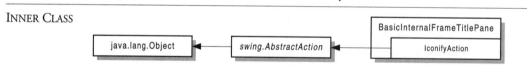

This `Action` is triggered by the `JInternalFrame`'s minimize button and System menu Minimize item.

As of Swing 1.1 this class was `public` due to a compiler bug in JDK 1.1.6. It should be treated as `protected`.

```
public class BasicInternalFrameTitlePane.IconifyAction
    extends AbstractAction
```

Constructors
```
public IconifyAction()
```
   Constructs an `IconifyAction`, setting its NAME to `BasicInternalFrameTitle-Pane.ICONIFY_CMD`.

Methods
`public void actionPerformed(java.awt.event.ActionEvent e)`

If the `JInternalFrame isIconifiable()`, this calls its `setIcon()` method with the opposite of its current `isIcon()` state. When restoring the `JInternalFrame` from its iconized state, this method will clear any previously maximized state.

See also AbstractAction (p.115).

swing.plaf.basic.BasicInternalFrameTitlePane.MaximizeAction

INNER CLASS

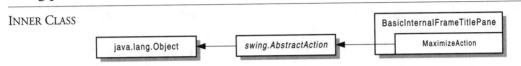

This `Action` is triggered by the `JInternalFrame`'s maximize button and System menu Maximize item.

As of Swing 1.1 this class was `public` due to a compiler bug in JDK 1.1.6. It should be treated as `protected`.

```
public class BasicInternalFrameTitlePane.MaximizeAction
    extends AbstractAction
```

Constructors
`public MaximizeAction()`

Constructs a `MaximizeAction` and sets its NAME to `BasicInternalFrameTitle-Pane.MAXIMIZE_CMD`.

Methods
`public void actionPerformed(java.awt.event.ActionEvent e)`

If the `JInternalFrame isMaximizable()`, this calls its `setmaximum()` method with the opposite of its current `isMaximum()` state. When restoring the `JInternalFrame` from its maximized state, this method will clear any previously iconified state.

See also AbstractAction (p.115).

swing.plaf.basic.BasicInternalFrameTitlePane.MoveAction

INNER CLASS

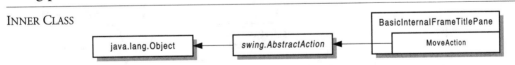

This `Action` is triggered by the `JInternalFrame`'s System menu Move item.

As of Swing 1.1 this class was `public` due to a compiler bug in JDK 1.1.6. It should be treated as `protected`.

```
public class BasicInternalFrameTitlePane.MoveAction
    extends AbstractAction
```

plaf.basic

Constructors

public MoveAction()

Constructs a MoveAction and sets its NAME to BasicInternalFrameTitlePane.MOVE_CMD.

Methods

public void actionPerformed(java.awt.event.ActionEvent e)

As of Swing 1.1, this method does nothing.

See also AbstractAction (p.115).

swing.plaf.basic.BasicInternalFrameTitlePane.PropertyChangeHandler

INNER CLASS

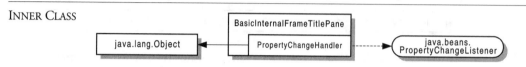

This inner class responds to property change events from the associated JInternalFrame.

As of Swing 1.1 this class was `public` due to a compiler bug in JDK 1.1.6. It should be treated as `protected`.

```
public class BasicInternalFrameTitlePane.MoveAction
    extends java.lang.Object
    implements java.beans.PropertyChangeListener
```

Constructors

public PropertyChangeHandler()

Default constructor.

Methods

public void propertyChanged(java.beans.PropertyChangeEvent e)

Updates the BasicInternalFrameTitlePane as needed based on the change in the JInternalFrame.

See also JInternalFrame (p.254).

swing.plaf.basic.BasicInternalFrameTitlePane.RestoreAction

INNER CLASS

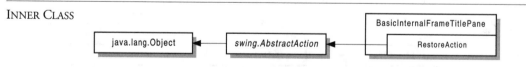

This Action is triggered by the JInternalFrame's System menu Restore item.

As of Swing 1.1 this class was `public` due to a compiler bug in JDK 1.1.6. It should be treated as `protected`.

```
public class BasicInternalFrameTitlePane.RestoreAction
    extends AbstractAction
```

plaf.basic

Constructors

`public RestoreAction()`

Constructs a `RestoreAction` and sets its NAME to `BasicInternalFrameTitle-Pane.RESTORE_CMD`.

Methods

`public void actionPerformed(java.awt.event.ActionEvent e)`

Restores the `JInternalFrame` from its maximized or iconized states.

See also   AbstractAction (p.115).

swing.plaf.basic.BasicInternalFrameTitlePane.SizeAction

INNER CLASS

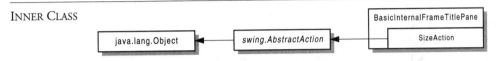

This `Action` is triggered by the `JInternalFrame`'s System menu Size item.

As of Swing 1.1 this class was `public` due to a compiler bug in JDK 1.1.6. It should be treated as `protected`.

`public class BasicInternalFrameTitlePane.SizeAction`
    `extends AbstractAction`

Constructors

`public SizeAction()`

Constructs a `SizeAction` and sets its NAME to `BasicInternalFrameTitlePane.SIZE_CMD`.

Methods

`public void actionPerformed(java.awt.event.ActionEvent e)`

As of Swing 1.1, this method does nothing.

See also   AbstractAction (p.115).

swing.plaf.basic.BasicInternalFrameTitlePane.SystemMenuBar

INNER CLASS

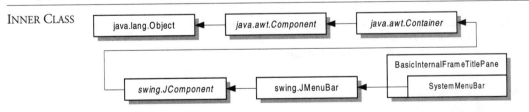

This inner class is a specialized `JMenuBar` used for the System menu on a `JInternalFrame`.

As of Swing 1.1 this class was `public` due to a compiler bug in JDK 1.1.6. It should be treated as `protected`.

`public class BasicInternalFrameTitlePane.SystemMenuBar`
    `extends JMenuBar`

plaf.basic

Constructors
public SystemMenuBar()
Default constructor.

Methods
public boolean isFocusTraversable()
Returns `false`, preventing this component from getting the focus through normal focus traversal.
Overrides: isFocusTraversable in class JComponent.

public boolean isOpaque()
Always returns `true`.
Overrides: isOpaque in class JComponent.

public void paint(java.awt.Graphics g)
Gets and paints the frame Icon, resizing it if necessary.
Overrides: paint in class JComponent.

public void requestFocus()
An empty method, which disables the ability of this component to request the focus.
Overrides: requestFocus in class JComponent.

See also   JComponent (p.207), JMenuBar (p.288).

swing.plaf.basic.BasicInternalFrameTitlePane.TitlePaneLayout

INNER CLASS

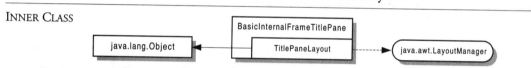

This inner class is the layout manager used by a `BasicInternalFrameTitlePane`. It directly manipulates the buttons contained in that class to place them in the title area. Due to this, its `addLayoutComponent()` and `removeLayoutComponent()` methods are nonfunctional. If a subclass of `BasicInternalFrameTitlePane` wishes to add more components to the layout, it must replace this layout manager.

As of Swing 1.1 this class was `public` due to a compiler bug in JDK 1.1.6. It should be treated as `protected`.

```
public class BasicInternalFrameTitlePane.TitlePaneLayout
    extends java.lang.Object
    implements java.awt.LayoutManager
```

Constructors
public TitlePaneLayout()
Default constructor.

Methods
public void addLayoutComponent(String name, java.awt.Component c)
An empty method.
Implements: addLayoutComponent in interface LayoutManager.

public void layoutContainer(java.awt.Container c)
    Implements: layoutContainer in interface LayoutManager.
public java.awt.Dimension minimumLayoutSize(java.awt.Container c)
    Implements: minimumLayoutSize in interface LayoutManager.
public java.awt.Dimension preferredLayoutSize(java.awt.Container c)
    Implements: preferredLayoutSize in interface LayoutManager.
public void removeLayoutComponent(java.awt.Component c)
    An empty method.
    Implements: removeLayoutComponent in interface LayoutManager.

swing.plaf.basic.BasicInternalFrameUI

CLASS

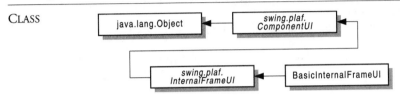

A Basic look and feel UI delegate for JInternalFrame.

BasicInternalFrameUI uses the following keys in the UIDefaults table.

Key name	Description
InternalFrame.icon	The Icon used for the JDesktopIcon.
InternalFrame.border	The JInternalFrame's Border.

public class BasicInternalFrameUI extends InternalFrameUI

Constructors
public BasicInternalFrameUI(JInternalFrame b)
    Constructs a new BasicInternalFrameUI for the given JInternalFrame.

Methods
public static ComponentUI createUI(JComponent b)
    Overrides: createUI in class ComponentUI.
public JComponent getEastPane()
    Returns the pane which is in the East (as specified by a BorderLayout).
public java.awt.Dimension getMaximumSize(JComponent x)
    Overrides: getMaximumSize in class ComponentUI.
public java.awt.Dimension getMinimumSize(JComponent x)
    Overrides: getMinimumSize in class ComponentUI.
public JComponent getNorthPane()
    Returns the pane which is in the North (as specified by a BorderLayout).
public java.awt.Dimension getPreferredSize(JComponent x)
    Overrides: getPreferredSize in class ComponentUI.
public JComponent getSouthPane()
    Returns the pane which is in the South (as specified by a BorderLayout).

public JComponent getWestPane()

Returns the pane which is in the West (as specified by a BorderLayout).

public void installUI(JComponent c)

Overrides: installUI in class ComponentUI.

public final boolean isKeyBindingActive()

Returns true if the keyBindings are registered with the associated JInternalFrame.

public void setEastPane(JComponent c)

Sets the pane which will occupy the East (as specified by a BorderLayout).

public void setNorthPane(JComponent c)

Sets the pane which will occupy the North (as specified by a BorderLayout).

public void setSouthPane(JComponent c)

Sets the pane which will occupy the North (as specified by a BorderLayout).

public void setWestPane(JComponent c)

Sets the pane which will occupy the North (as specified by a BorderLayout).

public void uninstallUI(JComponent c)

Overrides: uninstallUI in class ComponentUI.

Protected Fields

protected MouseInputAdapter borderListener

The listener which responds to MouseEvents and MouseMotionEvents on the frame border.

protected java.awt.ComponentListener componentListener

The listener used to match the size of a maximized JInternalFrame to its parent.

protected JComponent eastPane

The component occupying the BorderLayout.EAST.

protected JInternalFrame frame

The associated JInternalFrame.

protected MouseInputListener glassPaneDispatcher

The listener that forwards mouse events received by the glass pane.

protected java.awt.LayoutManager internalFrameLayout

The layout manager used for the internal frame.

protected KeyStroke openMenuKey

The KeyStroke that opens the System menu.

protected JComponent northPane

The component in the BorderLayout.NORTH, usually the title pane.

protected java.beans.PropertyChangeListener propertyChangeListener

The listener for property changes in the associated JInternalFrame.

protected JComponent southPane

The component in the BorderLayout.SOUTH.

protected BasicInternalFrameTitlePane titlePane

The associated BasicInternalFrameTitlePane component.

protected JComponent westPane

The component occupying the BorderLayout.WEST.

Protected Methods

protected void activateFrame(JInternalFrame f)

Called when the frame becomes selected. This action is delegated to the desktopManager.

protected void closeFrame(JInternalFrame f)

Called when the JInternalFrame wants to be closed. This action is delegated to the desktop-Manager.

protected MouseInputAdapter createBorderListener(JInternalFrame w)

Creates an instance of BasicInternalFrameUI.BorderListener.

protected java.awt.event.ComponentListener createComponentListener()

Creates the component listener to be attached to the JInternalFrame.

protected DesktopManager createDesktopManager()

Creates the desktop manager.

protected JComponent createEastPane(JInternalFrame w)

Creates the default pane to use in the East.

protected MouseInputListener createGlassPaneDispatcher()

Creates the handler that forwards mouse events received by the glass pane.

protected void createInternalFrameListener()

Creates the listener for internal frame-specific changes in the JInternalFrame.

protected java.awt.LayoutManager createLayoutManager()

Creates the layout manager.

protected JComponent createNorthPane(JInternalFrame w)

Creates the default pane to use in the North, which is a BasicInternalFrameTitlePane.

protected java.beans.PropertyChangeListener createPropertyChangeListener()

Creates the listener for property changes in the JInternalFrame.

protected JComponent createSouthPane(JInternalFrame w)

Creates the default pane to use in the South.

protected JComponent createWestPane(JInternalFrame w)

Creates the default pane to use in the West.

protected void deactivateFrame(JInternalFrame f)

Called when the frame is no longer selected. This action is delegated to the desktopManager.

protected void deiconifyFrame(JInternalFrame f)

Called when the user wants to deiconify the frame. This action is delegated to the desktopManager.

protected void deinstallMouseHandlers(JComponent c)

Removes all of the mouse listeners which were attached to the JInternalFrame.

protected DesktopManager getDesktopManager()

Returns the associated DesktopManager. This method attempts to find the desktop manager by finding an associated JDesktopPane. If it cannot find one this method returns a default desktop manager.

protected void iconifyFrame(JInternalFrame f)

Called when the user wants to iconify the frame. This action is delegated to the desktopManager.

protected void installComponents()

An empty method.

protected void installDefaults()

Installs the Icon and Border from the UIDefaults table.

protected void installKeyboardActions()

Installs CTRL-SPACE (COMMAND-SPACE on the Mac) as the key which will open the system menu.

protected void installListeners()

Installs the listeners and the glass pane dispatcher into the JInternalFrame.

protected void installMouseHandlers(JComponent c)
Installs mouse listeners and mouse motion listeners into the given JInternalFrame.

protected final boolean isKeyBindingRegistered()
Returns true if the open and close system menu key bindings have been registered with the JInternalFrame.

protected void maximizeFrame(JInternalFrame f)
Called when the user wants to maximize the frame. This action is delegated to the desktopManager.

protected void minimizeFrame(JInternalFrame f)
Called when the user wants to minimize the frame. This action is delegated to the desktopManager.

protected void replacePane(JComponent currentPane, JComponent newPane)
Adds the necessary mouseHandlers to currentPane and adds it to the frame. The reverse process occurs for the newPane.

protected final void setKeyBindingActive(boolean b)
Sets the isKeyBindingActive property to *b*.

protected final void setKeyBindingRegistered(boolean b)
Sets the isKeyBindingRegistered property to *b*.

protected void setupMenuCloseKey()
Registers the menu close key with the JInternalFrame.

protected void setupMenuOpenKey()
Registers the menu open key with the JInternalFrame.

protected void uninstallComponents()
An empty method.

protected void uninstallDefaults()
Uninstalls the Icon and the Border.

protected void uninstallKeyboardActions()
Uninstalls the menu open and close keys.

protected void uninstallListeners()
Uninstalls the listeners.

Inner Classes

protected class BasicInternalFrameUI.BasicInternalFrameListener
protected class BasicInternalFrameUI.BorderListener
protected class BasicInternalFrameUI.ComponentHandler
protected class BasicInternalFrameUI.GlassPaneDispatcher
public class BasicInternalFrameUI.InternalFramePropertyChangeListener
public class BasicInternalFrameUI.InternalFrameLayout

See also   ComponentUI (p.530), DesktopManager (p.180), JComponent (p.207), JInternalFrame (p.254), MouseInputAdapter (p.504), MouseInputListener (p.505).

plaf.basic

swing.plaf.basic.BasicInternalFrameUI.BasicInternalFrameListener

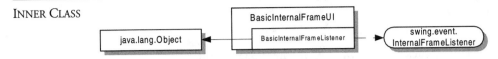

```
protected class BasicInternalFrameUI.BasicInternalFrameListener
    extends java.lang.Object
    implements InternalFrameListener
```

Constructors
`public BasicInternalFrameListener()`
Default constructor.

Methods
`public void internalFrameActivated(InternalFrameEvent e)`
Implements: internalFrameActivated in interface InternalFrameListener.
`public void internalFrameClosed(InternalFrameEvent e)`
Implements: internalFrameClosed in interface InternalFrameListener.
`public void internalFrameClosing(InternalFrameEvent e)`
Implements: internalFrameClosing in interface InternalFrameListener.
`public void internalFrameDeactivated(InternalFrameEvent e)`
Implements: internalFrameDeactivated in interface InternalFrameListener.
`public void internalFrameDeiconified(InternalFrameEvent e)`
Implements: internalFrameDeiconified in interface InternalFrameListener.
`public void internalFrameIconified(InternalFrameEvent e)`
Implements: internalFrameIconified in interface InternalFrameListener.
`public void internalFrameOpened(InternalFrameEvent e)`
Implements: internalFrameOpened in interface InternalFrameListener.

See also   InternalFrameEvent (p.497), InternalFrameListener (p.498).

swing.plaf.basic.BasicInternalFrameUI.BorderListener

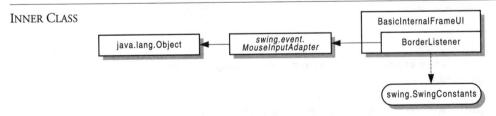

This class handles the various manipulations of a JInternalFrame that are done using its border, such as resizing or moving.

```
protected class BasicInternalFrameUI.BorderListener
    extends MouseInputAdapter
    implements SwingConstants
```

plaf.basic

Constructors

public BorderListener()
   Default constructor.

Methods

public void mouseDragged(java.awt.event.MouseEvent e)
   Overrides: mouseDragged in class MouseInputAdapter.
public void mouseExited(java.awt.event.MouseEvent e)
   Overrides: mouseExited in class MouseInputAdapter.
public void mouseMoved(java.awt.event.MouseEvent e)
   Overrides: mouseMoved in class MouseInputAdapter.
public void mousePressed(java.awt.event.MouseEvent e)
   Overrides: mousePressed in class MouseInputAdapter.
public void mouseReleased(java.awt.event.MouseEvent e)
   Overrides: mouseReleased in class MouseInputAdapter.

Protected Fields

protected final int RESIZE_NONE = 0

   See also   MouseInputAdapter (p.504), SwingConstants (p.442).

swing.plaf.basic.BasicInternalFrameUI.ComponentHandler

INNER CLASS

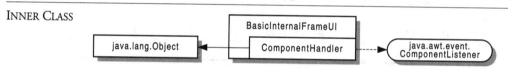

This inner class listens for changes in the JInternalFrame's parent.

```
protected class BasicInternalFrameUI.ComponentHandler
    extends java.lang.Object
    implements java.awt.event.ComponentListener
```

Constructors

public ComponentHandler()
   Default constructor.

Methods

public void componentHidden(java.awt.event.ComponentEvent e)
   An empty method.
   Implements: componentHidden in interface ComponentListener.
public void componentMoved(java.awt.event.ComponentEvent e)
   An empty method.
   Implements: componentMoved in interface ComponentListener.
public void componentResized(java.awt.event.ComponentEvent e)
   Matches the size of a maximized JInternalFrame to its parent when the parent resizes.
   Implements: componentResized in interface ComponentListener.

plaf.basic

public void componentShown(java.awt.event.ComponentEvent e)

An empty method.

Implements: componentShown in interface ComponentListener.

swing.plaf.basic.BasicInternalFrameUI.GlassPaneDispatcher

INNER CLASS

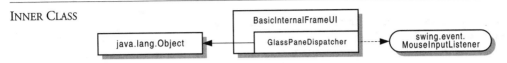

protected class BasicInternalFrameUI.GlassPaneDispatcher
extends java.lang.Object
implements MouseInputListener

Constructors

public GlassPaneDispatcher()

Default constructor.

Methods

public void mouseClicked(java.awt.event.MouseEvent e)

An empty method.

Implements: mouseClicked in interface MouseInputListener.

public void mouseDragged(java.awt.event.MouseEvent e)

An empty method.

Implements: mouseDragged in interface MouseInputListener.

public void mouseEntered(java.awt.event.MouseEvent e)

Forwards the mouseEntered event to the component in the content pane which is underneath the location of the event.

Implements: mouseEntered in interface MouseInputListener.

public void mouseExited(java.awt.event.MouseEvent e)

Forwards the mouseExited event to the component in the content pane which is underneath the location of the event.

Implements: mouseExited in interface MouseInputListener.

public void mouseMoved(java.awt.event.MouseEvent e)

Forwards the mouseMoved event to the component in the content pane which is underneath the location of the event.

Implements: mouseMoved in interface MouseInputListener.

public void mousePressed(java.awt.event.MouseEvent e)

If the BasicInternalFrameUI's borderListener is not null, this method forwards mouse-Pressed events to it. This allows the JInternalFrame to be enabled by clicking anywhere in the window, rather than just on the title area.

Implements: mousePressed in interface MouseInputListener.

public void mouseReleased(java.awt.event.MouseEvent e)

An empty method.

Implements: mouseReleased in interface MouseInputListener.

See also   MouseInputListener (p.505).

swing.plaf.basic.BasicInternalFrameUI.InternalFrameLayout

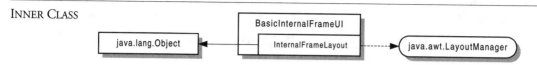

```
public class BasicInternalFrameUI.InternalFrameLayout
    extends java.lang.Object
    implements java.awt.LayoutManager
```

Constructors

```
public InternalFrameLayout()
```
Default constructor.

Methods

```
public void addLayoutComponent(String name, java.awt.Component c)
```
Implements: addLayoutComponent in interface LayoutManager.

```
public void layoutContainer(java.awt.Container c)
```
Implements: layoutContainer in interface LayoutManager.

```
public Dimension minimumLayoutSize(java.awt.Container c)
```
Implements: minimumLayoutSize in interface LayoutManager.

```
public Dimension preferredLayoutSize(java.awt.Container c)
```
Implements: preferredLayoutSize in interface LayoutManager.

```
public void removeLayoutComponent(java.awt.Component c)
```
Implements: removeLayoutComponent in interface LayoutManager.

swing.plaf.basic.BasicInternalFrameUI.InternalFramePropertyChangeListener

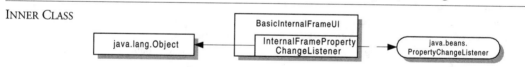

```
public class BasicInternalFrameUI.InternalFramePropertyChangeListener
    extends java.lang.Object
    implements java.beans.PropertyChangeListener
```

Constructors

```
public InternalFramePropertyChangeListener()
```
Default constructor.

Methods

```
public void propertyChange(java.beans.PropertyChangeEvent evt)
```
Updates the BasicInternalFrameUI based on changes in the JInternalFrame.
Implements: propertyChange in interface PropertyChangeListener.

See also JInternalFrame (p.254).

swing.plaf.basic.BasicLabelUI

CLASS

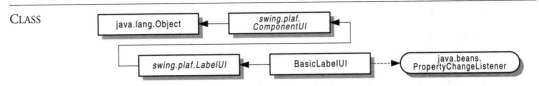

A Basic look and feel implementation of LabelUI. This class keeps a single shared instance of itself that is used by all JLabels.

UIDefaults table key	Description
Label.background	The background Color for the label.
Label.font	The Font for the text in the label.
Label.foreground	The text Color for the label.

public class BasicLabelUI extends LabelUI
    implements java.beans.PropertyChangeListener

Constructors
public BasicLabelUI()
    Default constructor.

Methods
public static ComponentUI createUI(JComponent c)
    Overrides: createUI in class ComponentUI.
public java.awt.Dimension getMaximumSize(JComponent c)
    Returns getPreferredSize(c).
    Overrides: getMaximumSize in class ComponentUI.
public java.awt.Dimension getMinimumSize(JComponent c)
    Returns getPreferredSize(c).
    Overrides: getMinimumSize in class ComponentUI.
public java.awt.Dimension getPreferredSize(JComponent c)
    Overrides: getPreferredSize in class ComponentUI.
public void installUI(JComponent c)
    Overrides: installUI in class ComponentUI.
public void paint(java.awt.Graphics g, JComponent c)
    Paints the text for the label using paintEnabledText or paintDisabledText, as appropriate. The label is laid out before being painted using layoutCL(). If the label is opaque, its background is painted here.
    Overrides: paint in class ComponentUI.
public void propertyChange(java.beans.PropertyChangeEvent e)
    Implements: propertyChange in interface PropertyChangeListener.
public void uninstallUI(JComponent c)
    Overrides: uninstallUI in class ComponentUI.

plaf.basic

Protected Fields

protected static BasicLabelUI labelUI

The single shared BasicLabelUI instance.

Protected Methods

protected void installComponents(JLabel c)

An empty method.

protected void installDefaults(JLabel c)

Installs the foreground and background Colors and the Font.

protected void installListeners(JLabel c)

Adds a PropertyChangeListener to the associated JLabel.

protected void installKeyboardActions(JLabel c)

Installs the default keyboard actions associated with labels. The default listeners shift the focus to the component set as this JLabel's labelFor() value, or the next component in the tab order, when the JLabel's mnemonic character is pressed.

protected String layoutCL(JLabel label, java.awt.FontMetrics fontMetrics, String text, Icon icon, java.awt.Rectangle viewR, java.awt.Rectangle iconR, java.awt.Rectangle textR)

Forwards the call to SwingUtilities.layoutCompoundLabel(). Subclasses can override this method to change how labels are laid out.

protected void paintDisabledText(JLabel l, java.awt.Graphics g, String s, int textX, int textY)

Paints s at textX, textY with background.lighter() and then shifted down and to the right by one pixel with background.darker().

protected void paintEnabledText(JLabel l, java.awt.Graphics g, String s, int textX, int textY)

Paints s at textX, textY with the label's foreground color.

protected void uninstallComponents(JLabel c)

An empty method.

protected void uninstallDefaults(JLabel c)

Uninstalls the resources installed by installDefaults().

protected void uninstallKeyboardActions(JLabel c)

Uninstalls the keyboard actions installed using installKeyboardActions().

protected void uninstallListeners(JLabel c)

Removes the PropertyChangeListener from the associated JLabel.

See also   Icon (p.183), JLabel (p.264).

swing.plaf.basic.BasicListUI

CLASS

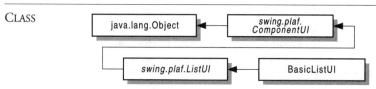

A Basic look and feel implementation of ListUI.

UIDefaults table key	Description
List.background	The background Color for the list.
List.border	The Border used around the list.
List.cellRenderer	The default CellRenderer to use for the list.
List.font	The Font to use by default for list items.
List.foreground	The foreground Color for the list.
List.selectionBackground	The background Color to use for selected items in the list.
List.selectionForeground	The foreground (text) Color to use for selected items in the list.

public class BasicListUI extends ListUI

Constructors
public BasicListUI()
> Default constructor.

Methods
public static ComponentUI createUI(JComponent list)
> Returns a new instance of BasicListUI. BasicListUI delegates are allocated one per JList.
> *Overrides:* createUI in class ComponentUI.

public java.awt.Rectangle getCellBounds(JList list, int index1, int index2)
> *Overrides:* getCellBounds in class ListUI.

public java.awt.Dimension getMaximumSize(JComponent c)
> *Overrides:* getMaximumSize in class ComponentUI.

public java.awt.Dimension getMinimumSize(JComponent c)
> *Overrides:* getMinimumSize in class ComponentUI.

public java.awt.Dimension getPreferredSize(JComponent c)
> The preferredSize of a JList is the total height of the rows and the maximum width of the cells, plus their respective margins.
> *Overrides:* getPreferredSize in class ComponentUI.

public java.awt.Point indexToLocation(JList list, int index)
> *Overrides:* indexToLocation in class ListUI.

public void installUI(JComponent list)
> Initializes the associated JList by calling configureList(), addListListeners(), and registerKeyboardActions() in order.
> *Overrides:* installUI in class ComponentUI.

public int locationToIndex(JList list, java.awt.Point location)
> *Overrides:* locationToIndex in class ListUI.

public void paint(java.awt.Graphics g, JComponent c)
> Paints any list cells that are in *g*'s clipping region.
> *Overrides:* paint in class ComponentUI.

public void uninstallUI(JComponent c)
> Uninitializes the associated JList by calling removeListListeners(), unregisterKeyboardActions(), and unconfigureList() in order. Sets list to null.
> *Overrides:* uninstallUI in class ComponentUI.

plaf.basic

Protected Fields

protected int cellHeight
protected int[] cellHeights
protected int cellWidth

> These three fields are set in updateLayoutState().

protected java.awt.FocusListener focusListener

> A listener for focus events from the associated JList.

protected JList list

> The associated JList.

protected ListDataListener listDataListener

> The listener for changes in the list data.

protected ListSelectionListener listSelectionListener

> The listener for changes in selection in the JList.

protected MouseInputListener mouseInputListener

> A listener for mouse events in the associated JList.

protected java.beans.PropertyChangeListnener propertyChangeListener

> The listener for property changes in the JList.

protected CellRendererPane rendererPane

> The cell renderer pane.

protected int updateLayoutStateNeeded

> An integer representing flags which indicate what aspects of the JList have changed.

protected final static int modelChanged = 1 << 0
protected final static int selectionModelChanged = 1 << 1
protected final static int fontChanged = 1 << 2
protected final static int fixedCellWidthChanged = 1 << 3
protected final static int fixedCellHeightChanged = 1 << 4
protected final static int prototypeCellValueChanged = 1 << 5
protected final static int cellRendererChanged = 1 << 6

> These fields are used as flags set in the updateLayoutStateNeeded field. When properties change in the JList, these fields are used to set bits in updateLayoutStateNeeded. When a repaint happens, maybeLayoutStateNeeded() is called and checks these flags.

Protected Methods

protected int convertRowToY(int row)

> Returns the Y coordinate of the origin of the given row. If row is invalid, this method returns −1.

protected int convertYToRow(int y0)

> Returns the row that contains the given Y coordinate. If no row contains the coordinate, this method returns −1.

protected java.awt.FocusListener createFocusListener()

> Returns an instance of BasicListUI.FocusHandler.

protected ListDataListener createListDataListener()

> Creates the ListDataListener used by this UIDelegate. This method can be overridden by subclasses to provide a listener that does look and feel specific processing.

protected ListSelectionListener createListSelectionListener()

> Creates the ListSelectionListener for selection changes in the JList. Subclasses can override this method to provide look and feel specific processing on list selection changes.

protected MouseInputListener createMouseInputListener()

Creates the MouseInputListener, which is a compound mouse and mouse motion listener. Subclasses can override this method to provide look and feel specific processing for those events.

protected java.beans.PropertyChangeListnener createPropertyListener()

Creates the PropertyChangeListener. Subclasses can override this method to provide look and feel specific processing for JList property changes.

protected int getRowHeight(int row)

Returns the height of the specified row based on the current layout.

protected void installDefaults()

Installs the Font, foreground, and background Colors, and the CellRendererPane.

protected void installKeyboardActions()

Registers keyboard actions for the VK_UP and VK_DOWN keys. The default actions call the select-NextIndex() or selectPreviousIndex() methods.

protected void installListeners()

Creates and installs the listeners for the JList, its model, and its selectionModel.

protected void maybeUpdateLayoutState()

If updateLayoutStateNeeded is non 0, calls updateLayoutState() and resets updateLayoutStateNeeded. This method must be called by methods that need sizing information, such as paint().

protected void paintCell(java.awt.Graphics g, int row,
java.awt.Rectangle rowBounds, ListCellRenderer cellRenderer,
ListModel dataModel, ListSelectionModel selModel, int leadIndex)

Paints one cell and then uses the computed information to configure the ListCellRenderer. The cellRenderer is used to paint all of the other cells in the list.

protected void selectNextIndex()

Selects the next row and ensures it is visible. Called by the KeyEvent.VK_DOWN keyboard action.

protected void selectPreviousIndex()

Selects the previous row and ensures it is visible. Called by the KeyEvent.VK_UP keyboard action.

protected void uninstallDefaults()

Sets the JList properties that haven't been explicitly overriden to null. A property is considered overridden if its current value is not a UIResource.

protected void uninstallKeyboardActions()

Unregisters the two keyboard actions. This method is called by uninstallUI.

protected void uninstallListeners()

Removes the listeners for the JList, its model, and its selectionModel. All of the listener fields are reset to null here. This method is called at uninstallUI() time, so it should be kept in sync with installListeners.

protected void updateLayoutState()

Replaces the cached values of cellHeight or cellHeights and cellWidth, based on the font and the current values of fixedCellWidth, fixedCellHeight, and prototypeCellValue.

Inner Classes

public class BasicListUI.FocusHandler
public class BasicListUI.ListDataHandler
public class BasicListUI.ListSelectionHandler
public class BasicListUI.MouseInputHandler
public class BasicListUI.PropertyChangeHandler

plaf.basic

See also   CellRendererPane (p.151), ComponentUI (p.530), JComponent (p.207), JList (p.271), ListCellRenderer (p.420), ListDataListener (p.499), ListModel (p.421), ListSelectionListener (p.500), ListUI (p.535), MouseInputListener (p.505).

swing.plaf.basic.BasicListUI.FocusHandler

<small>Inner Class</small>

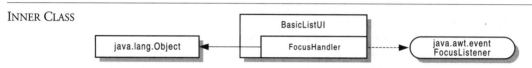

The listener which handles updating the `BasicListUI` for focus changes.

```
public class BasicListUI.FocusHandler extends java.lang.Object
    implements java.awt.event.FocusListener
```

Constructors
```
public FocusHandler()
```
    Default constructor.

Methods
```
public void focusGained(java.awt.event.FocusEvent e)
```
    Implements: `focusGained` in interface `FocusListener`.
```
public void focusLost(java.awt.event.FocusEvent e)
```
    Implements: `focusLost` in interface `FocusListener`.
```
protected void repaintCellFocus()
```
    Repaints the list to either show or hide the focus indicator when the list gains or loses the focus.

    Returned by   BasicListUI.createFocusListener() (p.614).

swing.plaf.basic.BasicListUI.ListDataHandler

<small>Inner Class</small>

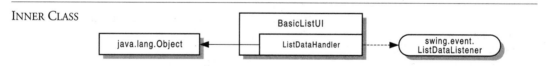

The listener that handles updating the `BasicListUI` for changes in the data contained in the `JList`.

```
protected class BasicListUI.ListDataHandler extends java.lang.Object
    implements ListDataListener
```

Constructors
```
public ListDataHandler()
```
    Default constructor.

Methods
```
public void contentsChanged(ListDataEvent e)
```
    Implements: `contentsChanged` in interface `ListDataListener`.

<small>plaf.basic</small>

public void intervalAdded(ListDataEvent e)
> *Implements:* intervalAdded in interface ListDataListener.

public void intervalRemoved(ListDataEvent e)
> *Implements:* intervalRemoved in interface ListDataListener.

> *Returned by*   BasicListUI.createListDataListener() (p.614).
> *See also*   ListDataEvent (p.498), ListDataListener (p.499).

swing.plaf.basic.BasicListUI.ListSelectionHandler

INNER CLASS

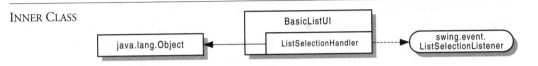

This class is added to the JList at installUI() time and repaints the selection highlight when the selection changes in the JList.

```
public class BasicListUI.ListSelectionHandler
    extends java.lang.Object
    implements ListSelectionListener
```

Constructors
public ListSelectionHandler()
> Default constructor.

Methods
public void valueChanged(ListSelectionEvent e)
> *Implements:* valueChanged in interface ListSelectionListener.

> *Returned by*   BasicListUI.createListSelectionListener() (p.614).
> *See also*   ListSelectionEvent (p.499), ListSelectionListener (p.500).

swing.plaf.basic.BasicListUI.MouseInputHandler

INNER CLASS

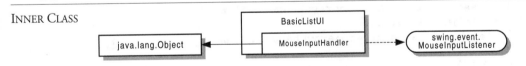

```
public class BasicListUI.MouseInputHandler extends java.lang.Object
    implements MouseInputListener
```

Constructors
public MouseInputHandler()
> Default constructor.

Methods
public void mouseClicked(java.awt.event.MouseEvent e)
> An empty method.

public void mouseDragged(java.awt.event.MouseEvent e)

If SHIFT or CTRL is pressed, does nothing. Otherwise, selects the cell under the mouse cursor and scrolls the list so that cell is fully visible.

public void mouseEntered(java.awt.event.MouseEvent e)

An empty method.

public void mouseExited(java.awt.event.MouseEvent e)

An empty method.

public void mouseMoved(java.awt.event.MouseEvent e)

An empty method.

public void mousePressed(java.awt.event.MouseEvent e)

Requests the focus, and then modifies the selection based on the state of the CTRL or SHIFT keys. If CTRL is held down when the mouse is pressed, it selects or deselects the single item under the mouse cursor. If SHIFT is held down, all items between the mouse cursor position and the anchor selection item will be selected or deselected as a group. The JList's ListSelectionModel may refuse these method calls, depending on its mode.

public void mouseReleased(java.awt.event.MouseEvent e)

If SHIFT or CTRL is pressed, does nothing. Otherwise, selects the cell under the current mouse cursor position.

Returned by   BasicListUI.createMouseInputListener (p.614).
See also   MouseInputListener (p.505).

swing.plaf.basic.BasicListUI.PropertyChangeHandler

INNER CLASS

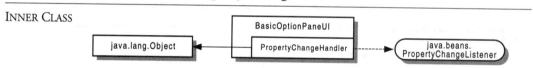

The PropertyChangeListener that's added to the JList at installUI() time. When the value of a JList property that affects layout changes, a flag bit is set in updateLayoutState-Needed.

```
public class BasicListUI.PropertyChangeHandler
    extends java.lang.Object
    implements java.beans.PropertyChangeListener
```

Constructors
public PropertyChangeHandler()

Default constructor.

Methods
public void propertyChange(java.beans.PropertyChangeEvent e)

Implements: propertyChange in interface PropertyChangeListener.

swing.plaf.basic.BasicLookAndFeel

CLASS

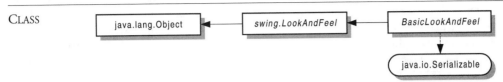

This abstract class provides support and some basic definitions for use by standard look and feels. The constants defined by this class provide the baseline to which application developers may safely code and still have their applications work with all of the look and feels supplied with Swing.

It should be used as the `LookAndFeel` superclass for any look and feel that is not highly specialized. A subclass of this class will also want to override the `getName()`, `getID()`, `getDescription()`, `isNativeLookAndFeel()`, and `isSupportedLookAndFeel()` methods of the `LookAndFeel` class.

A list of the keys this class defines can be found in appendix B, which lists the `UIDefaults` table standard keys (p.1013).

```
public abstract class BasicLookAndFeel extends LookAndFeel
    implements java.io.Serializable
```

Constructors
`public BasicLookAndFeel()`
> Default constructor.

Methods
`public UIDefaults getDefaults()`
> Creates, initializes, and returns the `UIDefaults` table for this look and feel. Subclasses will usually not override this method.
> *Overrides:* `getDefaults` in class `LookAndFeel`.

Protected Methods
`protected void initClassDefaults(UIDefaults table)`
> Initializes the `UIDefaults` table with the `uiClassID` to UI delegate class mapping. Each component (such as `JList`) defines a `uiClassID` (for `JList` it is "List"). The `uiClassID` is used as the key for the `UIDefaults` table to find the associated look and feel UI delegate for the component. Subclasses will want to override this method to install their own UI delegates.

`protected void initComponentDefaults(UIDefaults table)`
> Initializes the `UIDefaults` table with the resources (such as fonts or colors) needed by the various UI delegates and components. Where possible, subclasses should use the keys defined by this class (where appropriate), instead of creating new keys. Using new keys implies that application developers will have to write look and feel dependent code to support them. There is a naming convention for these keys. The convention is that all keys have the `uiClassID` of the associated component prepended to the descriptive name, separated by a '.'. So, the `JList` foreground color uses the key `"List.foreground."`. The `UIManager` class provides type-safe methods to retrieve the values associated with the keys.

plaf.basic

protected void initSystemColorDefaults(UIDefaults table)

Initializes the UIDefaults table with SystemColors. The key names for the colors are the same as the public field names in the SystemColor class. A subclass look and feel that is the native look and feel for a platform may want to override this method to load the appropriate system colors for the platform. This method uses the Windows default system colors on any non-Windows platform.

protected void loadSystemColors(UIDefaults table,
String[] systemColors, boolean useNative)

If useNative is true, this method loads the values of the SystemColors matching the names given in the systemColors array into table. Otherwise this method treats the values in the systemColors array as values to decode to get the colors to load into table.

Swing 1.1 always passes false for useNative, since the SystemColors are unreliable in JDK 1.1.x. JDK 1.2 passes the value of isNativeLookAndFeel() to this method, since it contains a fix for the SystemColors bug.

See also   LookAndFeel (p.423), UIDefaults (p.452).

swing.plaf.basic.BasicMenuBarUI

CLASS

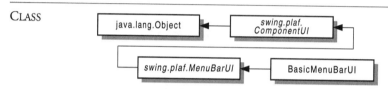

The Basic look and feel UI delegate for JMenuBar.

UIDefaults table key	Description
MenuBar.background	The background Color for the menu bar.
MenuBar.border	The Border for the menu bar.
MenuBar.font	The Font for the menu bar.
MenuBar.foreground	The foreground Color for the menu bar.

public class BasicMenuBarUI extends MenuBarUI

Constructors
public BasicMenuBarUI()
Default constructor.

Methods
public static ComponentUI createUI(JComponent x)
Overrides: createUI in class ComponentUI.
public java.awt.Dimension getMaximumSize(JComponent c)
Overrides: getMaximumSize in class ComponentUI.
public java.awt.Dimension getMinimumSize(JComponent c)
Overrides: getMinimumSize in class ComponentUI.

public java.awt.Dimension getPreferredSize(JComponent c)

> *Overrides:* getPreferredSize in class ComponentUI.

public void installUI(JComponent c)

> *Overrides:* installUI in class ComponentUI.

public void uninstallUI(JComponent c)

> *Overrides:* uninstallUI in class ComponentUI.

Protected Fields

protected ChangeListener changeListener

> Listens for changes in the models of the menus contained within the JMenuBar.

protected java.awt.event.ContainerListener containerListener

> Listens for new JMenus being added to or removed from the JMenuBar.

protected JMenuBar menuBar

> The associated JMenuBar.

Protected Methods

protected ChangeListener createChangeListener()

> Creates the change listener. Can be overridden by subclasses to return a ChangeListener that performs any additional work required by the subclass.

protected java.awt.event.ContainerListener createContainerListener()

> Creates the ContainerListener used to listen for JMenus being added or removed. Can be overridden by subclasses to change the actions taken when a JMenu is added or removed. The default handler installs or removes the ChangeListener from the affected JMenu.

protected void installDefaults()

> Installs the default Border into the JMenuBar.

protected void installKeyboardActions()

> An empty method.

protected void installListeners()

> Adds the ContainerListener to the JMenuBar and the ChangeListener to its contained JMenus.

protected void uninstallDefaults()

> Removes the default Border from the JMenuBar.

protected void uninstallKeyboardActions()

> An empty method.

protected void uninstallListeners()

> Removes the ContainerListener from the JMenuBar and the ChangeListener from its contained JMenus.

> *See also*   ChangeListener (p.488), JComponent (p.207), MenuBarUI (p.536).

swing.plaf.basic.BasicMenuItemUI

CLASS

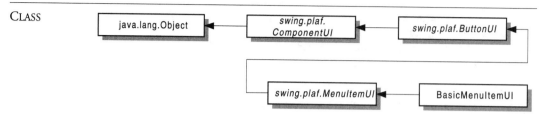

The Basic look and feel UI delegate for JMenuItems.

UIDefaults table key (without propertyPrefix)	Description
.acceleratorForeground	The foreground Color used for the accelerator text.
.acceleratorSelectionForeground	The foreground Color used for the accelerator text on a selected item.
.arrowIcon	The Icon used for items with submenus.
.background	The background Color.
.border	The Border.
.borderPainted	A Boolean indicating if the border should be painted.
.checkIcon	The Icon used for the "checked" menu items.
.disabledForeground	The foreground Color used when the item is disabled.
.font	The Font.
.foreground	The foreground Color.
.margin	The Insets around the menu item.
.selectionBackground	The Color used for the selected background.
.selectionForeground	The Color used for the selected foreground.
MenuItem.acceleratorFont	The only item specific to a MenuItem, the Font used for the accelerator text.

public class BasicMenuItemUI extends MenuItemUI

Constructors
public BasicMenuItemUI()
Default constructor.

Methods
public static ComponentUI createUI(JComponent c)
Overrides: createUI in class ComponentUI.
public java.awt.Dimension getMaximumSize(JComponent c)
Returns getPreferredSize().
Overrides: getMaximumSize in class ComponentUI.
public java.awt.Dimension getMinimumSize(JComponent c)
Returns getPreferredSize().
Overrides: getMinimumSize in class ComponentUI.

public MenuElement[] getPath()

Returns the path of MenuElements that leads to this menu item.

public java.awt.Dimension getPreferredSize(JComponent c)

Returns the preferred size of the component, which is based on the size of the check icon, arrow icon, the `defaultTextIconGap`, and the component. `BasicGraphicsUtils.getPreferred-MenuItemSize()` is used to perform the calculation.

Overrides: getPreferredSize in class ComponentUI.

public void installUI(JComponent c)

Overrides: installUI in class ComponentUI.

public void paint(java.awt.Graphics g, JComponent c)

Uses `BasicGraphicsUtils.paintMenuItem()` to paint the menu item. This method fills the background of the menu item as needed.

Overrides: paint in class ComponentUI.

public void uninstallUI(JComponent c)

Overrides: uninstallUI in class ComponentUI.

public void update(java.awt.Graphics g, JComponent c)

The background of a menu is filled as part of the normal painting procedure, so override update to just call paint().

Overrides: update in ComponentUI.

Protected Fields

protected java.awt.Font acceleratorFont

The Font used for rendering the accelerator key sequence on the menu item (for example, "CTRL+V" for a Paste menu item).

protected java.awt.Color acceleratorForeground

The Color used for the accelerator text.

protected java.awt.Color acceleratorSelectionForeground

The text Color to use for the accelerator text when the menu item is selected.

protected Icon arrowIcon

The Icon used for JMenuItems that are actually JMenus.

protected Icon checkIcon

The Icon used for two-state menu items (the item toggles between checked and unchecked).

protected static final int defaultTextIconGap = 4

The default space between the Icon and the text on a menu item.

protected java.awt.Color disabledForeground

The text Color to use when the menu item is disabled.

protected MenuDragMouseListener menuDragMouseListener

The listener that updates the menu selection in response to the mouse being dragged in the menu.

protected JMenuItem menuItem

The associated JMenuItem.

protected MenuKeyListener menuKeyListener

The handler for the associated mnemonic character.

protected MouseInputListener mouseInputListener

Updates the MenuSelectionManager as the mouse moves over this menu item.

protected boolean oldBorderPainted

Stores whether the look and feel used before this one was installed painted a border around JMenu-Items. This is used by uninstallUI().

```
protected java.awt.Color selectionBackground
```
The background `Color` when this menu item is selected.
```
protected java.awt.Color selectionForeground
```
The text `Color` when this menu item is selected.

Protected Methods

```
protected MenuDragMouseListener createMenuDragMouseListener(JComponent c)
```
Creates the listener which updates the `MenuSelectionManager` as the mouse is dragged within the menu hierarchy.
```
protected MenuKeyListener createMenuKeyListener(JComponent c)
```
Creates the listener which handles the menu item's mnemonic.
```
protected MouseInputListener createMouseInputListener(JComponent c)
```
Creates the listener which updates the `MenuSelectionManager` as the mouse moves into and out of this menu item.
```
protected java.awt.Dimension getPreferredMenuItemSize(JComponent c,
    Icon checkIcon, Icon arrowIcon, int defaultTextIconGap)
```
Calculates the preferred size of the menu item based on the given information.
```
protected String getPropertyPrefix()
```
Returns the prefix `String` used when retrieving information from the `UIDefaults` table. Returns "MenuItem."
```
protected void installDefaults()
```
Installs the Fonts, Colors, and Border into the `JMenuItem`.
```
protected void installKeyboardActions()
```
An empty method.
```
protected void installListeners()
```
Installs the three listeners into the associated `JMenuItem`. See the `createXListener()` methods.
```
protected void paintMenuItem(java.awt.Graphics g, JComponent c,
    Icon checkIcon, Icon arrowIcon, java.awt.Color background,
    java.awt.Color foreground, int defaultTextIconGap)
```
Paints the menu item.
```
protected void uninstallDefaults()
```
Uninstalls the resources installed in `installDefaults()`.
```
protected void uninstallKeyboardActions()
```
An empty method.
```
protected void uninstallListeners()
```
Uninstalls the three listeners from the associated `JMenuItem`.

Inner Classes

```
protected class BasicMenuItemUI.MouseInputHandler
```

Extended by   BasicCheckBoxMenuItemUI (p.559), BasicMenuUI (p.627), BasicRadioButtonMenuItemUI (p.640).

See also   ButtonUI (p.528), ComponentUI (p.530), Icon (p.183), JComponent (p.207), MenuDragMouseListener (p.502), MenuItemUI (p.536), MenuKeyListener (p.503), MouseInputListener (p.505).

plaf.basic

swing.plaf.basic.BasicMenuItemUI.MouseInputHandler

INNER CLASS

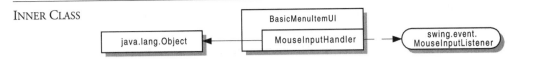

This listener updates the MenuSelectionManager in response to mouse events in the JMenu-Item.

```
protected class BasicMenuItemUI.MouseInputHandler
    extends java.lang.Object
    implements MouseInputListener
```

Constructors

public MouseInputHandler()
Default constructor.

Methods

public void mouseClicked(java.awt.event.MouseEvent e)
Implements: mouseClicked in interface MouseInputListener.

public void mouseDragged(java.awt.event.MouseEvent e)
Implements: mouseDragged in interface MouseInputListener.

public void mouseEntered(java.awt.event.MouseEvent e)
Implements: mouseEntered in interface MouseInputListener.

public void mouseExited(java.awt.event.MouseEvent e)
Implements: mouseExited in interface MouseInputListener.

public void mouseMoved(java.awt.event.MouseEvent e)
Implements: mouseMoved in interface MouseInputListener.

public void mousePressed(java.awt.event.MouseEvent e)
Implements: mousePressed in interface MouseInputListener.

public void mouseReleased(java.awt.event.MouseEvent e)
Implements: mouseReleased in interface MouseInputListener.

See also MouseInputListener (p.505).

swing.plaf.basic.BasicMenuUI

CLASS

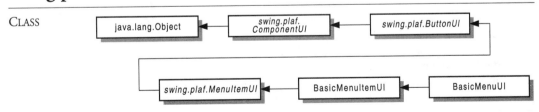

The Basic look and feel delegate for menus.

```
public class BasicMenuUI extends BasicMenuItemUI
```

Constructors

public BasicMenuUI()

Default constructor.

Methods

public static ComponentUI createUI(JComponent c)

Overrides: createUI in class BasicMenuItemUI.

public java.awt.Dimension getMaximumSize(JComponent c)

Overrides: getMaximumSize in class BasicMenuItemUI.

Protected Fields

protected ChangeListener changeListener

The listener that listens for changes in the JMenu.

protected MenuListener menuListener

The listener that listens for changes in the selection state of the associated JMenu.

protected java.beans.PropertyChangeListener propertyChangeListener

The listener that listens for property changes in the associated JMenu.

Protected Methods

protected ChangeListener createChangeListener(JComponent c)

Creates the listener used to handle ChangeEvents from the associated JMenu.

protected MenuDragMouseListener createMenuDragMouseListener(JComponent c)

Creates the listener used to update the MenuSelectionManager as the mouse is dragged into and out of this menu.

Overrides: createMenuDragMouseListener in class BasicMenuItemUI.

protected MenuKeyListener createMenuKeyListener(JComponent c)

Creates the listener used to handle the mnemonic character for this menu.

Overrides: createMenuKeyListener in class BasicMenuItemUI.

protected MenuListener createMenuListener(JComponent c)

Creates the listener used to handle selection state changes in the associated JMenu.

protected MouseInputListener createMouseInputListener(JComponent c)

Creates the listener used to update the MenuSelectionManager when the mouse is clicked or moved into or out of this JMenu.

Overrides: createMouseInputListener in class BasicMenuItemUI.

protected java.beans.PropertyChangeListener createPropertyChangeListener(JComponent c)

Creates the listener used to handle property changes in the associated JMenu.

protected String getPropertyPrefix()

Returns the prefix used to distinguish the entries for the different kinds of MenuElements in the UIDefaults table. The prefix for this class is "Menu."

Overrides: getPropertyPrefix in class BasicMenuItemUI.

protected void installDefaults()

Calls super.installDefaults, and then sets the menu posting delay to 200ms.

Overrides: installDefaults in class BasicMenuItemUI.

protected void installKeyboardActions()

Installs the ALT+mnemonic accelerator key sequence into the JMenu.

Overrides: installKeyboardActions in class BasicMenuItemUI.

plaf.basic

protected void installListeners()

Overrides: installListeners in class BasicMenuItemUI.

protected void setupPostTimer(JMenu menu)

Creates the timer used to trigger the delayed pop-up of the JMenu. The default time delay is 200ms.

protected void uninstallDefaults()

Overrides: uninstallDefaults in class BasicMenuItemUI.

protected void uninstallKeyboardActions()

Overrides: uninstallKeyboardActions in class BasicMenuItemUI.

protected void uninstallListeners()

Overrides: uninstallListeners in class BasicMenuItemUI.

Inner Classes

public class BasicMenuUI.ChangeHandler

> *See also* BasicMenuItemUI (p.624), ChangeListener (p.488), ComponentUI (p.530), JMenu (p.281), MenuDragMouseListener (p.502), MenuKeyListener (p.503), MenuListener (p.504), MouseInputListener (p.505).

swing.plaf.basic.BasicMenuUI.ChangeHandler

INNER CLASS

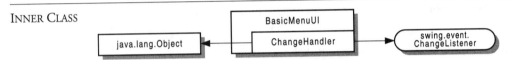

This inner class handles adding and removing keyboard support for the associated JMenu as the selection state of this menu changes.

public class BasicMenuUI.ChangeHandler extends java.lang.Object implements ChangeListener

Fields

public boolean isSelected

Caches the last known selection state of this menu.

public JMenu menu

The associated JMenu.

public BasicMenuUI ui

The associated ui.

public java.awt.Component wasFocused

Caches the component which had the focus before this menu was selected so the focus can be restored when the menu becomes unselected.

Constructors

public ChangeHandler(JMenu m, BasicMenuUI ui)

Sets up a change handler which listens to the given JMenu and updates the given BasicMenuUI.

Methods

public void stateChanged(ChangeEvent e)

Implements: stateChanged in interface ChangeListener.

swing.plaf.basic.BasicOptionPaneUI

CLASS

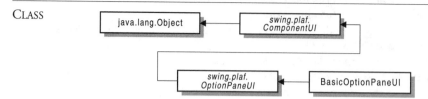

The Basic look and feel UI delegate for JOptionPane.

UIDefaults table key	Description
OptionPane.background	The background Color for the JOptionPane.
OptionPane.border	The Border to put around the JOptionPane.
OptionPane.font	The Font to use for the text in the JOptionPane.
OptionPane.foreground	The text Color for the JOptionPane.
OptionPane.minimumSize	The Dimension to use as the default minimum size.

public class BasicOptionPaneUI extends OptionPaneUI

Fields
public static final int MinimumHeight = 90
Minimum height for the component.
public static final int MinimumWidth = 262
Minimum width for the component.
public static final String[] defaultOptions = { "OK" }
Default option names to use when none are supplied.
public static final String[] okCancelOptions = { "OK", "Cancel" }
Option names for OK_CANCEL_OPTION.
public static final String[] yesNoCancelOptions = { "Yes", "No", "Cancel" }
Option names for YES_NO_CANCEL_OPTION.
public static final String[] yesNoOptions = { "Yes", "No" }
Option names for YES_NO_OPTION.

Constructors
public BasicOptionPaneUI()
Default constructor.

Methods
public boolean containsCustomComponents(JOptionPane op)
Returns true if the message or the buttons contain a custom component.
Overrides: containsCustomComponents in class OptionPaneUI.
public static ComponentUI createUI(JComponent x)
Overrides: createUI in class ComponentUI.
public java.awt.Dimension getMaximumSize(JComponent c)
Returns getPreferredSize().
Overrides: getMaximumSize in class ComponentUI.

plaf.basic

public java.awt.Dimension getMinimumOptionPaneSize()

Allows a subclass to override the hard-coded defaults in this class.

public java.awt.Dimension getMinimumSize(JComponent c)

Returns `getPreferredSize()`.

Overrides: `getMinimumSize` in class `ComponentUI`.

public java.awt.Dimension getPreferredSize(JComponent c)

Returns the greater of the preferred layout size of the `JOptionPane` or the minimum OptionPane size.

Overrides: `getPreferredSize` in class `ComponentUI`.

public void installUI(JComponent c)

Sets up the passed-in `JOptionPane` with the default resources supplied by this UI delegate.

Overrides: `installUI` in class `ComponentUI`.

public void selectInitialValue()

Requests the focus for the `inputComponent`. If the `inputComponent` is `null`, this method forwards the call along to `AbstractOptionPaneUI`.

Overrides: `selectInitialValue` in class `OptionPaneUI`.

public void uninstallUI(JComponent c)

Removes this UI delegate from the `JOptionPane`.

Overrides: `uninstallUI` in class `ComponentUI`.

Protected Fields

protected boolean hasCustomComponents

A flag set in `validateComponents()` to indicate whether the message or buttons contain a custom component.

protected java.awt.Component initialFocusComponent

The component which should initially get the focus in the `JOptionPane`.

protected JComponent inputComponent

`JComponent` provided for input if `optionPane.getWantsInput()` returns `true`. Depending on the number of selectionValues this component will be a list box, a combo box, or a text field.

protected java.awt.Dimension minimumSize

The cached minimum size of the `JOptionPane` based on the size of all contained components.

protected JOptionPane optionPane

The associated `JOptionPane`.

protected java.beans.PropertyChangeListener propertyChangeListener

The listener used to listen for changes in the `JOptionPane`.

Protected Methods

protected java.beans.PropertyChangeListener createPropertyChangeListener(JComponent c)

Creates the appropriate `PropertyChangeListener`.

protected Object[] getButtons()

Returns the buttons the look and feel should display. If the `JOptionPane` has custom options, they will be used. Otherwise, this method will return `yesNoOptions`, `yesNoCancelOptions`, or `defaultOptions` depending on the value of `JOptionPane`'s optionType.

protected Icon getIcon()

Returns the custom Icon from the associated `JOptionPane`, or the default Icon.

protected Icon getIconForType(int messageType)

Returns the Icon that matches the given `messageType`.

protected int getInitialValueIndex()
  Returns the initial button index that should be selected.
protected int getMaxCharactersPerLineCount()
  Returns the value from the associated JOptionPane.
protected Object getMessage()
  Returns the message to display from the JMessagePane that the receiver is providing the look and feel for.
protected boolean getSizeButtonsToSameWidth()
  Returns true.
protected void installComponents()
  Calls createMessageArea(), createSeparator(), and createButtonArea().
protected void installDefaults()
  Installs the font, border, and minimum size from the UIDefaults table. Also sets the component to be opaque.
protected void installKeyboardActions()
  Registers the ESCAPE key for the close button.
protected void installListeners()
  Installs the PropertyChangeListener for the JOptionPane.
protected void resetInputValue()
  Changes the inputValue of the JOptionPane to match the value in the inputComponent.
protected void uninstallComponents()
  Calls removeAll() on the option pane.
protected void uninstallDefaults(JComponent c)
  Removes the UI resources added to the JOptionPane.
protected void uninstallKeyboardActions()
  Uninstalls the ESCAPE key handler.
protected void uninstallListeners(JComponent c)
  Removes the listeners added to the JOptionPane.

Inner Classes

public class BasicOptionPaneUI.ButtonActionListener
public static class BasicOptionPaneUI.ButtonAreaLayout
public class BasicOptionPaneUI.PropertyChangeHandler

See also ComponentUI (p.530), Icon (p.183), JOptionPane (p.294), OptionPaneUI (p.537), UIDefaults (p.452).

swing.plaf.basic.BasicOptionPaneUI.ButtonActionListener

INNER CLASS

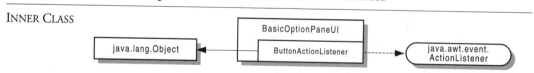

This inner class should be treated as if it were protected. It is only public due to a compiler bug, and it will be changed to protected.

```
public class BasicOptionPaneUI.ButtonActionListener
    extends java.lang.Object
    implements java.awt.event.ActionListener
```

Constructors
public ButtonActionListener(int buttonIndex)

Methods
public void actionPerformed(java.awt.event.ActionEvent e)
  Implements: actionPerformed in interface ActionListener.

Protected Fields
protected int buttonIndex

swing.plaf.basic.BasicOptionPaneUI.ButtonAreaLayout

INNER CLASS

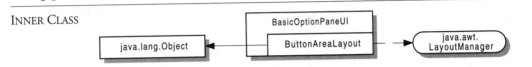

ButtonAreaLayout acts similiar to FlowLayout. It lays out all components from left to right. If syncAllWidths is true, the widths of each component will be set to the largest preferred size width. This inner class is marked public due to a compiler bug. This class should be treated as a protected inner class.

```
public static class BasicOptionPaneUI.ButtonAreaLayout
    extends java.lang.Object
    implements java.awt.LayoutManager
```

Constructors
public ButtonAreaLayout(boolean syncAllWidths, int padding)
  Constructs a new layout, setting the associated fields to the given values.

Methods
public void addLayoutComponent(String string, java.awt.Component comp)
  Implements: addLayoutComponent in interface LayoutManager.
public boolean getCentersChildren()
  Returns true if the children are centered in the area.
public int getPadding()
  Returns the padding used between components in the layout.
public boolean getSyncAllWidths()
  Returns true if the layout makes all of its children the same width.
public void layoutContainer(java.awt.Container container)
  Implements: layoutContainer in interface LayoutManager.
public java.awt.Dimension minimumLayoutSize(java.awt.Container c)
  Implements: minimumLayoutSize in interface LayoutManager.
public java.awt.Dimension preferredLayoutSize(java.awt.Container c)
  Implements: preferredLayoutSize in interface LayoutManager.
public void removeLayoutComponent(java.awt.Component c)
  Implements: removeLayoutComponent in interface LayoutManager.
public void setCentersChildren(boolean newValue)
  If newValue is true, the layout will center its children in the allotted area.

public void setPadding(int newPadding)

Sets the padding (in pixels) to use between components in the layout.

public void setSyncAllWidths(boolean newValue)

If newValue is true, the layout will make all of its contained components the same width.

Protected Fields

protected boolean centersChildren

Set to true if the layout centers all of its children.

protected int padding

The padding (in pixels) between components in the layout.

protected boolean syncAllWidths

Set to true if the layout makes all of its children the same width as the widest component in the layout.

swing.plaf.basic.BasicOptionPaneUI.PropertyChangeHandler

INNER CLASS

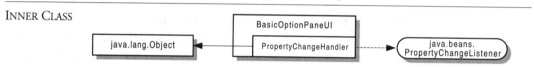

public class BasicOptionPaneUI.PropertyChangeHandler
    extends java.lang.Object
    implements java.beans.PropertyChangeListener

Constructors

public PropertyChangeHandler()

Default constructor.

Methods

public void propertyChange(java.beans.PropertyChangeEvent e)

Calls validateComponent() in BasicOptionPaneUI if the property change is ICON_PROPERTY, MESSAGE_PROPERTY, OPTIONS_PROPERTY, or INITIAL_VALUE_PROPERTY.
Implements: propertyChange in interface PropertyChangeListener.

See also JOptionPane (p.294).

swing.plaf.basic.BasicPanelUI

CLASS

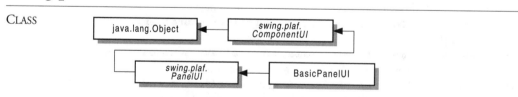

The Basic look and feel delegate for JPanels. Only one instance of this class is created and shared among all JPanel instances.

UIDefaults table key	Description
Panel.background	The default background Color for JPanels.
Panel.border	The default Border for JPanels.
Panel.font	The default Font for child components of the JPanel.
Panel.foreground	The default foreground Color for JPanels.

public class BasicPanelUI extends PanelUI

Constructors
public BasicPanelUI()
 Default constructor.

Methods
public static ComponentUI createUI(JComponent c)
 If the shared instance of this class has not been created, creates it and returns it. Otherwise, just returns it.
 Overrides: createUI in class ComponentUI.
protected void installDefaults(JPanel p)
 Installs the default foreground and background Colors, Font, and Border for the JPanel.
public void installUI(JComponent c)
 Overrides: installUI in class ComponentUI.
protected void uninstallDefaults(JPanel p)
 Uninstalls the default Border.
public void uninstallUI(JComponent c)
 Overrides: uninstallUI in class ComponentUI.

 See also ComponentUI (p.530), JComponent (p.207), JPanel (p.305), PanelUI (p.537).

swing.plaf.basic.BasicPasswordFieldUI

CLASS

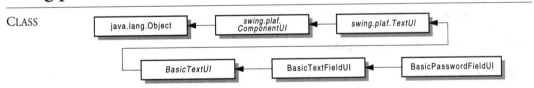

Overrides the BasicTextFieldUI class so that the text is drawn as a string of the echoChar defined in the associated JPasswordFieldUI.

public class BasicPasswordFieldUI extends BasicTextFieldUI

Constructors
public BasicPasswordFieldUI()
 Default constructor.

Methods
public View create(Element elem)
 Returns a new PasswordView for the Element.

Overrides: create in class `BasicTextFieldUI`.
Implements: create in interface `ViewFactory`.

public static ComponentUI createUI(JComponent c)

Creates a UI for a `JPasswordField`.
Overrides: createUI in class `BasicTextFieldUI`.

Protected Methods

protected String getPropertyPrefix()

Fetches the name used as a key to lookup properties through the `UIManager`. This is used as a prefix to all the standard text properties. Returns `PasswordField`.
Overrides: getPropertyPrefix in class `BasicTextFieldUI`.

See also   BasicTextFieldUI (p.694), ComponentUI (p.530), Element (p.830), PasswordView (p.856), View (p.893), ViewFactory (p.896).

swing.plaf.basic.BasicPopupMenuSeparatorUI

CLASS

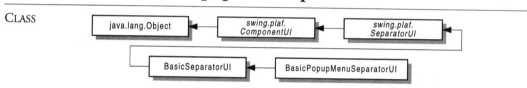

This class exists to allow the separators used in a `JPopupMenu` to be different from those in a `JMenu`.

public class BasicPopupMenuSeparatorUI extends BasicSeparatorUI

Constructors

public BasicPopupMenuSeparatorUI()

Default constructor.

Methods

public static ComponentUI createUI(JComponent c)

Overrides: createUI in class `BasicSeparatorUI`.

public java.awt.Dimension getPreferredSize(JComponent c)

Overrides: getPreferredSize in class `BasicSeparatorUI`.

public void paint(java.awt.Graphics g, JComponent c)

Overrides: paint in class `BasicSeparatorUI`.

See also   BasicSeparatorUI (p.654), ComponentUI (p.530), JComponent (p.207).

swing.plaf.basic.BasicPopupMenuUI

CLASS

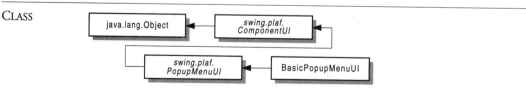

The Basic look and feel UI delegate for a JPopupMenu.

UIDefaults table key	Description
PopupMenu.background	The default background Color for a JPopupMenu.
PopupMenu.border	The default Border for a JPopupMenu.
PopupMenu.font	The default Font for a JPopupMenu.
PopupMenu.foreground	The default foreground Color for a JPopupMenu.

public class BasicPopupMenuUI extends PopupMenuUI

Constructors
public BasicPopupMenuUI()
Default constructor.

Methods
public static ComponentUI createUI(JComponent x)
Overrides: createUI in class ComponentUI.
public java.awt.Dimension getMaximumSize(JComponent c)
Returns getPreferredSize().
Overrides: getMaximumSize in class ComponentUI.
public java.awt.Dimension getMinimumSize(JComponent c)
Returns getPreferredSize().
Overrides: getMinimumSize in class ComponentUI.
public java.awt.Dimension getPreferredSize(JComponent c)
Returns null.
Overrides: getPreferredSize in class ComponentUI.
public void installDefaults()
Sets the layout to a GridBagLayout and installs the default Colors and Border into the associated JPopupMenu.
public void installUI(JComponent c)
Overrides: installUI in class ComponentUI.
public void uninstallUI(JComponent c)
Overrides: uninstallUI in class ComponentUI.

Protected Fields
protected JPopupMenu popupMenu
The associated JPopupMenu.

Protected Methods
protected void installKeyboardActions()
An empty method.
protected void installListeners()
An empty method.
protected void uninstallDefaults()
Uninstalls the resources installed in installDefaults().
protected void uninstallKeyboardActions()
An empty method.

plaf.basic

protected void uninstallListeners()

An empty method.

See also   ComponentUI (p.530), JComponent (p.207), JPopupMenu (p.309), PopupMenuUI (p.538).

swing.plaf.basic.BasicProgressBarUI

CLASS

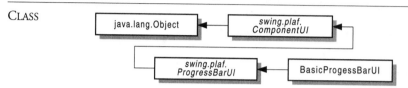

The Basic look and feel UI delegate for the JProgressBar class.

UIDefaults table key	Description
ProgressBar.background	The background Color for the JProgressBar.
ProgressBar.border	The Border used around the tray for the progress bar.
ProgressBar.cellLength	The Integer length in pixels of each segment of the progress bar.
ProgressBar.cellSpacing	The Integer gap in pixels between each segment of the progress bar.
ProgressBar.font	The Font used for any text in the JProgressBar.
ProgressBar.foreground	The foreground Color for the JProgressBar.
ProgressBar.selectionBackground	The Color used to draw any text when it is over an unfilled area of the progress bar.
ProgressBar.selectionForeground	The Color used to draw any text when it is over a filled area of the progress bar.

public class BasicProgressBarUI extends ProgressBarUI

Constructors
public BasicProgressBarUI()

Default constructor.

Methods
public static ComponentUI createUI(JComponent x)

Overrides: createUI in class ComponentUI.

public java.awt.Dimension getMaximumSize(JComponent c)

Returns Short.MAX_VALUE. A subclass might want to override this to return a better value.

Overrides: getMaximumSize in class ComponentUI.

public java.awt.Dimension getMinimumSize(JComponent c)

Returns 0. A subclass might want to override this to return a better value.

Overrides: getMinimumSize in class ComponentUI.

public java.awt.Dimension getPreferredSize(JComponent c)

Returns the sum of the border insets and either preferredInnerVertical or preferredInnerHorizontal, depending on the orientation of the JProgressBar.

Overrides: `getPreferredSize` in class `ComponentUI`.

public void installUI(JComponent c)

Overrides: `installUI` in class `ComponentUI`.

public void paint(java.awt.Graphics g, JComponent c)

This paint method should work correctly for most linear progress bars. To change the way it paints, change the values set into the UIDefaults table for the following keys: `ProgressBar.cellLength`, `ProgressBar.cellSpacing`, and the normal component keys.

Overrides: `paint` in class `ComponentUI`.

public void uninstallUI(JComponent c)

Overrides: `uninstallUI` in class `ComponentUI`.

Protected Fields

protected ChangeListener changeListener

The `ChangeListener` used to handle changes in the associated `JProgressBar`.

protected JProgressBar progressBar

The associated `JProgressBar`.

Protected Methods

protected int getAmountFull(java.awt.Insets insets, int width, int height)

Returns the length of the progress bar (in pixels) that should be filled based on information from the model. This method only returns results that apply to linear progress bars. Progress indicators of other shapes (for example, round) will want to override this method.

protected int getCellLength()

Returns the width or height (in pixels) of each segment of the progress bar. If text is being painted on the progress bar, this method will always return 1, which draws a completely filled progress bar.

protected int getCellSpacing()

Returns the gap (in pixels) between each segment of the progress bar. If text is being painted on the progress bar, this method will always return 0, which draws a completeley filled progress bar.

protected java.awt.Dimension getPreferredInnerHorizontal()

Used in calculating the preferred size. The value returned represents the preferred inside `Dimensions` for a horizontal progress bar.

protected java.awt.Dimension getPreferredInnerVertical()

Used in calculating the preferred size. The value returned represents the preferred inside `Dimensions` for a horizontal progress bar.

protected java.awt.Color getSelectionBackground()

The `selectionBackground` Color is used when text is drawn over an unfilled area of the progress bar.

protected java.awt.Color getSelectionForeground()

The `selectionForeground` Color is used when text is drawn over a filled area of the progress bar.

protected java.awt.Point getStringPlacement(java.awt.Graphics g, String progressString, int x, int y, int width, int height)

Returns the origin point to use when drawing the text. This method returns a `Point` which centers the text both horizontally and vertically inside the progress bar.

protected void installDefaults(JComponent c)

Installs this delegate's UI resources into the `JProgressBar`.

protected void installListeners(JComponent c)

Installs the listeners needed by this delegate into the `JProgressBar`.

plaf.basic

protected void paintString(java.awt.Graphics g, int x, int y,
int width, int height, int amountFull, java.awt.Insets b)
Paints the string representing the amount done as a percentage into the progress bar.
protected void setCellLength(int cellLen)
Sets the length (in pixels) of each segment of the progress bar.
protected void setCellSpacing(int cellSpace)
Sets the gap (in pixels) between each segment of the progress bar.
protected void uninstallDefaults(JComponent c)
Removes the UI resources installed by this delegate from the JProgressBar.
protected void uninstallListeners(JComponent c)
Removes the listeners installed in installListeners() from the JProgressBar.

Inner Classes
public class BasicProgressBarUI.ChangeHandler

See also   ChangeListener (p.488), JComponent (p.207), JProgressBar (p.315),
ProgressBarUI (p.538).

swing.plaf.basic.BasicProgressBarUI.ChangeHandler

INNER CLASS

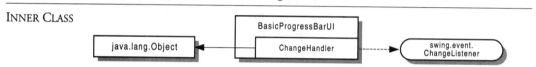

This inner class updates the progress bar when the value of the JProgressBar changes. This
class should be treated as if it were protected.

public class BasicProgressBarUI.ChangeHandler
**   extends java.lang.Object**
**   implements ChangeListener**

Constructors
public ChangeHandler()
Default constructor.

Methods
public void stateChanged(ChangeEvent e)
Implements: stateChanged in interface ChangeListener.

See also   ChangeEvent (p.487), ChangeListener (p.488), JProgressBar (p.315).

swing.plaf.basic.BasicRadioButtonMenuItemUI

CLASS

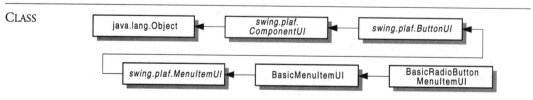

The Basic look and feel UI delegate for `JRadioButtonMenuItems`.

UIDefaults table key	Description
RadioButtonMenuItem.checkIcon	The Icon to use as the selected "dot".

public class BasicRadioButtonMenuItemUI extends BasicMenuItemUI

Constructors
public BasicRadioButtonMenuItemUI()
> Default constructor.

Methods
public static ComponentUI createUI(JComponent b)
> *Overrides:* createUI in class ComponentUI.

public void processMouseEvent(JMenuItem item, java.awt.event.MouseEvent e, MenuElement[] path, MenuSelectionManager manager)
> Selects the menu item on MOUSE_RELEASED.
> *Overrides:* processMouseEvent in class MenuItemUI.

Protected Methods
protected String getPropertyPrefix()
> Returns "RadioButtonMenuItem".
> *Overrides:* getPropertyPrefix in class BasicMenuItemUI.

protected void installDefaults()
> *Overrides:* installDefaults in class BasicMenuItemUI.

> *See also*   BasicMenuItemUI (p.624), ComponentUI (p.530), JRadioButtonMenuItem (p.321).

swing.plaf.basic.BasicRadioButtonUI

CLASS

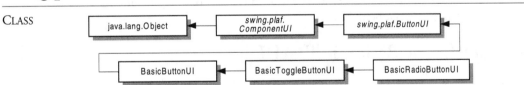

The Basic look and feel UI delegate for `JRadioButtons`. This class creates a single shared instance of itself for all `JRadioButtons`.

UIDefaults table key	Description
RadioButton.icon	The Icon used for the radio button "dot".

public class BasicRadioButtonUI extends BasicToggleButtonUI

Constructors
public BasicRadioButtonUI()
> Default constructor.

plaf.basic

Methods
public Icon getDefaultIcon()
Creates the radio button's "dot."
public static ComponentUI createUI(JComponent b)
Overrides: createUI in class BasicToggleButtonUI.
public java.awt.Dimension getPreferredSize(JComponent c)
Returns the preferred size of the radio button.
Overrides: getPreferredSize in class BasicButtonUI.
public synchronized void paint(java.awt.Graphics g, JComponent c)
Paints the radio button.
Overrides: paint in class BasicToggleButtonUI.

Protected Fields
protected Icon icon
The "dot" Icon for the JRadioButton.

Protected Methods
protected String getPropertyPrefix()
Returns "RadioButton".
Overrides: getPropertyPrefix in class BasicToggleButtonUI.
protected void installDefaults(AbstractButton c)
Overrides: installDefaults in BasicButtonUI.
protected void paintFocus(java.awt.Graphics g,
java.awt.Rectangle textRect, java.awt.Dimension size)
Paints the focus indicator for the JRadioButton.
protected void uninstallDefaults(AbstractButton b)
Overrides: uninstallDefaults in class BasicButtonUI.

Extended by BasicCheckBoxUI (p.560).
See also AbstractButton (p.118), BasicButtonUI (p.557), BasicToggleButtonUI (p.701), Icon (p.183), JRadioButton (p.319).

swing.plaf.basic.BasicScrollBarUI

CLASS

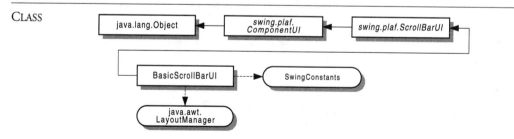

Implementation of ScrollBarUI for the Basic look and feel. The "thumb" is the button in the area in between the two arrow buttons that can be dragged to change the scroll bar's location. The "track" is the area where the thumb can move.

UIDefaults table key	Description
ScrollBar.border	The `Border` used around the whole scroll bar.
ScrollBar.maximumThumbSize	The maximum `Dimension` for the thumb.
ScrollBar.minimumThumbSize	The minimum allowed `Dimension` for the thumb.
ScrollBar.thumb	The `Color` used for the background of the thumb.
ScrollBar.thumbDarkShadow	The shadow `Color` used when the thumb is not pressed.
ScrollBar.thumbHighlight	The highlight `Color` when the thumb is not pressed.
ScrollBar.thumbLightShadow	The shadow `Color` used when the thumb is pressed.
ScrollBar.track	The `Color` used for the background of the track.
ScrollBar.trackHighlight	The highlight `Color` used when the thumb is pressed.

```
public class BasicScrollBarUI extends ScrollBarUI
    implements java.awt.LayoutManager, SwingConstants
```

Constructors
public BasicScrollBarUI()
Default constructor.

Methods
public void addLayoutComponent(String name, java.awt.Component child)
An empty method.
Implements: addLayoutComponent in interface LayoutManager.

public static ComponentUI createUI(JComponent c)
Overrides: createUI in class ComponentUI.

public java.awt.Dimension getMaximumSize(JComponent c)
Returns new Dimension(Integer.MAX_VALUE, Integer.MAX_VALUE).
Overrides: getMaximumSize in class ComponentUI.

public java.awt.Dimension getMinimumSize(JComponent c)
Returns the largest minimum size of the two arrow buttons and the thumb.
Overrides: getMinimumSize in class ComponentUI.
See also: getMaximumSize, getPreferredSize.

public java.awt.Dimension getPreferredSize(JComponent c)
Returns the larger of the preferred sizes for the arrow buttons or the minimum size for the thumb.
Overrides: getPreferredSize in class ComponentUI.

public void installUI(JComponent c)
Overrides: installUI in class ComponentUI.

public void layoutContainer(java.awt.Container scrollbarContainer)
Calls layoutHScrollbar or layoutVScrollbar, depending on the orientation of the JScrollBar.
Implements: layoutContainer in interface LayoutManager.

public java.awt.Dimension minimumLayoutSize(java.awt.Container scrollbarContainer)
Implements: minimumLayoutSize in interface LayoutManager.

public void paint(java.awt.Graphics g, JComponent c)
Overrides: paint in class ComponentUI.

plaf.basic

```
public java.awt.Dimension preferredLayoutSize(java.awt.Container
    scrollbarContainer)
```
Implements: preferredLayoutSize in interface LayoutManager.
```
public void removeLayoutComponent(java.awt.Component child)
```
An empty method.

Implements: removeLayoutComponent in interface LayoutManager.
```
public void uninstallUI(JComponent c)
```
Overrides: uninstallUI in class ComponentUI.

Protected Fields

```
protected static final int DECREASE_HIGHLIGHT = 1
protected static final int INCREASE_HIGHLIGHT = 2
protected static final int NO_HIGHLIGHT = 0
```
The values used to indicate the track should be drawn highlighted on the given side of the thumb.
```
protected BasicScrollBarUI.ArrowButtonListener buttonListener
```
The listener used for the arrow buttons.
```
protected JButton decrButton
```
The decrease arrow button.
```
protected JButton incrButton
```
The increase arrow button.
```
protected boolean isDragging
```
Returns true if the thumb is being dragged.
```
protected java.awt.Dimension maximumThumbSize
```
Stores the value of the maximum thumb size.
```
protected java.awt.Dimension minimumThumbSize
```
Stores the value of the minimum thumb size.
```
protected BasicScrollBarUI.ModelListener modelListener
```
The listener used to detect changes in the associated JScrollBar's model.
```
protected java.beans.PropertyChangeListener propertyChangeListener
```
The listener for property changes in the associated JScrollBar.
```
protected BasicScrollBarUI.ScrollListener scrollListener
```
The listener used to listen for scroll events triggered by the scrollTimer.
```
protected Timer scrollTimer
```
The delay between scrolls when the mouse button is held down on an arrow button or the track.
```
protected JScrollBar scrollbar
```
The associated JScrollBar.
```
protected java.awt.Color thumbColor
```
The color for the face (background) of the thumb.
```
protected java.awt.Color thumbDarkShadowColor
```
The dark shadow color to use on the thumb.
```
protected java.awt.Color thumbHighlightColor
```
The highlight color to use on the thumb.
```
protected java.awt.Color thumbLightShadowColor
```
The light shadow color to use on the thumb.
```
protected java.awt.Rectangle thumbRect
```
The bounding rectangle of the thumb.

protected java.awt.Color trackColor

The color to fill the background of the track.

protected int trackHighlight

Used during repaint, this field holds NO_HIGHLIGHT, DECREASE_HIGHLIGHT, or INCREASE_HIGHLIGHT.

protected java.awt.Color trackHighlightColor

The highlight color for the track's shadow effect.

protected BasicScrollBarUI.TrackListener trackListener

The listener used to detect clicks in the area of the track not occupied by the thumb.

protected java.awt.Rectangle trackRect

The bounding rectangle of the track.

Protected Methods

protected void configureScrollBarColors()

Loads the colors needed to paint the scroll bar's thumb and track from the UIDefaults table.

protected BasicScrollBarUI.ArrowButtonListener createArrowButtonListener()

Creates the listener used to handle events from the arrow buttons.

protected JButton createDecreaseButton(int orientation)

Returns a BasicArrowButton oriented in the given direction (usually SOUTH or WEST).

protected JButton createIncreaseButton(int orientation)

Returns a BasicArrowButton oriented in the given direction (usually NORTH or EAST).

protected BasicScrollBarUI.ModelListener createModelListener()

Creates the listener for changes in the associated JScrollBar's model.

protected java.beans.PropertyChangeListener createPropertyChangeListener()

Creates the listener for changes in the associated JScrollBar's properties.

protected BasicScrollBarUI.ScrollListener createScrollListener()

Creates the listener for scroll events generated by the scrollTimer.

protected BasicScrollBarUI.TrackListener createTrackListener()

Creates the listener for clicks in the track region not covered by the thumb.

protected java.awt.Dimension getMaximumThumbSize()

Returns a reference to a static final value containing Dimension(4096, 4096).

protected java.awt.Dimension getMinimumThumbSize()

Returns the acceptable size for the thumb. Below this size the thumb is simply hidden. Do not modify the value returned from this method, as it is a static final value shared among all scroll bars. For the Basic look and feel this value is Dimension (8,8).

protected java.awt.Rectangle getThumbBounds()

Returns a reference to the bounding rectangle of the thumb. Do not modify the value returned; use setThumbBounds instead.

protected java.awt.Rectangle getTrackBounds()

Returns the bounding rectangle of the track. Do not modify the value returned from this method, as it is a direct reference to the actual bounding rectangle of the track, not a copy.

protected void installComponents()

An empty method.

protected void installDefaults()

Creates the arrow buttons, sizes the thumb based on values from the UIDefaults table, and installs the border and colors from the UIDefaults table.

protected void installKeyboardActions()
An empty method.

protected void installListeners()
Creates the listeners using the createXListener() methods and installs them.

protected void layoutHScrollbar(JScrollBar sb)
Lays out a horizontal scroll bar.

protected void layoutVScrollbar(JScrollBar sb)
Lays out a vertical scroll bar.

protected void paintDecreaseHighlight(java.awt.Graphics g)
Paints the track when it is clicked outside the region of the thumb, on the SOUTH or WEST side.

protected void paintIncreaseHighlight(java.awt.Graphics g)
Paints the track when it is clicked outside the region of the thumb, on the NORTH or EAST side.

protected void paintThumb(java.awt.Graphics g, JComponent c, java.awt.Rectangle thumbBounds)
Paints the thumb at its current position and size.

protected void paintTrack(java.awt.Graphics g, JComponent c, java.awt.Rectangle trackBounds)
Paints the area of the track not occupied by the thumb.

protected void scrollByBlock(int direction)
Sets the new location of the scroll bar after scrolling by blockIncrement in the given direction and then repaints the scroll bar.

protected void scrollByUnit(int direction)
Sets the new location of the scroll bar after scrolling by unitIncrement in the given direction and then repaints the scroll bar.

protected void setThumbBounds(int x, int y, int width, int height)
Sets the bounds of the thumb and forces a repaint that includes the old thumbBounds and the new one.

protected void uninstallComponents()
An empty method.

protected void uninstallDefaults()
Uninstalls the values installed in installDefaults() if they haven't been overridden by an application defined value.

protected void uninstallKeyboardActions()
An empty method.

protected void uninstallListeners()
Uninstalls the listeners installed in installListeners().

Inner Classes

protected class BasicScrollBarUI.ArrowButtonListener
protected class BasicScrollBarUI.ModelListener
public class BasicScrollBarUI.PropertyChangeHandler
protected class BasicScrollBarUI.ScrollListener
protected class BasicScrollBarUI.TrackListener

See also   BasicArrowButton (p.550), JButton (p.191), JComponent (p.207), ScrollBarUI (p.538), SwingConstants (p.442), Timer (p.447).

plaf.basic

swing.plaf.basic.BasicScrollBarUI.ArrowButtonListener

INNER CLASS

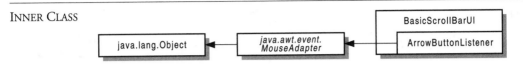

This class listens to the arrow buttons on a scroll bar and also for the cursor keys when the scroll bar has the focus.

```
protected class BasicScrollBarUI.ArrowButtonListener
    extends java.awt.event.MouseAdapter
```

Constructors
```
public ArrowButtonListener()
```
   Default constructor.

Methods
```
public void mousePressed(java.awt.event.MouseEvent e)
```
   Overrides: mousePressed in class MouseAdapter.
   Implements: mousePressed in interface MouseListener.
```
public void mouseReleased(java.awt.event.MouseEvent e)
```
   Overrides: mouseReleased in class MouseAdapter.
   Implements: mouseReleased in interface MouseListener.

   Returned by   BasicScrollBarUI.createArrowButtonListener() (p.642).

swing.plaf.basic.BasicScrollBarUI.ModelListener

INNER CLASS

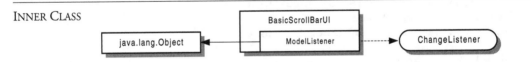

This class listens for changes in the JScrollBar's model and updates the UI delegate as appropriate.

```
protected class BasicScrollBarUI.ModelListener
    extends java.lang.Object
    implements ChangeListener
```

Constructors
```
public ModelListener()
```
   Default constructor.

Methods
```
public void stateChanged(ChangeEvent e)
```
   Implements: stateChanged in interface ChangeListener.

   Returned by   BasicScrollBarUI.createModelListener() (p.642).
   See also   ChangeEvent (p.487), ChangeListener (p.488).

plaf.basic

swing.plaf.basic.BasicScrollBarUI.PropertyChangeHandler

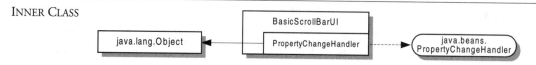

```
public class BasicScrollBarUI.PropertyChangeHandler
    extends java.lang.Object
    implements java.beans.PropertyChangeListener
```

Constructors

public PropertyChangeHandler()

    Default constructor.

Methods

public void propertyChange(java.beans.PropertyChangeEvent)

    Responds to changes to the JScrollBar's model and orientation properties.
    Implements: propertyChange in interface PropertyChangeListener.

swing.plaf.basic.BasicScrollBarUI.ScrollListener

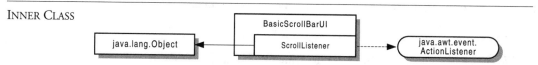

Listener for scroll events triggered by the associated scroll pane (usually autoscroll events).

```
protected class BasicScrollBarUI.ScrollListener
    extends java.lang.Object
    implements java.awt.event.ActionListener
```

Constructors

public ScrollListener()

public ScrollListener(int dir, boolean block)

    Constructs a new ScrollListener for the given direction. The default value for block is false.

Methods

public void actionPerformed(java.awt.event.ActionEvent e)

    Implements: actionPerformed in interface ActionListener.

public void setDirection(int direction)

    Changes the direction this scroll listener will scroll the associated scroll bar.

public void setScrollByBlock(boolean block)

    Changes whether this scroll listener will scroll the associated scroll bar by a unit increment or a block increment.

    Returned by   BasicScrollBarUI.createScrollListener() (p.642).

swing.plaf.basic.BasicScrollBarUI.TrackListener

INNER CLASS

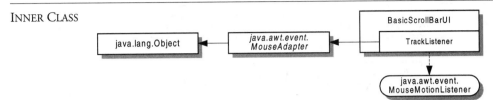

This class listens for events related to the area of the track not occupied by the thumb.

```
protected class BasicScrollBarUI.TrackListener
    extends java.awt.event.MouseAdapter
    implements java.awt.event.MouseMotionListener
```

Constructors
public TrackListener()
> Default constructor.

Methods
public void mouseDragged(java.awt.event.MouseEvent e)
> Sets the model's value to the position of the top/left of the thumb relative to the origin of the track.
> *Implements:* mouseDragged in interface MouseMotionListener.

public void mouseMoved(java.awt.event.MouseEvent e)
> *Implements:* mouseMoved in interface MouseMotionListener.

public void mousePressed(java.awt.event.MouseEvent e)
> If the mouse is pressed above the thumb, then this reduces the scroll bar's value by blockIncrement, otherwise increases it by blockIncrement. If there is no thumb, then it bases the decision on whether the click is in the top or bottom half of the track.
> *Overrides:* mousePressed in class MouseAdapter.
> *Implements:* mousePressed in interface MouseListener.

public void mouseReleased(java.awt.event.MouseEvent e)
> *Overrides:* mouseReleased in class MouseAdapter.
> *Implements:* mouseReleased in interface MouseListener.

Protected Fields
protected transient int currentMouseX
protected transient int currentMouseY
protected transient int offset
> These fields are used to calculate the distance that the thumb should move.

Returned by   BasicScrollBarUI.createTrackListener() (p.642).

swing.plaf.basic.BasicScrollPaneUI

CLASS

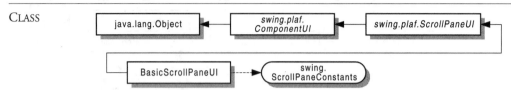

The Basic look and feel UI delegate for a JScrollPane.

UIDefaults table key	Description
ScrollPane.background	The background Color for the JScrollPane.
ScrollPane.border	The Border to use around the whole JScrollPane.
ScrollPane.font	The default Font for children of the JScrollPane.
ScrollPane.foreground	The foreground Color for the JScrollPane.
ScrollPane.viewportBorder	The Border to use around the viewport.

public class BasicScrollPaneUI extends ScrollPaneUI
    implements ScrollPaneConstants

Constructors
public BasicScrollPaneUI()
    Default constructor.

Methods
public static ComponentUI createUI(JComponent x)
    Overrides: createUI in class ComponentUI.
public java.awt.Dimension getMaximumSize(JComponent c)
    Overrides: getMaximumSize in class ComponentUI.
public java.awt.Dimension getMinimumSize(JComponent c)
    Overrides: getMinimumSize in class ComponentUI.
public java.awt.Dimension getPreferredSize(JComponent c)
    Overrides: getPreferredSize in class ComponentUI.
public void installUI(JComponent x)
    Overrides: installUI in class ComponentUI.
public void paint(java.awt.Graphics g, JComponent c)
    Overrides: paint in class ComponentUI.
public void uninstallUI(JComponent x)
    Overrides: uninstallUI in class ComponentUI.

Protected Fields
protected ChangeListener hsbChangeListener
    The listener used to track the horizontal scroll bar.
protected JScrollPane scrollpane
    The associated JScrollPane.

protected java.beans.PropertyChangeListener spPropertyChangeListener

The property change listener added to the associated JScrollPane.

protected ChangeListener viewportChangeListener

The listener used to track changes in the viewport.

protected ChangeListener vsbChangeListener

The listener used to track changes in the vertical scroll bar.

Protected Methods

protected ChangeListener createHSBChangeListener()

Creates the listener for the horizontal scroll bar.

protected java.beans.PropertyChangeListener createPropertyChangeListener()

Creates the property change listener that handles changes in the associated JScrollPane.

protected ChangeListener createVSBChangeListener()

Creates the listener used for handling events from the vertical scroll bar.

protected ChangeListener createViewportChangeListener()

Creates the listener for changes in the viewport.

protected void installDefaults(JScrollPane scrollpane)

Installs the border, background and foreground colors, and viewport border into the JScrollPane.

protected void installKeyboardActions(JScrollPane c)

An empty method.

protected void installListeners(JScrollPane c)

Installs the listeners into the JScrollPane.

protected void syncScrollPaneWithViewport()

Synchronizes the current state of the scroll pane with the state of the viewport.

protected void uninstallDefaults(JScrollPane c)

Uninstalls the colors, font, and borders.

protected void uninstallKeyboardActions(JScrollPane c)

An empty method.

protected void uninstallListeners(JComponent c)

Uninstalls the listeners.

protected void updateColumnHeader(java.beans.PropertyChangeEvent e)

Updates the column header when it changes in the JScrollPane.

protected void updateRowHeader(java.beans.PropertyChangeEvent e)

Updates the row header when it changes in the JScrollPane.

protected void updateScrollBarDisplayPolicy(
java.beans.PropertyChangeEvent e)

Updates the scroll bars to reflect a change in the JScrollPane's policy.

protected void updateViewport(java.beans.PropertyChangeEvent e)

Updates the viewport when it changes in the JScrollPane.

Inner Classes

public class BasicScrollPaneUI.HSBChangeListener
public class BasicScrollPaneUI.PropertyChangeHandler
public class BasicScrollPaneUI.ViewportChangeHandler
public class BasicScrollPaneUI.VSBChangeListener

See also ChangeListener (p.488), JScrollBar (p.328), JScrollPane (p.332), JViewport (p.410), ScrollPaneConstants (p.436), ScrollPaneLayout (p.437), ScrollPaneUI (p.539).

swing.plaf.basic.BasicScrollPaneUI.HSBChangeListener

INNER CLASS

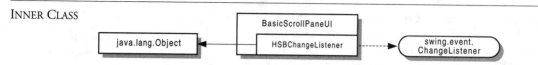

This class listens for changes in the horizontal scroll bar and updates the scroll pane appropriately.

```
protected class BasicScrollPaneUI.HSBListener
    extends java.lang.Object
    implements ChangeListener
```

Constructors
```
public HSBChangeListener()
```
Default constructor.

Methods
```
public void stateChanged(ChangeEvent e)
```
Implements: stateChanged in interface ChangeListener.

See also   ChangeEvent (p.487), ChangeListener (p.488).

swing.plaf.basic.BasicScrollPaneUI.PropertyChangeHandler

INNER CLASS

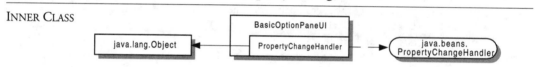

This inner class listens for property changes in the associated JScrollPane and updates the BasicScrollPaneUI appropriately. The properties handled by this inner class are verticalScrollBarDisplayPolicy, horizontalScrollBarDisplayPolicy, viewport, rowHeader, and columnHeader. This class simply forwards the PropertyChangeEvent to the appropriate method in BasicScrollPaneUI.

```
public class BasicScrollPaneUI.PropertyChangeHandler
    extends java.lang.Object
    implements java.beans.PropertyChangeListener
```

Constructors
```
public PropertyChangeHandler()
```
Default constructor.

Methods
```
public void propertyChange(java.beans.PropertyChangeEvent e)
```
Implements: propertyChange in interface PropertyChangeListener.

See also   JScrollPane (p.332).

swing.plaf.basic.BasicScrollPaneUI.ViewportChangeHandler

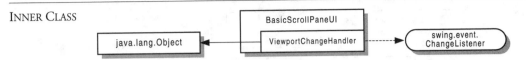

This class listens for changes in the viewport and updates the scroll pane appropriately.

```
protected class BasicScrollPaneUI.ViewportChangeHandler
    extends java.lang.Object
    implements ChangeListener
```

Constructors
```
public ViewportChangeHandler()
```
Default constructor.

Methods
```
public void stateChanged(ChangeEvent e)
```
Implements: stateChanged in interface ChangeListener.

See also   ChangeEvent (p.487), ChangeListener (p.488), JViewport (p.410).

swing.plaf.basic.BasicScrollPaneUI.VSBChangeListener

INNER CLASS

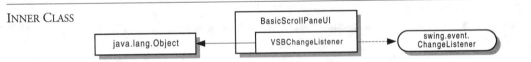

This class listens for changes in the vertical scroll bar and updates the scroll pane appropriately.

```
protected class BasicScrollPaneUI.VSBChangeListener
    extends java.lang.Object
    implements ChangeListener
```

Constructors
```
public VSBChangeListener()
```
Default constructor.

Methods
```
public void stateChanged(ChangeEvent e)
```
Implements: stateChanged in interface ChangeListener.

See also   ChangeEvent (p.487), ChangeListener (p.488), JScrollBar (p.328).

plaf.basic

swing.plaf.basic.BasicSeparatorUI

CLASS

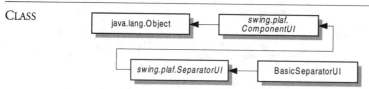

The basic look and feel UI delegate for the JSeparator component.

UIDefaults table key	Description
Separator.highlight	The Color to use for the JSeparator's highlight.
Separator.shadow	The Color to use for the JSeparator's shadow.

public class BasicSeparatorUI extends SeparatorUI

Constructors
public BasicSeparatorUI()
Default constructor.

Methods
public static ComponentUI createUI(JComponent x)
Overrides: createUI in class ComponentUI.

public java.awt.Dimension getMaximumSize(JComponent c)
Returns null.
Overrides: getMaximumSize in class ComponentUI.

public java.awt.Dimension getMinimumSize(JComponent c)
Returns null.
Overrides: getMinimumSize in class ComponentUI.

public java.awt.Dimension getPreferredSize(JComponent c)
Returns Dimension(0, 2).
Overrides: getPreferredSize in class ComponentUI.

public void installUI(JComponent c)
Overrides: installUI in class ComponentUI.

public void paint(java.awt.Graphics g, JComponent c)
Overrides: paint in class ComponentUI.

public void uninstallUI(JComponent c)
Overrides: uninstallUI in class ComponentUI.

Protected Fields
protected java.awt.Color highlight
The cached value of the highlight color.
protected java.awt.Color shadow
The cached value of the shadow color.

plaf.basic

Protected Methods

protected void installDefaults(JSeparator c)

Caches the highlight and shadow colors from the UIDefaults table into the `highlight` and `shadow` fields.

protected void installListeners(JSeparator s)

An empty method.

protected void uninstallDefaults(JSeparator c)

Sets the cached color fields to `null`.

protected void uninstallListeners(JSeparator s)

An empty method.

Extended by   BasicPopupMenuSeparatorUI (p.636), BasicToolBarSeparatorUI (p.702).

See also   ComponentUI (p.530), JComponent (p.207), JSeparator (p.338), SeparatorUI (p.539).

swing.plaf.basic.BasicSliderUI

CLASS

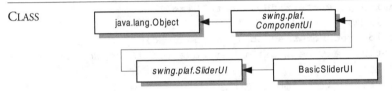

The Basic look and feel UI delegate for a `JSlider`.

UIDefaults table key	Description
Slider.background	The background `Color` used by the slider.
Slider.border	The `Border` for the slider.
Slider.focus	The `Color` used for the focus indicator.
Slider.focusInsets	The `Insets` for the focus indicator.
Slider.foreground	The foreground `Color` for the slider.
Slider.highlight	The highlight `Color` for the slider's 3D effect.
Slider.shadow	The shadow `Color` for the slider's 3D effect.

public class BasicSliderUI extends SliderUI

Fields

public final int MAX_SCROLL = +2
public final int MIN_SCROLL = -2
public final int NEGATIVE_SCROLL = -1
public final int POSITIVE_SCROLL = +1

Constants which are assigned to the keyboard actions for this UI delegate.

Constructors

public BasicSliderUI(JSlider b)

Constructs a new BasicSliderUI for the given JSlider.

Methods

public static ComponentUI createUI(JComponent b)

Overrides: createUI in class ComponentUI.

public java.awt.Dimension getMaximumSize(JComponent c)

Overrides: getMaximumSize in class ComponentUI.

public java.awt.Dimension getMinimumHorizontalSize()

Returns the minimum size when the slider is oriented horizontally.

public java.awt.Dimension getMinimumSize(JComponent c)

Calls getMinimumHorizontalSize or getMinimumVerticalsize, depending on the orientation of the slider.

Overrides: getMinimumSize in class ComponentUI.

public java.awt.Dimension getMinimumVerticalSize()

Returns the minimum size when the slider is oriented vertically.

public java.awt.Dimension getPreferredHorizontalSize()

Returns Dimension(200, 21).

public java.awt.Dimension getPreferredSize(JComponent c)

Calls getPreferredHorizontalSize or getPreferredVerticalSize, depending on the orientation of the slider.

Overrides: getPreferredSize in class ComponentUI.

public java.awt.Dimension getPreferredVerticalSize()

Returns Dimension(21, 200).

public void installUI(JComponent c)

Overrides: installUI in class ComponentUI.

public void paint(java.awt.Graphics g, JComponent c)

Overrides: paint in class ComponentUI.

public void paintFocus(java.awt.Graphics g)

Paints the focus indicator.

public void paintLabels(java.awt.Graphics g)

Paints the labels.

public void paintThumb(java.awt.Graphics g)

Paints the thumb.

public void paintTicks(java.awt.Graphics g)

Paints the ticks.

public void paintTrack(java.awt.Graphics g)

Paints the track.

public void scrollByBlock(int direction)

Updates the JScrollBar's model by incrementing it or decrementing it by a blockIncrement, and repaints it.

public void scrollByUnit(int direction)

Updates the JScrollBar's model by incrementing it or decrementing it by a unitIncrement, and repaints it.

public void setThumbLocation(int x, int y)

Sets the origin of the thumb.

public void uninstallUI(JComponent c)

Overrides: uninstallUI in class ComponentUI.

public int valueForXPosition(int xPos)

Returns the slider value which most closely matches the given *x* position. A position past either end of the slider (if the slider is horizontal) will return the maximum or minimum value of the slider, as appropriate.

public int valueForYPosition(int yPos)

Returns the slider value which most closely matches the given *y* position. A position past the top or the bottom of the slider (if the slider is vertical) will return the maximum or minimum value of the slider, as appropriate.

Protected Fields

protected ChangeListener changeListener

Listens for changes in the JSlider and updates the UI as appropriate.

protected java.awt.event.ComponentListener componentListener

Listens for resizing events from the JSlider and updates the UI as appropriate.

protected java.awt.Rectangle contentRect

Cached bounding box for the content of the JSlider. Updated in calculateGeometry().

protected java.awt.Insets focusInsets

The insets of the focus rectangle.

protected java.awt.event.FocusListener focusListener

Listens for FocusEvents and updates the focus rectangle as appropriate.

protected java.awt.Rectangle focusRect

Cached bounding box for the focus rectangle. Updated in calculateGeometry().

protected java.awt.Insets insetCache

The cached Insets for the slider.

protected java.awt.Rectangle labelRect

The rectangle used for the labels.

protected java.beans.PropertyChangeListener propertyChangeListener

Listens for property changes in the JSlider.

protected BasicSliderUI.ScrollListener scrollListener

Handles converting keystroke-triggered ActionEvents into the appropriate scroll.

protected Timer scrollTimer

The timer that controls the speed at which the slider scrolls.

protected JSlider slider

The associated JSlider.

protected java.awt.Rectangle thumbRect

The cached bounding rectangle for the thumb.

protected java.awt.Rectangle tickRect

The cached bounding rectangle for the ticks.

protected int trackBuffer

The distance (in pixels) that the slider track is from the edge of the component.

protected BasicSliderUI.TrackListener trackListener

Handles mouse events in the track, to control dragging and moving the thumb when the mouse is clicked in the track.

protected java.awt.Rectangle trackRect

The cached bounding rectangle for the track.

Protected Methods

protected void calculateContentRect()
Calculates the size of the content (track and thumb) area by insetting it in the focus rectangle.

protected void calculateFocusRect()
Calculates the size of the focus rectangle by insetting it in the total available area.

protected void calculateGeometry()
The wrapper method to call the other calculateX() methods.

protected void calculateLabelRect()
Calculates the bounding rectangle for the labels based on the location of the ticks.

protected void calculateThumbLocation()
Calculates the bounding rectangle for the thumb based on the JSlider's value and the track rectangle.

protected void calculateThumbSize()
Calls getThumbRect() and caches the value in thumbRect.

protected void calculateTickRect()
Calculates the bounding rectangle for the ticks based on the bounding rectangle for the track.

protected void calculateTrackBuffer()
Calculates the distance (in pixels) from the track edge to the edge of the component. This value is based on the sizes of the ticks, the labels, and the focus rectangle.

protected void calculateTrackRect()
Calculates the bounding rectangle for the track based on the content rectangle and the track-Buffer.

protected ChangeListener createChangeListener(JSlider slider)
Creates the handler for ChangeEvents from the JSlider.

**protected java.awt.event.ComponentListener
createComponentListener(JSlider slider)**
Creates the listener for ComponentEvents from the JSlider. The default handler only handles resizing.

protected java.awt.event.FocusListener createFocusListener(JSlider slider)
Creates the handler for FocusEvents.

**protected java.beans.PropertyChangeListener
createPropertyChangeListener(JSlider slider)**
Creates the handler for PropertyChangeEvents from the JSlider.

protected BasicSliderUI.ScrollListener createScrollListener(JSlider slider)
Creates the handler which converts key events into the appropriate scrolling behavior.

protected BasicSliderUI.TrackListener createTrackListener(JSlider slider)
Creates the handler for mouse events in the track area.

protected java.awt.Color getFocusColor()
Returns the color used for the focus indicator.

protected int getHeightOfHighValueLabel()
Returns the height of the label representing the highest value.

protected int getHeightOfLowValueLabel()
Returns the height of the label representing the lowest value.

protected int getHeightOfTallestLabel()
Returns the height of the tallest label.

protected java.awt.Component getHighestValueLabel()
Returns the label that corresponds to the highest slider value in the label table.

protected java.awt.Color getHighlightColor()
    Returns the color to use for the highlight of the track's 3D effect.

protected java.awt.Component getLowestValueLabel()
    Returns the label that corresponds to the lowest slider value in the label table.

protected java.awt.Color getShadowColor()
    Returns the color to use for the shadow of the track's 3D effect.

protected java.awt.Dimension getThumbSize()
    Returns the size (in pixels) of the thumb.

protected int getTickLength()
    Returns the height (or width, for vertical sliders) of the tick area.

protected int getWidthOfHighValueLabel()
    Returns the width of the label representing the highest value in the slider.

protected int getWidthOfLowValueLabel()
    Returns the width of the label representing the lowest value in the slider.

protected int getWidthOfWidestLabel()
    Returns the width of the widest label.

protected void installDefaults(JSlider slider)
    Installs the border and foreground and background colors. Also caches the shadow and highlight colors and the Insets for the focus rectangle.

protected void installKeyboardActions(JSlider slider)
    Installs handlers for VK_RIGHT, VK_LEFT, VK_UP, VK_DOWN, VK_PAGE_UP, VK_PAGE_DOWN, VK_HOME, and VK_END keys.

protected void installListeners(JSlider slider)
    Installs the listeners into the associated JSlider and its model.

protected void paintHorizontalLabel(java.awt.Graphics g, int value, java.awt.Component label)
    Paints a label for a horizontal slider. This method is called for each label.

protected void paintMajorTickForHorizSlider(java.awt.Graphics g, java.awt.Rectangle tickBounds, int x)
    Paints a major tick in a horizontal slider. Major ticks are usually longer than minor ticks.

protected void paintMajorTickForVertSlider(java.awt.Graphics g, java.awt.Rectangle tickBounds, int y)
    Paints a major tick in a vertical slider. Major ticks are usually longer than minor ticks.

protected void paintMinorTickForHorizSlider(java.awt.Graphics g, java.awt.Rectangle tickBounds, int x)
    Paints a minor tick in a horizontal slider. Minor ticks are usually shorter than major ticks.

protected void paintMinorTickForVertSlider(java.awt.Graphics g, java.awt.Rectangle tickBounds, int y)
    Paints a minor tick in a vertical slider. Minor ticks are usually shorter than major ticks.

protected void paintVerticalLabel(java.awt.Graphics g, int value, java.awt.Component label)
    Paints a label for a vertical slider. This method is called for each label.

protected void recalculateIfInsetsChanged()
    If the new Insets for the JSlider don't match the cached Insets, calls calculateGeometry().

protected void scrollDueToClickInTrack(int dir)
    Called when a mousePressed was detected in the track, not in the thumb. This method causes a block scroll.

plaf.basic

protected void uninstallKeyboardActions(JSlider slider)
Uninstalls the key handlers.

protected void uninstallListeners(JSlider slider)
Uninstalls the various listeners.

protected int xPositionForValue(int randomValue)
Returns the *x* position for a given value in the slider.

protected int yPositionForValue(int randomValue)
Returns the *y* position for a given value in the slider.

Inner Classes

public class BasicSliderUI.ActionScroller
public class BasicSliderUI.ChangeHandler
public class BasicSliderUI.ComponentHandler
public class BasicSliderUI.FocusHandler
public class BasicSliderUI.PropertyChangeHandler
public class BasicSliderUI.ScrollListener
public class BasicSliderUI.TrackListener

See also   ChangeListener (p.488), ComponentUI (p.530), JComponent (p.207),
JSlider (p.341), SliderUI (p.539), Timer (p.447).

swing.plaf.basic.BasicSliderUI.ActionScroller

INNER CLASS

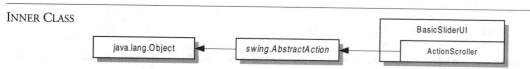

This class defines the action to perform when the slider is scrolled.

This inner class is `public` in Swing 1.1 due to a compiler bug. It will be changed to `protected` when the bug is fixed, so it should be treated as such.

public class BasicSliderUI.ActionScroller extends AbstractAction

Constructors

public ActionScroller(JSlider slider, int dir, boolean block)
Constructs an `ActionScroller` for the given `JSlider` that will scroll in the direction `dir`. If `block` is `true`, the `ActionScroller` will scroll by a `blockIncrement`, rather than the default `unitIncrement`.

Methods

public void actionPerformed(java.awt.event.ActionEvent e)
Causes the slider to scroll.

public boolean isEnabled()
Overrides: `isEnabled` in class `AbstractAction`.
Implements: `isEnabled` in interface `Action`.

See also   AbstractAction (p.115), JSlider (p.341).

swing.plaf.basic.BasicSliderUI.ChangeHandler

INNER CLASS

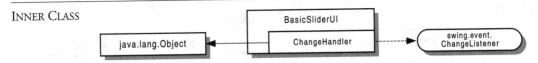

This inner class listens for changes in the associated JSlider's model.

This inner class is public in Swing 1.1 due to a compiler bug. It will be changed to protected when the bug is fixed, so it should be treated as such.

```
public class BasicSliderUI.ChangeHandler extends java.lang.Object
    implements ChangeListener
```

Constructors
```
public ChangeHandler()
```
Default constructor.

Methods
```
public void stateChanged(ChangeEvent e)
```
Implements: stateChanged in interface ChangeListener.

See also   ChangeEvent (p.487), ChangeListener (p.488).

swing.plaf.basic.BasicSliderUI.ComponentHandler

INNER CLASS

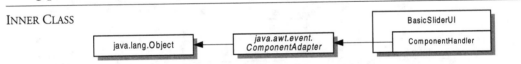

This inner class handles resizing events from the JSlider. This handler will cause the BasicSliderUI to recalculate its cached values and redraw the slider.

This inner class is public in Swing 1.1 due to a compiler bug. It will be changed to protected when the bug is fixed, so it should be treated as such.

```
public class BasicSliderUI.ComponentHandler
    extends java.awt.event.ComponentAdapter
```

Constructors
```
public ComponentHandler()
```
Default constructor.

Methods
```
public void componentResized(java.awt.event.ComponentEvent e)
```
Overrides: componentResized in class ComponentAdapter.
Implements: componentResized in interface ComponentListener.

plaf.basic

swing.plaf.basic.BasicSliderUI.FocusHandler

INNER CLASS

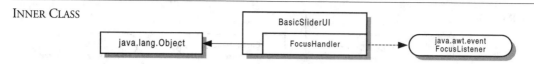

This class implements the focus listener for the JSlider.

This inner class is public in Swing 1.1 due to a compiler bug. It will be changed to protected when the bug is fixed, so it should be treated as such.

```
protected class BasicSliderUI.FListener extends java.lang.Object
    implements java.awt.event.FocusListener
```

Constructors
```
public FocusHandler()
```
Default constructor.

Methods
```
public void focusGained(java.awt.event.FocusEvent e)
```
Implements: focusGained in interface FocusListener.
```
public void focusLost(java.awt.event.FocusEvent e)
```
Implements: focusLost in interface FocusListener.

swing.plaf.basic.BasicSliderUI.PropertyChangeHandler

INNER CLASS

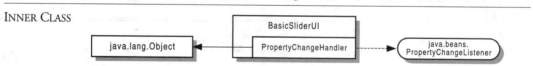

This inner class is public in Swing 1.1 due to a compiler bug. It will be changed to protected when the bug is fixed, so it should be treated as such.

```
public class BasicSliderUI.PropertyChangeHandler
    extends java.lang.Object
    implements java.beans.PropertyChangeListener
```

Constructors
```
public PropertyChangeHandler()
```
Default constructor.

Methods
```
public void propertyChange(java.beans.PropertyChangeEvent e)
```
Implements: propertyChange in interface PropertyChangeListener.

plaf.basic

swing.plaf.basic.BasicSliderUI.ScrollListener

INNER CLASS

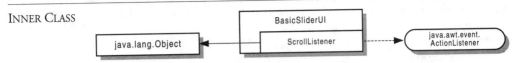

This class implements the listener for timed scroll events.

This inner class is `public` in Swing 1.1 due to a compiler bug. It will be changed to `protected` when the bug is fixed, so it should be treated as such.

```
public class BasicSliderUI.ScrollListener extends java.lang.Object
    implements java.awt.event.ActionListener
```

Constructors
```
public ScrollListener()
public ScrollListener(int dir, boolean block)
```
Constructs a `ScrollListener`. The default values for `dir` and `block` are `BasicSliderUI.POSITIVE_SCROLL` and `true`.

Methods
```
public void actionPerformed(java.awt.event.ActionEvent e)
```
Implements: `actionPerformed` in interface `ActionListener`.
```
public void setDirection(int direction)
```
Changes the direction of this `ScrollListener`.
```
public void setScrollByBlock(boolean block)
```
Changes whether the slider will be scrolled by a block or a unit increment.

swing.plaf.basic.BasicSliderUI.TrackListener

INNER CLASS

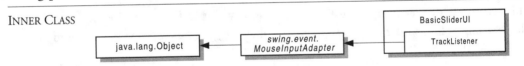

This class listens for mouse events in the track (which includes the thumb area).

```
protected class BasicSliderUI.TrackListener extends MouseInputAdapter
```

Constructors
```
public TrackListener()
```
Default constructor.

Methods
```
public void mouseDragged(java.awt.event.MouseEvent e)
```
Set the model's value to the position of the top/left of the thumb relative to the origin of the track.
Implements: `mouseDragged` in interface `MouseMotionListener`.
```
public void mouseMoved(java.awt.event.MouseEvent e)
```
Implements: `mouseMoved` in interface `MouseMotionListener`.

public void mousePressed(java.awt.event.MouseEvent e)

If the mouse is pressed above/to the right of the thumb, then this increases the scroll bar's value by a `blockIncrement`, otherwise, it reduces it by the `blockIncrement`. If there is no thumb, then it pages up if the mouse is in the upper half of the track.

Overrides: mousePressed in class `MouseInputAdapter`.

Implements: mousePressed in interface `MouseListener`.

public void mouseReleased(java.awt.event.MouseEvent e)

Stops any dragging and sets the `valueIsAdjusting` property in the `JSlider` to `false`.

Overrides: mouseReleased in class `MouseInputAdapter`.

Implements: mouseReleased in interface `MouseListener`.

public boolean shouldScroll(int direction)

Returns `true` if the slider can scroll in the given direction.

Protected Fields

protected transient int currentMouseX
protected transient int currentMouseY
protected transient int offset

Cached values used to figure out the distance the mouse has moved and whether a click was in the slider.

swing.plaf.basic.BasicSplitPaneDivider

CLASS

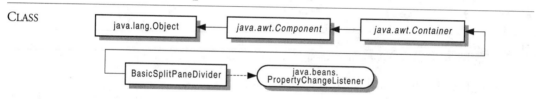

This class is the divider component for a `BasicSplitPaneUI`. This implementation is simply a filled rectangle. The border of this component is drawn by the `BasicSplitPaneUI`, and must be overridden there.

UIDefaults table key	Description
SplitPane.background	The background Color used to fill the divider.

public class BasicSplitPaneDivider extends java.awt.Container
    implements java.beans.PropertyChangeListener

Constructors

public BasicSplitPaneDivider(BasicSplitPaneUI ui)

Creates an instance of `BasicSplitPaneDivider`. Registers this instance for mouse events and mouse dragged events with the `JSplitPane`.

Methods

public BasicSplitPaneUI getBasicSplitPaneUI()

Returns the associated `BasicSplitPaneUI`.

public int getDividerSize()

Returns the width or the height of the divider, depending on the split pane orientation.

public java.awt.Dimension getPreferredSize()

Returns Dimension(dividerSize, dividerSize).

Overrides: getPreferredSize in class Container.

public void paint(java.awt.Graphics g)

Paints the divider.

Overrides: paint in class Container.

public void propertyChange(java.beans.PropertyChangeEvent e)

Called when a property change occurs in the associated JSplitPane.

Implements: propertyChange in interface PropertyChangeListener.

public void setBasicSplitPaneUI(BasicSplitPaneUI newUI)

Sets the associated JSplitPane.

public void setDividerSize(int newSize)

Sets the width or the height of the divider, depending on the orientation.

Protected Fields

protected static final int ONE_TOUCH_OFFSET = 2
protected static final int ONE_TOUCH_SIZE = 5

Constants related to the one touch expand/restore/shrink button.

protected int dividerSize

The size of the divider.

protected BasicSplitPaneDivider.DragController dragger

Handles mouse dragging message to do the actual dragging.

protected java.awt.Component hiddenDivider

The divider that is used for noncontinuous layout mode.

protected JButton leftButton

The button for quickly toggling the left component.

protected BasicSplitPaneDivider.MouseHandler mouseHandler

The handler for mouse events.

protected int orientation

The orientation of the JSplitPane.

protected JButton rightButton

The button for quickly toggling the right component.

protected JSplitPane splitPane

The JSplitPane this divider is in.

protected BasicSplitPaneUI splitPaneUI

The UI this instance was created from.

Protected Methods

protected JButton createLeftOneTouchButton()

Creates and returns a JButton that can be used to collapse the left component in the split pane.

protected JButton createRightOneTouchButton()

Creates and returns a JButton that can be used to collapse the right component in the split pane.

protected void dragDividerTo(int location)

Calls dragDividerTo() in the associated BasicSplitPaneUI.

protected void finishDraggingTo(int location)

Calls finishDraggingTo() in the associated BasicSplitPaneUI.

plaf.basic

```
protected void oneTouchExpandableChanged()
```
Called when the oneTouchExpandable property of the associated JSplitPane changes.
```
protected void prepareForDragging()
```
Calls startDragging() in the associated BasicSplitPaneUI.

Inner Classes

```
protected class BasicSplitPaneDivider.DividerLayout
protected class BasicSplitPaneDivider.DragController
protected class BasicSplitPaneDivider.MouseHandler
protected class BasicSplitPaneDivider.VerticalDragController
```

Returned by   BasicSplitPaneUI.createDefaultDivider() (p.668),
BasicSplitPaneUI.getDivider() (p.668).

See also   BasicSplitPaneUI (p.668), JButton (p.191), JSplitPane (p.346).

swing.plaf.basic.BasicSplitPaneDivider.DividerLayout

INNER CLASS

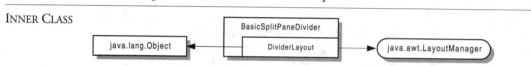

The layout manager for a BasicSplitPaneDivider. This class manages the location of the one touch buttons.

```
protected class BasicSplitPaneDivider.DividerLayout
    extends java.lang.Object
    implements java.awt.LayoutManager
```

Constructors
```
public DividerLayout()
```
Default constructor.

Methods
```
public void addLayoutComponent(String string, java.awt.Component c)
```
Implements: addLayoutComponent in interface LayoutManager.
```
public void layoutContainer(java.awt.Container c)
```
Implements: layoutContainer in interface LayoutManager.
```
public java.awt.Dimension minimumLayoutSize(java.awt.Container c)
```
Implements: minimumLayoutSize in interface LayoutManager.
```
public java.awt.Dimension preferredLayoutSize(java.awt.Container c)
```
Implements: preferredLayoutSize in interface LayoutManager.
```
public void removeLayoutComponent(java.awt.Component c)
```
Implements: removeLayoutComponent in interface LayoutManager.

swing.plaf.basic.BasicSplitPaneDivider.DragController

INNER CLASS

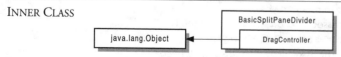

Handles the dragging for a horizontal split pane divider. This is the class that calls `dragDividerTo()`. When the dragging is done this class calls `finishDraggingTo()`. When this class is first created, `isValid()` must be called to confirm that dragging will happen.

protected class BasicSplitPaneDivider.DragController
extends java.lang.Object

Constructors
protected DragController(java.awt.event.MouseEvent e)
Starts dragging with the given MouseEvent's location as its origin.

Methods
protected void completeDrag(int x, int y)
Calls finishDraggingTo() with the *x* coordinate.
protected void completeDrag(java.awt.event.MouseEvent e)
Calls finishDraggingTo() with the *x* coordinate of the MouseEvent.
protected void continueDrag(int newX, int newY)
Calls dragDividerTo() with the *x* coordinate.
protected void continueDrag(java.awt.event.MouseEvent e)
Calls dragDividerTo() with the *x* coordinate of the MouseEvent.
protected int getNeededLocation(int x, int y)
Returns the *x* argument, since this is used for horizontal splits.
protected boolean isValid()
Returns true if the dragging session is valid.
protected int positionForMouseEvent(java.awt.event.MouseEvent e)
Returns the new position to put the divider at based on the passed in MouseEvent.

Extended by   BasicSplitPaneDivider.VerticalDragController (p.668).

swing.plaf.basic.BasicSplitPaneDivider.MouseHandler

INNER CLASS

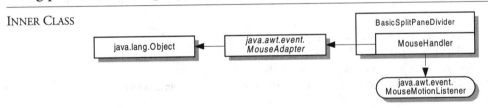

The `MouseHandler` inner class handles mouse events by calling the appropriate methods in the `DragController` inner class.

protected class BasicSplitPaneDivider.MouseHandler
extends java.awt.event.MouseAdapter
implements java.awt.event.MouseMotionListener

Constructors
public MouseHandler()
Default constructor.

Methods

public void mouseDragged(java.awt.event.MouseEvent e)

If dragger is not null it has its continueDrag() method called.
Implements: mouseDragged in interface MouseMotionListener.

public void mouseMoved(java.awt.event.MouseEvent e)

Resets the cursor based on the orientation.
Implements: mouseMoved in interface MouseMotionListener.

public void mousePressed(java.awt.event.MouseEvent e)

Starts the dragging session by creating the appropriate instance of DragController.
Overrides: mousePressed in class MouseAdapter.
Implements: mousePressed in interface MouseListener.

public void mouseReleased(java.awt.event.MouseEvent e)

If dragger is not null it has its completeDrag() method called.
Overrides: mouseReleased in class MouseAdapter.
Implements: mouseReleased in interface MouseListener.

swing.plaf.basic.BasicSplitPaneDivider.VerticalDragController

INNER CLASS

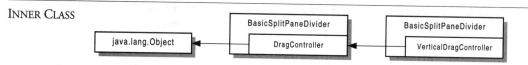

This class handles the dragging for vertical split panes.

protected class BasicSplitPaneDivider.VerticalDragController
**   extends BasicSplitPaneDivider.DragController**

Constructors

protected VerticalDragController(java.awt.event.MouseEvent e)

Constructs a new VerticalDragController starting at the location of the MouseEvent.

Methods

protected int getNeededLocation(int x, int y)

Returns the *y* argument, since this is used for vertical splits.
Overrides: getNeededLocation in class BasicSplitPaneDivider.DragController.

protected int positionForMouseEvent(java.awt.event.MouseEvent e)

Returns the new position to put the divider, based on the passed-in MouseEvent.
Overrides: positionForMouseEvent in class BasicSplitPaneDivider.DragController.

swing.plaf.basic.BasicSplitPaneUI

CLASS

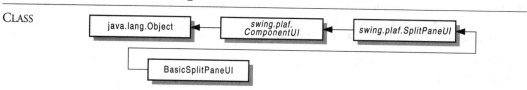

The Basic look and feel UI delegate for JSplitPanes.

UIDefaults table key	Description
SplitPane.border	The Border used around the split pane and its two children.
SplitPane.dividerSize	The Integer size of the divider.

public class BasicSplitPaneUI extends SplitPaneUI

Constructors
public BasicSplitPaneUI()
  Creates a new instance of BasicSplitPaneUI.

Methods
public BasicSplitPaneDivider createDefaultDivider()
  Creates the default divider.
public static ComponentUI createUI(JComponent x)
  Creates a new BasicSplitPaneUI instance.
  Overrides: createUI in class ComponentUI.
public void finishedPaintingChildren(JSplitPane jc,
  java.awt.Graphics g)
  Called after the JSplitPane has finished drawing its children.
  Overrides: finishedPaintingChildren in class SplitPaneUI.
public BasicSplitPaneDivider getDivider()
  Returns the divider between the two Components.
public int getDividerLocation()
  Returns the location of the divider.
  Overrides: getDividerLocation in class SplitPaneUI.
public java.awt.Insets getInsets(JComponent jc)
  Returns the insets of the current border.
public int getLastDragLocation()
  Returns the last position of the divider.
public int getMaximumDividerLocation()
  Gets the maximum location of the divider.
  Overrides: getMaximumDividerLocation in class SplitPaneUI.
public java.awt.Dimension getMaximumSize(JComponent jc)
  Returns the maximum size for the passed-in component.
  Overrides: getMaximumSize in class ComponentUI.
public int getMinimumDividerLocation()
  Gets the minimum location of the divider.
  Overrides: getMinimumDividerLocation in class SplitPaneUI.
public java.awt.Dimension getMinimumSize(JComponent jc)
  Returns the minimum size for the passed-in component.
  Overrides: getMinimumSize in class ComponentUI.
public java.awt.Component getNonContinuousLayoutDivider()
  Returns the divider to use when the continuousLayout property is set in the JSplitPane.
public int getOrientation()
  Returns the orientation of the split pane.

public java.awt.Dimension getPreferredSize(JComponent jc)

Returns the preferred size for the passed-in component.

Overrides: getPreferredSize in class ComponentUI.

public JSplitPane getSplitPane()

Returns the associated JSplitPane.

public void installUI(JComponent c)

Installs this UI delegate into the given component.

Overrides: installUI in class ComponentUI.

public boolean isContinuousLayout()

Returns true if the associated JSplitPane has its continuousLayout property set.

public void paint(java.awt.Graphics g, JComponent jc)

Paints the split pane.

Overrides: paint in class ComponentUI.

public void resetToPreferredSizes()

Resets the child components to their preferred sizes.

Overrides: resetToPreferredSizes in class SplitPaneUI.

public void setContinuousLayout(boolean b)

Sets the continuousLayout property.

public void setDividerLocation(int location)

Sets the location of the divider to location.

Overrides: setDividerLocation in class SplitPaneUI.

public void setLastDragLocation(int 1)

Sets the last position of the divider.

public void setOrientation(int orientation)

Sets the orientation of the split pane.

public void uninstallUI(JComponent c)

Calls uninstallDefaults and uninstallUI.

Overrides: uninstallUI in class ComponentUI.

Protected Fields

protected static int KEYBOARD_DIVIDER_MOVE_OFFSET = "keyboardDividerMoveOffset"

How far the divider moves when it is controlled by the keyboard.

protected static final String NON_CONTINUOUS_DIVIDER = "nonContinuousDivider"

The name used for the noncontinuous layout divider component.

protected int beginDragDividerLocation

The location of the divider when the dragging session began.

protected BasicSplitPaneDivider divider

The divider used to divide the two child components.

protected KeyStroke dividerResizeToggleKey

The KeyStroke registered for the VK_F8 key that toggles the one-touch expand-collapse button. Triggers keyboardResizeToggleListener.

protected int dividerSize

The size of the divider.

protected KeyStroke downKey

The KeyStroke registered for the VK_DOWN key. Triggers keyboardDownRightListener.

protected boolean draggingHW

Set to true in `startDragging()` if any of the children (not including the `nonContinuousLay-outDivider`) are heavyweights.

protected KeyStroke endKey

The `KeyStroke` registered for the `VK_END` key. Triggers `keyboardEndListener`.

protected FocusListener focusListener

The `FocusListener` registered with the associated `JSplitPane`.

protected KeyStroke homeKey

The `KeyStroke` registered for the `VK_HOME` key. Triggers `keyboardHomeListener`.

protected ActionListener keyboardDownRightListener

The listener that handles the `VK_DOWN` and `VK_RIGHT` keys.

protected ActionListener keyboardEndListener

The listener that handles the `VK_END` key.

protected ActionListener keyboardHomeListener

The listener that handles the `VK_HOME` key.

protected ActionListener keyboardResizeToggleListener

The listener that handles the resize-toggle key, `VK_F8`.

protected ActionListener keyboardUpLeftListener

The listener that handles the `VK_LEFT` and `VK_UP` keys.

protected BasicSplitPaneUI.BasicHorizontalLayoutManager layoutManager

The layout manager responsible for horizontal split panes.

protected KeyStroke leftKey

The `KeyStroke` registered for the `VK_LEFT` key. Triggers `keyboardUpLeftListener`.

protected java.awt.Component nonContinuousLayoutDivider

The component used for the divider when the `continuousLayout` property is not set.

protected java.beans.PropertyChangeListener propertyChangeListener

The listener for property changes in the associated `JSplitPane`.

protected KeyStroke rightKey

The `KeyStroke` registered for the `VK_RIGHT` key. Triggers `keyboardDownRightListener`.

protected JSplitPane splitPane

The associated `JSplitPane`.

protected KeyStroke upKey

The `KeyStroke` registered for the `VK_UP` key. Triggers `keyboardUpLeftListener`.

Protected Methods

protected java.awt.Component createDefaultNonContinuousLayoutDivider()

Returns the default non-continuous layout divider, which is an `instanceof Canvas` that fills the background in dark gray.

protected FocusListener createFocusListener()

Creates a `FocusListener` for the `JSplitPane`.

protected ActionListener createKeyboardDownRightListener()

Creates a handler for the `VK_DOWN` and `VK_RIGHT` keys.

protected ActionListener createKeyboardEndListener()

Creates a handler for the `VK_END` key.

protected ActionListener createKeyboardHomeListener()

Creates a handler for the `VK_HOME` key.

protected ActionListener createKeyboardResizeToggleListener()
Creates a handler for the VK_F8 key, which toggles the one-touch expand button.

protected ActionListener createKeyboardUpLeftListener()
Creates a handler for the VK_UP and VK_LEFT keys.

protected java.beans.PropertyChangeListener createPropertyChangeListener()
Creates a handler for property changes in the associated JSplitPane.

protected void dragDividerTo(int location)
Called while the divider is being dragged. If the continuousLayout property is set in the JSplitPane, this will also relayout and repaint the child panes.

protected void finishDraggingTo(int location)
Called when the divider stops being dragged. If the continuousLayout property is not set in the JSplitPane, this will set the divider location and relayout and repaint the child panes.

protected int getDividerBorderSize()
Returns the width of one side of the divider border.

protected void installDefaults()
Installs the resources for this UI delegate into the given component.

protected void installKeyboardActions()
Installs the keyboard actions for the UI into the associated JSplitPane.

protected void installListeners()
Installs the listeners into the associated JSplitPane.

protected void resetLayoutManager()
Resets the layout to its defaults.

protected void setNonContinuousLayoutDivider(java.awt.Component newDivider)
Sets the divider to use when the split pane is set to *not* continuously layout. For performance reasons this component should be a heavyweight component. This method call will not reset the relative sizes of the child components.

protected void setNonContinuousLayoutDivider(
java.awt.Component newDivider, boolean rememberSizes)
Sets the divider to use when the split pane is set to *not* continuously layout. If rememberSizes is false, this method will reset the sizes of the child components.

protected void startDragging()
Must be called before starting to drag the divider. This method resets lastDragLocation and dividerSize.

protected void uninstallDefaults()
Uninstalls the UI resources installed in installDefaults.

protected void uninstallKeyboardActions()
Uninstalls the keyboard actions for the UI from the associated JSplitPane.

protected void uninstallListeners()
Uninstalls the listeners installed in installListeners.

Inner Classes

public class BasicSplitPaneUI.BasicVerticalLayoutManager
public class BasicSplitPaneUI.BasicHorizontalLayoutManager
public class BasicSplitPaneUI.FocusHandler
public class BasicSplitPaneUI.KeyboardDownRightHandler
public class BasicSplitPaneUI.KeyboardEndHandler
public class BasicSplitPaneUI.KeyboardHomeHandler

```
public class BasicSplitPaneUI.KeyboardResizeToggleHandler
public class BasicSplitPaneUI.KeyboardUpLeftHandler
public class BasicSplitPaneUI.PropertyHandler
```

Returned by BasicSplitPaneDivider.getBasicSplitPaneUI() (p.664).

See also BasicSplitPaneDivider (p.664), ComponentUI (p.530), JComponent (p.207), JSplitPane (p.346), SplitPaneUI (p.540).

swing.plaf.basic.BasicSplitPaneUI.BasicHorizontalLayoutManager

INNER CLASS

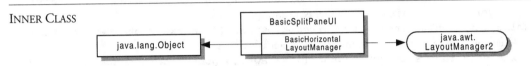

This class is the LayoutManager for JSplitPanes that have an orientation of HORIZONTAL_SPLIT.

This inner class is public in Swing 1.1 due to a compiler bug. It will be changed to protected when the bug is fixed, so it should be treated as such.

```
public class BasicSplitPaneUI.BasicHorizontalLayoutManager
    extends java.lang.Object
    implements java.awt.LayoutManager2
```

Methods

public void addLayoutComponent(java.awt.Component comp, Object constraints)
Adds the given component to the layout, using the specified constraints.
Implements: addLayoutComponent in interface LayoutManager2.

public void addLayoutComponent(String place, java.awt.Component component)
Adds the component at place, which must be JSplitPane.LEFT, RIGHT, TOP, BOTTOM, or null (for the divider).

protected int getAvailableSize(java.awt.Dimension containerSize, java.awt.Insets insets)
Returns the available width based on the containerSize and insets.

protected int getInitialLocation(java.awt.Insets insets)
Returns the left inset, unless insets is null, in which case 0 is returned.

public float getLayoutAlignmentX(java.awt.Container target)
Returns the alignment along the *x* axis.
Implements: getLayoutAlignmentX in interface LayoutManager2.

public float getLayoutAlignmentY(java.awt.Container target)
Returns the alignment along the *y* axis.
Implements: getLayoutAlignmentY in interface LayoutManager2.

protected int getPreferredSizeOfComponent(java.awt.Component c)
Returns the width of the given Component's preferred size.

protected int getSizeOfComponent(java.awt.Component c)
Returns the width of the given component.

protected int[] getSizes()
Returns the widths of the child components.

public void invalidateLayout(java.awt.Container c)
> An empty method. Use `JSplitPane.resetToPreferredSizes()` instead.
> *Implements:* invalidateLayout in interface `LayoutManager2`.

public void layoutContainer(java.awt.Container container)
> Lays out the split pane.

public java.awt.Dimension maximumLayoutSize(java.awt.Container target)
> Returns `Integer.MAX_VALUE`.
> *Implements:* maximumLayoutSize in interface `LayoutManager2`.

public java.awt.Dimension minimumLayoutSize(java.awt.Container container)
> Returns the total of the child components' minimum widths.

public java.awt.Dimension preferredLayoutSize(java.awt.Container container)
> Returns the total of the child components' preferred widths.

public void removeLayoutComponent(java.awt.Component component)
> Removes the given component from the layout.

protected void resetSizeAt(int location)
> Resets the size of the component occupying `location`, which will be `JSplitPane.LEFT`, `RIGHT`, `TOP`, `BOTTOM`, or `null` (for the divider).

public void resetToPreferredSizes()
> Resets the layout to its defaults.

protected void setComponentToSize(java.awt.Component c, int size,
**   int location, java.awt.Insets insets, java.awt.Dimension containerSize)**
> Sets the component to the given size and location.

protected void setSizes(int[] newSizes)
> Sets the sizes of the child components to the given sizes.

protected void updateComponents()
> Retrieves the child components from the associated `JSplitPane`.

Protected Fields

protected java.awt.Component[] components
> The child components.

protected int[] sizes
> The sizes of the child components.

Extended by BasicSplitPaneUI.BasicVerticalLayoutManager (p.674).

swing.plaf.basic.BasicSplitPaneUI.BasicVerticalLayoutManager

INNER CLASS

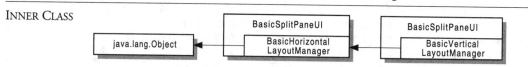

The LayoutManager used for `JSplitPanes` with an orientation of `VERTICAL_SPLIT`.

This inner class is `public` in Swing 1.1 due to a compiler bug. It will be changed to `protected` when the bug is fixed, so it should be treated as such.

public class BasicSplitPaneUI.BasicVerticalLayoutManager
**   extends BasicSplitPaneUI.BasicHorizontalLayoutManager**

Constructors

public BasicVerticalLayoutManager()

    Default constructor.

Methods

protected int getAvailableSize(java.awt.Dimension containerSize, java.awt.Insets insets)

    Returns the available height based on the container size and Insets.

    Overrides: getAvailableSize in class BasicSplitPaneUI.BasicHorizontalLayoutManager.

protected int getInitialLocation(java.awt.Insets insets)

    Returns the top inset, unless insets is null, in which case 0 is returned.

    Overrides: getInitialLocation in class BasicSplitPaneUI.BasicHorizontalLayoutManager.

protected int getPreferredSizeOfComponent(java.awt.Component c)

    Returns the height of the passed-in Component's preferred size.

    Overrides: getPreferredSizeOfComponent in class BasicSplitPaneUI.BasicHorizontalLayoutManager.

protected int getSizeOfComponent(java.awt.Component c)

    Returns the height of the passed-in component.

    Overrides: getSizeOfComponent in class BasicSplitPaneUI.BasicHorizontalLayoutManager.

public java.awt.Dimension minimumLayoutSize(java.awt.Container container)

    Returns the minimum size needed to contain the children. The height is the sum of all the children's minimum heights. The width is the widest minimum size of any component.

    Overrides: minimumLayoutSize in class BasicSplitPaneUI.BasicHorizontalLayoutManager.

public java.awt.Dimension preferredLayoutSize(java.awt.Container container)

    Returns the preferred size needed to contain the children. The height is the sum of the largest of the children's preferred heights. The width is the widest preferred size of any component.

    Overrides: preferredLayoutSize in class BasicSplitPaneUI.BasicHorizontalLayoutManager.

protected void setComponentToSize(java.awt.Component c, int size, int location, java.awt.Insets insets, java.awt.Dimension containerSize)

    Sets the component's size and location to the given values.

    Overrides: setComponentToSize in class BasicSplitPaneUI.BasicHorizontalLayoutManager.

swing.plaf.basic.BasicSplitPaneUI.FocusHandler

INNER CLASS

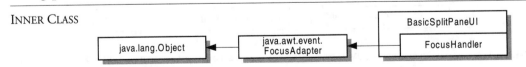

This inner class handles focus changes in the associated JSplitPane.

plaf.basic

This inner class is `public` in Swing 1.1 due to a compiler bug. It will be changed to `protected` when the bug is fixed, so it should be treated as such.

```
public class BasicSplitPaneUI.FocusHandler
    extends java.awt.event.FocusAdapter
```

Constructors
```
public FocusHandler()
```
Default constructor.

Methods
```
public void focusLost(java.awt.event.FocusEvent e)
```
Implements: propertyChange in interface PropertyChangeListener.

swing.plaf.basic.BasicSplitPaneUI.KeyboardDownRightHandler

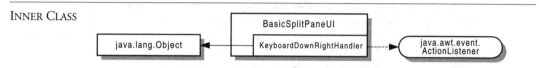

This inner class is used as a handler for VK_DOWN and VK_RIGHT key strokes. It is implemented to increment the divider location by `BasicSplitPaneUI.KEYBOARD_DIVIDER_MOVE_OFFSET` pixels.

This inner class is `public` in Swing 1.1 due to a compiler bug. When the bug is fixed, this class will be changed to `protected`, so it should be treated as such.

```
public class BasicSplitPaneUI.KeyboardDownRightHandler
    extends java.lang.Object
    implements java.awt.event.ActionListener
```

Constructors
```
public KeyboardDownRightHandler()
```
Default constructor.

Methods
```
public void actionPerformed(java.awt.event.ActionEvent e)
```
Implements: actionPerformed in interface ActionListener.

swing.plaf.basic.BasicSplitPaneUI.KeyboardEndHandler

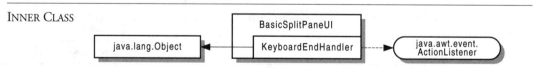

This inner class is used as a handler for VK_END key strokes. It is implemented to move the divider to its maximum position.

This inner class is `public` in Swing 1.1 due to a compiler bug. When the bug is fixed, this class will be changed to `protected`, so it should be treated as such.

```
public class BasicSplitPaneUI.KeyboardEndHandler
    extends java.lang.Object
    implements java.awt.event.ActionListener
```

Constructors
```
public KeyboardEndHandler()
```
    Default constructor.

Methods
```
public void actionPerformed(java.awt.event.ActionEvent e)
```
    Implements: actionPerformed in interface ActionListener.

swing.plaf.basic.BasicSplitPaneUI.KeyboardHomeHandler

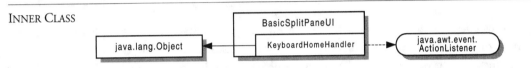

This inner class is used as a handler for VK_HOME key strokes. It is implemented to move the divider to its minimum location.

    This inner class is public in Swing 1.1 due to a compiler bug. When the bug is fixed, this class will be changed to protected, so it should be treated as such.

```
public class BasicSplitPaneUI.KeyboardHomeHandler
    extends java.lang.Object
    implements java.awt.event.ActionListener
```

Constructors
```
public KeyboardHomeHandler()
```
    Default constructor.

Methods
```
public void actionPerformed(java.awt.event.ActionEvent e)
```
    Implements: actionPerformed in interface ActionListener.

swing.plaf.basic.BasicSplitPaneUI.KeyboardResizeToggleHandler

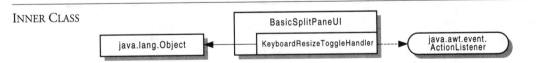

This inner class is used as a handler for the "toggle" VK_F8 key strokes. It is implemented to trigger the one-touch-expand button.

    This inner class is public in Swing 1.1 due to a compiler bug. When the bug is fixed, this class will be changed to protected, so it should be treated as such.

```
public class BasicSplitPaneUI.KeyboardResizeToggleHandler
    extends java.lang.Object
    implements java.awt.event.ActionListener
```

plaf.basic

Constructors
public KeyboardResizeToggleHandler()
> Default constructor.

Methods
public void actionPerformed(java.awt.event.ActionEvent e)
> *Implements:* actionPerformed in interface ActionListener.

swing.plaf.basic.BasicSplitPaneUI.KeyboardUpLeftHandler

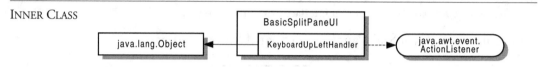

This inner class is used as a handler for VK_UP and VK_LEFT key strokes. It is implemented to decrement the divider location by BasicSplitPaneUI.KEYBOARD_DIVIDER_MOVE_OFFSET pixels.

This inner class is public in Swing 1.1 due to a compiler bug. When the bug is fixed, this class will be changed to protected, so it should be treated as such.

public class BasicSplitPaneUI.KeyboardUpLeftHandler
**   extends java.lang.Object**
**   implements java.awt.event.ActionListener**

Constructors
public KeyboardUpLeftHandler()
> Default constructor.

Methods
public void actionPerformed(java.awt.event.ActionEvent e)
> *Implements:* actionPerformed in interface ActionListener.

swing.plaf.basic.BasicSplitPaneUI.PropertyHandler

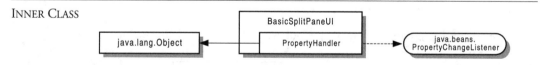

This inner class handles property changes in the JSplitPane.

This inner class is public in Swing 1.1 due to a compiler bug. It will be changed to protected when the bug is fixed, so it should be treated as such.

public class BasicSplitPaneUI.SplitBorder extends java.lang.Object
**   implements java.beans.PropertyChangeListener**

Constructors
public PropertyHandler()
> Default constructor.

Methods
public void propertyChange(java.beans.PropertyChangeEvent e)
 Implements: propertyChange in interface PropertyChangeListener.

swing.plaf.basic.BasicTabbedPaneUI

CLASS

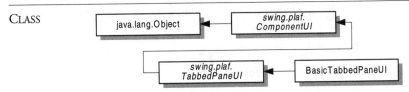

The Basic look and feel UI delegate for the JTabbedPane component.

UIDefaults table key	Description
TabbedPane.background	The background Color for the tabbed pane.
TabbedPane.contentBorderInsets	The Insets to use around the component contained in a tab.
TabbedPane.darkShadow	The shadow Color used on the emphasized selected tab.
TabbedPane.focus	The Color used for the focus indicator.
TabbedPane.font	The Font used on the tabs.
TabbedPane.foreground	The foreground Color for the tabbed pane.
TabbedPane.highlight	The highlight Color used on the non-selected tabs.
TabbedPane.lightHighlight	The highlight Color used on the emphasized selected tab.
TabbedPane.selectedTabPadInsets	The Insets amount to pad the selected tab to make it stand out.
TabbedPane.shadow	The shadow Color used on the nonselected tabs.
TabbedPane.tabAreaInsets	The Insets around the area where the tabs are drawn.
TabbedPane.tabInsets	The Insets for each tab.
TabbedPane.tabRunOverlay	The amount the "front" rows overlap the "back" rows.
TabbedPane.textIconGap	The gap between the text and the Icon on a tab.

```
public class BasicTabbedPaneUI extends TabbedPaneUI
    implements SwingConstants
```

Constructors
public BasicTabbedPaneUI()
 Default constructor.

Methods
public static ComponentUI createUI(JComponent c)
 Overrides: createUI in class ComponentUI.
public java.awt.Dimension getMaximumSize(JComponent c)
 Overrides: getMaximumSize in class ComponentUI.
public java.awt.Dimension getMinimumSize(JComponent c)
 Overrides: getMinimumSize in class ComponentUI.

public java.awt.Dimension getPreferredSize(JComponent c)

Overrides: getPreferredSize in class ComponentUI.

public java.awt.Rectangle getTabBounds(JTabbedPane pane, int i)

Returns the bounding Rectangle for the tab at the given index.

Overrides: getTabBounds in class TabbedPaneUI.

public int getTabRunCount(JTabbedPane pane)

Returns the number of rows of tabs needed to display all of the tabs in the JTabbedPane.

Overrides: getTabRunCount in class TabbedPaneUI.

public void installUI(JComponent c)

Overrides: installUI in class ComponentUI.

public void paint(java.awt.Graphics g, JComponent c)

Overrides: paint in class ComponentUI.

public int tabForCoordinate(JTabbedPane pane, int x, int y)

Returns the index of the tab that lies underneath the given coordinate, or –1 if none is found.

Overrides: tabForCoordinate in class TabbedPaneUI.

public void uninstallUI(JComponent c)

Overrides: uninstallUI in class ComponentUI.

Protected Fields

protected static java.awt.Insets contentBorderInsets

Returns the gap between the component on a page and the page border.

protected java.awt.Color darkShadow

The Color to use for the shadow of the deep 3D effect.

protected KeyStroke downKey

The KeyStroke that handles the VK_DOWN key.

protected java.awt.Color focus

The color used to render the focus highlight.

protected java.awt.event.FocusListener focusListener

The FocusListener.

protected java.awt.Color highlight

The highlight Color for the normal 3D shadow effect.

protected KeyStroke leftKey

The KeyStroke which handles the VK_LEFT key.

protected java.awt.Color lightHighlight

The highlight Color for the deep 3D effect.

protected int maxTabHeight

The maximum tab height.

protected int maxTabWidth

The maximum tab width.

protected java.awt.event.MouseListener mouseListener

The MouseListener for the tabs.

protected java.beans.PropertyChangeListener propertyChangeListener

The handler for PropertyChangeEvents in the JTabbedPane.

protected java.awt.Rectangle[] rects

The bounding Rectangles for the tabs.

protected KeyStroke rightKey

The KeyStroke which handles the VK_RIGHT key.

protected int runCount

The number of rows of tabs needed to display all of the tabs in the alloted width or height.

protected int selectedRun

The tab row that the currently selected tab occupies.

protected java.awt.Insets selectedTabPadInsets

The Insets to use around the content in the selected tab.

protected java.awt.Color shadow

The shadow color for the normal 3D effect.

protected java.awt.Insets tabAreaInsets

The Insets around the area occupied by the tabs.

protected ChangeListener tabChangeListener

The listener for changes in the tabs.

protected java.awt.Insets tabInsets

The Insets to use around the content in the nonselected tabs.

protected JTabbedPane tabPane

The associated JTabbedPane.

protected int tabRunOverlay

The amount (in pixels) to overlay the "front" tab row over the "back" tab rows.

protected int[] tabRuns

The index of the first tab in each run.

protected int textIconGap

The gap (in pixels) between the text and the Icon on a tab.

protected KeyStroke upKey

The KeyStroke which handles the VK_UP key.

Protected Methods

protected void assureRectsCreated(int tabCount)

Ensures that the cache array for the tab Rectangles is the same size as the number of tabs. If more array elements need to be added, they are pre-filled with new Rectangle().

protected int calculateMaxTabHeight(int tabPlacement)

Scans through the tabs looking for the tallest in the given orientation, then returns its height.

protected int calculateMaxTabWidth(int tabPlacement)

Scans through the tabs looking for the widest in the given orientation, then returns its width.

**protected int calculateTabAreaHeight(int tabPlacement,
    int horizRunCount, int maxTabHeight)**

Calculates the height needed to hold all of the tabs, given the number of runs and the maximum tab height.

**protected int calculateTabAreaWidth(int tabPlacement,
    int vertRunCount, int maxTabWidth)**

Calculates the width needed to hold all of the tabs, given the number of runs and the maximum tab width.

**protected int calculateTabHeight(int tabPlacement, int tabIndex,
    int fontHeight)**

Calculates the height of the given tab, using the given Font to render any text.

**protected int calculateTabWidth(int tabPlacement, int tabIndex,
    java.awt.FontMetrics metrics)**

Calculates the width of the given tab, using the given FontMetrics to calculate the width of any text.

protected ChangeListener createChangeListener()
Creates the appropriate ChangeListener.

protected java.awt.event.FocusListener createFocusListener()
Creates the appropriate FocusListener.

protected java.awt.LayoutManager createLayoutManager()
Creates the custom layout manager used to lay out the tabbed pane.

protected java.awt.event.MouseListener createMouseListener()
Creates the appropriate MouseListener.

protected java.beans.PropertyChangeListener createPropertyChangeListener()
Creates the PropertyChangeListener used to handle property changes in the JTabbedPane.

protected void expandTabRunsArray()
Increases the size of the tab runs array by 10.

protected java.awt.Insets getContentBorderInsets(int tabPlacement)
Returns the border insets of the page with the largest border insets.

protected java.awt.FontMetrics getFontMetrics()
Returns the FontMetrics for the JTabbedPane's font.

protected Icon getIconForTab(int tabIndex)
Returns the Icon for the given tab.

protected int getNextTabIndex(int base)
Returns the next higher tab index. If the index generated is past the last index in the tabbed pane, the return value will wrap around to the start of the tab indicies.

protected int getPreviousTabIndex(int base)
Returns the tab index before base. If the generated index is below zero, the return value will wrap around to the end of the tab indicies.

protected int getRunForTab(int tabCount, int tabIndex)
Returns the run that contains the given tab.

protected java.awt.Insets getSelectedTabPadInsets(int tabPlacement)
Returns the value of selectedTabPadInsets.

protected java.awt.Insets getTabAreaInsets(int tabPlacement)
Returns the Insets for the tab area, as opposed to the page area.

protected java.awt.Insets getTabInsets(int tabPlacement, int tabIndex)
Returns the Insets for the given tab.

**protected int getTabLabelShiftX(int tabPlacement, int tabIndex,
boolean isSelected)**
Returns the x-offset for any content in the given tab, using the given tabPlacement.

**protected int getTabLabelShiftY(int tabPlacement, int tabIndex,
boolean isSelected)**
Returns the y-offset for any content in the given tab, using the given tabPlacement.

public int getTabRunCount(JTabbedPane pane)
Overrides: getTabRunCount in class TabbedPaneUI.

protected int getTabRunIndent(int tabPlacement, int run)
Returns the amount (in pixels) to indent the start of the given run.

**protected int getTabRunOffset(int tabPlacement, int tabCount,
int tabIndex, boolean forward)**
Returns the amount to offset the tab run from the page area when painting.

protected int getTabRunOverlay(int tabPlacement)
Returns the amount (in pixels) that the front rows overlap the back rows.

protected java.awt.Component getVisibleComponent()
> Returns the component currently visible in the page area.

protected void installDefaults()
> Installs this UI delegate's resources into the associated JTabbedPane.

protected void installKeyboardActions()
> Installs keyboard accelerators for the tabbed pane.

protected void installListeners()
> Installs the listeners into the JTabbedPane.

protected int lastTabInRun(int tabCount, int run)
> Returns the last tab index in the current run.

protected void layoutLabel(int tabPlacement, java.awt.FontMetrics metrics, String title, Icon icon, java.awt.Rectangle tabRect, java.awt.Rectangle iconRect, java.awt.Rectangle textRect, boolean isSelected)
> Lays out the Icon and text on a tab.

protected void navigateSelectedTab(int direction)
> Handles keyboard navigation in the tabs.

protected void normalizeTabRuns(JTabbedPane pane, int tabPlacement, int tabCount, int start, int max)
> Tries to evenly distribute the tabs across the runs.

protected void paintContentBorder(java.awt.Graphics g, int tabPlacement, int selectedIndex)
> Paints the border of the component which is currently being shown.

protected void paintContentBorderBottomEdge(java.awt.Graphics g, int tabPlacement, int selectedIndex, int x, int y, int w, int h)
> Paints the bottom edge of the content border.

protected void paintContentBorderLeftEdge(java.awt.Graphics g, int tabPlacement, int selectedIndex, int x, int y, int w, int h)
> Paints the left edge of the content border.

protected void paintContentBorderRightEdge(java.awt.Graphics g, int tabPlacement, int selectedIndex, int x, int y, int w, int h)
> Paints the right edge of the content border.

protected void paintContentBorderTopEdge(java.awt.Graphics g, int tabPlacement, int selectedIndex, int x, int y, int w, int h)
> Paints the top edge of the content border.

protected void paintFocusIndicator(java.awt.Graphics g, int tabPlacement, java.awt.Rectangle[] rects, int tabIndex, java.awt.Rectangle iconRect, java.awt.Rectangle textRect, boolean isSelected)
> Paints the focus indicator in a tab.

protected void paintIcon(java.awt.Graphics g, int tabPlacement, int tabIndex, Icon icon, java.awt.Rectangle iconRect, boolean isSelected)
> Paints the Icon for a tab.

protected void paintTab(java.awt.Graphics g, int tabPlacement, java.awt.Rectangle[] rects, int tabIndex, java.awt.Rectangle iconRect, java.awt.Rectangle textRect)
> Paints the given tab.

protected void paintTabBackground(java.awt.Graphics g, int tabPlacement,
  int tabIndex, int x, int y, int w, int h, boolean isSelected)
Paints the background of a tab.

protected void paintTabBorder(java.awt.Graphics g, int tabPlacement,
  int tabIndex, int x, int y, int w, int h, boolean isSelected)
Paints the border around each tab.

protected void paintText(java.awt.Graphics g, int tabPlacement,
  java.awt.Font font, java.awt.FontMetrics metrics, int tabIndex,
  String title, java.awt.Rectangle textRect, boolean isSelected)
Paints the given tab's text.

protected static void rotateInsets(java.awt.Insets topInsets,
  java.awt.Insets targetInsets, int targetPlacement)
Switches the run with the selected tab to be the "front" run.

protected void selectAdjacentRunTab(int tabPlacement, int tabIndex,
  int offset)
Selects the tab in the run above or below that is directly next to the currently selected tab.

protected void selectNextTab(int current)
Selects the next tab after current. If necessary, the index of the tab to select will wrap around to the start of the tab indicies.

protected void selectPreviousTab(int current)
Selects the tab before current. If necessary, the index of the tab to select will wrap around to the end of the tab indicies.

protected void setVisibleComponent(java.awt.Component component)
Shows a new page.

protected boolean shouldPadTabRun(int tabPlacement, int run)
Returns true if there is more than one run.

protected boolean shouldRotateTabRuns(int tabPlacement)
Returns true, since Basic shuffles the run of the selected tab to the front. The Java look and feel allows you to turn off the shuffling of the rows.

protected void uninstallDefaults()
Uninstalls the resources installed in installDefaults().

protected void uninstallKeyboardActions()
Uninstalls the keyboard actions installed in installKeyboardActions().

protected void uninstallListeners()
Uninstalls the listeners installed in installListeners().

Inner Classes

public class BasicTabbedPaneUI.FocusHandler
public class BasicTabbedPaneUI.MouseHandler
public class BasicTabbedPaneUI.PropertyChangeHandler
public class BasicTabbedPaneUI.TabbedPaneLayout
public class BasicTabbedPaneUI.TabSelectionHandler

See also   ChangeListener (p.488), ComponentUI (p.530), JTabbedPane (p.351), KeyStroke (p.419), TabbedPaneUI (p.540).

swing.plaf.basic.BasicTabbedPaneUI.FocusHandler

INNER CLASS

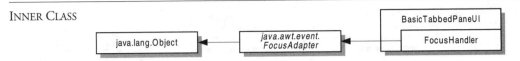

This inner class repaints the selected tab when the focus is gained or lost.

This inner class is `public` in Swing 1.1 due to a compiler bug. It will be changed to `protected` when the bug is fixed, so it should be treated as such.

```
public class BasicTabbedPaneUI.FocusHandler
    extends java.awt.event.FocusAdapter
```

Constructors
public FocusHandler()
Default constructor

Methods
public void focusGained(java.awt.event.FocusEvent e)
Overrides: focusGained in class FocusAdapter.
Implements: focusGained in interface FocusListener.
public void focusLost(java.awt.event.FocusEvent e)
Overrides: focusLost in class FocusAdapter.
Implements: focusLost in interface FocusListener.

swing.plaf.basic.BasicTabbedPaneUI.MouseHandler

INNER CLASS

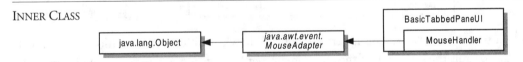

This inner class selects the tab which is under the mouse press and requests the focus.

This inner class is `public` in Swing 1.1 due to a compiler bug. It will be changed to `protected` when the bug is fixed, so it should be treated as such.

```
public class BasicTabbedPaneUI.MouseHandler
    extends java.awt.event.MouseAdapter
```

Constructors
public MouseHandler()
Default constructor

Methods
public void mousePressed(java.awt.event.MouseEvent e)
Overrides: mousePressed in class MouseAdapter.
Implements: mousePressed in interface MouseListener.

plaf.basic

swing.plaf.basic.BasicTabbedPaneUI.PropertyChangeHandler

INNER CLASS

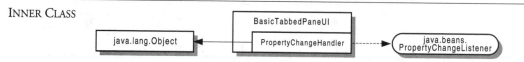

This inner class is a stub. It does not contain any code.

This inner class is `public` in Swing 1.1 due to a compiler bug. It will be changed to `protected` when the bug is fixed, so it should be treated as such.

```
public class BasicTabbedPaneUI.PropertyChangeHandler
    extends java.lang.Object
    implements java.beans.PropertyChangeListener
```

Constructors
public PropertyChangeHandler()
Default constructor.

Methods
public void propertyChange(java.beans.PropertyChangeEvent e)
An empty method.
Implements: propertyChange in interface PropertyChangeListener.

swing.plaf.basic.BasicTabbedPaneUI.TabbedPaneLayout

INNER CLASS

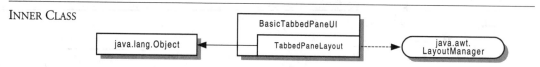

Lays out the JTabbedPane. This inner class controls how the different tab positions are handled, and also controls the swapping of the component that belongs to the selected tab with the previously selected tab's component.

This inner class is `public` in Swing 1.1 due to a compiler bug. It will be changed to `protected` when the bug is fixed, so it should be treated as such.

```
public class BasicTabbedPaneUI.TabbedPaneLayout
    extends java.lang.Object
    implements java.awt.LayoutManager
```

Constructors
public TabbedPaneLayout()
Default constructor.

Methods
public void addLayoutComponent(String name, java.awt.Component comp)
An empty method.
Implements: addLayoutComponent in interface LayoutManager.

plaf.basic

public void calculateLayoutInfo()

Calculates the required information for `layoutContainer()`.

public void layoutContainer(java.awt.Container parent)

Lays out the JTabbedPane based on the orientation of the tabs and which tab is the selected tab.

Implements: `layoutContainer` in interface `LayoutManager`.

public java.awt.Dimension minimumLayoutSize(java.awt.Container parent)

Returns `calculateLayoutSize(true)`.

Implements: `minimumLayoutSize` in interface `LayoutManager`.

public java.awt.Dimension preferredLayoutSize(java.awt.Container parent)

Returns `calculateLayoutSize(false)`.

Implements: `preferredLayoutSize` in interface `LayoutManager`.

public void removeLayoutComponent(java.awt.Component comp)

An empty method.

Implements: `removeLayoutComponent` in interface `LayoutManager`.

Protected Methods

protected java.awt.Dimension calculateSize(boolean minimum)

Returns the minimum or maximum size of the JTabbedPane and its contents based on the value of `minimum`.

protected void calculateTabRects(int tabPlacement, int tabCount)

Calculates the bounding Rectangles for the tabs in a run.

protected void normalizeTabRuns(int tabPlacement, int tabCount, int start, int max)

Tries to even out the sizes of the various tab runs.

protected void padSelectedTab(int tabPlacement, int selectedIndex)

Pads the selected tab to make it appear "in front" of the other tabs.

protected void padTabRun(int tabPlacement, int start, int end, int max)

Pads the given tab run to make it appear "in front" of the other runs.

protected int preferredTabAreaHeight(int tabPlacement, int width)

Calculates the tab area height, taking into account that the tabs may be split into runs.

protected int preferredTabAreaWidth(int tabPlacement, int height)

Calculates the tab area width, taking into account that the tabs may be split into runs.

protected void rotateTabRuns(int tabPlacement, int selectedRun)

Moves the selected run to the "front" run of tabs.

swing.plaf.basic.BasicTabbedPaneUI.TabSelectionHandler

INNER CLASS

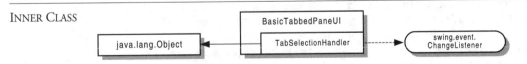

Revalidates and repaints the tabbed pane when the selected tab changes.

This inner class is `public` in Swing 1.1 due to a compiler bug. It will be changed to `protected` when the bug is fixed, so it should be treated as such.

```
public class BasicTabbedPaneUI.TabSelectionHandler
    extends java.lang.Object
    implements ChangeListener
```

plaf.basic

Constructors
`public TabSelectionHandler()`
   Default constructor.

Methods
`public void stateChanged(ChangeEvent e)`
   Implements: stateChanged in interface ChangeListener.

   See also   ChangeEvent (p.487), ChangeListener (p.488).

swing.plaf.basic.BasicTableHeaderUI

CLASS

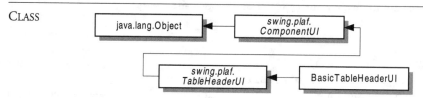

The Basic look and feel UI delegate for a JTableHeader.

UIDefaults table key	Description
TableHeader.background	The background Color of the table header.
TableHeader.font	The Font used for the table header.
TableHeader.foreground	The foreground Color of the table header.

`public class BasicTableHeaderUI extends TableHeaderUI`

Constructors
`public BasicTableHeaderUI()`
   Default constructor.

Methods
`public static ComponentUI createUI(JComponent h)`
   Overrides: createUI in class ComponentUI.
`public java.awt.Dimension getMaximumSize(JComponent c)`
   Overrides: getMaximumSize in class ComponentUI.
`public java.awt.Dimension getMinimumSize(JComponent c)`
   Overrides: getMinimumSize in class ComponentUI.
`public java.awt.Dimension getPreferredSize(JComponent c)`
   Overrides: getPreferredSize in class ComponentUI.
`public void installUI(JComponent c)`
   Overrides: installUI in class ComponentUI.
`public void paint(java.awt.Graphics g, JComponent c)`
   Overrides: paint in class ComponentUI.
`public void uninstallUI(JComponent c)`
   Overrides: uninstallUI in class ComponentUI.

Protected Fields

protected JTableHeader header

The associated JTableHeader.

protected MouseInputListener mouseInputListener

The combined Mouse and MouseMotionListener for the JTableHeader.

protected CellRendererPane rendererPane

The CellRendererPane for the JTableHeader.

Protected Methods

protected MouseInputListener createMouseInputListener()

Returns an instance of BasicTableHeaderUI.MouseInputHandler.

protected void installDefaults()

Installs the background and foreground Colors and the Font into the associated JTableHeader.

protected void installKeyboardActions()

An empty method.

protected void installListeners()

Installs the mouseInputListener into the JTableHeader.

Inner Classes

public class BasicTableHeaderUI.MouseInputHandler

See also   CellRendererPane (p.151), ComponentUI (p.530), JTableHeader (p.752), MouseInputListener (p.505), TableHeaderUI (p.541).

swing.plaf.basic.BasicTableHeaderUI.MouseInputHandler

INNER CLASS

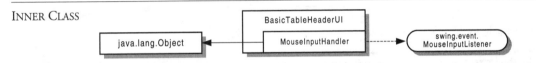

public class BasicTableHeaderUI.MouseInputHandler
    extends java.lang.Object
    implements MouseInputListener

Constructors

public MouseInputHandler()

Default constructor.

Methods

public void mouseClicked(java.awt.event.MouseEvent e)

An empty method.

Implements: mouseClicked in interface MouseInputListener.

public void mouseDragged(java.awt.event.MouseEvent e)

Handles resizing a column or dragging a column depending on where the mouse was during the previous mousePressed().

Implements: mouseDragged in interface MouseInputListener.

public void mouseEntered(java.awt.event.MouseEvent e)

An empty method.

Implements: mouseEntered in interface MouseInputListener.

public void mouseExited(java.awt.event.MouseEvent e)
An empty method.
Implements: mouseExited in interface MouseInputListener.

public void mouseMoved(java.awt.event.MouseEvent e)
Changes the cursor to a resize cursor if you're currently resizing a column. Otherwise sets it to the normal cursor.
Implements: mouseMoved in interface MouseInputListener.

public void mousePressed(java.awt.event.MouseEvent e)
Identifies whether the mouse was pressed over the column resizing region of a header cell. If it was, starts resizing the column. If it wasn't, begins dragging the column.
Implements: mousePressed in interface MouseInputListener.

public void mouseReleased(java.awt.event.MouseEvent e)
Ends resizing or dragging.
Implements: mouseReleased in interface MouseInputListener.

See also MouseInputListener (p.505).

swing.plaf.basic.BasicTableUI

CLASS

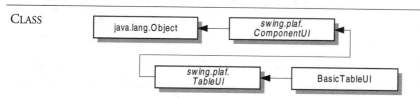

The Basic look and feel UI delegate for JTable.

UIDefaults table key	Description
Table.background	The background Color for the table.
Table.font	The Font for the table.
Table.foreground	The foreground Color for the table.
Table.gridColor	The Color for the grid lines.
Table.scrollPaneBorder	The Border to use if this table is in a JScrollPane.
Table.selectionBackground	The background Color for selected cells.
Table.selectionForeground	The foreground Color for selected cells.

public class BasicTableUI extends TableUI

Constructors
public BasicTableUI()
Default constructor.

Methods
public static ComponentUI createUI(JComponent c)
Overrides: createUI in class ComponentUI.

public java.awt.Dimension getMaximumSize(JComponent c)

Returns getPreferredSize().

Overrides: getMaximumSize in class ComponentUI.

public java.awt.Dimension getMinimumSize(JComponent c)

Returns getPreferredSize().

Overrides: getMinimumSize in class ComponentUI.

public java.awt.Dimension getPreferredSize(JComponent c)

If the JTable's autoResizeMode property is set to AUTO_RESIZE_OFF, the value returned is the total width of all columns, including the inter-cell spacing. If the autoResizeMode property is anything else, the width is the width of the containing JViewport. The height is always the number of rows times the preferred row height, including the inter-cell spacing.

Overrides: getPreferredSize in class ComponentUI.

public void installUI(JComponent c)

Overrides: installUI in class ComponentUI.

public void paint(java.awt.Graphics g, JComponent c)

Overrides: paint in class ComponentUI.

public void uninstallUI(JComponent c)

Overrides: uninstallUI in class ComponentUI.

Protected Fields

protected java.awt.event.FocusListener focusListener

A FocusListener that updates and repaints the selection when the focus is gained or lost.

protected java.awt.event.KeyListener keyListener

The handler for key events in the table.

protected MouseInputListener mouseInputListener

The handler for Mouse and MouseMotionEvents.

protected CellRendererPane rendererPane

The CellRendererPane.

protected JTable table

The associated JTable.

Protected Methods

protected java.awt.event.FocusListener createFocusListener()

Creates and returns an instance of BasicTableUI.FocusHandler.

protected java.awt.event.KeyListener createKeyListener()

Creates and returns an instance of BasicTableUI.KeyHandler.

protected MouseInputListener createMouseInputListener()

Creates and returns an instance of BasicTableUI.MouseInputHandler.

protected void installDefaults()

Installs the background, foreground, selectionBackground, selectionForeground, and grid Colors into the JTable. Also installs the Font and the Border for the parent JViewport, if there is one.

protected void installKeyboardActions()

Installs handlers for VK_RIGHT, VK_LEFT, VK_UP, and VK_DOWN.

protected void installListeners()

Adds the listeners to the associated JTable.

protected void uninstallDefaults()

Uninstalls the resources installed in installDefaults().

protected void uninstallKeyboardActions()
    Uninstalls the key handlers.
protected void uninstallListeners()
    Uninstalls the listeners.

Inner Classes
public class BasicTableUI.FocusHandler
public class BasicTableUI.KeyHandler
public class BasicTableUI.MouseInputHandler

See also   CellRendererPane (p.151), ComponentUI (p.530), JTable (p.357), MouseInputListener (p.505), TableUI (p.541).

swing.plaf.basic.BasicTableUI.FocusHandler

INNER CLASS

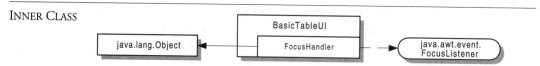

public class BasicTableUI.FocusHandler extends java.lang.Object
    implements java.awt.event.FocusListener

Constructors
public FocusHandler()
    Default constructor.

Methods
public void focusGained(java.awt.event.FocusEvent e)
    Ensures that the row and column selection values are sane (make sense) and then repaints the selection.
    Implements: focusGained in interface FocusListener.
public void focusLost(java.awt.event.FocusEvent e)
    Repaints the selection.
    Implements: focusLost in interface FocusListener.

swing.plaf.basic.BasicTableUI.KeyHandler

INNER CLASS

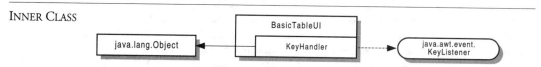

public class BasicTableUI.KeyHandler extends java.lang.Object
    implements java.awt.event.KeyListener

Constructors
public KeyHandler()
    Default constructor

Methods
public void keyPressed(java.awt.event.KeyEvent e)
    An empty method.

Implements: keyPressed in interface KeyListener.

public void keyReleased(java.awt.event.KeyEvent e)

An empty method.

Implements: keyReleased in interface KeyListener.

public void keyTyped(java.awt.event.KeyEvent e)

Attempts to start or continue editing in the current cell. If it is being edited, passes the key along to the editor.

Implements: keyTyped in interface KeyListener.

swing.plaf.basic.BasicTableUI.MouseInputHandler

INNER CLASS

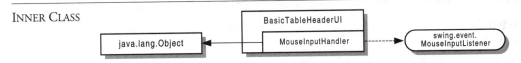

```
public class BasicTableUI.MouseInputHandler extends java.lang.Object
    implements MouseInputListener
```

Constructors
public MouseInputHandler()

Default constructor.

Methods
public void mouseClicked(java.awt.event.MouseEvent e)

An empty method.

Implements: mouseClicked in interface MouseInputListener.

public void mouseDragged(java.awt.event.MouseEvent e)

Passes this event along to any component in the table which is currently editing.

Implements: mouseDragged in interface MouseInputListener.

public void mouseEntered(java.awt.event.MouseEvent e)

Stops mouse events from being passed along to editors.

Implements: mouseEntered in interface MouseInputListener.

public void mouseExited(java.awt.event.MouseEvent e)

Stops mouse events from being passed along to editors.

Implements: mouseExited in interface MouseInputListener.

public void mouseMoved(java.awt.event.MouseEvent e)

Stops mouse events from being passed along to editors.

Implements: mouseMoved in interface MouseInputListener.

public void mousePressed(java.awt.event.MouseEvent e)

Attempts to start editing in the cell underneath the mouse press. If it can't, this method gets the focus for that cell.

Implements: mousePressed in interface MouseInputListener.

public void mouseReleased(java.awt.event.MouseEvent e)

Passes the event along to any component currently editing in the table.

Implements: mouseReleased in interface MouseInputListener.

See also　　MouseInputListener (p.505).

swing.plaf.basic.BasicTextAreaUI

CLASS

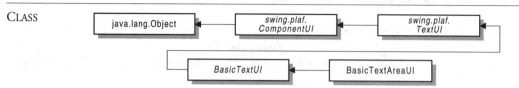

The Basic look and feel UI delegate for JTextArea.

```
public class BasicTextAreaUI extends BasicTextUI
```

Constructors
```
public BasicTextAreaUI()
```
Constructs a new BasicTextAreaUI object.

Methods
```
public View create(Element elem)
```
Creates the view for an element.
Overrides: create in class BasicTextUI.
Implements: create in interface ViewFactory.

```
public static ComponentUI createUI(JComponent ta)
```
Creates a UI for the given JTextArea.
Overrides: createUI in class ComponentUI.

Protected Methods
```
protected String getPropertyPrefix()
```
Returns TextArea. The propertyPrefix is used as a prefix to the name of all of the standard text
properties so the appropriate ones can be found in the UIDefaults table.
Overrides: getPropertyPrefix in class BasicTextUI.

```
protected void propertyChange(PropertyChangeEvent evt)
```
Rebuilds the View when the wrapLine or the wrapStyleWord properties change.
Overrides: propertyChange in class BasicTextUI.

See also   BasicTextUI (p.696), ComponentUI (p.530), Element (p.830), JTextArea (p.374),
View (p.893), ViewFactory (p.896).

swing.plaf.basic.BasicTextFieldUI

CLASS

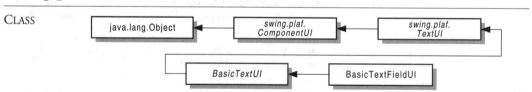

The Basic look and feel UI delegate for a JTextField.

```
public class BasicTextFieldUI extends BasicTextUI
```

Constructors
public BasicTextFieldUI()
> Creates a new BasicTextFieldUI.

Methods
public View create(Element elem)
> Creates a FieldView based on the given Element.
> *Overrides:* create in class BasicTextUI.
> *Implements:* create in interface ViewFactory.

public static ComponentUI createUI(swing.JComponent c)
> Creates a UI for a JTextField.
> *Overrides:* createUI in class ComponentUI.

Protected Methods
protected Caret createCaret()
> Creates the caret for a field.
> *Overrides:* createCaret in class BasicTextUI.

protected String getPropertyPrefix()
> Returns "TextField". The propertyPrefix is prepended to the standard text resource names to find the resources appropriate to this particular implementation.
> *Overrides:* getPropertyPrefix in class BasicTextUI.

> *Extended by*   BasicPasswordFieldUI (p.635).
> *See also*   BasicTextUI (p.696), Element (p.830), JTextField (p.379), View (p.893), ViewFactory (p.896).

swing.plaf.basic.BasicTextPaneUI

CLASS

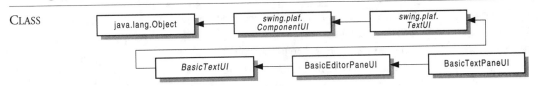

The basic look and feel UI delegate for a JTextPane.

```
public class BasicTextPaneUI extends BasicEditorPaneUI
```

Constructors
public BasicTextPaneUI()
> Creates a new BasicTextPaneUI.

Methods
public static ComponentUI createUI(JComponent c)
> Creates a UI for the given JTextPane.
> *Overrides:* createUI in class BasicTextAreaUI.

public EditorKit getEditorKit()

Returns the EditorKit currently set in the JTextPane.

Overrides: getEditorKit in class BasicEditorPaneUI.

Protected Methods

protected String getPropertyPrefix()

Returns "TextPane". The propertyPrefix is prepended to the standard text resource names so the appropriate resources for this implementation can be found.

Overrides: getPropertyPrefix in class BasicEditorPaneUI.

protected void propertyChange(PropertyChangeEvent evt)

If the font or foreground has changed, and the Document is a StyledDocument, the appropriate property is set in the default style.

Overrides: propertyChange in class BasicTextUI.

See also   BasicEditorPaneUI (p.586), BasicTextUI (p.696), EditorKit (p.829).

swing.plaf.basic.BasicTextUI

ABSTRACT
CLASS

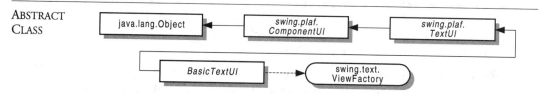

This class provides the basic functionality for all Basic look and feel text UI delegates.

UIDefaults table key (without propertyPrefix)	Description
.background	The background Color for this text component.
.border	The Border for this text component.
.caretBlinkRate	The Integer representing the number of milliseconds between Caret blinks.
.caretForeground	The foreground Color used for the Caret.
.font	The default Font for this text component.
.foreground	The foreground Color for this text component.
.inactiveForeground	The foreground Color to use when this text component is disabled.
.keyBindings	The array of additional JTextComponent.KeyBindings defined by this text component.
.margin	The default Insets around this text component.
.selectionBackground	The background Color to use for the selection highlight.
.selectionForeground	The foreground Color to use for the selection highlight.

**public abstract class BasicTextUI extends TextUI
    implements ViewFactory**

Constructors

public BasicTextUI()

Default constructor.

Methods

public View create(Element elem)

Creates a View for the given Element. If a subclass wishes to directly implement the factory producing the View(s), it should override this method. This method returns null to indicate it cannot create a View.

Implements: create in interface ViewFactory.

public View create(Element elem, int p0, int p1)

Creates the View for an Element that has been broken as a result of formatting. If subclasses support breakable Views they should override this method. This method returns null to indicate it does not support breakable Views.

public void damageRange(JTextComponent tc, int p0, int p1)

Causes the given range to be repainted if it is showing.

Overrides: damageRange in class TextUI.

public void damageRange(JTextComponent t, int p0, int p1,
Position.Bias p0Bias, Position.Bias p1Bias)

Causes the given range to be repainted if it is showing.

Overrides: damageRange in class TextUI.

public EditorKit getEditorKit()

Returns an instance of DefaultEditorKit.

Overrides: getEditorKit in class TextUI.

public java.awt.Dimension getMaximumSize(JComponent c)

Returns Integer.MAX_VALUE for each dimension in which the root View is resizable. If there are any dimensions which are not resizeable, this method returns the smaller of Integer.MAX_VALUE and the preferred span of the root View along the corresponding axis.

Overrides: getMaximumSize in class ComponentUI.

public java.awt.Dimension getMinimumSize(JComponent c)

Returns 1 for each dimension in which the root View is resizable. If there are any dimensions which are not resizeable, this method returns the smaller of Integer.MAX_VALUE and the preferred span of the root View along the corresponding axis.

Overrides: getMinimumSize in class ComponentUI.

public int getNextVisualPositionFrom(JTextComponent t, int pos,
Position.Bias b, int direction, Position.Bias[] biasRet)
throws BadLocationException

Returns the next offset in the model from the given offset pos that has a visual representation. An example of where this might be needed is in skipping over HTML tags that are in the model to get to the next text position. The direction may be SwingConstants.WEST, SwingConstants.EAST, SwingConstants.NORTH, or SwingConstants.SOUTH.

Throws: IllegalArgumentException for an invalid direction.

Overrides: getNextVisualPositionFrom in class TextUI.

public java.awt.Dimension getPreferredSize(JComponent c)

Sets the size of the root View to the size of the component, and then returns the preferred spans of the root View along the two axes.

plaf.basic

Overrides: getPreferredSize in class ComponentUI.

public View getRootView(JTextComponent tc)

Returns a View that matches the dimensions of the associated text component and which also forms the root of the view hierarchy.

Overrides: getRootView in class TextUI.

public void installUI(JComponent c)

Installs this UI delegate into the given component. By default, this sets the component to be opaque, installs the default Caret and Highlighter, attaches listeners to the component and the model, and creates the ViewFactory to use in creating the Views. If the text component does not already have an associated model, an appropriate empty default model will be created.

Overrides: installUI in class ComponentUI.

public java.awt.Rectangle modelToView(JTextComponent tc, int pos) throws BadLocationException

Converts the given Document offset into a bounding rectangle in the View.

Throws: BadLocationException if the given position does not represent a valid location in the associated document.

Overrides: modelToView in class TextUI.

public java.awt.Rectangle modelToView(JTextComponent tc, int pos, Position.Bias bias) throws BadLocationException

Converts the given Document offset into a bounding rectangle in the View.

Throws: BadLocationException if the given position does not represent a valid location in the associated document.

Overrides: modelToView in class TextUI.

public final void paint(java.awt.Graphics g, JComponent c)

Paints the component. This calls paintSafely() in a separate thread.

Overrides: paint in class ComponentUI.

public void uninstallUI(JComponent c)

Removes the listeners, Views, Highlighter, Caret, and Keymap from the component.

Overrides: uninstallUI in class ComponentUI.

public int viewToModel(JTextComponent tc, java.awt.Point pt)

Converts the given point in the View coordinate system to the offset in the model that best represents it.

Overrides: viewToModel in class TextUI.

public int viewToModel(JTextComponent tc, java.awt.Point pt, Position.Bias[] biasReturn)

Converts the given point in the View coordinate system to the offset in the model that best represents it.

Overrides: viewToModel in class TextUI.

Protected Methods

protected Caret createCaret()

Creates the object to use for a caret.

protected Highlighter createHighlighter()

Creates the object to use for selection highlights.

protected Keymap createKeymap()

Creates the keymap to use for the text component and installs key bindings into it. The Keymap name is returned by the getKeymapName() method. If a keymap matching the default name is not found in the UIDefaults table, the DEFAULT_KEYMAP defined in JTextComponent is used.

protected final JTextComponent getComponent()

Returns the associated JTextComponent.

protected String getKeymapName()

Returns the name of the Keymap to use. This method returns the name of the editor class without the package prefix.

protected abstract String getPropertyPrefix()

Returns the prefix String to prepend to the default resource names used in looking up resources in the UIDefaults table.

protected java.awt.Rectangle getVisibleEditorRect()

Returns the portion of the editor visible on the screen.

protected void installDefaults()

Installs the resources appropriate for this type of text editor (for example, the font, colors, etc.) into the associated text component.

protected void installKeyboardActions()

Installs the Keymap into the associated JTextComponent.

protected void installListeners()

Installs the listeners into the associated component.

protected void modelChanged()

Called when the model (the Document) changes.

protected void paintBackground(java.awt.Graphics g)

Paints a background for the View if the associated text component is opaque. By default this is the case.

protected void paintSafely(java.awt.Graphics g)

Locks the associated model and paints the View. First the background is painted, if needed. Next the selection highlights are painted, followed by the Views and then the Caret. This painting order is logically painting from "back" to "front."

protected void propertyChange(java.beans.PropertyChangeEvent evt)

Called when a bound property is changed on the associated JTextComponent.

protected final void setView(View v)

Sets the root View and calls invalidate().

protected void uninstallDefaults()

Uninstalls the resources installed in installDefaults.

protected void uninstallKeyboardActions()

Uninstalls the Keymap from the JTextComponent.

protected void uninstallListeners()

Uninstalls the listeners installed using installListeners.

Inner Classes

public static class BasicTextUI.BasicCaret
public static class BasicTextUI.BasicHighlighter

Extended by BasicEditorPaneUI (p.586), BasicTextAreaUI (p.694), BasicTextFieldUI (p.694), DefaultTextUI (p.826).

plaf.basic

See also   BadLocationException (p.796), Caret (p.800), EditorKit (p.829), Element (p.830), Highlighter (p.835), JComponent (p.207), JTextComponent (p.838), Keymap (p.846), View (p.893).

swing.plaf.basic.BasicTextUI.BasicCaret

INNER CLASS

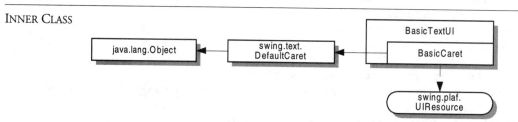

This inner class is a simple subclass of `DefaultCaret` that implements the `UIResource` interface so it can be used safely by a look and feel.

```
public static class BasicTextUI.BasicCaret extends DefaultCaret
    implements UIResource
```

Constructors
```
public BasicCaret()
```
     Default constructor.

See also   DefaultCaret (p.806), UIResource (p.544).

swing.plaf.basic.BasicTextUI.BasicHighlighter

INNER CLASS

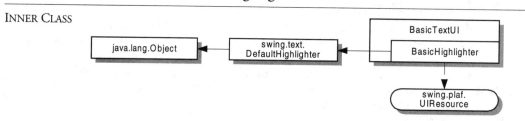

This inner class is a simple subclass of `DefaultHighlighter` that implements the `UIResource` interface so it can be used safely by a look and feel.

```
public static class BasicTextUI.BasicHighlighter
    extends DefaultHighlighter
    implements UIResource
```

Constructors
```
public BasicHighlighter()
```
     Default constructor.

See also   DefaultHighlighter (p.818), UIResource (p.544).

swing.plaf.basic.BasicToggleButtonUI

CLASS

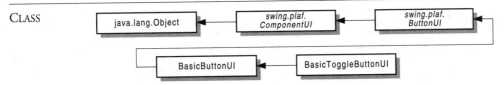

The Basic look and feel UI delegate for the `JToggleButton` component.

public class BasicToggleButtonUI extends BasicButtonUI

Constructors
public BasicToggleButtonUI()
> Default constructor.

Methods
public static ComponentUI createUI(JComponent b)
> *Overrides:* createUI in class BasicButtonUI.

public void paint(java.awt.Graphics g, JComponent c)
> *Overrides:* paint in class BasicButtonUI.

Protected Methods
protected int getPropertyPrefix()
> Returns "ToggleButton."
> *Overrides:* getPropertyPrefix in class BasicButtonUI.

protected void paintButtonPressed(java.awt.Graphics g, AbstractButton b)
> Paints the button in its pressed state.
> *Overrides:* paintButtonPressed in class BasicButtonUI.

protected void paintFocus(java.awt.Graphics g, AbstractButton b,
java.awt.Rectangle viewRect, java.awt.Rectangle textRect,
java.awt.Rectangle iconRect)
> Paints the focus indicator.
> *Overrides:* paintFocus in class BasicButtonUI.

protected void paintIcon(java.awt.Graphics g, AbstractButton b,
java.awt.Rectangle iconRect)
> Paints the button's Icon.

protected void paintText(java.awt.Graphics g, AbstractButton b,
java.awt.Rectangle textRect, String text)
> Paints the button's text.

> *Extended by* BasicRadioButtonUI (p.641).
> *See also* AbstractButton (p.118), BasicButtonUI (p.557), ComponentUI (p.530), JComponent (p.207).

plaf.basic

swing.plaf.basic.BasicToolBarSeparatorUI

CLASS

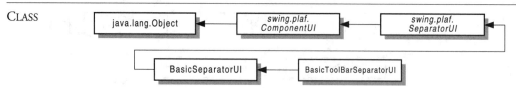

This class implements the look and feel for a `JSeparator` in a `JToolBar`.

UIDefaults table key	Description
`ToolBar.separatorSize`	The `Dimension` of the separator.

```
public class BasicToolBarSeparatorUI extends BasicSeparatorUI
```

Constructors
`public BasicToolBarSeparatorUI()`
Default constructor.

Methods
`public static ComponentUI createUI(JComponent c)`
Overrides: `createUI` in class `BasicSeparatorUI`.
`public java.awt.Dimension getMaximumSize(JComponent c)`
Overrides: `getMaximumSize` in class `BasicSeparatorUI`.
`public java.awt.Dimension getMinimumSize(JComponent c)`
Overrides: `getMinimumSize` in class `BasicSeparatorUI`.
`public java.awt.Dimension getPreferredSize(JComponent c)`
Overrides: `getPreferredSize` in class `BasicSeparatorUI`.
`public void paint(java.awt.Graphics g, JComponent c)`
Overrides: `paint` in class `BasicSeparatorUI`.

Protected Methods
`protected void installDefaults(JSeparator s)`
Overrides: `installDefaults` in class `BasicSeparatorUI`.

See also   BasicSeparatorUI (p.654), ComponentUI (p.530), JComponent (p.207), JSeparator (p.338).

swing.plaf.basic.BasicToolBarUI

CLASS

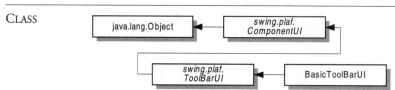

The Basic look and feel UI delegate for the `JToolBar` component.

UIDefaults table key	Description
`ToolBar.background`	The background `Color` for the toolbar.
`ToolBar.border`	The `Border` for the toolbar.
`ToolBar.dockingBackground`	The background `Color` to use for the docking-active border.
`ToolBar.dockingForeground`	The foreground `Color` to use for the docking-active border.
`ToolBar.floatingBackground`	The background `Color` used for the floating border.
`ToolBar.floatingForeground`	The foreground `Color` used for the floating border.
`ToolBar.font`	The `Font` used for the toolbar.
`ToolBar.foreground`	The foreground `Color` for the toolbar.

Client property	Description
`JToolBar.focusedCompIndex`	The component in the toolbar which has the focus.

`public class BasicToolBarUI extends ToolBarUI`

Constructors
`public BasicToolBarUI()`
    Default constructor.

Methods
`public boolean canDock(java.awt.Component c, java.awt.Point p)`
    Returns `true` if the toolbar can dock to the given component at the given point.

`public static ComponentUI createUI(JComponent x)`
    Overrides: `createUI` in class `ComponentUI`.

`public java.awt.Color getDockingColor()`
    Returns the color displayed when over a docking area.

`public java.awt.Color getFloatingColor()`
    Returns the color displayed when over a floating area.

`public java.awt.Dimension getMaximumSize(JComponent c)`
    Overrides: `getMaximumSize` in class `ComponentUI`.

`public java.awt.Dimension getMinimumSize(JComponent c)`
    Overrides: `getMinimumSize` in class `ComponentUI`.

`public java.awt.Dimension getPreferredSize(JComponent c)`
    Overrides: `getPreferredSize` in class `ComponentUI`.

`public void installUI(JComponent c)`
    Overrides: `installUI` in class `ComponentUI`.

`public boolean isFloating()`
    Returns `true` if the toolbar is floating.

`public void propertyChange(java.beans.PropertyChangeEvent e)`
    Called when a bound property changes in the associated `JToolBar`.

`public void setDockingColor(java.awt.Color c)`
    Sets the color displayed when over a docking area.

`public void setFloating(boolean b, java.awt.Point p)`
  Starts or stops the toolbar floating at the given point.

`public void setFloatingColor(java.awt.Color c)`
  Sets the color displayed when over a floating area.

`public void setFloatingLocation(int x, int y)`
  Sets the location of the floating frame.

`public void setOrientation(int orientation)`
  Changes the orientation of the toolbar.

`public void uninstallUI(JComponent c)`
  Overrides: `uninstallUI` in class `ComponentUI`.

Protected Fields

`protected java.awt.Color dockingBorderColor`
  The color to use for the drag window edge when it is in the docking region.

`protected java.awt.Color dockingColor`
  The color to use when the window is in the docking region.

`protected MouseInputListener dockingListener`
  The `MouseInputListener` used for detecting and handling docking situations.

`protected KeyStroke downKey`
  The `KeyStroke` for the `VK_DOWN` key.

`protected BasicToolBarUI.DragWindow dragWindow`
  The window to display as the dragging indicator.

`protected java.awt.Color floatingBorderColor`
  The border color of the toolbar when it is floating.

`protected java.awt.Color floatingColor`
  The color to use when the toolbar is floating.

`protected int focusedCompIndex`
  The index of the component in the toolbar that has the focus.

`protected KeyStroke leftKey`
  The `KeyStroke` for the `VK_LEFT` key.

`protected java.beans.PropertyChangeListener propertyListener`
  The handler for PropertyChangeEvents from the `JToolBar`.

`protected KeyStroke rightKey`
  The `KeyStroke` for the `VK_RIGHT` key.

`protected JToolBar toolBar`
  The associated `JToolBar`.

`protected java.awt.ContainerListener toolBarContListener`
  The listener attached to the container holding the toolbar.

`protected java.awt.FocusListener toolBarFocusListener`
  The focus listener attached to the associated `JToolBar`.

`protected KeyStroke upKey`
  The `KeyStroke` for the `VK_UP` key.

Protected Methods

`protected MouseInputListener createDockingListener()`
  Creates the `MouseInputListener` to handle the mouse events which would cause docking or undocking.

protected BasicToolBarUI.DragWindow createDragWindow(JToolBar toolbar)

Creates the DragWindow.

protected JFrame createFloatingFrame(JToolBar toolbar)

Creates the frame for the toolbar when it is floating.

protected java.awt.event.WindowListener createFrameListener()

Creates the listener for the floating frame.

protected java.beans.PropertyChangeListener createPropertyListener()

Creates the PropertyChangeListener which will handle events from the JToolBar.

protected java.awt.ContainerListener createToolBarContListener()

Creates the container listener to attach to the associated JToolBar.

protected FocusListener createToolBarFocusListener()

Creates the focus listener for the associated JToolBar.

protected void dragTo(java.awt.Point position, java.awt.Point origin)

Moves the floating window to the given position and tries to dock it if it can.

protected void floatAt(java.awt.Point position, java.awt.Point origin)

Moves the floating frame to the given position.

protected void installComponents()

An empty method.

protected void installDefaults()

Installs the UI resources into the toolbar.

protected void installKeyboardActions()

An empty method.

protected void installListeners()

Installs the listeners into the toolbar.

protected void navigateFocusedComp(int direction)

Moves the focus from the currently focused component in the toolbar to the next component in the toolbar in the given direction.

protected void uninstallComponents()

An empty method.

protected void uninstallDefaults()

Uninstalls the UI resources from the JToolBar.

protected void uninstallKeyboardActions()

An empty method.

protected void uninstallListeners(JComponent c)

Uninstalls the listeners from the toolbar.

Inner Classes

public class BasicToolBarUI.DockingListener
protected class BasicToolBarUI.DragWindow
protected class BasicToolBarUI.FrameListener
protected class BasicToolBarUI.PropertyListener
protected class BasicToolBarUI.ToolBarContListener
protected class BasicToolBarUI.ToolBarFocusListener

See also   ComponentUI (p.530), JComponent (p.207), JFrame (p.248), JToolBar (p.388), MouseInputListener (p.505), ToolBarUI (p.543).

plaf.basic

swing.plaf.basic.BasicToolBarUI.DockingListener

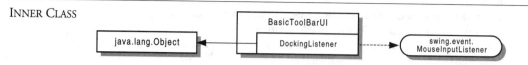

The listener that tracks mouse events to drag the toolbar.

This inner class is `public` in Swing 1.1 due to a compiler bug. When the bug is corrected this class will be changed to `protected`, so it should be treated as such.

```
public class BasicToolBarUI.DockingListener extends java.lang.Object
    implements MouseInputListener
```

Constructors

public DockingListener(JToolBar t)
Constructs a `DockingListener` that will listen to the given toolbar.

Methods

public void mouseClicked(java.awt.event.MouseEvent e)
An empty method.
Implements: mouseClicked in interface MouseInputListener.

public void mouseDragged(java.awt.event.MouseEvent e)
Sets `isDragging` to `true` and drags the toolbar to the position of this event.
Implements: mouseDragged in interface MouseInputListener.

public void mouseEntered(java.awt.event.MouseEvent e)
An empty method.
Implements: mouseEntered in interface MouseInputListener.

public void mouseExited(java.awt.event.MouseEvent e)
An empty method.
Implements: mouseExited in interface MouseInputListener.

public void mouseMoved(java.awt.event.MouseEvent e)
An empty method.
Implements: mouseMoved in interface MouseInputListener.

public void mousePressed(java.awt.event.MouseEvent e)
If the toolbar is enabled, sets `isDragging` to `false`.
Implements: mousePressed in interface MouseInputListener.

public void mouseReleased(java.awt.event.MouseEvent e)
If `isDragging` is `true`, calls `floatAt()` with the new position and the old location of the toolbar. Resets `isDragging` to `false`.
Implements: mouseReleased in interface MouseInputListener.

Protected Fields

protected boolean isDragging
Set to `true` if the window is being dragged.

protected java.awt.Point origin
The origin of the drag.

`protected JToolBar toolBar`

The associated `JToolBar`.

Returned by   BasicToolBarUI.createDockingListener() (p.702).
See also   MouseInputListener (p.505), JToolBar (p.388).

swing.plaf.basic.BasicToolBarUI.DragWindow

INNER CLASS

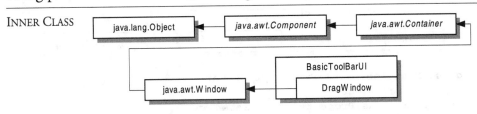

`protected class BasicToolBarUI.DragWindow extends java.awt.Window`

Methods

`public java.awt.Color getBorderColor()`

Returns the Color used to paint the dragging border.

`public java.awt.Insets getInsets()`

Overrides: `getInsets` in class `Container`.

`public java.awt.Point getOffset()`

Returns the location of the mouse cursor relative to the origin of the drag window.

`public void paint(java.awt.Graphics g)`

Overrides: `paint` in class `Container`.

`public void setBorderColor(java.awt.Color c)`

Sets the Color to paint the dragging border.

`public void setOffset(java.awt.Point p)`

Sets the location of the mouse cursor relative to the origin of the drag window.

`public void setOrientation(int o)`

Sets the horizontal or vertical orientation of the drag window.

Returned by   BasicToolBarUI.createDragWindow() (p.702).

swing.plaf.basic.BasicToolBarUI.FrameListener

INNER CLASS

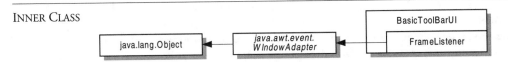

`protected class BasicToolBarUI.FrameListener extends WindowAdapter`

Constructors

`public FrameListener()`

Default constructor.

Methods
`public void windowClosing(java.awt.event.WindowEvent w)`
>   *Overrides:* windowClosing in class WindowAdapter.
>   *Implements:* windowClosing in interface WindowListener.

swing.plaf.basic.BasicToolBarUI.PropertyListener

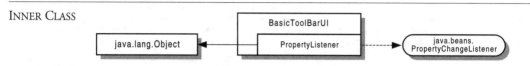

```
protected class BasicToolBarUI.PropertyListener
    extends java.lang.Object
    implements java.beans.PropertyChangeListener
```

Constructors
`public PropertyListener()`
>   Default constructor.

Methods
`public void propertyChange(java.beans.PropertyChangeEvent e)`
>   *Implements:* propertyChange in interface PropertyChangeListener.

swing.plaf.basic.BasicToolBarUI.ToolBarContListener

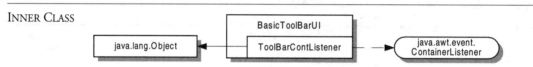

```
protected class BasicToolBarUI.ToolBarContListener
    extends java.lang.Object
    implements java.awt.event.ContainerListener
```

Constructors
`public ToolBarContListener()`
>   Default constructor.

Methods
`public void componentAdded(java.awt.event.ContainerEvent e)`
>   Adds the focus listener to the newly added component.
>   *Implements:* componentAdded in interface ContainerListener.

`public void componentRemoved(java.awt.event.ContainerEvent e)`
>   Removes the focus listener from the component.
>   *Implements:* componentRemoved in interface ContainerListener.

plaf.basic

swing.plaf.basic.BasicToolBarUI.ToolBarFocusListener

INNER CLASS

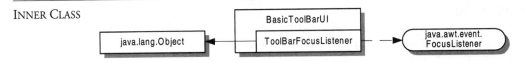

```
protected class BasicToolBarUI.ToolBarFocusListener
    extends java.lang.Object
    implements java.awt.event.FocusListener
```

Constructors
public ToolBarFocusListener()
  Default constructor.

Methods
public void focusGained(java.awt.event.FocusEvent e)
  Updates BasicToolBarUI.focusCompIndex to match the index of the focused component.
  Implements: componentAdded in interface ContainerListener.

public void focusLost(java.awt.event.FocusEvent e)
  An empty method.
  Implements: componentRemoved in interface ContainerListener.

swing.plaf.basic.BasicToolTipUI

CLASS

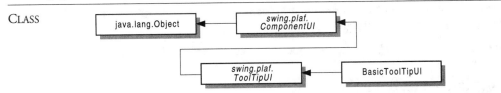

The Basic look and feel UI delegate for the JToolTip component. This class maintains a single shared instance that is used by all tool tips.

UIDefaults table key	Description
ToolTip.background	The background Color for the tool tip.
ToolTip.border	The Border to use around the tool tip.
ToolTip.font	The Font to use in the tool tip.
ToolTip.foreground	The foreground Color to use for the tool tip.

```
public class BasicToolTipUI extends ToolTipUI
```

Constructors
public BasicToolTipUI()
  Calls super().

Methods

public static ComponentUI createUI(JComponent c)
>   Returns the single shared instance.
>   *Overrides:* createUI in class ComponentUI.

public java.awt.Dimension getMaximumSize(JComponent c)
>   *Overrides:* getMaximumSize in class ComponentUI.

public java.awt.Dimension getMinimumSize(JComponent c)
>   *Overrides:* getMinimumSize in class ComponentUI.

public java.awt.Dimension getPreferredSize(JComponent c)
>   *Overrides:* getPreferredSize in class ComponentUI.

public void installUI(JComponent c)
>   *Overrides:* installUI in class ComponentUI.

public void paint(java.awt.Graphics g, JComponent c)
>   *Overrides:* paint in class ComponentUI.

public void uninstallUI(JComponent c)
>   *Overrides:* uninstallUI in class ComponentUI.

Protected Methods

protected void installDefaults(JComponent c)
>   Installs the color and font to use for the ToolTips into the given component.

protected void installListeners(JComponent c)
>   Installs the listeners into the given component.

protected void uninstallDefaults(JComponent c)
>   Removes the installed colors and font from the given component.

protected void uninstallListeners(JComponent c)
>   Removes the listeners from the given component.

>   *See also*   ComponentUI (p.530), JComponent (p.207), ToolTipUI (p.543).

swing.plaf.basic.BasicTreeUI

CLASS

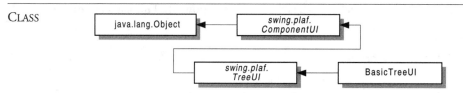

UIDefaults table key	Description
Tree.background	The background Color for the tree.
Tree.changeSelectionWithFocus	A Boolean indicating whether the tree will update the selection as the focus highlight is moved.
Tree.collapsedIcon	The Icon to be used for a collapsed node handle.
Tree.expandedIcon	The Icon to be used for an expanded node handle.
Tree.font	The default font for the tree.

plaf.basic

UIDefaults table key	Description
Tree.hash	The Color used for the lines connecting nodes.
Tree.leftChildIndent	The amount to indent the child rows of a node.
Tree.rightChildIndent	The offset between the right edge of a node handle and the node content area.
Tree.rowHeight	The default height to use for a row.
Tree.scrollsOnExpand	A Boolean indicating whether the tree will scroll so that the last child of a newly expanded node will be visible.

public class BasicTreeUI extends TreeUI

Constructors
public BasicTreeUI()

Calls super().

Methods
public void cancelEditing()

Cancels the current editing session, if there is one.

Overrides: cancelEditing in class TreeUI.

public static ComponentUI createUI(JComponent x)

Overrides: createUI in class ComponentUI.

public TreePath getClosestPathForLocation(JTree tree, int x, int y)

Returns the TreePath to the node closest to *x,y*. If the tree is empty this returns null; otherwise, it returns the node *closest* to the point, which may be the bottom-most node if the point is off the bottom of the tree. To find out if the returned node is *directly* underneath the point, use this method and then check to see if the Rectangle of the returned node contains the point.

Overrides: getClosestPathForLocation in class TreeUI.

public Icon getCollapsedIcon()

Returns the Icon used for the collapsed state of the expand/collapse buttons in the tree.

public TreePath getEditingPath()

Returns the path to the element that is being edited.

Overrides: getEditingPath in class TreeUI.

public Icon getExpandedIcon()

Returns the Icon used for the expanded state of the expand/collapse buttons in the tree.

public int getLeftChildIndent()

Returns the distance (in pixels) to indent child nodes relative to their parents. This distance is to the leftmost part of the expand/collapse button.

public java.awt.Dimension getMaximumSize(JComponent c)

Returns the maximum size. If this UI delegate has an associated JTree this method returns JTree.getPreferredSize(). Otherwise, this method returns the preferredMinSize if non-null, or as a last resort, it returns new Dimension(0,0).

Overrides: getMaximumSize in class ComponentUI.

public java.awt.Dimension getMinimumSize(JComponent c)

Returns the minimum size. If the preferredMinSize is non-null it will be returned. Otherwise, this method returns new Dimension(0,0).

Overrides: getMinimumSize in class ComponentUI.

public java.awt.Rectangle getPathBounds(JTree tree, TreePath path)

Uses the treeState LayoutCache (either a `FixedHeightLayoutCache` or a `VariableHeight-LayoutCache`) to retrieve the bounds of the renderer area for the node at the end of `path`.

Overrides: `getPathBounds` in class `TreeUI`.

public TreePath getPathForRow(JTree tree, int row)

Uses the treeState LayoutCache to return the `TreePath` for the node at `row`.

Overrides: `getPathForRow` in class `TreeUI`.

public java.awt.Dimension getPreferredMinSize()

Returns the minimum preferred size.

public java.awt.Dimension getPreferredSize(JComponent c)

Calls `getPreferredSize(c, false)`.

Overrides: `getPreferredSize` in class `ComponentUI`.

public java.awt.Dimension getPreferredSize(JComponent c,
boolean checkConsistency)

Returns the preferred size of the tree. The `checkConsistency` parameter is ignored. If the `cachedPerferredSize` field is invalid, this method uses the AbstractLayoutCache to update the field before calculating the preferred size.

public int getRightChildIndent()

Returns the amount (in pixels) to add to the leftChildIndent to calculate where to begin drawing with the node renderer.

public int getRowCount(JTree tree)

Returns the number of rows that are being displayed.

Overrides: `getRowCount` in class `TreeUI`.

public int getRowForPath(JTree tree, TreePath path)

Calls `treeState.getRowForPath(path)`. If `treeState` is `null`, this method returns −1.

Overrides: `getRowForPath` in class `TreeUI`.

public void installUI(JComponent c)

Overrides: `installUI` in class `ComponentUI`.

public boolean isEditing()

Returns `true` if a node in the tree is being edited. The node that is being edited can be returned by `getEditingPath()`.

Overrides: `isEditing` in class `TreeUI`.

public void paint(java.awt.Graphics g, JComponent c)

Overrides: `paint` in class `ComponentUI`.

public void setCollapsedIcon(Icon newG)

Sets the Icon to use for the collapsed state of the expand/collapse buttons in the tree.

public void setExpandedIcon(Icon newG)

Sets the Icon to use for the expanded state of the expand/collapse buttons in the tree.

public void setLeftChildIndent(int newAmount)

Sets the amount to indent child nodes from their parents.

public void setModel(TreeModel newModel)

Ends any editing, then updates the `BasicTreeUI` from the `newModel`. Also transfers any listeners from the old TreeModel to the `newModel`.

public void setPreferredMinSize(java.awt.Dimension newSize)

Sets the preferred minimum size.

public void setRightChildIndent(int newAmount)

Sets the distance (in pixels) to horizontally offset the cell renderer area from the leftChildIndent.

public void startEditingAtPath(JTree tree, TreePath path)

Selects the last item in path and tries to edit it. If the node cannot be edited this method silently does nothing.

Overrides: startEditingAtPath in class TreeUI.

public boolean stopEditing()

Stops any editing in the tree. This method returns true if the editor returns true from stop-CellEditing().

Overrides: stopEditing in class TreeUI.

public void uninstallUI(JComponent c)

Overrides: uninstallUI in class ComponentUI.

Protected Fields

protected transient TreeCellEditor cellEditor

The editor for the tree.

protected transient Icon collapsedIcon

The Icon used for the collapsed state of the expand/collapse buttons in the tree.

protected boolean createdCellEditor

Set to true if the editor renderer that is currently in the tree was created by this instance.

protected boolean createdRenderer

Set to true if the renderer that is currently in the tree was created by this instance.

protected transient TreeCellRenderer currentCellRenderer

The renderer being used by the tree.

protected int depthOffset

This value is the distance (in pixels) to shift the *x* coordinates of nodes to account for the root node being hidden/shown and the root handles being hidden/shown. The largest offset will occur when the root node and root handles are showing.

protected java.util.Hashtable drawingCache

Used to eliminate drawing vertical lines to a parent multiple times due to having multiple children.

protected java.awt.Component editingComponent

When editing, this will be the Component that is doing the actual editing.

protected TreePath editingPath

The path that is being edited.

protected int editingRow

The row that is being edited. Only valid if editingComponent is not null.

protected boolean editorHasDifferentSize

Set to true if the editor is a different size than the renderer.

protected transient Icon expandedIcon

The Icon used for the expanded state of the expand/collapse buttons in the tree.

protected boolean largeModel

Set to true when optimizing drawing for a large model. A FixedHeightLayoutCache does most of these optimizations.

protected int lastSelectedRow

The index of the row that was selected most recently.

protected int leftChildIndent

The distance (in pixels) to offset child nodes from their parents.

protected AbstractLayoutCache.NodeDimensions nodeDimensions
 A cache of the node sizes.
protected java.awt.Dimension preferredMinSize
 The minimum preferred size.
protected java.awt.Dimension preferredSize
 The size needed to display all of the visible nodes in the tree.
protected CellRendererPane rendererPane
 Used to paint the TreeCellRenderer.
protected int rightChildIndent
 The distance (in pixels) to offset the cell renderer from the leftChildIndent.
protected boolean stopEditingInCompleteEditing
 Set to false while editing is happening and shouldSelectCell() returns true.
protected int totalChildIndent
 The cached sum of leftChildIndent and rightChildIndent.
protected JTree tree
 The associated JTree.
protected TreeModel treeModel
 The associated JTree's model.
protected TreeSelectionModel treeSelectionModel
 The associated JTree's selection model.
protected AbstractLayoutCache treeState
 The class used to lay out the tree. Will be either a FixedHeightLayoutCache or a VariableHeightLayoutCache in the Basic look and feel.
protected boolean validCachedPreferredSize
 Set to true when the preferredSize is valid.

Protected Methods

protected void checkForClickInExpandControl(TreePath path,
 int mouseX, int mouseY)
 If (mouseX, mouseY) is in the expand/collapse button of the given node this method will expand or collapse the node as appropriate.
protected void completeEditing()
 Stops any editing. If the tree returns true from getInvokesStopCellEditing() this method calls stopCellEditing() on the editor. completeEditing(false, true, false) is called to finish all remaining cleanup.
protected void completeEditing(boolean messageStop,
 boolean messageCancel, boolean messageTree)
 Stops any editing. If messageStop is true, stopEditing() is called on the editor. If message-Cancel is true, cancelEditing() is called on the editor. If messageTree is true, the JTree's TreeModel has valueForPathChanged() called on it.
protected void completeUIInstall()
 Called from installUI after all the defaults/listeners have been installed.
protected void completeUIUninstall()
 Called from uninstallUI after all other cleanup tasks are complete.
protected void configureLayoutCache()
 Resets the LayoutCache for a new JTree.

protected CellEditorListener createCellEditorListener()
Creates the listener to handle events from the editor.

protected CellRendererPane createCellRendererPane(JComponent c)
Creates the `CellRendererPane`.

protected java.awt.ComponentListener createComponentListener()
Creates and returns an instance of `BasicTreeUI.ComponentHandler`. This handler is used for large model support to mark the `validCachedPreferredSize` as invalid when the component moves.

protected TreeCellEditor createDefaultCellEditor()
Creates a default cell editor.

protected TreeCellRenderer createDefaultCellRenderer()
Returns the default cell renderer that is used to do the painting of each node.

protected java.awt.event.FocusListener createFocusListener()
Repaints the tree when the focus is gained or lost.

protected java.awt.event.KeyListener createKeyListener()
Creates the handler for the keyboard navigation events. Returns an instance of `BasicTreeUI.Key-Handler`.

protected AbstractLayoutCache createLayoutCache()
Creates the object responsible for managing node expansion and node sizes.

protected java.awt.event.MouseListener createMouseListener()
Handles mouse events in the tree.

protected AbstractLayoutCache.NodeDimensions createNodeDimensions()
Creates an instance of `NodeDimensions` that is able to determine the size of a given node in the tree.

protected java.beans.PropertyChangeListnener createPropertyChangeListener()
Creates the handler for property changes in the JTree.

protected java.beans.PropertyChangeListener createSelectionModelPropertyChangeListener()
Creates the handler for property changes in the selection model.

protected TreeExpansionListener createTreeExpansionListener()
Creates the handler for changes in the tree's expansion state.

protected TreeModelListener createTreeModelListener()
Creates the handler for changes in the JTree's TreeModel.

protected TreeSelectionListener createTreeSelectionListener()
Creates the handler for changes in the JTree's selection.

protected void drawCentered(java.awt.Component c, java.awt.Graphics graphics, Icon icon, int x, int y)
Draws the given `Icon` centered around the given point. Used in drawing the expand/collapse button.

protected void drawDashedHorizontalLine(java.awt.Graphics g, int y, int x1, int x2)
Draws the horizontal part of the line connecting a parent to its child.

protected void drawDashedVerticalLine(java.awt.Graphics g, int x, int y1, int y2)
Draws the vertical part of the line connecting a parent to its child.

public void ensureRowsAreVisible(int beginRow, int endRow)
Scrolls the tree so that the given row range is visible..

protected TreeCellEditor getCellEditor()
Returns the cell editor for the tree.

protected TreeCellRenderer getCellRenderer()
Returns the cell renderer for the tree.

protected java.awt.Color getHashColor()
Returns the Color to use for the dotted connector lines.

protected int getHorizontalLegBuffer()
Returns the gap (in pixels) to leave between the end of the horizontal connector line and the child node.

protected TreePath getLastChildPath(TreePath parent)
Returns a path to the last child of `parent`.

protected TreeModel getModel()
Returns the cached `TreeModel` previously retrieved from the `JTree`.

protected int getRowHeight()
Returns the row height in the tree. Will return −1 for a tree with variable height nodes.

protected TreeSelectionModel getSelectionModel()
Returns the cached `TreeSelectionModel` previously retrieved from the `JTree`.

protected boolean getShowsRootHandles()
Returns `true` if the tree displays the handles of children connected to the root.

protected int getVerticalLegBuffer()
The gap (in pixels) to leave between the start of the vertical line and the parent node.

protected void handleExpandControlClick(TreePath path, int mouseX, int mouseY)
Toggles the selection state of the given `TreePath`.

protected void installComponents()
Installs the renderer pane.

protected void installDefaults()
Installs the `Colors` and `Font`. Also caches the `leftChildIndent` and `rightChildIndent` values.

protected void installKeyboardActions()
Installs the key handlers.

protected void installListeners()
Installs the other listeners into the `JTree` and its models.

protected boolean isEditable()
Returns `true` if the tree is editable.

protected boolean isLargeModel()
Returns `true` if the tree UI should optimize for a large tree.

protected boolean isLeaf(int row)
Returns `true` if the node at the given row is a leaf.

protected boolean isLocationInExpandControl(TreePath path, int mouseX, int mouseY)
Returns `true` if `mouseX` and `mouseY` fall in the area of `row` that is used to expand/collapse the node and the node at `row` does not represent a leaf.

protected boolean isMultiSelectEvent(java.awt.event.MouseEvent event)
Returns `true` if a MouseEvent on the node should select from the anchor point.

protected boolean isRootVisible()
Returns `true` if the root node is visible.

protected boolean isToggleEvent(java.awt.event.MouseEvent event)

Returns true if the row under the mouse should be toggled based on the event. This is invoked after checkForClickInExpandControl, implying the location is not in the expand (toggle) control. It is used to check for double clicking in the renderer area, which also expands a node in the Basic look and feel.

protected boolean isToggleSelectionEvent(java.awt.event.MouseEvent event)

Returns true if a mouse event on a node should toggle the selection of only the row under the mouse cursor.

protected void paintExpandControl(java.awt.Graphics g, java.awt.Rectangle clipBounds, java.awt.Insets insets,java.awt.Rectangle bounds, TreePath path, int row, boolean isExpanded, boolean hasBeenExpanded, boolean isLeaf)

Paints the expand/collapse button part of a row.

protected void paintHorizontalLine(java.awt.Graphics g, JComponent c, int y, int left, int right)

Paints a horizontal line.

protected void paintHorizontalPartOfLeg(java.awt.Graphics g, java.awt.Rectangle clipBounds, java.awt.Insets insets, java.awt.Rectangle bounds, TreePath path, int row, boolean isExpanded, boolean hasBeenExpanded, boolean isLeaf)

Paints the horizontal part of the line connecting a parent to a child.

protected void paintRow(java.awt.Graphics g, java.awt.Rectangle clipBounds, java.awt.Insets insets, java.awt.Rectangle bounds, TreePath path, int row, boolean isExpanded, boolean hasBeenExpanded, boolean isLeaf)

Paints the renderer part of a row.

protected void paintVerticalLine(java.awt.Graphics g, JComponent c, int x, int top, int bottom)

Paints a vertical line.

protected void paintVerticalPartOfLeg(java.awt.Graphics g, java.awt.Rectangle clipBounds, java.awt.Insets insets, TreePath path)

Paints the vertical part of the line connecting a parent and a child.

protected void pathWasCollapsed(TreePath path)

Called after the node at path has collapsed.

Overrides: pathWasCollapsed in class AbstractTreeUI.

protected void pathWasExpanded(TreePath path)

Called after the node at path has expanded.

Overrides: pathWasExpanded in class AbstractTreeUI.

protected void prepareForUIInstall()

Invoked after the tree instance variable has been set, but before any defaults/listeners have been installed.

protected void selectPathForEvent(TreePath path, java.awt.event.MouseEvent event)

Called to update the selection based on a MouseEvent over the given path. If the event is a toggle selection event, the row is either selected, or deselected. If the event identifies a multiselection event, the selection is updated from the anchor point. Otherwise, the row is selected and if the event specified a toggle event, the row is expanded/collapsed.

protected void setCellEditor(TreeCellEditor editor)
Sets the cellEditor.

protected void setCellRenderer(TreeCellRenderer tcr)
Sets the TreeCellRenderer.

protected void setEditable(boolean newValue)
Enables or disables editing in the tree.

protected void setHashColor(java.awt.Color color)
Sets the color for the connecting lines in the tree.

protected void setLargeModel(boolean largeModel)
Updates the componentListener, if necessary, and changes the treeState to a FixedHeight-LayoutCache.
Overrides: setLargeModel in class AbstractTreeUI.

protected void setRootVisible(boolean newValue)
Shows or hides the root node.

protected void setRowHeight(int rowHeight)
Sets the row height in the treeState.

protected void setSelectionModel(TreeSelectionModel newLSM)
Stops editing, calls super, and adds a listener to the new model.

protected void setShowsRootHandles(boolean newValue)
Shows or hides the handles of root level nodes.

protected boolean shouldPaintExpandControl(TreePath path, int row, boolean isExpanded, boolean hasBeenExpanded, boolean isLeaf)
Returns true if the expand (toggle) control should be drawn for the specified row.

protected boolean startEditing(TreePath path, java.awt.event.MouseEvent event)
Will start editing for node if there is a cellEditor and shouldSelectCell returns true. This assumes that path is valid and visible.

protected void toggleExpandState(TreePath path)
Toggles the expansion state of the node at the end of the given path.

protected void uninstallComponents()
Uninstalls the renderer pane.

protected void uninstallDefaults()
Uninstalls the resources installed by installDefaults.

protected void uninstallKeyboardActions()
Uninstalls the keyboard actions installed by installKeyboardActions.

protected void uninstallListeners()
Uninstalls the listeners added by installListeners.

protected void updateCachedPreferredSize()
Updates the preferredSize instance variable. The size is determined by the current Abstract-LayoutCache.

protected void updateCellEditor()
Updates the cellEditor based on the editability of the associated. If the tree is editable but doesn't have a cellEditor, a default one will be used.

protected void updateDepthOffset()
Updates how much each level of the tree should be offset.

protected void updateExpandedDescendants(TreePath path)

Updates the expanded state of all the descendants of `path` by getting the expanded descendants from the tree and forwarding them to the `treeState`.

protected void updateLayoutCacheExpandedNodes()

Makes all the nodes that are expanded in JTree expanded in `treeState`. This invokes `update-ExpandedDescendants()` with the root path.

protected void updateRenderer()

Called by the associated `JTree` when the renderer has changed.

protected void updateSize()

Marks the cached size as being invalid, and messages the tree with `treeDidChange`.

Inner Classes

public class BasicTreeUI.TreeExpansionHandler
public class BasicTreeUI.ComponentHandler
public class BasicTreeUI.TreeModelHandler
public class BasicTreeUI.TreeSelectionHandler
public class BasicTreeUI.CellEditorHandler
public class BasicTreeUI.KeyHandler
public class BasicTreeUI.FocusHandler
public class BasicTreeUI.NodeDimensionsHandler
public class BasicTreeUI.MouseHandler
public class BasicTreeUI.PropertyChangeHandler
public class BasicTreeUI.SelectionModelPropertyChangeHandler
public class BasicTreeUI.TreeTraverseAction
public class BasicTreeUI.TreePageAction
public class BasicTreeUI.TreeIncrementAction
public class BasicTreeUI.TreeHomeAction
public class BasicTreeUI.TreeToggleAction
public class BasicTreeUI.TreeCancelEditingAction
public class BasicTreeUI.MouseInputHandler

See also   AbstractLayoutCache (p.958), CellEditorListener (p.486), CellRendererPane (p.151), ComponentUI (p.530), Icon (p.183), JTree (p.393), TreeCellEditor (p.985), TreeCellRenderer (p.985), TreeExpansionListener (p.511), TreeModel (p.987), TreeModelListener (p.513), TreePath (p.989), TreeSelectionListener (p.514), TreeSelectionModel (p.990).

swing.plaf.basic.BasicTreeUI.CellEditorHandler

INNER CLASS

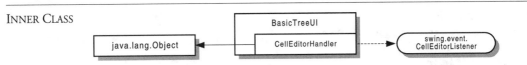

public class BasicTreeUI.CellEditorHandler extends java.lang.Object implements CellEditorListener

Constructors
public CellEditorHandler()
    Default constructor.

Methods
public void editingCanceled(ChangeEvent e)
    Implements: editingCanceled in interface CellEditorListener.
public void editingStopped(ChangeEvent e)
    Implements: editingStopped in interface CellEditorListener.

    See also   ChangeEvent (p.487), ChangeListener (p.488).

swing.plaf.basic.BasicTreeUI.ComponentHandler

INNER CLASS

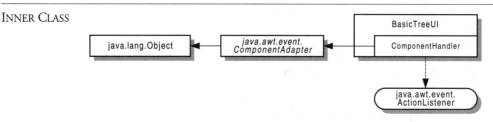

This inner class updates the preferred size to adapt for changes in the size of the parent component.

public class BasicTreeUI.ComponentHandler extends ComponentAdapter
    implements ActionListener

Constructors
public ComponentHandler()
    Default constructor.

Methods
public void actionPerformed(java.awt.event.ActionEvent ae)
    Public as a result of Timer. If the scrollBar is null, or not adjusting, this stops the timer and updates the sizing.
    Implements: actionPerformed in interface ActionListener.
public void componentMoved(java.awt.event.ComponentEvent e)
    Overrides: componentMoved in class ComponentAdapter.
    Implements: componentMoved in interface ComponentListener.

Protected Fields
protected JScrollBar scrollBar
    The scroll bar that is being adjusted.
protected Timer timer
    The timer used when inside a scrollpane and the scroll bar is adjusting.

Protected Methods
protected JScrollPane getScrollPane()
    Returns the JScrollPane housing the JTree, or null if one isn't found.

protected void startTimer()

Creates, if necessary, and starts a Timer to check if the bounds need to be resized.

See also   JScrollBar (p.328), JScrollPane (p.332), Timer (p.447).

swing.plaf.basic.BasicTreeUI.FocusHandler

INNER CLASS

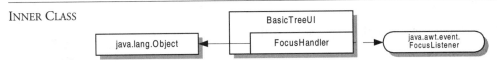

Repaints the lead selection row when focus is lost or gained.

**public class BasicTreeUI.FocusHandler extends java.lang.Object
    implements java.awt.event.FocusListener**

Constructors
public FocusHandler()

Default constructor.

Methods
public void focusGained(java.awt.event.FocusEvent e)

Redraws the lead row with the focus indicator.

Implements: focusGained in interface FocusListener.

public void focusLost(java.awt.FocusEvent e)

Redraws the lead row without the focus indicator.

Implements: focusLost in interface FocusListener.

swing.plaf.basic.BasicTreeUI.KeyHandler

INNER CLASS

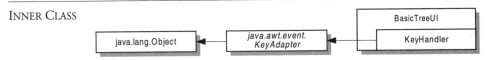

This inner class manages keyboard navigation in the tree.

public class BasicTreeUI.KeyHandler extends java.awt.event.KeyAdapter

Constructors
public KeyHandler()

Default constructor.

Methods
public void keyPressed(java.awt.event.KeyEvent e)

Overrides: keyPressed in class KeyAdapter.

Implements: keyPressed in interface KeyListener.

public void keyReleased(java.awt.event.KeyEvent e)

Overrides: keyReleased in class KeyAdapter.

Implements: keyReleased in interface KeyListener.

Protected Fields

protected boolean isKeyDown
Set to true while keyPressed is active.

protected Action repeatKeyAction
The key code that is being generated.

See also Action (p.128).

swing.plaf.basic.BasicTreeUI.MouseHandler

INNER CLASS

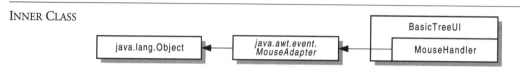

This inner class is responsible for updating the selection in the tree based on mouse events.

```
public class BasicTreeUI.MouseHandler
    extends java.awt.event.MouseAdapter
```

Constructors

public MouseHandler()
Default constructor.

Methods

public void mousePressed(java.awt.event.MouseEvent e)
Invoked when a mouse button has been pressed on a component.
Overrides: mousePressed in class MouseAdapter.
Implements: mousePressed in interface MouseListener.

swing.plaf.basic.BasicTreeUI.MouseInputHandler

INNER CLASS

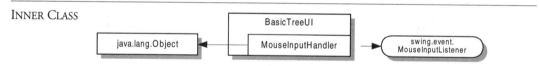

This inner class forwards mouseClicked and mouseReleased events that occur in the given source component to the destination component. All mouse events except for mouseClicked stop further redirection when they occur.

```
public class BasicTreeUI.MouseInputHandler extends java.lang.Object
    implements MouseInputListener
```

Constructors

public MouseInputHandler(java.awt.Component source,
java.awt.Component destination, java.awt.event.MouseEvent event)
Begins forwarding mouseClicked and mouseReleased events (including the given event) from source to destination.

Methods
public void mouseClicked(java.awt.event.MouseEvent e)
Forwards the event to the destination given in the constructor.
Implements: mouseClicked in interface MouseInputListener.

public void mouseDragged(java.awt.event.MouseEvent e)
Stops forwarding events.
Implements: mouseDragged in interface MouseInputListener.

public void mouseEntered(java.awt.event.MouseEvent e)
Stops forwarding events.
Implements: mouseEntered in interface MouseInputListener.

public void mouseExited(java.awt.event.MouseEvent e)
Stops forwarding events.
Implements: mouseExited in interface MouseInputListener.

public void mouseMoved(java.awt.event.MouseEvent e)
Stops forwarding events.
Implements: mouseMoved in interface MouseInputListener.

public void mousePressed(java.awt.event.MouseEvent e)
An empty method.
Implements: mousePressed in interface MouseInputListener.

public void mouseReleased(java.awt.event.MouseEvent e)
Forwards the event to the destination given in the constructor, then stops forwarding events.
Implements: mouseReleased in interface MouseInputListener.

Protected Fields
protected java.awt.Component destination
The destination that receives all events.
protected java.awt.Component source
The source that events are coming from.

Protected Methods
protected void removeFromSource()
Stops the forwarding of events by removing this class from the listener list of the source.

See also   MouseInputListener (p.505).

swing.plaf.basic.BasicTreeUI.NodeDimensionsHandler

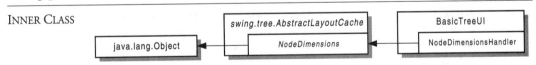

This inner class handles returning the size and position for a given node in the tree.

```
public class BasicTreeUI.NodeDimensionsHandler
    extends AbstractLayoutCache.NodeDimensions
```

plaf.basic

Constructors

`public NodeDimensionsHandler()`

 Default constructor.

Methods

`public java.awt.Rectangle getNodeDimensions(Object value, int row,`
 `int depth, boolean expanded, java.awt.Rectangle size)`

 This method behaves in one of two ways. The first way is when the row in question is being edited. If that is the case, this method simply asks the editor for its preferred size and then offsets its origin by the amount returned from getRowX(). The second way is when the row is just rendering. In this case, this method adds the renderer to the cell renderer pane and then validates it. It then reads the size values from the validated component. Again, the origin of the rectangle is then offset by the amount returned from getRowX().

 Overrides: getNodeDimensions in class AbstractLayoutCache.NodeDimensions.

Protected Methods

`protected int getRowX(int row, int depth)`

 Returns the amount to indent the given row.

 See also AbstractLayoutCache.NodeDimensions (p.961).

swing.plaf.basic.BasicTreeUI.PropertyChangeHandler

INNER CLASS

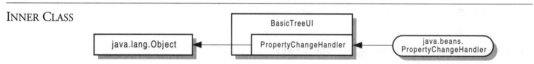

This inner class handles property changes in the associated JTree.

`public class BasicTreeUI.PropertyChangeHandler`
 `extends java.lang.Object`
 `implements java.beans.PropertyChangeListener`

Constructors

`public PropertyChangeHandler()`

 Default constructor.

Methods

`public void propertyChange(java.beans.PropertyChangeEvent event)`

 Updates the property in BasicTreeUI that matches the property that changed in JTree.
 Implements: propertyChange in interface PropertyChangeListener.

 See also JTree (p.393).

swing.plaf.basic.BasicTreeUI.SelectionModelPropertyChangeHandler

INNER CLASS

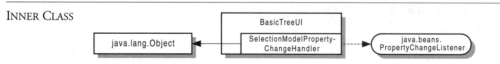

plaf.basic

This inner class handles changes in the `TreeSelectionModel`. If the selection changes, the UI is updated to reflect the change.

```
public class BasicTreeUI.SelectionModelPropertyChangeHandler
    extends java.lang.Object
    implements java.beans.PropertyChangeListener
```

Constructors
`public SelectionModelPropertyChangeHandler()`
Default constructor.

Methods
`public void propertyChange(java.beans.PropertyChangeEvent event)`
Implements: propertyChange in interface PropertyChangeListener.

See also   TreeSelectionModel (p.990).

swing.plaf.basic.BasicTreeUI.TreeCancelEditingAction

INNER CLASS

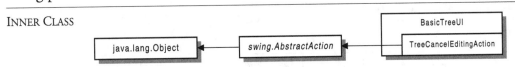

This inner class invokes `cancelEditing` when its `actionPerformed()` method is called.

```
public class BasicTreeUI.TreeCancelEditingAction
    extends AbstractAction
```

Constructors
`public TreeCancelEditingAction(String name)`
Creates a TreeCancelEditingAction which uses the given name for the Action.NAME property.

Methods
`public void actionPerformed(java.awt.event.ActionEvent e)`
Calls cancelEditing() in the associated JTree.
`public boolean isEnabled()`
Overrides: isEnabled in class AbstractAction.
Implements: isEnabled in interface Action.

See also   AbstractAction (p.115).

swing.plaf.basic.BasicTreeUI.TreeExpansionHandler

INNER CLASS

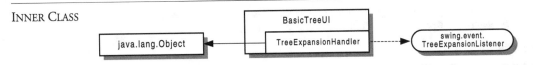

This inner class handles updating the UI as the tree's expansion state changes.

```
public class BasicTreeUI.TreeExpansionHandler
    extends java.lang.Object
    implements TreeExpansionListener
```

Constructors

public TreeExpansionHandler()
> Default constructor.

Methods

public void treeCollapsed(TreeExpansionEvent event)
> Called whenever an item in the tree has been collapsed.
> *Implements:* treeCollapsed in interface TreeExpansionListener.

public void treeExpanded(TreeExpansionEvent event)
> Called whenever an item in the tree has been expanded.
> *Implements:* treeExpanded in interface TreeExpansionListener.

> *See also*   TreeExpansionEvent (p.511), TreeExpansionListener (p.511).

swing.plaf.basic.BasicTreeUI.TreeHomeAction

INNER CLASS

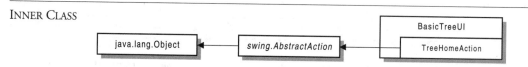

This inner class handles VK_END or VK_HOME KeyStrokes. It scrolls the tree to display either the first tree row or last tree row as appropriate. If the SHIFT or CONTROL keys are held down when the KeyStroke is triggered, this class will extend or change the selection as appropriate. The selection-changing variants are created through a private constructor so they cannot be created outside of BasicTreeUI.

public class BasicTreeUI.TreeHomeAction extends AbstractAction

Constructors

public TreeHomeAction(int direction, String name)
> Creates a TreeHomeAction with the given name. If direction is –1, it will scroll to the first row. If direction is 1, it will scroll to the last row.

Methods

public void actionPerformed(java.awt.event.ActionEvent e)
> Scrolls the tree in the appropriate direction, and extends or changes the selection if configured to do so.

public boolean isEnabled()
> *Overrides:* isEnabled in class AbstractAction.
> *Implements:* isEnabled in interface Action.

Protected Fields

protected int direction
> Holds –1 to scroll to the first row, 1 to scroll to the last row.

> *See also*   AbstractAction (p.115).

swing.plaf.basic.BasicTreeUI.TreeIncrementAction

INNER CLASS

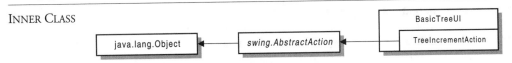

This inner class scrolls the tree one cell in the given direction when the VK_UP or VK_DOWN keys are pressed. BasicTreeUI configures this class to change the selection using a private constructor.

public class BasicTreeUI.TreeIncrementAction extends AbstractAction

Constructors
public TreeIncrementAction(int direction, String name)

Creates a TreeIncrementAction with the given name. Use 1 to indicate scrolling the tree up (the row with the next higher index than the bottommost one showing is scrolled so it is visible). Use −1 to indicate scrolling the tree down.

Methods
public void actionPerformed(java.awt.event.ActionEvent e)

Scroll the tree up or down as appropriate.

public boolean isEnabled()

Overrides: isEnabled in class AbstractAction.

Implements: isEnabled in interface Action.

Protected Fields
protected int direction

Holds the direction to scroll.

See also AbstractAction (p.115).

swing.plaf.basic.BasicTreeUI.TreeModelHandler

INNER CLASS

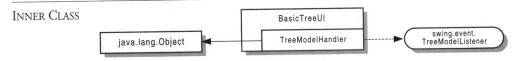

Updates the TreeState (layout cache) based on changes in the model.

public class BasicTreeUI.TreeModelHandler extends java.lang.Object implements TreeModelListener

Constructors
public TreeModelHandler()

Default constructor.

Methods
public void treeNodesChanged(TreeModelEvent e)

Implements: treeNodesChanged in interface TreeModelListener.

public void treeNodesInserted(TreeModelEvent e)
    Implements: treeNodesInserted in interface TreeModelListener.
public void treeNodesRemoved(TreeModelEvent e)
    Implements: treeNodesRemoved in interface TreeModelListener.
public void treeStructureChanged(TreeModelEvent e)
    Implements: treeStructureChanged in interface TreeModelListener.

    See also   TreeModelEvent (p.511), TreeModelListener (p.513).

swing.plaf.basic.BasicTreeUI.TreePageAction

INNER CLASS

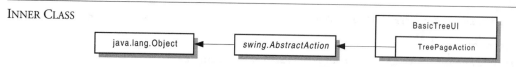

This inner class handles VK_PAGE_UP and VK_PAGE_DOWN KeyStrokes in much the same way as TreeHomeAction handles VK_HOME and VK_END. The only difference is this inner class increments by blocks the size of the visible region of the tree.

public class BasicTreeUI.TreePageAction extends AbstractAction

Constructors
public TreePageAction(int direction, String name)

Methods
public void actionPerformed(java.awt.event.ActionEvent e)
public boolean isEnabled()
    Overrides: isEnabled in class AbstractAction.
    Implements: isEnabled in interface Action.

Protected Fields
protected int direction

    See also   AbstractAction (p.115).

swing.plaf.basic.BasicTreeUI.TreeSelectionHandler

INNER CLASS

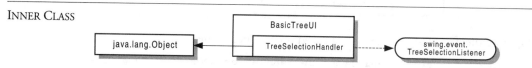

This inner class updates the UI based on changes in the tree's selection model.

public class BasicTreeUI.TreeSelectionHandler
    extends java.lang.Object
    implements TreeSelectionListener

Constructors
public TreeSelectionHandler()
    Default constructor.

Methods

`public void valueChanged(TreeSelectionEvent event)`

Called when the selection changes in the associated JTree. This method stops any editing, and updates the UI with the new selection.

Implements: valueChanged in interface TreeSelectionListener.

See also   TreeSelectionEvent (p.513), TreeSelectionListener (p.514).

swing.plaf.basic.BasicTreeUI.TreeToggleAction

INNER CLASS

This inner class toggles the expansion state of the lead selection row when the ENTER key is pressed.

`public class BasicTreeUI.TreeToggleAction extends AbstractAction`

Constructors

`public TreeToggleAction(String name)`

Constructs a TreeToggleAction with the given name.

Methods

`public void actionPerformed(java.awt.event.ActionEvent e)`

Toggles the lead selection row.

`public boolean isEnabled()`

Overrides: isEnabled in class AbstractAction.

Implements: isEnabled in interface Action.

See also   AbstractAction (p.115).

swing.plaf.basic.BasicTreeUI.TreeTraverseAction

INNER CLASS

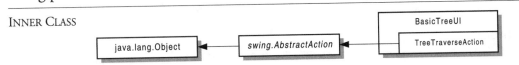

This inner class handles expanding nodes in the tree when the VK_LEFT and VK_RIGHT keys are pressed. As appropriate, this class will expand the current row and it will change the selection as needed.

`public class BasicTreeUI.TreeTraverseAction extends AbstractAction`

Constructors

`public TreeTraverseAction(int direction, String name)`

Creates a TreeTraverseAction with the given name for the given direction.

plaf.basic

Methods

`public void actionPerformed(ActionEvent e)`
> Expands or contracts the node as necessary.

`public boolean isEnabled()`
> *Overrides:* `isEnabled` in class `AbstractAction`.
> *Implements:* `isEnabled` in interface `Action`.

Protected Fields

`protected int direction`
> Holds the direction to traverse, where 1 means expand, −1 means collapse.

See also   AbstractAction (p.115).

swing.plaf.basic.BasicViewportUI

CLASS

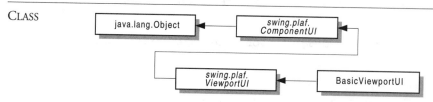

UIDefaults table key	Description
`Viewport.background`	The background `Color` for the viewport.
`Viewport.font`	The `font` used by default by children of the viewport.
`Viewport.foreground`	The foreground `Color` for the viewport.

`public class BasicViewportUI extends ViewportUI`

Constructors

`public BasicViewportUI()`
> Default constructor.

Methods

`public static ComponentUI createUI(JComponent c)`
> *Overrides:* `createUI` in class `ComponentUI`.

`public void installUI(JComponent c)`
> *Overrides:* `installUI` in class `ComponentUI`.

`public void uninstallUI(JComponent c)`
> *Overrides:* `uninstallUI` in class `ComponentUI`.

Protected Methods

`protected void installDefaults(JComponent c)`
> Installs the viewport background, foreground, and font.

`protected void uninstallDefaults(JComponent c)`

See also   ComponentUI (p.530), JComponent (p.207), ViewportUI (p.546).

swing.plaf.basic.ComboPopup

INTERFACE   (ComboPopup)

This interface defines the contract that has to be supported by the pop-up in `BasicComboBoxUI`. The only real limitation this interface places on an implementor is that it subclasses `JList` (or at least provides an adapter subclass of `JList` that will let it masquerade as a `JList`).

```
public interface ComboPopup
```

Methods

`public abstract java.awt.event.KeyListener getKeyListener()`
Returns a key listener that shows and hides the pop-up.

`public abstract JList getList()`
Returns the list that is being used to draw the items in the `JComboBox`.

`public abstract java.awt.event.MouseListener getMouseListener()`
Returns a mouse listener that shows and hides the pop-up.

`public abstract java.awt.event.MouseMotionListener getMouseMotionListener()`
Returns a mouse motion listener that makes the pop-up act like a menu.

`public abstract void hide()`
Hides the pop-up.

`public abstract boolean isVisible()`
Returns whether or not the pop-up is visible.

`public abstract void show()`
Shows the pop-up.

`public abstract void uninstallingUI()`
Called to inform the `ComboPopup` that the UI is uninstalling. If the `ComboPopup` added any listeners in the component, it should remove them here.

Returned by BasicComboBoxUI.createPopup() (p.565).
Implemented by BasicComboPopup (p.572).
See also JList (p.271).

swing.plaf.basic.DefaultMenuLayout

CLASS

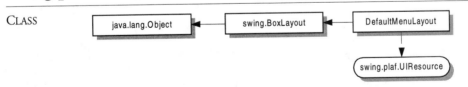

This class is the default layout used for menus and pop-up menus. It is a simple subclass of `BoxLayout` that implements `UIResource` so it can be used safely by a look and feel.

```
public class DefaultMenuLayout extends BoxLayout
    implements UIResource
```

plaf.basic

Constructors

public DefaultMenuLayout(java.awt.Container target, int axis)
Default constructor.

See also   BoxLayout (p.144), UIResource (p.544).

plaf.basic

Package swing.table

Swing's JTable is extremely powerful but it remains very easy to use. This package contains the classes that give JTable both its power and its ease of use.

It is important to remember that JTable is not designed to be a spreadsheet. It is designed to present tables of data where the columns contain data *all of the same type* (or related by a common superclass). So, a column may contain only all Strings, or all Booleans, or all instances of a custom class. An example of this would be a table which lists information about students: column 1 is always the last name String, column 2 is the first name String, column 3 is a Boolean indicating whether they are currently attending, and so forth. The closest you can come to mixing data types in a single column of a JTable is having the types all be related by a common superclass. The default behavior for a JTable is to use java.lang.Object as the common superclass, and render the data by using the toString() method in Object.

JTables can have custom TableCellRenderers (p.760) and TableCellEditors (p.758) assigned to the whole table, or on a column-by-column basis. A TableCellRenderer is an object that understands how to display a particular kind of data. Similarly, a TableCellEditor understands how to edit a particular kind of data. If a cell renderer or editor is assigned to the whole table, it is assigned using a method that also takes a parameter of type Class that indicates what kind of data the renderer or editor understands. The JTable later uses the getColumnClass() method of TableModel to choose the appropriate renderer or editor for the given column.

Table extends/implements hierarchy

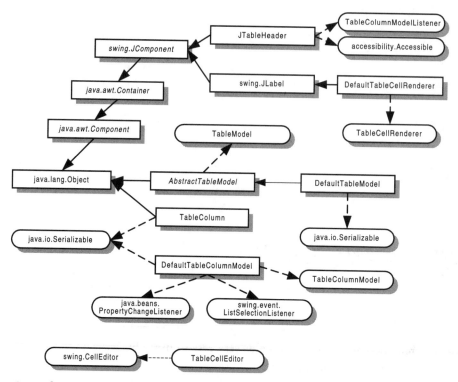

Quick summary

The model	`TableModel` (p.766) models the data. `TableColumnModel` (built from a series of `TableColumns`) models the columns (p.764).
The view	`JTable` (p.357). `JTableHeader` (p.752) manages and displays the column headers.
How to use	Provide a `TableModel` implementation, either by subclassing `AbstractTableModel` (p.735) or by using `DefaultTableModel` (p.747). You can subclass or use `DefaultTableColumnModel` (p.744) to provide a model for the columns (or let `JTable` build its own column model from the data).
Display and edit	The `TableCellRenderer` (p.760) interface defines how the table's cells are displayed. The `TableCellEditor` (p.758) interface defines how the cells are edited. Implement these interfaces (or use a `DefaultTableCellRenderer`) and install them on a `JTable` or a `TableColumn` to change rendering or editing.
Events	A `TableModelEvent` (p.508) describes changes in the table data. Its listener is `TableModelListener` (p.513). A `TableColumnModelEvent` (p.507) describes a change in the order or size of the columns. Its listener is `TableColumnModelListener` (p.508).

FAQs

How do I put my information in a table?

Either subclass `AbstractTableModel` and implement the required three methods, or use a `DefaultTableModel` (which has a built-in `Vector`). The three methods required by `Abstract-TableModel` are very simple to implement so subclassing it is the preferred method. Using `DefaultTableModel` requires copying your data from its native form into the `DefaultTable-Model`, so it is tremendously less efficient than `AbstractTableModel`.

How do I get different colored cells?

The look and feel is usually responsible for providing the appearance of the cells. You can install a `TableCellRenderer` that uses the row and column position to decide what color the cell should be.

How do I load cells on demand?

Subclass `AbstractTableModel`, and have your implementation of `getValueAt()` check whether the cell (or row) is loaded: if so, return it; if not, load it first and then return the value. A hash table using the row and column as a key can be used to store the loaded cells, or a sparse-matrix implementation may be used. Given the tabular (as opposed to spreadsheet) nature of a `JTable`, a reasonable solution would involve loading a full row of data at a time since the data on a row is usually all related.

How do I get a sorted table?

You can provide a sorting table model as a wrapper around a base table model. When the base table changes, the sorted table will re-sort. Operations involving the row will be translated according to the sorted order. See `AbstractTableModel` for an example.

swing.table.AbstractTableModel

CLASS

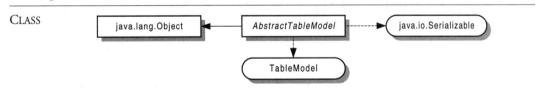

The `AbstractTableModel` provides a default implementation of the `TableModel` interface that should be used as the basis for almost all table models you implement. It supplies methods for managing the lists of listeners and simple (or empty) implementations of the other methods in the `TableModel` interface.

A minimal read-only table must implement `getColumnCount()`, `getRowCount()`, and `getValueAt()`. If you want to modify values, you will override `isCellEditable()` to support in-place editing in the table and `setValueAt()`. For most realistic applications you will want to override `getColumnClass()` and `getColumnName()`. `getColumnClass()` is used to identify the correct renderer and/or editor for the column. The implementation of `getColumnClass()` supplied by this class always returns `Object.class`. This causes the `JTable` to use the default `Object.class` renderer, which calls `toString()` on the value in the cell and displays the returned text. `getColumnName()` supplies the labels to be displayed in the `JTable`'s table header.

Example: Minimal work

```
// File atm\Example1.java
package atm;

import java.awt.*;
import java.awt.event.*;
import com.sun.java.swing.*;
import com.sun.java.swing.table.*;

public class Example1 extends JFrame {
    // Table of primes < 20 as the x coordinate, 2*x+1 as the y coordinate.
    public class CoordinateTableModel extends AbstractTableModel {
        private int[] x = {2, 3, 5, 7, 11, 13, 17, 19};   // x is prime < 20
        public int getColumnCount() {return 2;}     // Two columns, x and y
        public int getRowCount() {return x.length;}
        public Object getValueAt(int r, int c) {
            return (c == 0) ? new Integer(x[r]) : new Integer(2 * x[r] + 1);
        }
        public String getColumnName(int c) {return (c == 0) ? "x" : "2x+1";}
    }

    public Example1() {
        JTable table = new JTable(new CoordinateTableModel());
        getContentPane().add(new JScrollPane(table), BorderLayout.CENTER);
        pack();
    }

    public static void main (String arg[]) {
        Example1 ex1 = new Example1();
        ex1.setDefaultCloseOperation(JFrame.DISPOSE_ON_CLOSE);
        ex1.addWindowListener(new WindowAdapter() {
            public void windowClosed(WindowEvent e) {
                System.exit(0);
            }
        });
        ex1.setVisible(true);
    }
}
```

Example: Firing notifications

Suppose you want to change the contents of the table. If you just change values without telling anyone, views like `JTable`s won't be aware that a change has occurred, so they won't update. To prevent this problem, call the appropriate `fireTableXxx()` methods after your change. This simple example shows the update for `setValueAt()`.

```java
// File atm/Example2.java
package atm;

import java.awt.*;
import java.awt.event.*;
import com.sun.java.swing.*;
import com.sun.java.swing.table.*;

public class Example2 extends JFrame {
   private class Matrix3x3 extends AbstractTableModel {
      private int[][] table = {new int[3], new int[3], new int[3]};

      public Matrix3x3() {
         for (int i = 0; i < 3; i++) {
            for (int j = 0; j < 3; j++) {
               table[i][j] = i * j;
            }
         }
      }
      public int getColumnCount() {return table.length;}
      public int getRowCount() {return table[0].length;}
      public Object getValueAt(int r, int c) {
         return new Integer(table[r][c]);
      }
      public void setValueAt(Object obj, int r, int c) {
         table[r][c] = ((Integer)obj).intValue();
         // Inform the Views/listeners that the Model has changed
         // Since JTable is a listener of its model, this will cause the
         // JTable to update.
         fireTableCellUpdated(r,c);
      }

   }

   public Example2() {
      // declaring these final allows them to be accessed from the inner class
      final AbstractTableModel model = new Matrix3x3();
      final JTable table = new JTable(model);
      getContentPane().add(new JScrollPane(table), BorderLayout.CENTER);
      model.setValueAt(new Integer(1), 0, 0);

      NoFocusButton button = new NoFocusButton("Increment selected cell");
      getContentPane().add(button, BorderLayout.SOUTH);
      button.addActionListener (new ActionListener() {
         public void actionPerformed(ActionEvent e) {
            int row = table.getSelectedRow();
            // since Columns can be reordered by dragging the table headers
            // in the JTable without affecting the column ordering in the
            // model, we have to convert from the JTable ordering to
            // the model's.
            int column = table.convertColumnIndexToModel(
                        table.getSelectedColumn());
            int currentValue = ((Integer)model.getValueAt(
                          row,column)).intValue();
            model.setValueAt(new Integer(currentValue + 1), row, column);
         }
      });
```

```
        pack();
      }
   class NoFocusButton extends JButton {
      public NoFocusButton(String s) {
         super(s);
      }
      public boolean isRequestFocusEnabled()
      {
         return false;
      }
      public boolean isFocusTraversable() {
         return false;
      }
   }
   public static void main (String arg[]) {
      Example2 ex2 = new Example2();
      ex2.setDefaultCloseOperation(JFrame.DISPOSE_ON_CLOSE);
      ex2.addWindowListener(new WindowAdapter() {
         public void windowClosed(WindowEvent e) {
            System.exit(0);
         }
      });
      ex2.setVisible(true);
   }
}
```

Example: Sorting table

This example shows how a sorting table can act as a wrapper for a regular table. (See the Decorator pattern in the book *Design Patterns* by Gamma, et al.) This is a naive implementation: it uses a simple insertion sort, it always re-sorts on all table changes (even those that wouldn't affect the whole table), and it provides no mechanism for changing the sorting column.

```
// SortingTableModel.java
import java.awt.*;
import java.awt.event.*;
import com.sun.java.swing.*;
import com.sun.java.swing.event.*;
import com.sun.java.swing.table.*;
class SampleSortingTableModel extends AbstractTableModel
   implements TableModelListener
{
   protected TableModel base;
   protected int sortColumn;
   protected int[] row;
   public SampleSortingTableModel (TableModel tm, int sortColumn) {
      this.base = tm;
      this.sortColumn = sortColumn;
      tm.addTableModelListener(this);
      rebuild();
   }

   // These methods can be directly delegated to 'base'.
```

```
   public Class getColumnClass(int c) {return base.getColumnClass(c);}
   public int getColumnCount() {return base.getColumnCount();}
   public String getColumnName(int c) {return base.getColumnName(c);}
   public int getRowCount() {return base.getRowCount();}

   // These operations can be delegated to 'base' after row translation
   public Object getValueAt(int r, int c) {
      return base.getValueAt(row[r], c);
   }
   public boolean isCellEditable(int r, int c) {
      return base.isCellEditable(row[r], c);
   }
   public void setValueAt(Object value, int r, int c) {
      base.setValueAt(value, row[r], c);  // Notification will cause re-sort
   }

   // Notifications from base. Naive: always re-sorts & notifies
   public void tableChanged(TableModelEvent event) {
      rebuild();
   }

   // Utility methods
   protected void rebuild() {
      int size = base.getRowCount();
      row = new int[size];
      for (int i = 0; i < size; i++) {row[i] = i;}
      sort();
   }
   protected void sort() {     // Sort and notify listeners
      // Simple insertion sort, from Jon Bentley's "Programming Pearls",
      // p.108
      for (int i = 1; i < row.length; i++) {
         // Invariant: row[0] to row[i-1] sorted
         int j = i;
         while (j > 0 && compare(j-1, j) > 0) {
            int temp = row[j];
            row[j] = row[j-1];
            row[j-1] = temp;
            j--;
         }
      }
      fireTableStructureChanged();     // notify _our_ listeners
   }
   // Return <0 if row[i] < row[j], 0 if equal, >0 if row[i] > row[j]
   protected int compare(int i, int j) {
      String s1 = base.getValueAt(row[i], sortColumn).toString();
      String s2 = base.getValueAt(row[j], sortColumn).toString();
      return s1.compareTo(s2);
   }
}
public class SortingTableModel extends JFrame {
   DefaultTableModel model = new DefaultTableModel(
      new Object[][] { {"this", "1"}, {"text", "2"},
                       {"will", "3"}, {"be", "4"},
                       {"sorted", "5"} },
```

```
                        new Object[] {"Column 1", "Column 2"}
      );
   public SortingTableModel() {
      setDefaultCloseOperation(DISPOSE_ON_CLOSE);
      addWindowListener(new WindowAdapter() {
         public void windowClosed(WindowEvent e) {
            System.exit(0);
         }
      });
      getContentPane().add(new JLabel(
         "Original and Sorted on Column 1 Tables: edit a cell"),
         BorderLayout.NORTH);
      JTable tableOrig = new JTable(model);
      tableOrig.setAutoResizeMode(JTable.AUTO_RESIZE_ALL_COLUMNS);
      JTable tableSorted = new JTable(new SampleSortingTableModel(model,0));
      tableSorted.setAutoResizeMode(JTable.AUTO_RESIZE_ALL_COLUMNS);
      JPanel panel = new JPanel(new GridLayout(1,2));
      panel.add(new JScrollPane(tableOrig));
      panel.add(new JScrollPane(tableSorted));
      getContentPane().add(panel, BorderLayout.CENTER);
      pack();
   }
   public static void main (String arg[]) {
      new SortingTableModel().setVisible(true);
   }
}
```

public class AbstractTableModel extends java.lang.Object implements TableModel, java.io.Serializable

Constructors
public AbstractTableModel()
Creates an instance of this model.

Methods
public void addTableModelListener(TableModelListener listener)
Adds listener to the list of objects to be notified when the table changes.
Implements: addTableModelListener in interface TableModel.

public int findColumn(String columnName)
Returns the index of the (first) column whose name is equal to columnName, or –1 if there is no such column. This is the only public method of AbstractTableModel which is not in the TableModel interface.

protected void fireTableCellUpdated(int row, int column)
Creates a TableModelEvent, and uses it to notify listeners that the specified cell has changed.

protected void fireTableChanged(TableModelEvent event)
Uses event to notify listeners that the table has changed. See TableModelEvent for the full range of event possibilities.

protected void fireTableDataChanged()
Creates a TableModelEvent, and uses it to notify listeners that all data in the table may have changed, including the number of rows, but the table structure has not changed.

protected void `fireTableRowsDeleted(int row1, int row2)`

Creates a `TableModelEvent`, and uses it to notify listeners that the data from `row1` to `row2` inclusive has been deleted.

protected void `fireTableRowsInserted(int row1, int row2)`

Creates a `TableModelEvent`, and uses it to notify listeners that rows were inserted from `row1` to `row2` inclusive.

protected void `fireTableRowsUpdated(int row1, int row2)`

Creates a `TableModelEvent`, and uses it to notify listeners that the data (in all columns) from `row1` to `row2` (inclusive) may have changed.

protected void `fireTableStructureChanged()`

Creates a `TableModelEvent`, and uses it to notify listeners that the table structure and all data in it have changed. See `JTable`. A `JTable` regards this change as drastic; if its `autoCreateColumns-FromModel` flag is `true`, the column model will be rebuilt.

public Class `getColumnClass(int column)`

Gets the class for `column`. By providing this information, you help cause the most appropriate renderer to be used. (For example, an entry of type `Boolean` could be displayed as a checkbox, rather than the string `true` or `false`.) You should return the class that is common to all entries in the column. For example, if you have both Integer and Boolean items in the column, you would need to return `Object.class` (their only common superclass).

Implements: `getColumnClass` in interface `TableModel`.

public String `getColumnName(int column)`

Returns the name of the specified `column`. Two columns may have the same name. This usually has no impact because `JTable` works with column indexes rather than column names. This method supports the `TableModel` interface. (If you don't override this method, you get a series of labels A, B, C, ..., AA, ..., ZZ, etc.)

public boolean `isCellEditable(int row, int column)`

Returns `true` if the cell may be edited. If you don't override this method, it always returns `false`.

Implements: `isCellEditable` in interface `TableModel`.

public void `removeTableModelListener(TableModelListener listener)`

Removes `listener` from the list of objects notified when the table changes.

Implements: `removeTableModelListener` in interface `TableModel`.

public void `setValueAt(Object object, int row, int column)`

Stores `object` at the specified cell in the table. You should store a value only if `isCellEditable(row, column)` returns `true`. If you don't override this method, it does not store any values.

Implements: `setValueAt` in interface `TableModel`.

Protected Fields

protected EventListenerList `listenerList`

The list of listeners to be notified of changes in the table. See the `fireTableXxx()` methods.

Extended by   DefaultTableModel (p.747).
See also   EventListenerList (p.491), JTable (p.357), TableModel (p.766),
TableModelEvent (p.508), TableModelListener (p.510).

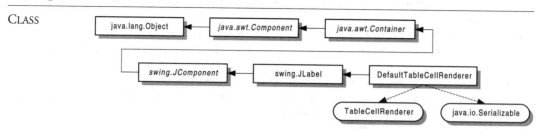

swing.table.DefaultTableCellRenderer

CLASS

This is the renderer used to display table cells when none is specified. It can also be used as a basis for custom renderer subclasses.

To support the `TableCellRenderer` interface this class must return a `Component` to render a cell. Since this class extends `JLabel`, it can return itself.

Example: a `DefaultTableCellRenderer` subclass that colors cells depending on their state and location.

```
package tablecr;

// Main.java - TableCellRenderer Example
import java.awt.*;
import java.awt.event.*;
import com.sun.java.swing.*;
import com.sun.java.swing.table.*;
public class Main extends JFrame {
   DefaultTableModel tmodel = new DefaultTableModel(
      new Object[][] {
         {"some", "text"}, {"any", "text"},
         {"even", "more"}, {"text", "strings"},
         {"and", "other"}, {"text", "values"}
      },
      new Object[] {"Column 1", "Column 2"}
   );

   class MyRenderer implements TableCellRenderer {
      public Component getTableCellRendererComponent(
         JTable table, Object value,
         boolean isSelected, boolean hasFocus,
         int row, int column)
      {
         JTextField editor = new JTextField();
         if (value != null) editor.setText(value.toString());
         editor.setBackground((row%2==0)?Color.white:Color.cyan);
         return editor;
      }
   }

   public Main() {
      addWindowListener(new WindowAdapter() {
         public void windowClosing(WindowEvent e) {
            Main.this.dispose();
```

```
            System.exit(0);
        }
    });
    JTable table = new JTable(tmodel);
    table.setDefaultRenderer(Object.class, new MyRenderer());
    getContentPane().add(new JScrollPane(table), BorderLayout.CENTER);
    pack();
  }
  public static void main (String arg[]) {
    new Main().setVisible(true);
  }
}
```

public class DefaultTableCellRenderer extends JLabel
    implements TableCellRenderer

Constructors
public DefaultTableCellRenderer()
    Creates a cell renderer.

Methods
public java.awt.Component getTableCellRendererComponent(JTable table,
    Object value, boolean isSelected, boolean hasFocus,
    int row, int column)
    Handles all rendering (display) of the table cells. The table and value may be null. If isSelected is true, the row is currently selected (and probably should be displayed in a highlight color). If hasFocus is true, the row has focus (and may be displayed with special highlight—for example, a dashed border). The row and column tell the location of the object in the table. The return value is a component configured to display the cell.
    Implements: getTableCellRendererComponent in interface TableCellRenderer.

public void setBackground(java.awt.Color color)
    Sets the background color of the renderer.
    Overrides: setBackground in class Component.

public void setForeground(java.awt.Color color)
    Sets the foreground color of the renderer.
    Overrides: setForeground in class Component.

public void updateUI()
    Tells the renderer to update itself according to the current look and feel.

Protected Fields
protected static Border noFocusBorder
    This is the border to use when the cell does not have the focus.
    Overrides: updateUI in class JLabel.

Protected Methods
protected void setValue(Object value)
    Sets the value that this renderer is supposed to display.

Inner Classes
public static class DefaultTableCellRenderer.UIResource

See also   Border (p.465), JLabel (p.264), JTable (p.357), TableCellRenderer (p.760).

swing.table.DefaultTableCellRenderer.UIResource

INNER CLASS

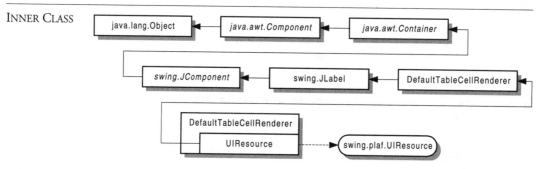

A subclass of `DefaultTableCellRenderer` that implements `UIResource`. This class can be placed in the `UIDefaults` table.

```
public static class DefaultTableCellRenderer.UIResource
    extends DefaultTableCellRenderer
    implements UIResource
```

Constructors
public UIResource()
> Default constructor.

See also   UIResource (p.544).

swing.table.DefaultTableColumnModel

CLASS

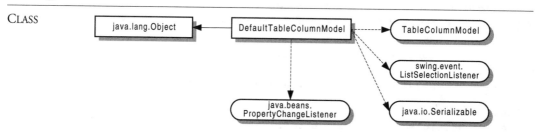

The `DefaultTableColumnModel` is an implementation of `TableColumnModel`. It tracks all columns in a table, and which ones are selected. This object will notify its listeners of changes in the columns, selection, or margins.

```
public class DefaultTableColumnModel extends java.lang.Object
    implements TableColumnModel, java.beans.PropertyChangeListener,
    ListSelectionListener, java.io.Serializable
```

Constructors

`public DefaultTableColumnModel()`

Creates a table column model.

Methods

`public void addColumn(TableColumn column)`

Makes `column` the new last column of the model. Notifies any listeners of the change using the `columnAdded()` method of `swing.event.TableColumnModelListener`.

Implements: `addColumn` in interface `TableColumnModel`.

`public void addColumnModelListener(TableColumnModelListener listener)`

Adds `listener` to the list of objects to be notified when the column model changes (for example, when columns are added or removed).

Implements: `addColumnModelListener` in interface `TableColumnModel`.

`public TableColumn getColumn(int column)`

Gets the column information for the specified `column`.

Implements: `getColumn` in interface `TableColumnModel`.

`public int getColumnCount()`

Returns the number of columns.

Implements: `getColumnCount` in interface `TableColumnModel`.

`public int getColumnIndex(Object columnName)`

Finds the index of the column for which `column.getIdentifier().equals(columnName)`.

Throws: `IllegalArgumentException` if `columnName` is null or no `TableColumn` has this name.

Implements: `getColumnIndex` in interface `TableColumnModel`.

`public int getColumnIndexAtX(int xPosition)`

Finds the index of the column at `xPosition`, or –1 if there is no such column.

Implements: `getColumnIndexAtX` in interface `TableColumnModel`.

`public int getColumnMargin()`

Gets the width (in pixels) of the margin between adjacent columns. Notifies any listeners of the change using the `columnMarginChanged()` method of `TableColumnModelListener`. The default `columnMargin` is 2.

Implements: `getColumnMargin` in interface `TableColumnModel`.

`public boolean getColumnSelectionAllowed()`

Returns `true` if columns may be selected.

Implements: `getColumnSelectionAllowed` in interface `TableColumnModel`.

`public java.util.Enumeration getColumns()`

Returns the list of columns, in order.

Implements: `getColumns` in interface `TableColumnModel`.

`public int getSelectedColumnCount()`

Returns the number of selected columns.

Implements: `getSelectedColumnCount` in interface `TableColumnModel`.

`public int[] getSelectedColumns()`

Returns a list of the selected columns. This never returns `null`, but may return an array of 0 elements.

Implements: `getSelectedColumns` in interface `TableColumnModel`.

`public ListSelectionModel getSelectionModel()`

Returns the `ListSelectionModel` that is used to maintain column selection state. This method returns `null` if row selection is not allowed. See also `setSelectionModel`.

Implements: `getSelectionModel` in interface `TableColumnModel`.

`public int getTotalColumnWidth()`

Returns the sum of all column widths.

Implements: `getTotalColumnWidth` in interface `TableColumnModel`.

`public void moveColumn(int fromIndex, int toIndex)`

Moves the column at `fromIndex` to be located at `toIndex` (other columns will be shifted to make room). For example, if you have columns 012345, and move column 2 to position 4, you will get 013425. If you have columns 012345, and move column 4 to position 2, you will get 014235.

Also notifies any listeners of the change using the `columnMoved()` method of `TableColumnModelListener`.

Throws: `IllegalArgumentException` if column or newIndex are not in the valid range.

Implements: `moveColumn` in interface `TableColumnModel`.

`public void propertyChange(java.beans.PropertyChangeEvent event)`

Supports the `PropertyChangeListener` interface, and lets the model listen for property changes.

Implements: `propertyChange` in interface `PropertyChangeListener`.

`public void removeColumn(TableColumn column)`

Removes the specified `column` if it is present. Shifts other columns to adjust for this removal and notifies any listeners of the change using the `columnRemoved()` method of `TableColumnModelListener`.

Implements: `removeColumn` in interface `TableColumnModel`.

`public void removeColumnModelListener(`
`TableColumnModelListener listener)`

Removes `listener` from the list of objects to be notified of column changes.

Implements: `removeColumnModelListener` in interface `TableColumnModel`.

`public void setColumnMargin(int width)`

Sets the margin between columns to width (in pixels) and notifies any listeners using a `columnMarginChanged()` event.

Implements: `setColumnMargin` in interface `TableColumnModel`.

`public void setColumnSelectionAllowed(boolean maySelect)`

Sets whether columns may be selected.

Implements: `setColumnSelectionAllowed` in interface `TableColumnModel`.

`public void setSelectionModel(ListSelectionModel selectionModel)`

Sets the selection model for the columns. This method also registers this `TableColumnModel` for event notifications from the new selection model. If `selectionModel` is null, columns are not selectable.

Implements: `setSelectionModel` in interface `TableColumnModel`.

`public void valueChanged(ListSelectionEvent event)`

Supports the `ListSelectionListener` interface, and lets the model listen for changes in the selection.

Implements: `valueChanged` in interface `ListSelectionListener`.

Protected Fields

`protected transient ChangeEvent changeEvent`

The event used to notify listeners of changes in the column model.

protected int columnMargin
> The margin between cells.

protected boolean columnSelectionAllowed
> Set to true if columns may be selected.

protected EventListenerList listenerList
> The list of listeners to be notified of changes in the column model.

protected ListSelectionModel selectionModel
> The selection model for the columns.

protected java.util.Vector tableColumns
> The list of columns. (Each element is a TableColumn.)

protected int totalColumnWidth
> The total of all column widths (including margins).

Protected Methods

protected ListSelectionModel createSelectionModel()
> Creates the default selection model for the column model.

protected void fireColumnAdded(TableColumnModelEvent event)
> Notifies listeners that a column has been added.

protected void fireColumnMarginChanged()
> Notifies listeners that the column margin has changed.

protected void fireColumnMoved(TableColumnModelEvent event)
> Notifies listeners that a column has been moved.

protected void fireColumnRemoved(TableColumnModelEvent event)
> Notifies listeners that a column has been removed.

protected void fireColumnSelectionChanged(ListSelectionEvent event)
> Notifies listeners that the selection has changed.

protected void recalcWidthCache()
> Recalculates the total width after a column or the margin changes its size.

See also   JTable (p.357), ListSelectionListener (p.500), ListSelectionModel (p.421), TableColumnModel (p.764), TableColumnModelListener (p.508).

swing.table.DefaultTableModel

CLASS

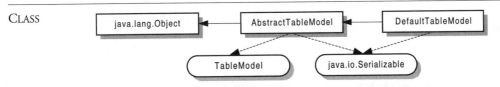

The DefaultTableModel is used by JTable when you don't provide a table model. It uses a Vector to manage a list of rows. Each row item is a Vector of the columns for that row. It is almost always preferable to subclass AbstractTableModel rather than use this class. Subclassing AbstractTableModel requires a minimal amount of code and allows your data to stay in its native data structure. Using DefaultTableModel forces the data in your application to be copied back and forth between the native data structure and the data structure used by DefaultTableModel. This is almost certainly not what you want to do due to its CPU and memory usage implications. The only time you might prefer DefaultTableModel is when your data is dynamic and has no data structure holding it, or when you need to implement a quick prototype.

Example

```
package dtm;

// Main.java - DefaultTableModel example
import java.awt.*;
import java.awt.event.*;
import com.sun.java.swing.*;
import com.sun.java.swing.table.*;
public class Main extends JFrame {
    DefaultTableModel model = new DefaultTableModel(
        new Object[][] {
            {"some", "text"}, {"any", "text"},
            {"even", "more"}, {"text", "strings"},
            {"and", "other"}, {"text", "values"}
        },
        new Object[] {"Column 1", "Column 2"}
    );
    public Main() {
        addWindowListener(new WindowAdapter() {
            public void windowClosing(WindowEvent e) {
                Main.this.dispose();
                System.exit(0);
            }
        });
        JTable table = new JTable(model);
        getContentPane().add(new JScrollPane(table), BorderLayout.CENTER);
        pack();
    }
    public static void main (String arg[]) {
        new Main().setVisible(true);
    }
}
```

public class DefaultTableModel extends AbstractTableModel
    implements java.io.Serializable

Constructors
public DefaultTableModel()
public DefaultTableModel(int rows, int columns)
    Creates a table, with the specified number of rows and columns. (*Default:* 0 rows, 0 columns; any cells default to null.)
public DefaultTableModel(Object[] columnNames, int rows)
public DefaultTableModel(java.util.Vector columnNames, int rows)
    Creates a table with the specified set of column names, and the specified number of rows. All data values default to null. If columnNames is null, the table has 0 columns.

public DefaultTableModel(Object[][] data, Object[] columnNames)

Creates a table with the specified `data` and column names. The value in `data[r][c]` will be returned as `getValueAt(r,c)`.

public DefaultTableModel(java.util.Vector data,
java.util.Vector columnNames)

Creates a table with the specified `data` and column names. The value in `data.element-At(r).elementAt(c)` will be returned by `getValueAt(r,c)`. (The data `Vector`'s elements are each a `Vector` of `Object`.)

Public Methods

public void addColumn(Object columnName)

Adds a new column to the table, with the specified name and all values `null`. The `columnName` may not be `null`. Notifies any listeners of the change.

Throws: `IllegalArgumentException` if `columnName` is `null`.

public void addColumn(Object columnName, Object[] data)

Adds a new column to the table, with the specified name, and all values filled from the `data` array. The `columnName` may not be `null`. If `data` is `null`, all values are set to `null`.

Throws: `IllegalArgumentException` if `columnIdentifier` is `null`.

public void addColumn(Object columnName, Vector data)

Adds a new column to the table, with the specified name, and all data values filled from the `data` vector. The `columnName` may not be `null`. If `data` is `null`, all values are set to `null`.

Throws: `IllegalArgumentException` if `columnIdentifier` is `null`.

public void addRow(Object[] rowData)

Puts `rowData` in a new Vector, and adds it as the new last row of the table. If `rowData` is `null`, all values are set to `null`. Notifies any listeners of the change.

public void addRow(java.util.Vector rowData)

Adds `rowData` as the new last row of the table. If `rowData` is `null`, all values are set to `null`. Notifies any listeners of the change.

public int getColumnCount()

Returns the number of columns.

Implements: `getColumnCount` in interface `TableModel`.

public String getColumnName(int column)

Returns the name of the specified `column`. Two columns may have the same name. This usually has no impact because `JTable` usually works with column indexes rather than column names. This method supports the `TableModel` interface. (If no value has been established for the column name, the `AbstractTableModel` method is called, giving a series of labels "A," "B," "C," etc.)

Overrides: `getColumnName` in class `AbstractTableModel`.

Implements: `getColumnName` in interface `TableModel`.

public java.util.Vector getDataVector()

Returns the data which is a `Vector` with each entry a `Vector` of `Object`. The number of items in the returned `Vector` is the number of rows. You may modify this data either by changing the data in a particular cell or by changing the number of rows, provided you call `newDataAvailable()`, `newRowsAdded()`, or `rowsRemoved()` with an appropriate event, so listeners will be notified. (You may not directly modify the number of columns; use `addColumn()` or `removeColumn()` to do that.)

public int getRowCount()

Returns the number of rows. This routine should be efficient because it is called by JTable very frequently.

Implements: getRowCount in interface TableModel.

public Object getValueAt(int row, int column)

Returns the value at the specified row and column.

Throws: ArrayIndexOutOfBoundsException if an invalid row or column was given.

Implements: getValueAt in interface TableModel.

public void insertRow(int rowIndex, Object[] rowData)

Inserts rowData at rowIndex. The rowData is first put into a new Vector. (If rowData is null, all values will be null.) Rows after rowIndex are moved down, and listeners are notified of the change.

Throws: ArrayIndexOutOfBoundsException if the row was invalid.

public void insertRow(int rowIndex, java.util.Vector rowData)

Inserts rowData at rowIndex. The rowData is a Vector of Objects, each object corresponding to the value at the corresponding column. (If rowData is null, all values will be null.) Rows after rowIndex are moved down, and listeners are notified of the change.

Throws: ArrayIndexOutOfBoundsException if the row was invalid.

public boolean isCellEditable(int row, int column)

Returns true if the cell may be edited. This method supports the TableModel interface. If this is false, setValueAt() has no effect. See also setValueAt.

Overrides: isCellEditable in class AbstractTableModel.

Implements: isCellEditable in interface TableModel.

public void moveRow(int startRow, int endRow, int newStartRow)

Moves the rows ranging from startRow to endRow so that they are at newStartRow. All rows must be in the range [0, getRowCount()-1], and you must have startRow <= endRow. All indexes are specified by their position *before* the move.

Throws: ArrayIndexOutOfBoundsException if any of the indices are out of range, or if endRow is less than startRow.

public void newDataAvailable(TableModelEvent event)

Notifies listeners of the change in the table using event. If event is null, or if the number of rows in the data Vector doesn't match the number of rows as tracked by the DefaultTableModel, an event is created that reports all data changed.

public void newRowsAdded(TableModelEvent event)

Notifies listeners of the change in the table using event.

public void removeRow(int row)

Removes the specified row. Notifies any listeners of the change.

Throws: ArrayIndexOutOfBoundsException if the row was invalid.

public void rowsRemoved(TableModelEvent event)

Notifies listeners of the change in the table using event. The event may not be null.

Throws: IllegalArgumentException if event is null.

public void setColumnIdentifiers(Object[] names)

Stores the names as the new column names.

public void setColumnIdentifiers(java.util.Vector names)

Stores the names as the new column names.

public void setDataVector(Object[][] data, Object[] columnNames)

Clears the table, and repopulates it with `data`. The number of rows and columns in the table is recalculated, the column names are reset, and any listeners are notified of the change.

Throws: `IllegalArgumentException` if `newData` is null or if the number of columns in `data` does not equal the number of the column identifiers in `columnNames`.

public void setDataVector(java.util.Vector data,
java.util.Vector columnNames)

Clears the table, and repopulates it with `data`. Each element of `data` should be a `Vector` of `Objects`. The `data` may not be `null`. (The number of rows and columns in the table is recalculated.) Each row should have the same number of values, the same as the number of `columnNames`. If `columnNames` is `null`, the old column names are retained. Notifies any listeners of the change.

Throws: `IllegalArgumentException` if `data` is null or if the number of columns in `data` does not equal the number of the column identifiers in `columnNames`.

public void setNumRows(int rows)

Sets the number of rows in the model to `rows`. If new rows are required, their values are `null`. Notifies any listeners of the change. See also `setColumnIdentifiers`.

public void setValueAt(Object object, int row, int column)

Stores `object` at the specified cell in the table. The value is stored only if `isCellEditable(row,column)` returns `true`. If you don't override this method, it does not store any values.

Throws: `ArrayIndexOutOfBoundsException` if an invalid row or column was given.

Overrides: `setValueAt` in class `AbstractTableModel`.

Implements: `setValueAt` in interface `TableModel`.

Protected Fields

protected java.util.Vector columnIdentifiers

A `Vector` of the column names.

protected java.util.Vector dataVector

The `Vector` of `Vector` of `Object` values, representing the data in the table.

Protected Methods

protected static java.util.Vector convertToVector(Object[] data)

Returns a `Vector`, populated from `data`.

protected static java.util.Vector convertToVector(Object[][] data)

Returns a `Vector` of `Vector` of `Object`. Each item in the outermost vector corresponds to `data[r]`, and each element in the inner vector corresponds to `data[r][c]`.

See also AbstractTableModel (p.735), TableModel (p.766).

swing.table.JTableHeader

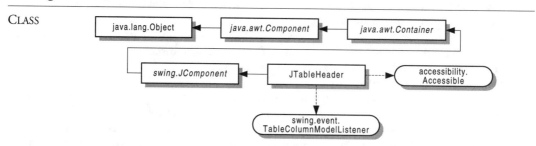

This component represents the table header—the label area at the top of the columns in a JTable. Its model is the same TableColumnModel that the associated JTable uses.

```
public class JTableHeader extends JComponent
    implements TableColumnModelListener, Accessible
```

Constructors
public JTableHeader()
public JTableHeader(TableColumnModel columnModel)
Creates the table header object. *Default:* column model created by createDefaultColumn-Model().

Methods
public void columnAdded(TableColumnModelEvent event)
Returns notification that a column has been added.
Implements: columnAdded in interface TableColumnModelListener.

public int columnAtPoint(java.awt.Point point)
Returns the column index corresponding to point, or –1 if none does.

public void columnMarginChanged(ChangeEvent event)
Returns notification that the margin of a column has changed.
Implements: columnMarginChanged in interface TableColumnModelListener.

public void columnMoved(TableColumnModelEvent event)
Returns notification that a column has moved.
Implements: columnMoved in interface TableColumnModelListener.

public void columnRemoved(TableColumnModelEvent event)
Returns notification that a column has been deleted.
Implements: columnRemoved in interface TableColumnModelListener.

public void columnSelectionChanged(ListSelectionEvent event)
Returns notification that the column selection has changed.
Implements: columnSelectionChanged in interface TableColumnModelListener.

public AccessibleContext getAccessibleContext()
Returns the accessible context for the table header.
Overrides: getAccessibleContext in class JComponent.
Implements: getAccessibleContext in interface Accessible.

public TableColumnModel getColumnModel()
Gets the column model used by the table header. See also setColumnModel.

public TableColumn getDraggedColumn()

If a column is being dragged, returns the index of that column (if no column is being dragged, returns null).

public int getDraggedDistance()

Returns the distance (in pixels along the *x* axis) that the column has been dragged. Defined only when a drag is in progress.

public java.awt.Rectangle getHeaderRect(int column)

Returns the rectangle corresponding to the header's location for column.

public boolean getReorderingAllowed()

Returns true if the user may rearrange the columns in the table by dragging (the application may rearrange the columns regardless of this value).

public boolean getResizingAllowed()

Returns true if the user may resize the table header columns by dragging (the application may resize the columns regardless of this value).

public TableColumn getResizingColumn()

Returns the index of the column being resized. If no column is being resized, this method returns null.

public JTable getTable()

Gets the table with which this object is associated.

public String getToolTipText(java.awt.event.MouseEvent event)

Gets the ToolTip text from the header's renderer.

Overrides: getToolTipText in class JComponent.

public TableHeaderUI getUI()

Returns the UI (look and feel) for this object.

public String getUIClassID()

Returns TableHeaderUI.

Overrides: getUIClassID in class JComponent.

public boolean getUpdateTableInRealTime()

Returns true if the table should be displayed during dragging and resizing. May be set false to improve performance (default value is true).

public void resizeAndRepaint()

Resets the sizes of the header columns and requests a repaint. Also resets rectangles for the header view and line scroll amounts for the Scrollable interface.

public void setColumnModel(TableColumnModel model)

Makes model the new column model for this view. Registers with the model as a TableColumnModelListener.

Throws: IllegalArgumentException if model is null.

public void setDraggedColumn(TableColumn column)

Sets the index of the column currently being dragged.

public void setDraggedDistance(int deltaX)

Sets the distance that the dragged column should be moved from its original position.

public void setReorderingAllowed(boolean mayReorder)

Sets whether the user can reorder columns by dragging column headers.

public void setResizingAllowed(boolean mayResize)

Sets whether the user can resize columns by dragging.

public void setResizingColumn(TableColumn column)

Sets the index of the column currently being resized.

public void setTable(JTable table)

Sets the table with which this table header is associated.

public void setUI(TableHeaderUI ui)

Sets the look and feel for this component.

public void setUpdateTableInRealTime(boolean shouldUpdateInRealTime)

Sets whether the table updates in real time when a column header is resized or dragged.

public void updateUI()

Updates the header using the current UI.

Overrides: updateUI in class JComponent.

Protected Fields

protected TableColumnModel columnModel

The TableColumnModel of the table header.

protected transient TableColumn draggedColumn

The column currently being dragged (or null if none).

protected transient int draggedDistance

The distance by which the currently dragged column has been moved (meaningful only during a drag).

protected boolean reorderingAllowed

Set to true if the user may rearrange the columns.

protected boolean resizingAllowed

Set to true if the user may resize the columns.

protected transient TableColumn resizingColumn

The column being resized (or null if no column is resizing)

protected JTable table

The table for which this is the header.

protected boolean updateTableInRealTime

If this flag is true, then the whole table will repaint as a column is dragged or resized. If this value is false, only the header will repaint.

Protected Methods

protected TableColumnModel createDefaultColumnModel()

Returns the default column model object which is a DefaultTableColumnModel. Subclasses can override this method to return a different column model object.

protected void initializeLocalVars()

Sets the default values for the fields.

protected String paramString()

Returns a string representation of the properties of this JTableHeader. The returned string may be empty but it will not be null.

Overrides: paramString in class JComponent.

Inner Classes

protected class JTableHeader.AccessibleJTableHeader

Returned by JTable.createDefaultTableHeader() (p.357), JTable.getTableHeader() (p.357).

See also Accessible (p.85), AccessibleContext (p.90), ChangeEvent (p.487), JComponent (p.207), JTable (p.357), ListSelectionEvent (p.499), TableColumnModel (p.764), TableColumnModelEvent (p.507), TableColumnModelListener (p.508), TableHeaderUI (p.541).

swing.table.JTableHeader.AccessibleJTableHeader

INNER CLASS

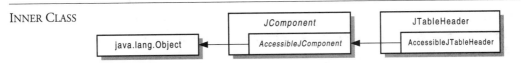

This inner class is the class returned when you call `getAccessibleContext().getAccessibleComponent()` on a `JTableHeader`.

```
protected class JTableHeader.AccessibleJTableHeader
    extends AccessibleJComponent
```

Constructors
public AccessibleJTableHeader()
   Default constructor.

Methods
public Accessible getAccessibleAt(java.awt.Point p)
   Returns the `Accessible` child, if one exists, contained at the local coordinate `Point`.
public Accessible getAccessibleChild(int index)
   Returns the `Accessible` child of the object at `index`.
public int getAccessibleChildrenCount()
   Returns the number of accessible children in the object. If all of the children of this object implement `Accessible`, then this method should return the number of children of this object.
public AccessibleRole getAccessibleRole()
   Returns `AccessibleRole.PANEL`.

Inner Classes
**protected class
   JTableHeader.AccessibleJTableHeader.AccessibleJTableHeaderEntry**

See also Accessible (p.85), AccessibleRole (p.95), JComponent.AccessibleJComponent (p.221).

swing.table.JTableHeader.AccessibleJTableHeader.AccessibleJTableHeaderEntry

INNER CLASS

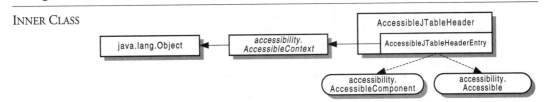

This inner class is the class that gets returned when `getAccessibleChild()` is called on a `JTableHeader`.

```
protected class
    JTableHeader.AccessibleJTableHeader.AccessibleJTableHeaderEntry
    extends AccessibleContext
    implements Accessible, AccessibleComponent
```

Constructors

public AccessibleJTableHeaderEntry(int index, JTableHeader header, JTable table)

Methods

public void addFocusListener(java.awt.event.FocusListener l)
 Implements: addFocusListener in interface AccessibleComponent.

public void addPropertyChangeListener(
 java.beans.PropertyChangeListnener l)
 Overrides: addPropertyChangeListener in class AccessibleContext.

public boolean contains(java.awt.Point p)
 Implements: contains in interface AccessibleComponent.

public AccessibleAction getAccessibleAction()
 Overrides: getAccessibleAction in class AccessibleContext.

public Accessible getAccessibleAt(Point p)
 Implements: getAccessibleAt in interface AccessibleComponent.

public Accessible getAccessibleChild(int i)
 Overrides: getAccessibleChild in class AccessibleContext.

public int getAccessibleChildrenCount()
 Overrides: getAccessibleChildrenCount in class AccessibleContext.

public AccessibleComponent getAccessibleComponent()
 Overrides: getAccessibleComponent in class AccessibleContext.

public AccessibleContext getAccessibleContext()
 Gets the AccessibleContext associated with this object.
 Implements: getAccessibleContext in interface Accessible.

public String getAccessibleDescription()
 Overrides: getAccessibleDescription in class AccessibleContext.

public int getAccessibleIndexInParent()
 Overrides: getAccessibleIndexInParent in class AccessibleContext.

public String getAccessibleName()
 Overrides: getAccessibleName in class AccessibleContext.

public AccessibleRole getAccessibleRole()
 Overrides: getAccessibleRole in class AccessibleContext.

public AccessibleSelection getAccessibleSelection()
 Overrides: getAccessibleSelection in class AccessibleContext.

public AccessibleStateSet getAccessibleStateSet()
 Overrides: getAccessibleStateSet in class AccessibleContext.

public AccessibleText getAccessibleText()
 Overrides: getAccessibleText in class AccessibleContext.

public AccessibleValue getAccessibleValue()
Overrides: getAccessibleValue in class AccessibleContext.

public java.awt.Color getBackground()
Implements: getBackground in interface AccessibleComponent.

public java.awt.Rectangle getBounds()
Implements: getBounds in interface AccessibleComponent.

public java.awt.Cursor getCursor()
Implements: getCursor in interface AccessibleComponent.

public java.awt.Font getFont()
Implements: getFont in interface AccessibleComponent.

public java.awt.FontMetrics getFontMetrics(java.awt.Font f)
Implements: getFontMetrics in interface AccessibleComponent.

public java.awt.Color getForeground()
Implements: getForeground in interface AccessibleComponent.

public java.util.Locale getLocale()
Overrides: getLocale in class AccessibleContext.

public java.awt.Point getLocation()
Implements: getLocation in interface AccessibleComponent.

public java.awt.Point getLocationOnScreen()
Implements: getLocationOnScreen in interface AccessibleComponent.

public java.awt.Dimension getSize()
Implements: getSize in interface AccessibleComponent.

public boolean isEnabled()
Implements: isEnabled in interface AccessibleComponent.

public boolean isFocusTraversable()
Implements: isFocusTraversable in interface AccessibleComponent.

public boolean isShowing()
Implements: isShowing in interface AccessibleComponent.

public boolean isVisible()
Implements: isVisible in interface AccessibleComponent.

public void removeFocusListener(java.awt.event.FocusListener l)
Implements: removeFocusListener in interface AccessibleComponent.

public void removePropertyChangeListener(
java.beans.PropertyChangeListnener l)
Overrides: removePropertyChangeListener in class AccessibleContext.

public void requestFocus()
Implements: requestFocus in interface AccessibleComponent.

public void setAccessibleDescription(String s)
Overrides: setAccessibleDescription in class AccessibleContext.

public void setAccessibleName(String s)
Overrides: setAccessibleName in class AccessibleContext.

public void setBackground(java.awt.Color c)
Implements: setBackground in interface AccessibleComponent.

public void setBounds(java.awt.Rectangle r)
Implements: setBounds in interface AccessibleComponent.

public void setCursor(java.awt.Cursor c)
Implements: setCursor in interface AccessibleComponent.

```
public void setEnabled(boolean b)
```
Implements: setEnabled in interface AccessibleComponent.
```
public void setFont(java.awt.Font f)
```
Implements: setFont in interface AccessibleComponent.
```
public void setForeground(java.awt.Color c)
```
Implements: setForeground in interface AccessibleComponent.
```
public void setLocation(java.awt.Point p)
```
Implements: setLocation in interface AccessibleComponent.
```
public void setSize(java.awt.Dimension d)
```
Implements: setSize in interface AccessibleComponent.
```
public void setVisible(boolean b)
```
Implements: setVisible in interface AccessibleComponent.

See also   Accessible (p.85), AccessibleAction (p.86), AccessibleComponent (p.87), AccessibleContext (p.90), AccessibleRole (p.95), AccessibleStateSet (p.101), AccessibleText (p.103), AccessibleValue (p.104), JTable (p.357), JTableHeader (p.752).

swing.table.TableCellEditor

INTERFACE   TableCellEditor

A TableCellEditor provides components to edit cells. One editor can serve as the editor for a whole table or just a particular column or cell.

See "Swing, color, and the UIDefaults table" on p.51 for information on selecting the right colors and borders to match the Component returned by this method to the defaults for the table.

Example: Setting a cell editor for an entire table

```
// File tablecelleditor/Main.java - TableCellEditor Example
package tablecelleditor;

import java.awt.*;
import java.awt.event.*;
import com.sun.java.swing.*;
import com.sun.java.swing.table.*;

public class Main extends JFrame {
   DefaultTableModel model = new DefaultTableModel(
      new Object[][] {
         {"some", "text"}, {"any", "text"},
         {"even", "more"}, {"text", "strings"},
         {"and", "other"}, {"text", "values"}
      },
      new Object[] {"Column 1", "Column 2"}
   );

   class MyEditor extends DefaultCellEditor {
      public MyEditor() {super(new JTextField());}
```

```
    public Component getTableCellEditorComponent(JTable table, Object value,
                                                 boolean isSelected,
                                                 int row, int column) {
        JTextField editor = (JTextField)super.getTableCellEditorComponent(
                                table, value, isSelected, row, column);

        if (value != null) editor.setText(value.toString());
        if (column == 0) {
            editor.setHorizontalAlignment(SwingConstants.CENTER);
            editor.setFont(new Font("Serif", Font.BOLD, 14));
        } else {
            editor.setHorizontalAlignment(SwingConstants.RIGHT);
            editor.setFont(new Font("Serif", Font.ITALIC, 12));
        }
        return editor;
    }
}
public Main() {
    this.addWindowListener(new WindowAdapter() {
        public void windowClosing(WindowEvent e) {
            Main.this.dispose();
            System.exit(0);
        }
    });
    JTable table = new JTable(model);
    table.setDefaultEditor(Object.class, new MyEditor());
    getContentPane().add(new JScrollPane(table), BorderLayout.CENTER);
    pack();
}
public static void main(String arg[]) {
    new Main().setVisible(true);
}
}
```

public interface TableCellEditor extends CellEditor

Methods
public abstract java.awt.Component getTableCellEditorComponent(
   JTable table, Object value, boolean isSelected, int row, int column)
   Handles all editing of table cells. The table and value may be null. If isSelected is true, the row is currently selected (and probably should be displayed in a highlight color). The row and column tell the location of the object in the table.

   The return value is a component configured to edit the cell. You can make the return value depend on whatever you want. For example, you might return a checkbox if value is Boolean, and a label for any other type.

   Cell editors can be established either on a table basis (see JTable) or a column basis (see Table-Column).

   Returned by JTable.getCellEditor() (p.357), JTable.getDefaultEditor() (p.357), TableColumn.getCellEditor() (p.761).

   Implemented by DefaultCellEditor (p.164).

swing.table.TableCellEditor   759

See also JTable (p.357), TableColumn (p.761).

swing.table.TableCellRenderer

INTERFACE (TableCellRenderer)

A `TableCellRenderer` draws the cell's representation on the screen. A single renderer can serve as the "cookie cutter" to display all cells of the table. You can set the renderer for a whole table, or for a particular column.

If no renderer has been provided, a `DefaultTableCellRenderer` will be created and used.

See "Swing, color, and the UIDefaults table" on p.51 for information on selecting the right colors and borders to match the `Component` returned by this method to the defaults for the table.

Example

```
package tablecr;

// Main.java - TableCellRenderer Example
import java.awt.*;
import java.awt.event.*;
import com.sun.java.swing.*;
import com.sun.java.swing.table.*;
public class Main extends JFrame {
   DefaultTableModel tmodel = new DefaultTableModel(
      new Object[][] {
         {"some", "text"}, {"any", "text"},
         {"even", "more"}, {"text", "strings"},
         {"and", "other"}, {"text", "values"}
      },
      new Object[] {"Column 1", "Column 2"}
   );

   class MyRenderer implements TableCellRenderer {
      public Component getTableCellRendererComponent(
         JTable table, Object value,
         boolean isSelected, boolean hasFocus,
         int row, int column)
      {
         JTextField editor = new JTextField();
         if (value != null) editor.setText(value.toString());
         editor.setBackground((row%2==0)?Color.white:Color.cyan);
         return editor;
      }
   }

   public Main() {
      addWindowListener(new WindowAdapter() {
         public void windowClosing(WindowEvent e) {
            Main.this.dispose();
            System.exit(0);
         }
```

```
    });
    JTable table = new JTable(tmodel);
    table.setDefaultRenderer(Object.class, new MyRenderer());
    getContentPane().add(new JScrollPane(table), BorderLayout.CENTER);
    pack();
  }
  public static void main (String arg[]) {
    new Main().setVisible(true);
  }
}
```

public interface TableCellRenderer

Methods
public abstract java.awt.Component getTableCellRendererComponent(
JTable table, Object value, boolean isSelected,
boolean hasFocus, int row, int column)
Handles all rendering (display) of the table cells. The table and value may be null. If isSelected is true, the row is currently selected (and probably should be displayed in a highlight
color). If hasFocus is true, the row has focus (and may be displayed with special highlight—a
dashed border, for example). The row and column tell the location of the object in the table.

The return value is a component configured to display the cell. You can make the return value
depend on whatever you want. For example, you might return a checkbox if value is Boolean, and
a label for any other type.

Renderers can be established either on a table basis (see JTable) or a column basis (see TableColumn).

Returned by   BasicTableUI.getCellRenderer() (p.690), JTable.getDefaultRenderer() (p.357),
TableColumn.createDefaultHeaderRenderer() (p.761), TableColumn.getCellRenderer() (p.761),
TableColumn.getHeaderRenderer() (p.761).

Implemented by   DefaultTableCellRenderer (p.742).

See also   JTable (p.357), TableColumn (p.761).

swing.table.TableColumn

This is the model for a single table column (TableColumnModel is the model for all columns in
a table). Note that tables are not symmetric: there is a model for the data and a model for the columns, but no model for the rows.

public class TableColumn extends java.lang.Object
implements java.io.Serializable

Fields
public static final String CELL_RENDERER_PROPERTY = "cellRenderer"
The property name for the renderer for nonheader cells.

```
public static final String COLUMN_WIDTH_PROPERTY = "columnWidth"
```
The property name for the width of the column (in pixels).
```
public static final String HEADER_RENDERER_PROPERTY = "headerRenderer"
```
The property name for the renderer for header cells.
```
public static final String HEADER_VALUE_PROPERTY = "headerValue"
```
The property name for the value of the header.

Constructors

```
public TableColumn()
```
Do not use this constructor. It is here for the use of Beans tools and Serialization.
```
public TableColumn(int modelIndex)
```
Creates a TableColumn for the given index in the model. The default renderer will be used (a JLabel subclass) and no editor will be assigned.
```
public TableColumn(int modelIndex, int width)
```
Creates a TableColumn of the given width for the given index in the model. The default renderer will be used (a JLabel subclass) and no editor will be assigned.
```
public TableColumn(int modelIndex, int width,
    TableCellRenderer renderer, TableCellEditor editor)
```
Creates a TableColumn of the given width for the given index in the model. This TableColumn will use the given renderer and editor. The value passed for editor may be null.

Methods

```
public synchronized void addPropertyChangeListener(
    java.beans.PropertyChangeListnener listener)
```
Adds listener to the list of objects to be notified when bound properties change.
```
public void disableResizedPosting()
```
Disables the posting of resize events while the table is resizing.
```
public void enableResizedPosting()
```
Enables the posting of resize events while the table is resizing.
```
public TableCellEditor getCellEditor()
```
Gets the editor responsible for displaying cells in this column (if this is null, JTable will use its default editor).
```
public TableCellRenderer getCellRenderer()
```
Gets the renderer responsible for displaying cells in this column (if this is null, JTable will see use its default renderer).
```
public TableCellRenderer getHeaderRenderer()
```
Gets the renderer responsible for displaying the header cell.
```
public Object getHeaderValue()
```
Gets the value of the header cell for this column.
```
public Object getIdentifier()
```
Gets the identifier for this column. If none has been set or it is null, it returns the header value. (See getHeaderValue().)
```
public int getMaxWidth()
```
Returns the maximum width of the column (in pixels). The default value is 2000 pixels.
```
public int getMinWidth()
```
Returns the minimum width of the column (in pixels). The default value is 15 pixels.

public int getModelIndex()

Returns the index in the model to which this `TableColumn` corresponds. The model index doesn't change as columns are moved around in the `JTable`. The simplest way to think about the relationship between a column in the model, the corresponding `TableColumn`, and how the columns are presented in the `JTable` is this:

A `TableColumn` is *associated* with a column in the model. A `JTable` contains a set of `TableColumns`, *not* columns from the model. As columns are moved around in a `JTable`, all that is being moved is the associated `TableColumn`, not the actual model column. So, the order of the `TableColumns` in the `JTable` may change, but the order of the columns in the model never changes.

public int getPreferredWidth()

Returns the preferred width of this `TableColumn`. The default preferred width is 75 pixels.

public boolean getResizable()

Returns `true` if the user may resize the column. The `setWidth()` method works even if this method returns `false`.

public int getWidth()

Returns the current width of the column.

public synchronized void removePropertyChangeListener(
java.beans.PropertyChangeListnener listener)

Removes `listener` from the list of objects to be notified of property changes.

public void setCellEditor(TableCellEditor anEditor)

Sets the editor that will edit the values in this column.

public void setCellRenderer(TableCellRenderer aRenderer)

Sets the renderer that will display values in this column.

public void setHeaderRenderer(TableCellRenderer aRenderer)

Sets the renderer responsible for displaying the header value. See `setHeaderValue()`.

Throws: `IllegalArgumentException` if a Renderer is `null`.

public void setHeaderValue(Object aValue)

Sets the header for the column (this value is displayed by the header renderer at the top of the column).

public void setIdentifier(Object anIdentifier)

Sets the identifier for this column. This value can be used as a string name of a column; for example, `DefaultTableModel` may use column identifiers.

public void setMaxWidth(int newMaxWidth)

Sets the maximum size (in pixels) the column may take (the current width is reduced to this width if it is greater). The default maximum width is 2000 pixels.

public void setMinWidth(int newMinWidth)

Sets the minimum size (in pixels) that the column may take. The default value is 15 pixels. The current width is increased to this width if it is smaller.

public void setModelIndex(int index)

Sets the model index—the column number in the model to which this column corresponds.

public void setPreferredWidth(int preferredWidth)

Sets this column's preferred width to `preferredWidth`. If the given size is outside the maximum or minimum allowed based on the resizing value of the `JTable`, it will be set to the maximum or minimum as appropriate.

public void setResizable(boolean mayResize)

Sets whether the column may be resized.

public void setWidth(int newWidth)

Sets the width of this column to newWidth.

public void sizeWidthToFit()

Tells the column to resize itself to fit the size of the header cell. (It will set the column's minimum size to at most the header's current size, and set its maximum size to at least the header's current size.)

Protected Fields

protected TableCellEditor cellEditor

The editor for cells.

protected TableCellRenderer cellRenderer

The renderer that displays cells.

protected TableCellRenderer headerRenderer

The renderer that displays the headerValue.

protected Object headerValue

The value for the header.

protected Object identifier

The name of the column. This name is not used by Swing per se, but may be used by the application program to keep track of the column.

protected boolean isResizable

Returns True if the column may be resized.

protected int maxWidth

The maximum width of the column.

protected int minWidth

The minimum width of the column.

protected int modelIndex

The index in the model with which this column model is associated. This is the mapping that lets the model maintain a consistent ordering: the view can maintain a sequence of TableColumns, while they map to the proper column in the model.

protected transient int resizedPostingDisableCount

Used to track whether the column should receive resize events during a resize operation.

protected int width

The current width of the column.

Protected Methods

protected TableCellRenderer createDefaultHeaderRenderer()

Creates a renderer for the header cell (used if none is provided in the constructor).

Returned by   DefaultTableColumnModel.getColumn() (p.744), JTable.getColumn() (p.357), JTableHeader.getDraggedColumn() (p.752), JTableHeader.getResizingColumn() (p.752), TableColumnModel.getColumn() (p.764).

See also   TableCellEditor (p.758), TableCellRenderer (p.760).

swing.table.TableColumnModel

INTERFACE   (TableColumnModel)

TableColumnModel is the model for *all* columns in a table, as a set. TableColumn is the model for an individual column.

```
public interface TableColumnModel
```

Public Methods

public abstract void addColumn(TableColumn column)

Makes column the new last column of the model. Notifies any listeners of the change using the columnAdded() method of TableColumnModelListener (p.508).

public abstract void addColumnModelListener(
TableColumnModelListener listener)

Adds listener to the list of objects to be notified when the column model changes (for example, when columns are added or removed).

public abstract TableColumn getColumn(int column)

Gets the column information for the specified column.

public abstract int getColumnCount()

Returns the number of columns.

public abstract int getColumnIndex(Object columnName)

Finds the index of the column for which column.getIdentifier().equals(columnName). This method will throw an IllegalArgumentException if columnName is null or if no column has that identifier.

public abstract int getColumnIndexAtX(int xCoordinate)

Finds the index of the column at xCoordinate, or –1 if there is no such column.

public abstract int getColumnMargin()

Gets the width (in pixels) of the margin between adjacent columns. Notifies any listeners of the change using the columnMarginChanged() method of swing.event.TableColumnModelListener (p.508).

public abstract boolean getColumnSelectionAllowed()

Returns true if columns may be selected.

public abstract java.util.Enumeration getColumns()

Returns the list of columns, in order.

public abstract int getSelectedColumnCount()

Returns the number of selected columns.

public abstract int[] getSelectedColumns()

Returns a list of the selected columns. This never returns null, but may return an array of 0 elements.

public abstract ListSelectionModel getSelectionModel()

Returns the model that tracks column selection.

public abstract int getTotalColumnWidth()

Returns the sum of all column widths (including margins).

public abstract void moveColumn(int fromIndex, int toIndex)

Moves the column at fromIndex to be located at toIndex. Notifies any listeners of the change using the columnMoved() method of TableColumnModelListener (p.508).

public abstract void removeColumn(TableColumn column)

Removes the specified column. Shifts other columns to adjust for this. Notifies any listeners of the change using the columnRemoved() method of TableColumnModelListener (p.508).

```
public abstract void removeColumnModelListener(
    TableColumnModelListener listener)
```
Removes listener from the list of objects to be notified of column changes.
```
public abstract void setColumnMargin(int width)
```
Sets the margin between columns to width (in pixels).
```
public abstract void setColumnSelectionAllowed(boolean maySelect)
```
Sets whether columns may be selected.
```
public abstract void setSelectionModel(ListSelectionModel selectionModel)
```
Sets the selection model for the columns.

Returned by JTable.createDefaultColumnModel() (p.357), JTable.getColumnModel() (p.357), JTableHeader.createDefaultColumnModel() (p.752), JTableHeader.getColumnModel() (p.752).

Implemented by DefaultTableColumnModel (p.744).

See also ListSelectionModel (p.421), TableColumnModelListener (p.508).

swing.table.TableModel

INTERFACE — TableModel

This is the fundamental interface for tables. This is the model used by JTable.

The easiest way to provide this interface is to override AbstractTableModel or use a DefaultTableModel. The preferred choice is to subclass AbstractTableModel.

```
public interface TableModel
```

Methods

```
public abstract void addTableModelListener(TableModelListener listener)
```
Adds listener to the list of objects to be notified when the table changes.
```
public abstract java.lang.Class getColumnClass(int column)
```
Gets the class for column. By providing this information, you help cause the most appropriate renderer to be used. (For example, an entry of type Boolean could be displayed as a checkbox, rather than the string "true" or "false.") You should return the class that is common to all entries in the column. For example, if you have both Integer and Boolean items, you would need to return Object.class (their only common superclass).
```
public abstract int getColumnCount()
```
Returns the number of columns.
```
public abstract String getColumnName(int column)
```
Returns the name of the specified column. Two columns may have the same name; this usually has no impact because JTable usually works with column indexes rather than column names. (When a JTable is created, it queries the model for the number of columns and their names; see JTable.createDefaultColumnsFromModel() and JTable.getAutoCreateColumns-FromModel().)
```
public abstract int getRowCount()
```
Returns the number of rows. This routine is called by JTable very frequently.
```
public abstract Object getValueAt(int row, int column)
```
Returns the value at the specified row and column.

public abstract boolean isCellEditable(int row, int column)
    Returns true if the cell may be edited.
public abstract void removeTableModelListener(TableModelListener listener)
    Removes listener from the list of objects to be notified when the table changes.
public abstract void setValueAt(Object object, int row, int column)
    Stores object at the specified cell in the table. (The value is stored only if isCellEditable(row,column) returns true.)

Returned by   JTable.createDefaultDataModel() (p.357), JTable.getModel() (p.357).
Implemented by   AbstractTableModel (p.735).
See also   DefaultTableModel (p.747), JTable (p.357), TableModelListener (p.510).

Package swing.text

The text package is easily the most complex package in Swing. This is understandable in that text formatting is far and away the most complex task a user interface needs to perform. A text editor that supports a single font and basic operations can be written in a few hundred lines of code. Add in complex styles and formatting and the code size grows exponentially.

The average developer will never experience most of the complexity in this package. The design of the Swing text support is very elegant in that the complexity is only uncovered as you need it, and for most uses it remains hidden. Most developers will need to examine only the `JEditorPane` component in the Swing package and the `StyledEditorKit` and `DefaultEditorKit` classes in this package to understand all they need to know.

Developers working on custom text editors will learn to appreciate the flexibility of this package. There are a considerable number of classes but they fit together cleanly, with clearly defined purposes. The `Document`, `Element`, and `View` implementing classes work together to translate from the raw text, through the text markup to the actual display of the text.

Text extends/implements hierarchy

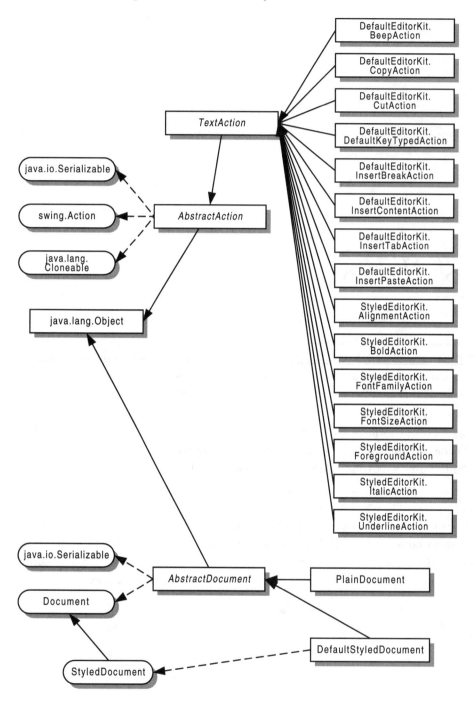

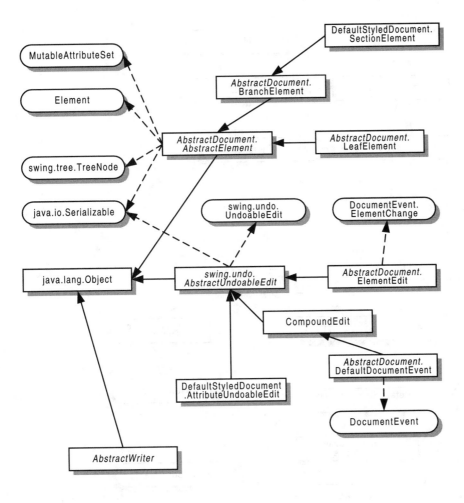

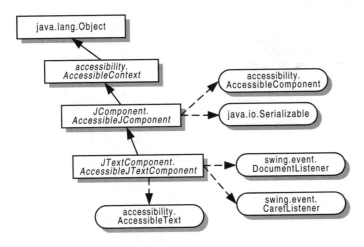

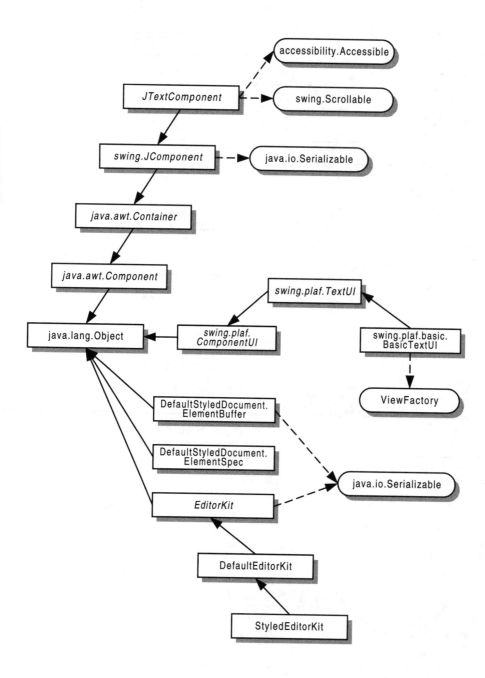

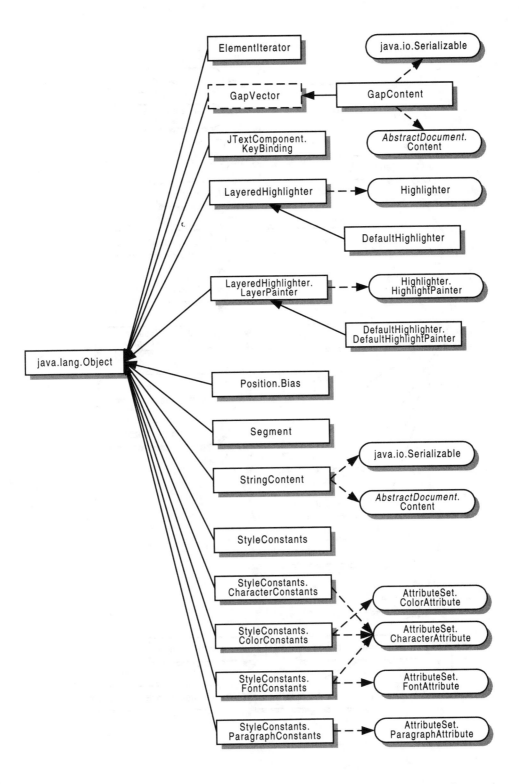

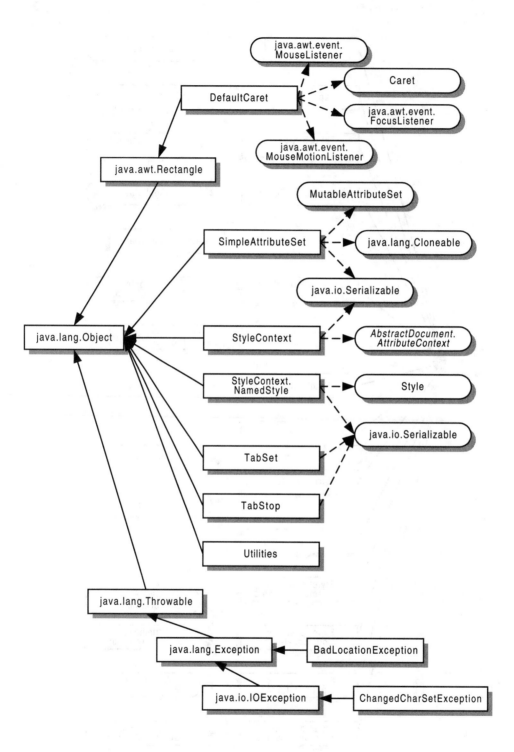

774   Text extends/implements hierarchy

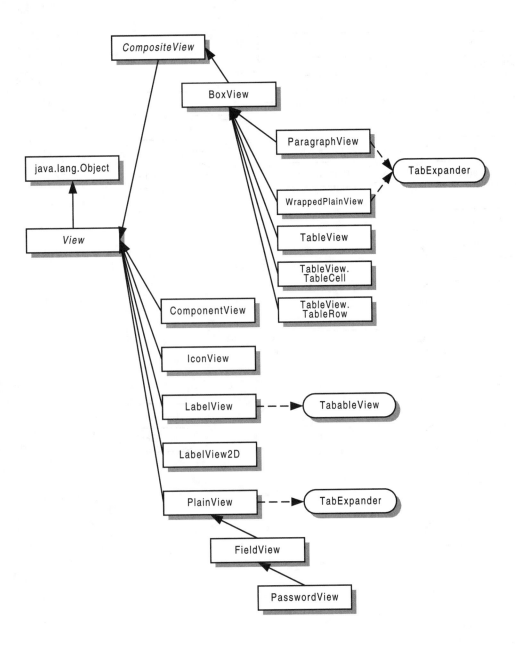

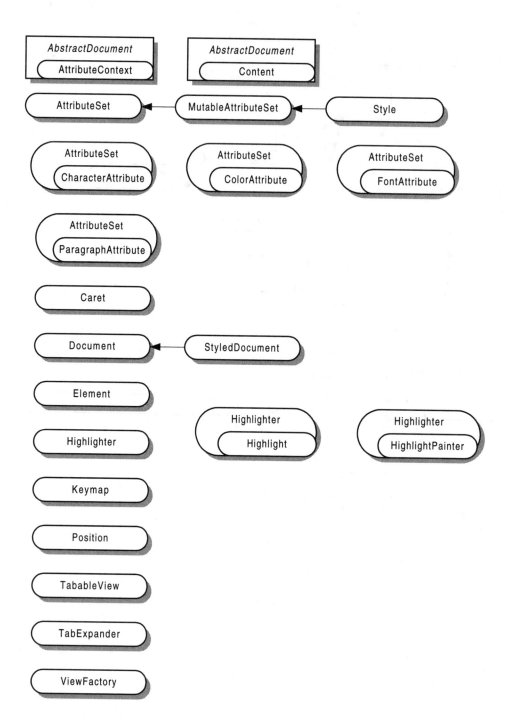

Quick summary

The view	Any component derived from `JTextComponent` (p.838). This includes `JTextField` (p.379), `JTextArea` (p.374), `JEditorPane` (p.232), and `JTextPane` (p.383).
The model	The `Document` interface is the basis for the model. An `AbstractDocument` is supplied as a base to derive your own documents. Generally, you will work with one of the supplied concrete document classes such as `PlainDocument` (p.857) and `DefaultStyledDocument` (p.820).
How to use	Generally, just choose the text component that best suits your needs. If you need custom editing capability, create a specialized `EditorKit` and `View` subclasses (usually subclasses of `LabelView`).
Coordinate system	The coordinate system used by the text package is the JDK 1.1 point-based coordinate system, which assumes there are 72 points per inch. The values are represented as floating point values because pixel locations generally don't map to an integer point value.
Display and edit	Use one of the following: `JTextField` (p.379), `JTextArea` (p.374), `JPasswordField` (p.306), `JEditorPane` (p.232), or `JTextPane` (p.383).
Events	`DocumentEvent` (p.489) and `CaretEvent` (p.485).

FAQs

What on earth do some of the terms used in this package mean?

Term	Simple definition
Attribute	A tag that can be assigned to a character or section of the document that Views use to decide how to draw the text.
Caret	The text cursor.
Document	The text being edited.
Dot	The current location of the `Caret` in the document.
Element	A piece of the `Document`, which can have associated attributes.
Mark	The position at the other end of a selection from the caret's current position. If there isn't a selection, the dot and the mark are at the same position.
Resolving parent	If an attribute can't be found in the current `AttributeSet`, look here.
Segment	A piece of text. It's important to remember that this may be a direct reference into the document, not a copy of text from the document. Don't modify the text in a `Segment`.
Span	Either the width or height, depending on the orientation.

How do I create a JTextField that only accepts numbers, phone numbers, and so forth?

Create a subclass of `PlainDocument` (or `DefaultStyledDocument`) and override the `insertString()` method. Inside the overridden method you can test the characters being inserted to see if they match the criteria you are using.

Example: A number-only field

```
// NumberDocumentTest.java
// For Swing 1.03 and before
//import com.sun.java.swing.text.*;
```

```
//import com.sun.java.swing.*;

// For Swing 1.1 and higher
import javax.swing.*;
import javax.swing.text.*

public class NumberDocumentTest {
  class NumberDocument extends PlainDocument
  {
    public void insertString(int offset,String str,AttributeSet a)
      throws BadLocationException
    {
      if (str.length() > 0)
      {
        // filter out any non-digit characters.
        if (Character.isDigit(str.charAt(0)))
        {
          super.insertString(offset,str,a);
        }
      }
    }
  }

  public NumberDocumentTest() {
    JFrame f = new JFrame();
    JTextField tf = new JTextField();
    f.getContentPane().add(new JTextField(new NumberDocument(), "", 30));
    f.setVisible(true);
  }
  public static void main(String[] args) {
    NumberDocumentTest ndt = new NumberDocumentTest();
  }
}
```

swing.text.AbstractDocument

ABSTRACT
CLASS

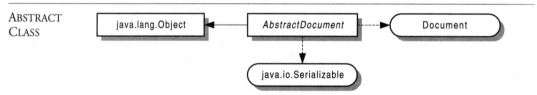

This class provides a basis for creating new kinds of Documents. One notable feature of this implementation is that it provides a readers-writers locking mechanism for the Document. The end result of this is that multiple threads can be reading the document at the same time, while writers lock out all other threads while they are making their updates.

While this policy greatly improves the efficiency of threaded access to a Document, it does mean that you must be aware of, and avoid, situations that can cause deadlock among threads.

```
public abstract class AbstractDocument
    implements Document, java.io.Serializable
```

Fields

`public static final String BidiElementName = "bidi level"`

The name used by Elements that represent a run of text in a single direction.

Since: Swing 1.1.

`public static final String ContentElementName = "content"`

The name used by Elements that represent content in the document, as opposed to formatting.

`public static final String ElementNameAttribute = "$ename"`

The attribute name used to identify Element names.

`public static final String ParagraphElementName = "paragraph"`

The name used by Elements that represent paragraphs.

`public static final String SectionElementName = "section"`

The name used by Elements that represent sections, which may be either lines or paragraphs.

Methods

`public void addDocumentListener(DocumentListener listener)`

Adds `listener` to the notification list for `DocumentEvents`.

Implements: addDocumentListener in interface Document.

`public void addUndoableEditListener(UndoableEditListener l)`

Adds `l` to the notification list for `UndoableEditEvents`. The `UndoableEdits` sent to the listeners will be configured to have their `undo()`/`redo()` methods send the correct `DocumentEvents` to keep the views of the document updated.

Implements: addUndoableEditListener in interface Document.

`public synchronized Position createPosition(int offset)`
`    throws BadLocationException`

Returns a `Position` for the given offset. `Positions` are different from plain offsets in that they are unaffected by changes in the document. The document segment they refer to will always remain the same. This method is thread safe.

Throws: BadLocationException if the given offset does not represent a valid location in the document.

Implements: createPosition in interface Document.

`public void dump(java.io.PrintStream out)`

Prints the contents of the document model to the given `PrintStream`. Used for debugging.

`public int getAsynchronousLoadPriority()`

Returns the priority of the background thread which will load the document. If the return value is less than zero, the document is loaded by the main thread.

Since: Swing 1.1.

`public Element getBidiRootElement()`

Returns the root `Element` of the bidirectional structure for this document. The child `Elements` of this root represent character runs with a given Unicode bidi level.

Since: Swing 1.1.

`public abstract Element getDefaultRootElement()`

Returns the root `Element` to be used in creating views of the document.

Implements: getDefaultRootElement in interface Document.

`public java.util.Dictionary getDocumentProperties()`

Returns the `documentProperties` dictionary. The `documentProperties` dictionary can be used to set document-wide properties.

public final Position getEndPosition()

Returns a `Position` that will always represent the end of the document, no matter what changes happen to the document.

Implements: getEndPosition in interface Document.

public int getLength()

Returns the number of characters in the document contents. The value returned is not the full size of the document, since formatting and other attributes are not included in the count.

Implements: getLength in interface Document.

public abstract Element getParagraphElement(int pos)

Returns the paragraph `Element` representing the given offset in the document. Subclasses will define the meaning of a "paragraph" in their representation. A paragraph should be, at a minimum, a unit of text appropriate for the Unicode bidirectional algorithm.

public final Object getProperty(Object key)

A convenience method provided to retrieve a value from the `documentProperties` dictionary. This method is equivalent to calling getDocumentProperties().get(key).

Implements: getProperty in interface Document.

public Element[] getRootElements()

Returns all of the root elements defined by the document. In almost all cases there will be only one root element.

Implements: getRootElements in interface Document.

public final Position getStartPosition()

Returns a `Position` that will always represent the start of the document, no matter what changes happen to the document.

Implements: getStartPosition in interface Document.

public String getText(int startOffset, int length)
throws BadLocationException

Returns the `length` characters of text starting at `startOffset` in the document.

Throws: BadLocationException if the range given includes a position outside the document.

Implements: getText in interface Document.

public void getText(int offset, int length, Segment txt)
throws BadLocationException

Causes `txt` to reference the section of text in the document starting at `offset` and running for `length` characters. This method may potentially make `txt` reference its own internal data, not a copy, so no assumptions should be made about the text remaining the same. This method is provided so that rendering can be more efficient, and should not be used anywhere else, nor should `txt` be used after the end of the rendering method.

Throws: BadLocationException if the range given includes a position that is outside the document.

Implements: getText in interface Document.

public void insertString(int offs, String str, AttributeSet a)
throws BadLocationException

Inserts the String `str` into the document at offset `offs`, using the `AttributeSet` a. Note that this method takes a write lock while it is inserting the text, and then a notification lock (which allows reading, but not writing) while listeners are notified of the change. This method is thread safe.

Throws: BadLocationException if the range refers to a position outside the document.

Implements: insertString in interface Document.

public boolean isLeftToRight(int p0, int p1)

Returns true if the text in the range p0 to p1 in the Document is left to right.

Since: Swing 1.1.

public final void putProperty(Object key, Object value)

A convenience method for placing a value in the documentProperties dictionary. It is equivalent to getDocumentProperties().put(key, value). To remove a property, associate a null value to key.

Implements: putProperty in interface Document.

public final synchronized void readLock()

Use to acquire a read lock on the document. There can be multiple simultaneous readers of a document, but writers are blocked while there are any active readers.

public final synchronized void readUnlock()

Use to release a read lock held on the document. If this read lock was the last read lock held on the document, a write lock can then be acquired.

public void remove(int startOffset, int len) throws BadLocationException

Removes the text starting at startOffset and running len characters from the document. Note that this method takes a write lock while it is inserting the text, and then a notification lock (which allows reading, but not writing) while listeners are notified of the change. This method is thread safe.

Throws: BadLocationException if the range refers to a position outside the document.

Implements: remove in interface Document.

public void removeDocumentListener(DocumentListener listener)

Removes the document listener listener.

Implements: removeDocumentListener in interface Document.

public void removeUndoableEditListener(UndoableEditListener l)

Removes the UndoableEditListener l.

Implements: removeUndoableEditListener in interface Document.

public void render(java.lang.Runnable r)

Allows the model to be rendered safely, even in the presence of other threads trying to modify it. The Runnable will be executed inside a read lock, which blocks any threads that want to write updates to the model until the Runnable completes. It is extremely important that the Runnable only read from the model, and not try to make any changes to it. If the Runnable tries to make a change, it will deadlock. It is also very important that any Runnable passed to this method eventually terminates. All updates to the model are blocked until all Runnables complete.

Implements: render in interface Document.

public void setAsynchronousLoadPriority(int p)

Sets the priority of the background thread which will load the document. If p is less than zero, the foreground thread will be used to load the document.

public void setDocumentProperties(java.util.Dictionary x)

Replaces the existing documentProperties dictionary with the given dictionary x.

Protected Fields

protected static final String BAD_LOCATION = "document location failure"

Error message to indicate a bad location.

protected EventListenerList listenerList

The event listener list for the document.

Protected Constructors

protected AbstractDocument(AbstractDocument.Content data)

Constructs a new `AbstractDocument` wrapping the contents stored in the given implementation of the `AbstractDocument.Content` interface.

protected AbstractDocument(AbstractDocument.Content data, AbstractDocument.AttributeContext context)

Constructs a new `AbstractDocument` wrapping the contents stored in the given implementation of the `AbstractDocument.Content` interface. An implementation of the `AbstractDocument.AttributeContext` interface is also passed in to manage the document's styles.

Protected Methods

protected Element createBranchElement(Element parent, AttributeSet a)

Creates and returns a branch element, one which can contain other elements.

protected Element createLeafElement(Element parent, AttributeSet a, int beginRange, int endRange)

Creates and returns a leaf element with the given attributes for the range in the document from `beginRange` to `endRange`.

protected void fireChangedUpdate(DocumentEvent e)

Notifies listeners of a change in the document.

protected void fireInsertUpdate(DocumentEvent e)

Notifies listeners of an insertion into the document.

protected void fireRemoveUpdate(DocumentEvent e)

Notifies listeners of a removal of elements from the document.

protected void fireUndoableEditUpdate(UndoableEditEvent e)

Notifies all listeners that an `UndoableEdit` has occurred.

Since: Swing 1.1.

protected final AbstractDocument.AttributeContext getAttributeContext()

Returns the `AbstractDocument.AttributeContext` implementation being used for managing the attributes in the document.

protected final AbstractDocument.Content getContent()

Returns the content for the document.

protected final synchronized java.lang.Thread getCurrentWriter()

Returns the `Thread` currently modifying the document, if there is one. The return value can be compared to the current `Thread` to determine if the write lock is already held by this thread, or if it needs to be acquired before an update can be made.

protected void insertUpdate(AbstractDocument.DefaultDocumentEvent chng, AttributeSet attr)

Updates the document structure after new text has been inserted. If this method is overridden, the subclass method should call `super.insertUpdate()` as part of its processing.

protected void postRemoveUpdate(AbstractDocument.DefaultDocumentEvent chng)

Called after the text has been removed from the Content. This method will only be called while a write lock is held. If a subclass overrides this method, it should delegate to the superclass.

protected void removeUpdate(AbstractDocument.DefaultDocumentEvent chng)

Updates the document structure after text has been removed from the document. If this method is overridden, the subclass method should call `super.removeUpdate()` as part of its processing.

`protected final synchronized void writeLock()`

Use to acquire a write lock on the document to allow modification to begin. This method will block until all existing readers and notifiers release their locks. Only one writer is allowed at a time.

`protected final synchronized void writeUnlock()`

Use to release the write lock on a document.

Inner Classes

`public abstract class AbstractDocument.AbstractElement`
`public static interface AbstractDocument.AttributeContext`
`public class AbstractDocument.BranchElement`
`public static interface AbstractDocument.Content`
`public class AbstractDocument.DefaultDocumentEvent`
`public static class AbstractDocument.ElementEdit`
`public class AbstractDocument.LeafElement`

Extended by DefaultStyledDocument (p.820), PlainDocument (p.857).
See also AbstractDocument.Content (p.788), BadLocationException (p.796), Document (p.826), DocumentEvent (p.489), DocumentListener (p.490), Element (p.830), EventListenerList (p.491), Position (p.860), Segment (p.861), UndoableEditListener (p.516).

swing.text.AbstractDocument.AbstractElement

ABSTRACT
INNER
CLASS

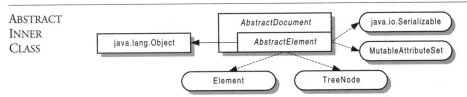

Provides the basic functionality for an `Element`. This implementation keeps the attributes in an immutable set. Any modifications to the set are in the form of copying an updated set from the `AttributeContext`. For example, an add to the set involves asking the `AttributeContext` for a new set which is created by adding the new attribute to the old set.

`public abstract class AbstractDocument.AbstractElement`
`    implements Element, MutableAttributeSet, TreeNode,`
`    java.io.Serializable`

Constructors

`public AbstractElement(Element parent, AttributeSet a)`

Constructs a new `AbstractElement` with the given attributes and the given Element as its parent.

Methods

`public void addAttribute(Object attribName, Object attribValue)`

Has the `AttributeContext` return a new set that is the old set with the given attribute added.
Implements: addAttribute in interface MutableAttributeSet.

`public void addAttributes(AttributeSet attr)`

Has the `AttributeContext` return a new set that is the old set merged with the attributes in `attr`.

Implements: addAttributes in interface MutableAttributeSet.

public abstract java.util.Enumeration children()

Returns the children of the Element as an Enumeration.

Implements: children in interface TreeNode.

public boolean containsAttribute(Object name, Object value)

Returns true if this AbstractElement contains the given name/value pair.

public boolean containsAttributes(AttributeSet attrs)

Returns true if this AbstractElement contains all of the attributes in attrs.

public AttributeSet copyAttributes()

Returns a copy of the current attribute set held by this AbstractElement.

public void dump(java.io.PrintStream out, int indentAmount)

Prints the element hierarchy to the given stream. Used for debugging.

public abstract boolean getAllowsChildren()

Returns true if the Element allows children.

Implements: getAllowsChildren in interface TreeNode.

public Object getAttribute(Object attrName)

Returns the value for the attribute named attrName.

public int getAttributeCount()

Returns the number of attributes in the current attribute set.

public java.util.Enumeration getAttributeNames()

Returns the names of all of the attributes in the current attribute set.

public AttributeSet getAttributes()

Returns the current attribute set.

Implements: getAttributes in interface Element.

public TreeNode getChildAt(int childIndex)

Returns the child Element at childIndex as a TreeNode.

Implements: getChildAt in interface TreeNode.

public int getChildCount()

Returns the number of child Elements.

Implements: getChildCount in interface TreeNode.

public Document getDocument()

Returns the Document associated with this Element.

Implements: getDocument in interface Element.

public abstract Element getElement(int index)

Returns the child element at index.

Implements: getElement in interface Element.

public abstract int getElementCount()

Returns the number of child elements this Element contains.

Implements: getElementCount in interface Element.

public abstract int getElementIndex(int offset)

Returns the index of the child Element which best represents the given offset in the Document.

Implements: getElementIndex in interface Element.

public abstract int getEndOffset()

Returns the offset in the Document which represents the end of this Element.

Implements: getEndOffset in interface Element.

`public int getIndex(TreeNode node)`

Returns the index of node in the list of child Elements. If node is not a child of this Element, this method returns −1.

Implements: getIndex in interface TreeNode.

`public String getName()`

Returns the name of this Element.

Implements: getName in interface Element.

`public TreeNode getParent()`

Returns the parent Element of this object as a TreeNode. If this object is the root Element, this method returns null.

Implements: getParent in interface TreeNode.

`public Element getParentElement()`

Returns the parent Element of this Element.

Implements: getParentElement in interface Element.

`public AttributeSet getResolveParent()`

Returns the attributes from the resolving Parent Element, or null if the parent doesn't have any attributes.

`public abstract int getStartOffset()`

Returns the offset in the Document that represents the beginning of this Element.

Implements: getStartOffset in interface Element.

`public boolean isDefined(Object attrName)`

Returns true if the attribute named attrName is defined.

`public boolean isEqual(AttributeSet attr)`

Returns true if the given attribute set matches this Element's attribute set.

`public abstract boolean isLeaf()`

Returns true if this Element is a leaf.

Implements: isLeaf in interface Element.

`public void removeAttribute(Object name)`

Uses the AttributeContext to remove an attribute from this Element's attribute set.

Implements: removeAttribute in interface MutableAttributeSet.

`public void removeAttributes(AttributeSet attrs)`

Uses the AttributeContext to remove a set of attributes from this Element's attribute set.

Implements: removeAttributes in interface MutableAttributeSet.

`public void removeAttributes(java.util.Enumeration names)`

Uses the AttributeContext to remove a set of attributes by name.

Implements: removeAttributes in interface MutableAttributeSet.

`public void setResolveParent(AttributeSet parent)`

Sets the parent to use for resolving missing attributes.

Implements: setResolveParent in interface MutableAttributeSet.

Protected Methods

`protected void finalize() throws java.lang.Throwable`

Overrides: finalize in class Object.

Extended by   AbstractDocument.BranchElement (p.786), AbstractDocument.LeafElement (p.791).

See also   AttributeSet (p.794), Document (p.826), Element (p.830), MutableAttributeSet (p.853).

swing.text.AbstractDocument.AttributeContext

INNER
INTERFACE

An interface which allows `MutableAttributeSet` implementations to perform attribute compression using a pluggable mechanism. By passing all modifications of a `MutableAttributeSet` through this interface, the attribute set may actually be immutable, with a new copy being returned. See `StyleContext` (p.872) for an implementation of this interface.

```
public static interface AbstractDocument.AttributeContext
```

Methods

```
public abstract AttributeSet addAttribute(AttributeSet oldSet,
    Object name, Object value)
```
Given an attribute set and an attribute, returns an `AttributeSet` which is equivalent to the result from adding the new attribute to the old set.

```
public abstract AttributeSet addAttributes(AttributeSet old,
    AttributeSet attr)
```
Returns an `AttributeSet` which is equivalent to the result from merging the `old` and `attr` `AttributeSets`.

```
public abstract AttributeSet getEmptySet()
```
Returns an empty `AttributeSet`.

```
public abstract void reclaim(AttributeSet a)
```
Garbage collects unnecessary `AttributeSets`. Only needed in JDK 1.1, where it emulates the JDK 1.2 concept of weak references.

```
public abstract AttributeSet removeAttribute(AttributeSet old, Object name)
```
Removes an attribute from the set.

```
public abstract AttributeSet removeAttributes(AttributeSet old,
    AttributeSet attrs)
```
Removes a set of attributes for the element.

```
public abstract AttributeSet removeAttributes(AttributeSet old,
    java.util.Enumeration names)
```
Removes a set of attributes for the element.

Implemented by   StyleContext (p.872).
See also   AttributeSet (p.794).

swing.text.AbstractDocument.BranchElement

INNER CLASS

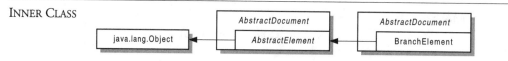

A `BranchElement` is an `Element` that can contain sub-`Elements`.

```
public class AbstractDocument.BranchElement
    extends AbstractDocument.AbstractElement
```

Constructors

public BranchElement(Element parent, AttributeSet a)

Constructs a `BranchElement` that initially doesn't have any sub-`Element`s and has the given `AttributeSet`.

Methods

public java.util.Enumeration children()

Returns the children of the `Element` as an `Enumeration`.

Overrides: `children` in class `AbstractDocument.AbstractElement`.

Implements: `children` in interface `TreeNode`.

public boolean getAllowsChildren()

Returns `true`.

Overrides: `getAllowsChildren` in class `AbstractDocument.AbstractElement`.

Implements: `getAllowsChildren` in interface `TreeNode`.

public Element getElement(int index)

Returns the child `Element` at the index.

Overrides: `getElement` in class `AbstractDocument.AbstractElement`.

Implements: `getElement` in interface `Element`.

public int getElementCount()

Returns the number of child `Element`s this `BranchElement` contains.

Overrides: `getElementCount` in class `AbstractDocument.AbstractElement`.

Implements: `getElementCount` in interface `Element`.

public int getElementIndex(int offset)

Returns the index of the child `Element` that best represents the given `Document` offset.

Overrides: `getElementIndex` in class `AbstractDocument.AbstractElement`.

Implements: `getElementIndex` in interface `Element`.

public int getEndOffset()

Returns the offset in the model that represents the end of this Element.

Overrides: `getEndOffset` in class `AbstractDocument.AbstractElement`.

Implements: `getEndOffset` in interface `Element`.

public String getName()

Returns the element name.

Overrides: `getName` in class `AbstractDocument.AbstractElement`.

Implements: `getName` in interface `Element`.

public int getStartOffset()

Returns the offset in the Document that represents the start of this Element.

Overrides: `getStartOffset` in class `AbstractDocument.AbstractElement`.

Implements: `getStartOffset` in interface `Element`.

public boolean isLeaf()

Returns `false`, since a `BranchElement` is never a leaf (it always *can* have children, even if it does not at the moment).

Overrides: `isLeaf` in class `AbstractDocument.AbstractElement`.

Implements: `isLeaf` in interface `Element`.

public Element positionToElement(int pos)

Returns the child `Element` that contains the given position in the `Document`.

public void replace(int startOffset, int length, Element[] elems)

Replaces content in the `Document` with new `Element`s.

public String toString()
> Converts the element to a string.
> *Overrides:* toString in class Object.

> *See also*   AbstractDocument.AbstractElement (p.783), AttributeSet (p.794), Element (p.830).

swing.text.AbstractDocument.Content

INNER
INTERFACE

This interface is used to describe Document content that can be edited. Implementors of this interface may or may not support undo/redo. If an implementation does not wish to support undo/redo, it simply needs to return null from all methods which have an UndoableEdit return type.

public static interface AbstractDocument.Content

Methods
public abstract Position createPosition(int offset)
> **throws BadLocationException**
> Creates a Position which maintains its relative position in the Document as best it can as the Document changes. Throws BadLocationException for an invalid offset.

public abstract void getChars(int startOffset, int len,
> **Segment copyIntoHere) throws BadLocationException**
> Copies a sequence of characters from the Document into copyIntoHere.
> *Throws:* BadLocationException if the area covered by the arguments is not contained in the character sequence.

public abstract String getString(int startOffset, int len)
> **throws BadLocationException**
> Returns a String containing the characters from the Document between startOffset and startOffset + len.

public abstract UndoableEdit insertString(int startOffset,
> **String str) throws BadLocationException**
> Inserts a String into the Document at startOffset. If the implementor of this interface supports undo/redo it should return an instance of UndoableEdit.
> *Throws:* BadLocationException if the startOffset is not in the content.

public abstract int length()
> Returns the length of the content.

public abstract UndoableEdit remove(int startOffset, int numItems)
> **throws BadLocationException**
> Removes the numItems items from the Document which start at startOffset. Otherwise, it returns null.

> *Implemented by*   StringContent (p.863).
> *See also*   AbstractDocument (p.778), BadLocationException (p.796), Position (p.860), Segment (p.861), UndoableEdit (p.1005).

INNER CLASS

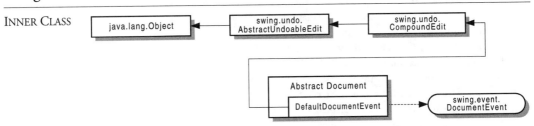

This class stores information about changes made to a Document. A single DocumentEvent may represent one or many changes to a Document. When the edit is complete the DocumentEvent may be sent to any DocumentListeners.

```
public class AbstractDocument.DefaultDocumentEvent
    extends CompoundEdit
    implements DocumentEvent
```

Constructors

public DefaultDocumentEvent(int offs, int len, DocumentEvent.EventType type)

Constructs a new DefaultDocumentEvent which represents a change starting at offs and running for len characters. The type can be DocumentEvent.EventType.CHANGE, DocumentEvent.EventType.INSERT, or DocumentEvent.EventType.REMOVE.

Methods

public boolean addEdit(UndoableEdit anEdit)

Adds anEdit to the list of edits. This implementation of this method will switch from a list of DocumentEvent.ElementChanges to a hash table if the number of edits becomes large.

Overrides: addEdit in class CompoundEdit.

Implements: addEdit in interface UndoableEdit.

public DocumentEvent.ElementChange getChange(Element elem)

Returns an object representing the changes that happened to elem.

Implements: getChange in interface DocumentEvent.

public Document getDocument()

Returns the Document that was the source of this event.

Implements: getDocument in interface DocumentEvent.

public int getLength()

Returns the length, in characters, of the change.

Implements: getLength in interface DocumentEvent.

public int getOffset()

Returns the offset into the Document content that represents the start of the changed section.

Implements: getOffset in interface DocumentEvent.

public String getPresentationName()

Returns a localized String describing the change.

Overrides: getPresentationName in class CompoundEdit.

Implements: getPresentationName in interface UndoableEdit.

public String getRedoPresentationName()

Returns a localized `String` describing the edit that can be redone.

Overrides: `getRedoPresentationName` in class `CompoundEdit`.

Implements: `getRedoPresentationName` in interface `UndoableEdit`.

public DocumentEvent.EventType getType()

Returns the type of this event.

Implements: `getType` in interface `DocumentEvent`.

public String getUndoPresentationName()

Returns a localized `String` describing the edit that can be undone.

Overrides: `getUndoPresentationName` in class `CompoundEdit`.

Implements: `getUndoPresentationName` in interface `UndoableEdit`.

public boolean isSignificant()

`DefaultDocumentEvents` are all significant. To combine multiple edits (such as the removal of text and the associated change in the selection) into one, use a `CompoundEdit`.

Overrides: `isSignificant` in class `CompoundEdit`.

Implements: `isSignificant` in interface `UndoableEdit`.

public void redo() throws CannotRedoException

Redoes an edit.

Throws: `CannotRedoException` if the change cannot be redone.

Overrides: `redo` in class `CompoundEdit`.

Implements: `redo` in interface `UndoableEdit`.

public String toString()

Returns a `String` describing the change.

Overrides: `toString` in class `CompoundEdit`.

public void undo() throws CannotUndoException

Undoes an edit.

Throws: `CannotUndoException` if the change cannot be undone.

Overrides: `undo` in class `CompoundEdit`.

Implements: `undo` in interface `UndoableEdit`.

See also   CannotRedoException (p.1000), CannotUndoException (p.1001), CompoundEdit (p.1001), Document (p.826), DocumentEvent (p.489), DocumentEvent.EventType (p.490), UndoableEdit (p.1005).

swing.text.AbstractDocument.ElementEdit

INNER CLASS

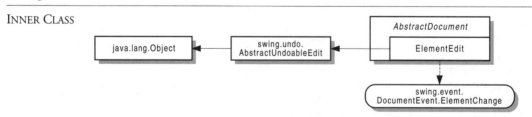

This class is an implementation of `DocumentEvent.ElementChange` as an `UndoableEdit`. Instances of this class can be added to a `DocumentEvent`.

```
public static class AbstractDocument.ElementEdit
    extends AbstractUndoableEdit
    implements DocumentEvent.ElementChange
```

Constructors
`public ElementEdit(Element e, int index, Element[] removed, Element[] added)`
Constructs an `ElementEdit` for the element at index `index` in the given parent Element e.

Methods
`public Element[] getChildrenAdded()`
Returns the child Elements that were added.
Implements: `getChildrenAdded` in interface `DocumentEvent.ElementChange`.

`public Element[] getChildrenRemoved()`
Returns the child Elements that were removed.
Implements: `getChildrenRemoved` in interface `DocumentEvent.ElementChange`.

`public Element getElement()`
Returns the parent Element of the Element this `ElementEdit` was created for.
Implements: `getElement` in interface `DocumentEvent.ElementChange`.

`public int getIndex()`
Returns the index of the represented Element in the parent's list of elements.
Implements: `getIndex` in interface `DocumentEvent.ElementChange`.

`public void redo() throws CannotRedoException`
Redoes a change.
Throws: `CannotRedoException` if the change cannot be redone.
Overrides: `redo` in class `AbstractUndoableEdit`.
Implements: `redo` in interface `UndoableEdit`.

`public void undo() throws CannotUndoException`
Undoes a change.
Throws: `CannotUndoException` if the change cannot be undone.
Overrides: `undo` in class `AbstractUndoableEdit`.
Implements: `undo` in interface `UndoableEdit`.

See also   CannotRedoException (p.1000), CannotUndoException (p.1001), DocumentEvent.ElementChange (p.489), Element (p.830).

swing.text.AbstractDocument.LeafElement

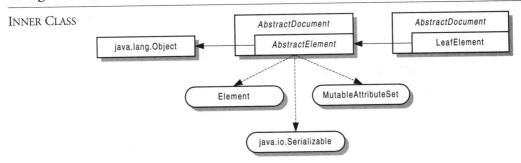

INNER CLASS

This class represents an `Element` that does not have any children, and as such, directly represents content in the `Document`.

```
public class AbstractDocument.LeafElement
    extends AbstractDocument.AbstractElement
```

Constructors

`public LeafElement(Element parent, AttributeSet a, int rangeBegin, int rangeEnd)`

Constructs a `LeafElement` that represents the content from `rangeBegin` to `rangeEnd` in the Document.

Methods

`public Element getElement(int index)`

Always returns `null`.

Overrides: `getElement` in class `AbstractDocument.AbstractElement`.

Implements: `getElement` in interface `Element`.

`public int getElementCount()`

Always returns 0.

Overrides: `getElementCount` in class `AbstractDocument.AbstractElement`.

Implements: `getElementCount` in interface `Element`.

`public int getElementIndex(int pos)`

Always returns −1, which represents no child found since this Element cannot have child elements.

Overrides: `getElementIndex` in class `AbstractDocument.AbstractElement`.

Implements: `getElementIndex` in interface `Element`.

`public int getEndOffset()`

Returns the end offset in the Document for this Element.

Overrides: `getEndOffset` in class `AbstractDocument.AbstractElement`.

Implements: `getEndOffset` in interface `Element`.

`public String getName()`

Returns this Element's name.

Overrides: `getName` in class `AbstractDocument.AbstractElement`.

Implements: `getName` in interface `Element`.

`public int getStartOffset()`

Returns the start offset in the Document for this Element.

Overrides: `getStartOffset` in class `AbstractDocument.AbstractElement`.

Implements: `getStartOffset` in interface `Element`.

`public boolean isLeaf()`

Returns `true`.

Overrides: `isLeaf` in class `AbstractDocument.AbstractElement`.

Implements: `isLeaf` in interface `Element`.

`public String toString()`

Returns a String representing the Element.

Overrides: `toString` in class `Object`.

See also AbstractDocument.AbstractElement (p.783), AttributeSet (p.794), Document (p.826), Element (p.830).

swing.text.AbstractWriter

ABSTRACT
CLASS

This abstract class provides basic support for text file formats that are tag-based and ignore new-line characters in their file formats (for example, HTML).

```
public abstract class AbstractWriter extends java.lang.Object
```

Protected Fields
protected static final char NEWLINE = '\n'
> The character used as a newline character in Java strings. Note that this is for comparing with characters in the in-memory content, not the content written to the `Writer`.

Protected Constructors
protected AbstractWriter(java.io.Writer w, Document doc)
> Creates a new `AbstractWriter` which will write out all `Elements` in the `Document`.

protected AbstractWriter(java.io.Writer w, Document doc, int pos, int len)
> Creates a new `AbstractWriter` which will write out the `Elements` in the `Document` starting at `pos` and running for `len` characters.

protected AbstractWriter(java.io.Writer w, Element root)
> Creates a new `AbstractWriter` which will write out the contents of the given `Element` and its children.

protected AbstractWriter(java.io.Writer w, Element root, int pos, int len)
> Creates a new `AbstractWriter` which will write out the contents of the given `Element` starting at `pos` and running for `len` characters.

Protected Methods
protected void decrIndent()
> Reduces the indent level by one.

protected Document getDocument()
> Returns the `Document`.

protected ElementIterator getElementIterator()
> Returns the `ElementIterator` being used to traverse the content.

protected String getText(Element elem) throws BadLocationException
> Returns the content of the given `Element`. This method assumes the `Element` is a leaf.
> *Throws:* `BadLocationException` if the start or end offsets of the `Element` represent an invalid location within the document.

protected boolean inRange(Element next)
> Returns `true` if the given `Element` either contains or is contained within the `Element` currently being written.

protected void incrIndent()
> Increments the indentation level by one.

protected void indent() throws IOException
> Writes out space characters equal in number to the indent level times the indent size.
> *Throws:* `IOException` on any I/O error.

protected void setIndentSpace(int space)

Sets the number of spaces to use for each indent level. The default is 2.

protected void setLineLength(int l)

Sets the maximum number of characters to write per line. The default is 100.

protected void text(Element elem) throws BadLocationException, IOException

Writes out the text in the Element. This method respects any ranges set using the constructor.

Throws: IOException on any I/O error, BadLocationException if any part of the Element (or the specified range) represents an invalid location within the document.

protected abstract void write() throws IOException, BadLocationException

Iterates over the content and uses the write() methods to output the content in the correct format.

protected void write(char ch) throws IOException

Writes out a single character. If the character is NEWLINE, this method resets the line length count to zero. If this character is the last character allowed on a single line by the maximum line length limit, a NEWLINE is automatically written out and the line length count is reset to zero.

Throws: IOException on any I/O error.

protected void write(String str) throws IOException

Writes out a string. If any part of the string will go past the maximum line length, a NEWLINE is written and the string is written to the new line. If the string itself is longer than the maximum line length, it will be written out in chunks which are the length of the maximum line length.

Throws: IOException on any I/O error.

protected void writeAttributes(AttributeSet attr) throws IOException

Writes out the Attributes in the set as name = value pairs.

Throws: IOException on any I/O error.

Extended by   HTMLWriter (p.931), MinimalHTMLWriter (p.934).

See also   BadLocationException (p.796), Document (p.826), Element (p.830), ElementIterator (p.831).

swing.text.AttributeSet

INTERFACE   (AttributeSet)

This interface defines methods for classes that represent a collection of unique attributes. An attribute is defined as being a (key, value) pair. There is no restriction on what the keys or the values may be. It is up to the Views to identify the attributes they understand and decide how they will be visually represented.

This interface also defines the concept of a resolving parent. If an attribute cannot be found in a table, the search will be continued in its parent table, which itself is defined as an attribute which has an AttributeSet as its value. This search continues until the attribute is found or the AttributeSet being searched does not have a parent.

public interface AttributeSet

Fields

public static final Object NameAttribute

Key used to find the value which represents the name of an `AttributeSet`.

public static final Object ResolveAttribute

Key used to find the value which represents the `AttributeSet` of the resolving parent.

Methods

public abstract boolean containsAttribute(Object name, Object value)

Returns `true` if the set already contains this (name, value) pair.

public abstract boolean containsAttributes(AttributeSet attributes)

Returns `true` if this set contains all of the attributes in `attributes`.

public abstract AttributeSet copyAttributes()

Returns a new copy of this `AttributeSet`.

public abstract Object getAttribute(Object key)

Returns the value associated with the given `key`. If the key is not found in the current set, the search will continue in the resolving parent's set, if there is a resolving parent.

public abstract int getAttributeCount()

Returns the number of attributes defined in this set.

public abstract java.util.Enumeration getAttributeNames()

Returns an Enumeration containing the results of calling `toString()` on all of the keys in the set.

public abstract AttributeSet getResolveParent()

Returns the resolving parent `AttributeSet`, if there is one.

public abstract boolean isDefined(Object attrName)

Returns `true` if the given `attrName` has an associated value in this set.

public abstract boolean isEqual(AttributeSet attr)

Returns `true` if the two `AttributeSet`s contain exactly the same set of (key, value) pairs.

Inner Classes

public static interface AttributeSet.FontAttribute
public static interface AttributeSet.ColorAttribute
public static interface AttributeSet.CharacterAttribute
public static interface AttributeSet.ParagraphAttribute

> *Extended by*   MutableAttributeSet (p.853).

swing.text.AttributeSet.CharacterAttribute

INNER
INTERFACE

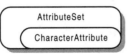

This interface is a tag or marker interface that must be present on the key object for any attribute that is to represent a character-level property.

public static interface AttributeSet.CharacterAttribute

> *Implemented by*   StyleConstants.CharacterConstants (p.869),
> StyleConstants.ColorConstants (p.870), StyleConstants.FontConstants (p.871).

swing.text.AttributeSet.ColorAttribute

INNER
INTERFACE

This interface is a tag or marker interface that must be present on the key object for any attribute that is to represent a color property.

`public static interface AttributeSet.ColorAttribute`

Implemented by   StyleConstants.ColorConstants (p.870).

swing.text.AttributeSet.FontAttribute

INNER
INTERFACE

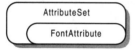

This interface is a tag or marker interface that must be present on the key object for any attribute that is to represent a font property.

`public static interface AttributeSet.FontAttribute`

Implemented by   StyleConstants.FontConstants (p.871).

swing.text.AttributeSet.ParagraphAttribute

INNER
INTERFACE

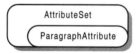

This interface is a tag or marker interface that must be present on the key object for any attribute that is to represent a paragraph-level property.

`public static interface AttributeSet.ParagraphAttribute`

Implemented by   StyleConstants.ParagraphConstants (p.872).

swing.text.BadLocationException

CLASS

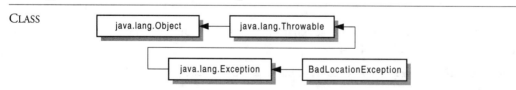

This exception is thrown when an attempt is made to reference a location in a Document that doesn't exist.

```
public class BadLocationException extends java.lang.Exception
```

Constructors
```
public BadLocationException(String explanation, int offsetInDocument)
```
Creates a new BadLocationException.

Methods
```
public int offsetRequested()
```
Returns the first offset into the Document that was invalid.

Thrown by AbstractDocument (p.778), AbstractDocument.Content (p.788), ComponentView (p.802), DefaultEditorKit (p.810), DefaultHighlighter (p.818), DefaultTextUI (p.826), Document (p.826), EditorKit (p.829), Highlighter (p.835), HTMLEditorKit (p.922), JTextArea (p.374), JTextComponent (p.838), PasswordView (p.856), PlainView (p.858), RTFEditorKit (p.952), StringContent (p.863), View (p.893), WrappedPlainView (p.897).

swing.text.BoxView

CLASS

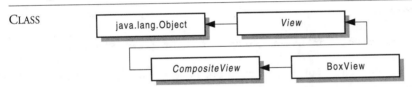

A View that arranges its children into the form of a box. As an example of where it can be used, it could be used to represent a whole page with multiple paragraphs.

```
public class BoxView extends CompositeView
```

Constructors
```
public BoxView(Element elem, int axis)
```
Constructs a BoxView which will arrange its children horizontally (when axis is View.X_AXIS) or vertically (when axis is View.Y_AXIS).

Methods
```
public void changedUpdate(DocumentEvent changeInfo, java.awt.Shape a,
    ViewFactory f)
```
Called when the Document has changed in an area this view is presenting.
Overrides: changedUpdate in class View.
```
public float getAlignment(int axis)
```
Returns the alignment of this View along the given axis (either View.X_AXIS or View.Y_AXIS). The alignment value is a float that must range between 0.0 and 1.0, with 0.5 being centered. The axis along which the children are being arranged will return 0.5 and the other axis will return the alignment needed to line up all of the children along their preferred alignments.
Throws: IllegalArgumentException for an invalid axis.
Overrides: getAlignment in class View.

public final int getHeight()

Returns the height of this BoxView.

public float getMaximumSpan(int axis)

Returns the maximum width or height for this view along axis.

Throws: IllegalArgumentException for an invalid axis.

Overrides: getMaximumSpan in class View.

public float getMinimumSpan(int axis)

Returns the minimum width or height for this view along axis.

Throws: IllegalArgumentException for an invalid axis.

Overrides: getMinimumSpan in class View.

public float getPreferredSpan(int axis)

Returns the preferred width or height for this view along the given axis.

Throws: IllegalArgumentException for an invalid axis.

Overrides: getPreferredSpan in class View.

public int getResizeWeight(int axis)

Determines the resizability of the view along the given axis. A value of 0 or less is not resizable. Returns the sum of the resizeWeights of this View's children.

Overrides: getResizeWeight in class View.

public final int getWidth()

Returns the last allocated width for this view.

public void insertUpdate(DocumentEvent changeInfo, java.awt.Shape a, ViewFactory f)

Called when content was inserted into the Document at a point being rendered by this View.

Overrides: insertUpdate in class View.

public java.awt.Shape modelToView(int pos, java.awt.Shape thisViewsAllocation) throws BadLocationException

Returns the bounding box of the View region that represents the given offset pos in the Document content.

Throws: BadLocationException if the given position does not represent a valid location in the associated document.

Overrides: modelToView in class CompositeView.

public void paint(java.awt.Graphics g, java.awt.Shape allocation)

Renders this View into the given graphics context using the given allocated area.

Overrides: paint in class View.

public void preferenceChanged(View child, boolean width, boolean height)

A child view calls this method when its preferred width, height, or both changes. The two boolean flags indicate which dimension(s) changed.

Overrides: preferenceChanged in class View.

public void removeUpdate(DocumentEvent e, java.awt.Shape a, ViewFactory f)

Called when content is removed from the portion of the Document that this View represents.

Overrides: removeUpdate in class View.

public void replace(int offset, int count, View[] elems)

Replaces the count child Views starting at offset in this View's list of children with the Views in elems.

Overrides: replace in class CompositeView.

public void setSize(float width, float height)

Sets the size of the View, including the area occupied by the insets around the View.

Overrides: setSize in class View.

public int viewToModel(float x, float y, java.awt.Shape a)

Returns the offset into the Document that represents the point at (x, y).

Overrides: viewToModel in class CompositeView.

Protected Methods

protected void baselineLayout(int targetSpan, int axis, int[] offsets, int[] spans)

Lays out views along a baseline. The offsets and spans parameters are output parameters. The returned offsets are the offset of the views below the baseline, and the spans are the total heights of the views.

protected SizeRequirements baselineRequirements(int axis, SizeRequirements r)

Calculates the space needed to fit views along a baseline.

protected SizeRequirements calculateMajorAxisRequirements(int axis, SizeRequirements r)

Calculates the space needed to fit the View along its major axis.

protected SizeRequirements calculateMinorAxisRequirements(int axis, SizeRequirements r)

Calculates the space needed to fit the View along its minor axis.

protected void childAllocation(int childIndex, java.awt.Rectangle allocatedRegion)

Allocates a region for the child View at childIndex.

Overrides: childAllocation in class CompositeView.

protected boolean flipEastAndWestAtEnds(int position, Position.Bias bias)

If the view at position is a CompositeView, returns the value from its flipEastAnd-WestAtEnds() method. Otherwise, returns false. See CompositeView for more details on what this method is for.

Overrides: flipEastAndWestAtEnds in class CompositeView.

protected final int getOffset(int axis, int childIndex)

Returns the offset to the given child along the given axis.

protected final int getSpan(int axis, int childIndex)

Returns the width or height of a child View, depending on the axis.

protected View getViewAtPoint(int x, int y, java.awt.Rectangle alloc)

Returns the child View whose display area includes the point (x, y). When calling this method, pass the parent's bounding box as alloc. When this method returns, alloc will be the child View's bounding box.

Overrides: getViewAtPoint in class CompositeView.

protected boolean isAfter(int x, int y, java.awt.Rectangle innerAlloc)

Returns true if the point (x, y) is logically after the given Rectangle.

Overrides: isAfter in class CompositeView.

protected boolean isAllocationValid()

Returns true if the regions allocated to this View's child Views are still valid. The allocations would be invalid after changes to the document.

protected boolean isBefore(int x, int y, java.awt.Rectangle innerAlloc)
Returns true if the point (x, y) is logically before the given Rectangle.
Overrides: isBefore in class CompositeView.

protected void layout(int width, int height)
Lays out the child Views of this View. The given width and height defines the width and height of the View less the area used by the insets. This method calls layoutMajorAxis() or layoutMinorAxis() as appropriate.

protected void layoutMajorAxis(int targetSpan, int axis,
int[] offsets, int[] spans)
Lays out the views along the major axis of the box. The calculated values are returned in the offsets and spans arrays. The offsets array is the offsets from the axis, and the spans array is the size of the views.

protected void layoutMinorAxis(int targetSpan, int axis,
int[] offsets, int[] spans)
Lays out the views along the minor axis of the box. The calculated values are returned in the offsets and spans arrays. The offsets array is the offsets from the axis, and the spans array is the size of the views.

protected void paintChild(java.awt.Graphics g, Rectangle alloc, int index)
Paints the child at index into the rectangular region alloc.

Extended by   BlockView (p.902), ParagraphView (p.853), TableView (p.886), TableView.TableCell (p.887), TableView.TableRow (p.888), WrappedPlainView (p.897).
See also   CompositeView (p.804), DocumentEvent (p.489), Element (p.830), View (p.893), ViewFactory (p.896).

swing.text.Caret

INTERFACE   (Caret)

A Caret is what people normally think of as a text cursor. From a technical standpoint, it really represents, in the View, the position at which insertions will occur into the Document. The Caret is also used to indicate and manage navigation through the Document contents so sections can be skipped over if necessary.

public interface Caret

Methods
public abstract void addChangeListener(ChangeListener l)
The listeners added through this method will be notified whenever the Caret position changes.
public abstract void deinstall(JTextComponent c)
Called when the Caret is being removed from a JTextComponent. This method should be used to remove the Caret from the listener lists it added itself to in install().

public abstract int getBlinkRate()

Returns the number of milliseconds between blinks of the Caret. Carets are usually made to blink while not moving so they can be found more easily by the user. If this method returns 0, the Caret is not blinking.

public abstract int getDot()

Returns the current postion of the Caret as an offset into the Document.

public abstract java.awt.Point getMagicCaretPosition()

Returns the last remembered position of the Caret. This is used in situations where the Caret is being moved between lines of text. When the Caret moves from a longer line to a line which is too short to represent the same position on the line, the `MagicCaretPosition` remembers the old position for when the Caret returns to a sufficiently long line.

public abstract int getMark()

Returns the mark. The mark represents the other end of a text selection relative to where the Caret currently is.

public abstract void install(JTextComponent c)

Called when the Caret is being added to a `JTextComponent`. This allows the Caret to discover the model to navigate and to add the Caret as a listener for various events in the component.

public abstract boolean isSelectionVisible()

Returns `true` if the selection is currently visible.

public abstract boolean isVisible()

Returns `true` if the Caret is currently visible. Note that this method will return `true` even if the Caret is in the off half of a blink, as long as the visible property is `true`.

public abstract void moveDot(int dot)

Moves the Caret to a new position, leaving behind the mark. This is used when making selections.

public abstract void paint(java.awt.Graphics g)

Paints the Caret.

public abstract void removeChangeListener(ChangeListener l)

Removes the listener from the list of listeners to notify when the Caret changes position.

public abstract void setBlinkRate(int rate)

Sets the number of milliseconds between blinks. If 0 is passed to this method, the Caret will not blink.

public abstract void setDot(int dot)

Sets the Caret position to the given position `dot`. This will also move the mark to match, clearing any selection.

public abstract void setMagicCaretPosition(java.awt.Point p)

Saves the current Caret position. This position is used to remember the Caret position when the Caret moves from a longer line to a line that is too short to allow the Caret to keep the same position. The position on the long line is saved in the magic position so it can be restored when the Caret returns to a sufficiently long line.

public abstract void setSelectionVisible(boolean v)

Sets the visibility of the selection.

public abstract void setVisible(boolean showCaret)

Sets the visibility of the Caret. Note that this is not related to the on-off cycle of a blinking Caret. If this is set to `false`, the Caret will not show at all.

Implemented by DefaultCaret (p.806).

See also ChangeListener (p.488), JTextComponent (p.838).

swing.text.ChangedCharSetException

CLASS

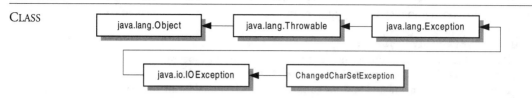

This exception is used by a parser reading an input file to indicate that the character set of the file is different than what is currently being used. The `EditorKit` can catch this exception and restart the `read()` of the file using the correct character set.

```
public class ChangedCharSetException extends java.io.IOException
```

Constructors
public ChangedCharSetException(String charSetSpec, boolean charSetKey)

Creates a `ChangedCharSetException`, passing the new character set name (or the full "content-type" attribute) as `charSetSpec`, and passing `true` for `charSetKey` if the `charSetSpec` came from a "charset" parameter on a MIME type.

Methods
public String getCharSetSpec()

Returns the name of the new charset (for example, "ISO-8859-1") or content type (for example, "text/plain" or "text/html; charset=Euc-jp").

public boolean keyEqualsCharSet()

Returns `true` if the returned `String` from `getCharSetSpec()` is a character set name. Returns `false` if the returned `String` from `getCharSetSpec()` is a full content-type string and the charset parameter will need to be searched for in the string.

Thrown by DocumentParser.handleEmptyTag() (p.944), Parser.handleEmptyTag() (p.948), Parser.startTag() (p.948).

swing.text.ComponentView

CLASS

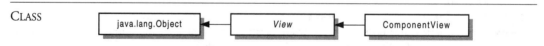

This `View` allows components to be embedded into a `View`. An example of this would be a Java button on a Web page, where there is an active button component surrounded by read-only text. The component used in this `View` occupies the whole `View` area, less the insets.

```
public class ComponentView extends View
```

Constructors
public ComponentView(Element elem)

Constructs a `ComponentView` for the given element.

Methods

public float getAlignment(int axis)

Returns the alignment property of the component.

Overrides: getAlignment in class View.

public final java.awt.Component getComponent()

Returns the component for the view.

public float getMaximumSpan(int axis)

Returns the maximum width or height for this view along an axis.

Throws: IllegalArgumentException for an invalid axis.

Overrides: getMaximumSpan in class View.

public float getMinimumSpan(int axis)

Returns the minimum width or height for this view along an axis.

Throws: IllegalArgumentException for an invalid axis.

Overrides: getMinimumSpan in class View.

public float getPreferredSpan(int axis)

Returns the preferred width or height for the component along the given axis. The axis parameter is either View.X_AXIS or View.Y_AXIS.

Overrides: getPreferredSpan in class View.

public java.awt.Shape modelToView(int pos, java.awt.Shape alloc, Position.Bias[] bias) throws BadLocationException

If pos is between the start postion and the end position of the Element used to construct this View, this method returns the bounding Rectangle of alloc after setting the width to 0. If pos is not inside the associated Element, this method returns null.

Throws: This implementation of this method will never throw a BadLocationException.

Overrides: modelToView in class View.

public void paint(java.awt.Graphics g, java.awt.Shape a)

Used to properly size and position the component. The actual painting of the component happens as a result of it being contained by the same container as the View.

Overrides: paint in class View.

public void setParent(View p)

Sets the parent for this View, and then adds the component to the container this View is in. If p is null, this will remove the View and detach the component from the View's parent container.

Overrides: setParent in class View.

public void setSize(float width, float height)

Sets the size of the component.

Overrides: setSize in class View.

public int viewToModel(float x, float y, java.awt.Shape a, Position.Bias[] bias)

Returns the start offset of the Element associated with this View.

Overrides: viewToModel in class View.

Protected Methods

protected java.awt.Component createComponent()

Creates and returns a new component to use. This method will be called when the parent container of the View changes or the attribute defining the component changes.

See also Element (p.830), View (p.893).

swing.text.CompositeView

A `View` that presents a set of child `Views`. This class can be used to create any subclass that contains a set of `Views`.

```
public abstract class CompositeView extends View
```

Constructors

public CompositeView(Element elem)

Creates a `CompositeView` associated with the given `Element`.

Methods

public void append(View v)

Appends v to the list of child elements.

public java.awt.Shape getChildAllocation(int index, java.awt.Shape a)

Returns the bounding box the child at `index` should render into.

Overrides: `getChildAllocation` in class `View`.

public int getNextVisualPositionFrom(int pos, Position.Bias b,
Shape a, int direction, Position.Bias[] biasRet)
throws BadLocationException

Uses `getNorthSouthVisualDirectionFrom()` and `getEastWestVisualDirection-From()` to decide the offset of the next visible location in the given direction. This test is required because all content in a document may not be visible, and the `Elements` and `Views` may not be in the same order as the content they represent in the `Document` (for example, in text which has mixed reading directions). The direction is one of `SwingConstants.WEST`, `SwingConstants.EAST`, `SwingConstants.NORTH`, or `SwingConstants.SOUTH`.

Throws: `IllegalArgumentException` for an invalid direction, `BadLocationException` if a position outside the `Document` is encountered.

Overrides: `getNextVisualPositionFrom` in class `View`.

public View getView(int n)

Returns the child `View` at index n.

Throws: `ArrayIndexOutOfBounds` if n >= `getViewCount()`.

Overrides: `getView` in class `View`.

public int getViewCount()

Returns the number of child `Views` contained by this `View`.

Overrides: `getViewCount` in class `View`.

public void insert(int offs, View v)

Inserts v into the list of child `Views` at `offs`.

public java.awt.Shape modelToView(int p0, Position.Bias b0, int p1,
Position.Bias b1, java.awt.Shape a) throws BadLocationException

Returns the bounding box of the given range of content when rendered by the `View`.

Throws: `BadLocationException` if the given range does not represent a valid location in the associated `Document`, `IllegalArgumentException` for an invalid `Bias` argument.

Overrides: `modelToView` in class `View`.

**public java.awt.Shape modelToView(int pos, java.awt.Shape a,
  Position.Bias b) throws BadLocationException**

Returns the bounding box of the given pos when rendered by the View.

Throws: BadLocationException if the given position does not represent a valid location in the associated Document.

Overrides: modelToView in class View.

public void removeAll()

Removes all child Views from this View.

public void replace(int offset, int length, View[] views)

Replaces the Views starting at offset and ending at offset + length in the child View list with the Views in views.

public void setParent(View parent)

Sets the parent of the View and loads the child Views.

Overrides: setParent in class View.

**public int viewToModel(float x, float y, java.awt.Shape a,
  Position.Bias[] b)**

Returns the position in the document which best represents the point (x, y) in the View.

Overrides: viewToModel in class View.

Protected Methods

**protected abstract void childAllocation(int index,
  java.awt.Rectangle a)**

Returns the allocation for the child Element at index in the passed-in Rectangle.

protected boolean flipEastAndWestAtEnds(int position, Position.Bias bias)

Returns false. A subclass which supported right-to-left text would return true from this method to indicate that when a View returned −1 from getNextVisualPositionFrom() (meaning the next visual position is in the next or previous View, depending on the direction), the View chosen would be currentViewIndex − 1 for SwingConstants.EAST and currentViewIndex + 1 for SwingConstants.WEST. Returning false causes the default left-to-right ordering of Views to be used, meaning SwingConstants.EAST would use currentViewIndex + 1 and SwingConstants.WEST would use currentViewIndex − 1.

protected final short getBottomInset()

Returns the inset at the bottom of the View.

protected java.awt.Rectangle getInsideAllocation(java.awt.Shape a)

Returns the Rectangle defining the region a less the margins on the four sides, if any.

protected final short getLeftInset()

Returns the inset at the left of the View.

**protected int getNextEastWestVisualPositionFrom(int pos,
  Position.Bias b, java.awt.Shape a, int direction,
  Position.Bias[] biasRet) throws BadLocationException**

Returns the next position for the Caret in either the EAST or the WEST.

**protected int getNextNorthSouthVisualPositionFrom(int pos,
  Position.Bias b, java.awt.Shape a, int direction,
  Position.Bias[] biasRet) throws BadLocationException**

Returns the next position for the Caret in either the NORTH or the SOUTH.

protected final short getRightInset()

Returns the inset at the right of the View.

protected final short getTopInset()
Returns the inset at the top of the View.

protected abstract View getViewAtPoint(int x, int y, Rectangle alloc)
Returns the child View which contains the point (x, y).

protected View getViewAtPosition(int pos, java.awt.Rectangle a)
Returns the child View which represents pos in the Document.

protected int getViewIndexAtPosition(int pos)
Returns the index of the child View which is responsible for the section of the Document which contains pos.

protected abstract boolean isAfter(int x, int y, java.awt.Rectangle alloc)
Returns true if the point (x, y) is logically after alloc.

protected abstract boolean isBefore(int x, int y, java.awt.Rectangle alloc)
Returns true if the point (x, y) is logically before alloc.

protected void loadChildren(ViewFactory f)
Loads the child Views representing the child Elements of the Element corresponding to this View. This method is called by the setParent() method.

protected final void setInsets(short top, short left, short bottom, short right)
Sets the insets for the view.

protected final void setParagraphInsets(AttributeSet attr)
Sets the insets for the child Views of this View from the paragraph attributes specified in attr.

Extended by   BoxView (p.797).

See also   AttributeSet (p.794), BadLocationException (p.796), View (p.893), ViewFactory (p.896).

swing.text.DefaultCaret

CLASS

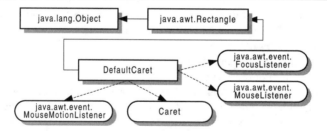

The default implementation of a text caret. This caret traverses the entire Document without skipping any sections. It draws the caret as a blinking vertical line, drawn using the caretColor property of the asociated JTextComponent. This caret uses the Highlighter defined by the look and feel to draw the selection highlight (which is usually some form of a shaded rectangle covering the selected text).

```
public class DefaultCaret extends java.lang.Object
    implements Caret, java.awt.event.FocusListener,
    java.awt.event.MouseListener,
    java.awt.event.MouseMotionListener
```

Constructors

public DefaultCaret()

Constructs a default caret.

Methods

public void addChangeListener(ChangeListener listener)

Adds `listener` to the list of listeners to notify when the caret's position changes.

Implements: addChangeListener in interface Caret.

public void deinstall(JTextComponent c)

Called when the caret is being removed from a JTextComponent. This allows the caret to unregister itself from all of the listener interfaces it added itself to in the `install()` method.

Implements: deinstall in interface Caret.

public void focusGained(java.awt.event.FocusEvent e)

Sets the caret to `visible` if the text component is editable, and sets the selection to `visible`.

Implements: focusGained in interface FocusListener.

public void focusLost(java.awt.event.FocusEvent e)

Sets the caret visibility to `false` and sets the selection visibility to `false`.

Implements: focusLost in interface FocusListener.

public int getBlinkRate()

Returns the number of milliseconds between the on and off parts of the blink cycle.

Implements: getBlinkRate in interface Caret.

public int getDot()

Returns the current position of the caret in the Document.

Implements: getDot in interface Caret.

public java.awt.Point getMagicCaretPosition()

Returns the saved caret position. The magic caret position is used when the caret is moved between lines of text and the line it is moving to is too short to allow the caret to be placed at the same line offset as the previous line. When the caret reaches a sufficiently long line, the caret position is restored from the magic caret position.

Implements: getMagicCaretPosition in interface Caret.

public int getMark()

Returns the mark, which is the other end of a selection from the caret. If there isn't a selection, the caret position (the `dot`) and the mark will be the same.

Implements: getMark in interface Caret.

public void install(JTextComponent c)

Called when the caret is being attached to a JTextComponent. Can be used to add this caret as a listener for various JTextComponent events (such as mouse events or key events) and to get the model for the JTextComponent.

Implements: install in interface Caret.

public boolean isSelectionVisible()

Returns `true` if the current selection is visible.

Implements: isSelectionVisible in interface Caret.

public boolean isVisible()

Returns `true` if the caret is visible. Note that this method returns `true` even if the caret is in the off/invisible half of a blink. If the caret is not visible, the caret will not show up at all.

Implements: isVisible in interface Caret.

public void mouseClicked(java.awt.event.MouseEvent e)

Called when the mouse is clicked. A double click selects a word; a triple click selects the current line.

Implements: mouseClicked in interface MouseListener.

public void mouseDragged(java.awt.event.MouseEvent e)

Moves the caret position according to the mouse pointer's current location. This effectively extends the selection since it does not move the mark.

Implements: mouseDragged in interface MouseMotionListener.

public void mouseEntered(java.awt.event.MouseEvent e)

An empty method.

Implements: mouseEntered in interface MouseListener.

public void mouseExited(java.awt.event.MouseEvent e)

An empty method.

Implements: mouseExited in interface MouseListener.

public void mouseMoved(java.awt.event.MouseEvent e)

An empty method.

Implements: mouseMoved in interface MouseMotionListener.

public void mousePressed(java.awt.event.MouseEvent e)

Requests focus on the associated text component, and tries to set the cursor position.

Implements: mousePressed in interface MouseListener.

public void mouseReleased(java.awt.event.MouseEvent e)

An empty method.

Implements: mouseReleased in interface MouseListener.

public void moveDot(int dot)

Moves the caret to another location, leaving the mark unchanged. This method is used to create a selection.

Implements: moveDot in interface Caret.

public void paint(java.awt.Graphics g)

Draws the caret. If the paint method is overridden to draw the caret as something other than a vertical single pixel line, the damage() method needs to be overridden as well to cause the repainting of the correct area when the caret moves.

Implements: paint in interface Caret.

public void removeChangeListener(ChangeListener l)

Removes the given ChangeListener.

Implements: removeChangeListener in interface Caret.

public void setBlinkRate(int rate)

Sets the time between the on and off parts of the blink cycle to rate milliseconds.

Implements: setBlinkRate in interface Caret.

public void setDot(int dot)

Moves the caret to the given position. This method also moves the mark to the same position, so it will get rid of any selection.

Implements: setDot in interface Caret.

public void setMagicCaretPosition(java.awt.Point p)

Saves the caret position when the caret moves from a long line to a shorter line, making it impossible to display the caret at the same position. When the caret returns to a sufficiently long line, the position will be restored from the magic position.

Implements: setMagicCaretPosition in interface Caret.

public void setSelectionVisible(boolean vis)

Changes the selection visibility.

Implements: setSelectionVisible in interface Caret.

public void setVisible(boolean e)

Sets the caret's visibility.

Implements: setVisible in interface Caret.

public String toString()

Overrides: toString in class Rectangle.

Protected Fields

protected transient ChangeEvent changeEvent

The ChangeEvent always used by the caret. Since a ChangeEvent doesn't have any state information that changes and the source for ChangeEvents sent by this caret is always this, it can use just one instance for all changes and listeners.

protected EventListenerList listenerList

The list of ChangeListeners.

Protected Methods

protected void adjustVisibility(java.awt.Rectangle newPosition)

If necessary, scrolls the View so the caret is visible. This implementation uses scrollRectToVisible(). A subclass could override this method to reduce the number of times the view has to be scrolled by scrolling more intelligently. For example, the subclass could center the View horizontally around the caret so it would have to move a half line before the View scrolled again.

protected void damage(java.awt.Rectangle r)

Causes the area around the caret to be repainted. If paint() is overridden, this method must also be overridden to cause a repaint of the area occupied by the new caret indicator.

protected void fireStateChanged()

Informs all ChangeListeners that the caret's position has changed.

protected final JTextComponent getComponent()

Returns the JTextComponent this caret is installed in.

protected Highlighter.HighlightPainter getSelectionPainter()

Returns the object used to paint the highlight (selection indicator).

protected void moveCaret(java.awt.event.MouseEvent e)

Tries to move the position of the caret from the coordinates of a mouse event, using viewToModel(). This will cause a selection if the dot and mark are different.

protected void positionCaret(java.awt.event.MouseEvent e)

Tries to set the position of the caret from the coordinates of a mouse event, using viewToModel(). This method moves the dot and mark to the new location, clearing any selection.

protected final synchronized void repaint()

Causes the caret indicator to be repainted.

See also   Caret (p.800), ChangeEvent (p.487), ChangeListener (p.488), EventListenerList (p.491), Highlighter.HighlightPainter (p.837), JTextComponent (p.838).

swing.text.DefaultEditorKit

CLASS

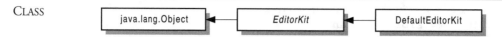

A default EditorKit that provides the minimal functionality required by any text editor. This EditorKit only supports plain text and the minimal set of Actions.

The Actions supported by a DefaultEditorKit are the following:

Actions supported by the DefaultEditorKit class

Constant name (in the form DefaultEditorKit.X)	String value of name	Purpose
backwardAction	"caret-backward"	Moves the caret logically backward one position.
beepAction	"beep"	Causes the system to emit a beep.
beginAction	"caret-begin"	Moves the caret to the beginning of the document.
beginLineAction	"caret-begin-line"	Moves the caret to the beginning of the current line.
beginParagraphAction	"caret-begin-paragraph"	Moves the caret to the beginning of the current paragraph.
beginWordAction	"caret-begin-word"	Moves the caret to the beginning of the current word (the position after the first white space to be found before the current caret position).
copyAction	"copy-to-clipboard"	Places a copy of the selected text into the system clipboard.
cutAction	"cut-to-clipboard"	Removes the selected text from the document and places it in the system clipboard.
defaultKeyTypedAction	"default-typed"	The action to perform when a key is typed and there isn't a Keymap entry for it.
deleteNextCharAction	"delete-next"	Deletes the character that is immediately after the current caret position.
deletePrevCharAction	"delete-previous"	Deletes the character that is immediately before the current caret position.
downAction	"caret-down"	Moves the caret logically downward one position (usually forward a line's worth of content).
endAction	"caret-end"	Moves the caret to the end of the document.
endLineAction	"caret-end-line"	Moves the caret to the end of the current line.
endParagraphAction	"caret-end-paragraph"	Moves the caret to the end of the current paragraph.
endWordAction	"caret-end-word"	Moves the caret to the end of the current word (the position before the first white space to be found after the current caret position).
forwardAction	"caret-forward"	Moves the caret logically forward one position.
insertBreakAction	"insert-break"	Inserts a line or paragraph break into the document, replacing the selected text, if there is any.
insertContentAction	"insert-content"	Inserts text into the document, replacing the selected text, if there is any.

Actions supported by the DefaultEditorKit class (continued)

Constant name (in the form DefaultEditorKit.X)	String value of name	Purpose
insertTabAction	"insert-tab"	Inserts a tab character into the document, replacing the selected text, if there is any.
nextWordAction	"caret-next-word"	Moves the caret to the beginning of the next word.
pageDownAction	"page-down"	Scrolls the View down a page.
pageUpAction	"page-up"	Scrolls the View up a page.
pasteAction	"paste-from-clipboard"	Inserts the contents of the system clipboard into the document, replacing the selected text if there is any.
previousWordAction	"caret-previous-word"	Moves the caret to the beginning of the previous word.
readOnlyAction	"set-read-only"	Makes the editor read only.
selectAllAction	"select-all"	Selects the entire document.
selectionBackwardAction	"selection-backward"	Changes the selection by moving the caret logically backward one position.
selectionBeginAction	"selection-begin"	Changes the selection by moving the caret to the beginning of the document.
selectionBeginLineAction	"selection-begin-line"	Changes the selection by moving the caret to the beginning of the current line.
selectionBeginParagraphAction	"selection-begin-paragraph"	Changes the selection by moving the caret to the beginning of the current paragraph.
selectionBeginWordAction	"selection-begin-word"	Changes the selection by moving the caret to the beginning of the current word.
selectionDownAction	"selection-down"	Changes the selection by moving the caret logically downward one position (usually forward a line's worth of content).
selectionEndAction	"selection-end"	Changes the selection by moving the caret to the end of the document.
selectionEndLineAction	"selection-end-line"	Changes the selection by moving the caret to the end of the current line.
selectionEndParagraphAction	"selection-end-paragraph"	Changes the selection by moving the caret to the end of the current paragraph.
selectionEndWordAction	"selection-end-word"	Changes the selection by moving the caret to the end of the current word.
selectionForwardAction	"selection-forward"	Changes the selection by moving the caret logically forward one position.
selectionNextWordAction	"selection-next-word"	Changes the selection by moving the caret to the beginning of the next word.
selectionPreviousWordAction	"selection-previous-word"	Changes the selection by moving the caret to the beginning of the previous word.
selectionUpAction	"selection-up"	Changes the selection by moving the caret logically upward one position (usually backward a line's worth of content).

text

Constant name (in the form DefaultEditorKit.X)	String value of name	Purpose
selectLineAction	"select-line"	Selects the line the caret is on.
selectParagraphAction	"select-paragraph"	Selects the paragraph the caret is in.
selectWordAction	"select-word"	Selects the word the caret is in.
upAction	"caret-up"	Moves the caret logically upward one position (usually backward a line's worth of content).
writableAction	"set-writable"	Makes the editor editable.

```
public class DefaultEditorKit extends EditorKit
```

Fields

```
public static final String EndOfLineStringProperty
```
    This property name is used to store the end-of-line character that was found when reading the document, so it can be used again when the document is written back out.

```
public static final String backwardAction
public static final String beepAction
public static final String beginAction
public static final String beginLineAction
public static final String beginParagraphAction
public static final String beginWordAction
public static final String copyAction
public static final String cutAction
public static final String defaultKeyTypedAction
public static final String deleteNextCharAction
public static final String deletePrevCharAction
public static final String downAction
public static final String endAction
public static final String endLineAction
public static final String endParagraphAction
public static final String endWordAction
public static final String forwardAction
public static final String insertBreakAction
public static final String insertContentAction
public static final String insertTabAction
public static final String nextWordAction
public static final String pageDownAction
public static final String pageUpAction
public static final String pasteAction
public static final String previousWordAction
public static final String readOnlyAction
public static final String selectAllAction
public static final String selectLineAction
public static final String selectParagraphAction
public static final String selectWordAction
public static final String selectionBackwardAction
public static final String selectionForwardAction
```

```
public static final String selectionBeginLineAction
public static final String selectionBeginParagraphAction
public static final String selectionBeginWordAction
public static final String selectionDownAction
public static final String selectionEndAction
public static final String selectionEndLineAction
public static final String selectionEndParagraphAction
public static final String selectionEndWordAction
public static final String selectionForwardAction
public static final String selectionNextWordAction
public static final String selectionPreviousWordAction
public static final String selectionUpAction
public static final String upAction
public static final String writableAction
```

Constant names that can be used to access the different Actions. These names can be used to find the corresponding Action in the array returned by the getActions() call. See the above table for descriptions of what each of the Actions does.

Constructors

public DefaultEditorKit()

Constructs a DefaultEditorKit.

Methods

public Object clone()

Creates a duplicate of the current instance.

Overrides: clone in class EditorKit.

public Caret createCaret()

Returns a Caret that knows how to display itself in the Views returned from this EditorKit's ViewFactory. This method returns null.

Overrides: createCaret in class EditorKit.

public Document createDefaultDocument()

Creates an empty Document appropriate for this type of EditorKit. This method returns a new instance of a PlainDocument.

Overrides: createDefaultDocument in class EditorKit.

public Action[] getActions()

Returns an array of the Actions supported by this EditorKit. See the above table for a list of the supported Actions.

Overrides: getActions in class EditorKit.

public String getContentType()

Returns the MIME type that this EditorKit supports, which is "text/plain."

Overrides: getContentType in class EditorKit.

public ViewFactory getViewFactory()

Returns null, since this EditorKit lets the UI supply the ViewFactory.

Overrides: getViewFactory in class EditorKit.

public void read(java.io.InputStream in, Document doc, int pos)
 throws IOException, BadLocationException

Reads from in and inserts the content into the Document starting at pos. The line separator character found is stored in the Document's property table using a name EndOfLineStringProperty.

Throws: `IOException` on any I/O error, `BadLocationException` if `pos` represents an invalid location within the document.

Overrides: `read` in class `EditorKit`.

`public void read(java.io.Reader in, Document doc, int pos)`
    `throws IOException, BadLocationException`

Reads from the `Reader` `in` and inserts the content into the `Document` starting at `pos`.

Throws: `IOException` on any I/O error, `BadLocationException` if `pos` represents an invalid location within the document.

Overrides: `read` in class `EditorKit`.

`public void write(java.io.OutputStream out, Document doc, int pos,`
    `int len) throws IOException, BadLocationException`

Writes the content starting at `pos` and running for `len` characters of the `Document` to `out`.

Throws: `IOException` on any I/O error, `BadLocationException` if `pos` represents an invalid location within the document.

Overrides: `write` in class `EditorKit`.

`public void write(java.io.Writer out, Document doc, int pos, int len)`
    `throws IOException, BadLocationException`

Writes the content starting at `pos` and running for `len` characters of the `Document` to `out`.

Throws: `IOException` on any I/O error, `BadLocationException` if `pos` represents an invalid location within the document.

Overrides: `write` in class `EditorKit`.

Inner Classes

`public static class DefaultEditorKit.BeepAction`
`public static class DefaultEditorKit.CopyAction`
`public static class DefaultEditorKit.CutAction`
`public static class DefaultEditorKit.DefaultKeyTypedAction`
`public static class DefaultEditorKit.InsertBreakAction`
`public static class DefaultEditorKit.InsertContentAction`
`public static class DefaultEditorKit.InsertTabAction`
`public static class DefaultEditorKit.PasteAction`

Extended by   StyledEditorKit (p.878).

See also   Action (p.128), Caret (p.800), Document (p.826), EditorKit (p.829), ViewFactory (p.896).

swing.text.DefaultEditorKit.BeepAction

INNER CLASS

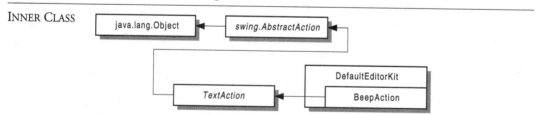

See `beepAction` in the table on page 810 for a full description.

`public static class DefaultEditorKit.BeepAction extends TextAction`

Constructors
`public BeepAction()`

Methods
`public void actionPerformed(java.awt.event.ActionEvent)`

See also   TextAction (p.891).

swing.text.DefaultEditorKit.CopyAction

INNER CLASS
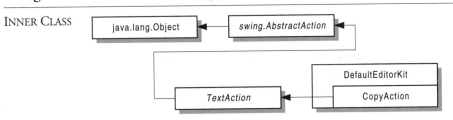

See `copyAction` in the table on page 810 for a full description.

`public static class DefaultEditorKit.CopyAction extends TextAction`

Constructors
`public CopyAction()`

Methods
`public void actionPerformed(java.awt.event.ActionEvent)`

See also   TextAction (p.891).

swing.text.DefaultEditorKit.CutAction

INNER CLASS
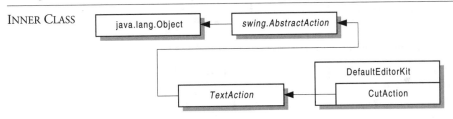

See `cutAction` in the table on page 810 for a full description.

`public static class DefaultEditorKit.CutAction extends TextAction`

Constructors
`public CutAction()`

Methods
`public void actionPerformed(java.awt.event.ActionEvent)`

See also   TextAction (p.891).

swing.text.DefaultEditorKit.DefaultKeyTypedAction

INNER CLASS

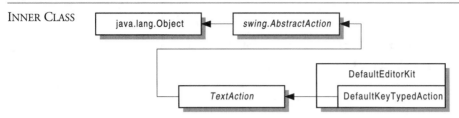

See defaultKeyTypedAction in the table on page 810 for a full description.

```
public static class DefaultEditorKit.DefaultKeyTypedAction
    extends TextAction
```

Constructors
```
public DefaultKeyTypedAction()
```

Methods
```
public void actionPerformed(java.awt.event.ActionEvent)
```

See also   TextAction (p.891).

swing.text.DefaultEditorKit.InsertBreakAction

INNER CLASS

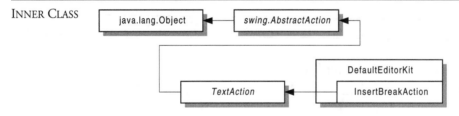

See insertBreakAction in the table on page 810 for a full description.

```
public static class DefaultEditorKit.InsertBreakAction
    extends TextAction
```

Constructors
```
public InsertBreakAction()
```

Methods
```
public void actionPerformed(java.awt.event.ActionEvent)
```

See also   TextAction (p.891).

swing.text.DefaultEditorKit.InsertContentAction

INNER CLASS

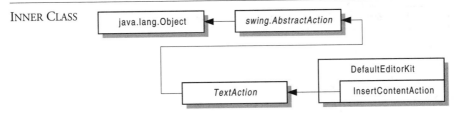

See `insertContentAction` in the table on page 810 for a full description.

```
public static class DefaultEditorKit.InsertContentAction
    extends TextAction
```

Constructors
```
public InsertContentAction()
```

Methods
```
public void actionPerformed(java.awt.event.ActionEvent)
```

> *See also*   TextAction (p.891).

swing.text.DefaultEditorKit.InsertTabAction

INNER CLASS

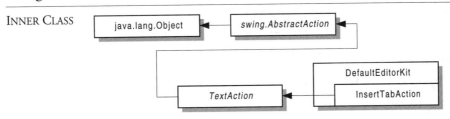

See `insertTabAction` in the table on page 810 for a full description.

```
public static class DefaultEditorKit.InsertTabAction
    extends TextAction
```

Constructors
```
public InsertTabAction()
```

Methods
```
public void actionPerformed(java.awt.event.ActionEvent)
```

> *See also*   TextAction (p.891).

swing.text.DefaultEditorKit.PasteAction

INNER CLASS

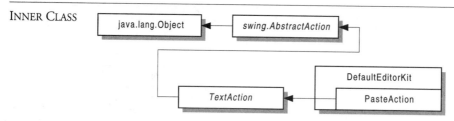

See `pasteAction` in the table on page 810 for a full description.

public static class DefaultEditorKit.PasteAction extends TextAction

Constructors
public PasteAction()

Methods
public void actionPerformed(java.awt.event.ActionEvent)

See also   TextAction (p.891).

swing.text.DefaultHighlighter

CLASS

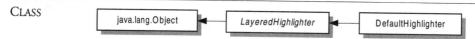

Provides a `Highlighter` that renders the selection highlight as a solid color rectangle.

public class DefaultHighlighter extends LayeredHighlighter

Constructors
public DefaultHighlighter()
Constructs a DefaultHighlighter.

Methods
public Object addHighlight(int startOffset, int endOffset,
Highlighter.HighlightPainter p) throws BadLocationException
Adds a selection highlight to the `View` for the area that represents the `Document` content between `startOffset` and `endOffset`. This method returns an `Object` that can be used in the change-`Highlight()` and `removeHighlight()` methods to refer to the highlight created.
Throws: BadLocationException if any part of the given range in the `Document` is invalid.
Implements: addHighlight in interface `Highlighter`.

public void changeHighlight(Object tag, int newStartOffset,
int newEndOffset) throws BadLocationException
Called to change a highlight when the selection changes.
Throws: BadLocationException if any part of the given range in the `Document` is invalid.
Implements: changeHighlight in interface `Highlighter`.

public void deinstall(JTextComponent c)

Called when the highlighter is being removed from the JTextComponent.

Implements: deinstall in interface Highlighter.

public boolean getDrawsLayeredHighlights()

Returns true if the highlight is painted as part of the View painting process.

public Highlighter.Highlight[] getHighlights()

Returns an array of the current highlights.

Implements: getHighlights in interface Highlighter.

public void install(JTextComponent c)

Called when the highlighter is being added to the JTextComponent. Used to get the associated Document.

Implements: install in interface Highlighter.

public void paint(java.awt.Graphics g)

Paints the highlights.

Implements: paint in interface Highlighter.

public void paintLayeredHighlights(java.awt.Graphics g, int p0, int p1, java.awt.Shape viewBounds, JTextComponent editor, View view)

Used by leaf Views (views which do not have child Views) to render the highlight for their region. The viewBounds parameter is the bounds of the given View, not the intended bounds of the highlight. The highlight should not go outside this given region. The highlight region needs to be calculated based on the p0 and p1 parameters.

Overrides: paintLayeredHighlights in class LayeredHighlighter.

public void removeAllHighlights()

Removes all currently defined highlights. After this call is made, any stored tag Objects are invalid.

Implements: removeAllHighlights in interface Highlighter.

public void removeHighlight(Object tag)

Removes the highlight which is associated with tag.

Implements: removeHighlight in interface Highlighter.

public void setDrawsLayeredHighlights(boolean newValue)

If newValue is set to true, Views will call the paintLayeredHighlights() method as they paint themselves.

Inner Classes
public static class DefaultHighlighter.DefaultHighlightPainter

See also   BadLocationException (p.796), JTextComponent (p.838), LayeredHighlighter (p.852).

swing.text.DefaultHighlighter.DefaultHighlightPainter

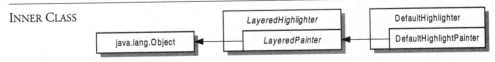

A class which actually paints the highlight.

```
public static class DefaultHighlighter.DefaultHighlightPainter
    extends java.lang.Object
    implements Highlighter.HighlightPainter
```

Constructors
`public DefaultHighlightPainter(java.awt.Color c)`
Constructs a `DefaultHighlightPainter`.

Methods
`public java.awt.Color getColor()`
Returns the Color used for the highlight.
`public void paint(java.awt.Graphics g, int offs0, int offs1,`
`java.awt.Shape bounds, JTextComponent c)`
Paints the whole highlight.
Implements: paint in interface `Highlighter.HighlightPainter`.
`public java.awt.Shape paintLayer(java.awt.Graphics g, int modelStart,`
`int modelEnd, java.awt.Shape viewBounds, JTextComponent c, View view)`
Paints a part of a highlight. This method will be called as part of the paint process for a single `View`.
Overrides: paintLayer in class `LayeredHighlighter.LayerPainter`.

See also JTextComponent (p.838), LayeredHighlighter.LayeredHighlightPainter (p.852).

swing.text.DefaultStyledDocument

CLASS

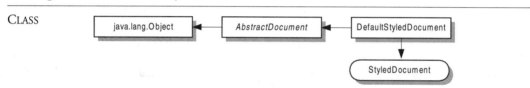

This class represents a `Document` that can have character, paragraph, and `Document` default syles. The `Element` structure for this `Document` is implemented so that `Elements` can overlap (for example, so a word can be both in bold and italics). Attribute runs cannot cross from one paragraph to another, since the breaks between paragraphs use document default syles.

`public class DefaultStyledDocument extends AbstractDocument`
`implements StyledDocument`

Fields
`public static final int BUFFER_SIZE_DEFAULT`
The default size of the content buffer for the `Document`.

Constructors
`public DefaultStyledDocument()`
Constructs a `DefaultStyledDocument`. It initially creates a content buffer of `BUFFER_SIZE_DEFAULT` characters and a `StyleContext` unique to this `Document`.
`public DefaultStyledDocument(Content c, StyleContext styles)`
Constructs a `DefaultStyledDocument` with the given `Content` and `StyleContext`.
`public DefaultStyledDocument(StyleContext styles)`
Constructs a `DefaultSyledDocument` with a content buffer of size `BUFFER_SIZE_DEFAULT` and the given `StyleContext`.

Methods

public void addDocumentListener(DocumentListener listener)

Adds a DocumentListener to the list to notify when this Document changes.

Overrides: addDocumentListener in class AbstractDocument.

Implements: addDocumentListener in interface Document.

public Style addStyle(String styleName, Style parent)

Adds a new Style to the Document. The Style is created and assigned the name styleName, which may be null. The created Style is returned from this method. If a Style is created with a null name, the caller must not lose the returned reference to it, since there is no other way to retrieve the Style. The parent is the Style to search if an attribute cannot be found in this Style. The parent parameter may also be null, if this Style does not have a resolving parent.

Implements: addStyle in interface StyledDocument.

public java.awt.Color getBackground(AttributeSet attr)

Returns the background color stored in an AttributeSet, if there is one.

Implements: getBackground in interface StyledDocument.

public Element getCharacterElement(int pos)

Returns an Element representing the given character in the Document.

Implements: getCharacterElement in interface StyledDocument.

public Element getDefaultRootElement()

Returns the default root Element, creating it if necessary.

Overrides: getDefaultRootElement in class AbstractDocument.

Implements: getDefaultRootElement in interface Document.

public java.awt.Font getFont(AttributeSet attr)

Returns the Font stored in the AttributeSet, if there is one.

Implements: getFont in interface StyledDocument.

public java.awt.Color getForeground(AttributeSet attr)

Returns the foreground color from the given AttributeSet.

Implements: getForeground in interface StyledDocument.

public Style getLogicalStyle(int p)

Returns the Style for the paragraph that contains the position p in the Document.

Implements: getLogicalStyle in interface StyledDocument.

public Element getParagraphElement(int pos)

Returns an Element representing the paragraph which contains the position pos in the Document.

Overrides: getParagraphElement in class AbstractDocument.

Implements: getParagraphElement in interface StyledDocument.

public Style getStyle(String styleName)

Returns the Style which was created with the name styleName.

Implements: getStyle in interface StyledDocument.

public java.util.Enumeration getStyleNames()

Returns the list of of defined style names.

public void removeDocumentListener(DocumentListener listener)

Removes the given DocumentListener.

Overrides: removeDocumentListener in class AbstractDocument.

Implements: removeDocumentListener in interface Document.

public void removeStyle(String styleName)

Removes the Style named styleName from the Document.

Implements: removeStyle in interface StyledDocument.

public void setCharacterAttributes(int offset, int length,
AttributeSet attrs, boolean replace)

If replace is true, this method changes the attributes on the given range of text to attrs. If replace is false, this method adds attrs to the existing attributes of the given range of text. This method is thread safe.

Implements: setCharacterAttributes in interface StyledDocument.

public void setLogicalStyle(int pos, Style s)

Sets the logical style for the paragraph that contains the content from the Document at pos. The logical style is the style used if attributes aren't explicitly set for the paragraph or a character in the paragraph. This method is thread safe.

Implements: setLogicalStyle in interface StyledDocument.

public void setParagraphAttributes(int offset, int length,
AttributeSet s, boolean replace)

Sets the attributes for the given paragraph. If replace is true, the attributes in s replace the current paragraph attributes. If replace is false, the attributes in s are added to the current AttributeSet. This method is thread safe.

Implements: setParagraphAttributes in interface StyledDocument.

Protected Methods

protected AbstractElement createDefaultRoot()

Creates and returns the root Element for the Document.

protected void insert(int offset, DefaultStyledDocument.ElementSpec[] data)
throws BadLocationException

Inserts new content into the Document starting at offset. The content to be inserted is stored in the ElementSpecs in the data array. This method is thread safe.

Throws: BadLocationException for an invalid starting offset.

protected void insertUpdate(DefaultDocumentEvent chng, AttributeSet attr)

Called when new content is inserted into the Document. This method updates the Document structure by building a set of ElementSpecs representing the lines of text separated by line breaks. It then inserts those ElementSpecs into the ElementBuffer. This method is thread safe.

Overrides: insertUpdate in class AbstractDocument.

protected void removeUpdate(DefaultDocumentEvent chng)

Updates the Document structure when content is removed from the Document.

Overrides: removeUpdate in class AbstractDocument.

protected void styleChanged(Style style)

Creates a DefaultDocumentEvent informing the listeners that the entire Document has changed. Subclasses should override this to be more specific about the range in the Document that changed.

Inner Classes

public static class DefaultStyledDocument.AttributeUndoableEdit
public class DefaultStyledDocument.ElementBuffer
public static class DefaultStyledDocument.ElementSpec
protected class DefaultStyledDocument.SectionElement

Extended by   HTMLDocument (p.912).

See also   AbstractDocument (p.778), Document (p.826), StyledDocument (p.877).

INNER CLASS

An UndoableEdit used when an Attribute (or Attributes) changes in an Element.

public static class DefaultStyledDocument.AttributeUndoableEdit
    extends AbstractUndoableEdit

Constructors

public AttributeUndoableEdit(Element element,
    AttributeSet newAttributes, boolean isReplacing)

Constructs a new AttributeUndoableEdit which stores the information needed to undo or redo the change. If isReplacing is true, the newAttributes completely replaced the Element's old AttributeSet.

Methods

public void redo() throws CannotRedoException

Redoes a change.

Throws: CannotRedoException if the change cannot be redone.

Overrides: redo in class AbstractUndoableEdit.

Implements: redo in interface UndoableEdit.

public void undo() throws CannotUndoException

Undoes a change.

Throws: CannotUndoException if the change cannot be undone.

Overrides: undo in class AbstractUndoableEdit.

Implements: undo in interface UndoableEdit.

Protected Fields

protected AttributeSet copy

A copy of the Attributes the Element had before the change.

protected Element element

The Element which was changed.

protected boolean isReplacing

If set to true, the new Attributes completely replace the old Attributes of the Element.

protected AttributeSet newAttributes

The new Attributes which were either added to or which replaced the Element's AttributeSet.

See also AbstractUndoableEdit (p.998), AttributeSet (p.794), CannotRedoException (p.1000), CannotUndoException (p.1001), Element (p.830).

swing.text.DefaultStyledDocument.ElementBuffer

INNER CLASS

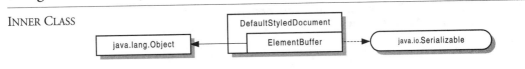

This class manages compound edits being made to the `Document`.

```
public class DefaultStyledDocument.ElementBuffer
    extends java.lang.Object
    implements java.io.Serializable
```

Constructors

`public ElementBuffer(Element root)`

Constructs a new `ElementBuffer` based on the given root `Element`.

Methods

`public void change(int offset, int length, DefaultDocumentEvent de)`

Changes the content starting at `offset` and running for `length` characters. Stores the edit in the given `DefaultDocumentEvent`.

`public Element clone(Element parent, Element clonee)`

Copies the `Element clonee`, making `parent` the parent of the new `Element`.

`public Element getRootElement()`

Returns the root element for the `Document`.

`public void insert(int offset, int length,`
`DefaultStyledDocument.ElementSpec[] data, DefaultDocumentEvent de)`

Inserts the content stored in `data` into the `Document` and sets `de` to represent the change.

`public void remove(int offset, int length, DefaultDocumentEvent de)`

Removes the content starting at `offset` and running for `length` characters from the `Document`, and sets `de` to represent the change.

Protected Methods

`protected void changeUpdate()`

Responds to a change event from the `Document`.

`protected void insertUpdate(DefaultStyledDocument.ElementSpec[] data)`

Inserts the content in `data` into the `Document`.

`protected void removeUpdate()`

Updates the buffer in response to a change in the associated section of the `Document`. Any Elements representing the section that was removed are also removed.

See also   AbstractDocument.DefaultDocumentEvent (p.789), Document (p.826), Element (p.830).

swing.text.DefaultStyledDocument.ElementSpec

INNER CLASS

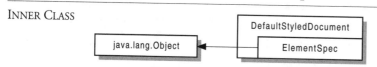

Defines how to build an `Element` for a future update.

```
public static class DefaultStyledDocument.ElementSpec
    extends java.lang.Object
```

Fields

public static final short ContentType = 3

This value means the ElementSpec represents content. See getType().

public static final short EndTagType = 2

This value means the ElementSpec represents the end of an Element. See getType().

public static final short JoinFractureDirection = 7

This value means the ElementSpec should be joined to the fractured element. A fractured Element is created when attributes are added that change the Attribute tree structure that currently exists. See getDirection().

public static final short JoinNextDirection = 5

This value means the ElementSpec should be joined with the ElementSpec that follows it. See getDirection().

public static final short JoinPreviousDirection = 4

This value means the ElementSpec should be joined with the ElementSpec that precedes it. See getDirection().

public static final short OriginateDirection = 6

This value means the ElementSpec should start a new Element. See getDirection().

public static final short StartTagType = 1

This value means the ElementSpec represents the start of an Element. See getType().

Constructors

public ElementSpec(AttributeSet a, short type)

Use this constructor to build an ElementSpec that is for markup and will not be stored in the Document. The type parameter is one of StartTagType, EndTagType, or ContentType.

public ElementSpec(AttributeSet a, short type, char[] txt, int offs, int len)

Use this constructor for creating an ElementSpec containing new content (given by txt) to be inserted into the Document starting at offs and running for len characters.

public ElementSpec(AttributeSet a, short type, int len)

Use this constructor when the data is already added to the Document and is being parsed, which needs the length information.

Methods

public char[] getArray()

Returns the array of characters in this ElementSpec.

public AttributeSet getAttributes()

Returns the AttributeSet for this ElementSpec.

public short getDirection()

Returns the direction this ElementSpec should be joined.

public int getLength()

Returns the length of the content in this ElementSpec.

public int getOffset()

Returns the offset into the Document.

public short getType()

Returns the type of this ElementSpec.

public void setDirection(short direction)

Sets the direction this ElementSpec should be joined.

public void setType(short type)
> Sets the type of this ElementSpec.

public String toString()
> Returns the contents of the ElementSpec as a String.
> *Overrides:* toString in class Object.

> *See also*   AttributeSet (p.794), Element (p.830).

swing.text.DefaultStyledDocument.SectionElement

This class is the default root Element of a DefaultStyledDocument.

protected class DefaultStyledDocument.SectionElement
   extends BranchElement

Constructors
public SectionElement()
> Creates a new SectionElement.

Methods
public String getName()
> Returns the name of this Element.

swing.text.DefaultTextUI

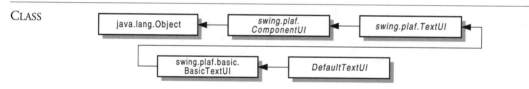

This class has been deprecated as of Swing 1.0.2. See the implementations of the various TextUIs in the swing.plaf.basic package (p.547) and BasicTextUI (p.696), which replaces this class.

public abstract class DefaultTextUI extends BasicTextUI

Constructors
public DefaultTextUI()

swing.text.Document

Document

The Document interface defines the model to be used for text components. This interface defines methods to support editing and notification of Views about changes in the Document.

A Document has several associated classes and interfaces. An Element (p.830) is a means of structuring the Document and providing markup of the Document content with attributes. Views (p.893) are usually tied to an Element, and provide for rendering the Document. A Position (p.860) is a special way of representing an offset into the Document so it always represents the same piece of the Document even if it changes.

Usually there will only be one Element structure per Document, but this interface does not prevent having more than one. Multiple Element structures are helpful in situations such as converting the Document from one format to another, representing annotations to the Document, or parsing the Document to provide color syntax highlighting for a programming language.

public interface Document

Fields
public static final String StreamDescriptionProperty = "stream"
The property name used for the property that holds the information about the stream used to create the Document, if the Document was created from a stream.

public static final String TitleProperty = "title"
The property name of the property that holds the title of the Document, if it has one.

Methods
public abstract void addDocumentListener(DocumentListener listener)
Adds listener to the list of listeners to be notified when this Document changes.

public abstract Position createPosition(int offs)
    throws BadLocationException
Returns a Position that will track changes in the Document so that it will always represent the same section of text that was at offs when it was created. Of course, if the section of text represented by the position is removed, the Position will not be able to represent it. In that situation, the Position should represent the offset in the Document just before the removal point.
Throws: BadLocationException if the given offset does not represent a valid location in the document.

public abstract Element getDefaultRootElement()
Returns the default root Element Views should be based on. A subclass is not bound by this, in that it may provide an alternate means to connect Views and Elements.

public abstract Position getEndPosition()
Returns a Position that always represents the end of the Document, no matter what changes occur.

public abstract int getLength()
Returns the number of characters in the Document.

public abstract Object getProperty(Object key)
Returns a value associated with the passed-in key. The Document properties can store any information about the Document that is not normally considered content, such as the author's name.

public abstract Element[] getRootElements()
Returns all of the root Elements for the Document.

public abstract Position getStartPosition()

Returns a `Position` that will always represent the start of the `Document`, no matter what changes occur.

public abstract String getText(int offset, int length)
throws BadLocationException

Returns a `String` containing the text in the `Document` between `offset` and `offset+length` (inclusive).

Throws: `BadLocationException` if some portion of the given range is invalid. The location in the exception is the first invalid position encountered.

public abstract void getText(int offset, int length, Segment txt)
throws BadLocationException

Returns the `Document` text in the given range in `txt`. This method does not have to create a copy of the text; it may allow direct access to the `Document` content. The `Segment` returned by this method should be treated as read-only.

Throws: `BadLocationException` if some portion of the given range is invalid. The location in the exception is the first invalid position encountered.

public abstract void insertString(int offset, String str,
AttributeSet attrSet) throws BadLocationException

Inserts the contents of `str` into the `Document` at `offset`. If the attributes in `attrSet` match the attributes already defined at the location, the `Element` for that location will be expanded to represent the section with the increased content. If the attributes are different, a new `Element` will be created to represent the new content and attributes. When the `Document` is updated, its listeners will be notified of the change.

Throws: `BadLocationException` if the given insert position is not a valid position within the document.

public abstract void putProperty(Object key, Object value)

Sets a new property (`key, value`) pair into the `Document` properties `Dictionary`.

public abstract void remove(int offs, int len) throws BadLocationException

Removes the range of content starting at `offset` and running for `len` characters from the `Document`. When the content has been removed, the `Document`'s listeners should be notified.

Throws: `BadLocationException` if some portion of the removal range was invalid. The location in the exception is the first invalid position encountered.

public abstract void removeDocumentListener(DocumentListener listener)

Removes `listener` from the list of listeners to notify when this `Document` changes.

public abstract void render(Runnable r)

Renders the `Document` in a thread-safe manner, if the `Document` allows concurrent updates to be performed. The implementing class may assume that the `Runnable` is not allowed to make any updates of its own to the `Document`.

Extended by StyledDocument (p.877).

Implemented by AbstractDocument (p.778).

Returned by AbstractDocument.AbstractElement.getDocument() (p.783),
AbstractDocument.DefaultDocumentEvent.getDocument() (p.789),
AbstractWriter.getDocument() (p.793), DefaultEditorKit.createDefaultDocument() (p.810),
DocumentEvent.getDocument() (p.489), EditorKit.createDefaultDocument() (p.829),
Element.getDocument() (p.830), HTMLEditorKit.createDefaultDocument() (p.922),

JTextArea.createDefaultModel() (p.374), JTextComponent.getDocument() (p.838), JTextField.createDefaultModel() (p.379), StyledEditorKit.createDefaultDocument() (p.878), View.getDocument() (p.893).

See also AttributeSet (p.794), DocumentEvent (p.489), DocumentListener (p.490), Element (p.830), Position (p.860).

swing.text.EditorKit

ABSTRACT
CLASS

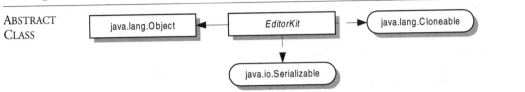

An `EditorKit` is a class that defines the set of behaviors required to make a text component into an editor. Each instance of an `EditorKit` will be associated with a single text component through the `setComponent()` method.

Since `EditorKit` provides access to the functionality, multiple different subclasses can implement the editing functionality for a specific type of content (such as HTML) and can be switched transparently.

```
public abstract class EditorKit extends java.lang.Object
    implements java.lang.Cloneable, java.io.Serializable
```

Constructors
public EditorKit()
  Default constructor.

Methods
public abstract Object clone()
  Creates and returns a copy of this `EditorKit`. This allows the rapid creation of new instances of a paricular subclass. This method is required since each text component gets its own `EditorKit`.
  Overrides: `clone` in class `Object`.

public abstract Caret createCaret()
  Creates and returns a `Caret` that can navigate the `Views` returned by the `getViewFactory()` method.

public abstract Document createDefaultDocument()
  Creates an empty `Document` appropriate for this `EditorKit`.

public void deinstall(JEditorPane c)
  Called when the `EditorKit` is being removed from the text component. This allows the `Editor-Kit` to remove itself from any listener lists in the text component.

public abstract Action[] getActions()
  Returns an array of the `Actions` supported by the `EditorKit`.

public abstract String getContentType()
  Returns the MIME type this `EditorKit` supports.

public abstract ViewFactory getViewFactory()

Returns a `ViewFactory` which can create the `View`s associated with this `EditorKit`.

public void install(JEditorPane c)

Called when the `EditorKit` is being added to the text component. This method allows the `EditorKit` to register itself as a listener on the text component.

public abstract void read(InputStream in, Document doc, int pos)
throws IOException, BadLocationException

Inserts the content from the stream into the `Document` starting at pos.

Throws: `IOException` on any I/O error, `BadLocationException` if pos represents an invalid location within the document.

public abstract void read(Reader in, Document doc, int pos)
throws IOException, BadLocationException

Inserts the content from the `Reader` into the `Document` starting at pos.

Throws: `IOException` on any I/O error, `BadLocationException` if pos represents an invalid location within the document.

public abstract void write(OutputStream out, Document doc, int pos,
int len) throws IOException, BadLocationException

Writes the contents of the `Document` starting at pos and running for len characters to the `OutputStream`.

Throws: `IOException` on any I/O error, `BadLocationException` if pos represents an invalid location within the document.

public abstract void write(Writer out, Document doc, int pos,
int len) throws IOException, BadLocationException

Writes the contents of the `Document` starting at pos and running for len characters to the given `Writer`.

Throws: `IOException` on any I/O error, `BadLocationException` if pos represents an invalid location within the document.

Extended by DefaultEditorKit (p.810).

Returned by BasicEditorPaneUI.getEditorKit() (p.586), BasicTextPaneUI.getEditorKit() (p.695), BasicTextUI.getEditorKit() (p.696), JEditorPane.createDefaultEditorKit() (p.232), JEditorPane.createEditorKitForContentType() (p.232), JEditorPane.getEditorKit() (p.232), JEditorPane.getEditorKitForContentType() (p.232), JTextPane.createDefaultEditorKit() (p.383), TextUI.getEditorKit() (p.542).

swing.text.Element

INTERFACE   Element

An `Element` describes a piece of `Document` structure, separate from the content. An `Element` may have associated attributes and be part of a hierarchy of `Element`s.

public interface Element

Methods

public abstract AttributeSet getAttributes()

Returns the AttributeSet associated with the Element. If there aren't any attributes associated with this Element, this method returns null.

public abstract Document getDocument()

Returns the Document that is associated with this Element.

public abstract Element getElement(int index)

Returns the child Element at index if this Element supports children and has a child at that index. If the Element does not support children, this method returns null.

public abstract int getElementCount()

Returns the number of child Elements contained by this Element.

public abstract int getElementIndex(int offset)

Returns the index of the child index that best represents the text at offset in the Document.

public abstract int getEndOffset()

Returns the offset in the Document that is the last piece of text represented by this element or one of is children.

public abstract String getName()

Returns the name of this Element. The name is usually descriptive of the type of Document structure this Element represents.

public abstract Element getParentElement()

Returns the parent Element of this Element. If this Element is the root Element of the Document, this method returns null.

public abstract int getStartOffset()

Returns the offset in the Document that is the earliest offset represented by this Element or one of its children.

public abstract boolean isLeaf()

Returns true if this Element does not have any children.

Returned by   Many.

Implemented by   AbstractDocument.AbstractElement (p.783).

swing.text.ElementIterator

CLASS

The ElementIterator class provides a mechanism for performing a depth-first, left-to-right iteration of the Element tree.

This class does not lock the tree while it is iterating, so it is up to the user to keep track of whether the tree changes.

```
public class ElementIterator extends java.lang.Object
    implements java.lang.Cloneable
```

Constructors

public ElementIterator(Document document)

Creates a new ElementIterator which will start at the default root Element of the document.

public ElementIterator(Element root)
>   Creates a new ElementIterator which will iterate across the subtree rooted at root.

Methods
public synchronized Object clone()
>   Clones the ElementIterator.
>   *Overrides:* clone in class Object.

public Element current()
>   Returns the current Element.

public int depth()
>   Returns the depth of the current Element in the tree.

public Element first()
>   Returns the first (root) Element.

public Element next()
>   Returns the next Element in the depth-first, left-to-right iteration order. If the current Element is the last Element, returns null.

public Element previous()
>   Returns the previous Element. If the current Element is the first Element, returns null.

>   *Returned by*   AbstractWriter.getElementIterator() (p.793).

swing.text.FieldView

CLASS

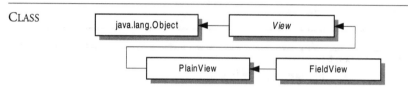

This View represents a single line editor. If this View is in a JTextField, it will manage the component's associated BoundedRangeModel, and it will adjust the View to match the size of the JTextField.

public class FieldView extends PlainView

Constructors
public FieldView(Element elem)
>   Constructs a new FieldView for the given Element.

Methods
public float getPreferredSpan(int axis)
>   Returns the preferred width or height for this view depending on the axis. The axis is either View.X_AXIS or View.Y_AXIS.
>   *Overrides:* getPreferredSpan in class PlainView.

public int getResizeWeight(int axis)
>   Returns an integer representing the resizability of the View along the given axis. A value of 0 or less means the View is not resizable.

Overrides: getResizeWeight in class View.

public void insertUpdate(DocumentEvent changes, java.awt.Shape a, ViewFactory f)

Called when the Document's contents change in a range represented by this View.

Overrides: insertUpdate in class PlainView.

public java.awt.Shape modelToView(int pos, java.awt.Shape a, Position.Bias nextOrPrevious) throws BadLocationException

Returns the bounding box of the character at pos in the Document when rendered into this View.

Throws: BadLocationException if the given position does not represent a valid location in the associated document.

Overrides: modelToView in class PlainView.

public void paint(java.awt.Graphics g, java.awt.Shape a)

Renders into the given area using the given graphics context.

Overrides: paint in class PlainView.

public void removeUpdate(DocumentEvent changes, java.awt.Shape a, ViewFactory f)

Called when content is removed from the Document at a point which is represented by this View.

Overrides: removeUpdate in class PlainView.

public int viewToModel(float fx, float fy, java.awt.Shape a, Position.Bias[] b)

Returns the offset into the Document that best represents the content that is at (fx, fy) when rendered.

Overrides: viewToModel in class PlainView.

Protected Methods

protected java.awt.Shape adjustAllocation(java.awt.Shape a)

Adjusts the allocation of the View to match the JTextField. If the area occupied by the JTextField becomes larger vertically than the preferred vertical span of the View, it will adjust the allocation to center the View in the area. If the area is larger horizontally, the View will adjust the allocation using the alignment property of the JTextField.

protected java.awt.FontMetrics getFontMetrics()

Returns the FontMetrics of the JTextField.

Extended by PasswordView (p.856).

swing.text.GapContent

CLASS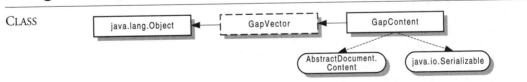

This class is an implementation of the AbstractDocument.Content interface. Of the two supplied Content classes in Swing (StringContent is the other), this class is the one to use as it is much more efficient.

This class stores its content as an array of characters, but with one important difference. It places a "gap" in the array at the location being modified. Because most modifications happen in the same general place in the text (around the Caret), the only part of the array that normally has to be updated is around the gap. Using the gap greatly reduces the burden of having to move content to make room, and also keeps maintaining `Positions` efficient.

```
public class GapContent extends GapVector
    implements AbstractDocument.Content, java.io.Serializable
```

Constructors

public GapContent()

Creates a new GapContent object using a buffer of size 10.

public GapContent(int initialLength)

Creates a new GapContent object, with a buffer of the length specified.

Methods

public Position createPosition(int offset) throws BadLocationException

Creates a position within the content that will track change as the content is mutated.

Throws: BadLocationException if the specified position is invalid.

Implements: createPosition in interface AbstractDocument.Content.

public void getChars(int where, int len, Segment chars)
throws BadLocationException

Retrieves a portion of the content. If the desired content spans the gap, we copy the content. If the desired content does not span the gap, the actual store is returned to avoid the copy since it is contiguous.

Throws: BadLocationException if the specified position is invalid.

Implements: getChars in interface AbstractDocument.Content.

public String getString(int where, int len) throws BadLocationException

Retrieves a portion of the content.

Throws: BadLocationException if the specified position is invalid.

Implements: getString in interface AbstractDocument.Content.

public UndoableEdit insertString(int where, String str)
throws BadLocationException

Inserts a string into the content.

Throws: BadLocationException if the specified position is invalid.

Implements: insertString in interface AbstractDocument.Content.

public int length()

Returns the length of the content.

Implements: length in interface AbstractDocument.Content.

public UndoableEdit remove(int where, int nitems)
throws BadLocationException

Removes part of the content.

Throws: BadLocationException if the specified position is invalid.

Implements: remove in interface AbstractDocument.Content.

Protected Methods

protected Object allocateArray(int len)

Returns an array of characters of the given length.

protected int getArrayLength()

Returns the length of the allocated array.

protected java.util.Vector getPositionsInRange(java.util.Vector v, int offset, int length)

Returns a Vector containing instances of UndoPosRef for the Positions in the range offset to offset + length. If v is not null the matching Positions are placed in there. The vector with the resulting Positions are returned. UndoPosRef is a package private class.

protected void resetMarksAtZero()

Resets all the marks that have an offset of 0 to have an index of 0 as well.

protected void shiftEnd(int newSize)

Makes the gap bigger, moving any content affected by this and updating the appropriate marks.

protected void shiftGap(int newGapStart)

Moves the gap so that it starts at newGapStart. This moves the content in the array and updates the marks.

protected void shiftGapEndUp(int newGapEnd)

Makes the gap bigger by moving the end to newGapEnd. This change doesn't affect any of the content, but the marks between the old gap end and the new gap end are all set to point to the new end of the gap.

protected void shiftGapStartDown(int newGapStart)

Makes the gap bigger by moving the start to newGapStart. This change doesn't affect any of the content, but the marks between the old gap start and the new gap start are all set to point to the new start of the gap.

protected void updateUndoPositions(java.util.Vector positions, int offset, int length)

Resets the location for all the UndoPosRef instances in positions.

See also AbstractDocument.Content (p.788).

swing.text.Highlighter

Highlighter

This interface defines an object that draws selection highlights by changing the background.

public interface Highlighter

Methods

public abstract Object addHighlight(int rangeBegin, int rangeEnd, Highlighter.HighlightPainter p) throws BadLocationException

Adds a selection highlight to the View over the area representing the Document content from rangeBegin to rangeEnd.

Throws: BadLocationException for an invalid range specification.

public abstract void changeHighlight(Object highlightTag,
   int rangeBegin, int rangeEnd) throws BadLocationException
   Changes the area highlighted. This may be more efficient than removing and readding the highlight if the new region is an extension or reduction of an existing highlight.
   Throws: BadLocationException for an invalid range specification.
public abstract void deinstall(JTextComponent c)
   Called when the highlight is being removed from a component. This allows the highlighter to remove itself from any listener lists it added itself to in the install() method.
public abstract Highlighter.Highlight[] getHighlights()
   Returns the list of currently defined highlights.
public abstract void install(JTextComponent c)
   Called when the Highlighter is being added to a JTextComponent. This allows the High-lighter to add itself as a listener to the JTextComponent and retrieve the model represented by the component.
public abstract void paint(java.awt.Graphics g)
   Called to paint the highlight.
public abstract void removeAllHighlights()
   Removes all highlights this Highlighter has created.
public abstract void removeHighlight(Object highlightTag)
   Removes the highlight identified by highlightTag.

Inner Classes
public static interface Highlighter.HighlightPainter
public static interface Highlighter.Highlight

   Returned by   BasicTextUI.createHighlighter() (p.696),
   JTextComponent.getHighlighter() (p.838).
   Implemented by   LayeredHighlighter (p.852).

swing.text.Highlighter.Highlight

INNER
INTERFACE
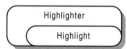

public static interface Highlighter.Highlight

Methods
public abstract int getEndOffset()
   Returns the end offset of the highlight in the model.
public abstract Highlighter.HighlightPainter getPainter()
   Returns the painter for the Highlighter.
public abstract int getStartOffset()
   Returns the start offset of the highlight in the model.

   Returned by   DefaultHighlighter.getHighlights() (p.818), Highlighter.getHighlights() (p.835).
   Implemented by   DefaultHighlighter.HighlightInfo (p.818).

swing.text.Highlighter.HighlightPainter

INNER
INTERFACE

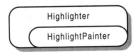

Highlight renderer.

```
public static interface Highlighter.HighlightPainter
```

Methods

```
public abstract void paint(java.awt.Graphics g, int start, int end,
    java.awt.Shape boundingBox, JTextComponent c)
```
Paints the highlight.

Returned by DefaultCaret.getSelectionPainter() (p.806),
Highlighter.Highlight.getPainter() (p.836).
Implemented by LayeredHighlighter.LayerPainter (p.852).

swing.text.IconView

CLASS

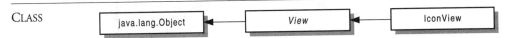

This `View` displays an `Icon`.

```
public class IconView extends View
```

Constructors

```
public IconView(Element elem)
```
Constructs an `IconView` for the given `Element`.

Methods

```
public float getAlignment(int axis)
```
Returns the alignment of the bottom of the `Icon` for the `Y_AXIS`, and the normal meaning of alignment for the `X_AXIS`.
Overrides: getAlignment in class `View`.

```
public float getPreferredSpan(int axis)
```
Returns the preferred height or width, depending on the given axis.
Overrides: getPreferredSpan in class `View`.

```
public java.awt.Shape modelToView(int pos, java.awt.Shape a,
    Position.Bias beforeOrAfterBias) throws BadLocationException
```
Returns the bounding box of the character at `pos` in the `Document` when rendered.
Throws: BadLocationException if the given position does not represent a valid location in the associated document.
Overrides: modelToView in class `View`.

swing.text.IconView   837

public void paint(java.awt.Graphics g, java.awt.Shape a)

Positions the Icon correctly. The actual painting of the Icon happens as a result of the Icon being contained in the parent Container of the View.

Overrides: paint in class View.

public void setSize(float width, float height)

Does nothing, since an icon cannot be resized.

Overrides: setSize in class View.

public int viewToModel(float x, float y, java.awt.Shape a,
**   Position.Bias[] bias)**

Returns the offset in the Document that best matches the point (x, y) when rendered into a. Returns the location within the model that best represents the given point in the View.

Overrides: viewToModel in class View.

swing.text.JTextComponent

CLASS

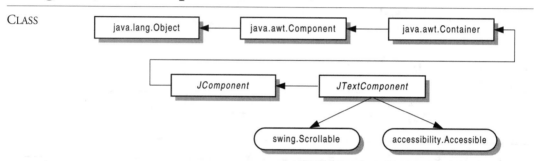

A JTextComponent defines the base functionality required by any text editing component.

Due to the nature of the Swing text API, JTextComponent mostly acts as a link between the different classes that make up an editor.

The main piece of a JTextComponent is the Document (p.826). The Document represents the text being edited by the component. The Document acts as the Model in the Model-View-Controller design, and can be shared among Views (for example, when the component is being printed, the print process will create its own View). When the Document changes, a Document-Event is sent to its DocumentListeners to describe the change. Documents may also send UndoableEditEvents at the same time as the DocumentEvents to help support undo/redo.

The next major piece of a JTextComponent is an EditorKit. This class does not provide a means to change the EditorKit; that responsibility is left up to the subclasses if they want to support it. By default all JTextComponents use a DefaultEditorKit (p.810). Text editing in a JTextComponent is provided through the use of *commands*, which are implementations of the Swing Action interface. The Actions supported are retrieved from the EditorKit. See DefaultEditorKit for a list of Actions supported by standard JTextComponents. An EditorKit also provides a means to get an appropriately initialized Document and to retrieve an appropriate ViewFactory (p.896).

The other pieces of `JTextComponent` are the `Keymap`, which allows for keyboard control of the editor, and the `Caret` (also known as a text cursor) that is used to mark the current editing position in the `Document` and provides the ability to highlight selections.

`JTextComponents` create a `Keymap` (named `DEFAULT_KEYMAP`) that provides the minimal keyboard handling for an editor. This default map will usually be modified by the look and feel to contain `Keymap` entries for standard keys in the look and feel (for example, `KeyEvent.CTRL_MASK-X`, `KeyEvent.CTRL_MASK-C`, `KeyEvent.CTRL_MASK-V` for cut, copy, and paste on Windows and the Macintosh). The order which `KeyStrokes` travel through the different AWT and component handlers and `Keymaps` is as follows:

1 The Focus manager

2 The registered `KeyListeners`

3 The `Keymap`

4 The keyboard handling in `JComponent` (for accelerators, component navigation, etc.)

```
public abstract class JTextComponent extends JComponent
    implements Scrollable, Accessible
```

Fields
`public static final String DEFAULT_KEYMAP = "default"`
The property name for the default keymap set by the look and feel.

`public static final String FOCUS_ACCELERATOR_KEY = "focusAcceleratorKey"`
The property name for the key used to change the focus.

Constructors
`public JTextComponent()`
Constructs a new `JTextComponent`. This constructor is generally not called directly, but is called by the constructor of one of its subclasses.

Methods
`public void addCaretListener(CaretListener listener)`
Adds a `CaretListener` to the list of listeners to notify when the `Caret` changes.

`public static Keymap addKeymap(String name, Keymap parent)`
Adds a new `Keymap` named name to the hierarchy of `Keymaps`. Any key defined in this `Keymap` will override the same key defined in a parent `Keymap`. The parent `Keymap` is the `Keymap` to search for keys not defined in the new `Keymap`. Note that name cannot be the same as a name already in use.

`public void copy()`
Copies the currently selected text in the `Document` to the system clipboard without changing the selection range.

`public void cut()`
Removes the currently selected text from the `Document` and places it in the system clipboard. Since the selected text is removed, this method also removes the selection.

`public AccessibleContext getAccessibleContext()`
Returns the `AccessibleContext` associated with this `JTextComponent`.

Implements: getAccessibleContext in interface Accessible.

public Action[] getActions()

Returns the Actions supported by this editor. The returned Actions can be bound to Keymaps, JMenus, or JToolbars, or simply called directly.

public Caret getCaret()

Returns the Caret to use in this editor.

public java.awt.Color getCaretColor()

Returns the color used to paint the Caret.

public int getCaretPosition()

Returns the current position of the Caret.

public java.awt.Color getDisabledTextColor()

Returns the color used to paint disabled text.

public Document getDocument()

Returns the Document associated with this editor.

public char getFocusAccelerator()

Returns the character that will cause this editor to get the focus. If a focus accelerator key has not been set, this method returns '\0', the null character.

public Highlighter getHighlighter()

Returns the object responsible for rendering text selection highlights in this editor.

public Keymap getKeymap()

Returns the current Keymap being used by this editor.

public static Keymap getKeymap(String name)

Returns a named Keymap previously added to the text component.

public java.awt.Insets getMargin()

Returns the gap between the edges of the editor component and the text it contains.

public java.awt.Dimension getPreferredScrollableViewportSize()

Returns the preferred size of the editor.

Implements: getPreferredScrollableViewportSize in interface Scrollable.

public int getScrollableBlockIncrement(
java.awt.Rectangle visibleRect, int orientation, int direction)

Returns the size of the visible area. Subclasses should override this to provide a more reasonable value, preferably one that leaves a portion of the previously viewed area visible so the user does not lose his or her place. The possible values for the orientation parameter are SwingConstants.VERTICAL and SwingConstants.HORIZONTAL. The direction parameter should be less than 0 to scroll up/left and greater than 0 to scroll down/right.

Implements: getScrollableBlockIncrement in interface Scrollable.

public boolean getScrollableTracksViewportHeight()

Returns false. A subclass should return false if it presents its content in a way where vertical scrolling doesn't make sense. For example, an editor that presents its content in a form such as a multicolumn list should override this to disable vertical scrolling.

Implements: getScrollableTracksViewportHeight in interface Scrollable.

public boolean getScrollableTracksViewportWidth()

Returns false. A subclass that presents its content in a form where horizontal scrolling doesn't make sense should override this and return true. An example of a subclass that would need to do this is one that supported word wrap.

Implements: getScrollableTracksViewportWidth in interface Scrollable.

public int getScrollableUnitIncrement(java.awt.Rectangle visibleRect, int orientation, int direction)

Returns 10 percent of the visible area. Subclasses should override this to provide a value that causes the view to scroll by one line or column. See also setUnitIncrement.

Implements: getScrollableUnitIncrement in interface Scrollable.

public String getSelectedText()

Returns the currently selected text, if there is any. See also setText.

Throws: IllegalArgumentException if the selection doesn't have a valid mapping into the document for some reason.

public java.awt.Color getSelectedTextColor()

Returns the color used to render the selected text.

public java.awt.Color getSelectionColor()

Returns the color used to render the selection highlight.

public synchronized int getSelectionEnd()

Returns the end offset of the selection (this is the same as the "mark" of the Caret). This method returns 0 if the Document is empty.

public int getSelectionEnd(Position.Bias[] bias)

Returns the end offset of the selection (this is the same as the "mark" of the Caret). This method returns 0 if the Document is empty.

public synchronized int getSelectionStart()

Returns the start offset of the selection.

public String getText()

Returns the text contained in this editor.

public String getText(int offs, int len) throws BadLocationException

Returns the text in the editor starting at offs and ending at offs+len.

Throws: BadLocationException if the offset or length are invalid.

public TextUI getUI()

Returns the UI delegate for this editor.

public boolean isEditable()

Returns true if this JTextComponent is editable. See also setEditable.

public boolean isFocusTraversable()

Returns true if this component can accept the focus.

Overrides: isFocusTraversable in class JComponent.

public boolean isOpaque()

Returns true if this component is opaque.

Overrides: isOpaque in class JComponent.

public static void loadKeymap(Keymap map, JTextComponent.KeyBinding[] bindings, Action[] actions)

Adds bindings to a Keymap from an array of KeyBindings and an array of Actions. This method is useful in loading a Keymap from a hard-coded set of KeyBindings.

public java.awt.Rectangle modelToView(int pos) throws BadLocationException

Returns the bounding box in the View that best represents the text at pos in the associated Document.

Throws: BadLocationException if the given position does not represent a valid location in the associated document.

public void moveCaretPosition(int pos)

Moves the Caret to a new postion, leaving the Caret's "mark" behind. This creates a selection between the new Caret position and the mark.

public void paste()

Pastes the contents of the system clipboard into the Document. If there is a selection, the pasted text replaces the selection. If there isn't a selection, the text is inserted before the current Caret position.

public void read(java.io.Reader in, Object desc) throws IOException

Initializes the JTextComponent from the Reader. This method creates a new Document using the current EditorKit (DefaultEditorKit in this class) and fills it with the contents for the Reader. The desc parameter is an arbitrary object that can be used to give additional information about the source of the stream, such as a filename, a document name, or a URL.

Throws: IOException if one is thrown by the Reader.

public void removeCaretListener(CaretListener listener)

Removes the given CaretListener from the notification list.

public static Keymap removeKeymap(String name)

Removes a Keymap named name from the text component.

public void removeNotify()

Called when the text component is removed from its container. The reason this method is overridden is to be able to null out any references which indicate this component is the last component to have the focus. Many of the TextActions use that particular piece of information.

Overrides: removeNotify in class JComponent.

public void replaceSelection(String content)

Replaces the current selection in the Document with the given String. If the String is empty, this is equivalent to deleting the selected text.

public void select(int selectionStart, int selectionEnd)

Provided for compatibility with the AWT Text components. The preferred way of setting a selected region is to move the Caret to one end of the selection using setCaretPosition() and then marking the text using moveCaretPosition().

public void selectAll()

Selects all of the text in the Document.

public void setCaret(Caret c)

Sets the Caret to be used by the text component. The default Caret is set by the UI to be appropriate to the look and feel.

public void setCaretColor(java.awt.Color c)

Sets the Color to use to paint the Caret.

public void setCaretPosition(int position)

Sets the position of the Caret, removing any selection currently set.

Throws: IllegalArgumentException if position is less than 0 or greater than the length of the associated document.

public void setDisabledTextColor(java.awt.Color c)

Sets the Color used to paint disabled text.

public void setDocument(Document doc)

Sets the Document associated with the editor. The editor's ViewFactory is used to create the initial View of the new Document.

public synchronized void setEditable(boolean b)

If b is true, this method makes the text editable; otherwise, it makes it read-only.

public void setEnabled(boolean b)

This method is overridden to repaint() after calling super.setEnabled().

Overrides: setEnabled in class JComponent.

public void setFocusAccelerator(char aKey)

Sets the key used to get this editor the focus. The actual keystroke to trigger the request for the focus is KeyEvent.ALT_MASK + aKey. The aKey parameter is used case-insensitively. By default no key is assigned.

public void setHighlighter(Highlighter h)

Sets the Highlighter to use to paint the selected region. By default this is set by the UI to be appropriate to the look and feel.

public void setKeymap(Keymap map)

Sets the Keymap to use for keyboard control of the editor.

public void setMargin(java.awt.Insets margin)

Sets the gap between the edge of the editor and the text it contains. Setting this value to null indicates the component should use the default margin. Margins in Swing are actually the responsibility of the component's Border. If a nonstandard Border is added to the component, it must manage the margin for the component. If it does not, this value will be ignored.

public void setOpaque(boolean isOpaque)

If isOpaque is true, the component will paint its background. If it is false, the component will allow whatever is underneath it to show through.

Overrides: setOpaque in class JComponent.

public void setSelectedTextColor(java.awt.Color c)

Sets the Color used to paint text which is in a selected region.

public void setSelectionColor(java.awt.Color c)

Paints the Color used to render the highlight.

public void setSelectionEnd(int selectionEnd)

Sets the end of the current selection to selectionEnd. Provided for compatibility; use setCaret-Position/moveCaretPosition instead.

public void setSelectionStart(int selectionStart)

Sets the start of the current selection to selectionStart. Provided for compatibility; use set-CaretPosition/moveCaretPosition instead.

public void setText(String t)

Sets the contents of this editor and its Document to t. This method is thread safe.

public void setUI(TextUI ui)

Sets the UI delegate for this editor.

public void updateUI()

Called when the UI has changed and needs to be reloaded.

Overrides: updateUI in class JComponent.

public int viewToModel(java.awt.Point pt)

Returns the offset into the Document that best represents the given point in the View.

public void write(Writer out) throws IOException

Writes the contents of this editor to the given Writer.

Throws: IOException on any I/O error.

Protected Methods

protected void fireCaretUpdate(CaretEvent e)

Notifies all added listeners that the Caret has changed.

protected String paramString()

Returns a String containing the properties of this JTextComponent. The returned String may be empty but it will not be null.

Overrides: paramString in class JComponent.

protected void processComponentKeyEvent(java.awt.event.KeyEvent e)

Converts KeyEvents into the appropriate Actions for this component.

Overrides: processComponentKeyEvent in class JComponent.

Inner Classes

public class JTextComponent.AccessibleJTextComponent

public static class JTextComponent.KeyBinding

Extended by   JEditorPane (p.232), JTextArea (p.374), JTextField (p.379).

Returned by   BasicTextUI.getComponent() (p.696), DefaultCaret.getComponent() (p.806), TextAction.getFocusedComponent() (p.891), TextAction.getTextComponent() (p.891).

See also   Caret (p.800), CaretEvent (p.485), CaretListener (p.486), Document (p.826), DocumentEvent (p.489), DocumentListener (p.490), TextUI (p.542), View (p.893), ViewFactory (p.896).

swing.text.JTextComponent.AccessibleJTextComponent

INNER CLASS

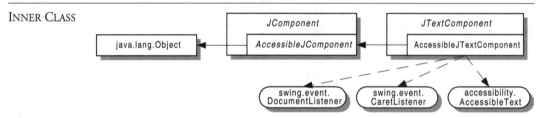

protected class JTextComponent.AccessibleJTextComponent
    extends AccessibleJComponent
    implements AccessibleText

Constructors

public AccessibleJTextComponent()

Default constructor.

Methods

public void caretUpdate(CaretEvent e)

Fires property changes for AccessibleContext.ACCESSIBLE_CARET_PROPERTY and AccessibleContext.ACCESSIBLE_SELECTION_PROPERTY as appropriate, based on the information in the CaretEvent.

Implements: caretUpdate in interface CaretListener.

public void changedUpdate(DocumentEvent e)

Fires AccessibleContext.ACCESSIBLE_TEXT_PROPERTY events.

Implements: changedUpdate in interface DocumentListener.

public AccessibleRole getAccessibleRole()

Returns AccessibleRole.TEXT.

public AccessibleStateSet getAccessibleStateSet()

Returns the state set of the text component.

public AccessibleText getAccessibleText()

Returns the AccessibleText for interacting with this editor.

public String getAfterIndex(int part, int index)

Returns the CHARACTER, WORD, or SENTENCE String after a given index.

Implements: getAfterIndex in interface AccessibleText.

public String getAtIndex(int part, int index)

Returns the CHARACTER, WORD, or SENTENCE String at a given index.

Implements: getAtIndex in interface AccessibleText.

public String getBeforeIndex(int part, int index)

Returns the String before a given index.

Implements: getBeforeIndex in interface AccessibleText.

public int getCaretPosition()

Implements: getCaretPosition in interface AccessibleText.

public int getCharCount()

Implements: getCharCount in interface AccessibleText.

public AttributeSet getCharacterAttribute(int i)

Implements: getCharacterAttribute in interface AccessibleText.

public java.awt.Rectangle getCharacterBounds(int i)

Implements: getCharacterBounds in interface AccessibleText.

public int getIndexAtPoint(java.awt.Point p)

Returns the index in the Document of the character under the Point p, or –1 if the location under p is empty.

Implements: getIndexAtPoint in interface AccessibleText.

public String getSelectedText()

Implements: getSelectedText in interface AccessibleText.

public int getSelectionEnd()

Implements: getSelectionEnd in interface AccessibleText.

public int getSelectionStart()

Implements: getSelectionStart in interface AccessibleText.

public void insertUpdate(DocumentEvent e)

Fires a PropertyChangeEvent for AccessibleContext.ACCESSIBLE_TEXT_PROPERTY.

Implements: insertUpdate in interface DocumentListener.

public void removeUpdate(DocumentEvent e)

Fires a PropertyChangeEvent for AccessibleContext.ACCESSIBLE_ TEXT_PROPERTY.

Implements: removeUpdate in interface DocumentListener.

See also   AccessibleText (p.103), DocumentEvent (p.489), JComponent.AccessibleJComponent (p.221).

swing.text.JTextComponent.KeyBinding

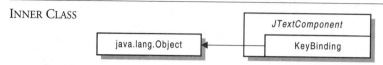

Stores the relationship between a `KeyStroke` and an `Action`.

```
public static class JTextComponent.KeyBinding
    extends java.lang.Object
```

Fields
public String actionName
The name of the action for the key.
public KeyStroke key
The key.

Constructors
public KeyBinding(KeyStroke key, String actionName)
Creates a new key binding.

Returned by   LookAndFeel.makeKeyBindings() (p.423).

swing.text.Keymap

Keymap

This interface defines a relationship between `KeyStrokes` and `Actions`. A `Keymap` may be part of a hierarchy of `Keymaps`, where if a binding isn't found in the current map, its parent will be searched.

```
public interface Keymap
```

Methods
public abstract void addActionForKeyStroke(KeyStroke key, Action action)
Adds a binding between `key` and `action` to the `Keymap`.
public abstract Action getAction(KeyStroke key)
Returns the `Action` associated with the given `KeyStroke`. If the `KeyStroke` cannot be found in the current `Keymap`, its parent may be searched for it. If the `KeyStroke` cannot be found, this method returns `null`.
public abstract Action[] getBoundActions()
Returns an array of all `Actions` in this `Keymap`. It is not guaranteed that the order of `Actions` in the array will correspond with the order of `KeyStrokes` in the array returned from `getBoundKey-Strokes()`.

public abstract KeyStroke[] getBoundKeyStrokes()

Returns an array of all KeyStrokes in this Keymap. It is not guaranteed that the order of Actions in the array will correspond with the order of KeyStrokes in the array returned from getBoundKeyStrokes().

public abstract KeyStroke[] getKeyStrokesForAction(Action a)

Returns an array of KeyStrokes that are bound to the same Action.

public abstract String getName()

Returns the name of this Keymap.

public abstract Keymap getResolveParent()

Returns the parent of this Keymap, if it has one.

public abstract boolean isLocallyDefined(KeyStroke key)

Returns true if this KeyStroke is contained in the current Keymap.

public abstract void removeBindings()

Empties the Keymap.

public abstract void removeKeyStrokeBinding(KeyStroke keys)

Removes the binding for KeyStroke from the Keymap.

public abstract void setResolveParent(Keymap parent)

Sets the parent Keymap, which will be seached for a KeyStroke that cannot be found in this Keymap.

Returned by : BasicTextUI.createKeymap() (p.696), JTextComponent.addKeymap() (p.838), JTextComponent.removeKeymap() (p.838), Keymap.getResolveParent() (p.846).

See also   Action (p.128), KeyStroke (p.419).

swing.text.LabelView

CLASS

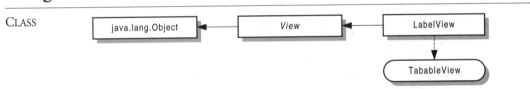

A LabelView is responsible for displaying attributes on characters. LabelView supports breaking into fragments if necessary during formatting. The fragments created are very lightweight Views that rely on the creating View for most of their state information.

Since LabelViews can contain tabs, LabelView implements the TabableView interface.

```
public class LabelView extends View
    implements TabableView
```

Constructors
public LabelView(Element elem)

Constructs a LabelView for the given Element.

Methods

public View breakView(int axis, int documentOffset, float pos, float len)

Breaks this view on the given axis (View.X_AXIS or View.Y_AXIS) at the given document offset. This implementation tries to break the View at a white space character. If it can't find a white space character near enough, it breaks on the nearest character.

Overrides: breakView in class View.

public void changedUpdate(DocumentEvent e, java.awt.Shape a, ViewFactory f)

Called when the Document changes in the section this View is responsible for.

Overrides: changedUpdate in class View.

public View createFragment(int beginRange, int endRange)

Returns a new View that represents the given range in the Element. A LabelView supports fragmenting, so this method returns a new View representing the range. The actual class of the View returned is very lightweight, depending on the creating Element for most of its state information.

Overrides: createFragment in class View.

public float getAlignment(int axis)

Returns the alignment for this View along an axis. For View.X_AXIS, this method returns the alignment of this View's parent. For View.Y_AXIS, this method returns the alignment of the baseline of the text.

Overrides: getAlignment in class View.

public int getBreakWeight(int axis, float pos, float len)

Returns a value representing how appropriate it is to break this View. When formatting the View, this can be used to decide which View would handle having breakView() called on it the best. A returned value less than or equal to View.BadBreakWeight means this View should not be broken. A returned value greater than or equal to View.ForcedBreakWeight should be broken.

The pos and len parameters together represent the position that needs the break. The pos parameter is given to use as a starting point for expanding any tabs that are near the break. The actual position where the break should happen is pos+len.

If this method is called with View.Y_AXIS, it will return the value from the superclass' getBreakWeight() method. If this method is called with View.X_AXIS, it can only return one of the following three values:

- View.ExcellentBreakWeight if there is white space sufficiently close in front of the desired break location.

- View.BadBreakWeight if the desired break location results in a break location of the starting offset.

- View.GoodBreakWeight otherwise.

Overrides: getBreakWeight in class View.

public int getNextVisualPositionFrom(int pos, Position.Bias b, java.awt.Shape a, int direction, Position.Bias[] biasRet) throws BadLocationException

Returns the next offset in the Document that represents a visible position in the given direction.

Throws: IllegalArgumentException for an invalid direction.

Overrides: getNextVisualPositionFrom in class View.

public float getPartialSpan(int beginRange, int endRange)

Called from getPreferredSpan and getTabbedSpan to help calculate the span of a section that does not have tabs. The axis assumed by this call is the axis being used in the calling method.

Implements: getPartialSpan in interface TabableView.

public float getPreferredSpan(int axis)

Returns the preferred height along the Y_AXIS and preferred width along the X_AXIS.

Overrides: getPreferredSpan in class View.

public float getTabbedSpan(float startPosition, TabExpander e)

Returns the span of the View after expanding any tabs using the given TabExpander. The start-Position is the position the View should be considered to be for the purpose of expanding the tabs correctly.

Implements: getTabbedSpan in interface TabableView.

public void insertUpdate(DocumentEvent e, java.awt.Shape a, ViewFactory f)

Overrides: insertUpdate in class View.

public java.awt.Shape modelToView(int pos, java.awt.Shape a, Position.Bias bias) throws BadLocationException

Returns the bounding box in the View that best represents the character in the Document at pos.

Throws: BadLocationException if the given position does not represent a valid location in the associated document.

Overrides: modelToView in class View.

public void paint(java.awt.Graphics g, java.awt.Shape a)

Paints the text for this View.

Overrides: paint in class View.

public int viewToModel(float x, float y, java.awt.Shape a, Position.Bias[] returnedBias)

Returns the offset into the Document that best represents the point (x, y) in the View.

Overrides: viewToModel in class View.

Protected Methods

protected java.awt.Font getFont()

Returns the Font used for this view.

protected java.awt.FontMetrics getFontMetrics()

Returns the cached FontMetrics used for this view.

protected void setPropertiesFromAttributes()

Fills in some convenience properties based on the Attributes of the associated Element.

protected void setStrikeThrough(boolean s)

A convenience method to set the strike property.

protected void setSubscript(boolean s)

A convenience method to set the subscript property.

protected void setSuperscript(boolean s)

A convenience method to set the superscript property.

protected void setUnderline(boolean u)

A convenience method to set the underline property.

See also TabableView (p885.), View (p.893), ViewFactory (p.896).

swing.text.LabelView2D

CLASS
(JDK 1.2 ONLY)

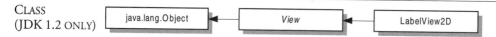

This class is an implementation of `LabelView` that makes use of features from JDK 1.2.

```
public class LabelView2D extends View
```

Constructors

public LabelView2D(Element elem)

Constructs a `LabelView2D` for the given `Element`.

Methods

public View breakView(int axis, int documentOffset, float pos, float len)

Breaks this view on the given axis (`View.X_AXIS` or `View.Y_AXIS`) at the given document offset. This implementation tries to break the `View` at a white space character. If it can't find a white space character near enough, it breaks on the nearest character.

Overrides: breakView in class `View`.

public void changedUpdate(DocumentEvent e, java.awt.Shape a, ViewFactory f)

Called when the `Document` changes in the section this `View` is responsible for.

Overrides: changedUpdate in class `View`.

public View createFragment(int beginRange, int endRange)

Returns a new `View` that represents the given range in the `Element`. A `LabelView` supports fragmenting, so this method returns a new `View` representing the range. The actual class of the `View` returned is very lightweight, depending on the creating `Element` for most of its state information.

Overrides: createFragment in class `View`.

public float getAlignment(int axis)

Returns the alignment for this `View` along an axis. For `View.X_AXIS`, this method returns the alignment of this `View`'s parent. For `View.Y_AXIS`, this method returns the alignment of the baseline of the text.

Overrides: getAlignment in class `View`.

public int getBreakWeight(int axis, float pos, float len)

Returns a value representing how appropriate it is to break this `View`. When formatting the `View`, this can be used to decide which `View` would handle having `breakView()` called on it the best. A returned value less than or equal to `View.BadBreakWeight` means this `View` should not be broken. A returned value greater than or equal to `View.ForcedBreakWeight` should be broken.

The `pos` and `len` parameters together represent the position that needs the break. The `pos` parameter is given to use as a starting point for expanding any tabs that are near the break. The actual position where the break should happen is `pos+len`.

If this method is called with `View.Y_AXIS`, it will return the value from the superclass' `getBreakWeight()` method. If this method is called with `View.X_AXIS`, it will return one of the following three values:

- `View.ExcellentBreakWeight` if there is white space sufficiently close in front of the desired break location.
- `View.BadBreakWeight` if the desired break location results in a break location of the starting offset.

- View.GoodBreakWeight otherwise.

Overrides: getBreakWeight in class View.

public int getNextVisualPositionFrom(int pos, Position.Bias b,
java.awt.Shape a, int direction, Position.Bias[] biasRet)
throws BadLocationException

Returns the next offset in the Document that represents a visible position in the given direction.

Throws: IllegalArgumentException for an invalid direction.

Overrides: getNextVisualPositionFrom in class View.

public float getPreferredSpan(int axis)

Returns the preferred height along the Y_AXIS and preferred width along the X_AXIS.

Overrides: getPreferredSpan in class View.

public void insertUpdate(DocumentEvent e, java.awt.Shape a, ViewFactory f)

Overrides: insertUpdate in class View.

public java.awt.Shape modelToView(int pos, java.awt.Shape a,
Position.Bias bias) throws BadLocationException

Returns the bounding box in the View that best represents the character in the Document at pos.

Throws: BadLocationException if the given position does not represent a valid location in the associated document.

Overrides: modelToView in class View.

public void paint(java.awt.Graphics g, java.awt.Shape a)

Paints the text for this View.

Overrides: paint in class View.

public String toString()

Overrides: toString in class Object.

public int viewToModel(float x, float y, java.awt.Shape a,
Position.Bias[] returnedBias)

Returns the offset into the Document that best represents the point (x, y) in the View.

Overrides: viewToModel in class View.

Protected Methods

protected java.awt.Font getFont()

Returns the Font used for this view.

protected java.awt.FontMetrics getFontMetrics()

Returns the cached FontMetrics used for this view.

protected void setPropertiesFromAttributes()

Fills in some convenience properties based on the Attributes of the associated Element.

protected void setStrikeThrough(boolean s)

A convenience method to set the strike property.

protected void setSubscript(boolean s)

A convenience method to set the subscript property.

protected void setSuperscript(boolean s)

A convenience method to set the superscript property.

protected void setUnderline(boolean u)

A convenience method to set the underline property.

See also TabableView (p885.), View (p.893), ViewFactory (p.896).

swing.text.LayeredHighlighter

ABSTRACT
CLASS

This class defines a `Highlighter` that can be used to paint just the portion of a highlight that is contained within a `View`.

```
public abstract class LayeredHighlighter extends java.lang.Object
    implements Highlighter
```

Constructors
```
public LayeredHighlighter()
```
Default constructor.

Methods
```
public abstract void paintLayeredHighlights(java.awt.Graphics g, int p0,
    int p1, java.awt.Shape viewBounds, JTextComponent editor, View view)
```
Paints a portion of the total highlight as part of the process of a `View` painting itself. The view-Bounds parameter is the bounding box for the surrounding `View`. The actual area that needs to have the highlight painted needs to be calculated using the offsets p0 and p1.

Inner Classes
```
public abstract static class LayeredHighlighter.LayerPainter
```

Extended by   DefaultHighlighter (p.818).
See also   Highlighter (p.835).

swing.text.LayeredHighlighter.LayerPainter

ABSTRACT
INNER CLASS

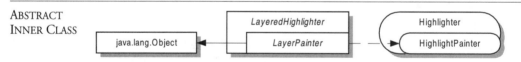

```
public abstract static class LayeredHighlighter.LayerPainter
    extends java.lang.Object
    implements Highlighter.HighlightPainter
```

Constructors
```
public LayerPainter()
```
Default constructor.

Methods
```
public abstract java.awt.Shape paintLayer(java.awt.Graphics g, int p0,
    int p1, java.awt.Shape viewBounds, JTextComponent editor, View view)
```
Paints the highlight for the `View` between the offsets p0 and p1.

Extended by   DefaultHighlighter.DefaultHighlightPainter (p.819).

swing.text.MutableAttributeSet

INTERFACE

This interface describes a modifiable `AttributeSet`.

```
public interface MutableAttributeSet extends AttributeSet
```

Methods
`public abstract void addAttribute(Object name, Object value)`
Adds the given attribute defined by (`name, value`) to the set. The `value` object must be immutable or at least an instance that is never modifed.
`public abstract void addAttributes(AttributeSet attributes)`
Adds the given attributes to the set.
`public abstract void removeAttribute(Object name)`
Removes the attribute identified by `name` from the set.
`public abstract void removeAttributes(AttributeSet attributes)`
Removes the given attributes from the set, if they are an exact match on *both* the name and the value.
`public abstract void removeAttributes(Enumeration names)`
Removes all attributes with the given names from the set.
`public abstract void setResolveParent(AttributeSet parent)`
Sets the parent to search if an attribute cannot be found in this set.

Extended by Style (p.865).
Implemented by AbstractDocument.AbstractElement (p.783), SimpleAttributeSet (p.862).
Returned by JTextPane.getInputAttributes() (p.383),
StyledEditorKit.getInputAttributes() (p.878).
See also AttributeSet (p.794).

swing.text.ParagraphView

CLASS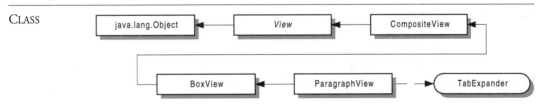

This class implements a `View` of a paragraph that supports line wrap, and multiple `Fonts`, `Colors`, `Icons`, and `Components`. This `View` lines up its children vertically.

```
public class ParagraphView extends BoxView
    implements TabExpander
```

Constructors
`public ParagraphView(Element elem)`
Constructs a `ParagraphView` for the given element.

Methods

public View breakView(int axis, float len, java.awt.Shape a)

Tries to break this View at the position given by len. ParagraphViews are only breakable along the Y_AXIS. Passing X_AXIS for the axis will always cause this method to return the current View, unbroken. This method is not implemented as of Swing 1.1.

Overrides: breakView in class View.

public void changedUpdate(DocumentEvent changes, java.awt.Shape a, ViewFactory f)

Called when the Document changes in a region this View is representing.

Overrides: changedUpdate in class BoxView.

public float getAlignment(int axis)

For X_AXIS, returns an alignment value which matches the ALIGN property for the paragraph. For the Y_AXIS, returns the value from the superclass getAlignment.

Overrides: getAlignment in class BoxView.

public int getBreakWeight(int axis, float len)

If the axis is X_AXIS or the len is less than a full line in the View, this method returns Bad-BreakWeight. If the axis is Y_AXIS and len is greater than one lines worth of text in the View this method returns an appropriate break weight. This method always returns BadBreakWeight for any values passed in as of Swing 1.1.

Overrides: getBreakPenalty in class View.

public void insertUpdate(DocumentEvent changes, java.awt.Shape a, ViewFactory f)

Called when the Document has content inserted into a range that this View represents.

Overrides: insertUpdate in class BoxView.

public float nextTabStop(float afterHere, int tabOffset)

Returns the position of the first tab stop after the position given by afterHere. This calls get-TabbedSpan() on each of the children. The children of this View can use this View to expand their tabs, since this View implements TabExpander. This implementation tries to find a TabSet in the paragraph Element's attribute set. If one is found it will be used. Otherwise, the default tab value will be used.

Implements: nextTabStop in interface TabExpander.

public void paint(java.awt.Graphics g, java.awt.Shape a)

Stores the starting coordinate so it can be used for tab expansions later and then calls the superclass paint method.

Overrides: paint in class BoxView.

public void removeUpdate(DocumentEvent changes, java.awt.Shape a, ViewFactory f)

Called when content is removed from the region of the Document that this View represents.

Overrides: removeUpdate in class BoxView.

Protected Fields

protected int firstLineIndent

The indent for the first line of the paragraph, relative to the left margin.

Protected Methods

protected void adjustRow(Row row, int desiredSpan, int startOfRow)

Tries to fit the `row` within the `desiredSpan`. This method tries to find the highest break weight, nearest the end of the line. A forced break will always be chosen, if found.

protected SizeRequirements calculateMinorAxisRequirements(int axis, SizeRequirements r)

Overrides: `calculateMinorAxisRequirements` in class `BoxView`.

protected int findOffsetToCharactersInString(char[] string, int startOffset)

Returns the offset in the `Document` of the first character from `string` which is found after `startOffset` in the `Document`. If none of the characters are found, this method returns –1.

protected boolean flipEastAndWestAtEnds(int position, Position.Bias bias)

Returns `true` if the first chracter for this `View` in the `Document` returns `false` from `AbstractDocument.isLeftToRight()`.

Overrides: `flipEastAndWestAtEnds` in class `BoxView`.

protected int getClosestPositionTo(int pos, Position.Bias b, java.awt.Shape a, int direction, Position.Bias[] biasRet, int rowIndex, int x) throws BadLocationException

Returns the closest offset into the `Document` to the given x coordinate. The `rowIndex` gives the index of the child view that should be used for the y position.

protected View getLayoutView(int index)

Returns the `View` responsible for managing the child `View` of the `Element` at index.

protected int getLayoutViewCount()

Returns the number of child views which are being used to manage the `View`s associated with this `View`'s child `Element`s.

protected int getNextNorthSouthVisualPositionFrom(int pos, Position.Bias b, java.awt.Shape a, int direction, Position.Bias[] biasRet) throws BadLocationException

Overrides: `getNextNorthSouthVisualPositionFrom` in class `CompositeView`.

protected float getPartialSize(int startOffset, int endOffset)

Returns the size, when rendered, of the region between `startOffset` and `endOffset` in the Document. If the region covers a child `View` that implements the `TabableView` interface, this method will use the `getPartialView` method. If the child does not support the `tabableView` interface, this method will use the `getPreferredSpan` method instead.

protected float getTabBase()

Returns where tabs are calculated from.

protected TabSet getTabSet()

Returns the `TabSet` which defines the tabs in this `View`.

protected View getViewAtPosition(int pos, Rectangle a)

Returns the child `View` which contains the given position pos. In this class this method examines the child `View`s, not the child `Element`s since `View`s and `Element`s do not have a 1-to-1 correspondence.

Overrides: `getViewAtPosition` in class `CompositeView`.

protected int getViewIndexAtPosition(int pos)

Returns the child view index representing the given position in the model.

Overrides: `getViewIndexAtPosition` in class `CompositeView`.

protected void layout(int width, int height)

Lays out the child Views of this View. If the horizontal span of the paragraph has changed, the rows are rebuilt. After the rows are rebuilt, the superclass layout method is called. If the vertical span of the paragraph has changed, the preferenceChanged() method in the parent View is called.

Overrides: layout in class BoxView.

protected void loadChildren(ViewFactory f)

Called from setParent(). This method is overridden to not actually load the children, just create Views for them which are used later when the formatting is done. The actual loading of the children occurs during the formatting of the paragraph.

Overrides: loadChildren in class CompositeView.

protected void setFirstLineIndent(float fi)

Sets the indent on the first line of the paragraph.

protected void setJustification(int j)

Sets the type of justification.

protected void setLineSpacing(float ls)

Sets the line spacing.

protected void setPropertiesFromAttributes()

Fills the properties from the attributes of the associated Element.

See also BoxView (p.797), DocumentEvent (p.489), TabExpander (p.885), ViewFactory (p.896).

swing.text.PasswordView

CLASS

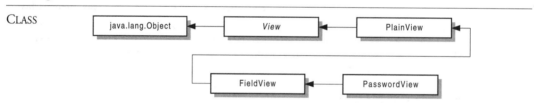

If this View can figure out that it is attached to a JPasswordField component, it will render all content using the echoChar from the component. If it cannot find an associated JPassword-Field, this View does not render anything.

public class PasswordView extends FieldView

Constructors

public PasswordView(Element elem)

Constructs a new PasswordView of the given Element.

Protected Methods

protected int drawEchoCharacter(java.awt.Graphics g, int x, int y, char c)

Draws the echo character. The correct text Color needs to be set into g before this method is called.

protected int drawSelectedText(java.awt.Graphics g, int x, int y, int p0, int p1) throws BadLocationException

Paints the given region with the echo character. This method leaves the background alone, assuming the highlighter will paint the background.

Throws: BadLocationException if p0 or p1 are out of range.

Overrides: drawSelectedText in class PlainView.

protected int drawUnselectedText(java.awt.Graphics g, int x, int y, int p0, int p1) throws BadLocationException

Paints the given region with the echo character.

Throws: BadLocationException if p0 or p1 are out of range.

Overrides: drawUnselectedText in class PlainView.

public Shape modelToView(int pos, java.awt.Shape a, Position.Bias b) throws BadLocationException

Overridden to handle the echo character being used instead of the actual text.

Throws: BadLocationException if the given position does not represent a valid location in the associated document.

Overrides: modelToView in class FieldView.

public int viewToModel(float fx, float fy, java.awt.Shape a, Position.Bias[] bias)

Overridden to handle the echo character being used instead of the actual text.

Overrides: viewToModel in class FieldView.

See also   BadLocationException (p.796), Element (p.830), FieldView (p.832), PlainView (p.858).

swing.text.PlainDocument

CLASS

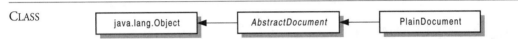

A Document that can use one Font and Color. The Element returned by getDefault-RootElement() is an Element that is the root of a tree of Elements representing the lines in the Document. The tab size used is 8.

public class PlainDocument extends AbstractDocument

Fields

public static final String lineLimitAttribute = "lineLimit"

The name of the property that represents the maximum line size.

public static final String tabSizeAttribute = "tabSize"

The name of the property that represents the tab size in this document.

Constructors

public PlainDocument()

Constructs a PlainDocument using a new GapContent instance.

Methods

public Element getDefaultRootElement()

Returns the default root Element of the Document, creating it if necessary.

Overrides: getDefaultRootElement in class AbstractDocument.

Implements: getDefaultRootElement in interface Document.

```
public Element getParagraphElement(int pos)
```
Returns the line containing the given position.

Overrides: getParagraphElement in class AbstractDocument.

Protected Constructors
```
protected PlainDocument(Content c)
```
Constructs a PlainDocument for the given Content.

Protected Methods
```
protected AbstractElement createDefaultRoot()
```
Creates and returns the Element which is the root of the document structure.
```
protected void insertUpdate(DefaultDocumentEvent chng, AttributeSet attr)
```
Updates the Document with the information in chng. This update will update the current line list inside a write lock.

Overrides: insertUpdate in class AbstractDocument.
```
protected void removeUpdate(DefaultDocumentEvent chng)
```
Updates the Document with the information in chng. This update will occur inside a write lock. If the removal spans more than one line, the partial line before the removed section and the partial line after the removed section will be joined into one line.

Overrides: removeUpdate in class AbstractDocument.

See also AbstractDocument (p.778), AbstractDocument.AbstractElement (p.783), AbstractDocument.Content (p.788), AbstractDocument.DefaultDocumentEvent (p.789), AttributeSet (p.794), Element (p.830).

swing.text.PlainView

CLASS

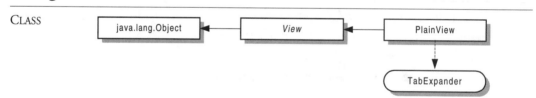

This View displays a simple multiline text view. The View only uses one Font and Color and renders each child Element as a new line.
```
public class PlainView extends View
    implements TabExpander
```

Constructors
```
public PlainView(Element elem)
```
Constructs a new View of elem.

Methods
```
public void changedUpdate(DocumentEvent changes, java.awt.Shape a,
    ViewFactory f)
```
Called when the Document changes in the region represented by this View.

Overrides: changedUpdate in class View.

public float getPreferredSpan(int axis)

Returns the preferred width or height for this view depending on which axis is given.

Overrides: getPreferredSpan in class View.

public void insertUpdate(DocumentEvent changes, java.awt.Shape a, ViewFactory f)

Called when content is inserted into the Document at a position this View represents.

Overrides: insertUpdate in class View.

public java.awt.Shape modelToView(int pos, java.awt.Shape a, Position.Bias b) throws BadLocationException

Returns the bounding box in the View of the character at pos in the Document.

Throws: BadLocationException if the given position does not represent a valid location in the associated document.

Overrides: modelToView in class View.

public float nextTabStop(float x, int tabOffset)

Returns the next tab stop position. PlainView does not support aligment attributes, so the tab-Offset parameter is unnecessary and ignored.

Implements: nextTabStop in interface TabExpander.

public void paint(java.awt.Graphics g, java.awt.Shape a)

Paints the View. This method may cause a layout to be done and create child Views as needed.

Overrides: paint in class View.

public void preferenceChanged(View child, boolean width, boolean height)

Called by this View's children if their preferred span changes.

Overrides: preferenceChanged in class View.

public void removeUpdate(DocumentEvent changes, java.awt.Shape a, ViewFactory f)

Called when content was removed from a region of the Document that this View represents.

Overrides: removeUpdate in class View.

public int viewToModel(float fx, float fy, java.awt.Shape a, Position.Bias[] returnBias)

Returns the offset in the Document that best represents the given point (fx, fy) in the View.

Overrides: viewToModel in class View.

Protected Fields

protected java.awt.FontMetrics metrics

Font metrics for the current font.

Protected Methods

protected void drawLine(int lineIndex, java.awt.Graphics g, int x, int y)

Draws a line of text. This method trims off any white space at the end of the line and expands any tabs in the line's content. This method makes calls to the drawUnselected and drawSelected methods so that a subclass can easily override the way selected and unselected text is drawn.

protected int drawSelectedText(java.awt.Graphics g, int x, int y, int beginRange, int endRange) throws BadLocationException

Draws the text as selected text. This method does not render the selection background, leaving that to the Highlighter.

Throws: badLocationException if the range is invalid.

```
protected int drawUnselectedText(java.awt.Graphics g, int x, int y,
    int p0, int p1) throws BadLocationException
```
Draws the text as normal text.

Throws: BadLocationException if the range is invalid.

protected final Segment getLineBuffer()

Returns a Segment which directly references the text in the Document. This method is faster than copying the content into a String, but the Segment's contents *must not* be modified.

protected int getTabSize()

Returns the tab size for the View, which defaults to 8.

Extended by FieldView (p.832).

See also BadLocationException (p.796), DocumentEvent (p.489), Element (p.830), Segment (p.861), TabExpander (p.885), View (p.893), ViewFactory (p.896).

swing.text.Position

INTERFACE

This interface is used for objects which track changes in the Document so that they always represent the same section of text in the Document.

public interface Position

Methods
public abstract int getOffset()

Returns the offset this Position currently represents.

Inner Classes
public static final class Position.Bias

Returned by AbstractDocument.Content.createPosition() (p.788), AbstractDocument.createPosition() (p.778), AbstractDocument.getEndPosition() (p.778), AbstractDocument.getStartPosition() (p.778), Document.createPosition() (p.826), Document.getEndPosition() (p.826), Document.getStartPosition() (p.826), GapContent.createPosition() (p.833), StringContent.createPosition() (p.863).

swing.text.Position.Bias

INNER CLASS

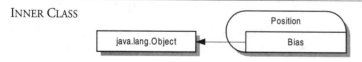

This class is an enumeration used to indicate which direction from a given offset is the preferred direction. This is used for situations where the position lies between two characters, to account for the possibility of bidirectional text.

public static final class Position.Bias
    extends java.lang.Object

Fields
public static final Position.Bias Backward
>This means that the preferred direction is toward the previous character in the Document.

public static final Position.Bias Forward
>This means that the preferred direction is toward the next character in the Document.

Methods
public String toString()
>Returns the String "Forward" or "Backward" depending on which of the two constants is being used.
>*Overrides:* toString in class Object.

swing.text.Segment

CLASS

This class provides direct access to a section of the content in a Document. The content represented by this object *must not* be modified through this object. If you need to modify the content, use the Document methods.

public class Segment

Fields
public char[] array
>This array contains the content referenced by this Segment.

public int count
>The number of characters in the array.

public int offset
>The offset into the array that is the start of the text that was requested when the Segment was created.

Constructors
public Segment()
>Constructs a new, empty Segment.

public Segment(char[] array, int offset, int count)
>Constructs a Segment representing an existing array of content.

Methods
public String toString()
>Returns a String copy of the content in this Segment.
>*Overrides:* toString in class Object.

>*Returned by*   PlainView.getLineBuffer() (p.858), WrappedPlainView.getLineBuffer() (p.897).

swing.text.SimpleAttributeSet

CLASS

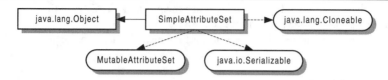

This class implements the `MutableAttributeSet` interface using a hash table.

```
public class SimpleAttributeSet extends java.lang.Object
    implements MutableAttributeSet, java.io.Serializable,
    java.lang.Cloneable
```

Fields
`public static final AttributeSet EMPTY`
    Represents an empty `AttributeSet`.

Constructors
`public SimpleAttributeSet()`
    Constructs a new, empty `AttributeSet`.
`public SimpleAttributeSet(AttributeSet source)`
    Constructs a new `AttributeSet` by copying `source`.

Methods
`public void addAttribute(Object name, Object value)`
    Adds an attribute given by (`name`, `value`) to the set.
    Implements: `addAttribute` in interface `MutableAttributeSet`.
`public void addAttributes(AttributeSet attributes)`
    Adds the attributes in the given `AttributeSet` to the set.
    Implements: `addAttributes` in interface `MutableAttributeSet`.
`public Object clone()`
    Clones this `AttributeSet`.
    Overrides: `clone` in class `Object`.
`public boolean containsAttribute(Object name, Object value)`
    Returns `true` if this `AttributeSet` contains an *exact* match for the given (`name`, `value`) pair.
`public boolean containsAttributes(AttributeSet attrs)`
    Returns `true` if this `AttributeSet` contains all of the attributes in `attrs`.
`public AttributeSet copyAttributes()`
    Returns a copy of this `AttributeSet`.
`public boolean equals(Object obj)`
    Returns `true` if the given object is an `AttributeSet` that matches this `AttributeSet`.
    Overrides: `equals` in class `Object`.
`public Object getAttribute(Object name)`
    Returns the value associated with the given `name`.
`public int getAttributeCount()`
    Returns the number of `Attributes` in this `AttributeSet`.
`public Enumeration getAttributeNames()`
    Returns an `Enumeration` of all of the names in this `AttributeSet`.

public AttributeSet getResolveParent()

Returns the parent AttributeSet to search if an attribute cannot be found in this Attribute-Set. If this set does not have a parent, this method returns null.

public int hashCode()

Returns a hash code for this AttributeSet. This method is required for "100 percent pure Java" status since the equals() method is defined.

Overrides: hashCode in class Object.

public boolean isDefined(Object attrName)

Returns true if there is an attribute with the given name in the set.

public boolean isEmpty()

Returns true if there aren't any attributes in the set.

public boolean isEqual(AttributeSet attr)

Returns true if the given AttributeSet exactly matched this one.

public void removeAttribute(Object name)

Removes the named attribute from the set.

Implements: removeAttribute in interface MutableAttributeSet.

public void removeAttributes(AttributeSet attributes)

Removes all of the attributes in the given AttributeSet from the set.

Implements: removeAttributes in interface MutableAttributeSet.

public void removeAttributes(java.util.Enumeration names)

Removes all attributes with the given names from the set.

Implements: removeAttributes in interface MutableAttributeSet.

public void setResolveParent(AttributeSet parent)

Sets the parent AttributeSet that should be searched if an attribute cannot be found in this set.

Implements: setResolveParent in interface MutableAttributeSet.

public String toString()

Returns a String representing this AttributeSet.

Overrides: toString in class Object.

Returned by   Parser.getAttributes() (p.948).

See also   AttributeSet (p.794), MutableAttributeSet (p.853).

swing.text.StringContent

CLASS

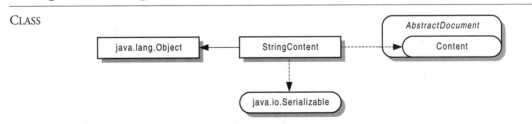

This class implements the AbstractDocument.Content interface using a simple character array. In Swing 1.1 this class has been largely superseded by GapContent.

```
public final class StringContent extends java.lang.Object
    implements AbstractDocument.Content, java.io.Serializable
```

Constructors

public StringContent()

Constructs a StringContent object using an initial array size of 10.

public StringContent(int initialLength)

Constructs a StringContent object using an initial array of the given size. If the array size given is less than 1, the array size is changed to 1.

Methods

public Position createPosition(int offset) throws BadLocationException

Creates and returns a Position which will try to always represent the same section of text.

Throws: BadLocationException if the specified position is invalid.

Implements: createPosition in interface AbstractDocument.Content.

**public void getChars(int where, int len, Segment chars)
throws BadLocationException**

Returns a Segment representing the given region in the content. The Segment should not be used to modify the content.

Throws: BadLocationException if the specified position is invalid.

Implements: getChars in interface AbstractDocument.Content.

public String getString(int where, int len) throws BadLocationException

Returns a String copy of the given region of content.

Throws: BadLocationException if the specified position is invalid.

Implements: getString in interface AbstractDocument.Content.

**public UndoableEdit insertString(int where, String str)
throws BadLocationException**

Inserts the given String into the content at where.

Throws: BadLocationException if the specified position is invalid.

Implements: insertString in interface AbstractDocument.Content.

public int length()

Returns the number of characters in the content array.

Implements: length in interface AbstractDocument.Content.

**public UndoableEdit remove(int where, int nitems)
throws BadLocationException**

Removes the content starting at where and running for nitems characters.

Throws: BadLocationException if the specified position is invalid.

Implements: remove in interface AbstractDocument.Content.

Protected Methods

**protected java.util.Vector getPositionsInRange(java.util.Vector v,
int offset, int length)**

Returns a Vector containing instances of UndoPosRef for the previously created Positions in the range offset to offset + length. If v is not null the Positions are added to that Vector. The Vector with the resulting Positions are returned. UndoPosRef is a package private inner class.

protected void updateUndoPositions(java.util.Vector positions)

Resets the location for all the UndoPosRef instances in positions. UndoPosRef is a package private inner class.

See also   BadLocationException (p.796), Position (p.860), Segment (p.861), UndoableEdit (p.1005).

swing.text.Style

INTERFACE

This interface represents a named set of attributes which can be assigned to `Elements` in a `Document`. `Views` using `Elements` which contain these `Styles` can attach themselves as listeners to be notified when the `Style` changes.

```
public interface Style extends MutableAttributeSet
```

Methods
```
public abstract void addChangeListener(ChangeListener l)
```
   Adds a listener to be notified whenever an attribute has been changed.
```
public abstract String getName()
```
   Returns the name associated with the `Style`. If the `Style` is unnamed, `null` will be returned.
```
public abstract void removeChangeListener(ChangeListener l)
```
   Removes a listener from the list to notify when an attribute changed.

   Returned by   DefaultStyledDocument.addStyle() (p.820),
   DefaultStyledDocument.getLogicalStyle() (p.820), DefaultStyledDocument.getStyle() (p.820),
   JTextPane.addStyle() (p.383), JTextPane.getLogicalStyle() (p.383), JTextPane.getStyle() (p.383),
   StyleContext.addStyle() (p.872), StyleContext.getStyle() (p.872),
   StyledDocument.addStyle() (p.877), StyledDocument.getLogicalStyle() (p.877),
   StyledDocument.getStyle() (p.877), StyleSheet.getRule() (p.938).
   Implemented by   StyleContext.NamedStyle (p.875).
   See also   ChangeListener (p.488), MutableAttributeSet (p.853).

swing.text.StyleConstants

CLASS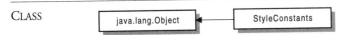

This class is a collection of predefined attribute names and methods for adding and removing attributes to an `AttributeSet` or `MutableAttributeSet` in a typesafe way. All sizes in this set of attributes are set using points, with the Java assumption of 72 points per inch.

```
public class StyleConstants extends java.lang.Object
```

Fields
```
public static final int ALIGN_CENTER
```
   A value for alignment. The paragraph with this alignment value should be placed in the center of the line with the white space split evenly between the front and the end of the line.

public static final int ALIGN_JUSTIFIED

A value indicating that the paragraph will have all lines except for the last line start flush with the left indent and end flush with the right indent. The last line will be left justified.

public static final int ALIGN_LEFT

A value for alignment. The paragraph with this alignment value should be placed flush with the left indent and have the excess white space on each line placed to the right of the line.

public static final int ALIGN_RIGHT

A value for alignment. The paragraph with this alignment value should be placed flush with the right indent and have the excess white space on each line placed to the left of the line.

public static final Object Alignment

The attribute name to use for paragraph alignment. The valid values for this key are ALIGN_LEFT, ALIGN_RIGHT, ALIGN_CENTER, and ALIGN_JUSTIFIED.

public static final Object Background

The attribute name used for the background color. The value should be a java.awt.Color.

public static final Object BidiLevel

The bidirectional level of a character as assigned by the Unicode algorithm for handling bidirectional text.

public static final Object Bold

The attribute name used for bold font characters.

public static final Object ComponentAttribute

The attribute name used for components in an Element.

public static final String ComponentElementName

The attribute name for Elements that contain java.awt.Components.

public static final Object FirstLineIndent

The attribute name used for the amount to indent the first line of a paragraph. The value is a float representing the distance in points. If the value is negative the first line is outdented (hanging).

public static final Object FontFamily

The attribute name used for specifying the font's family name.

public static final Object FontSize

The attribute name used for specifying the font size.

public static final Object Foreground

The attribute name used for specifying the foreground color. The value should be a java.awt.Color.

public static final Object IconAttribute

The attribute name used for specifying an Icon in an Element.

public static final String IconElementName

The attribute name used for Elements that contain Icons.

public static final Object Italic

The attribute name used for italicized characters.

public static final Object LeftIndent

The attribute name used for specifying the amount to indent the paragraph from the left. The value is a float and gives the distance in points.

public static final Object LineSpacing

The attribute name used for specifying the space between lines. The value is a float and gives the distance in points.

public static final Object ModelAttribute

The attribute name used for specifying the model for `Component` attributes that use a model.

public static final Object NameAttribute

The attribute name used to specify the name of a set of attributes.

public static final Object Orientation

The orientation for a paragraph.

public static final Object ResolveAttribute

The attribute name used to specify the resolving parent of this set. The value is an `AttributeSet`.

public static final Object RightIndent

The attribute name used for specifying the distance to indent the paragraph from the right. The value is a float and gives the distance in points.

public static final Object SpaceAbove

The attribute name used for specifying the amount of space above the paragraph. The value is a float and gives the distance in points.

public static final Object SpaceBelow

The attribute name used for specifying the amount of space below the paragraph. The value is a float and gives the distance in points.

public static final Object StrikeThrough

The attribute name used for specifying strikethrough characters.

public static final Object Subscript

The attribute name used for specifying subscripted characters.

public static final Object Superscript

The attribute name used for specifying superscripted characters.

public static final Object TabSet

The attribute name used for specifying the `TabSet` of a paragraph. The type this name is used with is a `TabSet` containing TabStops.

public static final Object Underline

The attribute name used for specifying underlined characters.

Methods

public static int getAlignment(AttributeSet a)

Returns the value of the `Alignment` attribute from the given `AttributeSet`.

public static Color getBackground(AttributeSet a)

Returns the value of the `Background` attribute from the given `AttributeSet`. Defaults to `Color.black`.

public static int getBidiLevel(AttributeSet a)

Returns the value of the `BidiLevel` from the given `AttributeSet`.

public static java.awt.Component getComponent(AttributeSet a)

Returns the value of the `ComponentAttribute` attribute from the given `AttributeSet`.

public static float getFirstLineIndent(AttributeSet a)

Returns the value of the `FirstLineIndent` attribute from the given `AttributeSet`.

public static String getFontFamily(AttributeSet a)

Returns the value of the `FontFamily` attribute from the given `AttributeSet`. Defaults to "Monospaced."

public static int getFontSize(AttributeSet a)

Returns the value of the `FontSize` attribute from the given `AttributeSet`. Defaults to 12.

public static java.awt.Color getForeground(AttributeSet a)
> Returns the value of the `Foreground` attribute from the given `AttributeSet`. Defaults to `Color.black`.

public static Icon getIcon(AttributeSet a)
> Returns the value of the `IconAttribute` attribute from the given `AttributeSet`.

public static float getLeftIndent(AttributeSet a)
> Returns the value of the `LeftIndent` attribute from the given `AttributeSet`.

public static float getLineSpacing(AttributeSet a)
> Returns the value of the `LineSpacing` attribute from the given `AttributeSet`.

public static float getRightIndent(AttributeSet a)
> Returns the value of the `RightIndent` attribute from the given `AttributeSet`.

public static float getSpaceAbove(AttributeSet a)
> Returns the value of the `SpaceAbove` attribute from the given `AttributeSet`.

public static float getSpaceBelow(AttributeSet a)
> Returns the value of the `SpaceBelow` attribute from the given `AttributeSet`.

public static TabSet getTabSet(AttributeSet a)
> Returns the value of the `TabSet` attribute from the given `AttributeSet`.

public static boolean isBold(AttributeSet a)
> Returns `true` if the `Bold` attribute is set in the given `AttributeSet`.

public static boolean isItalic(AttributeSet a)
> Returns `true` if the `Italic` attribute is set in the given `AttributeSet`.

public static boolean isStrikeThrough(AttributeSet a)
> Returns `true` if the `StrikeThrough` attribute is set in the given `AttributeSet`.

public static boolean isSubscript(AttributeSet a)
> Returns `true` if the `Subscript` attribute is set in the given `AttributeSet`.

public static boolean isSuperscript(AttributeSet a)
> Returns `true` if the `Superscript` attribute is set in the given `AttributeSet`.

public static boolean isUnderline(AttributeSet a)
> Returns `true` if the `Underline` attribute is set in the given `AttributeSet`.

public static void setAlignment(MutableAttributeSet a, int align)
> Sets the value of the `Alignment` attribute in the given `AttributeSet`.

public static void setBackground(MutableAttributeSet a, java.awt.Color bg)
> Sets the value of the `Background` attribute in the given `AttributeSet`.

public static void setBidiLevel(MutableAttributeSet a, int o)
> Sets the value of the `BidiLevel` attribute in the given `AttributeSet`.

public static void setBold(MutableAttributeSet a, boolean b)
> Sets the value of the `Bold` attribute in the given `AttributeSet`.

public static void setComponent(MutableAttributeSet a, Component c)
> Sets the value of the `Component` attribute in the given `AttributeSet`.

public static void setFirstLineIndent(MutableAttributeSet a, float i)
> Sets the value of the `FirstLineIndent` attribute in the given `AttributeSet`.

public static void setFontFamily(MutableAttributeSet a, String fam)
> Sets the value of the `FontFamily` attribute in the given `AttributeSet`.

public static void setFontSize(MutableAttributeSet a, int s)
> Sets the value of the `FontSize` attribute in the given `AttributeSet`.

public static void setForeground(MutableAttributeSet a, java.awt.Color fg)
> Sets the value of the `Foreground` attribute in the given `AttributeSet`.

```
public static void setIcon(MutableAttributeSet a, Icon c)
```
Sets the value of the Icon attribute in the given AttributeSet.
```
public static void setItalic(MutableAttributeSet a, boolean b)
```
Sets the value of the Italic attribute in the given AttributeSet.
```
public static void setLeftIndent(MutableAttributeSet a, float i)
```
Sets the value of the LeftIndent attribute in the given AttributeSet.
```
public static void setLineSpacing(MutableAttributeSet a, float i)
```
Sets the value of the LineSpacing attribute in the given AttributeSet.
```
public static void setRightIndent(MutableAttributeSet a, float i)
```
Sets the value of the RightIndent attribute in the given AttributeSet.
```
public static void setSpaceAbove(MutableAttributeSet a, float i)
```
Sets the value of the SpaceAbove attribute in the given AttributeSet.
```
public static void setSpaceBelow(MutableAttributeSet a, float i)
```
Sets the value of the SpaceBelow attribute in the given AttributeSet.
```
public static void setStrikeThrough(MutableAttributeSet a, boolean b)
```
Sets the value of the StrikeThrough attribute in the given AttributeSet.
```
public static void setSubscript(MutableAttributeSet a, boolean b)
```
Sets the value of the Subscript attribute in the given AttributeSet.
```
public static void setSuperscript(MutableAttributeSet a, boolean b)
```
Sets the value of the Superscript attribute in the given AttributeSet.
```
public static void setTabSet(MutableAttributeSet a, TabSet tabs)
```
Sets the value of the TabSet attribute in the given AttributeSet.
```
public static void setUnderline(MutableAttributeSet a, boolean b)
```
Sets the value of the Underline attribute in the given AttributeSet.
```
public String toString()
```
Overrides: toString in class Object.

Inner Classes
```
public static class StyleConstants.ParagraphConstants
public static class StyleConstants.CharacterConstants
public static class StyleConstants.ColorConstants
public static class StyleConstants.FontConstants
```

See also   AttributeSet (p.794), Icon (p.183), MutableAttributeSet (p.853).

swing.text.StyleConstants.CharacterConstants

INNER CLASS

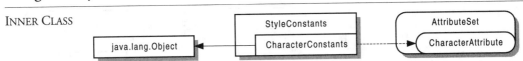

This class provides what acts as a typesafe enumeration of the attribute names used for character attributes.

```
public static class StyleConstants.CharacterConstants
    extends java.lang.Object
    implements AttributeSet.CharacterAttribute
```

Fields

public static final Object Background
> The name of the Background color attribute.

public static final Object BidiLevel
> The name of the BidiLevel attribute.

public static final Object Bold
> The name of the Bold attribute.

public static final Object ComponentAttribute
> The name of the Component attribute.

public static final Object Family
> The name of the font Family attribute.

public static final Object Foreground
> The name of the Foreground color attribute.

public static final Object IconAttribute
> The name of the Icon attribute.

public static final Object Italic
> The name of the Italic attribute.

public static final Object Size
> The name of the font Size attribute.

public static final Object StrikeThrough
> The name of the Strikethrough attribute.

public static final Object Subscript
> The name of the Subscript attribute.

public static final Object Superscript
> The name of the Superscript attribute.

public static final Object Underline
> The name of the Underline attribute.

Methods

public String toString()
> *Overrides:* toString in class Object.

> *See also*   AttributeSet.CharacterAttribute (p.795).

swing.text.StyleConstants.ColorConstants

INNER CLASS

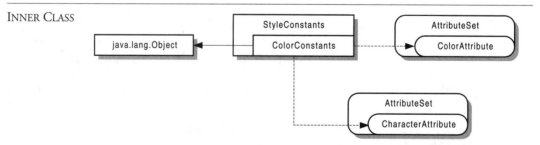

This class acts as a typesafe enumeration of the attribute names used for color attributes.

```
public static class StyleConstants.ColorConstants
    extends java.lang.Object
    implements AttributeSet.ColorAttribute,
    AttributeSet.CharacterAttribute
```

Fields

`public static final Object Background`
The name of the `Background` color attribute.
`public static final Object Foreground`
The name of the `Foreground` color attribute.

Methods

`public String toString()`
Overrides: `toString` in class `Object`.

See also   AttributeSet.CharacterAttribute (p.795), AttributeSet.ColorAttribute (p.796).

swing.text.StyleConstants.FontConstants

INNER CLASS

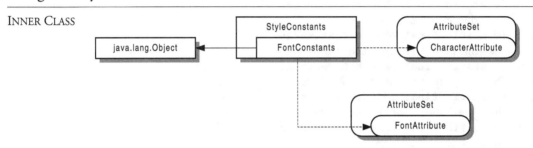

This class acts as a typesafe enumeration of the attribute names used for font attributes.

```
public static class StyleConstants.FontConstants
    extends java.lang.Object
    implements AttributeSet.FontAttribute,
    AttributeSet.CharacterAttribute
```

Fields

`public static final Object Bold`
The name of the `Bold` attribute.
`public static final Object Family`
The name of the font `Family` attribute.
`public static final Object Italic`
The name of the `Italic` attribute.
`public static final Object Size`
The name of the font `Size` attribute.

Methods

`public String toString()`
Overrides: `toString` in class `Object`.

See also   AttributeSet.CharacterAttribute (p.795), AttributeSet.FontAttribute (p.796).

swing.text.StyleConstants.ParagraphConstants

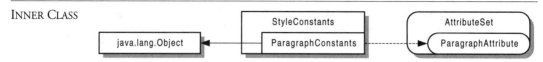

This class acts as a typesafe enumeration of the attribute names used for paragraph attributes.

```
public static class StyleConstants.ParagraphConstants
    implements AttributeSet.ParagraphAttribute
```

Fields

public static final Object Alignment
The name of the `Alignment` attribute. Valid values are `ALIGN_LEFT`, `ALIGN_RIGHT`, `ALIGN_CENTER`, and `ALIGN_JUSTIFED`.

public static final Object FirstLineIndent
The name of the `FirstLineIndent` attribute.

public static final Object LeftIndent
The name of the `LeftIndent` attribute.

public static final Object LineSpacing
The name of the `LineSpacing` attribute.

public static final Object Orientation
The name of the `Orientation` attribute.

public static final Object RightIndent
The name of the `RightIndent` attribute.

public static final Object SpaceAbove
The name of the `SpaceAbove` attribute.

public static final Object SpaceBelow
The name of the `SpaceBelow` attribute.

public static final Object TabSet
The name of the `TabSet` attribute.

Methods

public String toString()
Overrides: `toString` in class `Object`.

See also   AttributeSet.ParagraphAttribute (p.796).

swing.text.StyleContext

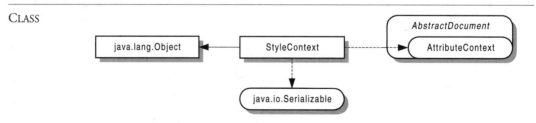

This class is an implementation of `AbstractDocument.AttributeContext` that manages a shared pool of `Style`s for a `Document`. This class takes advantage of the fact that `Attribute-Sets` are immutable to share instances when they can. Since a normal document uses a very small number of styles, the savings from sharing are very significant. A `StyleContext` may even be shared among documents.

```
public class StyleContext extends java.lang.Object
    implements java.io.Serializable,
    AbstractDocument.AttributeContext
```

Fields

`public static final String DEFAULT_STYLE = "default"`
> The `Style` name for the default style applied to paragraphs.

Constructors

`public StyleContext()`
> Constructs a `StyleContext` object.

Methods

`public synchronized AttributeSet addAttribute(AttributeSet old, Object name, Object value)`
> Creates a copy of the given `AttributeSet` and adds a new attribute (name, value) pair to it. The new set is then returned.
>
> *Implements:* addAttribute in interface `AbstractDocument.AttributeContext`.

`public synchronized AttributeSet addAttributes(AttributeSet old, AttributeSet attr)`
> Creates a copy of the given `AttributeSet` old and adds the attributes from `attr` to it. The new set is then returned.
>
> *Implements:* addAttributes in interface `AbstractDocument.AttributeContext`.

`public void addChangeListener(ChangeListener 1)`
> Adds a listener to be notified when styles are added or removed.

`public Style addStyle(String nm, Style parent)`
> Adds a new `Style` to the context named name. The `parent` parameter specifies the resolving parent of the new `Style` and may be `null`. If the `Style` is unnamed, the caller must retain a handle to the returned `Style` as there is no other way to refer to it.

`public java.awt.Color getBackground(AttributeSet attr)`
> Returns the value specified by the `StyleConstants.Background` attribute.

`public static final StyleContext getDefaultStyleContext()`
> Returns the default `StyleContext` used by all `Document`s that don't supply their own.

`public AttributeSet getEmptySet()`
> Returns an empty `AttributeSet`.
>
> *Implements:* getEmptySet in interface `AbstractDocument.AttributeContext`.

`public java.awt.Font getFont(AttributeSet attr)`
> Returns the `Font` attribute from the given set. If it cannot be found in the given set, it will be retrieved from a font cache.

public java.awt.Font getFont(String family, int style, int size)

Returns a `Font` for the given parameters. If a matching instance of the `Font` exists in the cache, that instance will be returned. If not, a new instance will be created and added to the cache, then returned.

public java.awt.FontMetrics getFontMetrics(java.awt.Font f)

Returns the `FontMetrics` for the given `Font`.

public java.awt.Color getForeground(AttributeSet attr)

Returns the value specified by the `StyleConstants.Foreground` attribute.

public static Object getStaticAttribute(Object key)

Returns an object previously registered with `registerStaticAttributeKey()`.

public static Object getStaticAttributeKey(Object key)

Returns the unique key which should be used to register the given `key` in the static table.

public Style getStyle(String nm)

Returns a named `Style` previously added to the `Document`.

public java.util.Enumeration getStyleNames()

Returns an `Enumeration` of all defined `Style` names.

public static void readAttributeSet(java.io.ObjectInputStream in, MutableAttributeSet a) throws ClassNotFoundException, IOException

Reads an `AttributeSet` from the given stream. Any static keys (those which had been registered with `registerStaticAttribute()` before they were serialized) will be restored to the static table. The `AttributeSet` read will be returned in the given `MutableAttributeSet`.

Throws: `ClassNotFoundException` if thrown while reading the object stream, `IOException` if thrown while reading the object stream.

public void readAttributes(java.io.ObjectInputStream in, MutableAttributeSet a) throws ClassNotFoundException, IOException

Calls `readAttributeSet()`.

public synchronized void reclaim(AttributeSet a)

Reclaims the resources of a no-longer-needed `AttributeSet`. Used in JDK 1.1 to imitate the JDK 1.2 concept of weak references. This method is thread safe.

Implements: `reclaim` in interface `AbstractDocument.AttributeContext`.

public static void registerStaticAttributeKey(Object key)

Registers an object as a static object that is being used as a key in attribute sets. When the set is serialized, these keys will be treated specially.

public synchronized AttributeSet removeAttribute(AttributeSet old, Object name)

Returns a copy of `old`, after removing the given attribute from it. This method is thread safe.

Implements: `removeAttribute` in interface `AbstractDocument.AttributeContext`

public synchronized AttributeSet removeAttributes(AttributeSet old, AttributeSet attrs)

Creates a copy of `old` and removes the attributes in `attrs` from it. The new copy is then returned. This method is thread safe.

Implements: `removeAttributes` in interface `AbstractDocument.AttributeContext`.

public synchronized AttributeSet removeAttributes(AttributeSet old, java.util.Enumeration names)

Creates a copy of `old` and removes the attributes matching the given names from the set. The new copy is then returned. This method is thread safe.

Implements: removeAttributes in interface AbstractDocument.AttributeContext.

public void removeChangeListener(ChangeListener 1)

Removes a listener that was listening for changes in the StyleContext.

public void removeStyle(String nm)

Removes a named Style from the Document.

public String toString()

Returns a StyleContext as a String.

Overrides: toString in class Object.

public static void writeAttributeSet(java.io.ObjectOutputStream out,
AttributeSet a) throws IOException

Serializes the given AttributeSet to the stream. Any keys registered with registerStaticAttributeKey() are specially encoded so that they can be successfully recreated after deserialization.

Throws: IOException on any I/O error.

public void writeAttributes(ObjectOutputStream out, AttributeSet a)
throws IOException

Calls writeAttributeSet().

Protected Methods

protected int getCompressionThreshold()

Returns the attribute limit above which AttributeSets are stored as independent MutableAttributeSets. Below that limit this class will try to compress the set into immutable, shared sets.

Inner Classes

public class StyleContext.NamedStyle

See also   AbstractDocument.AttributeContext (p.786), AttributeSet (p.794), ChangeListener (p.488), Style (p.865).

swing.text.StyleContext.NamedStyle

INNER CLASS

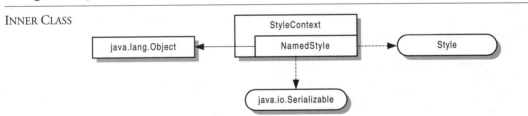

An implementation of Style that can be observed for changes. This class also takes advantage of immutability while the Style's set is small.

public class StyleContext.NamedStyle extends java.lang.Object
implements Style, java.io.Serializable

Constructors

public NamedStyle()

Constructs a new anonymous NamedStyle without a parent.

public NamedStyle(Style parent)

Constructs a new anonymous NamedStyle with the given parent.

public NamedStyle(String name, Style parent)

Constructs a new NamedStyle with the given name and parent.

Methods

public void addAttribute(Object name, Object value)

Adds the given (name, value) attribute pair to the Style.

public void addAttributes(AttributeSet attr)

Adds the given attibutes to the Style.

public void addChangeListener(ChangeListener l)

Makes l a ChangeListener for this object.

Implements: addChangeListener in interface Style.

public boolean containsAttribute(Object name, Object value)

Returns true if the given (name, value) attribute pair is defined in this Style.

public boolean containsAttributes(AttributeSet attrs)

Returns true if this Style contains an exact match for *all* of the given attributes.

public AttributeSet copyAttributes()

Returns a copy of this set of attributes.

public Object getAttribute(Object attrName)

Returns the value for the given attribute name.

public int getAttributeCount()

Returns the number of defined attributes.

public java.util.Enumeration getAttributeNames()

Returns an Enumeration of all attribute names in this Style.

public String getName()

Returns the name of this Style. This method returns null if this is an anonymous style.

Implements: getName in interface Style.

public AttributeSet getResolveParent()

Returns the resolving parent AttributeSet for this Style.

public boolean isDefined(Object attrName)

Returns true if there is an attribute in this Style that has the given name.

public boolean isEmpty()

Returns true if the Style does not have any attributes defined.

public boolean isEqual(AttributeSet attr)

Returns true if the two attribute sets contain the exact same set of attributes.

public void removeAttribute(Object name)

Removes the attribute named name from the Style.

public void removeAttributes(AttributeSet attrs)

Removes the attributes matching those in the given set from the Style.

public void removeAttributes(java.util.Enumeration names)

Removes the attributes with the given names from the Style.

public void removeChangeListener(ChangeListener l)

Removes the given ChangeListener.

Implements: removeChangeListener in interface Style.

public void setName(String name)

Sets the name of the Style.

public void setResolveParent(AttributeSet parent)

Sets the resolving parent of this Style.

public String toString()

    Returns a `String` representation of a `Style`.

    Overrides: `toString` in class `Object`.

Protected Fields

protected transient ChangeEvent changeEvent

    Cached `ChangeEvent` used for all changes and listeners. The source for this event is always `this`.

protected EventListenerList listenerList

    The listeners.

Protected Methods

protected void fireStateChanged()

    Notifies all listeners that the `Style` has changed.

    See also   AttributeSet (p.794), ChangeEvent (p.487), ChangeListener (p.488), EventListenerList (p.491), Style (p.865).

swing.text.StyledDocument

INTERFACE

This interface defines a basic styled `Document`.

public interface StyledDocument extends Document

Methods

public abstract Style addStyle(String nm, Style parent)

    Adds a new, empty `Style` to the `Document` using the given name and parent. Either or both of nm and parent may be `null` if they are not required.

public abstract java.awt.Color getBackground(AttributeSet attr)

    Returns the `Background` attribute from the given `AttributeSet`.

public abstract Element getCharacterElement(int pos)

    Returns the character `Element` that represents the character at pos in the `Document`.

public abstract java.awt.Font getFont(AttributeSet attr)

    Returns the `Font` attribute from the given `AttributeSet`.

public abstract java.awt.Color getForeground(AttributeSet attr)

    Returns the `Foreground` attribute from the given `AttributeSet`.

public abstract Style getLogicalStyle(int p)

    Returns the `Style` defined for the paragraph that contains the character at p in the `Document`.

public abstract Element getParagraphElement(int pos)

    Returns the `Element` that represents the paragraph that contains the character at pos in the `Document`.

public abstract Style getStyle(String nm)

    Returns a named `Style` that was previously added to the `Document`.

public abstract void removeStyle(String nm)

    Removes the named `Style` from the `Document`.

public abstract void setCharacterAttributes(int offset, int length, AttributeSet s, boolean replace)

Changes the character attributes used for the given range in the `Document`. If `replace` is `true`, the given `AttributeSet` replaces the current set. If `replace` is `false`, the given set is merged with the existing attributes.

public abstract void setLogicalStyle(int pos, Style s)

Sets the `Style` to use for the paragraph that contains the character at `pos` in the `Document`.

public abstract void setParagraphAttributes(int offset, int length, AttributeSet s, boolean replace)

Changes the attributes used for the paragraph which contains the given range in the `Document`. If `replace` is `true`, the given set replaces the existing attributes. If `replace` is `false`, the set is merged with the existing `AttributeSet`.

Returned by JTextPane.getStyledDocument() (p.383), StyledEditorKit.StyledTextAction.getStyledDocument() (p.883).
Implemented by DefaultStyledDocument (p.820).
See also AttributeSet (p.794), Element (p.830), Style (p.865), StyleConstants (p.865).

swing.text.StyledEditorKit

CLASS

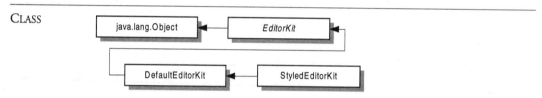

This class provides the basic functionality required to make an editor that handles styled text.

The `Actions` this `EditorKit` supplies are the `Actions` defined by `DefaultEditorKit` (p.810) and the new `Actions` shown in table 2

The Actions supplied by StyledEditorKit. See StyleConstants (p.865) for a description of the attributes.

Action class (of the form StyledEditorKit.X)	Action name	Purpose
FontFamilyAction	"font-family-SansSerif"	Sets the `FontFamily` character attribute to `SansSerif`.
FontFamilyAction	"font-family-Monospaced"	Sets the `FontFamily` character attribute to `Monospaced`.
FontFamilyAction	"font-family-Serif"	Sets the `FontFamily` character attribute to `Serif`.
FontSizeAction	"font-size-8"	Sets the `FontSize` attribute to `8`.
FontSizeAction	"font-size-10"	Sets the `FontSize` attribute to `10`.
FontSizeAction	"font-size-12"	Sets the `FontSize` attribute to `12`.
FontSizeAction	"font-size-14"	Sets the `FontSize` attribute to `14`.
FontSizeAction	"font-size-16"	Sets the `FontSize` attribute to `16`.
FontSizeAction	"font-size-18"	Sets the `FontSize` attribute to `18`.
FontSizeAction	"font-size-24"	Sets the `FontSize` attribute to `24`.
FontSizeAction	"font-size-36"	Sets the `FontSize` attribute to `36`.

The Actions supplied by StyledEditorKit. See StyleConstants (p.865) for a description of the attributes.

Action class (of the form StyledEditorKit.X)	Action name	Purpose
FontSizeAction	"font-size-48"	Sets the FontSize attribute to 48.
AlignmentAction	"left-justify"	Sets the Alignment attribute to ALIGN_LEFT.
AlignmentAction	"center-justify"	Sets the Alignment attribute to ALIGN_CENTER.
AlignmentAction	"right-justify"	Sets the Alignment attribute to ALIGN_RIGHT.
BoldAction	"font-bold"	Toggles the Bold character attribute.
ItalicAction	"font-italic"	Toggles the Italic character attribute.
UnderlineAction	"font-underline"	Toggles the Underline character atttribute.

Unlike DefaultEditorKit, StyledEditorKit does not define constants which can be used to represent its Actions. The Actions must be found by name in the array returned by getActions(). StyledEditorKit also supplies some additional Actions in the form of public inner classes which do not have instances in the getActions() array.

public class StyledEditorKit extends DefaultEditorKit

Constructors
public StyledEditorKit()
Constructs a StyledEditorKit.

Methods
public Object clone()
Returns a copy of this EditorKit.
Overrides: clone in class DefaultEditorKit.

public Document createDefaultDocument()
Creates an empty DefaultStyledDocument.
Overrides: createDefaultDocument in class DefaultEditorKit.

public void deinstall(JEditorPane c)
Called when the EditorKit is being removed from the editor. This particular implementation removes any listeners which were added.
Overrides: deinstall in class EditorKit.

public Action[] getActions()
Returns an array of Actions supported by this EditorKit.
Overrides: getActions in class DefaultEditorKit.

public Element getCharacterAttributeRun()
Returns the Element which defines the character attributes where the Caret is located.

public MutableAttributeSet getInputAttributes()
Returns the attributes which will be added to new text which is entered, As the Caret moves, the input attributes change to match the attributes defined in the text around the Caret.

public ViewFactory getViewFactory()
Fetches a factory that is suitable for producing views of any models that are produced by this kit. This is implemented to return View implementations for the following kinds of elements: AbstractDocument.ContentElementName, AbstractDocument.ParagraphElementName, Abstract-

Document.SectionElementName, StyleConstants.ComponentElementName, and StyleConstants.IconElementName.

Overrides: getViewFactory in class DefaultEditorKit.

public void install(JEditorPane c)

Called when the EditorKit is being installed into the editor.

Overrides: install in class EditorKit.

Protected Methods

protected void createInputAttributes(Element element, MutableAttributeSet set)

Called as the Caret moves to keep the input attributes up to date. It is implemented to copy the attributes which are applicable to new content from the given Element to the set.

Inner Classes

public static class StyledEditorKit.AlignmentAction
public static class StyledEditorKit.BoldAction
public static class StyledEditorKit.FontFamilyAction
public static class StyledEditorKit.FontSizeAction
public static class StyledEditorKit.ForegroundAction
public static class StyledEditorKit.ItalicAction
public abstract static class StyledEditorKit.StyledTextAction
public static class StyledEditorKit.UnderlineAction

> *Extended by*   HTMLEditorKit (p.922), RTFEditorKit (p.952).
> *Returned by*   JTextPane.getStyledEditorKit() (p.383),
> StyledEditorKit.StyledTextAction.getStyledEditorKit() (p.883).
> *See also*   Action (p.128), Document (p.826), ViewFactory (p.896).

swing.text.StyledEditorKit.AlignmentAction

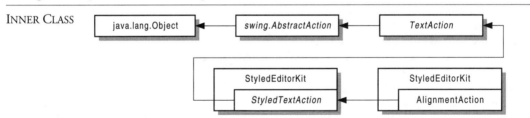

Sets the paragraph Alignment attribute.

public static class StyledEditorKit.AlignmentAction extends StyledEditorKit.StyledTextAction

Constructors

public AlignmentAction(String nm, int a)

Creates a new AlignmentAction.

Methods
`public void actionPerformed(java.awt.event.ActionEvent ae)`

Sets the alignment. The `commandString` of the event is interpreted as an integer representing one of the allowed alignment constants.

See also   StyledEditorKit.StyledTextAction (p.883).

swing.text.StyledEditorKit.BoldAction

INNER CLASS

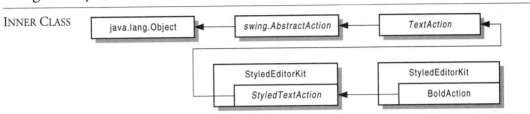

Toggles the `Bold` character attribute.

```
public static class StyledEditorKit.BoldAction
    extends StyledEditorKit.StyledTextAction
```

Constructors
`public BoldAction()`

Constructs a new `BoldAction`.

Methods
`public void actionPerformed(java.awt.event.ActionEvent ae)`

Toggles the `Bold` attribute.

See also   StyledEditorKit.StyledTextAction (p.883).

swing.text.StyledEditorKit.FontFamilyAction

INNER CLASS

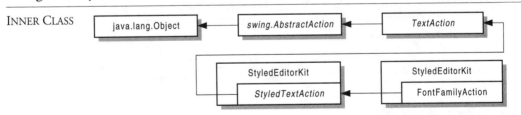

Sets the `FontFamily` character attribute.

```
public static class StyledEditorKit.FontFamilyAction
    extends StyledEditorKit.StyledTextAction
```

Constructors
`public FontFamilyAction(String actionName, String fontFamily)`

Methods

`public void actionPerformed(java.awt.event.ActionEvent e)`
> Sets the font family.

> *See also*   StyledEditorKit.StyledTextAction (p.883).

swing.text.StyledEditorKit.FontSizeAction

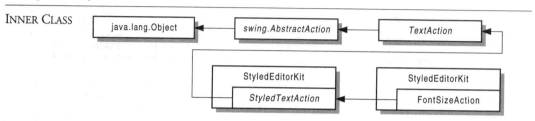

Sets the `FontSize` character attribute.

```
public static class StyledEditorKit.FontSizeAction
    extends StyledEditorKit.StyledTextAction
```

Constructors

`public FontSizeAction(String name, int size)`
> Creates a new `FontSizeAction`.

Methods

`public void actionPerformed(java.awt.event.ActionEvent e)`
> Sets the font size. The `commandString` of the event is interpreted as an integer giving the new size.

> *See also*   StyledEditorKit.StyledTextAction (p.883).

swing.text.StyledEditorKit.ForegroundAction

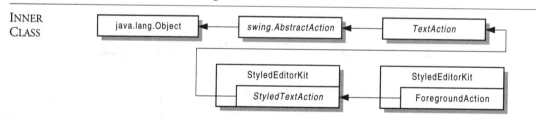

Sets the `Foreground` attribute.

```
public static class StyledEditorKit.ForegroundAction
    extends StyledEditorKit.StyledTextAction
```

Constructors

`public ForegroundAction(String nm, java.awt.Color fg)`
> Creates a new ForegroundAction.

Methods
`public void actionPerformed(java.awt.event.ActionEvent e)`
> Sets the foreground color. The `commandString` will be passed to `java.awt.Color.decode()`, so it must be a legal value for that method.

> *See also*   StyledEditorKit.StyledTextAction (p.883).

swing.text.StyledEditorKit.ItalicAction

INNER CLASS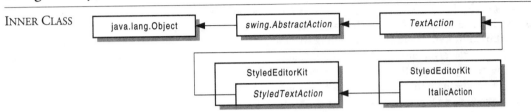

Toggles the `Italic` character attribute

`public static class StyledEditorKit.ItalicAction`
`    extends StyledEditorKit.StyledTextAction`

Constructors
`public ItalicAction()`

Methods
`public void actionPerformed(java.awt.event.ActionEvent ae)`
> Toggles the `Italic` attribute.

> *See also*   StyledEditorKit.StyledTextAction (p.883).

swing.text.StyledEditorKit.StyledTextAction

ABSTRACT
INNER CLASS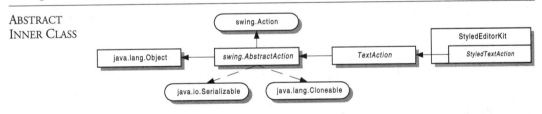

This class defines an `Action` that has some convenience methods for setting character or paragraph attributes.

`public abstract static class StyledEditorKit.StyledTextAction`
`    extends TextAction`

Constructors
`public StyledTextAction(String nm)`
> Creates a new `StyledTextAction` from a string action name.

Protected Methods

protected final JEditorPane getEditor(ActionEvent e)
   Gets the target editor for an action.

protected final StyledDocument getStyledDocument(JEditorPane e)
   Gets the document associated with an editor pane.
   Throws: IllegalArgumentException for the wrong document type.

protected final StyledEditorKit getStyledEditorKit(JEditorPane e)
   Gets the editor kit associated with an editor pane.
   Throws: IllegalArgumentException for the wrong document type.

protected final void setCharacterAttributes(JEditorPane editor,
   AttributeSet attr, boolean replace)
   Applies the given attributes to character content. If there is a selection, the attributes are applied to the selection range. If there is no selection, the attributes are applied to the input attribute set which defines the attributes for any new text that gets inserted.

protected final void setParagraphAttributes(JEditorPane editor,
   AttributeSet attr, boolean replace)
   Applies the given attributes to paragraphs. If there is a selection, the attributes are applied to the paragraphs that intersect the selection. If there is no selection, the attributes are applied to the paragraph at the current caret position.

Extended by   StyledEditorKit.AlignmentAction (p.880),
StyledEditorKit.BoldAction (p.881), StyledEditorKit.FontFamilyAction (p.881),
StyledEditorKit.FontSizeAction (p.882), StyledEditorKit.ForegroundAction (p.882),
StyledEditorKit.ItalicAction (p.883), StyledEditorKit.UnderlineAction (p.884).
See also   AttributeSet (p.794), JEditorPane (p.232), StyledDocument (p.877),
StyledEditorKit (p.878), TextAction (p.891).

swing.text.StyledEditorKit.UnderlineAction

INNER CLASS

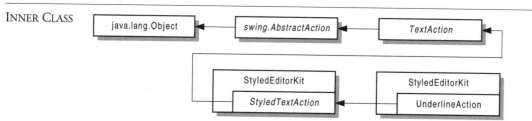

Toggles the Underline attribute.

public static class StyledEditorKit.UnderlineAction
   extends StyledEditorKit.StyledTextAction

Constructors

public UnderlineAction()
   Constructs a new UnderlineAction.

Methods

`public void actionPerformed(java.awt.event.ActionEvent e)`
Toggles the `Underline` attribute.

See also   StyledEditorKit.StyledTextAction (p.883).

swing.text.TabableView

INTERFACE   (TableView)

This interface defines a `View` that has a size dependent upon tabs.

`public interface TabableView`

Methods

`public abstract float getPartialSpan(int startOffset, int endOffset)`
Returns the span of the given range, assuming it doesn't have tabs. This method is used by a `TabExpander` when it has to line up a section of text based on a tab. The axis for the span is the same one currently being used by the `TabExpander`.

`public abstract float getTabbedSpan(float x, TabExpander e)`
Returns the preferred span of the `View` when its tabs are expanded by the given `TabExpander`. The `TabExpander` uses x as the starting position for its expansions.

Implemented by   LabelView (p.847).
See also   TabExpander (p.885), LabelView (p.847), ParagraphView (p.853).

swing.text.TabExpander

INTERFACE   (TabExpander)

This interface defines a class that implements a policy for expanding tabs.

`public interface TabExpander`

Methods

`public abstract float nextTabStop(float x, int tabOffset)`
Returns the position of the next tab stop using the given reference position x.

Implemented by   LabelView (p.847), PlainView (p.858).

swing.text.TableView

CLASS

```
java.lang.Object  ←  View  ←  CompositeView  ←

         BoxView  ←  TableView
```

Implements a `View` of a table (an HTML table, for example).

The `Element` structure needed by a `TableView` is very specific. The `Element` that defines the `TableView` must have children which represent the rows of the table. The grandchildren `Elements` (the children's children) represent the cells of the table. The cell `Elements` can have whatever child structures they want.

The `View` itself is implemented as a hierarchy of `BoxViews`, with the `TableView` being a vertical box, the row `Views` being horizontal boxes, and the cell `Views` being vertical boxes. Cells are allowed to fill more than one (`row`, `column`) location.

class TableView extends BoxView

Constructors
public TableView(Element elem)
Default constructor.

Protected Methods
protected SizeRequirements calculateMinorAxisRequirements(int axis, SizeRequirements r)
Returns the space requirements along the minor axis. This implementation sums the requirements of the columns.
Overrides: `calculateMinorAxisRequirements` in class `BoxView`.

protected TableView.TableCell createTableCell(Element elem)
Creates and returns a new table cell.

protected TableView.TableRow createTableRow(Element elem)
Creates and returns a new table row.

protected View getViewAtPosition(int pos, java.awt.Rectangle a)
Returns the child `View` which represents the given position in the model.
Overrides: `getViewAtPosition` in class `CompositeView`.

protected void layoutColumns(int targetSpan, int[] offsets, int[] spans, SizeRequirements[] reqs)
Lays out the columns to fit within the `targetSpan`. The other parameters are all returned values. The `offsets` are the offsets to the start of each column, the `spans` are their widths, and the `reqs` are the maximum requirements defined by the cells in each column.

protected void layoutMinorAxis(int targetSpan, int axis, int[] offsets, int[] spans)
Lays out the table along its minor axis (the axis of the columns). This method calls `layoutColumns()` and then passes the values to the superclass to actually have the layout performed.
Overrides: `layoutMinorAxis` in class `BoxView`.

protected void loadChildren(ViewFactory f)

Called by `setParent()` to initialize the table. This implementation creates rows using the `createTableRow()` method, and it also creates proxy cells for any cell that occupies more than one (row, column) location in the table.

Overrides: `loadChildren` in class `CompositeView`.

Inner Classes
public class TableView.TableRow
public class TableView.TableCell

See also   BoxView (p.797), Element (p.830), View (p.893), ViewFactory (p.896).

swing.text.TableView.TableCell

INNER CLASS

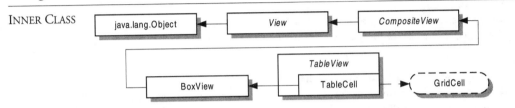

The `View` for a cell in a `TableView`.

public class TableCell extends BoxView

Constructors
public TableCell(Element elem)

Constructs a `TableCell` for the given element.

Methods
public int getColumnCount()

Returns the number of columns this cell occupies.

public int getGridColumn()

Returns the column that holds this cell.

public int getGridRow()

Returns the row that holds this cell.

public float getPreferredSpan(int axis)

Returns the preferred span of the cell. Subclasses can reimplement this method to allow cells to span columns and rows.

Overrides: `getPreferredSpan` in class `BoxView`.

public int getRowCount()

Returns the number of rows this cell occupies.

public void setGridLocation(int row, int col)

Sets the origin grid cell for this cell.

Returned by   TableView.createTableCell() (p.886).
See also   Element (p.830).

swing.text.TableView.TableRow

 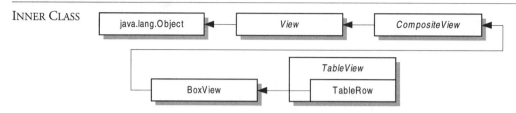

The `View` for a row in a `TableView`.

```
public class TableRow extends BoxView
```

Constructors
public TableRow(Element elem)
Constructs a `TableRow` for the given element.

Methods
public int getResizeWeight(int axis)
Returns an `int` indicating how much the `View` can be stretched or squished along the given axis to fit in a given area. Values zero or less mean that the `View` cannot be resized, while larger integers indicate more resizability.
Throws: `IllegalArgumentException` for an invalid `axis`.
Overrides: `getResizeWeight` in class `BoxView`.

Protected Methods
protected View getViewAtPosition(int pos, java.awt.Rectangle a)
Returns the `View` which is displaying the content at `pos` in the `Document`.
Overrides: `getViewAtPosition` in class `CompositeView`.

protected void layoutMajorAxis(int targetSpan, int axis,
int[] offsets, int[] spans)
Lays out the cells of the row along the given `axis` to fit into the given span. The `offsets` are the calculated offsets for each cell from the origin of the table. The `spans` are the width of each column. This method calculates the width by using the column width for the table, then multiplying it by how many columns the associated cell occupies.
Overrides: `layoutMajorAxis` in class `BoxView`.

protected void layoutMinorAxis(int targetSpan, int axis,
int[] offsets, int[] spans)
Lays out the cells along the given `axis`. This method calls `super.layoutMinorAxis()` to get the initial height of the row (which is assigned to each cell), and then adjusts the height of the cells which occupy more than one row.
Overrides: `layoutMinorAxis` in class `BoxView`.

protected void loadChildren(ViewFactory f)
Initializes the row.
Overrides: `loadChildren` in class `CompositeView`.

See also   BoxView (p.797), Element (p.830), ViewFactory (p.896).

swing.text.TabSet

This class provides an immutable set of TabStops.

```
public class TabSet extends java.lang.Object
    implements java.io.Serializable
```

Constructors
public TabSet(TabStop[] tabs)
Constructs a TabSet from the given TabStop array, which *must* be sorted in ascending order.

Methods
public TabStop getTab(int index)
Returns the TabStop at index.
public TabStop getTabAfter(float location)
Returns the first TabStop which will be reached after the given location. This method can return null if the location is after the last TabStop.
public int getTabCount()
Returns the number of TabStops in the set.
public int getTabIndex(TabStop tab)
Returns the index of the given TabStop. If the TabStop is not in this set, this method returns –1.
public int getTabIndexAfter(float location)
Returns the first TabStop that will be reached after the given location. This method returns –1 if the location is past the last TabStop.
public String toString()
Returns a String representing this TabSet.
Overrides: toString in class Object.

> *Returned by* ParagraphView.getTabSet() (p.853), StyleConstants.getTabSet() (p.865).

swing.text.TabStop

 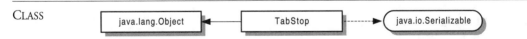

This class defines a TabStop. A TabStop has properties including how far it is from the left margin, how it aligns the text around the tab, and the leader used to fill the space created by the tab.

```
public class TabStop extends java.lang.Object
    implements java.io.Serializable
```

Fields
public static final int ALIGN_BAR = 5
public static final int ALIGN_CENTER = 2
This value indicates that the text up to the next tab or new line should be centered around the tab.

public static final int ALIGN_DECIMAL = 4
>This value indicates that the text should be aligned with the next decimal character, tab, or new line at the tab location.

public static final int ALIGN_LEFT = 0
>This value indicates that the character *following* the tab should be located at the tab position.

public static final int ALIGN_RIGHT = 1
>This value indicates that the characters following the tab are aligned so that the next tab or new line is at the tab position.

public static final int LEAD_DOTS = 1
>Fills the empty space created by the tab with dots.

public static final int LEAD_EQUALS = 5
>Fills the empty space created by the tab with equals symbols.

public static final int LEAD_HYPHENS = 2
>Fills the empty space created by the tab with hyphens.

public static final int LEAD_NONE = 0
>Leaves the empty space created by the tab empty.

public static final int LEAD_THICKLINE = 4
>Fills the empty space created by the tab with a thick line.

public static final int LEAD_UNDERLINE = 3
>Fills the empty space created by the tab with underlines.

Constructors

public TabStop(float pos)
>Constructs a tab at position pos with ALIGN_LEFT and LEADER_NONE.

public TabStop(float pos, int align, int leader)
>Constructs a tab with the specified position pos, alignment align, and leader leader.

Methods

public boolean equals(Object other)
>Returns true if other equals this TabStop.
>*Overrides:* equals in class Object.

public int getAlignment()
>Returns the alignment of the tab.

public int getLeader()
>Returns the leader of the tab.

public float getPosition()
>Returns the position of the tab.

public int hashCode()
>Returns the hashCode for the object. Required because equals() is defined.
>*Overrides:* hashCode in class Object.

public String toString()
>*Overrides:* toString in class Object.

Returned by   TabSet.getTab() (p.889), TabSet.getTabAfter() (p.889).

swing.text.TextAction

ABSTRACT
CLASS

This class defines an `Action` that can be shared among text components.

public abstract class TextAction extends AbstractAction

Constructor
public TextAction(String actionName)
> Constructs a `TextAction` with the given name. Never called directly; called from the subclass constructor.

Methods
public static final Action[] augmentList(Action[] basisList, Action[] extendingList)
> Merges two lists of commmands and returns the result. If an `Action` with the same name is defined in both lists, the `Action` from the `extendingList` will be the one included.

Protected Methods
protected final JTextComponent getFocusedComponent()
> Returns the `JTextComponent` which is currently focused.

protected final JTextComponent getTextComponent(java.awt.event.ActionEvent e)
> Returns the source of the event as a `JTextComponent` if the conversion can be made.

> *Extended by* : DefaultEditorKit.BeepAction (p.814), DefaultEditorKit.CopyAction (p.815), DefaultEditorKit.CutAction (p.815), DefaultEditorKit.DefaultKeyTypedAction (p.816), DefaultEditorKit.InsertBreakAction (p.816), DefaultEditorKit.InsertContentAction (p.817), DefaultEditorKit.InsertTabAction (p.817), DefaultEditorKit.PasteAction (p.818), StyledEditorKit.StyledTextAction (p.883).
> *See also*   AbstractAction (p.115), Action (p.128), JTextComponent (p.838).

swing.text.Utilities

CLASS

This class serves as a storehouse for utility methods used by the text classes.

public class Utilities

Constructors
public Utilities()
> Default constructor. Never construct an instance of this class since all of the methods are static.

Methods

public static final int drawTabbedText(Segment s, int x, int y,
java.awt.Graphics g, TabExpander e, int startOffset)

Draws the text in s, expanding any tabs using e. This particular implementation renders in a 1.1-style coordinate system where ints are used and 72 points per inch is assumed.

public static final int getBreakLocation(Segment s,
java.awt.FontMetrics metrics, int x0, int x, TabExpander e,
int startOffset)

Returns the offset of the best break location in the Segment. This method tries to find white space near the requested break location.

public static final int getNextWord(JTextComponent c, int offs)
throws BadLocationException

Returns the start of the next word after offs.

Throws: BadLocationException if the offset is out of range.

public static final Element getParagraphElement(JTextComponent c,
int offs)

Returns the Element to use for the paragraph around offs.

public static final int getPositionAbove(JTextComponent c, int offs,
int x) throws BadLocationException

Returns the postion in the Document that best represents the position directly above the current position.

Throws: BadLocationException if the offset is out of range.

public static final int getPositionBelow(JTextComponent c, int offs,
int x) throws BadLocationException

Returns the position in the Document that best represents the position directly below the current position.

Throws: BadLocationException if the offset is out of range.

public static final int getPreviousWord(JTextComponent c, int offs)
throws BadLocationException

Returns the offset in the Document for the start of the word previous to the given offset.

Throws: BadLocationException if the offset is out of range.

public static final int getRowEnd(JTextComponent c, int offs)
throws BadLocationException

Returns the end offset of the row that contains the given offset.

Throws: BadLocationException if the offset is out of range.

public static final int getRowStart(JTextComponent c, int offs)
throws BadLocationException

Returns the start offset of the row which contains the given location.

Throws: BadLocationException if the offset is out of range.

public static final int getTabbedTextOffset(Segment s,
java.awt.FontMetrics metrics, int x0, int x, TabExpander e,
int startOffset)

Returns the offset in s that best represents the given location. Uses the JDK 1.1 72-points-per-inch coordinate system.

```
public static final int getTabbedTextOffset(Segment s,
    java.awt.FontMetrics metrics, int x0, int x, TabExpander e,
    int startOffset, boolean round)
```
Similar to the other `getTabbedTextOffset()`, but this version allows the returned value to be rounded down. The other method calls this one with `true`, which causes the value to be rounded up.
```
public static final int getTabbedTextWidth(Segment s,
    java.awt.FontMetrics metrics, int x, TabExpander e, int startOffset)
```
Returns the full width of the given `Segment` with its tabs expanded. This is implemented in a 1.1-style coordinate system where `int`s are used and 72 points per inch is assumed.
```
public static final int getWordEnd(JTextComponent c, int offs)
    throws BadLocationException
```
Returns the end of the word immediately after the given offset.

Throws: `BadLocationException` if the offset is out of range.
```
public static final int getWordStart(JTextComponent c, int offs)
    throws BadLocationException
```
Returns the start of the word immediately before the given offset.

Throws: `BadLocationException` if the offset is out of range

See also   Segment (p.861), TabExpander (p.885).

swing.text.View

ABSTRACT
CLASS

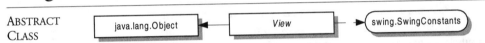

A view of a portion of a `Document`. This class provides utility methods for mapping to and from the `Document`'s coordinate system to the `View` coordinate system and utility methods to handle `Document` updates and layouts.

```
public abstract class View
    implements SwingConstants
```

Fields
```
public static final int BadBreakWeight = 0
```
The weight to indicate a view is a bad break opportunity for the purpose of formatting. This value indicates that no attempt should be made to break the view into fragments as the view has not been written to support fragmenting.
```
public static final int ExcellentBreakWeight = 2000
```
The weight to indicate a view supports breaking, and this represents a very attractive place to break.
```
public static final int ForcedBreakWeight = 3000
```
The weight to indicate a view supports breaking, and must be broken to be represented properly when placed in a view that formats its children by breaking them.
```
public static final int GoodBreakWeight = 1000
```
The weight to indicate a view supports breaking, but better opportunities probably exist.
```
public static final int X_AXIS = 0
```
The axis for format/break operations.

```
public static final int Y_AXIS = 1
```
The axis for format/break operations.

Constructors
```
public View(Element elementToView)
```
Creates a new View object for the given element.

Methods
```
public View breakView(int axis, int offset, float pos, float len)
```
Tries to break this view on the given `axis`. This class' implementation returns this `View`, indicating that it cannot be broken.
```
public void changedUpdate(DocumentEvent changeInfo,
    java.awt.Shape viewAlloc, ViewFactory f)
```
Called when the content of the `Document` changes in a location represented by this `View`.
```
public View createFragment(int p0, int p1)
```
Returns a `View` that represents the given portion of the `Element`. This class' implementation simply returns itself, indicating it cannot be fragmented.
```
public float getAlignment(int axis)
```
Returns the alignment for this `View` along the `X_AXIS` or the `Y_AXIS`. The default alignment is centered.
```
public AttributeSet getAttributes()
```
Returns the `Attributes` to use while rendering the `View`. This class simply returns the `Attributes` defined in the `Element`. This method should be used at all times when working with `Views`, in preference to getting `Attributes` from the `Element` directly. Using this method allows `View` subclasses to define `View`-specific `Attributes`.
```
public int getBreakWeight(int axis, float pos, float len)
```
Returns a value indicating how good a choice the given location `pos+len` would be for breaking. The possible return value is one of the `XBreakWeights` defined above.
```
public java.awt.Shape getChildAllocation(int childIndex,
    java.awt.Shape viewAllocation)
```
Returns the bounding box for the given child. This class's implementation returns `null` since it does not support child `Views`.
```
public java.awt.Container getContainer()
```
Returns the `Container` holding this `View`. This class's implementation simply asks its parent if its parent is not `null`.
```
public Document getDocument()
```
Returns the `Document` associated with this `View`.
```
public Element getElement()
```
Returns the `Element` this `View` is displaying all or part of.
```
public int getEndOffset()
```
Returns the end offset into the `Document` represented by this `View`.
```
public float getMaximumSpan(int axis)
```
Returns the maximum width or height for this view along the given `axis`.
```
public float getMinimumSpan(int axis)
```
Returns the minimum width or height for this view along the given `axis`.

public int getNextVisualPositionFrom(int pos, Position.Bias b, java.awt.Shape a, int direction, Position.Bias[] biasRet) throws BadLocationException

Returns the offset in the Document that represents the next place a Caret can move to. This method returns the next Document offset after pos. In Documents such as an HTML document, there are places where a Caret cannot be placed because the content is not visually displayed or it is read only.

Throws: IllegalArgumentException for an invalid direction.

public View getParent()

Returns the parent of the view.

public abstract float getPreferredSpan(int axis)

Returns the preferred width for the X_AXIS and the preferred height for the Y_AXIS.

public int getResizeWeight(int axis)

Returns an integer representing the extent to which this View can resize itself along the given axis. A return value of 0 or less indicates the View is not resizable.

public int getStartOffset()

Returns the offset into the Document which begins the region represented by this View.

public View getView(int index)

Returns the child View at index. This class's implementation returns null since it does not support children.

public int getViewCount()

Returns the number of child Views. This class's implementation returns 0 since it does not support children.

public ViewFactory getViewFactory()

Returns the ViewFactory used to create this View.

public void insertUpdate(DocumentEvent changeInfo, java.awt.Shape a, ViewFactory f)

Called when the content is inserted into the Document at a location this View represents.

public boolean isVisible()

Returns true, since by default all Views are visible.

public java.awt.Shape modelToView(int p0, Position.Bias b0, int p1, Position.Bias b1, Shape a) throws BadLocationException

Returns the bounding region in the View which represents the region in the Document defined by p0 and p1.

Throws: BadLocationException if the given position does not represent a valid location in the associated Document, throws IllegalArgumentException for an invalid bias argument.

public abstract java.awt.Shape modelToView(int pos, java.awt.Shape a, Position.Bias b) throws BadLocationException

Returns the bounding region of the View which contains the location in the Document indicated by pos.

Throws: BadLocationException if the given position does not represent a valid location in the associated Document, throws IllegalArgumentException for an invalid bias argument.

public abstract java.awt.Shape modelToView(int pos, java.awt.Shape a) throws BadLocationException

Deprecated. Use the other modelToView() methods.

public abstract void paint(java.awt.Graphics g, java.awt.Shape allocation)
Paints the View into the supplied Graphics object.

public void preferenceChanged(View child, boolean width, boolean height)
Child Views call this to indicate their preferred size has changed. This message gets forwarded upwards, where it eventually causes the text component to revalidate.

public void removeUpdate(DocumentEvent changeInfo, java.awt.Shape a, ViewFactory f)
Called when content has been removed from a location in the Document represented by this View.

public void setParent(View parent)
Sets the parent of this View. This method will also be called with null when the View is being removed.

public void setSize(float width, float height)
Sets the size of this View.

public abstract int viewToModel(float x, float y, java.awt.Shape a, Position.Bias[] biasReturn)
Returns the offset into the Document that best represents the given location in the View. The returned value indicates whether the offset refers to the character before the offset or after the offset.

public abstract int viewToModel(float x, float y, java.awt.Shape viewAllocation)
Deprecated. Use the other viewToModel().

Extended by   ComponentView (p.802), CompositeView (p.804), IconView (p.837), LabelView (p.847), LabelView2D (p.850), PlainView (p.858).

Returned by   BasicPasswordFieldUI.create() (p.635), BasicTextAreaUI.create() (p.694), BasicTextFieldUI.create() (p.694), BasicTextUI.create() (p.696), BasicTextUI.getRootView() (p.696), BoxView.getViewAtPoint() (p.797), CompositeView.getView() (p.804), CompositeView.getViewAtPoint() (p.804), CompositeView.getViewAtPosition() (p.804), HTMLEditorKit.HTMLFactory.create() (p.925), LabelView.breakView() (p.847), LabelView.createFragment (p.847), LabelView2D.breakView() (p.850), LabelView2D.createFragment() (p.850), ParagraphView.breakView() (p.853), ParagraphView.getLayoutView() (p.853), ParagraphView.getViewAtPosition() (p.853), TableView.getViewAtPosition() (p.886), TableView.TableRow.getViewAtPosition() (p.888), TextUI.getRootView() (p.542), View.breakView() (p.893), View.createFragment() (p.893), ViewFactory.create() (p.896), View.getParent() (p.893), View.getView() (p.893), View.getViewAtPosition() (p.853).

See also   BadLocationException (p.796), Document (p.826), DocumentEvent (p.489), Element (p.830), ViewFactory (p.896).

swing.text.ViewFactory

INTERFACE   ⬭ ViewFactory

A factory to create a View of a given Document or piece of a Document.

public interface ViewFactory

Methods
`public abstract View create(Element elem)`

Creates a view from the given structural element (piece) of a document.

Returned by DefaultEditorKit.getViewFactory() (p.810),
EditorKit.getViewFactory() (p.829), HTMLEditorKit.getViewFactory() (p.922),
StyledEditorKit.getViewFactory() (p.878), View.getViewFactory() (p.893).
Implemented by BasicTextUI (p.696), HTMLEditorKit.HTMLFactory (p.925).
See also Element (p.830), View (p.893).

swing.text.WrappedPlainView

CLASS

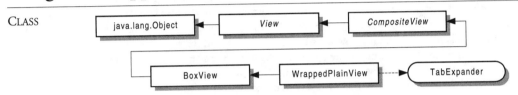

A View that supports line wrapping and allows a single font and color.

`public class WrappedPlainView extends BoxView implements TabExpander`

Constructors
`public WrappedPlainView(Element elem)`

Creates a new WrappedPlainView. All Lines will be wrapped on character boundaries.

`public WrappedPlainView(Element elem, boolean wrapOnWord)`

Creates a new WrappedPlainView. All Lines can be wrapped on either character or word boundaries, depending upon the setting of the wrapOnWord parameter.

Methods
`public void changedUpdate(DocumentEvent e, java.awt.Shape a, ViewFactory f)`

Called when the Document changes in a region represented by this View.
Overrides: changedUpdate in class BoxView.

`public float getPreferredSpan(int axis)`

Implemented to call the superclass after caching the current FontMetrics (for use by the nested lines).
Overrides: getPreferredSpan in class BoxView.

`public void insertUpdate(DocumentEvent e, java.awt.Shape a, ViewFactory f)`

Updates the child Views in response to content being inserted into the Document.
Overrides: insertUpdate in class BoxView.

`public float nextTabStop(float x, int tabOffset)`

Returns the next tab stop position after a given reference position. This implementation does not support things like centering so it ignores the tabOffset argument.
Implements: nextTabStop in interface TabExpander.

`public void paint(java.awt.Graphics g, java.awt.Shape a)`

Paints using the given rendering surface and area on that surface. This is implemented to stash the selection positions, selection colors, and font metrics for the nested lines to use.

Overrides: paint in class BoxView.

public void removeUpdate(DocumentEvent e, java.awt.Shape a, ViewFactory f)
Implemented to simply update the children.
Overrides: removeUpdate in class BoxView.

public void setSize(float width, float height)
Sets the size of the view. If the size has changed, layout is redone. The size includes the inset areas.
Overrides: setSize in class BoxView.

Protected Methods

protected int calculateBreakPosition(int p0, int p1)
Called by the nested wrapped line views to determine the break location. It will either break at word or character boundaries depending upon the wrapOnWord parameter given at construction time.

protected void drawLine(int p0, int p1, java.awt.Graphics g, int x, int y)
Draws a line of text, suppressing white space at the end and expanding any tabs. This is implemented to make calls to the methods drawUnselectedText() and drawSelectedText().

protected int drawSelectedText(java.awt.Graphics g, int x, int y, int p0, int p1) throws BadLocationException
Draws the given range in the model as selected text. This method assumes the Highlighter will render the selected background.
Throws: BadLocationException if the range is invalid.

protected int drawUnselectedText(java.awt.Graphics g, int x, int y, int p0, int p1) throws BadLocationException
Draws the given range in the model as normal unselected text.
Throws: BadLocationException if the range is invalid.

protected final Segment getLineBuffer()
Returns a buffer that can be used to directly access text in the associated document.

protected int getTabSize()
Returns the tab size set for the document, defaulting to 8.

protected void loadChildren(ViewFactory f)
Called by the setParent() method to load all of the children to initialize the view. Subclasses can reimplement this to initialize their child views in a different manner. The default implementation creates a child view for each child element.

See also   DocumentEvent (p.489), Element (p.830), Segment (p.861), View (p.893), ViewFactory (p.896).

Package swing.text.html

This package exists to support JEditorPane's HTML editing capabilities. The main class of the package is HTMLEditorKit. Generally, HTMLEditorKit is the only class which will be used directly, and it will usually be used indirectly through JEditorPane.

The rest of the classes in this package support HTML 3.2, including forms. The quality of the parser in Swing 1.1 is greatly improved over Swing 1.0 since it is the same parser used by the HotJava browser. This EditorKit is also being used for JavaHelp, so the implementation is much more robust than it was previously.

HTML extends/implements hierarchy

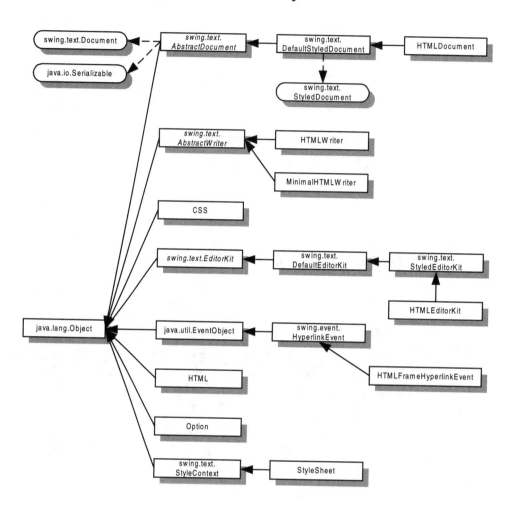

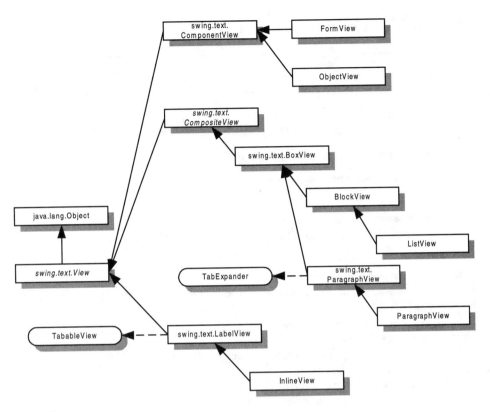

Quick summary

Main Class	`HTMLEditorKit` (p.922). Generally, that is the only class you will ever use directly unless you are creating a subclass for an extended set of HTML tags.

FAQs

Does the HTMLEditorKit support frames?

As of Swing 1.1, the answer is yes. The parser used is the same parser that is used by the HotJava browser, which supports HTML 3.2, including frames.

Does the HTMLEditorKit support Components?

Swing 1.1 introduces support for `Components`. The `HTMLEditorKit` can display most HTML forms, including their controls.

swing.text.html.BlockView

CLASS

```
java.lang.Object  ◄──  swing.text.View  ◄──  swing.text.CompositeView  ◄──
swing.text.BoxView  ◄──  BlockView
```

A view which can render an area marked up using a style sheet.

`public class BlockView extends BoxView`

Constructors
`public BlockView(Element elem, int axis)`
Constructs a new `BlockView` for `elem`. The box is oriented along the given `axis`.

Methods
`public float getAlignment(int axis)`
Returns 0 along the `X_AXIS`, and the alignment of the first child view adjusted by the preferred span along the `Y_AXIS`.
Overrides: `getAlignment` in class `BoxView`.
`public AttributeSet getAttributes()`
Returns the attributes to use for painting, retrieving the defaults from the style sheet.
Overrides: `getAttributes` in class `View`.
`public int getResizeWeight(int axis)`
Returns 1 along the `X_AXIS` and 0 along the `Y_AXIS`.
Throws: `IllegalArgumentException` for an invalid axis.
Overrides: `getResizeWeight` in class `BoxView`.
`public void paint(java.awt.Graphics g, java.awt.Shape allocation)`
Paints the view into the given area.
Overrides: `paint` in class `BoxView`.

Protected Methods
`protected StyleSheet getStyleSheet()`
Returns the style sheet from the `HTMLDocument` associated with this view.
`protected void setPropertiesFromAttributes()`
Resets the `Insets`.

Extended by ListView (p.933).
See also BoxView (p.797), Element (p.830), StyleSheet (p.938), View (p.893).

swing.text.html.CSS

CLASS

```
java.lang.Object  ◄──  CSS
```

This class provides an enumeration of the attributes defined in the CSS (cascading style sheet) standard.

```
public class CSS extends java.lang.Object
```

Constructors
```
public CSS()
```
    Default constructor.

Methods
```
public static final CSS.Attribute getAttribute(String name)
```
    Returns the attribute corresponding to the given string. If a match cannot be found, null is returned.

Inner Classes
```
public class CSS.Attribute
```

swing.text.html.CSS.Attribute

INNER CLASS

This class provides an enumeration of all tags defined in the CSS specification.

```
public static final class CSS.Attribute extends java.lang.Object
```

Fields
```
public static final CSS.Attribute BACKGROUND
public static final CSS.Attribute BACKGROUND_ATTACHMENT
public static final CSS.Attribute BACKGROUND_COLOR
public static final CSS.Attribute BACKGROUND_IMAGE
public static final CSS.Attribute BACKGROUND_POSITION
public static final CSS.Attribute BACKGROUND_REPEAT
public static final CSS.Attribute BORDER
public static final CSS.Attribute BORDER_BOTTOM
public static final CSS.Attribute BORDER_BOTTOM_WIDTH
public static final CSS.Attribute BORDER_COLOR
public static final CSS.Attribute BORDER_LEFT
public static final CSS.Attribute BORDER_LEFT_WIDTH
public static final CSS.Attribute BORDER_RIGHT
public static final CSS.Attribute BORDER_RIGHT_WIDTH
public static final CSS.Attribute BORDER_STYLE
public static final CSS.Attribute BORDER_TOP
public static final CSS.Attribute BORDER_TOP_WIDTH
public static final CSS.Attribute BORDER_WIDTH
public static final CSS.Attribute CLEAR
public static final CSS.Attribute COLOR
public static final CSS.Attribute DISPLAY
public static final CSS.Attribute FLOAT
```

```
public static final CSS.Attribute FONT
public static final CSS.Attribute FONT_FAMILY
public static final CSS.Attribute FONT_SIZE
public static final CSS.Attribute FONT_STYLE
public static final CSS.Attribute FONT_VARIANT
public static final CSS.Attribute FONT_WEIGHT
public static final CSS.Attribute HEIGHT
public static final CSS.Attribute LETTER_SPACING
public static final CSS.Attribute LINE_HEIGHT
public static final CSS.Attribute LIST_STYLE
public static final CSS.Attribute LIST_STYLE_IMAGE
public static final CSS.Attribute LIST_STYLE_POSITION
public static final CSS.Attribute LIST_STYLE_TYPE
public static final CSS.Attribute MARGIN
public static final CSS.Attribute MARGIN_BOTTOM
public static final CSS.Attribute MARGIN_LEFT
public static final CSS.Attribute MARGIN_RIGHT
public static final CSS.Attribute MARGIN_TOP
public static final CSS.Attribute PADDING
public static final CSS.Attribute PADDING_BOTTOM
public static final CSS.Attribute PADDING_LEFT
public static final CSS.Attribute PADDING_RIGHT
public static final CSS.Attribute PADDING_TOP
public static final CSS.Attribute TEXT_ALIGN
public static final CSS.Attribute TEXT_DECORATION
public static final CSS.Attribute TEXT_INDENT
public static final CSS.Attribute TEXT_TRANSFORM
public static final CSS.Attribute VERTICAL_ALIGN
public static final CSS.Attribute WHITE_SPACE
public static final CSS.Attribute WIDTH
public static final CSS.Attribute WORD_SPACING
public static final CSS.Attribute[] allAttributes
```
All attributes defined in the CSS specification.

Methods

```
public String getDefaultValue()
```
Returns the default value for an attribute.

```
public boolean isInherited()
```
If true, this attribute should also be used by child views of this view.

```
public String toString()
```
Returns the string from the CSS specification which this attribute represents.
Overrides: toString in class Object.

Returned by   CSS.getAttribute() (p.902).

swing.text.html.FormView

CLASS

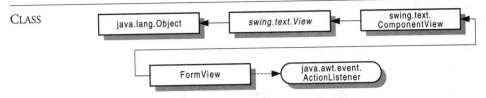

This class provides support for the components used in HTML forms.

HTML element type	Component created
input, type button	JButton
input, type checkbox	JCheckBox
input, type image	JButton
input, type password	JPasswordField
input, type radio	JRadioButton
input, type reset	JButton
input, type submit	JButton
input, type text	JTextField
select, size > 1 or multiple attributes defined	JList in a JScrollPane
select, size unspecified or 1	JComboBox
textarea	JTextArea in a JScrollPane

```
public class FormView extends ComponentView
    implements java.awt.event.ActionListener
```

Fields
```
public static final java.lang.String SUBMIT
public static final java.lang.String RESET
```
These strings are the defaults for the SUBMIT and RESET controls.

Constructors
```
public FormView(Element elem)
```
Creates a new FormView object.

Methods
```
public void actionPerformed(java.awt.event.ActionEvent evt)
```
Handles the ActionEvent.
Implements: actionPerformed in interface ActionListener.

Protected Methods
```
protected java.awt.Component createComponent()
```
Creates the component.
Overrides: createComponent in class ComponentView.

protected void submitData(String data)
Submits the form data using a background thread.
protected void imageSubmit(String imageData)
Submits results based on a click on an image.

Inner Classes
protected class FormView.MouseEventListener

swing.text.html.FormView.MouseEventListener

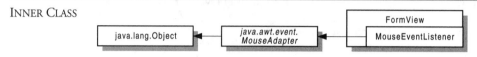

This inner class handles mouse clicks on images in forms.

protected class FormView.MouseEventListener
    extends java.awt.event.MouseAdapter

Methods
public void mouseReleased(java.awt.event.MouseEvent evt)
Overrides: mouseReleased in class MouseAdapter.

swing.text.html.HTML

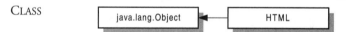

This class and its inner classes define attribute constants used by HTMLDocument.

public class HTML extends java.lang.Object

Fields
public static final String NULL_ATTRIBUTE_VALUE

Constructors
public HTML()
Default constructor.

Methods
public static HTML.Attribute getAttributeKey(String attName)
Returns the attribute matching the given string name.
public static int getIntegerAttributeValue(AttributeSet attr,
    HTML.Attribute key, int def)
A utility method that returns an attribute as an integer. All attributes defined in this class and its sub-classes are stored as Strings.
public static HTML.Tag getTag(String tagName)
Returns the tag matching the given string tag name.

Inner Classes
```
public static final class HTML.Attribute
public static class HTML.Tag
public static class HTML.UnknownTag
```

swing.text.html.HTML.Attribute

This inner class defines an enumeration of the standard HTML attributes. This class is final and cannot be extended.

```
public static final class HTML.Attribute extends java.lang.Object
```

Fields
```
public static final HTML.Attribute ACTION
public static final HTML.Attribute ALIGN
public static final HTML.Attribute ALINK
public static final HTML.Attribute ALT
public static final HTML.Attribute ARCHIVE
public static final HTML.Attribute BACKGROUND
public static final HTML.Attribute BGCOLOR
public static final HTML.Attribute BORDER
public static final HTML.Attribute CELLPADDING
public static final HTML.Attribute CELLSPACING
public static final HTML.Attribute CHECKED
public static final HTML.Attribute CLASS
public static final HTML.Attribute CLASSID
public static final HTML.Attribute CLEAR
public static final HTML.Attribute CODE
public static final HTML.Attribute CODEBASE
public static final HTML.Attribute CODETYPE
public static final HTML.Attribute COLOR
public static final HTML.Attribute COLS
public static final HTML.Attribute COLSPAN
public static final HTML.Attribute COMMENT
public static final HTML.Attribute COMPACT
public static final HTML.Attribute CONTENT
public static final HTML.Attribute COORDS
public static final HTML.Attribute DATA
public static final HTML.Attribute DECLARE
public static final HTML.Attribute DIR
public static final HTML.Attribute DUMMY
public static final HTML.Attribute ENCTYPE
public static final HTML.Attribute ENDTAG
public static final HTML.Attribute FACE
public static final HTML.Attribute FRAMEBORDER
```

```
public static final HTML.Attribute HALIGN
public static final HTML.Attribute HEIGHT
public static final HTML.Attribute HREF
public static final HTML.Attribute HSPACE
public static final HTML.Attribute HTTPEQUIV
public static final HTML.Attribute ID
public static final HTML.Attribute ISMAP
public static final HTML.Attribute LANG
public static final HTML.Attribute LANGUAGE
public static final HTML.Attribute LINK
public static final HTML.Attribute LOWSRC
public static final HTML.Attribute MARGINHEIGHT
public static final HTML.Attribute MARGINWIDTH
public static final HTML.Attribute MAXLENGTH
public static final HTML.Attribute METHOD
public static final HTML.Attribute MULTIPLE
public static final HTML.Attribute N
public static final HTML.Attribute NAME
public static final HTML.Attribute NOHREF
public static final HTML.Attribute NORESIZE
public static final HTML.Attribute NOSHADE
public static final HTML.Attribute NOWRAP
public static final HTML.Attribute PROMPT
public static final HTML.Attribute REL
public static final HTML.Attribute REV
public static final HTML.Attribute ROWS
public static final HTML.Attribute ROWSPAN
public static final HTML.Attribute SCROLLING
public static final HTML.Attribute SELECTED
public static final HTML.Attribute SHAPE
public static final HTML.Attribute SHAPES
public static final HTML.Attribute SIZE
public static final HTML.Attribute SRC
public static final HTML.Attribute STANDBY
public static final HTML.Attribute START
public static final HTML.Attribute STYLE
public static final HTML.Attribute TARGET
public static final HTML.Attribute TEXT
public static final HTML.Attribute TITLE
public static final HTML.Attribute TYPE
public static final HTML.Attribute USEMAP
public static final HTML.Attribute VALIGN
public static final HTML.Attribute VALUE
public static final HTML.Attribute VALUETYPE
public static final HTML.Attribute VERSION
public static final HTML.Attribute VLINK
public static final HTML.Attribute VSPACE
public static final HTML.Attribute WIDTH
public static HTML.Attribute[] allAttributes
```

Methods
public String toString()
> *Overrides:* toString in class Object.

> *Returned by*   HTML.getAttributeKey() (p.906).

swing.text.html.HTML.Tag

INNER CLASS

This inner class provides an enumeration of the standard HTML tags. This class can be extended to add support for additional tags, while still working with the standard HTML parser class.

public static class HTML.Tag extends java.lang.Object

Fields
public static final HTML.Tag A
public static final HTML.Tag ADDRESS
public static final HTML.Tag APPLET
public static final HTML.Tag AREA
public static final HTML.Tag B
public static final HTML.Tag BASE
public static final HTML.Tag BASEFONT
public static final HTML.Tag BIG
public static final HTML.Tag BLOCKQUOTE
public static final HTML.Tag BODY
public static final HTML.Tag BR
public static final HTML.Tag CAPTION
public static final HTML.Tag CENTER
public static final HTML.Tag CITE
public static final HTML.Tag CODE
public static final HTML.Tag COMMENT
> This tag is made up by the parser to indicate a comment (which obviously doesn't have an associated HTML tag).

public static final HTML.Tag CONTENT
> This tag is used by the parser to tag content in the HTML document (which is defined as text that doesn't have an associated tag and isn't a comment).

public static final HTML.Tag DD
public static final HTML.Tag DFN
public static final HTML.Tag DIR
public static final HTML.Tag DIV
public static final HTML.Tag DL
public static final HTML.Tag DT
public static final HTML.Tag EM
public static final HTML.Tag FONT
public static final HTML.Tag FORM
public static final HTML.Tag FRAME

```
public static final HTML.Tag FRAMESET
public static final HTML.Tag H1
public static final HTML.Tag H2
public static final HTML.Tag H3
public static final HTML.Tag H4
public static final HTML.Tag H5
public static final HTML.Tag H6
public static final HTML.Tag HEAD
public static final HTML.Tag HR
public static final HTML.Tag HTML
public static final HTML.Tag I
public static final HTML.Tag IMG
public static final HTML.Tag IMPLIED
```

This tag is created by the parser for implicit paragraphs, paragraphs of content that aren't begun by a <p> tag.

```
public static final HTML.Tag INPUT
public static final HTML.Tag ISINDEX
public static final HTML.Tag KBD
public static final HTML.Tag LI
public static final HTML.Tag LINK
public static final HTML.Tag MAP
public static final HTML.Tag MENU
public static final HTML.Tag META
public static final HTML.Tag NOFRAMES
public static final HTML.Tag OBJECT
public static final HTML.Tag OL
public static final HTML.Tag OPTION
public static final HTML.Tag P
public static final HTML.Tag PARAM
public static final HTML.Tag PRE
public static final HTML.Tag S
public static final HTML.Tag SAMP
public static final HTML.Tag SCRIPT
public static final HTML.Tag SELECT
public static final HTML.Tag SMALL
public static final HTML.Tag STRIKE
public static final HTML.Tag STRONG
public static final HTML.Tag STYLE
public static final HTML.Tag SUB
public static final HTML.Tag SUP
public static final HTML.Tag TABLE
public static final HTML.Tag TD
public static final HTML.Tag TEXTAREA
public static final HTML.Tag TH
public static final HTML.Tag TITLE
public static final HTML.Tag TR
public static final HTML.Tag TT
public static final HTML.Tag U
public static final HTML.Tag UL
```

```
public static final HTML.Tag VAR
public static HTML.Tag[] allTags
```
This array contains all of the standard HTML tags. COMMENT, CONTENT, and IMPLIED are not included, since they aren't standard.

Methods
```
public boolean breaksFlow()
```
Returns true if the tag causes a line break in the content.
```
public boolean isBlock()
```
Returns true if the tag is a structure tag (for example, <p>) rather than a formatting tag, such as <strike>.
```
public boolean isPreformatted()
```
Returns true if the content tagged with this tag provides its own line breaks and formatting.
```
public String toString()
```
Returns the String which this tag represents.
Overrides: toString in class Object.

Protected Constructors
```
protected Tag(String id)
```
Constructs a Tag for the given id. It defaults to not causing a break and not being a block.
```
protected Tag(String id, boolean causesBreak, boolean isBlock)
```
Constructs a Tag for the given id.

Extended by   HTML.UnknownTag (p.911).
Returned by   HTMLDocument.Iterator.getTag() (p.921), HTML.getTag() (p.906).

swing.text.html.HTML.UnknownTag

INNER CLASS

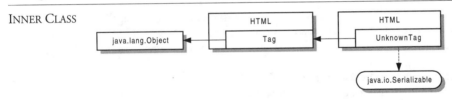

This inner class is used to maintain tags which aren't recognized by the parser when the Document is read, so they can be written back out if the Document is saved.

```
public static class HTML.UnknownTag extends HTML.Tag
    implements java.io.Serializable
```

Constructors
```
public UnknownTag(String id)
```
Constructs a holder for the given String.

Methods
```
public boolean equals(Object obj)
```
Returns true if obj is an UnknownTag storing the same id.
Overrides: equals in class Object.

```
public int hashCode()
```
Overrides: hashCode in class Object.

swing.text.html.HTMLDocument

CLASS

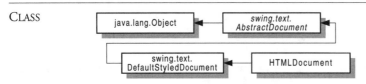

This class represents an HTML document. The structure of the representation is built using HTMLDocument.HTMLReader, which may be subclassed and replaced by overriding the getReader() method. The default document structure is designed primarily so a document may be read, edited, and then rewritten without losing any information (unless the user deletes it).

The Elements in the document are in 1-to-1 correspondence with the blocks defined by the tags in the HTML.

```
public class HTMLDocument extends DefaultStyledDocument
```

Fields
```
public static final java.lang.String AdditionalComments
```
A custom document property key which is used to store comments in the original HTML that are outside the <body>.

Constructors
```
public HTMLDocument()
```
Constructs an empty HTMLDocument which will use a GapBuffer for storage.
```
public HTMLDocument(AbstractDocument.Content c, StyleSheet styles)
```
Constructs an empty HTMLDocument which will use the given content storage and style storage mechanisms.
```
public HTMLDocument(StyleSheet styles)
```
Constructs an empty HTMLDocument which will use a GapBuffer to store the content and the given style storage mechanism.

Methods
```
public java.net.URL getBase()
```
Returns the base URL for any relative URLs in the document.
```
public HTMLDocument.Iterator getIterator(HTML.Tag t)
```
Returns an iterator which will find the tags of the given type in the document.
```
public boolean getPreservesUnknownTags()
```
Returns true if the parser should return tags that it can't identify.
```
public HTMLEditorKit.ParserCallback getReader(int pos)
```
Returns the class which will read and parse the HTML stream starting at the given position. Returns HTMLDocument.HTMLReader by default.

public HTMLEditorKit.ParserCallback getReader(int startOffset,
    int tagsToGenerateBeforeInserting, int
    tagsToStartBeforeInserting, HTML.Tag insertAtStartTag)

Returns the `ParserCallback` which handles the tags as they are read. The default class returned is `HTMLDocument.HTMLReader`.

public StyleSheet getStyleSheet()

Returns the `StyleSheet` defined by the document.

public int getTokenThreshold()

Returns how many tokens should be generated before it is worthwhile to try updating the document's structure to take them into account. Returns `Integer.MAX_VALUE`.

public void processHTMLFrameHyperlinkEvent(HTMLFrameHyperlinkEvent e)

Handles figuring out `HyperlinkEvents` which come from a document contained within a HTML frame.

public void setBase(java.net.URL u)

Sets the base URL for any relative URLs in the document.

public void setTokenThreshold(int n)

Sets the number of tokens to parse before updating the document while reading. This allows for incremental display of the document as it loads. By default the `tokenThreshold` is `Integer.MAX_VALUE`, which indicates that the document should not be updated until it is fully read.

public void setPreservesUnknownTags(boolean preservesTags)

Sets whether the document keeps track of tags it does not recognize. This should probably be left as the default `true`, since setting it to `false` causes information from the original document to be lost.

Protected Methods

protected void create(DefaultStyledDocument.ElementSpec[] data)

Replaces the current contents of the document with the given data.

Overrides: `create` in class `DefaultStyledDocument`.

protected Element createBranchElement(Element parent, AttributeSet a)

Returns an `Element` of type `HTMLDocument.BlockElement`.

Overrides: `createBranchElement` in class `AbstractDocument`.

protected AbstractElement createDefaultRoot()

Creates the root element for the document.

Overrides: `createDefaultRoot` in class `DefaultStyledDocument`.

protected Element createLeafElement(Element parent, AttributeSet a,
    int p0, int p1)

Returns an `Element` of type `HTMLDocument.RunElement`.

Overrides: `createLeafElement` in class `AbstractDocument`.

protected void insert(int offset, DefaultStyledDocument.ElementSpec[] data)
    throws BadLocationException

Inserts the given content into the document.

Throws: `BadLocationException` if any `Element` represents an invalid location.

Overrides: `insert` in class `DefaultStyledDocument`.

protected void insertUpdate(
    AbstractDocument.DefaultDocumentEvent chng, AttributeSet attr)

Regenerates the document structure after an insertion.

Overrides: `insertUpdate` in class `DefaultStyledDocument`.

Inner Classes

```
public class HTMLDocument.BlockElement
public class HTMLDocument.HTMLReader
public abstract static class HTMLDocument.Iterator
public class HTMLDocument.RunElement
```

See also   AbstractDocument.AbstractElement (p.783), AbstractDocument.Content (p.788), BadLocationException (p.796), StyleSheet (p.938).

swing.text.html.HTMLDocument.BlockElement

INNER CLASS

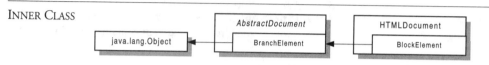

An `Element` that represents a block of HTML.

```
public class HTMLDocument.BlockElement
    extends AbstractDocument.BranchElement
```

Constructors

public BlockElement(Element parent, AttributeSet a)
Constructs a composite element that initially contains no children.

Methods

public String getName()
Gets the name of the element.

public AttributeSet getResolveParent()
Gets the resolving parent. HTML attributes are not inherited at the model level, so we override this to return `null`.

See also   AbstractDocument.BranchElement (p.786), AttributeSet (p.794), Element (p.830).

swing.text.html.HTMLDocument.HTMLReader

INNER CLASS

This class is called by the parser to build the document and then fill the HTMLDocument with the constructed content using the `insert()` method.

Action inner classes are provided to handle the various tags found in the HTML document.

- *BlockAction*—handle tags that create `Elements` that contain other `Elements`.
- *ParagraphAction*—a subclass of `BlockAction` that handles `Elements` inside paragraphs.
- *CharacterAction*—creates `Elements` for HTML text.
- *SpecialAction*—creates a special `Element`, usually for an image.
- *FormAction*—creates an `Element` that contains components.

- *HiddenAction*—creates an `Element` that is only visible if the document is being edited. An example of this would be comments or currently unsupported tags like `<APPLET>` and `<SCRIPT>`.
- *IsindexAction*—inserts the content within a block defined by the `HTML.Tag.IMPLIED` tag as a special `Element`.
- *PreAction*—a subclass of `BlockAction`, it handles preformatted (`<PRE>`) sections of content.

Tag	Associated action
`HTML.Tag.A`	`CharacterAction`
`HTML.Tag.ADDRESS`	`CharacterAction`
`HTML.Tag.APPLET`	`HiddenAction`
`HTML.Tag.AREA`	`HiddenAction`
`HTML.Tag.B`	`CharacterAction`
`HTML.Tag.BASE`	`BaseAction`
`HTML.Tag.BASEFONT`	`CharacterAction`
`HTML.Tag.BIG`	`CharacterAction`
`HTML.Tag.BLOCKQUOTE`	`BlockAction`
`HTML.Tag.BODY`	`BlockAction`
`HTML.Tag.BR`	`SpecialAction`
`HTML.Tag.CAPTION`	`BlockAction`
`HTML.Tag.CENTER`	`BlockAction`
`HTML.Tag.CITE`	`CharacterAction`
`HTML.Tag.CODE`	`CharacterAction`
`HTML.Tag.DD`	`BlockAction`
`HTML.Tag.DFN`	`CharacterAction`
`HTML.Tag.DIR`	`BlockAction`
`HTML.Tag.DIV`	`BlockAction`
`HTML.Tag.DL`	`BlockAction`
`HTML.Tag.DT`	`ParagraphAction`
`HTML.Tag.EM`	`CharacterAction`
`HTML.Tag.FONT`	`CharacterAction`
`HTML.Tag.FORM`	`CharacterAction`
`HTML.Tag.FRAME`	`SpecialAction`
`HTML.Tag.FRAMESET`	`BlockAction`
`HTML.Tag.H1`	`ParagraphAction`
`HTML.Tag.H2`	`ParagraphAction`
`HTML.Tag.H3`	`ParagraphAction`
`HTML.Tag.H4`	`ParagraphAction`
`HTML.Tag.H5`	`ParagraphAction`
`HTML.Tag.H6`	`ParagraphAction`
`HTML.Tag.HEAD`	`HiddenAction`
`HTML.Tag.HR`	`SpecialAction`

Tag	Associated action
HTML.Tag.HTML	BlockAction
HTML.Tag.I	CharacterAction
HTML.Tag.IMG	SpecialAction
HTML.Tag.INPUT	FormAction
HTML.Tag.ISINDEX	IsIndexAction
HTML.Tag.KBD	CharacterAction
HTML.Tag.LI	BlockAction
HTML.Tag.LINK	HiddenAction
HTML.Tag.MAP	HiddenAction
HTML.Tag.MENU	BlockAction
HTML.Tag.META	HiddenAction
HTML.Tag.NOFRAMES	BlockAction
HTML.Tag.OBJECT	SpecialAction
HTML.Tag.OL	BlockAction
HTML.Tag.OPTION	FormAction
HTML.Tag.P	ParagraphAction
HTML.Tag.PARAM	HiddenAction
HTML.Tag.PRE	PreAction
HTML.Tag.SAMP	CharacterAction
HTML.Tag.SCRIPT	HiddenAction
HTML.Tag.SELECT	FormAction
HTML.Tag.SMALL	CharacterAction
HTML.Tag.STRIKE	CharacterAction
HTML.Tag.S	CharacterAction
HTML.Tag.STRONG	CharacterAction
HTML.Tag.STYLE	HiddenAction
HTML.Tag.SUB	CharacterAction
HTML.Tag.SUP	CharacterAction
HTML.Tag.TABLE	BlockAction
HTML.Tag.TD	BlockAction
HTML.Tag.TEXTAREA	FormAction
HTML.Tag.TH	BlockAction
HTML.Tag.TITLE	TitleAction
HTML.Tag.TR	BlockAction
HTML.Tag.TT	CharacterAction
HTML.Tag.U	CharacterAction
HTML.Tag.UL	BlockAction
HTML.Tag.VAR	CharacterAction

```
public class HTMLDocument.HTMLReader
    extends HTMLEditorKit.ParserCallback
```

Constructors

public HTMLReader(int offset)

Creates a reader which will begin inserting text into the document at pos.

public HTMLReader(int offset, int popDepth, int pushDepth,
HTML.Tag insertTag)

Creates a reader which will begin inserting text into the document at pos. The popDepth and pushDepth parameters are only used if insertTag is not null.

Methods

public void flush() throws BadLocationException

Called to insert any buffered content into the Document.

Overrides: flush in class HTMLEditorKit.ParserCallback.

public void handleComment(char[] data, int pos)

Called to handle a comment tag. If the comment is outside the <body>, the tag will be stored as a Document property. Otherwise, it will be handled as a special tag.

public void handleEndTag(HTML.Tag t, int pos)

Callback from the parser. Route to the appropriate handler for the tag.

Overrides: handleEndTag in class HTMLEditorKit.ParserCallback.

public void handleSimpleTag(HTML.Tag t, MutableAttributeSet a, int pos)

Called by the parser. It is this method that decides which method to call based on the type of the simple single-element tag.

Overrides: handleSimpleTag in class HTMLEditorKit.ParserCallback.

public void handleStartTag(HTML.Tag t, MutableAttributeSet a, int pos)

Called by the parser to handle the start tag of a tag pair. It calls one of the other methods based on the type of tag.

Overrides: handleStartTag in class HTMLEditorKit.ParserCallback.

public void handleText(char[] data, int pos)

Handles a block of text in the content.

Overrides: handleText in class HTMLEditorKit.ParserCallback.

Protected Methods

protected void addContent(char[] data, int offs, int length)

Inserts the given text using the current character attributes.

protected void addContent(char[] data, int offs, int length,
boolean genImpliedParaIfNecessary)

Inserts the given text using the current character attributes. This method generates an IMPLIED tag if it needs to.

protected void addSpecialElement(HTML.Tag t, MutableAttributeSet a)

Inserts the content given in the MutableAttributeSet.

protected void blockClose(HTML.Tag t)

Ends a section of content bounded by the given tag.

protected void blockOpen(HTML.Tag t, MutableAttributeSet attr)

Begins a section of content bounded by the given tag. The content in the section will use the given attributes.

protected void popCharacterStyle()

Pops the current style off of the top of the stack, so that the new current style is the one which was used before the old current style was pushed onto the stack.

```
protected void preContent(char[] data)
```
Inserts preformatted content into the document.
```
protected void pushCharacterStyle()
```
Starts a new section of content with a new character style.
```
protected void registerTag(HTML.Tag t, HTMLDocument.HTMLReader.TagAction a)
```
Registers a handler for a given tag. All of the standard tags have handlers registered, so this method is used for overriding the default handler or adding a new tag.
```
protected void textAreaContent(char[] data)
```
Inserts the given text into an internal document for text areas.

Inner Classes
```
public class HTMLDocument.HTMLReader.TagAction
public class HTMLDocument.HTMLReader.BlockAction
public class HTMLDocument.HTMLReader.ParagraphAction
public class HTMLDocument.HTMLReader.SpecialAction
public class HTMLDocument.HTMLReader.PreAction
public class HTMLDocument.HTMLReader.CharacterAction
```

See also BadLocationException (p.796), HTMLEditorKit.ParserCallback (p.929), HTML.Tag (p.909), MutableAttributeSet (p.853).

swing.text.html.HTMLDocument.HTMLReader.BlockAction

INNER CLASS

```
public class HTMLDocument.HTMLReader.BlockAction
    extends HTMLDocument.HTMLReader.TagAction
```

Constructors
```
public BlockAction()
```
Default constructor.

Methods
```
public void end(HTML.Tag t)
```
Overrides: end in class `HTMLDocument.HTMLReader.TagAction`.
```
public void start(HTML.Tag t, MutableAttributeSet attr)
```
Overrides: start in class `HTMLDocument.HTMLReader.TagAction`.

Extended by HTMLDocument.HTMLReader.ParagraphAction (p.919), HTMLDocument.HTMLReader.PreAction (p.920).

See also HTMLDocument.HTMLReader.TagAction (p.921), HTML.Tag (p.909), MutableAttributeSet (p.853).

swing.text.html.HTMLDocument.HTMLReader.CharacterAction

INNER CLASS

```
public class HTMLDocument.HTMLReader.CharacterAction
    extends HTMLDocument.HTMLReader.TagAction
```

Constructors
public CharacterAction()

Default constructor.

Methods
public void end(HTML.Tag t)

Overrides: end in class HTMLDocument.HTMLReader.TagAction.

public void start(HTML.Tag t, MutableAttributeSet attr)

Overrides: start in class HTMLDocument.HTMLReader.TagAction.

See also   HTMLDocument.HTMLReader.TagAction (p.921), HTML.Tag (p.909), MutableAttributeSet (p.853).

swing.text.html.HTMLDocument.HTMLReader.ParagraphAction

INNER CLASS

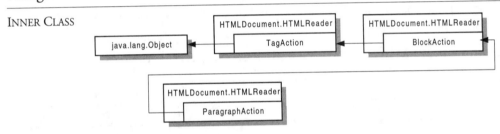

```
public class HTMLDocument.HTMLReader.ParagraphAction
    extends HTMLDocument.HTMLReader.BlockAction
```

Constructors
public ParagraphAction()

Default constructor.

Methods
public void end(HTML.Tag t)

Overrides: end in class HTMLDocument.HTMLReader.BlockAction.

public void start(HTML.Tag t, MutableAttributeSet a)

Overrides: start in class HTMLDocument.HTMLReader.BlockAction.

See also   HTMLDocument.HTMLReader.BlockAction (p.914), HTML.Tag (p.909), MutableAttributeSet (p.853).

swing.text.html.HTMLDocument.HTMLReader.PreAction

INNER CLASS

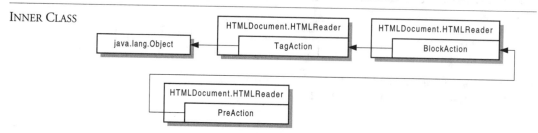

```
public class HTMLDocument.HTMLReader.PreAction
    extends HTMLDocument.HTMLReader.BlockAction
```

Constructors
```
public PreAction()
```
Default constructor.

Methods
```
public void end(HTML.Tag t)
```
Overrides: end in class HTMLDocument.HTMLReader.BlockAction.
```
public void start(HTML.Tag t, MutableAttributeSet attr)
```
Overrides: start in class HTMLDocument.HTMLReader.BlockAction.

See also   HTMLDocument.HTMLReader.BlockAction (p.914), HTML.Tag (p.909),
MutableAttributeSet (p.853).

swing.text.html.HTMLDocument.HTMLReader.SpecialAction

INNER CLASS

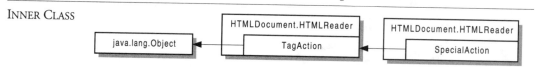

```
public class HTMLDocument.HTMLReader.SpecialAction
    extends HTMLDocument.HTMLReader.TagAction
```

Constructors
```
public SpecialAction()
```
Default constructor.

Methods
```
public void start(HTML.Tag t, MutableAttributeSet a)
```
Overrides: start in class HTMLDocument.HTMLReader.TagAction.

See also   HTMLDocument.HTMLReader.TagAction (p.921), HTML.Tag (p.909),
MutableAttributeSet (p.853).

swing.text.html.HTMLDocument.HTMLReader.TagAction

INNER CLASS

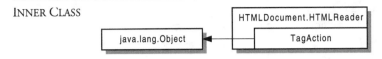

This class forms the basis for all other tag handlers.

```
public class HTMLDocument.HTMLReader.TagAction
    extends java.lang.Object
```

Constructors
public TagAction()
Default constructor.

Methods
public void end(HTML.Tag t)
Called when an end tag of the given type is found.
public void start(HTML.Tag t, MutableAttributeSet a)
Called when a start tag of the given type is found.

Extended by   HTMLDocument.HTMLReader.BlockAction (p.914),
HTMLDocument.HTMLReader.CharacterAction (p.918),
HTMLDocument.HTMLReader.SpecialAction (p.920).
See also   HTML.Tag (p.909), MutableAttributeSet (p.853).

swing.text.html.HTMLDocument.Iterator

INNER CLASS

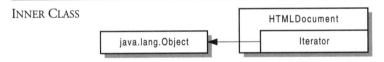

This class provides support for finding all tags of a given type in a document.

```
public abstract static class HTMLDocument.Iterator
    extends java.lang.Object
```

Constructors
public Iterator()
Default constructor.

Methods
public abstract AttributeSet getAttributes()
Returns the attributes associated with this tag.
public abstract int getEndOffset()
Returns the end offset of the range associated with the current tag.
public abstract int getStartOffset()
Returns the start offset of the range associated with the current tag.

```
public abstract HTML.Tag getTag()
```
Returns the tag being searched for.
```
public abstract boolean isValid()
```
Returns `false` when the iterator has moved past the last tag of the given type in the document.
```
public abstract void next()
```
Finds the next tag.

Returned by   HTMLDocument.getIterator() (p.912).

swing.text.html.HTMLDocument.RunElement

INNER CLASS

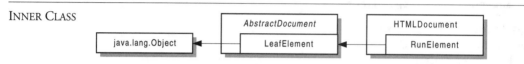

This `Element` represents a sequence of HTML content for a given tag that all has the same attributes.

```
public class HTMLDocument.RunElement extends LeafElement
```

Constructors
```
public RunElement(Element parent, AttributeSet a, int offs0, int offs1)
```
Constructs an `Element` that represents the content in the document between `offs0` and `offs1`.

Methods
```
public String getName()
```
Returns the name of the `Element`, which may be `null`.
```
public AttributeSet getResolveParent()
```
Returns `null`, because this class does not support inherited attributes.

See also   AttributeSet (p.794).

swing.text.html.HTMLEditorKit

CLASS

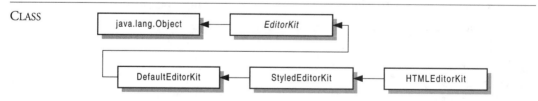

An `EditorKit` that supports editing HTML 3.2 including forms.

To extend or replace the parser you can override the `getParser()` method. A less drastic modification can be done by overriding the processing class for the parser, which is a subclass of `HTMLEditorKit.ParserCallback`. The default processing class is `HTMLDocument.HTMLReader`.

The `Views` generated by this `EditorKit` are all created through the `HTMLEditorKit.HTML-Factory` class. To change what `Views` are created, override that class.

```
public class HTMLEditorKit extends StyledEditorKit
```

Fields

public static final String BOLD_ACTION

The name of the bold `Action`.

public static final String COLOR_ACTION

The name of the color `Action`.

public static final String DEFAULT_CSS

The name of the default style sheet used to provide styles for the document.

public static final String FONT_CHANGE_BIGGER

The name of the font-bigger `Action`.

public static final String FONT_CHANGE_SMALLER

The name of the font-smaller `Action`.

public static final String IMG_ALIGN_BOTTOM

The name of the align-image-bottom `Action`.

public static final String IMG_ALIGN_MIDDLE

The name of the align-image-middle `Action`.

public static final String IMG_ALIGN_TOP

The name of the align-image-top `Action`.

public static final String IMG_BORDER

The name of the image border `Action`.

public static final String ITALIC_ACTION

The name of the italics `Action`.

public static final String LOGICAL_STYLE_ACTION

The name of the logical style `Action`.

public static final String PARA_INDENT_LEFT

The name of the indent-left `Action`.

public static final String PARA_INDENT_RIGHT

The name of the indent-right `Action`.

Constructors

public HTMLEditorKit()

Constructs an `HTMLEditorKit`, creates a `StyleContext`, and loads the default style sheet.

Methods

public Object clone()

Creates a copy of the editor kit.

public Document createDefaultDocument()

Creates an empty `Document` of the default type for this `EditorKit`.

Overrides: `createDefaultDocument` in class `StyledEditorKit`.

public void deinstall(JEditorPane c)

Unregisters any listeners when the `EditorKit` is being removed from the `JEditorPane`.

Overrides: `deinstall` in class `StyledEditorKit`.

public Action[] getActions()

Returns the `Actions` for this `EditorKit`.

Overrides: `getActions` in class `StyledEditorKit`.

public String getContentType()

Returns "text/html".

Overrides: getContentType in class DefaultEditorKit.

public StyleSheet getStyleSheet()

Returns the current StyleSheet.

public ViewFactory getViewFactory()

Returns an instance of HTMLEditorKit.HTMLFactory.

Overrides: getViewFactory in class StyledEditorKit.

public void insertHTML(HTMLDocument doc, int offset, java.lang.String html, int popDepth, int pushDepth, HTML.Tag insertTag) throws BadLocationException, java.io.IOException

Inserts HTML into an existing Document.

public void install(JEditorPane c)

Adds listeners to the JEditorPane when the EditorKit is added to the JEditorPane.

Overrides: install in class StyledEditorKit.

public void read(java.io.Reader in, Document doc, int pos) throws IOException, BadLocationException

Reads the HTML content from the Reader into the given Document starting at pos.

Throws: IOException on any I/O error, BadLocationException if pos represents an invalid location within the document.

Overrides: read in class DefaultEditorKit.

public void setStyleSheet(StyleSheet s)

Sets the StyleSheet to use for document attributes.

public void write(java.io.Writer out, Document doc, int pos, int len) throws IOException, BadLocationException

Writes the HTML content from pos to pos + len in the given Document to the given Writer.

Throws: IOException on any I/O error, BadLocationException if pos represents an invalid location within the document.

Overrides: write in class DefaultEditorKit.

Protected Methods

protected void createInputAttributes(Element element, MutableAttributeSet set)

Fills set with the attributes from element.

Overrides: createInputAttributes in class StyledEditorKit.

protected HTMLEditorKit.Parser getParser()

Returns the parser to use for processing HTML content.

Inner Classes

public static class HTMLEditorKit.HTMLFactory
public abstract static class HTMLEditorKit.HTMLTextAction
public static class HTMLEditorKit.InsertHTMLTextAction
public static class HTMLEditorKit.LinkController
public abstract static class HTMLEditorKit.Parser
public static class HTMLEditorKit.ParserCallback

swing.text.html.HTMLEditorKit.HTMLFactory

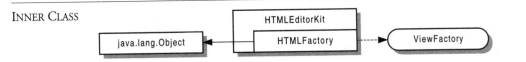

This inner class returns the `View` for a given tag.

Tag	View created
HTML.Tag.CONTENT	InlineView
HTML.Tag.IMPLIED	ParagraphView
HTML.Tag.P	ParagraphView
HTML.Tag.H1	ParagraphView
HTML.Tag.H2	ParagraphView
HTML.Tag.H3	ParagraphView
HTML.Tag.H4	ParagraphView
HTML.Tag.H5	ParagraphView
HTML.Tag.H6	ParagraphView
HTML.Tag.DT	ParagraphView
HTML.Tag.MENU	ListView
HTML.Tag.DIR	ListView
HTML.Tag.UL	ListView
HTML.Tag.OL	ListView
HTML.Tag.LI	BlockView
HTML.Tag.DL	BlockView
HTML.Tag.DD	BlockView
HTML.Tag.BODY	BlockView
HTML.Tag.HTML	BlockView
HTML.Tag.CENTER	BlockView
HTML.Tag.DIV	BlockView
HTML.Tag.BLOCKQUOTE	BlockView
HTML.Tag.PRE	BlockView
HTML.Tag.BLOCKQUOTE	BlockView
HTML.Tag.PRE	BlockView
HTML.Tag.IMG	ImageView
HTML.Tag.HR	HRuleView
HTML.Tag.BR	BRView
HTML.Tag.TABLE	TableView
HTML.Tag.INPUT	FormView
HTML.Tag.SELECT	FormView
HTML.Tag.TEXTAREA	FormView

Tag	View created
HTML.Tag.OBJECT	ObjectView
HTML.Tag.FRAMESET	FrameSetView
HTML.Tag.FRAME	FrameView

```
public static class HTMLEditorKit.HTMLFactory
    extends java.lang.Object
    implements ViewFactory
```

Constructors

`public HTMLFactory()`

Default constructor.

Methods

`public View create(Element elem)`

Creates a View representing the given Element.
Implements: create in interface ViewFactory.

See also   Element (p.830), View (p.893), ViewFactory (p.896).

swing.text.html.HTMLEditorKit.HTMLTextAction

INNER CLASS

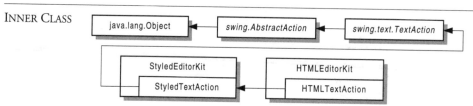

A utility class for implementing text Actions on HTML content. The methods defined by this class are not thread safe, so only one thread should be modifying the document if these methods are used.

```
public abstract static class HTMLEditorKit.HTMLTextAction
    extends StyledEditorKit.StyledTextAction
```

Constructors

`HTMLTextAction(java.lang.String name)`

Constructs an HTMLTextAction with the given name.

Protected Methods

`protected int elementCountToTag(HTMLDocument doc, int offset,HTML.Tag tag)`

Returns the number of Elements between the given offset and the first Element representing the given tag.

`protected Element findElementMatchingTag(HTMLDocument doc, int offset, HTML.Tag tag)`

Finds the nearest Element to offset representing the given tag.

protected Element[] getElementsAt(HTMLDocument doc, int offset)
Returns an array of Elements which form a hierarchy of all Elements which contain offset, ordered by depth in the hierarchy.

protected HTMLDocument getHTMLDocument(JEditorPane e)
Returns the associated Document.

protected HTMLEditorKit getHTMLEditorKit(JEditorPane e)
Returns the associated EditorKit.

Extended by   HTMLEditorKit.InsertHTMLTextAction (p.927).

swing.text.html.HTMLEditorKit.InsertHTMLTextAction

<small>INNER CLASS</small>

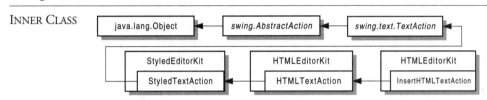

Inserts content into the Document. The parentTag is the containing tag, such as <body>. The addTag is the type of tag for the content being inserted.

```
public static class HTMLEditorKit.InsertHTMLTextAction
    extends HTMLEditorKit.HTMLTextAction
```

Constructors
InsertHTMLTextAction(java.lang.String name, java.lang.String html,
    HTML.Tag parentTag, HTML.Tag addTag)
Creates an Action of the given name to insert the HTML content given by html.

InsertHTMLTextAction(java.lang.String name, java.lang.String html,
    HTML.Tag parentTag, HTML.Tag addTag, HTML.Tag alternateParentTag,
    HTML.Tag alternateAddTag)
Creates an Action of the given name to insert the HTML content given by html. The alternateParentTag and alternateAddTag are used if the parentTag cannot be found in the document.

Methods
public void actionPerformed(java.awt.event.ActionEvent ae)
Inserts the content (passed to the constuctor as *html*) into the document.

Protected Fields
protected HTML.Tag addTag
The cached value of the addTag.

protected HTML.Tag alternateAddTag
The tag to use as the addTag if the given parentTag is not found, but the alternateParentTag is.

protected HTML.Tag alternateParentTag
If the parentTag is not found, this tag will be used as the parentTag.

protected java.lang.String html
The HTML content to insert when the `Action` is triggered.
protected HTML.Tag parentTag
The default `parentTag` to search for.

Protected Methods
protected void insertAtBoundry(JEditorPane editor, HTMLDocument doc,
int offset, Eement insertElement, java.lang.String html,
HTML.Tag parentTag, HTML.Tag addTag)
Called when inserting the content at a boundary between two tags in the document. It keeps track of the tag end additions and tag start additions needed to have the text after the insertion keep its same nesting depth in the document.
protected void insertHTML(JEditorPane editor, HTMLDocument doc,
int offset, java.lang.String html, int popDepth, int pushDepth,
HTML.Tag addTag)
Calls `HTMLEditorKit.insertHTML()`.

See also HTML.Tag (p.909), HTMLDocument (p.912), JEditorPane (p.232).

swing.text.html.HTMLEditorKit.LinkController

INNER CLASS

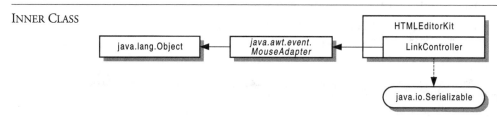

This inner class identifies clicks on hyperlinks and fires `HyperlinkEvents` in response.

public static class HTMLEditorKit.LinkController
extends java.awt.event.MouseAdapter
implements java.io.Serializable

Constructors
public LinkController()
Default constructor.

Methods
public void mouseClicked(java.awt.event.MouseEvent evt)
Calculates the offset into the `Document` based on the coordinates of the event and then calls `activateLink()`.
Overrides: mouseClicked in class `MouseAdapter`.
Implements: mouseClicked in interface `MouseListener`.

Protected Methods
protected void activateLink(int pos, JEditorPane html)
If `pos` is within a hyperlink in the document, this method calls `linkActivated()` in the given `JEditorPane`.

See also   JEditorPane (p.232).

swing.text.html.HTMLEditorKit.Parser

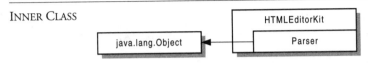

INNER CLASS

This inner class provides the interface which needs to be supported by the HTML parser.

```
public abstract static class HTMLEditorKit.Parser
    extends java.lang.Object
```

Constructors
```
public Parser()
```
Default constructor.

Methods
```
public abstract void parse(java.io.Reader r,
    HTMLEditorKit.ParserCallback cb) throws IOException
```
A thread-safe method to read the content from the `Reader` and call the `ParserCallback` to handle processing it.

Returned by   HTMLEditorKit.getParser() (p.922).

swing.text.html.HTMLEditorKit.ParserCallback

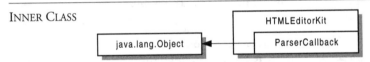

INNER CLASS

This inner class provides an interface for classes which process HTML content and insert it into a `Document`.

```
public static class HTMLEditorKit.ParserCallback
    extends java.lang.Object
```

Constructors
```
public ParserCallback()
```
Default constructor.

Methods
```
public void flush() throws BadLocationException
```
Forces any cached content to be inserted into the `Document`.
```
public void handleComment(char[] data, int pos)
```
Handles a comment in the HTML content.
```
public void handleEndTag(HTML.Tag t, int pos)
```
Handles an end tag of a tag pair (the '/' tags).

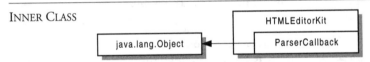

text.html

```
public void handleError(String errorMsg, int pos)
```
Handles an error condition while parsing.
```
public void handleSimpleTag(HTML.Tag t, MutableAttributeSet a,
    int pos)
```
Handles a tag which is complete by itself (such as <p>).
```
public void handleStartTag(HTML.Tag t, MutableAttributeSet a,
    int pos)
```
Handles the starting tag of a tag pair.
```
public void handleText(char[] data, int pos)
```
Handles regular, untagged content.

Extended by   HTMLDocument.HTMLReader (p.914).
Returned by   HTMLDocument.getReader() (p.912).

swing.text.html.HTMLFrameHyperlinkEvent

CLASS

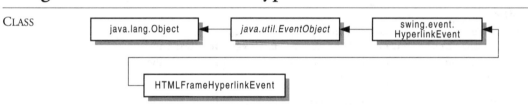

This event is generated when a link is clicked on a page which is inside a frame.

```
public class HTMLFrameHyperlinkEvent extends HyperlinkEvent
```

Constructors
```
public HTMLFrameHyperlinkEvent(java.lang.Object source,
    HyperlinkEvent.EventType type, java.net.URL targetURL,
    java.lang.String targetFrame)
```
Creates an event of the given type, linking to targetURL, and the resulting page should be placed in the frame named targetFrame.
```
public HTMLFrameHyperlinkEvent(java.lang.Object source,
    HyperlinkEvent.EventType type, java.net.URL targetURL,
    java.lang.String desc, java.lang.String targetFrame)
```
Creates an event of the given type, linking to targetURL, and the resulting page should be placed in the frame named targetFrame. The desc is a textual description of the hyperlink.
```
public HTMLFrameHyperlinkEvent(java.lang.Object source,
    HyperlinkEvent.EventType type, java.net.URL targetURL,
    Element sourceElement, java.lang.String targetFrame)
```
Creates an event of the given type, linking to targetURL, and the resulting page should be placed in the frame named targetFrame. The sourceElement is the Element which contains the originating hyperlink.
```
public HTMLFrameHyperlinkEvent(java.lang.Object source,
    HyperlinkEvent.EventType type, java.net.URL targetURL,
    java.lang.String desc, Element sourceElement,
    java.lang.String targetFrame)
```

Creates an event of the given `type`, linking to `targetURL`, and the resulting page should be placed in the frame named `targetFrame`. The `desc` is a textual description of the hyperlink.

Methods
public Element getSourceElement()

Returns the `Element` which represents the frame that was the origin of the hyperlink.

public java.lang.String getTarget()

Returns the target URL as a `String`.

swing.text.html.HTMLWriter

text.html

CLASS

This class provides a writer that knows how to generate HTML from a document structure.

public class HTMLWriter extends AbstractWriter

Constructors
public HTMLWriter(java.io.Writer w, HTMLDocument doc)

Creates a new `HTMLWriter` which will write out the given document to `w`.

Methods
public void write() throws IOException, BadLocationException

Writes the content in the document to the `Writer`.

Throws: `IOException` on any I/O error, `BadLocationException` if any `Element` in the document represents an invalid location.

Overrides: `write` in class `AbstractWriter`.

Protected Methods
protected void closeOutUnwantedEmbeddedTags(AttributeSet attr)
throws IOException

Clears out any tags in the document that aren't in `attr`.

Throws: `IOException` on any I/O error.

protected void comment(Element elem) throws BadLocationException,
IOException

Writes out a comment `Element`.

Throws: `IOException` on any I/O error, `BadLocationException` if the `Element` represents an invalid location within the document.

protected void emptyTag(Element elem) throws BadLocationException,
IOException

Writes out tags for `Elements` that don't have a matching end tag.

Throws: `IOException` on any I/O error, `BadLocationException` if the `Element` represents an invalid location within the document.

protected void endTag(Element elem) throws IOException

Writes out an appropriate end tag for the given `Element`.

Throws: `IOException` on any I/O error.

protected boolean isBlockTag(AttributeSet attr)

Returns true if the Tag for this Element is a block tag.

protected boolean matchNameAttribute(AttributeSet attr, HTML.Tag tag)

Returns true if the name of attr is the same as the name of the tag.

protected void selectContent(AttributeSet attr) throws IOException

Writes out a "select" for an HTML form Element.

Throws: IOException on any I/O error.

protected void startTag(Element elem) throws IOException

Writes out an appropriate start tag for the given Element.

Throws: IOException on any I/O error.

protected boolean synthesizedElement(Element elem)

Returns true if the Element is an implied tag.

protected void text(Element elem) throws BadLocationException, IOException

Writes out text content.

Throws: IOException on any I/O error, BadLocationException if the Element represents an invalid location within the document.

Overrides: text in class AbstractWriter.

protected void textAreaContent(AttributeSet attr)
throws BadLocationException, IOException

Writes out the content in a TEXTAREA form element.

Throws: IOException on any I/O error, BadLocationException if the Element represents an invalid location within the document.

protected void write(java.lang.String content) throws IOException

Writes out the given content.

Throws: IOException on any I/O error.

Overrides: write in class AbstractWriter.

protected void writeAttributes(AttributeSet attr) throws IOException

Writes out the given attribute set, ignoring any Tags.

Throws: IOException on any I/O error.

Overrides: writeAttributes in class AbstractWriter.

protected void writeEmbeddedTags(AttributeSet attr) throws IOException

Writes out any Tags in the attribute set. The closeOutUnwantedEmbeddedTags() method is called afterwards to provide matching end tags.

Throws: IOException on any I/O error.

protected void writeOption(Option option) throws IOException

Writes out an "option" HTML form element.

Throws: IOException on any I/O error.

See also AbstractWriter (p.793), AttributeSet (p.794), BadLocationException (p.796), Element (p.830), Option (p.936).

swing.text.html.InlineView

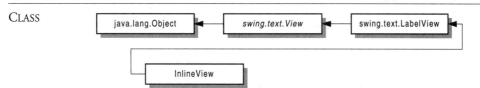

This `View` displays inline content based on the style sheet specifications. Inline content is content which does not cause a line break, such as `<strong>`.

`public class InlineView extends LabelView`

Constructors
`public InlineView(Element elem)`
    Constructs a new `View` for `elem`.

Methods
`public AttributeSet getAttributes()`
    Returns the attributes to use, based on the style sheet attributes.
    Overrides: `getAttributes` in class `View`.
`public boolean isVisible()`
    Returns `false` if the content for the `Element` is nonprinting white space.
    Overrides: `isVisible` in class `View`.

Protected Methods
`protected StyleSheet getStyleSheet()`
    Returns the style sheet to use.
`protected void setPropertiesFromAttributes()`
    Caches the properties to use based on the current attributes.
    Overrides: `setPropertiesFromAttributes` in class `LabelView`.

    See also   AttributeSet (p.794), LabelView (p.847), StyleSheet (p.938), View (p.893).

swing.text.html.ListView

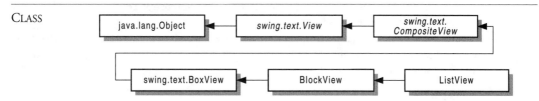

This `View` renders an HTML list element.

`public class ListView extends BlockView`

Constructors
public ListView(Element elem)
Creates a new view for elem.

Methods
public float getAlignment(int axis)
Overrides: getAlignment in class BlockView.
public void paint(java.awt.Graphics g, java.awt.Shape allocation)
Overrides: paint in class BlockView.

Protected Methods
protected void paintChild(java.awt.Graphics g,
java.awt.Rectangle alloc, int index)
Overrides: paintChild in class BoxView.

See also BlockView (p.902), BoxView (p.797), Element (p.830).

swing.text.html.MinimalHTMLWriter

CLASS

This class is used to write out document content that wasn't generated using an HTMLEditorKit (content from a StyledDocument). This class only writes out bold, italic, and underline tags. The other tags are written out as style tags.

public class MinimalHTMLWriter extends AbstractWriter

Constructors
public MinimalHTMLWriter(java.io.Writer w, StyledDocument doc)
Creates a new MinimalHTMLWriter.
public MinimalHTMLWriter(java.io.Writer w, StyledDocument doc,
int pos, int len)
Creates a new MinimalHTMLWriter for the given range in doc.

Methods
public void write() throws IOException, BadLocationException
Writes the content to the Writer.
Throws: IOException on any I/O error, BadLocationException if any Element in the document represents an invalid position.
Overrides: write in class AbstractWriter.

Protected Methods
protected void writeAttributes(AttributeSet attr) throws IOException
Writes out the given attributes if they are StyleConstants attributes. They are written out as (name:value) pairs, separated by a semicolon.
Throws: IOException on any I/O error.
Overrides: writeAttributes in class AbstractWriter.

protected void endFontTag() throws IOException

Writes out the end tag for a font.

Throws: IOException on any I/O error.

protected boolean inFontTag()

Returns true if the current position is inside a font tag pair.

protected boolean isText(Element elem)

Returns true if the Element contains text.

protected void startFontTag(String style) throws IOException

Writes a start font tag. Font tags cannot be nested, so if inFontTag() returns true, the current tag is closed before the start tag is written.

Throws: IOException on any I/O error.

protected void text(Element elem) throws IOException, BadLocationException

Writes out the text in the element.

Throws: IOException on any I/O error, BadLocationException if the Element represents an invalid position in the document.

Overrides: text in class AbstractWriter.

protected void writeBody() throws IOException, BadLocationException

Writes out all Elements in the document.

Throws: IOException on any I/O error, BadLocationException if any Element in the document represents an invalid position.

protected void writeComponent(Element elem) throws IOException

Handles Component Elements. This method is empty in this class.

protected void writeContent(Element elem, boolean needsIndenting) throws IOException, BadLocationException

Writes out text content.

Throws: IOException on any I/O error, BadLocationException if the Element represents an invalid location within the document.

protected void writeEndParagraph() throws IOException

Writes an end tag for a paragraph.

Throws: IOException on any I/O error.

protected void writeEndTag(String endTag) throws IOException

Writes out an end tag.

Throws: IOException on any I/O error.

protected void writeHTMLTags(AttributeSet attr) throws IOException

Writes out the bold, italic, and underline tags.

Throws: IOException on any I/O error.

protected void writeHeader() throws IOException

Writes out the <head> and <style> tags. After the style tag has been written, this method calls writeStyles().

Throws: IOException on any I/O error.

protected void writeImage(Element elem) throws IOException

Writes out Icon Elements. Left empty in this class.

protected void writeLeaf(Element elem) throws IOException

Writes out any leaf Elements which don't contain text.

Throws: IOException on any I/O error.

`protected void writeNonHTMLAttributes(AttributeSet attr) throws IOException`
Writes out any tags which aren't bold, underlined, or italics.
Throws: IOException on any I/O error.

`protected void writeStyles() throws IOException`
Writes out the styles for the style tag.
Throws: IOException on any I/O error.

See also   AbstractWriter (p.793), StyledDocument (p.877).

swing.text.html.ObjectView

CLASS

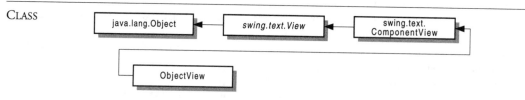

This View displays components from `<object>` tags.

`public class ObjectView extends ComponentView`

Constructors
`public ObjectView(Element elem)`
Creates a new ObjectView for the given Element.

Protected Methods
`protected java.awt.Component createComponent()`
Loads the component given by the classid parameter of the tag.
Overrides: createComponent in class ComponentView.

See also   Element (p.830).

swing.text.html.Option

CLASS

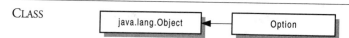

This class is used in the representation of `<option>` and `<select>`.

`public class Option extends java.lang.Object`

Constructors
`public Option(AttributeSet attr)`
Creates a new Option using the given attribute set.

Methods
`public AttributeSet getAttributes()`
Returns the attributes for this Option.

public String getLabel()
> Returns the Option's label.

public String getValue()
> Returns the String representation of the value.

public boolean isSelected()
> Returns the selection state of the Option.

public void setLabel(String label)
> Sets the label for the Option.

public String toString()
> *Overrides:* toString in class Object.

Protected Methods

protected void setSelection(boolean state)
> Sets the selection state of the Option.

> *See also*   AttributeSet (p.794).

swing.text.html.ParagraphView

CLASS

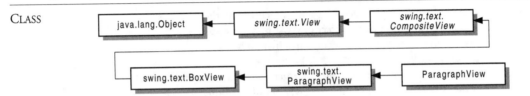

This View renders a paragraph using style sheet attributes.

public class ParagraphView extends swing.text.ParagraphView

Constructors

public ParagraphView(Element elem)
> Constructs a ParagraphView for the given element.

Methods

public AttributeSet getAttributes()
> Returns the attributes to use, based on the style sheet.
> *Overrides:* getAttributes in class View.

public void paint(java.awt.Graphics g, java.awt.Shape allocation)
> Uses the StyleSheet.BoxPainter to paint the border and the background, then calls super.paint().
> *Overrides:* paint in class ParagraphView.

Protected Methods

protected StyleSheet getStyleSheet()
> Returns the associated StyleSheet.

protected void setPropertiesFromAttributes()
> Sets the paragraph's properties from the style sheet.
> *Overrides:* setPropertiesFromAttributes in class ParagraphView.

See also AttributeSet (p.794), ParagraphView (p.853), StyleSheet (p.938).

swing.text.html.StyleSheet

CLASS

This class is an abstraction of an HTML CSS (style sheet). It contains attribute definitions based on the style sheet rules, and additionally provides support for painting `Views` based on the stored attributes.

```
public class StyleSheet extends StyleContext
```

Constructors
public StyleSheet()
> Constructs a `StyleSheet`.

Methods
public void addRule(String rule)
> Adds a CSS rule to the style sheet. Currently an empty method.

public java.awt.Color getBackground(AttributeSet a)
> Converts the given attributes into a color specification.
> *Overrides:* getBackground in class StyleContext.

public StyleSheet.BoxPainter getBoxPainter(AttributeSet a)
> Returns the `BoxPainter` to use for the given set of attributes.

public AttributeSet getDeclaration(String decl)
> Converts the given CSS declaration into a matching `AttributeSet`. Currently returns `null`.

public java.awt.Font getFont(AttributeSet a)
> Returns the font to use for the given set of attributes.
> *Overrides:* getFont in class StyleContext.

public java.awt.Color getForeground(AttributeSet a)
> Converts the given attributes into a color specification.
> *Overrides:* getForeground in class StyleContext.

public static int getIndexOfSize(float pt)
> Returns the index into the size map that matches the given point size.

public StyleSheet.ListPainter getListPainter(AttributeSet a)
> Returns the `ListPainter` used for the given attributes.

public float getPointSize(int index)
> Returns a point size, given an index into the size map.

public float getPointSize(String size)
> Given a string representing a relative font size change (for example, "+2", "–2", "2"), returns a point size.

public Style getRule(HTML.Tag t, Element e)
> Fetches the style to use to render the given type of HTML tag.

public Style getRule(String selector)
> Returns the rule that best matches the selector given in string form. Currently returns `null`.

public AttributeSet getViewAttributes(View v)
Returns the attributes to use for the given View.
public void loadRules(java.io.Reader in, java.net.URL baseURL)
  throws IOException
Loads CSS rules from the given Reader. The baseURL is used to resolve any relative URLs found.
public void setBaseFontSize(int sz)
Sets the default font size used in calculating the relative sizes.
public void setBaseFontSize(String size)
Sets the default font size from the given String.
public java.awt.Color stringToColor(String str)
Converts an HTML 3.2 color string or a hexidecimal color string to a Color.
public AttributeSet translateHTMLToCSS(AttributeSet htmlAttrSet)
Converts from HTML attributes to the matching CSS attributes.

Inner Classes
public static class StyleSheet.BoxPainter
public static class StyleSheet.ListPainter

Returned by   BlockView.getStyleSheet() (p.902), HTMLDocument.getStyleSheet() (p.912),
HTMLEditorKit.getStyleSheet() (p.922), InlineView.getStyleSheet() (p.933),
ParagraphView.getStyleSheet() (p.937).

swing.text.html.StyleSheet.BoxPainter

INNER CLASS

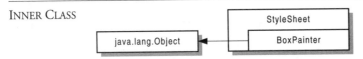

This class provides painting services for Views so they do not need to know anything about style sheets or how the style sheet attributes are stored.

public static class StyleSheet.BoxPainter extends java.lang.Object

Constructors
public BoxPainter()
Default constructor.

Methods
public float getInset(int viewSide, View v)
Returns the gap needed on the given side of the given View to allow space for the margin, border, and padding.
Throws: IllegalArgumentException for an invalid side.
public void paint(java.awt.Graphics g, float x, float y, float w,
  float h, View v)
Paints the border, padding, and background based on the style sheet attributes.

Returned by   StyleSheet.getBoxPainter() (p.938).

swing.text.html.StyleSheet.ListPainter

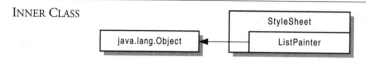

This class provides painting services for lists based on style sheet attributes.

```
public static class StyleSheet.ListPainter
    extends java.lang.Object
```

Methods

```
public void paint(java.awt.Graphics g, float x, float y, float w,
    float h, View v, int item)
```
Paints the list based on the style sheet attributes.

Returned by   StyleSheet.getListPainter() (p.938).

Package swing.html.parser

This package contains the implementation of the default HTML parser used by Swing. Documenting this package is really beyond the scope of this book; if you are going to be modifying or extending this package, the source is really the best documentation there is. Many of the concepts in this package are derived from SGML, especially the concept of a DTD.

Parser extends/implements hierarchy

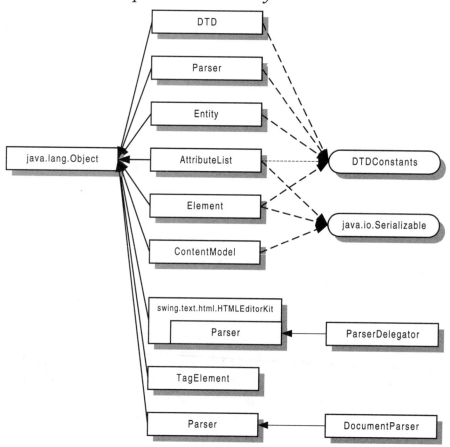

swing.text.html.parser.AttributeList

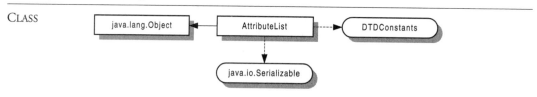

Returns the attributes for an `Element` (the version in this package, not the normal Swing text `Element`).

```
public final class AttributeList extends java.lang.Object
    implements DTDConstants, java.io.Serializable
```

Fields
```
public int modifier
```

```
public String name
public AttributeList next
public int type
public String value
public java.util.Vector values
```

Constructors
```
public AttributeList(String name)
public AttributeList(String name, int type, int modifier,
    String value, java.util.Vector values, AttributeList next)
```

Methods
```
public int getModifier()
public String getName()
public AttributeList getNext()
public int getType()
public String getValue()
public java.util.Enumeration getValues()
public static int name2type(String nm)
public String toString()
```
Overrides: toString in class Object.
```
public static String type2name(int tp)
```

Returned by AttributeList.getNext() (p.942), DTD.defAttributeList() (p.944), Element.getAttribute() (p.947), Element.getAttributeByValue() (p.947), Element.getAttributes() (p.947).

swing.text.html.parser.ContentModel

CLASS

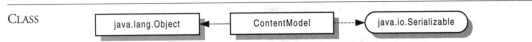

This class represents the document as a whole. It provides methods to return the first Element or all Elements.

```
public final class ContentModel extends java.lang.Object
    implements java.io.Serializable
```

Fields
```
public Object content
public ContentModel next
public int type
```

Constructors
```
public ContentModel()
public ContentModel(Element content)
public ContentModel(int type, ContentModel content)
public ContentModel(int type, Object content, ContentModel next)
```

Methods
```
public boolean empty()
public Element first()
public boolean first(Object token)
public void getElements(java.util.Vector elemVec)
public String toString()
```
Overrides: toString in class Object.

Returned by DTD.defContentModel() (p.944), Element.getContent() (p.947).

swing.text.html.parser.DocumentParser

CLASS

A Parser subclass that does its parsing based on a supplied SGML DTD.

```
public class DocumentParser extends Parser
```

Constructors
```
public DocumentParser(DTD dtd)
```

Methods
```
public void parse(java.io.Reader in, ParserCallback callback)
    throws IOException
```

Protected Methods
```
protected void handleComment(char[] text)
```
Overrides: handleComment in class Parser.
```
protected void handleEmptyTag(TagElement tag)
```
Overrides: handleEmptyTag in class Parser.
```
protected void handleEndTag(TagElement tag)
```
Overrides: handleEndTag in class Parser.
```
protected void handleError(int ln, String errorMsg)
```
Overrides: handleError in class Parser.
```
protected void handleStartTag(TagElement tag)
```
Overrides: handleStartTag in class Parser.
```
protected void handleText(char[] data)
```
Overrides: handleText in class Parser.

swing.text.html.parser.DTD

CLASS

This class defines a SGML DTD. It is used by DocumentParser to decide how to parse the content stream.

```
public class DTD extends java.lang.Object
    implements DTDConstants
```

Fields
```
public static int FILE_VERSION
public final Element applet
public final Element base
public final Element body
public java.util.Hashtable elementHash
public java.util.Vector elements
public java.util.Hashtable entityHash
public final Element head
public final Element html
public final Element isindex
public final Element meta
public String name
public final Element p
public final Element param
public final Element pcdata
public final Element title
```

Constructors
```
protected DTD(String name)
```

Methods
```
public Entity defEntity(String name, int type, int ch)
public void defineAttributes(String name, AttributeList atts)
public Element defineElement(String name, int type, boolean omitStart,
    boolean omitEnd, ContentModel content, java.util.BitSet exclusions,
    java.util.BitSet inclusions, AttributeList atts)
public Entity defineEntity(String name, int type, char[] data)
public static DTD getDTD(String name) throws IOException
public Element getElement(int index)
public Element getElement(String name)
public Entity getEntity(int ch)
public Entity getEntity(String name)
public String getName()
public static void putDTDHash(String name, DTD dtd)
public void read(java.io.DataInputStream in) throws IOException
public String toString()
```
Overrides: toString in class Object.

Protected Methods
```
protected AttributeList defAttributeList(String name, int type,
    int modifier, String value, String values, AttributeList atts)
protected ContentModel defContentModel(int type, Object obj,
    ContentModel next)
protected Element defElement(String name, int type,
    boolean omitStart, boolean omitEnd, ContentModel content,
```

```
               String[] exclusions, String[] inclusions, AttributeList atts)
      protected Entity defEntity(String name, int type, String str)
```

Returned by   DTD.getDTD() (p.944), ParserDelegator.createDTD() (p.949).

swing.text.html.parser.DTDConstants

INTERFACE ⬤ DTDConstants

This interface supplies the constants which match the tags used in a SGML DTD.

```
public interface  DTDConstants
```

Fields
```
public static final int ANY
public static final int CDATA
public static final int CONREF
public static final int CURRENT
public static final int DEFAULT
public static final int EMPTY
public static final int ENDTAG
public static final int ENTITIES
public static final int ENTITY
public static final int FIXED
public static final int GENERAL
public static final int ID
public static final int IDREF
public static final int IDREFS
public static final int IMPLIED
public static final int MD
public static final int MODEL
public static final int MS
public static final int NAME
public static final int NAMES
public static final int NMTOKEN
public static final int NMTOKENS
public static final int NOTATION
public static final int NUMBER
public static final int NUMBERS
public static final int NUTOKEN
public static final int NUTOKENS
public static final int PARAMETER
public static final int PI
public static final int PUBLIC
public static final int RCDATA
public static final int REQUIRED
public static final int SDATA
public static final int STARTTAG
```

```
public static final int SYSTEM
```

Implemented by   AttributeList (p.942), DTD (p.944), Element (p.947),
Entity (p.948), Parser (p.948).

swing.text.html.parser.Element

CLASS

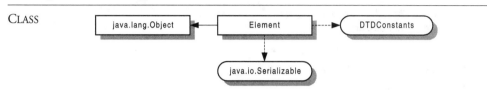

This class provides an abstraction of a DTD element so that it can be used by the parser.

```
public final class Element extends java.lang.Object
    implements DTDConstants, java.io.Serializable
```

Fields
```
public AttributeList atts
public ContentModel content
public Object data
public java.util.BitSet exclusions
public java.util.BitSet inclusions
public int index
public String name
public boolean oEnd
public boolean oStart
public int type
```

Methods
```
public AttributeList getAttribute(String name)
public AttributeList getAttributeByValue(String name)
public AttributeList getAttributes()
public ContentModel getContent()
public int getIndex()
public String getName()
public int getType()
public boolean isEmpty()
public static int name2type(String nm)
public boolean omitEnd()
public boolean omitStart()
public String toString()
```
Overrides: toString in class Object.

Returned by   ContentModel.first() (p.943), DTD.defElement() (p.944),
DTD.defineElement() (p.944), DTD.getElement() (p.944), TagElement.getElement() (p.950).

swing.text.html.parser.Entity

CLASS

This class provides an abstraction for a DTD entity.

```
public final class Entity extends java.lang.Object
    implements DTDConstants
```

Fields
```
public char[] data
public String name
public int type
```

Constructors
```
public Entity(String name, int type, char[] data)
```

Methods
```
public char[] getData()
public String getName()
public String getString()
public int getType()
public boolean isGeneral()
public boolean isParameter()
public static int name2type(String nm)
```

Returned by   DTD methods (p.944).

swing.text.html.parser.Parser

CLASS

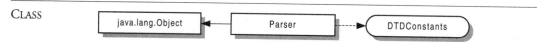

This class provides the main engine of a DTD-driven parser. Subclasses are responsible for handling particular tags as they are encountered.

```
public class Parser extends java.lang.Object
    implements DTDConstants
```

Constructors
```
public Parser(DTD dtd)
```

Methods
```
public synchronized void parse(java.io.Reader in) throws IOException
public String parseDTDMarkup() throws IOException
```

Protected Fields
```
protected DTD dtd
protected boolean strict
```

Protected Methods

```
protected void endTag(boolean omitted)
protected void error(String err)
protected void error(String err, String arg1)
protected void error(String err, String arg1, String arg2)
protected void error(String err, String arg1, String arg2, String arg3)
protected void flushAttributes()
protected SimpleAttributeSet getAttributes()
protected int getCurrentLine()
protected int getCurrentPos()
protected void handleComment(char[] text)
protected void handleEOFInComment()
protected void handleEmptyTag(TagElement tag)
protected void handleEndTag(TagElement tag)
protected void handleError(int ln, String msg)
protected void handleStartTag(TagElement tag)
protected void handleText(char[] text)
protected void handleTitle(char[] text)
protected TagElement makeTag(Element elem)
protected TagElement makeTag(Element elem, boolean fictional)
protected void markFirstTime(Element elem)
protected boolean parseMarkupDeclarations(StringBuffer strBuff)
    throws IOException
protected void startTag(TagElement tag)
```

Extended by   DocumentParser (p.944).

swing.text.html.parser.ParserDelegator

CLASS

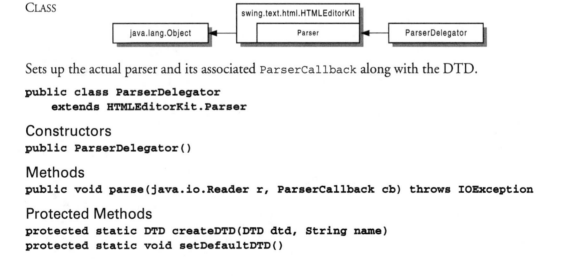

Sets up the actual parser and its associated `ParserCallback` along with the DTD.

```
public class ParserDelegator
    extends HTMLEditorKit.Parser
```

Constructors
```
public ParserDelegator()
```

Methods
```
public void parse(java.io.Reader r, ParserCallback cb) throws IOException
```

Protected Methods
```
protected static DTD createDTD(DTD dtd, String name)
protected static void setDefaultDTD()
```

swing.text.html.parser.TagElement

A `TagElement` is similar to an `Element`, but because it handles HTML tags, it also defines how white space is interpreted in and around itself.

```
public class TagElement extends java.lang.Object
```

Constructors
```
public TagElement(Element elem)
public TagElement(Element elem, boolean fictional)
```

Methods
```
public boolean fictional()
public Element getElement()
public Tag getHTMLTag()
public boolean isBlock()
public boolean isPreformatted()
```

> *Returned by*   Parser.makeTag() (p.948).

Package swing.text.rtf

This package contains the implementation of the RTFEditorKit. RTF is a portable document format popularized by Microsoft Word.

Rtf extends/implements hierarchy

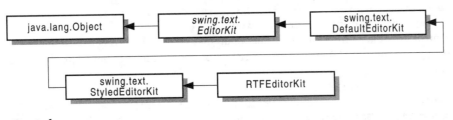

Quick summary

How to use	Create a JEditorPane for content type "text/rtf" (or the older "application/rtf").

FAQs

How do I use this EditorKit?

The easiest way to use this (or any other EditorKit) is to use it through a JEditorPane. For special purposes, like doing file format conversions, you can instantiate this EditorKit directly.

After instantiating the `EditorKit`, you can use its `createDefaultDocument()`, `read()`, and `write()` methods to manipulate a document directly.

swing.text.rtf.RTFEditorKit

CLASS

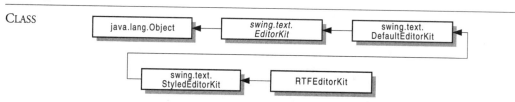

This `EditorKit` provides support for editing RTF content. The standard content type for this `EditorKit` is `text/rtf`. Most of the support for editing is provided through the `StyledEditorKit` class (since the editing concepts in that class are actually based on the RTF specification). This class adds support for reading and writing RTF.

```
public class RTFEditorKit extends StyledEditorKit
```

Constructors
public RTFEditorKit()
> Constructs an RTFEditorKit.

Methods
public Object clone()
> Returns a new copy of the `EditorKit`. This is much faster than instantiating a new instance.
> *Overrides:* `clone` in class `StyledEditorKit`.

public String getContentType()
> Returns `text/rtf`.
> *Overrides:* `getContentType` in class `DefaultEditorKit`.

public void read(java.io.InputStream in, Document doc, int pos)
> **throws IOException, BadLocationException**
> Reads RTF content from the given stream, inserting it into the `Document` starting at pos.
> *Throws:* `IOException` on any I/O error, `BadLocationException` if pos represents an invalid location within the `Document`.
> *Overrides:* read in class `DefaultEditorKit`.

public void read(java.io.Reader in, Document doc, int pos)
> **throws IOException, BadLocationException**
> Throws an `IOException` because RTF is an 8-bit ASCII format (a `Reader` may be trying to do character set translation, which cannot be supported).
> *Throws:* `IOException` on any I/O error, `BadLocationException` if pos represents an invalid location within the `Document`.
> *Overrides:* read in class `DefaultEditorKit`.

public void write(java.io.OutputStream out, Document doc, int pos,
> **int len) throws IOException, BadLocationException**
> Converts the content of the `Document` to RTF and writes it to the stream.

Throws: IOException on any I/O error, BadLocationException if pos represents an invalid location within the Document.

Overrides: write in class DefaultEditorKit.

public void write(java.io.Writer out, Document doc, int pos, int len)
 throws IOException, BadLocationException

Throws an IOException because RTF is an 8-bit ASCII format (a Writer may be trying to do character set translation, which cannot be supported).

Throws: IOException on any I/O error, BadLocationException if pos represents an invalid location within the Document.

Overrides: write in class DefaultEditorKit.

Package swing.tree

The tree package contains support classes and interfaces for the `JTree` component. The most important classes in this package are `DefaultMutableTreeNode` and `DefaultTreeModel`.

`DefaultMutableTreeNode` encapsulates a standard tree data-structure node. It implements all of the methods needed to assemble an N-ary tree (a tree where each node can have an arbitrary number of children).

It might seem that there is no need to think about a `DefaultTreeModel`, since all it does is provide a `Model` interface wrapper around a tree made up of `TreeNodes`. The catch is that `DefaultTreeModel` is the `Model` for the `JTree`, and if the model doesn't know about changes in the tree since the `TreeNodes` were modified directly, the `JTree` will not be properly notified of the change. The `TreeModelListener` methods implemented by `JTree` can be called directly, but it is much easier (and safer) to use the `DefaultTreeModel` methods to update the tree and have the event methods called automatically.

The `TreeCellEditor` and `TreeCellRenderer` interfaces are very useful in applications, since they allow you to implement classes to draw the nodes in the tree. By default, the look and feel draws the nodes and calls `toString()` on the user object stored in the node to get the text to display. This may not be what you want, especially if you are already using `toString()` to print debugging information. Implementing a `TreeCellEditor` and/or a `TreeCellRenderer` gives you total flexibility in how your data is displayed.

Tree extends/implements hierarchy

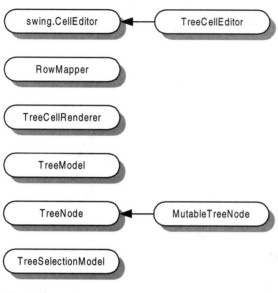

Quick summary

The model	TreeModel (p.987) (uses TreeNode (p.988) and/or MutableTreeNode (p.984)).
The view	JTree (p.393).
How to use	Create a DefaultTreeModel (p.975), built from DefaultMutableTreeNodes (p.961). (Or, define your own model implementing the TreeModel interface and/or your own nodes implementing TreeNode.)
Display and edit	The TreeCellRenderer (p.972) interface defines how the tree's rows are displayed. The TreeCellEditor (p.985) interface defines how the rows are edited. Implement these interfaces and install them on a JTree to change rendering or editing.
Other interfaces	TreePath (p.989) tracks the path from the root to a node. TreeSelectionModel (p.990) tracks the selection in a tree.

FAQs

How do I put my information in a tree?

Use DefaultMutableTreeNode (p.961). Use setUserObject() to include your information in the node. Make sure yourObject.toString() displays the information for your node if you are not going to implement a TreeCellRenderer (p.985).

How do I get different icons on my tree nodes?

The look and feel is usually responsible for providing the icons in a tree. To draw your own icons for a node, implement and install a custom TreeCellRenderer (p.985).

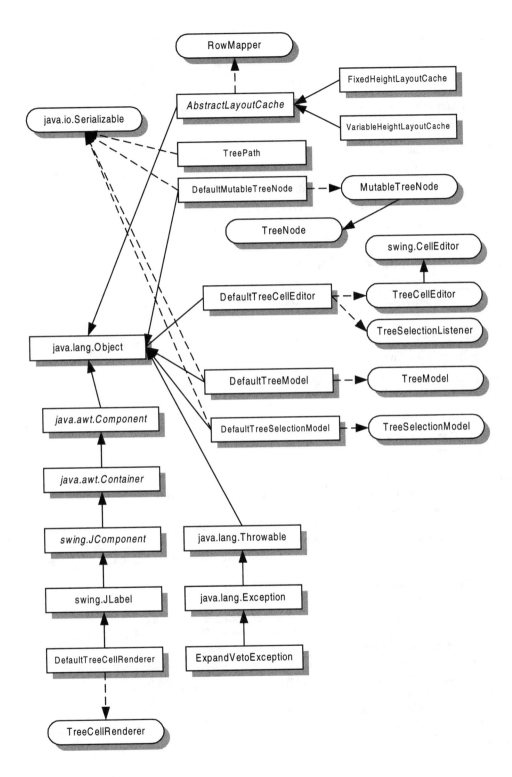

How do I load nodes on demand?

Make a subclass of `DefaultMutableTreeNode` (p.961). Override `getAllowsChildren()` and `getChildCount()` to load the tree beneath each node the first time they are called.

Why won't my folder/directory/container TreeNodes draw properly when they don't have any children?

Set `allowsChildren` to be `true` for all of your container nodes, and set `askAllowsChildren` to true in the `TreeModel`. By default, `askAllowsChildren` is `false`, which makes the model call `isLeaf()` to decide how to render a node. `isLeaf()` returns `true` if the node doesn't have any children at the moment. So, by default, all childless nodes are drawn as leaves regardless of whether they *could* have children.

swing.tree.AbstractLayoutCache

CLASS

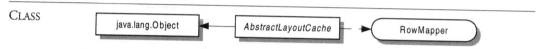

This class is used to store visual state information about a tree. It exists because it is used by `BasicTreeUI` to help in maintaining the layout of the tree.

```
public abstract class AbstractLayoutCache extends java.lang.Object
    implements RowMapper
```

Constructors
```
public AbstractLayoutCache()
```
Default constructor.

Methods
```
public abstract java.awt.Rectangle getBounds(TreePath path,
    java.awt.Rectangle placeIn)
```
Returns the bounding rectangle needed to render the given path into the given region, `placeIn`.
```
public abstract boolean getExpandedState(TreePath path)
```
Returns `true` if the node at the end of `path` is expanded and visible (all nodes in `path` leading to the last are also expanded).
```
public TreeModel getModel()
```
Returns the associated `TreeModel`.
```
public AbstractLayoutCache.NodeDimensions getNodeDimensions()
```
Returns the object which is responsible for calculating the dimensions of the nodes in the tree.
```
public abstract TreePath getPathClosestTo(int x, int y)
```
Returns the path to the node which is *closest* to (`x, y`). Note the emphasis on closest; the node does not need to contain the point (`x, y`). If nothing is currently visible in the tree (including the root node) this method returns `null`.
```
public abstract TreePath getPathForRow(int row)
```
Returns the path to the node that occupies the given row of the tree. If `row` is below the bottom of the tree, this method returns `null`.

public int getPreferredHeight()
Returns the preferred height of the tree.

public int getPreferredWidth(java.awt.Rectangle bounds)
Returns the preferred width of the tree in the given `bounds`, which usually should match the visible region of the tree. Pass `null` to get the preferred width for the entire tree.

public abstract int getRowCount()
Returns the number of rows currently being shown in the tree.

public abstract int getRowForPath(TreePath path)
Returns the row index occupied by the node at the end of the given path. If any of the nodes in the path before the end node are not expanded, this method returns −1, since the end node will not be visible.

public int getRowHeight()
Returns the row height for the tree. If the height is less than one, the `TreeCellRenderer` should be queried for the height of each row individually.

public int[] getRowsForPaths(TreePath[] paths)
Like `getRowForPath()`, this method just works on a whole set at once. The returned array should be the same size as the passed array, with −1 used for any paths which aren't visible.
Implements: `getRowsForPaths` in interface `RowMapper`.

public TreeSelectionModel getSelectionModel()
Returns the selection model for the tree.

public abstract int getVisibleChildCount(TreePath path)
Returns the number of visible children of the last node in `path`.

public abstract java.util.Enumeration getVisiblePathsFrom(TreePath path)
Returns an `Enumeration` which will return all of the visible paths rooted at the given `path`, including `path` itself as the first element. If `path` isn't visible, none of its children will be, so this method returns `null`.

public abstract void invalidatePathBounds(TreePath path)
Recalculates the cached bounds for the node at the end of `path`.

public abstract void invalidateSizes()
Recalculates all cached values the layout cache has.

public abstract boolean isExpanded(TreePath path)
Returns `true` if the node at the end of `path` is expanded.

public boolean isRootVisible()
Returns `true` if the root node of the tree is visible.

public abstract void setExpandedState(TreePath path, boolean isExpanded)
Sets the expansion state of the given node to `isExpanded`.

public void setModel(TreeModel newModel)
Sets the `TreeModel`.

public void setNodeDimensions(AbstractLayoutCache.NodeDimensions nd)
Sets the object which will be used to calculate the dimensions of the nodes in the tree.

public void setRootVisible(boolean rootVisible)
Sets the visibility of the root node to `rootVisible`.

public void setRowHeight(int rowHeight)
Sets a fixed height for the rows in the tree. If the `rowHeight` is less than one, the row height is variable, and is set by the `TreeCellRenderer`.

public void setSelectionModel(TreeSelectionModel newSM)

Sets the `TreeSelectionModel`.

public abstract void treeNodesChanged(TreeModelEvent e)

Called after a child node (or nodes) has changed. The nodes have not moved, but they have changed some facet of their visual appearance. Changing the text for a node would be an example of when this method would be called. The nodes which have changed can be retrieved by calling `e.getChild-Indices()`.

public abstract void treeNodesInserted(TreeModelEvent e)

Called after new nodes have been inserted into the tree. The parent node of the new nodes is returned by `e.getPath()`, and the indices of the new children are retrieved using `e.getChild-Indices()`.

public abstract void treeNodesRemoved(TreeModelEvent e)

Called after nodes (and their children) have been removed from the tree. The parent of the removed nodes is retrieved using `e.getPath()`, and the indices (before the deletion) of the removed children are returned from `e.getChildIndices()`.

public abstract void treeStructureChanged(TreeModelEvent e)

Called when the tree has dramatically changed. The root element of the subtree changed is returned by `e.getPath()`. If the path returned is only one node long, the path is the new root node for the whole tree.

Protected Fields

protected AbstractLayoutCache.NodeDimensions nodeDimensions

The object responsible for calculating the size of a node.

protected boolean rootVisible

Set to `true` if the root node is displayed.

protected int rowHeight

A fixed height to use for all nodes in the tree. If this value is less than one, the `TreeCellRenderer` will be used to get the row height for each node independently.

protected TreeModel treeModel

The model for the tree.

protected TreeSelectionModel treeSelectionModel

The selection model for the tree.

Protected Methods

protected java.awt.Rectangle getNodeDimensions(Object value, int row, int depth, boolean expanded, java.awt.Rectangle placeIn)

Returns the bounding rectangle for a node containing `value`, occupying `row` and of `depth` in the tree (how many ancestors the node has, to calculate the indent) when rendered into `placeIn`.

protected boolean isFixedRowHeight()

Returns `true` if `rowHeight` is greater than zero.

Inner Classes

public abstract static class AbstractLayoutCache.NodeDimensions

Extended by FixedHeightLayoutCache (p.982), VariableHeightLayoutCache (p.993).

Returned by BasicTreeUI.createLayoutCache() (p.710).

See also TreeModel (p.987), TreePath (p.989), TreeSelectionModel (p.990).

swing.tree.AbstractLayoutCache.NodeDimensions

INNER CLASS

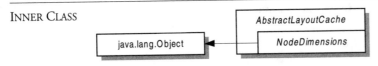

This class is used to calculate the dimensions and origin of nodes in the tree.

```
public abstract static class AbstractLayoutCache.NodeDimensions
    extends java.lang.Object
```

Constructors
```
public NodeDimensions()
```
Default constructor.

Methods
```
public abstract java.awt.Rectangle getNodeDimensions(Object value,
    int row, int depth, boolean expanded, java.awt.Rectangle bounds)
```
Returns the bounding box of the node occupying row in the tree. The depth indicates the number of ancestors this node has and is used to calculate the indent. This method will fill the Rectangle passed in as bounds and return it. This allows the re-use of the same Rectangle for calculating all nodes in the tree. If bounds is null, a new Rectangle will be allocated and returned.

Extended by   BasicTreeUI.NodeDimensionsHandler (p.723).
Returned by   AbstractLayoutCache.getNodeDimensions() (p.958),
BasicTreeUI.createNodeDimensions() (p.710).

swing.tree.DefaultMutableTreeNode

CLASS

A DefaultMutableTreeNode is the easiest basis for building a tree. It is default because it is the node used by DefaultTreeModel. The mutable in its name implies that these nodes can be changed after they have been created. If you want to build a tree model that cannot be modified, use an implementor of the TreeNode interface.

When you build a tree out of these nodes, you almost always want to use all DefaultMutableTreeNodes (or subclasses) because several routines depend on the tree nodes being all of that type.

DefaultMutableTreeNodes hold references to Objects. Unless you create a custom TreeCellRenderer for a subclass, JTree will display the result of calling toString() on the held Object.

This node type provides many enumerations to let you walk the tree in a predefined order. A returned Enumeration is valid until the tree is changed.

Note that this class is not thread-safe.

Example: Building and evaluating an expression tree

```
package defaulttreenode;
//uncomment the next two lines and comment out the javax lines for Swing 1.0.3
// and before.
//import com.sun.java.swing.*;
//import com.sun.java.swing.tree.*;
import javax.swing.*;
import javax.swing.tree.*;
import java.awt.event.*;
import java.util.*;

public class ExprTree extends JFrame {

    public ExprTree() {
        addWindowListener(new WindowAdapter() {
            public void windowClosing(WindowEvent e) {
                ExprTree.this.dispose();
                System.exit(0);
            }
        });

        // Build a tree for the expression "3 + (4 * 5)": a "+" node with its
        // first child 3, and its second child a "*" node with 4 and 5 beneath.
        // Notice we have to use Integer; we can't put raw int's in the tree.
        DefaultMutableTreeNode root = new DefaultMutableTreeNode("+");
        root.add(new DefaultMutableTreeNode(new Integer(3)));
        DefaultMutableTreeNode node = new DefaultMutableTreeNode("*");
        node.add(new DefaultMutableTreeNode(new Integer(4)));
        node.add(new DefaultMutableTreeNode(new Integer(5)));
        root.add(node);

        // Build TreeModel from nodes, and JTree from the TreeModel.
        // Display JTree.
        JTree tree = new JTree(root);
        getContentPane().add(tree);
        pack();
        setVisible(true);

        // Some facts about the tree
        System.out.println("The root has " + root.getChildCount() + " children");
        System.out.println("The tree's depth is " + root.getDepth());
        System.out.println("The tree has " + root.getLeafCount() + " leaves");
        System.out.println("'Root' is really a root? " + root.isRoot());
        System.out.println("Root's userObject: " + root.toString());

        // Evaluate the expression using a stack. Walk the tree in postorder:
        // numeric -> push on stack; operator -> pop 2 values, apply, push result
        Stack stack = new Stack(); // Stack of Integer
        Enumeration enum = root.postorderEnumeration();
        while (enum.hasMoreElements()) { // For each node:
            DefaultMutableTreeNode node1 =
                        (DefaultMutableTreeNode)(enum.nextElement());
            Object obj = node1.getUserObject();
            if (obj instanceof Integer) {
                stack.push(obj); // Integer: Push on stack
```

tree

```
      } else {
        // Operator:
        String operator = (String)obj;
        // Pop two values
        Integer v1 = (Integer) stack.pop();
        Integer v2 = (Integer) stack.pop();

        // Apply operator, push result
        if (operator.equals("+")) {
          stack.push(new Integer(v2.intValue() + v1.intValue()));
        } else { // "*"
          stack.push(new Integer(v2.intValue() * v1.intValue()));
        }
      }
    }
  }
  System.out.println ("\nResult is " + stack.pop());
}
public static void main(String[] args) {
  ExprTree t = new ExprTree();
}
}
```

Note that in the preceding example the JTree was constructed using the root TreeNode as its parameter. This is equivalent to using

```
DefaultTreeModel tm = new DefaultTreeModel(root);
JTree tree = new JTree(tm);
```

JTree internally constructs a DefaultTreeModel when a TreeNode is passed as a parameter.

If you are displaying a tree of DefaultTreeNodes through a JTree, you need to modify the tree structure using methods defined in DefaultTreeModel. If you modify the nodes directly, the JTree will not be notified of the change, since notifying the View is the responsibility of the Model. See the discussion in DefaultTreeModel (p.975) for more details.

public class DefaultMutableTreeNode extends java.lang.Object
    implements java.lang.Cloneable, MutableTreeNode,
    java.io.Serializable

Public Constants
public static final java.util.Enumeration EMPTY_ENUMERATION
    An enumeration with no contents.

Constructors
public DefaultMutableTreeNode()
public DefaultMutableTreeNode(Object userObject)
public DefaultMutableTreeNode(Object userObject, boolean allowsChildren)
    Constructs a node without a parent or any children. Passing in the userObject parameter sets the data value of this node. The boolean allowsChildren indicates whether this node can ever have child nodes. The boolean is used by JTree when its askAllowsChildren property is set true. It is used when the JTree is drawing the nodes of the tree so that nodes which can have children, but don't at the moment (an empty folder, for example), can be drawn like the nodes that do have children by setting this boolean to true.

Methods

public void add(MutableTreeNode childToAdd)

Adds `childToAdd` to the end of this node's `Vector` of children. If `childToAdd` was already the child of a node, it is removed from its old parent's `Vector`. The `childToAdd` argument may not be `null`.

Throws: `IllegalArgumentException` if `childToAdd` is `null` throws `IllegalStateException` if the `allowsChildren` property is `false`.

public java.util.Enumeration breadthFirstEnumeration()

Returns a breadth-first enumeration: it starts with the receiver node, then all its children, then all their children, level-by-level. The whole tree must be built of `DefaultMutableTreeNodes` for this to work, and the tree may not be modified while the enumeration is being used.

public java.util.Enumeration children()

Returns an enumeration of all children of this node. The node's children may not be modified (changed, added, or deleted) while the enumeration is being used.

Implements: `children` in interface `TreeNode`.

public Object clone()

Returns a copy of this node with its parent set to `null` and no children, but the `userObject` reference copied. Note that only the reference is copied, so the new node returned references the *exact same* object as this node.

Overrides: `clone` in class `Object`.

public java.util.Enumeration depthFirstEnumeration()

Returns a depth-first enumeration: it starts with the deepest leftmost leaf, then its siblings, and so on, before ending with this node. (For a binary tree, you can think of this as "left-right-root." This is the same as `postorderEnumeration()`.) The whole tree must be built of `DefaultMutable-TreeNodes` for this to work, and the tree may not be modified while the enumeration is being used.

public boolean getAllowsChildren()

Returns `true` if this node may have child nodes. The default value of `allowsChildren` is `true`.

Implements: `getAllowsChildren` in interface `TreeNode`.

public TreeNode getChildAfter(TreeNode node)

Gets the child node after `node`, or `null` if `node` is not a child of this node. This method searches the children of this node, but not their children. The search is a sequential search of the children, and may take time proportional to the number of children.

Throws: `IllegalArgumentException` if `node` is `null` or is not a child of this node.

public TreeNode getChildAt(int index)

Gets the node at the specified position. You must have `0 <= index < getChildCount()`.

Throws: `ArrayIndexOutOfBoundsException` if index is out of bounds.

Implements: `getChildAt` in interface `TreeNode`.

public TreeNode getChildBefore(TreeNode node)

Gets the child node just before `node`, or `null` if `node` is not a child of this node. This method searches the children of the receiver, but not their children. The search is a sequential search of the children, and may take time proportional to the number of children.

Throws: `IllegalArgumentException` if `node` is `null` or is not a child of this node.

public int getChildCount()

Returns the number of the children of the receiver.

Implements: `getChildCount` in interface `TreeNode`.

public int getDepth()

Gets the longest distance from this node to a leaf. (If the receiver is a leaf, the depth is 0; otherwise, it is the maximum of the depths of all of its children nodes, plus 1.) This method is expensive; it must search from this node to all leaves. (See also getLevel(), which works from this node to the root.)

public TreeNode getFirstChild()

Returns the first child node under the receiver. This method may only be called if getChild-Count() > 0.

Throws: NoSuchElementException if this node has no children.

public DefaultMutableTreeNode getFirstLeaf()

Returns the leftmost leaf under the receiver (or the receiver itself if it is a leaf).

public int getIndex(TreeNode node)

Returns the position of node in the list of children, or –1 if it is not present. The node may not be null. The search is a sequential search of the children, and may take time proportional to the number of children. (Supports TreeNode.)

Throws: IllegalArgumentException if node is null.

Implements: getIndex in interface TreeNode.

public TreeNode getLastChild()

Returns the last child node under the receiver. This method may only be called if getChild-Count()>0.

Throws: NoSuchElementException if this node has no children.

public DefaultMutableTreeNode getLastLeaf()

Returns the rightmost leaf node under the receiver, or the receiver itself if it is a leaf.

public int getLeafCount()

Returns the number of leaves under the receiver (or 1 if the receiver is a leaf). The search is a sequential search of all nodes beneath the receiver, and may take time proportional to the number of nodes.

public int getLevel()

Returns the number of nodes above the receiver. The value is 0 for the root.

public DefaultMutableTreeNode getNextLeaf()

Gets the next leaf to the right, or null if there is none. The search is a sequential search starting from the current leaf's parent, and may take time proportional to the number of nodes in the tree.

public DefaultMutableTreeNode getNextNode()

Gets the next node in a preorder traversal starting at this node. (In a binary tree, preorder is "root-left-right.")

public DefaultMutableTreeNode getNextSibling()

Returns the next sibling node following the receiver in the parent's list of children. The search is a sequential search of the parent's children, and may take time proportional to the number of children.

public TreeNode getParent()

Returns the parent of the receiver, or null if the receiver is the root.

Implements: getParent in interface TreeNode.

public TreeNode[] getPath()

Returns the path (of TreeNodes) from the root to the receiver. The receiver will be the last node in the path.

public DefaultMutableTreeNode getPreviousLeaf()

Gets the next leaf to the left, or null if there is none. The search is a sequential search starting from the current leaf's parent, and may take time proportional to the number of nodes in the tree.

public DefaultMutableTreeNode getPreviousNode()

Gets the preceding node in a preorder traversal starting at this node. (In a binary tree, preorder is "root-left-right.")

public DefaultMutableTreeNode getPreviousSibling()

Returns the sibling node preceding the receiver in the parent's list of children. The search is a sequential search of the parent's children, and may take time proportional to the number of children.

public TreeNode getRoot()

Returns the root of the tree that contains this node.

public TreeNode getSharedAncestor(DefaultMutableTreeNode aNode)

Returns the deepest node in the tree such that the receiver and node have the same ancestor. If the receiver is the same as node, the result is node. The result is null if node is null or in a different tree.

public int getSiblingCount()

Returns the number of siblings of this node (including this node).

public Object getUserObject()

Returns the user-defined object. You may use this to add your own information to a DefaultMutableTreeNode.

public Object[] getUserObjectPath()

Returns the path of userObject values to the receiver. Some elements of the path may be null if the corresponding node has no userObject. The last object in the path is the userObject of the receiver.

public void insert(MutableTreeNode node, int index)

Inserts node to become the new node at index. (The setParent() method is called on node to establish the new parent.) The node must not be null; the index must be valid (0 <= index <= getChildCount()). If node is in another tree, it is removed from that tree before being made a child of the receiver.

Throws: ArrayIndexOutOfBoundsException if index is out of bounds, IllegalArgument-Exception if node is null or is an ancestor of this node, or IllegalStateException if this node does not allow children.

Implements: insert in interface MutableTreeNode.

public boolean isLeaf()

Returns true if the receiver has no children. (Note that having no children is not the same as allowing no children; see getAllowsChildren().) This method is one way JTree has of deciding how to draw the nodes and leaves of the tree. getAllowsChildren() is the other way.

Implements: isLeaf in interface TreeNode.

public boolean isNodeAncestor(TreeNode node)

Returns true if the receiver is an ancestor of node. The search is sequential, and may take time proportional to the number of ancestors of node.

public boolean isNodeChild(TreeNode node)

Returns true if the receiver is the parent of node.

public boolean isNodeDescendant(DefaultMutableTreeNode anotherNode)

Returns true if node is a descendant of the receiver. The search is sequential, and may take time proportional to the number of ancestors of node.

public boolean isNodeRelated(DefaultMutableTreeNode aNode)

Returns true if node and the receiver have the same root.

public boolean isNodeSibling(TreeNode anotherNode)

Returns `true` if the receiver and `node` have the same parent.

public boolean isRoot()

Returns `true` if the receiver is the root of its tree.

public java.util.Enumeration pathFromAncestorEnumeration(TreeNode ancestor)

Returns the path from `ancestor` to this node as an enumeration of nodes.

Throws: `IllegalArgumentException` if `ancestor` is not an ancestor of this node.

public java.util.Enumeration postorderEnumeration()

Returns the list of nodes in postorder: the first child and all its children, the second child and all its children, and so forth, and then the receiving node. (In a binary tree, this is "left-right-root" order.) This is the same as `depthFirstEnumeration()`. The whole tree must be built of `DefaultMutableTreeNodes` for this to work, and the tree may not be modified while the enumeration is being used.

public java.util.Enumeration preorderEnumeration()

Returns the list of nodes in preorder: this node, then its first child and all its children, the second child and all its children, and so forth. (In a binary tree, this is "root-left-right" order.) The whole tree must be built of `DefaultMutableTreeNodes` for this to work, and the tree may not be modified while the enumeration is being used.

public void remove(MutableTreeNode node)

Removes `node` from the children of the receiver. The `node` may not be `null`, and it must be a child of the receiver.

Throws: `IllegalArgumentException` if `node` is `null` or is not a child of this node.

Implements: `remove` in interface `MutableTreeNode`.

public void remove(int index)

Removes the specified child. You must have `0 <= index < getChildCount()`. The child must be a `MutableTreeNode`, as its `setParent()` method will be called.

Throws: `ArrayIndexOutOfBoundsException` if `childIndex` is out of bounds.

Implements: `remove` in interface `MutableTreeNode`.

public void removeAllChildren()

Removes any children of this node from the tree (and sets each child's parent to `null`).

public void removeFromParent()

Removes the receiver and all its children from the tree. The receiver's parent is set to `null`. If the receiver is the root of the tree, this method is ignored.

Implements: `removeFromParent` in interface `MutableTreeNode`.

public void setAllowsChildren(boolean allowsChildren)

Sets whether or not the node is allowed to have children. By default the `allowsChildren` property is `true`. If `allowsChildren` is set `false` when the node has children, all its children are removed.

public void setParent(MutableTreeNode newParent)

Sets the parent of the receiver to `parent`. This method should only be called by the `insert()` and `remove()` methods.

Implements: `setParent` in interface `MutableTreeNode`.

public void setUserObject(Object userObject)

Sets the user-defined object of this node.

Implements: `setUserObject` in interface `MutableTreeNode`.

public String toString()

Returns `userObject.toString()`, or null if no `userObject` is defined.

Overrides: `toString` in class `Object`.

tree

Protected Fields

protected boolean allowsChildren
Returns `True` if the node is allowed to have children.

protected java.util.Vector children
The children of the node.

protected MutableTreeNode parent
The parent of the node. If this `node` is a root node (a node without a parent), this field will be `null`.

protected transient Object userObject
The object that holds the actual data that this `node` represents. The `toString()` method of this class returns the result of calling `toString()` on this object, or `null` if this field is `null`.

Protected Methods

protected TreeNode[] getPathToRoot(TreeNode node, int offsetFromEnd)
Computes the path from `node` toward the root, starting with `node` stored at `offsetFromEnd` from the right. Used in computing `getPath()`.

Extended by   JTree.DynamicUtilTreeNode (p.393).
Returned by   DefaultMutableTreeNode methods.
See also   MutableTreeNode (p.984), TreeNode (p.988).

swing.tree.DefaultTreeCellEditor

CLASS

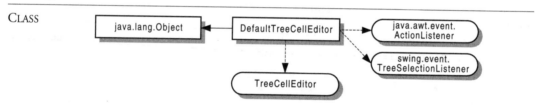

A default `TreeCellEditor`. The constructor of this class takes a `DefaultTreeCellRenderer` which will be used to get the correct `Icons` for the cells (note that the `Icon` appears *outside* the editor, not inside, so the editor itself does not need to supply an `Icon`). If an editor is not given, a `JTextField` will be used by default. You can specify a custom editor using the constructor that takes a `TreeCellEditor`.

```
public class DefaultTreeCellEditor extends java.lang.Object
    implements java.awt.event.ActionListener, TreeCellEditor,
    TreeSelectionListener
```

Constructors

public DefaultTreeCellEditor(JTree tree, DefaultTreeCellRenderer renderer)
Constructs a `DefaultTreeCellEditor` which will use the given renderer and a `JTextField` for editing.

**public DefaultTreeCellEditor(JTree tree,
    DefaultTreeCellRenderer renderer, TreeCellEditor editor)**
Constructs a `DefaultTreeCellEditor` which will use the given renderer and editor.

Methods

public void actionPerformed(java.awt.event.ActionEvent e)

Called after the timer expires and it will start the editing process. The timer is part of the sequence of events which will start the editor (either a triple-click, or a click-pause-click and then a delay which is timed by the timer).

Implements: actionPerformed in interface ActionListener.

public void addCellEditorListener(CellEditorListener l)

Adds the given CellEditorListener to the list to notify when editing is canceled or stopped.

public void cancelCellEditing()

Calls cancelCellEditing() on the actual TreeCellEditor component, and then disposes of it.

public java.awt.Color getBorderSelectionColor()

Returns the color to use for the border around the editor.

public Object getCellEditorValue()

Returns the value from the editor.

public java.awt.Font getFont()

Returns the font used by the editor.

public java.awt.Component getTreeCellEditorComponent(JTree tree, Object value, boolean isSelected, boolean expanded, boolean leaf, int row)

Forwarded to the actual TreeCellEditor component.

Implements: getTreeCellEditorComponent in interface TreeCellEditor.

public boolean isCellEditable(EventObject event)

Forwarded to the actual TreeCellEditor. If it returns true, prepareForEditing() is called, then true is returned.

public void removeCellEditorListener(CellEditorListener l)

Removes the given CellEditorListener from the listener list.

public void setBorderSelectionColor(java.awt.Color newColor)

Sets the color to use around the editor.

public void setFont(java.awt.Font font)

Sets the font used by the default JTextField editor.

public boolean shouldSelectCell(EventObject event)

Calls shouldSelectCell() on the actual TreeCellEditor.

public boolean stopCellEditing()

Forwarded to the actual TreeCellEditor. If it allows editing to stop, the editor is removed and true is returned.

public void valueChanged(TreeSelectionEvent e)

Stops editing.

Implements: valueChanged in interface TreeSelectionListener.

Protected Fields

protected java.awt.Color borderSelectionColor

The color to use for the border around the editor.

protected boolean canEdit

Caches the value returned by the real editor component.

protected transient java.awt.Component editingComponent

The component doing the editing.

protected java.awt.Container editingContainer
 The container which holds the editor.
protected transient Icon editingIcon
 The `Icon` which will be used when the editor is showing.
protected java.awt.Font font
 The font for the default `JTextField` editor.
protected transient TreePath lastPath
 The last path which was selected in the tree.
protected transient int lastRow
 The row value last used for `getTreeCellEditorComponent()`.
protected transient int offset
 The horizontal offset of the editor component.
protected TreeCellEditor realEditor
 The actual `TreeCellEditor` component.
protected DefaultTreeCellRenderer renderer
 The passed-in renderer, used to retrieve the border and colors for the editor.
protected transient Timer timer
 Used in the initial setup of the editing session.
protected transient JTree tree
 The associated `JTree`.

Protected Methods
protected boolean canEditImmediately(EventObject event)
 Returns `true` on a `null` event (which is generated by this object) or a triple-click.
protected java.awt.Container createContainer()
 Creates and configures the container which holds the actual editor.
protected TreeCellEditor createTreeCellEditor()
 Returns a `JTextField` editor, for when one is not supplied.
protected void determineOffset(JTree tree, Object value,
 boolean isSelected, boolean expanded, boolean leaf, int row)
 Calculates the horizontal offset of the editor in the tree and stores it in `offset`.
protected boolean inHitRegion(int x, int y)
 Returns `true` if the point is within the editable section of the tree cell.
protected void prepareForEditing()
 Sets up the editing component.
protected void setTree(JTree newTree)
 Sets the associated tree and adds a `TreeSelectionListener` to it.
protected boolean shouldStartEditingTimer(EventObject event)
 Returns `true` for a mouse event with a click count of one.
protected void startEditingTimer()
 Initializes and starts the timer.

Inner Classes
public class DefaultTreeCellEditor.DefaultTextField
public class DefaultTreeCellEditor.EditorContainer

swing.tree.DefaultTreeCellEditor.DefaultTextField

INNER CLASS

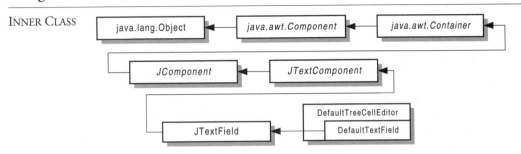

The default `TreeCellEditor` used when one is not supplied.

```
public class DefaultTreeCellEditor.DefaultTextField
    extends JTextField
```

Constructors
`public DefaultTextField(Border)`
> Constructs a `DefaultTextField` which will use the given border.

Methods
`public Border getBorder()`
> Returns the border.
> *Overrides:* `getBorder` in class `JComponent`.

`public java.awt.Font getFont()`
> Returns the font used by the editor.
> *Overrides:* `getFont` in class `Component`.

`public java.awt.Dimension getPreferredSize()`
> Adjusts the `preferredSize` for the current font, if set, or the renderer's font.
> *Overrides:* `getPreferredSize` in class `JTextField`.

Fields
`protected Border border`
> The border to put around the editor.

> *See also*   Border (p.465).

swing.tree.DefaultTreeCellEditor.EditorContainer

INNER CLASS

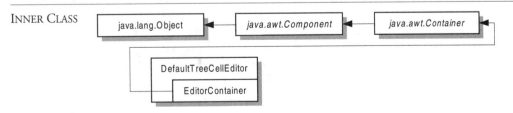

This inner class is responsible for positioning the editing component.

```
public class DefaultTreeCellEditor.EditorContainer
    extends java.awt.Container
```

Constructors
public EditorContainer()
>   Default constructor.

Methods
public void doLayout()
>   Lays out the editor at (DefaultTreeCellEditor.offset, 0).
>   *Overrides:* doLayout in class Container.

public java.awt.Dimension getPreferredSize()
>   Returns the size of the editor plus the offset.
>   *Overrides:* getPreferredSize in class Container.

public void paint(java.awt.Graphics g)
>   Paints the Icon as well as the editor.
>   *Overrides:* paint in class Container.

swing.tree.DefaultTreeCellRenderer

CLASS

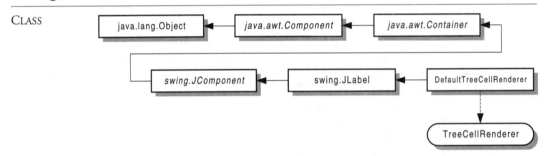

The default renderer for a JTree. This class uses the supplied Icon (if any) and the text returned from calling toString() on the userObject of the node it is rendering.

UIDefaults table key	Description
Tree.closedIcon	The Icon used for nodes which can have children and which are not expanded.
Tree.drawsFocusBorderAroundIcon	A Boolean indicating whether the focus indicator border is drawn surrounding the Icon and label area or just the label area.
Tree.leafIcon	The Icon for a node which cannot have child nodes.
Tree.openIcon	The Icon used for nodes which can have children and which are expanded.
Tree.selectionBackground	The background Color to use when the node is selected.
Tree.selectionBorderColor	The Color of the border when the node is selected.
Tree.selectionForeground	The foreground Color when the node is selected.
Tree.textBackground	The background Color of a node.
Tree.textForeground	The foreground Color of a node.

```
public class DefaultTreeCellRenderer extends JLabel
    implements TreeCellRenderer
```

Constructors
public DefaultTreeCellRenderer()

Constructs a DefaultTreeCellRenderer. Note that the default alignment is JLabel.LEFT.

Methods
public java.awt.Color getBackgroundNonSelectionColor()

Returns the background color of normal nodes.

public java.awt.Color getBackgroundSelectionColor()

Returns the background color of the selected node(s).

public java.awt.Color getBorderSelectionColor()

Returns the color of the border.

public Icon getClosedIcon()

Returns the icon for nodes which can/do have child nodes and which are currently not expanded.

public Icon getDefaultClosedIcon()

Returns the default icon for nodes which can/do have child nodes and which are currently not expanded.

public Icon getDefaultLeafIcon()

Returns the default icon for nodes which cannot have child nodes.

public Icon getDefaultOpenIcon()

Returns the default icon for nodes which can/do have child nodes and which are currently expanded.

public Icon getLeafIcon()

Returns the icon for nodes which cannot have child nodes.

public Icon getOpenIcon()

Returns the icon for nodes which can/do have child nodes and which are currently expanded.

public java.awt.Dimension getPreferredSize()

Makes the preferred size three pixels wider.

Overrides: getPreferredSize in class JComponent.

public java.awt.Color getTextNonSelectionColor()

Returns the text color used when a node is not selected.

public java.awt.Color getTextSelectionColor()

Returns the text color used when a node is selected.

public java.awt.Component getTreeCellRendererComponent(JTree tree,
Object value, boolean sel, boolean expanded, boolean leaf,
int row, boolean hasFocus)

Sets up the renderer based on the supplied information. The text used for the label is the String returned from calling toString() on the value.

Implements: getTreeCellRendererComponent in interface TreeCellRenderer.

public void paint(java.awt.Graphics g)

Paints the node. Note that this method ignores the opaque property and always fills in the background (unless the background color is set to null). The background color changes depending on whether the node is selected.

Overrides: paint in class JComponent.

public void setBackground(java.awt.Color color)

Overridden to accept color only if it is not a ColorUIResource.

Overrides: setBackground in class JComponent.

public void setBackgroundNonSelectionColor(java.awt.Color newColor)
Sets the background color for normal nodes.

public void setBackgroundSelectionColor(java.awt.Color newColor)
Sets the color for the background if the node is selected.

public void setBorderSelectionColor(java.awt.Color newColor)
Sets the color of the focus indicator border.

public void setClosedIcon(Icon newIcon)
Sets the icon used for nodes that can have child nodes and are not expanded.

public void setFont(java.awt.Font font)
Overridden to accept font only if it is not a FontUIResource.
Overrides: setFont in class JComponent.

public void setLeafIcon(Icon newIcon)
Sets the icon used to represent nodes which cannot have child nodes.

public void setOpenIcon(Icon newIcon)
Sets the icon used for nodes that can have child nodes and are expanded.

public void setTextNonSelectionColor(java.awt.Color newColor)
Sets the text color for normal nodes.

public void setTextSelectionColor(java.awt.Color newColor)
Sets the text color for selected nodes.

Protected Fields

protected java.awt.Color backgroundNonSelectionColor
The Color to use for the background when the node isn't selected.

protected java.awt.Color backgroundSelectionColor
The Color to use for the background when a node is selected.

protected java.awt.Color borderSelectionColor
The Color to use for the border when the node is selected.

protected transient Icon closedIcon
The Icon used to show nonleaf nodes that aren't expanded.

protected transient Icon leafIcon
The Icon used to show leaf nodes.

protected transient Icon openIcon
The Icon used to show nonleaf nodes that are expanded.

protected boolean selected
Set to true if the node is selected.

protected java.awt.Color textNonSelectionColor
The Color to use for the foreground of nonselected nodes.

protected java.awt.Color textSelectionColor
The Color to use for the foreground of selected nodes.

See also   ColorUIResource (p.529), FontUIResource (p.533), Icon (p.183), JLabel (p.264), JTree (p.393), TreeCellRenderer (p.985).

swing.tree.DefaultTreeModel

CLASS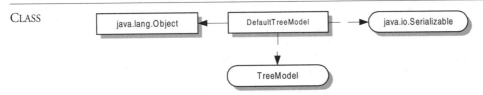

This is a basic implementation of the TreeModel interface.

The easiest way to modify the tree structure is to use insertNodeInto() and remove-NodeFromParent(). These methods ensure that any listeners are notified of changes. If you modify the TreeNode structure directly, you should call one of the nodeXxx() methods (for example, nodeChanged()). These will also notify listeners.

The other feature of this tree model is that it has some control over how "leafness" is defined. Rather than only using node.isLeaf() to determine leafness, it has a flag askAllows-Children that can be used to indicate that node.getAllowsChildren() should be used instead.

```
public class DefaultTreeModel extends java.lang.Object
    implements java.io.Serializable, TreeModel
```

Constructors
```
public DefaultTreeModel(TreeNode root)
public DefaultTreeModel(TreeNode root, boolean asksAllowsChildren)
```
> Creates a tree model from root. Uses askAllowsChildren to decide whether to ask a node if it is a leaf using getAllowsChildren() (if askAllowsChildren is true) or isLeaf() (if false). The default value is false.

Methods
```
public void addTreeModelListener(TreeModelListener listener)
```
> Adds listener to the list of objects to be notified when the tree changes.
> *Implements:* addTreeModelListener in interface TreeModel.

```
public boolean asksAllowsChildren()
```
> Returns true if nodes should be asked if they are children using getAllowsChildren(). Returns false if they should be asked using isLeaf().

```
public Object getChild(Object parent, int index)
```
> Finds the child of node located at index. You must have 0 <= index < getChildCount(node).
> *Implements:* getChild in interface TreeModel.

```
public int getChildCount(Object parent)
```
> Returns the number of children node has.
> *Implements:* getChildCount in interface TreeModel.

```
public int getIndexOfChild(Object parent, Object child)
```
> Gets the index for child (located under parent).
> *Implements:* getIndexOfChild in interface TreeModel.

tree

public TreeNode[] getPathToRoot(TreeNode node)

Returns the path of nodes from the root to node. (The root will be first, node last.)

public Object getRoot()

Gets the root of the tree (set in the constructor).

Implements: getRoot in interface TreeModel.

public void insertNodeInto(MutableTreeNode node,
MutableTreeNode parent, int index)

Inserts node beneath parent at index. After node is inserted, fireTreeNodesInserted() will be called, which will ensure that any listeners are notified of the change.

public boolean isLeaf(Object node)

Returns true if node is a leaf node. If askAllowsChildren is true, this is determined by asking node.getAllowsChildren(); if false, it is determined by node.isLeaf().

Implements: isLeaf in interface TreeModel.

public void nodeChanged(TreeNode node)

Call this method if you change the value of node (for example, its userObject field). This will cause the tree model to notify any of its listeners of the change.

public void nodeStructureChanged(TreeNode node)

Call this method if node has changed structure (for example, by changing its number of children). This will cause the tree model to notify any of its listeners of the change (affecting nodes from node down the tree).

public void nodesChanged(TreeNode node, int[] indices)

Call this method if node's children at indices have changed. (This is like nodeChanged(), but applies to a whole list of nodes.) This will cause the tree model to notify any of its listeners of the change.

public void nodesWereInserted(TreeNode node, int[] indices)

Call this method if node has had children inserted at indices (The indices must be in increasing numeric order.) This will cause the tree model to notify any of its listeners of the change.

public void nodesWereRemoved(TreeNode node, int[] indices, Object[]
removedChildren)

Vall this method if node has had children deleted from the positions indicated by indices. (The indices must be in increasing numeric order.) The nodes are the deleted nodes, in corresponding order to indices. This will cause the tree model to notify any of its listeners of the change.

public void reload()

Call this method to tell the TreeModel that the whole tree (all nodes) may have changed. This will cause the tree model to notify any of its listeners of the change.

public void reload(TreeNode node)

Call this method to tell the TreeModel that the tree has changed from node down. This will cause the tree model to notify any of its listeners of the change.

public void removeNodeFromParent(MutableTreeNode node)

Removes node from the tree. This will cause the tree model to notify any of its listeners of the change. Use this method instead of modifying the TreeNode structure directly, since this method sends the correct event to all listeners.

public void removeTreeModelListener(TreeModelListener l)

Removes listener from the list of objects to be notified of changes in the tree.

Implements: removeTreeModelListener in interface TreeModel.

public void setAsksAllowsChildren(boolean newValue)

Sets how the model determines that a node is a leaf. If `true`, it calls `getAllowsChildren()`; if `false`, it calls `isLeaf()`. *Default:* `false`.

public void setRoot(TreeNode root)

Sets the root of the model to `root`.

Throws: `IllegalArgumentException` if `root` is `null`.

public void valueForPathChanged(TreePath path, Object newValue)

Finds the node identified by path, and sets its `userObject` to `newValue`. It assumes that the node at the end of `path` is a `MutableTreeNode`.

Implements: `valueForPathChanged` in interface `TreeModel`.

Protected Fields

protected boolean asksAllowsChildren

If `true`, the model will ask a `TreeNode` whether it has children using the `getAllowsChildren()` method. If `false`, the model will ask a `TreeNode` whether it has children by using `isLeaf()`. *Default:* `false`.

protected EventListenerList listenerList

The list of listeners to be notified of tree changes.

protected TreeNode root

The root node of the tree for which this is the model.

Protected Methods

protected void fireTreeNodesChanged(Object source, Object[] path, int[] childIndices, Object[] children)

For each listener, calls its `treeNodesChanged()` method. (This requires the `source`, `path`, indexes, and `children` values.) This is called when the values of nodes have changed.

protected void fireTreeNodesInserted(Object source, Object[] path, int[] childIndices, Object[] children)

For each listener, calls its `treeNodesInserted()` method. (This requires the `source`, `path`, indexes, and `children` values.) This is called when nodes are inserted.

protected void fireTreeNodesRemoved(Object source, Object[] path, int[] childIndices, Object[] children)

For each listener, calls its `treeNodesRemoved()` method. (This requires the `source`, `path`, indexes, and `children` values.) This is called when nodes are removed.

protected void fireTreeStructureChanged(Object source, Object[] path, int[] childIndices, Object[] children)

For each listener, calls its `treeStructureChanged()` method. (This requires the `source`, `path`, indexes, and `children` values.) This is called when the tree structure is changed.

protected TreeNode[] getPathToRoot(TreeNode node, int depth)

This is an auxiliary method used by the public `getPathToRoot()`. It finds the path for node, storing the node at `offsetFromRight` (from the right), and calls the method on node's parent to fill in the rest of the array.

See also   EventListenerList (p.491), MutableTreeNode (p.984), TreeModel (p.987), TreeNode (p.988), TreePath (p.989).

swing.tree.DefaultTreeSelectionModel

CLASS

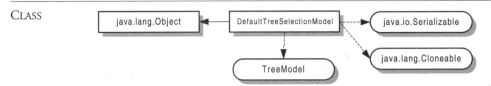

Simple implementation of `TreeSelectionModel`. Listeners of this model are only notified when *paths* in the selection change, not the rows as you might expect. Remember that this class is for selection in the `Model` and rows only make sense in a `View` of a tree. If you wish to keep track of selection changes on a row-by-row basis, you should also listen for `TreeExpansionEvents`.

A tree path is an array of `Objects` representing the `TreeNodes` from the root of the tree to the selected node.

public class DefaultTreeSelectionModel extends java.lang.Object
    implements java.lang.Cloneable, java.io.Serializable,
    TreeSelectionModel

Fields
public static final String SELECTION_MODE_PROPERTY = "selectionMode"
    Property name for `selectionMode`.

Constructors
public DefaultTreeSelectionModel()
    Constructs a selection model without a selection. The default selection mode is `DISCONTIGUOUS_TREE_SELECTION`.

Methods
public synchronized void addPropertyChangeListener(
    java.beans.PropertyChangeListener listener)
    Adds a `PropertyChangeListener`. The only property in this class is the `selectionMode`.
    Implements: addPropertyChangeListener in interface `TreeSelectionModel`.
public void addSelectionPath(TreePath path)
    Adds the given `path` to the current selection set, or replaces the current selection with `path`, depending on the selection mode. If this `path` was not selected already, the `TreeSelectionListeners` will be informed.
    Implements: addSelectionPath in interface `TreeSelectionModel`.
public void addSelectionPaths(TreePath[] paths)
    Adds the given `paths` to the selection. If the selection mode is `SINGLE_TREE_SELECTION`, the first path in the given array is made the new selection. If the selection mode is `CONTIGUOUS_TREE_SELECTION` and the paths are not contiguous, the first path in the given array is made the new selection. If this method changes the selection, the `TreeSelectionListeners` are notified.
    Implements: addSelectionPaths in interface `TreeSelectionModel`.
public void addTreeSelectionListener(TreeSelectionListener x)
    Adds a `TreeSelectionListener`.

tree

Implements: `addTreeSelectionListener` in interface `TreeSelectionModel`.

`public void clearSelection()`

Removes any selection. If this method changes the selection, the `TreeSelectionListeners` are notified.

Implements: `clearSelection` in interface `TreeSelectionModel`.

`public Object clone() throws CloneNotSupportedException`

Returns a duplicate of this object. Listener lists are not copied to the new object, but the selection and selection mode are.

Throws: `CloneNotSupportedException` if a subclass overrides this method to throw it.

Overrides: `clone` in class `Object`.

`public TreePath getLeadSelectionPath()`

Returns the last path that was added to the selection.

Implements: `getLeadSelectionPath` in interface `TreeSelectionModel`.

`public int getLeadSelectionRow()`

Returns the row index of the last path that was added to the selection.

Implements: `getLeadSelectionRow` in interface `TreeSelectionModel`.

`public int getMaxSelectionRow()`

Returns the row in the selection with the highest index.

Implements: `getMaxSelectionRow` in interface `TreeSelectionModel`.

`public int getMinSelectionRow()`

Returns the row in the selection with the lowest index.

Implements: `getMinSelectionRow` in interface `TreeSelectionModel`.

`public RowMapper getRowMapper()`

Returns an object that can be used to map from a path to a row index.

Implements: `getRowMapper` in interface `TreeSelectionModel`.

`public int getSelectionCount()`

Returns the number of paths that are selected.

Implements: `getSelectionCount` in interface `TreeSelectionModel`.

`public int getSelectionMode()`

Returns the selection mode.

Implements: `getSelectionMode` in interface `TreeSelectionModel`.

`public TreePath getSelectionPath()`

Returns the first path in the selection.

Implements: `getSelectionPath` in interface `TreeSelectionModel`.

`public TreePath[] getSelectionPaths()`

Returns the paths in the selection.

Implements: `getSelectionPaths` in interface `TreeSelectionModel`.

`public int[] getSelectionRows()`

Returns all of the currently selected row indices.

Implements: `getSelectionRows` in interface `TreeSelectionModel`.

`public boolean isPathSelected(TreePath path)`

Returns `true` if the path is in the selection.

Implements: `isPathSelected` in interface `TreeSelectionModel`.

`public boolean isRowSelected(int row)`

Returns `true` if the row is selected.

Implements: `isRowSelected` in interface `TreeSelectionModel`.

public boolean isSelectionEmpty()

Returns true if nothing is selected.

Implements: isSelectionEmpty in interface TreeSelectionModel.

public synchronized void removePropertyChangeListener(
java.beans.PropertyChangeListener listener)

Removes a PropertyChangeListener from the listener list. This removes a PropertyChange-Listener that was registered for all properties.

Implements: removePropertyChangeListener in interface TreeSelectionModel.

public void removeSelectionPath(TreePath path)

Removes path from the selection. If path is in the selection (and is therefore removed), the Tree-SelectionListeners are notified.

Implements: removeSelectionPath in interface TreeSelectionModel.

public void removeSelectionPaths(TreePath[] paths)

Removes paths from the selection. If any of the paths in paths are in the selection, the TreeSe-lectionListeners are notified.

Implements: removeSelectionPaths in interface TreeSelectionModel.

public void removeTreeSelectionListener(TreeSelectionListener x)

Removes x from the list of listeners that are notified each time the selection changes.

Implements: removeTreeSelectionListener in interface TreeSelectionModel.

public void resetRowSelection()

Uses the RowMapper to recalculate the selected row indices—for example, after a node is expanded or collapsed.

Implements: resetRowSelection in interface TreeSelectionModel.

public void setRowMapper(RowMapper newMapper)

Sets the RowMapper to use.

Implements: setRowMapper in interface TreeSelectionModel.

public void setSelectionMode(int mode)

Sets the selection mode, which must be one of SINGLE_TREE_SELECTION, CONTIGUOUS_TREE_SELECTION, or DISCONTIGUOUS_TREE_SELECTION.

Implements: setSelectionMode in interface TreeSelectionModel.

public void setSelectionPath(TreePath path)

Sets the selection to path. If this changes the selection, then the TreeSelectionListeners are notified.

Implements: setSelectionPath in interface TreeSelectionModel.

public void setSelectionPaths(TreePath[] paths)

Changes the selection to be the paths in paths. If this changes the selection, the TreeSelection-Listeners are notified. Potentially paths will be held by the receiver; in other words, don't change any of the objects in the array once passed in.

Implements: setSelectionPaths in interface TreeSelectionModel.

public String toString()

Overrides: toString in class Object.

Protected Fields

protected PropertyChangeSupport changeSupport

Maintains the list of registered PropertyChange listeners.

protected int leadIndex
The index of the lead path in the selection.
protected TreePath leadPath
The last path that was added to the selection.
protected int leadRow
The first row in the selection.
protected DefaultListSelectionModel listSelectionModel
Maintains the `ListSelectionModel` which masquerades as the `TreeSelectionModel`.
protected EventListenerList listenerList
Maintains the list of `TreeSelectionListeners`.
protected transient RowMapper rowMapper
Given a path, this class is used to return a row index.
protected TreePath[] selection
The list of paths that are currently selected in the tree, which may be `null`.
protected int selectionMode
The mode for the selection, which is SINGLE_TREE_SELECTION, CONTIGUOUS_TREE_SELEC-TION, or DISCONTIGUOUS_TREE_SELECTION.

Protected Methods
protected boolean arePathsContiguous(TreePath[] paths)
Returns `true` if the paths are contiguous.
protected boolean canPathsBeAdded(TreePath[] paths)
Returns `true` if the paths can be added without breaking the continuity of the model.
protected boolean canPathsBeRemoved(TreePath[] paths)
Returns `true` if the paths can be removed without breaking the continuity of the model. This is rather expensive.
protected void fireValueChanged(TreeSelectionEvent e)
Notifies listeners that the selection has changed.
protected void insureRowContinuity()
Makes sure the selected paths are represented by contiguous row indices.
protected void insureUniqueness()
Makes sure there aren't any duplicate entries in the selection.
protected void notifyPathChange(java.util.Vector changedPaths, TreePath oldLeadSelection)
Notifies listeners of a change in `changedPaths`. The `changedPaths` parameter should contain instances of `PathPlaceHolder`, which is a package-protection inner class.
protected void updateLeadIndex()
Updates the `leadIndex` instance variable.

Extended by   JTree.EmptySelectionModel (p.393).
See also   RowMapper (p.984), TreePath (p.989), TreeSelectionListener (p.514), TreeSelectionModel (p.990).

swing.tree.ExpandVetoException

CLASS

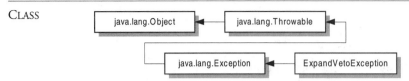

`TreeWillExpandListeners` can throw this exception to veto the expansion of a node.

public class ExpandVetoException extends java.lang.Exception

Constructors
public ExpandVetoException(TreeExpansionEvent event)
Constructs an `ExpandVetoException` object with no message.
public ExpandVetoException(TreeExpansionEvent event, String message)
Constructs an `ExpandVetoException` object with the specified `message`.

Protected Fields
protected TreeExpansionEvent event
The event that the exception was created for.

Thrown by   JTree.fireTreeWillCollapse() (p.393), JTree.fireTreeWillExpand() (p.393),
TreeWillExpandListener.treeWillCollapse() (p.515),
TreeWillExpandListener.treeWillExpand() (p.515).
See also   TreeExpansionEvent (p.511), TreeWillExpandListener (p.515).

swing.tree.FixedHeightLayoutCache

CLASS

A concrete implementation of `AbstractLayoutCache` for use with trees that have fixed height cells. A tree with fixed height cells is considerably more efficient than a variable height cell tree.

public class FixedHeightLayoutCache extends AbstractLayoutCache

Constructors
public FixedHeightLayoutCache()
Constructs a default layout cache for a tree with fixed height nodes.

Methods
public java.awt.Rectangle getBounds(TreePath path,
    java.awt.Rectangle placeIn)
Returns the bounding rectangle for `path` when rendered into `placeIn`.
Overrides: getBounds in class AbstractLayoutCache.
public boolean getExpandedState(TreePath path)
Returns `true` if all nodes in `path` are expanded.

Overrides: getExpandedState in class AbstractLayoutCache.

public TreePath getPathClosestTo(int x, int y)

Returns the path to the node that is *closest* to (x, y). Note the emphasis on closest; the node returned may not actually contain the point.

Overrides: getPathClosestTo in class AbstractLayoutCache.

public TreePath getPathForRow(int row)

Returns the path that leads to the given row index.

Overrides: getPathForRow in class AbstractLayoutCache.

public int getRowCount()

Returns the number of rows.

Overrides: getRowCount in class AbstractLayoutCache.

public int getRowForPath(TreePath path)

Returns the row index of the node at the end of path. If any part of path is not expanded, this method will return −1.

Overrides: getRowForPath in class AbstractLayoutCache.

public int getVisibleChildCount(TreePath path)

Returns the number of visible children that the node at the end of path has.

Overrides: getVisibleChildCount in class AbstractLayoutCache.

public java.awt.Enumeration getVisiblePathsFrom(TreePath path)

Returns an Enumeration which will return paths to all visible nodes starting at the given path.

Overrides: getVisiblePathsFrom in class AbstractLayoutCache.

public void invalidatePathBounds(TreePath path)

An empty method, because it doesn't apply to a fixed height cell tree.

Overrides: invalidatePathBounds in class AbstractLayoutCache.

public void invalidateSizes()

Calls visibleNodesChanged().

Overrides: invalidateSizes in class AbstractLayoutCache.

public boolean isExpanded(TreePath path)

Returns true if the node at the end of path is currently expanded.

Overrides: isExpanded in class AbstractLayoutCache.

public void setExpandedState(TreePath path, boolean isExpanded)

Changes the node at the end of path's expansion state to isExpanded.

Overrides: setExpandedState in class AbstractLayoutCache.

public void setModel(TreeModel newModel)

Sets the associated TreeModel.

Overrides: setModel in class AbstractLayoutCache.

public void setRootVisible(boolean rootVisible)

Changes whether the root node is shown.

Overrides: setRootVisible in class AbstractLayoutCache.

public void setRowHeight(int rowHeight)

Sets the height of the cells in the tree.

Throws: IllegalArgumentException if rowHeight is less than one.

Overrides: setRowHeight in class AbstractLayoutCache.

public void treeNodesChanged(TreeModelEvent e)

Overrides: treeNodesChanged in class AbstractLayoutCache.

tree

```
public void treeNodesInserted(TreeModelEvent e)
```
  Overrides: treeNodesInserted in class AbstractLayoutCache.
```
public void treeNodesRemoved(TreeModelEvent e)
```
  Overrides: treeNodesRemoved in class AbstractLayoutCache.
```
public void treeStructureChanged(TreeModelEvent e)
```
  Overrides: treeStructureChanged in class AbstractLayoutCache.

  See also AbstractLayoutCache (p.958), TreeModel (p.987), TreeModelEvent (p.511), TreePath (p.989).

swing.tree.MutableTreeNode

INTERFACE

A mutable tree node is a tree node that allows changes. (The TreeNode interface provides read-only access.) The mutable node also provides a user object: a field that can be set by the user of the node.

```
public interface MutableTreeNode extends TreeNode
```

Methods
```
public abstract void insert(MutableTreeNode node, int index)
```
  Inserts node as the new child at index. The node is notified of this change using setParent().
```
public abstract void remove(MutableTreeNode node)
```
  Removes node from the tree. The node is notified of its new (null) parent using setParent().
```
public abstract void remove(int index)
```
  Removes the child at position index from the node implementing this method.
```
public abstract void removeFromParent()
```
  Removes this node from its parent node.
```
public abstract void setParent(MutableTreeNode newParent)
```
  Notifies this node of its new parent newParent.
```
public abstract void setUserObject(Object object)
```
  Sets the user object for this node. (This provides a place to put your own content into a node.) Unfortunately, the corresponding getUserObject() method is in the DefaultMutable-TreeNode class.

  Implemented by DefaultMutableTreeNode (p.961).
  See also TreeNode (p.988).

swing.tree.RowMapper

INTERFACE   RowMapper

This class is used by TreeSelectionModels and subclasses of AbstractLayoutCache to map from paths to rows. (This way, given a selected path, they can highlight the corresponding row.)

tree

```
public interface RowMapper
```

Methods

```
public abstract int[] getRowsForPaths(TreePath[] paths)
```
Converts paths to their corresponding row number. Returns an array, for which each entry corresponds to the row position of the entry in `paths`. (Thus, the two arrays have the same length.) If one of the paths is not currently displayed, its row number is −1.

Returned by   DefaultTreeSelectionModel.getRowMapper() (p.978),
TreeSelectionModel.getRowMapper() (p.990).
Implemented by   AbstractLayoutCache (p.958).
See also   TreePath (p.989), TreeSelectionModel (p.990).

swing.tree.TreeCellEditor

INTERFACE

This interface describes how to edit a row in a `JTree`. To create a custom editor, implement this interface, and establish the editor in the tree with the `JTree.setCellEditor()` method.

This interface extends `CellEditor`; see that class for other methods.

```
public interface TreeCellEditor extends CellEditor
```

Methods

```
public abstract java.awt.Component getTreeCellEditorComponent(
    JTree tree, Object value, boolean isSelected, boolean isExpanded,
    boolean isLeaf, int row)
```
Returns a component that can act as an editor for this cell. The cell is from `tree` (which may be `null`), and has initial value `value`. The flags tell whether the tree node is selected, expanded, or a leaf. The `row` is the row number in the tree display.

Returned by   BasicTreeUI.createDefaultCellEditor() (p.710),
BasicTreeUI.getCellEditor() (p.710), DefaultTreeCellEditor.createTreeCellEditor() (p.968),
JTree.getCellEditor() (p.393).
Implemented by   DefaultCellEditor (p.164), DefaultTreeCellEditor (p.968).
See also   CellEditor (p.150), JTree (p.393).

swing.tree.TreeCellRenderer

INTERFACE   TreeCellRenderer

This interface describes how to display a row in a `JTree` (p.393). To create a custom renderer, implement this interface, and establish the renderer in the tree with the `JTree.setCellRenderer()` method.

Example: Show value and type

```java
package treecr;
import java.awt.*;
import java.awt.event.*;
import com.sun.java.swing.*;
import com.sun.java.swing.tree.*;

public class Main extends JFrame {
    public Main() {
        addWindowListener(new WindowAdapter() {
            public void windowClosing(WindowEvent e)
            {
                Main.this.dispose();
                System.exit(0);
            }
        });

        // Create a few nodes for the tree
        DefaultMutableTreeNode root = new DefaultMutableTreeNode("+");
        root.add(new DefaultMutableTreeNode(new Integer(3)));
        DefaultMutableTreeNode node = new DefaultMutableTreeNode("*");
        node.add(new DefaultMutableTreeNode("string"));
        node.add(new DefaultMutableTreeNode(new Short((short)5)));
        root.add(node);

        // Build TreeModel from nodes, and JTree from the TreeModel.
        // Display JTree.
        TreeModel tm = new DefaultTreeModel(root);
        JTree tree = new JTree(tm);
        tree.setShowsRootHandles(true);
        tree.setCellRenderer(new DemoRenderer());
        getContentPane().add(tree, BorderLayout.CENTER);
        setSize(400,300);
        setVisible(true);
    }

    // This renderer displays the type of the node as well as the value
    // You would probably want to add icons and set colors depending on
    // the flags.
    // (As it stands, there will be few visual clues for how to treat the node.)
    private class DemoRenderer extends JLabel implements TreeCellRenderer {
        public Component getTreeCellRendererComponent(JTree tree, Object value,
            boolean isSelected, boolean isExpanded, boolean isLeaf,
            int row, boolean hasFocus)
        {
            Object userObject = ((DefaultMutableTreeNode)value).getUserObject();
            setText(value.toString() + " [" + userObject.getClass().getName() +
                "]");
            return this;
        }
    }

    public static void main(String[] args) {
        Main m = new Main();
    }
}
```

public interface TreeCellRenderer

Methods
public abstract java.awt.Component getTreeCellRendererComponent(
    swing.JTree tree, Object value, boolean isSelected, boolean isExpanded,
    boolean isLeaf, int row, boolean hasFocus)

Returns a component that can act as an editor for this cell. The cell is from `tree` (which may be `null`), and has initial value `value`. The flags tell whether the tree node is selected, expanded, a leaf, or has the focus. The `row` is the row number in the tree display.

Returned by BasicTreeUI.createDefaultCellRenderer() (p.710),
BasicTreeUI.getCellRenderer() (p.710), JTree.getCellRenderer() (p.393).
Implemented by DefaultTreeCellRenderer (p.972).
See also JTree (p.393).

swing.tree.TreeModel

INTERFACE   (TreeModel)

This interface defines what it means to be a tree. The `JTree` class uses a `TreeModel` as its data model. See `DefaultTreeModel` and `DefaultMutableTreeNode` for an example of how to define your own tree.

public interface TreeModel

Methods
public abstract void addTreeModelListener(TreeModelListener l)

Adds `listener` to the list of objects to be notified when the tree model changes.

public abstract Object getChild(Object parent, int index)

Returns the child of `parent` at position `index`. The `parent` must have been obtained from this `TreeModel`.

public abstract int getChildCount(Object parent)

Returns the number of children that `parent` has. The `parent` must have been obtained from this `TreeModel`.

public abstract int getIndexOfChild(Object parent, Object child)

Returns the index position of `child` (contained in `parent`).

public abstract Object getRoot()

Returns the root node of the tree. (Its value is `null` only if the tree is empty.)

public abstract boolean isLeaf(Object node)

Returns `true` if `node` is a leaf. A leaf will never have children, but a node with no children is not necessarily a leaf. For example, a directory folder might be empty, but it could be later be filled, so we might not want to regard it as a leaf. (In contrast, in an expression tree the operators are never leaves, and the values are always leaves.)

public abstract void removeTreeModelListener(TreeModelListener l)

Removes `listener` from the list of objects to be notified of changes in the tree's data model. See also `addTreeModelListener`.

public abstract void valueForPathChanged(TreePath path, Object newValue)
   Tells the model that the node at the end of `path` has changed to `value`. If this is a change in the tree, listeners should be notified.

   Returned by   AbstractLayoutCache.getModel() (p.958), BasicTreeUI.getModel() (p.710), JTree.createTreeModel() (p.393), JTree.getDefaultTreeModel() (p.393), JTree.getModel() (p.393).
   Implemented by   DefaultTreeModel (p.975).
   See also   TreeModelListener (p.513), TreePath (p.989).

swing.tree.TreeNode

INTERFACE   ⊂ TreeNode ⊃

A node in a tree. The node is assumed to know most of the useful information needed to support the `TreeModel` interface. This interface provides read-only access to the tree. For nodes that can be changed, see `MutableTreeNode`.

public interface TreeNode

Methods
public abstract java.util.Enumeration children()
   Returns the list of all children of this node.
public abstract boolean getAllowsChildren()
   Returns `true` if the node can have children.
public abstract TreeNode getChildAt(int index)
   Returns the child of the node, at the specified `index`.
public abstract int getChildCount()
   Returns the number of children of the node.
public abstract int getIndex(TreeNode node)
   Returns the index of `node` in the list of children. (Returns –1 if `node` is not a child of the node.)
public abstract TreeNode getParent()
   Returns the parent of the current node.
public abstract boolean isLeaf()
   Returns `true` if this is a leaf node.

   Returned by   AbstractDocument.AbstractElement.getChildAt() (p.783), AbstractDocument.AbstractElement.getParent() (p.783), DefaultMutableTreeNode.getChildAfter() (p.961), DefaultMutableTreeNode.getChildAt() (p.961), DefaultMutableTreeNode.getChildBefore() (p.961), DefaultMutableTreeNode.getFirstChild() (p.961), DefaultMutableTreeNode.getLastChild() (p.961), DefaultMutableTreeNode.getParent() (p.961), DefaultMutableTreeNode.getPath() (p.961), DefaultMutableTreeNode.getPathToRoot() (p.961), DefaultMutableTreeNode.getRoot() (p.961), DefaultMutableTreeNode.getSharedAncestor() (p.961),

DefaultTreeModel.getPathToRoot() (p.975), JTree.DynamicUtilTreeNode.getChildAt() (p.407), TreeNode.getChildAt() (p.988), TreeNode.getParent() (p.988).
Extended by   MutableTreeNode (p.984).
See also   TreeModel (p.987).

swing.tree.TreePath

A `TreePath` identifies the path as a series of nodes from a root to a node. Each node in the list is the parent of the following node.

The objects making up the path should be regarded as abstract; a tree model could put anything in the array (provided it can use it again to locate the actual path). For `DefaultTree-Model`, the path is what you'd expect: a list of nodes from the root to the selected node.

Note that the path is marked serializable. It will truly be serializable only if the objects in the path array are serializable as well.

```
public class TreePath extends java.lang.Object
    implements java.io.Serializable
```

Constructors
public TreePath(Object singlePath)
public TreePath(Object[] path)
Creates a path object. The parameters may specify that this is a single node, or may provide some representation of the path as an array.

Methods
public boolean equals(Object o)
Returns `true` if the paths are equal (have the same length and the same components).
Overrides: `equals` in class `Object`.
public Object getLastPathComponent()
Returns the last component in the path.
public Object[] getPath()
Returns the array representation of the path (meaningful to the path's creator). See the constructors.
public Object getPathComponent(int index)
Returns the component at `index`. You should have `0 <= index < getPathCount()`.
Throws: `IllegalArgumentException` if the element is beyond the length of the path.
public int getPathCount()
Returns the number of items in the path.
public int hashCode()
Returns a hash value for the path.
public boolean isDescendant(TreePath path)
Returns `true` if `path` is descended from this object. (If paths are represented as arrays of nodes, this can be determined by comparing the arrays for common nodes.)

```
public String toString()
```
Overrides: toString in class Object.

Protected Constructors
```
protected TreePath()
```
Provided for the use of subclasses.
```
protected TreePath(TreePath parent, Object lastElement)
```
Constructs a TreePath by joining parent with lastElement.

See also DefaultTreeModel (p.975).

swing.tree.TreeSelectionModel

INTERFACE   (TreeSelectionModel)

This class tracks the selection in a tree. The selection is managed as a set of paths. You can find out the selection either as a path or a row index. The last selection added is known as the lead selection; see getLeadSelectionPath().

Example

```
package treesm;

import java.awt.*;
import java.awt.event.*;
import com.sun.java.swing.*;
import com.sun.java.swing.event.*;
import com.sun.java.swing.tree.*;

public class Main extends JFrame {
  JTextField text = new JTextField(10);

  public Main() {
    addWindowListener(new WindowAdapter() {
      public void windowClosing(WindowEvent e) {
        Main.this.dispose();
        System.exit(0);
      }
    });
    // Create a tree with several nodes
    DefaultMutableTreeNode root = new DefaultMutableTreeNode("abcde");
    DefaultMutableTreeNode node = new DefaultMutableTreeNode("1");
    node.add(new DefaultMutableTreeNode("12345"));
    node.add(new DefaultMutableTreeNode("testing"));
    root.add(node);
    root.add(new DefaultMutableTreeNode("1234567890"));

    // Build TreeModel from nodes, and JTree from the TreeModel.
    // Display JTree.
    TreeModel tm = new DefaultTreeModel(root);
    JTree tree = new JTree(tm);
    tree.getSelectionModel().addTreeSelectionListener(new Selector());
```

```
      tree.getSelectionModel().setSelectionMode(
                           TreeSelectionModel.SINGLE_TREE_SELECTION);
      getContentPane().add(tree, BorderLayout.CENTER);

      // Create a JTextField and put it in South.
      JPanel panel = new JPanel();
      panel.add(new JLabel("Size of node's string: "));
      panel.add(text);
      getContentPane().add(panel, BorderLayout.SOUTH);
      pack();
      setVisible(true);
   }
   private class Selector implements TreeSelectionListener {
      public void valueChanged(TreeSelectionEvent event) {
         Object obj = event.getNewLeadSelectionPath().getLastPathComponent();
         text.setText("" + obj.toString().length());
      }
   }
   public static void main(String[] args) {
      Main m = new Main();
   }
}
```

public interface TreeSelectionModel

Constants

public static final int CONTIGUOUS_TREE_SELECTION = 2
public static final int DISCONTIGUOUS_TREE_SELECTION = 4
public static final int SINGLE_TREE_SELECTION = 1

Defines the type of selection: either a range of rows (CONTIGUOUS_TREE_SELECTION), an arbitrary selection (DISCONTIGUOUS_TREE_SELECTION), or a single selection only (SINGLE_TREE_SELECTION). See getSelectionMode() and setSelectionMode().

Methods

public abstract void addPropertyChangeListener(
java.beans.PropertyChangeListener listener)

Adds listener to the list of objects to be notified when a property changes on the tree: font, background, or foreground.

public abstract void addSelectionPath(TreePath path)

Adds path to the selection. If path was not already in the selection, notifies any selection listeners.

public abstract void addSelectionPaths(TreePath[] paths)

Adds the paths to the selection. If any of them are new to the selection, notifies any selection listeners.

public abstract void addTreeSelectionListener(
TreeSelectionListener listener)

Adds listener to the list of objects to be notified when the selection changes.

public abstract void clearSelection()

Removes all paths from the selection. If this is a change, notifies any selection listeners.

public abstract TreePath getLeadSelectionPath()

Returns the path of the last selected node. (See also getLeadSelectionRow().)

public abstract int getLeadSelectionRow()

Returns the row index of the last selected node. (See also `getLeadSelectionPath()`.)

public abstract int getMaxSelectionRow()

Gets the maximum row index in the selection.

public abstract int getMinSelectionRow()

Gets the least row index in the selection.

public abstract RowMapper getRowMapper()

Returns the mapper that converts paths to row indexes..

public abstract int getSelectionCount()

Gets the number of paths in the selection.

public abstract int getSelectionMode()

Returns the selection style: `CONTIGUOUS_TREE_SELECTION`, `DISCONTIGUOUS_TREE_SELEC-TION`, or `SINGLE_TREE_SELECTION`.

public abstract TreePath getSelectionPath()

Returns the first path in the selection.

public abstract TreePath[] getSelectionPaths()

Returns all paths in the selection.

public abstract int[] getSelectionRows()

Returns the row indexes of all paths in the selection.

public abstract boolean isPathSelected(TreePath path)

Returns `true` if `path` is in the selection.

public abstract boolean isRowSelected(int row)

Returns `true` if the row at `index` is in the selection.

public abstract boolean isSelectionEmpty()

Returns `true` if nothing is selected.

public abstract void removePropertyChangeListener(
java.beans.PropertyChangeListener listener)

Removes `listener` from the list of objects to be notified of property changes.

public abstract void removeSelectionPath(TreePath path)

If `path` is in the selection, removes it from the selection and notifies any selection listeners.

public abstract void removeSelectionPaths(TreePath[] paths)

If `paths` are in the selection, removes them and notifies any selection listeners of the change.

public abstract void removeTreeSelectionListener(TreeSelectionListener x)

Removes `listener` from the list of nodes to be notified of selection changes.

public abstract void resetRowSelection()

Calls this method if the row indices of the selection changed, but the paths are the same. (The row indices will be remapped.)

public abstract void setRowMapper(RowMapper newMapper)

Sets the mapper that converts paths to row indexes.

public abstract void setSelectionMode(int mode)

Sets the selection style: `CONTIGUOUS_TREE_SELECTION`, `DISCONTIGUOUS_TREE_SELECTION`, or `SINGLE_TREE_SELECTION`.

public abstract void setSelectionPath(TreePath path)

Makes the selection consist only of `path`. If this changes the selection, notifies any selection listeners of the change.

public abstract void setSelectionPaths(TreePath[] paths)

Sets the selection to consist of all and only those paths in `paths`. If this changes the selection, notifies any selection listeners of the change.

Returned by   AbstractLayoutCache.getSelectionModel() (p.958),
BasicTreeUI.getSelectionModel() (p.710), JTree.getSelectionModel() (p.393).
Implemented by   DefaultTreeSelectionModel (p.978).
See also   RowMapper (p.984), TreePath (p.989), TreeSelectionListener (p.514).

swing.tree.VariableHeightLayoutCache

CLASS

A concrete implementation of `AbstractLayoutCache` for trees using variable row heights. See `AbstractLayoutCache` for details of these methods.

public class VariableHeightLayoutCache extends AbstractLayoutCache

Constructors
public VariableHeightLayoutCache()

Methods
public java.awt.Rectangle getBounds(TreePath path,
**   java.awt.Rectangle placeIn)**
Overrides: getBounds in class AbstractLayoutCache.
public boolean getExpandedState(TreePath path)
Overrides: getExpandedState in class AbstractLayoutCache.
public TreePath getPathClosestTo(int x, int y)
Overrides: getPathClosestTo in class AbstractLayoutCache.
public TreePath getPathForRow(int row)
Overrides: getPathForRow in class AbstractLayoutCache.
public int getPreferredWidth(java.awt.Rectangle bounds)
Overrides: getPreferredWidth in class AbstractLayoutCache.
public int getRowCount()
Overrides: getRowCount in class AbstractLayoutCache.
public int getRowForPath(TreePath path)
Overrides: getRowForPath in class AbstractLayoutCache.
public int getVisibleChildCount(TreePath path)
Overrides: getVisibleChildCount in class AbstractLayoutCache.
public java.util.Enumeration getVisiblePathsFrom(TreePath path)
Overrides: getVisiblePathsFrom in class AbstractLayoutCache.
public void invalidatePathBounds(TreePath path)
Overrides: invalidatePathBounds in class AbstractLayoutCache.
public void invalidateSizes()
Overrides: invalidateSizes in class AbstractLayoutCache.

public boolean isExpanded(TreePath path)

    Overrides: isExpanded in class AbstractLayoutCache.

public void setExpandedState(TreePath path, boolean isExpanded)

    Overrides: setExpandedState in class AbstractLayoutCache.

public void setModel(TreeModel newModel)

    Overrides: setModel in class AbstractLayoutCache.

public void setNodeDimensions(NodeDimensions nd)

    Sets the AbstractLayoutCache.NodeDimensions object to use.

public void setRootVisible(boolean rootVisible)

    Overrides: setRootVisible in class AbstractLayoutCache.

public void setRowHeight(int rowHeight)

    Throws: IllegalArgumentException if rowHeight is greater than zero, which would imply wanting a FixedHeightLayoutCache.

    Overrides: setRowHeight in class AbstractLayoutCache.

public void treeNodesChanged(TreeModelEvent e)

    Overrides: treeNodesChanged in class AbstractLayoutCache.

public void treeNodesInserted(TreeModelEvent e)

    Overrides: treeNodesInserted in class AbstractLayoutCache.

public void treeNodesRemoved(TreeModelEvent e)

    Overrides: treeNodesRemoved in class AbstractLayoutCache.

public void treeStructureChanged(TreeModelEvent e)

    Overrides: treeStructureChanged in class AbstractLayoutCache.

See also   AbstractLayoutCache (p.958), AbstractLayoutCache.NodeDimensions (p.961), TreeModelEvent (p.508), TreePath (p.989).

tree

Package swing.undo

Users love Undo. It is extremely rare to have a modern application without Undo, and when it is missing, it is guaranteed to be one of the first enhancements the users of the application ask for.

The Undo support in Swing comes as a result of its being used in the Swing text classes. Fortunately, the Swing team was thoughtful enough to use a generalized set of classes for the support, providing a clean undo/redo framework for all applications to use.

Using the undo support in an application will generally involve creating an appropriate `UndoableEdit` for the data which can be edited. As the model (or models, if there is a `SelectionModel`) representing the data is changed it will issue `UndoableEditEvents` to any listeners, which generally will be a single `UndoManager`. The application will then communicate with the `UndoManager` to display the current information about what can be undone or redone. For example, a menu that had Undo and Redo items would ask the `UndoManager` for the `undoPresentationName` and `redoPresentationName` whenever the menu was about to be shown. In response to a user choice, the application can then call the `undo()` or `redo()` methods on the `UndoManager` as appropriate.

undo

Undo extends/implements hierarchy

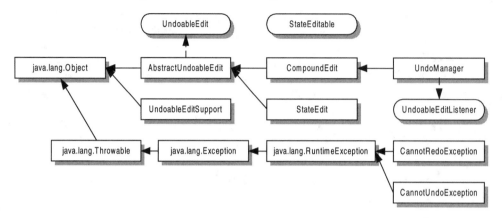

Quick summary

Main classes	`UndoManager` (p.1008), which maintains a list of `UndoableEdits` (p.1005). `AbstractUndoableEdit` (p.998), from which you can derive your own `UndoableEdits`.
Main interface	`UndoableEditListener` (p.516), which should be implemented by the class that wants to manage the undos.
How to use	Have a class implement `UndoableEditListener`.
Other	`UndoableEditSupport` (p.1006). `StateEditable` (p.1004), an interface which supports the `StateEdit` (p.1003) class. `CompoundEdit` (p.1001), which treats several edits as if they were one.

FAQs

How do I support Undo in my application?

Create an instance of `UndoManager` and have it listen for `UndoableEditEvents` from the model you want to support undo/redo. Use the information from the `UndoManager` to update the choices your application presents to the user. When the user chooses to perform an undo or redo, call the appropriate method on the `UndoManager`.

Example: Supporting Undo in an editor using a `JTextPane`.

```
// File undoexample\UndoEditor.java
package undoexample;

import java.awt.*;
import java.awt.event.*;
import com.sun.java.swing.*;
import com.sun.java.swing.undo.*;
import com.sun.java.swing.event.*;

public class UndoEditor extends JFrame {
    private UndoManager undoManager = new UndoManager();
    private JMenuBar menuBar = new JMenuBar();
```

```
private JMenu editMenu = new JMenu("Edit");
private UndoAction undoAction = new UndoAction();
private RedoAction redoAction = new RedoAction();

public UndoEditor() {
  this.addWindowListener(new WindowAdapter() {
    public void windowClosed(WindowEvent e) {
      System.exit(0);
    }
  });
  this.getContentPane().setLayout(new BorderLayout());
  this.setDefaultCloseOperation(JFrame.DISPOSE_ON_CLOSE);

  JTextPane editor = new JTextPane();
  // Add 'this' as a listener for undoable edits.
  editor.getDocument().addUndoableEditListener(new UndoListener());

  JScrollPane scroller = new JScrollPane(editor);
  editMenu.setMnemonic('e');
  menuBar.add(editMenu);
  JMenuItem undoMenu = editMenu.add(undoAction);
  undoMenu.setMnemonic('u');
  undoMenu.setAccelerator(KeyStroke.getKeyStroke(KeyEvent.VK_U,
                           Event.CTRL_MASK));
  JMenuItem redoMenu = editMenu.add(redoAction);
  redoMenu.setMnemonic('r');
  redoMenu.setAccelerator(KeyStroke.getKeyStroke(KeyEvent.VK_R,
                           Event.CTRL_MASK));
  this.setJMenuBar(menuBar);
  this.getContentPane().add(scroller);
}
public static void main(String[] args) {
  UndoEditor e = new UndoEditor();
  e.setSize(400,300);
  e.setVisible(true);
}
class UndoListener implements UndoableEditListener {
  public void undoableEditHappened(UndoableEditEvent e) {
    undoManager.addEdit(e.getEdit());
    undoAction.update();
    redoAction.update();
  }
} // end inner class UndoListener

class UndoAction extends AbstractAction {
  public UndoAction() {
    this.putValue(Action.NAME, undoManager.getUndoPresentationName());
    this.setEnabled(false);
  }

  public void actionPerformed(ActionEvent e) {
    if (this.isEnabled()) {
      undoManager.undo();
      // Must update the actions now since undo() does not create an
      // UndoableEditEvent for its change.
      undoAction.update();
```

undo

```
            redoAction.update();
        }
    }
    public void update() {
        this.putValue(Action.NAME, undoManager.getUndoPresentationName());
        this.setEnabled(undoManager.canUndo());
    }
} // end inner class UndoAction
class RedoAction extends AbstractAction {
    public RedoAction() {
        this.putValue(Action.NAME, undoManager.getRedoPresentationName());
        this.setEnabled(false);
    }
    public void actionPerformed(ActionEvent e) {
        if (this.isEnabled()) {
            undoManager.redo();
            // Must update the actions now since redo() does not create an
            // UndoableEditEvent for its change.
            undoAction.update();
            redoAction.update();
        }
    }
    public void update() {
        this.putValue(Action.NAME, undoManager.getRedoPresentationName());
        this.setEnabled(undoManager.canRedo());
    }
} // end inner class RedoAction
}
```

How do I create a custom UndoableEdit?

There are two ways to do this. The quicker way is to make your model `StateEditable` and use the `StateEdit` class. The more efficient way is to create a subclass of `AbstractUndoableEdit` to represent the changes that can happen to the data in your model.

swing.undo.AbstractUndoableEdit

CLASS

An implementation of `UndoableEdit` which provides default implementations for all of the methods. Subclasses will override `undo()` and `redo()` to provide the correct behavior. Subclasses should also override `getPresentationName()` to return a localized string describing the type of change that can be undone or redone.

```
public class AbstractUndoableEdit implements UndoableEdit
```

Constructors

public AbstractUndoableEdit()

Default constructor.

Methods

public boolean addEdit(UndoableEdit anEdit)

This default implementation returns false, which means that anEdit will not be merged with this UndoableEdit.

Implements: addEdit in interface UndoableEdit.

public boolean canRedo()

Returns true if this UndoableEdit has not had die() called on it and hasBeenDone is false.

Implements: canRedo() in interface UndoableEdit.

public boolean canUndo()

Returns true if this UndoableEdit has not had die() called on it and hasBeenDone is true.

Implements: canUndo() in interface UndoableEdit.

public void die()

Sets alive to false. Once this method has been called, this UndoableEdit cannot be used. Attempting to call undo() or redo() after calling die() causes a CannotUndoException or CannotRedoException to be thrown. Call this method when merging this UndoableEdit with another using addEdit() or replaceEdit(), or when removing the UndoableEdit from an UndoManager.

Implements: die() in interface UndoableEdit.

public String getPresentationName()

This default implementation returns an empty String. Subclasses should override this method to return a localized String describing the edit that can be undone or redone. This method is not usually called directly. The methods getRedoPresentationName() and getUndoPresentationName() call this method so they can return something better than just Undo or Redo.

Implements: getPresentationName in interface UndoableEdit.

public String getRedoPresentationName()

Returns RedoName concatenated with a space and the result of getPresentationName().

Implements: getRedoPresentationName() in interface UndoableEdit.

public String getUndoPresentationName()

Returns UndoName concatenated with a space and the result of getPresentationName().

Implements: getUndoPresentationName() in interface UndoableEdit.

public boolean isSignificant()

Returns true.

Implements: isSignificant() in interface UndoableEdit.

public void redo() throws CannotRedoException

Subclasses will override this method to redo the edit represented by this UndoableEdit. The overriding method should begin with a call to super(). The reason the subclass method should call super() is that this method checks canRedo() to see if the redo is possible and sets hasBeenDone to true if the edit can be redone. If canRedo() returns false, this method throws a CannotRedoException.

Throws: CannotRedoException if canRedo() returns false.

Implements: redo() in interface UndoableEdit.

public boolean replaceEdit(UndoableEdit anEdit)

Returns `false`, indicating that `anEdit` cannot replace this edit.

Implements: `replaceEdit()` in interface `UndoableEdit`.

public String toString()

Overrides: `toString()` in class `java.lang.Object`.

public void undo() throws CannotUndoException

Subclasses will override this method to undo the edit represented by this `UndoableEdit`. The overriding method should begin with a call to `super()`. The reason the subclass method should call `super()` is that this method checks `canUndo()` to see if the undo is possible and sets `hasBeenDone` to `false` if the edit can be undone. If `canUndo()` returns `false`, this method throws a `CannotUndoException`.

Throws: `CannotUndoException` if `canUndo()` returns `false`.

Implements: `undo()` in interface `UndoableEdit`.

Protected Fields

protected static final String RedoName = "Redo"

The string returned by `getRedoPresentationName()`.

protected static final String UndoName = "Undo"

The string returned by `getUndoPresentationName()`.

Extended by   AbstractDocument.ElementEdit (p.790), DefaultStyledDocument.AttributeUndoableEdit (p.823), CompoundEdit (p.1001), StateEdit (p.1003).

See also   CannotRedoException (p.1000), CannotUndoException (p.1001), UndoableEdit (p.1005).

swing.undo.CannotRedoException

CLASS

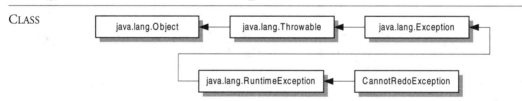

Thrown when `redo()` is called on an `UndoableEdit` and the edit it represents can't be redone.

public class CannotRedoException extends java.lang.RuntimeException

Constructors

public CannotRedoException()

Default constructor.

Thrown by   AbstractDocument.DefaultDocumentEvent.redo() (p.789), AbstractDocument.ElementEdit.redo() (p.790), AbstractUndoableEdit.redo() (p.998), CompoundEdit.redo() (p.1001), DefaultStyledDocument.AttributeUndoableEdit.redo() (p.823), UndoableEdit.redo() (p.1008), UndoManager.redo() (p.1008), UndoManager.redoTo() (p.1008), UndoManager.undoOrRedo() (p.1008).

swing.undo.CannotUndoException

CLASS

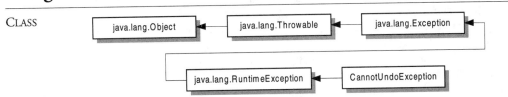

Thrown when undo() is called on an UndoableEdit and the edit it represents can't be undone.

public class CannotUndoException extends java.lang.RuntimeException

Constructors
public CannotUndoException()

Default constructor.

Thrown by   AbstractDocument.DefaultDocumentEvent.undo() (p.789),
AbstractDocument.ElementEdit.undo() (p.790), AbstractUndoableEdit.undo() (p.998),
DefaultStyledDocument.AttributeUndoableEdit.undo() (p.823),
CompoundEdit.undo() (p.1001), UndoableEdit.undo() (p.1005),
UndoManager.undo() (p.1008), UndoManager.undoOrRedo() (p.1008),
UndoManager.undoTo() (p.1008).

swing.undo.CompoundEdit

CLASS

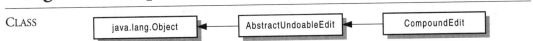

A concrete subclass of AbstractUndoableEdit. It is used to combine individual edits into one larger edit. An example of this would be combining the edits representing the deletion of characters in a word into an edit representing the deletion of the whole word when the user reached the white space around the word.

public class CompoundEdit extends AbstractUndoableEdit

Constructors
public CompoundEdit()

Constructs an empty edit.
public boolean addEdit(UndoableEdit anEdit)

If isInProgress() returns true, this method adds anEdit to the list of edits. The last edit in the list is asked if it wants to merge this edit into itself using lastEdit.addEdit(anEdit). If it returns false, anEdit is asked if it wants to replace the last edit using anEdit.replaceEdit(lastEdit). If both requests are refused, anEdit is simply added to the end of the list.
Overrides: addEdit() in class AbstractUndoableEdit.
Implements: addEdit() in interface UndoableEdit.
public boolean canRedo()

Returns false if isInProgress() returns true or if super.canRedo() does.

undo

Overrides: canRedo() in class AbstractUndoableEdit.

Implements: canRedo() in interface UndoableEdit.

public boolean canUndo()

Returns false if isInProgress() returns true or if super.canUndo() does.

Overrides: canUndo() in class AbstractUndoableEdit.

Implements: canUndo() in interface UndoableEdit.

public void die()

Calls die() on each subedit, from last to first.

Overrides: die() in class AbstractUndoableEdit.

Implements: die() in interface UndoableEdit.

public void end()

Sets inProgress to false, which prevents further edits from being added to this compound edit.

public String getPresentationName()

Returns the result of calling getPresentationName() on the last UndoableEdit added to the edit list. If the list of edits is empty, calls super.getPresentationName().

Overrides: getPresentationName() in class AbstractUndoableEdit.

Implements: getPresentationName() in interface UndoableEdit.

public String getRedoPresentationName()

Returns the result of calling getRedoPresentationName() on the last UndoableEdit added to the edit list. If the edit list is empty, calls super.getRedoPresentationName().

Overrides: getRedoPresentationName() in class AbstractUndoableEdit.

Implements: getRedoPresentationName() in interface UndoableEdit.

public String getUndoPresentationName()

Returns the result of calling getUndoPresentationName() on the last UndoableEdit added to the edit list. If the edit list is empty, calls super.getUndoPresentationName().

Overrides: getUndoPresentationName() in class AbstractUndoableEdit.

Implements: getUndoPresentationName in interface UndoableEdit.

public boolean isInProgress()

Returns true if end() has not been called.

public boolean isSignificant()

Asks all of the edits in the edit list if they are, and returns true if at least one returns true.

Overrides: isSignificant() in class AbstractUndoableEdit.

Implements: isSignificant() in interface UndoableEdit.

public void redo() throws CannotRedoException

Walks the edit list from last to first, calling redo() on each in turn.

Throws: CannotRedoException if any of the calls to redo() throw it.

Overrides: redo() in class AbstractUndoableEdit.

Implements: redo() in interface UndoableEdit.

public String toString()

Overrides: toString in class AbstractUndoableEdit.

public void undo() throws CannotUndoException

Walks the edit list from last to first, calling undo() on each in turn.

Throws: CannotUndoException if any of the calls to undo() do.

Overrides: undo() in class AbstractUndoableEdit.

Implements: undo() in interface UndoableEdit.

Protected Fields

protected java.util.Vector edits

    The list of edits.

Protected Methods

protected UndoableEdit lastEdit()

    Returns the last edit in the edits list, or `null` if the list is empty.

    Extended by   AbstractDocument.DefaultDocumentEvent (p.789), UndoManager (p.1008).

    Returned by   UndoableEditSupport.createCompoundEdit() (p.1006).

    See also   AbstractUndoableEdit (p.998), CannotRedoException (p.1000), CannotUndoException (p.1001), UndoableEdit (p.1005).

swing.undo.StateEdit

CLASS   java.lang.Object ← AbstractUndoableEdit ← StateEdit

`StateEdit` is a general edit for objects that change state. Objects being edited must conform to the `StateEditable` interface. This edit class works by asking an object to store its state in hash tables before and after editing occurs. Upon undo or redo, the object is told to restore its state from these hash tables.

    A `StateEdit` is used as follows:

```
// Create the edit during the "before" state of the object
StateEdit newEdit = new StateEdit(myObject);
// Modify the object
myObject.someStateModifyingMethod();
// "end" the edit when you are done modifying the object
newEdit.end();
```

    Note that when a `StateEdit` ends, it removes redundant state information from the hash tables. A state hash table is not guaranteed to contain all keys/values placed into it when the state is stored!

public class StateEdit extends AbstractUndoableEdit

Constructors

public StateEdit(StateEditable anObject)

    Constructs a new `StateEdit` for the `StateEditable` object.

public StateEdit(StateEditable anObject, String presentationName)

    Constructs a new `StateEdit` for the `StateEditable` object and sets its presentation name to `presentationName`.

Methods

public void end()

    Ends the edit by asking the associated `StateEditable` object for its postediting state using the `StateEditable.storeState()` method.

public String getPresentationName()

Returns the presentation name for this edit.

Overrides: getPresentationName() in class AbstractUndoableEdit.

Implements: getPresentationName() in interface UndoableEdit.

public void redo()

Calls the restoreState method of the associated StateEditable object with the saved postedit state information.

Overrides: redo() in class AbstractUndoableEdit.

Implements: redo() in interface UndoableEdit.

public void undo()

Calls the restoreState method of the associated StateEditable object with the saved preedit state information.

Overrides: undo() in class AbstractUndoableEdit.

Implements: undo() in interface UndoableEdit.

Protected Fields

protected static final String RCSID

Almost certainly included in interface StateEditable by mistake, the value of this field is an identifier from a version control system.

protected StateEditable object

The associated StateEditable object.

protected java.util.Hashtable postState

The state information saved from the StateEditable after the edit.

protected java.util.Hashtable preState

The state information saved from the StateEditable before the edit.

protected String undoRedoName

The undo/redo presentation name.

Protected Methods

protected void init(StateEditable anObject, String name)

Helper method to create the state information hash table and store the preedit state information from the StateEditable.

protected void removeRedundantState()

Removes any state information from the tables that didn't change as a result of the edit.

See also   AbstractUndoableEdit (p.998), StateEditable (p.1004), UndoableEdit (p.1005).

swing.undo.StateEditable

INTERFACE   (StateEditable)

StateEditable defines the interface for objects that can have their state undone/redone by a StateEdit.

public interface StateEditable

Fields

public static final String RCSID

This was almost certainly included by mistake, since its value is a string used in a version control system.

Methods

public abstract void restoreState(java.util.Hashtable state)

When this method is called, the receiving object should restore the state information from the `state` table, overwriting its current information.

public abstract void storeState(java.util.Hashtable state)

When this method is called, the receiving object should store any state information that may change during an edit to the `state` table.

See also StateEdit (p.1003).

swing.undo.UndoableEdit

INTERFACE   (UndoableEdit)

This interface allows the creation of objects that represent an edit that can be undone or redone. Usually implementations will be created by subclassing `AbstractUndoableEdit`.

public interface UndoableEdit

Methods

public abstract boolean addEdit(UndoableEdit anEdit)

Gives this `UndoableEdit` a chance to merge anEdit into itself. If the edit is absorbed, returns `true` from this method. If anEdit is absorbed, it must, in the future, return `false` from its `canRedo()` and `canUndo()` methods and throw an exception from `redo()` or `undo()`. This method is different from `replaceEdit` in that this method is called when a new edit is being added to an edit list to allow the new edit to absorb the last edit in the list. `replaceEdit()` is called on the edit already in the list to check if it wants to absorb the new edit.

public abstract boolean canRedo()

Returns `true` if this edit can be redone.

public abstract boolean canUndo()

Returns `true` if this edit can be undone.

public abstract void die()

Use to inform an `UndoableEdit` that it is no longer needed. The `UndoableEdit` can then perform cleanup of its resources and set the appropriate flags so that it cannot be undone or redone. `UndoManager` calls this before it discards edits.

public abstract String getPresentationName()

Returns a localized `String` to display to the user.

public abstract String getRedoPresentationName()

Returns a localized `String` for displaying to the user in a "redo" context, as on a Redo menu item or toolbar button ToolTip. This method should modify the result from `getPresentationName()` in preference to creating another unique text string.

public abstract String getUndoPresentationName()

Returns a localized `String` for displaying to the user in an "undo" context, as on an Undo menu item or toolbar button ToolTip. This method should modify the result from `getPresentation-Name()` in preference to creating another unique text string.

public abstract boolean isSignificant()

Returns `true` if the edit is significant in that it actually modifies the edited object's information state. An example of an insignificant edit is a change in the selection due to removing selected text. The removal of the text is a significant edit but the selection change is not. Both should be stored as edits.

public abstract void redo() throws CannotRedoException

Redoes the edit, if it has previously been undone.

public abstract boolean replaceEdit(UndoableEdit anEdit)

Returns `true` if this `UndoableEdit` should absorb `anEdit`. If `anEdit` is absorbed, it returns `false` from `canUndo()` and `canRedo()` and throws an exception from `undo()` or `redo()` when any of those methods are called in the future. This method is different from `addEdit` in that it is called on an existing edit to see if it wants to absorb the new edit. `addEdit()` is called on the new edit to check if it wants to absorb the existing edit.

public abstract void undo() throws CannotUndoException

Undoes the edit.

Implemented by AbstractUndoableEdit (p.998).

Returned by AbstractDocument.Content.insertString() (p.788), AbstractDocument.Content.remove() (p.788), CompoundEdit.lastEdit() (p.1001), GapContent.insertString() (p.833), GapContent.remove() (p.833), StringContent.insertString() (p.863), StringContent.remove() (p.863), UndoableEditEvent.getEdit() (p.515), UndoManager.editToBeRedone() (p.1008), UndoManager.editToBeUndone() (p.1008).

See also CannotRedoException (p.1000), CannotUndoException (p.1001).

swing.undo.UndoableEditSupport

CLASS

This class is similar in concept to `java.beans.PropertyChangeSupport` in that it supplies the basic support for managing `UndoableEditListeners`. This class uses a `CompoundEdit` to manage the list of edits. Because the `CompoundEdit` it creates is `protected`, you will need to create a subclass of this class to use it.

public class UndoableEditSupport extends java.lang.Object

Constructors

public UndoableEditSupport()

Constructs an `UndoableEditSupport` instance which will use itself as the source of the `UndoableEditEvents` it generates.

public UndoableEditSupport(Object eventSource)

Constructs an UndoableEditSupport instance which will use eventSource as the source of the UndoableEditEvents it generates.

Methods

public synchronized void addUndoableEditListener(UndoableEditListener l)

Adds an UndoableEditListener to the list of listeners.

public synchronized void beginUpdate()

Indicates the beginning of a series of edits that should be stored as a single edit before posting it to the listeners.

public synchronized void endUpdate()

Ends the compound edit started with the last call to beginUpdate(). Note that calling this method may call undoableEditHappened() in all listeners. If this method is called as part of a listener handling undoableEditHappened(), deadlock will occur since this method is synchronized.

public int getUpdateLevel()

Returns the number of beginUpdate() calls that have been made that have not been ended with a matching endUpdate().

public synchronized void postEdit(UndoableEdit e)

If there aren't any edits started with beginUpdate() which are still in progress, this method posts the compoundEdit to all listeners. Note that calling this method may call undoableEditHappened() in all listeners. If this method is called as part of a listener handling undoableEditHappened(), deadlock will occur since this method is synchronized.

public synchronized void removeUndoableEditListener(UndoableEditListener l)

Removes the given UndoableEditListener from the list of listeners.

public String toString()

Overrides: toString in class Object.

Protected Fields

protected CompoundEdit compoundEdit

The list of edits being managed by this instance.

protected java.util.Vector listeners

The list of UndoableEditListeners managed by this instance.

protected Object realSource

If the constructor was passed an eventSource, stores that value. Otherwise stores this.

protected int updateLevel

The number of nested calls to beginUpdate().

Protected Methods

protected void _postEdit(UndoableEdit e)

Calls undoableEditHappened in all listeners. This method should only be called indirectly by calling postEdit() or endUpdate().

protected CompoundEdit createCompoundEdit()

Called from beginUpdate() to create a compound edit to hold the edit sequence.

See also CompoundEdit (p.1001), UndoableEdit (p.1005), UndoableEditListener (p.515).

undo

swing.undo.UndoManager

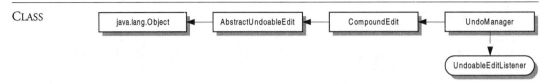

This class is provided to manage an edit list and its associated listeners. You'll generally use an instance of this class as your `UndoableEditListener`, since it provides the behavior you most often want.

```
public class UndoManager extends CompoundEdit
    implements UndoableEditListener
```

Constructors

`public UndoManager()`

Constructs a new `UndoManager`.

Methods

`public synchronized boolean addEdit(UndoableEdit anEdit)`

If `inProgress` is true, this method inserts `anEdit` at the location in the list marked as the next index for an add. Any edits in the list after the marked index will be discarded and have their `die()` methods called. If `inProgress` is `false`, this acts the same as the `addEdit` method in `CompoundEdit`.

Overrides: `addEdit` in class `CompoundEdit`.

Implements: `addEdit` in interface `UndoableEdit`.

`public synchronized boolean canRedo()`

Returns `true` if calling `redo()` would succeed.

Overrides: `canRedo` in class `CompoundEdit`.

Implements: `canRedo` in interface `UndoableEdit`.

`public synchronized boolean canUndo()`

Returns `true` if calling `undo()` would succeed.

Overrides: `canUndo` in class `CompoundEdit`.

Implements: `canUndo` in interface `UndoableEdit`.

`public synchronized boolean canUndoOrRedo()`

Returns `true` if calling `undoOrRedo()` would succeed.

`public synchronized void discardAllEdits()`

Discards all edits in this manager, calling `die()` on each as they are removed.

`public synchronized void end()`

Completes the work of the `UndoManager`. Calls `super.end()`, then calls `die()` on the unreachable edits starting at `indexOfNextAdd`.

Overrides: `end` in class `CompoundEdit`.

`public synchronized int getLimit()`

Sets the limit on the number of edits this manager will hold. The default value is `100`.

public synchronized String getRedoPresentationName()

If inProgress is true, returns the redoPresentationName of the significant edit in the manager that will be redone when redo() is called. If there aren't any edits, or if none are significant, this method returns AbstractUndoableEdit.RedoName. If inProgress is false, this method acts the same as the getRedoPresentationName method in CompoundEdit.

Overrides: getRedoPresentationName in class CompoundEdit.

Implements: getRedoPresentationName in interface UndoableEdit.

public synchronized String getUndoOrRedoPresentationName()

Returns the display string for the undoOrRedo command. That command makes sense only if the limit for this manager is one edit, which toggles between undo or redo.

public synchronized String getUndoPresentationName()

If inProgress is true, returns the undoPresentationName of the significant edit in the manager that will be undone when undo() is called. If there aren't any edits, or if none are significant, this method returns AbstractUndoableEdit.UndoName. If inProgress is false, this method acts the same as the getUndoPresentationName method in CompoundEdit.

Overrides: getUndoPresentationName in class CompoundEdit.

Implements: getUndoPresentationName in interface UndoableEdit.

public synchronized void redo() throws CannotRedoException

If inProgress is true, this method redoes all edits up to and including the first significant edit, starting from the position marked as the index of the next add operation. If inProgress is false, calls super.redo().

Overrides: redo in class CompoundEdit.

Implements: redo in interface UndoableEdit.

public synchronized void setLimit(int 1)

Sets the maximum number of edits this manager will hold. Will discard excess edits from the list if necessary, calling their die() method as they are removed.

public String toString()

Overrides: toString in class CompoundEdit.

public synchronized void undo() throws CannotUndoException

If inProgress is true, this method undoes all edits back to and including the first significant edit, starting from the position marked as the index of the next add operation. If inProgress is false, calls super.undo().

Overrides: undo in class CompoundEdit.

Implements: undo in interface UndoableEdit.

public synchronized void undoOrRedo()
    throws CannotRedoException, CannotUndoException

If the limit for this manager is one edit, calls undo() or redo() on the edit as appropriate.

public void undoableEditHappened(UndoableEditEvent e)

Called by the UndoableEdit sources this manager is listening to. Calls addEdit(e.getEdit()).

Implements: undoableEditHappened in interface UndoableEditListener.

Protected Methods

protected UndoableEdit editToBeRedone()

Returns the significant edit to redo when redo() is called. Returns null when the edit list is empty or if there aren't any significant edits.

protected UndoableEdit editToBeUndone()

Returns the significant edit to undo when undo() is called. Returns null when the edit list is empty or if there aren't any significant edits.

protected void redoTo(UndoableEdit edit) throws CannotRedoException

Redoes all edits from the index used for the next add operation to edit. Updates the next add index appropriately after it is done.

protected void trimEdits(int from, int to)

Removes the edits in the list from from to to. As the edits are removed their die() method will be called.

protected void trimForLimit()

Called when the new limit for this manager is smaller than the old limit, so edits need to be discarded. Will remove edits from *both* ends of the list to create a list of the proper size centered around the index used for the next add operation.

protected void undoTo(UndoableEdit edit) throws CannotUndoException

Undoes all edits from the index used for the next add operation to edit. Updates the next add index appropriately after it is done.

See also   AbstractUndoableEdit (p.998), CompoundEdit (p.1001), UndoableEdit (p.1005), UndoableEditListener (p.516).

A P P E N D I X   A

Related information sources

A.1 Web resources

- The Java Developer's Connection: `http://developer.javasoft.com`
- The Swing Connection:
  `http://java.sun.com/products/jfc/swingdoc-current/index.html`
- The Swing Tutorial:
  `http://java.sun.com/docs/books/tutorial/ui/swing/index.html`
- JavaSoft's Known Bugs in Swing Page: `http://www.javasoft.com/`
  `products/jdk/1.1/knownbugs/classes_swing.html`
- JavaWorld Online: `http://www.javaworld.com`
- JavaReport Online: `http://www.jro.com`
- Java Developer's Journal: `http://www.sys-con.com/java/index.cfm`

A.2 Newsgroups and mailing lists

- `comp.lang.java.gui`
- The Advanced Java mailing list:
  `http://MetaDigest.XCF.Berkeley.EDU/archive/advanced-java/`
- The Swing Mailing List: `http://www.eos.dk/archive/swing/index.html`

UIDefaults table standard keys

Important Note: Any of the keys in the UIDefaults table may have null for a value. Always check the returned value before using it.

B.1 Color keys

Here are the definitions for the color values not covered by the AWT SystemColor constants that are referenced in the table:

```
ColorUIResource red = new ColorUIResource(Color.red);
ColorUIResource black = new ColorUIResource(Color.black);
ColorUIResource white = new ColorUIResource(Color.white);
ColorUIResource yellow = new ColorUIResource(Color.yellow);
ColorUIResource gray = new ColorUIResource(Color.gray);
ColorUIResource lightGray = new ColorUIResource(Color.lightGray);
ColorUIResource darkGray = new ColorUIResource(Color.darkGray);
ColorUIResource scrollBarTrack = new ColorUIResource(224, 224, 224);
ColorUIResource treeSelection = new ColorUIResource(Color.red);
ColorUIResource menuItemPressedBackground = new ColorUIResource(0,0,128);
ColorUIResource menuItemPressedForeground =  new ColorUIResource(255,255,255);
```

UI color key (string)	Default assigned color
Button.background	table.get("control")
Button.foreground	table.get("controlText")
CheckBox.focus	black
ColorChooser.background	table.get("control")
ColorChooser.foreground	table.get("controlText")
ColorChooser.selectedColorBorder	selectedColorBorder
ComboBox.background	white
ComboBox.disabledBackground	table.get("control")
ComboBox.disabledForeground	table.get("textInactiveText")
ComboBox.foreground	black
ComboBox.selectedBackground	table.get("textHighlight")
ComboBox.selectedForeground	table.get("textHighlightText")
Desktop.background	table.get("desktop")
EditorPane.background	white
EditorPane.caretForeground	red
EditorPane.foreground	table.get("textText")
EditorPane.inactiveForeground	table.get("textInactiveText")
EditorPane.selectionBackground	lightGray
EditorPane.selectionForeground	table.get("textHighlightText")
Label.background	table.get("control")
Label.disabled	white
Label.disabledShadow	table.get("controlShadow")
Label.foreground	table.get("controlText")
List.background	table.get("window")
List.focusCellHighlightBorder	focusCellHighlightBorder
List.foreground	table.get("textText")
List.selectionBackground	table.get("textHighlight")
List.selectionForeground	table.get("textHighlightText")
Menu.background	table.get("menu")
Menu.foreground	table.get("menuText")
Menu.pressedBackground	menuItemPressedBackground
Menu.pressedForeground	menuItemPressedForeground
MenuBar.background	table.get("menu")
MenuBar.foreground	table.get("menuText")
MenuItem.acceleratorForeground	table.get("menuText")
MenuItem.acceleratorPressedForeground	menuItemPressedForeground
MenuItem.background	table.get("menu")
MenuItem.disabledForeground	null
MenuItem.foreground	table.get("menuText")

UI color key (string)	Default assigned color
MenuItem.pressedBackground	menuItemPressedBackground
MenuItem.pressedForeground	menuItemPressedForeground
OptionPane.background	table.get("control")
OptionPane.foreground	table.get("controlText")
Panel.background	table.get("control")
Panel.foreground	table.get("textText")
PasswordField.background	table.get("window")
PasswordField.caretForeground	black
PasswordField.foreground	table.get("textText")
PasswordField.inactiveForeground	table.get("textInactiveText")
PasswordField.selectionBackground	table.get("textHighlight")
PasswordField.selectionForeground	table.get("textHighlightText")
PopupMenu.background	table.get("menu")
PopupMenu.border	popupMenuBorder
PopupMenu.foreground	table.get("menuText")
ProgressBar.background	table.get("control")
ProgressBar.foreground	table.get("textHighlight")
RadioButton.background	table.get("control")
RadioButton.focus	black
RadioButton.foreground	table.get("controlText")
ScrollBar.background	scrollBarTrack
ScrollBar.foreground	table.get("control")
ScrollBar.thumb	table.get("control")
ScrollBar.thumbDarkShadow	table.get("controlDkShadow")
ScrollBar.thumbHighlight	table.get("controlHighlight")
ScrollBar.thumbLightShadow	table.get("controlShadow")
ScrollBar.track	scrollBarTrack
ScrollBar.trackHighlight	table.get("controlDkShadow")
ScrollPane.background	table.get("control")
ScrollPane.foreground	table.get("controlText")
Slider.background	table.get("control")
Slider.focus	table.get("controlDkShadow")
Slider.foreground	table.get("control")
Slider.highlight	table.get("controlHighlight")
Slider.shadow	table.get("controlShadow")
SplitPane.background	table.get("control")
SplitPane.highlight	table.get("controlHighlight")
SplitPane.shadow	table.get("controlShadow")
TabbedPane.focus	black

UI color key (string)	Default assigned color
TabbedPane.tabBackground	table.get("control")
TabbedPane.tabDarkShadow	table.get("controlDkShadow")
TabbedPane.tabForeground	table.get("controlText")
TabbedPane.tabHighlight	table.get("controlHighlight")
TabbedPane.tabShadow	table.get("controlShadow")
Table.background	table.get("window")
Table.focusCellBackground	table.get("window")
Table.focusCellForeground	table.get("controlText")
Table.focusCellHighlightBorder	focusCellHighlightBorder
Table.foreground	table.get("controlText")
Table.gridColor	gray
Table.selectionBackground	table.get("textHighlight")
Table.selectionForeground	table.get("textHighlightText")
TableHeader.background	table.get("control")
TableHeader.font	dialogPlain12
TableHeader.foreground	table.get("controlText")
TextArea.background	table.get("window")
TextArea.caretForeground	black
TextArea.foreground	table.get("textText")
TextArea.inactiveForeground	table.get("textInactiveText")
TextArea.selectionBackground	table.get("textHighlight")
TextArea.selectionForeground	table.get("textHighlightText")
TextField.background	table.get("window")
TextField.caretForeground	black
TextField.foreground	table.get("textText")
TextField.inactiveForeground	table.get("textInactiveText")
TextField.selectionBackground	table.get("textHighlight")
TextField.selectionForeground	table.get("textHighlightText")
TextPane.background	white
TextPane.caretForeground	black
TextPane.foreground	table.get("textText")
TextPane.inactiveForeground	table.get("textInactiveText")
TextPane.selectionBackground	lightGray
TextPane.selectionForeground	table.get("textHighlightText")
TitledBorder.titleColor	table.get("controlText")
ToggleButton.background	table.get("control")
ToggleButton.focus	table.get("controlText")
ToggleButton.foreground	table.get("controlText")
ToggleButton.pressed	table.get("control")

UI color key (string)	Default assigned color
ToolBar.background	table.get("control")
ToolBar.dockingBorderColor	red
ToolBar.dockingColor	table.get("control")
ToolBar.floatingBorderColor	darkGray
ToolBar.floatingColor	table.get("control")
ToolBar.foreground	table.get("controlText")
ToolTip.background	table.get("info")
ToolTip.foreground	table.get("infoText")
Tree.background	white
Tree.backgroundNonSelectionColor	white
Tree.backgroundSelectionColor	treeSelection
Tree.borderSelectionColor	black
Tree.hash	gray
Tree.textNonSelectionColor	black
Tree.textSelectionColor	white

B.2 Other keys

These are the other keys defined in the Basic look and feel that can be used in renderers and elsewhere.

UIDefaults table key	Description
Button.border	The Border to place around JButtons.
Button.font	The Font to use for JButton text.
Button.margin	The Insets between the edge of the button and its contents.
Button.textIconGap	The Integer for the gap (in pixels) between the Icon and the text on a JButton.
Button.textShiftOffset	The Integer for the amount to shift the text when the button is pressed.
CheckBox.border	The Border used for JCheckBoxes.
CheckBox.font	The Font used for JCheckBox text.
CheckBox.icon	The Icon used for the JCheckBox's "check".
CheckBox.margin	The Insets between the edge of the JCheckBox and its contents.
CheckBox.textIconGap	The Integer for the gap (in pixels) between the Icon and the text on a JButton.
CheckBox.textShiftOffset	The Integer for the amount to shift the text when the button is pressed.

UIDefaults table key	Description
CheckBoxMenuItem.acceleratorFont	The Font to use for the text displaying the accelerator for a JCheckBoxMenuItem.
CheckBoxMenuItem.arrowIcon	The arrow Icon for a JCheckBoxMenuItem.
CheckBoxMenuItem.border	The Border for a JCheckBoxMenuItem.
CheckBoxMenuItem.borderPainted	A Boolean representing whether the border should be painted.
CheckBoxMenuItem.checkIcon	The check Icon for a JCheckBoxMenuItem.
CheckBoxMenuItem.font	The Font for the text in a JCheckBoxMenuItem.
CheckBoxMenuItem.margin	The Insets between the border of a JCheckBoxMenuItem and its contents.
ColorChooser.font	The Font to use in a JColorChooser.
ColorChooser.rgbBlueMnemonic	The Integer representing the KeyEvent which moves the blue slider in a JColorChooser (settable because of internationalization).
ColorChooser.rgbGreenMnemonic	The Integer representing the KeyEvent which moves the green slider in a JColorChooser (settable because of internationalization).
ColorChooser.rgbRedMnemonic	The Integer representing the KeyEvent which moves the red slider in a JColorChooser (settable because of internationalization).
ColorChooser.swatchesRecentSwatchSize	The size (in pixels) of the component displaying the current color.
ColorChooser.swatchesSwatchSize	The size (in pixels) of the components displaying the colors.
ComboBox.font	The Font used in a JComboBox.
DesktopIcon.border	The Border used around a JDesktopIcon.
EditorPane.border	The Border around a JEditorPane.
EditorPane.caretBlinkRate	The Integer representing the time in milliseconds between blinks of the Caret.
EditorPane.font	The default Font for a JEditorPane.
EditorPane.keyBindings	The JTextComponent.KeyBinding array of KeyBindings for a JEditorPane.
EditorPane.margin	The Insets around a JEditorPane.
FileChooser.cancelButtonMnemonic	The Integer value representing the KeyEvent constant which will be used for the CANCEL button mnemonic.
FileChooser.detailsViewIcon	The Icon for the "switch to details view" button.
FileChooser.helpButtonMnemonic	The Integer value representing the KeyEvent constant which will be used for the help button mnemonic.
FileChooser.homeFolderIcon	The Icon for the "go home" button.
FileChooser.listViewIcon	The Icon for the "switch to list view" button.
FileChooser.newFolderIcon	The Icon for the "new folder" button.
FileChooser.openButtonMnemonic	The Integer value representing the KeyEvent constant which will be used for the open button mnemonic.

UIDefaults table key	Description
FileChooser.saveButtonMnemonic	The Integer value representing the KeyEvent constant which will be used for the save button mnemonic.
FileChooser.updateButtonMnemonic	The Integer value representing the KeyEvent constant which will be used for the update button mnemonic.
FileChooser.upFolderIcon	The Icon for the "go up one directory" button.
FileView.computerIcon	The Icon for "My Computer" on a Windows machine.
FileView.directoryIcon	The Icon used for a nonleaf node in the display.
FileView.fileIcon	The Icon used for a leaf node in the display.
FileView.floppyDriveIcon	The Icon for a floppy disk drive.
FileView.hardDriveIcon	The Icon for a hard drive.
InternalFrame.border	The Border to use around a JInternalFrame.
InternalFrame.closeIcon	The Icon used for the close button.
InternalFrame.icon	The default frame Icon.
InternalFrame.iconifyIcon	The Icon used for the iconify button.
InternalFrame.maximizeIcon	The Icon used for the maximize button.
InternalFrame.minimizeIcon	The Icon used for the minimize button.
InternalFrame.titleFont	The Font to use for the title of a JInternalFrame.
Label.border	The Border for a JLabel.
Label.font	The Font for a JLabel's text.
List.border	The Border for a JList.
List.cellRenderer	The default JList renderer.
List.focusCellHighlightBorder	The Border to use for the focused cell in the list.
List.font	The Font for the text of items in the list.
Menu.acceleratorFont	The Font to use for accelerator text in a JMenu.
Menu.arrowIcon	The arrow Icon for a JMenu.
Menu.border	The Border for a JMenu.
Menu.borderPainted	A Boolean indicating whether the border of a JMenu is painted.
Menu.checkIcon	The check Icon for a JMenu.
Menu.consumesTabs	A Boolean indicating if a JMenu consumes tabs so they won't switch to the next component.
Menu.font	The Font for JMenus.
Menu.margin	The Insets around a JMenu.
MenuBar.border	The Border for a JMenuBar.
MenuBar.font	The Font for text on the JMenuBar.
MenuItem.acceleratorFont	The Font used for accelerator text in a JMenuItem.
MenuItem.arrowIcon	The arrow Icon for a JMenuItem.
MenuItem.border	The Border for a JMenuItem.
MenuItem.borderPainted	A Boolean indicating whether the border of a JMenuItem is painted.
MenuItem.checkIcon	The check Icon for a JMenuItem.

UIDefaults table key	Description
MenuItem.font	The Font for text in a JMenuItem.
MenuItem.margin	The Insets around a JMenuItem.
OptionPane.border	The Border around a JOptionPane.
OptionPane.buttonAreaBorder	The Border around the section of a JOptionPane which contains the buttons.
OptionPane.errorIcon	The Icon for error JOptionPanes.
OptionPane.font	The Font for text in a JOptionPane.
OptionPane.informationIcon	The Icon for information JOptionPanes.
OptionPane.messageAreaBorder	The Border around the message area in a JOptionPane.
OptionPane.minimumSize	The Dimension for the smallest allowed JOptionPane.
OptionPane.questionIcon	The Icon for a prompt JOptionPane.
OptionPane.warningIcon	The Icon for a warning JOptionPane.
Panel.font	The Font for a JPanel (the default Font for its children).
PasswordField.border	The Border for a JPasswordField.
PasswordField.caretBlinkRate	The Integer delay in milliseconds between Caret blinks.
PasswordField.font	The Font for the echo character in a JPasswordField.
PasswordField.keyBindings	The default JTextComponent.KeyBindings for a JPasswordField. A password field needs its own so that cut/copy/paste can be removed.
PasswordField.margin	The Insets for a JPasswordField.
PopupMenu.border	The default Border for a JPopupMenu.
PopupMenu.font	The default Font for a JPopupMenu.
ProgressBar.border	The Border for a JProgressBar.
ProgressBar.cellLength	An Integer representing the default length of a "cell" in the painting of a JProgressBar.
ProgressBar.cellSpacing	An Integer representing the gap (in pixels) between cells in a JProgressBar.
ProgressBar.font	The default Font for a JProgressBar.
RadioButton.border	The default Border for a JRadioButton.
RadioButton.font	The default Font for a JRadioButton.
RadioButton.icon	The default Icon for a JRadioButton.
RadioButton.margin	The Insets around a JRadioButton.
RadioButton.textIconGap	An Integer representing the gap (in pixels) between the text and the Icon in a JRadioButton.
RadioButton.textShiftOffset	An Integer representing the distance (in pixels) to offset the text when the button is pressed.
RadioButtonMenuItem.acceleratorFont	The Font used for the text displaying the accelerator key in a JRadioButtonMenuItem.
RadioButtonMenuItem.arrowIcon	The arrow Icon for a JRadioButtonMenuItem.
RadioButtonMenuItem.background	The background Color for a JRadioButtonMenuItem.
RadioButtonMenuItem.border	The Border for a JRadioButtonMenuItem.

UIDefaults table key	Description
RadioButtonMenuItem.borderPainted	A `Boolean` indicating whether the border is painted.
RadioButtonMenuItem.checkIcon	The `Icon` to use when the `JRadioButtonMenuItem` is selected.
RadioButtonMenuItem.font	The `Font` for a `JRadioButtonMenuItem`.
RadioButtonMenuItem.margin	The `Insets` around a `JRadioButtonMenuItem`.
ScrollBar.background	The background `Color` for a `JScrollBar`.
ScrollBar.border	The `Border` for a `JScrollBar`.
ScrollBar.maximumThumbSize	A `Dimension` representing the largest size the scrollbar's thumb can grow to.
ScrollBar.minimumThumbSize	A `Dimension` representing the smallest size the thumb can get before it is simply not drawn.
ScrollPane.border	The `Border` for a `JScrollPane`.
ScrollPane.font	The default `Font` for children of a `JScrollPane`.
ScrollPane.viewportBorder	The `Border` for the viewport of a `JScrollPane`.
Slider.border	The `Border` for a slider.
Slider.focusInsets	The `Insets` representing the gap between the `JSlider`'s border and where the focus indicator is drawn.
SplitPane.border	The `Border` for a `JSplitPane`.
SplitPane.dividerSize	An `Integer` representing the default size (width or height, depending on its orientation) of the divider in a `JSplitPane`.
TabbedPane.contentBorderInsets	The `Insets` representing the gap between the edges of a `JTabbedPane` "page" and the component it holds.
TabbedPane.font	The `Font` for a `JTabbedPane`.
TabbedPane.selectedTabPadInsets	The `Insets` for the selected tab. These are added to the normal tab insets to allow the tab to appear emphasized relative to the other tabs.
TabbedPane.tabAreaInsets	The `Insets` around the area where all of the tabs are painted.
TabbedPane.tabInsets	The `Insets` between the edge of a normal tab and its text and `Icon`.
TabbedPane.tabRunOverlay	An `Integer` representing the distance (in pixels) that tab runs overlap the tab runs "behind" them.
TabbedPane.textIconGap	An `Integer` representing the gap (in pixels) between the text and the `Icon` on a tab.
Table.focusCellHighlightBorder	The `Border` to use for the focused cell in a `JTable`.
Table.font	The `Font` for a `JTable`.
Table.scrollPaneBorder	The `Border` to place around a `JTable` when it is added to a `JScrollPane`.
TableHeader.cellBorder	The `Border` of a cell in a `JTableHeader`.
TableHeader.font	The `Font` for `JTableHeader` cells.
TextArea.border	The `Border` around the content in a `JTextArea`.
TextArea.caretBlinkRate	An `Integer` representing the number of milliseconds between `Caret` blinks.

UIDefaults table key	Description
TextArea.font	The default Font for a JTextArea.
TextArea.keyBindings	The default JTextComponent.KeyBindings for a JTextArea.
TextArea.margin	The Insets around the JTextArea.
TextField.border	The Border for a JTextField.
TextField.caretBlinkRate	An Integer representing the number of milliseconds between Caret blinks.
TextField.font	The default Font for a JTextField.
TextField.keyBindings	The JTextComponent.KeyBindings for a JTextField.
TextField.margin	The Insets around a JTextField.
TextPane.border	The Border for a JTextField.
TextPane.caretBlinkRate	An Integer representing the number of milliseconds between Caret blinks.
TextPane.font	The default Font for a JTextPane.
TextPane.keyBindings	The JTextComponent.KeyBindings for a JTextPane.
TextPane.margin	The Insets around a JTextPane.
TitledBorder.border	The Border for the border part of a TitledBorder.
TitledBorder.font	The Font for a TitledBorder.
ToggleButton.border	The Border for a JToggleButton.
ToggleButton.font	The Font for a JToggleButton.
ToggleButton.margin	The Insets around a JToggleButton.
ToggleButton.textIconGap	An Integer representing the gap (in pixels) between the text and Icon on a JToggleButton.
ToggleButton.textShiftOffset	An Integer representing the distance (in pixels) to offset the text when the button is pressed.
ToolBar.background	The background Color for a JToolBar.
ToolBar.border	The Border for a JToolBar.
ToolBar.font	The Font for the button text in a JToolBar.
ToolBar.separatorSize	A Dimension representing the width or height of a separator in a JToolBar.
ToolTip.border	The Border around a JToolTip.
ToolTip.font	The Font for a JToolTip.
Tree.changeSelectionWithFocus	A Boolean indicating whether the selection should change as the focus is moved using the keyboard.
Tree.closedIcon	The default Icon used for a closed nonleaf node.
Tree.collapsedIcon	The Icon to use for the expand/collapse button for a collapsed node.
Tree.drawsFocusBorderAroundIcon	A Boolean indicating whether the focus indicator should be drawn around both the Icon and text, or just the text of a selected node.
Tree.editorBorder	The Border to use around a node being edited.
Tree.expandedIcon	The Icon to use for the expand/collapse button on an expanded node.

UIDefaults table key	Description
Tree.font	The default `Font` for nodes in the tree.
Tree.leafIcon	The default `Icon` for a leaf in the tree.
Tree.leftChildIndent	An `Integer` representing the amount to offset a child node along the x-axis from its parent. This distance is to the left edge of the expand/contract button.
Tree.openIcon	The default `Icon` for an expanded nonleaf node.
Tree.rightChildIndent	An `Integer` representing the amount to offset a child node along the x-axis from its parent. This distance is to the right edge of the renderer area of a node.
Tree.rowHeight	An `Integer` representing the default height (in pixels) for a row.
Tree.scrollsOnExpand	A `Boolean` indicating whether the tree should scroll to make as many newly expanded children visible as possible when a node is expanded.
Viewport.font	The default `Font` for children of a `JViewport`.

A P P E N D I X   C

Swing events, listener interfaces, and event sources

C.1 Event objects

Event object	Purpose
AncestorEvent (p.484)	Ancestor component added, moved, or removed.
CaretEvent (p.485)	Caret change.
ChangeEvent (p.487)	State change.
DocumentEvent (p.489)	Document state change.
HyperlinkEvent (p.494)	Hyperlink under cursor, chosen.
InternalFrameEvent (p.497)	InternalFrame state change.
ListDataEvent (p.498)	Contents of list change.
ListSelectionEvent (p.499)	Selection in list change.
MenuDragMouseEvent (p.501)	Used by the Basic look and feel when the mouse is being dragged inside a menu.
MenuEvent (p.502)	Menu selected, deselected, canceled.

Event object	Purpose
MenuKeyEvent (p.503)	Used by the Basic look and feel for key navigation events in a menu.
PopupMenuEvent (p.505)	PopupMenu state change.
TableColumnModelEvent (p.507)	Table column model change.
TableModelEvent (p.508)	Table model change.
TreeExpansionEvent (p.511)	Tree node expanded or collapsed.
TreeModelEvent (p.511)	Tree model change.
TreeSelectionEvent (p.513)	Tree selection change.
UndoableEditEvent (p.515)	Undoable edit made.

C.2 Listener interfaces

Listener interface	Methods
AncestorListener (p.485)	ancestorAdded(AncestorEvent e) ancestorMoved(AncestorEvent e) ancestorRemoved(AncestorEvent e)
CaretListener (p.486)	caretUpdate(CaretEvent e)
CellEditorListener (p.486)	editingCanceled(ChangeEvent e) editingStopped(ChangeEvent e)
ChangeListener (p.488)	stateChanged(ChangeEvent e)
DocumentListener (p.490)	changedUpdate(DocumentEvent e) insertUpdate(DocumentEvent e) removeUpdate(DocumentEvent e)
HyperlinkListener (p.495)	hyperlinkUpdate(HyperlinkEvent e)
InternalFrameListener (p.498)	internalFrameActivated(InternalFrameEvent e) internalFrameClosed(InternalFrameEvent e) internalFrameClosing(InternalFrameEvent e) internalFrameDeactivated(InternalFrameEvent e) internalFrameDeiconified(InternalFrameEvent e) internalFrameIconified(InternalFrameEvent e) internalFrameOpened(InternalFrameEvent e)
ListDataListener (p.499)	contentsChanged(ListDataEvent e) intervalAdded(ListDataEvent e) intervalRemoved(ListDataEvent e)
ListSelectionListener (p.500)	valueChanged(ListSelectionEvent e)
MenuListener (p.504)	menuCanceled(MenuEvent e) menuDeselected(MenuEvent e) menuSelected(MenuEvent e)
PopupMenuListener (p.506)	popupMenuCanceled(PopupMenuEvent e) popupMenuWillBecomeInvisible(PopupMenuEvent e) popupMenuWillBecomeVisible(PopupMenuEvent e)
TableColumnModelListener (p.508)	columnAdded(TableColumnModelEvent e) columnMarginChanged(TableColumnModelEvent e) columnMoved(TableColumnModelEvent e) columnRemoved(TableColumnModelEvent e) columnSelectionChanged(ListSelection e)

Listener interface	Methods

`TableModelListener` (p.510)	`tableChanged(TableModelEvent e)`
	`tableRowsInserted(TableModelEvent e)`
	`tableRowsRemoved(TableModelEvent e)`

`TreeExpansionListener` (p.511)	`treeCollapsed(TreeExpansionEvent e)` `treeExpanded(TreeExpansionEvent e)`

`TreeModelListener` (p.513)	`treeNodesChanged(TreeModelEvent e)`
	`treeNodesInserted(TreeModelEvent e)`
	`treeNodesRemoved(TreeModelEvent e)`
	`treeStructureChanged(TreeModelEvent e)`

`TreeSelectionListener` (p.514)	`valueChanged(TreeSelectionEvent e)`
`TreeWillExpandListener` (p.515)	`treeWillCollapse(TreeExpansionEvent e)` `treeWillExpand(TreeExpansionEvent e)`
`UndoableEditListener` (p.516)	`undoableEditHappened(UndoableEditEvent e)`

C.3 Event sources and their listeners

Event source	Listener interface
`AbstractButton` (p.118) `DefaultButtonModel` (p.161) `JTextField` (p.379) `Timer` (p.447)	`java.awt.event.ActionListener`
`JScrollBar` (p.328)	`java.awt.event.AdjustmentListener`
`JComponent` (p.207)	`AncestorListener` (p.485)
`JTextComponent` (p.838)	`CaretListener` (p.486)
`DefaultCellEditor` (p.164)	`CellEditorListener` (p.486)
`AbstractButton` (p.118) `DefaultBoundedRangeModel` (p.159) `DefaultButtonModel` (p.161) `DefaultCaret` (p.806) `DefaultSingleSelectionModel` (p.179) `JProgressBar` (p.315) `JSlider` (p.341) `JTabbedPane` (p.351) `JViewport` (p.410) `StyleContext` (p.872)	`ChangeListener` (p.488)
`Component`	`java.awt.event.ComponentListener`
`Container`	`java.awt.event.ContainerListener`
`AbstractDocument` (p.778)	`DocumentListener` (p490.)
`Component`	`java.awt.event.FocusListener`
`JEditorPane` (p.232)	`HyperlinkListener` (p.495)
`JInternalFrame` (p.254)	`InternalFrameListener` (p.498)
`AbstractButton` (p.118) `DefaultButtonModel` (p.161) `JComboBox` (p.200)	`java.awt.event.ItemListener`

Event source	Listener interface
`Component`	`java.awt.event.KeyListener`
`AbstractListModel` (p.127)	`ListDataListener` (p.499)
`DefaultListSelectionModel` (p.175) `JList` (p.271)	`ListSelectionListener` (p.500)
`JMenu` (p.281)	`MenuListener` (p.504)
`Component`	`java.awt.event.MouseListener`
`Component`	`java.awt.event.MouseMotionListener`
`JPopupMenu` (p.309)	`PopupMenuListener` (p.506)
`AbstractAction` (p.115) `DefaultTreeSelectionModel` (p.978) `JComponent` (p.207) `TableColumn` (p.761)	`java.beans.PropertyChangeListener`
`DefaultTableColumnModel` (p.744)	`TableColumnModelListener` (p.508)
`AbstractTableModel` (p.735)	`TableModelListener` (p.510)
`JTree` (p.393)	`TreeExpansionListener` (p.511) `TreeWillExpandListener` (p.515)
`DefaultTreeModel` (p.975)	`TreeModelListener` (p.513)
`DefaultTreeSelectionModel` (p.978) `JTree` (p.393)	`TreeSelectionListener` (p.514)
`UndoableEditSupport` (p.1006)	`UndoableEditListener` (p.516)
`JComponent` (p.207)	`java.beans.VetoableChangeListener`
`JPopupMenu` (p.309) `Window`	`java.awt.event.WindowListener`

index

1046

INDEX